Stats

Modeling the World

Teacher's Edition

Stats

Modeling the World

David E. Bock
Ithaca High School

Paul F. Velleman
Cornell University

Richard D. De Veaux
Williams College

PEARSON
Addison Wesley

Boston San Francisco New York
London Toronto Sydney Tokyo Singapore Madrid
Mexico City Munich Paris Cape Town Hong Kong Montreal

Publisher: Greg Tobin
Senior Acquisitions Editor: Deirdre Lynch
Managing Editor: Karen Guardino
Senior Project Editor: Rachel S. Reeve
Associate Project Editor: Joanne Ha
Editorial Assistant: Keren Blankfeld
Production Supervisor: Julie LaChance
Marketing Manager: Pamela Laskey
Senior Manufacturing Buyer: Evelyn Beaton
Senior Prepress Supervisor: Caroline Fell
Media Producer: Jennifer Kerber
Software Editors: Gail Light, Jan Wann
Compositor: Nesbitt Graphics, Inc.
Cover Design: Barbara T. Atkinson
Interior Design: Barbara T. Atkinson/Silvers Design
Cover Photo: Sandcastle on the beach © Mark M. Lawrence Photography/CORBIS

Library of Congress Cataloging-in-Publication Data

Bock, David E.
Stats: modeling the world / David E. Bock, Paul F. Velleman, Richard D. De Veaux.—1st ed.
p. cm.
Includes index.
ISBN 0-201-73735-3 (Student Edition) ISBN 0-321-18629-X (Teacher's Edition)
1. Statistics. I. Velleman, Paul F., 1949- II. DeVeaux, Richard D. III. Title.

QA276.12.B628 2004

519.5—dc22

2003057877

Printed in the United States of America.

2 3 4 5 6 7 8 9 10–QWT–06 05 04 03

To Greg and Becca, great fun as kids and great friends as adults, and especially to my wife and best friend, Joanna, for her understanding, encouragement, and love

—Dave

To my sons, David and Zevi, from whom I've learned so much

—Paul

To Sylvia, who has helped me in more ways than she'll ever know, and to Nicholas, Scyrine, Frederick, and Alexandra, who make me so proud in everything that they are and do

—Dick

Preface

About This Book

We've created *Stats: Modeling the World* with a new vision and a new spirit. Statistics is part of our lives. We are bombarded daily by data, by polls, by results of studies, and by assertions and claims made by people (including politicians) wanting to sell us things or convince us of something. A sound understanding of Statistics is an essential part of everyday life necessary in this age of information.

This text views Statistics through the framework of thinking about the world and telling what has been found. By leading with practical data analysis and graphics, the text gets students "doing statistics" quickly and "thinking statistically" from the start.

Our goal is to make this introduction to Statistics accessible to students pursuing careers in a variety of disciplines ranging from the social sciences of psychology and sociology to areas such as education, the allied health fields, business, economics, engineering, the humanities, the physical sciences, journalism, communications, and liberal arts. We use algebra as a tool, rather than a focus, of our approach. A couple of algebra courses should be sufficient background to this Statistics course.

Our Goal: Read This Book!

The best text in the world is of little value if students don't read it. Here are some of the ways we have tried to encourage students to read *Stats: Modeling the World:*

- *Readability.* You'll see immediately that this book doesn't read like other Statistics texts. The style is both colloquial and informative, engaging students to actually read the book to see what it says.
- *Humor.* We know that humor is the best way to promote learning. You will find quips and wry comments throughout the narrative, in margin notes, and in footnotes. If we sometimes cross the line and seem to trivialize something important, we apologize.

- *Informality.* We want to alert you to the fact that our informal diction does not mean that the subject matter is covered lightly or informally. We have tried to be precise and, wherever possible, to offer deeper explanations and justifications than those found in most introductory texts.
- *Focused lessons.* The chapters are shorter than in most other texts, so students can focus on one topic at a time.
- *The need to read.* Students who plan to just skim the book may find our presentation a bit frustrating. The important concepts, definitions, or sample solutions don't sit in little boxes. This is a book that needs to be read, so we've tried to make the reading experience enjoyable.

Technology and Data

To experience the world of Statistics, it's best to explore real data sets using modern technology.

- *Technology.* First, we assume that you are using some form of technology in your Statistics course. That could be a calculator, a spreadsheet, a statistics package, or some combination of these. We place little emphasis on calculating answers by hand, even though we often show students how. However, this is not a technology-heavy book. We discuss generic computer output rather than adopting any particular software. "TI Tips"—included in most chapters—show students how to use statistics features of the TI-83 series in a timely manner. The CD-ROM (optional for students) includes *ActivStats* and the software package *Data Desk*. We also offer general guidance to help students get started on five common software platforms (Excel®, Minitab®, Data Desk®, JMP®, and SPSS®) and on a TI-89 calculator. This guidance is gathered together in Appendix B, organized to correspond with the chapters.
- *Data.* Because we use technology for computing, we don't limit ourselves to small, artificial data sets. In addition to including small data sets, we have built examples on real data with moderate numbers of cases—usually more than you would want to enter by hand into a program or calculator. Machine-readable versions of the data are included on the CD-ROM. The *ActivStats* program includes a data set browser that lets you search through all of the data available in the book (and a few hundred others as well) by title or by the topics they can be used to teach. Once the data set is located, you can copy the data to paste into the software of your choice. The larger data sets are also available on the book's Web site.

Features

We have written *Stats: Modeling the World* with several basic features and themes in mind.

- *Think, Show, Tell.* The mantra of Think, Show, and Tell is repeated in every chapter. It emphasizes the importance of thinking about a Statistics question (What do we know? What do we hope to learn? Are the assumptions and conditions satisfied?) and of reporting our findings (the Tell step). The Show step contains only the mechanics of calculating results and we try to convey our belief that it is only one part of the process.

TI Tips

- *TI Tips.* We emphasize sound understanding of the formulas and methods, but want students to use technology for the actual calculations. Easy-to-read "TI Tips" in the chapters show students how to use the calculator's statistics functions as they become important. Help using common software packages (Data Desk, Excel, JMP, MiniTab, and SPSS) or a TI-89 is included in Appendix B. We do remind students, though, that calculators and computers are just for "Show"—they cannot Think about what to do nor Tell what it all means at the end.

Math Box

- *Math Boxes.* In many chapters we present the mathematical underpinnings of the statistical methods and concepts. By setting these proofs, derivations, and justifications apart from the narrative, we allow the student to continue to follow the logical development of the topic at hand, yet also refer to the underlying mathematics for greater depth.

What Can Go Wrong?

- *What Can Go Wrong?* The most common mistakes for the new user of statistical methods usually involve misusing a method or misinterpreting a result, not miscalculating a statistic. The slander that "you can prove anything with Statistics" arises from these mistakes. We acknowledge them with a "What Can Go Wrong?" section found near the end of each chapter. One of our goals is to arm students with the tools to detect statistical errors and to debunk misuses of statistics whether intentional or not. In this spirit, our exercises include some that probe the understanding of such failures.

Connections

- *Connections.* The book presents material in nearly 30 short, focused chapters. But they tell one overall story. Each chapter has a Connections section to link key terms and concepts with previous discussions, and to point out the continuing themes. The Connections help students fit newly learned concepts into their growing understanding of Statistics. The best way to retain new learning is to connect it with old understanding.
- *Key Concepts.* The critical concepts from the chapter are always collected at the end, to help students review and study.
- *Skills.* There's a list of skills at the end of each chapter. A student who knows the Key Concepts and has the Skills is ready for the exercises (and the exam).
- *Exercises.* Exercises in this book are almost never solved with a single numerical answer. Almost every answer requires writing a sentence or two. To create a complete solution a student needs to discuss the problem and justify the method (*Think*), to do some work by hand or technology (*Show*), and to draw a reasoned conclusion that responds to the initial motivation for the exercise (*Tell*). Exercise topics reflect issues that students are likely to encounter in everyday life, emphasizing the importance of having a clearly constructed conclusion.
- Data for marked exercises are available on the Web site.

Coverage

Textbooks are often defined more by what they choose not to cover than by what they do cover. We've been guided in the choice and order of topics by several fundamental principles. First, we have tried to ensure that each new topic fits into the growing structure of understanding that we hope students will build. We know that learning a new subject such as Statistics requires putting together many new ideas, and we have tried to facilitate that process.

That goal has led us to cover some topics in a different order than is found in other texts. As one example, we introduce inference by looking at a confidence interval for a proportion rather than the more traditional one-sample mean. Everyone has seen opinion polls. Most people understand that pollsters use a sample of voters to try to predict the preferences of the entire voting population, and that the result is an estimate with a margin of error. Showing how to construct and interpret a confidence interval in this context introduces key concepts of inference in a familiar setting. We next examine hypothesis tests for a proportion. The mechanics use formulas and a test statistic that are now familiar, so it is easier to focus on the logic and structure of a formal hypothesis test.

Next, we examine inference about the difference between two proportions. We build on students' understanding of confidence intervals and hypothesis tests as we introduce the added complexity of comparing two groups. When we then turn our attention to the more complicated topic of inference for means, the only new issue confronting students is the *t*-distribution.

We encourage you to try our presentation order.

We have been guided in our choices of topics and emphasis by the recommendations of the joint ASA/MAA Statistics Focus Group (Cobb, 1992), which included "Emphasize statistical thinking" and "More data and concepts: Less theory, fewer recipes." They urge using the computer to automate calculations and graphics. We have also been guided by the syllabus of the Advanced Placement Statistics course. We agree with the wisdom of those who designed that course in their selection of topics and their emphasis on statistics as a practical discipline.

A few topics deserve special mention

Chapters 3 to 5 emphasize the central role of statistical graphs in understanding the story data can tell. We follow the three rules of data analysis *(Make a picture. Make a picture. Make a picture.)* throughout the text.

Chapter 6 introduces the idea of standard deviation as a ruler, a universal yardstick for comparing measurements and results. This concept sets the stage for understanding sampling variability and eventually inference.

Chapter 10 on data re-expression may seem intimidating to some students because they'll find a logarithm and square root there. But with technology to do the mechanics, students can concentrate on when and why to use re-expression for the purposes of statistical analysis, and on correctly interpreting the results. They learn what a powerful tool re-expression can be.

Chapters 12 and 13 on sample surveys and experiments, respectively, provide greater depth on these topics than is often found in introductory books. Students will be interested to learn the concepts behind the surveys they read in the papers and the experiments that lead to approving pharmaceuticals.

Chapter 16 presents fundamental ideas about random variables. Armed with this understanding students are well equipped to deal with special probability distributions like the binomial (Chapter 17), the Central Limit Theorem (Chapter 18), and inference for independent groups (Chapters 22 and 24).

The CD-ROM includes two additional chapters covering Analysis of Variance and multiple regression. These topics point the way to further study in Statistics. They also discuss methods that require computers for calculation.

Mathematics

Mathematics traditionally appears in Statistics texts in several roles.

1. It can provide a concise, clear statement of important concepts.
2. It can embody proofs of fundamental results.
3. It can describe calculations to be performed with data.

Of these, we emphasize the first. Mathematics can make discussions of statistics concepts, probability, and inference clear and concise. We have tried to be sensitive to the student who is discouraged by equations by also providing verbal descriptions and numerical examples.

This book is not primarily concerned with proving theorems about statistics. Some of these theorems are quite interesting, and many are important. Often, though, their proofs are not enlightening to introductory Statistics students, and can distract the audience from the concepts we want them to understand. We have not shied away from the mathematics where we felt that it helped to clarify without intimidating. You will find some important proofs, derivations, and justifications in Math Boxes that accompany the development of many topics.

We also don't concentrate on calculations. Although statistics calculations are generally straightforward, they are also usually tedious. And, more to the point, they are unnecessary. Today, virtually all statistics are calculated with technology, so there is little need for students to spend time summing squared deviations by hand. Therefore, you'll find that the equations we use have been selected for their focus on understanding concepts and methods. Often these equations are unsuited to hand calculation. When that happens, we've provided more calculation-friendly versions, often in a marginal note that lays out the calculation for those who find following the process a better way to learn about the result.

Multimedia

The CD-ROM included with the Teacher's Edition includes the *ActivStats* multimedia program designed to match the book chapter by chapter. *ActivStats* extends the book with videos of real-world stories, worked examples, animated expositions of each of the major statistics topics, and tools for performing simulations, for performing hypothesis tests, and for visualizing confidence intervals. You can use *ActivStats* as a convenient way to work with standard distributions, for simulation exercises to help students understand probability and inference, and for training in statistics software. In addition, the expositions can serve students as an electronic "teaching assistant" who has infinite patience for reviewing topics.

Exercises from the book are integrated into *ActivStats* so that the associated data sets are easily available to students in the selected statistics software. *ActivStats* provides hundreds of additional exercises and datasets as well.

The CD-ROM also contains the additional chapters covering Analysis of Variance and multiple regression. You can bundle *ActivStats* with copies of the book at a deep discount to students. More information is available at **www.aw.com/activstats.**

Overview of Supplements

SUPPLEMENTS FOR THE INSTRUCTOR

Teacher's Edition contains answers to all exercises and a complimentary copy of the CD-ROM. The CD-ROM contains *ActivStats* and additional chapters covering Analysis of Variance and multiple regression. See also the multimedia discussion on the previous page and the *ActivStats* description on the following page. (ISBN 0-321-18629-X)

Teacher's Resource Guide, by Dave Bock, Paul Velleman, and Richard De Veaux. This guide will prove useful to the seasoned veteran and invaluable to those teaching a data-oriented Statistics course for the first time. This resource includes lesson plans, extensive teaching suggestions organized by chapter, including information to help you prepare for class and tips on presenting topics. It also contains AP practice questions, unit tests, investigative tasks, helpful Web sites, and lists of other helpful resources. (ISBN 0-321-18630-3)

Teacher's Solutions Manual, by William Craine (Ithaca High School), contains detailed solutions to all of the exercises. (ISBN 0-321-18632-X)

Testing System

Great care has been taken to ensure the strongest possible testing system for *Stats: Modeling the World.* Not only is there a Printed Test Bank, but there is also a computerized test generator. Available on dual-platform Windows™/Macintosh® CD-ROM, *TestGen* enables instructors to build, edit, print, and administer tests using a computerized test bank of questions. The program also offers many options for organizing and displaying test banks and tests according to text chapter content. Tests can be printed or saved for online testing via the Web or other network, and the software can generate a variety of grading reports for tests and quizzes. (ISBN 0-321-18628-1)

Printed Test Bank (ISBN 0-321-18627-3)

MathXL for Statistics

MathXL for Statistics is an online testing, homework, and tutorial system that uses algorithmically generated exercises correlated to your textbook. Teachers can assign tests and homework as well as track their students' results and tutorial work in an online gradebook. Students can take chapter tests and receive personalized study plans based on their test results. Students can also work unlimited practice exercises and receive tutorial instruction for areas in which they need improvement. Available to qualified adopters only. Contact your Pearson sales representative for further information.

SUPPLEMENTS FOR THE STUDENT

Stats: Modeling the World for-sale student edition: (ISBN 0-201-73735-3)

TI-83 Plus®/TI-89® Manual, by Pat Humphrey (Georgia Southern University), is organized to follow the sequence of topics in the text. It is an easy-to-follow, step-by-step guide to using the TI-83 Plus and TI-89 graphing calculators. It provides worked-out examples to help students fully understand and use the graphing calculator. This supplement is also suitable for use with a TI-83 calculator. (ISBN 0-321-19406-3)

Student AP Test Prep Guide, by Susan Peters, Janice Ricks, Ruth Carver, and Anne Carroll, was written specially to complement *Stats: Modeling the World.* This guide is intended to address students' AP Statistics test preparation needs. It contains test-taking strategies as well as several practice tests. This guide helps students review topics discussed in *Stats: Modeling the World* and likely to appear on the Advanced Placement exam. (ISBN 0-321-17344-9)

ActivStats (Mac and PC)

ActivStats provides an Introductory Statistics course on CD-ROM, using the full potential of multimedia. The CD-ROM integrates video, simulation, animation, narration, text, pictures, interactive experiments, and Web access into a rich learning environment. The course offers practice with real data via links to the Data Desk statistics package included on the disk. Using *ActivStats*, students develop a sound understanding of statistical concepts and methods. The CD-ROM follows a course scope and sequence consistent with the ASA/MAA guidelines for teaching introductory statistics and the Advanced Placement Statistics Course. *ActivStats* is designed to closely correlate with this text. It also can be used as a source of laboratory activities, a personal study guide, or the core of a self-paced or distance learning course. Add instructor extensions to each page to tailor the material to particular course needs. The *DataDesk* version of *ActivStats* is included in the Teacher's Edition of the book. *ActivStats* is also available separately in versions for Excel, JMP, Minitab, and SPSS. Contact your Addison-Wesley sales representative for special bundle pricing with the textbook.

The Web site **www.aw.com/bock** provides additional resources for instructors and students, including all of the large data sets.

Acknowledgments

This book would have never seen the light of day without the assistance of the incredible folks at AW. Our Senior Acquisitions Editor, Deirdre "Hey, I've got a great idea for a book" Lynch, was central to the genesis, development, and realization of the book from day one. Rachel "Superwoman" Reeve, Senior Project Editor, kept us on task as much as humanly possible with much needed humor and grace. Pam "High Priestess of Marketing" Laskey made sure that the message got out. Julie LaChance, Production Supervisor, kept the cogs from getting into the wheels, where they often wanted to wander. Joanne Ha, Associate Project Editor, and Keren Blankfeld, Editorial Assistant, were essential in managing all of the behind-the-scenes work that needed to be done. Jennifer Kerber, Media Producer, put together a top-notch media package for this book. Barbara Atkinson, Senior Designer, and Beth Anderson, Designer, are responsible for the wonderful way the final book looks. Joe Vetere, senior technical art specialist, made sure that could happen. Evelyn Beaton, Senior Manufacturing Buyer, and Ginny Michaud,

Manufacturing Buyer, worked miracles to get this book and CD in your hands, and Greg "Are you *sure* you want to keep that title?" Tobin, Publisher, was supportive and good-humored throughout all aspects of the project.

A few other folks at Pearson deserve special recognition too: Rich Williams, Tom Maksym, and Ellen Standafer for being encouraging and providing excellent suggestions for the book.

A special thanks goes to Nesbitt Graphics, the compositor, for the wonderful work they did on this book, and in particular to Bonnie Boehme, the project manager, for her close attention to detail and her amazing editorial skills.

We'd also like to thank our accuracy checkers, whose monumental task was to make sure we said what we thought we were saying. They are Mary Ellen Davis, Georgia Perimeter College; Jackie Miller, Drury University; Crista Lynn Coles, Elon University; and Sondra Perdue, University of Washington–Tacoma.

We'd like to single out Patricia Humphrey, Georgia Southern University, and Karen Estes, St. Petersburg Junior College, for their help with the answers to exercises and Ken Grace, Anoka-Ramsey Community College, whose detailed and timely feedback proved invaluable.

We applaud Bill Craine for class-testing chapters in their earliest forms, writing all the solutions, and offering countless suggestions.

We extend our sincere thanks for the suggestions and contributions made by the following reviewers, focus group participants, and class-testers:

John Arko, Glenbrook South High School, IL
Beverly Beemer, Ruben S. Ayala High School, CA
Judy Bevington, Santa Maria High School, CA
Walter Brown, Brackenridge High School, TX
Bill Craine, Ithaca High School, NY
Sybil Coley, Woodward Academy, GA
Laura Estersohn, Scarsdale High School, NY
Linda Gann, Sandra Day O'Conner High School, TX
Randall Groth, Illinois State University
Bill Hayes, Foothill High School, CA
Carol Huss, Independence High School, NC
Sam Jovell, Niskayuna High School, NY
Peter Kaczmar, Lower Merion High School, PA
John Kotmel, Lansing High School, NY
Beth Lazerick, St. Andrews School, FL
Michael Legacy, Greenhill School, TX
John Maceli, Ithaca College, NY
Jim Miller, Alta High School, UT
Timothy E. Mitchell, King Philip Regional High School, MA
Diana Podhrasky, Hillcrest High School, TX
Rochelle Robert, Nassau Community College, NY
Bruce Saathoff, Cenennial High School, CA
Murray Siegel, Sam Houston State University, TX
Chris Sollars, Alamo Heights High School, TX
Daren Starnes, The Webb Schools, CA

Meet the Authors

David E. Bock

David E. Bock has taught mathematics and statistics at Ithaca High School for 34 years. He holds degrees in Mathematics (B.A. summa cum laude, '69) and Statistics/Education (M.A., '71) from the University at Albany. Dave is a reader for the AP Statistics exam, a statistics consultant to the College Board, and leads workshops and institutes for AP Statistics teachers. He has taught statistics at Ithaca High School, Tompkins-Cortland Community College, Ithaca College, and Cornell University.

Dave has won numerous teaching awards, including the MAA's Edyth May Sliffe Award for Distinguished High School Mathematics Teaching (twice), Cornell University's Outstanding Educator Award (three times), and has been a finalist for New York State Teacher of the Year.

Dave relaxes by biking and hiking. He and his wife have enjoyed many days camping across Canada and through the Rockies. They have a son, a daughter, and twin granddaughters.

Paul F. Velleman

Paul F. Velleman has an international reputation for innovative Statistics education. He is the author and designer of the multimedia statistics CD-ROM, *ActivStats*, for which he was awarded the EDUCOM Medal for innovative uses of computers in teaching statistics, and the ICTCM Award for Innovation in Using Technology in College Mathematics. He also developed the award-winning statistics program, Data Desk and the Internet site Data And Story Library (DASL) (http://dasl.datadesk.com), which provides datasets for teaching statistics. Paul co-authored a book (with David Hoaglin), *ABCs of Exploratory Data Analysis.*

Paul has taught statistics at Cornell University since 1975. He holds an A.B. from Dartmouth College in Mathematics and Social Science, and M.S. and Ph.D. degrees from Princeton University in Statistics, where he studied with John Tukey. His research often deals with statistical graphics and data analysis methods.

Paul is a Fellow of the American Statistical Association and of the American Association for the Advancement of Science.

Out of class, Paul sings Baritone in a barbershop quartet and tries to keep up with his younger son on figure skates. He is the father of two boys.

Richard D. DeVeaux

Richard D. DeVeaux is an internationally known educator and lecturer. He has taught at the Wharton School and the Princeton University School of Engineering where he won a "Lifetime Award for Dedication and Excellence in Teaching". Since 1994, he has been Professor of Statistics at Williams College. Dick has won both the Wilcoxon and Shewell awards from the American Society for Quality. He is a fellow of the American Statistical Association. Dick is also well known in industry where for the past 20 years he has consulted for such companies as Hewlett-Packard, Alcoa, DuPont, Pillsbury, General Electric, and Chemical Bank. He is also the "Official Statistician for the Grateful Dead".

Dick holds degrees from Princeton University in Civil Engineering (B.S.E.) and Mathematics (A.B.) and from Stanford University in Dance Education (M.A.) and Statistics (Ph.D.) where he studied with Persi Diaconis. His research focuses on the analysis of large data sets and data mining in science and industry.

In his spare time he is an avid cyclist and swimmer. He also is the founder and bass for the "Diminished Faculty," an a cappella Doo-Wop quartet at Williams College. Dick is the father of four children.

Contents

Appendixes

Our world is awash in information,
more plentiful than the grains of sand in these dunes.

Hoping to understand the world, statisticians play in the
sand, our data. We collect it and inspect it.
We describe it and look for patterns.

We use it to create models. We hope that our models, like
the castle, are useful images of the real world.

Using tools based on the perfect curves of mathematics,
we compare our models to that reality.
Seeing where the models work
—and, more often, where they fail—
we discover truths about our world.

Part I

Exploring and Understanding Data

Chapter 1

Stats Starts Here[1]

"But where shall I begin?" asked Alice. "Begin at the beginning," the King said gravely, "and go on till you come to the end: then stop."
—Lewis Carroll, Alice's Adventures in Wonderland

Statistics gets no respect. People say things like "you can prove anything with Statistics." People will write off a claim based on data as "just a statistical trick." And Statistics courses don't have the reputation of being students' first choice for a fun elective.

But Statistics *is* fun. That's probably not what you heard on the street, but it's true. Statistics is about how to think clearly with data. A little practice thinking statistically is all it takes to start seeing the world more clearly and accurately.

So, What Is (Are?) Statistics?

Q: What is Statistics?
A: Statistics is a way of reasoning, along with a collection of tools and methods, designed to help us understand the world.
Q: What are statistics?
A: Statistics (plural) are particular calculations made from data.
Q: So what is data?
A: You mean, "what *are* data?" Data is the plural form. The singular is datum.
Q: OK, OK, so what are data?
A: Data are values along with their context.

It seems every time we turn around, someone is collecting data on us, from every purchase we make in the grocery store, to every click of our mouse as we surf the Web. The United Parcel Service (UPS) tracks every package it ships from one place to another around the world and stores these records in a giant database. You can access part of it if you send or receive a UPS package. The database is about 17 terabytes big—about the same size as a database that contained every book in the Library of Congress would be. (But, we suspect, not *quite* as interesting.) What can anyone hope to do with all these data?

Statistics plays a role in making sense of the complex world in which we live today. Statisticians assess the risk of genetically engineered foods or of a new drug being considered by the Food and Drug Administration (FDA). They predict the number of new cases of AIDS by regions of the country or the number of customers likely to respond to a sale at the market. And statisticians help scientists and social scientists understand how unemployment is related to environmental

[1]This chapter might have been called "Introduction," but nobody reads the introduction, and we wanted you to read this. We feel safe admitting this here, in the footnote, because nobody reads footnotes either.

The ads say, "Don't drink and drive; you don't want to be a statistic." But you can't be a statistic.

We say: "Don't be a datum."

controls, whether enriched early education affects later performance of school children, and whether vitamin C really prevents illness. Whenever there are data and a need for understanding the world, you need Statistics.

So our objectives in this book are to help you develop the insights to think clearly about the questions, use the tools to show what the data are saying, and acquire the skills to tell clearly what it all means.

FRAZZ reprinted by permission of United Feature Syndicate, Inc.

Statistics in a Word

Statistics is about variation.

Data vary because we don't see everything and because even what we do see and measure, we measure imperfectly.

So, in a very basic way, Statistics is about the real, imperfect world in which we live.

It can be fun, and sometimes useful, to summarize a discipline in only a few words. So,

Economics is about . . . *Money (and why it is good).*

Psychology: *Why we think what we think (we think).*

Biology: *Life.*

Anthropology: *Who?*

History: *What, where, and when?*

Philosophy: *Why?*

Engineering: *How?*

Accounting: *How much?*

In such a caricature, Statistics is about . . . ***Variation.***

Data vary. People are different. We can't see everything. And even what we do measure, we measure imperfectly. So the data we wind up looking at and basing our decisions on provide, at best, an imperfect picture of the world. This fact lies at the heart of what Statistics is all about. How to make sense of it is a central challenge of Statistics.

So, How Will This Book Help?

A fair question. Most likely, this book will not turn out to be quite what you expected.

What's different?

Close your eyes and open the book to a page at random. Is there an equation on that page? Do that again, say, 10 times. We'll bet you saw only a few pages with equations.

Equations are a great way of expressing a mathematical idea concisely. But they're not the main point of Statistics. Rather than just listing definitions and equations, this book leads you through the entire process of *thinking* about a problem, finding and *showing* results for the problem, and *telling* others about what you have discovered.

You looked at only a few randomly selected pages to get an impression of the entire book. We'll see soon that doing so was sound Statistics practice and reasoning.

Next, pick a chapter and read the first two sentences. (Go ahead; we'll wait.)

We'll bet you didn't see anything about Statistics. Why? Because the best way to understand Statistics is to see it at work. In this book, chapters usually start by presenting a story and posing questions. That's when Statistics really gets down to work.

There are three simple steps to doing Statistics right: *think, show,* and *tell:*

Think

Show

Tell

Think first. Know where you're headed and why. It will save you a lot of work.

Show is what most folks think Statistics is about. The *mechanics* of calculating statistics and making displays is important, but not the most important part of Statistics.

Tell what you've learned. Until you've explained your results so that someone else can understand your conclusions, the job is not done.

STEP-BY-STEP

Each chapter applies new concepts in a worked example called a **Step-by-Step.** These examples model the way statisticians attack and solve problems. They illustrate how to think about the problem, what to show, and how to tell what it all means. These step-by-step examples will show you how to produce the kind of solutions instructors hope to see.

Math Box

Knowing where the formulas and procedures of Statistics come from and why they work will help you understand the important concepts. We'll provide brief, clear explanations of the mathematics that supports many of the statistical methods in **Math Boxes** like this.

"Get your facts first, and then you can distort them as much as you please. (Facts are stubborn, but statistics are more pliable.)"
—Mark Twain

What Can Go Wrong?

One of the interesting challenges of Statistics is that, unlike some math and science courses, there can be more than one right answer. This is why two statisticians can testify honestly on opposite sides of a court case. And it's why some people think that you can prove anything with statistics. But that's not true. People make mistakes using statistics, sometimes on purpose in order to mislead others. Most of the unintentional mistakes people make, though, are avoidable. We're not talking about arithmetic. More often the mistakes come from using a method in the wrong situation or misinterpreting the results. Each chapter has a section called **What Can Go Wrong** to help you avoid some of the most common mistakes.

TI Tips

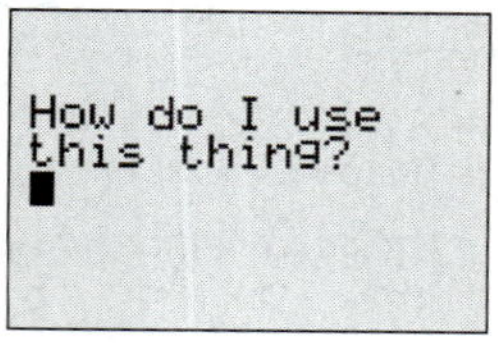

Although we'll show you all the formulas you need to understand the calculations, you will most often use a calculator or computer to perform the mechanics of a statistics problem. Your graphing calculator has a specialized program called a "statistics package." Each chapter contains **TI Tips** that teach you how to use it (and avoid doing most of the messy calculations).

There are a number of statistics packages for computers, too, and they differ widely in the details of how to use them and in how they present their results. But they all work from the same basic information and find the same results. Rather than adopt one package for this book, we'll present generic output and point out common features that you should look for in an . . . **And the Computer** section in most chapters. We'll also provide an Appendix showing tables of instructions to get you started on any of five commonly used packages.

...and the Computer

From time to time we'll take time out to discuss an interesting or important side issue. We indicate these by setting them apart like this.[2]

Doing it by hand

We'll show you how to calculate the simpler formulas by hand in a marginal note like this one. That way you can find it easily, but it won't be in the way.

We'll also highlight **Key Concepts** as they come up, and collect them at the end of each chapter, together with a summary of important **Skills.** Use these to check your knowledge of the important ideas in the chapter. If you have the skills and understand the key concepts, you should be well prepared for the exam—and ready to use Statistics!

Beware: No one can learn Statistics just by reading or listening. The only way to learn it is to do it. So, of course, at the end of each chapter (except this one) you'll find **Exercises** designed to help you learn to use the Statistics you've just read about.

You'll find all sorts of stuff in margin notes, such as stories and quotations. For example:

". . . geographers . . . crowd into the edges of their maps parts of the world which they do not know about, adding notes in the margin to the effect that beyond this lies nothing . . ."
—Plutarch, (46? C.E.–120 C.E.), A Life of Theseus

You'll find answers to the odd-numbered exercises at the back of the book. But these are only "answers" and not complete "solutions." Huh? What's the difference? The answers are sketches of the complete solutions. For most problems, your solution should follow the model of the Step-by-Step examples. If your calculations match the numerical parts of the "answer," and your argument contains the elements shown in the answer, you're on the right track. Your complete solution should explain the context, show your reasoning and calculations, and state your conclusions.

In the real world, there's no chapter just before the question. So in addition to the problems at the ends of chapters we've also collected more problems at the end of each part to make it more like the real world. This should help you to see whether you can sort out which methods to use when. If you can do that successfully, then you'll know you understand Statistics.

Onward!

It's only fair to warn you: You can't get there by just picking out the highlighted sentences and the summaries. This book is different. It's not about memorizing definitions and learning equations. It's deeper than that. And much more fun. But . . .

You have to read the book![3]

[2]Or in a footnote.

[3]So, turn the page.

Chapter 2

Data

"We did not have [data] at the beginning of our business, but find it invaluable now. We have history now, so we can make predictions and projections in a much more intelligent and reasoned manner."
—Amber Chand, Vice President for Vision, Eziba

Many years ago, most stores in small towns knew their customers personally. If you walked into the hobby shop, the owner might tell you about a new bridge that had come in for your Lionel train set. The tailor knew your dad's size, and the hairdresser knew how your mom liked her hair. There are still some stores like that around today, but we're increasingly likely to shop at large stores, by phone, or on the Internet. Even so, when you phone an 800 number to buy new running shoes, customer service representatives may call you by your first name, or ask about the socks you bought 6 weeks ago. Or the company may send an e-mail in October offering new head warmers for winter running. This company has millions of customers, and you called without identifying yourself. How did it know who you are, where you live, and what you had bought?

The answer to all these questions is data. Collecting data on their customers, transactions, and sales enables companies to know where their inventory is and what their customers prefer. These data can help them predict what their customers may buy in the future and how much of each item to stock. The store can use the data and what they learn from the data to improve customer service, mimicking the kind of personal attention a shopper had 50 years ago.

Eziba was founded in 1999 as an exclusively Web-based bazaar to forge a link between artisans in developing countries and customers in the West. To meet this challenge, they needed to collect and analyze data to track hundreds of inventory items from around the world, tens of thousands of customers, and marketing initiatives that include direct mail and print advertising. A small company must make smart decisions. How could Eziba compare the success of its print advertisement in the *New York Times* magazine with the effectiveness of its new Web site design?

Eziba designed its Web site to collect data on customer behavior. The company wanted to know how long a visitor to the site spent on each page and how likely she was to make a purchase. The Web site asked customers where they had heard of the company and recorded the number who mentioned the *Times* magazine ads. Analyses of these and other data have enabled Eziba to manage customer relationships and expand sales.

EZIBA

Amber Chand (foreground) co-founder of Eziba, with colleagues from Aid to Artisans, a nonprofit organization

But What *Are* Data?

> ***The W's:***
> ***WHO***
> ***WHAT***
> and in what units
> ***WHEN***
> ***WHERE***
> ***WHY***
> ***HOW***

We bet you thought you knew this instinctively. Think about it for a minute. What exactly *do* we mean by "data"?

You might say that data are numbers. The amount of your last purchase in dollars is numerical data, but some data record names or other labels. Your name in Eziba's database is data, but not numerical.

Sometimes, just to make things confusing, data can have values that look like numerical values but are just numerals serving as labels. The item stock numbers Eziba uses to track inventory are really just names.

Data values, no matter what kind, are useless without their context. Newspaper journalists know that the lead paragraph of a good story should establish the "Five W's": *Who, What, When, Where,* and (if possible) *Why.* Often, we add *How* to the list as well. Answering these questions can provide the **context** for data values. The answers to the first two questions are essential. If you can't answer those questions, you don't have **data,** and you don't have any useful information.

Data Tables

Here are some customer records from another company's database:

7O28YT	24		305	Boston	18	Kansas	5
Veterans		Orange	Y	CKJ245		413	Y
Garbage	43	Wrigley	Y	Chicago	N		Fenway
610		130		7TY734	368	JKN234	312

Try to guess what they represent. Why is that hard? Because these data have no *context.* It's impossible to know what they're about or what they refer to without knowing the W's. We can make the context clear if we organize the values into a **data table** such as this one.

Table 2.1

Name	Age (yr)	Time Since Last Purchase (days)	Area Code	Nearest Stadium	Internet Purchase?	Catalog Number of Last CD Bought	Artist
Katharine H.		130	312	Wrigley	Y	7TY734	Kansas
Samuel P.	24	18	305	Orange	N	CKJ245	Boston
Chris G.	43	368	610	Veterans	Y	JKN234	Chicago
Monique D.		5	413	Fenway	Y	7O28YT	Garbage

Now we can see that these are four customer records from an Internet CD store (that advertises at sporting events). The column titles tell *What* has been recorded. The rows tell us *Who.* The other W's might have to come from the company's database administrator.[1]

[1]In database management, this kind of information is called "metadata."

Who

In general, each row of a data table corresponds to an **individual** about whom (or about which—if they're not people) we record some characteristics. These individuals go by different names, depending on the situation. Individuals who answer a survey are referred to as **respondents.** People on whom we experiment are **subjects** or (in an attempt to acknowledge the importance of their role in the experiment) **participants,** but animals, plants, Web sites, and other inanimate subjects are often just called **experimental units.** In a database, rows are called **records**—in this example, **customer records.** Perhaps the most generic term is **cases.** In the table, the cases are the customers: Katharine, Samuel, Chris, and Monique.

Sometimes people just refer to data values as **observations** without being clear about the *Who.* Be sure you know the *Who* of the data or you may not know what the data say.

What

It is wise to be careful. The *What* and *Why* of area codes are not as simple as they may first seem. When area codes were first introduced, AT&T was still the source of all telephone equipment and phones had dials.

To reduce wear and tear on the dials, the area codes with the lowest digits (for which the dial would have to spin least) were assigned to the most populous regions—those with the most phone numbers and thus the area codes most likely to be dialed. New York City was assigned 212, Chicago 312, and Los Angeles 213, but rural upstate New York was given 607, Joliet was 815, and San Diego 619. For that reason, at one time, the numerical value of an area code could be used to guess something about the population of its region. Since the advent of push-button phones, area codes have finally become just categories.

The characteristics recorded about each individual are called **variables.** These are usually shown as the columns of a data table, and they should have a name that identifies *what* has been measured.

Whether a data value is a number or a name may depend on how we use it. Although area codes are numbers, do we use them that way? Is 610 twice 305? Of course it is, but is Allentown, PA (610), equal to 2 times Key West, FL (305)?

The numbers here are just labels and their values are arbitrary. They represent categories of the variables. We call such variables **categorical.**[2] A dog's gender, color, and breed are all categorical.

Variables recorded in numbers that we use as numbers are called **quantitative.** Familiar examples include incomes, heights, weights, ages, and counts.

Quantitative variables have measurement **units.** Units tell how a quantitative value has been measured. Units are such things as yen, cubits, carats, angstroms, nanoseconds, miles per hour, and degrees Celsius. Without units, the values of a quantitative variable have no meaning. It does little good to be promised a salary of 40,000 a year if you don't know whether it will be paid in euros, dollars, yen, or Estonian kroon. Knowing the attribute may not be sufficient. You might be surprised to see someone whose age is 72 listed in a database on childhood diseases until you find out that age is measured in months. No quantitative variable is complete without its units.

The International System of Units links together all systems of weights and measures by international agreement. There are seven base units from which all other physical units are derived:

• Distance	Meter
• Mass	Kilogram
• Time	Second
• Electric current	Ampere
• Temperature	Kelvin
• Amount of substance	Mole
• Intensity of light	Candela

[2]You may also see them called *qualitative.*

Often, just seeking the units can reveal a variable whose definition is dubious. For example, how should we measure "friendliness," "success," "study effort," or "commitment"? It may not be clear how to measure these concepts, yet people make scientific-sounding claims about such "variables." For example, a claim such as "Performance in school is highly correlated with self-esteem" might sound scientific—until we ask in what units one might measure "school performance" or "self-esteem."

Although we've described categorical and quantitative as if they were properties of variables, really they're properties of how we *use* a variable. For example, if we measure someone's age, we might measure it in years and use it as a quantitative variable. Taking the average age would make sense. But sometimes we treat age as categorical, as, for example, in the categories "child" and "adult." Many variables can be treated either way, depending on the use we want to put them to.

One tradition that hangs on in some quarters is to name variables with cryptic abbreviations written in uppercase letters. This can be traced back to the 1960s when the very first statistics computer programs were controlled with instructions punched on cards. The earliest punch card equipment used only uppercase letters, and the earliest statistics programs limited variable names to six or eight characters, so variables were called things like PRSRF3. Modern programs do not have such restrictive limits, so there is no reason for variable names that you wouldn't use in an ordinary sentence.

Some variables fall right in between categorical and quantitative. These are variables whose values are not categorical, but not quite quantitative either. For example, think about a survey that asks a question, "What did you think about the pace of the Statistics course you took?" 1 = Way too slow; 2 = A little too slow; 3 = About right; 4 = A little too fast; 5 = Way too fast. Is this variable categorical or quantitative? There is certainly an *order* of perceived speed here. Higher numbers indicate higher perceived speed. A course that averages 4.5 is perceived as going faster than one that averages 2, but we should be careful about treating them as purely quantitative. A course that averages 4.0 is not necessarily *twice* as fast as one that averages 2.0.

These variables are often called **ordinal** variables. Again, depending on what one wants to do with them, they might be treated as numerical (with caution) or categorical, or sometimes even both. For example, the figure numbers in this book can be categorical labels (as in "see Figure 2.1") or they could be quantitative and count the number of figures in a chapter, although there's little reason to want to know that.[3] The main point is to think about what the values mean and how they are being used. Be careful of automatically treating values as quantitative just because they look like numbers.

What is measured tells us the meaning of the values. In the Internet CD database, there are seven variables measuring various characteristics about the customers. The variable names often give a lot of information about the *What* if they are well chosen. For this reason, it's a good idea to avoid names like x_1, TEMP, or even XPECHR8 (as tempting as this may be). Use names that clearly show what the variable is about.

Where, When, How, and Why

We must know *Who* and *What* to analyze data. The more we know, the more we'll understand.

[3]Figure numbers are identifiers—a special type of categorical variable.

For example, we'd like to know the **When** and **Where** of data as well. Values recorded in 1803 may mean something different than similar values recorded last year. Values measured in Tanzania may differ in meaning from similar measurements made in Mexico.

How the data are collected can make the difference between insight and nonsense. As we'll see later, data that come from a voluntary survey on the Internet are almost always worthless. One primary concern of Statistics, discussed in Part III, is the design of sound methods for collecting data.

Often the most revealing W is **Why.** Knowing why data were collected can alert us to potential problems in *How* the data were measured or observed or in the decisions made about the *Who* and *What* of the data. For example, knowing that Levi Strauss conducted the survey may make us skeptical when we hear that 90% of students predicted Levi's 501 jeans to be the most popular clothing item on campus.[4]

Throughout this book, whenever we introduce data, we will provide a marginal note listing the W's (and H) of the data. It is a habit we recommend. Whenever you encounter data (or values masquerading as data) ask yourself whether you know the W's. You may be surprised to see how often this vital information is missing. That simple question will protect you from many of the most common misuses of Statistics.

An Example

A study compared the lifetimes of actors who had won Academy Awards (Oscars) with those of actors who had been nominated but had not won and with actors who had been in the movies that led to the awards but had not been nominated. The study found that actors who had won tended to live longer than the other actors considered.

What are the W's in this account? Pause for a moment and try to determine them to the extent that we can tell.

The *Who* are actors, and specifically actors who won Oscars, were nominated for Oscars, or acted in films for which others won Oscars. The *What* of concern in this study is the length of the lives of these actors (which suggests that we may need to modify the *Who* to be only dead actors who meet the other criteria). The *When* isn't clear, although the study may well have spanned the several decades of Academy Awards. *Where* is not really an issue here, although most of the actors nominated are American. The *Why* is, as far as we can tell, a scientific concern with whether fame, or winning, affects lifetimes.

Always refer to variables by name. Your conclusions from statistical analyses should be in clear sentences and about the variables. For example, here is a brief description of a study that was analyzed with Statistics:

> *Researchers gave 117 people either echinacea or a placebo (sugar pill) for two weeks, then exposed them to cold viruses. Those who took the echinacea were just as likely to develop a cold as those who took a placebo. The researchers concluded that echinacea treatments do not reduce the risk of catching colds.*

[4]Learning that these were the only jeans on the list just might increase our skepticism.

It is easy to tell the *Who* (117 people) and *What* (susceptibility to colds) from this description and to understand the conclusions of the study in terms of the variables (*treatment:* a categorical variable with values of either echinacea or placebo; and *cold:* a categorical variable recording whether the people got colds).

What Can Go Wrong?

- ***Just because your variable's values are numbers, don't assume that it's quantitative.*** Categories are often given numerical labels. Don't let that fool you into thinking they have quantitative meaning. Look at the context.
- ***Always be skeptical.*** One reason to analyze data is to discover the truth. Even when you are told a context for the data, it may turn out that the truth is a bit (or even a lot) different. The context colors our interpretation of the data, so those who want to influence what you think may slant the context. A survey that seems to be about all students may in fact report just the opinions of those who visited a fan Web site. The question that respondents answered may be slanted.

TI Tips

You'll need to be able to enter and edit data in your calculator. It's easy!

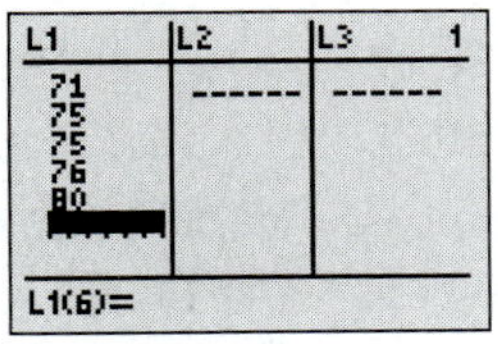

To enter data:

Hit the **STAT** button, and choose **EDIT** from the menu. You'll see a set of columns labeled **L1**, **L2**, and so on. Here is where you can enter, change, or delete a set of data.

Let's enter the heights (in inches) of the five starting players on a basketball team: 71, 75, 75, 76, and 80. Move the cursor to the space under **L1**, type in 71, and hit **ENTER** (or the down arrow). There's the first player. Now enter the data for the rest of the team.

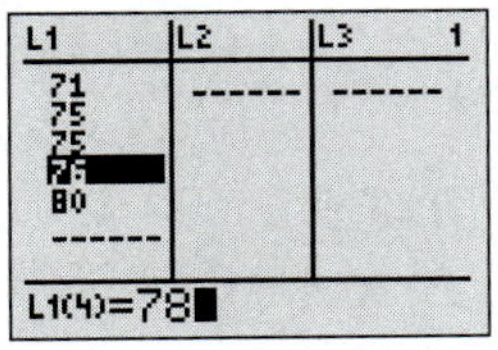

To change a datum:

Suppose the 76″ player grew since last season; his height should be listed as 78″. Use the arrow keys to move the cursor onto the 76, then change the value and **ENTER** the correction.

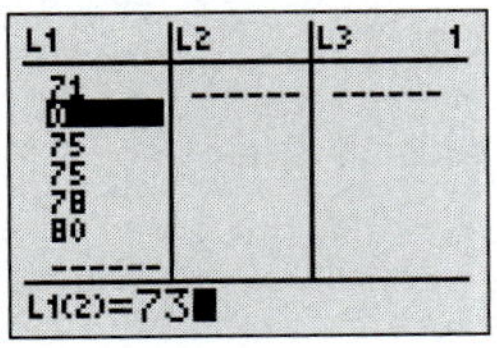

To add more data:

We want to include the sixth man, 73″ tall. It would be easy to simply add this new datum to the end of the list. However, sometimes the order of the data matters, so let's place this datum in numerical order. Move the cursor to the desired position (atop the first 75). Hit **2nd INS**, then **ENTER** the 73 in the new space.

To delete a datum:

The 78″ player just quit the team. Move the cursor there. Hit **DEL**. Bye.

To clear the datalist:

Finished playing basketball? Move the cursor atop the **L1**. Hit **CLEAR**, then **ENTER** (or down arrow). You should now have a blank datalist, ready for you to enter your next set of values.

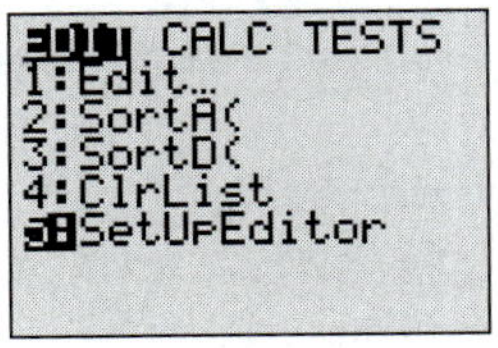

Lost a datalist?

Oops! Is **L1** now missing entirely? Did you *delete* **L1** by mistake, instead of just *clearing* it? Easy problem to fix: buy a new calculator. No? OK, then simply go to the **STAT EDIT** menu, and run **SetUpEditor** to recreate all the lists.

Data and the Computer

Most often we find statistics on a computer using a program, or *package,* designed for that purpose. There are many different statistics packages, but they all do essentially the same things. If you understand what the computer needs to know to do what you want and what it needs to show you in return, you can figure out the specific details of most packages pretty easily.

For example, to get your data into a computer statistics package you need to tell the computer:

- Where to find the data. This usually means directing the computer to a file stored on your computer's disk or to data on a database. Or it might just mean that you have copied the data from a spreadsheet program or Internet site, and it is currently on your computer's clipboard. Usually, the data should be in the form of a data table. Most computer statistics packages prefer the *delimiter* that marks the division between elements of a data table to be a *tab* character and the delimiter that marks the end of a case to be a *return* character.
- Where to put the data. (Usually this is handled automatically.)
- What to call the variables. Some data tables have variable names as the first row of the data, and often statistics packages can take the variable names from the first row automatically.

Key Concepts

Context The context ideally tells *Who* was measured, *What* was measured, *How* the data were collected, *Where* the data were collected, and *When* and *Why* the study was performed.

Data Systematically recorded information, whether numbers or labels, together with its context.

Data table An arrangement of data in which each row represents a case and each column represents a variable.

Case A case is an individual about whom or which we have data.

Variable A variable holds information about the same characteristic for many cases.

Categorical variable A variable that names categories (whether with words or numerals) is called categorical.

Quantitative variable A variable in which the numbers act as numerical values is called quantitative. Quantitative variables always have units.

Units A quantity or amount adopted as a standard of measurement, such as dollars, hours, or grams.

Skills

When you complete this lesson you should:

Think

- Be able to identify the *Who, What, When, Where, Why,* and *How* of data, or recognize when some of this information has not been provided.
- Be able to identify the cases and variables in any data set.
- Be able to classify a variable as categorical or quantitative.
- For any quantitative variable be able to identify the units in which the variable has been measured (or note that they have not been provided).

Tell

- Be able to describe a variable in terms of its *Who, What, When, Where, Why,* and *How* (and be prepared to remark when that information is not provided).

Exercises

For each description of data, identify the W's, name the variables, classify each variable as categorical or quantitative, and, for any quantitative variable, identify the units in which it was measured (or note that they were not provided).

1. **The News.** Find a newspaper or magazine article in which some data are reported. For the data discussed in the article answer the questions above. Include a copy of the article with your report.

2. **Investments.** According to an article in *Fortune* (Dec. 28, 1992), 401(k) plans permit employees to shift part of their before-tax salaries into investments such as mutual funds. Employers typically match 50% of the employees' contribution up to about 6% of salary. One company, concerned with what it believed was a low employee participation rate in its 401(k) plan, sampled 30 other companies with similar plans and asked for their 401(k) participation rates.

3. **Oil spills.** Owing to several major ocean oil spills by tank vessels, Congress passed the 1990 Oil Pollution Act, which requires all tankers to be designed with thicker hulls. Further improvements in the structural design of a tank vessel have been proposed since then, each with the objective of reducing the likelihood of an oil spill and decreasing the amount of outflow in the event of a hull puncture. To aid in this development, *Marine Technology* (Jan. 1995) reported on the spillage amount and cause of puncture for 50 recent major oil spills from tankers and carriers.

4. **Oscars.** *Ages of Oscar-Winning Best Actors and Actresses* by Richard Brown and Gretchen Davis gives the ages of actors and actresses at the time they won Oscars. We might use these data to see whether actors and actresses are likely to win Oscars at about the same age or not.

5. **Weighing bears.** Because of the difficulty of weighing a bear in the woods, researchers caught and measured 54 bears, recording their weight, neck size, length, and sex. They hoped to find a way to estimate weight from the other, more easily determined quantities.

6. **Molten iron.** The Cleveland Casting Plant is a large, highly automated producer of gray and nodular iron automotive castings for Ford Motor Company. According to an article in *Quality Engineering* (7 [1995]), Cleveland Casting is interested in keeping the pouring temperature of the molten iron (in degrees Fahrenheit) close to the specified value of 2550 degrees. Cleveland Casting measured the pouring temperature for a random sample of 10 crankshafts.

7. **Arby's menu.** A listing posted by the Arby's restaurant chain gives, for each of the sandwiches it sells, the type of meat in the sandwich, the number of calories, and the serving size in ounces. The data might be used to assess the nutritional value of the different sandwiches.

8. **Firefighters.** A study was conducted to compare the abilities of men and women to perform the strenuous tasks required of a shipboard firefighter (*Human Factors* 24 [1982]). The study reports the pulling force (in newtons) that a firefighter was able to exert in pulling the starter cord of a P-250 water pump. The study also gives the weight and, of course, the gender of the firefighters.

9. **Babies.** Medical researchers at a large city hospital investigating the impact of prenatal care on newborn health collected data from 882 births during 1998–2000. They kept track of the mother's age, the number of weeks the pregnancy lasted, the type of birth (cesarean, induced, natural), the level of prenatal care the mother had (none, minimal, adequate), the birth weight and gender of the baby, and whether the baby exhibited health problems (none, minor, major).

10. **Flowers.** In a study appearing in the journal *Science* a research team reports that plants in southern England are flowering earlier in the spring. Records of the first flowering dates for 385 species over a period of 47 years indicate that flowering has advanced an average of 15 days per decade, an indication of climate warming according to the authors.

11. **Fitness.** Are physically fit people less likely to die of cancer? An article in the May 2002 issue of *Medicine and Science in Sports and Exercise* reported results of a study that followed 25,892 men aged 30 to 87 for 10 years. The most physically fit men had a 55% lower risk of death from cancer than the least fit group.

12. **Schools.** The State Education Department requires local school districts to keep these records on all students: age, race or ethnicity, days absent, current grade level, standardized test scores in reading and mathematics, and any disabilities or special educational needs the student may have.

13. **Herbal medicine.** Scientists at a major pharmaceutical firm conducted an experiment to study the effectiveness of an herbal compound to treat the common cold. They exposed each patient to a cold virus, then gave them either the herbal compound or a sugar solution known to have no effect on colds. Several days later they assessed each patient's condition using a cold severity scale ranging 0–5. They found no evidence of the benefits of the compound.

14. **Tracking sales.** A start-up company is building a database of customers and sales information. For each

customer it records name, ID number, region of the country (1 = East, 2 = South, 3 = Midwest, 4 = West), date of last purchase, amount of purchase, and item purchased.

15. Cars. A survey of autos parked in student and staff lots at a large university recorded the make, country of origin, type of vehicle (car, van, SUV, etc.), and age.

16. Vineyards. Business analysts hoping to provide information helpful to grape growers compiled these data about vineyards: size (acres), number of years in existence, state, varieties of grapes grown, average case price, gross sales, and percent profit.

17. Streams. As research for an ecology class, students at a college in upstate New York collect data on streams each year. They record a number of biological, chemical, and physical variables, including the stream name, the substrate of the stream (limestone, shale, or mixed), the acidity of the water (pH), the temperature (°C), and the BCI (a numerical measure of biological diversity).

18. Age and party. The Gallup Poll conducted a representative telephone survey of 1180 American voters during the first quarter of 1999. Among the reported results were the voter's region (Northeast, South, etc.), age, party affiliation, and whether or not the person had voted in the 1998 midterm Congressional election.

19. Air travel. The Federal Aviation Administration (FAA) monitors airlines for safety and customer service. For each flight the carrier must report the type of aircraft, number of passengers, whether or not the flights departed and arrived on schedule, and any mechanical problems.

20. Fuel economy. The Environmental Protection Agency (EPA) tracks fuel economy of automobiles. Among the data they collect are the manufacturer (Ford, Toyota, etc.), vehicle type (car, SUV, etc.), weight, horsepower, and gas mileage (mpg) for city and highway driving.

21. Refrigerators. In 2002, *Consumer Reports* published an article evaluating refrigerators. It listed 41 models, giving the brand, cost, size (cu ft), type (such as top-freezer), estimated annual energy cost, an overall rating (good, excellent, etc.), and the repair history for that brand (percentage requiring repairs over the past 5 years).

Chapter 3

Displaying and Describing Categorical Data

WHO	People on the *Titanic*
WHAT	Survival status, age, sex, ticket class
WHEN	April 14, 1912
WHERE	North Atlantic
HOW	A variety of sources and Internet sites
WHY	Historical interest

What happened on the *Titanic* at 11:40 on the night of April 14, 1912, is well known. Frederick Fleet's cry of "Iceberg, right ahead" and the three accompanying pulls of the crow's nest bell signaled the beginning of a nightmare that has become legend. By 2:15 a.m. the *Titanic,* thought by many to be unsinkable, had sunk, leaving over 1500 passengers and crewmembers on board to meet their icy fate.

Here are some data about the passengers and crew aboard the *Titanic.* Each record of the data table (each row) shows the data for one person on board the ship. The variables are whether or not the person *Survived* (Dead or Alive), the person's *Age* (Adult or Child), *Sex* (Male or Female), and ticket *Class* (First, Second, Third, or Crew).

The problem with a data table like this—and in fact with all data tables—is that you can't *see* what's going on. And seeing is just what we want to do. We need ways to show the data so that we can see patterns, relationships, trends, and even exceptions.

Survived	Age	Sex	Class
Dead	Adult	Male	Third
Dead	Adult	Male	Crew
Dead	Adult	Male	Third
Dead	Adult	Male	Crew
Dead	Adult	Male	Crew
Dead	Adult	Male	Crew
Alive	Adult	Female	First
Dead	Adult	Male	Third
Dead	Adult	Male	Crew

Part of a data table showing four variables for nine passengers aboard the *Titanic.* **Table 3.1**

The Three Rules of Data Analysis

So, what should we do with data like these? There are three things you should always do first with data:

1. **Make a picture.** A display of your data will reveal things you are not likely to see in a table of numbers and will help you to *think* clearly about the patterns and relationships that may be hiding in your data.
2. **Make a picture.** A well-designed display will *show* the important features and patterns in your data. And a picture will show you the things you did not expect to see: the extraordinary (possibly wrong) data values or unexpected patterns.
3. **Make a picture.** The best way to *tell* others about your data is with a well-chosen picture.

These are the three rules of data analysis. There are pictures of data throughout the book, and new kinds keep showing up. These days, technology makes drawing pictures of data easy, so there is no reason not to follow the three rules.

A Picture to Tell a Story

Florence Nightingale, a founder of modern nursing, was also well versed in statistics. To argue forcefully for better hospital conditions for soldiers, she invented this display, which showed that in the Crimean War, far more soldiers died of illness and infection than died of battle wounds. Her campaign succeeded in improving hospital conditions and nursing for soldiers. **Figure 3.1**

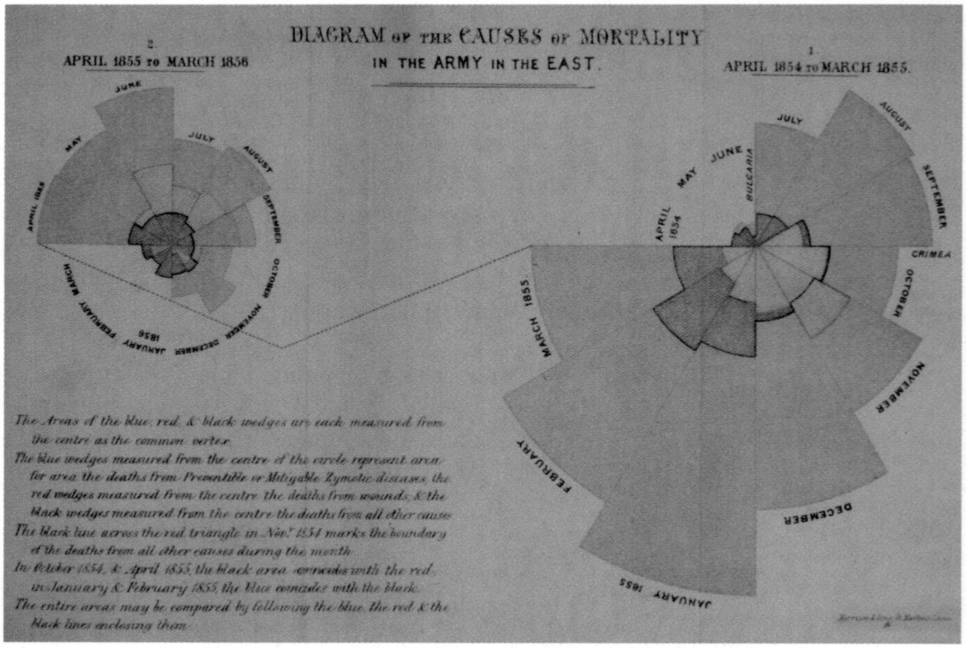

What to Do First: Make Piles

In order to make a picture, the first thing we have to do with data is to make piles. Believe it or not, making piles is the start of all science and the beginning of all understanding about data. We pile together things that seem to go together. Later we'll ask how they go together, why they go together, and how the piles relate and compare with one another. But first, we pile.

Frequency Tables

Class	Count
First	325
Second	285
Third	706
Crew	885

A frequency table of the *Titanic* passengers. **Table 3.2**

Class	%
First	14.766
Second	12.949
Third	32.076
Crew	40.209

The same data as a relative frequency table. **Table 3.3**

One way to put all 2201 people on the *Titanic* into piles is by ticket *Class,* counting up how many had each kind of ticket. We can organize these **counts** into a **frequency table,** which records the totals and the category names.

The variable ticket *Class* has only a few categories, so a frequency table is easy to read even though we have thousands of cases. A frequency table with dozens or hundreds of categories would be much harder to read. We use the names of the categories to label each row in the frequency table. For ticket *Class,* these are "First," "Second," "Third," and "Crew."

A **relative frequency table** is similar but gives the *percentages,* rather than the counts, of the values in each category. Both types of tables describe the **distribution** of a categorical variable because they name the possible categories and tell how frequently each occurs.

The Area Principle

How many people were in each class on the *Titanic?* From this display it looks as though the service must have been great, since most aboard were crew members. Although the *length* of each ship here corresponds to the correct number, the impression is all wrong. In fact, only 40% were crew. **Figure 3.2**

Now that we have the frequency table, we're ready to follow the three rules of data analysis and make a picture of the data. But a bad picture can distort our understanding rather than help it. Here's a graph of the *Titanic* data. What impression do you get about who was aboard the ship?

It sure looks like most of the people on the *Titanic* were crew members, with a few passengers along for the ride. That doesn't seem right. What's wrong? The lengths of the ships *do* match the totals in the table. (You can check the scale at the bottom.) However, experience and psychological tests show that our eyes tend to be more impressed by the *area* than by other aspects of each ship image. So, even though the *length* of each ship matches up with one of the totals, it's the associated *area* in the image that we notice. Since there were about 3 times as many crew as second-class passengers, the ship depicting the number of crew is about 3 times longer than the ship depicting second-class passengers, but it occupies about 9 times the area. As you can see from the frequency table (Table 3.2), that just isn't a correct impression.

The best data displays observe a fundamental principle of graphing data called the **area principle.** The area principle says that the area occupied by a part of the graph should correspond to the magnitude of the value it represents. Violations of the area principle are a common way to lie (or, since most mistakes are unintentional, we should say err) with Statistics.

Bar Charts

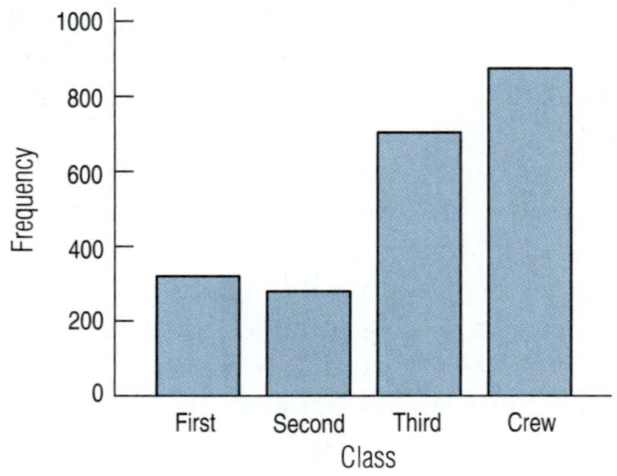

People on the *Titanic* by Ticket Class

With the area principle satisfied, we can see the true distribution more clearly. **Figure 3.3**

Here's a chart that obeys the area principle. It's not as visually entertaining as the ships, but it does give an *accurate* visual impression of the distribution. The height of each bar shows the count for its category. The bars are the same width, so their heights determine their areas, and the areas are proportional to the counts in each class. Now it's easy to see that the majority of people on board were *not* crew, as the ships picture led us to believe. We can also see that there were about 3 times as many crew as second-class passengers. And there were more than twice as many third-class passengers as either first- or second-class passengers, something you may have missed in the frequency table. Bar charts make these kinds of comparisons easy and natural.

A **bar chart** displays the distribution of a categorical variable, showing the counts for each category next to each other for easy comparison. Bar charts have small spaces between the bars to indicate that these are freestanding bars that could be rearranged into any order. The bars are lined up along a common base.

Usually they stick up like this 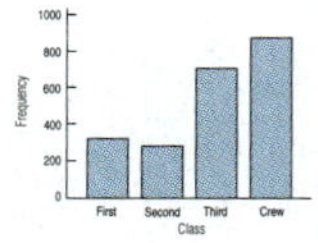, but sometimes they run sideways like this 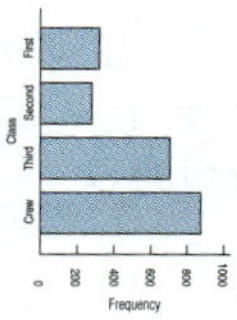.

For some reason, some computer programs give the name "bar chart" to any graph that uses bars. And others use different names according to whether the bars are horizontal or vertical. Don't be misled. "Bar chart" is the term for a *display of counts of a categorical variable* with bars.

Pie Charts

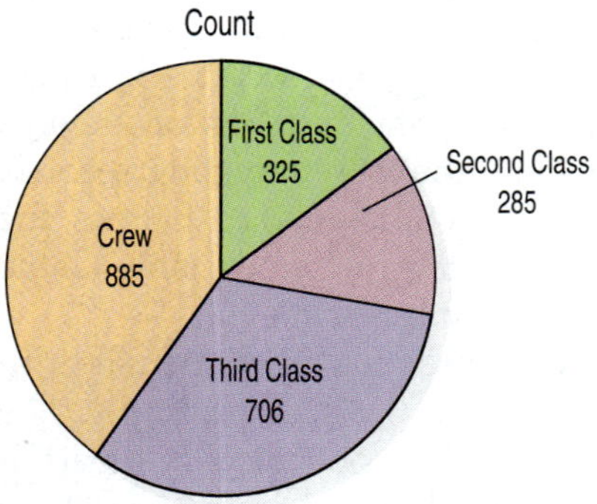

The number of *Titanic* passengers in each class. **Figure 3.4**

If we want to draw attention to the relative *proportion* of passengers falling into each of these classes, we could replace the counts with percentages in a bar chart. A better choice might be a pie chart. **Pie charts** show the whole group of cases as a circle. They slice the circle into pieces whose size is proportional to the fraction of the whole in each category.

Here again it's easy to see that the crew was the largest segment of those aboard. Pie charts give a quick impression of how a whole group is partitioned into smaller groups. Because we're used to cutting up pies into 2, 4, or 8 pieces, pie charts are good for seeing if the relative frequency of a category is near 1/2, 1/4, or 1/8. For example, you may be able to tell that the pink slice, representing the second-class passengers, is very close to 1/8 of the total. It's harder to see that there were about twice as many third-class as first-class passengers. Were there more crew or more third-class passengers? Comparisons such as these are easier in a bar chart.

Children and First-Class Ticket Holders First?

We know how many tickets of each class were sold on the *Titanic,* and we know that only 32% of all those aboard the *Titanic* survived. Was there a relationship between the kind of ticket a passenger held and the passenger's chances of making it into the lifeboat? To answer this question, we need to look at the two categorical variables *Class* and *Survival* together.

Contingency Tables

When we look at two categorical variables together, we often arrange the counts in a two-way table. Because the table shows how the individuals are distributed along each variable, contingent on the value of the other variable, such a table is called a **contingency table.**

Here is a contingency table of those aboard the *Titanic* classified according to class of ticket and whether they survived or didn't:

		Class				
		First	Second	Third	Crew	Total
Survival	Alive	202	118	178	212	710
	Dead	123	167	528	673	1491
	Total	325	285	706	885	2201

Contingency table of ticket *Class* and *Survival.* The bottom line of "Totals" is the same as the previous frequency table.
Table 3.4

The margins of the table, both on the right and at the bottom, give totals. The bottom line of the table is just the frequency distribution of ticket *Class.* A distribution, like this, of one of the variables in a contingency table is called its **marginal distribution.**

The **cells** of the table give the counts or frequencies for every combination of values for the two variables. If you look down the column for second-class passengers to the first cell, you can see that 118 second-class passengers survived. Looking at the third-class passengers, we see that more third-class passengers (178) survived. Those 118 surviving second-class passengers were nearly half of the 285 total in second class. But the 178 third-class survivors were a much smaller fraction of the total of 706 third-class passengers.

It might be more useful to have percentages, but to do that we have to make choices. We know that 118 second-class passengers survived. We could display this number as a percentage, but as a percentage of what? The total number of passengers (118 is 5.4% of the total, 2201)? The number of second-class passengers (118 is 41.4% of the 285 second-class passengers)? The number of survivors (118 is 16.6% of the 710 survivors)? All of these are possibilities, and all are potentially useful or interesting. You'll probably wind up calculating (or letting your technology

A bell-shaped artifact from the *Titanic.*

calculate) lots of percentages. Most statistics programs offer a choice of total percent, row percent, or column percent for contingency tables. Here are the counts and all three percentages displayed as they might be by a computer package:

Survival		Class: First	Second	Third	Crew	Total
Alive	**Count**	**202**	**118**	**178**	**212**	**710**
	% of Row	28.5%	16.6%	25.1%	29.9%	100%
	% of Column	62.2%	41.4%	25.2%	24.0%	32.3%
	% of Table	9.18%	5.36%	8.09%	9.63%	32.3%
Dead	**Count**	**123**	**167**	**528**	**673**	**1491**
	% of Row	8.25%	11.2%	35.4%	45.1%	100%
	% of Column	37.8%	58.6%	74.8%	76.0%	67.7%
	% of Table	5.59%	7.59%	24.0%	30.6%	67.7%
Total	**Count**	**325**	**285**	**706**	**885**	**2201**
	% of Row	14.8%	12.9%	32.1%	40.2%	100%
	% of Column	100%	100%	100%	100%	100%
	% of Table	14.8%	12.9%	32.1%	40.2%	100%

Another contingency table of ticket *Class*. This time we see not only the counts for each combination of *Class* and *Survival* (in bold) but the percentages these counts represent. For each count, there are three choices for the percentage: by row, by column, and by table total. There's probably too much information here for this table to be useful. **Table 3.5**

Each cell of this table gives the count, row percent, column percent, and table percent in that order. This is an example of why contingency tables can look so confusing. There's too much information to sort through at one glance. While it's fine to consider all these choices, it's probably better to look at them one at a time. In this table each row shows what percentage of passengers were in each class.

Survival		Class: First	Second	Third	Crew	Total
Alive	**Count**	**202**	**118**	**178**	**212**	**710**
	% of Row	28.5%	16.6%	25.1%	29.9%	100%
Dead	**Count**	**123**	**167**	**528**	**673**	**1491**
	% of Row	8.25%	11.2%	35.4%	45.1%	100%
Total	**Count**	**325**	**285**	**706**	**885**	**2201**

A contingency table of *Class* by *Survival* with only counts and row percentages. Notice how much easier this table is to read than the previous one. Of course, two other similar tables could be made for column percentages and table percentages. **Table 3.6**

Marginal and Conditional Distributions

Did the chance of surviving the *Titanic* sinking depend on ticket class? Does the distribution of survivors' ticket class look the same as that distribution for nonsurvivors? To answer the question, let's look at the table.

First we restrict our attention only to the survivors. This is like redefining the *Who* of the study. The *Who* we're interested in right now is only the survivors. Their numbers are in the first row of the contingency table. A distribution of one variable for only those individuals satisfying some condition on another variable is called a **conditional distribution.**

	Class				
	First	Second	Third	Crew	Total
Alive	202	118	178	212	710
	28.5%	16.6%	25.1%	29.9%	100%

The *conditional distribution* of ticket *Class*, conditional on having survived. **Table 3.7**

Now we do the same thing for the nonsurvivors. The numbers for the nonsurvivors are found in the following row:

	Class				
	First	Second	Third	Crew	Total
Dead	123	167	528	673	1491
	8.25%	11.2%	35.4%	45.1%	100%

The *conditional distribution* of ticket *Class*, conditional on having perished. **Table 3.8**

Let's compare these conditional distributions. Among survivors 28.5% held a first class ticket compared to only 8.25% among those who died. That looks like a big difference.

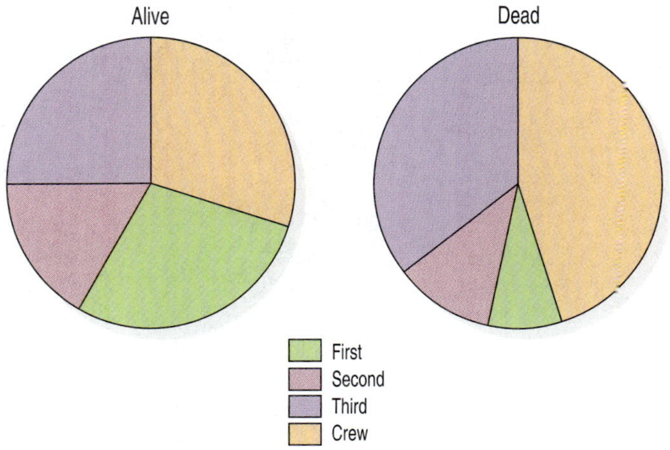

Pie charts of the distribution of *Class* for the survivors and nonsurvivors separately. Do the distributions appear to be the same? We're primarily concerned with percentages here, so pie charts are a good choice. **Figure 3.5**

The nonsurvivors are mostly crew and third-class passengers. The survivors, on the other hand, are more uniformly split up across all four classes. If the percentages of ticket class had been about the same across the two survival groups, we would have said that survival was independent of class. But it's not. The differences we see between the two conditional distributions suggest that survival may have depended on ticket class.

It is interesting to know that *Class* and *Survival* are associated. That's an important part of the *Titanic* story. And we know they're associated because we can see that the distribution of ticket classes differs between survivors and those who died.

Variables can be associated in many ways and to different degrees. The best way to tell whether two variables are associated is to ask whether they are *not*.[1] In a contingency table, when the distribution of *one* variable is the same for all categories of another, we say that the variables are **independent.** We'll see a way to check for independence formally later in the book. For now, we'll just compare the distributions.

Segmented Bar Charts

We could display the same information by dividing up bars rather than circles. The resulting **segmented bar chart** treats each bar as the "whole" and divides it proportionally into segments corresponding to the percentage in each group. We can clearly see that the distributions of ticket classes are different, indicating that survival was not independent of ticket class.

A segmented bar chart for *Class* by *Survival*

Notice that although the totals for survivors and nonsurvivors are quite different, the bars are the same height because we have converted the numbers to *percentages*. Compare this with the side-by-side pie charts of the same data.

Figure 3.6

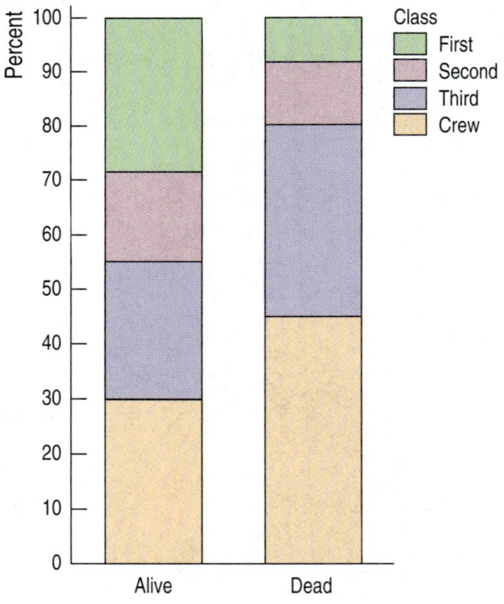

[1]This kind of "backwards" reasoning shows up surprisingly often in science—and in Statistics. We'll see it again.

Examining Contingency Tables STEP-BY-STEP

Medical researchers followed 6272 Swedish men for 30 years to see if there was any association between the amount of fish in their diet and prostate cancer ("Fatty Fish Consumption and Risk of Prostate Cancer," *Lancet*, June 2001). Their results are summarized in this table.

We asked for a picture of a "man eating fish." This is what we got.

Fish Consumption	Prostate Cancer: No	Prostate Cancer: Yes
Never/seldom	110	14
Small part of diet	2420	201
Moderate part	2769	209
Large part	507	42

Table 3.9

Is there an association between fish consumption and prostate cancer?

Think

Variables Identify the variables and report the W's. Be certain that the data are counts and that the categories do not overlap so that no individual is counted twice.

The individuals are 6272 Swedish men followed by medical researchers for 30 years. The variables record their fish consumption and whether or not they were diagnosed with prostate cancer. The data are reported as counts. The categories of diet do not overlap and the diagnoses do not overlap.

Show

Mechanics Make an appropriate display to see whether there is a difference in the relative proportions. Bar charts might have worked equally well.

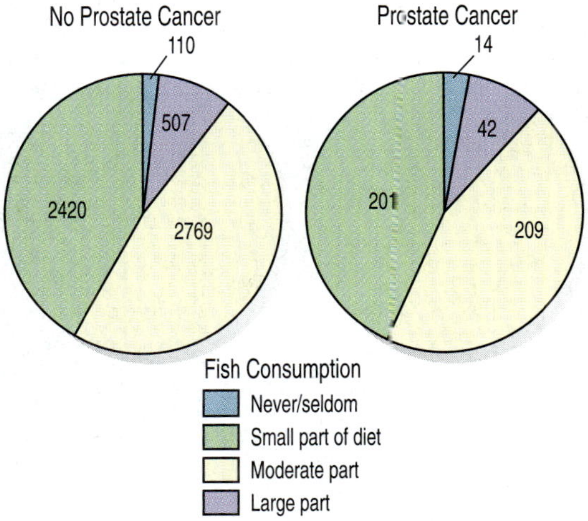

Tell

Interpretation Discuss the patterns in the table and displays.

There appears to be little difference between the two groups in terms of their fish consumption. Fish consumption appears to be independent of the incidence of prostate cancer.

If you can, discuss possible real-world consequences.

We see no reason for men to change their diets in an attempt to reduce their risk of prostate cancer based on this study.

What Can Go Wrong?

- ***Don't violate the area principle.*** This is probably the most common mistake in a graphical display. It is often made in the cause of artistic presentation. Here, for example, is a display of the pie chart of the *Titanic* passengers by class:

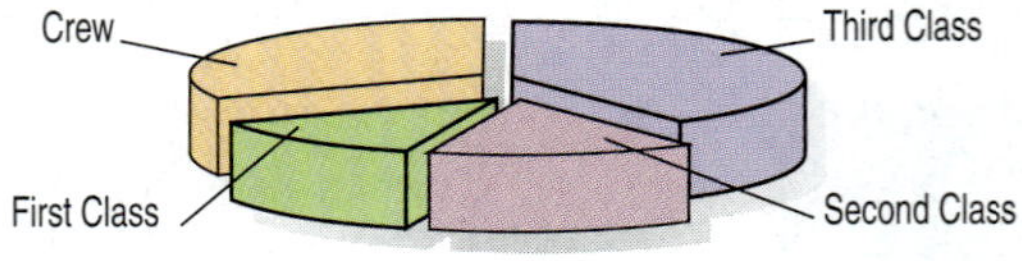

  Looks pretty, doesn't it? But showing the pie on a slant violates the area principle and makes it much more difficult to compare fractions of the whole made up of each class—the principal feature that a pie chart ought to show.

- ***Keep it honest.*** Here's a pie chart that displays data on the percentage of high school students who engage in specified dangerous behaviors as reported by the Centers for Disease Control. What's wrong with this plot?

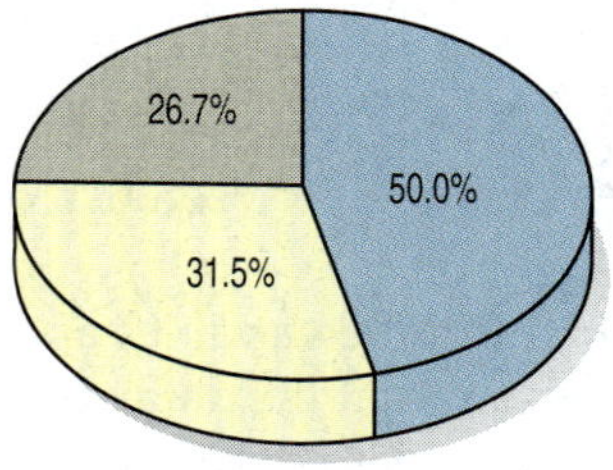

  Try adding up the percentages. Or look at the 50% slice. Does it look right? Then think: What are these percentages of? Is there a "whole" that has been sliced up? In a pie chart, the proportions shown by each slice of the pie must add up to 100% and each individual must fall into only one category. Of course, showing the pie on a slant makes it even harder to detect the error.

  Here's another. This bar chart shows the number of airline passengers searched by security screening.

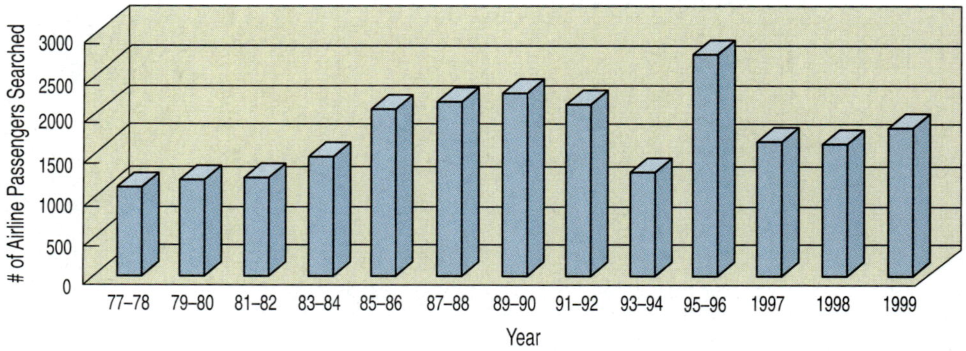

  Looks like things didn't change much in the final years of the 20th century—until you read the bar labels and see that the last three bars represent single years, while all the others are for *pairs* of years. Of course, the false depth makes it harder to see the problem.

- ***Don't confuse similar-sounding percentages.*** These percentages sound similar but are different:
  - The percentage of those who were both in first class and survived: This would be 202/2100, or 9.18%.

Survival	Class: First	Second	Third	Crew	Total
Alive	202	118	178	212	710
Dead	123	167	528	673	1491
Total	325	285	706	885	2201

- The percentage of those who survived among those who were in first class: This is 202/325, or 62.5%.
- The percentage of those who were in first class among those who survived: This is 202/710, or 28.5%.

  In each instance, pay attention to the *Who* implicitly defined by the phrase. Often there is a restriction to a smaller group (all aboard the *Titanic,* those in first class, and those who survived, respectively) before a percentage is found. Your discussion of results must make these differences clear.

- ***Be sure to use enough individuals.*** When you consider percentages, take care that they are based on a large enough number of individuals. Take care not to make a report such as this one:

  We found that 66.67% of the rats improved their performance with training. The other rat died.

- ***Don't overstate your case.*** Independence is an important concept, but it is rare for two variables to be *entirely* independent. We don't know, for example, that fish consumption has no effect whatever on prostate cancer. All we know is that no effect was observed in that study. Other studies of other groups under other circumstances could find different results.

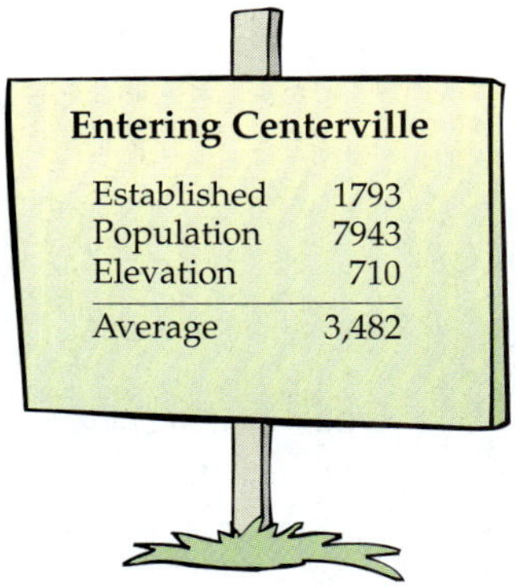

Simpson's Paradox

- ***Don't use unfair or silly averages.*** Sometimes averages can be misleading. Sometimes they just don't make sense at all. Be careful when averaging different variables that the quantities you're averaging are comparable. The Centerville sign says it all.

  When using averages of proportions across several different groups, it's important to make sure that the groups really are comparable.

It's easy to make up an example showing that averaging across very different values or groups can give absurd results. Here's how that might work. Suppose there are two pilots, Moe and Jill. Moe argues that he's the better pilot of the two, since he managed to land 83% of his last 120 flights on time compared with Jill's 78%. But let's look at the data a little more closely. Here are the results for each of their last 120 flights, broken down by the time of day they flew:

Pilot	Time of Day: Day	Night	Overall
Moe	90 out of 100 90%	10 out of 20 50%	100 out of 120 83%
Jill	19 out of 20 95%	75 out of 100 75%	94 out of 120 78%

On-time flights by Time of Day and Pilot. Look at the percentages within each Time of Day category. Who has a better on-time record during the day? At night? Who is better overall? **Table 3.10**

One famous example of Simpson's paradox arose during an investigation of admission rates for men and women at the University of California at Berkeley's graduate schools. As reported in an article in *Science*, about 45% of male applicants were admitted, but only about 30% of female applicants got in. It looked like a clear case of discrimination. However, when the data were broken down by school (Engineering, Law, Medicine, etc.) it turned out that within each school, the women were admitted at nearly the same or, in some cases, much *higher* rates than the men. How could this be? Women applied in large numbers to schools with very low admission rates (Law and Medicine, for example, admitted fewer than 10%). Men tended to apply to Engineering and Science. Those schools have admission rates above 50%. When the *average* was taken, the women had a much lower *overall* rate, but the average didn't really make sense.

Look at the day and nighttime flights separately. For day flights, Jill had a 95% on-time rate, and Moe only a 90% rate. At night, Jill was on time 75% of the time, and Moe only 50%. So Moe is better "overall," but Jill is better both during the day and at night. How can this be?

What's going on here is a problem known as **Simpson's paradox,** named for the statistician who discovered it in the 1960s. It comes up rarely in real life, but there have been several well-publicized cases of it. As we can see from the pilot example, the problem is *unfair averaging* over different groups. Jill has mostly night flights, which are more difficult, so her *overall average* is heavily influenced by her nighttime average. Moe, on the other hand, benefits from flying mostly during the day, with its higher on-time percentage. With their very different patterns of flying conditions, taking an overall average is misleading. It's not a fair comparison.

The moral of Simpson's paradox is to be careful when you average across different levels of a second variable. It's always better to compare percentages or other averages *within* each level of the other variable. The overall average may be misleading.

Displaying Categorical Data with a Computer

Although every package makes a slightly different bar chart, they all have similar features:

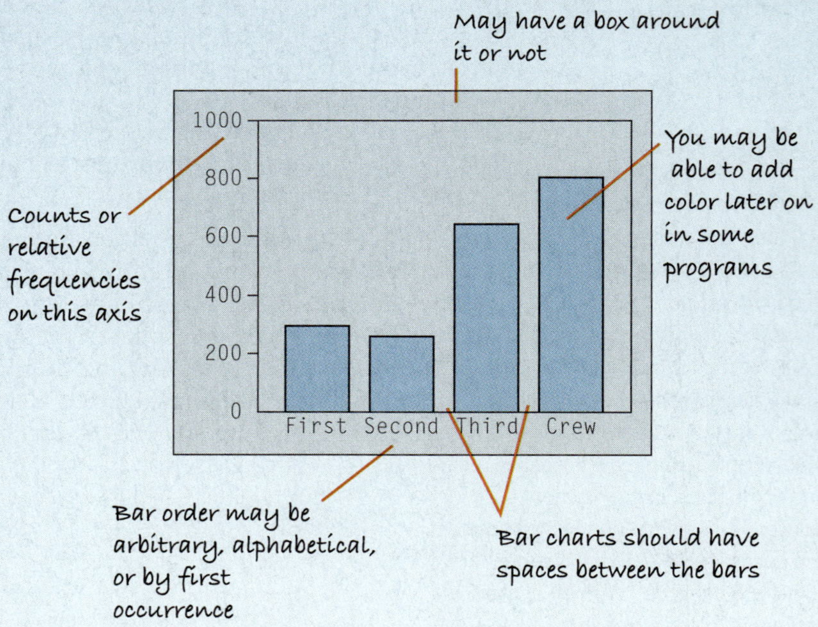

Sometimes the count or a percentage is printed above or on top of each bar to give some additional information. You may find that your statistics package sorts category names in annoying orders by default. For example, many packages sort categories alphabetically or by the order the categories are seen in the data set. Often, neither of these is the best choice.

Connections

All of the methods of this chapter work with *categorical variables.* You must know the *Who* of the data to know who is counted in each bar and the *What* of the variable to know where the categories come from.

Key Concepts

Frequency table A frequency table lists the categories in a categorical variable and gives the counts or percentage of observations of each category.

Distribution The distribution of a variable gives

- the possible values of the variable and
- the relative frequency of each value.

Area principle In a statistical display, each data value should be represented by the same amount of area.

Bar chart Bar charts show a bar representing the count of each category in a categorical variable.

Pie chart Pie charts show how a "whole" divides into categories by showing a wedge of a circle whose area corresponds to the proportion in each category.

Contingency table A contingency table displays counts and, sometimes, percentages of individuals falling into named categories on two or more variables. The table categorizes the individuals on all variables at once, to reveal possible patterns in one variable that may be contingent on the category of the other.

Marginal distribution In a contingency table, the distribution of either variable alone is called the marginal distribution. The counts or percentages are the totals found in the margins (last row or column) of the table.

Conditional distribution The distribution of a variable restricting the *Who* to consider only a smaller group of individuals is called a conditional distribution.

Independence Variables are said to be independent if the conditional distribution of one variable is the same for each category of the other. We'll show how to check for independence in a later chapter.

Simpson's paradox When averages are taken across different groups, they can appear to be contradictory. This is known as Simpson's paradox.

Skills

When you complete this lesson you should:

Think

- Be able to identify that a variable is categorical and choose an appropriate display for it.
- Understand how to examine the association between categorical variables by comparing conditional and marginal percentages.

Show

- Be able to summarize the distribution of a categorical variable with a frequency table.
- Be able to display the distribution of a categorical variable with a bar chart or pie chart.
- Know how to make and examine a contingency table.
- Know how to make and examine displays of the conditional distributions of one variable for two or more groups.

Tell

- Be able to describe the distribution of a categorical variable in terms of its possible values and relative frequencies.
- Know how to describe any anomalies or extraordinary features revealed by the display of a variable.
- Be able to describe and discuss patterns found in a contingency table and associated displays of conditional distributions.

Exercises

1. Graphs in the news. Find a bar graph of categorical data from a newspaper or magazine.
a) Is the graph clearly labeled?
b) Does it violate the area principle?
c) Does the accompanying article tell the W's of the variable?
d) Do you think the article correctly interprets the data? Explain.

2. Graphs in the news II. Find a pie chart of categorical data from a newspaper or magazine.
a) Is the graph clearly labeled?
b) Does it violate the area principle?
c) Does the accompanying article tell the W's of the variable?
d) Do you think the article correctly interprets the data? Explain.

3. Tables in the news. Find a frequency table of categorical data from a newspaper or magazine.
a) Is it clearly labeled?
b) Does it display percentages or counts?
c) Does the accompanying article tell the W's of the variable?
d) Do you think the article correctly interprets the data? Explain.

4. Tables in the news II. Find a contingency table of categorical data from a newspaper or magazine.
a) Is it clearly labeled?
b) Does it display percentages or counts?
c) Does the accompanying article tell the W's of the variables?
d) Do you think the article correctly interprets the data? Explain.

5. Causes of death. The Centers for Disease Control lists causes of death in the United States during 1999.

Cause of death	Percent
Heart disease	30.3
Cancer	23.0
Circulatory diseases and stroke	8.4
Respiratory diseases	7.9
Accidents	4.1

a) Is it reasonable to conclude that heart or respiratory diseases were the cause of approximately 38% of U.S. deaths in 1999?
b) What percent of deaths were from causes not listed here?
c) Create an appropriate display for these data.

6. Education. In a December 2000 report, the U.S. Census Bureau listed the levels of educational attainment for Americans over 65. Create an appropriate display for these data, and write a sentence or two that might appear in a newspaper article about the report.

Education level	Count (thousands)
No high school diploma	9,945
HS graduate, but no college	11,701
Some college, no degree	4,481
2-year degree	1,390
4-year degree	3,133
Master's degree	1,213
Ph.D. or professional degree	757

7. Ghosts. A May 2001 Gallup Poll found that many Americans believe in ghosts and other supernatural phenomena. The poll was based on telephone responses from 1012 randomly selected adults. The table shows the percentages of people who expressed belief in various phenomena.

Phenomenon	Percent expressing belief
Psychic healing	54
ESP	50
Ghosts	38
Astrology	28
Channeling	15

a) Is it reasonable to conclude that 66% of those polled expressed belief in either ghosts or astrology?
b) Can you tell what percent of people did not believe in any of these phenomena? Explain.
c) Create an appropriate display for these data.

8. Illegal guns. A study by the U.S. Bureau of Alcohol, Tobacco, and Firearms (BATF) (*USA Today*, 22 June 2000) surveyed 1530 investigations by the U.S. BATF into illegal gun trafficking from July 1996 through December 1998. The study reports the portion of cases that were the result of each of five gun trafficking violations:

46% Straw purchase (legal gun buyer acting on behalf of an illegal buyer.)

21% Unlicensed sellers

14% Gun shows and flea markets

14% Stolen from federally licensed dealers

10% Stolen from residences

a) State the W's for this study to the extent the story gives them.
b) What do you notice about the percentages listed? What does that probably mean?
c) Make a bar chart to display these results, and label it correctly.
d) Write a brief report on what they say about illegal gun trafficking. Note any possible problems with the data.
e) The study also noted that although corrupt licensed dealers accounted for 133 of the 1,530 investigations, they were linked to 40,365 of the 84,128 firearms involved in those investigations. How does this new information about the *Who* of the study affect your conclusions?

9. Oil spills. To improve the structural design of oil tankers with the objective of reducing the likelihood of an oil spill and decreasing the amount of outflow in the event of a hull puncture, a study (*Marine Technology*, Jan. 1995) reported the spillage amount and cause of puncture for 50 recent major oil spills from tankers and carriers. Here are displays. Write a brief report interpreting what the displays show. Is a pie chart an appropriate display for these data? Why or why not?

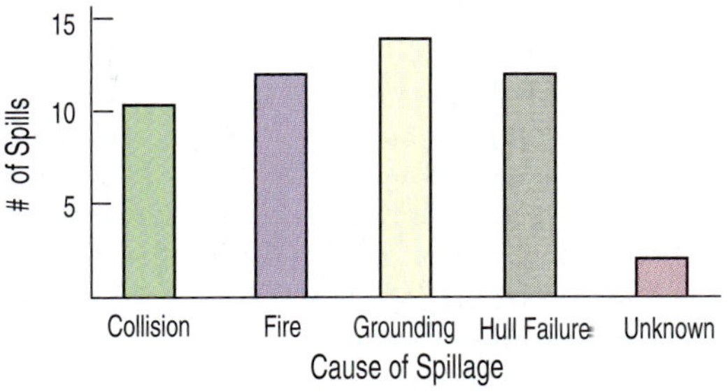

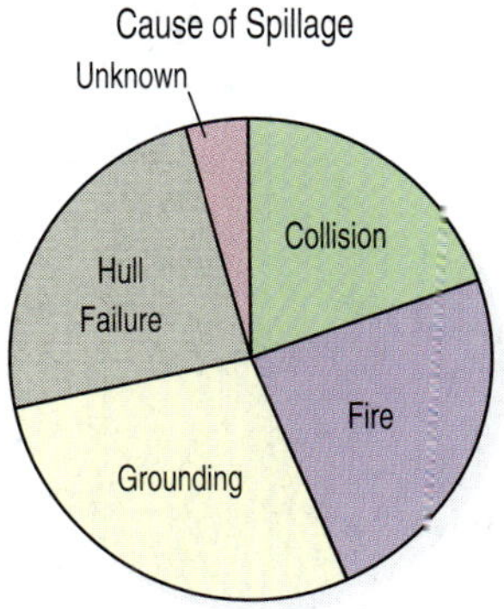

10. Winter Olympics 2002. 25 countries won medals in the 2002 Winter Olympics. The table lists them, along with the total number of medals each won:

Country	Medals	Country	Medals
Germany	35	Croatia	4
USA	34	Korea	4
Norway	24	Bulgaria	3
Canada	17	Estonia	3
Austria	16	Great Britain	3
Russia	16	Australia	2
Italy	12	Czech Republic	2
France	11	Japan	2
Switzerland	11	Poland	2
China	8	Spain	2
Netherlands	8	Belarus	1
Finland	7	Slovenia	1
Sweden	6		

a) Try to make a display of these data. What problems do you encounter?
b) Can you find a way to organize the data so that the graph is more successful?

11. Teens and technology. "The Gallup Organization, in conjunction with CNN, USA Today, and the National Science Foundation, conducted a national survey of 744 children in grades 7 through 12—mostly comprised of students in the 'teenage' years of 13 to 17. Telephone interviews were conducted from March 20–27, 1997 from Gallup interviewing centers throughout the country. The focus of the survey was on students' familiarity with and use of modern technology, with special attention given to use of computers and the Internet." The teenagers were asked if they used each of the following technologies on a daily basis and if the technology was critically important to own. For each question, the percentage of those responding yes is given. Gallup dubbed the difference between the two percentages the "Importance Gap." Here are the results:

Technology	Use daily	Critically important to own	Importance gap
Computer	44%	77%	33
Telephone answering machine	46%	62%	16
VCR	39%	51%	12
Calculator	67%	71%	4
Stereo/CDs/audio	85%	69%	−16
Video games	46%	18%	−28

Consider the following graphical display showing the percentages of teens that use each of the technologies on a daily basis.

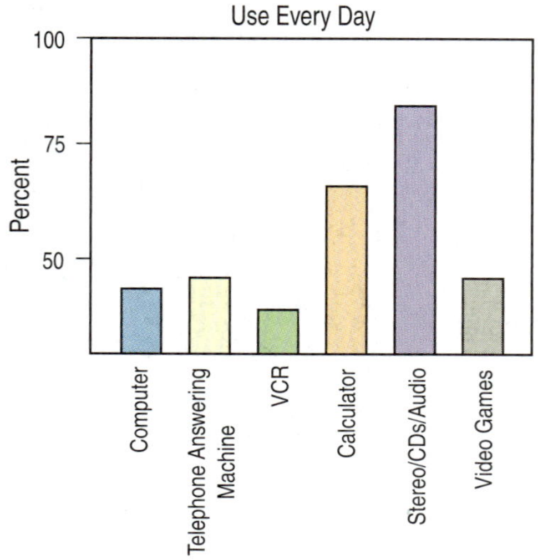

a) How much larger is the proportion of teens who use a calculator daily than the corresponding proportion for answering machines?

b) Is that the impression given by the display? Explain.

c) How would you improve this display?

d) Make an appropriate display for the Importance Gap. (*Hint:* Make the *y*-axis of your chart span the range from −30 to +35.)

e) Write a few sentences describing what you have learned about teens' attitudes toward technology.

12. Teens and technology II. Here's a display of the percentages of students who use the various technologies daily. List the errors in this display.

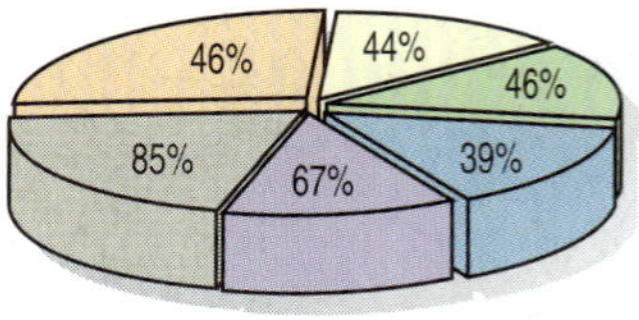

13. Auditing reform. In the wake of the Enron Corporation scandal, the Gallup Organization asked 1001 American adults what kind of changes, if any, are needed in the way major corporations are audited. Here is a display of the results.

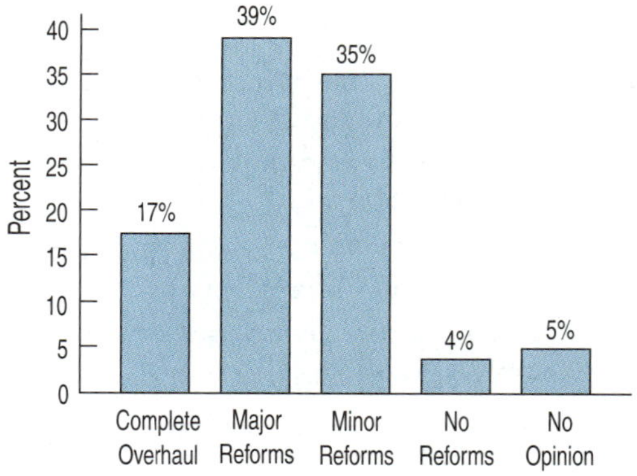

a) Make a pie chart of the same data.

b) Which chart works better to summarize the data? Why?

c) Summarize the findings of the poll in a few sentences that might appear in a newspaper article.

14. Cars. A survey of autos parked in student and staff lots at a large university classified the brands by country of origin, as seen in the table.

Origin	Driver: Student	Driver: Staff
American	107	105
European	33	12
Asian	55	47

a) What percent of all the cars surveyed were foreign?
b) What percent of the American cars were owned by students?
c) What percent of the students owned American cars?
d) What is the marginal distribution of origin?
e) What are the conditional distributions of origin by driver classification?
f) Do you think that origin of the car is independent of the type of driver? Explain.

15. Class of 2000. Prior to graduation a high school class of 2000 was surveyed about their plans. The table below displays the results for white and minority students. (The "Minority" group included African-American, Asian, Hispanic, and Native American students.)

Plans	White	Minority
4-year college	198	44
2-year college	36	6
Military	4	1
Employment	14	3
Other	16	3

a) What percent of the graduates are white?
b) What percent of the graduates are planning to attend a 2-year college?
c) What percent of the graduates are white and planning to attend a 2-year college?
d) What percent of the white graduates are planning to attend a 2-year college?
e) What percent of the graduates planning to attend a 2-year college are white?
f) Create a graph comparing the plans of white and minority students.
g) Do you see any important differences in the post-graduation plans of white and minority students? Write a brief summary of what these data show, including comparisons of conditional distributions.

16. After high school. The table below compares what Ithaca High School students did after graduation in 1959, 1970, and 1980.

What Graduates Did	1959	1970	1980
Continuing education	197	388	320
Employed	103	137	98
In the military	20	18	18
Other	13	58	45

a) What percent of all these graduates joined the military?
b) What percent of these students graduated in 1970?
c) What percent of the 1970 graduates joined the military?
d) Of the students in these surveys who joined the military, what percent graduated in 1970?
e) What is the marginal distribution of postgraduation activities?
f) What is the conditional distribution of postgraduation activities among the class of 1959?
g) Does this study present any evidence that post graduation plans have changed over this 21-year period? Write a brief description of these data. Include an appropriate graph.

17. Canadian languages. Statistics Canada provides, on its Web site, the following data on the Canadian population (in thousands). (Zeros indicate counts below 500.)
a) What percent of Canadian citizens speak only English?
b) What percent of Canadian citizens speak French?
c) What percent of Quebec residents speak French?
d) What percent of French-speaking Canadians live in Quebec?
e) Do you think that language knowledge and province of residence are independent for Canadians? Explain.

Province	English Only	French Only	Both	Neither	Total
Newfoundland	525	0	21	1	**547**
Prince Edward Island	118	0	15	0	**133**
Nova Scotia	813	1	84	1	**900**
New Brunswick	418	73	238	0	**730**
Quebec	359	3,952	2,661	74	**7,045**
Ontario	9,116	47	1,235	245	**10,643**
Manitoba	984	1	103	12	**1,100**
Saskatchewan	921	0	51	5	**977**
Alberta	2,455	2	179	34	**2,669**
British Columbia	3,342	2	249	97	**3,690**
Yukon Territory	27	0	3	0	**31**
Northwest Territories	36	0	3	1	**39**
Nunavut	20	0	1	4	**25**
Total	**19,134**	**4,078**	**4,843**	**474**	**28,529**

18. Tattoos. A study by the University of Texas Southwestern Medical Center examined 626 people to see if there was an increased risk of contracting hepatitis C associated with having a tattoo. If the subject had a tattoo, researchers asked whether it had been done in a commercial tattoo parlor or elsewhere. Write a brief description of the association between tattooing and hepatitis C, including an appropriate graphical display.

	Tattoo done in commercial parlor	Tattoo done elsewhere	No tattoo
Has hepatitis C	17	8	18
No hepatitis C	35	53	495

19. Weather forecasts. Just how accurate are the weather forecasts we hear every day? The table below compares the daily forecast with a city's actual weather for a year.

		Actual Weather	
		Rain	No rain
Forecast	Rain	27	63
	No rain	7	268

a) On what percent of days did it actually rain?
b) On what percent of days was rain predicted?
c) What percent of the time was the forecast correct?
d) Do you see evidence of an association between the type of weather and the ability of forecasters to make an accurate prediction? Write a brief explanation, including an appropriate graph.

20. Federal prisons. The table below shows the number of federal prison inmates serving sentences for various types of offenses in 1990 and 1998. Counts given are in thousands of prisoners.

		Year	
		1990	1998
Type of Offense	Violent (murder, robbery, etc.)	10	13
	Property (burglary, fraud, etc.)	8	9
	Drugs	30	63
	Public order (immigration, weapons, etc.)	9	22
	Other	1	2

a) Write a brief description of these data, in the proper context, highlighting any important changes you see in the prison population.

b) Do these data indicate that there was an increase in drug use in the United States during the 1990's? Explain.

21. Working parents. In July 1991 and again in April 2001 the Gallup Poll asked random samples of 1015 adults about their opinions on working parents. The table summarizes responses to this question:

"Considering the needs of both parents and children, which of the following do you see as the ideal family in today's society?"

Based upon these results, do you think there was a change in people's attitudes during the 10 years between these polls? Explain.

		Year	
		1991	2001
Response	Both work full time	142	131
	One works full time, other part time	274	244
	One works, other works at home	152	173
	One works, other stays home for kids	396	416
	No opinion	51	51

22. Twins. In 2000 the *Journal of the American Medical Association (JAMA)* published a study that examined pregnancies that resulted in the birth of twins. Births were classified as preterm with intervention (induced labor or cesarean), preterm without procedures, or term/post-term. Researchers also classified the pregnancies by the level of prenatal medical care the mother received (inadequate, adequate, or intensive). The data, from the years 1995–97, are summarized in the table below. Figures are in thousands of births. (*JAMA* 284 [2000]:335–341)

TWIN BIRTHS 1995–1997 (IN THOUSANDS)

		Preterm (induced or cesarean)	Preterm (without procedures)	Term or postterm	Total
Level of Prenatal Care	Intensive	18	15	28	61
	Adequate	46	43	65	154
	Inadequate	12	13	38	63
	Total	76	71	131	278

a) What percent of these mothers did not receive adequate medical care during their pregnancies?

b) What percent of all twin births were preterm?
c) Among the mothers who did not receive adequate medical care, what percent of the twin births were preterm?
d) Create an appropriate graph comparing the outcomes of these pregnancies by the level of medical care the mother received.
e) Write a few sentences describing the association between these two variables.

23. Blood pressure. A company held a blood pressure screening clinic for its employees. The results are summarized in the table below by age group and blood pressure level.

Blood Pressure	Under 30	30–49	Over 50
Low	27	37	31
Normal	48	91	93
High	23	51	73

(Columns: Age)

a) Find the marginal distribution of blood pressure level.
b) Find the conditional distribution of blood pressure level within each age group.
c) Compare these distributions with a segmented bar graph.
d) Write a brief description of the association between age and blood pressure among these employees.
e) Does this prove that people's blood pressure increases as they age? Explain.

24. Obesity and exercise. In the year 2000, the Centers for Disease Control (CDC) estimated that 19.8% of Americans over 15 years old were obese. The CDC conducts a survey on obesity and various behaviors. Here is a table on self-reported exercise classified by body mass index (BMI).
a) Are these percentages column percentages, row percentages, or table percentages?

Physical Activity	Body Mass Index: Normal (%)	Overweight (%)	Obese (%)
Inactive	23.8	26.0	35.6
Irregularly active	27.8	28.7	28.1
Regular, not intense	31.6	31.1	27.2
Regular, intense	16.8	14.2	9.1

b) Use graphical displays to show different percentages of physical activities for the three BMI groups.
c) Do these data prove that lack of exercise causes obesity? Explain.

25. Family planning. A 1954 study of 1438 pregnant women examined the association between the woman's education level and the occurrence of unplanned pregnancies, producing these data:

	Education Level: <3 yr HS	3+ yr HS	Some college
Number of Pregnancies	591	608	239
% Unplanned	66.2%	55.4%	42.7%

Does this indicate that more schooling taught young women better family planning? What other explanations for these data can you think of? (*Fertility Planning and Fertility Rates by Socio-Economic Status,* Social and Psychological Factors Affecting Fertility, 1954)

26. Pet ownership. The U.S. Census Bureau reports the number of households owning various types of pets. Specifically, they keep track of dogs, cats, birds, and horses.

Income Distribution of Households Owning Pets (Percent)

Income	Pet: Dog	Cat	Bird	Horse
Under $12,500	14	15	16	9
$12,500 to $24,999	20	20	21	21
$25,000 to $39,999	24	23	24	25
$40,000 to $59,999	22	22	21	22
$60,000 and over	20	20	18	23
Total	100	100	100	100

a) Do you think the income distributions of the households who own these different animals would be roughly the same? Why or why not?
b) The table shows the percentages of income levels for each type of animal owned. Are these row percentages, column percentages, or table percentages?
c) Do the data support your initial guess? Explain.

Regional Toy Sales by Channel of Distribution 1999

	Type of Outlet							
	Toy chains	General merchandise (including hypers and discounters)	Toy, hobby, and game retailers	Department stores	Food, drug, and misc. outlets	Catalog sales	E-Tailers	Total
World (Total)	17773.75	24883.25	10109.50	5987.60	12086.15	2843.80	710.95	**74395.00**
North America	6571.11	12516.40	1251.64	938.73	7822.75	1877.46	312.91	**31291.00**
Europe*	5105.40	5105.40	2552.70	2042.16	1701.80	510.54	0.00	**17018.00**
Asia	4294.75	4122.96	4981.91	2233.27	1546.11	0.00	0.00	**17179.00**
Latin and South America	440.80	1129.55	523.45	440.80	220.40	0.00	0.00	**2755.00**
Oceania	218.55	728.50	291.40	87.42	101.99	29.14	0.00	**1457.00**
Other	1143.14	1280.44	508.40	245.22	693.10	426.66	398.04	**4695.00**

27. Worldwide toy sales. Around the world, toys are sold through different channels. For example, in some parts of the world toys are sold primarily through large toy store chains, while in other countries, department stores sell more toys. The table at the top of the page shows the percentages by region of the distribution of toys sold through various channels in 1999.

a) What percent of all toys sold through department stores are sold in Europe?

b) What percent of all toys worldwide are sold through catalogs?

c) Compare the distribution of channels for Europe to North America.

d) Summarize the distribution of toy sales by channel in a few sentences.

28. Drivers' licenses. The following table shows the number of licensed U.S. drivers by age and by gender.

Age	Male drivers (number)	Female drivers (number)	Totals
19 and under	5,029,498	4,714,021	9,743,519
20–24	8,158,599	7,807,078	15,965,677
25–29	8,988,142	8,597,716	17,585,858
30–34	9,767,476	9,387,297	19,154,773
35–39	10,621,910	10,437,549	21,059,459
40–44	10,576,976	10,516,251	21,093,227
45–49	9,578,268	9,575,363	19,153,631
50–54	8,448,424	8,419,527	16,867,951
55–59	6,394,207	6,366,285	12,760,492
60–64	4,970,258	4,944,370	9,914,628
65–69	4,182,933	4,202,950	8,385,883
70–74	3,644,990	3,822,570	7,467,560
75–79	2,820,136	3,091,013	5,911,149
80–84	1,656,789	1,854,278	3,511,067
85 and over	957,463	1,092,687	2,050,150
Total	95,796,069	94,828,955	190,625,024

a) What percent of total drivers are under 20?

b) What percent of total drivers are male?

c) Write a few sentences comparing the number of male and female licensed drivers in each age group.

d) Do a driver's age and gender appear to be independent? Explain?

29. Hospitals. Most patients who undergo surgery make routine recoveries and are discharged as planned. Others suffer excessive bleeding, infection, or other postsurgical complications and have their discharges from the hospital delayed. Suppose your city has a large hospital and a small hospital, each performing major and minor surgeries. You collect data to see how many surgical patients have their discharges delayed by postsurgical complications, and find the results shown in the following table.

		Discharge Delayed	
		Large hospital	Small hospital
Procedure	Major surgery	120 of 800	10 of 50
	Minor surgery	10 of 200	20 of 250

a) Overall, for what percent of patients was discharge delayed?

b) Were the percentages different for major and minor surgery?

c) Overall, what were the discharge delay rates at each hospital?

d) What were the delay rates at each hospital for each kind of surgery?

e) The small hospital advertises that it has a lower rate of postsurgical complications. Do you agree?

f) Explain, in your own words, why this confusion occurs.

30. Delivery service. A company must decide which of two delivery services they will contract with. During a recent trial period they shipped numerous packages with each service, and have kept track of how often deliveries did not arrive on time. Here are the data:

Delivery service	Type of service	Number of deliveries	Number of late packages
Pack Rats	Regular	400	12
	Overnight	100	16
Boxes R Us	Regular	100	2
	Overnight	400	28

a) Compare the two services' overall percentage of late deliveries.
b) Based on the results in part a the company has decided to hire Pack Rats. Do you agree they deliver on time more often? Why or why not? Be specific.
c) The results here are an instance of what phenomenon?

31. Graduate admissions. A 1975 article in the magazine *Science* examined the graduate admissions process at Berkeley for evidence of gender bias. The table below shows the number of applicants accepted to each of four graduate programs.

Program	Males accepted (of applicants)	Females accepted (of applicants)
1	511 of 825	89 of 108
2	352 of 560	17 of 25
3	137 of 407	132 of 375
4	22 of 373	24 of 341
Total	1022 of 2165	262 of 849

a) What percent of total applicants were admitted?
b) Overall, were a higher percentage of males or females admitted?
c) Compare the percentage of males and females admitted in each program.
d) Which of the comparisons you made do you consider to be the most valid? Why?

Chapter 4

Displaying Quantitative Data

WHO	Months
WHAT	Changes in Enron's stock price in dollars
HOW	Difference of closing price on first day of each month minus the first day of previous month
WHEN	1997 to 2002
WHERE	New York Stock Exchange

Enron corporation was once one of the world's biggest corporations. From its humble beginnings as an interstate natural gas supply company in 1985, it grew steadily throughout the 1990s, diversifying into nearly every form of energy transaction and eventually dominating the energy trading business.

Its stock price followed this spectacular growth. In 1985 Enron stock sold for about $5 a share, but at the end of 2000, Enron stock closed at a 52-week high of $89.75 and the company's stock was worth more than $6 billion. Less than a year later it hit a low of $0.25 a share, having lost more than 99% of its value. Many employees who had taken advantage of generous stock plans lost retirement packages worth hundreds of thousands of dollars. Just how volatile was Enron stock? And were there hints of trouble that might have been seen?

Rather than look at the stock prices themselves, let's look at how much they changed from month to month. For example, on February 3 (the first trading day of the month) of 1997, Enron stock sold for $0.75 less than it had on January 2 (the first trading day of that month). Table 4.1 gives the monthly changes in stock price (in dollars) for the 5 years leading up to the company's failure.

	Jan.	Feb.	Mar.	Apr.	May	June	July	Aug.	Sept.	Oct.	Nov.	Dec.
1997	−$1.44	−0.75	−0.69	−0.88	0.12	0.75	0.81	−1.75	0.69	−0.22	−0.16	0.34
1998	0.78	0.62	2.44	−0.28	2.22	−0.50	2.06	−0.88	−4.50	4.12	1.16	−0.50
1999	3.28	3.34	−1.22	0.47	5.62	−1.59	4.31	1.47	−0.72	−0.38	−3.25	0.03
2000	5.72	21.06	4.50	4.56	−1.25	−1.19	−3.12	8.00	9.31	1.12	−3.19	−17.75
2001	14.38	−1.08	−10.11	−12.11	5.84	−9.37	−4.74	−2.69	−10.61	−5.85	−17.16	−11.59

Monthly stock price change in dollars of Enron stock for the period January 1997 to December 2001. **Table 4.1**

It's hard to tell very much from the data. Don't try too hard. Tables with lots of numbers are hard to understand by just reading them. You might get a rough idea of how much the stock changed from month to month, but even that would be approximate. "Looks like it's usually less than 10 dollars in either direction," you might say.

Instead, let's follow the first rule of data analysis and make a picture. What kind of picture should we make? It can't be a bar chart or a pie chart. Those are for categorical variables and the values here are in dollars. Price change is a *quantitative* variable, not a categorical one.

The Distribution of Price Changes

How can we display a quantitative variable? With a categorical variable life was easy. There were just a few values, and we could make one pile for each. Usually, though, we can't list all the individual values in a quantitative variable; there are just too many of them. So instead, we slice up the entire span of values covered by the quantitative variable into equal-width piles called **bins.** (For the Enron price changes we might try bins from −\$15 to −\$10, −\$10 to −\$5, −\$5 to \$0, and so on.) Then we count the number of values that fall into each bin. The bins and the counts in each bin give the **distribution** of the quantitative variable.

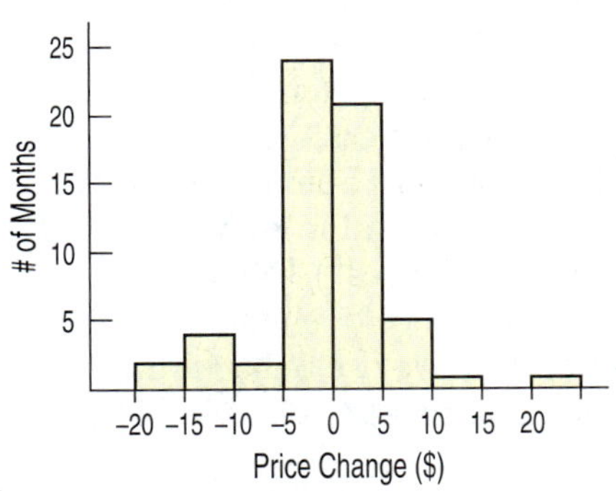

Monthly price changes of Enron stock.

Figure 4.1

> Some computer programs make a display they call a "histogram" with bars that have spaces between them. Because the bars represent bins that slice up the range of values so that every value is in a bin, spaces between them are not appropriate; they suggest that some values might "slip through the cracks." If you see an empty space in a histogram, it is a real "gap" where there are no data values.

We can display the bin counts in a display called a histogram. Like a bar chart, a **histogram** plots the bin counts as the heights of bars. For the Enron data, the cases are months, so the height of each bar is proportional to the number of months that have price changes falling into that bin. (We usually put values that fall exactly on a bin boundary in the bin to the right.)

Does the distribution of price change look as you expected? It's often a good idea to *imagine* what the distribution might look like before you ask a computer or calculator to make a picture for you. That way you'll be ready if the picture shows something unexpected, and less likely to let bad data or wrong data fool you.

The first bar, which counts changes from −\$20 to −\$15, has only two months in it. We can see that although they vary, most of the monthly price changes are less than \$5 in either direction. Only in a very few months were the changes larger than \$10 in either direction. There appear to be about as many positive as negative price changes.

A bar chart has spaces between the bars because the categories could appear in any order. But in a histogram, there are no gaps because the bins slice up *all the values* of a quantitative variable. Both kinds of display satisfy the area principle because the area covered by each bar corresponds to the count of the cases falling in the range covered by that bar. A **relative frequency histogram** is faithful to the area principle by displaying the *percentage* of cases in each bin instead of the count.

Stem-and-Leaf Displays

Stem-and-leaf displays show the distribution as well, and also give the individual values. They are easy to make by hand for data sets that aren't too large so let's look at just the first 3 years of price change data. Here are a histogram and stem-and-leaf display of those 36 values.

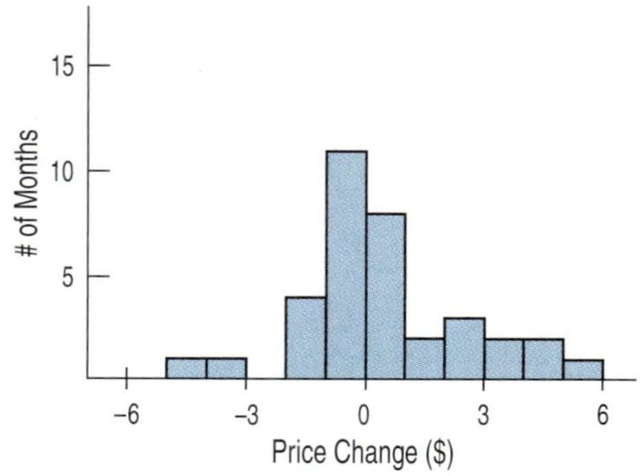

The first 36 months of Enron monthly stock price changes. **Figure 4.2**

-4	5
-3	2
-2	
-1	7642
-0	99777554322
0	13567888
1	25
2	124
3	33
4	13
5	6

Stem-and-leaf displays are best made by hand, so we are most likely to use them for small data sets. This much data is a typical number of data values for a stem-and-leaf display. For much larger data sets, use a histogram. **Figure 4.3**

The stem-and-leaf display is due to John W. Tukey, one of the greatest statisticians of the 20th century. It is called a "stemplot" in some texts and computer programs, but we prefer Tukey's original name for it. After all, he invented it, and an inventor has the right to name his own invention.

Turn the stem-and-leaf on its side (or turn your head to the right) and squint at it. It should look roughly like the histogram of the same data. Does it? Good. It's easy to see, for example, that the distribution has two separate groups of values.

What does the line that says **2 | 124** near the bottom of the display mean? It stands for the three numbers $2.1, $2.2, and $2.4. The histogram shows these same values as a bar of height 3 between $2 and $3. The stem-and-leaf uses the actual digits of the number to form the "bar." We can also easily see that the largest price change is $5.6—something we couldn't tell precisely from the histogram.

To make a stem-and-leaf display, we cut each data value into leading digits (which become the "stems") and trailing digits (the "leaves"). We use the stems to label the *bins*. For the Enron stock prices, the best choice of stem is the first digit (the $1 units). So $5.6 has a stem of 5 and a leaf of 6. We use only *one* digit for the leaf, so we round the data values to one decimal place after the stem before splitting them into stem and leaves.[1]

4	
5	
6	

Does a stem-and-leaf display satisfy the area principle? It does as long as each digit takes up the same amount of space. When doing this by hand, be careful to write a "1" and a "3" to take up the *same amount* of horizontal space. That way, each bar's length will be proportional to the number of observations that fall into its bin.

4	
5	2
6	

There are both positive and negative values in the price changes. Values of $0.3 and $0.5 are displayed as leaves of "**3**" and "**5**" on the "**0**" stem. But values of −$0.3 and −$0.5 must be plotted *below* zero. So the stem-and-leaf has a "**−0**" stem to hold them—again with leaves of "**3**" and "**5**." It may seem strange to see two zero stems, one labeled "**−0.**" If you think about it, though, you'll see that it is the sensible way to deal with negative values.

4	5
5	256
6	4

Stem-and-leaf displays contain all the information found in a histogram and, when carefully drawn, satisfy the area principle and show the distribution. In addition, stem-and-leaf displays preserve the individual data values. Few data displays can do this as effectively.

Unlike most other displays discussed in this book, stem-and-leaf displays are great pencil-and-paper constructions. They are well suited to moderate amounts of data—say, between 10 and a few hundred values. For larger data sets, histograms do a better job.

[1] It's equally good, and perhaps a bit easier, to truncate, just using the next digit regardless of the third digit. The shape of the stem-and-leaf display will not change and you'll still be able to identify any individual data value easily.

Dotplots

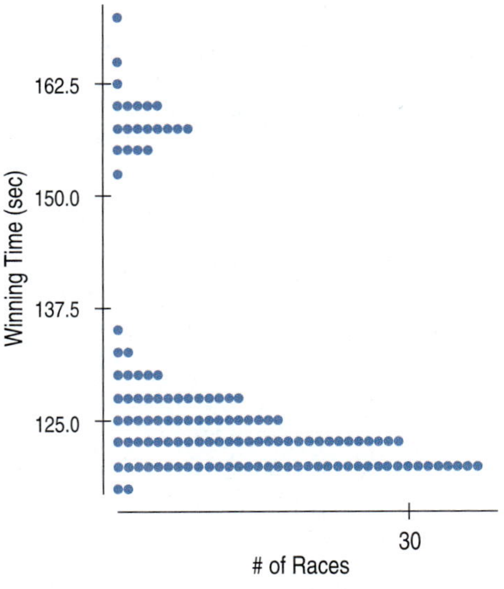

A dotplot of Kentucky Derby winning times shows the bimodal distribution but plots each race as its own dot. **Figure 4.4**

A **dotplot** is a simple display. It just places a dot for each case in the data. Dotplots are a great way to display a small data set (especially if you forget how to write the digits from 0 to 9). Here's a dotplot of the time (in seconds) that the winning horse took to win the Kentucky Derby in each race between the first Derby in 1875 and the 2001 Derby.

Dotplots show basic facts about the distribution. We can easily see the slowest and quickest races. It's also clear that there are two clusters of points, one at about 160 seconds and the other at about 126 seconds. Something strange happened to the Derby times. Once we know to look for it, we can find out that in 1896 the distance of the Derby race was changed from 1.5 miles to the current 1.25 miles. That explains the two clusters of winning times.

Some dotplots stretch out side-to-side. Others, such as the one shown here, run up-and-down. Some dotplots place points next to each other when they would otherwise overlap. Others just place them on top of one another. Newspapers sometimes offer dotplots with the dots made up of little pictures.

Shape, Center, and Spread

> The **mode** is sometimes defined as the single value that appears most often. That definition is fine for categorical variables because we need only to count the number of cases for each category. For quantitative variables, the mode is more ambiguous. What's the mode of the Enron data? No price change occurred more than twice, but two months had drops of $0.50. Should that be the mode? Probably not. It makes more sense to use the word "mode" in the more general sense of peak in a histogram, rather than as a single summary value.

Step back from a histogram or stem-and-leaf display. What can you say about the distribution? When you describe a distribution, you should always tell about three things: its **shape, center,** and **spread.**

What Is the Shape of the Distribution?

1. *Does the histogram have a single, central hump or several separated bumps?* These humps are called **modes.**[2] The Enron stock price changes have a single mode at just about $0. A histogram with one main peak, such as the price changes, is dubbed **unimodal;** histograms with two peaks are **bimodal,** and those with three or more are called **multimodal.** For example, here's a bimodal histogram.

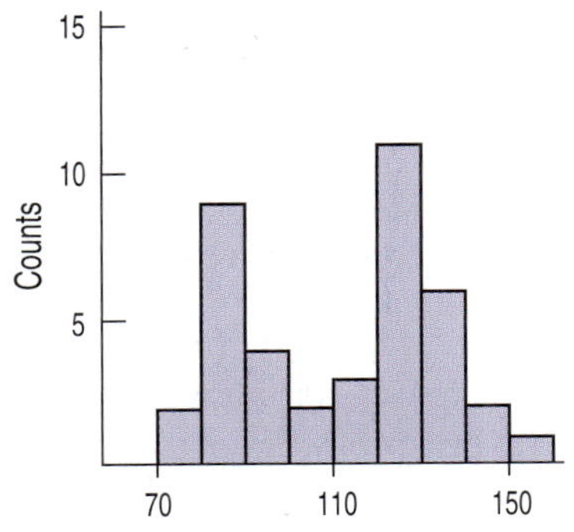

A bimodal histogram has two apparent peaks. **Figure 4.5**

[2]Well, technically, it's the value on the horizontal axis of the histogram that is the mode, but anyone asked to point to the mode would point to the hump.

You've heard of pie à la mode. Is there a connection between pie and the mode of a distribution? Actually, there is! The mode of a distribution is a *popular* value near which a lot of the data values gather. And à la mode means "in style"—*not* with ice cream. That just happened to be a *popular* way to have pie in Paris around 1900.

A histogram that doesn't appear to have any mode and in which all the bars are approximately the same height is called **uniform.**

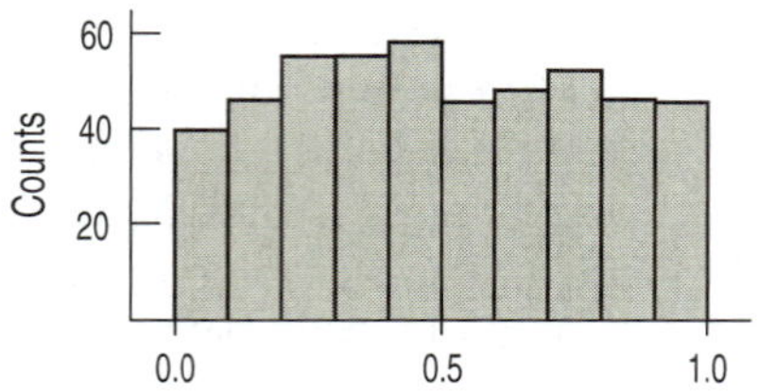

In a uniform histogram, the bars are all about the same height. The histogram doesn't appear to have a mode. **Figure 4.6**

2. *Is the histogram* ***symmetric?*** Can you fold it along a vertical line through the middle and have the edges match pretty closely, or are more of the values on one side?

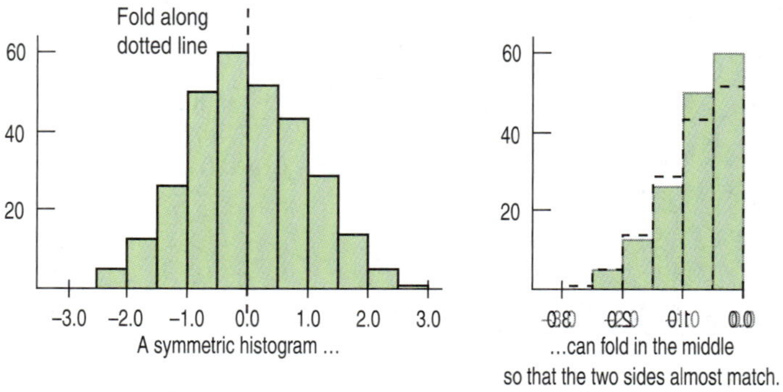

A symmetric histogram can fold in the middle so that the two sides almost match. **Figure 4.7**

The (usually) thinner ends of a distribution are called the **tails.** If one tail stretches out farther than the other, the histogram is said to be **skewed** to the side of the longer tail.

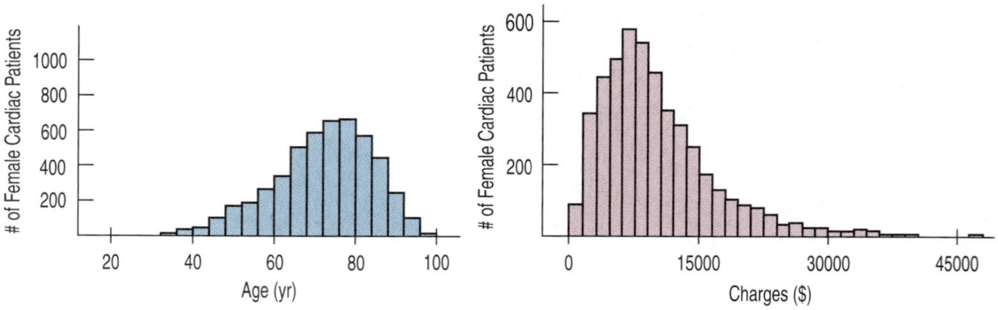

Two skewed histograms showing data for all female heart attack patients in New York state in one year. The blue one is skewed to the left. The purple one is skewed to the right. **Figure 4.8**

3. *Do any unusual features stick out?* Often such features tell us something interesting or exciting about the data. You should always mention any stragglers, or **outliers,** that stand off away from the body of the distribution. If you're collecting data on nose lengths and Pinocchio is in the group, you'd probably notice him, and you'd certainly want to mention it.

Outliers can affect almost every method we discuss in this course. So we'll always be on the lookout for them. An outlier can be the most informative

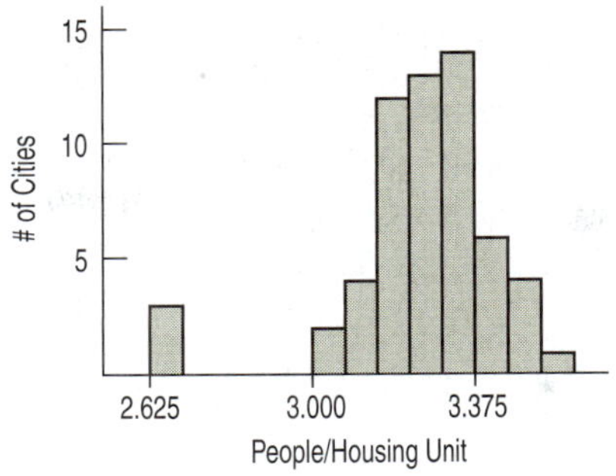

A histogram with outliers. There are three cities in the leftmost bar.
Figure 4.9

part of your data. (Or it might just be an error.) But don't throw it away without comment. Treat it specially and discuss it when you tell about your data. (Or find the error and fix it if you can.)

Are there any **gaps** in the distribution? The Kentucky Derby data that we saw in the dotplot on page 39 has a large gap between two groups, one near 120 seconds and one near 160. Gaps warn us that the data may not be homogeneous. They may come from different sources or contain more than one group.

How you characterize a distribution is often a judgment call. Some may see outliers where others just see a long tail on one side. Generally, we look at the main body of the data. If it seems roughly symmetric, then stragglers are best regarded as outliers. If the main part of the data is skewed, then the long tail that continues that skewness is part of the overall pattern and probably not full of outliers. Be sure to look for outliers. Always. The next chapter discusses a good rule of thumb for deciding when a point might be considered an outlier.

Where Is the Center of the Distribution?

If you had to pick a single number to describe all the data, what would you pick? The center is an easy description of a typical value and a concise summary of the whole batch of numbers. When a histogram is unimodal and symmetric, it's easy to find its center. It's right in the middle. (Where else would you look?) The center of the Enron price changes is about $0. That tells us that over the period we've examined, the stock went down about as often as it went up.

For distributions with other shapes, the situation isn't as clear. If the histogram is skewed, defining the center is more of a challenge. And if the histogram has more than one mode, the center might not even be a useful concept. You might be looking at two different groups thrown together, so it's probably a good idea to find out why you don't have a single mode.

The next chapter discusses some ways to locate centers numerically. For now we'll just eyeball a picture of the distribution and give a rough idea of where the center seems to be.

Why do banks favor a single line that feeds several teller windows rather than separate lines for each teller? The average waiting time is the same. But the time you can expect to wait is less variable when there is a single line, and people prefer consistency.

How Spread Out Is the Distribution?

The center gives a typical value, but not everyone is typical. Variation matters. Statistics is about variation, but how can we see it? We can look to see whether all the values of the distribution are tightly clustered around the center or spread out. Because distributions that vary a lot around the center are harder to predict or model, we often prefer distributions with less variability. Would you rather invest in a stock whose price gyrates wildly or one that grows steadily?

You're not finished describing a distribution until you discuss its spread.

Displaying Quantitative Data STEP-BY-STEP

WHO	CEOs
WHAT	Annual base salary in dollars
HOW	Survey from *Forbes* magazine
WHEN	1994
WHERE	United States
WHY	Inspiration?

With the current state of the economy,[3] more attention has been paid to the compensation of Chief Executive Officers (CEOs) of major companies. Let's look at the CEO salaries of the 800 largest corporations in 1994.

Think

Variable Identify the *variable* and how you wish to display it.

To identify a variable, report the W's.

Select an appropriate display based on the nature of the data and what you want to know about it.

We examine the base salaries of the CEOs of the 800 largest corporations in 1994, reported (in dollars) by *Forbes* magazine.

The data are quantitative and we are interested in how they are distributed, so we will make a histogram.

Show

Mechanics We almost always make histograms with a computer or graphing calculator.

Reality Check It is always a good idea to think about what we expected to see and to check whether the histogram is close to what we expected. Could CEOs really earn this much? Yes, six- to seven-figure salaries are about what we might expect.

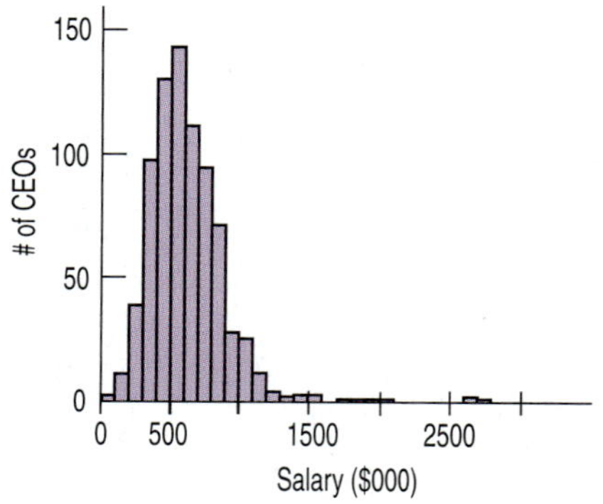

Tell

Interpretation Describe the shape, center, and spread of the distribution. Be sure to report on the symmetry, number of modes, and any gaps or outliers.

The main body of the distribution is unimodal and nearly symmetric,[4] centered around $500,000, with slightly more than half of CEOs earning salaries higher than that. But there are some high outliers. Some CEOs' salaries are higher than what is typical for most CEOs of large corporations. Even though the vast majority of CEOs have salaries below $1,000,000 a year, there are a few with salaries between $2,500,000 and $3,000,000 a year.

[3] In fact, we don't know what state the economy is in as you read this, but it really doesn't matter. People still want to know how much CEOs make and will use the economy as an excuse.

[4] Do you think it's skewed? Well, maybe. Here, if we cut off the tail, what's left behind is pretty symmetric. There is often more than one right answer. Just be prepared to defend your choice.

TI Tips

Your calculator can create histograms. First you need some data. Remember the Enron stock price changes at the start of the chapter? Relax—you don't have to type in all of those values to see how it works. We'll just use the Enron data for 1997 and 1998. Enter the 24 monthly values from these two rows of data into `L1`:

1997	−1.44	−0.75	−0.69	−0.88	0.12	0.75	0.81	−1.75	0.69	−0.22	−0.16	0.34
1998	0.78	0.62	2.44	−0.28	2.22	−0.50	2.06	−0.88	−4.50	4.12	1.16	−0.50

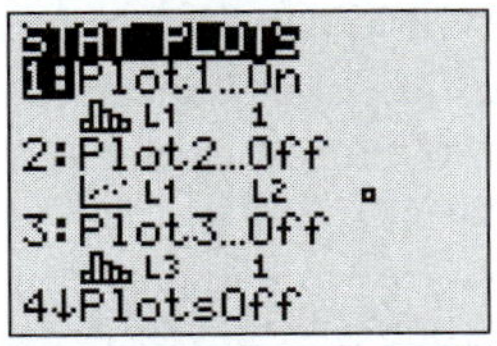

Now set up the calculator's plot:

- Go to `2nd STATPLOT`, choose `Plot1`, then `ENTER`.
- In the `Plot1` screen choose `On`, select the little histogram icon, then specify `Xlist:L1` and `Freq:1`.
- Be sure to turn off any other graphs the calculator may be set up for. Just hit the `Y=` button and deactivate any functions seen there.

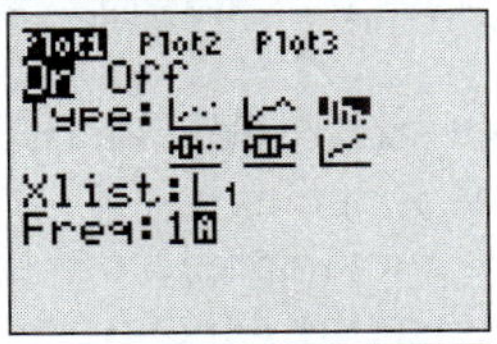

All set? To create your preliminary plot go to `ZOOM`, select `9:ZoomStat`, and then `ENTER`.

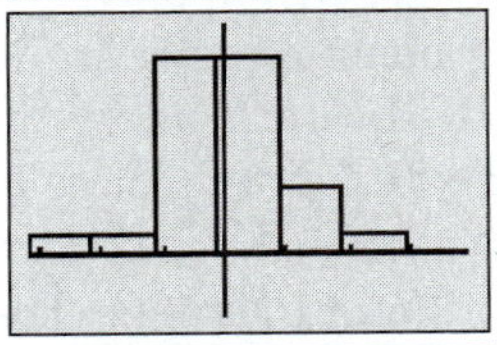

You now see the calculator's initial attempt to create a histogram of these data. Not bad. We can see that the distribution is roughly symmetric. But it's hard to tell exactly what this histogram shows, right? Let's fix it up a bit.

- Under `WINDOW`, let's reset the bins to convenient, sensible values. Try `Xmin=-6`, `Xmax=6`, and `Xscl=1`. That specifies the range of values along the *x*-axis, and makes each bar span one dollar.
- Hit `GRAPH` (*not* `ZoomStat`—this time we want control of the scale!).

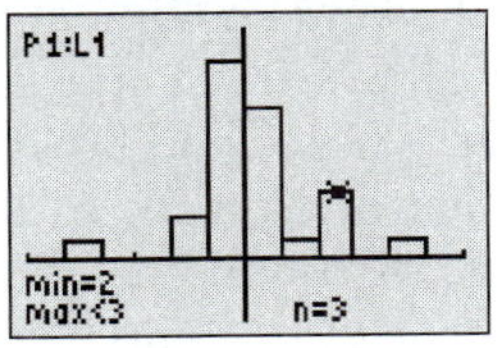

Look better? Note that you can now find out exactly what the bars indicate by activating `TRACE` and then moving across the histogram using the arrow keys. For each bar the calculator will indicate the range of values and the number of data values in that range. We see that the stock price increased between $2 and $3 during three of the months.

Play around with the `WINDOW` settings. A different `Ymax` will make the bars appear shorter or taller. What happens if you set the bar width (`Xscl`) smaller? Or larger? You don't want to lump lots of values into just a few bins, or make so many bins that the overall shape of the histogram is not clear. Choosing the best bar width takes practice.

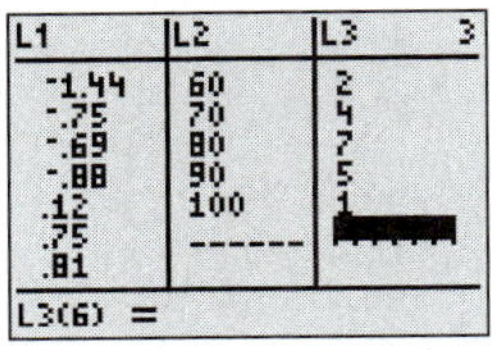

Finally, suppose the data are given as a frequency table. Consider a set of test scores, with two grades in the 60s, four in the 70s, seven in the 80s, five in the 90s, and one 100. Enter the group cutoffs 60, 70, 80, 90, 100 in `L2` and the corresponding frequencies 2, 4, 7, 5, 1 in `L3`. When you set up the histogram `STATPLOT`, specify `Xlist:L2` and `Freq:L3`. Can you specify the `WINDOW` settings to make this histogram look the way you want it? (By the way, if you get a `DIM MISMATCH` error, it means you can't count. Look at `L2` and `L3`; you'll see the two lists don't have the same number of entries. Fix the problem by correcting the data you entered.)

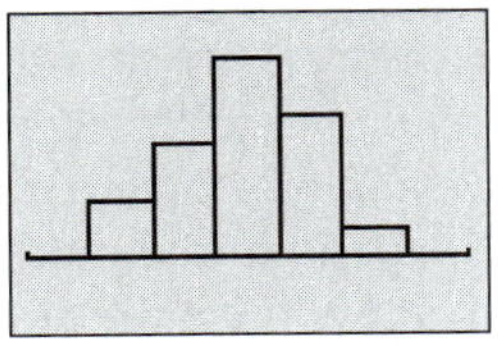

Comparing Distributions

Up to now, we've looked at one distribution at a time. But this route can take us only so far. While it may be interesting to know the distribution of CEO salaries, it might be more interesting to know how salaries in high-tech industries compare with those in manufacturing. The fact is that most interesting results about data involve making comparisons or modeling relationships.

Many common diseases show different patterns in women and men. In the past couple of decades, researchers have been more careful to collect data on women. What kinds of questions might we ask about these data? Here's one: Do men and women tend to get heart attacks at different ages? That's the kind of question that's well suited to investigating with a graph. Here are two histograms of the ages of every heart attack patient hospitalized during 1993 in New York State, one for women and one for men.

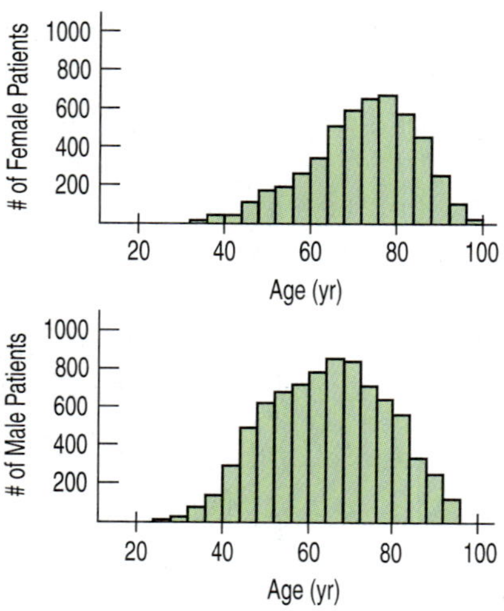

The distributions of ages for female and male heart attack patients differ in interesting ways. **Figure 4.10**

What can we tell from these histograms? We'll start, as usual, by looking at shape, center, and spread, but we'll reverse the order.

Notice first that the age distribution for men is more spread out than that for women. This is especially apparent if you look at the left sides of the histograms. The ages at which men tend to have heart attacks are less predictable than those for women because their distribution is more spread out. It's relatively easy to see this because the two histograms have been put on the *same scale.*

We can also see that the distributions have different centers. The men's histogram is centered to the left of the women's. Men tend to have heart attacks at younger ages.

What of the shapes of the distributions? The age distribution for women is unimodal and skewed to the low end. There is a broad peak just below 80 years old. For men, the picture is a little different. The histogram is more nearly symmetric, with a narrower peak near 70 years. Looking at the tails of the histograms, you see clearly that some men have heart attacks before they're 30 years old. And the percentage of men who've had heart attacks by the age of 50 is substantially higher than that of women. At the high end, there are clearly more women over the age of 90 who have heart attacks than men, but that may reflect the fact that there simply are more women than men alive in that age bracket to have heart attacks in the first place!

Order, Please!

The Enron price changes were collected over time; the changes are for *consecutive* months from January 1997 to December 2001. When data are collected in a specific order like that, you should check to see if they have a pattern when plotted in that order. We can array the dots of a dotplot across the page in the data's order. Often, connecting successive points with a line helps to show the pattern.

The Enron price changes show relatively stable stock prices until the middle of 1999. Then the stock price starts to oscillate wildly. (Remember that these are the *changes* in price, not the prices themselves.) Curiously, few stock analysts seem to have been concerned about this behavior at the time. Perhaps they weren't looking at a **timeplot** such as this one.

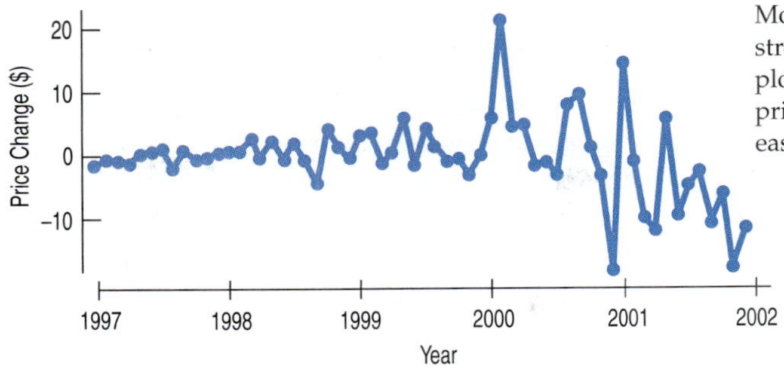

Monthly Enron stock price changes stretched out over time in a timeplot. The increased volatility in price that began in early 2000 is easy to see. **Figure 4.11**

Re-expressing Skewed Data to Improve Symmetry

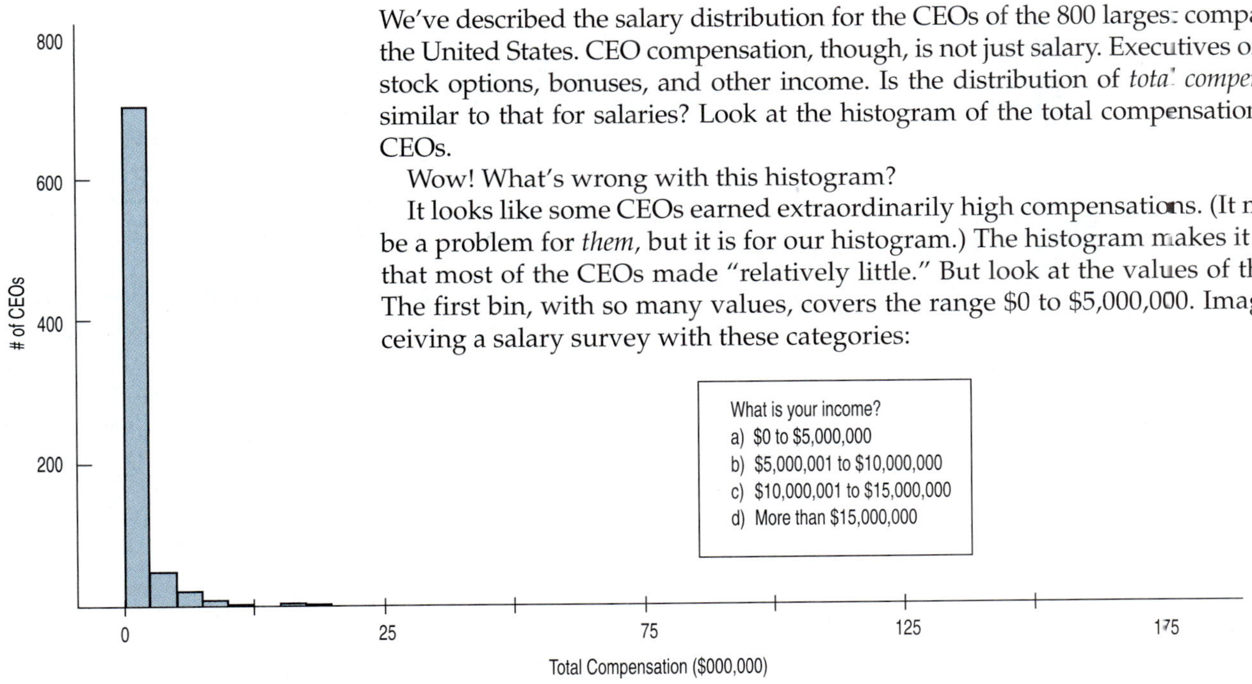

The total compensation for CEOs of 800 largest companies is extremely skewed and includes some extraordinarily large values. A few earned nearly $200 million (though the bars are too short to show up clearly). **Figure 4.12**

We've described the salary distribution for the CEOs of the 800 largest companies in the United States. CEO compensation, though, is not just salary. Executives often get stock options, bonuses, and other income. Is the distribution of *total compensations* similar to that for salaries? Look at the histogram of the total compensation of the CEOs.

Wow! What's wrong with this histogram?

It looks like some CEOs earned extraordinarily high compensations. (It may not be a problem for *them*, but it is for our histogram.) The histogram makes it appear that most of the CEOs made "relatively little." But look at the values of the bins. The first bin, with so many values, covers the range \$0 to \$5,000,000. Imagine receiving a salary survey with these categories:

> What is your income?
> a) \$0 to \$5,000,000
> b) \$5,000,001 to \$10,000,000
> c) \$10,000,001 to \$15,000,000
> d) More than \$15,000,000

As ridiculous as that first category appears, more than 10% of the CEOs had compensation too large to fit in that bin. In fact, 16 of them received more than \$15,000,000. The reason that the histogram seems to leave so much of the area blank is that these observations are spread all along the range from about \$15,000,000 to \$200,000,000. After \$20,000,000 there are so few for each bin that it's very hard to see the tiny bars. What we *can* see from this histogram is that this distribution is *very* skewed to the right.

Total compensation for CEOs consists of their base salaries, bonuses, and extra compensation, usually in the form of stock or stock options. Data that add together several variables, such as the compensation data, can easily have skewed distributions. It's often a good idea to separate the component variables and examine them individually to understand the data.

Dealing with logarithms

You have probably learned about logs in math courses and seen them in psychology or science classes. In this book, we use them only for making data behave better. Base 10 logs are the easiest to understand. You can think of them as roughly one less than the number of digits you need to write the number. So 100, which is the smallest number to require 3 digits, has a $\log_{10}$ of 2. And 1000 has a $\log_{10}$ of 3. The $\log_{10}$ of 500 has to be between 2 and 3, but you'd need a calculator to find that it's about 2.7. A salary of "six figures" has a $\log_{10}$ between 5 and 6. Logs are incredibly useful for making skewed data more symmetric. But don't worry. Nobody does logs without technology and neither should you. Often, remaking a histogram or other display using the logs of the data is as easy as pushing another button.

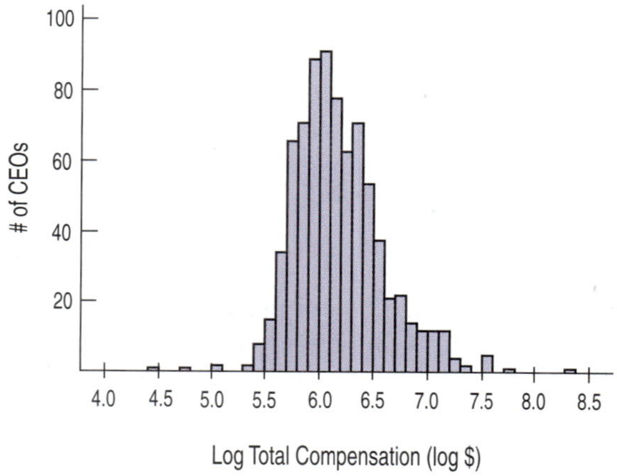

Taking logs makes the histogram of CEO total compensation nearly symmetric. The center of the distribution is around 6. How much money is that? It's 6 + 1 = "seven figures"—or $1,000,000. **Figure 4.13**

Skewed distributions are hard to summarize. It's hard to know what we mean by the "center" of a skewed distribution, so it's hard to pick a typical value to summarize the distribution. What would you say was a typical CEO total compensation?

One way to make a skewed distribution more symmetric is to **re-express** or **transform,** the data by applying a simple function. For example, we could take the square root or logarithm of each data value. Variables that have a distribution that is skewed to the right often benefit from a re-expression by logarithms or square roots. Those skewed to the left may benefit from squaring the data values.

The histogram of the logs of the total CEO compensations is much more nearly symmetric, so we can see that a typical *log compensation* is about 6.0, which corresponds to $1,000,000. Notice that nearly all the values are between 5.0 and 7.0—in other words, between six and eight figures. That's $100,000 to $10,000,000 a year, but who's counting? Because computers and calculators are available to do the calculating, you should consider re-expression as a helpful tool whenever you have skewed data.

What Can Go Wrong?

A data display should tell a story about the data. To do that it must speak in a clear language, making plain what variable is displayed, what any axis shows, and what the values of the data are. And it must be consistent in those decisions.

A display of quantitative data can go wrong in many ways. The most common failures arise from only a few basic errors:

- ***Don't make a histogram of a categorical variable.*** Just because the variable contains numbers doesn't mean it's quantitative. Here's a histogram of the insurance policy numbers of some workers. It's not very informative because the policy numbers are categorical. A histogram or stem-and-leaf display of a categorical variable makes no sense. A bar chart or pie chart may do better.
- ***Choose a scale appropriate to the data.*** Computer programs usually do a pretty good job of choosing histogram bin widths. Often, there's an easy way to adjust the width, sometimes interactively. Here is the Enron price change histogram with two other choices for the bin size.

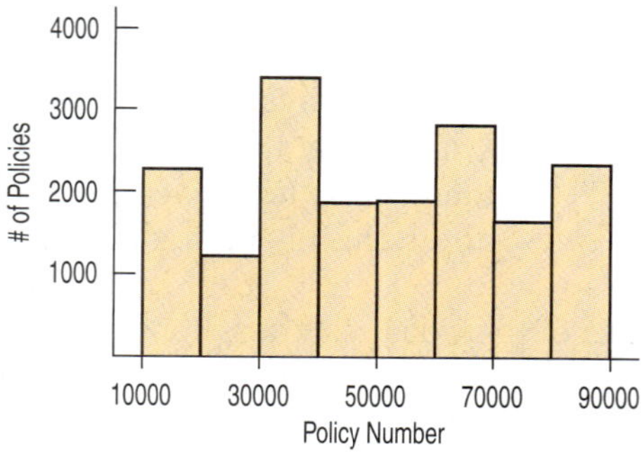

It's not appropriate to display these data with a histogram. **Figure 4.14**

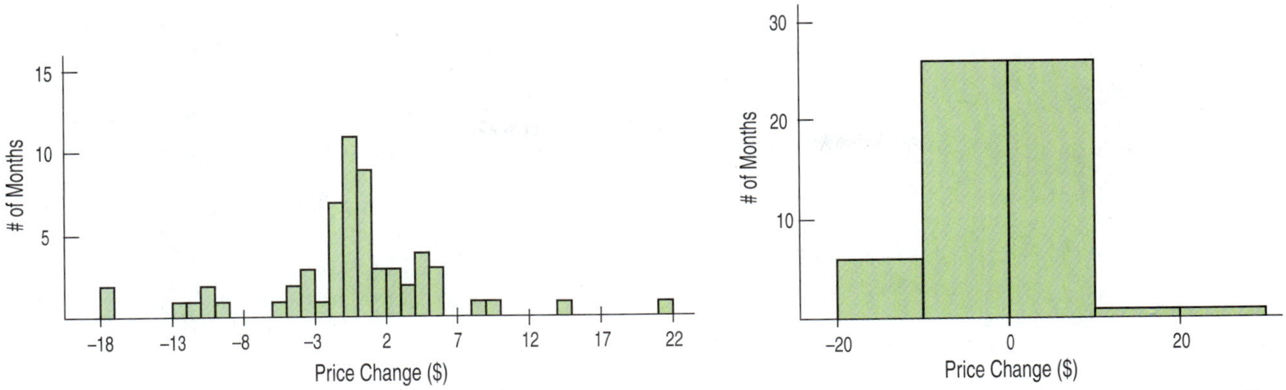

Changing the bin width changes how the histogram looks. The Enron stock price changes look different with these two choices. **Figure 4.15**

- ***Avoid inconsistent scales.*** Parts of displays should be mutually consistent—no fair changing scales in the middle or plotting two variables on different scales but on the same display. When comparing two groups, be sure to compare them on the same scale.
- ***Label clearly.*** Variables should be identified clearly and axes labeled so a reader knows what the plot displays.

Here's a remarkable example of a plot gone wrong. It illustrated a news story about rising college costs. It uses timeplots, but it gives a misleading impression. First think about the story you're being told by this display. Then try to figure out what has gone wrong.

What's wrong? Just about everything.

- The horizontal scales are inconsistent. Both lines show trends over time, but exactly for what years? The tuition sequence starts in 1965, but rankings are graphed from 1989. Plotting them on the same (invisible) scale makes it seem that they're for the same years.
- The vertical axis isn't labeled. That hides the fact that it's inconsistent. Does it graph dollars (of tuition) or ranking (of Cornell University)?

This display violates three of the rules. And it's even worse than that. It violates a rule that we didn't even bother to mention. The two inconsistent scales for the vertical axis don't point in the same direction! The line for Cornell's rank shows that it has "plummeted" from 15th place to 6th place in academic rank. Most of us think that's an *improvement*, but that's not the message of this graph.

Displaying Quantitative Data on a Computer

Almost any program that displays data can make a histogram, but some will do a better job of determining where the bars should start and how they should partition the range of the data.

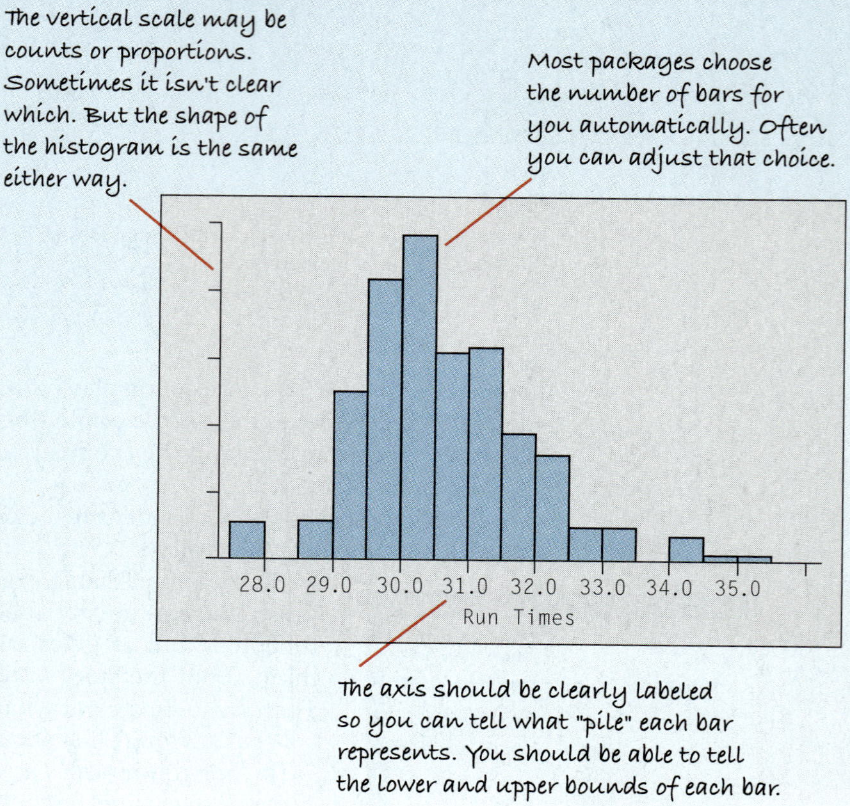

Connections

Distributions of quantitative variables, like those for categorical variables, show the possible values and their relative frequencies. A histogram shows the distribution of values in a quantitative variable with adjacent bars. Don't confuse them with bar charts, which display categorical variables. For categorical data, the mode is the category with the biggest count. For quantitative data, modes are peaks in the histogram.

The shape of the distribution of a quantitative variable is an important concept in most of the subsequent chapters. We will be especially interested in distributions that are unimodal and symmetric. And we will continue to check for outliers because we will need to deal with them specially.

Key Concepts

Distribution The distribution of a variable gives
- the possible values of the variable.
- the frequency or relative frequency of each value.

Histogram (relative frequency histogram) A histogram uses adjacent bars to show the distribution of values in a quantitative variable. Each bar represents the frequency (relative frequency) of values falling in an interval of values.

Stem-and-Leaf display A stem-and-leaf display shows quantitative data values in a way that sketches the distribution of the data. It's best described in detail by example.

Dotplot A dotplot graphs a dot for each case against a single axis.

Shape To describe the shape of a distribution, look for
- single vs. multiple modes.
- symmetry vs. skewness.
- outliers, clusters, or gaps.

Mode A hump or local high point in the shape of the distribution of a variable is called a "mode." The apparent location of modes can change as the scale of a histogram is changed.

Unimodal Having one mode. This is a useful term for describing the shape of a histogram when it's generally mound-shaped. Distributions with two modes are called **bimodal.** Those with more than two are **multimodal.** Statisticians don't like to count very high.

Uniform A distribution that's roughly flat is said to be uniform.

Symmetric A distribution is symmetric if the two halves on either side of the center look approximately like mirror images of each other.

Tails The tails of a distribution are the parts that typically trail off on either side. Distributions can be characterized as having long tails (if they straggle off for some distance) or short tails (if they don't).

Skewed A distribution is skewed if it's not symmetric and one tail stretches out farther than the other.

Outliers Outliers are extreme values that don't appear to belong with the rest of the data. They may be unusual values that deserve further investigation, or just mistakes; there's no obvious way to tell. Outliers can affect many statistical analyses, so you should always be alert for them.

Timeplot A timeplot displays data that change over time. Often, successive values are connected with lines to show trends more clearly.

Skills

When you complete this lesson you should:

Think

- Be able to identify an appropriate display for any quantitative variable.
- Be able to guess the shape of the distribution of a variable by knowing something about the data.

Show

- Know how to display the distribution of a quantitative variable with a stem-and-leaf display (by hand for smaller data sets), a dotplot, or a histogram (made by computer for larger data sets).
- Know how to make a timeplot of data that may vary over time.

Tell

- Be able to describe the distribution of a quantitative variable in terms of its shape, center, and spread.
- Be able to describe any anomalies or extraordinary features revealed by the display of a variable.
- Know how to compare the distributions of two or more groups by comparing their shapes, centers, and spreads.
- Know how to describe patterns over time shown in a timeplot.
- Be able to discuss any outliers in the data, noting how they deviate from the overall pattern of the data.

Exercises

1. Statistics in print. Find a histogram that shows the distribution of a variable in a newspaper or magazine article.
a) Does the article identify the W's?
b) Discuss whether the display is appropriate for the data.
c) Discuss what the display reveals about the variable and its distribution.
d) Does the article accurately describe and interpret the data? Explain.

2. Not a histogram. Find a graph other than a histogram that shows the distribution of a quantitative variable in a newspaper or magazine article.
a) Does the article identify the W's?
b) Discuss whether the display is appropriate for the data.
c) Discuss what the display reveals about the variable and its distribution.
d) Does the article accurately describe and interpret the data? Explain.

3. Thinking about shape. Would you expect distributions of these variables to be uniform, unimodal, or bimodal? Symmetric or skewed? Explain why.
a) The number of speeding tickets each student in the senior class of a college has ever had.
b) Players' scores (number of strokes) at the U.S. Open golf tournament in a given year.
c) Weights of female babies born in a particular hospital over the course of a year.
d) The length of the average hair on the heads of students in a large class.

4. More shapes. Would you expect distributions of these variables to be uniform, unimodal, or bimodal? Symmetric or skewed? Explain why.
a) Ages of people at a Little League game.
b) Number of siblings of people in your class.
c) Pulse rates of college-age males.
d) Number of times each face of a die shows in 100 tosses.

5. Heart attack stays. The histogram shows the lengths of hospital stays (in days) for all the female patients admitted to hospitals in New York in 1993 with a primary diagnosis of acute myocardial infarction (heart attack). Write a few sentences describing this distribution (shape, center, spread, unusual features).

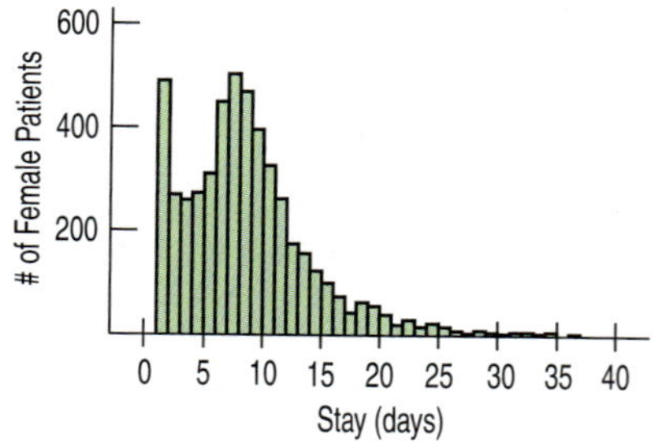

6. E-mails. A university teacher saved every e-mail received from students in a large Introductory Statistics class during an entire term. He then counted, for each student who had sent him at least one e-mail, how many e-mails each student had sent. Based on the histogram below, describe the distribution of e-mails.

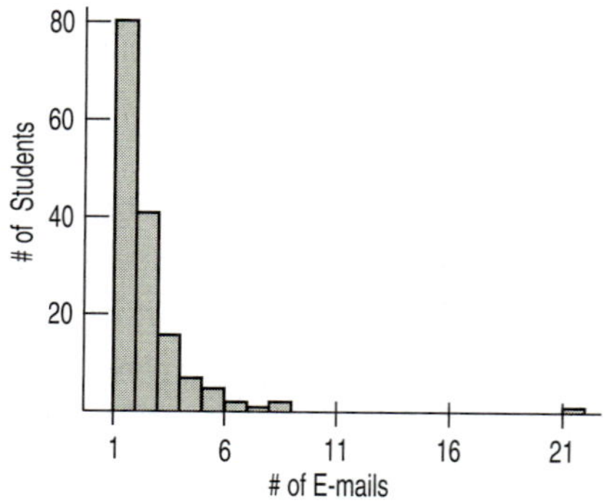

7. Sugar in cereals. The histogram displays the sugar content (as a percent of weight) of 49 brands of breakfast cereals.

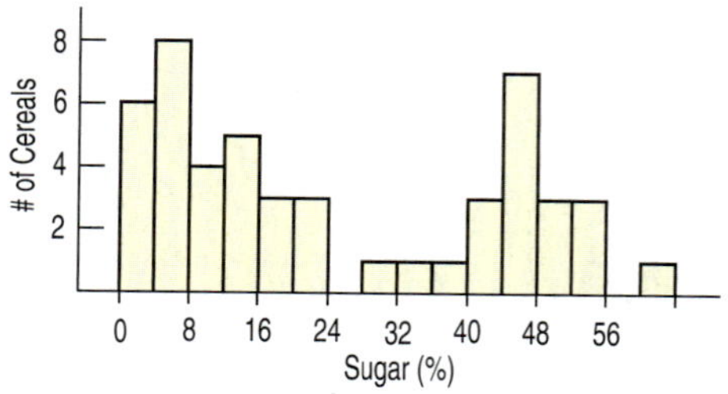

a) Describe this distribution.
b) What do you think might account for this shape?

8. Singers. The display shows the heights of some of the singers in a chorus, collected so that the singers could be positioned on stage with shorter ones in front and taller ones in back.

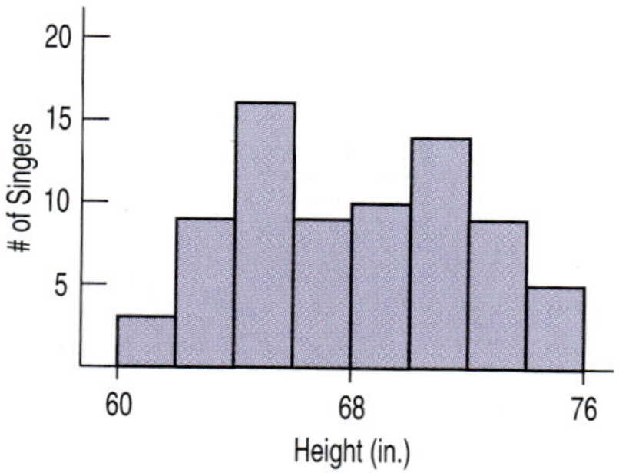

a) Describe the distribution.
b) Can you account for the features you see here?

9. Wineries. The histogram shows the sizes (in acres) of 36 wineries in the Finger Lakes region of New York.

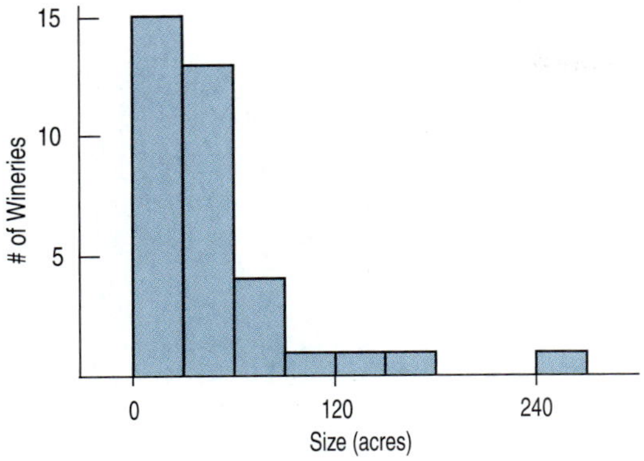

a) Approximately what percentage of these wineries are under 50 acres?

b) Write a brief description of this distribution (shape, center, spread, unusual features).

10. Run times. One of the authors collected the times (in minutes) it took him to run 4 miles on various courses during the period 1986 to 1997. Here is a histogram of the times.

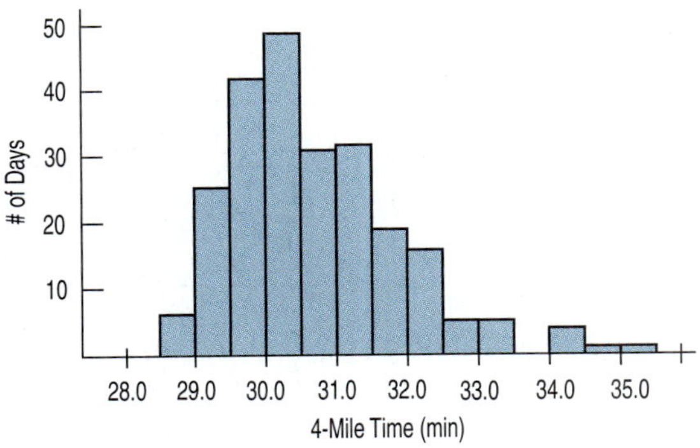

Describe the distribution and summarize the important features. What is it about running that might account for the shape you see?

11. Home runs. The stem-and-leaf display shows the number of home runs hit by Mark McGwire during the 1982–2001 seasons. Describe the distribution, mentioning its shape and any unusual features.

7	0
6	5
5	28
4	29
3	22399
2	29
1	
0	399

12. Bird species. The Laboratory of Ornithology holds an annual Christmas Bird Count, in which birdwatchers at various locations around the country see how many different species of birds they can spot. Here are some of the counts reported from sites in Texas during the 1999 event.

228	178	186	162	206	166	163
183	181	206	177	175	167	162
160	160	157	156	153	153	152

a) Create a stem-and-leaf display of these data.

b) Write a brief description of the distribution. Be sure to discuss the overall shape as well as any unusual features.

T 13. Horsepower. Create a stem-and-leaf display for these horsepowers of autos reviewed by *Consumer Reports* one year, and describe the distribution.

155	103	130	80	65
142	125	129	71	69
125	115	138	68	78
150	133	135	90	97
68	105	88	115	110
95	85	109	115	71
97	110	65	90	
75	120	80	70	

14. Population growth. Here is a "back-to-back" stem-and-leaf display that shows two data sets at once—one going to the left, one to the right. It compares the percent change in population for two regions of the United States (based on census figures for 1990 and 2000). The fastest growing states were Nevada at 66% and Arizona at 40%. Write a few sentences describing the difference in growth rates for the two regions of the United States. To show the distributions better, this display breaks each stem into two lines, putting leaves 0–4 on one stem and leaves 5–9 on the other.

NE/MW States		S/W States
	6	6
	6	
	5	
	5	
	4	
	4	0
	3	
	3	001
	2	6
	2	001134
	1	578
2100	1	001134444
99998876655	0	6999
4431	0	1

T 15. Hurricanes. The data below give the number of hurricanes that happened each year from 1944 through 2000 as reported by *Science* magazine.

3, 2, 1, 2, 4, 3, 7, 2, 3, 3, 2, 5, 2, 2, 4, 2, 2, 6, 0, 2, 5, 1, 3, 1, 0, 3, 2, 1, 0, 1, 2, 3, 2, 1, 2, 2, 2, 3, 1, 1, 1, 3, 0, 1, 3, 2, 1, 2, 1, 1, 0, 5, 6, 1, 3, 5, 3

a) Create a dotplot of these data.
b) Describe the distribution.

T 16. Hurricanes, again. A bimodal distribution usually indicates that there are actually two different behaviors present in the data. Investigating those two behaviors separately can produce important insights. Here are the data again, broken into two groups showing the number of hurricanes recorded annually before and after 1970. Create an appropriate visual display and write a few sentences comparing the two distributions.

1944–1969	1970–2000
3, 2, 1, 2, 4, 3, 7, 2, 3, 3, 2, 5, 2, 2, 4, 2, 2, 6, 0, 2, 5, 1, 3, 1, 0, 3	2, 1, 0, 1, 2, 3, 2, 1, 2, 2, 2, 3, 1, 1, 1, 3, 0, 1, 3, 2, 1, 2, 1, 1, 0, 5, 6, 1, 3, 5, 3

T 17. Acid rain. Two researchers measured the pH (a scale on which a value of 7 is neutral and values below 7 are acidic) of water collected from rain and snow over a 6-month period in Allegheny County, Pennsylvania. Describe their data with a graph and a few sentences.

4.57	5.62	4.12	5.29	4.64	4.31	4.30	4.39	4.45
5.67	4.39	4.52	4.26	4.26	4.40	5.78	4.73	4.56
5.08	4.41	4.12	5.51	4.82	4.63	4.29	4.60	

18. Marijuana. In 1995 the Council of Europe published a report entitled *The European School Survey Project on Alcohol and Other Drugs.* Among other issues, the survey investigated the percentages of 9th graders who had used marijuana. Here are the results for 20 Western European countries. Create an appropriate graph of these data, and describe the distribution.

Austria	10%	Italy	19%
Belgium	19%	Luxembourg	6%
Denmark	17%	Netherlands	31%
England	40%	No. Ireland	23%
Finland	5%	Norway	6%
France	12%	Portugal	7%
Germany	21%	Scotland	53%
Greece	2%	Spain	15%
Iceland	10%	Sweden	6%
Ireland	37%	Switzerland	27%

19. Hospital stays. The U.S. National Center for Health Statistics compiles data on the length of stay by patients in short-term hospitals, and publishes its finding in *Vital and Health Statistics.* Data from a sample of 39 male patients and 35 female patients on length of stay (in days) are displayed in these histograms.

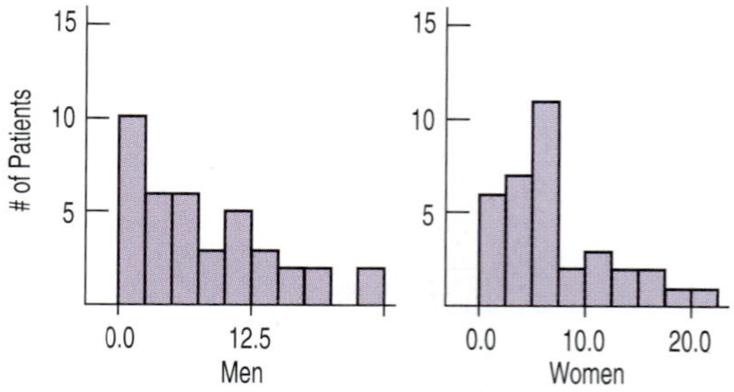

a) What would you suggest be changed about these histograms to make them easier to compare?
b) Describe these distributions by writing a few sentences comparing the duration of hospitalization for men and women.
c) Can you suggest a reason for the peak in women's length of stay?

20. Deaths. A National Vital Statistics Report indicated that nearly 300,000 black Americans died in 1999, compared with just over 2 million white Americans. Here are calculator histograms displaying the distributions of their ages at death.

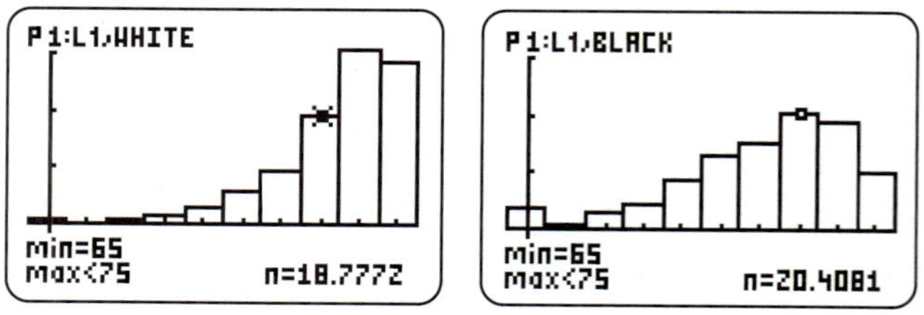

Most of the bars in these histograms display ten-year age groups. For example, the first histogram shows that for white Americans about 19% of the deaths were of people between 65 and 74 years old. The leftmost bars represent the percentage of total deaths that were children aged 0 through 4 years and the rightmost bars people over 85. Write a brief comparison of the distributions.

21. Final grades. A professor (of something other than Statistics!) distributed the following histogram to show the distribution of grades on his 200-point final exam. Comment on the display.

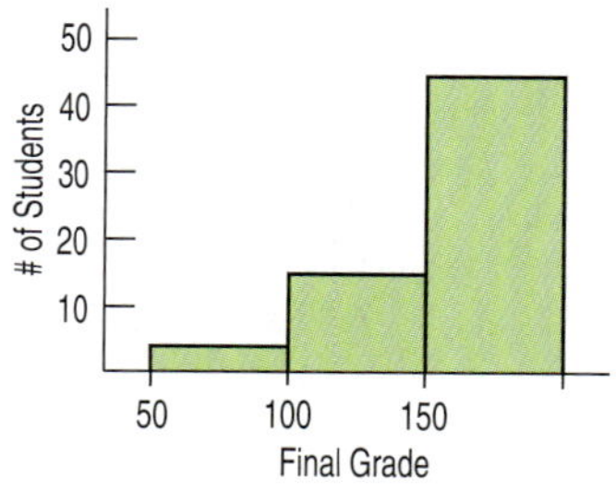

22. Final grades revisited. After receiving many complaints about his final grade histogram from students currently taking a Statistics course, the professor distributed the following revised histogram.

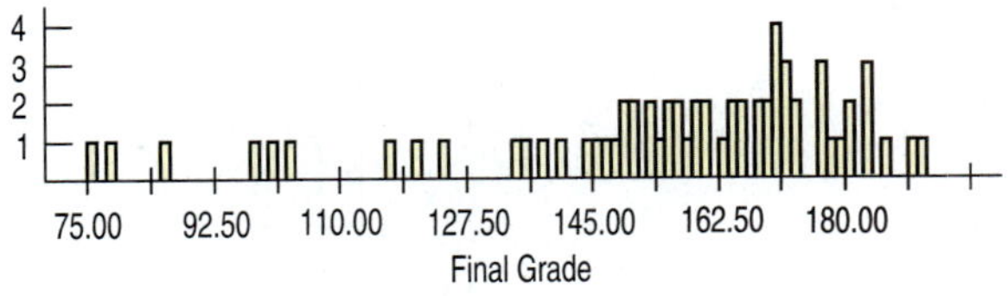

a) Comment on this display.
b) Describe the distribution of grades.

23. Zip codes. Holes R Us, an Internet company that sells piercing jewelry, keeps transaction records on its sales. At a recent sales meeting, one of the staff presented a histogram of the zip codes of the last 500 customers so that they might understand where sales are coming from. Comment on the usefulness and appropriateness of the display.

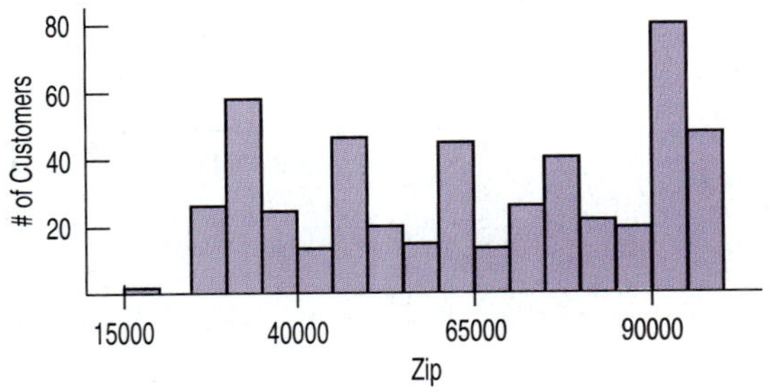

24. CEO data revisited. For each CEO, a code is listed that corresponds to the industry of the CEO's company. Here are a few of the codes and the industries to which they correspond.

Industry	Industry Code
Financial services	1
Food/drink/tobacco	2
Health	3
Insurance	4
Retailing	6
Forest products	9
Aerospace/defense	11
Energy	12
Capital goods	14
Computers/communications	16
Entertainment/information	17
Consumer nondurables	18
Electric utilities	19

A recently hired investment analyst has been assigned to examine the industries and the compensations of the CEOs. To start the analysis, he produces the following histogram of industry codes.

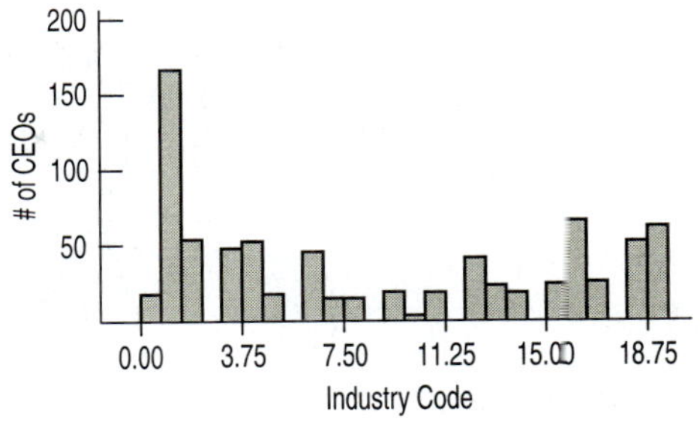

a) What might account for the gaps seen in the histogram?
b) Is the histogram unimodal?
c) What advice might you give the analyst about the appropriateness of this display?

25. Productivity study. The National Center for Productivity releases information on the efficiency of workers. In a recent report, they included the following graph showing a rapid rise in productivity. What questions do you have about this display?

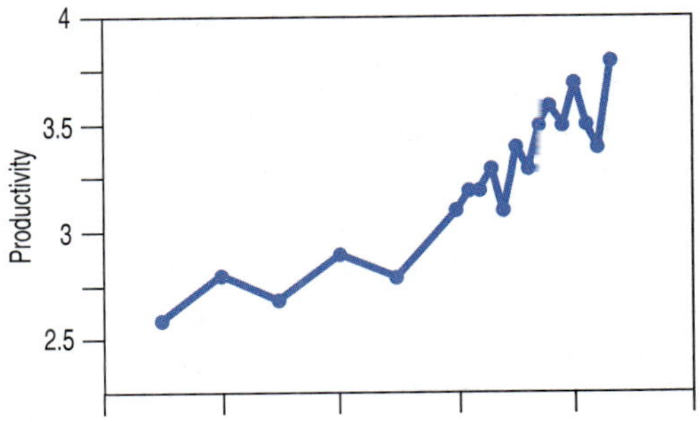

26. Productivity revisited. A second report by the National Center for Productivity analyzed the relationship between productivity and wages. Comment on the graph they used.

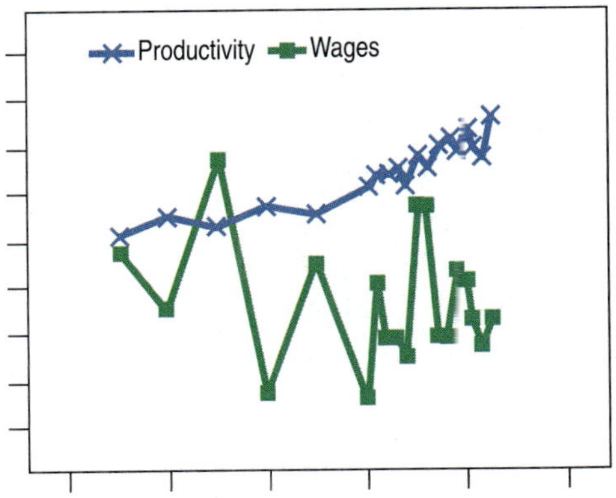

27. Law enforcement. Some federal employees have the authority to carry firearms and make arrests. Obviously some danger is associated with these jobs, but how much? The table below summarizes the rates of assault and injury (or death) for these employees for 5 years, 1995–1999.

Agency	Assaults (per 1000)	Killed-Injured (per 1000)
Bureau of Alcohol, Tobacco,and Firearms (BATF)	31.1	2.2
Capitol Police	5.0	3.6
Customs Service	9.7	5.1
Drug Enforcement Agency (DEA)	17.9	1.1
Federal Bureau of Investigation (FBI)	3.9	1.2
Immigration and Naturalization Services (INS)	14.1	2.5
Internal Revenue Service (IRS)	1.7	0.2
U.S. Marshal Service	9.7	3.0
National Park Service	38.7	15.0
Postal Service	5.7	2.9
Secret Service	9.7	3.0

a) Create a visual display of these data.
b) Describe these data (shape, center, spread, unusual features).
c) Which agencies are outliers?

T **28. Cholesterol.** A study examining the health risks of smoking measured the cholesterol levels of people who had smoked for at least 25 years and people of similar ages who had smoked for no more than 5 years and then stopped. Create histograms for both groups and write a brief report comparing their cholesterol levels.

Smokers				Ex-smokers		
225	211	209	284	250	134	300
258	216	196	288	249	213	310
250	200	209	280	175	174	328
225	256	243	200	160	188	321
213	246	225	237	213	257	292
232	267	232	216	200	271	227
216	243	200	155	238	163	263
216	271	230	309	192	242	249
183	280	217	305	242	267	243
287	217	246	351	217	267	218
200	280	209		217	183	228

29. MPG. A consumer organization compared gas mileage figures for several models of cars made in the United States with autos manufactured in other countries. The data are shown in the table.

U.S. Models	Others
16.9	16.2
15.5	20.3
19.2	31.5
18.5	30.5
30.0	21.5
30.9	31.9
20.6	37.3
20.8	27.5
18.6	27.2
18.1	34.1
17.0	35.1
17.6	29.5
16.5	31.8
18.2	22.0
26.5	17.0
21.9	21.6
27.4	
28.4	
28.8	
26.8	
33.5	
34.2	

a) Create a back-to-back stem-and-leaf display for these data.
b) Write a few sentences comparing the distributions.

30. Baseball. American League baseball teams play their games with the designated hitter rule, meaning that pitchers do not bat. The League believes that replacing the pitcher, traditionally a weak hitter, with another player in the batting order produces more runs and generates more interest among fans. Below are the average number of runs scored in American League and National League stadiums for the first half of the 2001 season.

American				National			
11.1	10.8	10.8	10.3	14.0	11.6	10.4	10.3
10.3	10.1	10.0	9.5	10.2	9.5	9.5	9.5
9.4	9.3	9.2	9.2	9.5	9.1	8.8	8.4
	9.0	8.3		8.3	8.2	8.1	7.9

a) Create a back-to-back stem-and-leaf display of these data.
b) Write a few sentences comparing the average number of runs scored per game in the two leagues. (Remember: shape, center, spread, unusual features!)
c) Coors Field, in Denver, stands a mile above sea level, an altitude far greater than that of any other major

league ball park. Some believe that the thinner air makes it harder for pitchers to throw curve balls and easier for batters to hit the ball a long way. Do you see any evidence that the 14 runs scored per game there is unusually high? Explain.

31. Nuclear power. For a while in the 20th century many nuclear-powered electrical generating plants were built, but then growing environmental concerns and construction costs led to increasing reliance on other forms of energy. The table shows the dates of completion (in months after January 1967) and costs (in thousands of dollars per megawatt) of 12 nuclear generators.

Time of completion (months after Jan 1, 1967)	Construction cost ($1000/mW)
2	35
3	28
10	32
12	60
17	56
19	63
21	62
26	81
30	84
32	79
41	88
47	80

a) Create a stem-and-leaf display of the costs.
b) Describe the distribution.
c) Create a timeplot of the costs.
d) What information about the construction of nuclear plants can you see from the timeplot that is not obvious in the stem-and-leaf display?

T **32. Drunk driving.** Accidents involving drunk drivers account for about 40% of all deaths on the nation's highways. The table tracks the number of alcohol-related fatalities for 20 years.

Year	Deaths (thousands)	Year	Deaths (thousands)
1982	25.2	1992	17.9
1983	23.6	1993	17.5
1984	23.8	1994	16.6
1985	22.7	1995	17.2
1986	24.0	1996	17.2
1987	23.6	1997	16.5
1988	23.6	1998	16.0
1989	22.4	1999	16.0
1990	22.0	2000	16.7
1991	19.9	2001	16.7

a) Create a stem-and-leaf display or a histogram of these data.
b) Create a timeplot.
c) Using features apparent in the stem-and-leaf display and the timeplot, write a few sentences about deaths caused by drunk driving.

33. Assets. Here is a histogram of the assets (in millions of dollars) of 79 companies chosen from the *Forbes* list of the nation's top corporations.

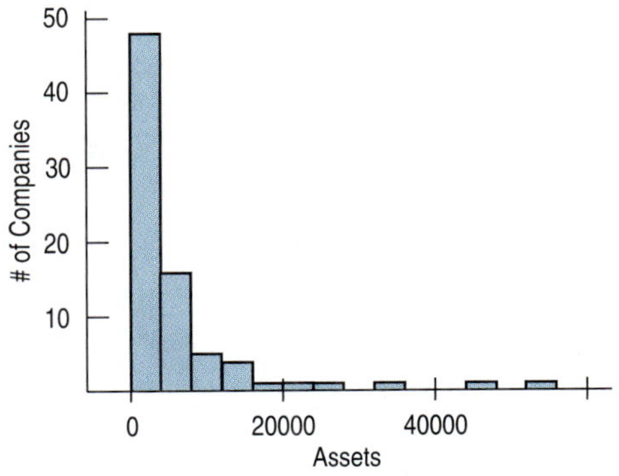

a) What aspect of this distribution makes it difficult to summarize, or to discuss, center and spread?
b) Here are the same data after re-expressions as the square root of assets and the logarithm of assets. Which re-expression do you prefer? Why?

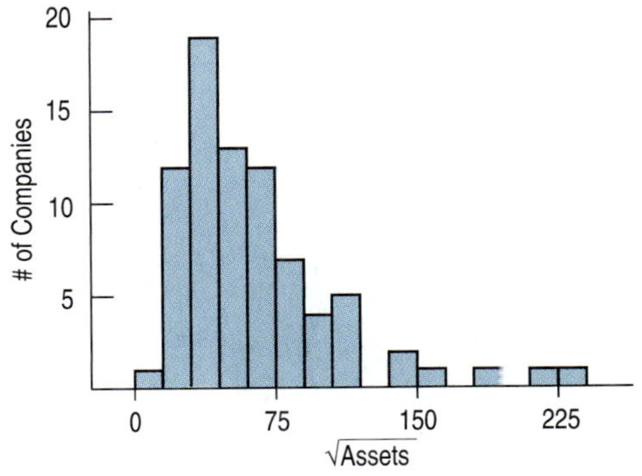

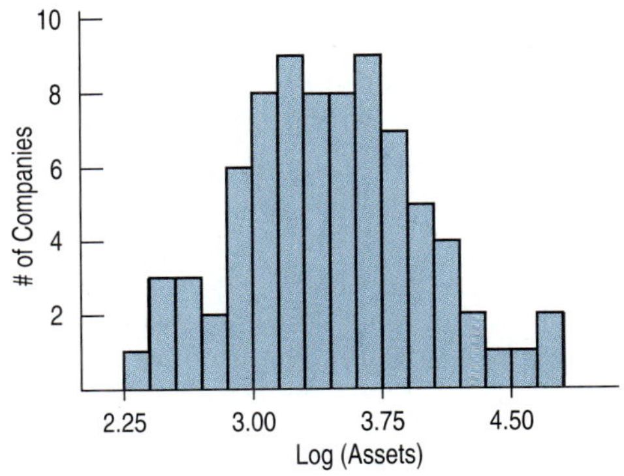

c) In the square root re-expression, what does the value 50 actually indicate about the company's assets?
d) In the logarithm re-expression, what does the value 3 actually indicate about the company's assets?

34. Rainmakers. The table lists the amount of rainfall (in acre-feet) from 26 clouds seeded with silver iodide.

2745	200
1697	198
1656	129
978	119
703	118
489	115
430	92
334	40
302	32
274	31
274	17
255	7
242	4

a) Why is "acre-feet" a good way to measure the amount of precipitation produced by cloud seeding?
b) Plot these data, and describe the distribution.
c) Create a re-expression of these data that produces a more advantageous distribution.
d) Explain what your re-expressed scale means.

Chapter 5

Describing Distributions Numerically

WHO	191 countries (not WHO!)
WHAT	DALE (disability adjusted life expectancy)
UNIT	Years
WHEN	Data are for babies born in 1999
WHERE	Earth
WHY	Annual report by World Health Organization

When distributions are mixed together the result is often a multimodal and/or skewed distribution. These data are combined from countries of different economic and social conditions, so a skewed distribution is no surprise.

The world health organization (WHO) collects health data worldwide on every member country of the United Nations. One traditional measure of the overall health of a country has been the life expectancy of its citizens—the number of years that a newborn can expect to live. Starting in 1999, WHO scientists introduced a revised measure to take account of the fact that illness and injuries can affect the quality of life. The disability adjusted life expectancy (DALE) adjusts for years of ill health to give a measure of years of healthy life.

Here is a histogram of the DALEs for all 191 United Nations countries:

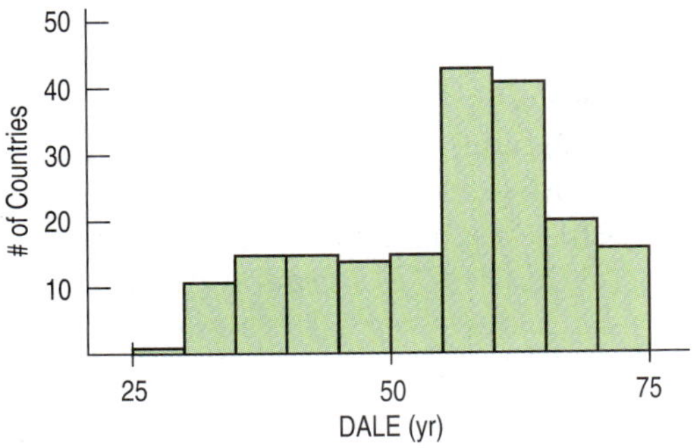

DALEs for the 191 United Nations countries. In 1999, Japan had the top DALE of 73.8 years, while Sierra Leone had the lowest at 29.5 years. **Figure 5.1**

The distribution may be bimodal and is clearly skewed to the left.

Center: Finding the Median

What is a typical DALE? Try to put your finger on the histogram at the value you think is typical. (Read the value from the horizontal axis and remember it.) When we think of a typical value, we usually look for the **center** of the distribution. Where do you think the center of this distribution is? For a unimodal, symmetric distribution, it's easy. We'd all agree on the center of symmetry, where we would

NOTATION ALERT:

We always use n to indicate the number of values. Some people even say, "how big is the n?" when they mean the number of data values.

Using the Midrange

There actually is *one* everyday use of the midrange. Whenever you make a plot of data, you're likely to center the plot at the midrange, exactly halfway between the two extremes of the data.

fold the histogram to match the two sides. But when the distribution is skewed as this one is, it's not immediately clear what we even mean by the center.

You might think of taking the average of the maximum and minimum values as a way of finding the center. This is called the **midrange,** but it's too sensitive to the outlying values to be safe for summarizing the whole distribution. A more reasonable choice of typical value is the value that is literally in the middle, with half the values below it and half above it.

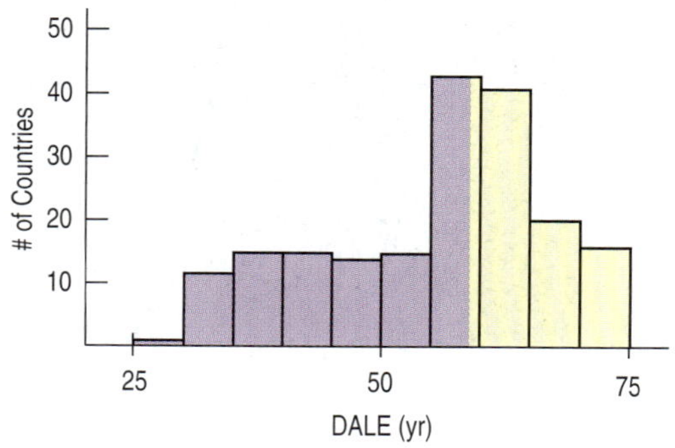

The median splits the histogram into two halves of equal area. Notice that the halves of this histogram have very different shapes.
Figure 5.2

Histograms follow the area principle, and each half of the data has about 95 countries, so each colored region has the same area in the display. The middle value that divides the histogram into two equal areas is called the **median.**

The median has the same units as the data. Be sure to include the units whenever you discuss the median.

For the DALE data, there are 191 countries, so the median is found at the $(191 + 1)/2 = 96$th place in the sorted data. This median DALE is 58.5 years.

The median is one way to find the center of the data. But there are many others. We'll look at an even more important measure later in this chapter.

Knowing the median, we could say that a typical life expectancy, worldwide, was about 58.5 years. How much does that really say? How well does the median describe the data? After all, not all countries have DALEs near 58.5 years. Whenever we find the center of data, the next step is always to ask how well it actually summarizes the data.

Finding the median by hand

Finding the median of a batch of n numbers is easy as long as you remember to order the values first. If n is odd, the median is the middle value. Counting in from the ends, we find this value in the $\frac{n+1}{2}$ position.

When n is even, there are two middle values. So, in this case, the median is the average of the two values in positions $\frac{n}{2}$ and $\frac{n}{2} + 1$.

Here are two examples:

Suppose the batch has the values 14.1, 3.2, 25.3, 2.8, −17.5, 13.9, and 45.8. First we order the values: −17.5, 2.8, 3.2, 13.9, 14.1, 25.3, and 45.8. Since there are 7 values, the median is the $(7 + 1)/2 = 4$th value counting from the top or bottom: 13.9.

Suppose we had the same batch with another value at 35.7. Then the ordered values are −17.5, 2.8, 3.2, 13.9, 14.1, 25.3, 35.7, and 45.8. The median is the average of the 8/2, or 4th and the (8/2) + 1, or 5th, values. So the median is $(13.9 + 14.1)/2 = 14.0$.

Spread: Home on the Range

If every country had a DALE of 58.5, knowing the median would tell us everything about the distribution of life expectancy worldwide. The more the data vary, however, the less the median alone can tell us. So we need to measure how much the data values vary around the center. In other words, how spread out are they? When we describe a distribution numerically, we always report a measure of its **spread** along with its center.

How should we measure the spread? We could simply look at the extent of the data. How far apart are the two extremes? The **range** of the data is defined as the *difference* between the maximum and minimum values,

$$\text{Range} = max - min.$$

Statistics pays close attention to what we *don't* know as well as what we do know. Understanding how spread out the data are is a first step in understanding what a summary *cannot* tell us about the data. It's the beginning of telling us what we don't know.

Notice that the range is a *single number, not* an interval of values, as you might think from its use in common speech. The maximum DALE is 73.8 years and the minimum is 29.5 years, so the *range* is 73.8 − 29.5 = 44.3 years.

The range (like the midrange) has the disadvantage that a single extreme value can make it very large, giving a value that doesn't really represent the data overall. For example, in the CEO compensations from Chapter 4, the range is \$202,991,184 − \$28,816 = \$202,962,368! Most of the compensations were between \$0 and \$5,000,000, so the range doesn't give a very accurate impression of the spread.

The Interquartile Range

A better way to describe the spread of a variable might be to ignore the extremes and concentrate on the middle of the data. We could, for example, find the range of just the middle half of the data. So, where's the middle half? First, split the sorted data at the median and then find the medians of each half. These values are the **quartiles,** and they border the middle half of the data. (When n is odd one of the data values *is* the median; include the median with each of the halves.)

The difference between the quartiles is the **interquartile range,** commonly abbreviated IQR (and pronounced "eye-cue-are," not "ikker"):

$$IQR = \textit{upper quartile} - \textit{lower quartile}.$$

Finding quartiles by hand

A simple way to find the quartiles is to split the batch into two halves at the median. (When n is odd, include the median in both halves.)The lower quartile is the median of the lower half, and the upper quartile is the median of the upper half.

Here are our two examples again.

The ordered values of the first batch were −17.5, 2.8, 3.2, 13.9, 14.1, 25.3, and 45.8, with a median of 13.9. Since 7 is odd, we include the median in both halves to get

−17.5, 2.8, 3.2, 13.9 and
13.9, 14.1, 25.3, 45.8.

Each half has 4 values, so the median of each is the average of its 2nd and 3rd values. So, the lower quartile is (2.8 + 3.2)/2 = 3.0 and the upper quartile is (14.1 + 25.3)/2 = 19.7.

The second batch has the ordered values −17.5, 2.8, 3.2, 13.9, 14.1, 25.3, 35.7, and 45.8.

Here n is even, so the two halves of 4 are −17.5, 2.8, 3.2, 13.9 and
14.1, 25.3, 35.7, 45.8.

Now the lower quartile is (2.8 + 3.2)/2 = 3.0 and the upper quartile is (25.3 + 35.7)/2 = 30.5.

For the DALE data, there are 95 values below and 95 values above the median. Including the median with each half of the data gives 96 values in each half. In each half, we'd average the 48th and 49th values. For the DALEs, the lower quartile is 46.9 years and the upper quartile is 63.6 years. The *difference* between the quartiles gives the IQR:

$$IQR = 63.6 - 46.9 \textit{ years} = 16.7 \textit{ years}.$$

Now we know that the middle half of the countries (in terms of DALE) extend for a (interquartile) range of 16.7 years. This seems like a reasonable summary of the spread of the distribution, as we can see from the histogram:

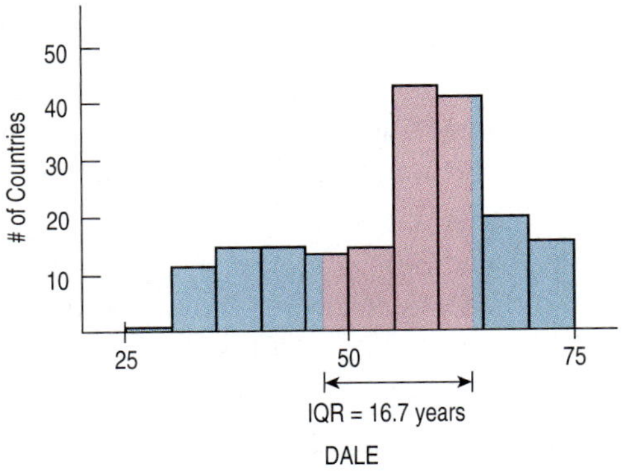

The IQR contains the middle 50% of the values of the distribution. It also gives a visual indication of the spread of the data. Here we see that the IQR is 16.7 years. **Figure 5.3**

The IQR is often a reasonable summary of the spread of a distribution. For the CEO compensations, the median is \$1,304,470 and the quartiles are at $787,304 and $2,518,628, so the IQR is $2,518,628 − $787,304 = $1,731,324. The IQR gives a different impression of how spread out CEOs' salaries are than we might get from the range of $202,962,368.

The lower and upper quartiles are also known as the 25th and 75th **percentiles** of the data, respectively, since the lower quartile falls above 25% of the data and the upper quartile falls above 75% of the data. If we count this way, the median is the 50th percentile. We could, of course, define and calculate any percentile that we want. For example, the 10th percentile would be the number that falls above 10% of the data values.

Five-Number Summary

NOTATION ALERT:

We will always use Q1 to label the lower (25%) quartile and Q3 to label the upper (75%) quartile. The skipped number is because the median would, by this system, naturally be labeled Q2—but we don't usually do that.

The **five-number summary** of a distribution reports its median, quartiles, and extremes (maximum and minimum). The five-number summary for the DALE data looks like this.

Max	73.8 years
Q3	63.6
Median	58.5
Q1	46.9
Min	29.5

It's a good idea to report the number of data values and the identity of the cases (the *Who*). Here there are 191 countries.

Rock Concert Deaths: Making Boxplots

WHO	Rock concert goers who died from being crushed
WHAT	Age at death
UNITS	Years
WHERE	Internationally
WHEN	The period 1999–2000
WHY	To think twice about going to concerts?

Whenever we have a five-number summary of a (quantitative) variable, we can put the information together in one graphical display called a **boxplot.** Here's another example. During the two years 1999 and 2000 there were 66 deaths recorded internationally at rock concerts attributed to "crowd crush." How old were these crowd crush victims? Here's a five-number summary of their ages.

Max	47 years
Q3	22
Median	19
Q1	17
Min	13

To make a boxplot of the ages of rock concert victims, follow these steps:

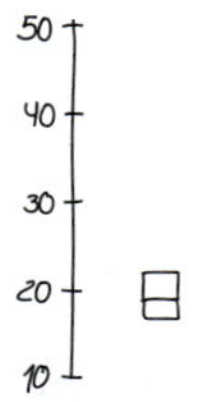

1. Draw a single vertical axis spanning the range of the data.[1] Draw short horizontal lines at the lower and upper quartiles and at the median. Then connect them with vertical lines to form a box. The box can have any width that looks OK.

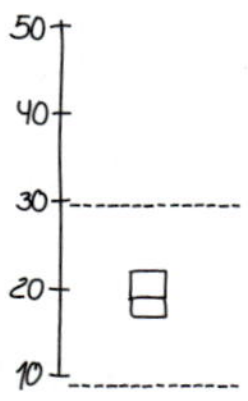

2. To help us construct the boxplot, we erect "fences" around the main part of the data. We place the upper fence 1.5 IQRs above the upper quartile and the lower fence 1.5 IQRs below the lower quartile. For the rock concert data, we compute

$$\textit{Upper fence} = Q3 + 1.5\ \textit{IQRs} = 22 + 1.5 \times 5 = 29.5\ \textit{years}$$

[1] The axis could also run horizontally.

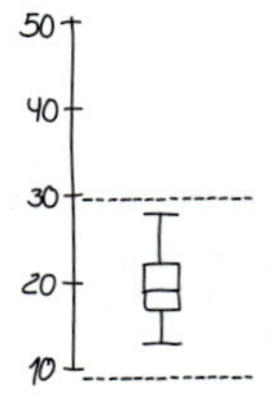

and

$$\textit{Lower fence} = Q1 - 1.5\ \textit{IQRs} = 17 - 1.5 \times 5 = 9.5\ \textit{years}.$$

The fences are just for construction and are not part of the display. We show them here with dotted lines for illustration. You should never include them in your boxplot.

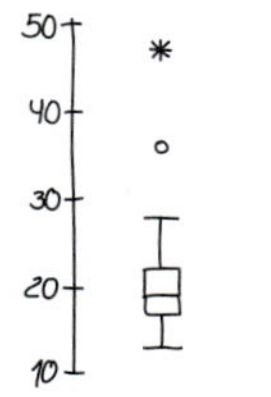

3. We use the fences to grow "whiskers." Draw lines from the ends of the box up and down to *the most extreme data values found within the fences.* If a data value falls outside one of the fences, we do *not* connect it with a whisker.
4. Finally, we add the outliers by displaying any data values beyond the fences with special symbols. (We often use a different symbol for "far outliers"—data values farther than 3 IQRs from the quartiles.)

Now that we've drawn the boxplot, let's summarize what it shows. The center of a boxplot is (remarkably enough) a box that shows the middle half of the data, between the quartiles. The height of the box is equal to the IQR. If the median is roughly centered between the quartiles, then the middle half of the data is roughly symmetric. If it is not centered, the distribution is skewed. The whiskers show skewness as well if they are not roughly the same length. Any outliers are displayed individually, both to keep them out of the way for judging skewness and to encourage you to give them special attention. They may be mistakes, but they may be the most interesting cases in your data.

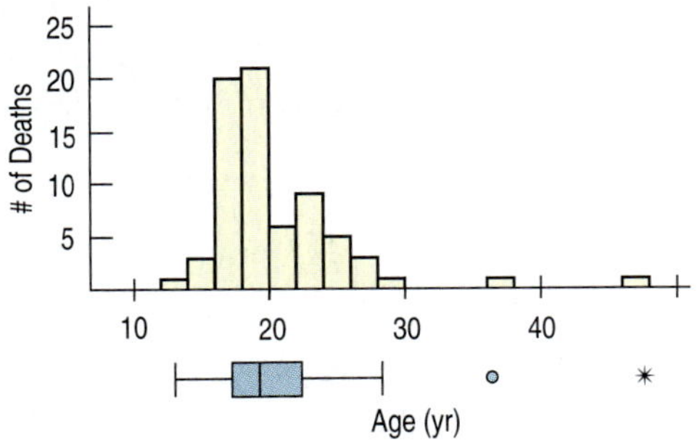

By turning a boxplot and putting it on the same scale, we can compare the boxplot and histogram of the rock concert deaths and see how each represents the distribution. **Figure 5.4**

From the boxplot we see that half of the victims were between 17 and 22 years old. The boxplot makes it look like the distribution of ages is roughly symmetric, with most of the victims between about 13 and 28 years old, but the histogram shows that the distribution is slightly skewed to the right. It is both an advantage and a disadvantage of boxplots that they simplify our view of the distribution like this. Boxplots are particularly good at pointing out outliers. Here, there are two victims who were substantially older. In a careful analysis of these data we'd want to learn more about them.

Boxplots complement histograms by providing more specific information about the center, the quartiles, and outliers. When looking at one variable, it's a good idea to look at the boxplot and histogram together. When *comparing* groups, boxplots really start to shine.

The prominent statistician John W. Tukey, the originator of the boxplot, was asked (by one of the authors) why the outlier nomination rule cut at 1.5 IQRs beyond each quartile. He answered that the reason was that 1 IQR would be too small and 2 IQRs would be too large. In the next chapter, we'll see some more reasons why 1.5 works well for nominating outliers.

Comparing Groups with Boxplots

Histograms show a lot about the shape of the distribution, but get a little unwieldy when we want to look at more than one group at a time. Boxplots work well for comparing groups because they let the fundamental story show through. When we place them side-by-side, we can easily see which group has the higher median, which has the greater IQR, where the central 50% of the data is located, and which has the greater overall range. And we can get a general idea of symmetry from whether the medians are centered within their boxes and whether the whiskers extend roughly the same distance on either side of the boxes. Equally important, we can see past any outliers in making these comparisons because they've been separated from the rest of the data.

Comparing Groups STEP-BY-STEP

A student designed an experiment to test the efficiency of various coffee containers by placing hot (180 °F) liquid in each of four different container types 8 different times. After 30 minutes she measured the temperature again and recorded the difference in temperature. Because these are temperature *differences*, smaller differences mean that the liquid stayed hot—what we probably want in a coffee mug.

What can we say about the effectiveness of these four mugs? Let's see what story the data tell us.

Think

Variable Identify the *variable* and report the W's.

The student placed 180 °F water in each of four mugs and measured the difference in temperature (in °F) of the water after 30 minutes to see which mug was more effective at maintaining temperature. She repeated the procedure 8 times.

Show

Mechanics Report the five-number summaries of the four groups. Including the IQR is a good idea as well.

	Min	Q1	Median	Q3	Max	IQR
CUPPS	6 °F	6	8.25	14.25	18.5	8.25
Nissan	0	1	2	4.5	7	3.50
SIGG	9	11.5	14.25	21.75	24.5	10.25
Starbucks	6	6.50	8.50	14.25	17.5	7.75

Display Because we want to compare the distributions for four groups, boxplots are an obvious choice.

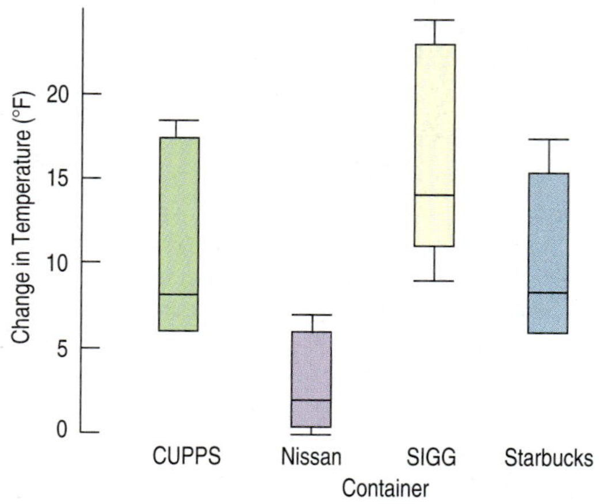

Tell

Interpretation Describe what the boxplots and summaries say about the ability of these mugs to maintain heat. Compare the shapes, centers, and spreads, and note any outliers.

The individual distributions are all slightly skewed to the high end. The Nissan cup does the best job of keeping liquids hot, with a median loss of only 2 °F, and the SIGG cup does the worst, typically losing 14 °F. The difference is large enough to be important; a coffee drinker would be likely to notice a 14° drop in temperature. And the mugs are clearly different; 75% of the Nissan tests showed less heat loss than any of the other mugs in the study. The IQR of results for the Nissan cup is also the smallest of these test cups, indicating that it is a consistent performer.

TI Tips

Let's make comparative boxplots for the performances of fourth grade boys and girls on an agility test. The test asks them to jump from side to side across a set of parallel lines, counting the number of lines they can clear in 30 seconds. Here are the results:

Boys:	22, 17, 18, 29, 22, 22, 23, 24, 23, 17, 21
Girls:	25, 20, 12, 19, 28, 24, 22, 21, 25, 26, 25, 16, 27, 22

Enter these data in `L1` (boys) and `L2` (girls).

Set up `STATPLOT`'s `Plot1` to make a boxplot of the boys' data:

- turn the plot `On`;
- choose the first boxplot icon (you want your plot to indicate outliers);
- specify `Xlist:L1` and `Freq:1`, and select the `Mark` you want the calculator to use for displaying any outliers.

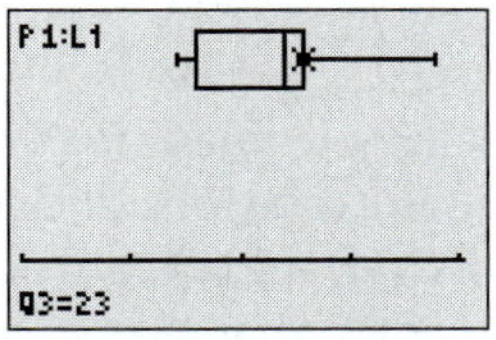

Use `ZoomStat` to display the boys' boxplot. You can now `TRACE` to see the statistics in the five-number summary. Try it!

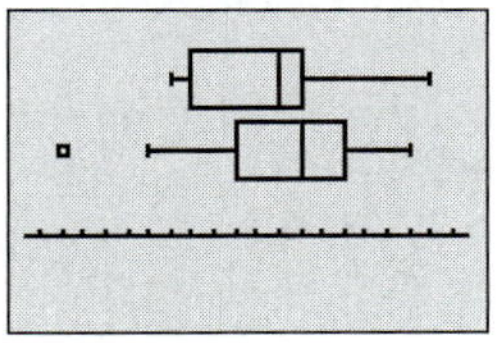

As you did for the boys, set up `Plot2` to display the girls' data. This time when you use `ZoomStat` with both plots turned on, the display shows the parallel boxplots. See the outlier?

This is a great opportunity to practice your "Tell" skills. How do these fourth graders compare in terms of agility?

Summarizing Symmetric Distributions

In everyday language, sometimes "average" *does* mean what we want it to mean. We don't talk about your grade point mean or a baseball player's batting mean or the Dow Jones Industrial mean. So, we'll continue to say "average" when that seems most natural. When we do, though, you may assume that what we mean is the mean.

Medians do a good job of locating the center of a distribution when the shape is skewed. But when we have symmetric data, there's another alternative. You probably already know how to average values. In fact, to find the median when n is even, we said you should average the two middle values, and you didn't even flinch. In general, to average values, add them up and divide by n, the number of values.

Averaging is a common thing to do with data. Once we've averaged some data, what do you think the result is called? The *average?* No, that would be too easy. Informally, we talk about the "average person" or the "average family," but we don't actually add up families and divide by n. So, to be more precise we call this summary the mean.

Pulse rates are useful for monitoring medical conditions. Resting heart rates depend on age. For children more than 10 years old and for adults 60 to 100 beats per minute is considered normal. Here are a histogram and summaries for the pulse rates of 52 adults.

WHO	52 adults
WHAT	Resting heart rates
UNITS	Beats per minute

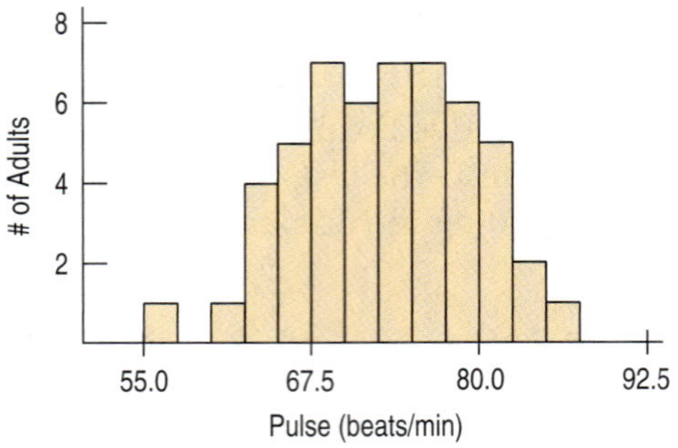

Mean	72.7 beats/min
Min	57
Q1	68
Median	73
Q3	78
Max	86
IQR	10

Pulse rates of 52 adults. **Figure 5.5**

The histogram shows a generally symmetric distribution, and the mean and median agree quite closely. That's what we expect for symmetric data. When the shape of the distribution is symmetric, there's no numerical reason to prefer the median or the mean. As we'll see, it turns out that there's more we can do and say with the mean than with the median. The mean is appropriate, however, only when the shape is symmetric and there are no outliers. (How do you check? Plot the data!)

Math Box

The median is the center of the data in the sense that half the values are bigger and half smaller. The median defines the center by counting the data, but does not care how big or small the actual values may be. Often, however, we do care about the size of the data values; then we need a measure of center that takes each data value into account.

If there are only 2 data values, say 10 and 20, where's the center? In some sense we could call 12 the median. After all, half of the data (the 10) is smaller than 12 and half is larger. But that feels wrong. Saying the center is 15 feels right. Why? Well, one reason might be because then the sizes of the data (not just the counts) are in balance; 20 is 5 points above the center, and 10 is 5 points below the center. We call these distances from the center *deviations*, and write them +5 and −5. Notice that these deviations add up to 0. This means that the distances above center balance the distances below center. The median only balances counts; we also want a center statistic that balances deviations.

In general, consider any set of n data values represented by y's. We want to find a center value (call it M for "middle") that balances these data by size. Let's look at the deviations (distances from this center), represented by the difference between each datum and the center: $y - M$.

We want to find M so that the sum of these deviations is 0:

$$\sum(y - M) = 0$$

Let's solve for M:

$$\sum y - \sum M = 0$$

$$\sum y = \sum M$$

Notice that $\sum M$ actually means adding M's repeatedly, n times:

$$\sum y = M + M + M + \cdots + M$$

$$\sum y = nM$$

When we divide by n, we see how to calculate M:

$$\frac{\sum y}{n} = M$$

That's the answer! To find the magic "middle value" that balances the data by size rather than count, we simply add up all the data and then divide by the number of data values. Sound familiar?

NOTATION ALERT:

In Algebra you used letters to represent values in a problem, but it didn't matter what letter you picked. You could call the width of a rectangle *X* or you could call it *w* (or Fred for that matter). But in Statistics, the notation is part of the vocabulary. For example, in Statistics *n* is always the number of data values. Always.

We will point out such special notation conventions. Think of them as part of the terminology you need to learn in this course.

Here's another one. Whenever we put a bar over a symbol, it means "find the mean."

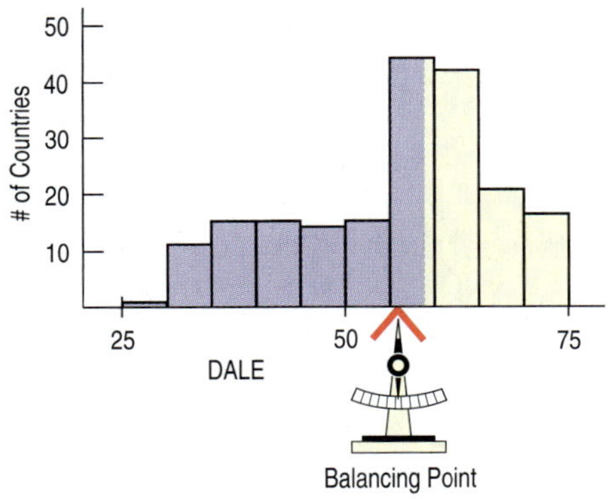

The mean is located at the *balancing point* of the histogram. Since this distribution is skewed to the left, the mean is *lower* than the median. The points at the left have pulled the mean toward them, away from the median. **Figure 5.6**

The Formula for Averaging (Say It in Greek)

You already know how to average values, and the Math Box explains why we want to. This is a good opportunity to introduce some notation that will make it easier to describe calculations later on. Here's the formula:

$$\bar{y} = \frac{Total}{n} = \frac{\sum y}{n}$$

The y with a line over it is pronounced "y-bar." In general, a bar over any symbol or variable name in Statistics denotes finding its mean. The symbol Σ is the Greek letter capital sigma—equivalent to an "S," as in "sum"—and means just that; add up all the observations. The formula says that to find the **mean,** add up all the numbers and divide by n—but you knew that.

Mean or Median?

Does it make a difference whether we choose a mean or a median? Well, sometimes it does. The median of the DALEs is 58.5 years. The mean is only 55.5 years. Why are they different? The answer lies in the shape of the distribution. The **mean** is the point at which the histogram would balance.

Just like a child who moves away from the center of a see-saw, a bar of the histogram far from the center has more leverage, pulling the mean in its direction. If the skewness is strong or if there are straggling outliers, the mean can be pulled quite far from the median. The skewness on the left pulls the mean somewhat to the left of the median here. For the CEO compensation data from Chapter 4, the skewness was to the right. The median compensation is $1,304,470, but the mean is $2,818,743—more than *twice* the median. It's hard to argue that a value pulled in this way is what we meant by the center of the data. For skewed data, it's better to report the median than the mean as a measure of center.

The median splits a histogram so that the *areas* of the bars on either side of the median are equal—regardless of how far they are from the center. The mean balances the histogram, taking into account both the size of the bars and their distance from the center, but as a result it may not have equal numbers of data values on either side.

What About Spread? The Standard Deviation

The IQR is always a reasonable summary of spread, but because it uses only the two quartiles of the data, it ignores much of the information about how individual values vary. A more powerful approach uses the standard deviation, which takes into account how far *each* value is from the mean. Like the mean, the standard deviation is appropriate only for symmetric data.

One way to think about spread is to examine how far each data value is from the mean. This difference is called a *deviation.* We could just average the deviations, but the positive and negative differences always cancel each other out. So the average deviation is always zero—not very helpful.

How to Say "Square Root"

We usually write a square root with the $\sqrt{\ }$ symbol. Especially on computers, though, you may see it as a special function, usually called SQRT(y).

You might recall from Algebra that we can also write the square root as the 1/2 power. On the computer, powers are indicated with an up arrow or carat: y^0.5.

That may not look like a square root at first, but it is, and you should recognize it if you happen to see it written like this.

NOTATION ALERT:

S^2 always means the variance, and s always denotes the standard deviation.

Finding the standard deviation by hand

To find the standard deviation, you start with the mean, $\bar{y}$. Then you find the *deviations* by taking $\bar{y}$ from each value: $(y - \bar{y})$. Square each deviation: $(y - \bar{y})^2$.

Now you're nearly home. Just add these up and divide by $n - 1$. That gives you the variance, s^2. To find the standard deviation, s, take the square root. Here we go:

Suppose the batch of values is 4, 3, 10, 12, 8, 9, and 3.

The mean is $\bar{y} = 7$. So the deviations are found by subtracting 7 from each value:

Original Values	Deviations	Squared Deviations
4	$4 - 7 = -3$	$(-3)^2 = 9$
3	$3 - 7 = -4$	$(-4)^2 = 16$
10	$10 - 7 = 3$	9
12	$12 - 7 = 5$	25
8	$8 - 7 = 1$	1
9	$9 - 7 = 2$	4
3	$3 - 7 = -4$	16

Add up the squared deviations: $9 + 16 + 9 + 25 + 1 + 4 + 16 = 80$.

Now, divide by $n - 1$: $80/6 = 13.33$.

Finally, take the square root:

$s = \sqrt{13.33} = 3.65$

Instead, we *square* each deviation. Squaring always gives a positive value, so the sum won't be zero. That's great. Squaring also emphasizes larger differences—a feature that turns out to be both good and bad.

When we add up these squared deviations and find their average (almost), we call the result the **variance:**

$$s^2 = \frac{\sum(y - \bar{y})^2}{n - 1}$$

Why almost? It would be a mean if we divided the sum by n. But instead we divide by $n - 1$. Why? The simplest explanation is "to drive you crazy." But there are good technical reasons, some of which we'll see later.

The variance will play an important role later in this book, but it has a problem as a measure of spread. Whatever the units of the original data are, the variance is in *squared* units. We want measures of spread to have the same units as the data. And we probably don't want to talk about squared dollars, or mpg^2. So, to get back to the original units, we take the square root of s^2. The result, s, is the **standard deviation.**

Putting it all together, the standard deviation of the data is found by the following formula:

$$s = \sqrt{\frac{\Sigma(y - \bar{y})^2}{n - 1}}$$

You will almost always rely on a calculator or computer to do the calculating.

Thinking about Variation

Statistics is about variation, so spread is an important fundamental concept in Statistics. Measures of spread help us to be precise about what we *don't* know. If many data values are scattered far from the center, the IQR and the standard deviation will be large. If the data values are close to the center, then these measures of spread will be small. If all our data values were exactly the same, we'd have no question about summarizing the center, and all measures of spread would be zero—and we wouldn't need Statistics. You might think this would be a big plus, but it would be a boring world. Fortunately (at least for Statistics), data do vary.

Measures of spread tell how well other summaries describe the data. That's why we always (always!) report a spread along with any summary of the center.

Shape, Center, and Spread

What should you tell about a quantitative variable? Report the shape of its distribution, and include a center and a spread. But which measure of center and which measure of spread? The rules are pretty easy:

- If the shape is skewed, report the median and IQR. You may want to include the mean and standard deviation, but you should point out why the mean and median differ. The fact that the mean and median do not agree is a sign that the distribution may be skewed. A histogram will help you make that point.
- If the shape is symmetric, report the mean and standard deviation and possibly the median and IQR as well.
- If there are any clear outliers and you are reporting the mean and standard deviation, report them with the outliers present and with the outliers removed. The differences may be revealing. (Of course, the median and IQR are not likely to be affected by the outliers.)

We always pair the median with the IQR and the mean with the standard deviation. It's not useful to report one without the other. Reporting a center without a spread is dangerous. You may think you know more than you do about the distribution. Reporting only the spread leaves us wondering where we are.

Summarizing a Distribution STEP-BY-STEP

One of the authors owned a 1989 Nissan Maxima for 8 years. Being a statistician, he recorded the car's fuel efficiency (in mpg) each time he filled the tank.[2] He wanted to know what fuel efficiency to expect as "ordinary" for his car. (Hey, he's a statistician, what would you expect?) Knowing this, he was able to predict when he'd need to fill the tank again, and to notice if the fuel efficiency suddenly got worse, which could be a sign of trouble. What do the data say?

Think

Variable Identify the variable and report the W's.

The data are the fuel efficiency values in miles per gallon for 100 fill-ups of a 1989 Nissan Maxima between 1989 and 1997.

Show

Mechanics Make a histogram. Based on its shape, choose appropriate numerical summaries.

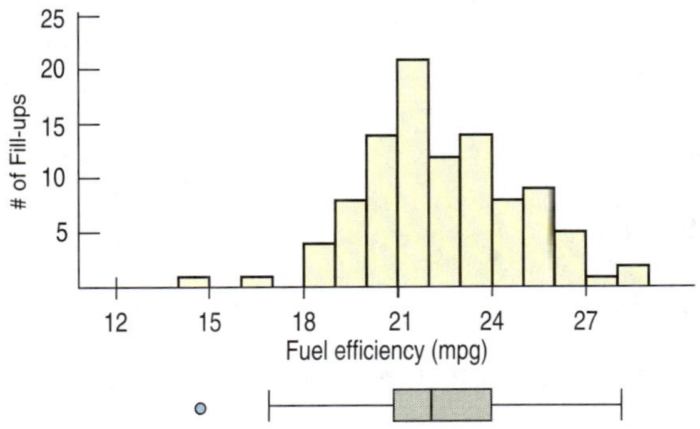

A histogram of the data shows a fairly symmetric distribution with a low outlier.

✓ Reality Check A value of 22 mpg seems reasonable for such a car. The spread is reasonable, although the range looks a bit large.

Count	100
Mean	22.4 mpg
StdDev	2.45
Median	22.0
IQR	3.2
Q1	20.8
Q3	24.0

[2]He also recorded the time of day, temperature, price of gas, and phase of the moon, but we won't go there.

The mean and median are close, so the outlier doesn't seem to be a problem. We can use the mean and standard deviation.

Tell **Interpretation** Summarize and interpret your findings.

The distribution of mileage is unimodal and symmetric with a mean of 22.4 mpg. There is a low outlier that should be investigated, but it does not influence the mean very much. The standard deviation is 2.4 mpg. The boxplot shows that half of the time, the car had a fuel efficiency between about 21 and 24 mpg.

TI Tips

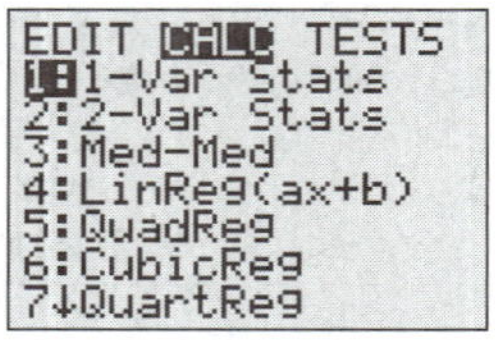

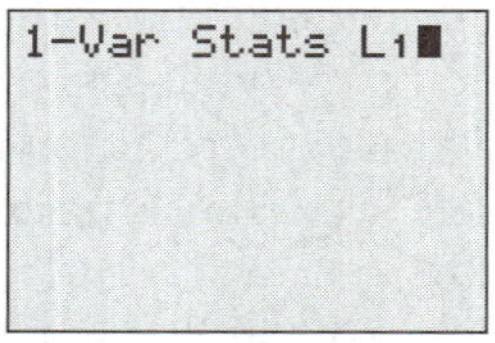

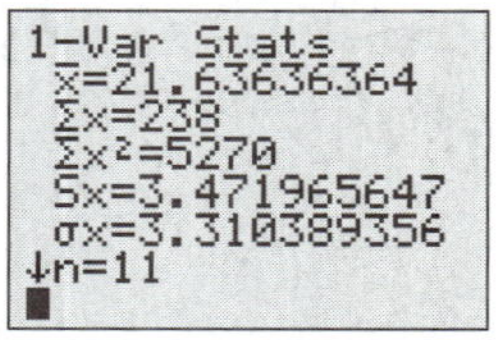

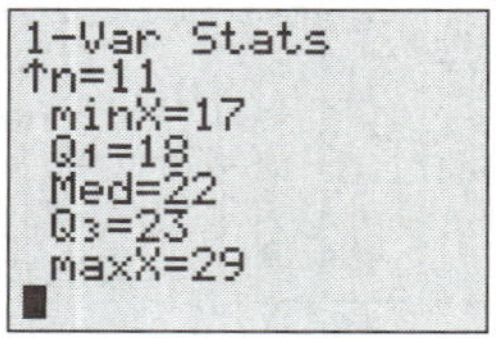

Your calculator can easily find all the numerical summaries of data. To try it out, you simply need a set of values in one of your datalists. We'll illustrate using the boys' agility test results from this chapter's earlier TI Tips (still in L1), but you can use any data currently stored in your calculator.

- Under the STAT CALC menu, select 1-Var Stats and hit ENTER.
- Specify the location of your data, creating a command like 1-Var Stats L1.
- Hit ENTER again.

Voila! Everything you wanted to know, and more. Among all of the information shown, you are primarily interested in these statistics: $\bar{x}$ (the mean), Sx (the standard deviation), n (the count), and—scrolling down—minX (the smallest datum), Q_1 (the first quartile), Med (the median), Q_3 (the third quartile), and maxX (the largest datum).

Sorry, but the TI doesn't explicitly tell you the range or the IQR. Just subtract: $IQR = Q_3 - Q_1 = 23 - 18 = 5$. What's the range?

By the way, if the data come as a frequency table with the values stored in, say, L4 and the corresponding frequencies in L5, all you have to do is ask for 1-Var Stats L4,L5.

What Can Go Wrong?

The task of summarizing a quantitative variable is relatively simple, and there is a simple path to follow. However, you need to watch out for certain features of the data that make summarizing them with a number dangerous. Here's some advice:

- ***Do a reality check.*** Don't let the computer (or calculator) do your thinking for you. Make sure the calculated summaries make sense. For example, does the mean look like it is in the center of the histogram? Think about the spread: An IQR of 50 mpg would clearly be wrong for a family car. And no measure of spread can be negative. The standard deviation can take the value 0, but only in the very unusual case that all the data values equal the same number. If you see the IQR or standard deviation equal to 0, it's probably a sign that something's wrong with the data.
- ***Don't forget to sort the values before finding the median or percentiles.*** It seems obvious, but when you work by hand, it's easy to forget to sort the data first before counting in to find medians, quartiles, or other percentiles. Don't

report that the median of the five values 194, 5, 1, 17, 893 is 1 just because 1 is the middle number.

- ***Don't compute numerical summaries of a categorical variable.*** The mean zip code or the standard deviation of social security numbers is not meaningful. If the variable is categorical, you should instead report summaries such as percentages. It is easy to make this mistake when using technology to do the summaries for you. After all, the computer doesn't care what the numbers mean.
- ***Watch out for multiple modes.*** If the distribution—as seen in a histogram, for example—has multiple modes, consider separating the data into different groups. If you cannot separate the data in a meaningful way, you should not summarize the center and spread of the variable.
- ***Be aware of slightly different methods.*** Finding the 10th percentile in a data set sounds easy enough. But it turns out that the practical definition of a percentile is not exactly clear. There are at least six reasonable definitions of quartiles alone.[3] If you compare different statistics packages or calculators, you may find that they give slightly different answers for the same data. These differences, though, are unlikely to be important in interpreting the data, the quartiles, or the IQR. So don't let them worry you.
- ***Beware of outliers.*** If the data have outliers but are otherwise unimodal, consider holding the outliers out of the further calculations and reporting them individually. If you can find a simple reason for the outlier (for instance, a data transcription error) you should remove or correct it. If you cannot do either of these, then choose the median and IQR to summarize the center and spread.
- ***Make a picture (make a picture, make a picture).*** The sensitivity of the mean and standard deviation to outliers is one reason why you should *always* make a picture of the data. Summarizing a variable with its mean and standard deviation when you have not looked at a histogram or dotplot to check for outliers invites disaster. You may find yourself drawing absurd or dangerously wrong conclusions about the data. And, of course, you should demand no less of others. Don't accept a mean and standard deviation blindly without some evidence that the variable they summarize has no outliers or severe skewness.
- ***Be careful when comparing groups that have very different spreads.*** For example, look at this boxplot. Researchers measured the concentration (nanograms per milliliter) of cotinine in the blood of three groups of people: nonsmokers who have not been exposed to smoke, nonsmokers who have been exposed to smoke (ETS), and smokers. Cotinine is left in the blood when the body metabolizes nicotine, so this measure gives a direct measurement of the effect of

WHO	Smokers, nonsmokers, and passive smokers
WHAT	Blood cotinine levels
UNITS	nanograms per milliliter (ng/mL)

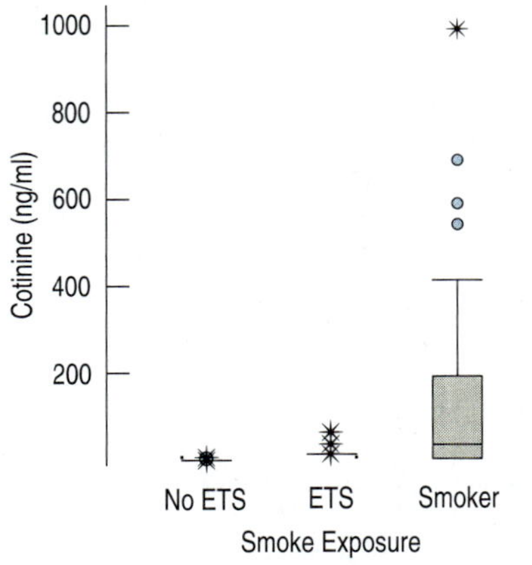

Cotinine levels (nanograms per milliliter) for three groups with different exposures to tobacco smoke. Can you compare the ETS and No ETS groups? **Figure 5.7**

[3]The method we give works well and is easy to do by hand. A similar method that omits the median before finding medians of each half of the data works a bit less well, sometimes making the IQR appear to be slightly larger. Both methods are commonly used, however. If you are willing to do a bit more calculating, there are several other methods of counting in that include interpolating between adjacent values. All of the definitions agree pretty closely anyway unless there are very few data values (in which case there's no need to summarize them).

passive smoke exposure. The boxplots of the cotinine levels of the three groups tell us that the smokers have higher cotinine levels, but if we want to compare the levels of the passive smokers to the nonsmokers, we're in trouble, because on this scale, the cotinine levels for both nonsmoking groups are too low to be seen.

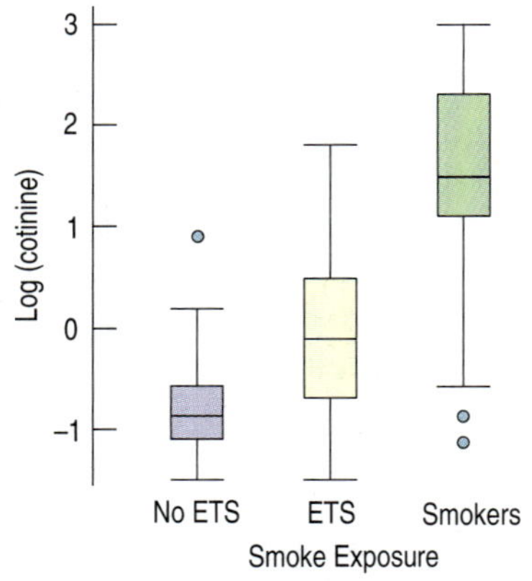

Blood cotinine levels after taking logs. What a difference a log makes! **Figure 5.8**

Re-expressing to Equalize the Spread of Groups

We can often alleviate the problem of comparing groups that have very different spreads by re-expressing the data values. For measurements like the cotinine data, whose values can't be negative and whose distributions are skewed to the high end, a good first guess at a re-expression is the logarithm.

After taking logs we can compare the groups and see that the nonsmokers exposed to environmental smoke (the ETS group) do show increased levels of (log) cotinine, although not the high levels found in the blood of smokers. Notice that the same re-expression has also improved the symmetry of the cotinine distribution for smokers and pulled in most of the apparent outliers in all of the groups. It is not unusual for a re-expression that improves one aspect of data to improve others as well. We'll talk about other ways to re-express data as the need arises throughout the book.

Numerical Summaries and the Computer

Many statistics packages offer a pre-packaged collection of summary measures. The result might look like this:

```
Variable: Weight
N = 234
Mean = 143.3          Median = 139
St. Dev = 11.1        IQR = 14
```

Alternatively, a package might make a table for several variables and summary measures.

Variable	N	mean	median	stdev	IQR
Weight	234	143.3	139	11.1	14
Height	234	68.3	68.1	4.3	5
Score	234	86	88	9	5

It is usually easy to read the results and identify each computed summary. You should be able to read the summary statistics produced by any computer package.

Packages often provide many more summary statistics than you need. Of course, some of these may not be appropriate when the data are skewed or have outliers. It is your responsibility to check a histogram or stem-and-leaf display and decide which summary statistics to use.

It is common for packages to report summary statistics to many decimal places of "accuracy." Of course, it is rare data that have such accuracy in the original measurements. The ability to calculate to six or seven digits beyond the decimal point doesn't mean that those digits have any meaning. Generally, it's a good idea to round these values, allowing perhaps one more digit of precision than was given in the original data.

Summary statistics are easy to find in most packages.

Connections

We discussed the value of summarizing a distribution with shape, center, and spread in Chapter 4. Now we have numerical summaries for center and spread to go with our general observations. The shape of the distribution helps us to decide which numerical summaries are most appropriate.

We compared distributions in Chapter 4 by just looking at histograms. Working with numerical summaries and boxplots adds depth to our comparisons.

Key Concepts

Center We summarize the center of a distribution with the mean or the median.

Median The median is the middle value with half of the data above and half below it.

Spread We summarize the spread of a distribution with the standard deviation, interquartile range, and range.

Range The difference between the lowest and highest values in a data set. Range = max − min.

Quartile The lower quartile (Q1) is the value with a quarter of the data below it. The upper quartile (Q3) has a quarter of the data above it. The median and quartiles divide data into four equal parts.

Interquartile range (IQR) The IQR is the difference between the first and third quartiles. IQR = Q3 − Q1.

Percentile The ith percentile is the number that falls above i% of the data.

Five-number summary A five-number summary for a variable consists of:

- The minimum and maximum
- The quartiles: Q1 and Q3
- The median

Boxplot A boxplot displays the five-number summary as a central box with whiskers that extend to the nonoutlying data values. Boxplots are particularly effective for comparing groups.

Mean The mean is found by summing all the data values and dividing by the count.

Variance The variance is the sum of squared deviations from the mean, divided by the count minus one.

Standard deviation The standard deviation is the square root of the variance.

Comparing distributions When comparing the distribution of several groups, consider their
- Shape
- Center
- Spread

Comparing boxplots When comparing groups with boxplots,
- Compare the medians; which group has the higher center?
- Compare the IQRs; which group is more spread out?
- On the scale of the IQRs are the medians very different?
- Check for possible outliers. Identify them if you can.

Skills

When you complete this lesson you should:

Think

- Be able to select a suitable measure of center and a suitable measure of spread for a variable based on information about its distribution.
- Know the basic properties of the median: The median divides the data into the half of the data values that are below the median and the half that are above the median.
- Know the basic properties of the mean: The mean is the point at which the histogram balances.
- Know that the standard deviation summarizes how spread out all the data are around the mean.

Show

- Know how to compute the mean and median of a set of data.
- Know how to compute the standard deviation and IQR of a set of data.
- Be able to create a five-number summary of a variable.
- Be able to construct a boxplot by hand from a five-number summary.
- Understand that the median and IQR resist the effects of outliers, while the mean and standard deviation do not.
- Understand that in a skewed distribution, the mean is pulled in the direction of the skewness (toward the longer tail) relative to the median.

Tell

- Know how to describe summary measures in a sentence. In particular, know that the common measures of center and spread have the same units as the variable that they summarize, and should be described in those units.
- Be able to describe the distribution of a quantitative variable with a description of the shape of the distribution, a numerical measure of center, and a numerical measure of spread.
- Know how to compare the distributions of two or more groups by comparing their shapes, centers, and spreads.
- Be able to compare two or more groups by comparing their boxplots.
- Know how to use the 1.5 IQR rule to identify possible outliers. Interpret outliers found in boxplots made on a computer.

Exercises

1. In the news. Find an article in a newspaper or a magazine that discusses an "average."
a) Does the article discuss the W's for the data?
b) What are the units for the variable?
c) Is the average used the median or the mean? How can you tell?
d) Is the choice of median or mean appropriate for the situation? Explain.

2. In the news II. Find an article in a newspaper or a magazine that discusses a measure of spread.
a) Does the article discuss the W's for the data?
b) What are the units for the variable?
c) Does the article use the range, IQR, or standard deviation?
d) Is the choice of measure of spread appropriate for the situation? Explain.

3. Summaries. Here are costs of 10 electric smoothtop ranges rated very good or excellent by *Consumer Reports* in August 2002.

$850 900 1400 1200 1050 1000 750 1250 1050 565

Find these statistics *by hand* (no calculator!):
a) mean
b) median and quartiles
c) range and IQR

4. More summaries. Here are the annual numbers of deaths from tornadoes in the United States from 1990 through 2000. (Source: NOAA)

53 39 39 33 69 30 25 67 130 94 40

Find these statistics *by hand* (no calculator!):
a) mean
b) median and quartiles
c) range and IQR

5. Mistake. A clerk entering salary data into a company spreadsheet accidentally put an extra "0" in the boss's salary, listing it as $2,000,000 instead of $200,000. Explain how this error will affect these summary statistics for the company payroll:
a) measures of center: median and mean.
b) measures of spread: range, IQR, and standard deviation.

6. Sick days. During contract negotiations a company seeks to change the number of sick days employees may take, saying that the annual "average" is 7 days of absence per employee. The union negotiators counter that the "average" employee misses only 3 days of work each year. Explain how both sides might be correct, identifying the measure of center you think each side is using and why the stated difference might exist.

7. Payroll. A small warehouse employs a supervisor at $1200 a week, an inventory manager at $700 a week, six stock boys at $400 a week, and four drivers at $500 a week.
a) Find the mean and median wage.
b) How many employees earn more than the mean wage?
c) Which measure of center best describes a typical wage at this company, the mean or the median?
d) Which measure of spread would best describe the payroll, the range, the IQR, or the standard deviation? Why?

8. Singers. The frequency table shows the heights (in inches) of 130 members of a choir.

Height	Count	Height	Count
60	2	69	5
61	6	70	11
62	9	71	8
63	7	72	9
64	5	73	4
65	20	74	2
66	18	75	4
67	7	76	1
68	12		

a) Find the five-number summary for these data.
b) Display these data with a boxplot.
c) Find the mean and standard deviation.
d) Display these data with a histogram.
e) Write a few sentences describing the distribution of heights.

9. Standard deviation. For each lettered part, a through c, examine the two given sets of numbers. Without doing any calculations, decide which set has the larger standard deviation and explain why. Then check by finding the standard deviations *by hand.*

	Set 1	Set 2
a)	3, 5, 6, 7, 9	2, 4, 6, 8, 10
b)	10, 14, 15, 16, 20	10, 11, 15, 19, 20
c)	2, 6, 6, 9, 11, 14	82, 86, 86, 89, 91, 94

10. Standard deviation. For each lettered part, a through c, examine the two given sets of numbers. Without doing any calculations, decide which set has the larger standard deviation and explain why. Then check by finding the standard deviations *by hand.*

	Set 1	Set 2
a)	4, 7, 7, 7, 10	4, 6, 7, 8, 10
b)	100, 140, 150, 160, 200	10, 50, 60, 70, 110
c)	10, 16, 18, 20, 22, 28	48, 56, 58, 60, 62, 70

11. Home runs. In 1961 Roger Maris made baseball headlines by hitting 61 home runs, breaking a famous record held by Babe Ruth. Here are Maris's home run totals for his 10 seasons in the American League. Would you consider his record-setting year to be an outlier? Explain.

8, 13, 14, 16, 23, 26, 28, 33, 39, 61

12. Camp sites. Shown below are the histogram and summary statistics for the number of camp sites at public parks in Vermont.

a) Which statistics would you use to identify the center and spread of this distribution? Why?
b) How many parks would you classify as outliers? Explain.
c) Create a boxplot for these data.
d) Write a few sentences describing the distribution.

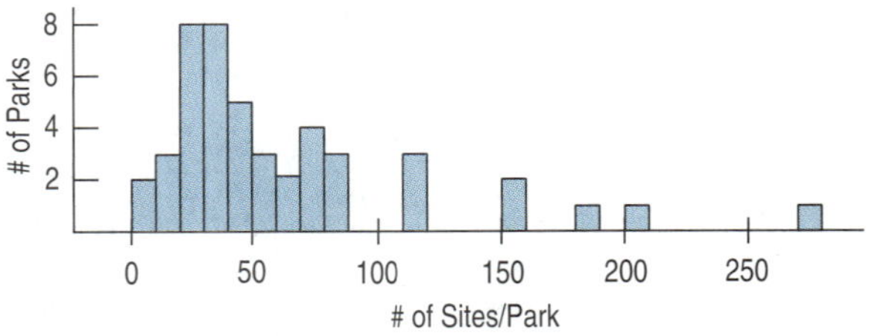

Count	46
Mean	62.78 sites
Median	43.50
StdDev	56.196
Min	0
Max	275
Lower Q	28
Upper Q	78

13. Marriage age. Do men and women marry at the same age? Here are boxplots of the age at first marriage for a sample of U.S. citizens. Write a brief report discussing what these data show.

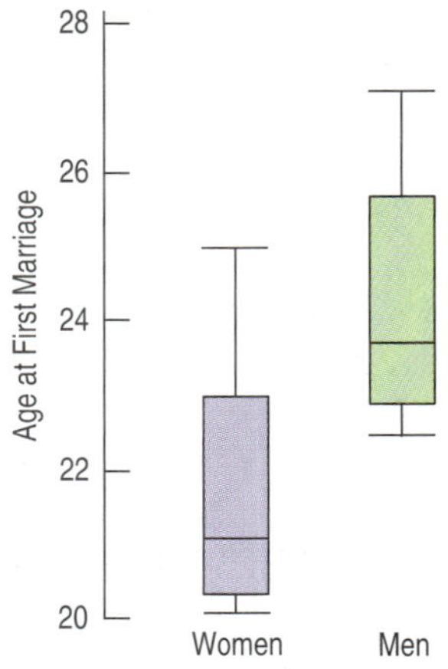

14. Fuel economy. Describe what these boxplots tell you about the relationship between the number of cylinders a car's engine has and the car's fuel economy (mpg).

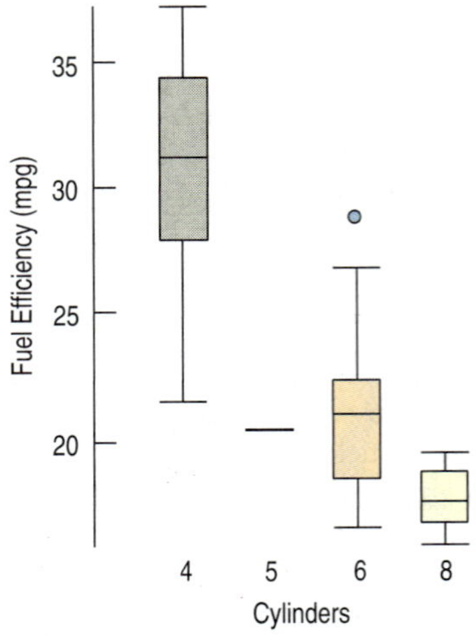

15. Grapes. The boxplots display case prices (in dollars) of varieties of grapes produced by vineyards along three of the Finger Lakes.

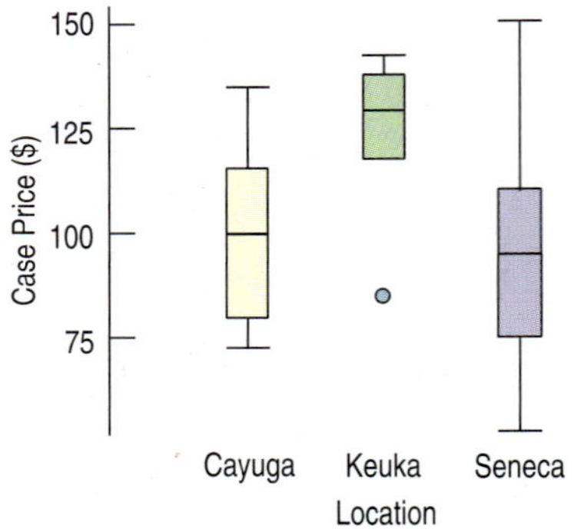

a) Which lake region produces the most expensive grape?
b) Which lake region produces the cheapest grape?
c) In which region are the grapes generally more expensive?
d) Write a few sentences describing these grape prices.

16. Ozone. Ozone levels (in parts per million, ppm) were recorded at sites in New Jersey monthly between 1926 and 1971. Here are boxplots of the data for each month (over the 46 years) lined up in order (January = 1).

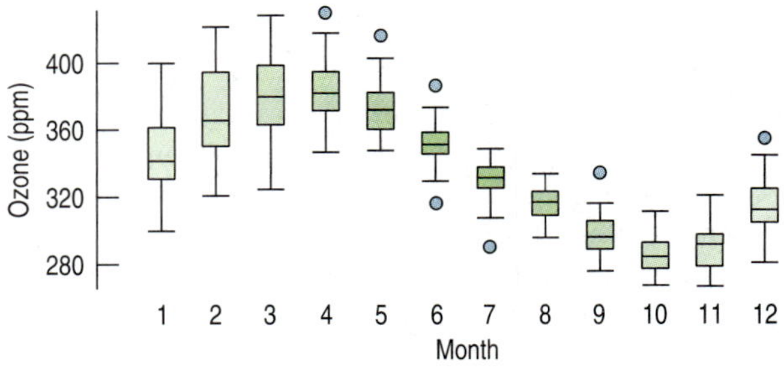

a) In what month was the highest ozone level ever recorded?
b) Which month has the largest IQR?
c) Which month has the smallest range?
d) Write a brief comparison of the ozone levels in January and June.
e) Write a report on the annual patterns you see in the ozone levels.

17. Wild card Summer Olympics. Seventy-one swimmers finished the qualifying first day of the men's 100-m swim in Sydney. The average time was 52.65 seconds with a standard deviation of 7.66 seconds. The median time was 51.34 seconds and the IQR was 2.58 seconds.
a) Without looking at a graphical display, what shape would you expect the distributions of times to have?
b) What might account for the difference between these two sets of statistics?
c) Here is the histogram of the actual times. Write a couple of sentences summarizing what you see.[4]

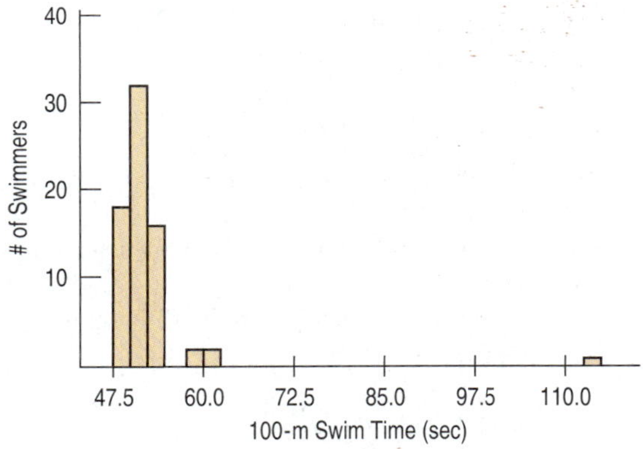

Eric Moussambani of Equatorial Guinea was eligible for the 100-m swim in the 2000 Olympics, thanks to a special program.

[4]IOC president Juan Antonio Samaranch initiated a special program in the 2000 Olympics. As a way of spreading sports around the world, a handful of athletes were allowed to compete even though they didn't meet qualifying standards. Moussambani, who trains in a 20-m pool with no lane markers in his African homeland, became an international celebrity after completing his swim in more than twice the time of the next slowest competitor. He carried the national flag in the opening ceremony, leading an 11-person team that also included a female swimmer. He actually won his heat of 3 swimmers when the other two failed to qualify.

18. Unemployment. In May of 2001, the U.S. Bureau of Labor Statistics (BLS) issued a news release that said, in part:

In April, 223 metropolitan areas recorded unemployment rates below the U.S. average of 4.2 percent (not seasonally adjusted), while 99 areas registered higher rates.

Sketch what the distribution of unemployment rates for the 322 metropolitan areas reported on by BLS probably looks like.

19. Test scores. Three Statistics classes all took the same test. Histograms of the scores for each class are shown below.

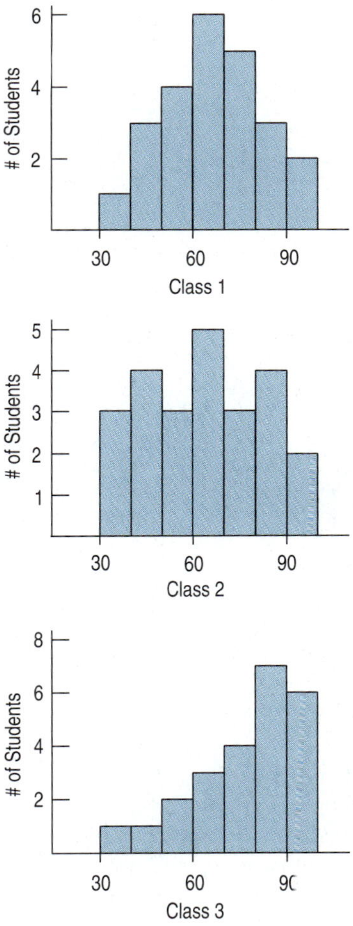

a) Which class had the highest mean score?
b) Which class had the highest median score?
c) For which class are the mean and median most different? Which is higher? Why?
d) Which class had the smallest standard deviation?
e) Which class had the smallest IQR?

20. Test scores. Look again at the histograms of test scores for the three Statistics classes in Exercise 19.

a) Overall, which class do you think performed better on the test? Why?
b) How would you describe the shape of each distribution?
c) Match each class with the corresponding boxplot below.

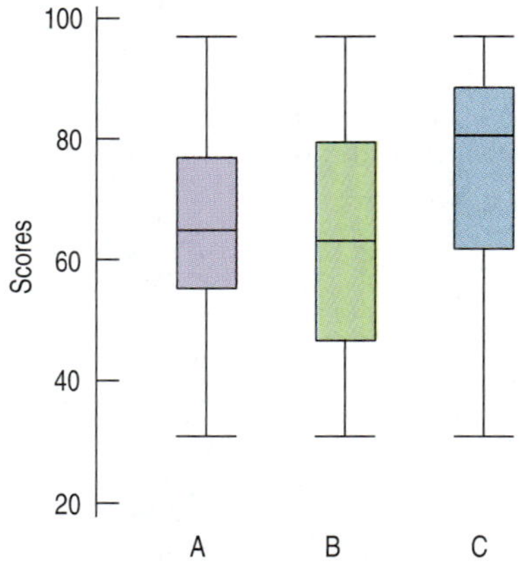

21. Still rockin'. On page 60, you read about the 66 deaths attributed to "crowd crush" at rock concerts during the years 1999 and 2000. Here are the histogram and boxplot of the victims' ages that we saw earlier:

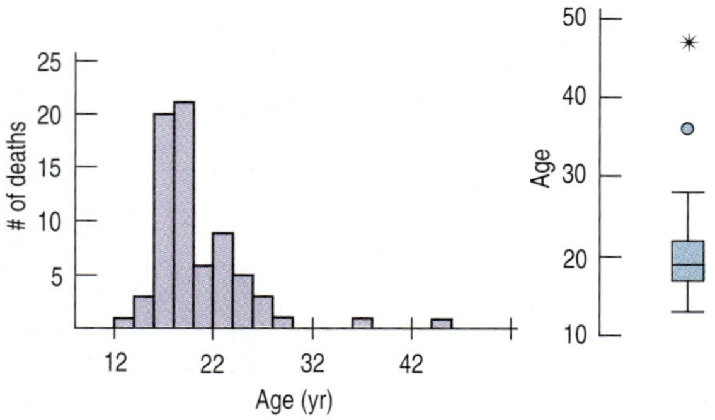

a) What features of the distribution can you see in both the histogram and the boxplot?
b) What features of the distribution can you see in the histogram that you could not see in the boxplot?
c) What summary statistic would you choose to summarize the center of this distribution? Why?
d) What summary statistic would you choose to summarize the spread of this distribution? Why?

22. Golf courses. One measure of the difficulty of a golf course is its length: the total distance (in yards) from tee to hole for all 18 holes. Below are the histogram and summary statistics for the lengths of all the golf courses in Vermont.

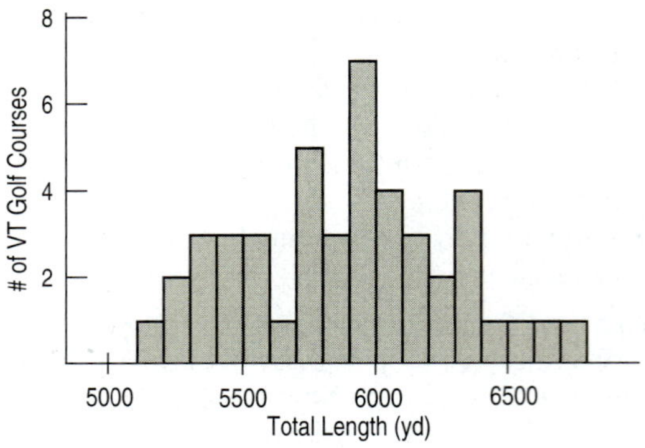

Count	45
Mean	5892.91 yd
StdDev	386.591
Min	5185
Q1	5585.75
Median	5928
Q3	6131
Max	6796

a) What is the range of these lengths?
b) Between what lengths do the central 50% of these courses lie?
c) What summary statistics would you use to describe these data?
d) Write a brief description of these data (shape, center, and spread).

23. Graduation? A survey of major universities asked what percentage of incoming freshmen usually graduate in 4 years. Use the summary statistics given to answer these questions.

	% on time
Count	48
Mean	68.35
Median	69.90
StdDev	10.196
Min	43.20
Max	87.40
Range	44.20
25th %tile	59.15
75th %tile	74.75

a) Would you describe this distribution as symmetric or skewed? Explain.
b) Are there any outliers? Explain.
c) Create a boxplot of these data.
d) Write a few sentences about the graduation rates.

24. Vineyards. Here are summary statistics for the sizes (in acres) of Finger Lakes vineyards.

Count	36
Mean	46.50 acres
StdDev	47.76
Median	33.50
IQR	36.50
Min	6
Q1	18.50
Q3	55
Max	250

a) Would you describe this distribution as symmetric or skewed? Explain.
b) Are there any outliers? Explain.
c) Create a boxplot of these data.
d) Write a few sentences about the sizes of the vineyards.

25. Caffeine. A student study of the effects of caffeine asked volunteers to take a memory test 2 hours after drinking soda. Some drank caffeine-free cola, some drank regular cola (with caffeine), and others drank a mixture of the two (getting a half-dose of caffeine). Here are the five-number summaries for each group's scores (number of items recalled correctly) on the memory test:

	n	Min	Q1	Median	Q3	Max
No caffeine	15	16	20	21	24	26
Low caffeine	15	16	18	21	24	27
High caffeine	15	12	17	19	22	24

a) Describe the W's for these data: Who, What, When, Where, Why, How.
b) Name the variables and classify each as categorical or quantitative.
c) Create parallel boxplots to display these results as best you can with this information.
d) Write a few sentences comparing the performances of the three groups.

26. Rainmakers? In an experiment to determine whether seeding clouds with silver iodide increases rainfall, 52 clouds were randomly assigned to be seeded or not. The amount of rain they generated was then measured (in acre-feet).

	n	Mean	Median	SD	IQR	Q1	Q3
Unseeded	26	164.59	44.20	278.43	138.60	24.40	163
Seeded	26	441.98	221.60	650.79	337.60	92.40	430

a) Which of the summary statistics are most appropriate for describing these distributions. Why?
b) Do you see any evidence that seeding clouds may be effective? Explain.

27. States. The stem-and-leaf display shows populations of the 50 states and Washington, D.C., in millions of people, according to the 2000 census.

3	4
2	
2	1
1	69
1	0122
0	5555666667888
0	111111111111122222333333344444

State Populations (1|2 means 12 million)

a) What measures of center and spread are most appropriate?
b) Without doing any calculations, which must be larger—the median or the mean? Explain how you know.
c) From the stem-and-leaf display, find the median and the interquartile range.
d) Write a few sentences describing this distribution.

28. Population growth. The back-to-back stem-and-leaf display compares the percentage change between the 1990 census and 2000 census in the populations of northeastern and midwestern states with the changes in population of southern and western states. The fastest growing states were Nevada at 66% and Arizona at 40%. Use the data displayed in the stem-and-leaf display to construct comparative boxplots.

NE/MW States		S/W States
	6	6
	6	
	5	
	5	
	4	
	4	0
	3	
	3	001
	2	6
	2	001134
	1	578
2100	1	001134444
99998876655	0	6999
1344	0	1

29. Derby speeds. How fast do horses run? Kentucky Derby winners top 30 miles per hour, as shown in the graph below. In fact, this graph shows the percentage of Derby winners that have run *slower* than a given speed.

Note that few have won running less than 33 miles per hour, but about 95% of the winning horses have run less than 37 miles per hour. (A cumulative frequency graph like this is called an "ogive.")

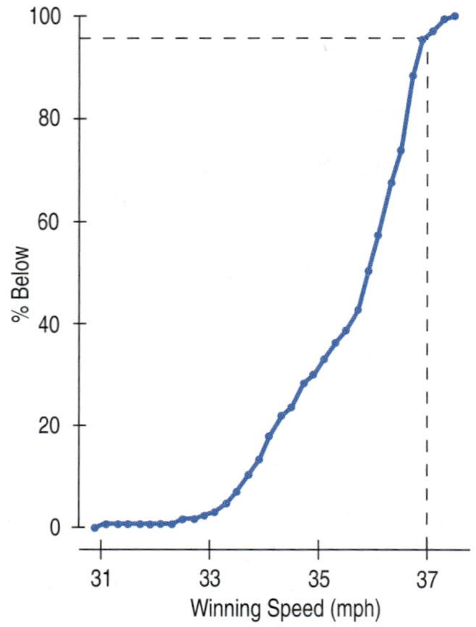

a) Estimate the median winning speed.
b) Estimate the quartiles.
c) Estimate the range and the IQR.
d) Create a boxplot of these speeds.
e) Write a few sentences about the speeds of the Kentucky Derby winners.

30. Cholesterol. The Framingham Heart Study recorded the cholesterol levels of more than 1400 men. Here is an ogive of the distribution of these cholesterol measures. (Recall that an ogive shows the percentage of cases at or below a certain value.) Construct a boxplot for these data and write a few sentences describing the distribution.

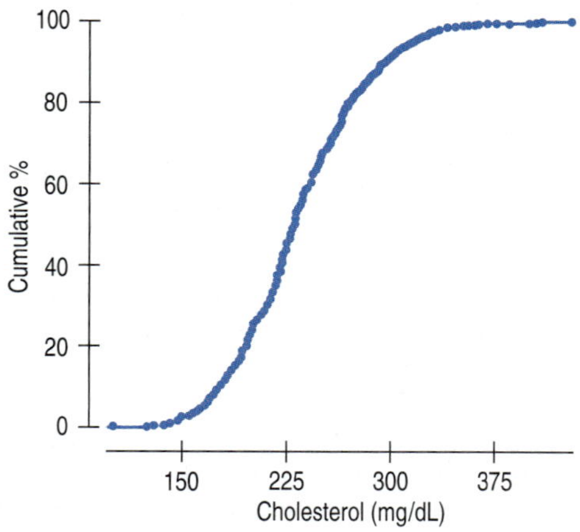

31. Reading scores. A class of fourth graders takes a diagnostic reading test, and the scores are reported by reading grade level. The five-number summaries for the 14 boys and 11 girls are shown:

Boys:	2.0	3.9	4.3	4.9	6.0
Girls:	2.8	3.8	4.5	5.2	5.9

a) Which group had the highest score?
b) Which group had the greatest range?
c) Which group had the greatest interquartile range?
d) Which group's scores appear to be more skewed? Explain.
e) Which group generally did better on the test? Explain.
f) If the mean reading level for boys was 4.2 and for girls was 4.6, what is the overall mean for the class?

32. SAT scores. Here are the summary statistics for Verbal SAT scores for a high school graduating class.

	n	Mean	Median	SD	Min	Max	Q1	Q3
Male	80	590	600	97.2	310	800	515	650
Female	82	602	625	102.0	360	770	530	680

a) Create parallel boxplots comparing the scores of boys and girls as best you can from the information given.
b) Write a brief report on these results. Be sure to discuss shape, center, and spread of the scores.

T **33. Phone calls.** In an advertisement in *USA Today* (July 9, 2001), the company Net2Phone listed its long distance rates to 24 of the 250 countries to which it offers service.

Country	Cost per minute (cents)	Country	Cost per minute (cents)
Belgium	7.9	Italy	9.9
Chile	17	Japan	7.9
Canada	3.9	Mexico	16
Colombia	9.9	Pakistan	49
Dominican Republic	15	Philippines	21
		Puerto Rico	6.9
Finland	9.9	Singapore	11
France	7.9	South Korea	9.9
Germany	7.9	Taiwan	9.9
Hong Kong	7.9	United Kingdom	7.9
India	49	United States	3.9
Ireland	7.9	Venezuela	22
Israel	8.9		

a) Make a display of these rates.
b) Find the mean and the median. Which is a more appropriate measure of center?

c) Find the IQR and the standard deviation. Which is the more appropriate measure of spread?
d) Would you consider any of these to be outliers? Carefully explain how you reached your decision.
e) Write a brief description of these rates. Don't forget to mention shape, center, and spread as well as any unusual features of the distribution.
f) What can you conclude about Net2Phone's rates to the 250 countries the ad says they service?

T **34. Job growth.** In 1996 the firm Standard and Poor's DRI predicted that the cities listed below would experience the fastest growing job markets in the United States over the next 3 years and predicted their growth rates, given here.

City	Growth(%)
Las Vegas, NV-AZ	3.72
Raleigh-Durham-Chapel Hill, NC	2.69
Austin-San Marcos, TX	2.64
Riverside-San Bernardino, CA	2.62
Boise, ID	2.61
Orlando, FL	2.51
Phoenix-Mesa, AZ	2.44
West Palm Beach-Boca Raton, FL	2.37
Sacramento, CA	2.26
Atlanta, GA	2.25
Sarasota-Bradenton, FL	2.22
Portland-Vancouver, OR-WA	2.16
Fort Lauderdale, FL	2.13
Charlotte-Gastonia-Rock Hill, NC-SC	2.07
Tucson, AZ	2.07
Vallejo-Fairfield-Napa, CA	2.02
Omaha, NE-IA	1.93
Salt Lake City-Ogden, UT	1.90
Albuquerque, NM	1.87
Fort Worth-Arlington, TX	1.86

a) Make a suitable display of the growth rates.
b) Summarize the central growth rate with a median and mean. Why do they differ?
c) Given what you know about the distribution, which of these measures does the better job of summarizing the growth rates? Why?
d) Summarize the spread of the growth rate distribution with a standard deviation and with an IQR.
e) Given what you know about the distribution, which of these measures does the better job of summarizing the growth rates? Why?
f) Suppose we subtract from each of these growth rates the predicted U.S. average growth rate of 1.20%, so that we could look at how much these growth rates exceed the U.S. rate. How would this change the values of the summary statistics you calculated above? (*Hint:* You need not recompute any of the summary statistics from scratch.)
g) If we were to omit Las Vegas from the data, how would you expect the mean, median, standard deviation, and IQR to change? Explain your expectations for each.
h) Write a brief report about these growth rates.

T **35. Math scores.** The National Center for Education Statistics reported 1999 average mathematics achievement scores for eighth graders in 38 nations. Singapore led the group, with an average score of 604, while South Africa had the lowest average of 275. The United States scored 502. The average score for each nation are given below.

604	587	585	582	579	558	540	534	532	531
530	526	525	520	520	519	511	505	502	496
491	482	479	476	472	469	467	466	448	447
429	428	422	403	392	345	337	275		

a) Find the five-number summary, the IQR, the mean, and the standard deviation of these national averages.
b) Write a brief summary of the performance of eighth graders worldwide. Be sure to comment on the performance of the United States.

36. Prisons. A report from the U.S. Department of Justice gave the following percent increases in federal prison populations in 20 northeastern and midwestern states during 1999.

5.9, 1.3, 3.0, 5.9, 4.5, 5.6, 2.1, 6.3, 4.8, 6.9, 4.5, 3.5, 7.2, 6.4, 5.5, 5.3, 8.0, 4.4, 7.2, 3.2

a) Graph these data.
b) Calculate appropriate summary statistics.
c) Write a few sentences about these data. (Remember: shape, center, spread, unusual features.)

T **37. Gasoline usage.** The U.S. Department of Transportation collects data on the amount of gasoline sold in each state. The following data show the per capita (gallons used per person) consumption in the year 2000. Using appropriate graphical displays and summary statistics, write a report on the gasoline use by state in the year 2000. (See table at top of next page.)

Alabama	544.71	Hawaii	327.27	Mass	438.1	NM	474.28	SD	555.06
Alaska	433.08	Idaho	500.34	Michigan	502.77	New York	551.18	TN	586.58
Arizona	452.82	Illinois	406.66	MN	528.06	NC	296.66	Texas	515.17
Arkansas	532.96	Indiana	518.7	MS	559.29	ND	513.3	Utah	498.66
CA	422.65	Iowa	534.7	Missouri	563.56	Ohio	574.83	Vermont	456.27
Colorado	461.90	Kansas	511.34	Montana	548.5	OK	457.63	Virginia	584.03
CT	431.04	Kentucky	510.9	Nebraska	508.28	Oregon	520.42	WA	506.92
Delaware	481.45	LA	522.12	Nevada	446.17	PA	441.44	WV	450.4
Florida	542.36	Maine	542.36	NH	542.86	RI	410.31	WI	462
Georgia	452.82	Maryland	452.82	NJ	474.28	SC	381.86	Wyoming	462.67

T 38. **Industrial experiment.** Engineers at a computer production plant tested two methods for accuracy in drilling holes into a PC board. They tested how fast they could set the drilling machine by running 10 boards at each of two different speeds. To assess the results, they measured the distance (in inches) from the center of a target on the board to the center of the hole. The data and summary statistics are shown in the table:

	Fast	Slow
	0.000101	0.000098
	0.000102	0.000096
	0.000100	0.000097
	0.000102	0.000095
	0.000101	0.000094
	0.000103	0.000098
	0.000104	0.000096
	0.000102	0.975600
	0.000102	0.000097
	0.000100	0.000096
Mean	0.000102	0.097647
StdDev	0.000001	0.308481

Write a report summarizing the findings of the experiment. Include appropriate visual and verbal displays of the distributions, and make a recommendation to the engineers if they are most interested in the accuracy of the method.

39. **Customer Database.** A philanthropic organization has a database of millions of donors that they contact by mail to raise money for charities. One of the variables in the database, *Title,* contains the title of the person or persons printed on the address label. The most common are Mr., Ms., Miss, and Mrs., but there are also Ambassador and Mrs., Your Imperial Majesty, and Cardinal to name a few others. In all there are over 100 different titles, each with a corresponding numeric code. Here are a few of them:

Code	Title
000	MR.
001	MRS.
002	MR. and MRS.
003	MISS
004	DR.
005	MADAME
006	SERGEANT
009	RABBI
010	PROFESSOR
126	PRINCE
127	PRINCESS
128	CHIEF
129	BARON
130	SHEIK
131	PRINCE AND PRINCESS
132	YOUR IMPERIAL MAJESTY
1035	M. ET MME.
1210	PROF.

An intern who was asked to analyze the organization's fundraising efforts presented these summary statistics for the variable *Title:*

Mean	54.41
StdDev	957.5
Median	1
IQR	2
n	94649

a) What does the mean of 54.41 mean?
b) What are the typical reasons that cause measures of center and spread to be as different as those in this table?
c) Is that why these are so different?

40. Zip codes revisited. Here are some summary statistics to go with the histogram of the zip codes of 500 customers from the Holes R Us Internet Jewelry Salon that we saw in Exercise 23 of Chapter 4.

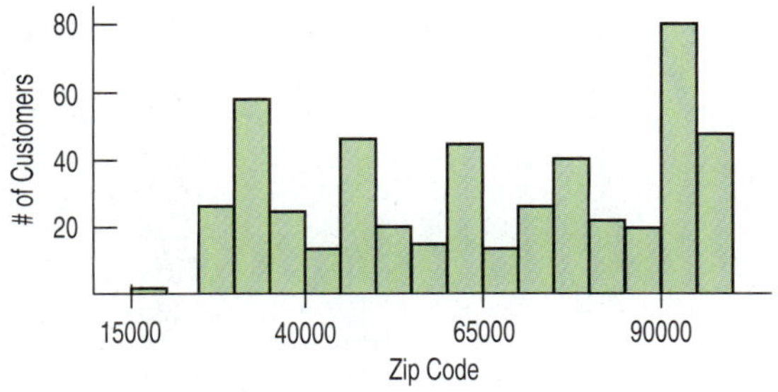

Count	500
Mean	64970.0
StdDev	23523.0
Median	64871
IQR	44183
Q1	46050
Q3	90233

a) Is the mean or median a "better" summary of the center of the zip code distribution?
b) Is the standard deviation or the IQR a better summary of the spread?
c) What can these statistics tell you about the company's sales?

41. Eye and hair color. A survey of 1021 school-age children was conducted by randomly selecting children from several large urban elementary schools. Two of the questions concerned eye and hair color. In the survey, the following codes were used:

Hair color:	Eye color:
1 = Blond	1 = Blue
2 = Brown	2 = Green
3 = Black	3 = Brown
4 = Red	4 = Grey
5 = Other	5 = Other

The statistics students analyzing the data were asked to study the relationship between eye and hair color. They produced this plot:

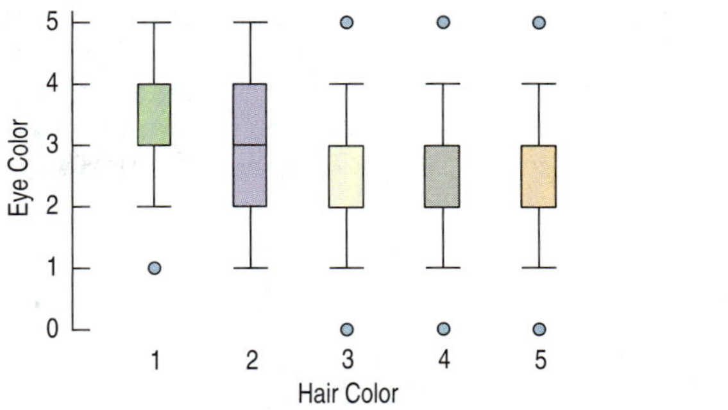

Is their graph appropriate? If so, summarize the findings. If not, explain why not.

42. Stereograms. Stereograms appear to be composed entirely of random dots. However, they contain separate images that a viewer can "fuse" into a three-dimensional (3D) image by staring at the dots while defocusing the eyes. An experiment was performed to determine whether knowledge of the embedded image affected the time required for subjects to fuse the images. One group of subjects (group NV) received no information or just verbal information about the shape of the embedded object. A second group (group VV) received both verbal information and visual information (specifically, a drawing of the object). The experimenters measured how many seconds it took for the subject to report that he or she saw the 3D image.

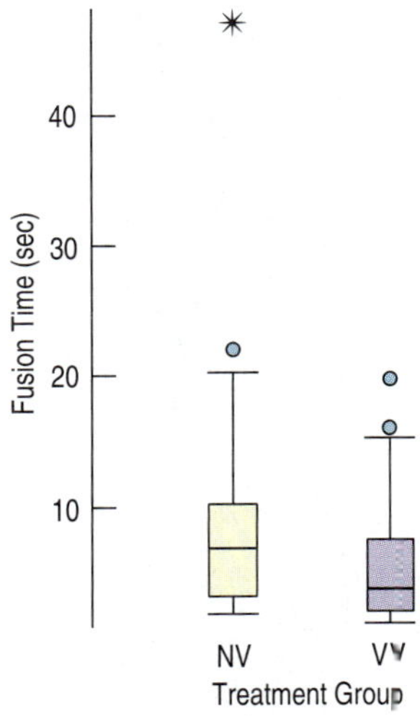

a) What two variables are discussed in this description?
b) For each variable, is it quantitative or categorical? If quantitative, what are the units?
c) Here are boxplots comparing the fusion times for the two treatment groups. Write a few sentences comparing these distributions. What does the experiment show?

43. Stereograms, revisited. Because of the skewness of the distributions of fusion times, we might consider a re-expression. Here are the boxplots of the *log* of fusion times. Is it better to analyze the original fusion times or the log fusion times? Explain.

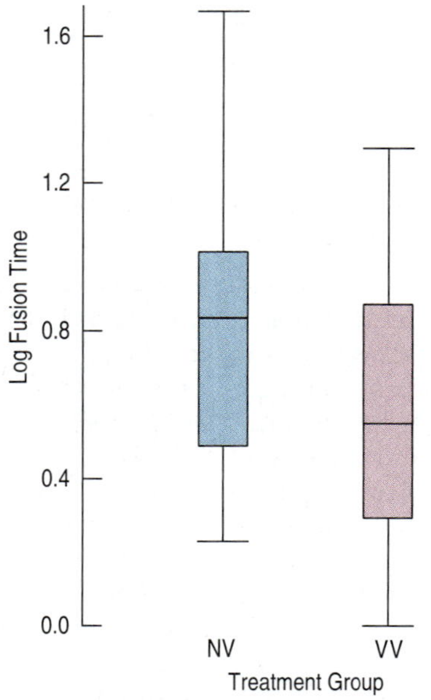

44. Stereograms, yet again. Here are the boxplots of the *reciprocal* of fusion times. Is it better to analyze the original fusion times, the log fusion times, or the reciprocal? Explain.

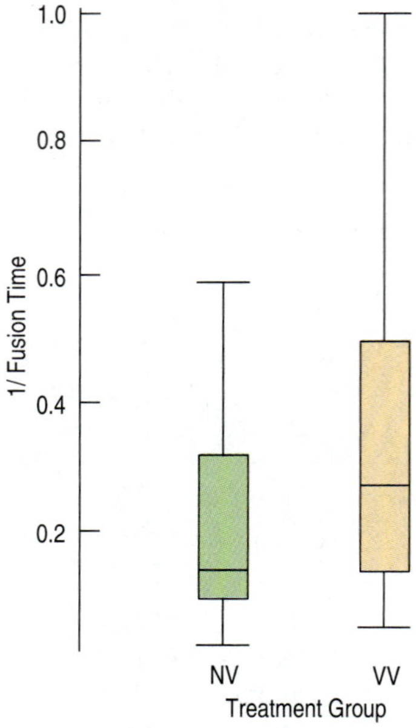

Chapter 6

The Standard Deviation as a Ruler and the Normal Model

The women's heptathlon in the Olympics consists of seven track and field events: the 200-m and 800-m runs, 100-m high hurdles, shot put, javelin, high jump, and long jump. Somehow, the performances in all seven events have to be combined into one score. How can performances in such different events be compared? They don't even have the same units; the races are recorded in seconds and the throwing and jumping events in meters. The best 800-m time, run by Getrud Bacher of Italy, was 8 seconds faster than the mean. The winning long jump by the Russian Yelena Prokhorova was 60 centimeters longer than the mean. Which performance deserves more points?

You might think at first that this is a silly question, but it's exactly the kind of question that has to be answered to compute heptathlon scores. And comparisons of values with different units show up in many places.

The Standard Deviation as a Ruler

The trick in comparing very different-looking values is to use the standard deviations as our rulers. The standard deviation is the most common measure of variation. So it should come as no surprise that the standard deviation plays a crucial role in how we look at data. Over and over during this course, we will ask questions such as "How far is this value from the mean?" or "How different are these two statistics?" The answer in every case will be to measure the distance or difference in standard deviations.

> **Grading on a Curve**
> A similar issue arises in grading a class. If you score 79% on an exam, what grade should you get? One teaching philosophy looks only at the raw percentage, 79, and bases the grade on that alone. Another looks at your *relative* performance and bases the grade on how you did compared with the rest of the class. Teachers and students still debate which method is better.

The concept of the standard deviation as a ruler is not special to this course. You'll find statistical distances measured in standard deviations throughout Statistics, up to the most advanced levels. This approach is one of the basic tools of statistical thinking.

Bacher's winning 800-m time of 129 seconds was 8 seconds faster than the mean of 137 seconds. How many *standard deviations* better than the mean is that? The standard deviation of all 27 qualifying times was 5.0 seconds. Her time was $(129 - 137)/5 = -8/5 = -1.6$, or 1.6

standard deviations better than the mean. Prokhorova's winning long jump was 60 cm *longer* than the average 6-m jump. The standard deviation was 30 cm, so the winning jump was (60/30) = 2.0 standard deviations better than the mean. The long jump performance was a greater improvement over its mean than was the winning 800-m time, since it was further away in *standard deviations.*

Standardizing

We compared the heptathlon results by asking how many standard deviations they were from the event means. We can write this as

$$z = \frac{(y - \bar{y})}{s}.$$

We call the resulting values **standardized values,** and denote them with the letter z. Usually we just call them **z-scores.**

Standardized values have no units. (The numerator has the same units as the data, but so does the denominator. Dividing one by the other "cancels out" the units.) That makes all z-scores comparable regardless of the original units of the data.

NOTATION ALERT:

There goes another letter. We always use the letter z to denote values that have been standardized with the mean and standard deviation.

In place of real-world units, z-scores measure the distance of each data value from the mean in standard deviations. A z-score of 2.0 indicates that a data value is 2 standard deviations above the mean. Data values below the mean have negative z-scores, so a z-score of -1.6 means that the data value was one and six tenths standard deviations *below* the mean. (Of course, racers want to achieve a negative z-score.) We are using the standard deviation as a ruler to measure statistical distance from the mean.

Benefits of Standardizing

Standardizing data brings several benefits. Standardized values have been converted from their original units to the standard statistical unit of *standard deviations from the mean.* This makes it possible to compare values that are measured on different scales, with different units, or for different populations. As we'll soon see, it also offers a useful rule of thumb about distributions.

We have already seen a comparison of values on two quite different variables. To determine the winner of the heptathlon, the judges must combine performances on the seven events. Although they use predetermined tables, they could have combined scores by standardizing each and then adding the z-scores together to reach a total score.

As an example, let's compare Bacher and Prokhorova in *both* the long jump and the 800-m run. We've seen that Bacher ran the 800-m in 129 seconds, 1.6 standard deviations better than the mean. But her long jump of 5.84 m fell below the mean, with a z-score of -0.44. We'd give her a total of $1.6 - 0.44 = 0.94$, then, for the two events. Prokhorova ran the 800 m in 130.32 seconds, 1.34 standard deviations better than the mean, and her long jump was 2.0 standard deviations better than the mean. So her total is $1.34 + 2.0 = 3.34$ for the two events. Not coincidentally, Prokhorova went on to win the silver medal while Bacher finished 14th.

When we standardize data to get a *z*-score, we do two things. First, we *shift* the data by subtracting the mean. Then, we *rescale* the values by dividing by their standard deviation. We often shift and rescale data. What happens to the grade distribution if *everyone* gets a five-point bonus? If we switch from feet to meters, what happens to the distribution of heights of students in your class? Before we can talk more about using *z*-scores, we need to see exactly how shifting and scaling work.

Shifting Data

The Trinidad and Tobago Stock Exchange Ltd. was formally opened on October 26, 1981. By the end of the year 2000, it listed the stocks of 28 companies. During that year, the average dividend paid by the stocks was 4.58%, with a standard deviation of 3.77%. However, inflation averaged about 4% during this period, so the *real* return of these stocks from their dividends is the dividend paid minus 4%. If we subtract 4% from the dividends of the 28 stocks, what will this do to the center and spread of the distribution?

When we shift data values by subtracting or adding the same number to all the data values, does the distribution change? How about its numerical summaries?

Here are the histograms of the dividends of the 28 stocks, and the same values with 4% subtracted from them.

WHO	The 28 companies listed on the stock exchange of Trinidad and Tobago
WHAT	Dividends paid in the year 2000
UNIT	Percent
WHEN	Calendar year 2000
WHERE	Trinidad and Tobago
WHY	Annual report of stock exchange

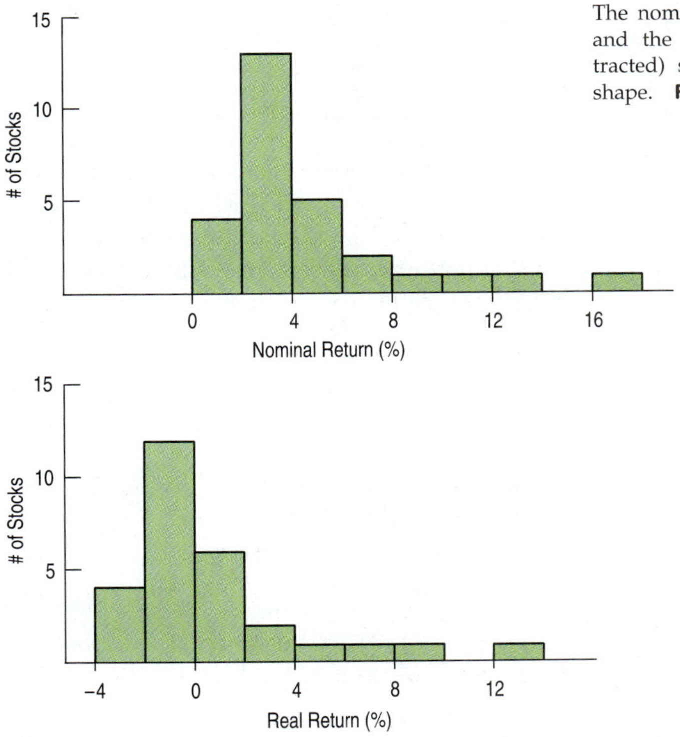

The nominal return on the 28 stocks and the real return (with 4% subtracted) show the same distribution shape. **Figure 6.1**

Doctors' height and weight charts sometimes give ideal weights for various heights that include 2-inch heels. If the mean height of adult women is 66 inches including 2-inch heels, what is the mean height of women without shoes? Each woman is shorter by 2 inches when barefoot, so the mean is decreased by 2 inches, to 64 inches.

What is the mean now that we've subtracted 4% from each? If you said the mean minus 4% you've got it right. Adding (or subtracting) a *constant* amount to each value just adds (or subtracts) the same constant to the mean. The same is true for the median. And the quartiles. (Did we mention maximum and minimum?) It's natural (and correct!) to expect such measures of location to decrease by exactly 4 when we subtract 4 from all the data values.

What about the spread? What does adding a constant value do to the spread of the distribution? Look at the two histograms again. Because adding a constant increases all the data values equally, the distribution just shifts. Its shape doesn't change and neither does the spread. None of the measures of spread we've discussed—not the range, not the IQR, not the standard deviation—changes.

Adding a constant to every data value adds the same constant to measures of center and percentiles, but leaves measures of spread unchanged.

Rescaling Data

Now suppose we *rescale* the data by multiplying or dividing all the values by the same number. Such an operation changes the measurement units. It's exactly how we would convert from fortnights to seconds or from meters to yards. The average price of the 28 stocks on December 31, 2000, was TT$9.12. (TT$ is a Trinidad and Tobago dollar.) If we want to convert the prices from TT$ to US$, we have to divide by 6.24, the exchange rate on December 31, 2000.

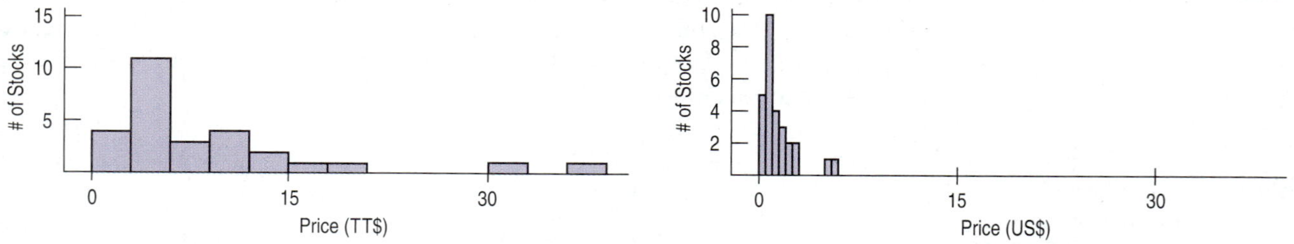

Stock prices in both TT and US dollars. How do the distribution and the numerical summaries change? **Figure 6.2**

What happens to the mean price? Not too surprisingly, it gets divided by 6.24 as well. The mean price of TT$9.21 becomes TT$9.21/6.24 = US$1.48. The median is also divided by 6.24. (The quartiles are, too.)

What happens to the spread? Take a look at the histograms. Clearly the spread in US$ is smaller. Consider the range, for example. Since we divided each value by 6.24, we divided the maximum and minimum values by 6.24.

$$\frac{max}{6.24} - \frac{min}{6.24} = \frac{max - min}{6.24} = \frac{range}{6.24}$$

So their difference, the range, is divided by 6.24.

What about the other measures of spread? The same thing happened to them and for much the same reasons.

When we divide or multiply all the data values by any constant value, both measures of location (such as the mean and median) and measures of spread (such as the range, the IQR, and the standard deviation) are divided or multiplied by that same value.

Back to *z*-scores

Standardizing data into *z*-scores is just shifting them by the mean and rescaling them by the standard deviation. Now we can see how standardizing affects the distribution. When we subtract the mean of the data from every data value, we shift the mean to zero. As we have seen, such a shift doesn't change the standard deviation.

When we *divide* each of these shifted values by s, however, the standard deviation should be divided by s as well. Since the standard deviation was s to start with, the new standard deviation becomes 1.

How, then, does standardizing affect the distribution of a variable? Let's consider the three aspects of a distribution: the shape, center, and spread.

z-scores have mean 0 and standard deviation 1.

- *Standardizing does not change the* ***shape*** *of the distribution of a variable.*
- *Standardizing changes the* ***center*** *by making the mean 0.*
- *Standardizing changes the* ***spread*** *by making the standard deviation 1.*

When Is a *z*-score BIG?

Is Normal normal?
Don't be misled. The name "Normal" doesn't mean that these are the *usual* shapes for histograms. The name follows a tradition of positive thinking in Mathematics and Statistics in which functions, equations, and relationships that are easy to work with or have other nice properties are called "normal," "common," "regular," "natural," or similar terms. It's as if by calling them ordinary we could make them actually occur more often and simplify our lives.

Here's a trick for writing the symbol σ. Start from the inside top and go clockwise, making sure the top is flat and parallel to the line you're writing on. If you started at the far right end and go backward counterclockwise, your σ would look like a 6 instead. Try it!

NOTATION ALERT:
$N(\mu, \sigma)$ always denotes a Normal model. The μ, pronounced "mew," is the Greek letter for "m," and always represents the mean in a model. The σ is the lowercase Greek letter for "s," sigma, and always represents the standard deviation in a model.

Is the Standard Normal a standard?
Yes. We call it the "Standard Normal," because it models standardized values. It is also a "standard" because this is the particular Normal model that we almost always use.

A z-score gives us an indication of how unusual a value is because it tells us how far it is from the mean. A standardized value of 0 tells us that the data value is right at the mean. A standardized value of +1 tells us that the value is 1 standard deviation above the mean. How far from 0 does a z-score have to be to be interesting or unusual? There is no universal standard, but there is a model that shows up over and over in Statistics. You may have heard of "bell-shaped curves." Statisticians call them Normal distributions.

Normal models are appropriate for distributions whose shapes are unimodal and roughly symmetric. For these distributions, they provide a measure of how extreme a z-score is. Fortunately, there is a Normal distribution for every possible combination of mean and standard deviation. We write $N(\mu, \sigma)$ to represent a Normal model with a mean of μ and a standard deviation of σ. Why the Greek? Well, *this* mean and standard deviation are not numerical summaries of data. They are part of the model. They don't come from the data, but rather they are numbers that we choose to help specify the model. Such numbers are called **parameters** of the model.

We don't want to confuse the parameters with summaries of the data such as $\bar{y}$ and s, so we use special symbols. In Statistics, we almost always use Greek letters for parameters. By contrast, summaries of data are called **statistics** and are usually written with Latin letters.

If we model data with a Normal model and standardize them using the corresponding μ and σ, we still call the standardized value a **z-score,** and we write

$$z = \frac{y - \mu}{\sigma}.$$

Usually it's easier to standardize data first (using its mean and standard deviation). Then we need only the model $N(0, 1)$. The Normal model with mean 0 and standard deviation 1 is called the **standard Normal model** (or the **standard Normal distribution**).

But be careful. You shouldn't use a Normal model for just any data set. Remember that standardizing won't change the shape of the distribution. If the distribution is not unimodal and symmetric to begin with, standardizing won't make it Normal.

The 68-95-99.7 Rule

These magic 68, 95, 99.7 values come from the Normal model. As a model, it can give us corresponding values for any *z*-score. For example, it tells us that fewer than 1 out of a million values have *z*-scores smaller than −5.0 or larger than 5.0. So if someone tells you you're "one in a million" they must really admire your *z*-score.

Normal models give us an idea of how extreme a value is by telling us how likely it is to find one that far from the mean. We'll soon show how to find these numbers precisely—but there's a simple rule that's usually all we need.

It turns out that in a Normal model about 68% of the values fall within one standard deviation of the mean, about 95% of the values fall within two standard deviations of the mean, and about 99.7%—almost all—of the values fall within three standard deviations of the mean. These facts are summarized in a rule that we call (let's see . . .) the **68-95-99.7 Rule.**[1]

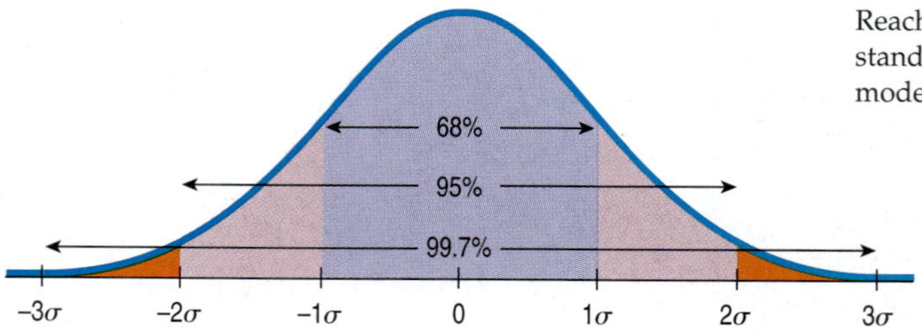

Reaching out one, two, and three standard deviations on a Normal model gives the 68-95-99.7 Rule.
Figure 6.3

The First Three Rules for Working with Normal Models

Make a picture.
Make a picture.
Make a picture.

Although we're thinking about models, not histograms of data, the three rules don't change. To help you think clearly, a simple hand-drawn sketch is all you need. Even experienced statisticians sketch pictures to help them think about Normal models. You should too.

Working with the 68-95-99.7 Rule STEP-BY-STEP

Scholastic Aptitude Test (SAT) scores have a distribution that is roughly unimodal and symmetric, and are designed to have an overall mean of 500 and a standard deviation of 100. In any one year, the mean and standard deviation may differ from these target values by a small amount, but they are a good overall approximation.

Suppose you earned a 600 on an SAT test. From that information and the 68-95-99.7 Rule, where do you stand among all students who took the SAT?

[1]This rule is called the "Empirical Rule" in older texts, because it originally came from observation. The rule was first published by Abraham De Moivre in 1733, 75 years before the Normal model was discovered. Maybe it should be called "De Moivre's Rule." But that wouldn't help us remember the important numbers, 68, 95, and 99.7.

Think

Variable Identify the variable; report the W's.

Let y = SAT score. Scores are quantitative but have no meaningful units.

Plan Check that a Normal model is appropriate in order to use the 68-95-99.7 Rule.

We have no data, so we cannot make a histogram, but we are told that SAT scores are roughly unimodal and symmetric.

Specify μ and σ.

We will model *SAT score* with a N(500, 100) model.

Show

Mechanics Make a picture of this Normal model. (A simple sketch is all you need.)

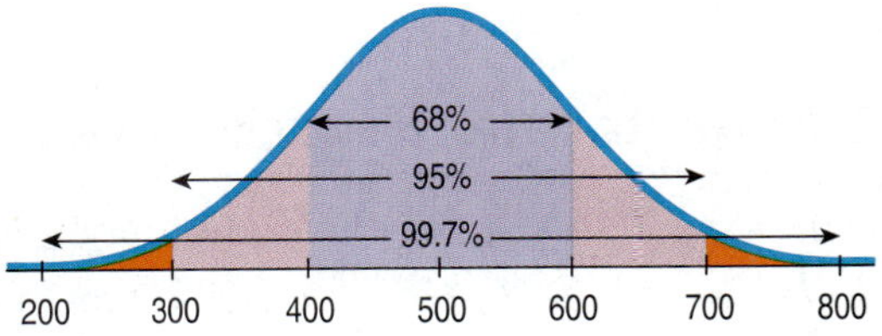

Locate your score.

A score of 600 is one standard deviation above the mean. That corresponds to one of the points in the 68-95-99.7% Rule.

Tell

Interpretation State your conclusion.

About 32% (100% − 68%) of those who took the test were more than one standard deviation from the mean, but only half of those were on the high side. So about 16% (half of 32%) of the test scores were better than 600.

The bounds of SAT scoring at 200 and 800 can also be explained by the 68-95-99.7 Rule. Since 200 and 800 are three standard deviations from 500, it hardly pays to extend the scoring any farther on either side. We'd get more information only on 100 − 99.7 = 0.3% of students.

Finding Normal Percentiles by Hand

An SAT score of 600 is easy to assess, because we can think of it as one standard deviation above the mean. If your score was 680, though, where do you stand among the rest of the people tested? Your z-score is 1.80, so you're somewhere between 1 and 2 standard deviations above the mean. We figured out that no more than 16% of people score better than 600. By the same logic, no more than 2.5% of people score better than 700. Can we be more specific than "between 16% and 2.5%"?

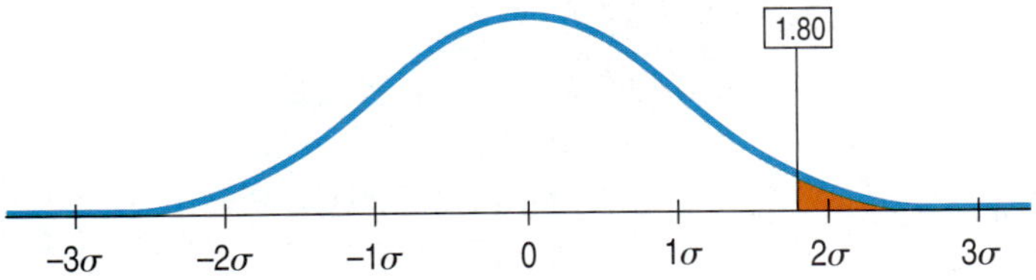

z	.00	.01
⋮	⋮	⋮
1.7	.9554	.9564
1.8	.9641	.9649
1.9	.9713	.9719
⋮	⋮	⋮

A table of Normal percentiles (Table Z in Appendix E) lets us find the percentage of individuals in a Standard Normal distribution falling below any specified z-score value. **Figure 6.4**

When the value doesn't fall exactly 1, 2, or 3 standard deviations from the mean, we can look it up in a table of **Normal percentiles.**[2] Nobody wants to lug around a bunch of tables, so we always use the *standard Normal.* That means we have to convert our data to *z*-scores before using the table. Your score of 680 has a *z*-score of $(680 - 500)/100 = 1.80$. In the piece of the table shown, we find your *z*-score by looking down the left column for the first two digits, 1.8, and across the top row for the third digit, 0. The table gives the percentile as 0.9641. That means that 96.4% of the *z*-scores are less than 1.80. Only 3.6% of people, then, scored better than 680 on the SAT.

Finding Normal Percentiles Using Technology

These days, finding percentiles from a Normal probability table is a "desert island" method—something we might do if we desperately needed a Normal percentile and were stranded miles from the mainland with only a Normal probability table. (Of course, you might feel just that way during a Statistics exam, so it's a good idea to know how to do it.) Fortunately, most of the time, we can use a calculator or computer. Graphing calculators, such as the TI-83, find Normal percentiles and offer to draw the picture as well. And most statistics programs have functions to find Normal percentiles.

TI Tips

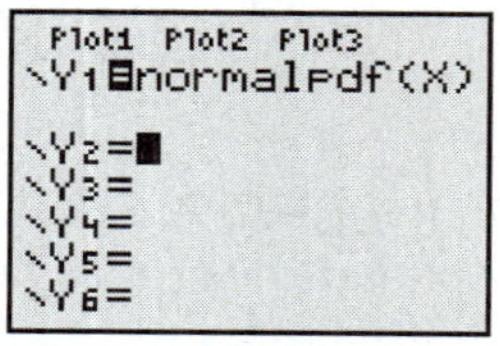

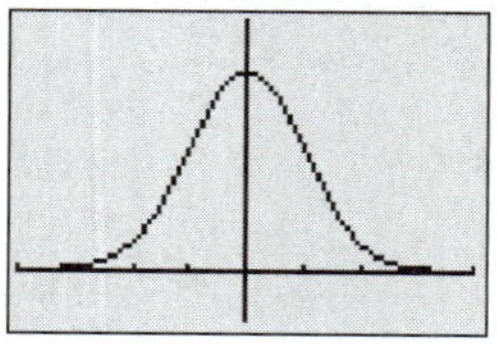

Your calculator knows the Normal model. Have a look under **2nd DISTR**. There you will see three "norm" functions, **normalpdf(**, **normalcdf(**, and **invNorm(**. Let's play with the first two.

- **normalpdf(** calculates *y*-values for graphing a Normal curve. You probably won't use this very often, if at all. If you want to try it, graph **Y1=normalpdf(X)** in a graphing **WINDOW** with **Xmin=-4**, **Xmax=4**, **Ymin=-0.1**, and **Ymax=0.5**.
- **normalcdf(** finds the area between two *z*-score cut points, by specifying **normalcdf(zLeft,zRight)**. Do make friends with this function; you will use it often!

Example 1

The Normal model shown shades the region between $z = -0.5$ and $z = 1.0$.

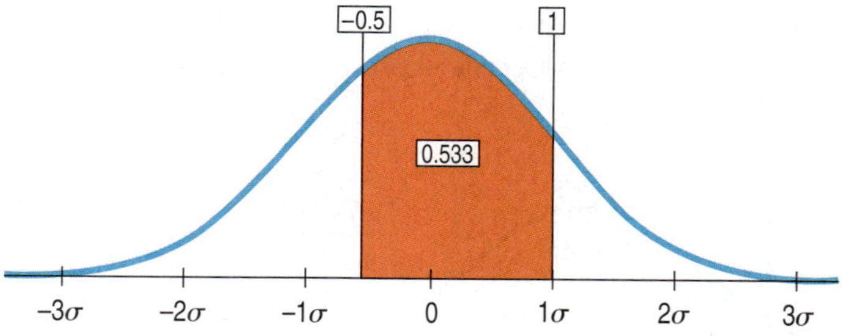

Figure 6.5

---

[2] See Table Z in Appendix E. Many calculators and statistics computer packages do this too.

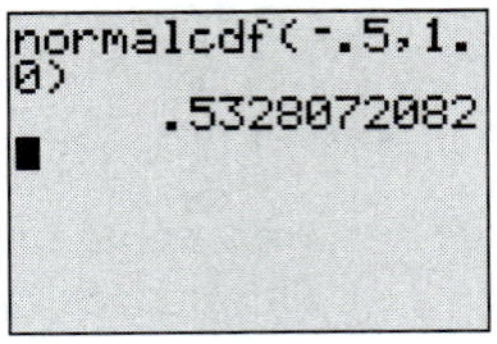

To find the shaded area:

Under `2nd DISTR` select `normalcdf(`; hit `ENTER`.

Specify the cut points: `normalcdf(-.5,1.0)` and hit `ENTER` again.

There's the area. Approximately 53% of a Normal model lies between half a standard deviation below and one standard deviation above the mean.

Example 2

In our "by hand" example we used Table Z to determine the fraction of SAT scores above your score of 680. Now let's do it again, this time using your TI.

First we need *z*-scores for the cut points:

- Since 680 is 1.8 standard deviations above the mean, your *z*-score is 1.8; that's the left cut point.
- Theoretically the standard Normal model extends rightward forever, but you can't tell the calculator to use infinity as the right cut point. Recall that for a Normal model almost all the area lies within ±3 standard deviations of the mean, so any upper cut point beyond, say, $z = 5$ does not cut off anything very important. We suggest you always use 99 (or −99) when you really want infinity as your cut point—it's easy to remember and way beyond any meaningful area.

Now you're ready. Use the command `normalcdf(1.8,99)`.

There you are! The Normal model estimates that approximately 3.6% of SAT scores are higher than 680.

Working with Normal Percentiles I STEP-BY-STEP

What proportion of SAT scores fall between 450 and 600?

Think

Variable Name the variable.

Let y = SAT score.

Plan Check to see if a Normal model is appropriate.

We are told that SAT scores are nearly Normal.

Specify which Normal model to use.

We'll model SAT scores with $N(500, 100)$ model, using the mean and standard deviation specified for them.

Show

Mechanics Make a picture of this Normal model. Locate the desired values and shade the region of interest.

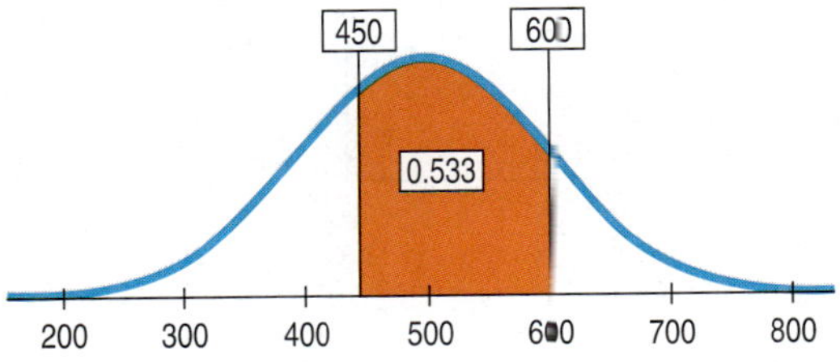

Find the *z*-scores for the cut points.

$$z = \frac{y - \mu}{\sigma} = \frac{450 - 500}{100} = -0.5$$

$$z = \frac{600 - 500}{100} = 1.0$$

Use technology to find the area. (This was Example 1 in the TI Tips—take another look.)

$\text{Area}(450 < y < 600) = \text{Area}(-0.5 < z < 1.0)$

$= 0.5328$

If you use a table, then you need to subtract the two areas to find the area *between* the cut points.

(**OR:** From Table Z, we find that area $(z < 1.0) = 0.8413$ and area $(z < -0.5) = 0.3085$, so the proportion of z-scores *between* them is: $0.8413 - 0.3085 = 0.5328$, or 53.28%.)

Tell — **Interpretation** State your conclusion.

The Normal model estimates that about 53.3% of SAT scores fall between 450 and 600.

From Percentiles to Scores: *z* in Reverse

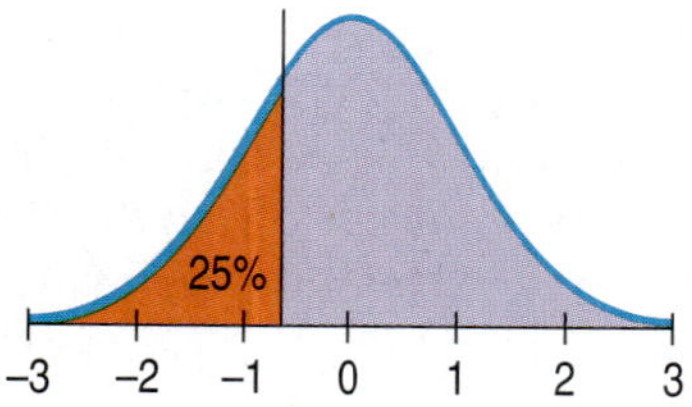

Finding areas from z-scores is the simplest way to work with the Normal model. But sometimes we start with areas and are asked to work backward to find the corresponding z-score or even the original data value.

For instance, what z-score represents the first quartile in a Normal model? In our first set of examples we knew the z-score and used the table or technology to find the percentile. Now we want to find the cut point for the 25th percentile.

Make a picture, shading the leftmost 25% of the area. Look in Table Z for an area of 0.2500. The exact area is not there, but 0.2514 is pretty close. That shows up in the table with −0.6 in the left margin and .07 in the top margin. The z-score for Q1, then, is approximately $z = -0.67$.

Computers and calculators will determine the cut point more precisely (and more easily).

TI Tips

To find the z-score at the 25th percentile, go to `2nd DISTR` again. This time we'll use the third of the "norm" functions, `invNorm(`.

Just specify the desired percentile with the command `invNorm(.25)` and hit **ENTER**. The calculator says that the cut point for the leftmost 25% of a Normal model is approximately $z = -0.674$.

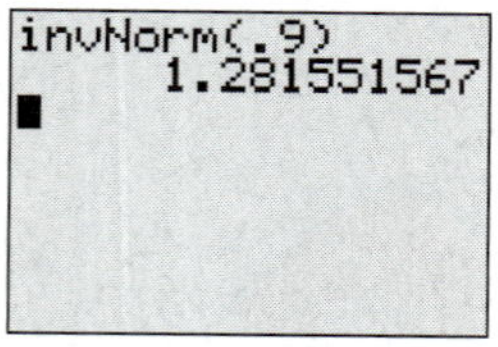

One more example: What z-score cuts off the highest 10% of a Normal model? That's easily done—just remember to specify the *percentile*. Since we want the cut point for the *highest* 10%, we know that the other 90% must be *below* that z-score. The cut point, then, must stand at the 90th percentile, so specify `invNorm(.90)`.

Only 10% of the area in a Normal model is more than about 1.28 standard deviations above the mean.

Working with Normal Percentiles II — STEP-BY-STEP

Suppose a college says they admit only people with SAT scores among the top 10%. How high an SAT score does it take to be eligible?

Think

Variable Define the variable.

Let y = SAT score.

Plan Check to see if a Normal model is appropriate, and specify which Normal model to use.

We are told that SAT scores are nearly Normal. We'll model them with $N(500, 100)$.

Show

Mechanics Make a Picture of this Normal model. Locate the desired percentile approximately by shading the rightmost 10% of the area.

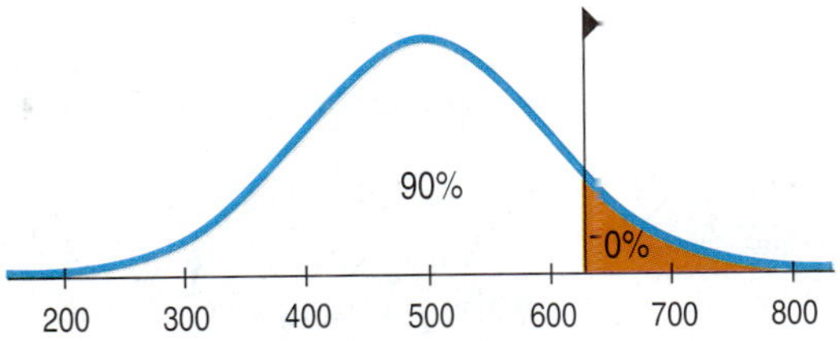

The college takes the top 10%, so their cutoff score is the 90th percentile. Find that z-score using a table or your calculator. (See our last TI Tips example.)

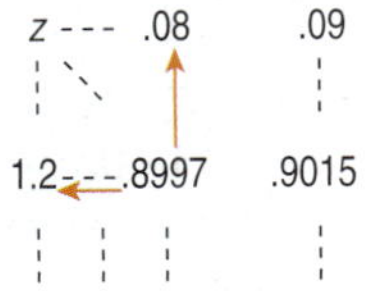

The cut point is $z = 1.28$

Convert the z-score back to the original units.

A z-score of 1.28 is 1.28 standard deviations above the mean. Since the SD is 100, that's 128 SAT points. The cutoff is 128 points above the mean of 500, or 628.

Tell

Interpretation State your conclusion.

Because the school wants SAT scores in the top 10%, the cutoff is 628. (Actually since SAT scores are reported only in multiples of 10, you'd have to score at least a 630.)

More Working with Normal Percentiles STEP-BY-STEP

Working with Normal percentiles can be a little tricky, depending on how the problem is stated. Here are a few more worked examples of the kind you're likely to see.

A cereal manufacturer has a machine that fills the boxes. Boxes are labeled "16 ounces," so the company wants to have that much cereal in each box, but since no packaging process is perfect, there will be minor variations. If the machine is set at exactly 16 ounces and the Normal model applies (or at least the distribution is roughly symmetric), then about half of the boxes will be underweight, making consumers unhappy and exposing the company to bad publicity and possible lawsuits. To prevent underweight boxes, the manufacturer has to set the mean a little higher than 16.0 ounces.

Based on their experience with the packaging machine, the company believes that the amount of cereal in the boxes fits a Normal model with a standard deviation of 0.2 ounces. The manufacturer decides to set the machine to put an average of 16.3 ounces in each box. Let's use that model to answer a series of questions about these cereal boxes.

Question 1: What fraction of the boxes will be underweight?

Think

Variable Name the variable.

Let y = weight of cereal in a box.

Plan Check to see if a Normal model is appropriate.

We have no data, so we cannot make a histogram, but we are told that the company believes the distribution of weights from the machine is Normal.

Specify which Normal model to use.

We use an $N(16.3, 0.2)$ model.

Show

Mechanics Make a picture of this Normal model. Locate the value you're interested in on the picture, label it, and shade the appropriate region.

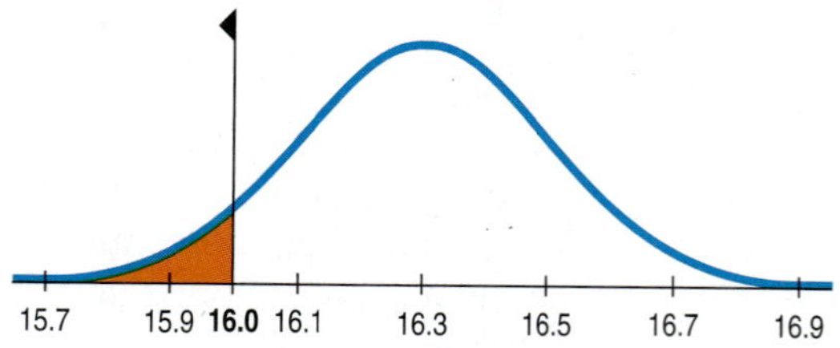

Reality Check Estimate from the picture the percentage of boxes that are underweight. (This will be useful later to check that your answer makes sense.)

(It looks like a low percentage. Less than 20% for sure.)

We want to know what fraction of the boxes will weigh less than 16 ounces.

Convert your cutoff value into a *z*-score.

$$z = \frac{y - \mu}{\sigma} = \frac{16 - 16.3}{0.2} = -1.50.$$

Look up the area in the Normal table, or use your calculator.

$$\text{Area } (y < 16) = \text{Area } (z < -1.50) = 0.0668.$$

Tell

Interpretation State your conclusion. (Check that it's consistent with your earlier guess.)

We estimate that approximately 6.7% of the boxes will contain less than 16 ounces of cereal.

Question 2: The company's lawyers say that 6.7% is too high. They insist that no more than 4% of the boxes can be underweight. So the company needs to set the machine to put a little more cereal in each box. What mean setting do they need?

Think

Variable Name the variable.

Let y = weight of cereal in a box.

Plan Check to see if a Normal model is appropriate.

We have no data, so we cannot make a histogram, but we are told that a Normal model applies.

Specify which Normal model to use. This time you are not given a value for the mean!

We don't know μ, the mean amount of cereal. The standard deviation for this machine is 0.2 oz. The model, then, is $N(\mu, 0.2)$.

Reality Check We found out earlier that setting the machine to $\mu = 16.3$ ounces made 6.7% of the boxes too light. We'll need to raise the mean a bit to reduce this fraction.

We are told that no more than 4% of the boxes can be below 16 ounces.

Show

Mechanics Make a picture of this Normal model. Center it at μ (since you don't know the mean) and shade the region below 16 ounces.

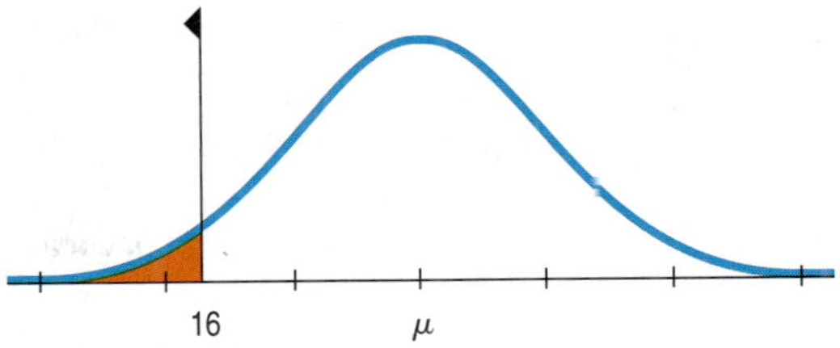

Using the Normal table or a calculator, find the z-score that cuts off the lowest 4%.

The z-score that has 0.04 area to the left of it is $z = -1.75$.

Use this information to find μ. It's located 1.75 standard deviations to the right of 16. Since σ is 0.2, that's 1.75×0.2, or 0.35 ounces more than 16.

Since 16 must be 1.75 standard deviations below the mean, we need to set the mean at $16 + 1.75 \times 0.2 = 16.35$.

Tell

Interpretation State your conclusion.

(This makes sense; we knew it would have to be just a bit higher than 16.3.)

The company must set the machine to average 16.35 ounces of cereal per box.

Question 3: The company president vetoes that plan, saying the company should give away less free cereal, not more. Her goal is to set the machine no higher than 16.2 ounces and still have only 4% underweight boxes. The only way to accomplish this is to reduce the standard deviation. What standard deviation must the company achieve, and what does that mean about the machine?

Think

Variable Name the variable.

Let y = weight of cereal in a box.

Plan Check that a Normal model is appropriate.

The company believes that the weights are described by a Normal model.

Specify which Normal model to use. This time you don't know σ.

✔ Reality Check We know the new standard deviation must be less than 0.2 ounces.

Now we know the mean, but we don't know the standard deviation. The model is therefore $N(16.2, \sigma)$.

Show

Mechanics Make a picture of this Normal model. Center it at 16.2, and shade the area you're interested in. We want 4% of the area to the left of 16 ounces.

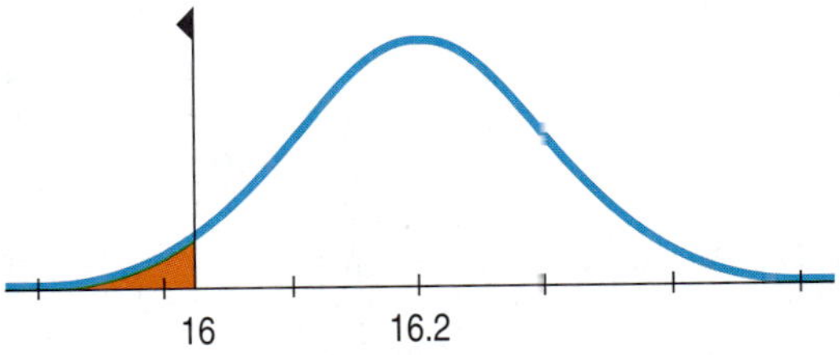

Find the z-score that cuts off the lowest 4%.

We already know that the z-score with 4% below it is $z = -1.75$.

Solve for σ. (Note that we need 16 to be 1.75 σ's below 16.2, so 1.75σ must be 0.2 ounces. You could just start with that equation.)

$$z = \frac{y - \mu}{\sigma}$$

$$-1.75 = \frac{16 - 16.2}{\sigma}$$

$$1.75\sigma = 0.2$$

$$\sigma = 0.114.$$

Tell **Interpretation** State your conclusion.

As we expected, the standard deviation is lower than before—actually, quite a bit lower.

The company must get the machine to box cereal with a standard deviation of only 0.114 ounces. This means the machine must be more consistent (by nearly a factor of 2) in filling the boxes.

Are You Normal? How Can You Tell?

In the examples we've just worked through, we've assumed that the underlying data distribution was roughly unimodal and symmetric, so that using a Normal model makes sense. When you actually have your own data, you must *check* to see whether a Normal model is reasonable. But how? Make a picture, of course! Drawing a histogram of the data and looking at the shape is one good way to see if a Normal model might work.

There's a more specialized graphical display that can help you to decide whether the Normal model is appropriate: the **Normal probability plot.** If the distribution of the data is roughly Normal, the plot approximates a diagonal straight line. Deviations from a straight line indicate that the distribution is not Normal. This plot is usually able to show deviations from Normality more clearly than the corresponding histogram, but it's usually easier to understand how a distribution fails to be Normal by looking at its histogram.

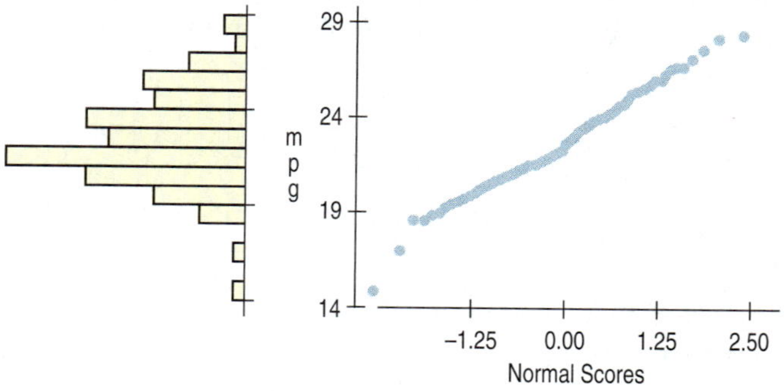

Histogram and Normal probability plot for the Nissan gas mileage data we saw in Chapter 5 (p. 66). The vertical axes are the same, so each dot in the probability plot would fall into the bar of the histogram immediately to its left. **Figure 6.6**

The Nissan car gas mileage data provide an example of data that are nearly Normal.

Most of the plot is straight. The two trailing low values correspond to the values in the histogram that trail off the low end. They're not quite in line with the rest of the data set. The Normal probability plot shows us that they're a bit lower than we'd expect of the lowest two values in a Normal model.

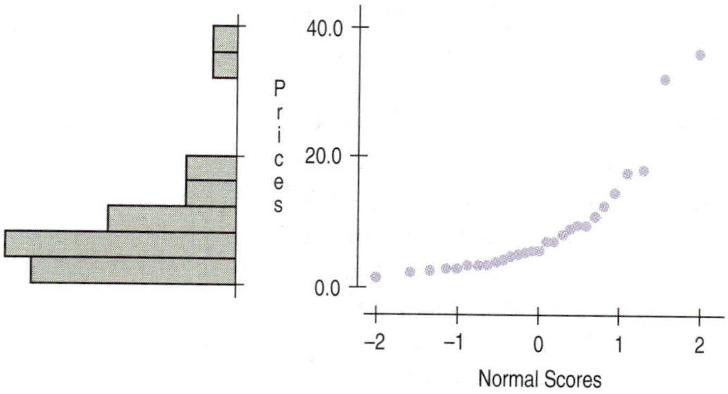

Histogram and probability plot for the Trinidad stock prices. Note how a skewed distribution corresponds to a bent probability plot.
Figure 6.7

By contrast, the Trinidad stock prices plot is far from straight. The prices are skewed to the high end, and the Normal probability plot is curved. We'd conclude from these pictures that approximations using the 68-95-99.7% Rule for the stock data would not be very accurate.

TI Tips

Let's make a Normal probability plot with the calculator. Here are the boys' agility test scores we looked at in Chapter 5; enter them in `L1`:

22, 17, 18, 29, 22, 23, 24, 23, 17, 21

Now you can create the plot:

- Turn a `STATPLOT On`.
- Tell it to make a Normal probability plot by choosing the last of the icons.
- Specify your datalist and which axis you want the data on. (We'll use `Y` so the plot looks like the others we showed you.)
- Specify the `Mark` you want the plot to use.
- Now `ZoomStat` does the rest.

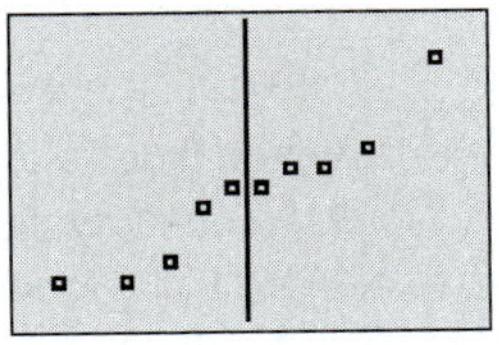

The plot doesn't look very straight. Normality is certainly questionable here.

(Not that it matters in making this decision, but that vertical line is the y-axis. Points to the left have negative z-scores and points to the right have positive z-scores.)

How Does a Normal Probability Plot Work?

Why does the Normal probability plot work like that? We have 100 fuel efficiency measures for the Nissan car. The smallest of these has a z-score of -3.16. The Normal model can tell us what value to expect for the smallest z-score in a batch of 100. That turns out to be -2.48. So our first data value is smaller than we would expect from the Normal.

We can continue this and ask a similar question for each value. For example, the 14th smallest fuel efficiency has a z-score of almost exactly -1, and that's just what we should expect (well, -1.1 to be exact). A Normal probability plot makes all of these comparisons and plots them so it is easy to see how they come out.

When the values match up well, the line is straight. If one or two points are surprising from the Normal's point of view, they don't line up. When the entire distribution is skewed or different from the Normal in some other way, the values don't match up very well at all and the plot bends.

It turns out to be tricky to find the values we expect. They're called "Normal scores," but you can't just look them up in the tables. That's why probability plots are best made with technology and not by hand.

The best advice on using Normal probability plots is to see whether they are straight. If so, then your data look like data from a Normal model. If not, make a histogram to understand how they differ from the model.

What Can Go Wrong?

- ***Don't use Normal models when the distribution is not unimodal and symmetric.*** Normal models are so easy and useful that it is tempting to use them even when they don't describe the data very well. That can lead to wrong conclusions. Don't use a Normal model without first looking at a picture of the data to check that it is unimodal and symmetric. A histogram, or better yet a Normal probability plot, can help us tell whether a Normal model is appropriate.

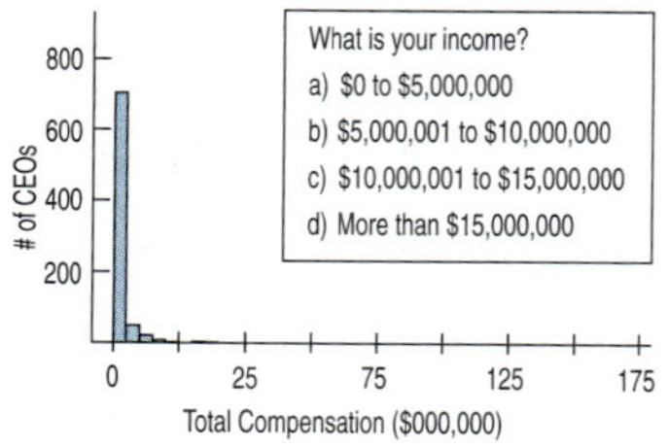

The CEOs (p. 45) had a mean total compensation of $2,818,743.10 and a standard deviation of $8,320,052.70. Using the Normal model rule, we should expect about 68% of the CEOs to have compensations between −$5,501,309.60 and $11,138,795.80. In fact, fewer than 5% of the CEOs' total compensations fall outside this range. What went wrong? The distribution is *skewed*, not symmetric. Using the 68–95–99.7% Rule on data like this will lead to silly results.

- ***Don't use the mean and standard deviation when outliers are present.*** Both means and standard deviations can be distorted by outliers, and no model based on distorted values will do a good job. It's a good idea, then, to always check for outliers. How? Make a picture.

Normal Plots and the Computer

The best way to tell whether your data can be modeled well by a Normal model is to make a picture or two. We've already talked about making histograms. Normal probability plots are almost never made by hand because the values of the normal scores are tricky to find. But most statistics software makes Normal plots, though various packages call the same plot by different names and array the information differently.

Connections

Changing the center and spread of a variable is equivalent to changing its *units.* Indeed, the only part of the data's context changed by standardizing is the *units.* All other aspects of the context do not depend on the choice or modification of measurement units. This fact points out an important distinction between the numbers the data provide for calculation and the meaning of the variables and the relationships among them. Standardizing can make the numbers easier to work with, but it does not alter the meaning.

Another way to look at this is to note that standardizing may change the center and spread values, but it does not affect the *shape* of a distribution. A histogram or boxplot of standardized values looks just the same as the histogram or boxplot of the original values except, perhaps, for the numbers on the axes.

When we summarized *shape, center,* and *spread* for histograms, we compared them to unimodal, symmetric shapes. You couldn't ask for a nicer example than the Normal model. And if the shape *is* like a Normal, we'll use the the mean and standard deviation to standardize the values.

Key Concepts

Changing the center Adding a constant to each data value adds the same constant to the mean, the median, and the quartiles, but does not change the standard deviation or IQR.

Changing the scale Multiplying each data value by a constant multiplies both the measures of position (mean, median, and quartiles) and the measures of spread (standard deviation and IQR) by that constant.

Standardizing We standardize to eliminate units. Standardized values can be compared and combined even if the original variables had different units and magnitudes.

Standardized value A value found by subtracting the mean and dividing by the standard deviation.

Normal model A useful family of models for unimodal, symmetric distributions.

Parameter A numerically valued attribute of a model. For example, the values of μ and σ in a $N(\mu, \sigma)$ model are parameters.

Statistic A value calculated from data to summarize aspects of the data. For example, the mean, $\bar{y}$, and standard deviation, s, are statistics.

***z*-score** A *z*-score tells how many standard deviations a value is from the mean; *z*-scores have a mean of zero and a standard deviation of one.

Standard Normal model A normal model, $N(\mu, \sigma)$, with mean $\mu = 0$ and standard deviation $\sigma = 1$.

68-95-99.7 Rule In a Normal model, 68% of values fall within one standard deviation of the mean, 95% fall within two standard deviations of the mean, and 99.7% fall within three standard deviations of the mean.

Normal percentile The Normal percentile corresponding to a *z*-score gives the percentage of values in a standard Normal distribution found at that *z*-score or below.

Normal probability plot A display to help assess whether a distribution of data is approximately Normal. If the plot is nearly straight, a Normal model is appropriate.

Changing center and spread Changing the center and spread of a variable is equivalent to changing its *units*.

Skills — When you complete this lesson you should:

Think

- Understand how adding a constant and multiplying by a constant changes the center or spread of a variable.
- Recognize when standardization can be used to compare values.
- Understand that standardizing uses the standard deviation as a ruler.
- Recognize when a Normal model is appropriate.

Show

- Know how to calculate the *z*-score of an observation.
- Know how to compare values from two different distributions using their *z*-scores.
- Be able to use Normal models and the 68-95-99.7 Rule to estimate the percentage of observations falling within one, two, or three standard deviations of the mean.
- Know how to find the percentage of observations falling below any value in a Normal model using a Normal table or appropriate technology.
- Know how to check whether a variable follows a Normal model by making a Normal probability plot.

Tell

- Know what *z*-scores mean.
- Be able to explain how extraordinary a standardized value may be by using a Normal model.

Exercises

1. **Payroll.** Here are the summary statistics for the weekly payroll of a small company: lowest salary = \$300, mean salary = \$700, median = \$500, range = \$1200, IQR = \$600, first quartile = \$350, standard deviation = \$400.
   a) Do you think the distribution of salaries is symmetric, skewed to the left, or skewed to the right? Explain why.
   b) Between what two values are the middle 50% of the salaries found?
   c) Suppose business has been good and the company gives every employee a \$50 raise. Tell the new value of each of the summary statistics.
   d) Instead, suppose the company gives each employee a 10% raise. Tell the new value of each of the summary statistics.

2. **Hams.** A specialty foods company sells "gourmet hams" by mail order. The hams vary in size from 4.15 to 7.45 pounds, with a mean weight of 6 pounds and standard deviation of 0.65 pounds. The quartiles and median weights are 5.6, 6.2, and 6.55 pounds.
   a) Find the range and the IQR of the weights.
   b) Do you think the distribution of the weights is symmetric or skewed? If skewed, which way? Why?
   c) If these weights were expressed in ounces (1 pound = 16 ounces) what would the mean, standard deviation, quartiles, median, IQR, and range be?
   d) When the company ships these hams, the box and packing materials add 30 ounces. What are the mean, standard deviation, quartiles, median, IQR, and range of weights of boxes shipped (in ounces)?
   e) One customer made a special order of a 10-pound ham. Which of the summary statistics of part d might *not* change if that data value were added to the distribution?

3. **SAT or ACT?** Each year thousands of high school students take either the SAT or the ACT, standardized tests used in the college admissions process. Combined SAT scores can go as high as 1600, while the maximum ACT composite score is 36. Since the two exams use very different scales, comparisons of performance are difficult. A convenient rule of thumb is $SAT = 40 \times ACT + 150$; that is, multiply an ACT score by 40 and add 150 points to estimate the equivalent SAT score.

   An admissions officer reports the following statistics about the ACT scores of 2355 students who applied to her college. Find the summaries of equivalent SAT scores.

Lowest score = 19	Mean = 27	Standard deviation = 3
Q3 = 30	Median = 28	IQR = 6

4. **Cold U?** A high school senior uses the Internet to get information on February temperatures in the town where he'll be going to college. He finds a Web site with some statistics, but they are given in degrees Celsius. The conversion formula is $F° = 9/5\ C° + 32$. Determine the Fahrenheit equivalents for the summary information below.

Maximum temperature = 11°C	Range = 33°	Mean = 1°
Standard deviation = 7°	Median = 2°	IQR = 16°

5. **Temperatures.** A town's January high temperatures average 36°F with a standard deviation of 10°, while in July the mean high temperature is 74° and the standard deviation is 8°. In which month is it more unusual to have a day with a high temperature of 55°? Explain.

6. **Placement exams.** An incoming freshman took her college's placement exams in French and mathematics. In French, she scored 82 and in math, 86. The overall results on the French exam had a mean of 72 and a standard deviation of 8, while the mean math score was 68 with a standard deviation of 12. On which exam did she do better compared with the other freshmen?

7. **Final exams.** Anna, a language major, took final exams in both French and Spanish and scored 83 on both. Her roommate Megan, also taking both courses, scored 77 on the French exam and 95 on the Spanish exam. Overall, student scores on the French exam had a mean of 81 and a standard deviation of 5, and the Spanish scores had a mean of 74 and a standard deviation of 15.
   a) To qualify for language honors, a major must maintain at least an 85 average for all language courses taken. So far, which student qualifies?
   b) Which student's overall performance was better?

8. **MP3s.** Two companies market new batteries targeted at owners of personal music players. DuraTunes claims a mean battery life of 11 hours, while RockReady advertises 12 hours.
   a) Explain why you would also like to know the standard deviations of the battery lifespans before deciding which brand to buy.
   b) Suppose those standard deviations are 2 hours for DuraTunes and 1.5 hours for RockReady. You are headed for 8 hours at the beach. Which battery is most likely to last all day? Explain.
   c) If your beach trip is all weekend, and you probably will have the music on for 16 hours, which battery is most likely to last? Explain.

9. **Professors.** A friend tells you about a recent study dealing with the number of years of teaching experience among current college professors. He remembers the mean but can't recall whether the standard deviation was 6 months, 6 years, or 16 years. Tell him which one it must have been, and why.

10. Rock concerts. A popular band on tour played a series of concerts in large venues. They always drew a large crowd, averaging 21,359 fans. While the band did not announce (and probably never calculated) the standard deviation, which of these values do you think is most likely to be correct: 20, 200, 2000, or 20,000 fans? Explain your choice.

11. Guzzlers? Environmental Protection Agency (EPA) fuel economy estimates for automobile models tested recently predicted a mean of 24.8 mpg and a standard deviation of 6.2 mpg for highway driving. Assume that a Normal model can be applied.

a) Draw the model for auto fuel economy. Clearly label it, showing what the 68-95-99.7 Rule predicts about miles per gallon.
b) In what interval would you expect the central 68% of autos to be found?
c) About what percent of autos should get more than 31 mpg?
d) About what percent of cars should get between 31 and 37 mpg?
e) Describe the gas mileage of the worst 2.5% of all cars.

12. IQ. Some IQ tests are standardized to a Normal model with a mean of 100 and a standard deviation of 16.

a) Draw the model for these IQ scores. Clearly label it, showing what the 68-95-99.7 Rule predicts about the scores.
b) In what interval would you expect the central 95% of IQ scores to be found?
c) About what percent of people should have IQ scores above 116?
d) About what percent of people should have IQ scores between 68 and 84?
e) About what percent of people should have IQ scores above 132?

T **13. Winter Olympics 2002 downhill.** Fifty-three men qualified for the men's alpine downhill race in Salt Lake City. The gold medal winner finished in 1 minute 39.13 seconds. All competitors' times (in seconds) are found in the following table:

99.13	99.35	99.41	99.78	99.96
100.00	100.30	100.31	100.37	100.39
100.58	100.74	100.74	100.76	100.81
100.84	100.85	101.05	101.24	101.25
101.27	101.56	101.66	101.69	101.70
101.76	101.84	101.85	101.86	101.86
101.88	102.15	102.31	102.52	102.54
103.04	103.19	103.20	103.33	103.63
103.73	103.75	104.35	105.25	105.34
105.49	106.36	107.63	107.65	108.37
108.84	109.75	114.42		

a) The mean time was 102.71 seconds, with a standard deviation of 3.01 seconds. If the normal model is appropriate, what percent of times will be less than 99.7 seconds?
b) What is the actual percent of times less than 99.7 seconds?
c) Why do you think the two percentages don't agree?
d) Create a histogram of these times. What do you see?

14. Rivets. A company that manufactures rivets believes the shear strength (in pounds) is modeled by $N(800, 50)$.

a) Draw and label the Normal model.
b) Would it be safe to use these rivets in a situation requiring a shear strength of 750 pounds? Explain.
c) About what percent of these rivets would you expect to fail below 900 pounds?
d) Rivets are used in a variety of applications with varying shear strength requirements. What is the maximum shear strength for which you would feel comfortable approving this company's rivets? Explain your reasoning.

15. Trees. A forester measured 27 of the trees in a large woods that is up for sale. He found a mean diameter of 10.4 inches and a standard deviation of 4.7 inches. Suppose that these trees provide an accurate description of the whole forest and that a Normal model applies.

a) Draw the Normal model for tree diameters.
b) What size would you expect the central 95% of all trees to be?
c) About what percent of the trees should be less than an inch in diameter?
d) About what percent of the trees should be between 5.7 and 10.4 inches in diameter?
e) About what percent of the trees should be over 15 inches in diameter?

16. Trees, part II. Later on the forester shows you a histogram of the tree diameters he used in analyzing the woods that was for sale. Do you think he was justified in using a Normal model? Explain, citing some specific concerns.

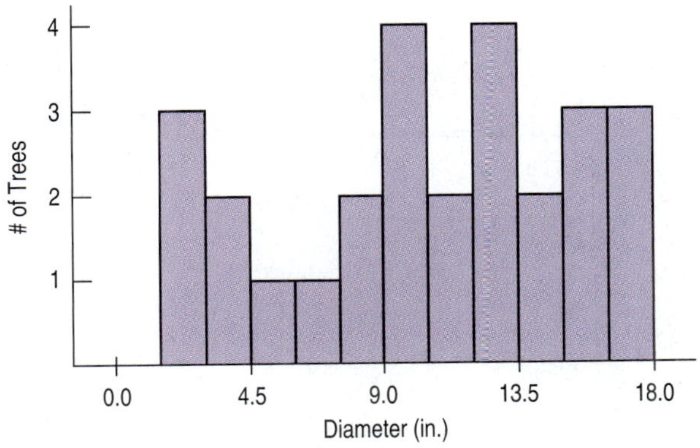

17. TV watching. A survey of 200 college students conducted during the week of March 15, 1999, showed the following distribution of the number of hours of TV watched per week:

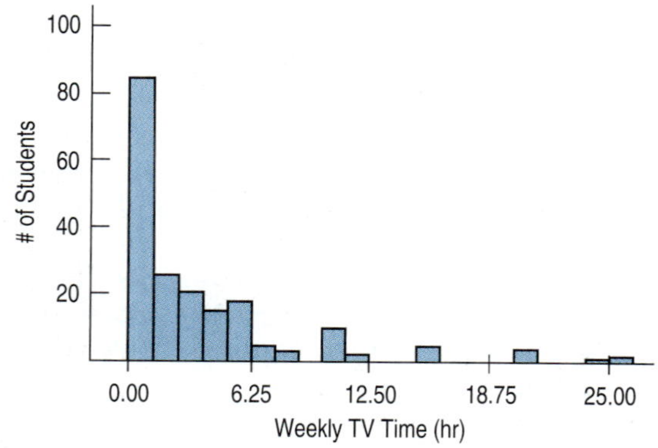

The mean is 3.66 hours with a standard deviation of 4.93 hours.

a) According to the Normal model, what percent of students will watch fewer than one standard deviation below the mean number of hours?
b) For these data, what does that mean? Explain.
c) Explain the problem in using the Normal model for these data.

18. Customer Database. A large philanthropic organization keeps records on the people who have contributed to their cause. In addition to keeping records of past giving, the organization buys demographic data on neighborhoods from the U.S. Census Bureau. Eighteen of these variables concern the ethnicity of the neighborhood of the donor. Here is a histogram and summary statistics for the percentage of whites in the neighborhoods of 500 donors:

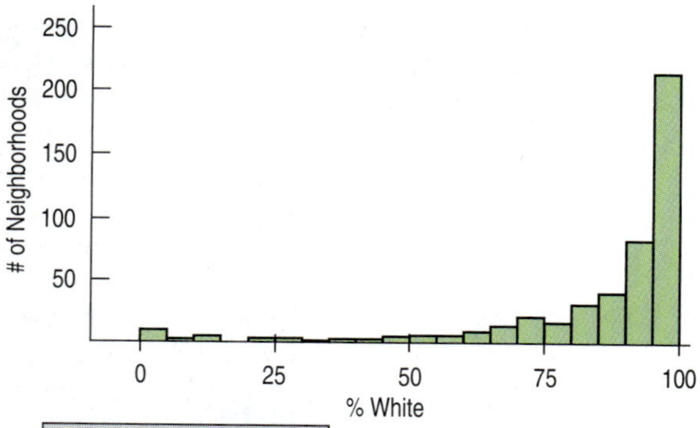

Count	500
Mean	83.59
Median	93
StdDev	22.26
IQR	17
Q1	80
Q3	97

a) Which is a better summary of the percentage of white residents in the neighborhoods, the mean or the median? Explain.
b) Which is a better summary of the spread, the IQR or the standard deviation? Explain.
c) From a Normal model, about what percentage of neighborhoods should have a percent white within one standard deviation of the mean?
d) What percentage of neighborhoods actually have a percent white within one standard deviation of the mean?
e) Explain the discrepancy between parts c and d.

19. Normal models. What percent of a standard Normal model is found in each region? Be sure to draw a picture first.

a) $z > 1.5$
b) $z < 2.25$
c) $-1 < z < 1.15$
d) $|z| > 0.5$

20. Normal models, again. What percent of a standard Normal model is found in each region? Draw a picture first.

a) $z > -2.05$
b) $z < -0.33$
c) $1.2 < z < 1.8$
d) $|z| < 1.28$

21. More Normal models. In a standard Normal model, what value(s) of z cut(s) off the region described? Don't forget to draw a picture.

a) the highest 20%
b) the highest 75%
c) the lowest 3%
d) the middle 90%

22. Yet another Normal model. In a standard Normal model, what value(s) of z cut(s) off the region described? Remember to draw a picture first.

a) the lowest 12%
b) the highest 30%
c) the highest 7%
d) the middle 50%

23. Parameters. Every Normal model is defined by its parameters, the mean and the standard deviation. For each model described below, find the missing parameter. As always, start by drawing a picture.

a) $\mu = 20$, 45% above 30; $\sigma = ?$
b) $\mu = 88$, 2% below 50; $\sigma = ?$
c) $\sigma = 5$, 80% below 100; $\mu = ?$
d) $\sigma = 15.6$, 10% above 17.2; $\mu = ?$

24. Parameters II. Every Normal model is defined by its parameters, the mean and the standard deviation. For each model described below, find the missing parameter. Don't forget to draw a picture.

a) $\mu = 1250$, 35% below 1200; $\sigma = ?$
b) $\mu = 0.64$, 12% above 0.70; $\sigma = ?$
c) $\sigma = 0.5$, 90% above 10.0; $\mu = ?$
d) $\sigma = 220$, 3% below 202; $\mu = ?$

25. Cholesterol. Assume the cholesterol levels of adult American women can be described by a Normal model with a mean of 188 mg/dL and a standard deviation of 24.
a) Draw and label the Normal model.
b) What percent of adult women do you expect to have cholesterol levels over 200 mg/dL?
c) What percent of adult women do you expect to have cholesterol levels between 150 and 170 mg/dL?
d) Estimate the interquartile range of the cholesterol levels.
e) Above what value are the highest 15% of women's cholesterol levels?

26. Tires. A tire manufacturer believes that the treadlife of its snow tires can be described by a Normal model with a mean of 32,000 miles and standard deviation of 2500 miles.
a) If you buy a set of these tires, would it be reasonable for you hope they'll last 40,000 miles? Explain.
b) Approximately what fraction of these tires can be expected to last less than 30,000 miles?
c) Approximately what fraction of these tires can be expected to last between 30,000 and 35,000 miles?
d) Estimate the IQR of the treadlifes.
e) In planning a marketing strategy, a local tire dealer wants to offer a refund to any customer whose tires fail to last a certain number of miles. However, the dealer does not want to take too big a risk. If the dealer is willing to give refunds to no more than 1 of every 25 customers, for what mileage can he guarantee these tires to last?

27. Kindergarten. Companies who design furniture for elementary school classrooms produce a variety of sizes for kids of different ages. Suppose the heights of kindergarten children can be described by a Normal model with a mean of 38.2 inches and standard deviation of 1.8 inches.
a) What fraction of kindergarten kids should the company expect to be less than 3 feet tall?
b) In what height interval should the company expect to find the middle 80% of kindergarteners?
c) At least how tall are the biggest 10% of kindergarteners?

28. Body temperatures. Most people think that the "normal" adult body temperature is 98.6°F. That figure, based on a 19th century study, has recently been challenged. In a 1992 article in the *Journal of the American Medical Association*, researchers reported that a more accurate figure may be 98.2°F. Furthermore, the standard deviation appeared to be around 0.7°F. Assume that a Normal model is appropriate.
a) In what interval would you expect most people's body temperatures to be? Explain.
b) What fraction of people would be expected to have body temperatures above 98.6°F?
c) Below what body temperature are the coolest 20% of all people?

29. First steps. While only 5% of babies have learned to walk by the age of 10 months, 75% are walking by 13 months of age. If the age at which babies develop the ability to walk can be described by a Normal model, find the parameters (mean and standard deviation).

30. Trout. Wildlife biologists believe that the weights of adult trout can be described by a Normal model. They collect data from fishermen, finding that 22% of the trout caught were thrown back because they were below the 2-pound minimum, and only 6% weighed over 5 pounds. What mean and standard deviation should define the model?

31. Eggs. Hens usually begin laying eggs when they are about 6 months old. Young hens tend to lay smaller eggs, often weighing less than the desired minimum weight of 54 grams.
a) The average weight of the eggs produced by the young hens is 50.9 grams, and only 28% of their eggs exceed the desired minimum weight. If a Normal model is appropriate, what would the standard deviation of the egg weights be?
b) By the time these hens have reached the age of 1 year, the eggs they produce average 67.1 grams, and 98% of them are above the minimum weight. What is the standard deviation for the appropriate Normal model for these older hens?
c) Are egg sizes more consistent for the younger hens or the older ones? Explain.
d) A certain poultry farmer finds that 3% of his eggs are underweight and that 12% weigh over 70 grams. Estimate the mean and standard deviation of his eggs.

32. Tomatoes. Agricultural scientists are working on developing an improved variety of Roma tomatoes. Marketing research indicates that customers are likely to bypass Romas that weigh less than 70 grams. The current variety of Roma plants produces fruit that average 74 grams, but 11% of the tomatoes are too small It is reasonable to assume that a Normal model applies.
a) What is the standard deviation of the weights of Romas now being grown?
b) Scientists hope to reduce the frequency of undersized tomatoes to no more than 4%. One way to accomplish this is to raise the average size of the fruit. If the standard deviation remains the same, what target mean should they have as a goal?
c) The researchers produce a new variety with a mean weight of 75 grams, which meets the 4% goal. What is the standard deviation of the weights of these new Romas?
d) Based on their standard deviations, compare the tomatoes produced by the two varieties.

Review of Part I Exploring and Understanding Data

Quick Review

It's time to put it all together. Real data don't come tagged with instructions for use. So let's step back and look at how the key concepts and skills we've seen work together. This brief list and the review exercises that follow should help you check your understanding of Statistics so far.

- Data come in two flavors: categorical and quantitative.
- To describe categorical data:
  - Make a picture. Bar graphs work well for comparing counts in categories.
  - Summarize the distribution with a table of counts or relative frequencies (percents) in each category.
  - Pie charts and segmented bar charts display divisions of a whole.
  - Compare distributions with plots side-by-side.
  - Look for associations between variables by comparing marginal and conditional distributions.
- To describe quantitative data:
  - Make a picture. Use histograms, boxplots, stem-and-leaf displays, or dotplots. Stem-and-leaf's are great for doing by hand and good for small data sets. Histograms are a good way to see the distribution. Boxplots are best for comparing several distributions.
  - Describe distributions in terms of their shape, center, and spread, and note any unusual features such as gaps or outliers.
  - The shape of most distributions you'll see will likely be uniform, unimodal, or bimodal. It may be multimodal. If it is unimodal, then it may be symmetric or skewed.
  - A five-number summary makes a good numerical description of a distribution: min, Q1, median, Q3, and max.
  - If the distribution is skewed, be sure to include the median and interquartile range (IQR) when you describe its center and spread.
  - A distribution that is severely skewed may benefit from re-expressing the data. If it is skewed to the high end, taking logs often works well.
  - If the distribution is unimodal and symmetric, describe its center and spread with the mean and standard deviation.
  - Use the standard deviation as a ruler to tell how unusual an observed value may be, or to compare or combine measurements made on different scales.
  - Changing scales by adding or subtracting a constant affects measures of position but not measures of spread. Multiplying or dividing by a constant affects both.
  - When a distribution is roughly unimodal and symmetric, it may approximate a Normal model. For Normal models the 68-95-99.7 Rule is a good rule of thumb.
  - If the Normal model fits well (check a histogram or Normal probability plot), then Normal percentile tables or functions found in most statistics technology can provide more detailed values.

Need more help with some of this? It never hurts to reread sections of the chapters! And in the following pages we offer you more opportunities[1] to review these concepts and skills.

The exercises that follow use the concepts and skills you've learned in the first six chapters. To be more realistic and more useful for your review, they don't tell you which of the concepts or methods you need. But neither will the exam.

[1]If you doubted that we are teachers, this should convince you. Only a teacher would call additional homework exercises an "opportunity."

Review Exercises

1. Bananas. Here are the prices (in cents per pound) of bananas reported from 15 markets surveyed by the U.S. Department of Agriculture.

51	52	45
48	53	52
50	49	52
48	43	46
45	42	50

a) Display these data with an appropriate graph.
b) Report appropriate summary statistics.
c) Write a few sentences about this distribution.

2. Prenatal care. Results of a 1996 American Medical Association report about the infant mortality rate for twins carried for the full term of a normal pregnancy are shown below, broken down by the level of prenatal care the mother had received.

Full-Term Pregnancies, Level of Prenatal Care	Infant Mortality Rate among Twins (deaths per thousand live births)
Intensive	5.4
Adequate	3.9
Inadequate	6.1
Overall	5.1

a) Is the overall rate the average of the other three rates? Should it be? Explain.
b) Do these results indicate that adequate prenatal care is important for pregnant women? Explain.
c) Do these results suggest that a woman pregnant with twins should be wary of seeking too much medical care? Explain.

3. Singers. The boxplots shown display the heights (in inches) of 130 members of a choir.

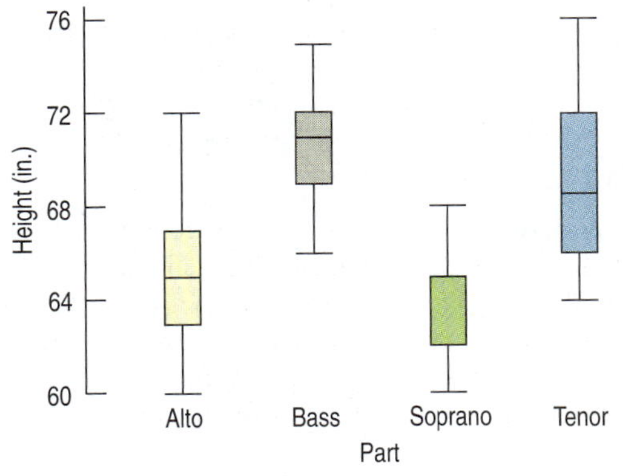

a) It appears that the median height for sopranos is missing, but actually the median and the upper quartile are equal. How could that happen?
b) Write a few sentences describing what you see.

4. Dialysis. In a study of dialysis, researchers found that "of the three patients who were currently on dialysis, 67% had developed blindness and 33% had their toes amputated." What kind of display might be appropriate for these data? Explain.

5. Beanstalks. Beanstalk Clubs are social clubs for very tall people. To join, a man must be over 6′2″ tall, and a woman over 5′10″. The National Health Survey suggests that heights of adults may be normally distributed with mean heights of 69.1″ for men and 64.0″ for women. The respective standard deviations are 2.8″ and 2.5″.
a) You are probably not surprised to learn that men are generally taller than women, but what does the greater standard deviation for men's heights indicate?
b) Who are more likely to qualify for Beanstalk membership, men or women?

6. Bread. Clarksburg Bakery is trying to predict how many loaves to bake. In the last 100 days, they have sold between 95 and 140 loaves per day. Here is a histogram of the number of loaves they sold for the last 100 days.

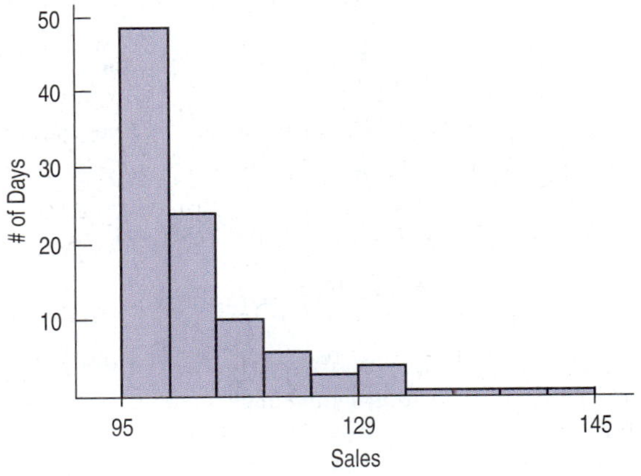

a) Describe the distribution.
b) Which should be larger, the mean number of sales or the median? Explain.
c) Here are the summary statistics for Clarksburg Bakery's bread sales. Use these statistics and the histogram above to create a boxplot. You may approximate the values of any outliers.

Summary of Sales	
Median	100
Min	95
Max	140
25th %tile	97
75th %tile	105.5

d) For these data the mean was 103 loaves sold per day, with a standard deviation of 9 loaves. Do these statistics suggest that Clarksburg Bakery should expect to sell between 94 and 112 loaves on about 68% of the days? Explain.

7. Watsamatta University. Public relations staff at Watsamatta U. collected data on people's opinions of various colleges and universities in their state. They phoned 850 local residents. After identifying themselves, the callers asked the survey participants their ages, whether they had attended college, and whether they had a favorable opinion of the university. The official report to the university's directors claimed that, in general, people had very favorable opinions about Watsamatta U.

a) Identify the W's of these data.
b) Identify the variables, classify each as categorical or quantitative, and specify units if relevant.
c) Are you confident about the report's conclusion? Explain.

8. Acid rain. Based on long-term investigation, researchers have suggested that the acidity (pH) of rainfall in the Shenandoah Mountains can be described by the Normal model $N(4.9, 0.6)$.

a) Draw and carefully label the model.
b) What percent of storms produce rain with pH over 6?
c) What percent of storms produce rainfall with pH under 4?
d) The lower the pH, the more acidic the rain. What is the pH level for the most acidic 20% of all storms?
e) What is the pH level for the least acidic 5% of all storms?
f) What is the IQR for the pH of rainfall?

9. Fraud detection. A credit card bank is investigating the incidence of fraudulent card use. The bank suspects that the type of product bought may provide clues to the fraud. To examine this situation, the bank looks at the Standard Industrial Code (SIC) of the business related to the transaction. This is a code that was used by the U.S. Census Bureau and Statistics Canada to identify the type of business of every registered business in North America.[2] For example, 1011 designates Meat and Meat Products (except Poultry), 1012 is Poultry Products, 1021 is Fish Products, 1031 is Canned and Preserved Fruits and Vegetables, and 1032 is Frozen Fruits and Vegetables.

A company intern produces the following histogram of the SIC codes for 1536 transactions:

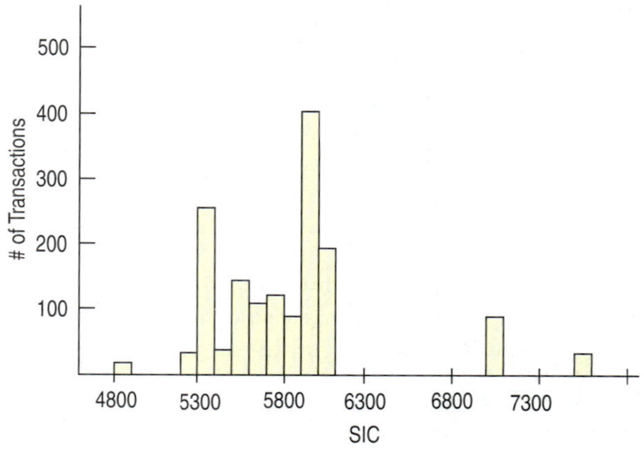

He also reports that the mean SIC is 5823.13 with a standard deviation of 488.17.

a) Comment on any problems you see with the use of the mean and standard deviation as summary statistics.
b) How well do you think the Normal model will work on these data? Explain.

10. Streams. As part of the coursework, a class at an upstate NY college collects data on streams each year. Students record a number of biological, chemical, and physical variables, including the stream name, the substrate of the stream (*limestone, shale,* or *mixed*), the pH, the temperature (°C), and BCI, a measure of biological diversity.

Group	Count	%
Limestone	77	44.8
Mixed	26	15.1
Shale	69	40.1

a) Name each variable, indicating whether it is categorical or quantitative, and giving the units if available.
b) These streams have been classified according to their substrate—the composition of soil and rock over which they flow—as summarized in the table. What kind of graph might be used to display these data?

11. Cramming. One Thursday researchers gave students enrolled in a section of basic Spanish a set of 50 new vocabulary words to memorize. On Friday the students took a vocabulary test. When they returned to class the following Monday they were retested—without advance warning. Both sets of test scores for the 28 students are shown.

[2] Since 1997 the SIC has been replaced by the NASIC, a code of six letters.

Fri	Mon	Fri	Mon
42	36	50	47
44	44	34	34
45	46	38	31
48	38	43	40
44	40	39	41
43	38	46	32
41	37	37	36
35	31	40	31
43	32	41	32
48	37	48	39
43	41	37	31
45	32	36	41
47	44		

a) Create a graphical display to compare the two distributions of scores.
b) Write a few sentences about the scores reported on Friday and Monday.
c) Create a graphical display showing the distribution of the *changes* in student scores.
d) Describe the distribution of changes.

12. Computers and Internet. A U.S. Census Bureau report (August 2000, *Current Population Survey*) found that 51.0% of homes had a personal computer and 41.5% had access to the Internet. A newspaper concluded that 92.5% of homes had either a computer or access to the Internet. Do you agree? Explain.

13. Let's play cards. You pick a card from a deck (see, for example, p. 213) and record its denomination (7, say) and its suit (maybe spades).
a) Is the variable *suit* categorical or quantitative?
b) Name a game you might be playing for which you would consider the variable *denomination* to be categorical. Explain.
c) Name a game you might be playing for which you would consider the variable *denomination* to be quantitative. Explain.

14. Accidents. In 2001, Progressive Insurance asked customers who had been involved in auto accidents how far they were from home when the accident happened. The data are summarized in the table.

Miles from Home	% of Accidents
Less than 1	23
1 to 5	29
6 to 10	17
11 to 15	8
16 to 20	6
Over 20	17

a) Create an appropriate graph of these data.
b) Do these data indicate that driving near home is particularly dangerous? Explain.

15. Hard water. In an investigation of environmental causes of disease, data were collected on the annual mortality rate (deaths per 100,000) for males in 61 large towns in England and Wales. In addition, the water hardness was recorded as the calcium concentration (parts per million, ppm) in the drinking water.
a) What are the variables in this study? For each, indicate whether it is quantitative or categorical and what the units are.
b) Here are histograms of calcium concentration and mortality. Describe the distributions of the two variables.

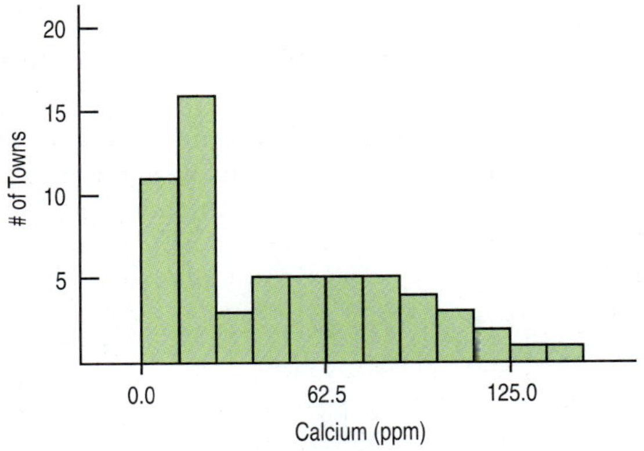

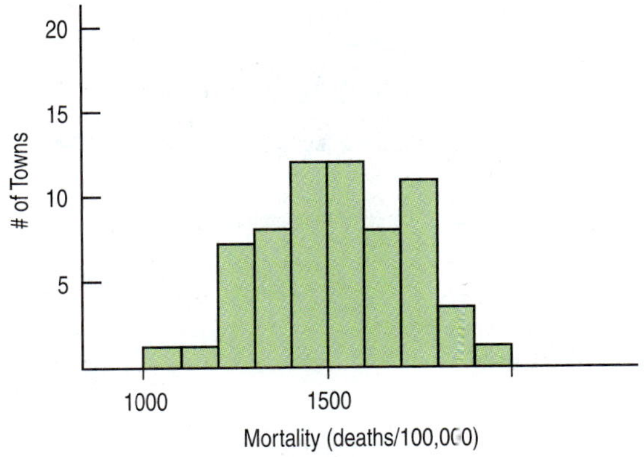

16. Hard water II. The data set from England and Wales also notes for each town whether it was south or north of Derby. Here are some summary statistics and a comparative boxplot for the two regions.

Summary of Mortality

Group	Count	Mean	Median	StdDev
North	34	1631.59	1631	138.470
South	27	1388.85	1369	151.114

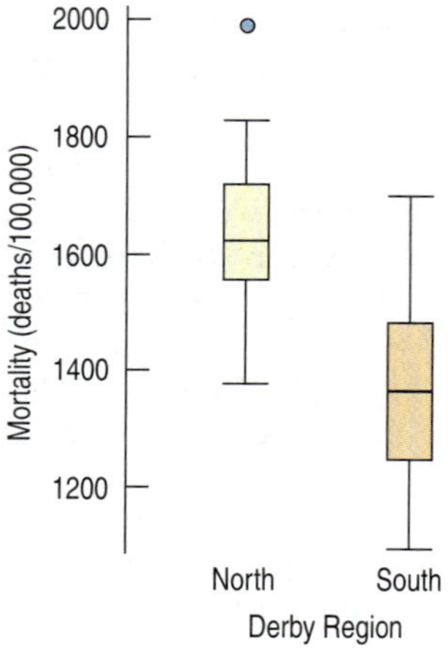

a) What is the overall mean mortality rate for the two regions?

b) Do you see evidence of a difference in mortality rates? Explain.

17. Seasons. Average daily temperatures in January and July for 60 large U.S. cities are graphed in the histograms below.

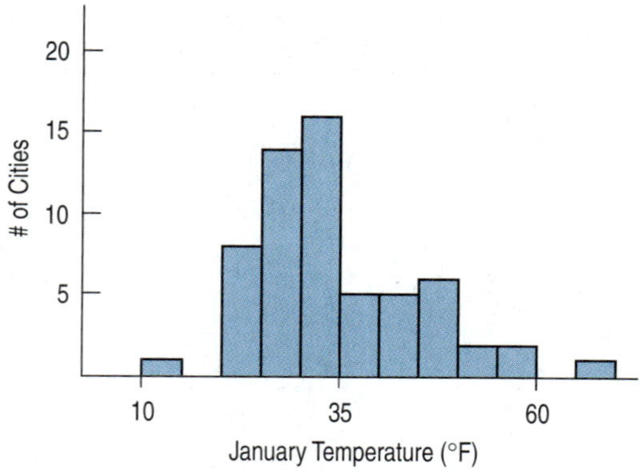

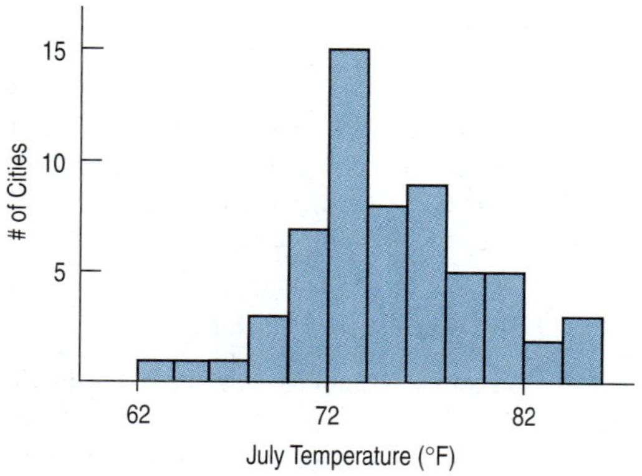

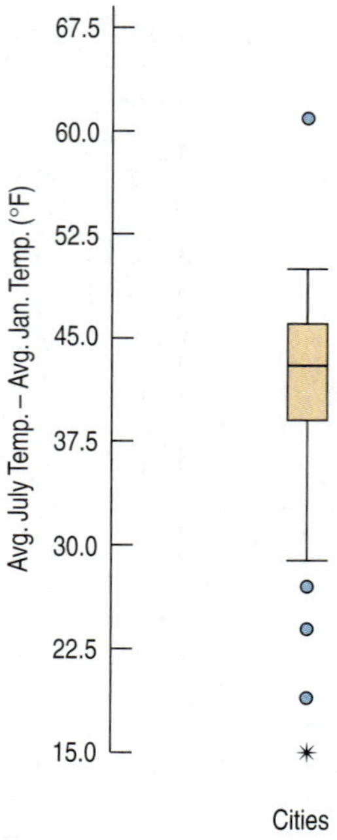

a) What aspect of these histograms makes it difficult to compare the distributions?

b) What differences do you see between the distributions of January and July average temperatures?

c) Differences in temperatures (July–January) for each of the cities are displayed in the boxplot above. Write a few sentences describing what you see.

18. Old Faithful. It is a common belief that Yellowstone's most famous geyser erupts once an hour at very predictable intervals. The histogram below shows the time gaps (in minutes) between 222 successive eruptions. Describe this distribution.

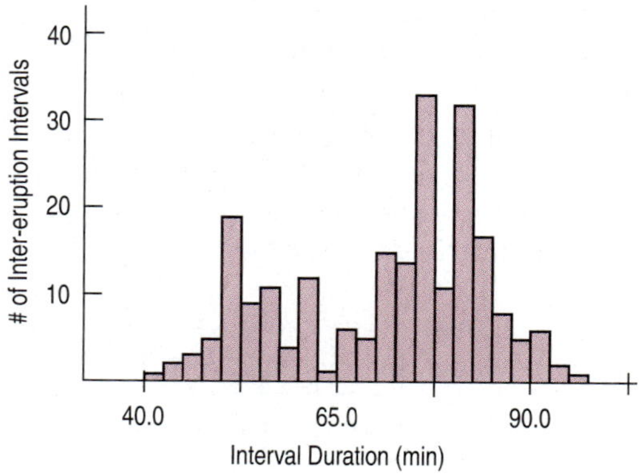

19. Old Faithful? Does the duration of an eruption have an effect on the length of time that elapses before the next eruption? *(continued)*

a) The histogram below shows the duration (in minutes) of those 222 eruptions. Describe this distribution.

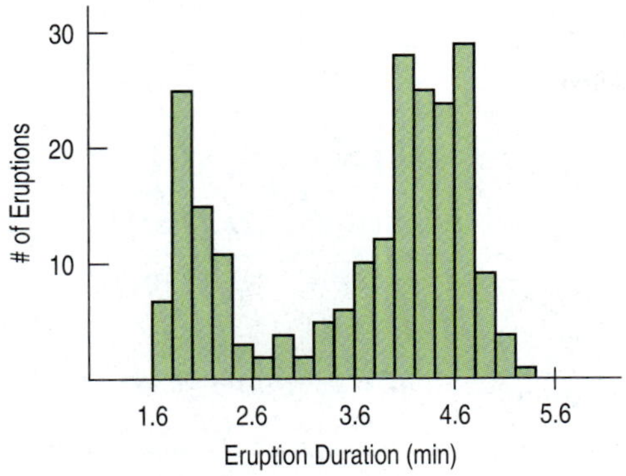

b) Explain why it is not appropriate to find summary statistics for this distribution.

c) Let's classify the eruptions as "long" or "short," depending upon whether or not they last at least 3 minutes. Describe what you see in the comparative boxplots.

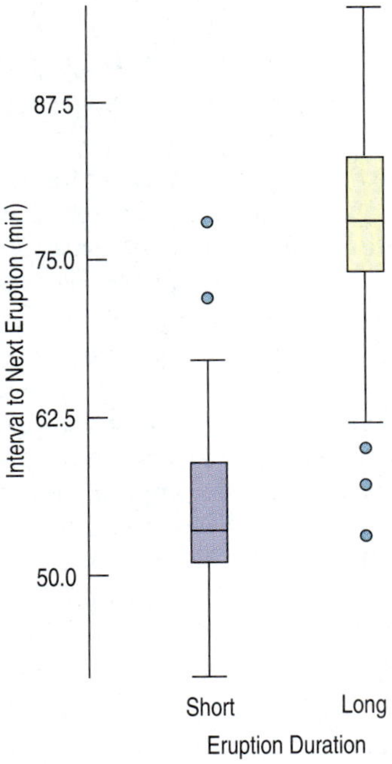

20. Teen drivers. In its *Traffic Safety Facts 2000*, the U.S. Department of Transportation reported that 6.8% of licensed drivers are between the ages of 15 and 20, yet this age group is behind the wheel in 14% of all fatal crashes. Use these statistics to explain the concept of independence.

T **21. Liberty's nose.** Is the Statue of Liberty's nose too long? Her nose measures 4′6″, but she is a large statue after all. Her arm is 42 feet long. That means her arm is 42/4.5 = 9.3 times as long as her nose. Is that a reasonable ratio? Shown in the table are arm and nose lengths of 18 girls in a Statistics class, and the ratio of arm to nose length for each.

Arm (cm)	Nose (cm)	Arm/Nose Ratio
73.8	5	14.8
74	4.5	16.4
69.5	4.5	15.4
62.5	4.7	13.3
68.6	4.4	15.6
64.5	4.8	13.4
68.2	4.8	14.2
63.5	4.4	14.4
63.5	5.4	11.8
67	4.6	14.6
67.4	4.4	15.3
70.7	4.3	16.4
69.4	4.1	16.9
71.7	4.5	15.9
69	4.4	15.7
69.8	4.5	15.5
71	4.8	14.8
71.3	4.7	15.2

a) Make an appropriate plot and describe the distribution of the ratios.

b) Summarize the ratios numerically, choosing appropriate measures of center and spread.

c) Is the ratio of 9.3 for the Statue of Liberty unrealistically low? Explain.

T **22. Winter Olympics 2002 speed skating.** The top 25 men's and 25 women's 500-m speed skating times are listed in the table below:

Skater	Country	Time
Casey FitzRandolph	USA	69.23
Hiroyasu Shimizu	Japan	69.26
Kip Carpenter	USA	69.47
Gerard van Velde	Netherlands	69.49
Lee Kyu-Hyuk	South Korea	69.59
Joey Cheek	USA	69.6
Mike Ireland	Canada	69.6
Toyoki Takeda	Japan	69.81
Jan Bos	Netherlands	69.86
Erben Wennemars	Netherlands	69.89
Dmitry Lobkov	Russia	70.1
Kuniomi Haneishi	Japan	70.11
Sergey Klevchenya	Russia	70.28
Manabu Horii	Japan	70.32

(continued)

Janne Hanninen	Finland	70.33
Pawel Abratkiewicz	Poland	70.44
Choi Jae-Bong	South Korea	70.57
Dmitry Dorofeyev	Russia	70.75
Michael Kuenzel	Germany	70.84
Patrick Bouchard	Canada	70.88
Li Yu	China	70.97
Tomasz Swist	Poland	71.27
Davide Carta	Italy	71.39
Eric Brisson	Canada	71.54
Park Jae-Man	South Korea	71.96
Catriona LeMay Doan	Canada	74.75
Monique Garbrecht-Enfeldt	Germany	74.94
Sabine Voelker	Germany	75.19
Andrea Nuyt	Netherlands	75.37
Anzhelika Kotyuga	Belarus	75.39
Tomomi Okazaki	Japan	75.64
Svetlana Zhurova	Russia	75.64
Marianne Timmer	Netherlands	76.17
Yukari Watanabe	Japan	76.2
Svetlana Kaykan	Russia	76.31
Eriko Sannmiya	Japan	76.37
Sayuri Osuga	Japan	76.42
Wang Manli	China	76.62
Chris Witty	USA	76.73
Jenny Wolf	Germany	76.73
Chiara Simionato	Italy	76.92
Marieke Wijsman	Netherlands	77.1
Choi Seung-Yong	South Korea	77.14
Marion Wohlrab	Germany	77.37
Becky Sundstrom	USA	77.6
Susan Auch	Canada	77.6
Eli Ochowicz	USA	77.71
Jin Hua	China	78.26
Yang Chunyuan	China	78.63
Cho Seon-Yeon	South Korea	78.78

a) The mean finishing time was 73.46 seconds with a standard deviation of 3.33 seconds. If the Normal model is appropriate, what percent of the times should be within 1.67 seconds of 73.46?
b) What percent of the times actually fall within this range?
c) Explain.

23. Sample. A study in South Africa focusing on the impact of health insurance identified 1590 children at birth and then sought to conduct follow-up health studies 5 years later. Only 416 of the original group participated in the 5-year follow-up study. This made researchers concerned that the follow-up group might not accurately resemble the total group in terms of health insurance. The table below summarizes the two groups by race and by presence of medical insurance when the child was born. Carefully explain how this study demonstrates Simpson's paradox. (*Birth to Ten Study,* Medical Research Council, South Africa)

Number (%) Insured

	Follow-up	Not Traced
Black	36 of 404 (8.9%)	91 of 1048 (8.7%)
White	10 of 12 (83.3%)	104 of 126 (82.5%)
Overall	46 of 416 (11.1%)	195 of 1174 (16.6%)

24. Sluggers. Roger Maris's 1961 home run record stood until Mark McGwire hit 70 in 1998. Listed below are the home run totals for each season McGwire played. Also listed are Babe Ruth's home run totals.

McGwire: 3*, 49, 32, 33, 39, 22, 42, 9*, 9*, 39, 52, 58, 70, 65, 32*,27*
Ruth: 54, 59, 35, 41, 46, 25, 47, 60, 54, 46, 49, 46, 41, 34, 22

a) Find the five-number summary for McGwire's career.
b) Do any of his seasons appear to be outliers? Explain.
c) McGwire played in only 18 games at the end of his first big league season, and missed major portions of some other seasons because of injuries to his back and knees. Those seasons might not be representative of his abilities. They are marked with asterisks in the list above. Omit these values and make parallel boxplots comparing McGwire's career to Babe Ruth's.
d) Write a few sentences comparing the two sluggers.
e) Create a side-by-side stem-and-leaf display comparing the careers of the two players.
f) What aspects of the distributions are apparent in the stem-and-leaf displays that did not clearly show in the boxplots?

25. Be quick! Avoiding an accident when driving can depend on reaction time. That time, measured from the moment the driver first sees the danger until he or she gets his foot on the brake pedal, is thought to follow a Normal model with a mean of 1.5 seconds and a standard deviation of 0.18 seconds.
a) Use the 68-95-99.7 Rule to draw the Normal model.
b) Write a few sentences describing driver reaction times.
c) What percent of drivers have a reaction time less than 1.25 seconds?

(continued)

d) What percent of drivers have reaction times between 1.6 and 1.8 seconds?
e) What is the interquartile range of reaction times?
f) Describe the reaction times of the slowest 1/3 of all drivers.

26. Music and memory. Is it a good idea to listen to music when studying for a big test? In a study conducted by some Statistics students, 62 people were randomly assigned to listen to rap music, Mozart, or no music while attempting to memorize objects pictured on a page. They were then asked to list all the objects they could remember. Here are the five-number summaries for each group:

	n	Min	Q1	Median	Q3	Max
Rap	29	5	8	10	12	25
Mozart	20	4	7	10	12	27
None	13	8	9.5	13	17	24

a) Describe the W's for these data: *Who, What, Where, Why, When, How.*
b) Name the variables and classify each as categorical or quantitative.
c) Create parallel boxplots as best you can from these summary statistics to display these results.
d) Write a few sentences comparing the performances of the three groups.

T **27. Mail.** Here are the number of pieces of mail received at a school office for 36 days.

123	70	90
80	78	72
52	103	138
112	92	93
118	118	106
95	131	59
151	115	97
100	128	130
66	135	76
143	100	88
110	75	60
115	105	85

a) Plot these data.
b) Find appropriate summary statistics.
c) Write a brief description of the school's mail deliveries.
d) What percent of the days actually lie within one standard deviation of the mean? Comment.

28. Pay. According to the *1999 National Occupational Employment and Wage Estimates for Management Occupations,* the mean hourly wage for Chief Executives was \$48.67 and the median hourly wage was \$52.08. By contrast, for General and Operations Managers, the mean hourly wage was \$31.69 and the median was \$27.23. Are these wage distributions likely to be symmetric, skewed left, or skewed right? Explain. (Bureau of Labor Statistics)

29. Engines. One measure of the size of an automobile engine is its "displacement," the total volume (in liters or cubic inches) of its cylinders. Summary statistics for several models of new cars are shown. These displacements were measured in cubic inches.

Summary of Displacement

Count	38
Mean	177.289
Median	148.500
StdDev	88.8767
Range	275
25th %tile	105
75th %tile	231

a) How many cars were measured?
b) Why might the mean be so much larger than the median?
c) Describe the center and spread of this distribution with appropriate statistics.
d) Your neighbor is bragging about the 227-cubic-inch engine he bought in his new car. Is that engine unusually large? Explain.
e) Are there any engines in this data set that you would consider to be outliers? Explain.
f) Is it reasonable to expect that about 68% of car engines measure between 88 and 266 cubic inches? (That's 177.289 ± 88.8767.) Explain.
g) We can convert all the data from cubic inches to cubic centimeters (cc) by multiplying by 16.4. For example, a 200-cubic-inch engine has a displacement of 3280 cc. How would such a conversion affect each of the summary statistics?

30. Engines, again. Horsepower is another measure commonly used to describe auto engines. Here are the summary statistics and histogram displaying horsepowers of the same group of 38 cars.

Summary of Horsepower

Count	38
Mean	101.737
Median	100
StdDev	26.4449
Range	90
25th %tile	78
75th %tile	125

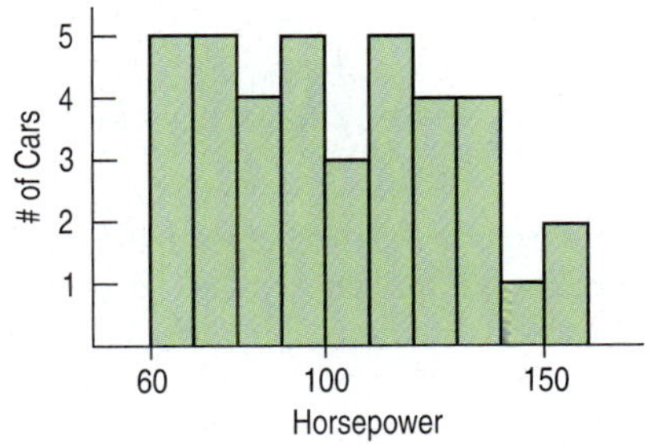

a) Describe the shape, center, and spread of this distribution.
b) What is the interquartile range?
c) Are any of these engines outliers in terms of horsepower? Explain.
d) Do you think the 68-95-99.7 Rule applies to the horsepower of auto engines? Explain.
e) From the histogram make a rough estimate of the percentage of these engines whose horsepower is within one standard deviation of the mean.
f) A fuel additive boasts in its advertising that it can "add 10 horsepower to any car." Assuming that is true, what would happen to each of these summary statistics if this additive were used in all the cars?

31. Age and party. The Gallup Poll conducted a representative telephone survey during the first quarter of 1999. Among their reported results was the following table concerning the preferred political party affiliation of respondents and their ages.

Age	Party: Rep.	Dem.	Ind.	Total
18–29	241	351	409	1001
30–49	299	330	370	999
50–64	282	341	375	998
65+	279	382	343	1004
Total	1101	1404	1497	4002

a) What percent of people surveyed were Republicans?
b) Do you think this might be a reasonable estimate of the percentage of all voters who are Republicans? Explain.
c) What percent of people surveyed were under 30 or over 65?
d) What percent of people were Independents under the age of 30?
e) What percent of Independents were under 30?
f) What percent of people under 30 were Independents?

32. Age and party II. Consider again the Gallup Poll results on age and political party in Exercise 31.
a) What is the marginal distribution of party affiliation?
b) Create segmented bar graphs displaying the conditional distribution of party affiliation for each age group.
c) Summarize these poll results in a few sentences that might appear in a newspaper article about party affiliation in the United States.
d) Do you think party affiliation is independent of the voter's age? Explain.

33. Herbal medicine. Researchers for the Herbal Medicine Council collected information on people's experiences with a new herbal remedy for colds. They went to a store selling natural health products. There they asked 100 customers whether they had taken the cold remedy and, if so, to rate its effectiveness (on a scale from 1 to 10) in curing their symptoms. The Council concluded that this product was highly effective in treating the common cold.
a) Identify the W's of these data.
b) Identify the variables, classify each as categorical or quantitative, and specify units if relevant.
c) Are you confident about the Council's conclusion? Explain.

34. Public opinion. For many years Martha Stewart was a popular expert in home decorating, an arbiter of good taste, and a very successful businesswoman. In June 2002 she came under attack amidst rumors of insider stock trading. A series of Gallup polls each contacted over 1000 people to ask about their overall opinion of her. Those polled could answer favorable, unfavorable, or that they did not know who she was. Results are summarized in the table.

	Oct. 1999	June 2002	July 2002
Favorable	49%	46%	30%
Unfavorable	16%	27%	39%
Don't know	32%	23%	27%

a) Each poll should total 100%. Can you think of a reason why these do not?
b) How could the number of people who do not know who Martha Stewart is *increase* from June to July? Did people forget her? Or perhaps the poll is flawed? Explain how these results could be valid.
c) Display these results in a bar graph.
d) Display these results with pie charts.
e) Display these results with a timeplot.
f) Which display do you think best depicts these data? Why?
g) Write a few sentences describing Martha Stewart's public image.

35. Bike safety. The Massachusetts Governor's Highway Safety Bureau's report on bicycle injuries for the years 1991–2000 included the counts shown in the table.

Year	Bicycle Injuries Reported
1991	1763
1992	1522
1993	1452
1994	1370
1995	1380
1996	1343
1997	1312
1998	1275
1999	1030
2000	1118

a) What are the W's for these data?
b) Display the data in a stem-and-leaf display.
c) Display the data in a timeplot.
d) What is apparent in the stem-and-leaf display that is hard to see in the timeplot?
e) What is apparent in the timeplot that is hard to see in the stem-and-leaf display?
f) Write a few sentences about bicycle injuries in Massachusetts.

36. Profits. Here is a stem-and-leaf display showing profits as a percent of sales for 29 of the *Forbes* 500 largest U.S. corporations. The stems are split; each stem represents a span of 5%, from a loss of 9% to a profit of 25%.

−0	9 9
−0	1 2 3 4
0	1 1 1 1 2 3 4 4 4
0	5 5 5 5 6 7 9
1	0 0 1 1 3
1	
2	2
2	5

Profits (% of sales)

(−0|3 means a loss of 3%)

a) Find the five-number summary.
b) Draw a boxplot for these data.
c) Find the mean and standard deviation.
d) Describe the distribution of profits for these corporations.

37. Some assembly required. A company that markets build-it-yourself furniture sells a computer desk that is advertised with the claim "less than an hour to assemble." However, through postpurchase surveys the company has learned that only 25% of their customers succeeded in building the desk in under an hour; 5% said it took them over 2 hours. The company assumes that consumer assembly time follows a Normal model.

a) Find the mean and standard deviation of the assembly time model.
b) One way the company could solve this problem would be to change the advertising claim. What assembly time should the company quote in order that 60% of customers succeed in finishing the desk by then?
c) Wishing to maintain the "less than an hour" claim, the company hopes that revising the instructions and labeling the parts more clearly can improve the 1-hour success rate to 60%. If the standard deviation stays the same, what new lower mean time does the company need to achieve?
d) Months later, another postpurchase survey shows that new instructions and part labeling did lower the mean assembly time, but only to 50 minutes. Nonetheless, the company did achieve the 60%-in-an-hour goal, too. How was that possible?

38. Crime and punishment. Because of the development of statistics and the methods of analysis you are learning about in this book, the 20th century has been called "The First Measured Century" in a series of documentaries on PBS. Here are two of their graphs.

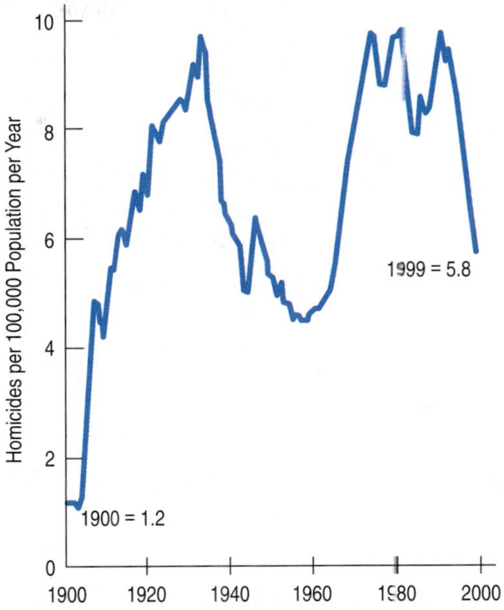

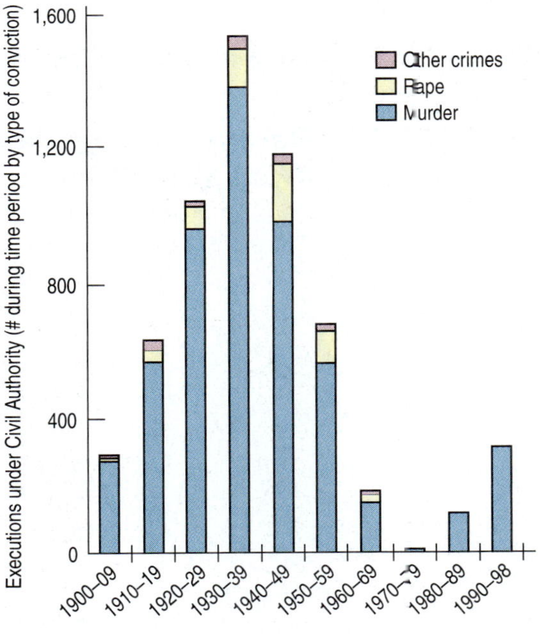

a) Write a few sentences describing the homicide rate in the United States during the 20th century.
b) Write a few sentences describing the use of capital punishment in the United States.
c) Could these two graphs be used to support the argument that capital punishment serves as a deterrent? If yes, explain how the graphs demonstrate that support. If no, explain why not.

Part II

Exploring Relationships Between Variables

Chapter 7

Scatterplots, Association, and Correlation

WHO	U.S. voters
WHAT	Percentage saying they would vote for a woman for president
WHEN	1937–1999
WHERE	United States
HOW	Gallup Poll

Regularly, since 1937, the Gallup Poll has asked likely U.S. voters whether they would vote for a qualified woman for president if their preferred political party nominated one. Are people more likely to say yes to this question now than they were 70 years ago? If so, has the increase been consistent, or do you think there might have been periods when the "yes's" didn't increase at all, or even decreased? Here's a plot of the percentage saying they would vote for a woman, plotted against the year in which the survey took place:

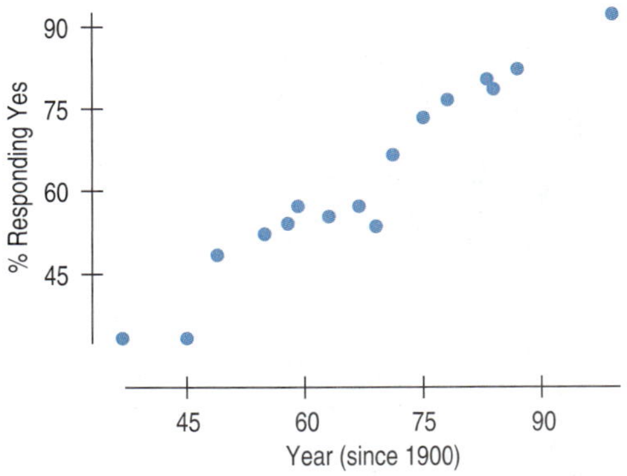

A scatterplot of percentage saying they would vote for a woman plotted against the year of the survey. Has the increase in willingness to vote for a woman been constant over the entire time period? What features in the trend do you see? **Figure 7.1**

Clearly, attitudes have changed. The plot shows fairly steady growth since 1937, reaching a level of 90% of voters saying "yes" by the year 1999. We can also see that there was a period of no growth in the 1960s and early 1970s.

This timeplot is an example of a more general kind of display called a **scatterplot.** Scatterplots may be the most common and most effective display for data. By just looking at them, you can see patterns, trends, relationships, and even the occasional extraordinary value sitting apart from the others. As the great philosopher Yogi Berra[1] once said, "You can observe a lot by watching."[2] Scatterplots

[1]Hall of Fame catcher and manager of the New York Mets.

[2]But then he also said "I really didn't say everything I said." So we can't really be sure.

are the best way to start observing the relationship between two *quantitative* variables.

Relationships between variables are often at the heart of what we'd like to learn from data:

- Are grades actually higher now than they used to be?
- Do people tend to reach puberty at a younger age than in previous generations?
- Does applying strong magnets to parts of the body relieve pain? If so, are stronger magnets more effective?
- Do students learn better with the use of computer technology?

Questions such as these relate two quantitative variables and ask whether there is an **association** between them. Scatterplots are the ideal way to *picture* such associations.

Looking at Scatterplots

WHO	70 U.S. cities
WHAT	Cost per person of traffic delays and peak period freeway speed
UNITS	$ per person per year and miles per hour
WHEN	2000
WHY	Annual report from the Texas Transportation Institute

The Texas Transportation Institute studies the mobility provided by the nation's transportation system. It issues an annual report on traffic congestion and its costs. Here's a scatterplot of the annual cost per person of traffic delays (in dollars) in 70 cities in the United States against the peak period freeway speed (mph).

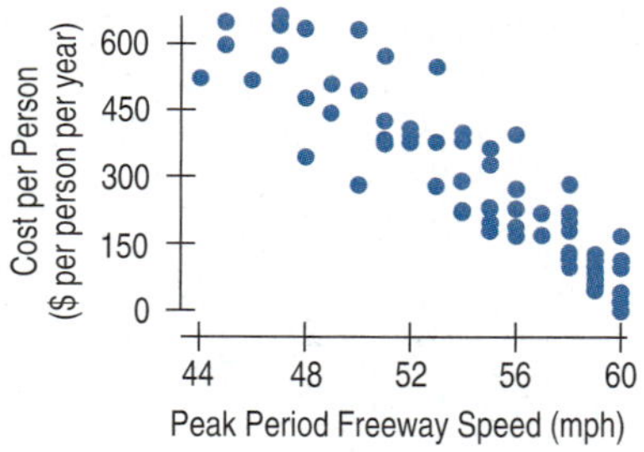

Cost per person ($ per year) of traffic delays vs. peak period freeway speed (mph) for 70 U.S. cities.

Figure 7.2

Everyone looks at scatterplots. But, if asked, most people would find it hard to say what to look for in a scatterplot. What do *you* see? Try to describe the scatterplot congestion cost against freeway speed.

Look for: Direction

Probably, you would say that the **direction** of the relationship is important. As the peak freeway speed goes up, the cost of congestion goes down. A pattern that runs from the upper left to the lower right  is said to have a **negative** direction. A pattern running the other way has a **positive** direction. 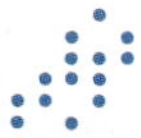

The second thing to look for in a scatterplot is its **form.** If there is a straight line relationship, it will appear as a cloud or swarm of points stretched out in a generally consistent, straight form. For example, the scatterplot of traffic congestion has such an underlying **linear** form with some points that stray away from it.

Look for: Form (especially straightness)

If the relationship isn't straight, but curves gently, while still increasing or decreasing steadily,  we can often find ways to make it more nearly straight. But if it curves sharply—up and then down, for example, 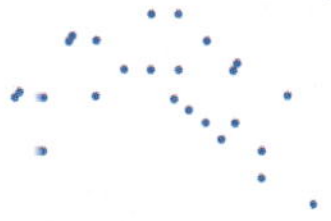, —there is much less we can say about it with the methods of this book.

Look for: Scatter

The third thing to look for in a scatterplot is how much **scatter** it has. At one extreme, do the points appear to follow a single stream 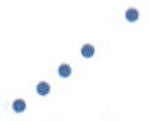 (whether straight, curved, or bending all over the place)? Or, at the other extreme, does the swarm of points seem to form a vague cloud through which we can barely discern any trend or pattern?  We are especially interested in the scatter when the underlying form is straight. We'll develop tools for *quantifying* the amount of scatter soon, but for now we just want to be aware of whether there seems to be a large or small amount of scatter. The traffic congestion plot shows little scatter, so we conclude that there's a strong relationship between cost and speed.

Finally, you should always look for the unexpected. Often the most interesting thing to see in a scatterplot is the thing you never thought to look for. One example of such a surprise is an **outlier** standing away from the overall pattern of the scatterplot. Such a point is almost always interesting and always deserves special attention. Clusters or subgroups that stand away from the rest of the plot or show a trend in a different direction than the rest of the plot should raise questions about why they are different. They may be a clue that you should split the data into subgroups rather than looking at it all together.

Scatterplot Details

Descartes was a philosopher, famous for his statement *cogito ergo sum:* I think, therefore I am.

Scatterplots were among the first modern mathematical displays. The idea of using two axes at right angles to define a field on which to display values can be traced back to René Descartes (1596–1650), and the playing field he defined in this way is formally called a *Cartesian plane* in his honor.

The two axes Descartes specified characterize the scatterplot. The axis that runs up and down is, by convention, called the y-axis, and the one that runs from side to side is called the x-axis. You can count on these names. If someone refers to the y-axis, you may be sure they mean the vertical, up-and-down axis, and similarly with the x-axis.[3]

[3] The axes are also called the "ordinate" and the "abscissa"—often by people who want to impress you. In Statistics (and in all statistics computer programs), the axes are always called "y" and "x."

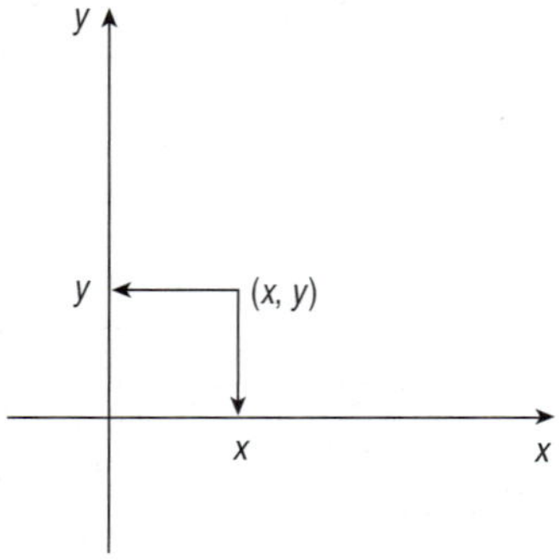

To make a scatterplot of two quantitative variables, assign one to the y-axis and the other to the x-axis. Be sure to label the axes clearly and indicate the scale of the axes with numbers. Scatterplots display **quantitative** variables. Each variable has units, which should appear with the display to define what it's showing.

Each point is placed on a scatterplot at a position that corresponds to values on these two variables. Its horizontal location is specified by its value on the x-axis variable and its vertical location is specified by its value on the y-axis variable. Together, these are known as *coordinates* and written (x, y).

Scatterplots made by computer programs (such as the two we've seen in this chapter) often do not—and usually should not—show the *origin:* the point at $x = 0, y = 0$ where the axes meet. If both variables have values that are near to or on both sides of zero, then the origin will be part of the display. If the values are far from zero, though, there's no reason to include the origin. In fact, it's far better to focus on the part of the Cartesian plane that contains the data. (For example, we're not interested in the likely cost of delays if the freeways had a peak period speed of 0 mph.) Often, programs indicate this choice by drawing the axes so that they don't quite meet.

TI Tips

Let's use your calculator to make a scatterplot. First you need some data. It's okay to just enter the data in any two lists, but let's get fancy. When you are handling lots of data and several variables (as you will be soon), remembering what you stored in L1, L2, and so on can become confusing. You can—and should—give your variables meaningful names. To see how, let's store some data that you will use several times in this chapter and the next. They show the change in tuition costs at Arizona State University during the 1990s.

Naming the Lists

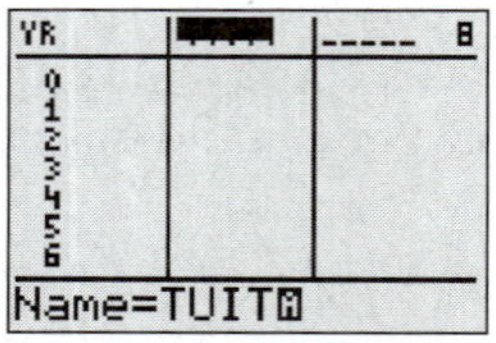

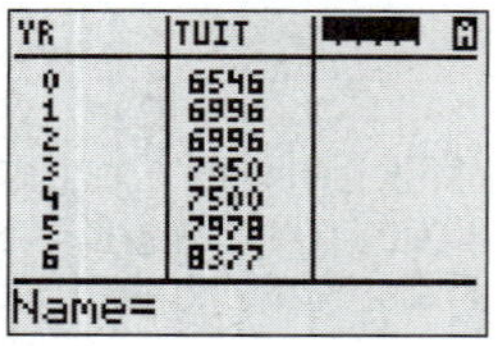

- Go into STAT Edit, place the cursor on one of the list names (L1, say), and use the arrow key to move to the right across all the lists until you encounter a blank column.
- Type YR to name this first variable, then hit ENTER.
- Often when we work with years it makes sense to use values like "90" (or even "0") rather than big numbers like "1990." For these data enter the years 1990 through 2000 as 0, 1, 2, . . ., 10.
- Now go to the next blank column, name this variable TUIT, and enter these values: 6546, 6996, 6996, 7350, 7500, 7978, 8377, 8710, 9110, 9411, 9800.

Making the Scatterplot

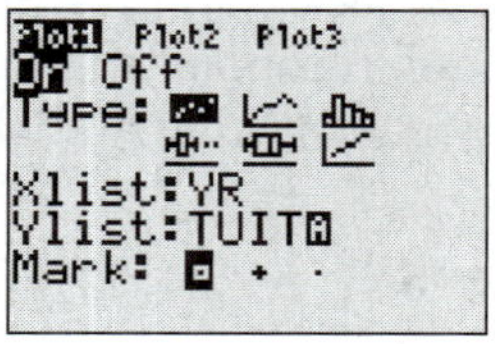

- Set up the STATPLOT by choosing the scatterplot icon (the first option).
- Identify which lists you want as Xlist and Ylist. If the data are in L1 and L2, that's easy to do—but your data are stored in lists with special names. To specify your Xlist, go to 2nd LIST NAMES, scroll down the list of variables until you find YR, then hit ENTER.
- Use LIST NAMES again to specify Ylist:TUIT.
- Pick a symbol for displaying the points.

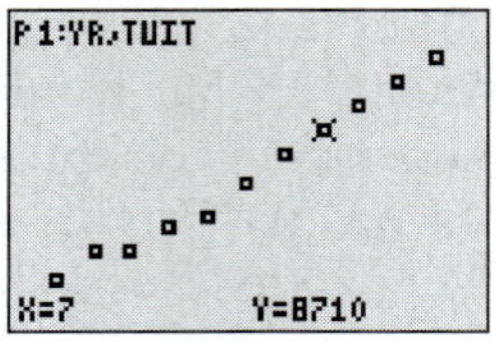

- Now ZoomStat to see your scatterplot. (Didn't work? ERR:DIM MISMATCH means you don't have the same number of *x*'s and *y*'s. Go to STAT Edit and look carefully at your two datalists. You can easily fix the problem once you find it.)
- Notice that if you TRACE the scatterplot the calculator will tell you the *x*- and *y*-value at each point.

What can you Tell about the trend in tuition costs at ASU? (Remember: direction, form, and scatter!)

Roles for Variables

Which variable should go on the *x*-axis and which on the *y*-axis? What we want to know about the relationship can tell us how to make the plot. We often have questions such as:

- Are people who smoke heavily more likely to get lung cancer?
- Is birth order an important factor in predicting future income?
- Can we estimate a person's % body fat more simply by just measuring girth or wrist size?

NOTATION ALERT:

So *x* and *y* are reserved letters as well, but not just for labeling the axes of a scatterplot. In Statistics, the assignment of variables to the *x*- and *y*-axes (and choice of notation for them in formulas) often conveys information about their roles as predictor or response.

In each of these examples, the two variables play different roles. One plays the role of the **explanatory** or **predictor** variable, while the other takes on the role of the **response** variable. When the roles are clear, we place the explanatory variable on the *x*-axis and the response variable on the *y*-axis. When you make a scatterplot, you can assume that those who view it will think this way, so take care in choosing which variables to assign to which axes.

The roles that we choose for variables are more about how we *think* about them than about the variables themselves. Just placing a variable on the *x*-axis doesn't necessarily mean that it explains or predicts *anything*. And the variable on the *y*-axis may not respond to it in any way. We plotted cost per person against peak freeway speed, thinking that the slower you go, the more it costs in delays. But maybe *spending* $500 per person in freeway improvement would increase speed. If we were examining that option, we might choose to plot cost per person as the explanatory variable and speed as the response.

Older textbooks and disciplines other than statistics sometimes refer to the *x*- and *y*-variables as the *independent* and *dependent* variables, respectively. The idea was that the *y*-variable depended on the *x*-variable and the *x*-variable acted independently to make *y* respond. But these names conflict with other uses of the same terms in Statistics. We'll use the terms "explanatory" and "response" when we're thinking about a relationship in those terms, but we'll often just say *x-variable* and *y-variable.*

Correlation

WHO	Students
WHAT	Height (inches), weight (pounds)
WHERE	Ithaca, NY
WHY	Data for class
HOW	Survey

Data collected from students in Statistics classes included their height (in inches) and weight (in pounds). It's no great surprise to discover that there is a positive association between the two. As you might suspect, taller students tend to weigh more. (If we had reversed the roles and chosen height as the explanatory variable, we might say that heavier students tend to be taller.) And the form of the scatterplot is fairly linear as well, although there seems to be a high outlier, as the plot on the next page shows.

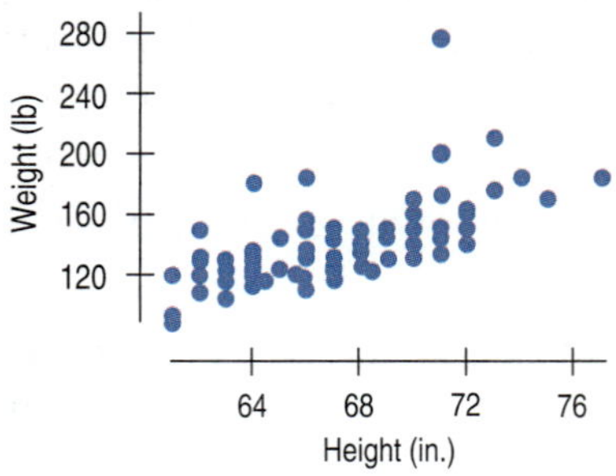

Weight vs. height of Statistics students.
Figure 7.3

We could have measured the weight in stones—a stone is a measure in the now outdated UK system of measures equal to 14 pounds.
And we could measure your height in hands—hands are still commonly used to measure the heights of horses. A hand is 4 inches.
But no matter what *units* we use to measure the two variables, the *correlation* stays the same.

There is clearly a positive association, but how strong is it? If you had to put a number (say, between 0 and 1) on the strength, what would it be? Clearly, whatever measure we use shouldn't depend on the units of the variables. After all, if we had measured heights and weights in different units, it wouldn't change the direction, form, or scatter, so it shouldn't change the strength.

Since the units don't matter, why not just remove them altogether? If we standardize both variables, we'll turn the coordinates of each point into a pair of z-scores. Now the center of the scatterplot is at the origin and the axes are in standard deviation units. (Look at Figure 7.5.)

Is this the only difference between these plots? Well, no. The underlying linear pattern seems steeper in the standardized plot. That's because we made the scales of the axes the same. Now the length of one standard deviation is the same vertically and horizontally. When we worked in the original units, we were free to make the plot as tall and thin

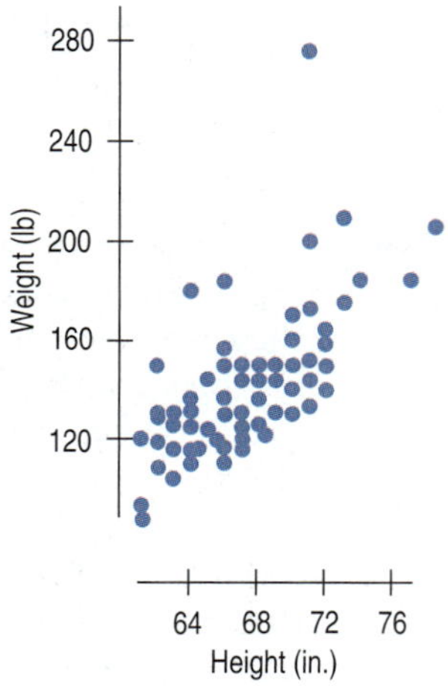

or as squat and wide

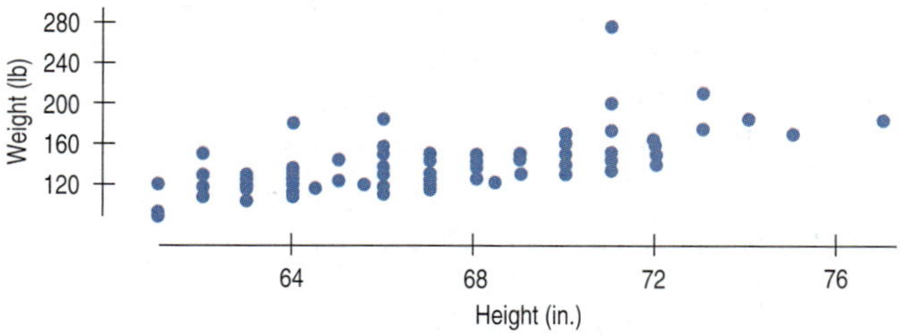

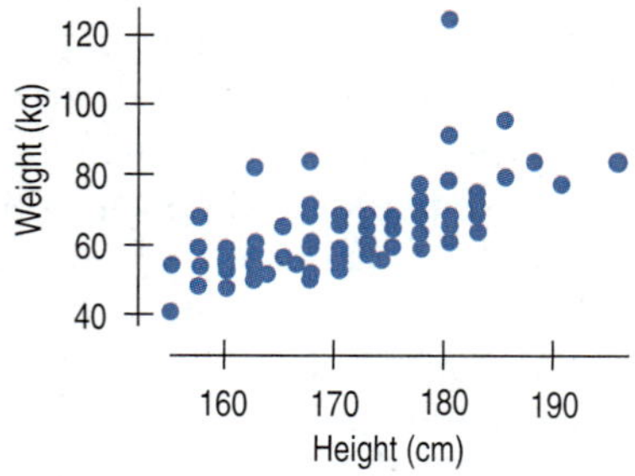

Plotting weight vs. height in different units doesn't change the shape of the pattern.
Figure 7.4

as we wanted to. Equal scaling gives a neutral way of drawing the scatterplot and a fairer impression of the strength of the association.[4]

Now we are plotting standardized values, so we should label them as z-scores. Since we have z-scores for each variable, we can distinguish them by calling them z_x and z_y. We can write the coordinates of a point as (z_x, z_y).

[4]When we're free to choose how to draw a scatterplot, what often looks best is to make the range of the x-axis slightly larger than the range of the y-axis. This is an aesthetic choice and is probably related to the Golden Ratio of the Greeks.

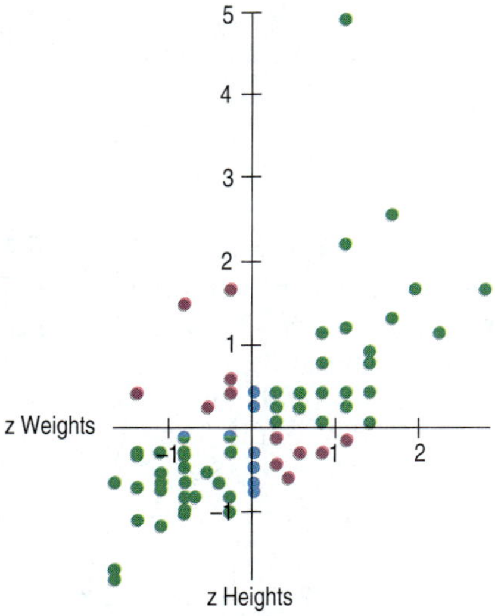

A scatterplot of standardized heights and weights with points colored by how they affect the association: green for positive, red for negative, and blue for neutral. **Figure 7.5**

Which points in the scatterplot of the *z*-scores give the impression of a positive association? The points in the upper right and lower left colored green strengthen the impression of a pattern with a positive direction. For points in these quadrants, z_x and z_y have the same sign. If we multiplied them together, every point would have a positive product. Points far from the origin (which make the association look more positive) have a bigger product.

The red points in the upper left and lower right quadrants tend to weaken the positive association. For these points, z_x and z_y have opposite signs. So the product $z_x z_y$ for these points is always negative. Points far from the origin (which make the association look more negative) have an even more negative product.

Points with *z*-scores of zero on either variable don't vote either way, and $z_x z_y = 0$. We've colored them blue.

We can turn these products into a measure of the strength of the association. We just add up the $z_x z_y$ products for every point in the scatterplot:

$$\sum z_x z_y$$

This summarizes the direction *and* strength of the association for all the points. If most of the points are in the green quadrants, the sum will tend to be positive. If most are in the red quadrants, it will tend to be negative.

Finding the correlation coefficient by hand

To find the correlation coefficient by hand, start with the summary statistics for both variables: $\bar{x}$, $\bar{y}$, s_x, and s_y. Then find the deviations as we did for the standard deviation, but now in both *x* and *y*: $(x - \bar{x})$ and $(y - \bar{y})$. For each data pair, multiply these deviations together: $(x - \bar{x})(y - \bar{y})$. Add the products up for all data pairs. Finally, divide the sum by the product of $(n - 1) \times s_x \times s_y$ to get the correlation coefficient.

Here we go:

Suppose the data pairs are:

x	6	10	14	19	21
y	5	3	7	8	12

Then $\bar{x} = 14$, $\bar{y} = 7$, $s_x = 6.20$, and $s_y = 3.39$

Deviations in *x*	Deviations in *y*	Product
$6 - 14 = -8$	$5 - 7 = -2$	$-8 \times -2 = 16$
$10 - 14 = -4$	$3 - 7 = -4$	16
$14 - 14 = 0$	$7 - 7 = 0$	0
$19 - 14 = 5$	$8 - 7 = 1$	5
$21 - 14 = 7$	$12 - 7 = 5$	35

Add the products up: $16 + 16 + 0 + 5 + 35 = 72$

Finally, we divide by $(n - 1) \times s_x \times s_y = (5 - 1) \times 6.20 \times 3.39 = 84.07$

The ratio is the correlation coefficient:

$r = 72/84.07 = 0.856$.

But the *size* of this sum gets bigger the more data we have. To adjust for this we divide the sum by $n - 1$.[5] The ratio is the famous **correlation coefficient**:

$$r = \frac{\sum z_x z_y}{n - 1}.$$

NOTATION ALERT:

The letter r is always used for correlation, so you can't use it for anything else in Statistics. Whenever you see an "r," it's safe to assume it's a correlation.

For the students' heights and weights, the correlation comes out to 0.644. There are a number of alternative formulas for the correlation coefficient, using x and y in their original units. You may find them written elsewhere.[6] They can be more convenient when you want to compute correlation by hand. But the form given above is best for understanding what it means.

Correlation Conditions

Correlation measures the strength of the *linear* association between two *quantitative* variables. Before you use correlation, you must check several *conditions:*

- **Quantitative variables condition.** Correlation applies only to quantitative variables. Don't apply correlation to categorical data masquerading as quantitative. Check that you know the variables' units and what they measure.
- **Straight enough condition.** Sure, you can *calculate* a correlation coefficient for any pair of variables. But correlation measures the strength only of the *linear* association, and will be misleading if the relationship is not linear.
- **Outlier condition.** Outliers can distort the correlation dramatically. An outlier can make an otherwise small correlation look big or hide a large correlation. It can even give an otherwise positive association a negative correlation coefficient (and vice versa). When you see an outlier, it's often a good idea to report the correlations with and without the point.

Each of these conditions is easy to check with a scatterplot. Many correlations are reported without supporting data or plots. You should still think about the conditions. And you should be cautious in interpreting (or accepting others' interpretations of) the correlation when you can't check the conditions for yourself.

Looking at Association STEP-BY-STEP

When your blood pressure is measured, it is reported as two values, systolic blood pressure and diastolic blood pressure. How are these variables related to each other? Do they tend to both be high or low? Let's examine their relationship with a scatterplot.

Think

Variables Identify two quantitative variables whose relationship we wish to examine. Report the W's and be sure both variables are recorded for the same individuals.

The variables are systolic and diastolic blood pressure (SBP and DBP) recorded (in millimeters of mercury, or mmHg) for each of 1406 participants in a famous health study in Framingham, MA.

---

[5]Yes, the same $n - 1$ we saw for the standard deviation. And we offer the same promise to explain it later.

[6]Like here, for example: $r = \frac{\sum(x - \bar{x})(y - \bar{y})}{\sqrt{\sum(x - \bar{x})^2 \sum(y - \bar{y})^2}} = \frac{\sum(x - \bar{x})(y - \bar{y})}{(n - 1)\sqrt{s_x^2 s_y^2}}.$

Plan Check the conditions.

Make the scatterplot. Use a computer program or graphing calculator if you can.

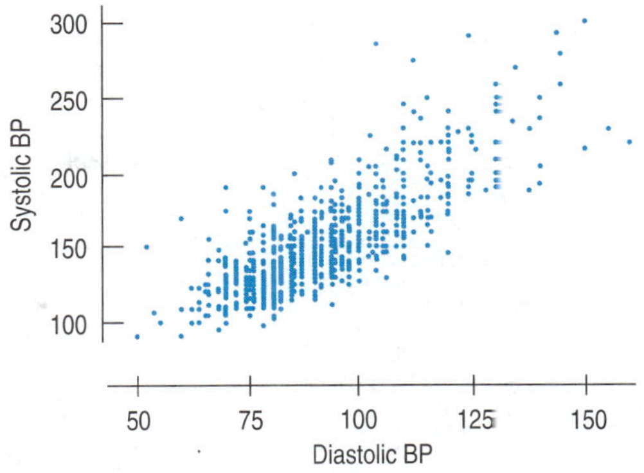

✓ Reality Check Looks like a strong positive linear association. We shouldn't be surprised if the correlation coefficient is positive and fairly large.

✓ **Quantitative variables condition:** Both SBP and DBP are quantitative and measured in mmHg.

✓ **Straight enough condition:** The scatterplot looks straight.

✓ **Outlier condition:** There are a few straggling points, but none far enough from the body of the data to be called outliers.

We have two quantitative variables that satisfy our conditions, so a correlation would be a suitable measure of association.

Show

Mechanics We usually calculate correlations with technology. Here we have 1406 cases, so we'd never try it by hand.

The correlation coefficient is $r = 0.792$.

Tell

Interpretation Describe the direction, form, and scatter you see in the plot, along with any unusual points or features.

The scatterplot shows a positive direction, with higher SBP going with higher DBP. The plot is generally straight with a moderate amount of scatter. The correlation of 0.792 indicates a strong linear association. A few cases stand out with unusually high SBP compared with their DBP. It seems far less common for the DBP to be high by itself.

TI Tips

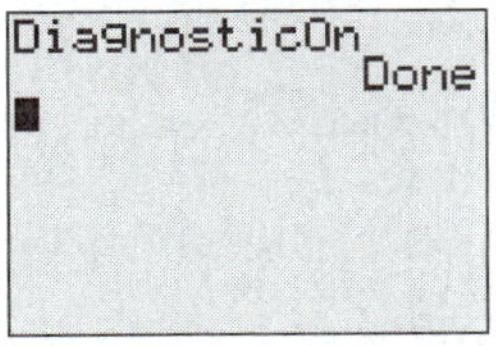

Now let's use the calculator to find a correlation. Unfortunately, the statistics package on your **TI-83** does not automatically do that. (Correlations are one of the most important things we might want to do, so here's how to fix that, once and for all.)

- Hit **2nd CATALOG** (on the zero key). You now see a list of everything the calculator knows how to do. Impressive, huh?
- Scroll down until you find **DiagnosticOn**. Hit **ENTER**. Again. It should say **Done**.

Now and forevermore (or perhaps until you change batteries) your calculator can find correlations.

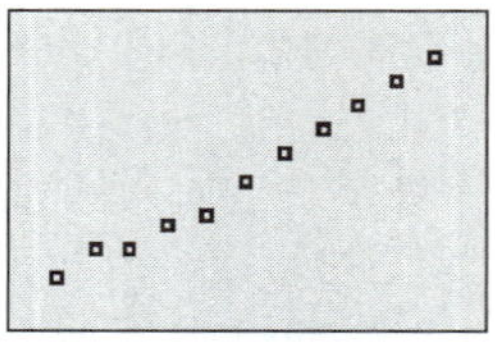

Finding the Correlation

- *Always* check the conditions first. Look at the scatterplot for the Arizona State tuition data again. Does this association look linear? Are there outliers? This plot looks fine, but remember that correlation can be used to describe the strength of linear associations only, and outliers can distort the results. Eyeballing the scatterplot is an essential first step. (You should get used to checking on assumptions and conditions before jumping into a statistical procedure—you'll be doing that a lot!)
- Under the `STAT CALC` menu, select `8:LinReg(a+bx)` and hit `ENTER`.
- Now specify x and y by importing the names of your variables from the `LIST NAMES` menu. First name your x-variable followed by a comma, then your y-variable, creating the command

`LinReg(a+bx) ʟYR,ʟTUIT`.

Wow! A lot of stuff happened. If you suspect all those other numbers are important, too, you'll really enjoy the next chapter. But for now, it's the value of `r` you care about. What does this correlation, $r = 0.993$, say about the trend in tuition costs?

Correlation Properties

Here's a useful list of facts about the correlation coefficient:

- The sign of a correlation coefficient gives the direction of the association.
- Correlation is always between -1 and $+1$.[7] Correlation *can* be exactly equal to -1.0 or $+1.0$, but these values are unusual in real data because they mean that all the data points fall *exactly* on a single straight line.
  A correlation near zero corresponds to a weak linear association.
- Correlation treats x and y symmetrically. The correlation of x with y is the same as the correlation of y with x.
- Correlation has no units. This fact can be especially appropriate when the data's units are somewhat vague to begin with (IQ score, personality index, socialization, and so on). Correlation is sometimes given as a percentage, but we discourage that because it suggests a percentage of *something*—and correlation, lacking units, has no "something" of which to be a percentage.
- Correlation is not affected by changes in the center or scale of either variable. Changing the units or baseline of either variable has no effect on the correlation coefficient. Correlation depends only on the z-scores, and they are unaffected by changes in center or scale.
- Correlation measures the strength of the *linear* association between the two variables. Variables can have a strong association but still have a small correlation if the association isn't linear.
- Correlation is sensitive to outliers. A single outlying value can make a small correlation large or make a large one small.

[7] If it is not obvious to you that $-1 \leq r \leq 1$, relax. There's a proof coming soon to a textbook near you.

Correlation Tables

It is common in some fields to compute the correlations between each pair of variables in a collection of variables and arrange these correlations in a table. The rows and columns of the table name the variables, and the cells hold the correlations.

Correlation tables are compact, and give a lot of summary information at a glance. They can be an efficient way to start to look at a large data set, but a dangerous one. By presenting all of these correlations without any checks for linearity and outliers, the correlation table risks showing truly small correlations that have been inflated by outliers, truly large correlations that are hidden by outliers, and correlations of any size that may be meaningless because the underlying form is not linear.

A correlation table of data reported by *Forbes* magazine for large companies. From this table, can you be sure that the variables are linearly associated and free from outliers?

Table 7.1

	Assets	Sales	Market Value	Profits	Cash Flow	Employees
Assets	1.000					
Sales	0.746	1.000				
Market Value	0.682	0.879	1.000			
Profits	0.602	0.814	0.968	1.000		
Cash Flow	0.641	0.855	0.970	0.989	1.000	
Employees	0.594	0.924	0.818	0.762	0.787	1.000

The diagonal cells of a correlation table always show correlations of exactly 1 (can you see why?). Correlation tables are commonly offered by statistics packages on computers. These same packages often offer simple ways to make all the scatterplots you need to look at.[8]

Straightening Scatterplots

Straight line relationships are the ones that we can measure with correlation. When a scatterplot shows a bent form that consistently increases or decreases, we can often straighten the form of the plot by re-expressing one or both variables.

Some camera lenses have an adjustable aperture, the hole that lets the light through. The size of the aperture is expressed in a mysterious number called the f/stop. Each increase of one f/stop number corresponds to a halving of the light that is allowed to come through. The f/stops of one 35-mm camera are

f/stop:	2.8	4	5.6	8	11	16	22	32

When you increase the f/stop one notch, you cut down the light, so you have to increase the time the shutter is open. We could experiment to find the best shutter

[8]A table of scatterplots arranged just like a correlation table is sometimes called a *scatterplot matrix*, sometimes abbreviated to *SPLOM*. You might see these terms in a statistics package.

speed for each f/stop value. A table of recommended shutter speeds and f/stops for a camera lists the relationship like this:

f/stop:	2.8	4	5.6	8	11	16	22	32
Shutter speed:	1/1000	1/500	1/250	1/125	1/60	1/30	1/15	1/8

The correlation of these f/stops and shutter speeds is 0.979. That sounds pretty high. You might assume that there must be a strong linear relationship. But when we check the scatterplot (we *always* check the scatterplot) it shows that something is not quite right:

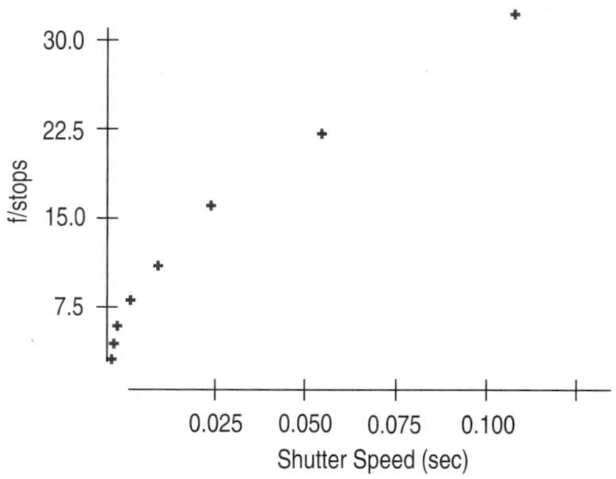

A scatterplot of f/stop vs. shutter speed shows a bent relationship. **Figure 7.6**

We can see that the f/stop is not *linearly* related to the shutter speed. Can we find a transformation of f/stop that straightens out the line? What if we look at the *square* of the f/stop against the shutter speed?

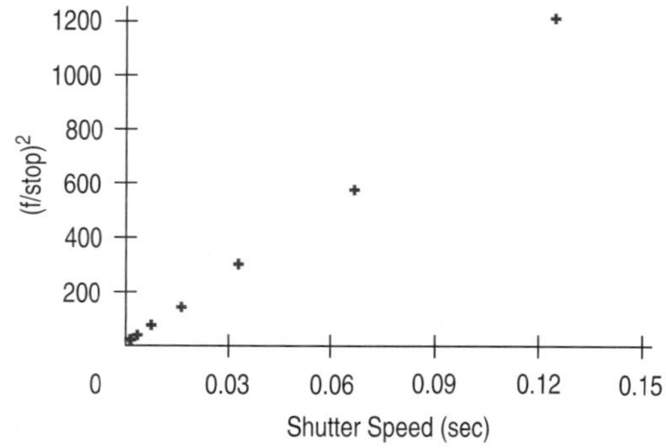

Re-expressing f/stop speed by squaring straightens the plot. **Figure 7.7**

The second plot looks much more nearly straight. In fact, the correlation is now 0.998, but the increase in correlation is not important. (The original value of 0.979 should please almost anyone who sought a large correlation.) What is important is that the *form* of the plot is now straight, so the correlation is now an appropriate measure of association.[9]

We can often find transformations that straighten out lines. Here, we found the square. Chapter 10 discusses simple ways to find a good re-expression.

---

[9] Sometimes we can do a "reality check" on our choice of re-expression. In this case, a bit of research reveals that f/stops are related to the diameter of the open shutter. Since the amount of light that enters is determined by the *area* of the open shutter, which is related to the diameter by squaring, the square re-expression seems reasonable. Not all re-expressions have such nice explanations, but it's a good idea to think about them.

TI Tips

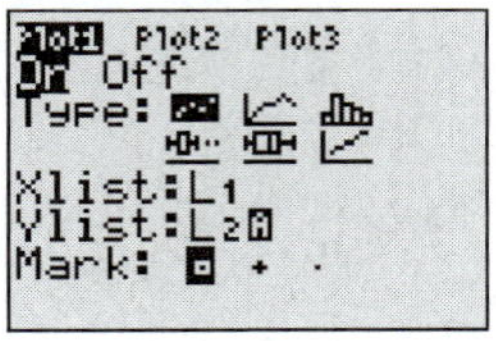

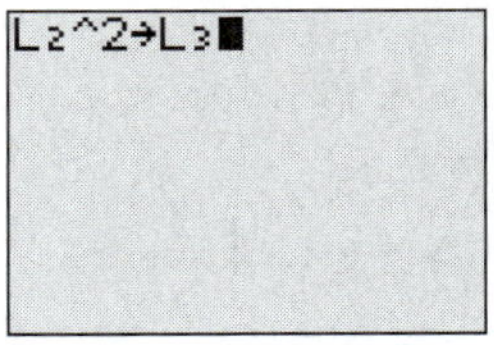

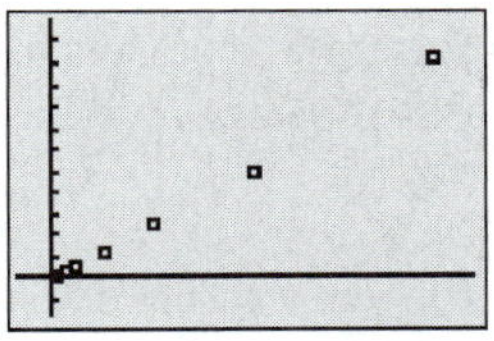

Let's straighten the f/stop scatterplot with your calculator.

- Enter the data in two lists, shutterspeed in `L1` and f/stop in `L2`.
- Set up a `STAT PLOT` to create a scatterplot with `Xlist:L1` and `Ylist:L2`.
- Hit `ZoomStat`. See the curve?

We want to find the squares of all the f/stops, and save those re-expressed values in another datalist. That's easy to do.

- Create the command to square all the values in `L2` and `STO`re those results in `L3`, then hit `ENTER`.

Now make the new scatterplot.

- Go back to `STAT PLOT` and change the setup. `Xlist` is still `L1`, but this time specify `Ylist:L3`.
- `ZoomStat` again.

You now see the straightened plot for these data. On deck: drawing the best line through those points!

What Can Go Wrong?

Don't Say "Correlation" When You Mean "Association"

How often have you heard the word "correlation"? Chances are pretty good that when you've heard the term, it's been misused. When people want to sound scientific, they often say "correlation" when talking about the relationship between two variables. It's one of the most widely misused Statistics terms, and given how often statistics are misused, that's saying a lot. One of the problems is that many people use the specific term *correlation* when they really mean the more general term *association*. Association is a deliberately vague term describing the relationship between two variables.

Correlation is a very precise term describing a linear relationship between quantitative variables.

Did you know that there's a strong correlation between playing an instrument and drinking coffee? No? One reason might be that the statement doesn't make sense. Correlation is valid only for *quantitative* variables.

Don't Forget to Check the Conditions

- ***Don't correlate categorical variables.*** People who misuse "correlation" to mean "association" often fail to notice whether the variables they discuss are quantitative.
- ***Be sure the association is linear.*** A student project evaluating the quality of brownies baked at different temperatures reports a correlation of -0.05 between judges' scores and baking temperature. That seems to say there is no relationship until we look at the scatterplot:

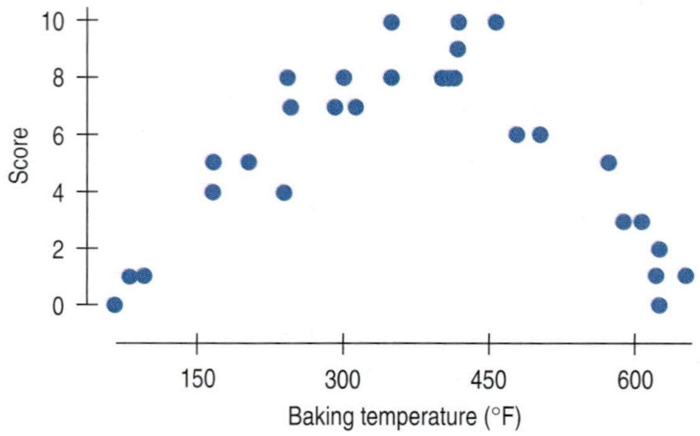

The relationship between brownie taste score and baking temperature is strong, but not at all linear. **Figure 7.8**

There is a strong association, but the relationship is not linear.

- ***Beware of outliers.*** You can't interpret a correlation coefficient safely without a background check for outliers. Here's a silly example:

  The relationship between IQ and shoe size among comedians shows a surprisingly strong positive correlation of 0.50. To check assumptions, we look at the scatterplot.

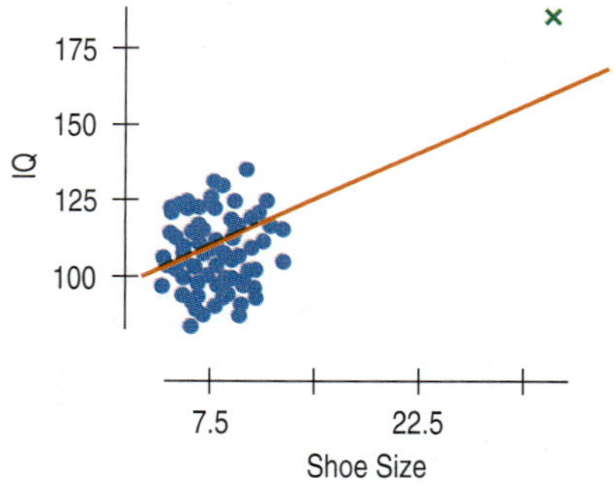

A scatterplot of IQ scores vs. shoe size. From this "study," what is the relationship between the two? The correlation is 0.50. Who *does* that point in the upper right-hand corner belong to? **Figure 7.9**

The outlier is Bozo the Clown, known for his large shoes, and widely acknowledged to be a comic "genius." Without Bozo the correlation is near zero.

Even a single outlier can dominate the correlation value.

Don't Confuse Correlation with Causation

Once we have a strong correlation, it's tempting to try to explain it by imagining that the predictor variable has *caused* the response to change. Humans are like that; we tend to see causes and effects in everything.

Sometimes we can play with this tendency. On the next page is a scatterplot that shows the human population (y) of Oldenburg, Germany, in the beginning of the 1930s plotted against the number of storks nesting in the town (x).

Anyone who has seen the beginning of the movie *Dumbo* remembers Mrs. Jumbo anxiously awaiting the arrival of the stork to bring her new baby. Even though you know it's silly, you can't help but think for a minute that this plot shows that storks are the culprits. The two variables are obviously related to each other (the correlation is 0.97!), but that doesn't prove that storks bring babies.

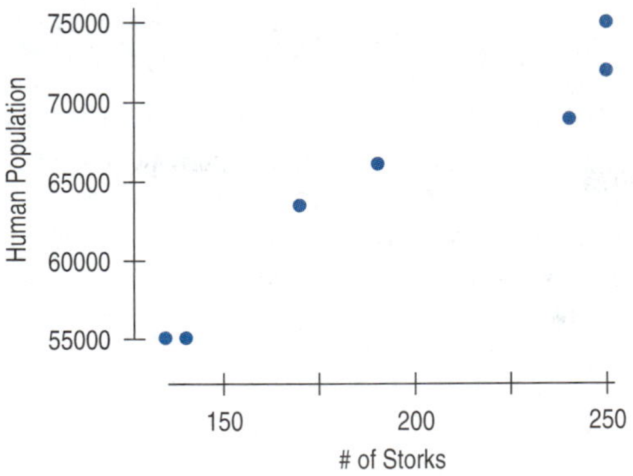

A scatterplot of the number of storks in Oldenburg, Germany, plotted against the population of the town for 7 years in the 1930s. The association is clear. How about the causation? (*Ornithologishe Monatsberichte,* 44, no. 2) **Figure 7.10**

It turns out that storks nest on house chimneys. More people means more houses, more nesting sites, and so more storks. The causation is actually in the *opposite* direction, but you can't tell from the scatterplot or correlation. You need additional information—not just the data—to determine the real mechanism.

Does cancer cause smoking?

Even if the correlation of two variables is due to a causal relationship, the correlation itself cannot tell us what causes what.

Sir Ronald Aylmer Fisher (1890–1962) was one of the greatest statisticians of the 20th century. Fisher testified in court (paid by the tobacco companies) that a causal relationship might underlie the correlation of smoking and cancer:

"Is it possible, then, that lung cancer . . . is one of the causes of smoking cigarettes? I don't think it can be excluded . . . the pre-cancerous condition is one involving a certain amount of slight chronic inflammation . . .

A slight cause of irritation . . . is commonly accompanied by pulling out a cigarette, and getting a little compensation for life's minor ills in that way. And . . . is not unlikely to be associated with smoking more frequently."

Ironically, the proof that smoking indeed is the cause of many cancers came from experiments conducted following the principles of experiment design and analysis that Fisher himself developed—and that we'll see in Chapter 13.

Scatterplots and correlation coefficients *never* prove causation. This is, for example, one part of the story of why it took so long for the U.S. Surgeon General to get warning labels on cigarettes. Although there was plenty of evidence that increased smoking was *associated* with increased levels of lung cancer, it took years to provide evidence that smoking actually *causes* lung cancer. (The tobacco companies used this to great advantage.)

Watch Out for Lurking Variables

A scatterplot of the damage (in dollars) caused to a house by fire would show a strong correlation with the number of firefighters at the scene. Surely the damage doesn't cause firefighters. And firefighters do seem to cause damage, spraying water all around and chopping holes. Does that mean we shouldn't call the fire department? Of course not. There is an underlying variable that leads to both damage and firefighters—the size of the blaze.

A hidden variable that stands behind a relationship and determines it by simultaneously affecting both variables is called a *lurking variable.* You can often debunk claims made about data by finding the lurking variable behind the scenes.

Scatterplots and Correlation on the Computer

Statistics packages generally make it easy to look at a scatterplot to check whether the correlation is appropriate. Some packages make this easier than others.

Many packages allow you to modify or enhance a scatterplot, altering the axis labels, the axis numbering, the plot symbols, or the colors used. Some options, such as color and symbol choice, can be used to display additional information on the scatterplot.

Connections

Scatterplots are the basic tool for examining the relationship between two quantitative variables. We start with a picture when we want to understand the distribution of a single variable, and we always make a scatterplot to begin to understand the relationship between two quantitative variables.

We used *z*-scores as a way to measure the statistical distance of data values from their means. Now we've seen the *z*-scores of x and y working together to build the correlation coefficient. Correlation is a summary statistic like the mean and standard deviation—only it summarizes the strength of a linear relationship. And we interpret it as we did *z*-scores, using the standard deviations as our rulers in both x and y.

Key Concepts

Scatterplots — A scatterplot shows the relationship between two quantitative variables measured on the same cases.

Looking at scatterplots
- direction
- form
- scatter

explanatory-variable, response variable *x*-variable, *y*-variable — In a scatterplot, you must choose a role for each variable. Assign to the *y*-axis the variable that you hope to predict or explain. Assign to the *x*-axis the variable that accounts for, explains, predicts, or is otherwise responsible for the *y*-variable.

Correlation — Correlation is a numerical measure of the direction and strength of a linear association.

Skills

When you complete this lesson you should:

Think

- Recognize when interest in the pattern of possible relationship between two quantitative variables suggests making a scatterplot.
- Know how to identify the roles of the variables and to place the response variable on the *y*-axis and the explanatory variable on the *x*-axis.
- Know the conditions for correlation and how to check them.
- Know that correlations are between -1 and $+1$, and that each extreme indicates a perfect linear association.

- Understand how the magnitude of the correlation reflects the strength of a linear association as viewed in a scatterplot.
- Know that the correlation has no units.
- Know that the correlation coefficient is not changed by changing the center or scale of either variable.
- Understand that causation cannot be demonstrated by a scatterplot or correlation.

Show

- Know how to make a scatterplot by hand (for a small set of data) or with technology.
- Know how to compute the correlation of two variables.
- Know how to read a correlation table produced by a statistics program.

Tell

- Be able to describe the direction, form, and scatter of a scatterplot.
- Be prepared to identify and describe points that deviate from the overall pattern.
- Be able to use correlation as part of the description of a scatterplot.
- Be alert to misinterpretations of correlation.
- Understand that finding a correlation between two variables does not indicate a causal relationship between them. Beware the dangers of suggesting causal relationships when describing correlations.

Exercises

1. Association. Suppose you were to collect data for each pair of variables. You want to make a scatterplot. Which variable would you use as the explanatory variable, and which as the response variable? Why? What would you expect to see in the scatterplot? Discuss the likely direction, form, and scatter.

a) Apples: weight in grams, weight in ounces
b) Apples: circumference (inches), weight (ounces)
c) College freshmen: shoe size, grade point average
d) Gasoline: number of miles you drove since filling up, gallons remaining in your tank

2. Association. Suppose you were to collect data for each pair of variables. You want to make a scatterplot. Which variable would you use as the explanatory variable, and which as the response variable? Why? What would you expect to see in the scatterplot? Discuss the likely direction, form, and scatter.

a) T- shirts at a store: price each, number sold
b) Skin diving: depth, water pressure
c) Skin diving: depth, visibility
d) All elementary school students: weight, score on a reading test

3. Association. Suppose you were to collect data for each pair of variables. You want to make a scatterplot. Which variable would you use as the explanatory variable, and which as the response variable? Why? What would you expect to see in the scatterplot? Discuss the likely direction, form, and scatter.

a) When climbing a mountain: altitude, temperature
b) For each week: Ice cream cone sales, air conditioner sales
c) People: age, grip strength
d) Drivers: blood alcohol level, reaction time

4. Association. Suppose you were to collect data for each pair of variables. You want to make a scatterplot. Which variable would you use as the explanatory variable, and which as the response variable? Why? What would you expect to see in the scatterplot? Discuss the likely direction, form, and scatter.

a) Long-distance calls: time (minutes), cost
b) Lightning strikes: Distance from lightning, time delay of the thunder
c) A streetlight: its apparent brightness, your distance from it
d) Cars: weight of car, age of owner

5. Scatterplots. Which of the scatterplots below show
a) little or no association?
b) a negative association?
c) a linear association?
d) a moderately strong association?
e) a very strong association?

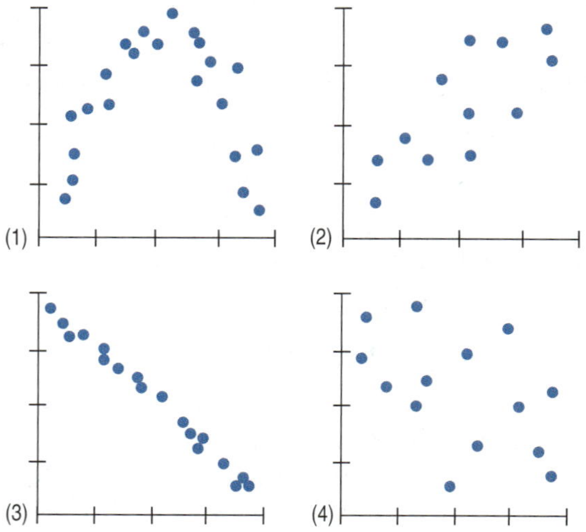

6. Scatterplots. Which of the scatterplots below show
a) little or no association?
b) a negative association?
c) a linear association?
d) a moderately strong association?
e) a very strong association?

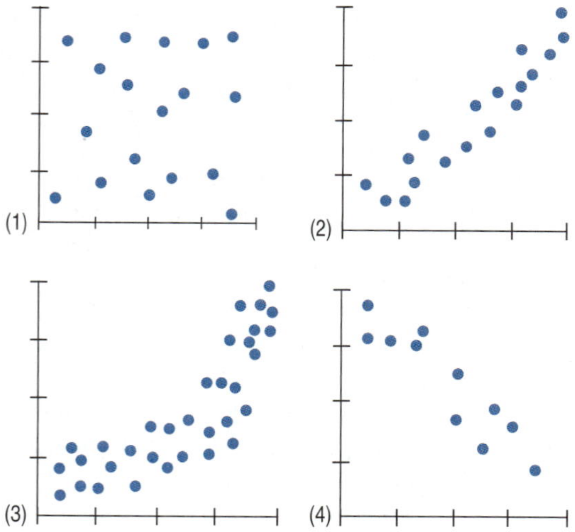

7. Performance IQ scores vs. brain size. A study examined brain size (measured as pixels counted in a digitized magnetic resonance image [MRI] of a cross-section of the brain) and IQ (4 Performance scales of the Weschler IQ test) for college students. The scatterplot shows the Performance IQ scores vs. the brain size. Comment on the association between brain size and IQ as seen in this scatterplot.

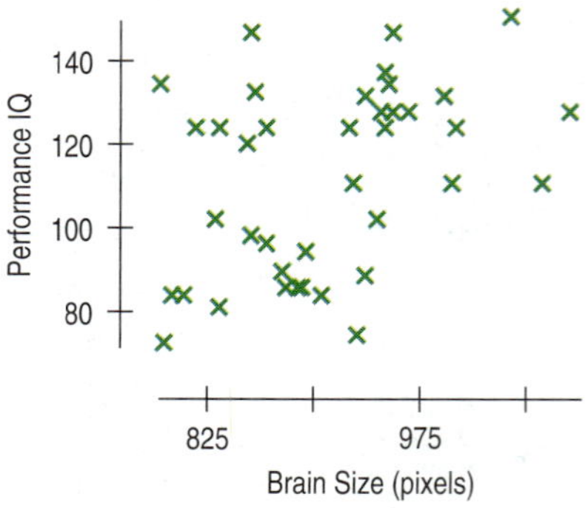

8. Kentucky Derby. The fastest horse in Kentucky Derby history was Secretariat in 1973. The scatterplot shows speed (in miles per hour) of the winning horses each year. What do you see? In most sporting events, performances have improved and continue to improve, so surely we anticipate a positive direction. But what of the form? Has the performance increased at the same rate throughout the last 125 years?

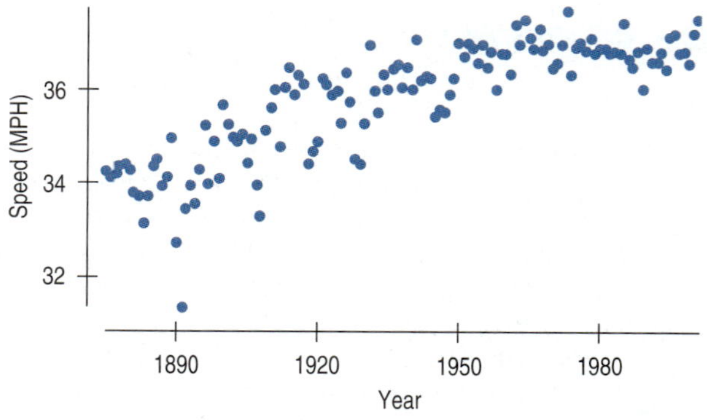

9. Firing pottery. A ceramics factory can fire eight large batches of pottery a day. Sometimes in the process a few of the pieces break. In order to understand the problem better, the factory records the number of broken pieces in each batch for 3 days and then creates the scatterplot shown.
a) Make a histogram showing the distribution of the number of broken pieces in the 24 batches of pottery examined.
b) Describe the distribution as shown in the histogram. What feature of the problem is more apparent in the histogram than in the scatterplot?

c) What aspect of the company's problem is more apparent in the scatterplot?

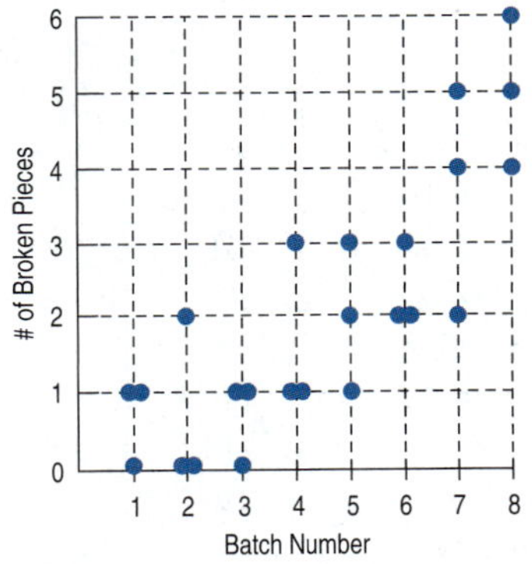

10. Coffee sales. Owners of a new coffee shop tracked sales for the first 20 days, and displayed the data in a scatterplot (by day):

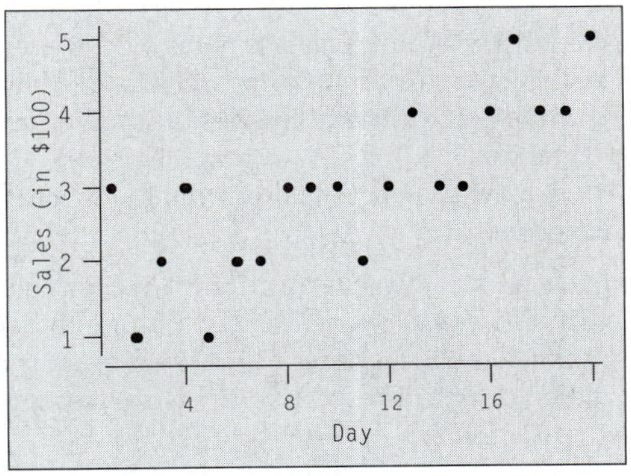

a) Make a histogram of the daily sales since the shop has been in business.
b) State one fact that is obvious from the scatterplot, but not from the histogram.
c) State one fact that is obvious from the histogram, but not from the scatterplot.

11. Matching. Here are several scatterplots. The calculated correlations are −0.923, −0.487, 0.006, and 0.777. Which is which?

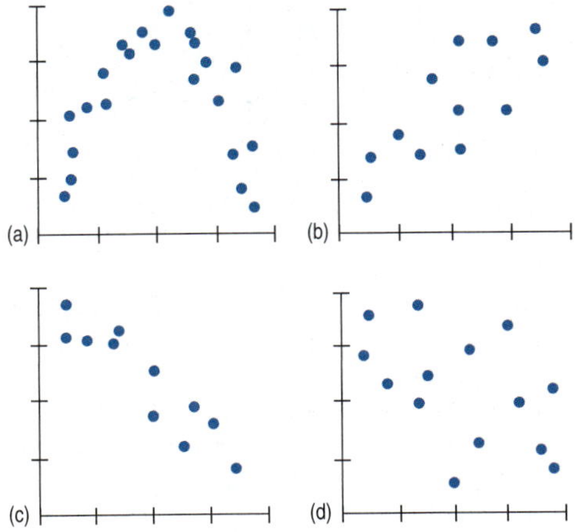

12. Matching. Here are several scatterplots. The calculated correlations are −0.977, −0.021, 0.736, and 0.951. Which is which?

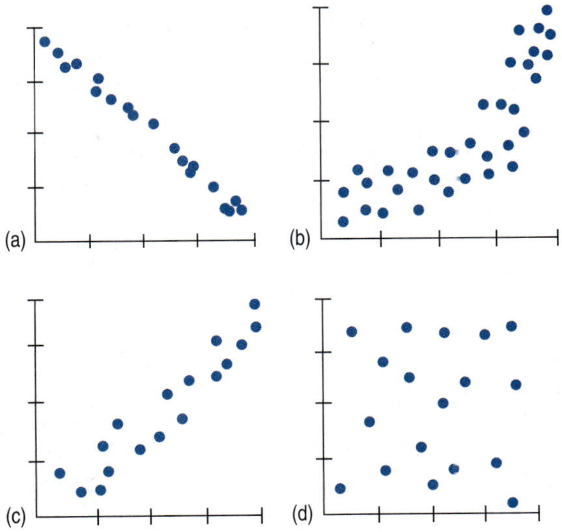

T **13. Lunchtime.** Does how long children remain at the lunch table help predict how much they eat? The table gives data on 20 toddlers observed over several months at a nursery school. "Time" is the average number of minutes a child spent at the table when lunch was served. "Calories" is the average number of calories the child consumed during lunch, calculated from careful observation of what the child ate each day.

Calories	Time
472	21.4
498	30.8
465	37.7
456	33.5
423	32.8
437	39.5
508	22.8
431	34.1
479	33.9
454	43.8
450	42.4
410	43.1
504	29.2
437	31.3
489	28.6
436	32.9
480	30.6
439	35.1
444	33.0
408	43.7

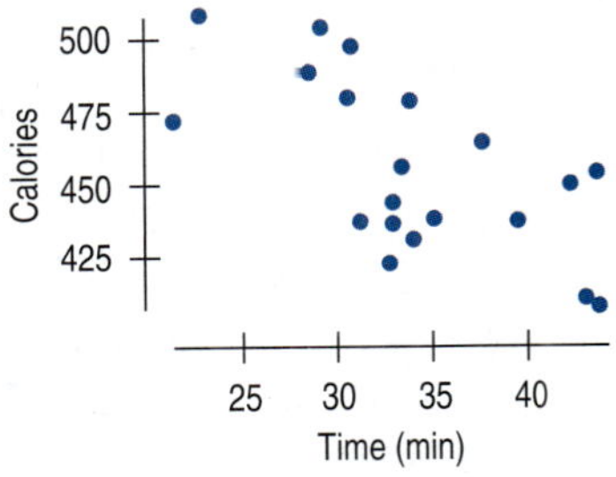

a) Find the correlation for these data.
b) Suppose we were to record time at the table in hours rather than in minutes. How would the correlation change? Why?
c) Write a sentence or two explaining what this correlation means for these data. Remember to write about food consumption in toddlers rather than about correlation coefficients.
d) One analyst concluded, "It is clear from this correlation that toddlers who spend more time at the table eat less. Evidently something about being at the table causes them to lose their appetites." Explain why this explanation is not an appropriate conclusion from what we know about the data.

T **14. Vehicle weights.** The Minnesota Department of Transportation hoped that they could measure the weights of big trucks without actually stopping the vehicles by using a newly developed "weigh-in-motion" scale. To see if the new device was accurate, they conducted a calibration test. They weighed several trucks when stopped (static weight), assuming that this weight was correct. They they weighed them again while the trucks were moving to see how well the new scale could estimate the actual weight. Their data are given in the table.

WEIGHT OF A TRUCK (THOUSANDS OF POUNDS)

Weight-in-Motion	Static Weight
26	27.9
29.9	29.1
39.5	38
25.1	27
31.6	30.3
36.2	34.5
25.1	27.8
31	29.6
35.6	33.1
40.2	35.5

a) Make a scatterplot for these data.
b) Describe the direction, form and scatter of the plot.
c) Write a few sentences telling what the plot says about the data. (*Note:* The sentences should be about weighing trucks, not about scatterplots.)
d) Find the correlation.
e) If the trucks were weighed in kilograms, how would this change the correlation? (1 kilogram = 2.2 pounds)
f) Do any points deviate from the overall pattern? What does the plot say about a possible recalibration of the weigh-in-motion scale?

15. Fuel economy. Here are advertised horsepower ratings and expected gas mileage for several 2001 vehicles.

Audi A4	170 hp	22 mpg
Buick LeSabre	205	20
Chevy Blazer	190	15
Chevy Prizm	125	31
Ford Excursion	310	10
GMC Yukon	285	13
Honda Civic	127	29
Hyundai Elantra	140	25
Lexus 300	215	21
Lincoln LS	210	23
Mazda MPV	170	18
Olds Alero	140	23
Toyota Camry	194	21
VW Beetle	115	29

a) Make a scatterplot for these data.
b) Describe the direction, form, and scatter of the plot.
c) Find the correlation between horsepower and miles per gallon.
d) Write a few sentences telling what the plot says about fuel economy.

16. Drug abuse. A survey was conducted in the United States and 10 countries of Western Europe to determine the percentage of teenagers who had used marijuana and other drugs. The results are summarized in the table.

	Percent Who Have Used	
Country	Marijuana	Other Drugs
Czech Rep.	22	4
Denmark	17	3
England	40	21
Finland	5	1
Ireland	37	16
Italy	19	8
No. Ireland	23	14
Norway	6	3
Portugal	7	3
Scotland	53	31
USA	34	24

a) Create a scatterplot.
b) What is the correlation between the percent of teens who have used marijuana and the percent who have used other drugs?
c) Write a brief description of the association.
d) Do these results confirm that marijuana is a "gateway drug," that is, that marijuana use leads to the use of other drugs? Explain.

17. Burgers. Fast food is often considered unhealthy because much fast food is high in both fat and sodium. But are the two related? Here are the fat and sodium contents of several brands of burgers. Create a scatterplot and find the correlation between fat content and sodium content. Write a description of the association.

Fat (g)	19	31	34	35	39	39	43
Sodium (mg)	920	1500	1310	860	1180	940	1260

18. Burgers. In the previous exercise you examined association between the amounts of fat and sodium in fast food hamburgers. What about fat and calories? Here are data for the same burgers.

Fat (g)	19	31	34	35	39	39	43
Calories	410	580	590	570	640	680	660

a) Create a scatterplot.
b) Find the correlation.
c) Describe the association.

19. Attendance. American League baseball games are played under the designated hitter rule, meaning that weak-hitting pitchers do not come to bat. Baseball owners believe that the designated hitter rule means more runs scored, which in turn means higher attendance. Is there evidence that more fans attend games if the teams score more runs? Data collected midway through the 2001 season indicate a correlation of 0.74 between runs scored and the number of people at the game.

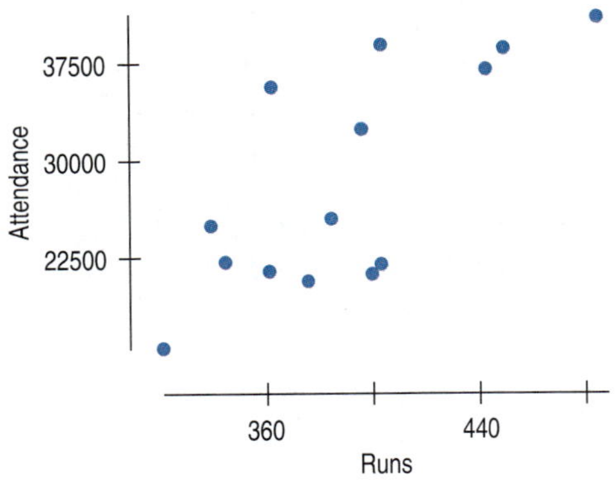

a) Does the scatterplot indicate that it's appropriate to calculate a correlation? Explain.
b) Describe the association between attendance and runs scored.
c) Does this prove that the owners are right, that more fans will come to games if the teams score more runs?

20. Second inning. Perhaps fans are just more interested in teams that win? Are the teams that win necessarily those that score the most runs?

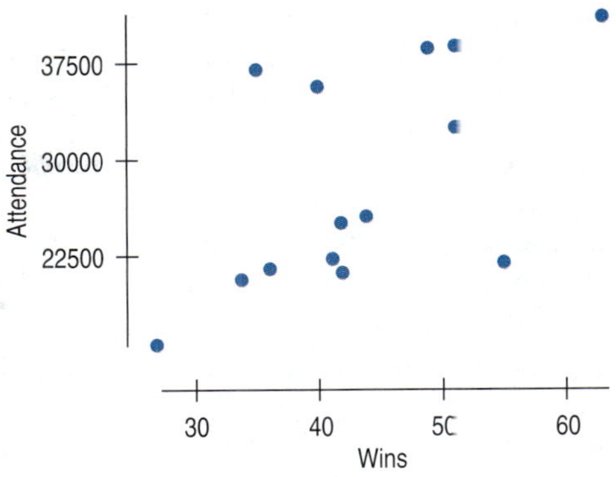

	Correlation		
	Wins	**Runs**	**Attend**
Wins	1.000		
Runs	0.680	1.000	
Attend	0.557	0.740	1.000

a) Do winning teams generally enjoy greater attendance at their home games? Describe the association.
b) Is attendance more strongly associated with winning or scoring runs? Explain.
c) How strongly is scoring more runs associated with winning more games?

21. Politics. A candidate for office claims that "there is a correlation between television watching and crime." Criticize this statement in statistical terms.

22. Association. A researcher investigating the association between two variables collected some data and was surprised when he calculated the correlation. He had expected to find a fairly strong association, yet the correlation was near 0. Discouraged, he didn't bother making a scatterplot. Explain to him how the scatterplot could still reveal the strong association he anticipated.

23. Correlation errors. Your economics instructor assigns your class to investigate factors associated with the gross domestic product (GDP) of nations. Each student examines a different factor (such as life expectancy, literacy rate, etc.) for a few countries and reports to the class. Apparently some of your classmates do not understand Statistics very well because you know several of their conclusions are incorrect. Explain the mistakes in their statements below.

a) "My correlation of −0.772 shows that there is almost no association between GDP and infant mortality rate."
b) "There was a correlation of 0.44 between GDP and continent."
c) "There was a very strong correlation of 1.22 between life expectancy and GDP."
d) "The correlation between literacy rate and GDP was 0.83. This shows that countries wanting to increase their standard of living should invest heavily in education."

24. Sample survey. A polling organization is checking its database to see if the two data sources they used sampled the same zip codes. The variable *datasource* = 1 if the data source is MetroMedia, 2 if the data source is DataQwest, and 3 if it's RollingPoll. The organization finds that the correlation between five digit zip code and *datasource* is −.0229. It concludes that the correlation is low enough to state that there is no dependency between zip code and source of data. Comment.

25. Baldness and heart disease. Medical researchers followed 1435 middle-aged men for a period of 5 years, measuring the amount of baldness present (none = 1, little = 2, some = 3, much = 4, extreme = 5) and presence of heart disease (No = 0, Yes = 1). They found a correlation of 0.089 between the two variables. Comment on their conclusion that this shows that baldness is not a possible cause of heart disease.

T **26. Oil production.** The following table shows the oil production of the United States from 1949 to 2000 (in millions of barrels per year).

a) Find the correlation between year and production.
b) A reporter concludes that a low correlation between year and production shows that oil production has remained steady over the 50-year period. Do you agree with this interpretation? Explain.

Year	Oil	Year	Oil
1949	1,841,940	1975	3,056,779
1950	1,973,574	1976	2,976,180
1951	2,247,711	1977	3,009,265
1952	2,289,836	1978	3,178,216
1953	2,357,082	1979	3,121,310
1954	2,314,988	1980	3,146,365
1955	2,484,428	1981	3,128,624
1956	2,617,283	1982	3,156,715
1957	2,616,901	1983	3,170,999
1958	2,448,987	1984	3,249,696
1959	2,574,590	1985	3,274,553
1960	2,574,933	1986	3,168,252
1961	2,621,758	1987	3,047,378
1962	2,676,189	1988	2,979,123
1963	2,752,723	1989	2,778,773
1964	2,786,822	1990	2,684,687
1965	2,848,514	1991	2,707,039
1966	3,027,763	1992	2,624,632
1967	3,215,742	1993	2,499,033
1968	3,329,042	1994	2,431,476
1969	3,371,751	1995	2,394,268
1970	3,517,450	1996	2,366,017
1971	3,453,914	1997	2,354,831
1972	3,455,368	1998	2,281,919
1973	3,360,903	1999	2,146,732
1974	3,202,585	2000	2,135,062

27. Planets. Is there any pattern to the locations of the planets in our solar system? The table shows the average distance of each of the nine planets from the sun.

Planet	Position Number	Distance from Sun (million miles)
Mercury	1	36
Venus	2	67
Earth	3	93
Mars	4	142
Jupiter	5	484
Saturn	6	887
Uranus	7	1784
Neptune	8	2796
Pluto	9	3666

a) Make a scatterplot and describe the association. (Remember: direction, form, scatter!)
b) Why would you not want to talk about the correlation between planet position and distance from the sun?
c) Make a scatterplot showing the logarithm of distance vs. position. What is better about this scatterplot?

28. Internet journals. The rapid growth of Internet publishing is seen in a number of electronic academic journals made available during the last decade.

Year	Number of Journals
1991	27
1992	36
1993	45
1994	181
1995	306
1996	1093
1997	2459

a) Make a scatterplot and describe the trend.
b) Re-express the data in order to make the association more nearly linear.

Chapter 8

Linear Regression

WHO	Items on the Burger King menu
WHAT	Protein content (g) and total fat content (g)
HOW	Supplied by BK on request or at their Web site.

Whoppers have been sold at Burger Kings for years. One Double Whopper with cheese provides 53 grams of protein—all the protein you need in a day. It also supplies 1020 calories and 65 grams of fat. The Daily Value (based on a 2000-calorie diet) for fat is 65 grams. So after a double Whopper you'll want the rest of your calories that day to be fat-free.[1]

There are other items on the Burger King menu. How are their fat and protein related? The scatterplot of the fat (in grams) versus the protein (in grams) for foods sold at Burger King shows a positive, linear relationship with relatively little scatter.

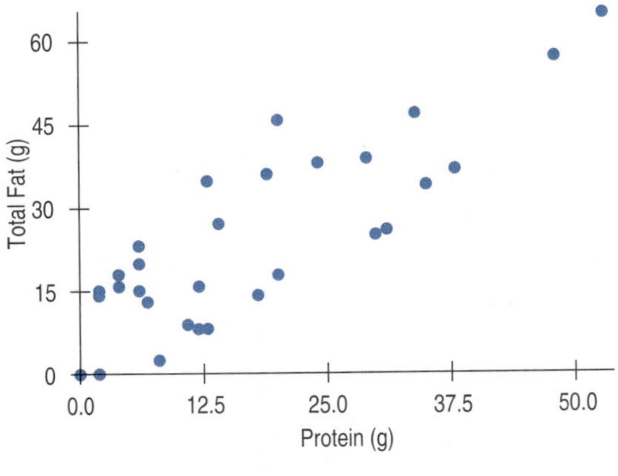

Total fat (grams) versus protein (grams) for 30 items on the Burger King menu. The Double Whopper is in the upper right corner. It's extreme, but is it out of line? **Figure 8.1**

If you want to get 25 grams of protein in your lunch, how much fat should you expect to consume at Burger King? The correlation between fat and protein is 0.83. That tells you that there's a strong linear association. But *strength* of the relationship is only part of the picture. The correlation says "There seems to be a linear association between these two variables," but it doesn't tell *what that association is.*

---

[1] Sorry about the fries.

Models for Data

"All models are wrong—but some are useful."

George Box, famous statistician

Of course, we *can* say more. We can **model** the relationship with a line and give its equation. The equation will let us predict the fat content for any Burger King food, given its amount of protein. Clearly no line can go through all the points. Like all models of the real world, the line will be wrong—wrong in the sense that it can't match reality *exactly*. But it can still be useful. Like a physical model, it's something we can look at and manipulate in order to learn more about the real world.

Models help our understanding in many ways. Just as a model of an airplane in a wind tunnel can give insights even though it doesn't have every rivet, models of data give us summaries that we can learn from and use even though they don't fit each data value exactly. It's important to remember that they're only models of reality and not reality itself. But without models, what we can learn about the world at large is limited to only what we can say about the data we have at hand.

A model simplifies reality in order to help us to understand underlying patterns and relationships. Models require numbers, called **parameters**, to specify them. Choosing values for the parameters helps us mold the model to fit a particular situation. We often estimate parameter values from the data.

We met our first model, the Normal model, in Chapter 6. We saw there that we can specify a Normal model with its mean (μ) and standard deviation (σ). These are the parameters of the Normal model.

For the Burger King foods, we might choose a linear model to describe the relationship between protein and fat. The **linear model** is just an equation of a straight line through the data. The points in the scatterplot don't all line up, but a straight line can summarize the general pattern with only a few parameters. This model can help us understand how the variables are associated.

Residuals

NOTATION ALERT:

More reserved symbols:

y is the **actual** value;

$\hat{y}$ is the value **predicted** by the model.

Of course, the model won't be perfect. No matter what line we draw, it won't go through many of the points. The best line might not even hit any of the points. Then how can it be the "best" line? We want to find the line that somehow comes *closer* to all the points than any other line. Some of the points will be above the line and some below. For example, the line might suggest that a BK Broiler chicken sandwich with 30 g of protein should have 36 g of fat when, in fact, it actually has only 25 g of fat. We call the estimate made from a model the **predicted value,** and write it as $\hat{y}$ (called *y-hat*) to distinguish it from the true value y (called, well, y). The difference between the observed value and its associated predicted value is called the **residual.** The residual value tells us how far off the model's prediction is at that point. The BK Broiler chicken residual would be $y - \hat{y} = 25 - 36 = -11$ g of fat.

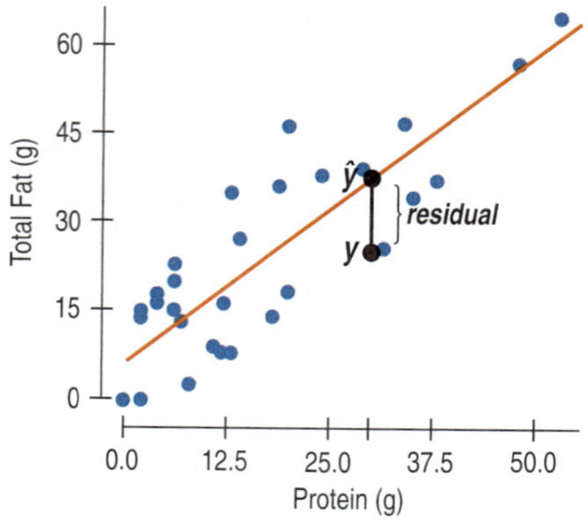

We always subtract the predicted value from the observed one. The negative residual tells us that the actual fat content of the BK Broiler chicken is about 11 g *less* than the model predicts for a typical Burger King menu item with 30 g of protein.

Our question now is how to find the right line to use.

"Best Fit" Means Least Squares

A *negative* residual from a model means that the predicted value is larger than the actual data value. In other words, it is an **overestimate.**

Likewise, a *positive* residual shows a model value that is an **underestimate.**

These may seem backwards until you think about them.

When we draw a line through a scatterplot, some residuals are positive and some negative. We can't assess how well the line fits by adding the residuals—the positive and negative ones would just cancel each other out. We faced the same issue when we calculated a standard deviation to measure spread. We deal with it the same way here: We square the residuals. Squaring makes them all positive. Now we can add them up. Squaring also emphasizes the large residuals. After all, points near the line are consistent with the model, but we are worried about points far from the line. When we add all the squared residuals together, that sum indicates how well the line we drew fits the data—the smaller the sum, the better the fit. A different line will produce a different sum, maybe bigger, maybe smaller. The **line of best fit** is the line for which the sum of the squared residuals is smallest.

Our line has the special property that the variation of the data from the model, as seen in the residuals, is the smallest it can be for any straight line model for these data. No other line has this property. Speaking mathematically, we say that this line minimizes the sum of the squared residuals.

You might think that finding this "least squares line of best fit" would be pretty hard. Surprisingly, it's not.

Correlation and the Line

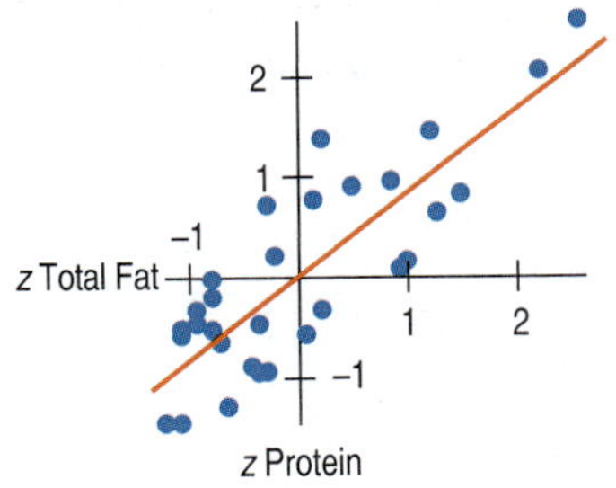

The Burger King scatterplot in z-scores. **Figure 8.2**

The same approach that worked for correlation can lead us to the equation of the linear model for the association. It turns out that it's not a very big step.

We'll start by standardizing the variables. We don't know μ and σ for either variable, but we can use the means and standard deviations of the data. What line would you choose to model the relationship of the standardized values? Let's start at the center of the scatterplot. How much protein and fat does a *typical* Burger King food item provide? If it has average protein content, $\bar{x}$, what about its fat content? If you guessed that its fat content should be about average, $\bar{y}$, as well, then you've discovered the first property of the line we're looking for. The line must go through the point $(\bar{x}, \bar{y})$. In the plot of z-scores, then, the line passes through the origin (0, 0).

You might recall that the equation for a line that passes through the origin can be written with just a slope and no intercept:

$$y = mx.$$

NOTATION ALERT:

"Putting a hat on it" is standard Statistics notation to indicate that something has been predicted by a model. Whenever you see a hat over a variable name or symbol, you can assume it is the predicted version of that variable or symbol (and look around for the model).

The coordinates of our standardized points aren't written (x, y); their coordinates are z-scores: (z_x, z_y). We'll need to change our equation to show that. And we'll need to indicate that the point on the line corresponding to a particular z_x is $\hat{z}_y$, the model's estimate of the actual value of z_y. So our equation becomes

$$\hat{z}_y = mz_x.$$

The value m is the **slope;** larger magnitude m's indicate steeper slopes, negative slopes show a negative association, and a slope of zero gives a horizontal line. Moving over one unit in z_x corresponds on the line to moving up m units in $\hat{z}_y$.

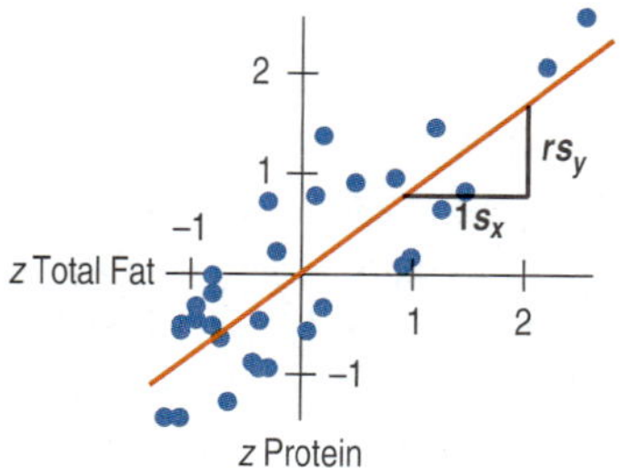

Standardized fat vs. standardized protein with the regression line. Each one standard deviation increase of *protein* results in a predicted increase of r standard deviations in *fat* from the model.

Figure 8.3

protein	*fat*
$\bar{x} = 17.2$ g	$\bar{y} = 23.5$ g
$s_x = 14.0$ g	$s_y = 16.4$ g

Many lines with different slopes pass through the origin. Which one fits our data the best? That is, which slope determines the line that minimizes the sum of the squared residuals? It turns out that the best choice for m is the correlation coefficient itself, r! (You must really wonder where that stunning assertion comes from! Check the Math Box.)

Now we can write

$$\hat{z}_y = rz_x.$$

Since the correlation between fat content and protein content is 0.83, the equation of the line drawn on the scatterplot of z-scores is

$$\hat{z}_y = 0.83z_x.$$

We can use this model for prediction. For example, the double hamburger has 31 g of protein. That's about 1 standard deviation (SD) above the mean. How much fat should you expect it to have? Putting 1.0 in for z_x in the model gives a $\hat{z}_y$ value of 0.83. If you trust the model, you'd expect the fat content to be about 0.83 fat SDs above the mean fat level. Moving one standard deviation away from the mean in x moves us r standard deviations away from the mean in y.

If $r = 0$ there's no linear relationship. The line is horizontal, and no matter how many standard deviations you move in x, the predicted value for y doesn't change. On the other hand, if $r = 1.0$ or -1.0, there's a perfect linear association. In that case, moving any number of standard deviations in x moves exactly the same number of standard deviations in y. In general, moving any number of standard deviations in x moves r times that number of standard deviations in y.

How Big Can Predicted Values Get?

Sir Francis Galton was the first to speak of "regression," although others had fit lines to data by the same method.

Suppose you were told that a new male student was about to join the class, and you were asked to guess his height in inches. What would be your guess? A good guess would be the mean height of male students. Now suppose you are also told that this student has a grade point average (GPA) of 3.9—about 2 SDs above the mean GPA. Would that change your guess? Probably not. There's no correlation between GPA and height, so knowing the GPA value doesn't tell you anything and doesn't move your guess. (And the formula tells us that as well, since it says that we should move 0 times 2 SDs from the mean.)

On the other hand, if you were told that, measured in centimeters, the student's height was 2 SDs above the mean, you'd know his height in inches. There's a perfect correlation between height in inches and height in centimeters, so you know he's 2 SDs above mean height in inches as well. (The formula would tell us to move 1.0 times 2 SDs from the mean.)

What if you're told that the student is 2 SDs above the mean in shoe size? Would you still guess that he's of average height? No, you'd probably guess that he's taller than average, since there's a positive correlation between height and shoe size. But would you guess that he's 2 SDs above the mean? When there was no correlation, we didn't move away from the mean at all. With a perfect correlation, we moved our guess the full 2 SDs. Any correlation between these extremes should lead us to move somewhere between 0 and 2 SDs above the mean. (To be exact, the formula tells us to move $2 \times r$ standard deviations away from the mean.)

Notice that we can't ever move more than 2 SDs away, since r can't be bigger than 1.0.[2] So, each predicted y tends to be closer to its mean (in standard deviations) than its corresponding x was. This property of the linear model is called **regression to the mean,** and the line is called the **regression line.**

The First Regression

Sir Francis Galton related the heights of sons to the heights of their fathers with a regression line. The slope of his line was less than 1. That is, sons of tall fathers were tall, but not as much above the average height as their fathers had been above their mean. Sons of short fathers were short, but generally not as far from their mean as their fathers. Galton interpreted the slope correctly as indicating a "regression" toward the mean height—and "regression" stuck as a description of the method he had used to find the line.

Math Box

Where does the equation of the line of best fit come from? To write the equation of any line, we need to know a point on the line and the slope. The point is easy. Consider the protein-fat example. Since it is logical to predict that a sandwich with average protein will contain average fat, the line passes through the point $(\bar{x}, \bar{y})$.

To think about the slope, we look once again at the z-scores. We need to remember a few things.

1. The mean of any set of z-scores is 0. This tells us that the line that best fits the z-scores passes through the origin (0, 0).
2. The standard deviation of a set of z-scores is 1, so the variance is also 1. This means that $\frac{\sum(z_y - \bar{z}_y)^2}{n-1} = \frac{\sum(z_y - 0)^2}{n-1} = \frac{\sum z_y^2}{n-1} = 1$, a fact that will be important soon.
3. The correlation is $r = \frac{\sum z_x z_y}{n-1}$, also important soon.

Ready? Remember that our objective is to find the slope of the best fit line. Because it passes through the origin, its equation will be of the form $\hat{z}_y = mz_x$. We want to find the value for m that will minimize the sum of the squared residuals. Actually we'll divide that sum by $n - 1$ and minimize this "mean squared residual," or *MSR*. Here goes:

Minimize: $$MSR = \frac{\sum(z_y - \hat{z}_y)^2}{n-1}.$$

Since $\hat{z}_y = mz_x$: $$MSR = \frac{\sum(z_y - mz_x)^2}{n-1}$$

Square the binomial: $$= \frac{\sum(z_y^2 - 2mz_xz_y + m^2z_x^2)}{n-1}$$

Rewrite the summation: $$= \frac{\sum z_y^2}{n-1} - 2m\frac{\sum z_xz_y}{n-1} + m^2\frac{\sum z_x^2}{n-1}$$

4. Substituting from (2) and (3): $$= 1 - 2mr + m^2$$

[2] In the last chapter we asserted that correlations max out at 1, but we never actually *proved* that. There's yet another reason to check out the Math Box.

Wow! That simplified nicely! And as a bonus, the last expression is quadratic. Remember parabolas from algebra class? A parabola in the form $y = ax^2 + bx + c$ reaches its minimum at its turning point, which occurs when $x = \frac{-b}{2a}$. We can minimize the mean of squared residuals by choosing $m = \frac{-(-2r)}{2(1)} = r$.

Wow, again! The slope of the best fit line for *z*-scores is the correlation, *r*. This stunning fact leads us immediately to two important additional results, listed below. As you read on in the text, we explain them in the context of our continuing discussion of Burger King foods.

- A slope of r for z-scores means that for every increase of 1 standard deviation in z_x there is an increase of r standard deviations in $z_{\hat{y}}$. "Over one, up r," as you probably said in algebra class. Translate that back to the x and y values: "Over one standard deviation in x, up r standard deviations in $\hat{y}$."

  That's it! The slope of the regression line is $b = \frac{rs_y}{s_x}$.

- We know choosing $m = r$ minimizes the sum of the squared residuals, but how small does that sum get? Equation (4) told us that the mean of the squared residuals is $1 - 2mr + m^2$. When $m = r$, $1 - 2mr + m^2 = 1 - 2r^2 + r^2 = 1 - r^2$. This is the percentage of variability *not* explained by the regression line. Since $1 - r^2$ of the variability is *not* explained, the percentage of variability in y that *is* explained by x is r^2. This important fact will help us assess the strength of our models.

And there's still another bonus. Because r^2 is the percent of variability explained by our model, r^2 is at most 100%. If $r^2 \leq 1$, then $-1 \leq r \leq 1$, proving that correlations are always between -1 and $+1$. (Told you so!)

Working in Real Units

Why Is Correlation "*r*"?

In his original paper on correlation, Galton used *r* for the "index of correlation" that we now call the correlation coefficient. He calculated it from the regression of *y* on *x* or of *x* on *y* after standardizing the variables, just as we have done. It's fairly clear from the text that he used *r* to stand for (standardized) regression.

When you read the Burger King menu, you probably don't think in *z*-scores. But you might want to know the fat content in grams for a specific amount of protein in grams.

How much fat should we predict for a double hamburger with 31 grams of protein? The mean protein content is 17 grams and the standard deviation is 14, so that item is 1 SD above the mean. Since $r = 0.83$, we predict the fat content will be 0.83 SDs above the mean fat content. Great. How much fat is that? Well, the mean fat content is 23.5 grams and the standard deviation of fat content is 16.4, so we predict that the double hamburger will have $23.5 + 0.83 \times 16.4 = 37.11$ grams of fat.

We can always convert both x and y to z-scores, find the correlation, use $\hat{z}_y = rz_x$, and then convert $\hat{z}_y$ back to its original units so that we can understand the prediction. But can't we do this more simply?

Yes. Let's write the equation of the line for protein and fat—that is, the actual x and y values rather than their z-scores. In Algebra class you may have once seen lines written in the form $y = mx + b$. Statisticians do exactly the same thing, but with different notation:

$$\hat{y} = b_0 + b_1 x.$$

In this equation, b_0 is the ***y*-intercept,** the value of y where the line crosses the y-axis, and b_1 is the **slope.**

First we find the slope, using the formula we developed in the Math Box.[3] Remember? We know that our model predicts that for each increase of one standard deviation in protein we'll see an increase of about 0.83 standard deviations in fat.

protein	*fat*
$\bar{x} = 17.2$ g	$\bar{y} = 23.5$ g
$s_x = 14.0$ g	$s_y = 16.4$ g

$$b_1 = \frac{rs_y}{s_x}$$

In other words, the slope of the line in original units is

$$b_1 = \frac{rs_y}{s_x} = \frac{0.83 \times 16 \text{ g fat}}{14 \text{ g protein}} = 0.97 \text{ grams of fat per gram of protein.}$$

We mean this literally. Get in the habit of identifying the units and writing down "y-units *per* x-unit" with the unit names put in place. You'll find it'll really help you to tell about the line.

The correlation coefficient, r, has no units, but the standard deviations carry the units of their respective variables, so this slope has units. To understand the slope, start with the phrase "y-units per x-unit" and put the units into the expression. In our example, the slope is in *grams of fat* per *gram of protein.*

Next, how do we find the y-intercept, b_0? Remember that the line has to go through the mean-mean point $(\bar{x}, \bar{y})$. In other words, the model predicts $\bar{y}$ to be the value that corresponds to $\bar{x}$. We can put the means into the equation and write $\bar{y} = b_0 + b_1\bar{x}$.

Solving for b_0, we see that the intercept is just $b_0 = \bar{y} - b_1\bar{x}$.

For the Burger King foods, that comes out to

If the correlation were zero, the slope b_1 would be zero, and the intercept, b_0, would be just $\bar{y}$. And so the model would ignore x completely and just predict y to be its mean: $\hat{y} = \bar{y}$.

$$b_0 = 23.5 \text{ g fat} - 0.97 \frac{\text{g fat}}{\text{g protein}} \times 17.2 \text{ g protein} = 6.8 \text{ g fat.}$$

Putting this back into the regression equation gives:

$$\widehat{fat} = 6.8 + 0.97\,protein.$$

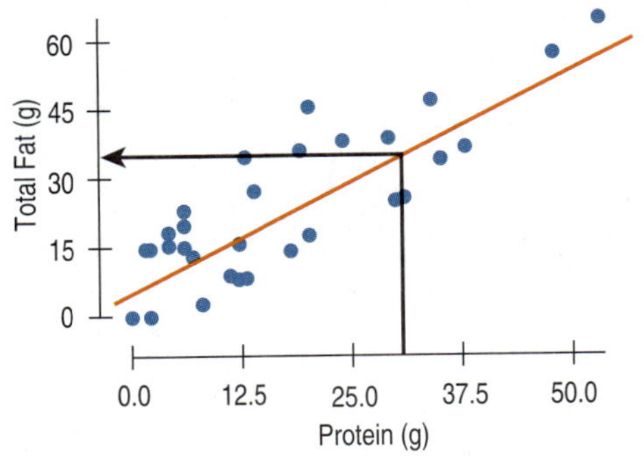

Burger King menu items in their natural units with the regression line. **Figure 8.4**

With the regression model equation it's easy to answer the question for any menu item we want. For example, if we wanted to know the *predicted* fat content of the BK Broiler chicken sandwich, which has 30 grams of protein, we could plug in 30 grams for the amount of protein and see that the predicted fat content is $6.8 + 0.97 \times 30 = 35.9$ grams of fat.

[3] Several important results popped up in that Math Box. Check it out!

Calculating a Regression Equation STEP-BY-STEP

In Chapter 7 we examined a scatterplot of annual cost per person due to traffic delays against peak period freeway speed and saw that slower speeds were linearly associated with higher costs. That's all very well, but it doesn't answer the all-important (when in comes to costs) question "how much?" Given the peak period freeway speeds, what would we predict the annual cost per person to be? That's the kind of question that might be raised when a city considers budget items for highway improvement or for public transportation. The answer lies in the regression model.

So let's find it.

Think

Variables Identify the variables and report the W's.

Let *speed* = peak period freeway speed (mph)
cost = annual cost per person ($)
These data for 70 U.S. cities come from the 2002 Urban Mobility Report issued by the Texas Transportation Institute.

Plan The condition we need to check is the one required for correlation—that we have a straight enough relationship. That's simple. We make a scatterplot.

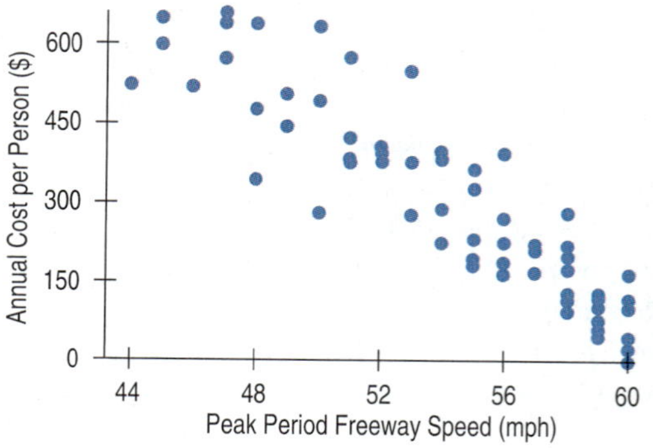

The **straight enough condition** is satisfied, as we can see from the scatterplot. We can reasonably fit a line to model this relationship.

Show

Mechanics Find the equation of the regression line. Summary statistics give the building blocks of the calculation.

(We generally report summary statistics to one more digit of accuracy than the data. We do the same for intercepts and predicted values, but for slopes we usually report an additional digit. Remember, though, not to round off until you finish computing an answer.)

Annual cost per person:

Mean = $298.96

Std dev = $180.830

Peak period freeway speed:

Mean = 54.34 mph

Std dev = 4.494 mph

Correlation: $r = -0.90$

Find the slope, b_1.

$$b_1 = \frac{rs_y}{s_x} = \frac{(-0.90)(180.83)}{4.494} = -36.21$$

Find the intercept, b_0.

$$b_0 = \bar{y} - b_1\bar{x}$$

$$= 298.96 - (-36.21)(54.34) = \$2266.61$$

Write the equation of the model using meaningful variable names.

The model is

$$\widehat{cost} = 2266.61 - 36.21\ speed.$$

Tell

Interpretation Discuss what you have found.

The model suggests traffic delays cost each urban area resident about $36 per year for each mile per hour the freeways are slowed at peak periods.

Residuals Revisited

The linear model we are using assumes that the relationship between the two variables is a perfect straight line. The residuals are the part of the data that *hasn't* been modeled. We can write

Data = Model + Residual
or, equivalently,

Residual = Data − Model.
Or, in symbols, $e = y - \hat{y}$.

We find the standard deviation of the residuals in almost the way you'd expect:

$$s_e = \sqrt{\frac{\sum e^2}{n-2}}$$

We don't need to subtract the mean because $\bar{e} = 0$.

Why $n - 2$ rather than $n - 1$? We used $n - 1$ for s when we estimated the mean. Now we're estimating both a slope and an intercept. Looks like a pattern. We subtract one more for each parameter we estimate.

When we want to know how well the model fits, we can ask instead what the model missed. To see that, we look at the residuals.

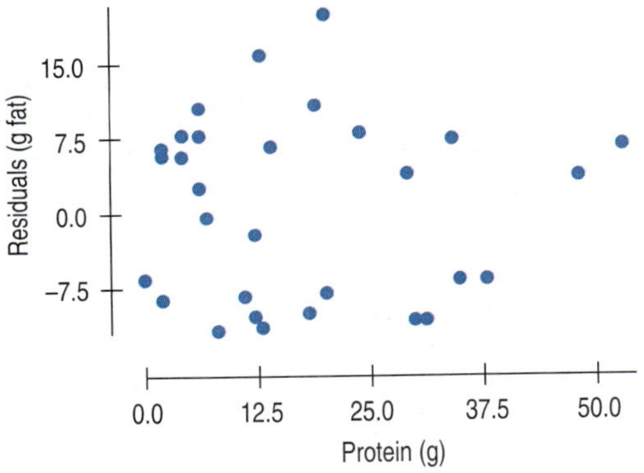

The residuals for the BK menu regression look appropriately boring. **Figure 8.5**

Residuals also help us to see whether the model makes sense. When a regression model is appropriate, it should model the underlying relationship. Nothing interesting should be left behind. So after we fit a regression model, we usually plot the residuals in the hope of finding . . . nothing.

A scatterplot of the residuals versus the x-values should be the most boring scatterplot you've seen. It shouldn't have any interesting features, like a direction or shape. It should stretch horizontally, with about the same amount of scatter throughout. It should show no bends, and it should have no outliers. If you see any of these features, you need to follow up to find out what the regression model missed.

If the residuals show no interesting pattern when we plot them against x, we can look at how big they are. After all, we're trying to make them as small as possible. Since their mean is always zero, though, it's only sensible to look at how much they vary. The standard deviation of the residuals, s_e, gives us a measure of how much the points spread out around the regression line.

For the Burger King foods, the standard deviation of the residuals is 9.2 grams of fat. That looks about right in the scatterplot of residuals. The residual for the BK Broiler chicken was −10.9 grams, just about what we'd expect.

R^2—The Variation Accounted For

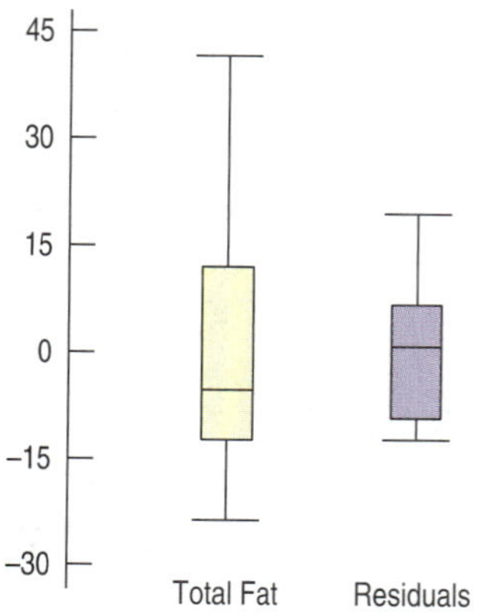

Compare the variability of total fat with the residuals from the regression. The means have been subtracted to make it easier to compare spreads. The variation left in the residuals is unaccounted for by the model, but it's less than the variation in the original data. **Figure 8.6**

Is a correlation of 0.80 twice as strong as a correlation of 0.40? Not if you think in terms of R^2. A correlation of 0.80 means an R^2 of $0.80^2 = 64\%$. A correlation of 0.40 means an R^2 of $0.40^2 = 16\%$—only a quarter as much of the variability accounted for. A correlation of 0.80 gives an R^2 *four* times as strong as a correlation of 0.40 and accounts for four times as much of the variability.

The variation in the residuals is the key to assessing how well the model fits. Let's compare the variation of the response variable with the variation of the residuals. The total fat has a standard deviation of 16.3 grams. The standard deviation of the residuals is 9.2 grams. If the correlation were 1.0 and the model predicted the fat values perfectly, the residuals would all be zero and have no variation. We couldn't possibly do any better than that.

On the other hand, if the correlation were zero, the model would simply predict 23.5 grams of fat (the mean) for all menu items. The residuals from that prediction would just be the observed fat values minus their mean. These residuals would have the same variation as the original data because, as we know, just subtracting the mean doesn't change the spread.

How well does the BK model do? Look at the boxplots. The variation in the residuals is smaller than in the data, but certainly bigger than zero. That's nice to know, but how much of the variation is still left in the residuals? If you had to put a number between 0% and 100% on the fraction of the variation left in the residuals, what would you say?

All regression models fall somewhere between the two extremes of zero correlation and perfect correlation. We'd like to gauge where our model falls. Can we use the correlation to do that? Well, a model with correlation −0.5 is doing as well as one with correlation +0.5. They just have different directions. But if we *square* the correlation coefficient, we'll get a value between 0 and 1, and the direction won't matter. It turns out, as we showed you in the Math Box,[4] that this works perfectly. The squared correlation, r^2, gives the fraction of the data's variance accounted for by the model and $1 - r^2$ is the fraction of the original variance left in the residuals. For the Burger King model, $r^2 = 0.83^2 = 0.69$, and $1 - r^2$ is 0.31, so 31% of the variance in total fat has been left in the residuals. How close was that to your guess?

All regression analyses include this statistic, although by tradition, it is written with a capital letter, R^2, and pronounced "*R*-squared." An R^2 of 0 means that none of the variance in the data is in the model; all of it is still in the residuals. It would be hard to imagine using that model for anything.

Because R^2 is a fraction of a whole, it is often given as a percentage.[5] For the Burger King data, R^2 is 69%.

When interpreting a regression model, you need to Tell what R^2 means. According to our linear model, 69% of the variability in the fat content of Burger King sandwiches is accounted for by variations in the protein content.

How can we see that R^2 is really the fraction of variance accounted for by the model?

It's a simple calculation. The variance of the fat content of the Burger King foods is $16.4^2 = 268.42$. The variance of the residuals is 83.195. As a fraction, that's $83.195/268.42 = 0.31$, or 31%. That's the fraction of the variance that is *not* accounted for by the model. The fraction that is accounted for is 100% − 31% = 69%, just the value we got for R^2.

[4] Have you looked yet? Please do.

[5] By contrast, we usually give correlation coefficients as decimal values between −1.0 and 1.0.

How Big Should R^2 Be?

Some Extreme Tales

One major company developed a method to differentiate between proteins. To do so, they had to distinguish between regressions with R^2 of 99.99% and 99.98%. For this application, 99.98% was not high enough.

The president of a financial services company reports that although his regressions give R^2 below 2%, they are highly successful because those used by his competition are even lower.

R^2 is always between 0% and 100%. But what's a "good" R^2 value? The answer depends on the kind of data you are analyzing and on what you want to do with it. There is no value for R^2 that automatically determines that the regression is "good." Data from scientific experiments often have R^2 in the 80% to 90% range and even higher. Data from observational studies and surveys, though, often show relatively weak associations because it's so difficult to measure reliable responses. An R^2 of 50% to 30% or even lower might be taken as evidence of a useful regression. The standard deviation of the residuals can give us more information about the usefulness of the regression by telling us how much scatter there is around the line.

As we've seen, an R^2 of 100% is a perfect fit with no scatter around the line. The s_e would be zero. All of the variance is accounted for by the model and none is left in the residuals at all. This sounds great, but it's too good to be true for real data.[6]

Along with the slope and intercept for a regression, you should always report R^2 so that readers can judge for themselves how successful the regression is at fitting the data. Statistics is about variation, and R^2 measures the success of the regression model in terms of the fraction of the variation of y accounted for by the regression. R^2 is the first part of a regression that many people look at because, along with the scatterplot, it tells whether the regression model is even worth thinking about.

Assumptions and Conditions

The linear regression model is perhaps the most widely used model in all of Statistics. It has everything we could want in a model: two easily estimated parameters, a meaningful measure of how well the model fits the data, and the ability to predict new values. It even provides a self-check in plots of the residuals, to help us avoid silly mistakes.

Like all models, though, linear models apply only when certain assumptions are true, so we'd better think about whether they're reasonable. Fortunately, we can check the conditions just by looking at simple plots.

Linearity Assumption

The linear model assumes that the relationship between the variables is linear. If you try to model a curved relationship with a straight line, you'll usually get exactly what you deserve. But a scatterplot will let you check that the assumption is reasonable.

Check the scatterplot. The shape must be linear or we can't use regression at all. And watch out for outliers.

The **straight enough condition** is satisfied if the scatterplot looks reasonably straight. It's a good idea to check linearity again *after* computing the regression when we can examine the residuals. You should also check for outliers, which could change the regression. If the data seem to clump or cluster in the scatterplot, that could be a sign of trouble worth looking into further.

[6] If you see an R^2 of 100%, it's a good idea to figure out what happened. You may have discovered a new law of Physics, but it's much more likely that you accidentally regressed two variables that measure the same thing.

If the scatterplot is not straight enough, stop here. You can't use a linear model for *any* two variables, even if they are related. They must have a *linear* association or the model won't mean a thing. Some nonlinear relationships can be saved by re-expressing the data to make the scatterplot more linear.

And you must watch out for outliers. Outlying values may have large residuals, and squaring makes their influence that much greater. Outlying points can dramatically change a regression model. Outliers can even change the sign of the slope, misleading us about the underlying relationship between the variables. We'll see examples in the next chapter.

Regression STEP-BY-STEP

Even if you hit the fast food joints for lunch, you should have a good breakfast. Researchers recorded facts about 77 breakfast cereals, including the calories and sugar content (in grams) of a serving. Let's build a linear model to understand how calories are related to sugar content.

Think

Variables Name the variables, report the W's, and specify the questions of interest.

Let x = sugar content of cereals (grams)
y = calories

We have two quantitative variables measured on 77 breakfast cereals.

We are interested in the relationship between these two variables.

Plan To check the conditions for a regression, always make a picture. Never fit a regression without looking at the scatterplot first.

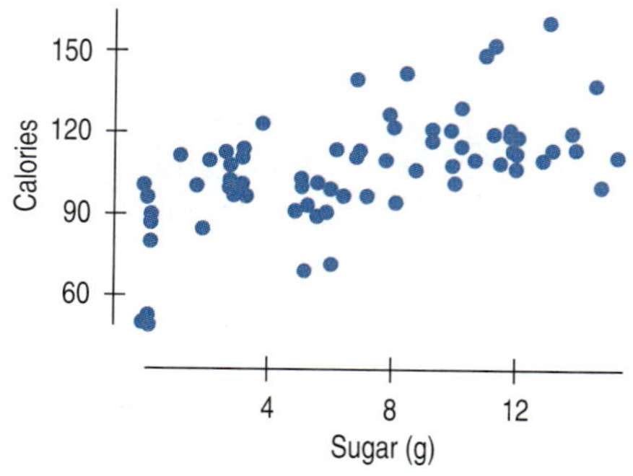

We can see from the scatterplot that the direction of the relationship is positive and the form of the association is straight enough.

There are no obvious outliers or groups.

Because the **straight enough condition** is satisfied, we can fit a regression model to these data.

Show

Mechanics If there are no clear violations of the condition, fit a straight line model of the form $\hat{y} = b_0 + b_1x$ to the data. Summary statistics give the building blocks of the calculation.

Calories
$\bar{y}$ = 107.0 calories
s_y = 19.5 calories

Sugars
$\bar{x} = 7.0$ grams
$s_x = 4.4$ grams

Correlation
$r = 0.564$

Find the slope.

$$b_1 = \frac{rs_y}{s_x} = \frac{0.564(19.5)}{4.4}$$

$= 2.50$ calories per gram of sugar.

Find the intercept.

$b_0 = \bar{y} - b_1\bar{x} = 107 - 2.50(7) = 89.5$ calories.

Write the equation using meaningful variable names.

So the least squares line is
$\hat{y} = 89.5 + 2.50\,x$,
or $\widehat{calories} = 89.5 + 2.50\ sugar$.

State the value of R^2.

Squaring the correlation gives
$R^2 = 0.564^2 = 0.318$ or 31.8%.

Tell

Interpretation Describe what the model says in words and numbers. Be sure to use the names of the variables and their units.

The key to interpreting a regression model is to start with the phrase "b_1 y-units per x-unit," substituting the estimated value of the slope for b_1 and the names of the respective units. The intercept is then a starting or base value.

R^2 gives the fraction of the variability of y accounted for by the linear regression model.

The scatterplot shows a positive, linear relationship and no outliers. The least squares regression line fit through these data has the equation

$\widehat{calories} = 89.5 + 2.50\ sugar$.

The slope says that cereals gain about 2.50 calories per gram of sugar.

The intercept predicts that sugar-free cereals would average about 89.5 calories.

The R^2 says that 31.8% of the variability in calories is accounted for by variation in sugar content.

Think Again

Check Again Even though we looked at the scatterplot *before* fitting a regression model, a plot of the residuals is an essential part of any regression analysis because it is the best check for additional patterns and interesting quirks in the data.

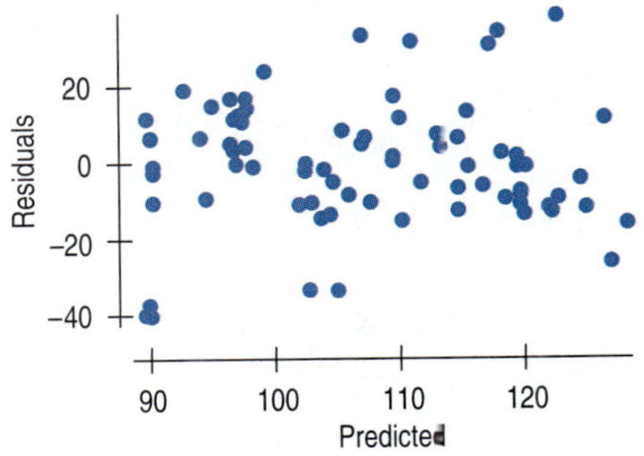

The residuals show a horizontal direction, a shapeless form, and roughly equal scatter for all predicted values. Our linear model appears to be appropriate.

TI Tips

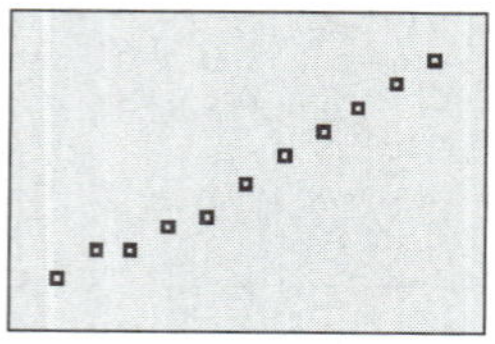

By now you will not be surprised to learn that your calculator can do it all: scatterplot, regression line, and residuals plot. Let's try it using the Arizona State tuition data from the last chapter. You should still have that saved in lists named **YR** and **TUIT**. First, recreate the scatterplot.

1. Find the equation of the regression line.

Actually, you already found the line when you used the calculator to get the correlation. But this time we'll be a little fancier so that we can display the line on our scatterplot. We want to tell the calculator to do the regression and save the equation of the model as a graphing variable.

- Under **STAT CALC** choose **LinReg(a+bx)**.
- Specify that x and y are **YR** and **TUIT**, as before, but . . .
- Now add a comma and one more specification. Press **VARS**, go to the **Y-VARS** menu, choose **1:Function**, and finally(!) choose **Y1**.
- Hit **ENTER**.

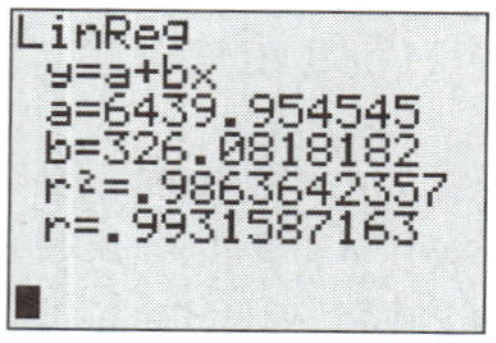

There's the equation. The calculator tells you that the regression line is $\widehat{tuit} = 6440 + 326\,year$. Can you explain what the slope and y-intercept mean?

2. Add the line to the plot.

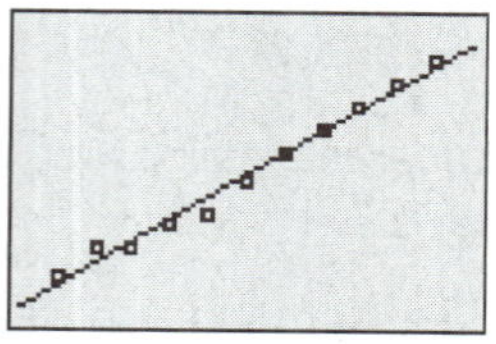

When you entered this command, the calculator automatically saved the equation as **Y1**. Just hit **GRAPH** to see the line drawn across your scatterplot.

3. Check the residuals.

Remember, you are not finished until you check to see if a linear model is appropriate. That means you need to see if the residuals appear to be randomly distributed. To do that, you need to look at the residuals plot.

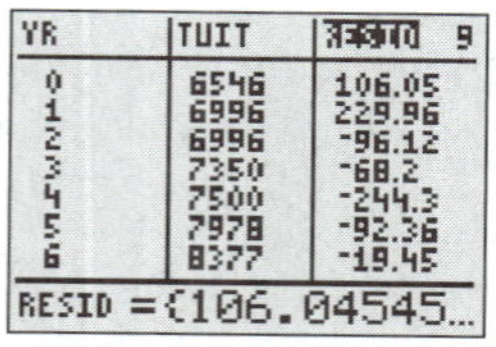

This is made easy by the fact that the calculator has already placed the residuals in a list named **RESID**. Want to see them? Go to **STAT EDIT** and look through the lists. (If **RESID** is not already there, go to the first blank list and import the name **RESID** from your **LIST NAMES** menu. The residuals should appear.) Every time you have the calculator compute a regression analysis, it will automatically save this list of residuals for you.

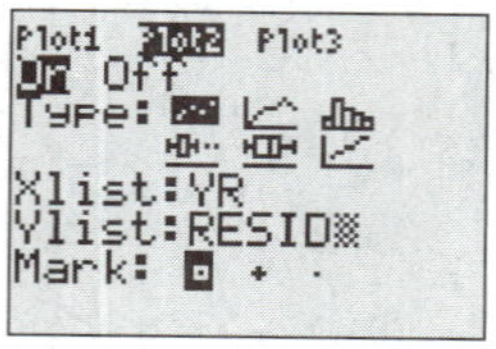

4. Now create the residuals plot:

- Set up **STATPLOT Plot2** as a scatterplot with **Xlist:YR** and **Ylist:RESID**.

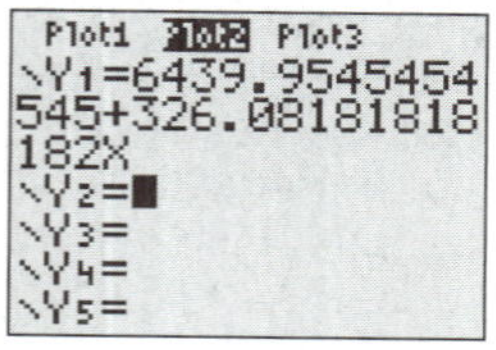

- Before you try to see the plot, go to the **Y=** screen. By moving the cursor around and hitting **ENTER** in the appropriate places you can turn off the regression line and **Plot1**, and turn on **Plot2**.
- **ZoomStat** will now graph the residuals plot.

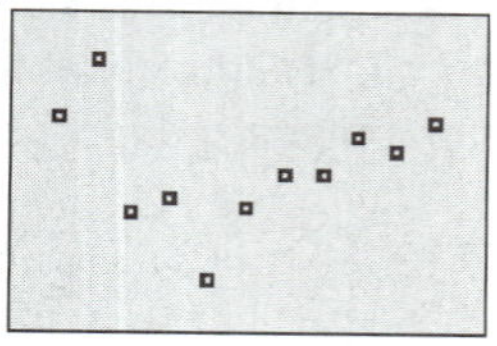

Uh-oh! See the curve? The residuals are high at both ends, low in the middle. Looks like a linear model may not be appropriate after all. Notice that the residuals plot makes the curvature much clearer than the original scatterplot did.

Moral: Always check the residuals plot!

So a linear model might not be appropriate here. What now? The next two chapters provide techniques for dealing with data like these.

Reality Check: Is the Regression Reasonable?

Statistics don't come out of nowhere. They are based on data. The results of a statistical analysis should reinforce your common sense, not fly in its face. If the results are surprising, then either you've learned something new about the world or your analysis is wrong.

Whenever you perform a regression, think about the coefficients and ask whether they make sense. Is a slope of 2.5 calories per gram of sugar reasonable? That's hard to say right off. We know from the summary statistics that a typical cereal has about 100 calories and 7 grams of sugar. A gram of sugar contributes some calories (actually, 4, but you don't need to know that), so calories should go up with increasing sugar. The direction of the slope seems right.

To see if the *size* of the slope is reasonable, a useful trick is to consider its order of magnitude. We'll start by asking if decreasing the slope by a factor of 10 seems reasonable. Is 0.25 calories per gram of sugar enough? The 7 grams of sugar found in the average cereal would contribute less than 2 calories. That seems too small.

Now let's try inflating the slope by a factor of 10. Is 25 calories per gram reasonable? Then the average cereal would have 175 calories from sugar alone. The average cereal has only 100 calories per serving, though, so that slope seems too big.

We have tried inflating the slope by a factor of 10 and deflating it by 10 and found both to be unreasonable. So, like Goldilocks, we're left with the value in the middle that's just right. And an increase of 2.5 calories per gram of sugar is certainly *plausible.*

The small effort of asking yourself whether the regression equation is plausible is repaid whenever you catch errors or avoid saying something silly or absurd about the data. It's too easy to take something that comes out of a computer at face value and assume that it makes sense.

Always be skeptical and ask yourself if the answer is reasonable.

What Can Go Wrong?

There are many ways in which data that appear at first to be good candidates for regression analysis may be unsuitable. And there are ways that people use regression that can lead them astray. Here's an overview of the most common problems. We'll discuss these at length in the next chapter.

- ***Don't fit a straight line to a nonlinear relationship.*** Linear regression is suited only to relationships that are, well, *linear.* Fortunately, we can often improve the linearity easily by using re-expression. We'll come back to this topic in Chapter 10.
- ***Beware extraordinary points.*** Data values can be extraordinary in a regression in two ways. They can have y-values that stand off from the linear pattern suggested by the bulk of the data, or extreme x-values. Both kinds of extraordinary points require attention.
- ***Don't extrapolate beyond the data.*** A linear model will often do a reasonable job of summarizing a relationship in the narrow range of observed x-values. Once we have a working model for the relationship, it's tempting to use it. But beware of predicting y-values for x-values that lie outside the range of the original data. The model may no longer hold there, so such **extrapolations** too far from the data are dangerous.

- ***Don't infer that x causes y just because there is a good linear model for their relationship.*** We have seen that when two variables are strongly correlated, it is often tempting to assume a causal relationship between them. Putting a regression line on a scatterplot tempts us even further, but it doesn't make the assumption of causation any more valid.

The R^2 does **not** mean that protein accounts for 69% of the fat in a BK food item. It is the *variation* in weight that is accounted for by the linear model.

Although R^2 measures the *strength* of the linear association, a high R^2 does not demonstrate the *appropriateness* of the regression. A single outlier, or data that separate into two groups rather than a single cloud of points, can make the R^2 seem quite large when, in fact, the linear regression model is simply inappropriate. Conversely, a low R^2 value may be due to a single outlier as well. It may be that most of the data fall roughly along a straight line with the exception of a single point.

Regression and the Computer

All statistics packages make a table of results for a regression. These tables may differ slightly from one package to another, but all are essentially the same—and all include much more than we need to know for now. Every computer regression table includes a section that looks something like this:

```
Dependent variable is: Total Fat
R squared = 69.0%
s = 9.277

Variable     Coefficient   SE(Coeff)   t-ratio   P-value
Constant     6.83077       2.664       2.56      0.0158
Protein      0.971381      0.1209      8.04      ≤0.0001
```

R squared

Standard dev of residuals

The "dependent" or y-variable

The "independent" or x-variable

The slope

The intercept

We'll deal with all of these later in the book. You may ignore them for now.

The slope and intercept coefficient are given in a table such as this one. Usually the slope is labeled with the name of the *x*-variable, and the intercept is labeled "Intercept" or "Constant." So the regression equation shown here is

$$\widehat{Fat} = 6.83077 + 0.97138\ protein.$$

It is not unusual for statistics packages to give many more digits of the estimated slope and intercept than could possibly be estimated from the data. (The original data were reported to the nearest pound and inch.) Ordinarily, you should round the reported numbers to one digit more than the precision of the data, and the slope to two. We will learn about the other numbers in the regression table later in the book. For now, all you need to be able to do is find the coefficients and the R^2 value.

Connections

We've talked about the importance of models before, but have seen only the Normal model as an example. The linear model is one of the most important models in Statistics. Chapter 7 talked about the assignment of variables to the y- and x-axes. It didn't matter to correlation, but it does matter to regression because y is predicted by x in the regression model.

The connection of R^2 to correlation is obvious, although it may not be immediately clear that just by squaring the correlation we can learn the fraction of the variability of y accounted for by a regression on x. We'll return to this in subsequent chapters.

We made a big fuss about knowing the units of your quantitative variables. We didn't need units for correlation, but without the units we can't define the slope of a regression. A regression makes no sense if you don't know the *Who*, the *What*, and the *Units* of both your variables.

We've summed squared deviations before when we computed the standard deviation and variance. That's not coincidental. They are closely connected to regression.

When we first talked about models, we noted that deviations away from a model were often interesting. Now we have a formal definition of these deviations as residuals.

Key Concepts

Model An equation or formula that simplifies and represents reality.

Parameters The numbers in the model that have to be chosen to explicitly determine the value of the model.

Linear model A linear model is an equation of the form

$$\hat{y} = b_0 + b_1x.$$

To interpret a linear model we need to know the variables (along with their "W's") and their units.

Predicted value The value of $\hat{y}$ found for each x value in the data. A predicted value is found by substituting the x-value in the regression equation. The predicted values are the values on the fitted line; the points $(x, \hat{y})$ all lie exactly on the fitted line.

Slope The slope gives a value in "y-units per x-unit." Changes of one standard deviation in x are associated with changes of r standard deviations in predicted values of y.

Regression to the mean Because the correlation is always less than 1.0 in magnitude each predicted $\hat{y}$ tends to be fewer standard deviations from its mean than its corresponding x was from its mean. This is called regression to the mean.

Regression line The particular linear equation

$$\hat{y} = b_0 + b_1x$$

that satisfies the least squares criterion is called the least squares regression line. Casually, we often just call it the regression line.

Intercept The intercept gives a starting value in y-units. It's the $\hat{y}$-value when x is 0.

Residuals Residuals are the differences between data values and the corresponding values predicted by the regression model—or, more generally, values predicted by any model.

$$\text{Residual} = \text{observed value} - \text{predicted value} = y - \hat{y}$$

R^2
- R^2 is the square of the correlation between *y* and *x*.
- R^2 gives the fraction of the variability of *y* accounted for by the least squares linear regression on *x*.
- R^2 is an overall measure of how successful the regression is in linearly relating *y* to *x*.

Least squares The least squares criterion specifies the unique line that minimizes the variance of the residuals or, equivalently, the sum of the squared residuals.

Examining Residuals To check whether a linear model is appropriate, it is usually best to plot the residuals. A histogram of the residuals can be checked for multiple modes and *y*-outliers. A scatterplot of residuals against predicted values can reveal bends, groups, and model outliers.

Skills

When you complete this lesson you should:

Think

- Be able to identify response (*y*) and explanatory (*x*) variables in context.
- Understand how a linear equation summarizes the relationship between two variables.
- Recognize when a regression should be used to summarize a linear relationship between two quantitative variables.
- Be able to judge whether the slope of a regression makes sense.
- Know how to examine your data for violations of the straight enough condition that would make it inappropriate to compute a regression.
- Understand that the least squares slope is easily affected by extreme values.
- Know that residuals are the differences between the data values and the corresponding values predicted by the line and that the *least squares criterion* finds the line that minimizes the sum of the squared residuals.
- Know how to use a plot of residuals against predicted values to check the straight enough condition or look for outliers.

Show

- Know how to find a regression equation from the summary statistics for each variable and the correlation between the variables.
- Know how to find a regression equation using your statistics software and how to find the slope and intercept values in the regression output table.
- Know how to use regression to predict a value of *y* for a given *x*.
- Know how to compute the residual for each data value and how to display them.

Tell

- Be able to write a sentence explaining what a linear equation says about the relationship between *y* and *x*, basing it on the fact that the slope is given in *y-units per x-unit*.
- Understand how the correlation coefficient and the regression slope are related. Know how R^2 describes how much variation in *y* is accounted for by its linear relationship with *x*.
- Be able to describe a prediction made from a regression equation, relating the predicted value to the specified *x*-value.

Exercises

1. Regression equations. Fill in the missing information in the table below.

	$\bar{x}$	s_x	$\bar{y}$	s_y	r	$\hat{y} = b_0 + b_1x$
a)	10	2	20	3	0.5	
b)	2	0.06	7.2	1.2	−0.4	
c)	12	6			−0.8	$\hat{y} = 200 - 4x$
d)	2.5	1.2		100		$\hat{y} = -100 + 50x$

2. More regression equations. Fill in the missing information in the table below.

	$\bar{x}$	s_x	$\bar{y}$	s_y	r	$\hat{y} = b_0 + b_1x$
a)	30	4	18	6	−0.2	
b)	100	18	60	10	0.9	
c)		0.8	50	15		$\hat{y} = -10 + 15x$
d)			18	4	−0.6	$\hat{y} = 30 - 2x$

3. Residuals. Tell what each of the residual plots below indicates about the appropriateness of the linear model that was fit to the data.

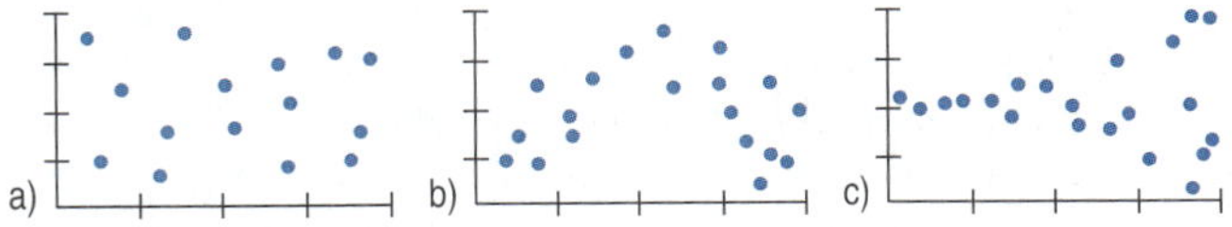

4. Residuals. Tell what each of the residual plots below indicates about the appropriateness of the linear model that was fit to the data.

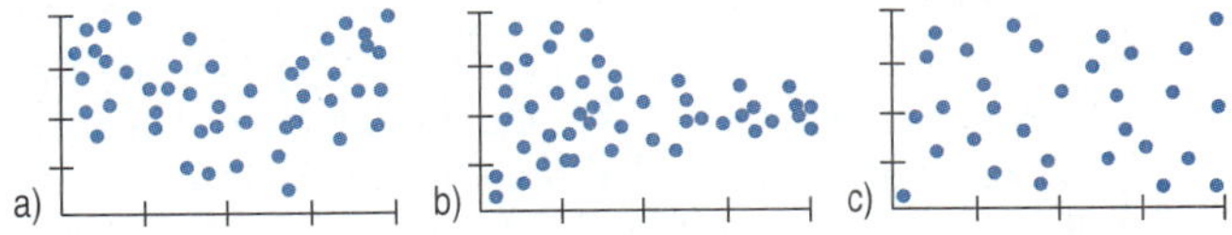

5. Least squares. Consider the four points (10, 10), (20, 50), (40, 20), and (50, 80). The line of best fit is $\hat{y} = 7.0 + 1.1x$. Explain what "least squares" means using these data as a specific example.

6. Least squares. Consider the four points (200, 1950), (400, 1650), (600, 1800), and (800, 1600). The line of best fit is $\hat{y} = 1975 - 0.45x$. Explain what "least squares" means using these data as a specific example.

7. Real estate. A random sample of records of sales of homes from Feb. 15 to Apr. 30, 1993, from the files maintained by the Albuquerque Board of Realtors gives the price and size (in square feet) of 117 homes. A regression to predict price (in thousands of dollars) from size has an R-squared of 71.4%. The residuals plot indicated that a linear model is appropriate.

a) What are the variables and units in this regression? What units does the slope have?
b) Write a sentence summarizing what the R-squared value says about this regression.
c) Do you think the slope is positive or negative? Explain.
d) What is the correlation between size and price?
e) What would you predict about the price of a home one standard deviation above average in size?
f) What would you predict about the price of a home two standard deviations below average in size?

8. Baseball. In the last chapter you looked at the relationship between the number of games won by American League baseball teams and the average attendance at their home games for the first half of the 2001 season. Here are the scatterplot, the residuals plot, and part of the regression analysis.

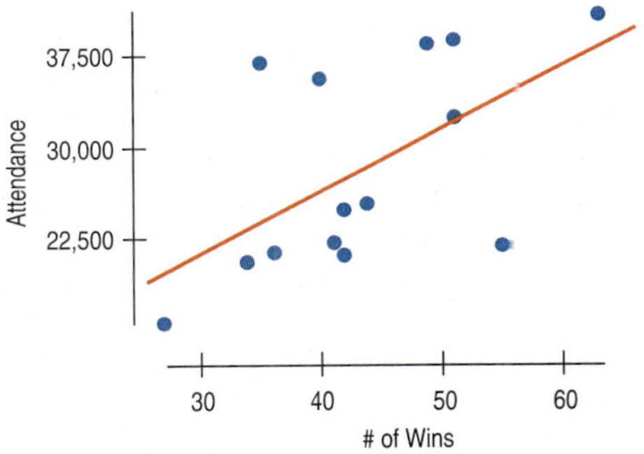

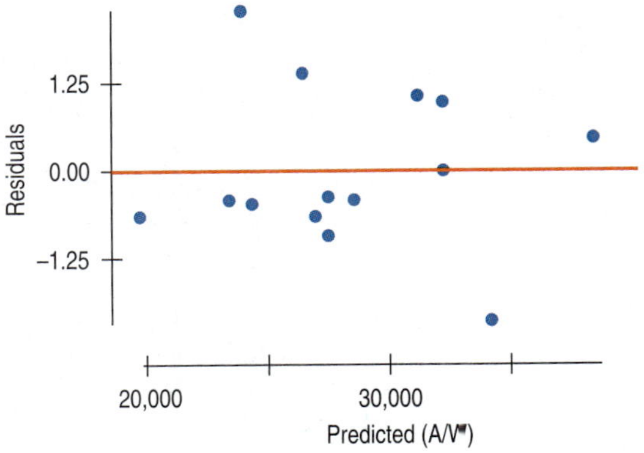

Dependent variable is: Attend
$R^2 = 33.3\%$

Variable	**Coefficient**
Constant	5773.27
Wins	517.609

a) Do you think a linear model is appropriate here? Explain.

b) Interpret the meaning of R^2 in this context.
c) What is the correlation between wins and average attendance?
d) What would you predict about the average attendance for a team that is two standard deviations above average in games won?
e) If a team is one standard deviation below average in attendance, what would you predict about the number of games the team has won?

9. More real estate. Consider the Albuquerque home sales from Exercise 7 again. The regression analysis gives the model $\widehat{price} = 47.82 + 0.061\ size$.
a) Explain what the slope of the line says about housing prices and house size.
b) What price would you predict for a 3000-square-foot house in this market?
c) A real estate agent shows a potential buyer a 1200-square-foot home, saying that the asking price is \$6000 less than what one would expect to pay for a house of this size. What is the asking price, and what is the \$6000 called?

10. Second inning. Refer again to the regression analysis for attendance and games won by American League baseball teams, seen in Exercise 8.
a) Write the equation of the regression line.
b) Estimate the average attendance for a team with 50 wins.
c) Interpret the meaning of the slope of the regression line in this context.
d) In general, what would a negative residual mean in this context?
e) The St. Louis Cardinals are not included in these data because they are a National League team. At the time these data were collected, the Cardinals had won 43 games and averaged 38,988 fans at their home games. Calculate the residual for this team, and explain what it means.

11. What slope? If you create a regression model for predicting the weight of a car (in pounds) from its length (in feet), is the slope most likely to be 3, 30, 300, or 3000? Explain.

12. What slope? If you create a regression model for estimating the height of a pine tree (in feet) based upon the circumference of its trunk (in inches), is the slope most likely to be 0.1, 1, 10, or 100? Explain.

13. Misinterpretations. A Biology student who created a regression model to use a bird's height when perched for predicting its wingspan made these two statements. Assuming the calculations were done correctly, explain what is wrong with each interpretation.
a) My R^2 of 93% shows that this linear model is appropriate.
b) A bird 10 inches tall will have a wingspan of 17 inches.

14. More misinterpretations. A Sociology student investigated the association between a country's literacy rate and life expectancy, then drew the conclusions listed below. Explain why each statement is incorrect. (Assume that all the calculations were done properly.)
a) The literacy rate determines 64% of the life expectancy for a country.
b) The slope of the line shows that an increase of 5% in literacy rate will produce a 2-year improvement in life expectancy.

15. ESP. People who claim to "have ESP" participate in a screening test in which they have to guess which of several images someone is thinking of. You and a friend both took the test. You scored two standard deviations above the mean, and your friend scored one standard deviation below the mean. The researchers offer everyone the opportunity to take a retest.
a) Should you choose to take this retest? Explain.
b) Now explain to your friend what his decision should be and why.

16. *SI* jinx. Players in any sport who are having great seasons, turning in performances that are much better than anyone might have anticipated, often are pictured on the cover of *Sports Illustrated.* Frequently, their performances then falter somewhat, leading some athletes to believe in a "*Sports Illustrated* jinx." Similarly, it is common for phenomenal rookies to have less stellar second seasons—the so-called "sophomore slump." While fans, athletes, and analysts put forth many theories about what leads to such declines, a statistician might simply argue that this is an example of regression to the mean. Explain.

17. SAT scores. The SAT is a test often used as part of an application to college. SAT scores are between 200 and 800, but have no units. Tests are given in both Math and Verbal areas. Because doing the SAT-Math problems also involves the ability to read and understand the questions, can a person's verbal score be used to predict the math score? Verbal and math SAT scores of a high school graduating class are displayed in the scatterplot, with the line of best fit added.

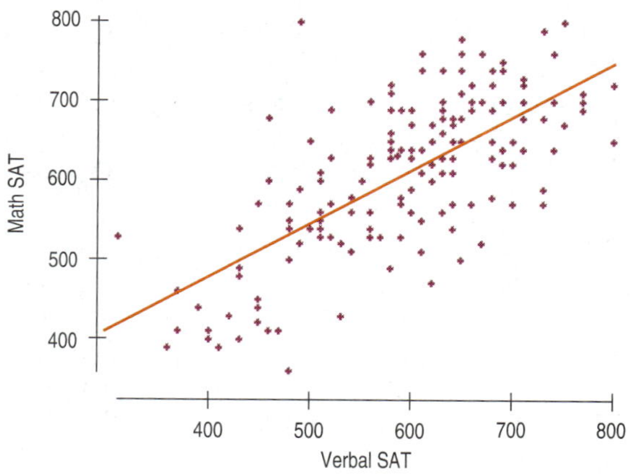

a) Describe the relationship.
b) Are there any students whose scores do not seem to fit the overall pattern?
c) For these data, $r = 0.685$. Interpret this statistic.
d) These verbal scores averaged 596.3 with a standard deviation of 99.5, and the math scores averaged 612.2 with a standard deviation of 96.1. Write the equation of the regression line.
e) Interpret the slope of this line.
f) Predict the math score of a student with a verbal score of 500.
g) A few students every year score a perfect 1600. Based on this model, what would that student's residual be for her math score?

18. Success in college. Colleges use SAT scores in the admissions process because they believe these scores provide some insight into how a high school student will perform at the college level. Suppose the entering freshmen at a certain college have mean combined SAT scores of 1222 with a standard deviation of 83. In the first semester these students attained a mean GPA of 2.66 with a standard deviation of 0.56. A scatterplot showed the association to be reasonably linear, and the correlation between SAT score and GPA was 0.47.

a) Write the equation of the regression line.
b) Explain what the y-intercept of the regression line indicates.
c) Interpret the slope of the regression line.
d) Predict the GPA of a freshman who scored a combined 1400.
e) Based upon these statistics, how effective do you think SAT scores would be in predicting academic success during first semester of the freshman year at this college? Explain.
f) As a student, would you rather have a positive or a negative residual in this context? Explain.

19. SAT, take 2. Suppose we wanted to use SAT math scores to estimate verbal scores based on the information in Exercise 17.

a) What is the correlation?
b) Write the equation of the line of regression predicting verbal scores from math scores.
c) In general, what would a positive residual mean in this context?
d) A person tells you her math score was 500. Predict her verbal score.
e) Using that predicted verbal score and the equation you created in Exercise 17, predict her math score.
f) Why doesn't the result in part e come out to 500?

20. Success, part 2. Based on the statistics for college freshmen given in Exercise 18, what SAT score might be expected among freshmen who attained a first-semester GPA of 3.0?

T **21. Used cars.** Classified ads in the *Ithaca Journal* offered several used Toyota Corollas for sale. Listed below are the ages of the cars and the advertised prices.

Age (yr)	Prices Advertised ($)
1	12995, 10950
2	10495
3	10995, 10995
4	6995, 7990
5	8700, 6995
6	5990, 4995
9	3200, 2250, 3995
11	2900, 2995
13	1750

a) Make a scatterplot for these data.
b) Describe the association between age and price of a used Corolla.
c) Do you think a linear model is appropriate?
d) Computer software says that $R^2 = 0.894$. What is the correlation between age and price?
e) Explain the meaning of R^2 in this context.
f) Why doesn't this model explain 100% of the variability in the price of a used Corolla?

22. Drug abuse. In the exercises of the last chapter you examined results of a survey conducted in the United States and 10 countries of Western Europe to determine the percentage of teenagers who had used marijuana and other drugs. Here is the scatterplot. Summary statistics showed that the mean percent that had used marijuana was 23.9%, with a standard deviation of 11.6%. An average of 15.6% of teens had used other drugs, with a standard deviation of 10.2%.

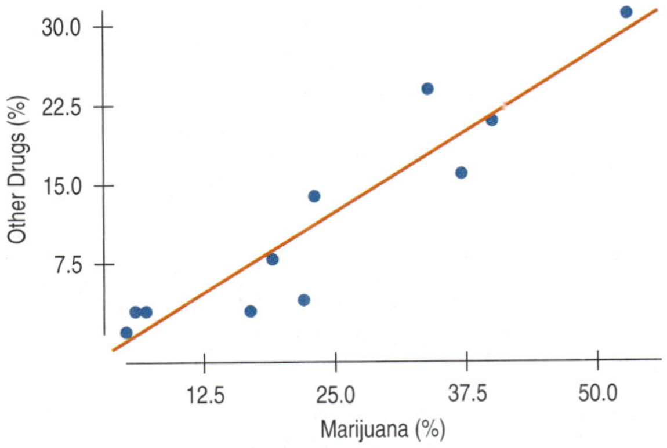

a) Do you think a linear model is appropriate? Explain.
b) For this regression, R^2 is 87.3%. Interpret this statistic in this context.
c) Write the equation you would use to estimate the percentage of teens who use other drugs from the percentage who have used marijuana.

d) Explain in context what the slope of this line means.
e) Do these results confirm that marijuana is a "gateway drug," that is, that marijuana use leads to the use of other drugs?

23. More used cars. Use the advertised prices for Toyota Corollas given in Exercise 21 to create a linear model for the relationship between a car's age and its price.
a) Find the equation of the regression line.
b) Explain the meaning of the slope of the line.
c) Explain the meaning of the y-intercept of the line.
d) If you want to sell a 7-year-old Corolla, what price seems appropriate?
e) You have a chance to buy one of two cars. They are about the same age and appear to be in equally good condition. Would you rather buy the one with a positive residual or a negative residual? Explain.
f) You see a "For Sale" sign on a 10-year old Corolla stating the asking price as $1500. What is the residual?
g) Would this regression model be useful in establishing a fair price for a 20-year-old car? Explain.

24. Veggie burgers. Recently Burger King introduced a meat-free burger. The nutrition label is shown here.

Nutrition Facts

Calories	330
Fat	10g*
Sodium	760g
Sugars	5g
Protein	14g
Carbohydrates	43g
Dietary Fiber	4g
Cholesterol	0

* (2 grams of saturated fat)

RECOMMENDED DAILY VALUES*
(based on a 2,000-calorie/day diet)

Iron	20%
Vitamin A	10%
Vitamin C	10%
Calcium	6%

a) Use the regression model created in this chapter, $\widehat{fat} = 6.8 + 0.97\ protein$, to predict the fat content of this burger from its protein content.
b) What is its residual? How would you explain the residual?
c) Write a brief report about the fat and protein content of this new menu item. Be sure to talk about the variables by name and in the correct units.

25. Burgers. In the last chapter you examined the association between the amounts of fat and calories in fast food hamburgers. Here are the data:

Fat (g)	19	31	34	35	39	39	43
Calories	410	580	590	570	640	680	660

a) Create a scatterplot of calories vs. fat content.
b) Interpret the value of R^2 in this context.
c) Write the equation of the line of regression.
d) Use the residuals plot to explain whether your linear model is appropriate.
e) Explain the meaning of the y-intercept of the line.
f) Explain the meaning of the slope of the line.
g) A new burger containing 28 grams of fat is introduced. According to this model, its residual for calories is +33. How many calories does the burger have?

26. Chicken. Chicken sandwiches are often advertised as a healthier alternative to beef because many are lower in fat. Tests on 11 brands of fast food chicken sandwiches produced the following summary statistics and scatterplot from a graphing calculator:

	Fat (g)	Calories
Mean	20.6	472.7
St. Dev.	9.8	144.2
Correlation	0.947	

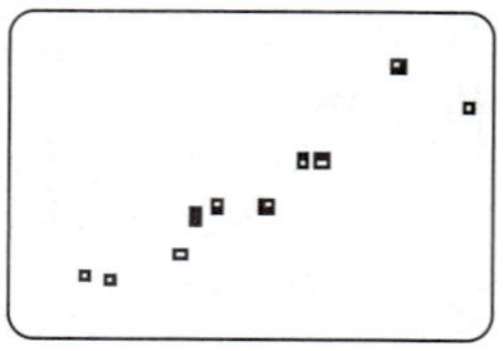

a) Do you think a linear model is appropriate in this situation?
b) Describe the strength of this association.
c) Write the equation of the regression line.
d) Explain the meaning of the slope.
e) Explain the meaning of the y-intercept.
f) What does it mean if a certain sandwich has a negative residual?
g) If a chicken sandwich and a burger each advertised 35 grams of fat, which would you expect to have more calories? (See Exercise 25.)
h) McDonald's Filet-O-Fish sandwich has 26 grams of fat and 470 calories. Does the fat/calorie relationship in this sandwich appear to be very different from that found in chicken sandwiches or in burgers (see Exercise 25)? Explain.

27. A second helping of burgers. In Exercise 25 you created a model that can estimate the number of calories in a burger when the fat content is known.
a) Explain why you cannot use that model to estimate the fat content of a burger with 600 calories.
b) Using an appropriate model, estimate the fat content of a burger with 600 calories.

T **28. Cost of living.** The *Worldwide Cost of Living Survey City Rankings* determine the cost of living in the 25 most expensive cities in the world. These rankings scale New

York City as 100, and express the cost of living in other cities as a percentage of the New York cost. For example, the table indicates that in Tokyo the cost of living was 65% higher than New York in 2000, but dropped to only 34% higher than NY in 2001.

City	2001	2000	City	2001	2000
Tokyo	134.0	164.9	Shenzhen	90.8	100.1
Moscow	132.4	136.1	Ho Chi Minh City	90.4	92.7
Hong Kong	130.0	141.5	Singapore	86.4	94.7
Beijing	124.4	138.3	White Plains, NY	85.5	84.0
Osaka	116.7	143.6	Tel Aviv	85.0	88.7
Shanghai	114.3	128.0	San Francisco	84.4	83.7
St. Petersburg	106.5	109.7	Chicago	84.3	82.7
New York	100.0	100.0	Kiev	83.8	78.2
Guangzhou	97.4	107.9	Beirut	83.8	86.2
Seoul	95.3	111.1	Buenos Aires	83.6	91.0
Hanoi	94.3	94.9	Los Angeles	83.4	83.1
Taipei	92.9	102.8	Miami	83.0	83.8
London	92.9	106.9			

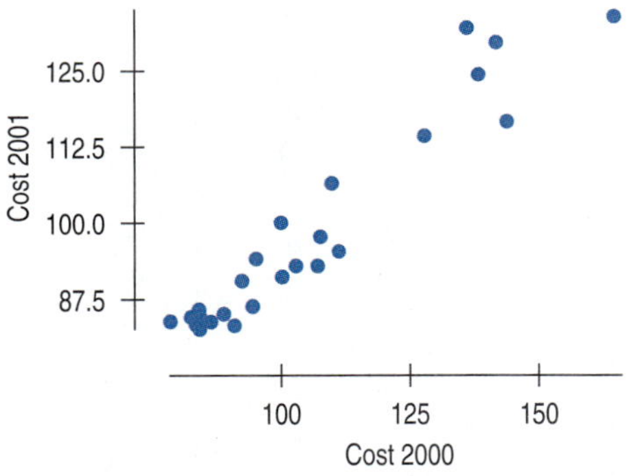

a) Here is a scatterplot. Describe the association between costs of living in 2000 and 2001.
b) The correlation is 0.957. Find and interpret the value of R^2.
c) The regression equation predicting the 2001 cost of living from the 2000 figure is $\widehat{cost01} = 25.41 + 0.69 \times cost00$. Use this equation to find the residual for Moscow.
d) Explain what the residual means.

29. Cell phones. Most people prefer digital cell phone service to analog because it is clearer and more private. Nonetheless, many calls are switched to analog channels because digital lines are busy, or because the calls are between people with different carriers. These analog calls require more power, so they are harder on phone batteries. How much battery time do you lose when making analog calls?

Consumer Reports tested seven popular brands of cell phones, comparing digital and analog talk times. The scatterplot appears to show a linear relationship with $r = 0.94$ and regression equation $\widehat{An} = -5.1 + 0.44dig$.

a) If you have a cell phone claiming to provide 200 minutes of digital calls between battery chargings, how many minutes of analog calling would you expect to get?
b) How much faith do you place in that prediction? Explain.
c) Explain what the slope of the line means in this context.
d) If a certain brand of battery has a positive residual, what does that mean in this context?

30. Candy. The table shows the increase in Halloween candy sales over a 7-year period. Using these data, predict the amount of sales for 2002. Discuss the appropriateness of your model and your faith in the prediction. (National Confectioners Association)

Year	Halloween Candy Sales (millions of dollars)
1995	1.474
1996	1.660
1997	1.708
1998	1.787
1999	1.896
2000	1.985
2001	2.035

31. El Niño. Concern over the weather associated with El Niño has increased interest in the possibility that the climate on earth is getting warmer. The most common theory relates an increase in atmospheric levels of carbon dioxide (CO_2), a greenhouse gas, to increases in temperature. Here is a scatterplot showing the mean annual CO_2 concentration in the atmosphere measured in parts per million (ppm) at the top of Mauna Loa in Hawaii, and the mean annual air temperature over both land and sea across the globe, in degrees Celsius (°C).

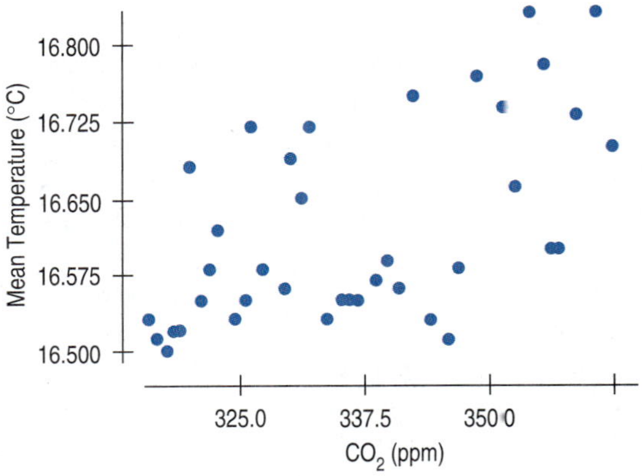

A regression predicting temperature from CO_2 level produces the following output table (in part):

Dependent variable is: Temperature
R-squared = 33.4%

Variable	Coefficient
Constant	15.3066
CO2	0.004

a) What is the correlation between CO_2 level and temperature?
b) Explain the meaning of *R*-squared in this context.
c) Give the regression equation.
d) What is the meaning of the slope in this equation?
e) What is the meaning of the *y*-intercept of this equation?
f) Here is a scatterplot of the residuals vs. CO_2 level. Does this plot show evidence of the violation of any assumptions behind the regression? If so, which ones?

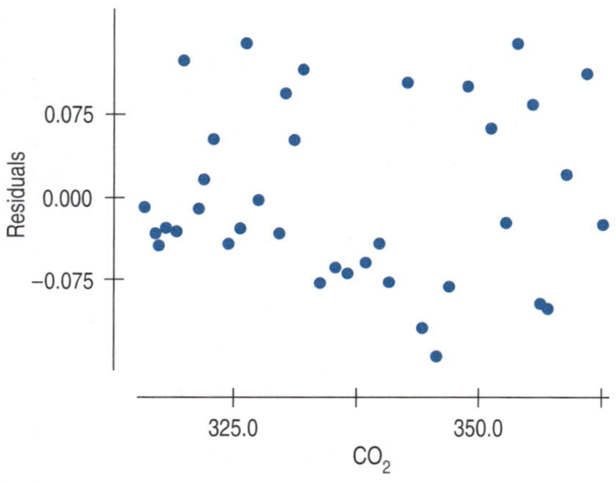

g) CO_2 levels will probably reach 364 ppm this year. What mean temperature does the regression predict from that information?

32. Birth rates. The table shows the number of live births per 1000 women aged 15–44 years in the United States, starting in 1965. (*National Vital Statistics Report*, April 2001)

Year	1965	1970	1975	1980	1985	1990	1995	1999
Rate	19.4	18.4	14.8	15.9	15.6	16.4	14.8	14.5

a) Make a scatterplot and describe the general trend in birth rates.
b) Find the equation of the regression line.
c) Check to see if the line is an appropriate model. Explain.
d) Interpret the slope of the line.
e) The table gives rates only at 5-year intervals. Estimate what the rate was in 1978.
f) In 1978 the birth rate was actually 15.0. How close did your model come?
g) Predict what the birth rate will be in 2005. Comment on your faith in this prediction.
h) Predict the birth rate for 2020. Comment on your faith in this prediction.

T **33. Body fat.** It is difficult to accurately determine a person's body fat percentage without immersing him or her in water. Researchers hoping to find ways to make a good estimate immersed 20 male subjects, then measured their waists and recorded their weights.

Waist (in.)	Weight (lb)	Body Fat (%)
32	175	6
36	181	21
38	200	15
33	159	6
39	196	22
40	192	31
41	205	32
35	173	21
38	187	25
38	188	30
33	188	10
40	240	20
36	175	22
32	168	9
44	246	38
33	160	10
41	215	27
34	159	12
34	146	10
44	219	28

a) Create a model to predict body fat from weight.
b) Do you think a linear model is appropriate? Explain.
c) Interpret the slope of your model.
d) Is your model likely to make reliable estimates? Explain.
e) What is the residual for a person who weighs 190 pounds and has 21% body fat?

34. Body fat, again. Would a model that uses the person's waist size be able to predict the percentage of body fat more accurately than one that uses weight? Using the data in Exercise 33, create and analyze that model.

35. Hard water. In an investigation of environmental causes of disease, data were collected on the annual mortality rate (deaths per 100,000) for males in 61 large towns in England and Wales. In addition, the water hardness was recorded as the calcium concentration (parts per million, ppm) in the drinking water. The following display shows the relationship between mortality and calcium concentration for these towns:

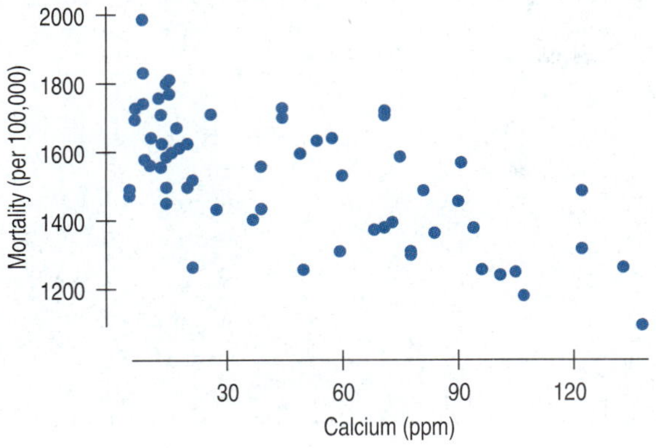

a) Describe what you see in this scatterplot, in context.
b) Here is the regression analysis of mortality and calcium concentration. What is the regression equation?

Dependent variable is: Mortality
R-squared = 43%
s = 143.0

Variable	Coefficient	SE(Coeff)	t-ratio	P-Value
Constant	1676	29.30	57.2	≤0.0001
Calcium	3.23	0.48	−6.66	≤0.0001

c) Interpret the slope and y-intercept of the line, in context.
d) The largest residual, with a value of −348.6, is for the town of Exeter. Explain what this value means.
e) The hardness of Derby's municipal water is about 100 ppm of calcium. Use this equation to predict the mortality rate in Derby.
f) Explain the meaning of R-squared in this situation.

36. Gators. Wildlife researchers monitor many wildlife populations by taking aerial photographs. Can they estimate the weights of alligators accurately from the air? Here is a regression analysis of the weight of alligators (in pounds) and their length (in inches) based on data collected from captured alligators.

Dependent variable is: Weight
R-squared = 83.6%
s = 54.01

Variable	Coefficient	SE(Coeff)	t-ratio	P-Value
Constant	−393	47.53	−8.27	≤0.0001
Length	5.9	0.5448	10.8	≤0.0001

a) Did they choose the correct variable to use as the dependent variable and the predictor? Explain.
b) What is the correlation between an alligator's length and weight?
c) Write the regression equation.
d) Interpret the slope of the equation in this context.
e) Do you think this equation will allow the scientists to make accurate predictions about alligators? What part of the regression analysis indicates this? What additional concerns do you have?

37. Internet. The rapid growth of Internet publishing is seen in the number of electronic academic journals made available during the last decade. Explain why you cannot use the methods of this chapter to model this growth.

Year	Number of Journals
1991	27
1992	36
1993	45
1994	181
1995	306
1996	1093
1997	2459

T **38. Oil production.** In the exercises for Chapter 7, you looked at the oil production of the United States from 1949 to 2000. Here are the data again:
a) Fit a least squares regression line to oil production by year.
b) Using this regression line, predict U.S. oil production in the year 2001.
c) Does the prediction in part b look reasonable? Comment.
d) Do you think the regression line is an appropriate model? Comment.

Year	Oil	Year	Oil
1949	1,841,940	1975	3,056,779
1950	1,973,574	1976	2,976,180
1951	2,247,711	1977	3,009,265
1952	2,289,836	1978	3,178,216
1953	2,357,082	1979	3,121,310
1954	2,314,988	1980	3,146,365
1955	2,484,428	1981	3,128,624
1956	2,617,283	1982	3,156,715
1957	2,616,901	1983	3,170,999
1958	2,448,987	1984	3,249,696
1959	2,574,590	1985	3,274,553
1960	2,574,933	1986	3,168,252
1961	2,621,758	1987	3,047,378
1962	2,676,189	1988	2,979,123
1963	2,752,723	1989	2,778,773
1964	2,786,822	1990	2,684,687
1965	2,848,514	1991	2,707,039
1966	3,027,763	1992	2,624,632
1967	3,215,742	1993	2,499,033
1968	3,329,042	1994	2,431,476
1969	3,371,751	1995	2,394,268
1970	3,517,450	1996	2,366,017
1971	3,453,914	1997	2,354,831
1972	3,455,368	1998	2,281,919
1973	3,360,903	1999	2,146,732
1974	3,202,585	2000	2,135,062

Chapter 9

Regression Wisdom

Regression may be the most widely used statistics method. It is used every day throughout the world to predict customer loyalty, numbers of admissions at hospitals, sales of automobiles, and many other things. Because regression is so widely used, it's also widely abused and misinterpreted. This chapter presents examples of regressions in which things are not quite as simple as they may have seemed at first, and shows how you can still use regression to discover what the data have to say.

Sifting Residuals for Groups

No regression analysis is complete without a display of the residuals to check that the linear model is reasonable. Because the residuals are what is "left over" after the model describes the relationship, they often reveal subtleties that were not clear from a plot of the original data. Sometimes these are additional details that help confirm or refine our understanding. Sometimes they reveal violations of the regression conditions that require our attention.

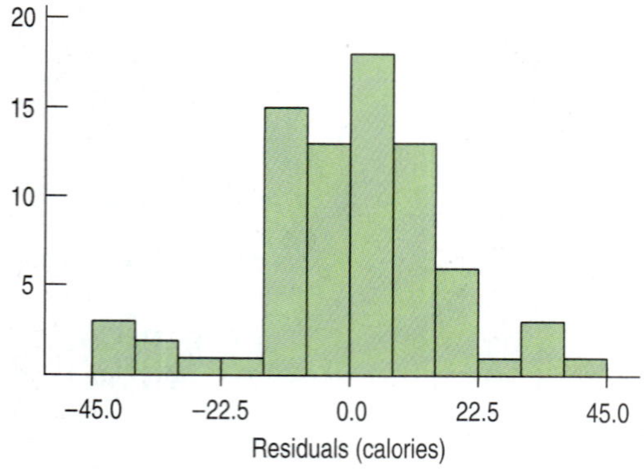

A histogram of the regression residuals shows small modes both above and below the central large mode. These may be worth a second look. **Figure 9.1**

In the Step-by-Step analysis of the cereal data from Chapter 8, we examined a scatterplot of the residuals. Our first impression was that it had no particular structure—a conclusion that supported using the regression model. But let's look again.

It's often a good idea to look at a histogram of the residuals. How would you describe its shape? It looks like there might be small modes at both sides of the central body of the data. There is a group of cereals that seem to stand out as having large negative residuals, with fewer calories than we might have predicted. The calories in these cereals were overestimated by the model. Whenever we suspect multiple modes, we ask whether they are somehow different.

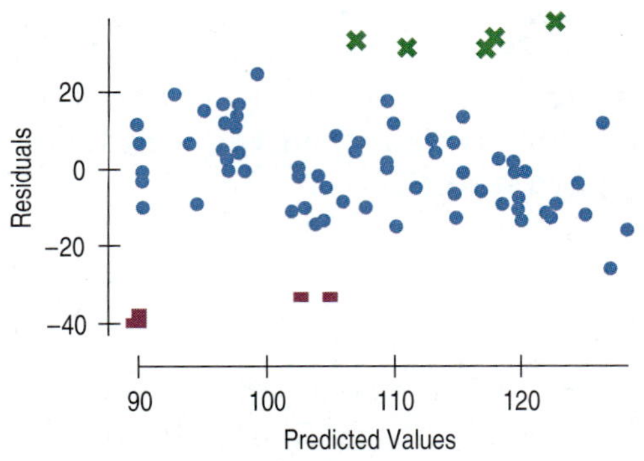

A scatterplot of the residuals vs. predicted values for the cereal regression. The green "x" points are cereals whose calorie content is higher than the linear model predicts. The red "–" points show cereals with fewer calories than the model predicts. Is there something special about these cereals?

Figure 9.2

Let's look more carefully at the residual scatterplot. Here's the same residual plot from Chapter 8, with the points in those modes marked. Now we can see that those two groups stand away from the central pattern in the scatterplot. If we examine the data set, we find that the high-residual cereals are Just Right Fruit & Nut; Muesli Raisins, Dates & Almonds; Muesli Raisins, Peaches, & Pecans; Mueslix Crispy Blend; and Nutri-Grain Almond Raisin. Do these cereals seem to have something in common? These high-calorie cereals all present themselves as "healthy." This might be surprising, but in fact, "healthy" cereals often contain more fat and therefore more calories than we might expect from looking at their sugar content alone.

The low-residual cereals are Puffed Rice, Puffed Wheat, three bran cereals, and Golden Crisps. These cereals have fewer calories than we would expect based on their sugar content. We might not have grouped these cereals together before. What they have in common is a low calorie count *relative to their sugar content*—even though their sugar contents are quite different.

These observations may not lead us to question the overall linear model, but they do help us understand that other factors may be part of the story. An examination of residuals often leads us to discover groups of observations that are different from the rest.

When we discover that there is more than one group in a regression, we may decide to analyze the groups separately, using a different model for each group. Or we can stick with the original model and simply note that there are groups that are a little different. Either way, the model will be wrong, but useful, and so it will improve our understanding of the data.

Subsets

Here's an important unstated condition for fitting models: **All the data must come from the same group.**

The residuals plot suggests that there may be different "types" of breakfast cereals. Cereal manufacturers aim cereals at different segments of the market. Supermarkets and cereal manufacturers try to attract different customers by placing different types on each shelf. Cereals for kids tend to be at kids' eye level. Toddlers wouldn't be likely to grab a box from the shelf and beg, "Mom, can we please get this All-Bran with Extra Fiber?"

Calories and sugars colored according to the shelf on which the cereal was found in a supermarket, with regression lines fit for each shelf individually. Do these data appear homogeneous? That is, do the cereals seem to all be from the same population of cereals? Or are there different kinds of cereals that we might want to consider separately?

Figure 9.3

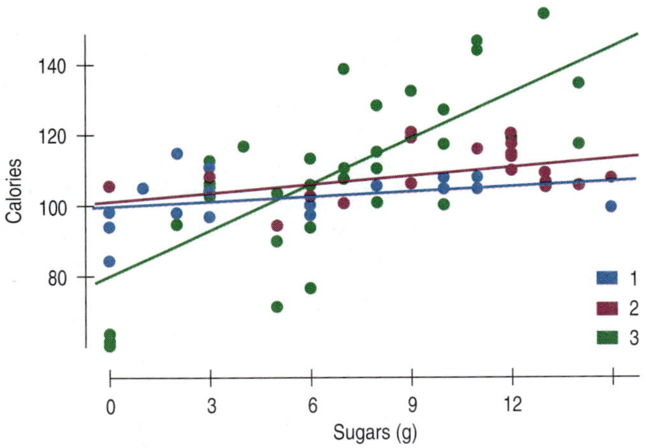

Should we take this extra information into account in our analysis? Figure 9.3 shows a scatterplot of calories and sugar, colored according to the shelf on which the cereals were found and with a separate regression line fit for each. Now we can see that the top shelf is different. We might want to report two regressions, one for the top shelf and one for the bottom two shelves.

Getting the "Bends"

The fundamental assumption for working with a linear model is that the relationship you are modeling is, in fact, linear. That sounds obvious, but when you fit a regression, you can't take it for granted. Often it's hard to tell from the scatterplot you looked at before you fit the regression model. Sometimes you can't see a bend in the relationship until you plot the residuals.

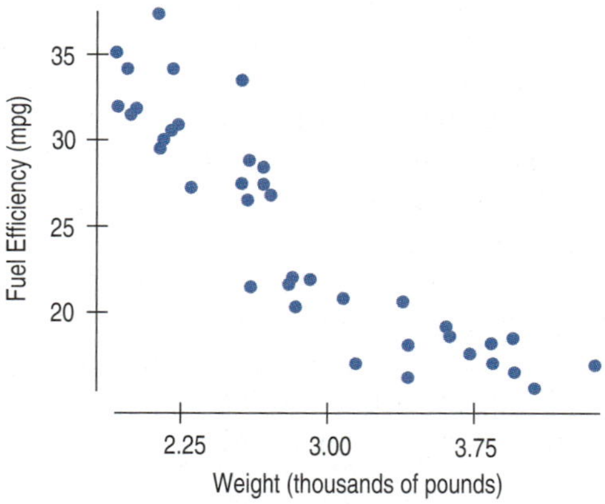

Fuel efficiency (mpg) vs. weight (thousands of pounds) shows a strong, apparently linear, negative trend. **Figure 9.4**

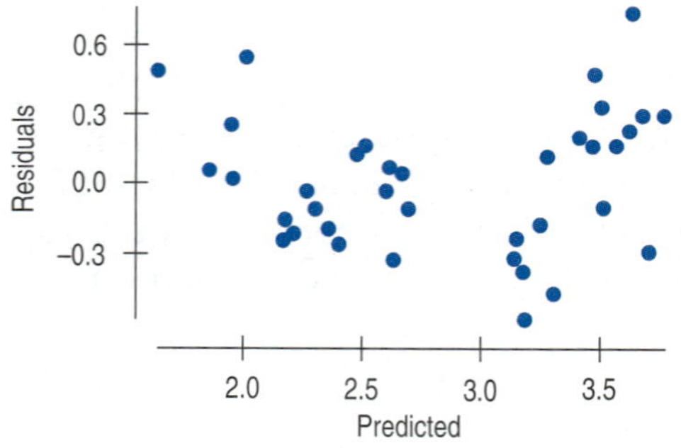

Plotting regression residuals against predicted values reveals a bend. It was in the original plot, but is easier to see here. **Figure 9.5**

Here are the weights (in thousands of pounds) and fuel efficiencies (measured in miles per gallon) of 38 cars. We know, from common sense and from physics, that heavier cars generally need more fuel to move. The scatterplot looks sort of linear with a moderately strong negative association (R^2 = 81.6%). The linear regression equation

$$\widehat{mpg} = 48.7 - 8.4\, weight$$

says that fuel efficiency drops by 8.4 mpg per 1000 pounds of weight, starting from a value of 48.7 mpg (presumably for a weightless car).

The scatterplot of the residuals against the predicted values holds a surprise. This plot should have no pattern. Instead, there's a bend, starting high on the left, dropping down in the middle of the display, and then rising again at the right. Graphs of residuals often reveal patterns such as this that were hard to see in the original scatterplot.

Look back at the original scatterplot. The scatter of points isn't really straight. There's a slight bend to the plot, but the bend is much easier to see in the residuals. Even though it means checking the straight enough condition *after* we find the regression, it's always a good idea to plot the residuals.

Extrapolation: Reaching Beyond the Data

Linear models give a predicted value for each case in the data. Put a new x-value into the equation and it gives a predicted value, $\hat{y}$, to go with it. But when the new x-value lies far from the data we used to build the regression, how trustworthy is the prediction?

The simple answer is that the farther the new x-value is from $\bar{x}$, the less trust we should place in the predicted value. Once we venture into new x territory, such a prediction is called an **extrapolation.** Extrapolations are dubious because they require the additional—and very questionable—assumption that nothing about the relationship between x and y changes even at extreme values of x.

Extrapolations can get you into deep trouble. The U.S. Census Bureau reports the median age at first marriage for men and women. Here's a regression of age at first marriage for men against year of the century (1900 is 0) for selected years reported on for the first part of the 20th century, 1900 to 1940:

R-squared = 92.6%
s = 0.2417

Variable	Coefficient
Constant	25.7
Year	−0.04

The regression equation is

$$\widehat{age} = 25.7 - 0.04\ year.$$

The slope of −0.04 years of age per year of the century shows that first marriage age for men was falling at a rate of about 4 years per century. That is, men were getting married for the first time at younger and younger ages. In these data, the intercept can be interpreted as the predicted mean age of men at first marriage in 1900 (year 0). The high R^2 suggests a strong linear pattern. Can we extrapolate?

When *year* counts from 0 in 1900, the year 2000 is "100." Substituting 100 for year, we find that the model predicts a first marriage age of $25.7 - 0.04 \times 100 = 21.7$ years old. In fact, though, by the year 2000, the median age at first marriage for men was almost 27 years. What's gone wrong?

Here's a scatterplot of the mean age at first marriage for men for the *entire* 20th century:

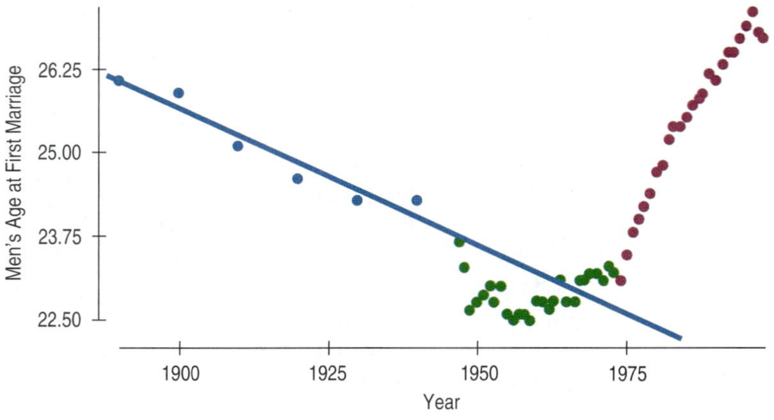

Mean age at first marriage (years of age) for men in the United States vs. year. The regression line is fit only to the first 4 decades of the 20th century, which looked nicely linear. But the linear pattern could not have continued, and in fact it changed in direction, steepness, and strength. **Figure 9.6**

Now we can see why the extrapolation failed. Although the trend in age at first marriage was linear for parts of the century, it did not follow the same linear pattern over the entire century.

Predicting the Future

"Prediction is difficult, especially about the future."
—Niels Bohr, Danish physicist

Extrapolation is always dangerous. But when, as in the marriage age predictions, the *x*-variable in a linear model is *time,* extrapolation becomes an attempt to peer into the future. People have always wanted to see into the future. We can foresee that they will always want to see into the future. In the past, seers, oracles, and wizards were called on to predict the future, and mediums, fortune-tellers, and Tarot card readers still find many customers. The clever ones usually phrase their predictions ambiguously in such a way that they can claim to be right no matter how things actually turn out.

Those with a more scientific turn of mind may spurn such methods—and then turn around and use a linear model based on time to predict into the future. That's just using a digital crystal ball. Linear models are based on the *x*-values of the data at hand and cannot be trusted beyond that span. Some phenomena do exhibit a kind of "inertia" that allows us to guess that current systematic behavior will continue outside this range. When *x* is time, though, you should be especially wary. Such regularity can't be counted on in phenomena such as stock prices, sales figures, hurricane tracks, or public opinion.

Extrapolating from current trends is a mistake made not only by regression beginners or the naïve. Professional forecasters are prone to the same mistakes, and sometimes the errors are striking. In the mid 1970s, in the midst of an energy crisis, oil prices surged and long lines at gas stations were common. In 1970, oil cost about $3 a barrel. A few years later it had surged to $15. In 1975, a survey of 15 top econometric forecasting models (built by groups that included Nobel prize–winning economists) found predictions for 1985 oil prices that ranged from $50 to $200 a barrel (in 1975 dollars). How close were these forecasts? Well, oil prices were actually *lower* in 1985 than in 1975, after accounting for inflation. No one predicted that. No one. The forecasts had all been made *assuming* oil prices would continue to rise at the same rate or even faster. By the year 2000, oil prices averaged about $7 a barrel in 1975 dollars ($28 a barrel in 2000 dollars).

Of course, knowing that extrapolation is dangerous doesn't stop people. The temptation to see into the future is hard to resist. So our more realistic advice is this:

If you must extrapolate into the future, at least don't believe that the prediction will come true.

Outliers

The outcome of the year 2000 U.S. presidential election was determined in Florida amid much controversy. The main race was between George W. Bush and Al Gore, but two minor candidates played a significant role. To the political right of the main party candidates was Pat Buchanan, while to the political left could be found Ralph Nader. Generally, Nader earned more votes than Buchanan throughout the state. We would expect counties with larger vote totals to give more votes to each candidate. Here's a regression relating Buchanan's vote totals by county in the state of Florida to Nader's:

Dependent variable is: Buchanan vote
R-squared = 42.8%
s = 343.0

Variable	**Coefficient**
Constant	50.3
Nader vote	0.14

The regression model,

$$\widehat{Buchanan} = 50.3 + 0.14\ Nader,$$

says that in each county, Buchanan received about 0.14 times (or 14% of) the vote Nader received, starting from a base of 50.3 votes.

This seems like a reasonable regression with an R^2 of almost 43%. But we've violated all three Laws of Data Analysis by going straight to the regression table without making a picture.

Here's a scatterplot that shows the vote for Buchanan in each county of Florida plotted against the vote for Nader. The outlying point is Palm Beach County.

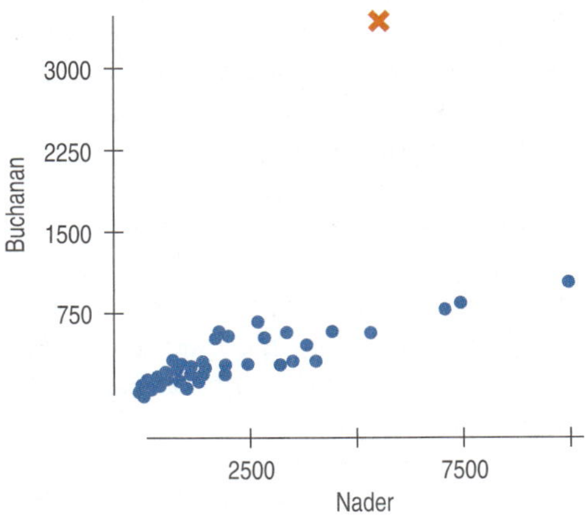

Votes received by Buchanan against votes for Nader in all Florida counties in the presidential election of 2000. The red "x" point is Palm Beach County, home of the "butterfly ballot." **Figure 9.7**

The so-called "butterfly ballot," used only in Palm Beach County, was a source of controversy. It has been claimed that the format of this ballot confused voters so that some who intended to vote for the Democrat, Al Gore, punched the wrong hole next to his name and, as a result, voted for Buchanan.

The scatterplot shows a strong, positive, linear association, and one striking point. With Palm Beach removed from the regression, the R^2 jumps from 42.8% to 82.1% and the slope of the line changes to 0.1, suggesting that Buchanan received only about 10% of the vote that Nader received. With more than 82% of the variability of the Buchanan vote accounted for, the model when Palm Beach is omitted certainly fits better. Palm Beach County now stands out, not as a Buchanan stronghold, but rather as a clear violation of the model that begs for explanation.

"Nature is no where accustomed more openly to display her secret mysteries than in cases where she shows traces of her workings apart from the beaten path."
—William Harvey (1657)

Outlying points can strongly influence a regression. Even a single point far from the body of the data can dominate the analysis. Points can be outliers because their x-value is extraordinary, because their y-value is extraordinary, or because they deviate from the regression model. A point can stand away from the regression model without being an outlier in either x or y. Any point that stands away from the others can be called an **outlier** and deserves your special attention. We sometimes speak of x-outliers, y-outliers, and *model* outliers as a shorthand way of emphasizing how a point is extraordinary, but in real data, it's not always clear that a particular point falls in one or another of these categories.

The Palm Beach County data point is an outlier in y because the Buchanan vote is far greater than for any other county. It's also a model outlier because it is far from the regression line. Model outliers are usually easy to see in a scatterplot of the residuals against either x or predicted values. That's another reason to never consider a regression analysis complete until a scatterplot of the residuals against the predicted values has been made and looked at. As with this example, removing a model outlier usually increases the R^2.

"For whoever knows the ways of Nature will more easily notice her deviations; and, on the other hand, whoever knows her deviations will more accurately describe her ways."
—Francis Bacon (1561–1626)

Whenever you have—or suspect that you have—model outliers, you should fit the linear model to the *other* points alone and then compare the resulting regression models to understand how the outlying points affect the model. On one hand, a model dominated by a single point is unlikely to be useful for understanding the rest of the cases. On the other hand, the best way to understand outliers is against the background of the model established by the other data values. (That insight's at least 400 years old. See the sidebar.) But don't give into the temptation to simply delete points that don't fit the line without examining and discussing them. Outliers—and especially model outliers—often tell us more about the data and the model than any other points. Arbitrarily deleting outliers will artificially inflate the R^2 and give a false sense of how well the model fits the data.

Points that are extraordinary in their x-value can especially influence a regression model. We say that they have high **leverage.** The physical image of a lever is exactly right. We know the line must pass through $(\bar{x}, \bar{y})$, so you can picture that point as the fulcrum of the lever. Just as sitting farther from the hinge on a see-saw gives you more leverage to pull it your way, points with values far from the mean of x pull more strongly on the regression line.

When a point with high leverage lines up with the rest of the data, it doesn't influence the slope but it does increase the R^2. Removing a point that is an x-outlier (high leverage) but not a model outlier can actually *decrease* your R^2. But even a single high-leverage point that's also a model outlier can change the regression model radically.

George W. Bush won Florida (and thus the presidency) by only a few hundred votes, so the Palm Beach County residual is big enough to be meaningful. Most outliers don't determine a presidency, but all are worth examining and trying to understand. When we investigate an outlier, we often learn more about the situation than we could have learned from the model alone.

Influential Points

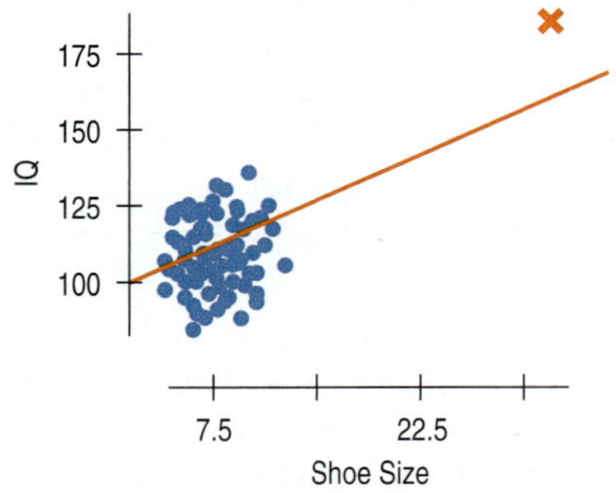

Bozo's extraordinarily large shoes give his data point high leverage in the regression. Wherever Bozo's IQ falls, the regression line will follow. **Figure 9.8**

High leverage points that are also model outliers can have a shocking effect on the regression. Here's a plot of IQ against shoe size again from the fanciful study of intelligence and foot size in comedians we saw in Chapter 7. The linear regression output shows:

Dependent variable is: IQ
R-squared = 24.8%

Variable	**Coefficient**
Constant	93.3265
Shoe size	2.08318

Although this is a silly example, it illustrates an important and common potential problem. Almost all of the variance accounted for (R^2 = 24.8%) is due to *one* point, namely, Bozo. Without Bozo, there is little correlation between shoe size and IQ. Look what happens to the regression when we take him out:

Response variable is: IQ
R-squared = 0.7%

Variable	**Coefficient**
Constant	105.458
Shoe size	0.460194

The R^2 value is now 0.7%—a very weak linear relationship (as one might expect!). One single point exhibits a great influence on the regression analysis.

What would have happened if Bozo hadn't shown his comic genius on IQ tests? Suppose his measured IQ had been only 50. The slope of the line drops from 0.96 points/shoe size to −0.69 points/shoe size. No matter where Bozo's IQ is, the line tends to follow it because his shoe size, being so far from the mean shoe size, makes this a high leverage point.

You can often see high leverage points best in the original scatterplot of the data. But it isn't always clear what to do with them. Sometimes these are data values that you had to work hard to get, and they may say more about the relationship between y and x than any of the other data values. At other times, high leverage points are values that really don't belong with the rest of the data. Such points should probably be omitted, and a linear model found without them for comparison. The situation may lie between these two extremes. A data value may be far from the other x-values, and therefore a point with high leverage, but it may not be clear whether it belongs. When it doubt, it's usually best to perform and compare the two regressions.

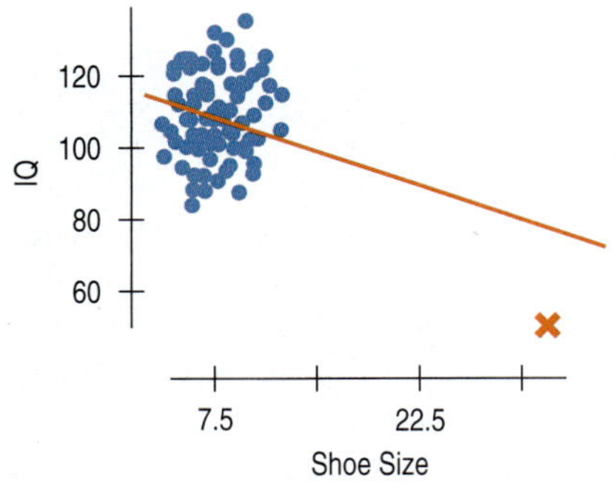

If Bozo's IQ were low, the regression slope would change from positive to negative. A single influential point can change a regression model drastically. **Figure 9.9**

Warning:

Influential points can hide in plots of residuals. Points with high leverage pull the line close to them, so they often have small residuals. You'll see influential points more easily in scatterplots of the original data or by finding a regression model with and without the points.

Lurking Variables and Causation

One common way to interpret a regression slope is to say that "a change of 1 unit in *x* *results* in a change of b_1 units in *y*." This way of saying things encourages causal thinking. Beware.

In Chapter 7, we tried to make it clear that no matter how strong the correlation is between two variables, there's no simple way to show that one variable causes the other. Putting a regression line through a cloud of points just increases the temptation to think and to say that the *x*-variable *causes* the *y*-variable. Just to make sure, let's repeat the point again. No matter how strong the association, no matter how large the R^2 value, no matter how straight the line, there is no way to conclude from a regression alone that one variable *causes* the other. There's always the possibility that some third variable is driving both of the variables you have observed. With observational data, as opposed to data from a designed experiment, there is no way to be sure that a **lurking variable** is not the cause of any apparent association.

Here's an example. The scatterplot shows the life expectancy (average between men and women, in years) for each of 41 countries of the world, plotted against the square root of the number of doctors per person in the country. (We've taken the square root to make the relationship linear. It's not a big deal. Without the re-expression, the plot is too curved to fit a straight line. The square root is not the point. The point is that life expectancy goes up with availability of doctors. You can learn more about re-expression in regression in more detail in the next chapter.)

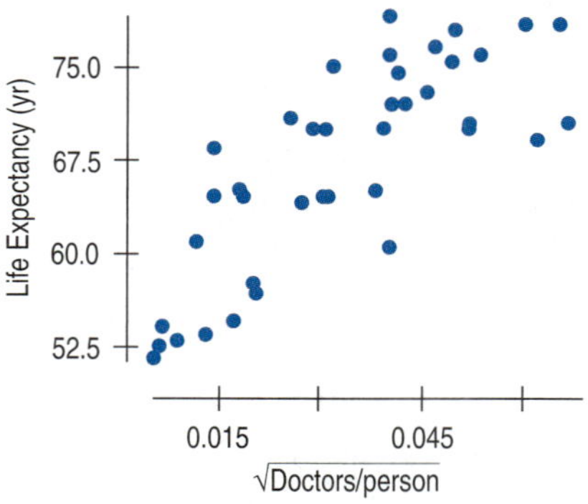

The relationship between life expectancy (years) and availability of doctors (measured as $\sqrt{\text{doctors per person}}$) for countries of the world shows a strong, positive, linear association. **Figure 9.10**

The strong positive association ($r = 0.79$; $R^2 = 62.4\%$) seems to confirm our expectation that more doctors per person improves healthcare, leading to longer lifetimes and a larger life expectancy. The strength of the association would *seem* to argue that we should send more doctors to developing countries to increase life expectancy.

That conclusion is about the consequences of a change. If we increase the number of doctors, should we predict that the life expectancy will increase? This is a *causal* explanation, arguing that adding doctors *causes* greater life expectancy. But these are observed data. Could there be another explanation of the association?

Let's consider another variable. Here's a very similar-looking scatterplot, again with life expectancy as the *y*-variable, but this time the *x*-variable is the square root of the number of televisions per person in each country. The positive association shown in this scatterplot is even *stronger* than the association in the previous plot ($r = 0.85$; $R^2 = 72.3\%$). We can fit the linear model, and quite possibly use the number of TVs as a way to predict life expectancy. Should we conclude, however, that increasing the number of TVs actually extends lifetimes? If so, we should send TVs instead of doctors to developing countries.

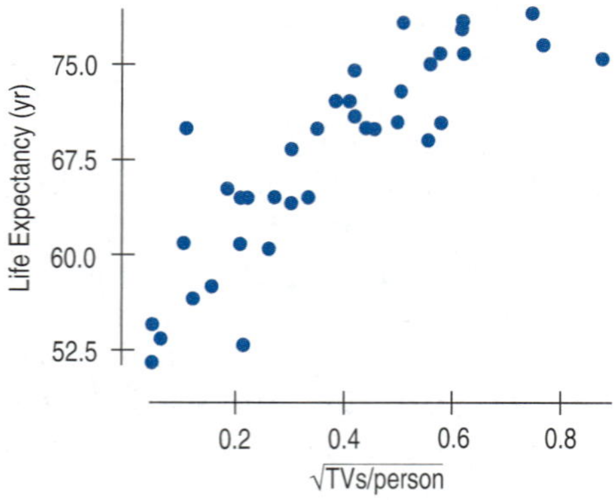

To increase life expectancy, don't send doctors, send TVs; they're cheaper and more fun. Or maybe that's not the right interpretation of this scatterplot of life expectancy against availability of TVs (as $\sqrt{\text{TVs per capita}}$). **Figure 9.11**

Not only is the correlation with life expectancy higher, but TVs are much cheaper than doctors.

What's wrong with this reasoning? Maybe we were a bit hasty earlier when we concluded that doctors *cause* longer lives. Maybe there's a lurking variable here. Countries with higher standards of living have both longer life expectancies *and* more doctors. Could higher living standards *cause* the other variables? If so, then improving living standards might be expected to prolong lives, increase the number of doctors, and increase the number of TVs.

From this example, you can see how easy it is to fall into the trap of mistakenly inferring causality from a regression. For all we know, doctors (or TVs!) *do* increase life expectancy. But we can't tell that from these data no matter how much we'd like to. Resist the temptation to conclude that x causes y from a regression, no matter how obvious that conclusion seems to you.

Working with Summary Values

Scatterplots of statistics summarized over groups tend to show less variability than we would see if we measured the same variable on individuals. This is because the summary statistics themselves vary less than the data on the individuals do, a fact we will make more specific in coming chapters.

In Chapter 7 we looked at the heights and weights of individual students. There we saw a correlation of 0.644, so R^2 is 41.5%.

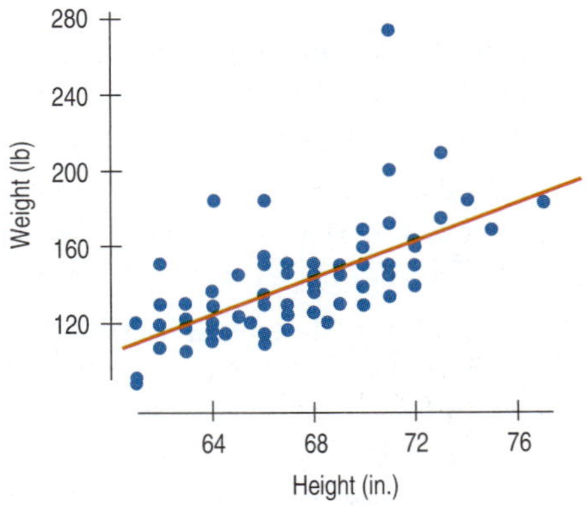

Weight (lb) against height (in.) for a sample of men. There's a strong, positive, linear association. **Figure 9.12**

Suppose, instead of data on individuals, we had been given only the mean weight for each height value. The scatterplot of mean weight by height would show less scatter. And the R^2 would increase to 80.1%.

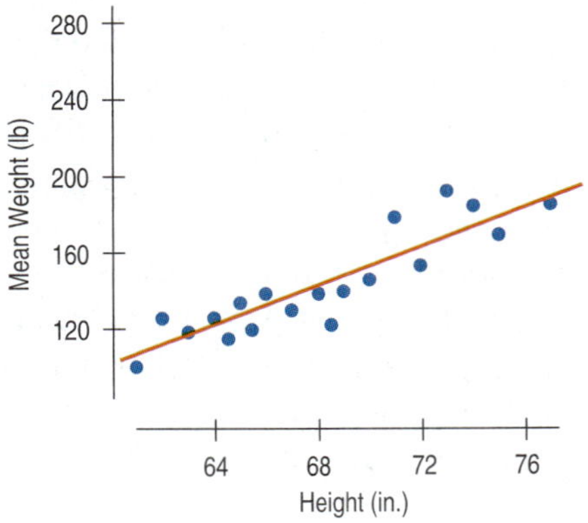

Mean weight (lb) shows a stronger linear association with height than do the weights of individuals. Means vary less than individual values. **Figure 9.13**

Scatterplots of summary statistics show less scatter than the baseline data on individuals, and can give a false impression of how well a line summarizes the data. There's no simple correction for this phenomenon. Once we're given summary data, there's no simple way to get the original values back.

In the life expectancy and TVs example, we have no good measure of exposure to doctors or to TV on an individual basis. But if we did, we should expect the scatterplot to show more variability and the corresponding R^2 to be smaller. The bottom line is that you should be a bit suspicious of conclusions based on regressions of summary data. They may look better than they really are.

What Can Go Wrong?

This entire chapter has held warnings about things that can go wrong in a regression analysis. So let's just recap. When you make a linear model:

- ***Make sure the relationship is straight.*** Check the straight enough condition. Always examine the residuals, and pay special attention to the most extreme residuals because they may have something to add to the story told by the linear model. Check the residuals for evidence that the linearity condition has failed. It's often easier to see deviations from a straight line in the residual plot than in the scatterplot of the original data.
- ***Beware of extrapolating.*** Beware of extrapolation beyond the x-values that were used to fit the model. Although it's common to use linear models to extrapolate, the practice is dangerous.
- ***Beware especially of extrapolating into the future!*** Be especially cautious about extrapolating into the future with linear models in which the x-variable is time. Predicting the future is particularly tempting and particularly dangerous.
- ***Be on guard for different groups in your regression.*** Check for evidence that the data consist of separate subsets. If you find subsets that behave differently, consider fitting a different linear model to each subset.
- ***Look for outliers.*** Outliers are special points that always deserve attention and that may well reveal more about your data than the rest of the points combined. Always look for them and try to understand why they stand apart. A scatterplot of the data is a good way to see outliers in y and x. A scatterplot of the residuals against the predicted values is a good tool for finding model outliers.
- ***Beware of high leverage points, and especially of those that are influential.*** High leverage points (x-outliers) that are also model outliers can alter the regression model a great deal. The resulting model may say more about one or two points than about the overall relationship.
- ***Consider comparing two regressions.*** To see the impact on a regression of outliers, it's often wise to run two regressions, one with and one without the extraordinary points and then to discuss the differences.
- ***Treat outliers honestly.*** If you remove enough carefully selected points, you can always get a regression with a high R^2, eventually. But it won't give you much understanding. Some data are just not simple enough for a linear model to fit very well. When that happens, report the failure and stop.
- ***Beware of lurking variables.*** Think about lurking variables before interpreting a linear model. It's particularly tempting to explain a strong regression by thinking that the x-variable *causes* the y-variable. A linear model fitted to

observational data can never demonstrate such causation, in part because it cannot eliminate the chance that a lurking variable has caused the variation in both *x* and *y*.

- ***Watch out when dealing with data that are summaries.*** Be cautious in working with data values that are themselves summaries, such as means or medians. Summary statistics are less variable than the raw data on which they are based, so they tend to inflate the impression of the strength of a relationship.

Regression Diagnosis and the Computer

Most Statistics technology offers simple ways to check whether your data satisfy the conditions for regression. We have already seen that these programs can make a simple scatterplot. They can also help us check the assumptions; we do that best by plotting residuals.

Connections

We are always alert to things that can go wrong if we use statistics without thinking carefully. Regression opens new vistas of potential problems. But each one relates to issues we've thought about before.

It is always important that our data be from a single homogeneous group and not made up of disparate groups. We looked for multiple modes in single variables. Now we check scatterplots for evidence of subgroups in our data. As with modes, it's often best to split the data and analyze the groups separately.

Our concern with outliers and their potential influence also harks back to our earlier concern with outliers in histograms and boxplots. And for many of the same reasons. As we've seen here, regression offers outliers new scope for mischief.

The risks of interpreting linear models as causal or predictive arose in Chapters 7 and 8. And they're important enough to mention again in later chapters.

Key Concepts

Subset One unstated condition for finding a linear model is that the data be homogeneous. If, instead, the data consist of two or more groups that have been thrown together, it is usually best to fit different linear models to each group than to try to fit a single model to all of the data. Displays of the residuals can often help you find subsets in the data.

Extrapolation Although linear models provide an easy way to predict values of *y* for a given value of *x*, it is unsafe to predict for values of *x* far from the ones used to find the linear model equation. Such extrapolation may pretend to see into the future, but the predictions should not be trusted.

Outlier Any data point that stands away from the others can be called an outlier. In regression, outliers can be extraordinary in *x*, in *y*, and in failing to fit the model.

Leverage Data points that are outliers in *x* because their *x*-value is far from the mean of *x* are said to exert leverage on a linear model. High leverage points pull the line close to them, and so they can have a large effect on the line, sometimes completely determining the slope and intercept.

Influential point A point that has high leverage and is also a model outlier is called an influential point. Omitting an influential point from the data usually results in a very different regression model.

Lurking variable A variable that is not explicitly part of a model but affects the way the variable in the model appears to be related is called a lurking variable. Because we can never be certain that observational data are not hiding a lurking variable that influences both *x* and *y*, it is never safe to conclude that a linear model demonstrates a causal relationship, no matter how strong the linear association.

Skills

When you complete this lesson you should:

Think

- Understand that we cannot fit linear models or use linear regression if the underlying relationship between the variables is not itself linear.
- Understand that data used to find a model must be homogeneous. Look for subgroups in data before you find a regression, and analyze each separately.
- Know the danger of extrapolating beyond the range of the *x*-values used to find the linear model, and especially when the extrapolation tries to predict into the future.
- Understand that outliers can be in the *x* or *y* direction, and can also be deviations from the regression model. Understand that points that are outliers in different ways can have different effects on the regression model.
- Look for lurking variables whenever considering the association between two variables. Understand that a strong association does not mean that the variables are causally related.

Show

- Know how to display residuals from a linear model by making a scatterplot of residuals against predicted values or against the *x*-variable, and know what patterns to look for in the picture.
- Know how to look for outliers in a regression by examining a scatterplot of the data, and how to look for model outliers by examining a scatterplot of the residuals against the predicted values. Understand how removing outliers can affect the regression model.
- Know how to look for high leverage points by examining the distribution of the *x*-values or by recognizing them in a scatterplot of the data, and understand how they can affect a linear model.

Tell

- Include diagnostic information as part of your report of a regression.
- Report any high leverage points.
- Report any outliers. Consider reporting analyses with and without outliers included to assess their influence on the regression.

- Include appropriate cautions about extrapolation when reporting predictions from a linear model.
- Discuss any possible lurking variables.

Exercises

1. Marriage age. We've looked at the ages of men at first marriage. How about women? Is there evidence that the age at which women get married has changed over the past 100 years? The scatterplot shows the trend in age at first marriage for American women.

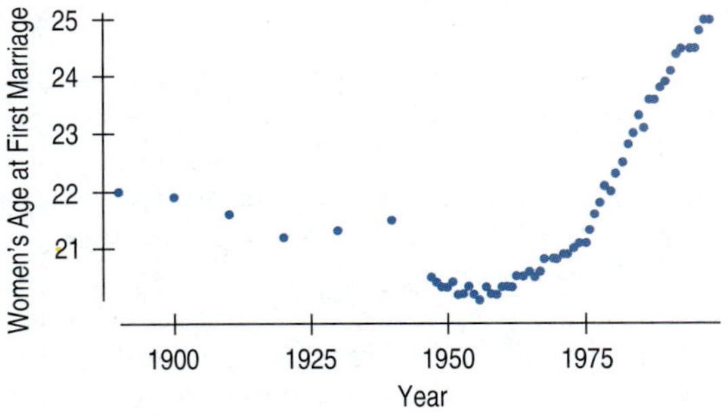

a) Do you think there is a clear pattern? Describe the trend.
b) Is the association strong?
c) Is the correlation high? Explain.
d) Do you think a linear model is appropriate for these data? Explain.

2. Ages of couples. The graph shows the ages of both men and women at first marriage.

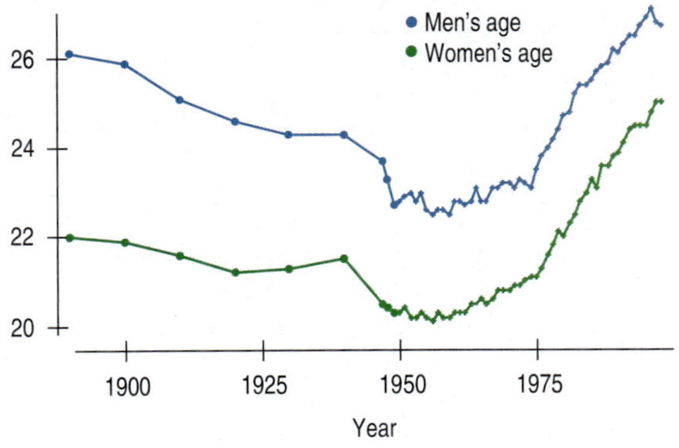

Clearly, the pattern for men is very similar to the pattern for women. But are the two lines getting closer together?

Here's a timeplot showing the *difference* in average age (men's age − women's age) at first marriage, the regression analysis, and the associated residuals plot.

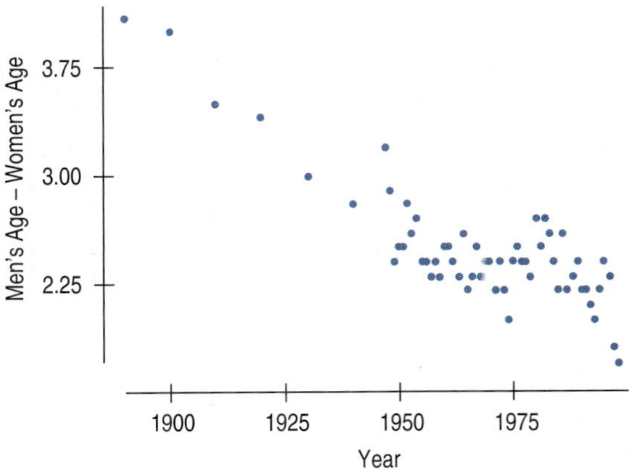

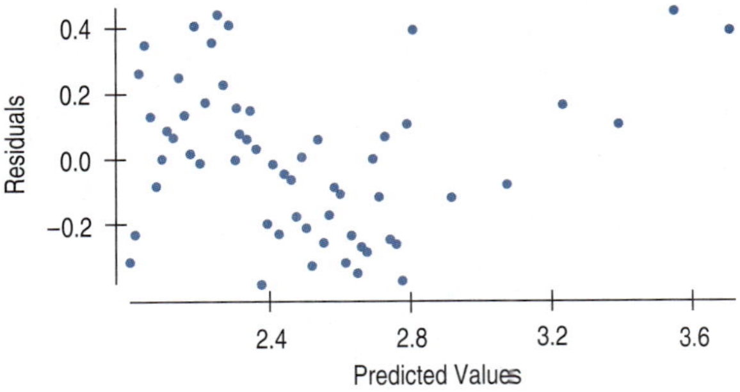

Dependent variable is: Men − Women
R-squared = 71.6%

Variable	Coefficient	SE(Coeff)
Constant	33.4830	2.606
Year	−0.015756	0.0013

a) What is the correlation between age difference and year?
b) Interpret the slope of this line.
c) Predict the average age difference in 2010.
d) Describe reasons why you might not place much faith in that prediction.

3. Marriage age revisited. Suppose you wanted to predict the trend in marriage age for American women into the early part of this century.

a) How could you use the data graphed in Exercise 1 to get a good prediction? Marriage ages in selected years starting in 1900 are listed below. Use all or part of these data to create an appropriate model for predicting the average age at which women will first marry in 2005.

1900–1940 (10-yr intervals): 21.9, 21.6, 21.2, 21.3, 21.5, 20.3
1955–1995 (5-yr intervals): 20.2, 20.2, 20.6, 20.8, 21.1, 22.0, 23.3, 23.9, 24.5

b) How much faith do you place in this prediction? Explain.
c) Do you think your model would produce an accurate prediction about your grandchildren, say, 50 years from now? Explain.

4. Ages of couples, again. Is the trend of decreasing difference in age at first marriage seen in Exercise 2 stronger recently? Here are the scatterplot and residual plot for all the data, and a regression analysis using only the data from 1975 through 1998.

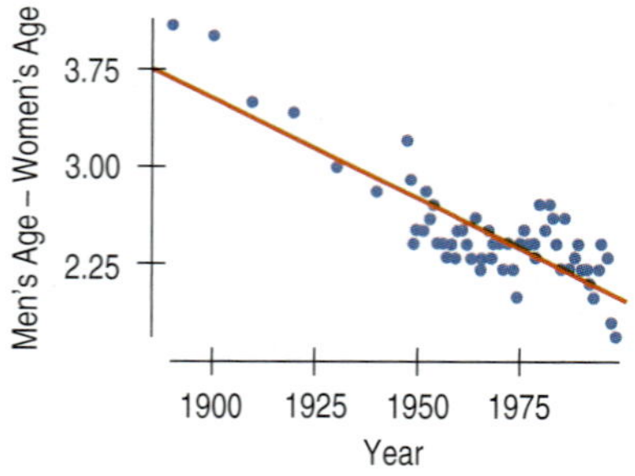

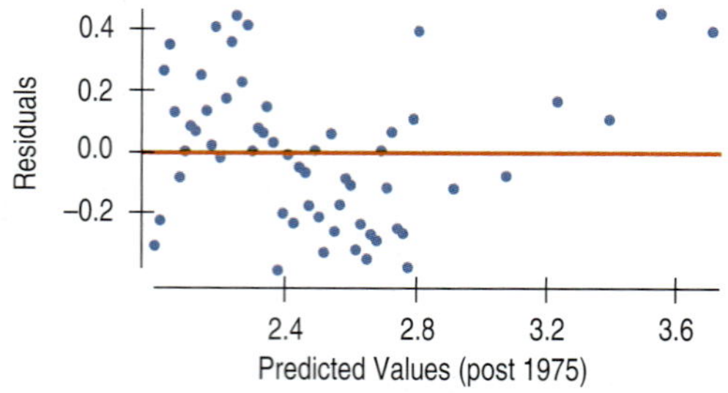

Dependent variable is: Men – Women
Cases selected according to post75
R-squared = 46.3%

Variable	Coefficient	SE(Coeff)
Constant	49.9021	10.93
Year	−0.023957	0.0055

a) Why is R^2 higher for the first model (in Exercise 2)?
b) Is the new linear model appropriate for the post-1975 data? Explain.
c) What does the slope say about marriage ages since 1975?
d) Explain why it's not reasonable to interpret the y-intercept.

5. Good model? In justifying his choice of a model, a student wrote, "I know this is the correct model because $R^2 = 99.4\%$."

a) Is this reasoning correct? Explain.
b) Does this model allow the student to make accurate predictions? Explain.

6. Bad model? A student who has created a linear model is disappointed to find that her R^2 value is a very low 13%.

c) Does this mean that a linear model is not appropriate? Explain.
d) Does this model allow the student to make accurate predictions? Explain.

7. Reading. To measure progress in reading ability, students at an elementary school take a reading comprehension test every year. Scores are measured in "grade level" units; that is, a score of 4.2 means that a student is reading at slightly above the expected level for a fourth grader. The school principal prepares a report to parents that includes a graph showing the mean reading score for each grade. In his comments he points out that the strong positive trend demonstrates the success of the school's reading program.

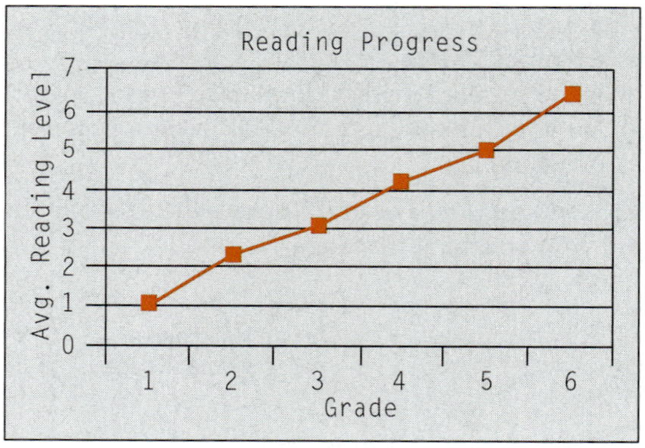

a) Does this graph indicate that students are making satisfactory progress in reading? Explain.
b) What would you estimate the correlation between grade and average reading level to be?
c) If, instead of this plot showing average reading levels, the principal had produced a scatterplot of the reading levels for all the individual students, would you expect the correlation to be the same, higher, or lower? Explain.

d) While the principal did not do a regression analysis, someone as statistically astute as you might do that. (But don't bother.) What value of the slope of that line would you view as demonstrating acceptable progress in reading comprehension? Explain.

8. Grades. A college admissions officer, defending the college's use of SAT scores in the admissions process, produced the graph below. It shows the mean GPAs for last year's freshmen, grouped by SAT scores. How strong is the evidence that SAT score is a good predictor of GPA? What concerns you about the graph, the statistical methodology, or the conclusions reached?

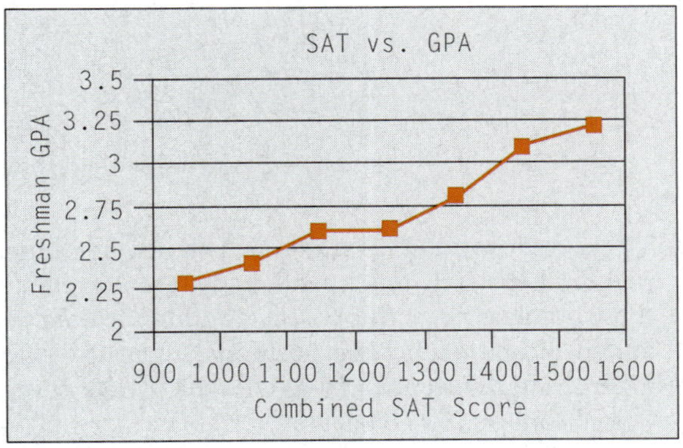

9. Heating. After keeping track of his heating expenses for several winters, a homeowner believes he can estimate the monthly cost C from the average daily Fahrenheit temperature using the model $\hat{C} = 133 - 2.13\ temp$. The residuals plot for his data is shown.

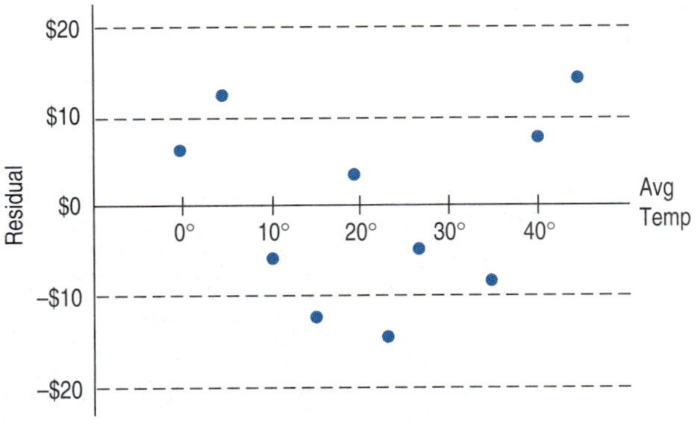

a) Interpret the slope of the line in this context.
b) Interpret the y-intercept of the line in this context.
c) During months when the temperature stays around freezing, would you expect cost predictions based on this model to be accurate, too low, or too high? Explain.
d) What heating cost does the model predict for a month that averages 10°?
e) During one of the months on which the model was based, the temperature did average 10°. What were the actual heating costs for that month?

f) Do you think the homeowner should use this model? Explain.
g) Would this model be more successful if created using degrees Celsius? Explain.

10. Speed. How does the speed at which you drive impact your fuel economy? To find out, researchers drove a compact car for 200 miles at speeds ranging from 35 to 75 miles per hour. From their data they created the model $\widehat{mpg} = 32 - 0.1\ mph$ and created this residuals plot:

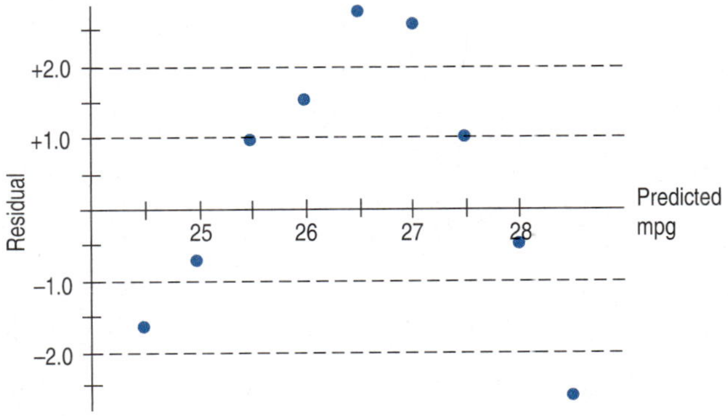

a) Interpret the slope of this line in context.
b) Explain why it's silly to attach any meaning to the y-intercept.
c) When this model predicts high gas mileage, what can you say about those predictions?
d) What gas mileage does the model predict when the car is driven at 50 mph?
e) What was the actual gas mileage when the car was driven at 45 mph?
f) Do you think there appears to be a strong association between speed and fuel economy? Explain.
g) Do you think this is the appropriate model for that association? Explain.

11. Unusual points. Each of the scatterplots below shows a cluster of points and one "stray" point. For each, answer these questions:
1) Do you think that point is an outlier?
2) Do you think that point is an influential point?
3) If that point were removed from the data, would the correlation become stronger or weaker? Explain.
4) If that point were removed from the data, would the slope of the regression line increase or decrease? Explain.

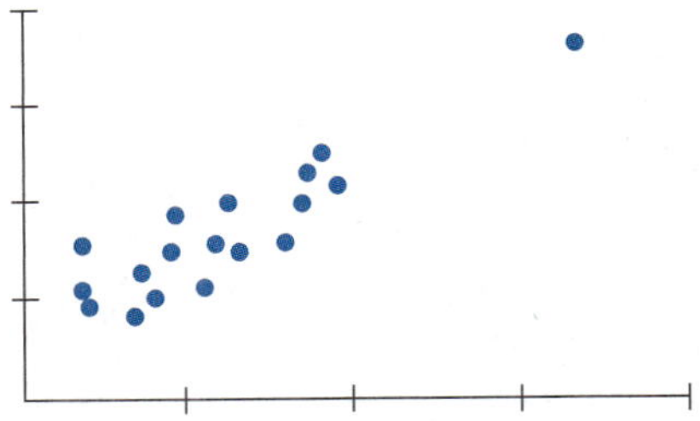

a)

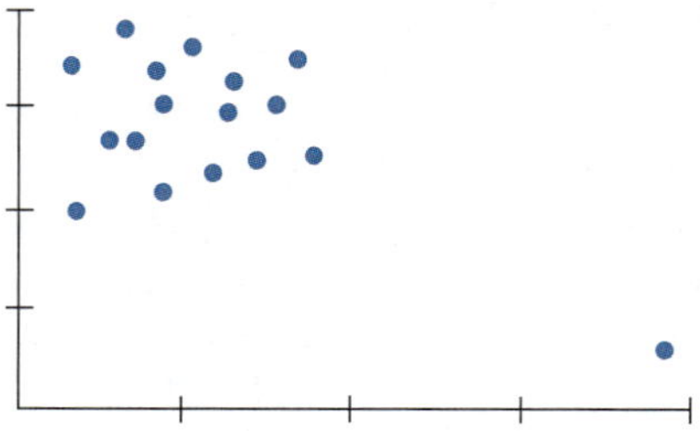

b)

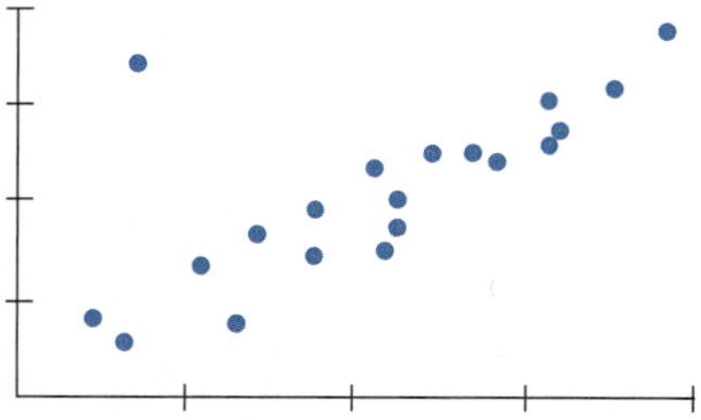

c)

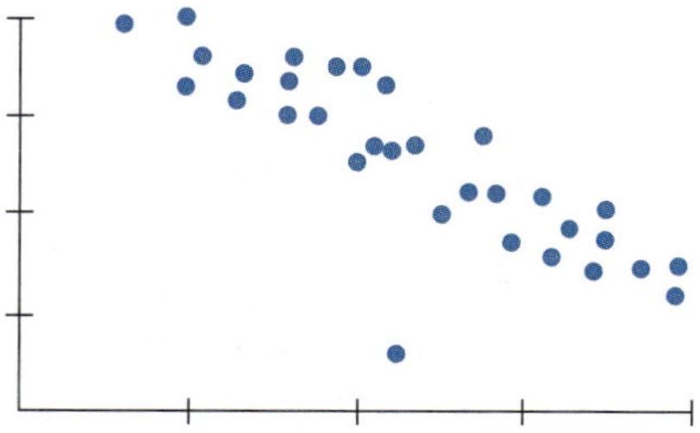

d)

12. More unusual points. Each of the scatterplots below shows a cluster of points and one "stray" point. For each, answer these questions:

1) Do you think that point is an outlier?
2) Do you think that point is an influential point?
3) If that point were removed from the data, would the correlation become stronger or weaker? Explain.
4) If that point were removed from the data, would the slope of the regression line increase or decrease? Explain.

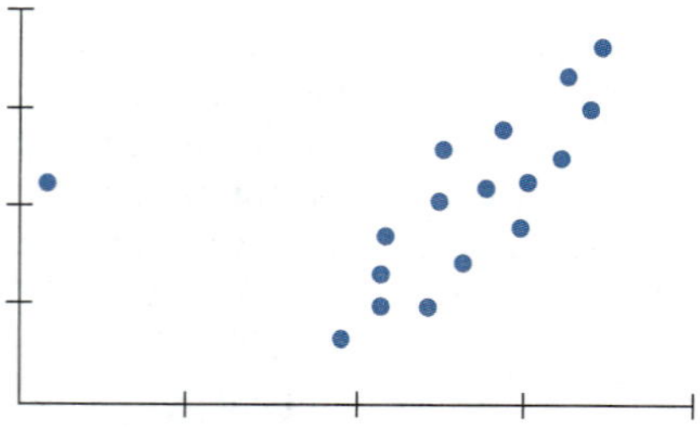

a)

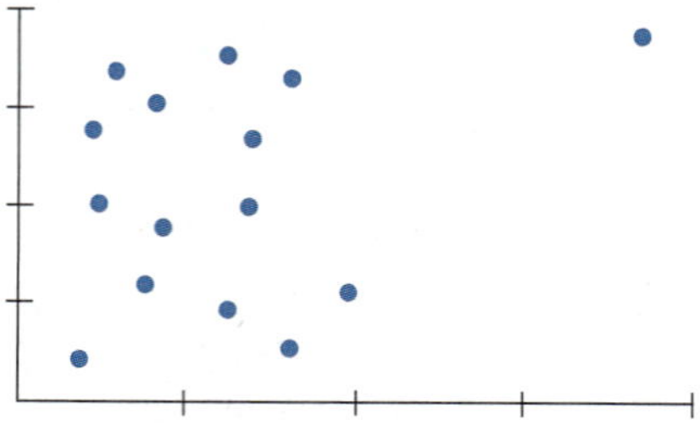

b)

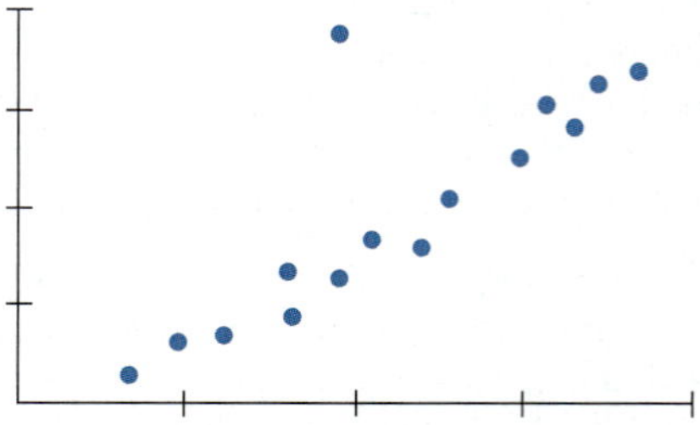

c)

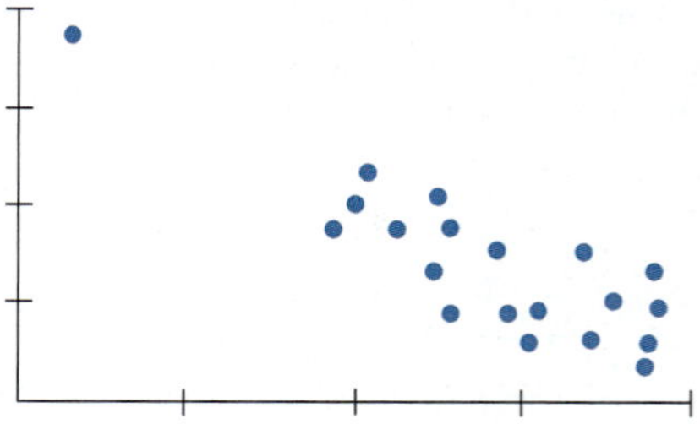

d)

13. The extra point. The scatterplot shows five blue data points at the left. Not surprisingly, the correlation for these points is $r = 0$. Suppose *one* additional data point is added at one of the five positions suggested below in green. Match each point (a–e) with the correct new correlation from the list given.

1) -0.90
2) -0.40
3) 0.00
4) 0.05
5) 0.75

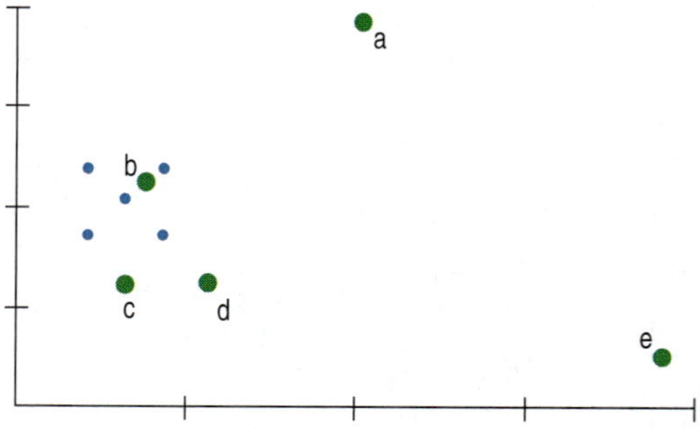

14. The extra point revisited. The original five points in Exercise 13 produce a regression line with slope 0. Match each of the green points (a–e) with the slope of the line after that one point is added.

1) -0.45
2) -0.30
3) 0.00
4) 0.05
5) 0.85

15. Gestation. For women, pregnancy lasts about 9 months. In other species of animals, the length of time from conception to birth varies. Is there any evidence that gestation period is related to the animal's lifespan? The first scatterplot shows gestation period (in days) vs. lifespan (in years) for 18 species of mammals. The highlighted point at the far right represents humans.

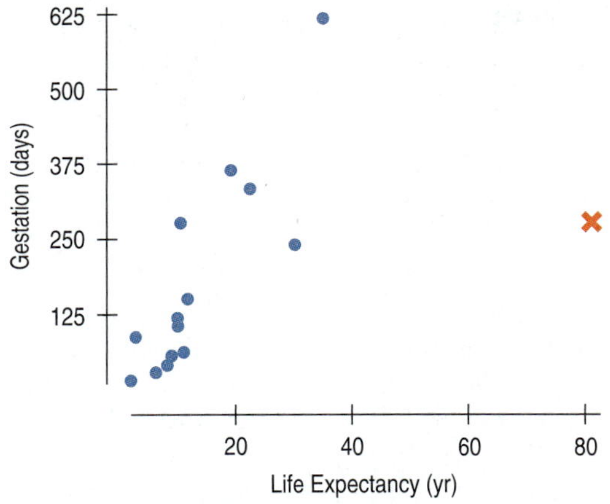

a) For these data $r = 0.54$, not a very strong relationship. Do you think the association would be stronger or weaker if humans were removed? Explain.
b) Is there reasonable justification for removing humans from the data set? Explain.
c) Here are the scatterplot and regression analysis for the 17 nonhuman species. Comment on the strength of the association.

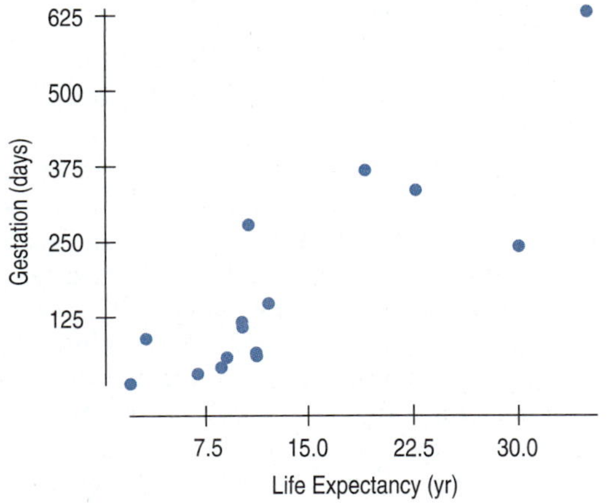

Dependent variable is: Gestation
R-squared = 72.2%

Variable	Coefficient
Constant	−39.5172
LifExp	15.4980

d) Interpret the slope of the line.
e) Some species of monkeys have a life expectancy of about 20 years. Estimate the expected gestation period of one of these monkeys.

16. Elephants and hippos. We removed humans from the scatterplot in Exercise 15 because our species was an outlier in life expectancy. The resulting scatterplot shows two points that now may be of concern. The point in the upper right corner of this scatterplot is for elephants, and the other point at the far right is for hippos.

a) By removing one of these points, we could make the association appear to be stronger. Which point? Explain.
b) Would the slope of the line increase or decrease?
c) Should we just keep removing animals to increase the strength of the model? Explain.
d) If we remove elephants from the scatterplot, the slope of the regression line becomes 11.6 days per year. Do you think elephants were an influential point? Explain.

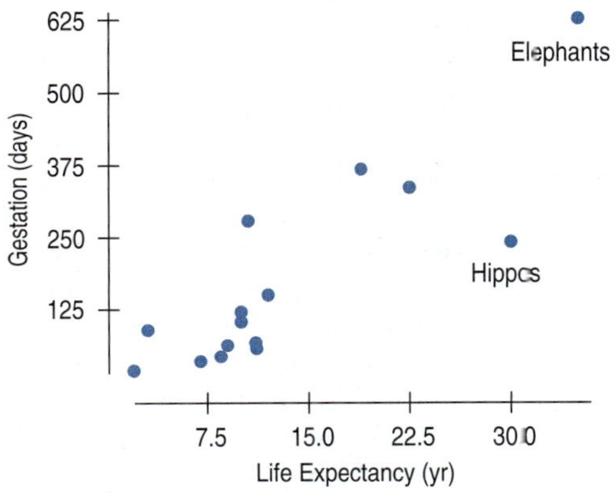

T **17. Law enforcement.** Federal employees with the authority to carry firearms and make arrests are sometimes assaulted, injured, or killed. The table below summarizes the rates of assault and injury (or death) for these employees for 5 years, 1995–1999. Can the assault rate be used to predict injuries or deaths?

Agency	Assaults (per 1000)	Killed or Injured (per 1000)
Bureau of Alcohol, Tobacco, and Firearms (BATF)	31.1	2.2
Capitol Police	5.0	3.6
Customs Service	9.7	5.1
Drug Enforcement Agency (DEA)	17.9	1.1
Federal Bureau of Investigation (FBI)	3.9	1.2
Immigration and Naturalization Service (INS)	14.1	2.5
Internal Revenue Service (IRS)	1.7	0.2
U.S. Marshal Service	9.7	3.0
National Park Service	38.7	15.0
Postal Service	5.7	2.9
Secret Service	9.7	3.0

T **18. Smoking.** The Centers for Disease Control and Prevention track cigarette smoking in the United States. How has the percentage of people who smoke changed since the danger became clear during the last half of the 20th century? The table below shows percentages of smokers among men 18–24 years of age, as estimated by surveys. Create a model to describe the changes in smoking rate. Justify decisions you make in using these data to construct your model.

Year	Percent	Year	Percent
1965	54.1	1992	28.0
1974	42.1	1993	28.8
1979	35.0	1994	29.8
1983	32.9	1995	27.8
1985	28.0	1997	31.7
1990	26.6	1998	31.3

19. Illegitimate births. The National Center for Health Statistics reported the data below, showing the percentage of all births that are to unmarried women for selected years between 1980 and 1998. Create a model that describes this trend. Justify decisions you make about how to best use these data.

Year	1980	1985	1990	1991	1992	1993	1994	1995	1996	1997	1998
%	18.4	22.0	28.0	29.5	30.1	31.0	32.6	32.2	32.4	32.4	32.8

T **20. Life expectancy.** Data from the World Bank for 26 Western Hemisphere countries can be used to examine the association between female life expectancy and the average number of children women give birth to.

Country	Births/ Woman	Life Exp.	Country	Births/ Woman	Life Exp.
Argentina	2.5	77	Guatemala	4.7	68
Bahamas	2.2	77	Honduras	4.0	72
Barbados	1.8	78	Jamaica	2.5	77
Belize	3.5	74	Mexico	2.8	75
Bolivia	4.0	64	Nicaragua	3.6	71
Brazil	2.2	71	Panama	2.5	76
Canada	1.5	82	Paraguay	4.0	72
Chile	2.2	79	Peru	3.1	71
Colombia	2.7	74	Puerto Rico	3.1	71
Costa Rica	25.0	79	U. S.	2.1	80
Dom. Rep.	2.8	73	Uruguay	2.3	78
Ecuador	3.1	71	Venezuela	2.9	76
El Salvador	3.2	72	Virgin Is.	2.4	79

a) Create a scatterplot relating these two variables and describe the association.
b) Are there any countries that do not seem to fit the overall pattern?
c) Find the correlation, and interpret the value of R^2.
d) Find the equation of the regression line.
e) Is the line an appropriate model? Describe what you see in the residuals plot.
f) Interpret the slope and the y-intercept of the line.
g) If government leaders wanted to increase life expectancy, in their country, should they encourage women to have fewer children? Explain.

T **21. Inflation.** The Consumer Price Index (CPI) tracks the prices of consumer goods in the United States, as shown in the table. It indicates, for example, that the average item costing $17.90 in 1928 cost $168.80 in the year 2000.

Year	CPI	Year	CPI
1916	10.4	1960	29.3
1920	16.5	1964	30.9
1924	17.3	1968	34.1
1928	17.9	1972	41.1
1932	12.9	1976	55.6
1936	14.2	1980	77.8
1940	13.9	1984	101.9
1944	17.4	1988	115.7
1948	23.7	1992	138.1
1952	26.5	1996	154.4
1956	26.8	2000	168.8

a) Make a scatterplot showing the trend in consumer prices. Describe what you see.
b) Be an economic forecaster: Project increases in the cost of living over the next decade. Justify decisions you make in creating your model.
c) Sometimes re-expressing the data can reveal interesting information concealed there. Create a new variable containing the logarithm of the CPI. Plot log(CPI) against year. What historical events had a clear impact on the cost of living? (The next chapter explores more advantages that may arise by re-expressing data.)

Chapter 10

Re-expressing Data: It's Easier Than You Think

We have seen several cases in which a simple re-expression of the data, such as taking a logarithm or looking at the reciprocal ($1/y$), makes the data much easier to understand. Many of our tools for displaying and summarizing data work only when the data meet certain conditions. Linear models raise the stakes even further. We cannot use a linear model unless the relationship between the two variables is linear. Often re-expression can save the day, straightening bent relationships so that we can fit and use a simple linear model. It turns out that finding a useful re-expression is probably easier than you think. This chapter shows how to find re-expressions in a simple, systematic way.

Sometimes when we use re-expressions, we hear people say, "Wait a minute. If you're allowed to do anything you want to the data, you can make them show anything you want. The original data weren't measured in square roots! You're cheating." The fact is, it's not cheating, and re-expression is something that you do everyday. The point of this chapter is to show you how to find re-expressions easily and to show you that not only is it incredibly useful, but it's easy and natural as well. The material in this chapter is not needed explicitly for any subsequent chapter. But it makes all of them more useful by allowing more data to satisfy the conditions of each method we will discuss.

Straightening Relationships

The relationship between *fuel efficiency* measured in miles per gallon and *weight* measured in pounds looks fairly linear at first. It isn't surprising that lighter cars get better gas mileage. With an R^2 of 81.6%, the regression line might seem like a good fit. A look at the residual plot, though, shows a problem.

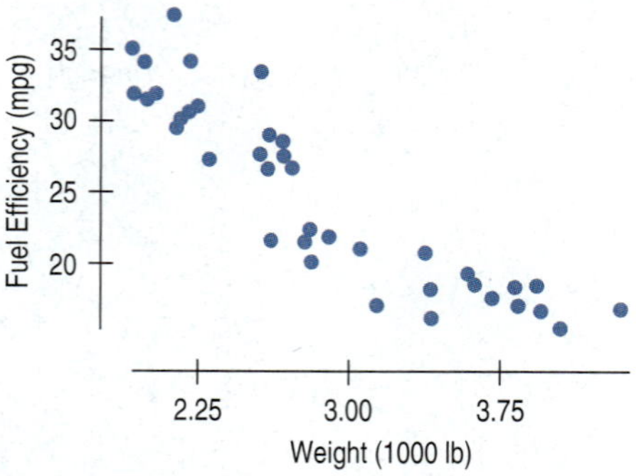

Fuel efficiency vs. weight for 38 cars as reported by *Consumer Reports.* The plot shows a negative direction, roughly linear shape, and strong relationship. **Figure 10.1**

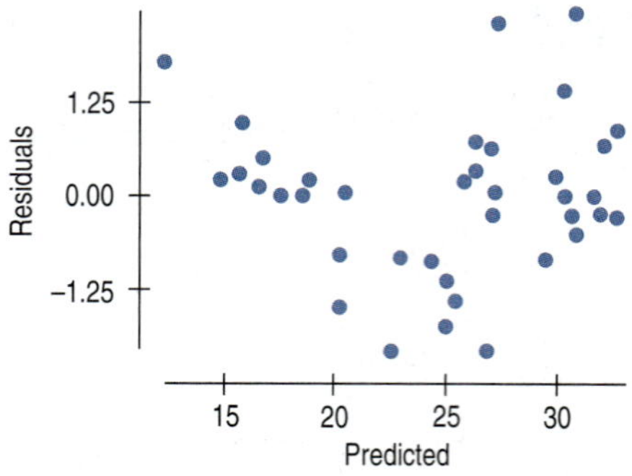

The residuals from a regression of fuel efficiency on weight reveal a bent shape when plotted against the predicted values. Looking back at the original scatterplot, you may be able to see the bend. **Figure 10.2**

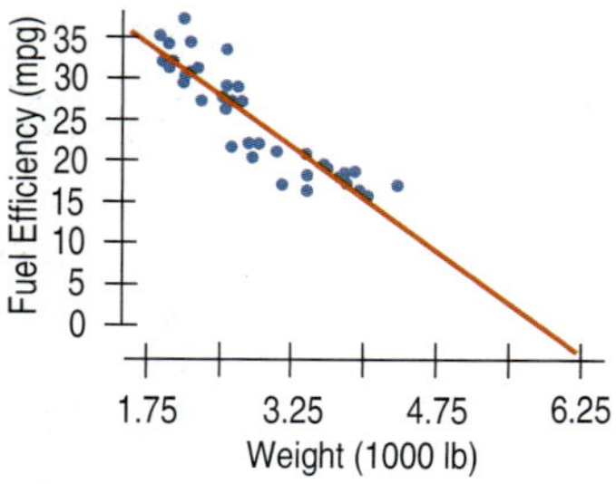

Extrapolating the regression line gives an absurd answer for vehicles that weigh as little as 6000 pounds. **Figure 10.3**

The shape is clearly bent. Looking back at the first scatterplot, you can probably see the slight bending. Think about the regression line through the points. How heavy would a car have to be to have a predicted gas mileage of 0? It looks like the fuel efficiency would go negative at about 6.00 (6000 pounds). The Lincoln Navigator 4-door wagon weighs in at 5994 pounds. It is hardly known for fuel efficiency, but it does get more than the *minus* 1 mpg this regression would predict. Extrapolation is always dangerous, but it's more dangerous the more the model is wrong, because wrong models tend to do even worse the farther you get from the middle of the data.

The bend in the relationship between *fuel efficiency* and *weight* is the kind of failure to satisfy the conditions for an analysis that we have repaired before by re-expressing the data. That method works here too. Instead of looking at miles per gallon, we can take the reciprocal and work with gallons per hundred miles.[1]

"Gallons per hundred miles—what an absurd way to measure fuel efficiency! Who would ever do it that way?"

Not all re-expressions are easy to understand, but in this case, the answer is "Everyone except U.S. drivers." Most of the world measures fuel efficiency in liters per 100 kilometers (L/100 km). This is the same reciprocal form (fuel amount per distance driven) and differs from gal/100 mi only by a constant multiple of about 2.38.

It has been suggested that most of the world says, "I've got to go 100 km, how much gas do I need?" But Americans say, "I've got 10 gallons in the tank. How far can I drive?"

In much the same way, re-expressions "think" about the data differently but don't change what they mean.

[1] The reciprocal is the part of this re-expression that makes the relationship more linear. Multiplying by 100 to get gallons per 100 miles simply makes the numbers easier to think about. You might have a good idea of how many gallons your car needs to drive 100 miles, but probably a much poorer sense of how much gas you need to go just 1 mile.

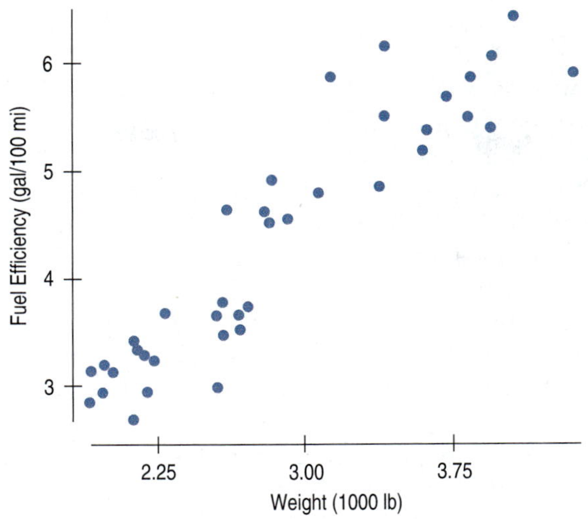

The reciprocal $(1/y)$ is measured in gallons per mile. Gallons per 100 miles gives more meaningful numbers. The reciprocal is more nearly linear against *weight* than the original variable, but the re-expression changes the direction of the relationship. **Figure 10.4**

The direction of the association is positive now, since we're measuring gas consumption and heavier cars consume more gas per mile. The R^2 is now 85.8%, but the real gain is that the relationship is much straighter, as we can see from a scatterplot of the regression residuals.

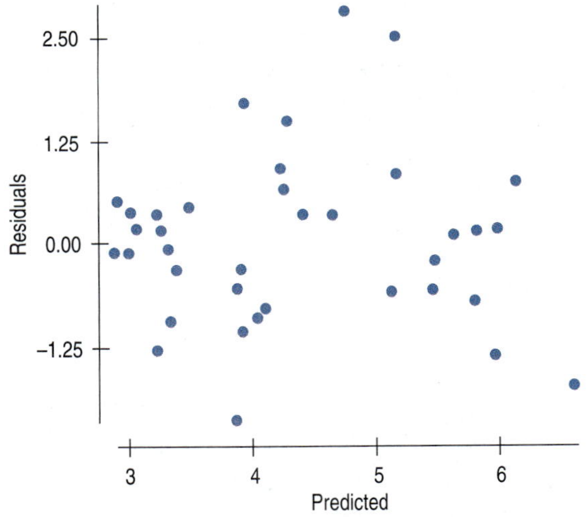

The residuals from the regression of *gallons per 100 miles* on *weight* show little pattern or trend. **Figure 10.5**

This is more the kind of boring scatterplot (no direction, no particular shape, no outliers, no bends) that we hope to see in a scatterplot of residuals, so we have reason to think that the straight enough condition is now satisfied.

What does the reciprocal model say about the Navigator? The regression line fit to the scatterplot of *gallons per 100 miles* vs. *weight* predicts somewhere near 9.1 for a car weighing 5995 pounds. What does this mean? It means the car is predicted to use 9.1 gallons for every 100 miles, or in other words

$$\frac{100 \text{ miles}}{9.1 \text{ gallons}} = 11.0 \text{ mpg}.$$

That's a much more reasonable prediction.

Everybody Does It

Scientific laws often include simple re-expressions. For example, in Psychology, Fechner's Law states that sensation increases as the logarithm of stimulus intensity, $S = k \log R$.

Scan through any Physics book. You're unlikely to see equations that don't have powers, reciprocals, or logs.

How Fast Can a Human Being Run?
The world record for 200 meters is 19.32 seconds (Michael Johnson, 1996). That's 23.4 mph (37.3 kph)! Most people can't even *bicycle* faster than about 19 or 20 mph. Of course, sprinters can't keep up that speed for very long. If they could, they could run a 2:34 mile.

You may not think about it, but you use re-expressions in everyday life. How fast can you go on a bicycle? If you measure your speed, you probably do it in distance per time (miles per hour or kilometers per hour). In 2000, during a 25-mile-long time trial in the Tour de France, Lance Armstrong *averaged* over 33.5 mph (53.9 kph). You probably realize that's a tough act to follow. It's fast. You can tell that at a glance because you have no trouble thinking in terms of distance covered per time.

OK, then, if you averaged 12.5 mph (20.1 kph) for a mile *run,* would that be fast? Would it be fast for a 100-m dash? Even if you run the mile often, you probably have to stop and calculate. Although we measure speed of bicycles in distance per time, we don't usually measure running speed that way. Instead, we use the *reciprocal,* time per distance (minutes per mile, seconds per 100 meters, etc.). Running a mile in under 5 minutes (12 mph) is fast. A mile at 16 mph would be a world record (that's a 3 minute 45 second mile).

The point is that there is no single *natural* way to measure speed. In some cases we use distance traveled per time, and in other cases we use the reciprocal. It's just because we're used to thinking that way in each case, not because one way is correct. The important fact to realize is that the way these quantities are measured is not sacred. It's usually just convenience or custom. When we re-express a quantity to make it satisfy certain conditions, we may either leave it in those new units when we explain the analysis to others, or convert back to the original units.

Other examples of common variables that re-express a crude measurement include the Richter scale of earthquake strength, the decibel scale for sound intensity, the f/stop scale for camera aperture openings, and the gauges of shotguns.

Careful re-expression is a common practice that can simplify patterns and relationships.

Goals of Re-expression

WHO	77 large companies
WHAT	Assets, sales, and market sector
HOW	Public records
WHEN	1986
WHY	By *Forbes* magazine in reporting on the Forbes 500 for that year

We re-express data for several reasons. Each of these goals is an aspect of the larger goal of making the data more suitable for analysis by our methods. We'll illustrate each goal with an example from data about large companies.

Goal 1

Make the distribution of a variable (as seen in its histogram, for example) more symmetric. It's easier to summarize the center of a symmetric distribution, and for nearly symmetric distributions we can use the mean and standard deviation. If the distribution is unimodal, then the resulting distribution may be closer to the Normal model, allowing us to use the 68-95-99.7 Rule.

Here are the assets of the companies we first saw in Chapter 4 (in $100,000):

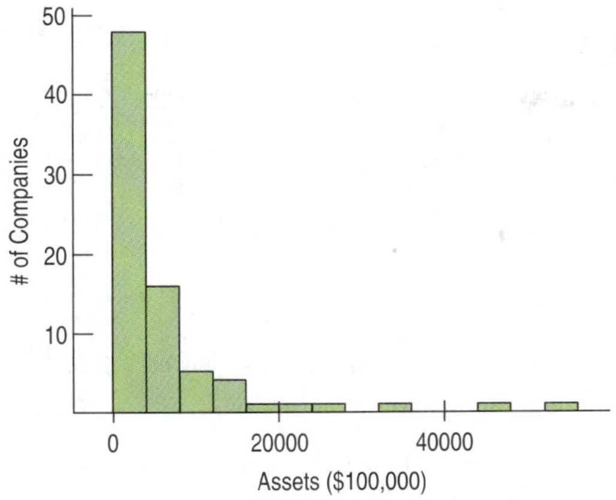

The distribution of the assets of large companies is skewed to the right. Data on wealth often look like this. **Figure 10.6**

The skewed distribution is made much more symmetric by taking logs.

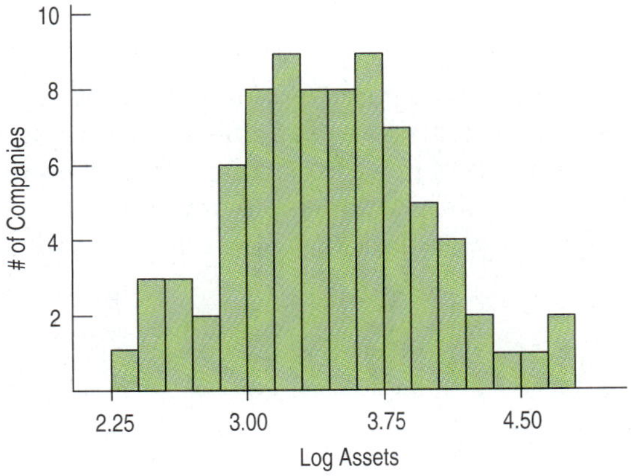

Taking logs makes the distribution more nearly symmetric. **Figure 10.7**

Goal 2

Make the spread of several groups (as seen in side-by-side boxplots) more alike, even if their centers differ. Groups that share a common spread are easier to compare. We'll see analysis methods later in the book that can be applied only to groups with a common standard deviation. We saw an example of re-expression for comparing groups with boxplots in Chapter 5.

Here are the assets of these companies by market sector:

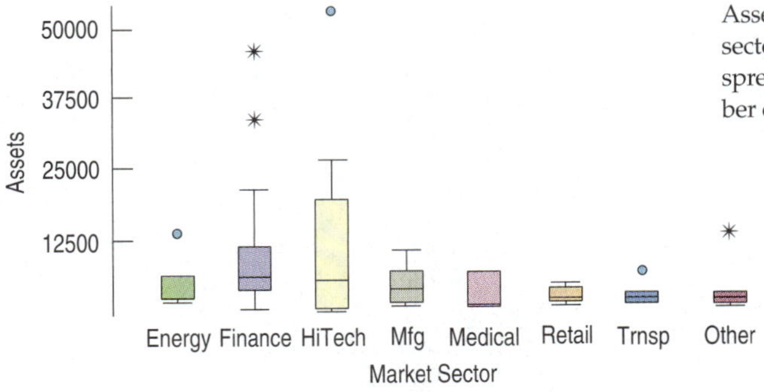

Assets of large companies by market sector. It's hard to compare centers or spreads, and there seem to be a number of high outliers. **Figure 10.8**

Taking logs makes the individual boxplots more symmetric and gives them spreads that are more nearly equal.

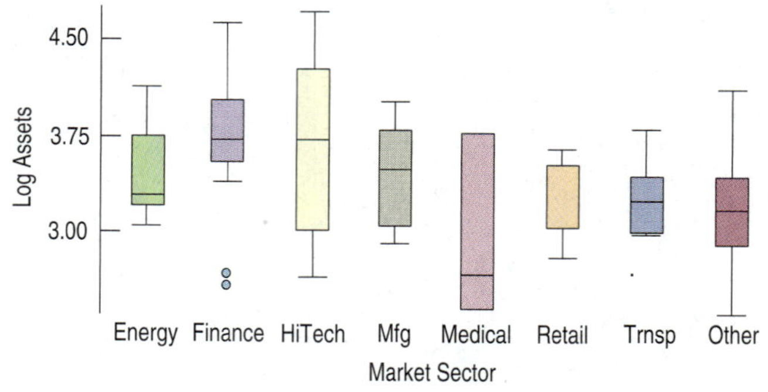

After re-expressing by logs, it's much easier to compare across market sectors. The boxplots are symmetric, most have similar spreads, and the companies that seemed to be outliers before are no longer extraordinary. Two new outliers have appeared in the finance sector. They are the only companies in that sector that are not banks. Perhaps they don't belong there. **Figure 10.9**

This makes it easier to compare assets across market sectors. It can also reveal problems in the data. Some companies that looked like outliers on the high end turned out to be more typical. But two companies in the Finance sector now stick out. They are not banks. Unlike the rest of the companies in that sector, they may have been placed in the wrong sector, but we couldn't see that in the original data.

Goal 3

Make the form of a scatterplot more nearly linear. Linear scatterplots are easier to describe. We saw an example of scatterplot straightening in Chapter 7. The greater value of re-expression to straighten a relationship is that we can fit a linear model once the relationship is straight.

Here are *assets* plotted against the logarithm of *sales*:

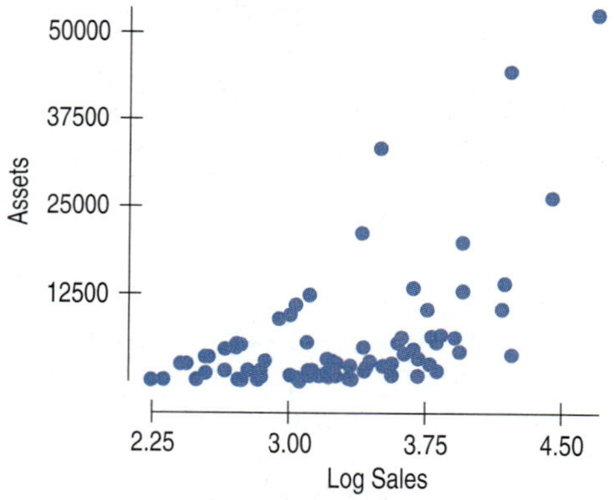

Assets vs. log *sales* shows a positive association (bigger sales goes with bigger assets) but a bent shape. Note also that the points go from tightly bunched at the left to widely scattered at the right—a "fan" shape. **Figure 10.10**

The plot's shape is bent. Taking logs makes things much more linear.

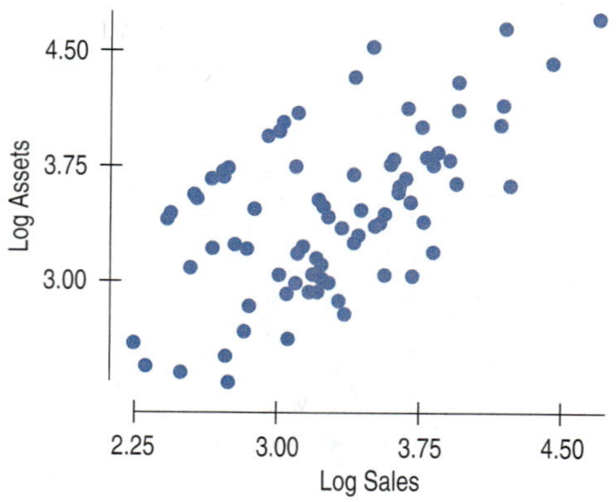

Log *assets* vs. log *sales* shows a clean, positive, linear association. And the variability at each value of x is about the same. **Figure 10.11**

Goal 4

Make the scatter in a scatterplot spread out evenly rather than following a fan shape. Having an even scatter is a condition of many methods of Statistics, as we'll see in later chapters. This goal is closely related to Goal 2, but it often comes along with Goal 3. Indeed, a glance back at the scatterplots shows that the plot for *assets* is much more spread out on the right than on the left, while the plot for log *assets* has roughly the same variation in log *assets* for any x-value.

The Ladder of Powers

We've seen that taking logs or reciprocals can really simplify an analysis. How do we know which re-expression to use? We could use trial and error to choose a re-expression, but there's an easier way. We can choose our re-expressions from a family of simple re-expressions that move data toward our goals in a consistent way. This family includes the most common ways to re-express data. More important, the members of the family line up in order, so that the farther you move away from the original data (the "1" position), the greater the effect on the data. This fact lets you search systematically for a re-expression that works, stepping a bit farther from "1" or taking a step back toward "1" as you see the results.

Where to start? It turns out that certain kinds of data are more likely to be helped by particular re-expressions. Knowing that gives you a good place to start your search for a re-expression.

We call this collection of re-expressions the **Ladder of Powers.** Each power is specified as a single value, as follows:

Power	Name	Comment
2	The square of the data values, y^2.	Try this for unimodal distributions that are skewed to the left.
1	The raw data—no change at all. This is "home base." The farther you step from here up or down the ladder, the greater the effect.	Data that can take on both positive and negative values with no bounds are less likely to benefit from re-expression.
1/2	The square root of the data values, $\sqrt{y}$.	Counts often benefit from a square root re-expression. For counted data, start here.
"0"	Although mathematicians define the "0th" power differently,[2] for us the place is held by the logarithm. You may feel uneasy about logarithms. Don't worry, the computer or calculator does the work.[3]	Measurements that cannot be negative, and especially values that grow by percentage increases such as salaries or populations, often benefit from a log re-expression. When in doubt, start here. If your data have zeros, try adding a small constant to all values before finding the logs.

(continued)

[2] You may remember that for any number, y, $y^0 = 1$. This is not a very exciting transformation for data; every data value would be the same. We use the logarithm in its place.

[3] Your calculator or software package probably gives you a choice between "base 10" logarithms and "natural (base e)" logarithms. Don't worry about that. It doesn't matter at all which you use; they have exactly the same effect on the data. If you want to choose, then base 10 logarithms can be a bit easier to interpret.

Power	Name	Comment
−1/2	The reciprocal square root $-1/\sqrt{y}$.	An uncommon re-expression, but sometimes useful. Changing the sign to take the *negative* of the reciprocal square root preserves the direction of relationships, which can be a bit simpler.
−1	The reciprocal, $-1/y$.	Ratios of two quantities (miles per hour, for example) often benefit from a reciprocal. (You have about a 50-50 chance that the original ratio was taken in the "wrong" order for simple statistical analysis and would benefit from re-expression.) Often, the reciprocal will have simple units (hours per mile). Change the sign if you want to preserve the direction of relationships. If your data have zeros, try adding a small constant to all values before finding the reciprocal.

The Ladder of Powers orders the *effects* that the re-expressions have on data. If you try, say, taking the square roots of all the values in a variable and it helps, but not enough, then moving farther down the ladder to the logarithm or reciprocal root will have a similar effect on your data, but even stronger. If you go too far, you can always back up. But don't forget—once you take a negative power, the *direction* of the relationship will change. That's OK. You can always change the sign of the response if you want to keep the same direction.

A generation ago, before desktop computers and powerful calculators were available, finding a suitable re-expression was a major undertaking, often given as an end-of-semester project. Now, it's usually no harder than the push of a button, making it easy to search for a suitable re-expression.

Re-expressing to Straighten a Scatterplot — STEP-BY-STEP

We have noted that scatterplots that have been re-expressed to have a linear shape let us fit linear models. Here's a simple example.

Standard (monofilament) fishing line comes in a range of strengths, usually expressed as "test pounds." Five-pound test line, for example, can be expected to withstand a pull of up to five pounds without breaking. The convention in selling fishing line is that the price of a spool doesn't vary with strength. Instead, the length of line on the spool varies. Because higher test pound line is thicker, though, spools of fishing line hold about the same amount of material. Some spools hold line that is thinner and longer, some fatter and shorter. Let's look at the length and strength of spools of monofilament line manufactured by the same company and sold for the same price at one store. How are the length on the spool and the strength related? And what re-expression will straighten the relationship?

Think

Variables Name the variables, report the W's, and specify the questions of interest.

We have the length and "pound test" of monofilament fishing line sold by a single vendor at a particular store. Each case is a different strength of line, but all spools of line sell for the same price.

Let *length* = length (in yards) of fishing line on the spool

test = the strength (in pounds).

Plan Examine the relationship for bends.

Check that even if there is a curve, the overall pattern does not reach a minimum or maximum, and then turn around and go back. An up-and-down curve can't be fixed by re-expression.

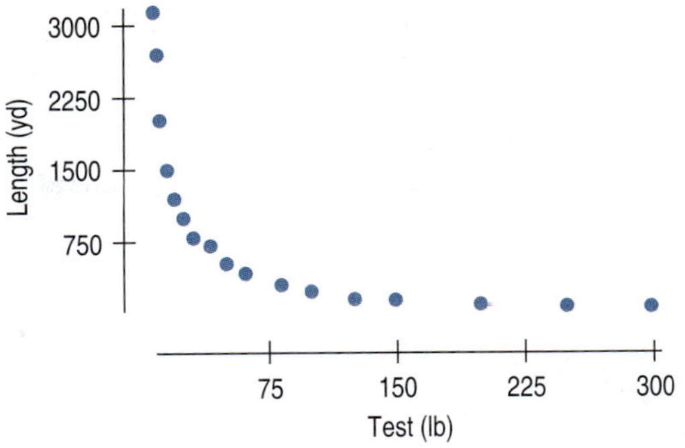

The plot shows a negative direction and an association that has little scatter but is not straight.

Show

Mechanics

Try a re-expression.

The lesson of the Ladder of Powers is that if we're moving in the right direction but have not had sufficient effect, we should go farther along the ladder. This example shows improvement, but is still not straight.

(Because length is an amount of something and cannot be negative, we probably should have started with logs. This plot is here in part to illustrate how the Ladder of Powers works.)

Here's a plot of the square root of length against strength:

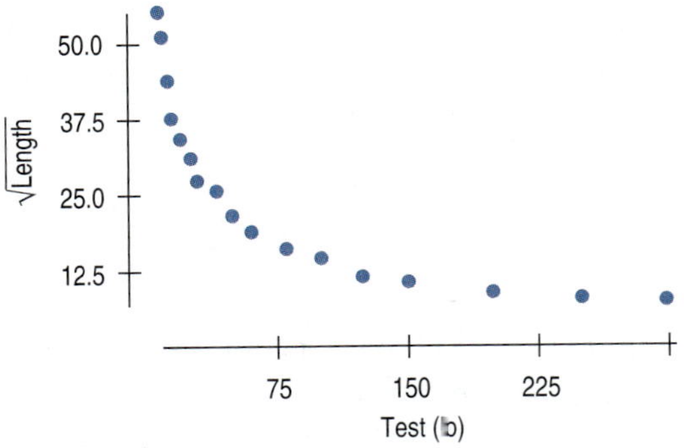

The plot is less bent, but still not straight.

Stepping from the 1/2 power to the "0" power, we try the logarithm of length against strength.

The scatterplot of the logarithm of length against test weight is still less bent:

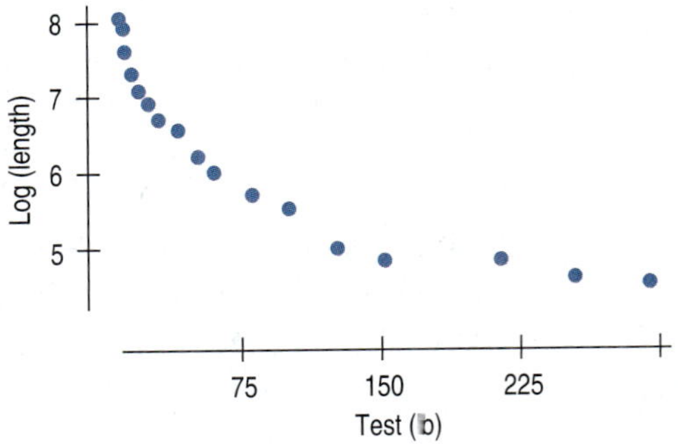

The straightness is improving, so we know we're moving in the right direction. But since the plot of the logarithms is not yet straight, we know we haven't gone far enough.

This is much better, but still not straight, so we take another step to the "−1" power, or reciprocal. (To keep the direction consistent, we'll change the sign and re-express to −1/length.)

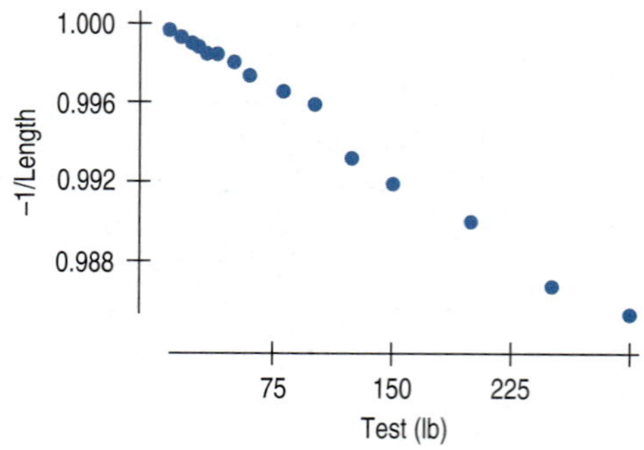

Maybe now we moved too far along the ladder.

We may have to choose between two adjacent re-expressions. For most data analyses, it really doesn't matter which we choose.

A half-step back is the −1/2 power: the reciprocal square root. Let's try it:

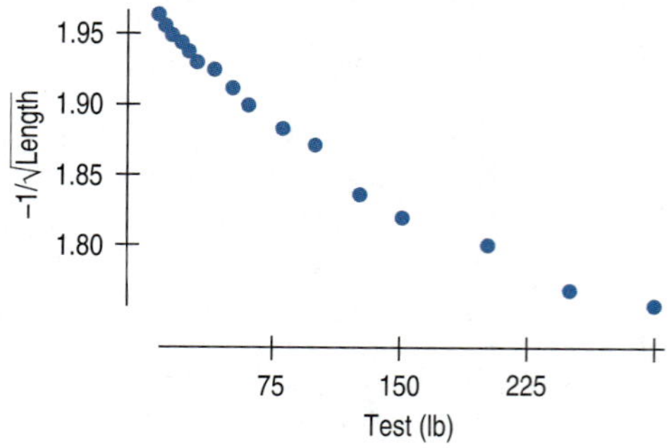

Tell

Discussion Specify your choice of re-expression. If there's some natural interpretation (as for gallons per 100 miles), give that.

It's hard to choose between the last two alternatives. Either of the last two choices is good enough for our purposes. We'll choose the −1/2 power.

Now that the re-expressed data satisfy the straight enough condition, we can fit a linear model by least squares. We find

$$\frac{-1}{\sqrt{length}} = -0.023 - 0.000373\,test.$$

We can use this model to predict the length of a spool of, say, 35-pound test line:

$$\frac{-1}{\sqrt{length}} = -0.023 - 0.000373 \times 35 = -0.036.$$

We could leave the result in these units ($-1/\sqrt{\text{yards}}$). Sometimes the new units may be as meaningful as the original, but here we want to transform the predicted value back into yards. Fortunately, each of the re-expressions in the Ladder of Powers can be reversed.

To reverse the process, we first take the reciprocal: $\sqrt{length} = 1/0.036 = 27.778$. Then squaring gets us back to the original units:

$$length = 27.778^2 = 771.6 \text{ yards.}$$

This may be the most painful part of the re-expression. Getting back to the original units can sometimes be a little work. Nevertheless, it's worth the effort to always consider re-expression. Re-expressions can often vastly improve a statistical analysis or model.

TI Tips

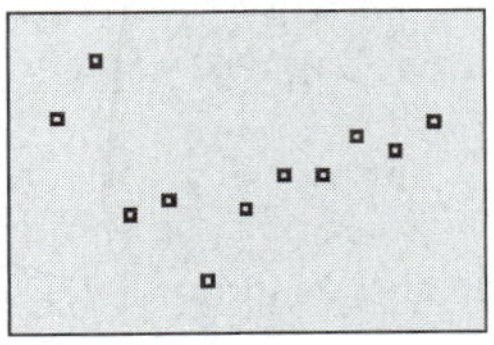

Let's revisit the Arizona State tuition data. Recall that back in Chapter 8 when we tried to fit a linear model to the yearly tuition costs the residuals plot showed a distinct curve. Residuals are high (positive) at the left, low in the middle of the decade, and high again at the right.

This curved pattern indicates that data re-expression may be in order. If you have no clue what re-expression to try, the Ladder of Powers may help. We just used that approach in the fishing line example. Here, though, we can play a hunch. It is reasonable to suspect that tuition increases at a relatively consistent percentage year by year. This suggests that using the logarithm of tuition may help.

- Tell the calculator to find the logs of the tuitions, and store them as a new list. Remember that you must import the name `TUIT` from the `LIST NAMES` menu. The command is `log(ʟTUIT) STO L1`.
- Check the scatterplot for the re-expressed data by changing your `STATPLOT` specifications to `Xlist:YR` and `Ylist:L1`. (Don't forget to use `9:ZoomStat` to resize the window properly.)

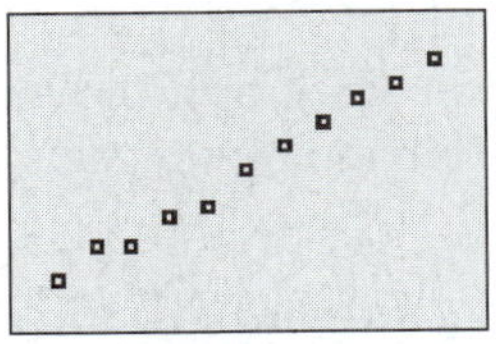

The new scatterplot looks quite linear, but it's really the residuals plot that will tell the story. Remember that the TI automatically finds and stores the residuals whenever you ask it to calculate a regression.

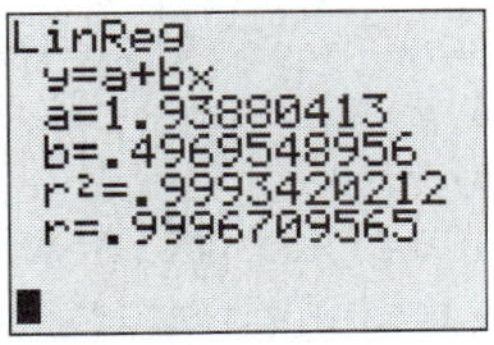

- Perform the regression for the logarithm of *tuition* vs. *year* with the command `LinReg(a+bx) ʟYR,L1`. That both creates the residuals and reports details about the model.
- Now that the residuals are stored in `RESID`, set up a new scatterplot, this time specifying `Xlist:YR` and `Ylist:RESID`.

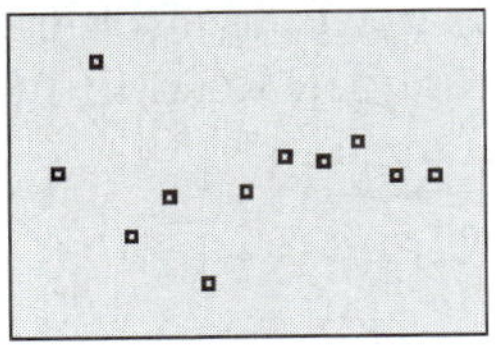

While the residual for the second and fifth years are comparatively large, the curvature we saw above is gone. The pattern in these residuals seems essentially horizontal and random. This re-expressed model is probably more useful than the original linear model.

Do you know what the model's equation is? Remember, it involves a log re-expression. The calculator does not indicate that; be sure to Think when you write your model!

$$\log \widehat{tuit} = 3.816 + 0.018\ yr$$

Plan B: Attack of the Logarithms

We've suggested using the Ladder of Powers as one approach to finding a re-expression that straightens a curved scatterplot. That's often successful. Sometimes, though, the curvature is more stubborn, and we're not satisfied with any of the residuals plots. What then?

When none of the data values is zero or negative, logarithms can be a helpful ally in the search for a useful model. Try taking the logs of both x and y variables. Then model the association between some combination of x or $\log(x)$ vs. y or $\log(y)$. You may find that one of these works pretty well.

Model Name	x-axis	y-axis	Comment
Exponential	x	$\log(y)$	This model is the "0" power in the ladder approach, useful for values that grow by percentage increases.
Logarithmic	$\log(x)$	y	A wide range of x values, or a scatterplot descending rapidly at the left but leveling off toward the right, may benefit from trying this model.
Power	$\log(x)$	$\log(y)$	The Goldilocks model: When one of the ladder's powers is too big and the next is too small, this one may be just right.

When we tried to model the relationship between the length of fishing line and its strength, we were torn between the "-1" power and the "$-1/2$" power. The first showed slight upward curvature, and the second downward. Maybe there's a better power between those values.

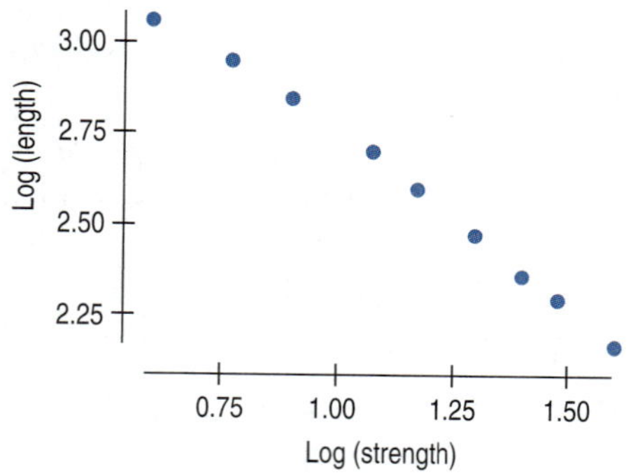

The scatterplot shows what happens when we graph the logarithm of length against the logarithm of strength. Technology reveals that the equation of our log-log model is

$$\log(\widehat{length}) = 3.65 - 0.90\log(strength).$$

It's interesting that the slope of this line (-0.90) is a power we didn't try. After all, the ladder can't have every imaginable rung.

A warning, though! Don't expect to be able to straighten every curved scatterplot you find. It may be that there just isn't a very effective re-expression to be had. You'll certainly encounter situations when nothing seems to work the way you wish it would. Don't set your sights too high—you won't find a perfect model. Keep in mind: We seek a *useful* model, not perfection (or even "the best").

TI Tips

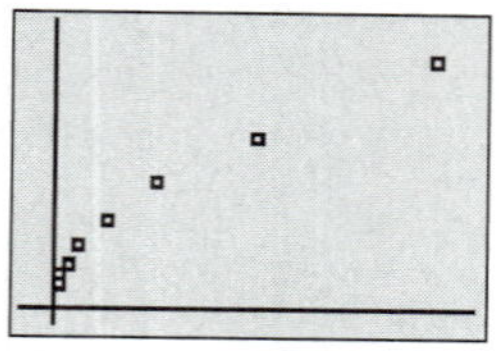

In Chapter 7 we looked at data showing the relationship between a camera's shutter speed and the f/stop of the lens. Let's use the attack of the logarithms to model this situation.

***f*/stop:**	2.8	4	5.6	8	11	16	22	32
Shutter speed:	1/1000	1/500	1/250	1/125	1/60	1/30	1/15	1/8

- Enter these data into your calculator, shutter *speed* in `L1` and *f/stop* in `L2`.
- Create the scatterplot with `Xlist:L1` and `Ylist:L2`. See the curve?
- Find the logarithms of each variable's values. Keep track of where you store everything so you don't get confused! We put log(*speed*) in `L3` and log(*f/stop*) in `L4`.
- Make three scatterplots:
  - *f/stop* vs. log(*speed*) using `Xlist:L3` and `Ylist:L2`
  - log(*f/stop*) vs. *speed* using `Xlist:L1` and `Ylist:L4`
  - log(*f/stop*) vs. log(*speed*) using `Xlist:L3` and `Ylist:L4`

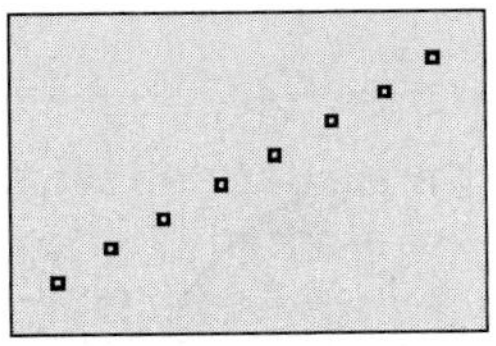

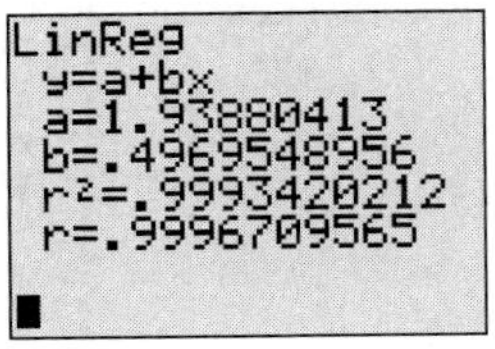

- Pick your favorite. We liked log(*f*/*stop*) vs. log(*speed*) a lot! It appears to be very straight. (Don't be misled—this is a situation governed by the laws of Physics. Real data are not so cooperative. Don't expect to achieve this level of perfection often!)
- Remember that before you check the residuals plot, you first have to calculate the regression. In this situation all the errors in the residuals are just round-off errors in the original *f*/stops. (More on that issue below)
- Use your regression to write the equation of the model. Remember: The calculator does not know there were logarithms involved. You have to Think about that to be sure you write your model correctly.

$$\log(\widehat{f/stop}) = 1.94 + 0.497\log(speed)^4$$

Multiple Benefits

We often choose a re-expression for one reason and then discover that it has helped other aspects of an analysis. For example, we might re-express a variable to make its histogram more nearly symmetric. It wouldn't be surprising to find that the same re-expression also straightens scatterplots or makes spreads more nearly equal. This phenomenon is one reason we encourage that data re-expression be used more often. Sometimes there's an obvious "best" or "right" re-expression for a variable. For example, it makes sense that things that tend to grow by a constant percentage, so that larger values grow faster (populations, bacteria counts, wealth), will grow exponentially. Logarithms straighten out the exponential trend and pull in the long right tail in the histogram.

We saw just this phenomenon in the companies example earlier. Each of our goals was met by re-expressing assets with logarithms. That single re-expression improved all four of the goals at the same time. That turns out not to be all that unusual.

If you think that simpler explanations and simpler models are more likely to give a true picture of the way things work, then you should look for opportunities to re-express your data and simplify your analyses. The general principle that simpler explanations are likely to be the better ones is known as Occam's Razor after the English philosopher and theologian William of Occam (1284–1347).

Measurement errors are often larger when measuring larger quantities than when measuring smaller ones. (The error in your height may be only a centimeter or two, but the error in the height of a tree could be ten times that much.) Again, logarithms are likely to help. Measurements of rates (time to complete a task) are often plagued by infinities for those who just never finish. The reciprocal of "minutes per task" is "tasks per minute"—a speed measure. And the unfinished tasks that once took "infinite" time now simply rate a zero speed. Here once more the re-expression seems natural.

In other cases, the only evidence we have to favor re-expression is that it seems to work well and that it leads to simpler models. Often we can find a re-expression for a variable that simplifies its analysis in several ways at once, making its distribution symmetric, making it linear in terms of other variables of interest, or stabilizing its variance. If so, re-expressing it certainly simplifies our efforts to analyze and understand it.

[4] See the slope, 0.497? Just about 0.5. That's because the actual relationship involves the square root of shutter speeds. Technically the *f*/stop listed as 2.8 should be $2\sqrt{2} \approx 2.8284$. Rounding off to 2.8 makes sense for photographers, but it's what led to the minor errors you saw in the residuals plot.

Why Not Just Use a Curve?

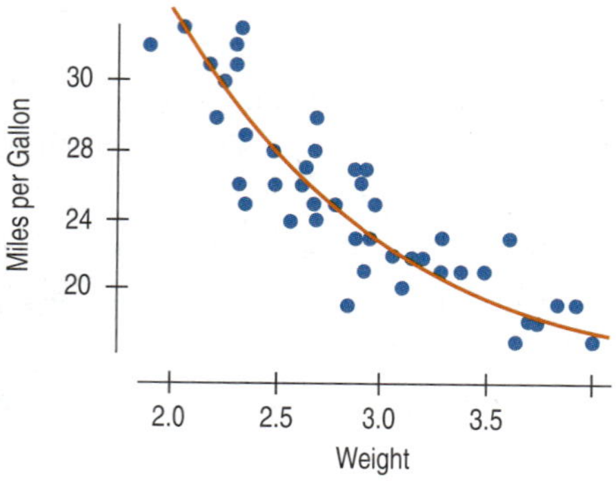

When a clearly curved pattern shows up in the scatterplot, why not just fit a curve to the data? We saw earlier that the association between the weight of a car and its fuel economy was not a straight line. Instead of trying to find a way to straighten the plot, why not find a curve that seems to describe the pattern well?

That's actually a reasonable idea. We can find "curves of best fit" using essentially the same approach that led us to linear models. You won't be surprised, though, to learn that the mathematics and the calculations are considerably more difficult for curved models. Fortunately, many calculators and computer packages do have the ability to fit curves to data.

This approach has many drawbacks, though. Lines are easy to understand. We know how to think about the slope and the *y*-intercept, for example. We often want some of the other benefits mentioned above. And in later chapters you will learn more advanced statistical methods for analyzing linear associations. We give all of that up when we create a model that is not linear. For many reasons, then, it is usually better to re-express the data to straighten the plot.

TI Tips

Your calculator offers many regression options in the **STAT CALC** menu. There are three that automate fitting simple re-expressions of *y* or *x*:

- **9:LnReg**—fits a logarithmic model ($\hat{y} = a + b\ln x$)
- **0:ExpReg**—fits an exponential model ($\hat{y} = ab^x$)
- **A:PwrReg**—fits a power model ($y = ax^b$)

In addition, the calculator offers two other functions:

- **5:QuadReg**—fits a quadratic model ($\hat{y} = ax^2 + bx + c$)
- **6:CubicReg**—fits a cubic (third-degree polynomial) model ($\hat{y} = ax^3 + bx^2 + cx + d$)

These two models have a form we haven't seen, with several *x*-terms. Because x, x^2, and x^3 are likely to be highly correlated with each other, the quadratic and cubic models are almost sure to be unreliable to fit, difficult to understand, and dangerous to use for predictions even slightly outside the range of the data. We recommend that you be very wary of models of this type.

Let's try out one of the calculator shortcuts; we'll use the Arizona State tuition data. (For the last time, we promise!) This time, instead of re-expressing *tuition* to straighten the scatterplot, we'll have the calculator do more of the work.

Which model should you use? You could always just play hit-and-miss, but knowing something about the data can save a lot of time. If tuition increases by a consistent percentage each year, then the growth is exponential.

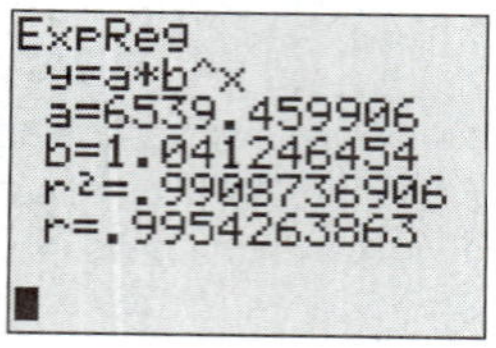

- Choose the exponential model, and specify your variables by importing **YR** and **TUIT** from the list names menu. And, because you'll want to graph the curve later, save its equation by adding **Y1** (from **VARS**, **Y-VARS**, **Function**) to create the command

ExpReg ʟYR,ʟTUIT,Y1.

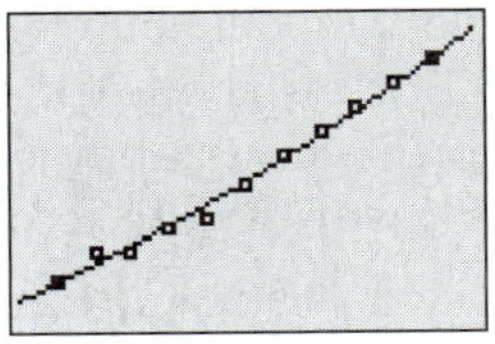

- Set up the scatterplot. When you hit `ZoomStat` it should show you the curve, too.
- Graph the residuals plot.

This all looks very good. R^2 is high, the curve appears to fit the points quite well, and the residuals plot is acceptably random.

The equation of the model is

$$\widehat{tuit} = 6539.46(1.041^{year}).$$

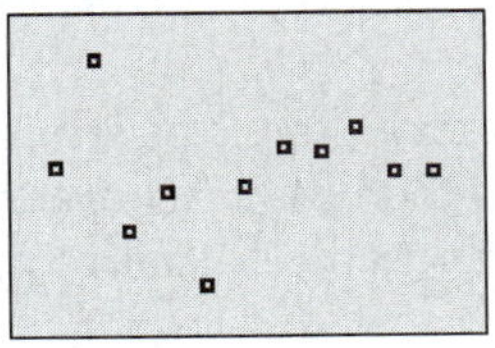

Notice that this is the same residuals plot we saw when we re-expressed the data and fit a line to the logarithm of *tuition*. That's because what the calculator just did is mathematically the very same thing. This new equation may look different, but it is equivalent to our earlier model:

$$\log \widehat{tuit} = 3.816 + 0.018\, year.$$

Not easy to see that, is it? Here's how it works:

Initially we used a logarithmic re-expression to create a linear model:	$\log \hat{y} = a + bx$
Rewrite that equation in exponential form:	$\hat{y} = 10^{a + bx}$
Simplify, using the laws of exponents:	$\hat{y} = 10^a (10^b)^x$
Let $10^a = a$ and $10^b = b$ (different a and b!)	$\hat{y} = ab^x$

See? Your linear model created by logarithmic re-expression is the same as the calculator model created by `ExpReg`.

Three of the special TI functions correspond to a simple regression model involving re-expression. The calculator presents the results in an equation of a different form, but it doesn't actually fit that equation. Instead it is just doing the re-expression for you automatically.

Here are the equivalent models for the two approaches.

Type of Model	Re-expression Equation	Calculator's Curve: Command	Calculator's Curve: Equation
Logarithmic	$\hat{y} = a + b\log x$	`LnReg`	$\hat{y} = a + b\ln x$
Exponential	$\log \hat{y} = a + bx$	`ExpReg`	$\hat{y} = ab^x$
Power	$\log \hat{y} = a + b\log x$	`PwrReg`	$\hat{y} = ax^b$

Be careful. It may look like the calculator is fitting these equations to the data by minimizing the sum of squared residuals, but it isn't really doing that. It handles the residuals differently, and the difference matters. If you use a statistics program to fit an "exponential model," it will probably fit the exponential form of the equation and give you a different answer. So think of these TI functions as just shortcuts for fitting linear regressions to re-expressed versions of your data.

You've seen two ways to handle bent relationships:

- straighten the data, then fit a line, or
- use the calculator shortcut to create a curve.

Note that the calculator does not have a shortcut for every model you might want to use—models involving square roots or reciprocals, for instance. And remember: The calculator may be quick, but there are real advantages to finding models by actually re-expressing the data. That's the approach we strongly recommend you use.

What Can Go Wrong?

- ***Beware of multiple modes.*** Re-expression can often make a skewed unimodal histogram more nearly symmetric, but it cannot pull separate modes together. A suitable re-expression may, however, make the separation of the modes clearer, simplifying their interpretation.
- ***Watch out for scatterplots that turn around.*** Re-expression can straighten many bent relationships, but not those that go up and then down or down and then up. You should refuse to analyze such data with methods that require a linear form.

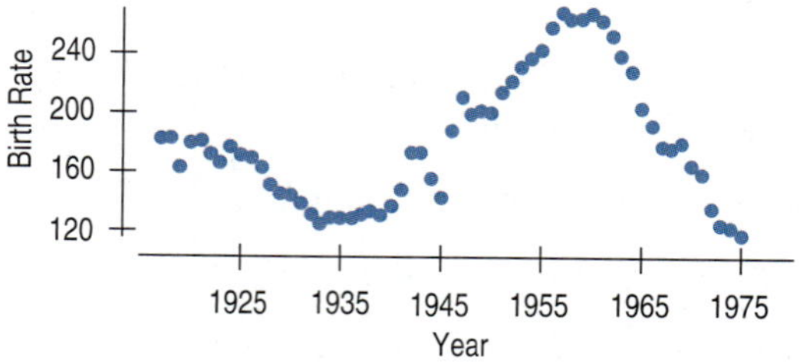

The shape of the scatterplot of birth rates (births per 100,000 women) in the United States shows an oscillation that cannot be straightened by re-expressing the data. **Figure 10.9**

- ***Watch out for negative data values.*** It's impossible to re-express negative values by any power that is not positive on the Ladder of Powers or to re-express values that are zero for powers between 0 and −1. Most statistics programs will just mark such values "missing" if they can't be re-expressed. But that might mean that when you try a re-expression, you inadvertently lose a bunch of data values. The effect of that loss may be surprising and may substantially change your analysis. Because you are likely to be working with a computer package or calculator, take special care that you do not lose otherwise good data values when you choose a re-expression.

  One possible cure if the negative values are not very far below zero is to add a small constant (1/2 and 1/6 are both used) to all the data values to bring the minimum up above zero.
- ***Watch for data far from one.*** Data values that are all very far from 1 may not be much affected by re-expression unless the range is very large. Re-expressing numbers between 1 and 100 will have a much greater effect than re-expressing numbers between 100,001 and 100,100. If all the data values are large (for example, working with years), consider subtracting a constant to bring them back near 1. (For example, consider "years since 1950" as an alternative variable to re-express.)
- ***Don't stray too far from the ladder.*** Finally, it's wise not to stray too far from the powers that we suggest in the Ladder of Powers. Taking the y-values to an extremely high power may artificially inflate R^2, but it won't give a useful or meaningful model, so it doesn't really simplify anything. It's better to stick to powers between 2 and −2. Even in that range, you should prefer the simpler powers in the ladder to those in the cracks. A square root is easier to understand than the 0.413 power. That simplicity may compensate for a slightly less straight relationship.

Re-expression and the Computer

Computers and calculators make it easy to re-express data. Most statistics packages offer a way to re-express and compute with variables. Some packages permit you to specify the power of a re-expression with a slider or other moveable control, possibly while watching the consequences of the re-expression on a plot or analysis. This, of course, is a very effective way to find a good re-expression.

Connections

We have seen several ways to model or summarize data. Each requires that the data have a particular simple structure. We seek symmetry for summaries of center and spread and to use a Normal model. We seek equal variation across groups when we compare groups with boxplots or want to compare their centers. We seek linear shape in a scatterplot so that we can use correlation to summarize the scatter and regression to fit a linear model.

Data do often satisfy the requirements to use statistics methods. But often they do not. Our choice is to stop with just displays, to use much more complex methods, or to re-express the data so that we can use the simpler methods we have developed.

In this fundamental sense, this chapter connects to everything we have done thus far and to all of the methods we will introduce throughout the rest of the book. Re-expression greatly extends the reach and applicability of all of these methods.

Key Concepts

Re-express data

To improve symmetry.
To make several groups have more nearly equal spreads.
To make the form of a scatterplot more nearly linear.
To make a scatterplot have a more nearly consistent spread throughout.

Skills

When you complete this lesson you should:

Think

- Recognize when a well-chosen re-expression may help you improve and simplify your analysis.
- Understand the value of re-expressing data to improve symmetry, constant variance, or linearity.
- Recognize when the pattern of the data indicates that no re-expression can improve the structure of the data.

Show

- Know how to re-express data with powers and how to find an effective re-expression for your data using your statistics software or calculator.
- Be able to reverse any of the common re-expressions to put a predicted value or residual back into the original units.

Tell

- Be able to describe a summary or display of a re-expressed variable making clear how it was re-expressed and giving its re-expressed units.
- Be able to describe a regression model fit to re-expressed data in terms of the re-expressed variables.

Exercises

1. Models. For each of the models listed below, predict y when $x = 2$.

a) $\hat{y} = 1.2 + 0.8x$

b) $\ln \hat{y} = 1.2 + 0.8x$

c) $\sqrt{\hat{y}} = 1.2 + 0.8x$

d) $\frac{1}{\hat{y}} = 1.2 + 0.8x$

e) $\hat{y} = 1.2x^{0.8}$

2. More models. For each of the models listed below, predict y when $x = 2$.

a) $\hat{y} = 1.2 + 0.8 \log x$

b) $\log \hat{y} = 1.2 + 0.8x$

c) $\hat{y} = 1.2 + 0.8\sqrt{x}$

d) $\hat{y} = 1.2(0.8^x)$

e) $\hat{y} = 0.8x^2 + 1.2x + 1$

3. Gas mileage. As the example in the chapter indicates, one of the important factors determining a car's fuel efficiency is its weight. Let's examine this relationship again, for 11 cars.

a) Describe the association between these variables shown in the scatterplot.

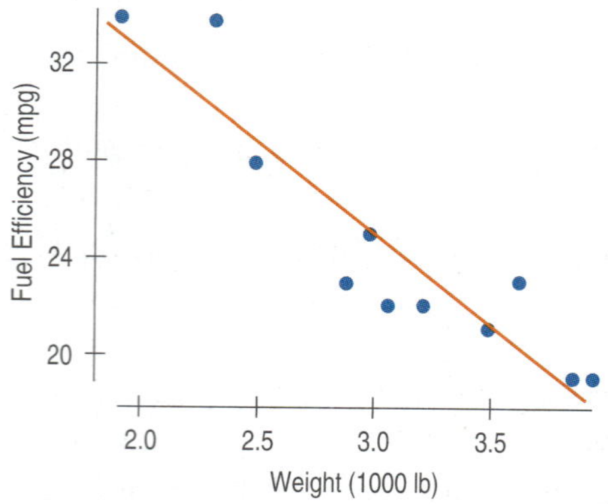

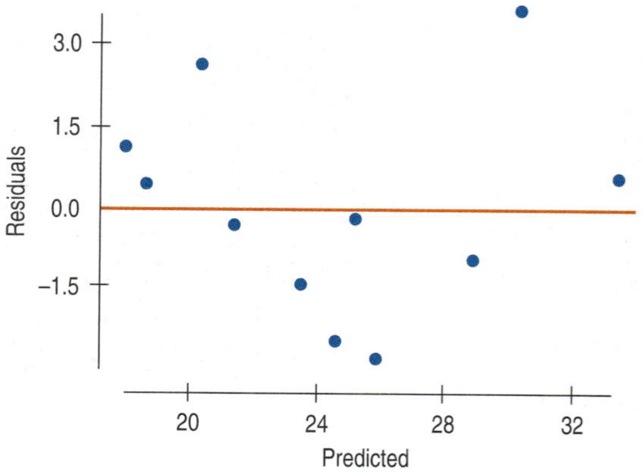

b) Here is the regression analysis for the linear model. What does the slope of the line say about this relationship?

Dependent variable is: MPG
R-squared = 85.9%

Variable	**Coefficient**
Constant	47.9636
WT(1000)	−7.65184

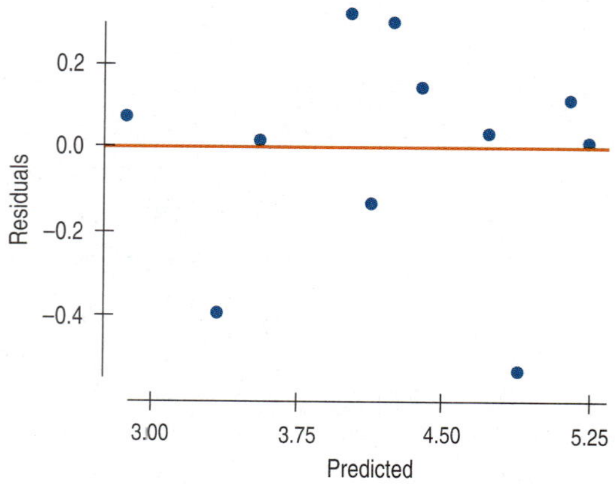

c) Do you think this linear model is appropriate? Use the residuals plot in part a to explain your decision.

d) Let's try a re-expressed variable: *gallons per hundred miles*. Use the new residuals plot to explain why this model appears to be better.

Dependent variable is: Gal/100
R-squared = 89.2%

Variable	Coefficient
Constant	0.624932
WT(1000)	1.17791

e) Using the regression analysis above, write an equation of this model.

f) Interpret the slope of this line.

g) Based on this model, how many miles per gallon would you expect a 3500-pound car to get?

T **4. Pressure.** Scientist Robert Boyle examined the relationship between the volume in which a gas is contained and the pressure in that container. He used a cylindrical container with a moveable top that could be raised or lowered to change the volume. He measured the *height* in inches by counting equally spaced marks on the cylinder, and measured the *pressure* in inches of mercury (as in a barometer). Some of his data are listed below. Create an appropriate model.

Height	48	44	40	36	32	28
Pressure	29.1	31.9	35.3	39.3	44.2	50.3
Height	24	20	18	16	14	12
Pressure	58.8	70.7	77.9	87.9	100.4	117.6

T **5. Brakes.** The table below shows stopping distances in feet for a car tested 3 times at each of 5 speeds. We hope to create a model that predicts stopping distance from the speed of the car.

Speed (mph)	Stopping Distance (ft)
20	64, 62, 59
30	114, 118, 105
40	153, 171, 165
50	231, 203, 238
60	317, 321, 276

a) Explain why a linear model is not appropriate.

b) Re-express the data to straighten the scatterplot.

c) Create an appropriate model.

d) Estimate the stopping distance for a car traveling 55 mph.

e) Estimate the stopping distance for a car traveling 70 mph.

f) How much confidence do you place in these predictions? Why?

6. Pendulum. A student experimenting with a pendulum counted the number of full swings the pendulum made in 20 seconds for various lengths of string. Her data are shown below.

Length (in.)	6.5	9	11.5	14.5	18	21	24	27	30	37.5
Number of Swings	22	20	17	16	14	13	13	12	11	10

a) Explain why a linear model is not appropriate for using the length of a pendulum to predict the number of swings in 20 seconds.

b) Re-express the data to straighten the scatterplot.

c) Create an appropriate model.

d) Estimate the number of swings for a pendulum with a 4″ string.

e) Estimate the number of swings for a pendulum with a 48″ string.

f) How much confidence do you place in these predictions? Why?

T **7. Baseball salaries.** Ball players have been signing ever larger contracts. The highest salaries (in million of dollars per season) for some notable players are given in the table below.

Player	Year	Salary (million $)
Nolan Ryan	1980	1
George Foster	1982	2.04
Kirby Puckett	1990	3
Jose Canseco	1990	4.7
Roger Clemens	1991	5.3
Ken Griffey, Jr.	1996	8.5
Albert Belle	1997	11
Pedro Martinez	1998	12.5
Mike Piazza	1999	12.5
Mo Vaughn	1999	13.3
Kevin Brown	1999	15
Carlos Delgado	2001	17
Alex Rodriguez	2001	25.2

a) Re-express the data to straighten the scatterplot.

b) Create an appropriate model for the trend in salaries.

c) Predict a superstar salary for 2005.

T **8. Planet distances and years.** The table shows the average distance of each of the nine planets from the sun, and the length of the year (in earth years).

	Position Number	Distance from Sun (million miles)	Length of Year (earth years)
Mercury	1	36	0.24
Venus	2	67	0.61
Earth	3	93	1.0
Mars	4	142	1.88
Jupiter	5	484	11.86
Saturn	6	887	29.46
Uranus	7	1784	84.07
Neptune	8	2796	164.82
Pluto	9	3666	247.68

a) Plot the length of the year against the distance from the sun. Describe the shape of your plot.

b) Re-express one or both variables to straighten the plot. Use the re-expressed data to create a model describing the length of a planet's year based on its distance from the sun.

c) Comment on how well your model fits the data.

T **9. Planet distances and order.** Let's look again at the pattern in the locations of the planets in our solar system seen in the table in Exercise 8.

a) Use re-expressed data to create a model for the distance from the sun based on the planet's position.

b) There is some debate among astronomers as to whether Pluto is truly a planet or actually a large member of the Kuiper Belt of comets and other icy bodies. Does your model suggest that Pluto may not belong in the planet group? Explain.

T **10. Planets, part 3.** The asteroid belt between Mars and Jupiter may be the remnants of a failed planet. If so, then Jupiter is really in position 6, Saturn is in 7, and so on. Repeat Exercise 9, using this revised method of numbering the positions. Which method seems to work better?

T **11. Quaoar, planets, part 4.** In June 2002, Caltech astronomers Chad Trujillo and Mike Brown discovered a new large body in orbit about the sun, a billion miles beyond Jupiter. Named Quaoar (pronounced "kwa-whar") after a Native American god, it is about one-tenth the diameter of earth. Quaoar orbits the sun once every 288 years at a distance of about 4 billion miles. Astronomers have classified it as a member of the Kuiper Belt, rather than as a planet.

There are reasons for suspecting that Pluto is unlike other planets. For example, its orbit is tilted relative to the plane in which other planetary orbits are found. And its orbit is very eccentric, passing both inside the orbit of Neptune and outside the orbit of Quaoar. Omit Pluto from your count of planets, and consider Quaoar as a candidate for the next planet beyond Neptune.

a) Based on its position, how does Quaoar's distance from the sun (re-expressed to logs) compare with the prediction made by your model from Exercise 9.

b) Refit the model using Quaoar's distance and position in the model instead of Pluto's. Now how well does your model to predict (re-expressed) distance from position number fit?

12. Models and laws, planets part 5. The model you found in Exercise 8 is a relationship noted in the 17th century by Kepler as his Third Law of Planetary Motion. It was subsequently explained as a consequence of Newton's Law of Gravitation. The models for Exercises 9–11 relate to what is sometimes called the Titius-Bode "law," a pattern noticed in the 18th century but lacking any scientific explanation.

Compare how well the re-expressed data are described by their respective linear models. What aspect of the model of Exercise 8 suggests that we have found a physical law? In the future, we may learn enough about a planetary system around another star to tell whether the Titius-Bode pattern applies there. If you discovered that another planetary system followed the same pattern, how would it change your opinion about whether this is a real natural "law"? What would you think if the next system we find does not follow this pattern?

13–18. Curved models. Use technology to create curved models for Exercises 4–9.

19. Logs (not logarithms). The value of a log is based on the number of "board feet" of lumber the log may contain. (A board foot is the equivalent of a piece of wood 1 inch thick, 12 inches wide, and 1 foot long. For example, a 2″ × 4″ piece that is 12 feet long contains 8 board feet.) To estimate the amount of lumber in a log, buyers measure the diameter inside the bark at the smaller end. Then they look in a table based on the Doyle Log Scale. The table below shows the estimates for logs 16 feet long.

Diameter of Log	8″	12″	16″	20″	24″	28″
Board Feet	16	64	144	256	400	576

a) What model does this scale use?

b) How much lumber would you estimate that a log 10″ in diameter contains?

c) What does this model suggest about logs 36″ in diameter?

20. Weight lifting. Listed below are the gold medal-winning men's weightlifting performances at the 2000 Olympics.

Weight Class (kg)	Winner (country)	Weight Lifted (kg)
56	Mutli (Turkey)	305
62	Pechalov (Croatia)	325
69	Boevski (Bulgaria)	357.5
77	Xugang (China)	367.5
85	Dimas (Greece)	390
94	Kakiasvilas (Greece)	405
105	Tavakoli (Iran)	425

a) Create a linear model for the amount lifted in each weight class.

b) Check the residuals plot. Is your linear model appropriate?

c) Create a better model.

d) Explain why you think your model is better.

e) Based on your model, which of the medalists turned in the most surprising performance? Explain.

f) Consider that competitor to be an outlier. Eliminate that data point and recreate your model.

g) Using this revised model, how much would you have expected the outlier competitor to lift?

h) Explain the meaning of the residual from your new model for that competitor.

21. Life expectancy. The data below list the life expectancy for white males in the United States every 10 years during the last century (1910, 1920, etc.). Create a model to predict future increases in life expectancy. (National Vital Statistics Report)

48.6, 54.4, 59.7, 62.1, 66.5, 67.4, 68.0, 70.7, 72.7, 74.9

22. Tree growth. A 1996 study examined the growth of grapefruit trees in Texas, determining the average trunk diameter (in inches) for trees of varying ages.

Age (yr)	2	4	6	8	10	12	14	16	18	20
Diameter (in.)	2.1	3.9	5.2	6.2	6.9	7.6	8.3	9.1	10.0	11.4

a) Fit a linear model to these data. What concerns do you have about the model?

b) If data had been given for individual trees instead of averages, would you expect the fit to be stronger, less strong, or about the same? Explain.

23. Slower is cheaper? Researchers studying how a car's gas mileage varies with its speed drove a compact car 200 miles at various speeds on a test track. Their data are shown in the table.

Speed (mph)	35	40	45	50	55	60	65	70	75
Miles per gal	25.9	27.7	28.5	29.5	29.2	27.4	26.4	24.2	22.8

a) Create a model for these data.

b) Do you think this model is appropriate? Why?

c) Discuss the strength of your model.

d) Do you think this model will produce accurate predictions about the gas mileage people may get in daily driving? Explain.

T **24. Orange production.** The table below shows that as the number of oranges on a tree increases, the fruit tend to get smaller. Create a model for this relationship, and express any concerns you may have.

Number of Oranges/Tree	Average Weight/Fruit (lb)
50	.60
100	.58
150	.56
200	.55
250	.53
300	.52
350	.50
400	.49
450	.48
500	.46
600	.44
700	.42
800	.40
900	.38

25. Years to live. Insurance companies and other organizations use actuarial tables to estimate the remaining lifespan of their customers. Below are the estimated additional years of life for black males in the United States, according to a 1999 National Vital Statistics Report.

Age	10	20	30	40	50	60	70	80	90	100
Years Left	59.2	49.6	40.7	31.9	24.0	17.2	11.6	7.2	4.4	2.8

a) Create an appropriate model.

b) Predict the lifespan of an 18-year-old black man.

T **26. Oil production (again).** Here are the data on U.S. oil production first seen in Exercise 26 of Chapter 7.

How successfully might a model based on these data predict the future of U.S. oil production? Explain.

Year	Oil	Year	Oil
1949	1,841,940	1975	3,056,779
1950	1,973,574	1976	2,976,180
1951	2,247,711	1977	3,009,265
1952	2,289,836	1978	3,178,216
1953	2,357,082	1979	3,121,310
1954	2,314,988	1980	3,146,365
1955	2,484,428	1981	3,128,624
1956	2,617,283	1982	3,156,715
1957	2,616,901	1983	3,170,999
1958	2,448,987	1984	3,249,696
1959	2,574,590	1985	3,274,553
1960	2,574,933	1986	3,168,252
1961	2,621,758	1987	3,047,378
1962	2,676,189	1988	2,979,123
1963	2,752,723	1989	2,778,773
1964	2,786,822	1990	2,684,687
1965	2,848,514	1991	2,707,039
1966	3,027,763	1992	2,624,632
1967	3,215,742	1993	2,499,033
1968	3,329,042	1994	2,431,476
1969	3,371,751	1995	2,394,268
1970	3,517,450	1996	2366,017
1971	3,453,914	1997	2,354,831
1972	3,455,368	1998	2,281,919
1973	3,360,903	1999	2,146,732
1974	3,202,585	2000	2,135,062

27. Internet. It's often difficult to find the ideal model for situations in which the data are strongly curved. The table below shows the rapid growth of the number of academic journals published on the Internet during the last decade.

Year	Number of Journals
1991	27
1992	36
1993	45
1994	181
1995	306
1996	1093
1997	2459

a) Try to create a good model to describe this growth.
b) Use your model to estimate the number of electronic journals in the year 2000.
c) Comment on your faith in this estimate.

Review of Part II Exploring and Understanding Data

Quick Review

You have now survived your second major unit of Statistics. Here's a brief summary of the key concepts and skills:

- Data come in two flavors: categorical and quantitative.
- To explore relationships in categorical data, check out Chapter 3.
- To explore relationships in quantitative data:
  - Make a picture. Use a scatterplot. Put the explanatory variable on the *x*-axis and the response variable on the *y*-axis.
  - Describe the association in terms of direction, form, and scatter.
  - The amount of scatter determines the strength of the association.
  - If as one variable increases so does the other, the association is positive. If one increases as the other decreases, it's negative.
  - If the form of the association is linear, calculate a correlation to measure its strength numerically, and do a regression analysis to model it.
  - Correlations closer to −1 or +1 indicate stronger linear associations. Correlations near 0 indicate weak linear relationships, but other forms of association may still be present.
  - The least squares regression line estimates values of the response variable from values of the explanatory variable.
  - A residual is the difference between the true value of the response variable and the value predicted by the regression model.
  - The slope of the line is a rate of change, best described in "*y*-units" per "*x*-unit."
  - R^2 gives the percentage of the variation in the response variable that is accounted for by the model.
  - The standard deviation of the residuals measures the amount of scatter around the line.
  - Outliers and influential points can distort any of our models.
  - If you see a pattern (a curve) in the residuals plot, your chosen model is not appropriate; use a different model. You may, for example, straighten the relationship by re-expressing one of the variables.
  - To straighten bent relationships, re-express the data using logarithms or a power (squares, square roots, reciprocals, etc.).
  - Always remember that an association is not necessarily an indication that one of the variables causes the other.

Need more help with some of this? Try rereading some sections of Chapters 7 through 10. And turn this page for more opportunities to review these concepts and skills.

"One must learn by doing the thing; though you think you know it, you have no certainty until you try."
—Sophocles (495–406 B.C.E.)

Review Exercises

1. College. Every year *US News and World Report* publishes a special issue on many U.S. colleges and universities. The scatterplots below have *student/faculty ratio* (number of students per faculty member) for the colleges and universities on the y-axes plotted against 4 other variables. The correct correlations for these scatterplots appear in this list. Match them.

-0.98 -0.71 -0.51 0.09 0.23 0.69

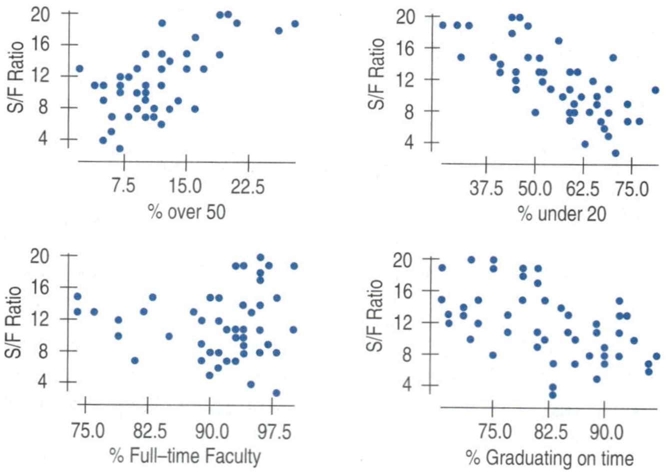

2. Togetherness. Are good grades in high school associated with family togetherness? A simple random sample of 142 high school students was asked how many meals per week their families ate together. Their responses produced a mean of 3.78 meals per week, with a standard deviation of 2.2. Researchers then matched these responses against the students' grade point averages (GPA). The scatterplot appeared to be reasonably linear, so they created a line of regression. No apparent pattern emerged in the residuals plot. The equation of the line was $\widehat{gpa} = 2.73 + 0.11 meals$.

a) Interpret the y-intercept in this context.
b) Interpret the slope in this context.
c) What was the mean GPA for the students in this study?
d) If a student in this study had a negative residual, what did that mean?
e) Upon hearing of this study, a counselor recommended that parents who want to improve the grades their children get should get the family to eat together more often. Do you agree with this interpretation? Explain.

3. Vineyards. Shown below are the scatterplot and regression analysis for case prices of 36 products from vineyards in the Finger Lakes region of New York State and the ages of the vineyards.

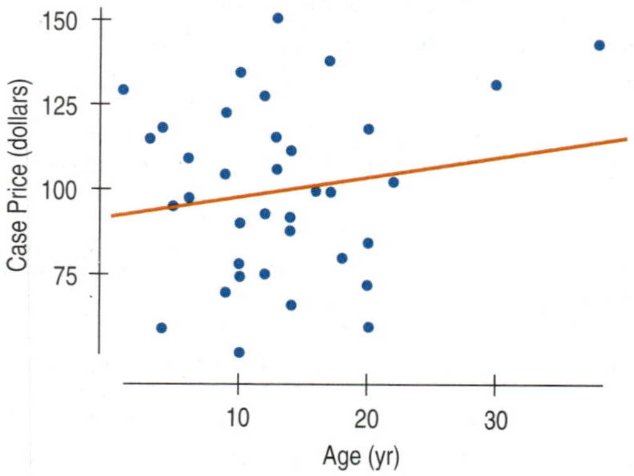

Dependent variable is: Case Price
R-squared = 2.7%

Variable	Coefficient
Constant	92.7650
Age	0.567284

a) Does it appear that vineyards in business longer get higher prices for their products? Explain.
b) What does this analysis tell us about vineyards in the rest of the world?
c) Write the regression equation.
d) Explain why that equation is essentially useless.

4. Vineyards again. Instead of age, perhaps the size of the vineyard (in acres) is associated with the value of the produce. Look at the scatterplot:

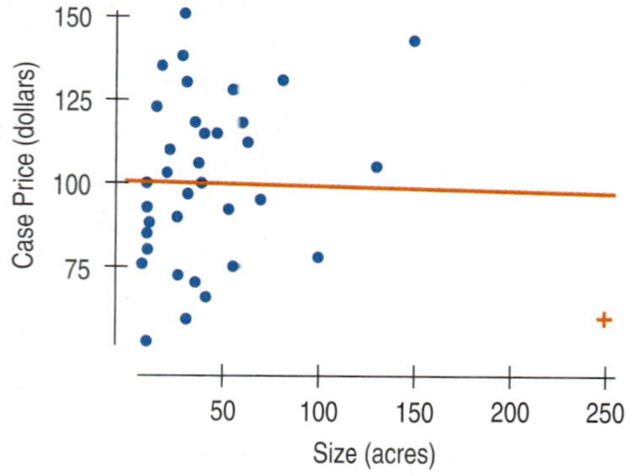

a) Do you see any evidence of an association?
b) What concern do you have about this scatterplot?
c) If the red "+" data point is removed, would you expect the correlation to become stronger or weaker? Explain.
d) If the red "+" data point is removed, would you expect the slope of the line to go up or down? Explain.

5. More twins? As the table shows, the number of twins born in the United States has been increasing.

Year	Twin births	Year	Twin births
1981	70,049	1990	93,865
1982	71,631	1991	94,779
1983	72,287	1992	95,372
1984	72,949	1993	96,445
1985	77,102	1994	97,064
1986	79,485	1995	96,736
1987	81,778	1996	100,750
1988	85,315	1997	104,137
1989	90,118		

a) Find the equation of the regression line for predicting the number of twin births.
b) Explain in this context what the slope of this line means.
c) Predict the number of twin births in the United States for the year 2002. Comment on your faith in that prediction.
d) Comment on the residuals plot.

6. Dow Jones. When the Dow Jones stock index first reached 10,000, the *New York Times* reported the dates on which the Dow first crossed each of the "thousand" marks, starting with reaching 1000 in 1972. A regression of the Dow prices on year looks (in part) like this:

```
Dependent variable is: Dow
R-squared = 65.8%

Variable     Coefficient
Constant     -603335
Year            305.471
```

a) What is the correlation between the Dow index and the year?
b) Write the regression equation.
c) Explain in this context what the equation says.
d) Here's a scatterplot of the residuals. Which assumption(s) of the regression analysis appear to be violated?

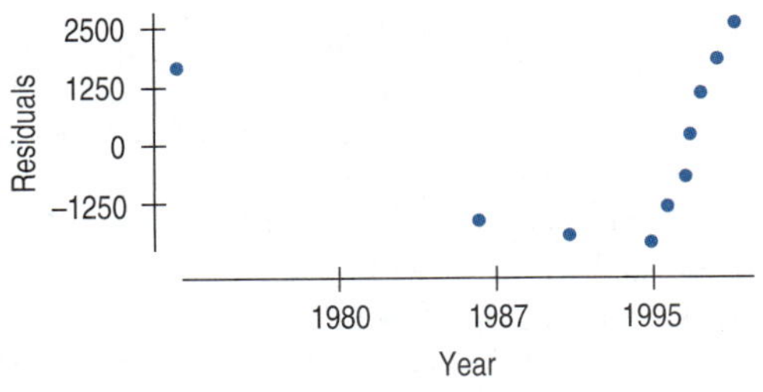

7. Acid rain. Biologists studying the effects of acid rain on wildlife collected data from 163 streams in the Adirondack Mountains. They recorded the pH (acidity) of the water and the BCI, a measure of biological diversity, and they calculated $R^2 = 27\%$. Here's a scatterplot of BCI against pH.

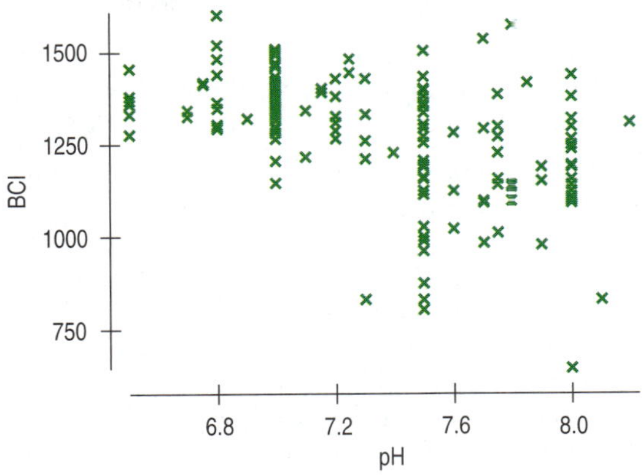

a) What is the correlation between pH and BCI?
b) Describe the association between these two variables.
c) If a stream has average pH, what would you predict about the BCI?
d) In a stream where the pH is 3 standard deviations above average, what would you predict about the BCI?

8. Manatees. Marine biologists warn that the growing number of powerboats registered in Florida threatens the existence of manatees. The February 12, 2002 *New York Times* reported these data:

Year	Manatees Killed	Powerboat Registrations (in 1000s)
1982	13	447.0
1983	21	459.6
1984	24	481.0
1985	16	497.9
1986	24	512.6
1987	20	512.3
1988	15	526.5
1989	34	558.6
1990	33	585.3
1992	33	613.5
1993	39	645.5
1994	43	675
1995	50	711
1996	47	719
1997	53	716
1998	38	716
1999	35	716
2000	49	735
2001	81	860

a) In this context, which do you think is the explanatory variable?
b) Make a scatterplot of these data and describe the association you see.
c) Find the correlation between boat registrations and manatee deaths.
d) Interpret the value of R^2.
e) Does your analysis prove that powerboats are killing manatees?

T **9. A Manatee model.** Continue your analysis of the manatee situation from the previous exercise.
a) Create a linear model of the association between manatee deaths and powerboat registrations.
b) Interpret the slope of your model.
c) Interpret the y-intercept of your model.
d) How accurately did your model predict the high number of manatee deaths in 2001?
e) Which is better for the manatees, positive residuals or negative residuals? Explain.
f) What does your model suggest about the future for the manatee?

10. Grades. A Statistics instructor created a linear regression equation to predict students' final exam scores from their midterm exam scores. The regression equation was $\widehat{fin} = 10 + 0.9mid$.
a) If Susan scored a 70 on the midterm, what did the instructor predict for her score on the final?
b) Susan got an 80 on the final. How big is her residual?
c) Suppose that the standard deviation of the final was 12 points and the standard deviation of the midterm was 10 points. What is the correlation between the two tests?
d) How many points would someone need to score on the midterm to have a predicted final score of 100?
e) Suppose someone scored 100 on the final. Explain why you can't estimate this student's midterm score from the information given.
f) One of the students in the class scored 100 on the midterm but got overconfident, slacked off, and scored only 15 on the final exam. What is the residual for this student?
g) No other student in the class "achieved" such a dramatic turnaround. If the instructor decides not to include this student's scores when constructing a new regression model, will the R^2 value of the regression increase, decrease, or remain the same? Explain briefly.
h) Will the slope of the new line increase or decrease?

11. Traffic. Highway planners investigated the relationship between traffic density (number of automobiles per mile) and the average speed of the traffic on a moderately large city thoroughfare. The data were collected at the same location at 10 different times over a span of 3 months. They found a mean traffic density of 68.6 cars per mile (cpm) with standard deviation of 27.07 cpm. Overall the cars' average speed was 26.38 mph with standard deviation of 9.68 mph. These researchers found the regression line for these data to be $\widehat{speed} = 50.55 - 0.352cars$.
a) What is the value of the correlation coefficient between *speed* and *cars?*
b) What percent of the variation in average speed is explained by traffic density?
c) Predict the average speed of traffic on the thoroughfare when the traffic density is 50 cpm.
d) What is the value of the residual for a traffic density of 56 cpm with an observed speed of 32.5 mph?
e) The data set initially included the point *cars* = 125 cpm, *speed* = 55 mph. This point was considered an outlier and was not included in the analysis. Will the slope increase, decrease, or remain the same if we redo the analysis and include this point?
f) Will the correlation become stronger, weaker, or remain the same if we redo the analysis and include this point (125, 55)?
g) A European member of the research team measured the speed of the cars in kilometers per hour (1 km ≈ 0.62 miles) and the traffic density in cars per kilometer. Find the value of his calculated correlation between speed and density.

T **12. Cramming.** One Thursday, researchers gave students enrolled in a section of basic Spanish a set of 50 new vocabulary words to memorize. On Friday the students took a vocabulary test. When they returned to class the following Monday, they were retested—without advance warning. Both sets of test scores for the 28 students are shown.

Fri.	Mon.	Fri.	Mon.	Fri.	Mon.
42	36	48	37	39	41
44	44	43	41	46	32
45	46	45	32	37	36
48	38	47	44	40	31
44	40	50	47	41	32
43	38	34	34	48	39
41	37	38	31	37	31
35	31	43	40	36	41
43	32				

a) What is the correlation between Friday and Monday scores?
b) What does a scatterplot show about the association between the scores?
c) What does it mean for a student to have a positive residual?
d) What would you predict about a student whose Friday score was one standard deviation below average?
e) Write the equation of the regression line.
f) Predict the Monday score of a student who earned a 40 on Friday.

13. Correlations. What factor most explains differences in gas mileage among cars? Here's a correlation matrix exploring that relationship for the car's weight, horsepower, engine size (displacement), and number of cylinders.

	MPG	Weight	Horse-power	Displace-ment	Cylinders
MPG	1.000				
Weight	−0.903	1.000			
Horsepower	−0.871	0.917	1.000		
Displacement	−0.786	0.951	0.872	1.000	
Cylinders	−0.806	0.917	0.864	0.940	1.000

a) Which factor seems most strongly associated with fuel economy (miles per gallon)?
b) What does the negative correlation indicate?
c) Explain the meaning of R^2 for that relationship.

14. Autos revisited. Look again at the correlation table for cars in the last exercise.
a) Which two variables in the table exhibit the strongest association?
b) Is that strong association necessarily cause-and-effect? Offer at least two explanations why that association might be so strong.
c) Engine displacements for U.S.-made cars are often measured in cubic inches. For many foreign cars the units are either cubic centimeters or liters. How would changing from cubic inches to liters affect the calculated correlations involving displacement?
d) What would you predict about the fuel economy of a car whose engine displacement is one standard deviation above the mean?

15. Cars, one more time! Can we predict the horsepower of the engine manufacturers will put in a car by knowing the weight of the car? Here are the regression analysis and residuals plot.

Dependent variable is: Horsepower
R-squared = 84.1%
s = 10.68

Variable	Coefficient
Constant	3.49834
Weight	34.3144

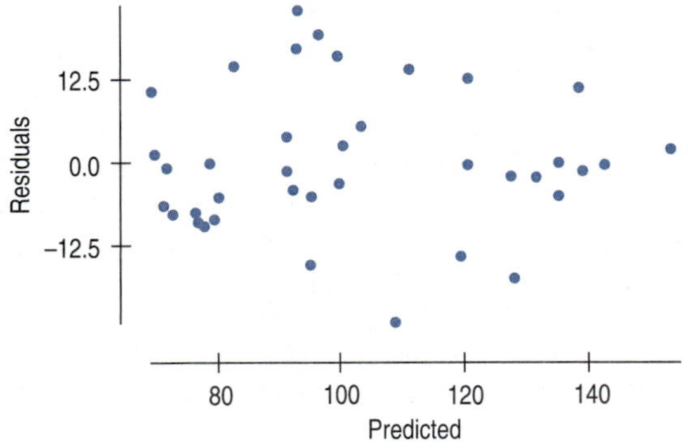

a) Write the equation of the regression line.
b) Do you think the car's weight is measured in pounds, or thousands of pounds? Explain.
c) Do you think this linear model is appropriate? Explain.
d) The highest point in the residuals plot representing a residual of 22.5 horsepower, is for a Chevy weighing 2595 pounds. How many horsepower does this car have?

16. Colorblind. Although some women are colorblind, this condition is primarily found in men. Why is it wrong to say there's a strong correlation between gender and colorblindness?

17. Old Faithful. There is evidence that eruptions of Old Faithful can best be predicted by knowing the duration of the previous eruption.
a) Describe what you see in the scatterplot of intervals between eruptions vs. duration of the previous eruption.

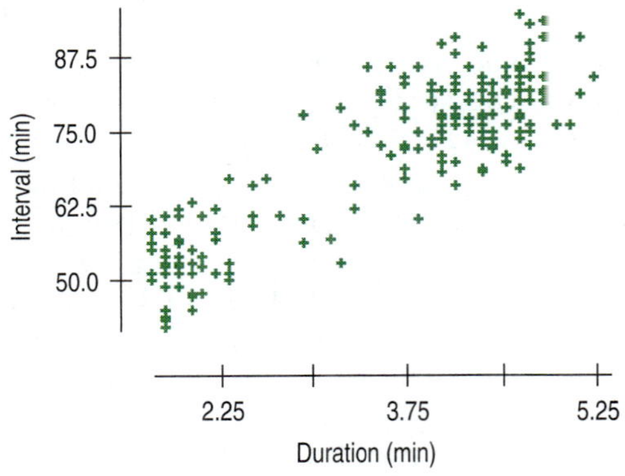

b) Write the equation of the line of best fit. Here's the regression analysis:

Dependent variable is: Interval
R-squared = 77.0%
s = 6.159

Variable	Coefficient
Constant	33.9668
Duration	10.3582

c) Carefully explain what the slope of the line means in this context.
d) How accurate do you expect predictions based on this model to be? Cite evidence from the regression analysis.
e) If you just witnessed an eruption that lasted 4 minutes, how long do you predict you'll have to wait to see the next eruption?
f) So you waited, and the next eruption came in 79 minutes. Use this as an example to explain what a residual is.

18. Which croc? The ranges inhabited by the Indian gharial crocodile and the Australian saltwater crocodile overlap in Bangladesh. Suppose a very large crocodile skeleton is found there, and we wish to determine which species the animal was. Wildlife scientists have measured the lengths of the heads and the complete bodies of several crocs (in centimeters) of each species, creating the regression analyses below:

Indian Crocodile		Australian Crocodile	
Dependent variable is: IBody		Dependent variable is: ABody	
R-squared = 97.2%		R-squared = 98.0%	
Variable	**Coefficient**	**Variable**	**Coefficient**
Constant	−69.3693	Constant	−20.2245
IHead	7.40004	A Head	7.71726

a) Do the associations between the sizes of the heads and bodies of the two species appear to be strong? Explain.
b) In what ways are the two relationships similar? Explain.
c) What is different about the two models? What does that mean?
d) The crocodile skeleton found had a head length of 62 cm and a body length of 380 cm. Which species do you think it was? Explain why.

T **19. How old is that tree?** One can determine how old a tree is by counting its rings, but that requires cutting the tree down. Can we estimate the age simply from its diameter? A forester measured 27 trees of the same species that had been cut down, and counted the rings to determine the ages of the trees.

Diameter (in.)	Age (yr)	Diameter (in.)	Age (yr)
1.8	4	10.3	23
1.8	5	14.3	25
2.2	8	13.2	28
4.4	8	9.9	29
6.6	8	13.2	30
4.4	10	15.4	30
7.7	10	17.6	33
10.8	12	14.3	34
7.7	13	15.4	35
5.5	14	11	38
9.9	16	15.4	38
10.1	18	16.5	40
12.1	20	16.5	42
12.8	22		

a) Find the correlation between diameter and age. Does this suggest that a linear model may be appropriate? Explain.
b) Create a scatterplot and describe the association.
c) Create the linear model.
d) Check the residuals. Explain why a linear model is probably not appropriate.
e) If you used this model, would it generally overestimate or underestimate the ages of very large trees? Explain.

T **20. Improving trees.** In the last exercise you saw that the linear model had some deficiencies. Let's create a better model.
a) Perhaps the cross-sectional area of a tree would be a better predictor of its age. Since area is measured in square units, try re-expressing the data by squaring the diameters. Does the scatterplot look better?
b) Create a model that predicts age from the square of diameter.
c) Check the residuals plot for this new model. Is this model more appropriate? Why?
d) Estimate the age of a tree 18″ in diameter.

21. New homes. A real estate agent collects data to develop a model that will use the size of a new home (in square feet) to predict its sale price (in thousands of dollars). Which of these is most likely to be the slope of the regression line: 0.008, 0.08, 0.8, or 8? Explain.

22. Smoking and pregnancy. The organization *KidsCount* monitors issues related to children. The table shows a 50-city average of the percent of expectant mothers who smoked cigarettes during their pregnancies.

Year	% Smoking while pregnant	Year	% Smoking while pregnant
1990	17.7	1995	12.7
1991	17.0	1996	11.9
1992	16.0	1997	11.2
1993	14.9	1998	10.8
1994	13.9	1999	10.4

a) Create a scatterplot and describe the trend you see.
b) Find the correlation.
c) How is the value of the correlation affected by the fact that the data are averages rather than percentages for each of the 50 cities?
d) Write a linear model and interpret the slope in this context.

23. No smoking? The downward trend in smoking you saw in the last exercise is good news for the health of babies, but will it ever stop?
a) Explain why you can't use the linear model you created in Exercise 22 to see when smoking during pregnancy will cease altogether.
b) Create a model that could estimate the year in which the level of smoking would be 0%.
c) Comment on the reliability of such a prediction.

24. Tips. It's commonly believed that people use tips to reward good service. A researcher for the hospitality industry examined tips and ratings of service quality from 2645 dining parties at 21 different restaurants. The correlation between ratings of service and tip percentages was 0.11. ("Gratitude and Gratuity." *Journal of Socio-Economics* 29: 203–214.)

a) Describe the relationship between quality of service and tip size.
b) Find and interpret the value of R^2 in this context.

25. Move south? Data from 50 large U.S. cities show the mean January temperature and the latitude. Describe what you see in the scatterplot.

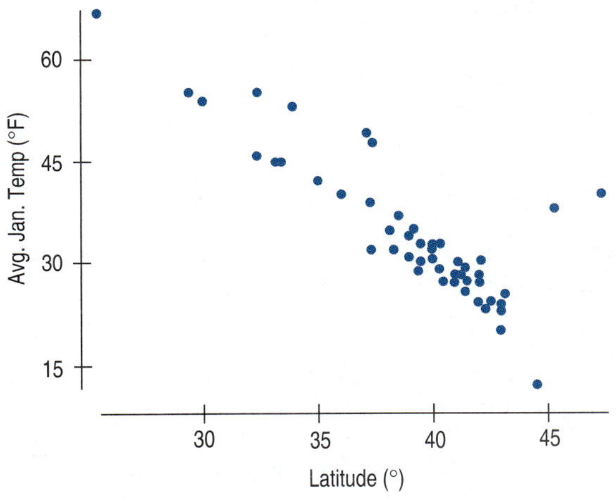

26. Correlations. A study of living conditions in 55 large U.S. cities found the mean January temperature (degrees Fahrenheit), altitude (feet above sea level), and latitude (degrees north of the equator). Here's the correlation matrix.

	Jan. Temp	Latitude	Altitude
Jan. Temp	1.000		
Latitude	−0.848	1.000	
Altitude	−0.369	0.184	1.000

a) Which seems to be more useful in predicting January temperature—altitude or latitude? Explain.
b) If the temperature were measured in degrees Celsius, what would be the correlation between temperature and latitude?
c) If the temperature were measured in degrees Celsius and the altitude in meters, what would be the correlation? Explain.
d) What would you predict about the January temperatures in a city that whose altitude is two standard deviations higher than the average altitude?

27. Winter in the city. Summary statistics for the data relating the latitude and average January temperature for 55 large U.S. cities are given below.

Variable	Mean	StdDev
Latitude	39.02	5.42
JanTemp	26.44	13.49

Correlation = −0.848

a) What percent of the variation in January temperatures can be explained by variation in latitude?
b) What is indicated by the fact that the correlation is negative?
c) Write the equation of the line of regression for predicting January temperature from latitude.
d) Explain what the slope of the line means.
e) Do you think the *y*-intercept of the line is meaningful? Explain.
f) The latitude of Denver is 40° N. Predict the mean January temperature there.
g) If the residual for a city is positive, what does that mean?

28. Depression. The September 1998 issue of the *American Psychologist* published an article by Kraut *et al.* that reported on an experiment examining "the social and psychological impact of the Internet on 169 people in 73 households during their first 1 to 2 years on-line." In the experiment, 73 households were offered free Internet access for one or two years in return for allowing their time and activity on-line to be tracked. The members of the households who participated in the study were also given a battery of tests at the beginning and again at the end of the study. The conclusion of the study made news headlines: Those who spent more time on-line tended to be more depressed at the end of the experiment. Although the paper reports a more complex model, the basic result can be summarized in the following regression of *Depression* (at the end of the study, in "depression scale units") vs. *Internet use* (in mean hours per week.)

Dependent variable is: Depression
R-squared = 4.6%
s = 0.4563

Variable	Coefficient
Constant	0.5655
Internet use	0.0199

The news reports about this study clearly concluded that using the Internet causes depression. Discuss whether such a conclusion can be drawn from this regression. If so, discuss the supporting evidence. If not, say why not.

29. Jumps. How are Olympic performances in various events related? The plot shows winning long jump and high jump distances, in inches, for the 20th century Olympic Games.

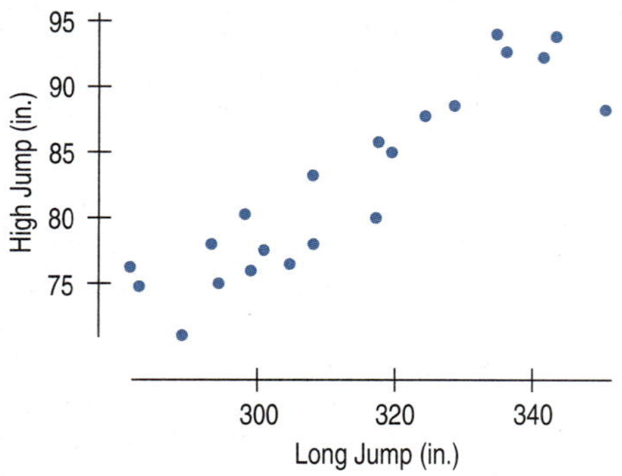

a) Describe the association.
b) Do long jump performances somehow influence the high jumpers? How do you account for the relationship you see?
c) The correlation for the given scatterplot is 0.92, but at the Olympics these jumps are actually measured in meters rather than inches. Does that make the actual correlation higher or lower?
d) What would you predict about the long jump in a year when the high jumper jumped one standard deviation better than the average high jump?

30. Modeling jumps. Here are the summary statistics for the Olympic long jumps and high jumps displayed in the scatterplot above.

Event	Mean	StdDev
Long Jump	314.10	20.71
High Jump	83.04	7.26

Correlation = 0.917

a) Write the equation of the line of regression for estimating high jump from long jump.
b) Interpret the slope of the line.
c) In a year when the long jump is 340 inches, what high jump would you predict?
d) Why can't you use this line to estimate the long jump for a year when you know the high jump was 85 inches?
e) Write the equation of the line you need to make that prediction.

31. French. Consider the association between a student's score on a French vocabulary test and the weight of the student. What direction and strength of correlation would you expect in each of the following situations? Explain.
a) The students are all in third grade.
b) The students are in third through twelfth grades in the same school district.
c) The students are in tenth grade in France.
d) The students are in third through twelfth grades in France.

32. Twins. Twins are often born after a pregnancy that lasts less than 9 months. The graph from the *Journal of the American Medical Association* (*JAMA*) shows the rate of pre-term twin births in the United States over the past 20 years. In this study, *JAMA* categorized mothers by the level of prenatal medical care they received: inadequate, adequate, or intensive.
a) Describe the overall trend in preterm twin births.
b) Describe any differences you see in this trend, depending on the level of prenatal medical care the mother received.
c) Should expectant mothers be advised to cut back on the level of medical care they seek in the hope of avoiding preterm births? Explain.

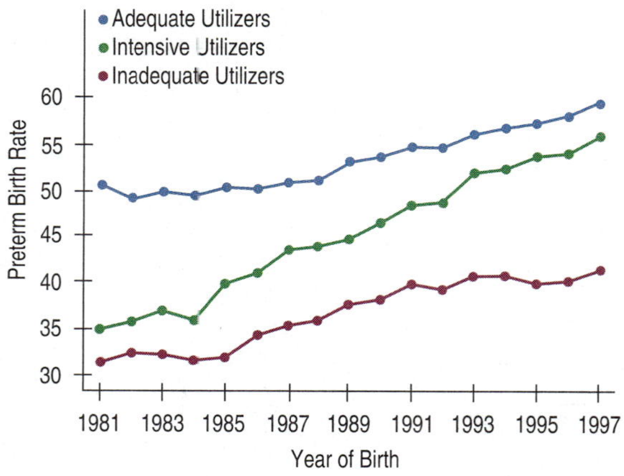

Preterm birth rate per 100 live twin births among U.S. twins by intensive, adequate, and less than adequate prenatal care utilization, 1981–1997. (*JAMA* 284[2000]:335–341)

T **33. Lunchtime.** Create and interpret a model for the toddlers' lunchtime data presented in Chapter 7. The table shows the number of minutes the kids stayed at the table and the number of calories they consumed for lunch.

Calories	Time	Calories	Time
472	21.4	450	42.4
498	30.8	410	43.1
465	37.7	504	29.2
456	33.5	437	31.3
423	32.8	489	28.6
437	39.5	436	32.9
508	22.8	480	30.6
431	34.1	439	35.1
479	33.9	444	33.0
454	43.8	408	43.7

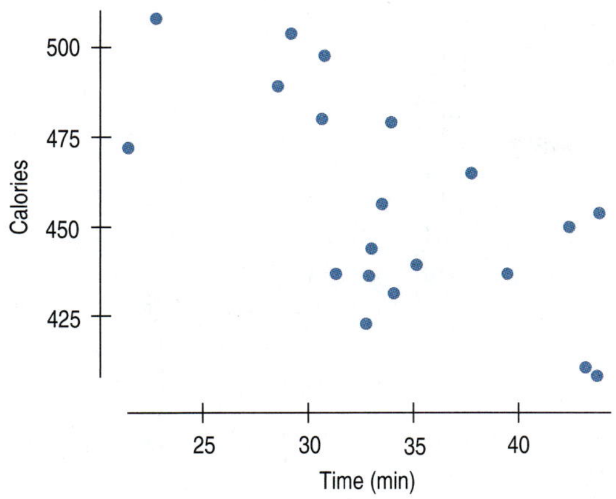

34. Gasoline. Since clean air regulations have dictated the use of unleaded gasoline, the supply of leaded gas in New York state has diminished. The table below was given on the August 2001 New York State Math B exam, a statewide achievement test for high school students.

Year	1984	1988	1992	1996	2000
Gallons (1000s)	150	124	104	76	50

a) Create a linear model to predict the number of gallons that will be available in 2005.
b) The exam then asked students to estimate the year when leaded gasoline will first become unavailable, expecting them to use the model from part (a) to answer the question. Explain why that method is incorrect.
c) Create a model that *would* be appropriate for that task, and make the estimate.
d) The "wrong" answer from the other model is fairly accurate in this case. Why?

35. Tobacco and alcohol. Are people who use tobacco products more likely to consume alcohol? Here are data on household spending (in pounds) taken by the British Government on 11 regions in Great Britain. Do tobacco and alcohol spending appear to be related? What questions do you have about these data? What conclusions can you draw?

Region	Alcohol	Tobacco
North	6.47	4.03
Yorkshire	6.13	3.76
Northeast	6.19	3.77
East Midlands	4.89	3.34
West Midlands	5.63	3.47
East Anglia	4.52	2.92
Southeast	5.89	3.2
Southwest	4.79	2.71
Wales	5.27	3.53
Scotland	6.08	4.51
Northern Ireland	4.02	4.56

36. Football weights. The Sears Cup was established in 1993 to honor institutions that maintain a broad-based athletic program, achieving success in many sports, both men's and women's. Since its Division III inception in 1995, the cup has been won by Williams College in every year except one. Their football team has a 85.3% winning record under their current coach. Why does the football team win so much? Is it because they're heavier than their opponents? The table shows the average team weights for selected years from 1973 to 1993.

Year	Weight (lb)	Year	Weight (lb)
1973	185.5	1983	192.0
1975	182.4	1987	196.9
1977	182.1	1989	202.9
1979	191.1	1991	206.0
1981	189.4	1993	198.7

a) Fit a straight line to the relationship between weight and year.
b) Does a straight line seem reasonable?
c) Predict the average weight of the team for the year 2003. Does this seem reasonable?
d) What about the prediction for the year 2103? Explain.
e) What about the prediction for the year 3003? Explain.

37. Models. Find the predicted value of y using each model for $x = 10$.

a) $\hat{y} = 2 + 0.8 \ln x$
b) $\log \hat{y} = 5 - 0.23x$
c) $\frac{1}{\sqrt{\hat{y}}} = 17.1 - 1.66x$

38. Williams vs. Texas. Here are the average weights of the football team for the University of Texas for various years in the 20th century.

Year	Weight (lb)
1905	164
1919	163
1932	181
1945	192
1955	195
1965	199

a) Fit a straight line to the relationship of weight by year for Texas footballers.
b) According to these models, in what year will the predicted weight of the Williams College team from Exercise 36 first be more than the University of Texas team?
c) Do you believe this? Explain.

39. Vehicle weights. The Minnesota Department of Transportation hoped that they could measure the weights of big trucks without actually stopping the vehicles by using a newly developed "weigh-in-motion" scale. After installation of the scale, a study was conducted to find out whether the scale's readings correspond to the true weights of the trucks being monitored. In Exercise 14 of Chapter 7, you examined the scatterplot for the data they collected, finding the association to be approximately linear with $R^2 = 93\%$. Their regression equation is $\widehat{Wt} = 10.85 + 0.64scale$, where both the scale reading and the predicted weight of the truck are measured in thousands of pounds.

a) Estimate the weight of a truck if this scale read 31,200 pounds.

b) If that truck actually weighed 32,120 pounds, what was the residual?

c) If the scale reads 35,590 pounds, and the truck has a residual of −2440 pounds, how much does it actually weigh?

d) In general, do you expect estimates made using this equation to be reasonably accurate? Explain.

e) If the police plan to use this scale to issue tickets to trucks that appear to be overloaded, will negative or positive residuals be a greater problem? Explain.

40. Profit. How are a company's profits related to its sales. Let's examine data from 71 large U.S. corporations. All amounts are in millions of dollars.

a) Here are histograms of profits and sales and histograms of the logarithms of profits and sales. Why are the re-expressed data better for regression?

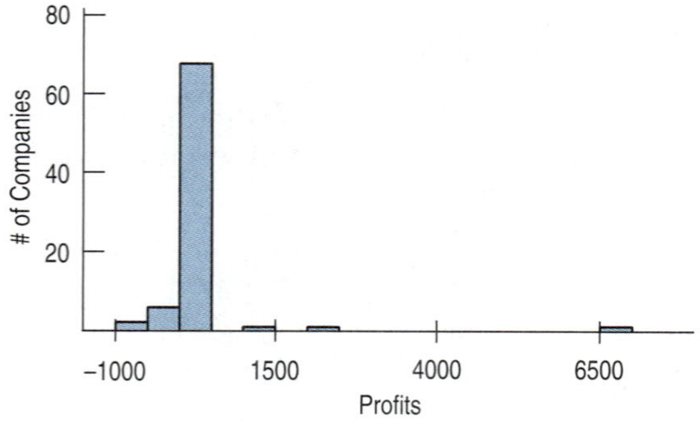

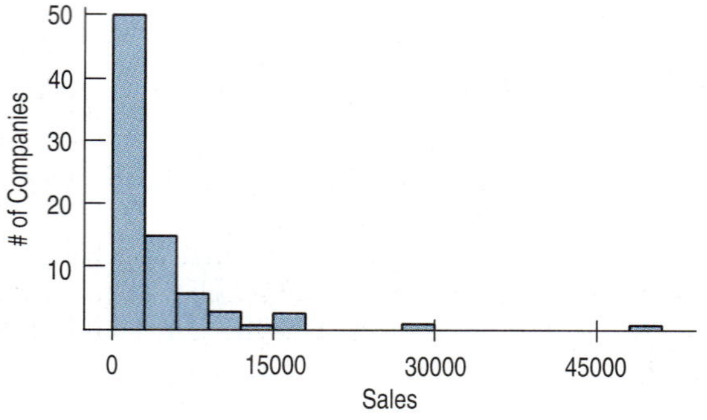

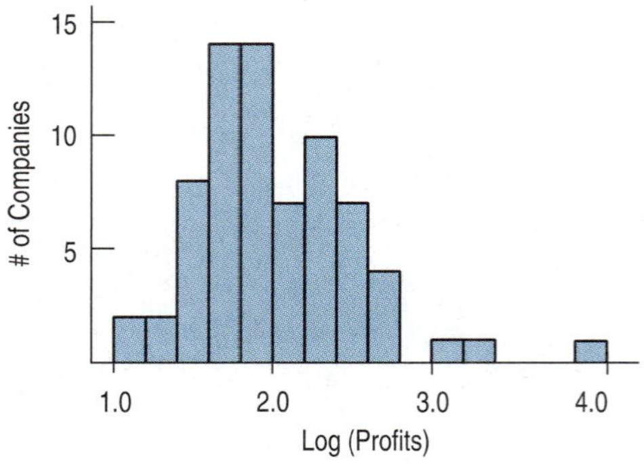

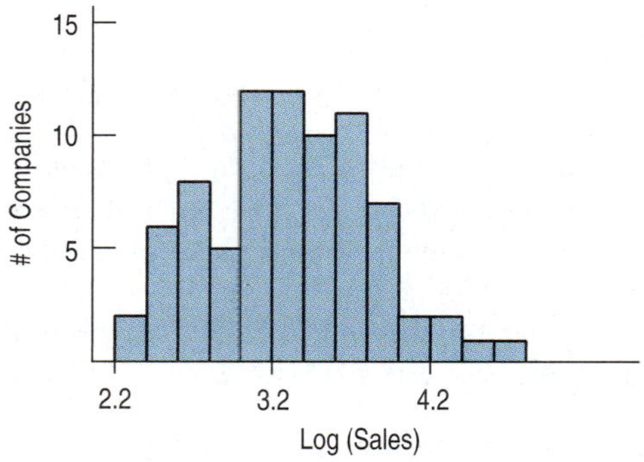

b) Here are the scatterplot and residuals plot for the regression of logarithm of profits vs. log of sales. Do you think this model is appropriate? Explain.

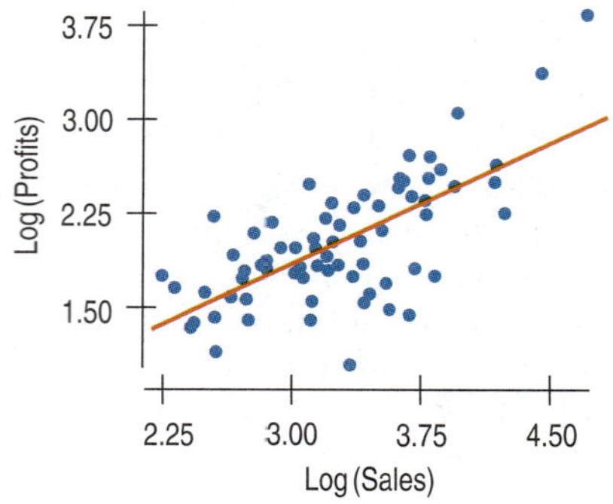

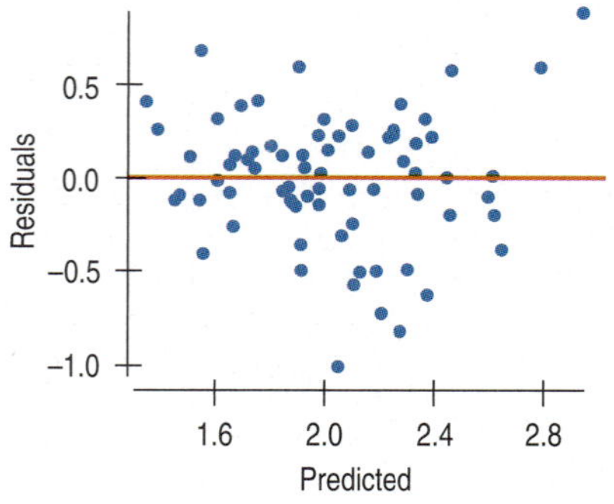

c) Here's the regression analysis. Write the equation.

Dependent variable is: Log Profit
R-squared = 48.1%

Variable	Coefficient
Constant	−0.106259
LogSales	0.647798

d) Use your equation to estimate profits earned by a company with sales of 2.5 billion dollars. (That's 2500 million.)

41. Down the drain. Most water tanks have a drain plug so that the tank may be emptied when it's to be moved or repaired. How long it takes a certain size tank to drain depends on the size of the plug, as shown in the table. Create a model.

Diameter of plug (in.)	Drain time (min.)
$\frac{3}{8}$	140
$\frac{1}{2}$	80
$\frac{3}{4}$	35
1	20
$1\frac{1}{4}$	13
$1\frac{1}{2}$	10
2	5

T **42. Chips.** A start-up company has developed an improved electronic chip for use in laboratory equipment. The company needs to project the manufacturing cost, so it develops a spreadsheet model that takes into account the purchase of production equipment, overhead, raw materials, depreciation, maintenance, and other business costs. The spreadsheet estimates the cost of producing 10,000 to 200,000 chips per year, as seen in the table. Develop a regression model to predict costs based on the level of production.

Chips produced (1000s)	Cost per chip ($)
10	146.10
20	105.80
30	85.75
40	77.02
50	66.10
60	63.92
70	58.80
80	50.91
90	47.22
100	44.31
120	42.88
140	39.05
160	37.47
180	35.09
200	34.04

43. Least squares. Consider the four points (12, 800), (24, 680), (36, 740), and (48, 660). The line of best fit is $\hat{y} = 810 - 3x$. Use these data to explain what "least squares" means.

Part III

Gathering Data

Chapter 11

Understanding Randomness

We all know what it means for something to be random. Or do we? Many children play games that rely on chance outcomes. Rolling dice, spinning spinners, and shuffling cards, all select at random. Adult games use randomness as well, from card games to lotteries to Bingo. What's the most important aspect of the randomness in these games? It must be fair.

What is it about the outcomes being random that makes random selection seem fair? It's really two things. First, part of what helps make it fair is that nobody can guess the outcome before it happens. Second, when we want things to be fair, usually some underlying set of outcomes will be equally likely (although in many games some combinations of outcomes are more likely than others).

Randomness is not always what we might think of as "at random." Random outcomes have a lot of structure, especially when viewed in the long run. As we will see, randomness is an essential tool of Statistics. Statisticians don't think of randomness as the annoying tendency of things to be unpredictable or haphazard. Statisticians use randomness as a tool. In fact, without deliberately applying randomness we could not do most of Statistics and this book would stop right about here.[1]

But truly random values are surprisingly hard to get. Just to see how fair humans are at selecting, pick a number at random from the top of the next page. Go ahead. Turn the page, look at the numbers quickly, and pick a number at random.

Ready?

Go.

[1]Don't get your hopes up.

1 2 3 4

Did you pick 3? If so, you've got company. Almost 75% of all people pick the number 3. About 20% pick either 2 or 4. If you picked 1, well, consider yourself a little different. Only about 5% choose 1. Psychologists have proposed reasons for this phenomenon, but for us, it simply serves as a lesson that we've got to find a better way to choose things at random.

It's Not Easy Being Random

So how should we generate random numbers? It's surprisingly difficult to generate random values even when they're equally likely.

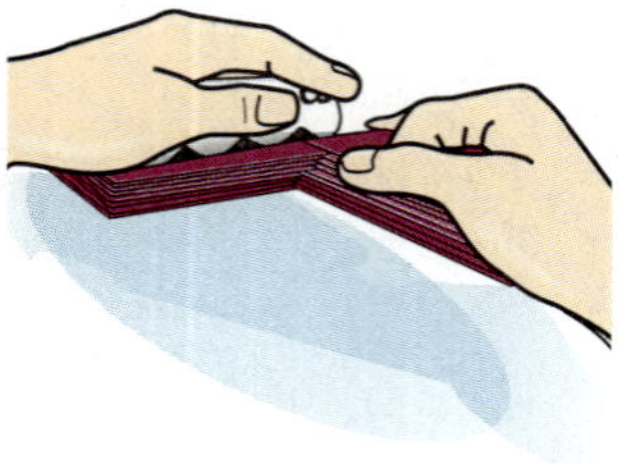

Aren't you done shuffling yet?

Even something as common as card shuffling may not be as random as you might think. If you shuffle cards by the usual method in which you split the deck in half and try to let cards fall roughly alternately from each half, you're doing a "riffle shuffle."

How many times should you shuffle cards to make the deck random? A surprising fact was discovered by statisticians Persi Diaconis, Ronald Graham, and W. M. Kantor. It takes seven shuffles. Fewer than seven leaves order in the deck, but after that, more shuffling does little good. Most people, though, don't shuffle that many times.

When computers were first used to generate hands in bridge tournaments, some professional bridge players complained that the computer was making too many "weird" hands—hands with 10 cards of one suit, for example. Suddenly these hands were appearing more often than players were used to when cards were shuffled by hand. The players assumed that the computer was doing something wrong. But it turns out that it's humans who hadn't been shuffling enough to make the decks really random and have those "weird" hands appear as often as they should.

An ordinary deck of playing cards, like the ones used in bridge and many other card games, consists of 52 cards. There are numbered cards (2 through 10), and face cards (Jack, Queen, King, Ace) whose value depends on the game you are playing. Each card is also marked by one of four suits (clubs, diamonds, hearts, or spades) whose significance is also game-specific.

Computers have become a popular way to generate random numbers. Even though they often do much better than humans, computers can't generate truly random numbers either. Computers follow programs. Start a computer from the same place, and it will always follow exactly the same path. So numbers generated by a computer program are not truly random. Technically, "random" numbers generated this way are *pseudorandom* numbers. Pseudorandom values are generated in a fixed sequence and because computers can represent only a finite number of distinct values, the sequence of pseudorandom numbers must eventually repeat itself. Fortunately, pseudorandom values are good enough for most purposes because they are virtually indistinguishable from truly random numbers.

There *are* ways to generate random numbers so that they are both equally likely and truly random. In the past, entire books of carefully generated random numbers were published. The books never made the best-seller lists and probably didn't make for great reading, but they were quite valuable to those who needed truly random values.[2] Today, we have a choice. We can use these books or find genuinely random digits from several Internet sites. The sites use methods like timing of the decay of a radioactive element or even the random changes of lava lamps to generate truly random digits. (See this book's Web site for URLs.) In either case, a string of random digits might look like this:

2217726304387410092537086270581997622725849795907032825001108963

3217535822643800292254644943760642389043766557204107354186024508

8906427308645681412198226653885873285801699027843110380420067664

8740522639824530519902027044464984322000946238678577902639002954

8887003319933147508331265192321413908608674496383528968974910533

6944182713168919406022181281304751019321546303870481407676636740

6070204916508913632855351361361043794293428486909462881431793360

7706356513310563210508993624272872250535395513645991015328128202

You probably have more interesting things to download than a few million random digits, but we'll discuss ways to use such random digits to apply randomness to real situations soon. The best ways we know to generate data that give a fair and accurate picture of the world rely on randomness, and the ways in which we draw conclusions from those data depend on the randomness, too.

[2]You'll find a table of random digits of this kind in the back of this book.

Practical Randomness

Suppose a cereal manufacturer puts pictures of famous athletes on cards in boxes of cereal in the hope of boosting sales. The manufacturer announces that 20% of the boxes contain a picture of Tiger Woods, 30% a picture of Lance Armstrong, and the rest a picture of Serena Williams. You want all three pictures. How many boxes of cereal do you expect to have to buy in order to get the complete set?

How can we answer questions like this? Well, one way is to go buy hundreds of boxes of cereal to see what might happen. But let's not. Instead, we'll consider using a random model. Why random? When we pick a box of cereal off the shelf we don't know what picture is inside. We'll assume that the pictures are randomly placed in the boxes and then the boxes are distributed randomly to stores around the country.

Why a model? We'll use a model to generate random values. To do that we'll need to make some assumptions about how they work. The assumption we'll work with here is that the underlying random events (we'll use random digits from 0 to 9) are equally likely to occur. With this model we can pretend we've bought sequences of cereal boxes and simulate the outcomes—even though these outcomes (which card we get) are not equally likely—to see what happens.

A Simulation

We want to use this simulation to give us some insight into how many boxes of cereal we might have to open until we get all three cards. We'll pretend to buy cereal, and the random numbers will tell us what happened. Like any model, the simulation will be imperfect, but we hope the results we get will help us understand the situation. A **simulation** consists of a collection of things that happen at random. There is a situation that is repeated. These situations are called the **components** of the simulation. Each component has a set of possible outcomes. In our cereal example, the component is the selection of a particular box of cereal and the outcome is the type of card in the box. Here are the steps for making a simulation in general:

1. **Identify the component to be repeated.** In this case, our component is the selection of a box of cereal.

2. **Explain how you will model the outcome.** The digits from 0 to 9 are equally likely to occur. Because 20% of the boxes contain Tiger's picture, we'll use 2 of the 10 digits to represent that outcome. Three of the 10 digits can model the 30% of boxes with Lance Armstrong cards, and the remaining 5 digits can represent the 50% of boxes with Serena. One possible assignment of the digits is

   0, 1 = Woods   2, 3, 4 = Armstrong   5, 6, 7, 8, 9 = Williams

3. **Explain how you will simulate the trial.** A **trial** is the sequence of events that we are pretending will take place. In this case we want to pretend to open cereal boxes until we have one of each picture. We do this by looking at each random number and indicating what outcome it represents. We continue until we've encountered all three pictures.

For example, the random number sequences 29240 would mean you get Lance's picture (2) in the first box you open, Serena's picture (9) in the next box, two more Armstrong pictures (2, 4) in the next two boxes, and then the Tiger Woods picture (0) you need to complete your collection. Since we've gotten all three pictures, we've finished one trial of the simulation.

4. **State clearly what the response variable is.** What are we interested in? We want to know how many boxes it takes to get all three pictures. This is the response variable. In the sample trial above, the response value is 5 boxes.
5. **Run several trials.** A simulation is cheaper than really buying cereal, and the more trials you run the better. For example, consider the third line of random digits shown earlier.

   89064 2730 8645681 41219 822665388587328580 169902784311 0380420067. . .

   Let's create a chart to keep track of what happened.

Trial number	Outcomes	y = Number of boxes
1	89064 = **Serena,** Serena, **Tiger,** Serena, **Lance**	5
2	2730 = **Lance, Serena,** Lance, **Tiger**	4
3	8645681 = **Serena,** Serena, **Lance, . . . , Tiger**	7
4	41219 = **Lance, Tiger,** Lance, Tiger, **Serena**	5
5	822665388587328580 = **Serena, Lance, . . . , Tiger**	18

6. **Analyze the response variable.** We wanted to know how many boxes we might expect to buy. To answer the question, we need to analyze the response variable in a number of ways. We know how to do this. In our first 5 trials we needed 5, 4, 7, 5, and then 18 for an average of 7.8 boxes.
7. **State your conclusion (in the context of the problem, as always).** Based on our simulation, we estimate that customers who want the complete set of sports star pictures will buy an average of 7.8 boxes of cereal.

If you fear that this may not be an accurate estimate because we only ran five trials, you are absolutely correct. The more trials the better, and five is woefully inadequate. Twenty trials is probably a reasonable minimum if you are doing this by hand. Even better, use a computer and do a few hundred trials.

Simulation STEP-BY-STEP

Fifty-seven students participated in a lottery for a particularly desirable dorm room—a triple with a fireplace and private bath in the tower. Twenty of the participants were members of the same varsity team. When all three winners were members of the team, the other students cried foul. Use a simulation to determine whether an all-team outcome could reasonably be expected to happen if everyone had a fair shot at the room.

Think

Components

Identify the components.

A component is the selection of a student.

Outcomes

State how you will model the random occurrence of an outcome. You can't just use the digits from 0 to 9 because the outcomes you are simulating are not multiples of 10%.

There are 20 and 37 students in the two groups. This time you must use *pairs* of random digits (and ignore some of them) to represent the 57 students.

Look at two-digit random numbers.

Let 00–19 represent the 20 varsity applicants.

Let 20–56 represent the other 37 applicants.

Skip 57–99. If we get a number in this range, we'll throw it away and go back for another two-digit random number.

Trial

Define a trial. Be sure that you don't use a repeated number.

Each trial consists of identifying pairs of digits as V (varsity) or N (non-varsity) until 3 people are chosen, ignoring out-of-range or repeated numbers (X)—we can't put the same person in the room twice.

Define the response variable.

The response variable is whether or not all selected students are on the Varsity team.

Show

Mechanics

Run several trials. Carefully record the random numbers, indicating what each represents. Indicate the value of the response variable for each trial.

Trial Number	Outcomes	All Varsity?
1	74 02 94 39 02 77 55 X V X N X X N	No
2	18 63 33 25 V X N N	No
3	05 45 88 91 56 V N X X N	No
4	39 09 07 N V V	No
5	65 39 45 95 43 X N N X N	No
6	98 95 11 68 77 12 17 X X V X X V V	Yes
7	26 19 89 93 77 27 N V X X X N	No
8	23 52 37 N N N	No
9	16 50 83 44 V N X N	No
10	74 17 46 85 09 X V N X V	No

Estimate

Summarize the results across all trials.

"All varsity" occurred once, or 10% of the time.

Tell

Interpretation

Describe what the simulation shows and draw your conclusions about the real world.

In our simulation of "fair" room draws the three people chosen were all varsity team members only 10% of the time. While this result *could* happen, it is not particularly likely. We might be suspicious, but we'd need many more trials and a smaller chance of the all-varsity outcome before we would make an accusation of unfairness.

TI Tips

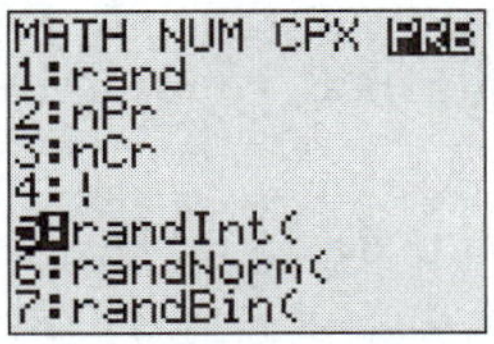

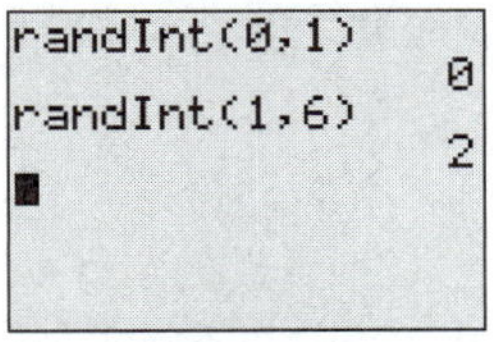

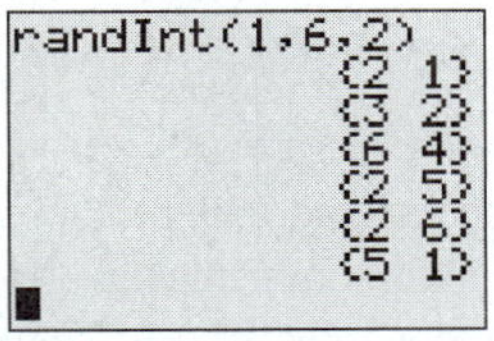

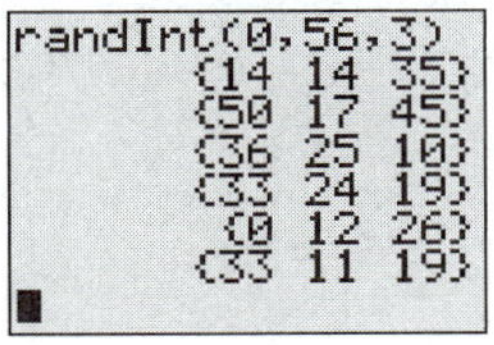

Instead of using coins, dice, cards, or tables of random numbers, you may decide to use your calculator for simulations. There are several random number generators offered in the MATH PRB menu.

`5:randInt(` is of particular importance. This command will produce any number of random integers in a specified range.

Here are some examples showing how to use `randInt` for simulations:

- `randInt(0,1)` randomly chooses a 0 or a 1. This is an effective simulation of a coin toss. You could let 0 represent tails and 1 represent heads.
- `randInt(1,6)` produces a random integer from 1 to 6, a good way to simulate rolling a die.
- `randInt(1,6,2)` simulates rolling *two* dice. To do several rolls in a row, just hit ENTER repeatedly.
- `randInt(0,9,5)` produces five random integers that might represent the pictures in the cereal boxes. Our run gave us two Tigers (0, 1), no Armstrongs (2, 3, 4), and three Serenas (5–9).
- `randInt(0,56,3)` produces three random integers between 0 and 56, a nice way to simulate the dorm room lottery. The window shows 6 trials, but we would skip the first one because one student was chosen twice. In none of the remaining 5 trials did three athletes (0–19) win.

What Can Go Wrong?

- ***Don't overstate your case.*** Let's face it: In some sense a simulation is *always* wrong. After all, it's not the real thing. We didn't buy any cereal, or run a room draw. So beware of confusing what really *happens* with what a simulation suggests *might* happen. Always be sure to indicate that future results will not match your simulated results exactly.
- ***Model the outcome chances accurately.*** A common mistake in constructing a simulation is to adopt a strategy that may appear to produce the right kind of results, but that does not accurately model the situation. For example, in our room

draw we could have gotten 0, 1, 2, or 3 team members. Why not just see how often these digits occur in random digits from 0 to 9, ignoring the digits 4 and up?

3 2 1 7 9 0 0 5 9 7 3 7 9 2 5 2 4 1 3 8

3 2 1 x x 0 0 x x x 3 x x 2 x 2 x 1 3 x

This "simulation" makes it seem fairly likely that three team members would be chosen. There's a big problem with this approach, though. The digits 0, 1, 2, and 3 occur with equal frequency among random digits, making each outcome appear to happen 25% of the time. In fact, the selection of 0, 1, 2, or all 3 team members are not all equally likely outcomes. In our correct simulation we estimated that all 3 would be chosen only about 10% of the time. If your simulation overlooks important aspects of the real situation, your model will not be accurate.

- ***Run enough trials.*** Simulation is cheap and fairly easy to do. Don't try to draw conclusions based on 5 or 10 trials (even though we did for illustration purposes here). We'll make precise how many trials to use in later chapters. For now, err on the side of large numbers of trials.

Simulation and the Computer

Simulations are best done with the help of technology simply because more trials makes a better simulation, and computers are fast. There are special computer programs designed for simulation, but most statistics packages can generate random numbers and support a simulation.

All technology-generated random numbers are *pseudorandom.* The random numbers available on the Internet may technically be better, but the differences won't matter for any simulation of modest size. Pseudorandom numbers generate the next random value from the previous one by a specified algorithm. But they have to start somewhere. This starting point is called the "seed." Most programs let you set the seed. There's usually little reason to do this, but if you wish to, go ahead. If you reset the seed to the same value, the programs will generate the same sequence of "random" numbers.

Connections

Simulations often generate many outcomes of a response variable, and we are often interested in the distribution of these responses. The tools we use to display and summarize the distribution of any real variable are appropriate for displaying and summarizing randomly generated responses as well.

Make histograms, boxplots, and Normal probability plots of the response variables from simulations and summarize them with measures of center and spread. Be especially careful to report the variation of your response variable.

Don't forget to think about your analyses. Simulations can hide subtle errors. A careful analysis of the responses can save you from erroneous conclusions based on a faulty simulation.

You may be less likely to find an outlier in simulated responses, but if you find one, you should certainly determine how it happened.

Key Concepts

Random An event is random if we know what outcomes could happen, but not which particular values did or will happen.

Random numbers Random numbers are hard to generate. Nevertheless, several Internet sites offer an unlimited supply of equally likely random values.

Simulation A simulation models random events by using random numbers to specify event outcomes with relative frequencies that correspond to the true real-world relative frequencies we are trying to model.

Simulation component A situation in a simulation in which something happens at random.

Outcome An individual result of a simulated component of a simulation is its outcome.

Trial The sequence of events that we are pretending will take place.

Skills

When you complete this lesson you should:

Think

- Be able to recognize random outcomes in a real-world situation.
- Be able to recognize when a simulation might usefully model random behavior in the real world.

Show

- Know how to perform a simulation either by generating random numbers on a computer or calculator, or by using some other source of random values such as dice, a spinner, or a table of random numbers.

Tell

- Be able to describe a simulation so that others could repeat it.
- Be able to discuss the results of a simulation study and draw conclusions about the question being investigated.

Exercises

1. **Coin toss.** Is a coin flip random? Why or why not, in your opinion?

2. **Casino.** A casino claims that its electronic "video roulette" machine is truly random. What should that claim mean?

3. **The lottery.** Many states run lotteries, giving away millions of dollars if you match a certain set of winning numbers. How are those numbers determined? Do you think this method guarantees randomness? Explain.

4. Games. Many kinds of games people play rely on randomness. Cite three different methods commonly used in the attempt to achieve this randomness, and discuss the effectiveness of each.

5. Bad simulations. Explain why each simulation described below fails to model the real situation properly.
a) Use a random integer from 0 through 9 to represent the number of heads that appear when 9 coins are tossed.
b) A basketball player takes a foul shot. Look at a random digit, using an odd digit to represent a good shot and an even digit to represent a miss.
c) Use five random digits from 1 through 13 to represent the denominations of the cards in a poker hand.

6. More bad simulations. Explain why each simulation described below fails to model the real situation properly.
a) Use random numbers 2 through 12 to represent the sum of the faces when two dice are rolled.
b) Use a random integer from 0 through 5 to represent the number of boys in a family of 5 children.
c) Simulate a baseball player's time at bat by letting 0 = an out, 1 = a single, 2 = a double, 3 = a triple, and 4 = a home run.

7. Wrong conclusion. A Statistics student properly simulated the length of checkout lines in a grocery store and then reported, "The average length of the line will be 3.2 people." What's wrong with this conclusion?

8. Another wrong conclusion. After simulating the spread of a disease, a researcher wrote, "24% of the people contracted the disease." What should the correct conclusion be?

9. Cereal. In the chapter's example, 20% of the cereal boxes contained a picture of Tiger Woods, 30% Lance Armstrong, and the rest Serena Williams. Suppose you buy five boxes of cereal. Estimate the probability that you end up with a complete set of the pictures. Your simulation should have at least 20 runs.

10. Cereal, again. Suppose you really want the Tiger Woods picture. How many boxes of cereal do you need to buy to be pretty sure of getting at least one? Your simulation should use at least 10 runs.

11. Multiple choice. You take a quiz with 6 multiple choice questions. After you studied, you estimated that you would have about an 80% chance of getting any individual question right. What are your chances of getting them all right? Your simulation should use at least 20 runs.

12. Lucky guessing? A friend of yours who took that same multiple choice quiz got all 6 questions right, but now claims to have guessed blindly on every question. If each question offered 4 possible answers, do you believe her? Explain, basing your argument on a simulation involving at least 10 runs.

13. Driving test. You are about to take the road test for your driver's license. You hear that only 34% of candidates pass the test the first time, but the percentage rises to 72% on retests. Estimate the average number of tests drivers take in order to get a license. Your simulation should use at least 20 runs.

14. Still learning? As in Exercise 13, assume that your chance of passing the driver's test is 34% the first time and 72% for retests. Estimate the percentage of those tested who still do not have a driver's license after two attempts.

15. Basketball strategy. Late in a basketball game, the team that is behind often fouls someone in an attempt to get the ball back. Usually the opposing player will get to shoot foul shots "one and one," meaning he gets a shot, and then a second shot if he makes the first one. Suppose the opposing player has made 72% of his foul shots this season. Estimate the number of points he will score in a one on one situation.

16. Blood donors. A person with type O-positive blood can receive blood only from other type O donors. About 44% of the U.S. population has type O blood. At a blood drive, how many potential donors do you expect to examine in order to get three units of type O blood?

17. Free groceries. To attract shoppers, a supermarket runs a weekly contest that involves "scratch-off" cards. With each purchase, customers get a card with a black spot obscuring a message. When the spot is scratched away, most of the cards simply say, "Sorry—please try again." But during the week, 100 customers will get cards that make them eligible for a drawing for free groceries. Ten of the cards say they may be worth $200, 10 others say $100, 20 may be worth $50, and the rest could be worth $20. To register those cards, customers write their names on them and put them in a barrel at the front of the store. At the end of the week the store manager draws cards at random, awarding the lucky customers free groceries in the amount specified on their card. The drawings continue until the store has given away more than $500 of free groceries. Estimate the average number of winners each week.

18. Find the ace. A new electronics store holds a contest to attract shoppers. Once an hour someone in the store is chosen at random to play the Music Game. Here's how it works. An ace and four other cards are shuffled and placed face down on a table. The customer gets to turn cards over one at a time, looking for the ace. The person wins $100 worth of free CDs or DVDs if the ace is the first card, $50 if it is the second card and $20, $10, or $5 if it is the third, fourth, or fifth card chosen. What is the average dollar amount of music the store will give away?

19. The family. Many couples want to have both a boy and a girl. If they decide to continue to have children until they have one child of each gender, what would the average family size be? Assume that boys and girls are equally likely.

20. A bigger family. Suppose a couple will continue having children until they have at least two children of each gender (two boys *and* two girls). How many children might they expect to have?

21. Dice game. You are playing a children's game in which the number of spaces you get to move is determined by rolling a die. You must land exactly on the final space in order to win. If you are 10 spaces away, how many turns might it take you to win?

22. Parcheesi. You are three spaces from a win in Parcheesi. On each turn you will roll two dice. To win, you must roll a total of 3, or roll a 3 on one of the dice. How many turns might you expect this to take?

23. The hot hand. A basketball player with a 65% shooting percentage has just made 6 shots in a row. The announcer says this player "is hot tonight! She's in the zone!" Assume the player takes about 20 shots per game. Is it unusual for her to make 6 or more shots in a row during a game?

24. The World Series. The World Series ends when a team wins 4 games. Suppose that sports analysts consider one team a bit stronger, with a 55% chance to win any individual game. Estimate the likelihood that the underdog wins the series.

25. Teammates. Four couples at a dinner party play a board game after the meal. They decide to play as teams of two and to select the teams randomly. All eight people write their names on slips of paper. The slips are thoroughly mixed, then drawn two at a time. How likely is it that every person will be teamed with someone other than the person he or she came to the party with?

26. Second team. Suppose the couples in Exercise 25 choose the teams by having one member of each couple write their names on the cards and the other people each pick a card at random. How likely is it that every person will be teamed with someone other than the person he or she came with?

27. Job discrimination? A company with a large sales staff announces openings for three positions as regional managers. Twenty-two of the current salespersons apply, 12 men and 10 women. After the interviews, when the company announces the newly appointed managers, all three positions go to women. The men complain of job discrimination. Do they have a case? Simulate a random selection of three people from the applicant pool and make a decision about the likelihood that a fair process would result in hiring all women.

28. Tires. A tire manufacturer believes that the treadlife of its snow tires can be described by a Normal model with mean of 32,000 miles and a standard deviation of 2500 miles. You buy four of these tires, hoping to drive them at least 30,000 miles. Estimate the chances that all four last at least that long.

29. Freshmen. A certain college estimates that SAT scores of students who apply for admission can be described by a Normal model with a mean of 1050 and a standard deviation of 120. Admissions officers search the pile of envelopes, opening them at random to look for three applicants with SAT scores over 1200. How many envelopes do you think they will need to open?

Chapter 12

Sample Surveys

We have learned ways to display, describe, and summarize data. Up to now, though, our conclusions have been limited to the particular batch of data we are examining. That's OK as far as it goes, but it doesn't go very far. We usually aren't satisfied with conclusions based only on *this* group of customers, or the people who answered the survey on *this* particular day. To make business decisions, to do science, to choose wise investments, or to understand what voters think they'll do in the next election, we need to stretch beyond the data at hand to the world at large.

To make that stretch, we need three ideas. You'll find the first one natural. The second may be more surprising. The third is one of the strange but true facts that often confuse those who don't know Statistics.

Idea 1: Examine a Part of the Whole

The first idea is to draw a sample. We'd like to know about an entire **population** of individuals, but examining all of them is usually impractical if not impossible. So we settle for examining a smaller group of individuals—a **sample**—selected from the population.

You do this every day. For example, suppose you wonder how the vegetable soup you're cooking for dinner tonight is going to go over with your friends. To decide whether it meets your standards, you only need to try a small amount. You might taste just a spoonful or two. You certainly don't have to consume the whole pot. You trust that the taste will *represent* the flavor of the entire pot. The idea behind your tasting is that a small sample, if selected properly, can represent the entire population.

It's hard to go a day without hearing about the latest opinion poll. These polls are examples of **sample surveys,** designed to ask questions of a small group of people in the hope of learning something about the entire population. Most likely, you've never been selected to be part of one of these national opinion polls. That's true of most people. So how can the pollsters claim that a sample is representative

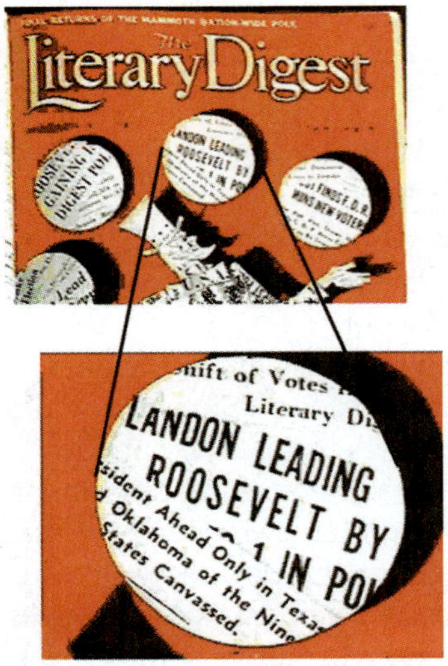

In 1936, a young pollster named George Gallup used a subsample of only 3000 of the 2.4 million reponses that the *Literary Digest* received to reproduce the wrong prediction of Landon's victory over Roosevelt. He then used an entirely different sample of 50,000 and predicted that Roosevelt would get 56% of the vote to Landon's 44%. His sample was apparently much more ***representative*** of the actual voting populace. The Gallup Organization went on to become one of the leading polling companies.

of the entire population? The answer is that professional pollsters work quite hard to ensure that the "taste"—the sample that they take—represents the population. If not, the sample can give misleading information about the population.

What are the basic techniques for making sure that a sample is representative? Sometimes it's instructive to see how to do something by studying a really dismal failure. Here's a famous one. By the beginning of the 20th century, it was common for newspapers to ask readers to return "straw" ballots on a variety of topics. (Today's Internet surveys are the same idea gone electronic.) The earliest known example of such a straw vote in the United States dates back to 1824.

The success of these regional polls in the early 1900s inspired national magazines to try their luck. Although the *Farm Journal* was probably the first, the *Literary Digest* was at the top of the heap. During the period 1916 to 1935, it regularly surveyed public opinion, and forecast election results correctly. During the 1936 presidential campaign between Alf Landon and Franklin Delano Roosevelt, the *Literary Digest* mailed more than 10 million ballots. The magazine got back an astonishing 2.4 million. (Polls were still a relatively novel idea and many people thought it was important to send back their opinions.) The results from the millions of responses were clear. Alf Landon would be the next president by a landslide: 57% to 43%. You remember President Landon, don't you? In fact, Landon carried only two states. Roosevelt won 62% to 37% and, perhaps coincidentally, the *Digest* went bankrupt soon afterward.

What went wrong? The problem was that the *Digest* sample was not representative. The pollsters made some mistakes that are now considered classics. First, let's look at how they got the list of 10 million names to start with. Where would you go to get such a list? You might think of using phone numbers as a way to select people—and that's just what the *Digest* did. But in 1936, at the height of the Great Depression, telephones were real luxuries. Any list of phone owners would include far more rich than poor people. In fact, it wasn't until 1986 that enough families in the United States had telephones so that phoning became a reliable way of surveying people.[1] The other lists available to the *Digest* were even less representative—drivers' registrations and memberships in organizations such as country clubs.

The main campaign issue in 1936 was the economy. Roosevelt's core supporters, who tended to be less well off, were not well represented in the *Digest*'s sample, so the results of a survey based on that sample did not reflect the opinions of the overall population. It did not matter how well it was measured, nor how many people responded. A sample that does not represent the population in some important way, such as one that overlooks an important group, is said to be **biased.** Bias is the bane of sampling—the one thing above all to avoid. There is usually no way to fix a biased sample and no way to salvage useful information from it.

How can we avoid the *Digest*'s errors? To make the sample as representative as possible, you might be tempted to handpick the individuals included in the sample with care and precision. The best strategy is to do something quite different. Instead, we should select individuals for the sample *at random.* The value of deliberately introducing randomness is one of the great insights of Statistics.

---

[1]Even today, phone numbers must be computer-generated to make sure that the phone owners are representative. Using only phone book listings would miss both people with unlisted numbers and those who have recently moved. Leaving these groups out may make the sample unrepresentative.

Idea 2: Randomize

Think back to the soup sample. Suppose you add some salt to the pot. If you sample it from the top before stirring, what will happen? With the salt sitting on top, you'll get the misleading idea that the whole pot is salty. If you sample from the bottom, you'll get an equally misleading idea that the whole pot is bland. By stirring, you *randomize* the amount of salt throughout the pot, making each taste more typical in terms of the amount of salt in the whole pot.

Randomization can protect you against factors that you know are in the data. It can also help protect against factors that you aren't even aware of. Suppose, while you weren't looking, a friend added a handful of peas to the soup. They are down at the bottom of the pot, mixing with the other vegetables. If you don't randomize the soup by stirring, your test spoonful from the top won't have any peas. By stirring in the salt, you *also* randomize the peas throughout the pot, making your sample taste more typical of the overall pot *even though you didn't know the peas were there.* So **randomizing** protects us by giving us a representative sample even over effects we were unaware of.

How would we "stir" people in our survey? We'd try to select them at random. **Randomizing** protects us from the influences of *all* the features of our population, even ones that we may not have thought about. It does that by making sure that *on the average* the sample looks like the rest of the population.

Why not match the sample to the population?

Rather than randomizing, we could try to design our sample so that the people we choose are typical in terms of every characteristic we can think of. In the 1936 vote, rich and poor voted differently as in no previous election. So, we'd like the income levels of those we sample to match the population. How about age? Do young and old vote alike? Political affiliation? Marital status? Having children? Living in the suburbs? We can't possibly think of all the things that might be important. Even if we could, we wouldn't be able to match our sample to the population for all these characteristics.

Not only does randomizing protect us from bias, it actually makes it possible for us to draw inferences about the population when we see only a sample. Such inferences are among the most powerful things we can do with Statistics, and we'll spend much of the rest of the book discussing them. Keep in mind, though, that it's all made possible because we deliberately choose things randomly.

Here's an example from a company's database of 3.5 million customers. We've taken two samples of size 8000 at random from the population. Here's how the means and proportions match up on seven variables.

Age (yr)	White (%)	Female (%)	# of Children	Income bracket (1–7)	Wealth bracket (1–9)	Homeowner? (% Yes)
61.4	85.12	56.2	1.54	3.91	5.29	71.36
61.2	84.44	56.4	1.51	3.88	5.33	72.30

Notice how well randomizing has stirred the population. We didn't look at these variables when we drew the samples, but randomizing has automatically matched them pretty closely. We can reasonably assume that since the two samples don't differ too much from each other, they don't differ much from the rest of the population either.

Idea 3: It's the Sample Size

A friend who knows that you are taking Statistics asks your advice on her study. What can you possibly say that won't sound stupid or be wrong? Just say: "If you could just get a larger sample size it would probably improve your study." Even though a larger sample might not be worth the cost, it will almost always make the results more precise.

How large a random sample do we need for the sample to be reasonably representative of the population? Obviously, if your sample is too small, it can't give much information. You might think that we need a large percentage, or *fraction*, of the population. That's what most people think, but it turns out that all that matters is the *number* of individuals in the sample. The size of the population doesn't matter at all.[2] A random sample of 100 students in a college represents the student body just about as well as a random sample of 100 voters represents the entire electorate of the United States. This is the *third* idea and probably the most surprising one in designing surveys.

How can it be that only the number in the sample, and not how big the population is, matters? Well, let's return one last time to that pot of soup. If you're cooking for a banquet rather than just for a few people, your pot will be bigger, but do you need a bigger spoon to decide how the soup tastes? Of course not. The same size spoonful is probably enough to make a decision about the entire pot, no matter how large the pot. The *fraction* of the population that you've sampled doesn't matter. It's the *sample size* itself that's important.

This somewhat surprising idea is of key importance to the design of any sample survey, because it determines the balance between how well the survey can measure the population and how much the survey costs.

How big a sample do you need? That depends on what you're estimating. If you're just interested in the broth, then you can just taste a sip from a spoon. But to get an idea of what's really in the soup, you need a large enough taste to be a *representative* sample from the pot, including a selection of the vegetables. For a survey that tries to find the proportion of the population that fall into a category, you'll usually need a large enough sample to see several respondents in each category—usually at least several hundred respondents—to say anything precise enough to be useful.[3]

Does a Census Make Sense?

Why bother determining the right sample size? Wouldn't it be better to just include everyone and "sample" the entire population? Such a special sample is called a **census.** Although a census would appear to provide the best possible information about the population, there are a number of reasons why it might not.

First, it can be difficult to complete a census. There always seem to be some individuals who are hard to locate or hard to measure. The cost of locating the last few cases may far exceed your budget. It can also be just plain impractical to take a census. If you were a taste tester for the Hostess Company, you probably wouldn't want to census *all* the Twinkies on the production line. Aside from the fact that you couldn't possibly eat that many Twinkies, it would defeat the

[2]Well, that's not exactly true. If the population is small enough and the sample is more than 10% of the whole population, it *can* matter. It doesn't matter whenever, as usual, our sample is a very small fraction of the population.

[3]Chapter 19 gives the details behind this statement and shows how to decide on a sample size for a survey.

purpose of your job. You wouldn't have any left to sell. And a wine tasting wouldn't be very practical if we needed to drink the whole bottle to get an idea of its quality. So, it's often not practical to attempt a census.

Second, populations rarely stand still. In populations of people, babies are born and folks die or leave the country. In opinion surveys, events may cause a shift in opinion during the survey. Even if you could take a census, the population changes while you work, so it's never possible to get a perfect measure. A sample surveyed in less time may give more accurate information.

Third, taking a census can be more complex than sampling. Often a census requires a team effort or the cooperation of the population members. Because it tries to count everyone, the U.S. Census records too many college students. Many are included by their families and are then also counted a second time in a report filed by their schools. Other errors of this sort can be found throughout the Census.

It's particularly difficult to compile a complete census of all members of a population as large, complex, and spread out as the U.S. population. The U.S. Census is known to miss some residents. On occasion the undercount has been striking. For example, there have been blocks in inner cities in which the number of residents recorded by the Census was smaller than the number of electric meters for which bills were being paid. What makes the problem particularly important is that some groups have a higher probability of being missed than others—the homeless, the poor, the indigent. The Census Bureau proposed the use of random sampling to estimate the number of residents missed by the ordinary census. Unfortunately, the resulting debate has become more political than statistical.

Populations and Parameters

Any quantity that we calculate from data could be called a "statistic." But in practice, we usually use a statistic to estimate a population parameter.

A study found that teens were less likely to "buckle up." The National Center for Chronic Disease Prevention and Health Promotion reports that 21.7% of U.S. teens never or rarely wear seatbelts. What does this statement mean? We're sure they didn't take a census. Even if they had, they must have missed some teens. So what *does* the 21.7% mean? We can't possibly know how many teenagers wear seatbelts. Reality is just too complex. But, as we've seen many times before, we can simplify the question by building a model.

We can simplify further by focusing on the *parameters* of the model rather than specifying the entire model. A parameter that is part of a model for a population is called a **population parameter.**

But let's not forget about the data. We use the data to try to estimate the population parameters. As we know, any summary found from the data is a **statistic.** Those statistics that estimate population parameters are particularly interesting. Sometimes—and especially when we match statistics with the parameters they estimate—you'll see the (redundant) term **sample statistic.**[4]

We've already met two parameters in Chapter 6: the mean, μ, and the standard deviation, σ. We'll try to keep denoting population model parameters with Greek letters and the corresponding statistics with Latin letters. Usually, but not always, the letter used for the statistic and the parameter correspond in a natural way. So

[4]Where else besides a sample *could* a statistic come from?

the standard deviation of the data is s, and the corresponding parameter is σ (Greek for s). We used r to denote the sample correlation. The corresponding correlation in a model for the population would be called ρ (rho). The slope of a linear regression estimated from the data is b_1. But if we think about a (linear) *model* for the population, we'd denote the slope parameter β_1 (beta).

Get the pattern? Good. Now it breaks down. We denote the mean of a population model with μ (because μ is the Greek letter for m). It might make sense to denote the sample mean with m, but longstanding convention is to put a bar over anything when we average it, so we write $\bar{y}$. What about proportions? Suppose we want to talk about the proportion of teens who don't wear seatbelts. If we use p to denote the proportion from the data, what is the corresponding model parameter? By all rights it should be π. Some books do this, but statements like $\pi = 0.25$ might be confusing because π has been equal to 3.1415926... for so long, and it's worked so *well*. So, once again we violate the rule. We'll use p for the population model parameter and $\hat{p}$ for the proportion from the data. Here's a table summarizing the notation:

NOTATION ALERT:

This entire table is a notation alert.

Name	Statistic	Parameter
Mean	$\bar{y}$	μ (mu, pronounced "meeoo," not "moo")
Standard deviation	s	σ (sigma)
Correlation	r	ρ (rho, pronounced "row")
Regression coefficient	b	β (beta, pronounced "baytah"[5])
Proportion	$\hat{p}$	p (pee)

Simple Random Samples

We draw samples because we can't work with the entire population. We need to be sure that the statistics we compute from the sample reflect the corresponding parameters accurately. A sample that does this is said to be **representative.**

How would you select a representative sample? Most people would say that every individual in the population should have an equal chance to be selected, and certainly that seems fair. But it's not sufficient. There are many ways to give everyone an equal chance that still wouldn't give a representative sample. Consider, for example, a school that has equal numbers of males and females. We could sample like this. Flip a coin. If it comes up heads, select 100 female students at random. If it comes up tails, select 100 males at random. Everyone has an equal chance of selection, but every sample is of only a single sex—hardly representative.

We need to do better. Suppose we insist that every possible *sample* of the size we plan to draw has an equal chance to be selected. This ensures that situations like the one just described are not likely to occur and still guarantees that each person has an equal chance of being selected. What's different is that with this method each *combination* of people has an equal chance of being selected as well. A sample drawn in this way is called a **Simple Random Sample,** usually abbreviated **SRS.** An SRS is the standard against which we measure other sampling methods, and the sampling method on which the theory of working with sampled data is based.

[5]If you're American. If you're British, it's "beetah."

To select a sample at random, we first need to define where the sample will come from. The **sampling frame** is a list of individuals from which the sample is drawn. For example, to draw a random sample of students at a college, we might obtain a list of all registered full-time students and sample from that list. In defining the sampling frame, we must deal with the details of defining the population. Are part-time students included? How about those who are attending school elsewhere and transferring credits back to the college?

Now that we have a sampling frame, the easiest way to choose an SRS is with random numbers. We have already seen good ways to obtain these. We can assign a random number to each individual in the sampling frame. As in a simulation, we then select only those whose random numbers satisfy some rule. Let's look at a couple of examples:

- We want to select 5 students from the 80 enrolled in an Introductory Statistics class. We start by numbering the students from 00 to 79. Now we look at a table of random numbers, finding 05166 29305 77482. Taking those random numbers two digits at a time gives us 05, 16, 62, 93, 05, 77, and 48. We ignore 93 because no one had a number that high. And we don't want to pick the same person twice, so we also skip the repeated number 05. Our simple random sample consists of students with the numbers 05, 16, 62, 77, and 48.
- Often the sampling frame is so large that it's too tedious to number everyone consecutively. If we want to sample approximately 10% of the sampling frame, we assign each individual a single random digit 0 to 9. Then we select only those with a specific random digit, say, 5.

When we draw a sample at random, each sample we draw will be different. We call these sample-to-sample differences **sampling variability.** Sampling variability is the price we must pay for working with a sample rather than the entire population. Fortunately, we can often estimate how large the sampling variability is and allow for it when we draw conclusions about the sampled population. We'll devote a lot of attention to this idea in the coming chapters.

Other Sampling Designs

Simple random sampling is not the only fair way to sample. More complicated designs may save time or money or help avoid sampling problems. All **statistical sampling** designs have in common the idea that chance, rather than human choice, is used to select the sample.

Designs that are used to sample from large populations—especially those residing across large areas—are often more complicated than simple random samples. Sometimes the population is first split up into homogeneous groups, called **strata,** before the sample is selected. Then simple random sampling is used within each stratum before the results are combined. This is the essence of **stratified random sampling.**

Why would we want to complicate things? Here's an example. Suppose we want to survey how students feel about funding for the football team at a large university. The campus is 60% men and 40% women. We suspect that men and women have different views on the funding and we want to protect ourselves from getting a really bad sample, one that has too many men or women, by chance. If we select 100 people for the survey at random we might get 35 men and 65 women, which might bias our result. To avoid this, we can decide to force a representative gender balance. Then we could select 60 men at random and

40 women at random. This would guarantee that the proportions of men and women within the sample match the proportions in the population. You can imagine the importance of stratifying by race, income, age, and other characteristics depending on the questions in the survey.

In addition to reducing bias, stratifying can reduce the variability of our results. When we restrict by strata, additional samples are more like one another, so statistics calculated for the sampled values will vary less from one sample to another. This reduced variability is an important added benefit of stratifying

Here's a different challenge. Suppose you wanted to assess the reading level of this textbook based on a random sample of the words used. A simple random sample would be very difficult to obtain. Just number each word from the beginning to the end of the book, then randomly choose, say, the 70,383rd word, the 567th word, and so on. Doesn't sound like much fun, does it? A logical alternative might be to pick *one* page at random and use every word on that page. When the population is split up into heterogeneous groups, selecting one group or **cluster,** can be an effective sampling method. This sampling design is called **cluster sampling.** In the case of our textbook each page is a cluster. This method will provide a useful sample if you believe that the pages of the book are all pretty similar in terms of reading level. If each page represents fairly the full range of variability to be found in the text, then choosing a page or two as a cluster sample will work well.

Perhaps, however, the reading level varies from chapter to chapter depending on the difficulty of the concepts presented there. Or maybe the book starts out easy and gets harder as it goes along. In that case you could randomly select one chapter from each of the seven units, then one page from each of those chapters. And if altogether that makes too many words, then you might select only a few words at random from each of those chosen pages. First you have stratified by section of the book, then chosen a cluster from each stratum—and perhaps an SRS within each cluster. Most surveys conducted by professional polling organizations use some combination of stratified and cluster sampling as well as simple random samples. Sampling schemes that combine several methods are called **multistage samples.**

Systematic Samples

Sometimes we draw a sample by selecting individuals systematically. For example, you might survey every 10th person on an alphabetical list of students. To make it random, you still must start the systematic selection from a randomly selected individual. When there is no reason to believe that the order of the list could be associated in any way with the responses sought, **systematic sampling** can give a representative sample. Systematic sampling can be much less expensive than true random sampling. When you use a systematic sample, you should justify the assumption that the systematic method is not associated with any of the measured variables.

Think about the reading level sampling example again. Suppose you have chosen a chapter of the book at random, then a page from that chapter, and now you want to select a sample of 20 words from the 573 words found on that page. Instead of numbering each word so you can pick a simple random sample, it would be easier to sample systematically. A quick calculation shows $573 \div 20 = 28.65$, so you can get your sample by picking every 28th word on the page. But where should you start? Essentially you have divided the page into 20 groups of 28 words each. Since $20 \times 28 = 560$, those groups span 560 of the 573 words. That leaves 13 "extra" words that should also have a chance to be part of your sample.

To include these extra words in the sampling frame, add them to the first group, making 13 + 28 = 41 words there. Use a random number to select your first word from those 41, say, the 33rd word. Now just count every 28th word from that random starting point (the 33 + 28 = 61st word, the 89th, and so on) and you will have your systematic sample of 20 words.

Sampling STEP-BY-STEP

The assignment says, "Conduct your own sample survey to find out how many hours per week students at your school spend watching TV during the school year." Let's see how we might do this step-by-step.

Think

Population and Parameter

Identify the W's of the study. The *Who* is the population and the associated sampling frame. The *What* identifies the parameter of interest and the variables measured. The *How, When,* and *Where* are given by the sampling plan.

Often thinking about the *Why* will help us see whether the sampling frame and plan are adequate to learn about the population.

The population studied was students at our school. We obtained a list of all students currently enrolled and used it as the sampling frame. The parameter of interest was the number of TV hours watched per week during the school year, which we attempted to measure by asking students how much TV they watched during the previous week.

Sampling Plan

Specify sampling method and the sample size, *n*. Specify how the sample was actually drawn. What is the sampling frame?

The description should, if possible, be complete enough to allow someone to replicate the procedure, drawing another sample from the same population in the same manner. A good description of the procedure is essential even if it could never practically be repeated.

Terms like simple random sample, cluster sample, and stratified sample often appear in this part of the discussion. You must also describe how the randomization was performed.

We decided against stratifying by class or sex. We selected a simple random sample of 200 students from our list. We obtained a list of random digits, matched it to an alphabetically arranged list of students, and selected all students who were assigned a "4." This method generated a sample of 212 students from the population of 2133 students.

Show

Sampling Practice

Specify when, where, and how the sampling was performed. Specify any other details of your survey, such as how respondents were contacted, what incentives were offered to encourage them to respond, how nonrespondents were treated, and so on.

The survey was taken over the period Oct. 15 to Oct. 25. Surveys were sent to selected students by e-mail with the request that they respond by e-mail as well. Students who could not be reached by email were handed the survey in person.

Tell

Summary and Interpretation

This report should include a discussion of all the elements. In addition, it's good practice to

During the period Oct. 15 to Oct. 25 2003, 212 students were randomly selected, using a simple random sample from a list of all students discuss any special circumstances. Professional polling organizations report the *When* of their samples, but will also note, for example, any important news that might have changed respondents' opinions during the sampling process. For example, in this survey a major news story or sporting event might change students' TV viewing behavior.

The report should include the statistics from the sample and the conclusions that you reached about the population.

currently enrolled. The survey they received asked the following question: "How many hours did you spend watching television last week?"

Of the 212 students surveyed, 110 responded. It's possible that the nonrespondents differ in the number of TV hours watched from those who responded, but we were unable to follow them up due to limited time and funds. The 110 respondents reported an average 3.62 hours of TV watching per week. The median was only 2 hours per week. A histogram of the data (below) shows that the data are highly right-skewed, indicating that the median might be a more appropriate summary of the typical TV watching of the students. Most of the students (90%) watch between 0 and 10 hours per week, while 30% reported watching less than 1 hour per week. A few watch much more. About 3% reported watching more than 20 hours per week.

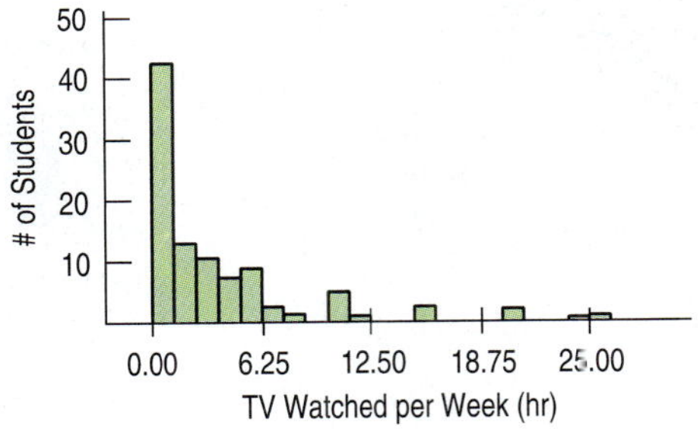

Who's Who?

The *Who* of a survey can refer to different groups, and the resulting ambiguity can tell you a lot about the success of a study. To start, you should think about the population of interest. Often, you'll find that this is not really a well-defined group (who, exactly, is a student?). Even if the population is clear, it may not be a practical group to study. For example, election polls want to sample all those who will vote in the next election—a population that is particularly tricky to identify before election day.

> The population is determined by the *Why* of the study. Unfortunately, the sample is just those we can reach to obtain responses—the *Who* of the study. This difference could undermine even a well-designed study.

Second, you must specify the sampling frame. (Do you have a list of students to sample from? How about a list of registered voters?) Usually, the sampling frame is not the group you *really* want to know about. (All those registered to vote are not equally likely to show up.) The sampling frame limits what your survey can find out.

Then there's the sample itself. These are the individuals for whom we *intend* to measure responses. We may not even succeed with all of them. Nonresponse is a problem in many surveys. ("I know it's dinner time, but I'm sure you wouldn't mind answering a few questions. It'll only take 20 minutes or so. Oh, you're busy?")

Finally, there are the actual respondents. These are the individuals about whom we *can* get data and draw conclusions. Unfortunately, they might not be representative of the sample, the sampling frame, or the population.

At each step, the group we can study may be constrained further. The *Who* keeps changing, and each constraint can introduce biases. A careful study should address the question of how well each group matches the population of interest. One of the main benefits of simple random sampling is that it never loses its sense of who's *Who*. The *Who* in an SRS is the population of interest from which we've drawn a representative sample. That's not always true for other kinds of samples.

What Can Go Wrong?—or, How to Sample Badly

Bad sample designs yield worthless data. And there is no way to correct for a bad sample. So it's wise to pay attention to sample design—and to beware of reports based on poor samples.

Sample Badly with Volunteers

Many of the most convenient forms of sampling can be seriously biased. One of the most common dangerous sampling methods is a voluntary response sample. In a **voluntary response sample,** a large group of individuals is invited to respond, and all who do respond are counted. This method is used by call-in shows, 900 numbers, Internet polls, and letters written to members of Congress. Voluntary response samples are almost always biased, and so conclusions drawn from them are almost always wrong.

A voluntary response sample is often biased toward those with strong opinions or those who are strongly motivated. People with very negative opinions tend to respond more often than those with equally strong positive opinions. The sample is not representative, even though every individual in the population may have been offered the chance to respond. The resulting **voluntary response bias** invalidates the survey.

How often do people write to their congressional representative when they're pretty happy about how things are going? Which survey would *you* be more likely to respond to—one that asked, "Should the minimum age to drive a car be raised to 25?" or one that asked, "Should shoe sizes be adjusted so women's and men's sizes correspond?"

If you had it to do over again, would you have children?

Ann Landers, the advice columnist, asked parents this question. The overwhelming majority—70% of the more than 10,000 people who wrote in—said no, kids weren't worth it. A more carefully designed survey later showed that about 90% of parents actually are happy with their decision to have children. What accounts for the striking difference in these two results? What kind of parents do you think are most likely to respond to the original question?

Sample Badly, but Conveniently

Another sampling method that doesn't work is convenience sampling. As the name suggests in **convenience sampling** we simply include the individuals who are at hand. Unfortunately, this group may not be representative of the population. A recent survey of 437 potential home buyers in Orange County, California, found, among other things that

Do you use the Internet?
Click here ○ for yes
Click here ○ for no

> *All but 2 percent of the buyers have at least one computer at home, and 62 percent have two or more. Of those with a computer, 99 percent are connected to the Internet (Jennifer Hieger, "Portrait of Homebuyer Household: 2 Kids and a PC,"* Orange County Register, *27 July 2001).*

Later in the article, we learn that the survey was conducted via the Internet! That was a convenient way to collect data and surely easier than drawing a simple random sample, but perhaps home builders shouldn't conclude from this study that *every* family has a computer and an Internet connection.

Internet convenience surveys are worthless. As voluntary response surveys, they have no well-defined sampling frame (all those who use the Internet and visit their site?) and thus report no useful information. Do not believe them.

Many surveys conducted at shopping malls suffer from the same problem. People in shopping malls are not necessarily representative of the population of interest. Mall shoppers tend to be more affluent and include a larger percentage of teenagers and retirees than the population at large. To make matters worse, survey interviewers tend to select individuals who look "safe," or easy to interview.

You may think that convenience sampling is only a problem for students or other beginning samplers. In fact, convenience sampling is a widespread problem in the business world. When a company wants to find out what people think about its products or services, whom does it survey? The easiest people to sample are its own customers. After all, the company has a list of its own customers with addresses, phone numbers, and other information—or at least a list of those customers who bothered to send in their registration cards. The company can easily stratify by age, sex, or other information it has, but no matter how it selects a sample from its customers, the sample is still a convenience sample. The company will find out only how its own customers feel about its services and, unless it takes the extra cost and effort to go outside its own customer base, will never learn how those who *don't* buy its product feel about it.

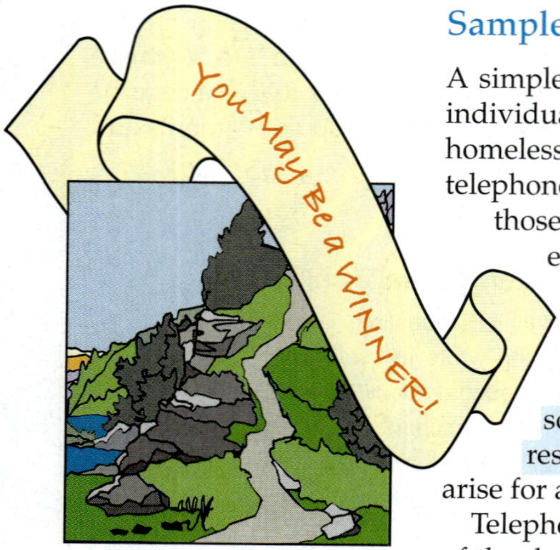

You may have already won a trip.

Sample from a Bad Sampling Frame

A simple SRS from an incomplete sampling frame introduces bias because the individuals included may differ from the ones not in the frame. People in prison, homeless people, students, and long-term travelers are all likely to be missed. In telephone surveys, selecting numbers at random from the phone book misses those with unlisted numbers (who might be wealthier), so pollsters often generate phone numbers randomly from *all* possible numbers.

Undercoverage

Many of these survey designs suffer from **undercoverage,** in which some portion of the population is not sampled at all or has a smaller representation in the sample than it has in the population. Undercoverage can arise for a number of reasons, but it's always a potential problem.

Telephone survey takers used to be able to find someone at home in the middle of the day. But now that most people work outside the home, telephone surveys are more likely to be conducted when you are likely to be home, interrupting your dinner. Of course, if you eat out often you may be less likely to be surveyed, a possible source of undercoverage.

What Else Can Go Wrong?

- ***Watch out for nonrespondents.*** A common and serious potential source of bias for most surveys is **nonresponse bias.** No survey succeeds in getting responses from everyone. The problem is that those who don't respond may differ from those who do. And they may differ on just the variables we care about. The lack of response will bias the results. Rather than sending out a large number of surveys for which the response rate will be low, it may be better to design a smaller randomized survey for which you have the resources to ensure a high response rate. One of the problems with nonresponse bias is that it's usually impossible to tell what the nonrespondents might have said.

Do people like filling out questionnaires?

A business school student wanted to study how people feel about filling out questionnaires. To do this, he designed—you guessed it—a questionnaire and gave it to a sample of all the other students at his business school. He was surprised and happy to learn that nearly all the questionnaires he got back indicated a positive attitude toward answering surveys. From this he concluded that people in general must not mind filling out questionnaires.

- ***Don't bore respondents with surveys that go on and on and on and on . . .*** Surveys that are too long are more likely to be refused, reducing the response rate and biasing *all* the results. When designing a survey, always keep in mind the purpose (the *Why*) of the survey and the population to be sampled (and about whom you hope to draw conclusions). For each question you consider including in the survey, ask yourself, "What would I do if I knew the answer to this question?" If you don't have a use for the answer, then don't ask the question.

- ***Work hard to avoid influencing responses.*** **Response bias** refers to anything in the survey design that influences the responses. Response bias is not the opposite of nonresponse bias. (We don't make these terms up, just try to explain them.) Response biases include the tendency of respondents to tailor their responses to try to please the interviewer, the ways in which the wording of the questions can change responses, and the natural unwillingness of respondents to reveal personal facts or admit to illegal or unapproved behavior.

  People responding to the survey questions often want to please the interviewer either consciously or unconsciously. The sex, race, attire, or behavior of the interviewer can influence the answers by subtle (or not so subtle) indications that certain answers are more desirable than others.

The **wording** of the question can influence the responses. This is often the most serious problem in a survey. Asking a question with a leading statement is a good way to bias the response. Many surveys, especially those conducted by special interest groups, present one side of an issue before the question itself. For example, asking a question like

> *Given that the threat of nuclear war is higher now than it has ever been in human history, and the fact that a nuclear war poses a threat to the very existence of the human race, would you favor an all-out nuclear test ban?*

will probably result in a higher percentage of people in favor of the ban than the simpler

> *Are you in favor of or opposed to a nuclear test ban?*

A Short Survey
Given the fact that those who understand Statistics are smarter and better looking than those who don't, don't you think it is important to take a course in Statistics?

Remember the *Literary Digest* survey?

It turns out that they were wrong on *two* counts. First, their list of 10 million people was not representative. There was a selection bias in their sampling frame. There was also a nonresponse bias. We know this because the *Digest* also surveyed a *systematic* sample in Chicago, sending the same question used in the larger survey to every 3rd registered voter. They *still* got a result in favor of Landon, even though Chicago voted overwhelmingly for Roosevelt in the election. This suggests that the Roosevelt supporters were less likely to respond to the *Digest* survey. There's a modern version of this problem. It's been suggested that those who screen their calls with caller ID or an answering machine, and so might not talk to a pollster, may differ in wealth or political views from those who just answer the phone.

How to Think About Biases

- ***Look for biases in any survey you encounter.*** If you design one of your own, ask someone else to help look for biases that may not be obvious to you. And do this *before* you collect your data. There's no way to recover from a biased sample or a survey that asks biased questions. Sorry, can't be done.
  A bigger sample size for a biased study just gives you a bigger useless study. A really big sample gives you an even bigger useless study. (Think of the 2.4 million *Literary Digest* responses.)
- ***Spend your time and resources reducing biases.*** No other use of resources is as worthwhile as reducing the biases.
- ***If you possibly can, pretest your survey.*** Administer the survey in the exact form that you intend to use it to a small sample drawn from the population you intend to sample. Look for misunderstandings, misinterpretation, confusion, or other possible biases. Then redesign your survey instrument.
- ***Always report your sampling methods in detail.*** Others may be able to detect biases where you did not expect to find them.

Sampling and the Computer

Computer-generated pseudorandom numbers are usually quite good enough for drawing random samples. But there is little reason not to use the truly random values available on the Internet.

Here's a convenient way to draw an SRS of a specified size using a computer-based sampling frame. The sampling frame can be a list of names or of identification numbers arrayed, for example, as a column in a spreadsheet, statistics program, or database:

1. Generate random numbers of enough digits that each exceeds the size of the sampling frame list by several digits. This makes duplication unlikely.
2. Assign the random numbers arbitrarily to individuals in the sampling frame list. For example, put them in an adjacent column.
3. Sort the list of random numbers, *carrying along* the sampling frame list.
4. Now the first n values in the sorted sampling frame column are an SRS of n values from the entire sampling frame.

Connections

With this chapter we take our first formal steps to relate our sample data to a larger population. Some of these ideas have been lurking in the background as we sought patterns and summaries for data. Even when we only worked with the data at hand, we often thought about implications for a larger population of individuals.

Be sure to notice the ongoing central importance of models. We've seen models in several ways in previous chapters. Here we recognize the value of a model for a population. The parameters of such a model are values we will often want to estimate using statistics such as those we've been calculating. The connections to summary statistics for center, spread, correlation, and slope are obvious.

We now have a specific application for random numbers. The idea of applying randomness deliberately showed up in Chapter 11 for simulation. Now we need randomization to get good quality data from the real world.

Key Concepts

Population The entire group of individuals or instances about whom we hope to learn.

Sample A representative subset of a population, examined in hope of learning about the population.

Sample survey A study that asks questions of a sample drawn from some population in the hope of learning something about the entire population. Polls taken to assess voter preferences are common sample surveys.

Bias Any systematic failure of a sample to represent its population is bias. It is almost impossible to recover from a biased sample, so any efforts to avoid bias are well spent. Common errors include

- relying on voluntary response.
- undercoverage of the population.
- nonresponse bias.
- response bias.

Randomization The best defense against bias is randomization, in which each individual is given a fair, random chance of selection.

Matching Any attempt to force a sample to resemble specified attributes is a form of matching. Matching may help make better samples, but it is no substitute for randomizing.

Sample size The number of individuals in a sample. The sample size determines how well the sample represents the population, not the fraction of the population sampled.

Census A sample that consists of the entire population is called a census.

Population parameter A numerically valued attribute of a model for a population. We rarely expect to know the true value of a population parameter, but we do hope to estimate it from sampled data. For example, the mean income of all employed people in the country is a population parameter.

Statistic, sample statistic Statistics are values calculated for sampled data. Those that correspond to, and thus estimate, a population parameter, are of particular interest. For example, the mean income of all employed people in a representative sample can provide a good estimate of the corresponding population parameter. The term "sample statistic" is sometimes used, usually to parallel the corresponding term, "population parameter."

Representative A sample is said to be representative if the statistics computed from it accurately reflect the corresponding population parameters.

Simple random sample A simple random sample of sample size *n* is one in which each set of *n* elements in the population has an equal chance of selection.

Sampling frame A list of individuals from whom the sample is drawn is called the sampling frame. Individuals who may be in the population of interest but who are not in the sampling frame cannot be included in any sample.

Stratified random sample A sampling design in which the population is divided into several subpopulations, or **strata,** and random samples then drawn from each stratum. If the strata are homogeneous but are different from each other, a stratified sample may yield more consistent results.

Cluster sample A sampling design in which entire groups or **clusters** are chosen at random. Cluster sampling is usually selected as a matter of convenience, practicality, or cost. Each cluster should be heterogeneous (representative of the population), and all the clusters should be similar to each other.

Systematic sample A sample drawn by selecting individuals systematically from a sampling frame. When there is no relationship between the order of the sampling frame and the variables of interest, a systematic sample can be representative.

Multistage sample Sampling schemes that combine several sampling methods are called multistage samples. For example, a national polling service may stratify the country by geographical regions, select a random sample of cities from each region, and then interview a cluster of residents in each city.

Voluntary response bias Bias introduced to a sample when individuals can choose on their own whether to participate in the sample. Samples based on voluntary response are always invalid and cannot be recovered, no matter how large the sample size.

Convenience sample A convenience sample consists of the individuals who are conveniently available. Convenience samples often fail to be representative because every individual in the population is not equally convenient to sample.

Undercoverage A sampling scheme that fails to sample from some part of the population or that samples in a way that gives a part of the population less representation than it has in the population, suffers from undercoverage.

Nonresponse bias Bias introduced to a sample when a large fraction of those sampled fail to respond. Those who do respond are likely to not represent the entire sample. Voluntary response bias is a form of nonresponse bias, but nonresponsive may occur for other reasons. For example, those who are at work during the day won't respond to a telephone survey conducted only during working hours.

Response bias Anything in a survey design that influences responses falls under the heading of response bias. One typical response bias arises from the wording of questions, which may suggest a favored response. Voters, for example, are more likely to express support of "the president" than support of the particular person holding that office at the moment.

Sampling variability The natural tendency of randomly drawn samples to differ, one from another. Sometimes, unfortunately, called *sampling error,* sampling variability is no error at all, but just the natural result of random sampling.

Skills

When you complete this lesson you should:

Think

- Know the basic concepts and terminology of sampling (see the preceding list, for example).
- Recognize population parameters in descriptions of populations and samples.
- Understand the value of randomization as a defense against bias.
- Understand the value of sampling to estimate population parameters from statistics calculated on representative samples drawn from the population.

Show

- Know how to draw a simple random sample from a master list of a population, using a computer or a table of random numbers.

Tell

- Know what to report about a sample as part of your account of a statistical analysis.
- Report possible sources of bias in samples. Recognize voluntary response and nonresponse as sources of bias in a sample survey.

Exercises

1–10. *What did they do? For the following reports about statistical studies, identify the following items (if possible). If you can't tell, then say so—this often happens when we read about a survey.*

a) The population
b) The population parameter of interest
c) The sampling frame
d) The sample
e) The sampling method, including whether or not randomization was employed
f) Any potential sources of bias you can detect and any problems you see in generalizing to the population of interest

1. A business magazine mailed a questionnaire to the human resource directors of all of the Fortune 500 companies, and received responses from 23% of them. Those responding reported that they did not find that such surveys intruded significantly on their workday.

2. A question posted on the Lycos Web site on 18 June 2000 asked visitors to the site to say whether they thought that marijuana should be legally available for medicinal purposes.

3. Consumers Union asked all subscribers whether they had used alternative medical treatments and, if so, whether they had benefited from them. For almost all of the treatments, approximately 20% of those responding reported cures or substantial improvement in their condition.

4. The Gallup Poll interviewed 1423 randomly selected American citizens September 10–14, 1999 and reported that when "asked which type of content bothers them most on TV, 44% of Americans identify 'violence,' 23% choose 'lewd and profane language,' while 22% say 'sexual situations.'"

5. Researchers waited outside a bar they had randomly selected from a list of such establishments. They stopped every 10th person who came out of the bar and asked whether he or she thought drinking and driving was a serious problem.

6. Hoping to learn what issues may resonate with voters in the coming election, the campaign director for a mayoral candidate selects one block from each of the city's election districts. Staff members go there and interview all the residents they can find.

7. The Environmental Protection Agency took soil samples at 16 locations near a former industrial waste dump and checked each for evidence of toxic chemicals. They found no elevated levels of any harmful substances.

8. State police set up a roadblock to check cars for up-to-date registration, insurance, and safety inspections. They usually find problems with about 10% of the cars they stop.

9. A company packaging snack foods maintains quality control by randomly selecting 10 cases from each day's production and weighing the bags. Then they open one bag from each case and inspect the contents.

10. Dairy inspectors visit farms unannounced and take samples of the milk to test for contamination. If the milk is found to contain dirt, antibiotics, or other foreign matter, the milk will be destroyed and the farm re-inspected until purity is restored.

11. Parent opinion, part 1. In a large city school system with 20 elementary schools, the school board is considering the adoption of a new policy that would require elementary students to pass a test in order to be promoted to the next grade. The PTA wants to find out whether parents agree with this plan. Listed below are some of the ideas proposed for gathering data. For each, indicate what kind of sampling strategy is involved and what (if any) biases might result.

a) Put a big ad in the newspaper asking people to log their opinions on the PTA Web site.
b) Randomly select one of the elementary schools and contact every parent by phone.
c) Send a survey home with every student, and ask parents to fill it out and return it the next day.
d) Randomly select 20 parents from each elementary school. Send them a survey, and follow up with a phone call if they do not return the survey within a week.

12. Parent opinion, part 2. Let's revisit the school system described in Exercise 11. Four new sampling strategies have been proposed to help the PTA determine whether parents favor requiring elementary students to pass a test in order to be promoted to the next grade. For each, indicate what kind of sampling strategy is involved and what (if any) biases might result.

a) Run a poll on the local TV news, asking people to dial one of two phone numbers to indicate whether they favor or oppose the plan.
b) Hold a PTA meeting at each of the 20 elementary schools and tally the opinions expressed by those who attend the meetings.
c) Randomly select one class at each elementary school and contact each of those parents.
d) Go through the district's enrollment records, selecting every 40th parent. PTA volunteers will go to those homes to interview the people chosen.

13. Wording the survey. Two members of the PTA committee in Exercises 11 and 12 have proposed different questions to ask in seeking parents' opinions.

Question 1: Should elementary school–age children have to pass high stakes tests in order to remain with their classmates?

Question 2: Should schools and students be held accountable for meeting yearly learning goals by testing students before they advance to the next grade?

a) Do you think responses to these two questions might differ? How? What kind of bias is this?
b) Propose a question with more neutral wording that might better assess parental opinion.

14. Survey questions. Examine each of the following questions for possible bias. If you think the question is biased, indicate how and propose a better question.
a) Should companies that pollute the environment be compelled to pay the costs of cleanup?
b) Given that 18-year-olds are old enough to vote and to serve in the military, is it fair to set the drinking age at 21?
c) Do you think high school students should be required to wear uniforms?
d) Given humanity's great tradition of exploration, do you favor continued funding for space flights?

15. Phone surveys. Anytime we conduct a survey we must take care to avoid undercoverage. Suppose we plan to select 500 names from the city phone book, call their homes between noon and 4 p.m., and interview whoever answers, anticipating contacts with at least 200 people.
a) Why is it difficult to use a simple random sample here?
b) Describe a more convenient, but still random, sampling strategy.
c) What kinds of households are likely to be included in the eventual sample of opinion? Who will be excluded?
d) Suppose, instead, that we continue calling each number, perhaps in the morning or evening, until an adult is contacted and interviewed. How does this improve the sampling design?
e) Random digit dialing machines can generate the phone calls for us. How would this improve our design? Is anyone still excluded?

16. Cell phone survey. What about drawing a random sample only from cell phone exchanges? Discuss the advantages and disadvantages of such a sampling method as compared with surveying randomly generated telephone numbers from non–cell phone exchanges. Do you think these advantages and disadvantages have changed over time? How do you expect they'll change in the future?

17. Arm length. How long is your arm compared with your hand size? Put your right thumb at your left shoulder bone, stretch your hand open wide, and extend your hand down your arm. Put your thumb at the place where your little finger is and extend down the arm again. Repeat this a third time. Now your little finger will probably have reached the back of your left hand. If the fourth hand width goes past the end of your middle finger, turn your hand sideways and count finger widths to get there.
a) How many hand and finger widths is your arm?
b) Suppose you repeat your measurement 10 times and average your results. What parameter would this average estimate? What is the population?
c) Suppose you now collect arm lengths measured in this way from 9 friends and average these 10 measurements. What is the population now? What parameter would this average estimate?
d) Do you think these 10 arm lengths are likely to be representative of the population of arm lengths in your community? In the country? Why or why not?

18. Fuel economy. Occasionally when I fill my car with gas, I figure out how many miles per gallon my car got. I wrote down those results after 6 fill-ups in the past few months. Overall, it appears my car gets 28.8 miles per gallon.
a) What statistic have I calculated?
b) What is the parameter I'm trying to estimate?
c) How might my results be biased?
d) When the Environmental Protection Agency (EPA) checks a car like mine to predict its fuel economy, what parameter is it trying to estimate?

19. Accounting. Between quarterly audits, a company likes to check on its accounting procedures to address any problems before they become serious. The accounting staff processes payments on about 120 orders each day. The next day the supervisor rechecks 10 of the transactions to be sure they were processed properly.
a) Propose a sampling strategy for the supervisor.
b) How would you modify that strategy if the company makes both wholesale and retail sales, requiring different bookkeeping procedures?

20. Happy workers? A manufacturing company employs 14 project managers, 48 foremen, and 377 laborers. In an effort to keep informed about any possible sources of employee discontent, management wants to conduct job satisfaction interviews with a sample of employees every month.
a) Do you see any danger of bias in the company's plan? Explain.
b) Propose a sampling strategy that uses a simple random sample.
c) Why do you think a simple random sample might not provide the representative opinion the company seeks?
d) Propose a better sampling strategy.
e) Listed below are the last names of the project managers. Use random numbers to select two people to be interviewed. Be sure to explain your method carefully.

Barrett	Bowman	Chen
DeLara	DeRoos	Grigorov
Maceli	Mulvaney	Pagliarulo
Rosica	Smithson	Tadros
Williams	Yamamoto	

21. Quality control. Sammy's Salsa, a small local company, produces 20 cases of salsa a day. Each case contains 12 jars, and is imprinted with a code indicating the date and batch number. To help maintain consistency, at the end of each day Sammy selects three bottles of salsa, weighs the contents, and tastes the product. Help Sammy select the sample jars. Today's cases are coded 07N61 through 07N80.

a) Carefully explain your sampling strategy.

b) Show how to use random numbers to pick the three jars for testing.

c) Did you use a simple random sample? Explain.

22. A fish story. Concerned about reports of discolored scales on fish caught downstream from a newly sited chemical plant, scientists set up a field station in a shoreline public park. For one week they asked fisherman there to bring any fish they caught to the field station for a brief inspection. At the end of the week, the scientists said that 18% of the 234 fish that were submitted for inspection displayed the discoloration. From this information, can the researchers estimate what proportion of fish in the river have discolored scales? Explain.

23. Sampling methods. Consider each of these situations. Do you think the proposed sampling method is appropriate? Explain.

a) We want to know what percentage of local doctors accept Medicaid patients. We call the offices of 50 doctors randomly selected from local Yellow Page listings.

b) We want to know what percentage of local businesses anticipate hiring additional employees in the upcoming month. We randomly select a page in the Yellow Pages, and call every business listed there.

24. More sampling methods. Consider each of these situations. Do you think the proposed sampling method is appropriate? Explain.

a) We want to know if there is neighborhood support to turn a vacant lot into a playground. We spend a Saturday afternoon going door-to-door in the neighborhood, asking people to sign a petition.

b) We want to know if students at our college are satisfied with the selection of food available on campus. We go to the largest cafeteria and interview every 10th person in line.

Chapter 13

Experiments

Who gets good grades? And, more importantly, why? Is there something schools and parents could do to help weaker students improve their grades? Some people think they have an answer: music! No, not your portable MP3 player, but an instrument. In a 1981 study conducted at Mission Viejo High School, in California, researchers compared the scholastic performance of music students with that of non-music students. Guess what? The music students had a much higher overall grade point average than the non-music students, 3.59 to 2.91. Not only that, a whopping 16% of the music students had all A's compared with only 5% of the non-music students.

As a result of this study and others, many parent groups and educators pressed for expanded music programs in the nation's schools. They argued that the work ethic, discipline, and feeling of accomplishment fostered by learning to play an instrument also enhance a person's ability to succeed in school. They thought that involving more students in music would raise academic performance. What do you think? Does this study provide solid evidence? Or are there other possible explanations for the difference in grades? Is there any way to really prove such a conjecture?

Observational Studies

For rare illnesses, it's not practical to draw a large enough sample to see many ill respondents, so the only option remaining is to develop retrospective data. For example, researchers can interview those who have become ill. The likely causes of both Legionnaires' disease and HIV were initially identified from such retrospective studies of the small populations who were initially infected. But to confirm the causes, researchers needed laboratory-based experiments.

This research tried to show an association between music, education and grades. But it wasn't a survey. Nor did it assign students to get music education. Instead, it simply observed students "in the wild," recording the choices they made and the outcome. Such studies are called **observational studies.** In observational studies, researchers don't *assign* choices; they simply observe them. In addition, this was a **retrospective study,** because researchers identified subjects who studied music and then collected data on their past grades.

What's wrong with concluding that music education causes good grades? One high school during one academic year may not be representative of the whole United States. That's true, but the real problem is that the claim that music study *caused* higher grades depends on there being *no other differences* between the groups that could account for the differences in grades, and studying music was not the *only* difference between the two groups of students.

We can think of lots of other reasons why the groups might perform differently. Students who study music may have better work habits to start with, and this makes them successful in both music and course work. Music students may have more parental support (someone had to pay for all those lessons) and that support enhanced their academic performance, too. Maybe they came from wealthier homes and had other advantages. Or it could be that smarter kids just like to play musical instruments.

No drug can be sold in the United States without first showing, in a suitably designed experiment approved by the FDA (Food and Drug Administration), that it's safe and effective. The small print on the booklet that comes with many prescription drugs usually describes the outcomes of that experiment.

This study can't be used to prove that music lessons *cause* grades to improve. How can we do better? We might start by selecting young students who have not begun music lessons. We could then track their academic performance over several years, comparing those who later choose to study music with those who do not. Identifying subjects in advance and collecting data as events unfold would make this a **prospective study.**

Students who choose to study an instrument might still differ from the others in some important way. It may be this difference—whether we know what it is or not—rather than music itself that leads to better grades.

Is it *ever* possible to prove a cause-and-effect relationship? Well, yes it is, but we would have to take a different approach. We could take a group of third graders, randomly assign half to take music lessons, and forbid the other half to do so. Then we could compare their grades several years later. This kind of study design is called an **experiment.**

"He that leaves nothing to chance will do few things ill, but he will do very few things."
—Lord Halifax (1633–1695)

An experiment requires a **random assignment** of subjects to treatments. Only an experiment can justify a claim like "music lessons cause higher grades." Questions such as "Does taking vitamin C reduce the chance of getting a cold?" and "Does working with computers improve performance in Statistics class?" and "Is this drug a safe and effective treatment for that disease?" require a designed experiment to establish cause and effect.

Randomized, Comparative Experiments

An Experiment:
Manipulates the factor levels to create treatments.
Randomly assigns subjects to these treatment levels.
Compares the responses of the subject groups across treatment levels.

Experiments study the relationship between two or more variables. An experimenter must identify at least one explanatory variable, called a **factor,** to manipulate and at least one **response** variable to measure. What distinguishes an experiment from other types of investigation is that the experimenter actively and deliberately manipulates the factors to control the details of the possible treatments, and assigns the subjects to those treatments *at random.* The experimenter then observes the response variable and *compares* responses for different groups of subjects who have been treated differently. For example, we might design an experiment to see whether the amount of sleep and exercise you get affects your performance.

The individuals on whom or which we experiment are known by a variety of terms. Humans who are experimented on are commonly called **subjects** or **participants.** Other individuals (rats, days, petri dishes of bacteria) are commonly referred to by the more generic term **experimental unit.** We'll recruit subjects for our sleep deprivation experiment by advertising in Statistics class. We'll probably

Experimental design was advanced in the 19th century by work in psychophysics by Gustav Fechner (1801–1887), the founder of experimental psychology. Fechner designed ingenious experiments that exhibited many of the features of modern designed experiments. Fechner was careful to control for the effects of factors that might affect his results. For example, he cautioned readers in his 1860 book *Elemente der Psychophysik* to group experiment trials together to minimize the possible effects of time of day and fatigue.

have better luck if we invite them to be participants than if we advertise our need for experimental units.

The specific values that the experimenter chooses for a factor are called the **levels** of the factor. We might assign our participants to sleep for 4, 6, or 8 hours. Often there are several factors at a variety of levels. (Our subjects will also be assigned to a treadmill for 0 or 30 minutes.) The combination of specific levels from all the factors that an experimental unit receives is known as its **treatment.** (Our subjects could have six different treatments—three sleep levels, each at two exercise levels.)

How should we assign our participants to these treatments? Some students prefer 4 hours of sleep, while others need 8. Some exercise regularly; others are couch potatoes. Should we let the students choose the treatments they'd prefer? No. That would not be a good idea. To have any hope of drawing a fair conclusion, we must assign our participants to their treatments *at random.*

It may be obvious to you that we shouldn't let the students choose the treatment they'd prefer, but the need for random assignment is a lesson that was once hard for some to accept. For example, physicians might naturally prefer to assign patients to the therapy that they think best rather than have a random element such as a coin flip determine the treatment. But we've known for more than a century that for the results of an experiment to be valid, there is no way to avoid deliberate randomization.

The Four Principles of Experimental Design

The deep insight that experiments should use random assignment is quite an old one. It is due to the American philosopher and scientist C. S. Peirce in his experiments with J. Jastrow, published in 1885.

1. **Control.** We control sources of variation other than the factors we are testing by making conditions as similar as possible for all treatment groups. For human subjects, we try to treat them alike. However, there is always a question of degree and practicality. Controlling extraneous sources of variation reduces the variability of the responses, making it easier to detect differences among the treatment groups.

   Making generalizations from the experiment to other levels of the controlled factor can be risky. For example, suppose we test two laundry detergents and carefully control the water temperature at 180° F. This would reduce the variation in our results due to water temperature, but what could we say about the detergents' performance in cold water? Not much. It would be hard to justify extrapolating the results to other temperatures.

2. **Randomize.** As in sample surveys, **randomization** allows us to equalize the effects of unknown or uncontrollable sources of variation. It does not eliminate the effects of these sources, but it spreads them out across the treatment levels so that we can see past them. If experimental units are not assigned to treatments at random, you will not be able to use the powerful methods of Statistics to draw conclusions from your study. Assigning subjects to treatments at random reduces bias due to uncontrolled sources of variation. Randomization protects us even from effects we didn't know about. There's an adage that says "control what you can, and randomize the rest." This may be

good advice, but we should be sure when we control that we don't want to generalize to other conditions.

3. **Replicate.** Two kinds of replication show up in comparative experiments. First, we should repeat the experiment, applying the treatments to a number of subjects. Only with such replication can we estimate the variability of responses. If we have not assessed the variation, the experiment is not complete. The outcome of an experiment on a single subject is an anecdote, not data.

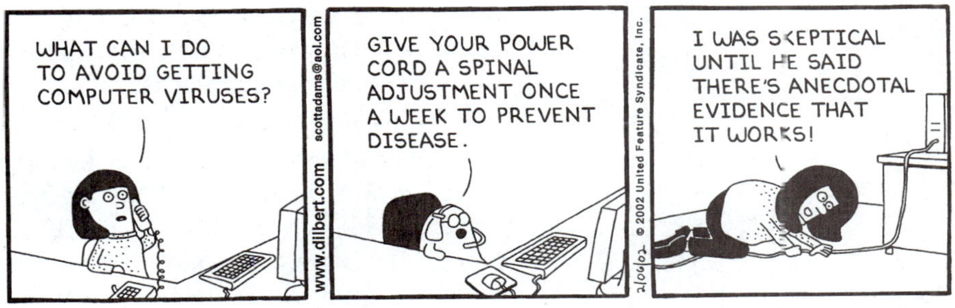

A second kind of replication shows up when the experimental units are not a representative sample from the population of interest. We may believe that what is true of the students in Psych 101 who volunteered for the sleep experiment is true of all humans, but we'll feel more confident of our conclusions after the experiment is *replicated* in another part of the country, with people of different ages, and at different times of the year. **Replication** of an entire experiment with the controlled sources of variation at different levels is an essential step in science.

Replicating Cold Fusion

"The origins of Cold Fusion have been loudly and widely documented in the press and popular literature. Pons and Fleischmann, fearing they were about to be scooped by a competitor named Steven Jones from nearby Brigham Young University, and with the encouragement of their own administration, held a press conference on March 23, 1989, at the University of Utah, to announce what seemed to be the scientific discovery of the century. Nuclear fusion, producing usable amounts of heat, could be induced to take place on a table-top by electrolyzing heavy water, using electrodes made of palladium and platinum, two precious metals. If so, the world's energy problems were at an end, to say nothing of the fiscal difficulties of the University of Utah. What followed was a kind of feeding frenzy, science by press conference and e-mail, confirmations and disconfirmations, claims and retractions, ugly charges and obfuscation, science gone berserk. For all practical purposes, it ended a mere 5 weeks after it began, on May 1st, 1989, at a dramatic session of The American Physical Society, in Baltimore. Although there were numerous presentations at this session, only two really counted. Steven Koonin and Nathan Lewis, speaking for himself and Charles Barnes, all three from Caltech, executed between them a perfect slam-dunk that cast Cold Fusion right out of the arena of mainstream science. . . . seasoned experimentalists like Lewis and Barnes refused to believe what they couldn't reproduce in their own laboratories."—David Goodstein, "Whatever Happened to Cold Fusion?"

4. **Block.** The ability of randomizing to equalize variation across treatment groups works best in the long run. For example, if we're allocating players to two 6-player soccer teams from a pool of 12 children, we might do so at random to equalize the talent. But what if there were two 12-year-olds and ten 6-year-olds in the group? Randomizing may place both 12-year-olds on the same team. In the long run, if we did this over and over, it would all equalize. Wouldn't it be better to assign one 12-year-old to each group (at random) and five 6-year-olds to each team (at random)? By doing this we would improve fairness in the short run. This approach makes the division more fair by recognizing the variation in *age* and allocating the players at random *within* each age level. When we do this, we call the variable *age* a **blocking variable.** The levels of *age* are called blocks.

   Sometimes, attributes of the experimental units that we are not studying and that we can't control may nevertheless affect the outcomes of an experiment. If we group similar individuals together and then randomize within each of these **blocks,** we can remove much of the variability due to the difference among the blocks. Blocking is an important compromise between randomization and control. However, unlike the first three principles, blocking is not *required* in an experimental design.

Designing an Experiment STEP-BY-STEP

A **completely randomized experiment** is the ideal simple design, just as a *simple random sample* is the ideal simple sample—and for many of the same reasons.

An ad for OptiGro plant fertilizer claims that with this product you will grow "juicier, tastier" tomatoes. You'd like to test this claim, and wonder whether you might be able to get by with half the specified dose. How can you set up an experiment to check out the claim?

Of course, you'll have to get some tomatoes, try growing some plants with the product and some without, and see what happens. But you'll need a clearer plan than that. How should you design your experiment?

Let's work through the design, step-by-step. We'll design the simplest kind of experiment, a **completely randomized experiment in one factor.** Since this is a *design* for an experiment, most of the steps are part of the Think stage. The statements in the right column are the kinds of things you would need to say in *proposing* an experiment. You'd need to include them in the "methods" section of a report once the experiment is run.

Think

Goal State what you want to know.

We want to know whether tomato plants grown with OptiGro yield juicier, tastier tomatoes than plants raised in otherwise similar circumstances but without the fertilizer.

Response Specify the response variable.

We will evaluate the juiciness and taste of the tomatoes by asking a panel of judges to rate them on a scale from 1 to 7 in juiciness and in taste.

Treatments Specify the factor levels and the treatments.

The factor is fertilizer, specifically *OptiGro* fertilizer. We will grow tomatoes at three different factor levels: some with no fertilizer, some with half the specified amount of *OptiGro*, and some with the full dose of *OptiGro*. These are the three treatments.

Experimental units Specify the experimental units.

We will obtain 24 tomato plants of the same variety from a local garden store.

Experimental Design Observe the principles of design:

Control any sources of variability you know of and can control.

We will locate the farm plots near each other so that the plants get similar amounts of sun and rain and experience similar temperatures. We will weed the plots equally and otherwise treat the plants alike.

Randomly assign experimental units to treatments, to equalize the effects of unknown or uncontrollable sources of variation.

Specify how the random numbers needed for randomization will be obtained.

We will randomly divide the plants into three groups. We will use random numbers from a table to determine the assignment.

Replicate results by placing more than one plant in each treatment group.

There are 8 plants in each treatment group.

Specify any other experiment details. You must give enough details so that another experimenter could exactly replicate your experiment. It's generally better to include details that might seem irrelevant than to leave out matters that could turn out to make a difference.

We will grow the plants until the tomatoes are mature, as judged by reaching a standard color.

We will harvest the tomatoes when ripe and store them for evaluation.

Specify how to **measure the response.**

We will set up a numerical scale of juiciness and one of tastiness for our taste testers. Several people will taste slices of tomato and rate them.

Show

Once you collect the data, you'll need to display it and compare the results for the three treatment groups.

We will display our results in side-by-side boxplots to compare the three treatment groups.

We will compare the means of the groups.

Tell

To answer the initial question, we ask whether the differences we observe in the means of the three groups are meaningful.

Because this is a randomized experiment, we can attribute significant differences to the treatments. To do this properly, we'll need methods from what is called "statistical inference," the subject of the rest of this book.

If the differences in taste and juiciness among the groups are greater than we would expect by knowing the usual variation among tomatoes, we may be able to conclude that these differences are due to treatment with the fertilizer.

Does the Difference Make a Difference?

We've said that if the differences among the treatment groups are big enough, we'll attribute the differences to the treatments. How will we know whether the differences are big enough?

Would we expect the group means to be identical? Not really. Even if the treatment made no difference whatever, there would still be some variation. We assigned the plants to treatments at random. But a different random assignment would have led to different results. Even a repeat of the *same* treatment on a different randomly assigned set of plants would lead to a different mean. The real question is whether the differences we observed are about as big as we'd get just from the randomization alone, or whether they're bigger than that. If we decide that they're bigger, we'll attribute the differences to the treatments. In that case we say the differences are **statistically significant.**

How will we decide if something is different enough to be considered statistically significant? We'll answer that question precisely in a later chapter, but to get some intuition, think about deciding whether a coin is fair. If we flip a fair coin 100 times, we expect, *on average* to get 50 heads. Suppose we get 54 heads out of 100. That doesn't seem very surprising. It's well within the bounds of ordinary random fluctuations. What if we'd seen 94 heads? That's clearly outside the bounds. We'd be pretty sure that the coin flips were not random. But what about 74 heads? Is that far enough from 50% to arouse our suspicions? That's the sort of question we need to ask of our experiment results.

In Statistics terminology, 94 heads would be a statistically significant difference from 50 and 54 heads would not. Whether 74 is statistically significant or not would depend on the chance of getting 74 heads in 100 flips of a fair coin and on our tolerance for believing that rare events can happen to us. We'll make that reasoning clear in later chapters.

Back at the tomato stand, we ask whether the differences we see among the treatment groups are the kind of differences we'd expect from randomization. A good way to get a feeling for that is to look at how much our results vary among plants that get the same treatment. Boxplots of our results by treatment group can give us a general idea.

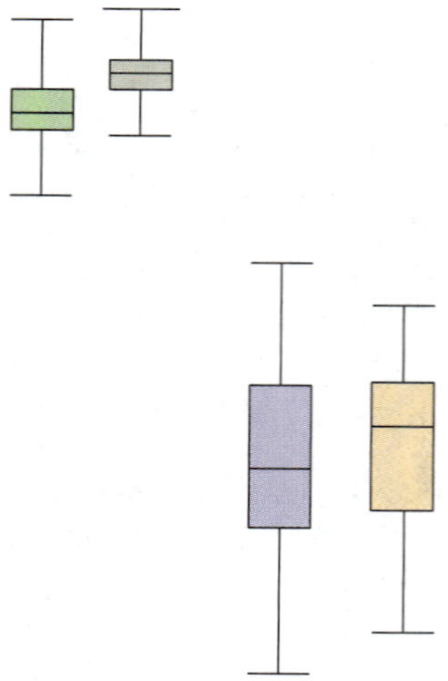

The boxplots in both pairs have centers the same distance apart, but when the spreads are large, the observed difference may be just from random fluctuation. **Figure 13.1**

For example, here are two pairs of boxplots whose centers differ by exactly the same amount. In the upper set, that difference appears to be larger than we'd expect just by chance. Why? Because the variation is quite small within treatment groups, so the larger difference between the groups is unlikely to be just from the randomization. In the bottom pair, that same difference between the centers looks less impressive. There the variation *within* each group swamps the difference *between* the two means. We'd say the difference is statistically significant in the upper pair and not statistically significant in the lower pair.

Later we'll see statistical tests that quantify this intuition. For now, the important point is that a difference is statistically significant if we don't believe that it's likely to have occurred only by chance.

Diagrams

An experiment is carried out over time with specific actions occurring in a specified order. A diagram of the procedure can help in thinking about experiments.[1]

[1]Diagrams of this sort were introduced by David Moore in his textbooks and are widely used.

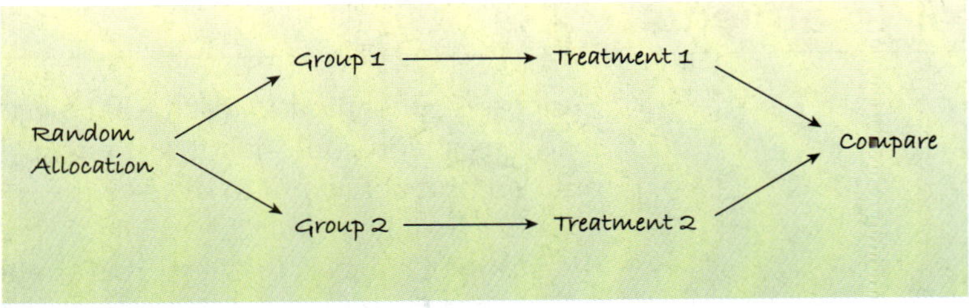

The diagram emphasizes the random allocation of subjects to treatment groups, the separate treatments applied to these groups, and the ultimate comparison of results. It's best to specify the responses that will be compared. A good way to start comparing results for the treatment groups is with boxplots.

We can diagram our tomato experiment like this:

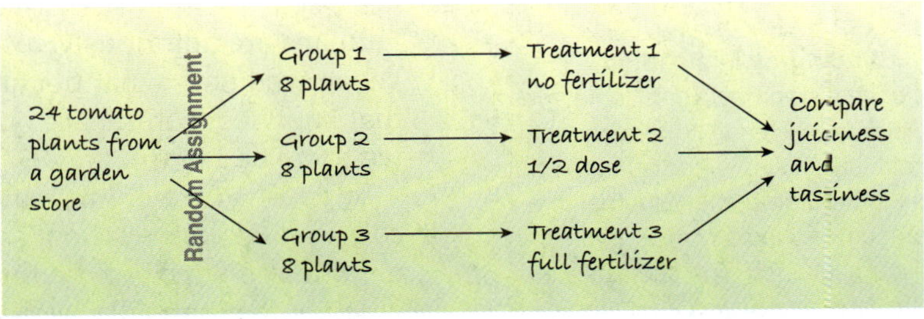

Experiments and Samples

Experiments are rarely performed on random samples from a population. Don't describe the subjects in an experiment as a random sample unless they really are. More likely, the randomization was in assigning subjects to treatments.

Both experiments and sample surveys use randomization to get unbiased data. But they do so in different ways and for different purposes. Sample surveys try to estimate population parameters, so the sample needs to be as representative of the population as possible. By contrast, experiments try to assess the effects of treatments. Experimental units are not always drawn randomly from a population. For example, a medical experiment may deal only with patients who have the disease under study. The randomization is in the assignment of their therapy. This is appropriate because our focus is on differences in the effects of the treatments.

Unless the experimental units are chosen from the population at random, you cannot immediately generalize experiment results to larger populations until the experiment has been repeated under different circumstances. An experiment result that is shown also to be true in a different season, in a different country, for a different species, and so on, is much more persuasive.

Even without choosing experimental units from a population at random, experiments can draw stronger conclusions than surveys. By looking only at the differences across treatment groups, experiments cancel out many sources of bias. For example, the entire pool of subjects may be biased and not representative of the population. (College students may need more sleep on average than the general population.) When we assign subjects randomly to treatment groups, all the groups are still biased, but *in the same way.* When we consider the differences in their responses, these biases cancel out, allowing us to see the differences due to treatment effects more clearly.

Control Treatments

Suppose you wanted to test a $300 piece of software designed to speed up download times. You could just try it on several files and record the download times, but you probably want to *compare* the speed with what would happen *without* the software installed. Such a baseline measurement is called a **control** treatment, and the group of subjects to whom it is applied is called a **control group.**

This is a use of the word "control" in an entirely different context. Previously, we controlled extraneous sources of variation by keeping them constant. Here, we use a control treatment as another *level* of the factor in order to compare the treatment results to a situation in which "nothing happens." That's what we did in the tomato experiment when we used no fertilizer on the 8 tomatoes in Group 1.

Blinding

Blinding by Misleading
Social science experiments can sometimes blind subjects by misleading them about the purpose of a study. One of the authors participated as an undergraduate volunteer in a (now infamous) psychology experiment using such a blinding method. The subjects were told that the experiment was about three-dimensional spatial perception and were assigned to draw a model of a horse. While they were busy drawing, a loud noise and then groaning were heard coming from the room next door. The *real* purpose of the experiment was to see how people reacted to the apparent disaster. The experimenters wanted to see whether the social pressure of being in groups made people react to the disaster differently. Subjects had been randomly assigned to draw either in groups or alone. The experimenter had no interest in how well the subjects could draw the horse, but the subjects were blinded to the treatment because they were misled.

Humans are notoriously susceptible to errors in judgment.[2] All of us. When we know what treatment was assigned, it's difficult not to let that knowledge influence our assessment of the response, even when we try to be careful.

Suppose you were trying to advise your school on which brand of cola to stock in the school's vending machines. You set up an experiment to see which of the three competing brands students prefer (or whether they can tell the difference at all). But people have brand loyalties. You probably prefer one brand already. So if you knew which brand you were tasting, it might influence your rating. To avoid this bias, it would be better to disguise the brands as much as possible. This strategy is called **blinding** the participants to the treatment.[3]

But it isn't just the subjects who should be blind. Experimenters themselves often subconsciously behave in ways that favor what they believe. Even technicians may treat plants or test animals differently if, for example, they expect them to die. An animal that starts doing a little better than others by showing an increased appetite may get fed a bit more than the experimental protocol specifies.

People are so good at picking up subtle cues about treatments that the best (in fact, the *only*) defense against such biases in experiments on human subjects is to keep *anyone* who could affect the outcome or the measurement of the response from knowing which subjects have been assigned to which treatments. So not only should your cola-tasting subjects be blinded, but also *you*, as the experimenter, shouldn't know which drink is which either—at least until you're ready to analyze the results.

There are two main classes of individuals who can affect the outcome of the experiment:

- those who could influence the results (the subjects, treatment administrators, or technicians)
- those who evaluate the results (judges, treating physicians, etc.)

When every individual in *either* of these classes is blinded, an experiment is said to be **single-blind.** When everyone in *both* classes is blinded, we call the experiment

---

[2]For example, here we are in Chapter 13 and you're still reading the footnotes.

[3]C. S. Peirce, in the same 1885 work in which he introduced randomization, also recommended blinding.

double-blind. Even if several individuals in one class are blinded—for example, both the patients and the technicians who administer the treatment—the study would still be just single-blind. If only some of the individuals in a class are blind—for example, if subjects are not told of their treatment, but the administering technician is not blind—there is a substantial risk that subjects can discern their treatment from subtle cues in the technician's behavior or that the technician might inadvertently treat subjects differently. Such experiments cannot be considered truly blind.

In our tomato experiment we certainly don't want the people judging the taste to know which tomatoes got the fertilizer. That makes the experiment single-blind. We might also not want the people caring for the tomatoes to know which ones were being fertilized in case they might treat them differently in other ways, too. We can accomplish this double-blinding by having some fake fertilizer for them to put on the other plants. Read on.

Placebos

The placebo effect is stronger when placebo treatments are administered with authority or by a figure who appears to be an authority. "Doctors" in white coats generate a stronger effect than salespeople in polyester suits. But the placebo effect is not reduced much even when subjects know that the effect exists. People often suspect that they've gotten the placebo if nothing at all happens. So, recently, drug manufacturers have gone so far in making placebos realistic that they sometimes even give them the same side effects as the drug being tested! Such "active placebos" are usually more effective. But when those side effects include loss of appetite or hair, the practice may raise ethical questions.

Often simply applying *any* treatment can induce an improvement. Every parent knows the medicinal value of a kiss to make a toddler's scrape or bump stop hurting. Some of the improvement seen with a treatment—even an effective treatment—can be due to the simple act of treating. To separate these two effects, we can use a control treatment that mimics the treatment itself.

A "fake" treatment that looks just like the treatments being tested is called a **placebo.** Placebos are the best way to blind subjects from knowing whether they are receiving the treatment or not. One common version of a placebo in drug testing is a "sugar pill." Especially when psychological attitude can affect the results, control group subjects treated with a placebo may show an improvement.

The fact is that subjects treated with a placebo sometimes improve. It's not unusual for 20% or more of subjects given a placebo to report reduction in pain, improved movement, or greater alertness, or even to demonstrate improved health or performance. This **placebo effect** highlights both the importance of effective blinding and the importance of comparing treatments with a control. Placebo controls are so effective that you should use them as an essential tool for blinding whenever possible.

The best experiments are usually

- randomized.
- comparative.
- double-blind.
- placebo-controlled.

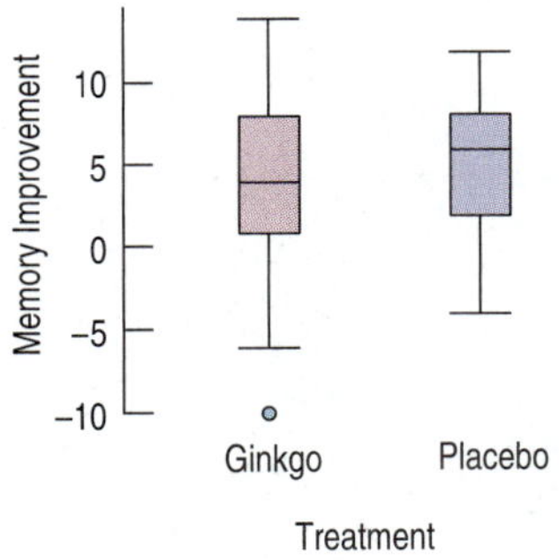

Does ginkgo biloba improve memory?

Researchers investigated the purported memory-enhancing effect of ginkgo biloba tree extract (P. R. Solomon, F. Adams, A. Silver, J. Zimmer, R. De Veaux, "Ginkgo for Memory Enhancement. A Randomized Controlled Trial." *JAMA* 285 [2002]:835S–840S). In a randomized comparative, double-blind, placebo-controlled study, they administered treatments to 230 elderly community members. One group received Ginkoba™ according to the manufacturer's instructions. The other received a similar-looking placebo. Thirteen different tests of memory were administered before and after treatment. The placebo group showed greater improvement on 7 of the tests; the treatment group on the other 6. None showed any significant differences. Here are boxplots of one measure.

Blocking

Suppose we wanted to use 18 tomato plants of the same variety for our experiment, but the garden store had only 12 plants left. So we drove down to the nursery and bought 6 more plants of that variety. We worry that the tomato plants from the two stores are different somehow, and, in fact, they don't really look the same.

How can we design the experiment so that the differences between the stores don't mess up our attempts to see differences among fertilizer levels? We can't treat the store the same way as the fertilizer because we can't assign it as we would a factor in the experiment. You can't tell a tomato what store to come from.

Because stores vary in the care they give and the sources of seeds, the plants from each store will be more like each other than like the plants from the other store. When groups of experimental units are similar, it's often a good idea to gather them together into **blocks.** By blocking we isolate the variability due to the differences between the blocks so that we can see the differences due to the treatments more clearly. Here, we would define the plants from each store to be a block. The randomization is introduced when we randomly assign treatments within each block.

In a retrospective or prospective study, subjects are sometimes paired because they are similar in ways *not* under study. **Matching** subjects in this way can reduce variation in much the same way as blocking. For example, a retrospective study of music education and grades might match each student who studies an instrument with one who is similar in family income and gender but didn't study an instrument. When we compare grades of music students with those of non-music students, the matching would reduce the variation due to income and gender differences.

In a completely randomized design, each of the 18 plants would have an equal chance to land in each of the three treatment groups. But we realize that the store may have an effect. To isolate the store effect, we assign the plants to treatments at random *within* each block. So we now have six treatment groups, three for each block. Within each block, we'll randomly assign the same number of plants to each of the three treatments. The experiment is still fair because each treatment is still applied (at random) to the same number of plants and to the same proportion from each store: 4 from store A and 2 from store B. Because the randomization occurs only within the blocks (plants from one store cannot be assigned to treatment groups for the other), we call it a **randomized block design.**

In effect, we conduct two parallel experiments, one for tomatoes from each store, and then combine the results. The picture tells the story.

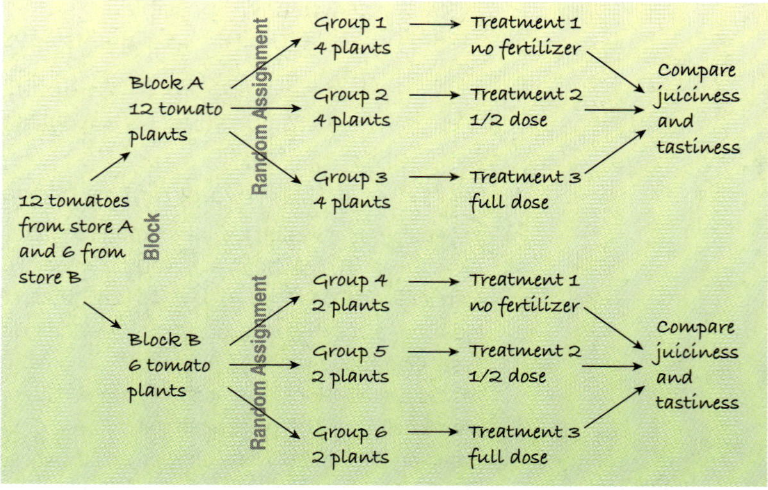

Blocking is the same idea for experiments as stratifying is for sampling. Both methods group together subjects that are similar and randomize within those groups as a way to remove unwanted variation. (But be careful to keep the terms straight. Don't say that we "stratify" an experiment or "block" a sample.) We use blocks to reduce variability so we can see the effects of the factors, not as factors to be studied themselves.

Adding More Factors

There are two kinds of gardeners. Some water frequently, making sure that the plants are never dry. Others let Mother Nature take her course and leave the watering to her. The makers of OptiGro want to ensure that their product will work under a wide variety of watering conditions. Maybe we should include the amount of watering as part of our experiment. Can we study a second factor at the same time and still learn as much about fertilizer?

We now have two factors (fertilizer at three levels and irrigation at two levels). We combine them in all possible ways to yield six treatments:

	No fertilizer	Half fertilizer	Full fertilizer
No added water	1	2	3
Daily watering	4	5	6

If we allocate the original 12 plants, the experiment now assigns 2 plants to each of these six treatments at random. This experiment is a **completely randomized two-factor experiment** because any plant could end up assigned at random to any of the six treatments (and we have two factors).

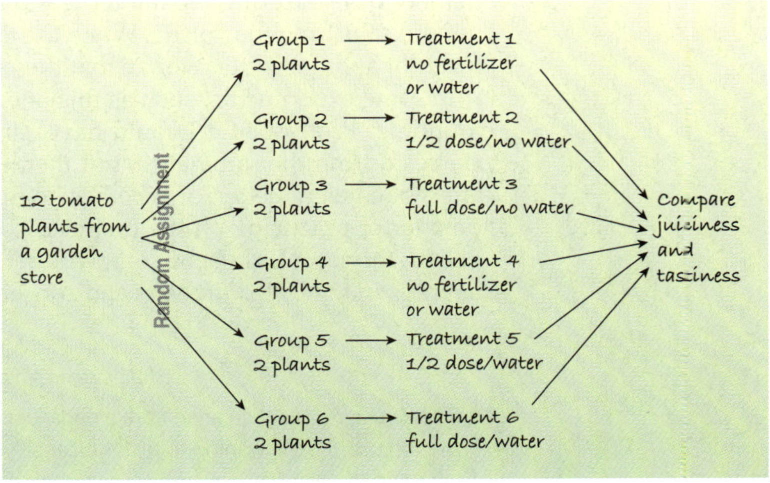

It's often important to include several factors in the same experiment in order to see what happens when the factor levels are applied in different *combinations*. A common misconception is that applying several factors at once makes it difficult to separate out the effects of the individual factors. You may hear people say that experiments should always be run "one factor at a time." In fact, just the opposite is true. Experiments with more than one factor are both more efficient and provide more information than one-at-a-time experiments. There are many ways to design efficient multifactor experiments, and you can take a whole course on the design and analysis of such experiments.

Confounding

Professor Stephen Ceci of Cornell University performed an experiment to investigate the effect of a teacher's classroom style on student evaluations. He taught a class in developmental psychology during two successive terms to a total of 472 students in two very similar classes. He kept everything about his teaching identical (same text, same syllabus, same office hours, etc.) and modified only his style in class. During the fall term he maintained a subdued demeanor. During the spring term, he used expansive gestures and lectured with more enthusiasm, varying his vocal pitch and using more hand gestures. He administered a standard student evaluation form at the end of each term.

The students in the fall term class rated him only an average teacher. Those in the spring term class rated him an excellent teacher, praising his knowledge and accessibility, and even the quality of the textbook. On the question "How much did you learn in the course?" the average response changed from 2.93 to 4.05 on a 5-point scale.[4]

How much of the difference he observed was due to his difference in manner and how much might have been due to the season of the year? Fall term in Ithaca, NY (home of Cornell University), starts out colorful and pleasantly warm but ends cold and bleak. Spring term starts out bitter and snowy and ends with blooming flowers and singing birds. Might students' overall happiness have been affected by the season and reflected in their evaluations?

Unfortunately, there's no way to tell. Nothing in the data enables us to tease apart these two effects because all of the students who experienced the subdued manner did so during the fall term and all who experienced the expansive manner did so during the Spring. When the levels of one factor are associated with the levels of another factor, we say that these two factors are **confounded.**

In some experiments, such as this one, it's just not possible to avoid some confounding. Professor Ceci could have randomly assigned students to one of two classes during the same term, but then we might question whether mornings or afternoons were better, or whether he really delivered the same class the second time (after practicing on the first class). Or he could have had another professor deliver the second class, but that would have raised more serious issues about differences in the two professors and concern over more serious confounding.

A two-factor example

Confounding can also arise from a badly designed multifactor experiment. Here's a classic. A credit card bank wanted to test the sensitivity of the market to two factors: the annual fee charged for a card and the annual percentage rate charged. Not wanting to scrimp on sample size, the bank selected 100,000 people at random from a mailing list. It sent out 50,000 offers with a low rate and no fee, and 50,000 offers with a higher rate and a $50 annual fee.

[4]But the two classes performed almost identically well on the final exam.

Guess what happened? That's right—people preferred the low-rate, no-fee card. No surprise. In fact, they signed up for that card at over twice the rate as the other offer. And because of the large sample size, the bank was able to estimate the difference precisely. But the question the bank really wanted to answer was "How much of the change was due to the rate, and how much was due to the fee?" Unfortunately, there's simply no way to separate out the two effects. If the bank had sent out all four possible different treatments—low rate with no fee; low rate with $50 fee; high rate with no fee, and high rate with $50 fee—each to 25,000 people, it could have learned about both factors and could have also seen what happens when the two factors occur in combination.

What Can Go Wrong?

- ***Beware of confounding.*** Use randomization whenever possible to ensure that the factors not in your experiment are not confounded with your treatment levels. Be alert to confounding that cannot be avoided, and report it along with your results.
- ***Bad things can happen even to good experiments.*** Protect yourself by recording additional information. An experiment in which the air conditioning failed for 2 weeks, affecting the results, was saved by recording the temperature (although that was not originally one of the factors) and estimating the effect the higher temperature had on the response (R. D. DeVeaux and M. Szelewski, "Optimizing Automatic Splitless Injection Parameters for Gas Chromatographic Environmental Analysis." *Journal of Chromatographic Science* 27, no. 9 [1989]:513–518).

  It's generally good practice to collect as much information as possible about your experimental units and the circumstances of the experiment. For example, in the tomato experiment, it would be wise to record details of the weather (temperature, rainfall, sunlight) that might affect the plants and any facts available about their growing situation. (Is one side of the field in shade sooner than the other as the day proceeds? Is one area lower and a bit wetter?) Sometimes we can use this extra information during the analysis to reduce biases.
- ***Don't spend your entire budget on the first run.*** Just as it's a good idea to pretest a survey, it's always wise to try a small pilot experiment before running the full-scale experiment. You may learn, for example, how to choose factor levels more effectively, about effects you forgot to control, and about unanticipated confoundings.

Experiments and the Computer

Most experiments are analyzed with a statistics package. You should almost always display the results of a comparative experiment with side-by-side boxplots. You may also want to display the means and standard deviations of the treatment groups in a table.

The analyses offered by statistics packages for comparative randomized experiments fall under the general heading of Analysis of Variance, usually abbreviated ANOVA. These analyses are beyond the scope of this chapter.

Connections

The fundamental role of randomization in experiments clearly points back to our discussions of randomization, to our experiments with simulations, and to our use of randomization in sampling. The similarities and differences between experiments and samples are important to keep in mind and can make each concept clearer.

If you think that blocking in an experimental sample resembles stratifying in a sample, you're quite right. Both are ways of removing variation we can identify to help us see past the variation in the data.

Experiments compare groups of subjects that have been treated differently. Graphics such as boxplots that help us compare groups are closely related to these ideas. Think about what we look for in a boxplot to tell whether two groups look really different and you'll be thinking about the same issues as experiment designers.

Generally, we're going to consider how different the mean responses are for different treatment groups. And we're going to judge whether those differences are large by using standard deviations as rulers. (That's why we needed to replicate results for each treatment; we need to be able to estimate those standard deviations.) The discussion in Chapter 6 introduced this fundamental statistical thought, and it's going to keep coming back over and over again. Statistics is about variation.

We'll see a number of ways to analyze results from experiments in subsequent chapters.

Key Concepts

Observational study A study based on data in which no manipulation of factors has been employed.

Retrospective study An observational study in which subjects are selected and then their previous conditions or behaviors are determined. Because retrospective studies are not based on random samples, they usually focus on estimating differences between groups or associations between variables.

Prospective study An observational study in which subjects are followed to observe future outcomes. Because no treatments are deliberately applied, a prospective study is not an experiment. Nevertheless, prospective studies typically focus on estimating differences among groups that might appear as the groups are followed during the course of the study.

Experiment An experiment *manipulates* factor levels to create treatments, *randomly assigns* subjects to these treatment levels, and then *compares* the responses of the subject groups across treatment levels.

Random assignment To be valid, an experiment must assign experimental units to treatment groups at random. This is called random assignment.

Factor A variable whose levels are controlled by the experimenter. Experiments attempt to discover the effects that differences in factor levels may have on the responses of the experimental units.

Response A variable whose values are compared across different treatments. In a randomized experiment, large response differences can be attributed to the effect of differences in treatment level.

Experimental units Individuals on whom an experiment is performed. Usually called **subjects** or **participants** when they are human.

Level The specific values that the experimenter chooses for a factor are called the levels of the factor.

Treatment The process, intervention, or other controlled circumstance applied to randomly assigned experimental units. Treatments are the different levels of a single factor or are made up of combinations of levels of two or more factors.

Principles of experimental design

- **Control** aspects of the experiment that we know may have an effect on the response, but that are not the factors being studied.
- **Randomize** subjects to treatments to even out effects for which we cannot control.
- **Replicate** over as many subjects as possible. Results for a single subject are just anecdotes. If, as often happens, the subjects of the experiment are not a representative sample from the population of interest, replicate the entire study with a different group of subjects, preferably from a different part of the population.
- **Block** to reduce the effects of identifiable attributes of the subjects that cannot be controlled.

Statistically significant When an observed difference is too large for us to believe that it is likely to have occurred naturally, we consider the difference to be statistically significant. Subsequent chapters will show specific calculations and give rules, but the principle remains the same.

Control group The experimental units assigned to a baseline treatment level, typically either the default treatment, which is well understood, or a null, placebo treatment. Their responses provide a basis for comparison.

Blinding Any individual associated with an experiment who is not aware of how subjects have been allocated to treatment groups is said to be blind.

Single-blind Double-blind There are two main classes of individuals who can affect the outcome of an experiment:

- those who could *influence the results* (the subjects, treatment administrators, or technicians).
- those who *evaluate the results* (judges, treating physicians, etc.).

When every individual in *either* of these classes is blinded, an experiment is said to be **single-blind.** When everyone in *both* classes is blinded, we call the experiment **double-blind.**

Placebo A null treatment known to have no effect, administered for comparison because many subjects respond to such a null treatment (a response known as a placebo effect). Only by comparing with a placebo can we be sure that the observed effect of a treatment is not due simply to the placebo effect.

Placebo effect The tendency of many human subjects (often 20% or more of experiment subjects) to show a response even when administered a placebo.

Block When groups of experimental units are similar, it is often a good idea to gather them together into blocks. By blocking we isolate the variability due to the differences between the blocks so that we can see the differences due to the treatments more clearly.

Matching In a retrospective or prospective study, subjects who are similar in ways not under study may be matched and then compared with each other on the variables of interest. Matching, like blocking, reduces unwanted variation.

Designs In a **completely randomized design,** all experimental units have an equal chance of receiving any treatment.

In a **randomized block design,** the randomization occurs only within blocks.

Confounding When the levels of one factor are associated with the levels of another factor, we say that these two factors are confounded.

Skills

When you complete this lesson you should:

Think

- Know the four basic principles of sound experiment design: control, randomize, replicate, and block, and be able to explain each.
- Be able to recognize the factors, the treatments, and the response variable in a description of a designed experiment.
- Understand the essential importance of randomization in assigning treatments to experimental units.
- Understand the importance of replication to move from anecdotes to general conclusions.
- Understand the value of blocking so that variability due to differences in attributes of the subjects can be removed.
- Understand the importance of a control group and the need for a placebo treatment in some studies.
- Understand the importance of blinding and double-blinding in studies on human subjects, and be able to identify blinding and the need for blinding in experiments.
- Understand the value of a placebo in experiments with human participants.

Show

- Be able to design a completely randomized experiment to test the effect of a single factor.
- Be able to design an experiment in which blocking is used to reduce variation.
- Know how to use graphs to compare responses for different treatment groups. Understand that you should *never* proceed with any other analysis of a designed experiment without first looking at boxplots or other graphical displays.

Tell

- Know how to compare the responses in different treatment groups to assess whether the differences are larger than could be reasonably expected from ordinary sampling variability.
- Know how to report the results of an experiment. Tell who the subjects are and how their assignment to treatments was determined. Report on how the response variable was measured and in what measurement units.
- Understand that your description of an experiment should be sufficient for another researcher to replicate the study with the same methods.
- Be able to report on the statistical significance of the result in terms of whether the observed group-to-group differences are larger than could be expected from ordinary sampling variation.

Exercises

1–18. What's the design? Read each brief report of statistical research, and identify:

a) whether it was an observational study or an experiment.

If it was an investigative study, identify (if possible)

b) whether it was retrospective or prospective.
c) the subjects studied, and how they were selected.
d) the parameter of interest.
e) the nature and scope of the conclusion the study can reach.

If it was an experiment, identify (if possible)

b) the subjects studied.
c) the factor(s) in the experiment, and the number of levels for each.

d) the number of treatments.
e) the response variable measured.
f) the design (completely randomized, blocked, or matched).
g) whether it was blind (or double-blind).
h) the nature and scope of the conclusion the experiment can reach.

1. Over a 4-month period, among 30 people with bipolar disorder, patients who were given a high dose (10 g/day) of omega-3 fats from fish oil improved more than those given a placebo. (*Archives of General Psychiatry* 56 [1999]: 407)

2. The leg muscles of men aged 60 to 75 were 50% to 80% stronger after they participated in a 16-week, high-intensity resistance-training program twice a week. (*Journal of Gerontology* 55A [2000]: B336)

3. In a test of roughly 200 men and women, those with moderately high blood pressure (averaging 164/89 mm Hg) did worse on tests of memory and reaction time than those with normal blood pressure. (*Hypertension* 36 [2000]: 1079)

4. Among a group of disabled women aged 65 and older who were tracked for several years, those who had a vitamin B_{12} deficiency were twice as likely to suffer severe depression as those who did not. (*American Journal of Psychology* 157 [2000]: 715)

5. An examination of the medical records of more than 360,000 Swedish men showed that those who were overweight or who had high blood pressure had a higher risk of kidney cancer. (*New England Journal of Medicine* 3434 [2000]: 1305)

6. To research the effects of "dietary patterns" on blood pressure in 459 subjects, subjects were randomly assigned to three groups and had their meals prepared by dieticians. Those who were fed a diet low in fat and cholesterol and high in fruits, vegetables, and low-fat dairy foods (known as the DASH diet) lowered their systolic blood pressure by an average of 6.7 points when compared with subjects fed a control diet.

7. After menopause many women take supplemental estrogen. There is some concern that if these women also drink alcohol their estrogen levels will rise too high. Twenty-four volunteers, 12 who were receiving supplemental estrogen and 12 who were not, were randomly divided into two groups. One group drank an alcoholic beverage, the other a nonalcoholic beverage. An hour later everyone's estrogen level was checked. Only these on supplemental estrogen who drank alcohol showed a marked increase.

8. Is diet or exercise effective in combating insomnia? Some believe that cutting out desserts can help alleviate the problem, while others recommend exercise. Forty volunteers suffering from insomnia agreed to participate in a month-long experiment. Half were randomly assigned to a special no-desserts diet; the others continued desserts as usual. Half of the people in each of these groups were randomly assigned to an exercise program, while the others did not exercise. Those who ate no desserts and engaged in exercise showed the most improvement.

9. Some gardeners prefer to use nonchemical methods to control insect pests in their gardens. Researchers have designed two kinds of traps, and want to know which design will be more effective. They randomly choose 10 locations in a large garden and place one of each kind of trap at each location. After a week they count the number of bugs in each trap.

10. Researchers have linked an increase in the incidence of breast cancer in Italy to dioxin released by an industrial accident in 1976. The study identified 981 women who lived near the site of the industrial explosion and were under age 40 at the time. Fifteen of the women had developed breast cancer, at an unusually young average age of 45. Medical records showed that these women had heightened concentrations of dioxin in their blood, and that each 10-fold increase in dioxin level was associated with a doubling of the risk of breast cancer. (*Science News*, Aug. 3, 2002)

11. In 2002 the journal *Science* reported that a study of women in Finland indicated that having sons shortened the lifespans of mothers by about 34 weeks per son, but that daughters helped to lengthen the mothers' lives. The data came from church records from the period 1640 to 1870.

12. In 2001 a report in the *Journal of the American Cancer Institute* indicated that women who work nights have a 60% greater risk of developing breast cancer. Researchers based these findings on the work histories of 763 women with breast cancer and 741 women without the disease.

13. The May 4, 2000, issue of *Science News* reported that, contrary to popular belief, depressed individuals cry no more often in response to sad situations than nondepressed people. Researchers studied 23 men and 48 women with major depression, and 9 men and 24 women with no depression. They showed the subjects a sad film about a boy whose father has died, noting whether or not the subjects cried. Women cried more often than men, but there were no significant differences between the depressed and nondepressed groups.

14. Scientists at a major pharmaceutical firm investigated the effectiveness of an herbal compound to treat the common cold. They exposed each subject to a cold virus, then gave him or her either the herbal compound or a sugar solution known to have no effect on colds. Several days later they assessed the patient's condition, using a cold severity scale ranging 0 to 5. They found no evidence of benefits associated with the compound.

15. Scientists examined the glycogen content of rats' brains at the rats' normal bedtimes and after they had been kept awake for an extra 6, 12, or 24 hours. The scientists found that glycogen was 38% lower among rats that had been sleep-deprived for 12 hours or more, and that the levels recovered during subsequent sleep. These researchers speculate that we may need to sleep in order to restore the brain's energy fuel. (*Science News,* July 20, 2002)

16. Some people who race greyhounds give the dogs large doses of vitamin C in the belief that the dogs will run faster. Investigators at the University of Florida tried three different diets in random order on each of five racing greyhounds. They were surprised to find that when the dogs ate high amounts of vitamin C they ran more slowly. (*Science News,* July 20, 2002)

17. Some people claim they can get relief from migraine headache pain by drinking a large glass of ice water. Researchers plan to enlist several people who suffer from migraines in a test. When a participant experiences a migraine headache, he or she will take a pill that may be a standard pain reliever or a placebo. Half of each group will also drink ice water. Participants will then report the level of pain relief they experience.

18. Weight is an issue for both humans and their pets. A dog food company wants to compare a new lower-calorie food with their standard dog food to see if it's effective in helping inactive dogs maintain a healthy weight. They have found several dog owners willing to participate in the trial. The dogs have been classified as small, medium, or large breeds, and the company will supply some owners of each size of dog with one of the two foods. The owners have agreed not to feed their dogs anything else for a period of 6 months, after which the dogs' weights will be checked.

19. Tomatoes. Describe a strategy to randomly split the 24 tomatoes into the three groups for the chapter's completely randomized single factor test of OptiGro fertilizer.

20. Tomatoes II. The chapter also described a completely randomized two-factor experiment testing OptiGro fertilizer in conjunction with two different routines for watering the plants. Describe a strategy to randomly assign the 24 tomato plants to the six treatments.

21. Mozart. Will listening to a Mozart piano sonata make you smarter? In a 1995 study, Rauscher, Shaw, and Ky reported that when students were given a spatial reasoning section of a standard IQ test, those who listened to Mozart for 10 minutes improved their scores more than those who simply sat quietly.

a) These researchers said the differences were statistically significant. Explain what that means in this context.

b) Steele, Bass, and Crook tried to replicate the original study. The subjects were 125 college students who participated in the experiment for course credit. Subjects first took the test. Then they were assigned to one of three groups: listening to a Mozart piano sonata, listening to music by Philip Glass, and sitting for 10 minutes in silence. Three days after the treatments, they were retested. Draw a diagram displaying the design of this experiment.

c) The boxplots show the differences in score before and after treatment for the three groups. Did the Mozart group show improvement?

d) Do you think the results prove that listening to Mozart is beneficial? Explain.

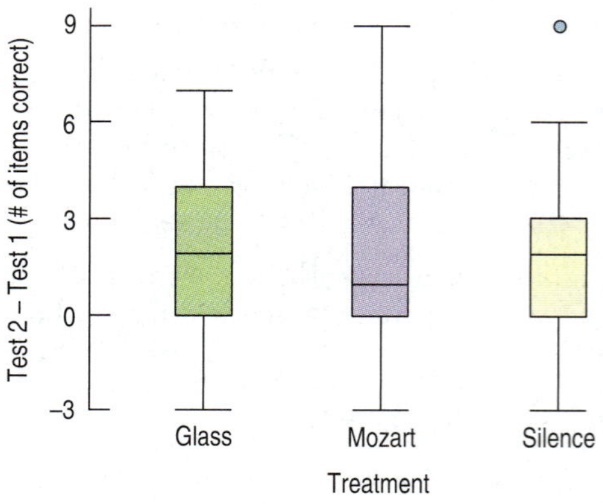

22. More Mozart. An advertisement selling specially designed music CDs of Mozart's music specifically because they will "strengthen your mind, heal your body, and unlock your creative spirit" claims (we *swear!*) that "In Japan, a brewery reports that their best sake is made when Mozart is played near the yeast." Suppose, just for the sake (as it were) of discussion, you wished to design an experiment to test whether this is true. Assume you have the full cooperation of the sake brewery. Specify how you would design the experiment. Indicate factors and response and how they would be measured, controlled, or randomized.

23. Frumpies. The makers of Frumpies, "the breakfast of rug rats," want to improve their marketing, so they consult you:

a) They first want to know what fraction of children, ages 10 to 13, like their celery-flavored cereal. What kind of study should they perform?

b) They are thinking of introducing a new flavor, maple-marshmallow Frumpies, and want to know whether children will prefer the new flavor to the old one. Design a completely randomized experiment to investigate this question.

c) They suspect that children who regularly watch the Saturday morning cartoon show staring Frump, the flying teenage warrior rabbit who eats Frumpies in every episode, may respond differently to the new flavor. How would you take that into account in your design?

24. Full moon. It's a common belief that people behave strangely when there's a full moon, and that as a result police and emergency rooms are busier than usual. Design a way you could find out if there is any merit to this belief. Will you use an observational study or an experiment? Why?

25. Health. A 2001 Danish study published in the *Archives of Internal Medicine* casts significant doubt on suggestions that adults who drink wine have higher levels of "good" cholesterol and fewer heart attacks. These researchers followed a group of individuals born at a Copenhagen hospital between 1959 and 1961 for 40 years. Their study found that in this group the adults who drank wine were richer and better educated than those who did not.

a) What kind of study was this?

b) It is generally true that people with high levels of education and high socioeconomic status are healthier than others. How does this call into question the supposed health benefits of wine?

c) Can studies such as these prove causation (that wine helps prevent heart attacks, that drinking wine makes one richer, that being rich helps prevent heart attacks, etc.)? Explain.

26. Swimming. Recently, a group of adults who swim regularly for exercise were evaluated for depression. It turned out that these swimmers were less likely to be depressed than the general population. The researchers said the difference was statistically significant.

a) What does "statistically significant" mean in this context?

b) Is this an experiment or an observational study? Explain.

c) News reports claimed this study proved that swimming can prevent depression. Explain why this conclusion is not justified by the study. Include an example of a possible confounding variable.

d) But perhaps it is true. We wonder if exercise can ward off depression, and whether anaerobic exercise (like weight training) is as effective as aerobic exercise (like swimming). We find 120 volunteers not currently engaged in a regular program of exercise. Design an appropriate experiment.

27. Dowsing. A water dowser claims to be able to sense the presence of water using a forked stick. Suppose we wish to set up an experiment to test his ability. We get 20 identical containers, fill some with water, and ask the dowser to tell which ones are full and which empty.

a) How will we randomize this procedure?

b) The dowser correctly identifies the contents of 12 out of 20 containers. Do you think this level of success is statistically significant? Explain.

c) How many correct identifications (out of 20) would the dowser have to make to convince you that the forked stick trick works? Explain.

28. Healing. A medical researcher suspects that giving post-surgical patients large doses of vitamin E will speed their recovery time by helping their incisions heal more quickly. Design an experiment to test this conjecture. Be sure to identify the factors, levels, treatments, response variable, and the role of randomization.

29. Reading. Some schools teach reading using phonics (the sounds made by letters) and others using whole language (word recognition). Suppose a school district wants to know which method works better. Suggest a design for an appropriate experiment.

30. Gas mileage. Do cars get better gas mileage with premium instead of regular unleaded gasoline? While it might be possible to test some engines in a laboratory setting, we'd rather use real cars and real drivers in real day-to-day driving, so we get 20 volunteers. Design the experiment.

31. Weekend deaths. A study published in the *New England Journal of Medicine* (Aug. 2001) suggests that it's dangerous to enter a hospital on a weekend. During a 10-year period, researchers tracked over 4 million emergency admissions to hospitals in Ontario, Canada. Their findings revealed that patients admitted on weekends had a much higher risk of death than those who went to the emergency room on weekdays.

a) The researchers said the difference in death rates was "statistically significant." Explain in this context what that means.

b) What kind of study was this? Explain

c) If you think you're quite ill on a Saturday, should you wait until Monday to seek medical help? Explain.

d) Suggest some possible explanations for this troubling finding.

32. Shingles. A research doctor has discovered a new ointment that she believes will be more effective than the current medication in the treatment of shingles (a painful skin rash). Eight patients have volunteered to participate in the initial trials of this ointment. You are the statistician hired as a consultant to help design a completely randomized experiment.

a) Describe how you will conduct this experiment.

b) Suppose the eight patients' last names start with the letters A to H. Using the random numbers listed below, show which patients you will assign to each treatment. Explain your randomization procedure clearly.

41098 18329 78458 31685 55259

c) Can you make this experiment double blind? If so, explain how.

d) The initial experiment revealed that males and females may respond differently to the ointment. Further testing of the drug's effectiveness is now planned, and many patients have volunteered. What changes in your first design, if any, would you make for this second stage of testing?

33. Beetles. Hoping to learn how to control crop damage by a certain species of beetle, a researcher plans to test two different pesticides in small plots of corn. A few days after application of the chemicals, he'll check the number of beetle larvae found on each plant. The researcher wants to know if either pesticide works, and whether there is a significant difference in effectiveness between them. Design an appropriate experiment.

34. SAT Prep. Can special study courses actually help raise SAT scores? One organization says that the 30 students they tutored achieved an average gain of 60 points when they retook the test.

a) Explain why this does not necessarily prove that the special course caused the scores to go up.

b) Propose a design for an experiment that could test the effectiveness of the tutorial course.

c) Suppose you suspect that the tutorial course might be more helpful for students whose initial scores were particularly low. How would this affect your proposed design?

35. Safety switch. An industrial machine requires an emergency shutoff switch that must be designed so that it can be easily operated with either hand. Design an experiment to find out whether workers will be able to deactivate the machine as quickly with their left hands as with their right hands. Be sure to explain the role of randomization in your design.

36. Washing clothes. A consumer group wants to test the effectiveness of a new "organic" laundry detergent and make recommendations to customers about how to best use the product. They intentionally get grass stains on 30 white t-shirts in order to see how well the detergent will clean them. They want to try the detergent in cold water and in hot water on both the "regular" and "delicates" wash cycles. Design an appropriate experiment, indicating the number of factors, levels, and treatments. Explain the role of randomization in your experiment.

Review of Part III Gathering Data

Quick Review

Before you can make a boxplot, calculate a mean, describe a distribution, or fit a line, you must have meaningful data to work with. Getting good data is essential to any investigation. No amount of clever analysis can make up for badly collected data. Here's a brief summary of the key concepts and skills:

- The way you gather depends both on what you want to discover and on what is practical.
- To get some insight into what might happen in a real situation, model it with a **simulation** using random numbers.
- To answer questions about a target population, collect information from a sample with a **survey** or poll.
  - Choose the sample randomly. Random sampling designs include simple, stratified, systematic, cluster, and multistage.
  - A simple random sample draws without restriction from the entire target population.
  - When there are subgroups within the population that may respond differently, use a stratified sample.
  - Avoid bias, a systematic distortion of the results. Sample designs that allow undercoverage or response bias and designs such as voluntary response or convenience samples don't faithfully represent the population.
  - Samples will naturally vary one from another. This sample-to-sample variation is called sampling error. Each sample only approximates the target population.
- **Observational studies** collect information from a sample drawn from a target population.
  - Retrospective studies examine existing data. Prospective studies identify subjects in advance, then follow them to collect data as the data are created, perhaps over many years.
  - Observational studies can spot associations between variables, but cannot establish cause and effect. It's impossible to eliminate the possibility of lurking or confounding variables.
- To see how different treatments influence a response variable, design an **experiment**.
  - Assign subjects to treatments randomly. If you don't assign treatments randomly, your experiment is not likely to yield valid results.
  - Control known sources of variation as much as possible. Reduce variation that cannot be controlled by using blocking if possible.
  - Replicate the experiment, assigning several subjects to each treatment level.
  - If possible, replicate the entire experiment with an entirely different collection of subjects.
  - A well-designed experiment can provide evidence that changes in the factors cause changes in the response variable.

Now for more opportunities to review these concepts and skills . . .

Review Exercises

*1–18. **What design?** Analyze the design of each research example reported. Is it a sample, a study, or an experiment? If a sample, what are the population, the parameter of interest, and the sampling procedure? If a study, was it retrospective or prospective? If an experiment, describe the factors, treatments, randomization, response variable, and any blocking, matching, or blinding that may be present. In each, what kind of conclusions can be reached?*

1. Researchers identified 242 children in the Cleveland area who had been born prematurely (at about 29 weeks). They examined these children at age 8 and again at age 20, comparing them to another group of 233 children not born prematurely. According to their report, published in the *New England Journal of Medicine*, the "preemies" engaged in significantly less risky behavior than the others. Differences between the groups showed up in the use of alcohol and marijuana, conviction of crimes, and teenage pregnancy.

2. The journal *Circulation* reported that among 1900 people who had heart attacks, those who drank an average of 19 cups of tea a week were 44% more likely than nondrinkers to survive at least 3 years after the attack.

3. Researchers at the Purina Pet Institute studied Labrador retrievers for evidence of a relationship between diet and longevity. At 8 weeks of age, two puppies of the same gender and weight were randomly assigned to one of two groups—a total of 48 dogs in all. One group was allowed to eat all they wanted, while the other group was fed a low-calorie diet (about 75% as much as the others). The median lifespan of dogs fed the restricted diet was 22 months longer than other dogs. (*Science News* 161, no. 19)

4. Radon is a radioactive gas found in some homes that poses a health risk to residents. To assess the level of contamination in their area, a county health department wants to test a few homes. If the risk seems high, they will publicize the results to emphasize the need for home testing. Officials plan to use the local property tax list to randomly choose 25 homes from various areas of the county.

5. Almost 90,000 women participated in a 16-year study of the role of the vitamin folate in preventing colon cancer. Some of the women had family histories of colon cancer in close relatives. In this at-risk group the incidence of colon cancer was cut in half among those who maintained a high folate intake. No such difference was observed in those with no family-based risk. (*Science News* Feb. 9, 2002)

6. In a study appearing in the journal *Science*, a research team reports that plants in southern England are flowering earlier in the spring. Records of the first flowering dates for 385 species over a period of 47 years indicate that flowering has advanced an average of 15 days per decade, an indication of climate warming, according to the authors.

7. Fireworks manufacturers face a dilemma. They must be sure that the rockets work properly, but test firing a rocket essentially destroys it. On the other hand, not testing the product leaves open the danger that they sell a bunch of duds, leading to unhappy customers and loss of future sales. The solution, of course, is to test a few of the rockets produced each day, assuming that if those tested work properly the others are ready for sale.

8. Can makeup damage fetal development? Many cosmetics contain a class of chemicals called phthalates. Studies that exposed some laboratory animals to these chemicals found a heightened incidence of damage to male reproductive systems. Since traces of phthalates are found in the urine of women who use beauty products, there is growing concern that they may present a risk to male fetuses. (*Science News,* July 20, 2002)

9. Can long-term exposure to strong electromagnetic fields cause cancer? Researchers in Italy tracked down 13 years of medical records for people living near Vatican Radio's powerful broadcast antennas. A disproportionate share of the leukemia cases occurred among men and children who lived within 6 kilometers of the antennas. (*Science News*, July 20, 2002)

10. Some doctors have expressed concern that men who have vasectomies seemed more likely to develop prostate cancer. Medical researchers used a national cancer registry to identify 923 men who had had prostate cancer and 1224 men of similar ages who had not. Roughly one quarter of the men in each group had undergone a vasectomy, many more than 25 years before the study. The study's authors concluded that there is strong evidence that having the operation presents no long-term risk for developing prostate cancer. (*Science News*, July 20, 2002)

11. Researchers investigating appetite control as a means of losing weight found that female rats ate less and lost weight after injections of the hormone leptin, while male rats responded better to insulin. (*Science News*, July 20, 2002)

12. An artisan wants to create pottery that has the appearance of age. He prepares several samples of clay with four different glazes and test fires them in a kiln at three different temperature settings.

13. Tests of gene therapy on laboratory rats have raised hopes of stopping the degeneration of tissue that characterizes chronic heart failure. Researchers at the University of California, San Diego, used hamsters with cardiac disease, randomly assigning 30 to receive the gene therapy and leaving the other 28 untreated. Five weeks after treatment the gene therapy group's heart muscles stabilized, while those of the untreated hamsters continued to weaken. (*Science News,* July 27, 2002)

14. Researchers at the University of Bristol (England) investigated reasons why different species of birds begin to sing at different times in the morning. They captured and examined birds of 57 species at seven different sites. They measured the diameter of the birds' eyes and also recorded the time of day at which each species began to sing. These researchers reported a strong relationship between eye diameter and time of singing, saying that birds with bigger eyes tended to sing earlier. (*Science News,* 161, no. 16 [2002])

15. An orange juice processing plant will accept a shipment of fruit only after several hundred oranges selected from various locations within the truck are carefully inspected. If too many of those checked show signs of unsuitability for juice (bruised, rotten, unripe, etc.) the whole truckload is rejected.

16. A soft drink manufacturer must be sure the bottle caps on the soda are fully sealed and will not come off easily. Inspectors pull a few bottles off the production line at regular intervals and test the caps. If they detect any problems, they will stop the bottling process to adjust or repair the machine that caps the bottles.

17. Physically fit people are less likely to die of cancer. A report in the May 2002 issue of *Medicine and Science in Sports and Exercise* followed 25,892 men aged 30 to 87 for 10 years. The most physically fit men had a 55% lower risk of death from cancer than the least fit group.

18. Does the use of computer software in Introductory Statistics classes lead to better understanding of the concepts? A professor teaching two sections of Statistics decides to investigate. She teaches both sections using the same lectures and assignments, but gives one class statistics software to help them with their homework. The classes take the same final exam, and graders do not know which students used computers during the semester. The professor is also concerned that students who have had calculus may perform differently from those who have not, so she plans to compare software vs. no-software scores separately for these two groups of students.

19. Point spread. When taking bets on sporting events, bookmakers often include a "point spread" that awards the weaker team extra points. In theory this makes the outcome of the bet a toss-up. Suppose a gambler places a \$10 bet and picks the winners of five games. If he's right about fewer than three of the games, he loses. If he gets three, four, or all five correct, he's paid \$10, \$20, or \$50 respectively. Estimate the amount such a bettor might expect to lose over many weeks of gambling.

20. The lottery. Many people spend a lot of money trying to win huge jackpots in state lotteries. Let's play a simplified version using only the numbers from 1 to 20. You bet on three numbers. The state picks five winning numbers. If your three are all among the winners, you are rich!

a) Simulate repeated plays. How long did it take you to win?
b) In real lotteries there are many more choices (often 54), and you must match all five winning numbers. Explain how these changes affect your chances of hitting the jackpot.

21. Everyday randomness. Aside from casinos, lotteries, and games, there are other situations you encounter in which something is described as "random" in some way. Give three different examples. Describe how randomness is (or is not) achieved in each.

22. Cell phone risks. Researchers at the Washington University School of Medicine randomly placed 480 rats into one of three chambers containing radio antennas. One group was exposed to digital cell phone radio waves, the second to analog cell phone waves, and the third group to no radio waves. Two years later the rats were examined for signs of brain tumors. In June 2002 the scientists said that differences among the three groups were not statistically significant.

a) Is this a study or an experiment? Explain.
b) Explain in this context what "statistically significant" means.
c) Comment on the fact that this research was supported by funding from Motorola, a manufacturer of cell phones.

23. Tips. In restaurants, servers rely on tips as a major source of income. Does serving candy after the meal produce larger tips? To find out, two waiters determined randomly whether or not to give candy to 92 dining parties. They recorded the sizes of the tips and reported that guests getting candy tipped an average of 17.8% of the bill, compared with an average tip of only 15.1% from those who got no candy. ("Sweetening the Till: The Use of Candy to Increase Restaurant Tipping." *Journal of Applied Social Psychology* 32, no. 2 [2002]: 300–309)

a) Was this an experiment or an observational study? Explain.
b) Is it reasonable to conclude that the candy caused guests to tip more? Explain.
c) The researchers said the difference was statistically significant. Explain in this context what that means.

24. Tips, take 2. In another experiment to see if getting candy after a meal would induce customers to leave a bigger tip, a waitress randomly decided what to do with 80 dining parties. Some parties received no candy, some just one piece, and some two pieces. Others initially got just one piece of candy, and then the waitress suggested that they take another piece. She recorded the tips received, finding that, in general, the more candy the higher the tip, but the highest tips (23%) came from the parties who got one piece and then were offered more. ("Sweetening the Till: The Use of Candy to Increase Restaurant Tipping." *Journal of Applied Social Psychology* 32, no. 2 [2002]: 300–309)

a) Diagram this experiment.
b) How many factors are there? How many levels?
c) How many treatments are there?
d) What is the response variable?
e) Did this experiment involve blinding? Double blinding?
f) In what way might the waitress, perhaps unintentionally, have biased the results?

25. Cloning. In September 1998, *USA Weekend* magazine asked, "Should humans be cloned?" Readers were invited to register a "Yes" or "No" answer by calling one of two different 900 numbers. Based on 38,023 responses, the magazine reported that "9 out of 10 readers oppose cloning."

a) Explain why you think the conclusion is not justified. Describe the types of bias that may be present.
b) Reword the question in a way that you think might create a more positive response.

26. Laundry. An experiment to test a new laundry detergent, SparkleKleen, is being conducted by a consumer advocate group. They would like to compare its performance with that of a laboratory standard detergent they have used in previous experiments. They can stain 16 swatches of cloth with 2 tsp of a common staining compound and then use a well-calibrated optical scanner to detect the amount of the stain that is left after washing with detergent. To save time in the experiment, several suggestions have been made. Comment on the possible merits and drawbacks of each one.

a) Since data for the laboratory standard detergent are already available from previous experiments, for this experiment wash all 16 swatches with SparkleKleen, and compare the results with the previous data.
b) Use both detergents with eight separate runs each, but to save time, use only a 10-second wash time with very hot water.
c) To ease bookkeeping, run successively all of the standard detergent washes on eight swatches, then run all of the SparkleKleen washes on the other eight swatches.
d) Rather than run the experiment, use data from the company that produced SparkleKleen, and compare them with past data from the standard detergent.

27. When to Stop? You play a game that involves rolling a die. You can roll as many times as you want, and your score is the total for all the rolls. But . . . if you roll a 6 your score is 0 and your turn is over. What might be a good strategy for a game like this?

a) One of your opponents decides to roll 4 times, then stop (hoping not to get the dreaded 6 before then). Use a simulation to estimate his average score.
b) Another opponent decides to roll until she gets at least 12 points, then stop. Use a simulation to estimate her average score.
c) Propose another strategy that you would use to play this game. Using your strategy, simulate several turns. Do you think you would beat the two opponents?

28. Rivets. A company that manufactures rivets believes the shear strength of the rivets they manufacture follows a Normal model with a mean breaking strength of 950 pounds and a standard deviation of 40 pounds.

a) What is the probability that a rivet selected at random will break when tested under a 900-pound load?
b) You're trying to improve the rivets and want to examine some that fail. Use a simulation to estimate how many rivets you might need to test in order to find three that fail at 900 pounds (or below).

29. Homecoming. A college Statistics class conducted a survey concerning community attitudes about the college's large homecoming celebration. That survey drew its sample in the following manner: Telephone numbers were generated at random by selecting one of the local telephone exchanges (first three digits) at random and then generating a random four-digit number to follow the exchange. If a person answered the phone and the call was to a residence, then that person was taken to be the subject for interview. (Undergraduate students and those under voting age were excluded, as was anyone who could not speak English.) Calls were placed until a sample of 200 eligible respondents had been reached.

a) Did every telephone number that could possibly occur in that community have an equal chance of being generated?
b) Did this method of generating telephone numbers result in a simple random sample (SRS) of local residences? Explain.
c) Did this method generate a SRS of local voters? Explain.
d) Did this method generate an unbiased sample of households? Explain.

30. Youthful appearance. *Readers' Digest* reported results of several surveys that asked graduate students to examine photographs of men and women and try to guess their ages. Researchers compared these guesses with information gathered from the people in the pictures. It turned out that those who had been more sexually active were judged as looking younger, and that the difference was described as "statistically significant." Psychologist David Weeks, who compiled the research, speculated that lovemaking boosts hormones that "reduce fatty tissue and increase lean muscle, giving a more youthful appearance."

a) What does "statistically significant" mean in this context?
b) Explain in statistical terms why you might be skeptical about Dr. Weeks' conclusion. Propose an alternative explanation for these results.

31. Smoking and Alzheimer's. Medical studies indicate that smokers are less likely to develop Alzheimer's disease than people who never smoked.

a) Does this prove that smoking may offer some protection against Alzheimer's? Explain.
b) Offer an alternative explanation for this association.
c) How would you conduct a study to investigate this issue?

32. Antacids. A researcher wants to compare the performance of three types of antacid in volunteers suffering from acid reflux disease. Because men and women may react differently to this medication, the subjects are split into two groups by gender. Subjects in each group are randomly assigned to take one of the antacids or to take a sugar pill made to look the same. The subjects will rate their level of discomfort 30 minutes after eating.

a) What kind of design is this?
b) The experiment uses volunteers rather than a random sample of all people suffering from acid reflux disease. Does this make the results invalid? Explain.
c) How may the use of the placebo confound this experiment? Explain.

33. Sex and violence. Does the content of a television program impact viewers' memory of the products advertised in commercials? Design an experiment to compare the ability of viewers to recall brand names of items featured in commercials during programs with violent content, sexual content, or neutral content.

34. Pubs. In England, Leeds University researcher, Dr. Colin Gill said that the welcoming atmosphere of a pub helps men get rid of the stresses of modern life and is vital for their psychological well-being. Dr. Gill's report, commissioned by alcohol-free beer brand Kaliber, surveyed 900 men on their reasons for going to the pub. More than 40% said they went for the conversation, with relaxation and a friendly atmosphere being the other most common reasons. Only 1 in 10 listed alcohol as the overriding reason.

Let's examine this news story from a statistical perspective.

a) What are the W's: Who, What, When, Where, Why?
b) What population does the researcher think the study applies to?
c) What is the most important thing about the selection process that the article does *not* tell us?
d) How do *you* think the 900 respondents were selected? (Name a method of drawing a sample that is likely to have been used.)
e) Do you think the report that only 10% of respondents listed alcohol as an important reason for going to the pub might be a biased result? Why?

35. Age and party. The Gallup Poll conducted a representative telephone survey during the first quarter of 1999. Among its reported results was the following table concerning the preferred political party affiliation of respondents and their ages.

Age	Republican	Democratic	Independent	Total
18–29	241	351	409	1001
30–49	299	330	370	999
50–64	282	341	375	998
65+	279	382	343	1004
Total	1101	1404	1497	**4002**

a) What sampling strategy do you think the pollsters used? Explain.
b) What percentage of the people surveyed were Democrats?
c) Do you think this is a good estimate of the percentage of voters in the United States who are registered Democrats? Why or why not?
d) In creating this sample design, what question do you think the pollsters were trying to answer?

36. Bias? Political analyst Michael Barone has written that "conservatives are more likely than others to refuse to respond to polls, particularly those polls taken by media outlets that conservatives consider biased" (*The Weekly Standard*, March 10, 1997). The Pew Research Foundation tested this assertion by asking the same questions in a national survey run by standard methods and in a more rigorous survey that was a true SRS with careful follow-up to encourage participation. The response rate in the "standard survey" was 42%. The response rate in the "rigorous survey" was 71%.

a) What kind of bias does Barone claim may exist in polls?
b) What is the population for these surveys?
c) On the question of political position, the Pew researchers report the following table:

	Standard Survey	Rigorous Survey
Conservative	37%	35%
Moderate	40%	41%
Liberal	19%	20%

What makes you think these results are incomplete?

d) The Pew researchers report that differences between opinions expressed on the two surveys were not statistically significant. Explain what "statistically significant" means in this context.

37. Save the grapes. Vineyard owners have problems with birds that like to eat the ripening grapes. Grapes damaged by birds cannot be used for winemaking (or much of anything else). Some vineyards use scarecrows to try to keep birds away. Others use netting that covers the plants. Owners really would like to know if either method works and, if so, which one is better. One owner has offered to let you use his vineyard this year for an experiment. Propose a design. Carefully indicate how you would set up the experiment, specifying the factor(s) and response variable.

38. Bats. It's generally believed that baseball players can hit the ball farther with aluminum bats than with the traditional wooden ones. Is that true? And, if so, how much farther? Players on your local high school baseball team have agreed to help you find out. Design an appropriate experiment.

39. Knees. Research reported in the spring of 2002 cast doubt on the effectiveness of arthroscopic knee surgery for patients with arthritis. Patients suffering from arthritis pain who volunteered to participate in the study were randomly divided into groups. One group received arthroscopic knee surgery. The other group underwent "placebo surgery" during which incisions were made in their knees, but no surgery was actually performed. Follow-up evaluations over a period of 2 years found that differences in the amount of pain relief experienced by the two groups were not statistically significant.

a) Why did the researchers feel it was necessary to have some of the patients undergo "placebo surgery"?

b) Because patients had to consent to participate in this experiment, the subjects were essentially self-selected—a kind of voluntary response group. Explain why that does not invalidate the findings of the experiment.

c) What does "statistically significant" mean in this context?

40. NBA draft lottery. Professional basketball teams hold a "draft" each year in which they get to pick the best available college and high school players. In an effort to promote competition, teams with the worst records get to pick first, theoretically allowing them to add better players. To combat the fear that teams with no chance to make the playoffs might try to get better draft picks by intentionally losing late-season games, the NBA's Board of Governors adopted a weighted lottery system in 1990. Under this system the 11 teams that did not make the playoffs were eligible for the lottery. The NBA prepared 66 cards, each naming one of the teams. The team with the worst win-loss record was named on 11 of the cards, the second-worst team on 10 cards, and so on, with the team having the best record among the nonplayoff clubs getting only one chance at having the first pick. The cards were mixed, then drawn randomly to determine the order in which the teams could draft players. (Since 1995, 13 teams have been involved in the lottery, using a complicated system with 14 numbered Ping-Pong balls drawn in groups of four.) Suppose there are two exceptional players available in this year's draft and your favorite team had the third-worst record. Use a simulation to find out how likely it is that your team gets to pick first or second. Describe your simulation carefully.

41. Security. There are 20 first-class passengers and 120 coach passengers scheduled on a flight. In addition to the usual security screening, 10% of the passengers will be subjected to a more complete search.

a) Describe a sampling strategy to randomly select those to be searched.

b) Here is the first-class passenger list and a set of random digits. Select two passengers to be searched, carefully demonstrating your process.

65436 71127 04879 41516 20451 02227 94769 23593

Bergman	Cox	Fontana	Perl
Bowman	DeLara	Forester	Rabkin
Burkhauser	Delli-Bovi	Frongillo	Roufaiel
Castillo	Dugan	Furnas	Swafford
Clancy	Febo	LePage	Testut

c) Explain how you would use a random number table to select the coach passengers to be searched.

42. Profiling? Among the 20 first-class passengers on the flight described in Exercise 41 there were four businessmen from the Middle East. Two of them were the two passengers selected to be searched. They complained of profiling, but the airline claims that the selection was random. What do you think? Support your conclusion with a simulation.

43. Par 4. In theory, a golfer playing a par 4-hole tees off, hitting the ball in the fairway, then hits an approach shot onto the green. The first putt (usually long) probably won't go in, but the second putt (usually much shorter) should. Sounds simple enough, but how many strokes might it really take? Use a simulation to estimate a pretty good golfer's score based on these assumptions:

- The tee shot hits the fairway 70% of the time.
- A first approach shot lands on the green 80% of the time from the fairway, but only 40% of the time otherwise.
- Subsequent approach shots land on the green 90% of the time.
- The first putt goes in 20% of the time, and subsequent putts go in 90% of the time.

44. The back nine. Use simulations to estimate more golf scores, similar to the procedure in Exercise 43.

a) On a par 3, the golfer hopes the tee shot lands on the green. Assume that the tee shot behaves like the first approach shot described in Exercise 43.

b) On a par 5, the second shot will reach the green 10% of the time and hit the fairway 60% of the time. If it does not hit the green, the golfer must play an approach shot as described in Exercise 43.

c) Create a list of assumptions that describe your golfing ability and then simulate your score on a few holes. Explain your simulation clearly.

Part IV

Randomness and Probability

Chapter 14

From Randomness to Probability

What's the difference between randomness and chaos? At first glance they might seem to be the same. Neither of their outcomes can be anticipated with certainty, but random phenomena have another important feature. In the long run, they settle down in a way that's actually consistent and predictable. Chaotic processes don't do this. It's this property of randomness that enables us to do Statistics. We'll show what we mean in this chapter and the next as we tame randomness and turn it into something that we can use.

Dealing with Random Phenomena

Every day you drive through the intersection at College and Main. Even though it may seem that the light is always red when you get there, you know this can't really be true. In fact, if you try really hard, you can recall just sailing through the green light once in a while.

What's random here? The light itself is governed by a timer. Its pattern isn't haphazard. In fact, the light may even be red at precisely the same times each day. It's the pattern of *your driving* that is random. No, we're certainly not insinuating that you can't keep the car on the road. At the precision level of the 30 seconds or so that the light spends being red or green, the time you arrive at the light *is random*. Even if you try to leave your house at exactly the same time every day, whether the light is red or green as *you* reach the intersection is a **random phenomenon.**

Is the color of the light completely unpredictable? When you stop to think about it (maybe while waiting for the green light), it's clear that we do expect some kind of *regularity* in your long-run experience. Some *fraction* of the time the light will be red as you get to the intersection. How can we figure out what that fraction is?

You might record what happens at the intersection each day and graph the *accumulated percentage* of red lights like this:

The overall percentage of times the light is red settles down as we see more outcomes. **Figure 14.1**

Day	Light	% Red
1	Red	100
2	Green	50
3	Red	66.7
4	Red	75
5	Green	60
6	Green	50
⋮	⋮	⋮

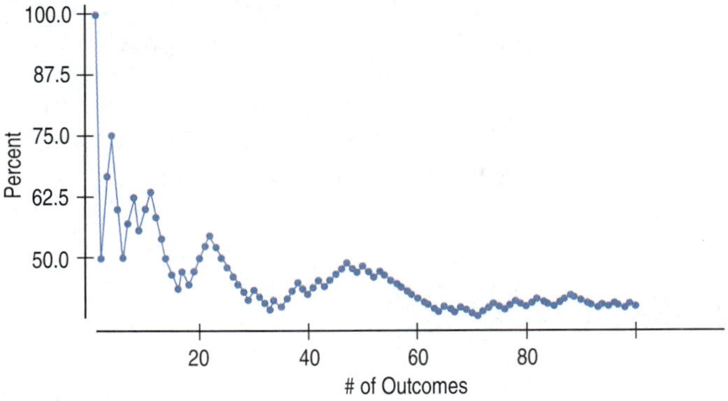

The first day you recorded the light it was red. Then on the next five days, it was green, then red again, then red, green, and green. If we plot the percentage red against the day, the graph would start at 100% because the first time the light was red (1 out of 1, for 100%). Then the next time it was green, so the accumulated percentage drops to 50% (1 out of 2). The third day it was red again (2 out of 3, or 66% red), then red (3 out of 4, or 75%), then green twice in a row (3 out of 5, for 60% red, and then 3 out of 6, for 50%), and so on. As you collect a new data point for each day, this new datum becomes a smaller and smaller *fraction* of the accumulated experience, so, in the long run, the graph settles down. As it settles down, we can see that, in fact, the light is red only about 35% of the time.

Probability

If you were asked for the *probability* that you would be stopped at the traffic light at College and Main, you might say that it was 35%. You would base that on knowing (from your data collection) that, in the long run, the fraction of the time the light is red is 35%. We could also say that the long-run *relative frequency* of red lights settles down to about 35%.

A **phenomenon** consists of **trials.**
Each **trial** has an **outcome.**
Outcomes combine to make **events.**

That's exactly what we mean by probability. The **probability** of an event is its long-run relative frequency.

Although we may not be able to predict a *particular* individual outcome, such as how a flipped coin will land, we're reasonably sure that a fair coin will fall heads about half the time *in the long run.* Of course, in the real world, we usually can't see the "true" proportions hiding behind the random outcomes. This forces us to reason backwards, as we did with the traffic light.

When talking about long-run behavior, it helps to define our terms. For any random phenomenon, each attempt, or **trial,** generates an **outcome.** Something happens on each trial, and we call whatever happens the outcome. These outcomes are *individual* possibilities such as the number we see on top when we roll a die. Often, instead of individual possibilities, we want to talk about *combinations* of outcomes such as "The number on the die is less than 4 (that is, it is 1, 2, or 3)." We call such a combination an **event.**

In order to think about what happens with combinations of outcomes, it really simplifies things if the individual trials are **independent.** Roughly speaking, this means that the outcome of one trial doesn't influence or change the outcome of another. (In Chapter 3, we called two *variables* independent for similar reasons.)

For example, if you drove to work with a friend in another car right behind you, you couldn't just add his observations to yours. Most of the time, his experience will just duplicate yours. Except for those few times when the light turns red just after you enter the intersection, the light will be the same for him as for you. So his observations would not be independent of yours. Because they're almost repeats of your observations, they wouldn't supply much more information. In order for us to make statements about the long-run behavior of random phenomena, the trials have to be independent.

The Law of Large Numbers

Do random phenomena always behave so well? If we're going to use long-run relative frequency as our definition of probability, we should first be sure that it will, in fact, settle down to a particular value. Couldn't it be that the probability will just bounce back and forth between two values forever, never settling on just one number? Fortunately, a principle called the **Law of Large Numbers** (LLN) gives us the guarantee that we need. It says that the long-run *relative frequency* of repeated independent events gets closer and closer to the *true* relative frequency as the number of trials increases.

Don't let yourself think that there's a Law of Averages that promises short-term compensation for recent deviations from expected behavior. A belief in such a "Law" can lead to money lost in gambling and to poor business decisions.

Although the LLN wasn't proven until the 18th century, everyone expects the kind of long-run regularity that the Law describes from everyday experience. If the light at College and Main is set by the traffic engineers to be red 35% of the time for the drivers on College Avenue, then no one is surprised to find out that in the long run, if you arrive at the intersection from College Avenue, *you'll* encounter a red light 35% of the time.

Yet the Law is often misunderstood because the idea of the *long run* is hard to grasp. Many gamblers believe, for example, that a number that has not come up on the roulette wheel or in a lottery for a long time, is "due" to occur—and they give the Law of Large Numbers as their reason. (Well, they usually call it the "Law of Averages" or some similar term, but the LLN is what they really mean.) But the LLN doesn't apply to short-run behavior. The problem is that probabilities even out *only in the long run.* And (according to the LLN) the long run must be *infinitely* long to give them enough time to even out.

The Law of Averages in Everyday Life

"Dear Abby: My husband and I just had our eighth child. Another girl, and I am really one disappointed woman. I suppose I should thank God she was healthy, but, Abby, this one was supposed to have been a boy. Even the doctor told me that the law of averages was in our favor 100 to one." (Abigail Van Buren, 1974. Quoted in Karl Smith, *The Nature of Mathematics.* 6TH ed. Pacific Grove, CA: Brooks/Cole, 1991, p. 589)

In fact, the so-called Law of Averages doesn't exist at all. The common (mis)understanding of this "Law" is that random phenomena are supposed to *compensate* somehow for whatever happened in the past. So if recent results have fallen to one side of what is expected, somehow results on the other side are "due" because the results must "average out" to the right value. Is a .300 hitter in baseball who has struck out the last 6 times *due* for a hit his next time up? If you've just flipped a fair coin 5 heads in a row, is the next flip more likely to be tails because the coin *owes us* a tail?

No. This is not the way random phenomena work. The coin can't *remember* what happened and make things come out right. In fact, if you flipped a fair coin several thousand times, you would find lots of long streaks of all heads. And if we looked at *all* streaks of 5 (or 6 or 10 . . .) heads, we'd see that, on the average, the next flip is *just as likely to be heads or tails* even after a streak. The Law of Large Numbers promises that given a very large number of trials (a *long run*), the distribution of subsequent results will *eventually* overwhelm any recent drift away from what is expected. The long run is a long time.

"For even the most stupid of men . . . is convinced that the more observations have been made, the less danger there is of wandering from one's goal."
—Jacob Bernoulli, 1713, discoverer of the LLN

If a fair coin has landed heads five times in a row, is the next flip more likely to be a tail? Five heads and no tails looks lopsided. In flipping a fair coin, shouldn't we expect about 50% heads and 50% tails? Doesn't the coin "owe" us some tails in the next few flips? Let's flip it another 100 times. In the next 100 flips, we'd expect to get about 50 more heads and 50 more tails. So after 105 flips we'd have about 55 Heads and 50 Tails—close enough to 50/50 for comfort. The lesson of the LLN is that random processes don't need to compensate in the *short* run to get back to the right long-run probabilities.

To test this, we ran a simulation of 100,000 flips of a fair coin. We collected 100,000 random numbers, letting the numbers 0 to 4 represent heads and the numbers 5 to 9 represent tails. In our 100,000 "flips," there were 2981 streaks of at least 5 heads. If the Law of Averages, were true, the next flip should be tails more often, to even things out. Actually the next flip was heads 1550 times and tails 1431 times (heads 51.9% of the time). If the probabilities don't change and the events are independent, the probability of the next trial is *always* the same, no matter what has happened up to then. There is *no* Law of Averages for short runs.

Keno and the Law of Averages

Of course, sometimes an apparent drift from what we expect means that the probabilities are, in fact, *not* what we thought. If you get 10 heads in a row, maybe the coin has heads on both sides!

Keno is a simple casino game in which numbers from 1 to 80 are chosen. The numbers, as in most lottery games, are supposed to be equally likely. Payoffs are made depending on how many of those numbers you match on your card. A group of graduate students from a Statistics department decided to take a field trip to Reno. They (*very* discreetly) wrote down the outcomes of the games for a couple of days, then drove back to test whether the numbers were, in fact, equally likely. It turned out that some numbers were *more likely* to come up than others. Rather than bet on the Law of Averages and put their money on the numbers that were "due," the students put their faith in the LLN—and all their (and their friend's) money on the numbers that had come up before. After they pocketed more than $50,000, they were escorted off the premises and invited never to show their faces in that casino again.

Probability

Now that we know, thanks to the Law of Large Numbers, that relative frequencies settle down in the long run, we can officially give the name **probability** to that value. If the relative frequency of red lights settles down to 35%, we say that the *probability* of a red light is 0.35, and write

$$P(Red) = 0.35$$

We can't record more "red lights" than the number of times we hit the intersection (or fewer than none) so our probability must be a value between 0 and 1:

$$0 \leq P \leq 1.$$

A probability of zero indicates impossibility. A probability of one indicates certainty. Remember that we said "in the long run." So we have to wait infinitely long to be sure that an event is impossible or certain.

Probability was first studied by a group of French mathematicians interested in games of chance (OK, gambling). To make things simple, they started by looking at games in which all the possible outcomes were *equally likely.* It's easy to think of situations where this is true, especially in gambling. It's equally likely to get any one of six outcomes from the roll of a fair die. Any of the 52 cards is equally likely to be picked from a well-shuffled deck. Each slot of a roulette wheel is equally likely (or at least it *should* be).

When outcomes are equally likely, the probability of their occurrence is easy to compute—it's just 1 divided by the number of possible outcomes. So, the probability of rolling a 3 from a fair die is 1/6. The probability of picking the ace of spades from the top of a well-shuffled deck is 1/52.

But don't get trapped into thinking that random events are always equally likely. The chance of winning a lottery—especially lotteries with very large payoffs—is small. Regardless, people continue to buy tickets. In an attempt to understand why, an interviewer asked someone who had just purchased a lottery ticket, "What do you think your chances are of winning the lottery?" The reply was, "Oh, about 50–50." The shocked interviewer asked, "How do you get that?" to which the response was, "Well, the way I figure it, either I win or I don't!"

The moral of this story is that events are *not* always equally likely.

Personal Probability

What's the probability that your grade in this Statistics course will be an A? You may be able to come up with a number that seems reasonable. Of course, no matter how confident or depressed you feel about your chances for success, your probability should be between 0 and 1. How did you come up with this probability? From our discussion of probability, we've said that probability represents the relative frequency, or the fraction of times that the event occurs in the long run. Is that what you meant? We doubt that you plan on taking this course over and over and over, so that can't be it.

We use the language of probability in everyday speech to express a degree of uncertainty *without* basing it on long-run relative frequencies. Your personal assessment of the probability of getting an A expresses your uncertainty about the outcome. That uncertainty may be based on how comfortable you're feeling in the course, or on your midterm grade, but it can't be based on long-run behavior. We call this kind of probability a subjective or **personal probability.**

Although personal probabilities may be based on experience, they're not based either on long-run relative frequencies or on equally likely events. So they don't display the kind of consistency that we'll need probabilities to have. For that reason, we'll stick to formally defined probabilities. You should be alert to the difference.

The line between personal probability and relative frequency probability can be a fuzzy one. When a weather forecaster predicts a 40% probability of rain, is this a personal probability or a relative frequency probability? The claim may be that 40% of the time, when the map looks like this, it has rained (over some period of time). Or the forecaster may be stating a personal opinion that is based on years of experience and reflects a sense of what has happened in the past in similar situations. When you hear a probability stated, it's good to try to ascertain what kind of probability is intended.

Formal Probability

1. If the probability is 0, the event *never* occurs, and likewise if it has probability 1, it *always* occurs. Even if you think an event is very unlikely, its probability can't be negative, and even if you're sure it will happen, its probability can't be greater than 1. So we require that

A probability is a number between 0 and 1.

For any event A, $0 \le P(A) \le 1$.

2. If a random phenomenon has only one possible outcome, it's not very interesting (or very random). So we need to distribute the probabilities among all the outcomes a trial can have. How can we do that so that it makes sense? For example, consider what you're doing as you read this book. The possible outcomes might be:

   A: you read to the end of this chapter before stopping.

   B: you finish this section but stop reading before the end of the chapter.

   C: you bail out before the end of this section.

   When we assign probabilities to these outcomes, the first thing to be sure of is that we distribute all of the available probability. Something always occurs, so the probability of *something* happening is 1.

   We put all the possible outcomes into a big event called the sample space.

   Making this more formal gives the **"Something has to happen rule":**

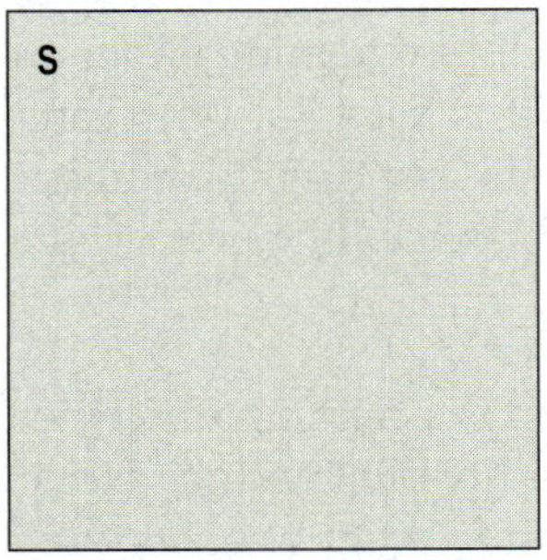

The sample space **S**.

The probability of the set of all possible outcomes of a trial must be 1.

$P(\mathbf{S}) = 1$. (**S** represents the set of all possible outcomes.)

3. Suppose the probability of getting an A in this course is 0.4. What's the probability of not getting an A? Yes, it's 0.6. The set of outcomes that are *not* in the event **A** is called the **complement** of **A**, and is denoted $\mathbf{A^C}$. This leads to the **Complement Rule:**

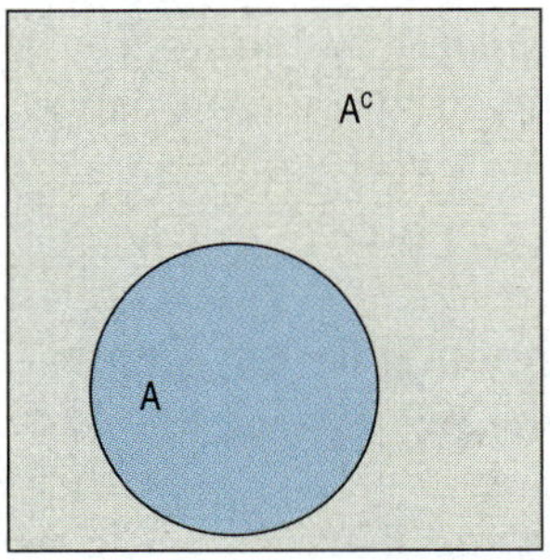

The set **A** and its complement.

The probability of an event occurring is 1 minus the probability that it doesn't occur.

$P(\mathbf{A}) = 1 - P(\mathbf{A^C})$

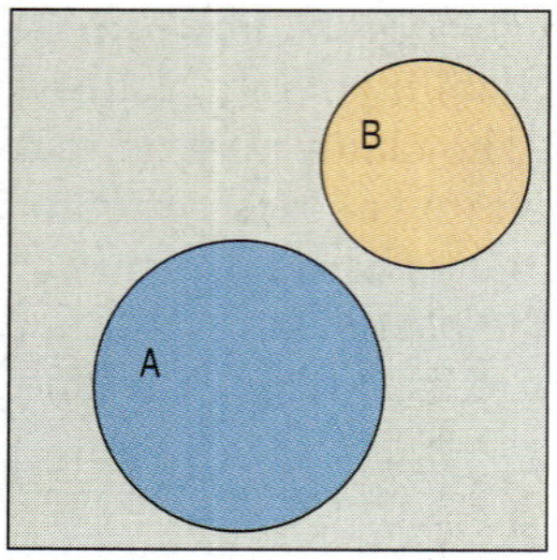

Two disjoint sets, **A** and **B**.

4. Suppose the probability that a randomly selected student is a sophomore **(A)** is 0.20 and the probability that he or she is a junior **(B)** is 0.30. What is the probability that the student is *either* a sophomore *or* a junior, written **(A ∪ B)**? If you guessed 0.50 you've deduced the **Addition Rule,** which says that you can add the probabilities of events that have no outcomes in common. Events like this, that can't occur together, are called **disjoint (or mutually exclusive).** The **Addition Rule** states

For two disjoint events A and B, the probability that one *or* the other occurs is the sum of the probabilities of the two events.

***P*(A ∪ B) = P(A) + P(B), provided that A and B are disjoint.**

NOTATION ALERT:

We write *P*(**A** *or* **B**) as *P*(**A** ∪ **B**). The symbol ∪ means "union," representing the outcomes in event **A** *or* event **B** (or both).

The symbol ∩ means "intersection," representing outcomes that are in both event **A** *and* event **B.** We write *P*(**A** *and* **B**) as *P*(**A** ∩ **B**).

We can always add the probabilities of outcomes because they are always disjoint. A trial can't come out in two different ways at the same time. This gives us an easy way to check whether the probabilities we've assigned are **legitimate.**

By the Something has to happen rule, the total of the probabilities of all possible outcomes must be exactly one. No more, no less. And because they are disjoint, we can add them up to check. For example, if we were told the probabilities of selecting at random a freshman, sophomore, junior, or senior from all the undergraduates at a school were 0.25, 0.23, 0.22, and 0.20, respectively, and that there were no other possibilities, we would know that something was wrong. These "probabilities" sum to only 0.90, so this is not a legitimate probability assignment. Similarly, a claim that the probabilities were 0.26, 0.27, 0.29. and 0.30 would be wrong because these "probabilities" sum to more than 1.

But be careful. The Addition Rule doesn't work for events that aren't mutually exclusive. If the probability of owning an MP3 player is 0.50 and the probability of owning a computer is 0.90, the probability of owning either an MP3 player or a computer may be pretty high, but it is *not* 1.40! Why can't you add probabilities like this? Because these events are not disjoint. You *can* own both. In the next chapter, we'll see how to add probabilities for events like these, but we'll need another rule.

5. The color of a traffic light as you reach an intersection is a random outcome. Suppose the light spends 35% of its time red in your direction and the other 65% either green or yellow. What's the chance of finding it red two days in a row? That's the same as asking the probability of finding it red today *and* finding it red tomorrow. For independent events, the answer is very simple. And the color of the light today *is* independent of the color yesterday. The **Multiplication Rule** says that for independent events, to find the probability that both events occur, we just multiply the probabilities together. Formally:

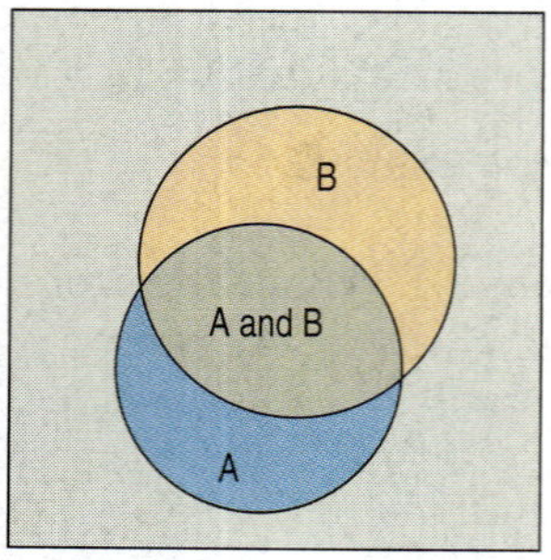

Two sets **A** and **B** that are not disjoint. The event **(A ∩ B)** is their intersection.

For two independent events A and B, the probability that both A *and* B occur is the product of the probabilities of the two events.

***P*(A ∩ B) = *P*(A) × *P*(B), provided that A and B are independent.**

This rule can be extended to more than two independent events. What's the chance of finding the light red every day this week? We can multiply the probability of it happening each day, so it's

$$0.35 \times 0.35 \times 0.35 \times 0.35 \times 0.35 = 0.00525$$

or about 5 times in a thousand. Of course, to calculate this probability we have used the assumption that the events are independent.

Many Statistics methods assume independence, but *assuming* independence doesn't make it true. We'll talk about conditions to check in data to help judge whether the independence assumption is reasonable.

Putting the Rules to Work

In informal English, you may see "some" used to mean "at least one." "What's the probability that some of the eggs in that carton are broken?" means at least one.

In most situations where we want to find a probability, we'll use the rules in combination.

For example, what's the chance that we'll hit a red light *at least once* during the week? Hitting at least one red light means that we hit either 1, 2, 3, 4 or 5 red lights during the week. So, we could calculate the probability of hitting at least one red light by first calculating the probability of hitting exactly 1 red light during the week, then exactly 2, then 3, 4, and 5. Then we just add them up. Aarrgghh! There must be an easier way to do this, and there is.

It can be easier to work with the *complement* of the event we're really interested in. Once we have the complement's probability, we know (from Rule 3) that the probability of the event we're interested in is 1 minus the probability of the complement. What's the complement of getting at least one red light? It's getting *no* red lights, five days in a row. We know the probability of hitting a red light is 0.35 each day, so by the Complement Rule, the probability of *not* hitting a red light is $1 - 0.35$, or 0.65 each day. So, the probability of making it through five consecutive days without hitting a red light is $(0.65)^5$. This is the probability of the complement of what we wanted. Now, taking the complement of this compound event, we find the probability that it *doesn't* happen (*not* 0 red lights) is $1 - (0.65)^5 = 1 - 0.116 = 0.884$.

Probability STEP-BY-STEP

The five rules we've seen can be used in a number of different combinations to answer a surprising number of questions. Let's try one to see how we might go about it.

In 2001, Masterfoods, the manufacturers of M&M's® milk chocolate candies, decided to add another color to the standard color lineup of brown, yellow, red, orange, blue, and green. To decide which color, they surveyed kids in nearly every country of the world and asked them to vote among purple, pink, and teal. The global winner was purple! In the United States, 42% of those who voted said purple, 37% said teal, and only 19% said pink. But in Japan the percentages were 38% pink, 36% teal, and only 16% purple. Let's use Japan's percentages to ask some questions.

1. What's the probability that a Japanese M&M's survey respondent selected at random preferred either pink or teal?

2. If we pick two respondents at random, what's the probability that they *both* selected purple?
3. If we pick three respondents at random, what's the probability that *at least one* preferred purple?

Think The probability of an event is its long-term relative frequency. It can be determined in several ways: by looking at many replications of an event, by deducing it from equally likely events, or by using some other information. Here, we are told the relative frequencies of the three responses.

The M&M's Web site reports the proportions of Japanese votes by color. These give us the probability of selecting a voter who preferred each of the colors:

$P(\text{pink}) = 0.38$
$P(\text{teal}) = 0.36$
$P(\text{purple}) = 0.16$

Make sure the probabilities are legitimate. Here, they're not. Either there was a mistake or the other voters must have chosen a color other than the three given. A check of other countries shows a similar deficit, so probably we're seeing those who had no preference or who wrote in another color.

Each is between 0 and 1, but these don't add up to 1. The remaining 10% of the voters must have not expressed a preference or written in another color. We'll put them together into "no preference" and add:

$P(\text{no preference}) = 0.10$. With this addition, we have a legitimate assignment of probabilities.

1. What's the probability that a Japanese M&M's survey respondent selected at random preferred either pink or teal?

Think Events must be disjoint to use the Addition Rule.

A respondent can't choose both pink and teal, so these events are disjoint and we can apply the Addition Rule.

Show

$$P(\text{pink} \cup \text{teal}) = P(\text{pink}) + P(\text{teal}) = 0.38 + 0.36 = 0.74$$

Tell State your conclusion.

The probability that the respondent said pink or teal is 0.74.

2. If we pick two respondents at random, what's the probability that they both said purple?

Think To use the Multiplication Rule, we'll need independent events. Independence seems like a reasonable assumption here. The choice of one respondent is not likely to have affected the choice of another.

We'll assume the events are independent because the choice of one respondent is unlikely to affect the choice of another.

Show For both respondents to pick purple, each one has to pick purple.

$$\begin{aligned} P(\text{both purple}) &= P(\text{first respondent picks purple} \cap \text{second respondent picks purple}) \\ &= P(\text{first respondent picks purple}) \times P(\text{second respondent picks purple}) \\ &= 0.16 \times 0.16 = 0.0256 \end{aligned}$$

Tell State your conclusion.

The probability that both respondents pick purple is 0.0256.

3. If we pick three respondents at random, what's the probability that at least one preferred purple?

$P(\text{at least one picked purple})$
$= P(\{\text{none picked purple}\}^C)$
$= 1 - P(\text{none picked purple}).$

Think The phrase "at least . . ." often flags a question best answered by looking at the complement, and that's the best approach here. The complement of "at least one preferred purple" is "none of them preferred purple."

$P(\text{none picked purple}) = P(\text{not purple} \cap \text{not purple} \cap \text{not purple}).$

These are independent events because they are choices by 3 independent respondents, so

Show We calculate P(none purple) by using the Multiplication Rule.

$P(\text{none picked purple}) = P(\text{first not purple}) \times P(\text{second not purple}) \times P(\text{third not purple}) = [P(\text{not purple})]^3.$

$P(\text{not purple}) = 1 - P(\text{purple})$
$= 1 - 0.16 = 0.84.$

So $P(\text{none picked purple}) = (0.84)^3 = 0.5927.$

Then we can use the Complement Rule to get the probability we want.

$P(\text{at least 1 picked purple})$
$= 1 - P(\text{none picked purple})$
$= 1 - 0.5927 = 0.4073.$

Tell State your conclusion.

The chance that at least one of the respondents picked purple is about 40.7%.

What Can Go Wrong?

- ***Beware of probabilities that don't add up to 1.*** To be a legitimate probability distribution, the sum of the probabilities for all possible outcomes must total 1. If the sum is less than 1, you may need to add another category ("other,") and assign the remaining probability to that outcome. If the sum is more than 1, check that the outcomes are disjoint. If they're not, then you can't assign probabilities by just counting relative frequencies.
- ***Don't add probabilities of events if they're not disjoint.*** Events must be disjoint to use the Addition Rule. The probability of being under 80 *or* a female is not the probability of being under 80 *plus* the probability of being female. That sum may be more than 1.
- ***Don't multiply probabilities of events if they're not independent.*** The probability of selecting a student at random who is over 6′10″ tall *and* on the basketball team is *not* the probability the student is 6′10″ tall *times* the probability he's on the basketball team. Knowing that the student is over 6′10″ changes the probability of his being on the basketball team. You can't multiply these probabilities. The multiplication of probabilities of events that are not independent is one of the most common errors in dealing with probabilities.
- ***Don't confuse disjoint and independent.*** Disjoint events *can't* be independent. If **A** = {you get an A in this class} and **B** = {you get a B in this class}, **A** and **B** are disjoint. Are they independent? If you find out that **A** is true, does that change the probability of **B**? You bet it does! So they can't be independent.

Connections

We saw in the previous three chapters that randomness plays a critical role in gathering data. That fact alone makes understanding how random events behave important. The rules and concepts of probability give us a language to talk and think about random phenomena. From here on, randomness will be fundamental to how we think about data, and probabilities will show up in every chapter.

Our interest in probability extends back to the start of the book. We've talked about "relative frequencies" often. But—let's be frank—that's just a casual term for probability. For example, you can now rephrase the 68-95-99.7 Rule to talk about the *probability* that a random value selected from a Normal model will fall within 1, 2, or 3 standard deviations of the mean.

Why not just say "probability" from the start? Well, we didn't need any of the formal rules of this chapter (or the next one), so there was no point to weighing down the discussion with those rules. And "relative frequency" is the right intuitive way to think about probability in this course, so you've been thinking right all along.

Keep it up.

Key Concepts

Random phenomenon A phenomenon is random if we know what outcomes could happen, but not which particular values did or will happen.

Trial A single attempt or realization of a random phenomenon.

Outcome The outcome of a trial is the value measured, observed, or reported for an individual instance of that trial.

Outcomes are considered to be either

- discrete if they have distinct values such as heads or tails (even if those values are labeled with numerals
- continuous if they take on numeric values in some range of possible values

Event A collection of outcomes. Usually, we identify events in order to attach probabilities to them. We denote events with bold capital letters such as **A, B,** or **C.**

Independence (informally) Two events are *independent* if knowing whether one event occurs does not alter the probability that the other event occurs.

Law of Large Numbers The Law of Large Numbers states that the long-run *relative frequency* of repeated independent events gets closer and closer to the *true* relative frequency as the number of trials increases.

Probability The probability of an event is a number between 0 and 1 that reports the likelihood of the event's occurrence. A probability can be derived from equally likely outcomes, from the long-run proportion of the event's occurrence, or from known proportions. We write $P(\mathbf{A})$ for the probability of the event **A.**

"Something has to happen rule" The sum of the probabilities of all possible outcomes of a trial must be 1.

Complement Rule The probability of an event occurring is 1 minus the probability that it doesn't occur.

$$P(\mathbf{A}) = 1 - P(\mathbf{A}^C)$$

Disjoint (mutually exclusive) Two events are disjoint if they share no outcomes in common. If **A** and **B** are disjoint, then knowing that **A** occurs tells us that **B** cannot occur. Disjoint events are also called "mutually exclusive."

Addition Rule If **A** and **B** are disjoint events, then the probability of **A** *or* **B** is

$$P(\mathbf{A} \cup \mathbf{B}) = P(\mathbf{A}) + P(\mathbf{B}).$$

Legitimate probability assignment An assignment of probabilities to outcomes is legitimate if
- each probability is between 0 and 1 (inclusive).
- the sum of the probabilities is 1.

Multiplication Rule If **A** and **B** are independent events, then the probability of **A** *and* **B** is

$$P(\mathbf{A} \cap \mathbf{B}) = P(\mathbf{A}) \times P(\mathbf{B}).$$

Skills

When you complete this lesson you should:

Think

- Understand that random phenomena are unpredictable in the short term but show long-run regularity.
- Be able to recognize random outcomes in a real-world situation.
- Know that the relative frequency of an outcome of a random phenomenon settles down as we gather more random outcomes. Be able to state the Law of Large Numbers.
- Know the basic definitions and rules of probability.
- Recognize when events are disjoint and when events are independent. Understand the difference, and that disjoint events cannot be independent.

Show

- Be able to use the facts about probability to determine whether an assignment of probabilities is legitimate. Each probability must be a number between 0 and 1 and the sum of the probabilities assigned to all possible outcomes must be 1.
- Know how and when to apply the Addition Rule. Know that events must be disjoint for the Addition rule to apply.
- Know how and when to apply the Multiplication Rule. Know that events must be independent for the Multiplication Rule to apply. Be able to use the Multiplication Rule to find probabilities for combinations of independent events.
- Know how to use the Complement Rule to make calculating probabilities simpler. Recognize that probabilities of "at least . . ." are likely to be simplified in this way.

Tell

- Be able to use statements about probability in describing a random phenomenon. You will need this skill soon for making statements about statistical inference
- Know and be able to use correctly the terms sample space, disjoint events, and independent events.

Exercises

1. Roulette. A casino claims that its roulette wheel is truly random. What should that claim mean?

2. Rain. The weather reporter on TV makes predictions such as a 25% chance of rain. What do you think is the meaning of such a phrase?

3. Winter. Comment on the following quotation:

"What I think is our best determination is it will be a colder than normal winter," said Pamela Naber Knox, a Wisconsin state climatologist. "I'm basing that on a couple of different things. First, in looking at the past few winters, there has been a

lack of really cold weather. Even though we are not supposed to use the law of averages, we are due." (Associated Press, fall 1992, quoted by Schaeffer et al.)

4. Rain. After an unusually dry autumn, a radio announcer is heard to say, "Watch out! We'll pay for these sunny days later on this winter." Explain what he's trying to say, and comment on the validity of his reasoning.

5. Cold streak. A batter who had failed to get a hit in seven consecutive times at bat then hits a game-winning home run. When talking to reporters afterward, he says he was very confident that last time at bat because he knew he was "due for a hit." Comment on his reasoning.

6. Crash. Commercial airplanes have an excellent safety record. Nevertheless, there are crashes occasionally, with the loss of many lives. In the weeks following a crash, airlines often report a drop in the number of passengers, probably because people are afraid to risk flying.

a) A travel agent suggests that, since the law of averages makes it highly unlikely to have two plane crashes within a few weeks of each other, flying soon after a crash is the safest time. What do you think?

b) If the airline industry proudly announces that it has set a new record for the longest period of safe flights, would you be reluctant to fly? Are the airlines due to have a crash?

7. Fire insurance. Insurance companies collect annual payments from homeowners in exchange for paying to rebuild houses that burn down.

a) Why should you be reluctant to accept a $300 payment from your neighbor to replace his house should it burn down during the coming year?

b) Why can the insurance company make that offer?

8. Jackpot. On January 20, 2000, the International Gaming Technology company issued a press release:

(LAS VEGAS, Nev.)—Cynthia Jay was smiling ear to ear as she walked into the news conference at The Desert Inn Resort in Las Vegas today, and well she should. Last night, the 37-year-old cocktail waitress won the world's largest slot jackpot—$34,959,458—on a Megabucks machine. She said she had played $27 in the machine when the jackpot hit. Nevada Megabucks has produced 49 major winners in its 14-year history. The top jackpot builds from a base amount of $7 million and can be won with a 3-coin ($3) bet.

a) How can the Desert Inn afford to give away millions of dollars on a $3 bet?

b) Why did the company issue a press release? Wouldn't most businesses want to keep such a huge loss quiet?

9. Spinner. The plastic arrow on a spinner for a child's game stops rotating to point at a color that will determine what happens next. Which of the following probability assignments are possible?

	Probabilities of . . .			
	Red	Yellow	Green	Blue
a)	0.25	0.25	0.25	0.25
b)	0.1	0.2	0.3	0.4
c)	0.2	0.3	0.4	0.5
d)	0	0	1	0
e)	0.1	0.2	1.2	−1.5

10. Scratch off. Many stores run "secret sales": Shoppers receive cards that determine how large a discount they get, but the percentage is revealed by scratching off that black stuff (what *is* that?) only after the purchase has been totaled at the cash register. The store is required to reveal (in the fine print) the distribution of discounts available. Which of these probability assignments are plausible?

	Probabilities of . . .			
	10% off	20% off	30% off	50% off
a)	0.2	0.2	0.2	0.2
b)	0.5	0.3	0.2	0.1
c)	0.80	0.10	0.05	0.05
d)	0.75	0.25	0.25	−0.25
e)	1	0	0	0

11. Car repairs. A consumer organization estimates that over a 1-year period 17% of cars will need to be repaired once, 7% will need repairs twice, and 4% will require three or more repairs.

a) What is the probability that a car chosen at random will need
   1. no repairs?
   2. no more than one repair?
   3. some repairs?

b) If you own two cars, what is the probability that
   1. neither will need repair?
   2. both will need repair?

12. Stats projects. In a large Introductory Statistics lecture hall, the professor reports that 55% of the students enrolled have never taken a Calculus course, 32% have taken only one semester of Calculus, and the rest have taken two or more semesters of Calculus. The professor randomly assigns students to groups of three to work on a project for the course.

a) What is the probability that the first groupmate you meet has studied
   1. some Calculus?
   2. no more than one semester of Calculus.

b) What is the probability that, of your other two groupmates,
   1. neither has studied Calculus?
   2. both have studied at least one semester of Calculus.
   3. at least one has had more than one semester of Calculus?

13. **M&M's.** The Masterfoods company says that before the introduction of purple, yellow candies made up 20% of their plain M&M's, red another 20%, and orange, blue, and green each made up 10%. The rest were brown.
   a) If you pick an M&M at random, what is the probability that
      1. it is brown?
      2. it is yellow or orange?
      3. it is not green?
      4. it is striped?
   b) If you pick three M&M's in a row, what is the probability that
      1. they are all brown?
      2. the third one is the first one that's red?
      3. none are yellow?
      4. at least one is green?

14. **Blood.** The American Red Cross says that about 45% of the U.S. population has Type O blood, 40 % Type A, 11% Type B, and the rest Type AB.
   a) Someone volunteers to give blood. What is the probability that this donor
      1. has Type AB blood?
      2. has Type A or Type B?
      3. is not Type O?
   b) Among four potential donors, what is the probability that
      1. all are Type O?
      2. no one is Type AB?
      3. they are not all Type A?
      4. at least one person is Type B?

15. **Disjoint or independent?** In Exercise 13 you calculated probabilities of getting various M&Ms. Some of your answers depended on the assumption that the outcomes described were *disjoint;* that is, they could not both happen at the same time. Other answers depended on the assumption that the events were *independent;* that is, the occurrence of one of them doesn't affect the probability of the other. Do you understand the difference between disjoint and independent?
   a) If you draw one M&M, are the events of getting a red one and getting an orange one disjoint or independent or neither?
   b) If you draw two M&M's one after the other, are the events of getting a red on the first and a red on the second disjoint or independent or neither?
   c) Can disjoint events ever be independent? Explain.

16. **Disjoint or independent?** In Exercise 14 you calculated probabilities involving various blood types. Some of your answers depended on the assumption that the outcomes described were *disjoint;* that is, they could not both happen at the same time. Other answers depended on the assumption that the events were *independent;* that is, the occurrence of one of them doesn't affect the probability of the other. Do you understand the difference between disjoint and independent?
   a) If you examine one person, are the events that the person is Type A and that the person is Type B disjoint or independent or neither?
   b) If you examine two people, are the events that the first is Type A and the second Type B disjoint or independent or neither?
   c) Can disjoint events ever be independent? Explain.

17. **Dice.** You roll a fair die three times. What is the probability that
   a) you roll all 6's?
   b) you roll all odd numbers?
   c) none of your rolls gets a number divisible by 3?
   d) you roll at least one 5?
   e) the numbers you roll are not all 5's?

18. **Slot machine.** A slot machine has three wheels that spin independently. Each has 10 equally likely symbols: 4 bars, 3 lemons, 2 cherries, and a bell. If you play, what is the probability
   a) you get 3 lemons?
   b) you get no fruit symbols?
   c) you get 3 bells (the jackpot)?
   d) you get no bells?
   e) you get at least one bar (an automatic loser)?

19. **Champion bowler.** A certain bowler can bowl a strike 70% of the time. What is the probability that she
   a) goes three consecutive frames without a strike?
   b) makes her first strike in the third frame?
   c) has at least one strike in the first three frames?
   d) bowls a perfect game (12 consecutive strikes)?

20. **The train.** To get to work, a commuter must cross train tracks. The time the train arrives varies slightly from day to day, but the commuter estimates he'll get stopped on about 15% of work days. During a certain 5-day work week, what is the probability that he
   a) gets stopped on Monday and again on Tuesday?
   b) gets stopped for the first time on Thursday?
   c) gets stopped every day?
   d) gets stopped at least once during the week?

21. **Voters.** Suppose that in your city 37% of the voters are registered as Democrats, 29% as Republicans, and 11% as members of other parties (Liberal, Right to Life, Green, etc.). Voters not aligned with any official party are termed "Independent." You are conducting a poll by calling registered voters at random. In your first three calls, what is the probability you talk to
   a) all Republicans?
   b) no Democrats?
   c) at least one Independent?

22. **Religion.** Census reports for a city indicate that 62% of residents classify themselves as Christian, 12% as Jewish, and 16% as members of other religions (Muslims, Buddhists, etc.). The remaining residents classify themselves as nonreligious. A polling organization seeking information about public opinions wants to be sure to talk with

people holding a variety of religious views, and makes random phone calls. Among the first four people they call, what is the probability they reach

a) all Christians?
b) no Jews?
c) at least one person who is nonreligious?

23. Tires. You bought a new set of four tires from a manufacturer who just announced a recall because 2% of those tires are defective. What is the probability that at least one of yours is defective?

24. Pepsi. For a sales promotion the manufacturer places winning symbols under the caps of 10% of all Pepsi bottles. You buy a six-pack. What is the probability that you win something?

25. 9/11? On September 11, 2002, the first anniversary of the terrorist attack on the World Trade Center, the New York State Lottery's daily number came up 9-1-1. An interesting coincidence or a cosmic sign?

a) What is the probability that the winning three numbers match the date on any given day?
b) What is the probability that a whole year passes without this happening?
c) What is the probability that the date and winning lottery number match at least once during any year?
d) If every one of the 50 states has a three-digit lottery, what is the probability that at least one of them will come up 9-1-1 on September 11?

Chapter 15

Probability Rules!

Let's face it. Probabilities of simple events are just not that interesting. When we combine events and think about conditional outcomes, though, things get juicier. We saw back in Chapter 3 that the chance of surviving the *Titanic* changed depending on the ticket class of the passenger. To navigate the stormy seas of probability, we'll need some rules to steer by.

Remember, for any random phenomenon, each **trial** generates an **outcome.** An **event** is *any* set or collection of outcomes. The collection of *all possible* outcomes is called the **sample space,** and denoted *S*.[1]

If you flip a coin, what is the sample space? All you can get is heads or tails (we'll ignore the possibility that it lands on the edge). So the sample space is just the set {H, T}, H for heads and T for tails. It's no big deal. To make it seem more important, some books use the Greek letter Ω instead of *S*. But whatever the symbol, the **sample space** is just the collection of *all the possible outcomes*.

Events

Pull a bill from your wallet or pocket without looking at it. An outcome of this trial is the bill you select. The sample space is all the bills in circulation: **S** = {$1 bill, $2 bill, $5 bill, $10 bill, $20 bill, $50 bill, $100 bill}. These are *all* the possible outcomes. (In spite of what you may have seen in bank robbery movies, there are no $500 or $1000 bills.)

We can combine possible outcomes of such a trial into events. For example, the event **A** = {$1, $5, $10} represents selecting a $1, $5, or $10 bill. The event **B** = {a bill that does not have a president on it} is the collection of outcomes (Don't look! Can you name them?): {$10 (Hamilton), $100 (Franklin)}. The event **C** =

[1]Mathematicians like to use the term "space" as a fancy name for a set. Sort of like referring to that closet colleges call a dorm room as your "living space." But remember that it's really just a bunch of outcomes.

{enough money to pay for a $12 meal with one bill} is the set of outcomes {$20, $50, $100}.

Notice that outcomes don't have to be equally likely. You'd no doubt be more surprised (and pleased) to pull out a $100 bill than a $1 bill—it's not very likely, though. You probably carry many more $1 than $100 bills, but without information about the probability of each outcome, we can't calculate the probability of such events.

When outcomes *are* equally likely, probabilities for events are easy to find just by counting. When the k possible outcomes are equally likely, each has a probability of $1/k$. For example, consider the final digit of the serial number of that bill you extracted at random. Final digits are equally likely to be any digit from 0 to 9.

What's the probability of randomly selecting a bill whose serial number ends in an odd digit? We could simulate this event by simply assigning the digits to the random numbers 0 through 9. Because half of the digits from 0 to 9 are odd, you wouldn't be surprised to learn that the probability of finding a bill whose last digit is odd is 5/10. We can make this more formal by saying that for any event, **A**, that is made up of *equally likely* outcomes,

$$P(\mathbf{A}) = \frac{\textit{count of outcomes in } \mathbf{A}}{\textit{count of all possible outcomes}}.$$

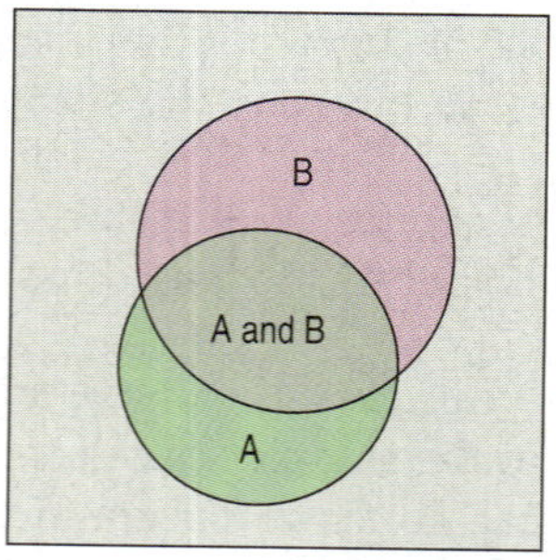

Events **A** and **B** and their intersection.

Be careful! This rule won't work unless the outcomes are *equally likely*. The probability of the event **C** (getting a bill worth more than $12) is *not* 3/7. There are 7 possible outcomes, and 3 of them exceed $12, but they are *not equally* likely. (Remember the probability that your lottery ticket will win rather than lose still isn't 1/2.)

Let's think about a randomly drawn bill again. There are images of famous buildings in the center of the backs of all but two bills in circulation. The $1 bill has the word ONE in the center, and the $2 bill shows the signing of the Declaration of Independence.

What's the probability of randomly selecting **A** = {a bill with an odd-numbered value} or **B** = {a bill with a building on the reverse}? We know **A** = {$1, $5} and **B** = {$5, $10, $20, $50, $100}. But we know *P* (**A** or **B**) is not simply the sum *P*(**A**) + *P*(**B**), because the events **A** and **B** are not disjoint. So what can we do? We'll need some new probability rules.

The First Three Rules for Working with Probability Rules

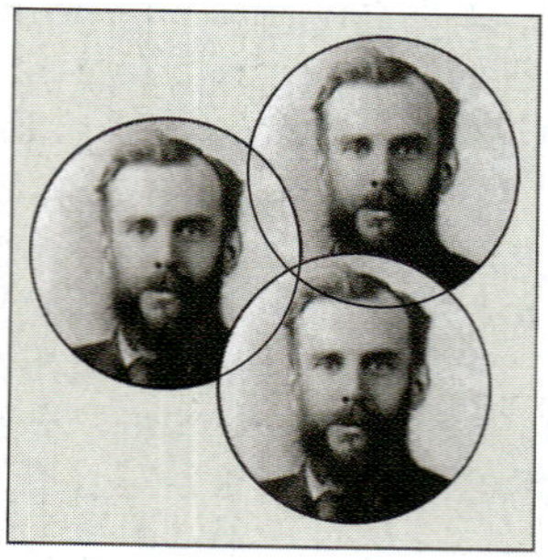

John Venn (1834–1923) created the Venn diagram. His book on probability, *The Logic of Chance,* was "strikingly original and considerably influenced the development of the theory of Statistics," according to John Maynard Keynes, one of the founders of Economics.

Make a picture.
Make a picture.
Make a picture.

We're dealing with probabilities now, not data, but the three rules don't change. The most common kind of picture to make is one like we just used, called a Venn diagram. Even experienced statisticians make Venn diagrams to help them think about probabilities of compound and overlapping events. You should, too.

The General Addition Rule

So, what is the probability of randomly selecting a bill with an odd-numbered value *or* a building on the reverse? As the diagram shows, we can't use the **Addition Rule** and add the two probabilities because the events are not **disjoint;** they overlap. There are outcomes in the *intersection* of **A** and **B.** Let's put the actual outcomes on the Venn diagram. The box represents the sample space. Notice that the $2 bill has neither a building nor an odd denomination, so it sits outside both circles.

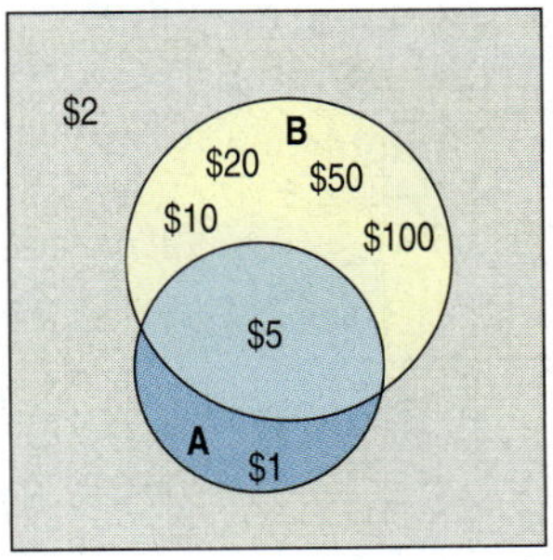

Denominations of bills that are odd (**A**) or that have a building on the reverse side (**B**). The two sets both include the $5 bill and both exclude the $2 bill.

It's the $5 bill that plays a crucial role here because it is both odd *and* has a building on the reverse. It's in both **A** and **B,** which places it in the *intersection* of the two circles. The reason we can't simply add the probabilities of **A** and **B** is that we'd count the $5 bill twice.

If we did add the two probabilities, we could compensate by *subtracting* out the probability of that $5 bill. So,

$$\begin{aligned} &P(\text{odd number value } \textit{or} \text{ building}) \\ &\quad = P(\text{odd number value}) + P(\text{building}) - P(\text{odd number value } \textit{and} \text{ building}) \\ &\quad = P(\$1, \$5) + P(\$5, \$10, \$20, \$50, \$100) - P(\$5). \end{aligned}$$

This rule works in general. We add the probabilities of two events and then subtract out the probability of their intersection. This approach gives us The **General Addition Rule,** which does not require disjoint events:

$$P(\mathbf{A} \cup \mathbf{B}) = P(\mathbf{A}) + P(\mathbf{B}) - P(\mathbf{A} \cap \mathbf{B}).$$

Would you like dessert or coffee?

Natural language can be ambiguous. In this question, is the answer one of the two alternatives, or simply "yes"? That kind of ambiguity can confuse our probabilities.

Suppose we had been asked the different question: What is the probability that the bill we draw has *either* an odd value or a building but *not both*? Which bills are we talking about now? The set we're interested in would be {$1, $10, $20, $50, $100}. We don't include the $5 bill in the set because it has both characteristics.

Why isn't this the same answer as before? The problem is that when we say the word "or," we usually mean *either* one *or* both. We don't usually mean the *exclusive* version of "or" as in, "Would you like the steak *or* the vegetarian entrée?" Ordinarily when we ask for the probability that **A** *or* **B** occurs, we mean **A** or **B** or both. And we know that probability is $P(\mathbf{A}) + P(\mathbf{B}) - P(\mathbf{A} \textit{ and } \mathbf{B})$. The General Rule subtracts the probability of the outcomes in **A** *and* **B** because we've counted those outcomes *twice.* But they're still there.

If we really mean **A** or **B,** but NOT both, then we have to get rid of the outcomes in {**A** and **B**}. So $P(\mathbf{A} \textit{ or } \mathbf{B}, \text{ but } \textit{not} \text{ both}) = P(\mathbf{A} \textit{ or } \mathbf{B}) - P(\mathbf{A} \textit{ and } \mathbf{B}) = P(\mathbf{A}) + P(\mathbf{B}) - 2 \times P(\mathbf{A} \cap \mathbf{B})$. Now we've subtracted $P(\mathbf{A} \textit{ and } \mathbf{B})$ twice: once because we don't want to double-count these events and a second time because we really didn't want to count them at all. At this point, it would be a good idea to make a picture to be sure you see how this works!

It Depends . . .

Two psychologists surveyed 478 children in grades 4, 5, and 6 in elementary schools in Michigan. They stratified their sample, drawing roughly 1/3 from rural, 1/3 from suburban, and 1/3 from urban schools. Among other questions, they asked the students whether their primary goal was to get good grades, to be popular, or to be good at sports. One question of interest was whether boys and girls at this age had similar goals.

Here's a *contingency table* giving counts of the students by their goals and gender.

Gender	Goals: Grades	Popular	Sports	Total
Boy	117	50	60	227
Girl	130	91	30	251
Total	247	141	90	478

The distribution of goals for boys and girls. **Table 15.1**

The distribution of goals for boys and girls. **Figure 15.1**

We looked at contingency tables and graphed the *conditional distributions* back in Chapter 3. The graphs show the *relative frequencies* with which boys and girls named the three goals. It's only a short step from these relative frequencies to probabilities.

Let's focus on this study and make the sample space just the set of these 478 students. If we select a student at random from this study, the probability we select a girl is just the corresponding relative frequency (since we're equally likely to select any of the 478 students). There are 251 girls in the data out of a total of 478, giving a probability of

$$P(\text{girl}) = 251/478 = 0.525$$

The same method works for more complicated events like intersections. For example, what's the probability of selecting a girl whose goal is to be popular? Well, 91 girls named popularity as their goal, so the probability is

$$P(\text{girl } \textit{and} \text{ popular}) = 91/478 = 0.190$$

The probability of selecting a student whose goal is to excel at sports is

$$P(\text{sports}) = 90/478 = 0.188$$

We can now build on what we did in Chapter 3. Now that we've defined the sample space as these 478 students, we can recognize the relative frequencies as probabilities.

What if we are given the information that the selected student is a girl? Would that change the probability that the selected student's goal is sports? You bet it would! The pie charts show that girls are much less likely to say their goal is to excel at sports than are boys. When we restrict our focus to girls, we look only at the girls' row of the table, which gives the conditional distribution of goals given "girl." Of the 251 girls, only 30 of them said their goal was to excel at sports.

We write the probability that a selected student wants to excel at sports *given that we have selected a girl* as

$$P(\text{sports} \mid \text{girl}) = 30/251 = 0.120$$

For boys, we look at the conditional distribution of goals given "boy" shown in the top row of the table. There, of the 227 boys, 60 said their goal was to excel at sports. So, $P(\text{sports}|\text{boy}) = 60/227 = 0.264$, more than twice the girls' probability.

		Goals			
		Grades	Popular	Sports	Total
Gender	Boy	117	50	60	227
	Girl	130	91	30	251
	Total	247	141	90	478

In general, when we want the probability of an event from a *conditional* distribution, we write $P(\mathbf{B}|\mathbf{A})$ and pronounce it "the probability of **B** *given* **A**." A probability that takes into account a given *condition* such as this is called a **conditional probability.**

Let's look at what we did. We worked with the counts, but we could work with the probabilities just as well. There were 30 students who both were girls and had sports as their goal, and there are 251 girls. So we found the probability to be 30/251. To find the probability of the event **B** *given* the event **A,** we restrict our attention to the outcomes in **A.** We then find in what fraction of *these* outcomes **B** also occurred. Formally, we write:

NOTATION ALERT:

$P(\mathbf{B}|\mathbf{A})$ is the conditional probability of **B** *given* **A.**

$$P(\mathbf{B}|\mathbf{A}) = \frac{P(\mathbf{A} \cap \mathbf{B})}{P(\mathbf{A})}.$$

Thinking this through, we can see that it's just what we've been doing, but with counts. Look back at the girls for whom sports was the goal. How did we calculate $P(\text{sports}|\text{girl})$?

The rule says to use probabilities. It says to take $P(\mathbf{A} \cap \mathbf{B})/P(\mathbf{A})$. The result is the same whether we use counts or probabilities because the total in the sample cancels out:

$$\frac{P(\text{sports} \cap \text{girl})}{P(\text{girl})} = \frac{30/478}{251/478} = \frac{30}{251}.$$

To use the formula for conditional probability, we're supposed to insist on one restriction. The formula doesn't work if $P(\mathbf{A})$ is 0. That would mean that that we were "given" the fact that **A** was true even though the probability of **A** is 0, which would be a contradiction. The formula works only when the event that's given has probability greater than 0.

Let's take our rule out for a spin. What's the probability that we have selected a girl *given* that the selected student's goal is popularity? Applying the rule, we get

$$P(\text{girl}|\text{popular}) = \frac{P(\text{girl} \cap \text{popular})}{P(\text{popular})}$$
$$= \frac{91/478}{141/478} = \frac{91}{141}$$

The General Multiplication Rule

Remember the Multiplication Rule for the probability of **A** *and* **B**? It said

$$P(\mathbf{A} \cap \mathbf{B}) = P(\mathbf{A})\,P(\mathbf{B}) \text{ when } \mathbf{A} \text{ and } \mathbf{B} \text{ are independent.}$$

Now we can write a more general rule that doesn't require independence. In fact, we've *already* written it down. We just need to rearrange the equation a bit.

The equation in the definition for conditional probability contains the probability of **A** *and* **B.** Rearranging the equation gives

$$P(\mathbf{A} \cap \mathbf{B}) = P(\mathbf{A}) \times P(\mathbf{B}|\mathbf{A}).$$

This is a **General Multiplication Rule** for compound events that does not require the events to be independent. Better than that, it even makes sense. The probability that two events, **A** and **B,** *both* occur is the probability that event **A** occurs multiplied by the probability that event **B** *also* occurs—that is, by the probability that event **B** occurs *given* that event **A** occurs.

Of course, there's nothing special about which set we call **A** and which one we call **B.** We should be able to state this the other way around. And indeed we can. It is equally true that

$$P(\mathbf{A} \cap \mathbf{B}) = P(\mathbf{B}) \times P(\mathbf{A}|\mathbf{B}).$$

Probability Rules STEP-BY-STEP

Police report that 78% of drivers stopped on suspicion of drunk driving are given a breath test, 36% a blood test, and 22% both tests. What is the probability that a randomly selected DWI suspect is given

1. a test?
2. a blood test or a breath test, but not both?
3. neither test?

Think

Define the events we're interested in.

Let A = {suspect is given a breath test}.
Let B = {suspect is given a blood test}.

Make a picture, and use the given probabilities to find the probability for each region.

We are told that

$$P(A) = 0.78$$
$$P(B) = 0.36$$
$$P(A \cap B) = 0.22$$

Show

The green region represents **A** but not **B.** Note that since $P(\mathbf{A}) = 0.78$ and $P(\mathbf{A}$ *and* $\mathbf{B}) = 0.22$, the probability of **A** but not **B** must be $0.78 - 0.22 = 0.56$.

The pale orange region is **B** but not **A.**

The gray region outside both circles represents the outcome neither **A** nor **B.** All the probabilities must total 1, so you can determine the probability of that region by subtraction.

So

$$P(A \cap B^C) = 0.78 - 0.22 = 0.56$$
$$P(B \cap A^C) = 0.36 - 0.22 = 0.14$$
$$P(A^C \cap B^C) = 1 - (0.56 + 0.22 + 0.14) = 0.08$$

Then, figure out what you want to know. The probabilities can come from the diagram or a formula. Sometimes translating the words to equations is the trickiest step.

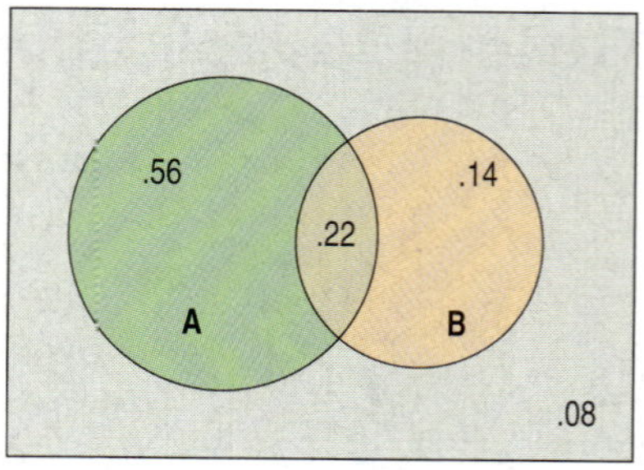

1. What is the probability that the suspect is given a test?

Show The probability the suspect is given a test is $P(\mathbf{A} \text{ or } \mathbf{B})$. You can use the General Addition Rule, or we can add the probabilities seen in the diagram.

$$P(A \cup B) = P(A) + P(B) - P(A \cap B)$$
$$= 0.78 + 0.36 - 0.22$$
$$= 0.92$$

OR

$$P(A \cup B) = 0.56 + 0.22 + 0.14 = 0.92$$

Tell Don't forget to state a conclusion.

92% of all suspects get a test.

2. What is the probability that the suspect gets either a blood test or a breath test but NOT both?

Show We can use the formula, or just add the appropriate probabilities seen in the Venn diagram.

$$P(A \text{ or } B \text{ but NOT both}) = P(A \cup B) - P(A \cap B)$$
$$= 0.92 - 0.22 = 0.70$$

OR

$$P(A \text{ or } B \text{ but NOT both}) = P(A \cap B^C) + P(B \cap A^C)$$
$$= 0.56 + 0.14 = 0.70$$

Tell State your conclusion.

70% of the suspects get exactly one of the tests.

3. What is the probability that the suspect gets neither test?

Show Getting neither test is the complement of getting one or the other. Use a formula, or just notice that "neither test" is represented by the region outside both circles.

$$P(\text{neither test}) = 1 - P(\text{either test})$$
$$= 1 - P(A \cup B)$$
$$= 1 - 0.92 = 0.08$$

OR

$$P(A^C \cap B^C) = 0.08$$

Tell State your conclusion.

Only 8% of the suspects get no test.

Independence

Let's return to the question of just what it means for events to be independent. We've said informally that what we mean by independence is that the outcome of one event does not influence the probability of the other. With our new notation for conditional probabilities, we can write a formal definition: Events **A** and **B** are **independent** whenever

$$P(\mathbf{B} \mid \mathbf{A}) = P(\mathbf{B}).$$

If we had to pick one idea in this chapter that you should understand and remember, it's the definition and meaning of independence. We'll need this idea in every one of the chapters that follow.

Now we can see that the Multiplication Rule for independent events we saw in Chapter 14 is just a special case of the general Multiplication Rule. The general rule says

$$P(\mathbf{A} \cap \mathbf{B}) = P(\mathbf{A}) \times P(\mathbf{B} \mid \mathbf{A})$$

whether the events are independent or not. But when events **A** and **B** are independent, we can write $P(\mathbf{B})$ for $P(\mathbf{B} \mid \mathbf{A})$ and we get back our simple rule:

$$P(\mathbf{A} \cap \mathbf{B}) = P(\mathbf{A}) \times P(\mathbf{B}).$$

Sometimes people use this statement as the definition of independent, but we find the other definition more intuitive. It doesn't really matter—the idea is that the probabilities of independent events don't change when you find out that one of them has occurred.

Is the probability of having good grades as a goal independent of the gender of the responding student? Looks like it might be. We need to check whether

$$P(\text{grades}|\text{girl}) = P(\text{grades})$$

$$\frac{130}{251} = 0.52 \stackrel{?}{=} \frac{247}{478} = 0.52.$$

To two decimal place accuracy, it looks like we can consider the events independent.

Independent ≠ Disjoint

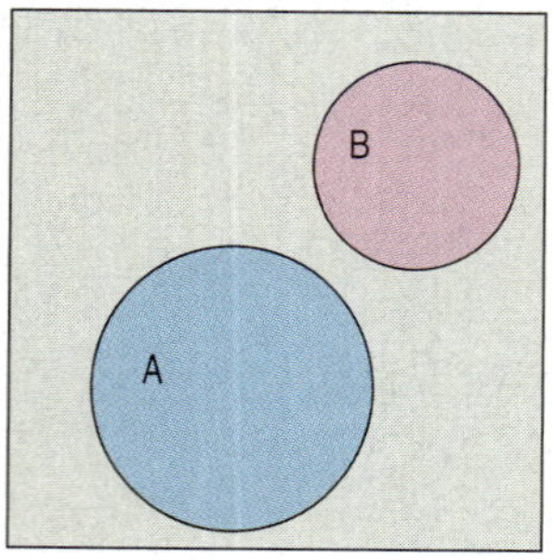

Disjoint events **A** and **B**. These events are mutually exclusive.

Are disjoint events independent? Both concepts seem to have similar ideas of separation and distinctness about them, but in fact disjoint events *cannot* be independent. Let's see why. Consider the two disjoint events {you get an A in this course} and {you get a B in this course}. They're disjoint because they have no outcomes in common. Suppose you learn that you *did* get an A in the course. What is the probability that you got a B now? You can't get both grades, so it must be 0.

Think about what that means. Knowing that the first event (getting an A) occurred changed your probability for the second event (down to 0). So the events aren't independent.

Mutually exclusive events can't be independent. They have no outcomes in common, so knowing that one occurred means the other didn't. A common error is to treat disjoint events as if they were independent, and apply the multiplication rule for independent events. Don't make that mistake.

Depending on Independence

It's much easier to think about independent events than to deal with conditional probabilities. It seems that most people's natural intuition for probabilities breaks down when it comes to conditional probabilities. Someone may estimate the probability of a compound event by multiplying the probabilities of its component events together without asking seriously whether those probabilities are independent.

For example, experts have assured us that the probability of a major commercial nuclear plant failure is so small that we should not expect such a failure to occur even in a span of hundreds of years. After only a few decades of commercial nuclear power, however, the world has seen two failures (Chernobyl and Three Mile Island). How could the estimates have been so wrong?

One simple part of the failure calculation is to test a particular valve and determine that valves such as this one fail only once in, say, 100 years of normal use. For a coolant failure to occur, several valves must fail. So we need the compound probability, *P*(valve 1 fails *and* valve 2 fails *and* . . .). A simple risk assessment might multiply the small probability of one valve failure together as many times as needed.

But if the valves all came from the same manufacturer, a flaw in one might be found in the others. And maybe when the first fails, it puts additional pressure on the next one in line. In either case, the events aren't independent and so we can't simply multiply the probabilities together.

Whenever you see probabilities multiplied together, stop and ask whether you think they are really independent.

Are the Events Disjoint? Independent? STEP-BY-STEP

Let's take another look at the drunk driving situation. Police report that 78% of drivers are given a breath test, 36% a blood test, and 22% both tests.

1. Are giving a DWI suspect a blood test and a breath test mutually exclusive?
2. Are giving the two tests independent?

Think Define the events we're interested in.

Let A = {suspect is given a breath test}.
Let B = {suspect is given a blood test}.

State the given probabilities.

We are told that

$$P(\mathbf{A}) = 0.78$$
$$P(\mathbf{B}) = 0.36$$
$$P(\mathbf{A} \cap \mathbf{B}) = 0.22$$

1. Are giving a DWI suspect a blood test and a breath test mutually exclusive?

Show Disjoint events cannot *both* happen at the same time, so check to see if $P(\mathbf{A}\ and\ \mathbf{B}) = 0$.

$P(\mathbf{A} \cap \mathbf{B}) = 0.22$. Since $P(\mathbf{A} \cap \mathbf{B}) \neq 0$, the events are *not* mutually exclusive.

Tell State your conclusion.

22% of all suspects get both tests, so a breath test and a blood test are *not* disjoint events.

2. Are the two tests independent?

Show Does getting a breath test change the probability of getting a blood test? That is, does $P(\mathbf{B}|\mathbf{A}) = P(\mathbf{B})$?

$$P(\mathbf{B}|\mathbf{A}) = \frac{P(\mathbf{A} \cap \mathbf{B})}{P(\mathbf{A})} = \frac{0.22}{0.78} \approx 0.28$$
$$P(\mathbf{B}) = 0.36$$
$$P(\mathbf{B}|\mathbf{A}) \neq P(\mathbf{B})$$

Because the two probabilities are *not* the same, the events are not independent.

Tell State your conclusion.

Overall, 36% of the drivers get blood tests, but only 22% of those who get a breath test do. Since suspects who get a breath test are less likely to have a blood test, the two events are not independent.

Drawing Without Replacement

Room draw is a process for assigning dormitory rooms to students. Sometimes, when students have equal priority, they are randomly assigned to the currently available dorm rooms. When it's time for you and your friend to draw, there are 12 rooms left. Three are in Gold Hall, a very desirable dorm with spacious wood-paneled rooms. Four are in Silver Hall, centrally located, but not quite as desirable. And five are in Wood Hall, a new dorm with cramped rooms, located half a mile from the center of campus on the edge of the woods.

Naturally, you and your friend would both like to score rooms in Gold. What are your chances? In particular, what's the chance that you *both* can get rooms in Gold?

If you go first, the chance that *you* will draw one of the Gold rooms is 3/12. Now, with you clutching your prized room assignment, what chance does your friend have? At this point there are now only 11 rooms left and just 2 left in Gold, so your friend's chance is now 2/11.

Using our notation, we write

$$P(\text{friend draws Gold} \mid \text{you draw Gold}) = 2/11.$$

The reason the denominator changes is that we draw these rooms *without replacement.* That is, once one is drawn, it doesn't go back into the pool.

We often sample without replacement. When we draw from a very large population, the change in the denominator is too small to worry about. But when there's a small population to draw from, as in this case, we need to take note and adjust the probabilities.

What are the chances that *both* of you will luck out? Well, now we've calculated the two probabilities we need for the General Multiplication Rule, so we can write:

$$\begin{aligned} P(\text{you} = \text{Gold} \cap \text{friend} = \text{Gold}) \\ &= P(\text{you} = \text{Gold}) \times P(\text{friend} = \text{Gold} \mid \text{you} = \text{Gold}) \\ &= 3/12 \times 2/11 = 1/22 = 0.045 \end{aligned}$$

In this instance, it doesn't matter who went first, or even if the rooms were drawn simultaneously. Even if the room draw was accomplished by shuffling cards containing the names of the dormitories and then dealing them out to 12 applicants (rather than by each student drawing a room in turn) we can still *think* of the calculation as having taken place in two steps:

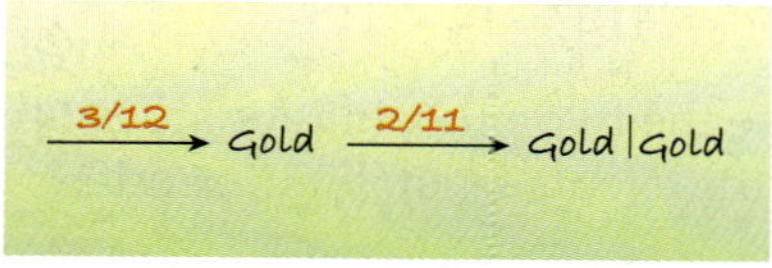

That is, one of you has a probability of 3/12 of drawing a Gold room and the other then has a probability of 2/11 of also drawing a Gold room. It doesn't matter whose draw we think of first. The probability changes for the second person nonetheless. The diagram shows this ordering of our thoughts.

Diagramming conditional probabilities leads to a more general way of helping us think with pictures—one that works for calculating conditional probabilities even when they involve different variables.

Tree Diagrams

For men, binge drinking is defined as having five or more drinks in a row, and for women as having four or more drinks in a row. (The difference is due to the average difference in weight.) According to a study by the Harvard School of Public Health (H. Wechsler, G. W. Dowdall, A. Davenport, and W. DeJong, "Binge Drinking on Campus: Results of a National Study"), 44% of college students engage in binge drinking, 37% drink moderately, and 19% abstain entirely. Another study, published in the *American Journal of Health Behavior,* finds that among binge drinkers aged 21 to 34, 17% have been involved in an alcohol-related automobile accident, while among non-bingers of the same age, only 9% have been involved in such accidents.

"Why," said the Dodo, "the best way to explain it is to do it."
—Lewis Carroll

With these statistics, what's the probability that a randomly selected college student will be a binge drinker who has had an alcohol-related car accident?

To start, we see that the probability of selecting a binge drinker is about 44%. To find the probability of selecting someone who is both a binge drinker and a driver with an alcohol-related accident, we would need to pull out the General Multiplication Rule and multiply the probability of one of the events by the conditional probability of the other given the first.

Or we *could* make a picture. Which would you prefer?

We thought so.

The kind of picture that helps us think through this kind of reasoning is called a **tree diagram,** because it shows sequences of events, like those we had in room draw, as paths that look like branches of a tree. The number of different paths we can take can get large, so we usually draw the tree starting from the left and growing vine-like across the page, although sometimes you'll see them drawn from the bottom up or top down.

The first branch of our tree separates students according to their drinking habits. We label each branch of the tree with a possible outcome and its corresponding probability.

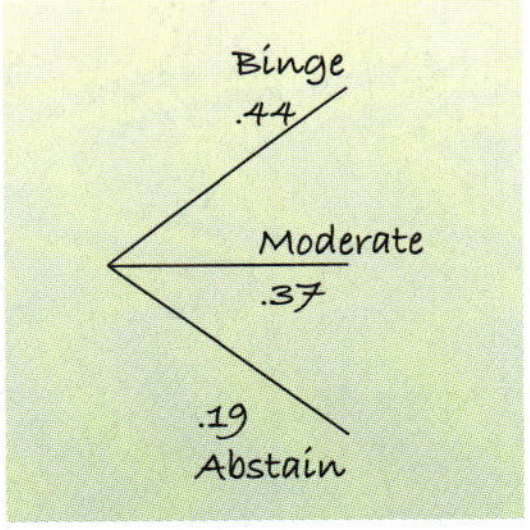

We can diagram the three outcomes of drinking and indicate their respective probabilities with a simple tree diagram. **Figure 15.2**

Notice that we cover all possible outcomes with the branches. The probabilities add up to one. But we're also interested in car accidents. The probability of having an alcohol-related accident *depends* on one's drinking behavior. Because the probabilities are *conditional,* we draw the alternatives separately on each branch of the tree:

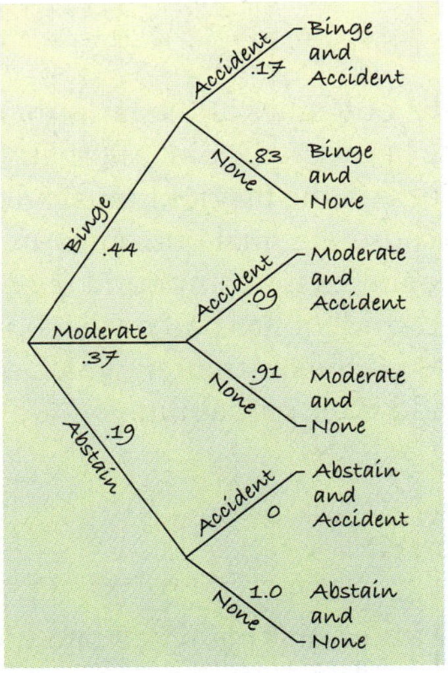

Extending the tree diagram, we can show both drinking and accident outcomes. The accident probabilities are conditional on the drinking outcomes, and they change depending on which branch we follow. Because we are concerned only with *alcohol-related* accidents, the conditional probability *P*(accident | abstinence) must be 0. **Figure 15.3**

On each of the second set of branches, we write the possible outcomes associated with having an alcohol-related car accident (having an accident or not) and the associated probability. These probabilities are different because they are *conditional* depending on the student's drinking behavior. (It shouldn't be too surprising that those who binge drink have a higher probability of alcohol-related accidents.) The probabilities add up to one, because given the outcome on the first branch, these outcomes cover all the possibilities. Looking back at the General Multiplication Rule, we can see how the tree depicts the calculation. To find the probability that a randomly selected student will be a binge drinker who has had an alcohol-related car accident, we follow the top branches. The probability of selecting a binger is 0.44. The conditional probability of an accident *given* binge drinking is 0.17. The General Multiplication Rule tells us that to find the *joint* probability of being a binge drinker and having an accident, we multiply these two probabilities together:

$$P(\text{binge } \textit{and} \text{ accident}) = P(\text{binge}) \times P(\text{accident} \mid \text{binge})$$
$$= 0.44 \times 0.17 = 0.075$$

And we can do the same for each combination of outcomes:

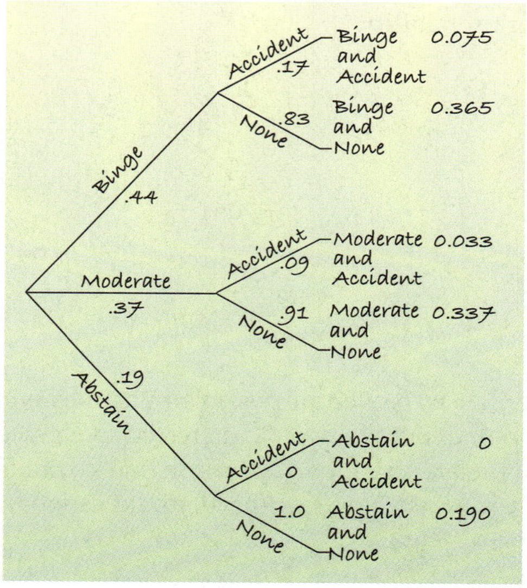

We can find the probabilities of compound events by multiplying the probabilities along the branch of the tree that leads to the event, just the way the General Multiplication Rule specifies. **Figure 15.4**

All the outcomes at the far right are disjoint because at each branch of the tree we chose between disjoint alternatives. And they are *all* the possibilities, so the probabilities on the far right must add up to one.

Because the final outcomes are disjoint, we can add up their probabilities to get probabilities for compound events. For example, what's the probability that a selected student has had an alcohol-related car accident? We simply find *all* the outcomes on the far right in which an accident has happened. There are three and we can add their probabilities: 0.075 + 0.033 + 0 = 0.108, or 10.8%.

Reversing the Conditioning

If we know a student has had an alcohol-related accident, what's the probability that the student is a binge drinker? That's an interesting question, but we can't just read it from the tree. The tree gives us $P(\text{accident} \mid \text{binge})$, but we want $P(\text{binge} \mid \text{accident})$—the conditioning in the other direction. The two probabilities are definitely *not* the same. We have reversed the conditioning.

We may not have the conditional probability we want, but we do know everything we need to know to find it. To find a conditional probability, we need the probability that both events happen divided by the probability that the given event occurs. We have already found the probability of an accident: $0.075 + 0.033 + 0 = 0.108$.

The joint probability that a student is both a binge drinker and someone who's had an accident is found at the top branch: 0.075. We've restricted the *Who* of the problem to the students with alcohol-related accidents, so we divide the two to find the conditional probability:

$$P(\text{binge} \mid \text{accident}) = \frac{P(\text{binge} \cap \text{accident})}{P(\text{accident})}$$
$$= \frac{0.075}{0.108} = 0.694.$$

The chance that a student who has an alcohol-related car accident is a binge drinker is more than 69%! As we said, reversing the conditioning is rarely intuitive, but tree diagrams help us keep track of the calculation when there aren't too many alternatives to consider.

Reversing the Conditioning STEP-BY-STEP

When the authors were in college, there were only three requirements for graduation that were the same for all students: You had to be able to tread water for 2 minutes, you had to learn a foreign language, and you had to be free of tuberculosis. For the last requirement, all freshmen had to take a TB screening test that consisted of a nurse jabbing what looked like a corn cob holder into your forearm. You were then expected to report back in 48 hours to have it checked. If you were healthy and TB-free, your arm was supposed to look as though you'd never had the test.

Sometime during the 48 hours, one of us had a reaction. When he finally saw the nurse, his arm was about 50% bigger than normal and a very unhealthy red. Did he have TB? The nurse had said that the test was about 99% effective, so it seemed that the chances must be pretty high that he had TB. How high do you think the chances were? Go ahead and guess. Guess low.

We'll call **TB** the event of actually having TB and + the event of testing positive. To start a tree, we need to know $P(\textbf{TB})$, the probability of having TB. This isn't given, so we looked it up. Even today TB is a fairly uncommon disease with an incidence of about 5 cases per 10,000 in the United States, so $P(\textbf{TB}) = 0.0005$. We also need to know the conditional probabilities $P(+ \mid \textbf{TB})$ and $P(+ \mid \textbf{No TB})$. Diagnostic tests can make two kinds of errors. They can give a positive result for a healthy person (a *false positive*) or a negative result for a sick person (a *false negative*). Being 99% accurate usually means a false-positive rate of 1%. That is, someone who doesn't have the disease has a 1% chance of testing positive anyway. We can write $P(+ \mid \textbf{No TB}) = 0.01$.

Since a false negative is more serious (because a sick person might not get treatment), tests are usually constructed to have a lower false-negative rate. We don't know exactly, but let's assume a 0.1% false-negative rate. So only 0.1% of sick people test negative. We can write $P(- \mid \textbf{TB}) = 0.001$.

Think

Define the events we're interested in and their probabilities.

Let **TB** = {having TB} and **No** = {no TB}
+ = {testing positive} and
− = {testing negative}

We know that $P(+ \mid \textbf{No}) = 0.01$ and $P(- \mid \textbf{TB}) = 0.001$. We are also given that $P(\textbf{TB}) = 0.0005$.

Figure out what you want to know in terms of the events. Use the definition of conditional probability to write the event whose probability you want to find.

We're interested in the probability that the author had TB given that he tested positive: $P(\textbf{TB} \mid +)$.

Show

Draw the tree diagram. When probabilities are very small like these are, be careful to keep all the significant digits.

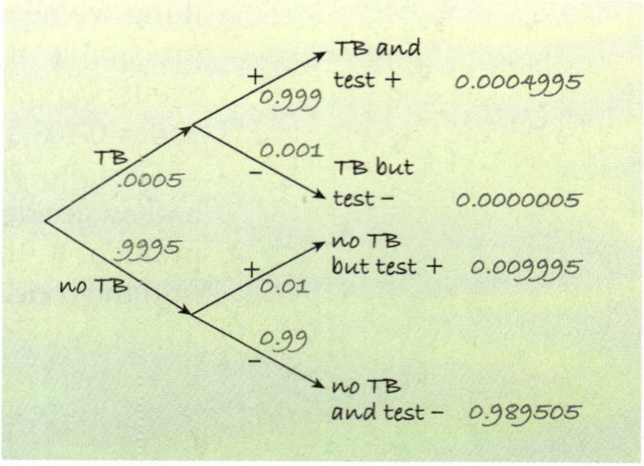

To finish the tree we need $P(\text{No})$, $P(-|\text{No})$ and $P(-|\textbf{TB})$. We can find each of these from the Complement Rule:

$$P(\textbf{No}) = 1 - P(\textbf{TB}) = 0.9995$$

$$P(-|\text{No}) = 1 - P(+|\text{No}) = 1 - 0.01 = 0.99 \text{ and}$$

$$P(+|\text{TB}) = 1 - P(-|\text{TB}) = 1 - 0.001. = 0.999$$

Multiply along the branches to find the probabilities of the four possible outcomes. It's a good idea to check your work by seeing if they total 1.

(Check: $0.0004995 + 0.0000005 + 0.0099950 + 0.9895050 = 1$)

Add up the probabilities corresponding to the condition of interest—in this case, testing positive. We can add the probabilities from the tree twigs that correspond to testing positive because the tree shows disjoint events.

$$P(+) = P(\text{TB} \cap +) + P(\text{No} \cap +)$$
$$P(+) = 0.0004995 + 0.009995 = 0.010495$$

Divide the probability of both events occuring (here, having TB given a positive test) by the probability (or frequency) of satisfying the condition (testing positive).

$$P(\text{TB}|+) = \frac{P(\text{TB} \cap +)}{P(+)} = \frac{0.0004995}{0.010495} = 0.047$$

Tell

State your conclusion.

The chance of having TB even after you test positive is less than 5%.

When we reverse the order of conditioning, we change the *Who* we are concerned with. With events of low probability, the result can be surprising. That's the reason patients who test positive for HIV, for example, are always told to seek medical counseling. They may have only a small chance of actually being infected. That's why global drug or disease testing can have unexpected consequences if people interpret *testing* positive as *being* positive.

Bayes' Rule

When we have $P(\textbf{A}|\textbf{B})$ but want the *reverse* probability $P(\textbf{B}|\textbf{A})$, we need to find $P(\textbf{A} \cap \textbf{B})$ and $P(\textbf{A})$. A tree is often a convenient way of finding these probabilities. It can work even when we have more than two possible events, as we saw in the binge drinking example. Instead of using the tree, we *could* write the calculation algebraically, showing exactly how we found the quantities that we needed: $P(\textbf{A} \cap \textbf{B})$ and $P(\textbf{A})$. The result is a formula known as Bayes' Rule after the

Reverend Thomas Bayes (1702?–1761), who was credited with the rule after his death, when he could no longer defend himself. Bayes' Rule is quite important in Statistics and is the foundation of an approach to Statistical analysis known as Bayesian Statistics. Although the simple rule deals with two alternative outcomes, the rule can be extended to the situation in which there are more than two branches to the first split of the tree. The principle remains the same (although the math gets more difficult). Bayes' Rule is just a formula for reversing the probability from the conditional probability that you're originally given.[2]

Who discovered Bayes' Rule?

Stigler's "Law of Eponymy" states that discoveries named for someone (eponyms) are usually named for the wrong person. Steven Stigler, who admits he didn't originate the law, is an expert on the history of Statistics, and he suspected that the law might apply to Bayes's Rule. He looked at the possibility that another candidate—one Nicholas Saunderson—was the real discoverer, not the Reverend Bayes. He assembled historical evidence and compared probabilities that the historical events would have happened *given* that Bayes was the discoverer of the rule, with the corresponding probabilities *given* that Saunderson was the discoverer. Of course, what he really wanted to know were the probabilities that Bayes or Saunderson was the discoverer *given* the historical events. How did he *reverse* the conditional probabilities? He used Bayes' Rule and concluded that, actually, it's more likely that Saunderson is the real originator of the rule.

But that doesn't change our tradition of naming the rule for Bayes and calling the branch of Statistics arising from this approach Bayesian Statistics. The Bayesians would never stand for being called Saundersonians anyway.

What Can Go Wrong?

- ***Don't use a simple probability rule where a general rule is appropriate.*** Don't assume independence without reason to believe it. Don't assume that outcomes are disjoint without checking that they are. Remember that the general rules always apply even when outcomes are in fact independent or disjoint.
- ***Don't find probabilities for samples drawn without replacement as if they had been drawn with replacement.*** Remember to adjust the denominator of your probabilities. This warning applies only when we draw from small populations or draw a large fraction of a finite population. When the population is very large relative to the sample size, the adjustments make no difference, and we ignore them.
- ***Don't reverse conditioning naively.*** As we have seen, the probability of **A** given **B** may not, and, in general does not, resemble the probability of **B** given **A.** The true probability may be counterintuitive.
- ***Don't confuse "disjoint" with "independent."*** Disjoint events *cannot* happen at the same time. When one happens, you know the other did not, so $P(\mathbf{B}|\mathbf{A}) = 0$. Independent events *must* be able to happen at the same time. When one happens, you know it has no effect on the other, so $P(\mathbf{B}|\mathbf{A}) = P(\mathbf{B})$.

---

[2]Bayes' Rule for two events says that $P(\mathbf{B}|\mathbf{A}) = \dfrac{P(\mathbf{A}|\mathbf{B})P(\mathbf{B})}{P(\mathbf{A}|\mathbf{B})P(\mathbf{B}) + P(\mathbf{A}|\mathbf{B}^C)P(\mathbf{B}^C)}$. Try it with the TB testing probabilities.

Connections

This chapter shows the unintuitive side of probability. If you've been thinking, "My mind doesn't work this way," you're probably right. Humans don't seem to find conditional and compound probabilities natural and often have trouble with such questions. Even statisticians make mistakes with conditional probability.

Our central connection is to the guiding principle that Statistics is about understanding the world. The events discussed in this chapter are close to the kinds of real-world situations in which understanding probabilities matters. The methods and concepts of this chapter are the tools you need to understand the part of the real world that deals with the outcomes of complex, uncertain events.

Key Concepts

Sample space The collection of all possible outcome values. The sample space has a probability of 1.

Disjoint events Two events are *disjoint* (or *mutually exclusive*) if they have no outcomes in common.

Addition Rule If **A** and **B** are disjoint events, then the probability of **A** *or* **B** is

$$P(\mathbf{A} \cup \mathbf{B}) = P(\mathbf{A}) + P(\mathbf{B}).$$

General Addition Rule For any two events, **A** and **B,** the probability of **A** *or* **B** is

$$P(\mathbf{A} \cup \mathbf{B}) = P(\mathbf{A}) + P(\mathbf{B}) - P(\mathbf{A} \cap \mathbf{B}).$$

Independence (used casually) Two events are *independent* if knowing whether one event occurs does not alter the probability that the other event occurs.

Conditional probability $P(\mathbf{B} \mid \mathbf{A}) = \dfrac{P(\mathbf{A} \cap \mathbf{B})}{P(\mathbf{A})}$

$P(\mathbf{B} \mid \mathbf{A})$ is read "the probability of **B** *given* **A.**"

Multiplication Rule If **A** and **B** are independent events, then the probability of **A** *and* **B** is

$$P(\mathbf{A} \cap \mathbf{B}) = P(\mathbf{A}) \times P(\mathbf{B}).$$

General Multiplication Rule For any two events, **A** and **B,** the probability of **A** *and* **B** is

$$P(\mathbf{A} \cap \mathbf{B}) = P(\mathbf{A}) \times P(\mathbf{B} \mid \mathbf{A}).$$

Independence (used formally) $P(\mathbf{B} \mid \mathbf{A}) = P(\mathbf{B})$ *when* **A** *and* **B** *are independent.*

Tree diagram A display of conditional events or probabilities that is helpful in thinking through conditioning.

Skills

When you complete this lesson you should:

Think

- Understand that the probability of an event is the proportion of times it occurs in many repetitions of a random phenomenon.
- Understand the concept of conditional probability as redefining the *Who* of concern according to the information about the event that is *given.*
- Understand the concept of independence.

Show

- Know how and when to apply the General Addition Rule.
- Know how to find probabilities for compound events as fractions of counts of occurrences in a two-way table.
- Know how and when to apply the General Multiplication Rule.
- Know how to make and use a tree diagram to understand conditional probabilities and reverse conditioning.

Tell

- Be able to make a clear statement about a conditional probability that makes clear how the condition affects the probability.
- Avoid making statements that assume independence of events when there is no clear evidence that they are in fact independent.

Exercises

1. Sample spaces. For each of the following, list the sample space and tell whether you think the events are equally likely.
   a) Toss 2 coins; record the order of heads and tails.
   b) A family has 3 children; record the number of boys.
   c) Flip a coin until you get a head or 3 consecutive tails.
   d) Roll two dice; record the larger number.

2. Sample spaces. For each of the following, list the sample space and tell whether you think the events are equally likely.
   a) Roll two dice; record the sum of the numbers.
   b) A family has 3 children; record the genders in order of birth.
   c) Toss four coins; record the number of tails.
   d) Toss a coin 10 times; record the longest run of heads.

3. Homes. Real estate ads suggest that 64% of homes for sale have garages, 21% have swimming pools, and 17% have both features. What is the probability that a home for sale has
   a) a pool or a garage?
   b) neither a pool nor a garage?
   c) a pool but no garage?

4. Travel. Suppose the probability that a U.S. resident has traveled to Canada is 0.18, to Mexico is 0.09, and to both countries is 0.04. What's the probability that an American chosen at random has
   a) traveled to Canada but not Mexico?
   b) traveled to either Canada or Mexico?
   c) not traveled to either country?

5. Amenities. A check of dorm rooms on a large college campus revealed that 38% had refrigerators, 52% had TVs, and 21% had both a TV and a refrigerator. What's the probability that a randomly selected dorm room has
   a) a TV but no refrigerator?
   b) a TV or a refrigerator, but not both?
   c) neither a TV nor a refrigerator?

6. Workers. Employment data at a large company reveal that 72% of the workers are married, that 44% are college graduates, and that half of the college grads are married. What's the probability that a randomly chosen worker
   a) is neither married nor a college graduate?
   b) is married but not a college graduate?
   c) is married or a college graduate?

7. Cards. You draw a card at random from a standard deck of 52 cards. Find each of the following conditional probabilities:
   a) The card is a heart, given that it is red.
   b) The card is red, given that it is a heart.
   c) The card is an ace, given that it is red.
   d) The card is a queen, given that it is a face card.

8. Pets. In its monthly report, the local animal shelter states that it currently has 24 dogs and 18 cats available for adoption. Eight of the dogs and 6 of the cats are male. Find each of the following conditional probabilities if an animal is selected at random:
   a) The pet is male, given that it is a cat.
   b) The pet is a cat, given that it is female.
   c) The pet is female, given that it is a dog.

9. Health. The probabilities that an adult American man has high blood pressure and/or high cholesterol are shown in the table.

		Blood Pressure	
		High	OK
Cholesterol	High	0.11	0.21
	OK	0.16	0.52

a) What's the probability that a man has both conditions?
b) What's the probability that he has high blood pressure?
c) What's the probability that a man with high blood pressure has high cholesterol?
d) What's the probability that a man has high blood pressure if it's known that he has high cholesterol?

10. Death penalty. The table shows the political affiliation of American voters and their positions on the death penalty.

		Death Penalty	
		Favor	Oppose
Party	Republican	0.26	0.04
	Democrat	0.12	0.24
	Other	0.24	0.10

a) What's the probability that a randomly chosen voter favors the death penalty?
b) What's the probability that a Republican favors the death penalty?
c) What's the probability that a voter who favors the death penalty is a Democrat?
d) A candidate thinks she has a good chance of gaining the votes of anyone who is a Republican or in favor of the death penalty. What portion of the voters is that?

11. Sick kids. Seventy percent of kids who visit a doctor have a fever, and 30% of kids with a fever have sore throats. What's the probability that a kid who goes to the doctor has a fever and a sore throat?

12. Sick cars. Twenty percent of cars that are inspected have faulty pollution control systems. The cost of repairing a pollution control system exceeds $100 about 40% of the time. When a driver takes her car in for inspection, what's the probability that she will end up paying more than $100 to repair the pollution control system?

13. Cards. You are dealt a hand of three cards, one at a time. Find the probability of each of the following.
a) The first heart you get is the third card dealt.
b) Your cards are all red (that is, all diamonds or hearts).
c) You get no spades.
d) You have at least one ace.

14. Another hand. You pick three cards at random from a deck. Find the probability of each event described below.
a) You get no aces.
b) You get all hearts.
c) The third card is your first red card.
d) You have at least one diamond.

15. Batteries. A junk box in your room contains a dozen old batteries, five of which are totally dead. You start picking batteries one at a time and testing them. Find the probability of each outcome.
a) The first two you choose are both good.
b) At least one of the first three works.
c) The first four you pick all work.
d) You have to pick 5 batteries in order to find one that works.

16. Shirts. The soccer team's shirts have arrived in a big box, and people just start grabbing them, looking for the right size. The box contains 4 medium, 10 large, and 6 extra-large shirts. You want a medium for you and one for your sister. Find the probability of each event described.
a) The first two you grab are the wrong sizes.
b) The first medium shirt you find is the third one you check.
c) The first four shirts you pick are all extra-large.
d) At least one of the first four shirts you check is a medium.

17. Eligibility. A university requires its biology majors to take a course called BioResearch. The prerequisite for this course is that students must have taken either a Statistics course or a computer course. By the time they are juniors, 52% of the Biology majors have taken Statistics, 23% have had a computer course, and 7% have done both.
a) What percent of the junior Biology majors are ineligible for BioResearch?
b) What's the probability that a junior Biology major who has taken Statistics has also taken a computer course?
c) Are taking these two courses disjoint events? Explain.
d) Are taking these two courses independent events? Explain.

18. Benefits. Fifty-six percent of all American workers have a workplace retirement plan, 68% have health insurance, and 49% have both benefits. We select a worker at random.
a) What's the probability he has neither employer-sponsored health insurance nor a retirement plan?
b) What's the probability he has health insurance if he has a retirement plan?
c) Are having health insurance and a retirement plan independent events? Explain.
d) Are having these two benefits mutually exclusive? Explain.

19. For sale. In the real estate ads described in Exercise 3, 64% of homes for sale have garages, 21% have swimming pools, and 17% have both features.
a) If a home for sale has a garage, what's the probability that it has a pool, too?
b) Are having a garage and a pool independent events? Explain.
c) Are having a garage and a pool mutually exclusive? Explain.

20. On the road again. According to Exercise 4, the probability that a U.S. resident has traveled to Canada is 0.18, to Mexico is 0.09, and to both countries is 0.04.
a) What's the probability that someone who has traveled to Mexico has visited Canada, too?
b) Are travel to Mexico and Canada disjoint events? Explain.
c) Are travel to Mexico and Canada independent events? Explain.

21. Cards. If you draw a card at random from a well-shuffled deck, is getting an ace independent of the suit? Explain.

22. Pets again. The local animal shelter in Exercise 8 reported that it currently has 24 dogs and 18 cats available for adoption; 8 of the dogs and 6 of the cats are male. Are the species and gender of the animals independent? Explain.

23. Men's health, again. Given the table of probabilities from Exercise 9, are high blood pressure and high cholesterol independent? Explain.

		Blood Pressure	
		High	OK
Cholesterol	High	0.11	0.21
	OK	0.16	0.52

24. Politics. Given the table of probabilities from Exercise 10, are party affiliation and position on the death penalty independent? Explain.

		Death Penalty	
		Favor	Oppose
Party	Republican	0.26	0.04
	Democrat	0.12	0.24
	Other	0.24	0.10

25. Luggage. Leah is flying from Boston to Denver with a connection in Chicago. The probability her first flight leaves on time is 0.15. If the flight is on time, the probability that her luggage will make the connecting flight in Chicago is 0.95, but if the first flight is delayed, the probability that the luggage will make it is only 0.65.
a) Are the first flight leaving on time and the luggage making the connection independent events? Explain.
b) What is the probability that her luggage arrives in Denver with her?

26. Graduation. A private college report contains these statistics:

70% of incoming freshmen attended public schools.

75% of public school students who enroll as freshmen eventually graduate.

90% of other freshmen eventually graduate.

a) Is there any evidence that a freshman's chances to graduate may depend upon what kind of high school the student attended? Explain.
b) What percent of freshmen eventually graduate?

27. Late luggage. Remember Leah (Exercise 25)? Suppose you pick her up at the Denver airport, and her luggage is not there. What is the probability that Leah's first flight was delayed?

28. Graduation, part II. What percent of students who graduate from the college in Exercise 26 attended a public high school?

29. Absenteeism. A company's records indicate that on any given day about 1% of their day shift employees and 2% of the night shift employees will miss work. Sixty percent of the employees work the day shift.
a) Is absenteeism independent of shift worked? Explain.
b) What percent of employees are absent on any given day?

30. Lungs and smoke. Suppose that 23% of adults smoke cigarettes. It's known that 57% of smokers and 13% of nonsmokers develop a certain lung condition by age 60.
a) Explain how these statistics indicate that lung condition and smoking are not independent.
b) What's the probability that a randomly selected 60-year-old has this lung condition?

31. Absenteeism, part II. At the company described in Exercise 29, what percent of the absent employees are on the night shift?

32. Lungs and smoke, again. Based on the statistics in Exercise 30, what's the probability that someone with the lung condition was a smoker?

33. Checkpoints. Police often set up sobriety checkpoints—roadblocks where drivers are asked a few brief questions to allow the officer to judge whether or not the person may have been drinking. If the officer does not suspect a problem, drivers are released to go on their way. Otherwise, drivers are detained for a Breathalyzer test that will determine whether or not they are arrested. The police say that based on the brief initial stop, trained officers can make the right decision 80% of the time. Suppose the police operate a sobriety checkpoint after 9 p.m. on a Saturday night, a time when national traffic safety experts suspect that about 12% of drivers have been drinking.

a) You are stopped at the checkpoint and, of course, have not been drinking. What's the probability that you are detained for further testing?
b) What's the probability that any given driver will be detained?
c) What's the probability that a driver who is detained has actually been drinking?
d) What's the probability that a driver who was released had actually been drinking?

34. Polygraphs. Lie detectors are controversial instruments, barred from use as evidence in many courts. Nonetheless, many employers use lie detector screening as part of their hiring process in the hope that they can avoid hiring people who might be dishonest. There has been some research, but no agreement, about the reliability of polygraph tests. Based on this research, suppose that a polygraph can detect 65% of lies, but incorrectly identifies 15% of true statements as lies.

A certain company believes that 95% of its job applicants are trustworthy. The company gives everyone a polygraph test, asking, "Have you ever stolen anything from your place of work?" Naturally, all the applicants answer "No," but the polygraph identifies some of those answers as lies, making the person ineligible for a job. What's the probability that a job applicant rejected under suspicion of dishonesty was actually trustworthy?

35. Dishwashers. Dan's Diner employs three dishwashers. Al washes 40% of the dishes and breaks only 1% of those he handles. Betty and Chuck each wash 30% of the dishes, and Betty breaks only 1% of hers, but Chuck breaks 3% of the dishes he washes. (He, of course, will need a new job soon. . . .)You go to Dan's for supper one night and hear a dish break at the sink. What's the probability that Chuck is on the job?

36. Parts. A company manufacturing electronic components for home entertainment systems buys electrical connectors from three suppliers. The company prefers to use supplier A because only 1% of those connectors prove to be defective, but supplier A can deliver only 70% of the connectors needed. The company also must purchase connectors from two other suppliers, 20% from supplier B and the rest from supplier C. The rates of defective connectors from B and C are 2% and 4%, respectively. You buy one of these components, and when you try to use it you find that the connector is defective. What's the probability that your component came from supplier A?

Chapter 16

Random Variables

What Is an Actuary?

Actuaries are the daring people who put a price on risk, estimating the likelihood and costs of rare events so they can be insured. That takes financial, statistical, and business skills. It also makes them invaluable to many businesses. Actuaries are rather rare themselves; only about 19,000 work in North America. Perhaps because of this, they are well paid. If you're enjoying this course, you may want to look into a career as an actuary. Contact the Society of Actuaries or the Casualty Actuarial Society (who, despite what you may think, did not pay for this blurb).

Insurance companies make bets. They bet that you're going to live a long life. You bet that you're going to die sooner. Both you and the insurance company want the company to stay in business, so it's important to find a "fair price" for your bet. Of course, the right price for *you* depends on many factors, and nobody can predict exactly how long you'll live. But when the company averages over enough customers, it can make reasonably accurate estimates of the amount it can expect to collect on a policy before it has to pay its benefit.

Here's a simple example. An insurance company offers a "death and disability" policy that pays $10,000 when you die or $5000 if you are permanently disabled. It charges a premium of only $50 a year for this benefit. Is the company likely to make a profit selling such a plan? To answer this question, the company needs to know the *probability* that its clients will die or be disabled in any year. From actuarial information like this, the company can calculate the expected value of this policy.

Expected Value: Center

NOTATION ALERT:

Are we now taking over all capital letters? Not really. The most common letters for random variables are X, Y, and Z. But be cautious. If you see a capital letter, it might denote a random variable.

We'll want to build a probability model in order to answer the questions about the insurance company's risk. First we need to define a few terms. The amount the company pays out on an individual policy is called a **random variable** because its value is based on the outcome of a random event. We use a capital letter, like X, to denote a random variable. A particular value that it can have we'll denote by the corresponding lower-case letter, in this case x. For the insurance company, x can be $10,000 (if you die that year), $5000 (if you are disabled), or $0 (if neither occurs). Because we can list all the outcomes, we might formally call this random variable a **discrete** random variable. Otherwise, we'd call it a **continuous** random variable. The collection of all the possible values and the probabilities that they occur is called the **probability model** for the random variable.

Suppose, for example, that the death rate in any year is 1 out of every 1000 people, and that another 2 out of 1000 suffer some kind of disability. Then we can display the probability model for this insurance policy in a table like this:

Policyholder outcome	Payout x	Probability P(X = x)
Death	10,000	$\frac{1}{1000}$
Disability	5000	$\frac{2}{1000}$
Neither	0	$\frac{997}{1000}$

To see what the insurance company can expect, imagine that it insures exactly 1000 people. Further imagine that, in perfect accordance with the probabilities, 1 of the policyholders dies, 2 are disabled, and the remaining 997 survive the year unscathed. The company would pay \$10,000 to one client and \$5000 to each of 2 clients. That's a total of \$20,000, or an average of 20000/1000 = \$20 per policy. Since it is charging people \$50 for the policy, the company expects to make a profit of \$30 per customer. Not bad!

NOTATION ALERT:

The expected value (or mean) of a random variable is written $E(X)$ or μ.

We can't predict what *will* happen during any given year, but we can say what we *expect* to happen. To do this, we (or, rather, the insurance company) need the probability model. The expected value of a policy is a parameter of this model. In fact, it's the mean. We'll signify this with the notation μ (for population mean) or $E(X)$ for expected value. This isn't an average of some data values, so we won't estimate it. Instead, we assume that the probabilities are known and simply calculate the expected value from them.

How did we come up with \$20 as the expected value of a policy? Here's the calculation. As we've seen, it often simplifies probability calculations to think about some (convenient) number of outcomes. For example, we could imagine that we have exactly 1000 clients. Of those, exactly 1 died and 2 were disabled, corresponding to what the probabilities would say.

$$\mu = E(X) = \frac{10{,}000(1) + 5000(2) + 0(997)}{1000}$$

So our total payout comes to \$20,000, or \$20 per policy.

Instead of writing the expected value as one big fraction, we can rewrite it as separate terms each divided by 1000.

$$\begin{aligned}\mu &= E(X)\\ &= \$10{,}000\left(\frac{1}{1000}\right) + \$5000\left(\frac{2}{1000}\right) + \$0\left(\frac{997}{1000}\right)\\ &= \$20\end{aligned}$$

How convenient! See the probabilities? For each policy, there's a 1/1000 chance that we'll have to pay \$10,000 for a death and a 2/1000 chance that we'll have to pay \$5000 for a disability. Of course, there's a 997/1000 chance that we won't have to pay anything.

Take a good look at the expression now. It's easy to calculate the **expected value** of a random variable—just multiply each possible value by the probability that it occurs, and find the sum.

$$\mu = E(X) = \sum x \cdot P(X = x)$$

Be sure that every possible outcome is included in the sum. And verify that you have a valid probability model to start with—the probabilities should each be between 0 and 1 and should sum to one.

First Center, Now Spread . . .

Of course, this expected value (or mean) is not what actually happens to any *particular* policyholder. No individual policy actually costs the company \$20. We are dealing with random events, so some policyholders receive big payouts, others nothing. Because the insurance company must anticipate this variability, it needs to know the *standard deviation* of the random variable.

For data, we calculated the **standard deviation** by first computing the deviation from the mean and squaring it. We do that with random variables as well. First, we find the deviation of each payout from the mean (expected value):

Policyholder outcome	Payout x	Probability $P(X = x)$	Deviation $(x - \mu)$
Death	10,000	$\frac{1}{1000}$	$(10{,}000 - 20) = 9980$
Disability	5,000	$\frac{2}{1000}$	$(5{,}000 - 20) = 4980$
Neither	0	$\frac{997}{1000}$	$(0 - 20) = -20$

Next we square each deviation. The variance is the expected value of those squared deviations. We multiply each by the appropriate probability and sum those products. That gives us the variance of X. Here's what it looks like:

$$Var(X) = 9980^2\left(\frac{1}{1000}\right) + 4980^2\left(\frac{2}{1000}\right) + (-20)^2\left(\frac{997}{1000}\right) = 149{,}600.$$

Finally, we take the square root to get the standard deviation:

$$SD(X) = \sqrt{149{,}600} \approx \$386.78.$$

The insurance company can expect an average payout of \$20 per policy, with a standard deviation of \$386.78.

Think about that. The company charges \$50 for each policy and expects to pay out \$20 per policy. Sounds like an easy way to make \$30. In fact, most of the time (probability 997/1000) the company pockets the entire \$50. But would you consider selling your roommate such a policy? The problem is that occasionally the company loses big. With probability 1/1000 it will pay out \$10,000, and with probability 2/1000 it will pay out \$5000. That may be more risk than you're willing to take on. The standard deviation of \$386.78 gives an indication that it's no sure thing. That's a pretty big spread (and risk) for an average profit of \$20.

Here are the formulas for what we just did. Because these are parameters of our probability model, the variance and standard deviation can also be written as σ^2 and σ. You should recognize both kinds of notation.

$$\sigma^2 = Var(X) = \sum(x - \mu)^2 \cdot P(X = x)$$

$$\sigma = SD(X) = \sqrt{Var(X)}$$

Expected Values and Standard Deviations for Random Variables STEP-BY-STEP

As the head of inventory for Knowway computer company, you were thrilled that you had managed to ship 2 computers to your biggest client the day the order arrived. You are horrified, though, to find out that someone restocked refurbished computers in with the new computers in your storeroom. The shipped computers were selected randomly from the 15 computers in stock, but 4 of those were actually refurbished.

If your client gets 2 new computers, things are fine. If the client gets a refurbished computer, it will be sent back at your expense—\$100—and you can replace it. However, if both computers are refurbished, the client will cancel the order this month and you'll lose \$1000. What's the expected value and the standard deviation of your loss?

Think

Define the random variable.

Let X = amount of loss.

Make a picture. This is another job for tree diagrams.

If you prefer calculation to drawing, find $P(NN)$ and $P(RR)$, then use the Complement Rule to find $P(NR \text{ or } RN)$.

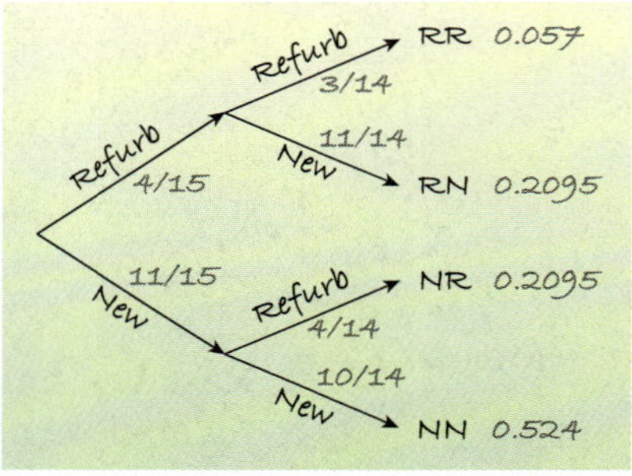

List the possible values of the random variable, and determine the probability model.

Outcome	x	P(X = x)
Two refurbs	1000	P(RR) = 0.057
One refurb	100	P(NR or RN) = 0.2095 + 0.2095 = 0.419
New/new	0	P(NN) = 0.524

Show

Find the expected value.

$$E(X) = 0(0.524) + 100(0.419) + 1000(0.057) = \$98.90$$

Find the variance.

$$Var(X) = (0 - 98.90)^2 \times 0.524 + (100 - 98.90)^2 \times 0.419 + (1000 - 98.90)^2 \times 0.057 = 51{,}408.80$$

Find the standard deviation.

$$SD(X) = \sqrt{51{,}408.79} = \$226.735$$

Tell State your conclusion.

I expect this mistake to cost the firm \$98.90 with a standard deviation of \$226.74.

Reality Check

Both numbers seem reasonable. The expected value of \$98.90 is between the extreme values of \$0 and \$1000. The standard deviation of \$226.74 reflects the fact that there's a pretty large range of outcome values.

TI Tips

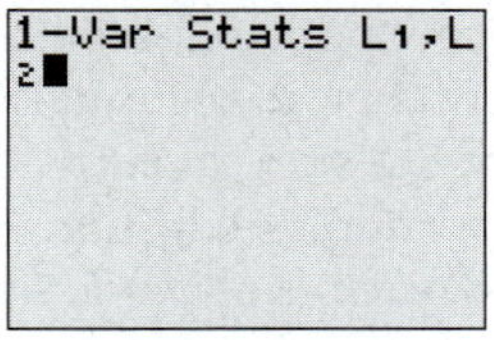

You can easily calculate means and standard deviations for a random variable with your TI. Let's do the Knowway computer example.

- Enter the values of the variable in a list, say, `L1`: 0, 100, 1000.
- Enter the probability model in another list, say, `L2`. Notice that you can enter the probabilities as fractions. For example, multiplying along the bottom branches of the tree gives the probability $\frac{11}{15} \cdot \frac{10}{14} = \frac{110}{210}$. When you enter that value, the TI will automatically change the fraction to a decimal!
- Under the `STAT CALC` menu, ask for `1-VarStats L1,L2`.

Now you see the mean and standard deviation (along with some other things). Don't fret that the calculator's mean and standard deviation aren't precisely the same as the ones we found. Such minor differences can arise whenever we round off probabilities to do the work by hand.

Beware: Although the calculator knows enough to call the standard deviation σ, it uses $\bar{x}$ where it should say μ. Make sure you don't make that mistake!

More About Means and Variances

Our insurance company expected to pay out an average of \$20 per policy, with a standard deviation of about \$387. If we take the \$50 premium into account, we see the company makes a profit of $50 - 20 = \$30$ per policy. Suppose the company lowers the premium by \$5 to \$45. It's pretty clear that the expected profit also drops an average of \$5 per policy, to $45 - 20 = \$25$.

What about the standard deviation? We know that adding or subtracting a constant from data shifts the mean but doesn't change the variance or standard deviation. The same is true of random variables.[1]

$$E(X \pm c) = E(X) \pm c \qquad Var(X \pm c) = Var(X)$$

What if the company decides to double all the payouts—that is, pay \$20,000 for deaths and \$10,000 for disability? This would double the average payout per policy and also increase the variability in payouts. We have seen that multiplying or

[1]The rules in this section are true for both discrete *and* continuous random variables.

dividing all data values by a constant changes both the mean and the standard deviation by the same factor. Variance, being the square of standard deviation, changes by the square of the constant. The same is true of random variables. In general, multiplying each value of a random variable by a constant multiplies the mean by that constant and the variance by the *square* of the constant.

$$E(aX) = aE(X) \qquad Var(aX) = a^2Var(X)$$

This insurance company sells policies to more than just one person. How can we figure means and variances for a collection of customers? For example, how can the company find the total expected value (and standard deviation) of policies taken over all policyholders? Consider a simple case: just two customers, Mr. Ecks and Ms. Wye. With an expected payout of \$20 on each policy, we might expect a total of \$20 + \$20 = \$40 to be paid out on the two policies. Nothing surprising there. The expected value of the sum is the sum of the expected values.

The variability is another matter. Is the risk of insuring two people the same as the risk of insuring one person for twice as much? We wouldn't expect both clients to die or become disabled in the same year. Because we've spread the risk, the standard deviation should be smaller. Indeed, this is the fundamental principle behind insurance. By spreading the risk among many policies, a company can keep the standard deviation quite small and predict costs more accurately.

But how much smaller is the standard deviation of the sum? It turns out that, if the random variables are independent, there is a simple Addition Rule for variances: *The variance of the sum of two independent random variables is the sum of their variances.*

For Mr. Ecks and Ms. Wye, the insurance company can expect their outcomes to be independent, so (using X for Mr. Ecks's payout and Y for Ms. Wye's)

$$Var(X + Y) = Var(X) + Var(Y) = 149{,}600 + 149{,}600 = 299{,}200.$$

If they had insured only Mr. Ecks for twice as much, there would only be one outcome rather than two *independent* outcomes, so the variance would have been

$$Var(2X) = 2^2Var(X) = 4 \times 149{,}600 = 598{,}400, \text{ or}$$

twice as big as with two independent policies.

Of course, variances are in squared units. The company would prefer to know standard deviations, which are in dollars. The standard deviation of the payout for two independent policies is $\sqrt{299{,}200} = \$547$. But the standard deviation of the payout for a single policy of twice the size is $\sqrt{598{,}400} = \$773.5$, or about 40% more.

If the company has two customers, then, it will have an expected annual total payout of \$40 with a standard deviation of \$547.

In general,

- *The mean of the sum of two random variables is the sum of the means.*
- *The mean of the difference of two random variables is the difference of the means.*
- *If the random variables are independent, the variance of their sum* or *difference is always the sum of the variances.*

$$E(X \pm Y) = E(X) \pm E(Y) \qquad Var(X \pm Y) = Var(X) + Var(Y)$$

Wait a minute! Is that third part correct? Do we always *add* variances? Yes. Think about the two insurance policies. Suppose we want to know the mean and standard deviation of the *difference* in payouts to the two clients. Since each policy has an expected payout of \$20, the expected difference is 20 − 20 = \$0. If we also subtract variances we get \$0, too, and that surely doesn't make sense. Note that if the outcomes for the two clients are independent, the difference in payouts could range from \$10,000 − \$0 = \$10,000 to \$0 − \$10,000 = −\$10,000, a spread of \$20,000. The variability in differences increases as much as the variability in sums. If the company has two customers, the difference in payouts has a mean of \$0 and a standard deviation of \$547 (again).

For random variables
$X + X + X \neq 3X$

As we've just seen, insuring one person for \$30,000 is not the same risk as insuring three people for \$10,000 each. When each instance is an instance of the same kind of random variable, though, it's easy to fall into the trap of writing all of them with the same symbol. Don't make this common mistake. Make sure you write each instance as a *different* random variable. Just because each random variable describes a similar situation doesn't mean that each random outcome will be the same.

These are *random* variables, not the variables you saw in Algebra. Being random, they take on different values each time they're evaluated. So what you really mean is $X_1 + X_2 + X_3$. Written this way, it's clear that the sum shouldn't necessarily equal 3 times *anything.*

Hitting the Road STEP-BY-STEP

You're planning to spend next year wandering through the mountains of Kyrgyzstan. You plan to sell your used Isuzu Trooper and purchase an off-road Honda motor scooter when you get there. Used Isuzus of the year and mileage of yours are selling for a mean of \$6940 with a standard deviation of \$250. Your research shows that scooters in Kyrgyzstan are going for about 65,000 Kyrgyzstan soms with a standard deviation of 500 soms. You have to survive on your profit, so you want to estimate what you can expect in your pocket after the sale and subsequent purchase. One U.S. dollar is worth about 46 Kyrgyzstan soms.

Think Define your variables.

Let A = sale price of your Isuzu (in dollars),
B = purchase of a scooter (in soms), and
D = profit (in soms).

Write an appropriate equation.

$D = 46A - B$

Check the conditions.

The sale and purchase are independent.

Show Find the expected value, using the appropriate rules.

$$E(D) = E(46A - B)$$
$$= 46E(A) - E(B)$$
$$= 46(6{,}940) - (65{,}000)$$
$$E(D) = 254{,}240 \text{ soms}$$

Find the variance, using the appropriate rules. Be sure to check the conditions first!

Since the sale and purchase are independent,

$$Var(D) = Var(46A - B).$$
$$= (46)^2 Var(A) + Var(B)$$
$$= 2{,}116(250)^2 + (500)^2$$
$$Var(D) = 132{,}500{,}000$$

Find the standard deviation.

$$SD(D) = \sqrt{132{,}500{,}000} = 11{,}511 \text{ soms}$$

Tell State your conclusion.

You can expect to clear about 254,240 soms with a standard deviation of 11,511 soms.

✓ Reality Check

We'd better convert back to dollars to get some sense of whether this result is plausible. We calculate a mean of about \$5527 with a standard deviation of about \$250. That seems reasonable.

Combining Normal Random Variables

When two random variables have Normal models, so does their sum or difference. This simple fact is very important. It allows us to apply our knowledge of Normal probabilities to questions about the sum or difference of independent random variables

Packaging Stereos STEP-BY-STEP

A company manufactures small stereo systems. At the end of the production line, the stereos are packaged and prepared for shipping. Stage 1 of this process is called "packing." Workers must collect all the system components (a main unit, two speakers, a power cord, an antenna, and some wires), put each in plastic bags, and then place everything inside a protective styrofoam form. The packed form then moves on to Stage 2, called "boxing." There workers place the form and a packet of instructions in a cardboard box, close it, then seal and label the box for shipping.

The company says that times required by the packing stage can be described by a Normal model with a mean of 9 minutes and standard deviation of 1.5 minutes. The times for the boxing stage can also be modeled as Normal, with a mean of 6 minutes and standard deviation of 1 minute.

Two questions:

1. What is the probability that packing two consecutive systems takes over 20 minutes?
2. What percentage of the stereo systems take longer to pack than to box?

Think

1. What is the probability that packing two consecutive systems takes over 20 minutes?

Define your variables

Let P_1 = time for packing the first system

P_2 = time for packing the second

T = total time to pack two systems

Write an appropriate equation.

$T = P_1 + P_2$

Check the conditions.

We are told that a Normal model applies, and can assume the times it takes to pack these systems are independent.

Show

Find the expected value.

$$E(T) = E(P_1 + P_2) = E(P_1) + E(P_2) = 9 + 9 = 18 \text{ minutes}$$

For sums of independent random variables, variances add.

Since the times are independent,

$$Var(T) = Var(P_1 + P_2) = Var(P_1) + Var(P_2) = 1.5^2 + 1.5^2$$

$$Var(T) = 4.50$$

Find the standard deviation.

$$SD(T) = \sqrt{4.50} \approx 2.12 \text{ minutes}$$

We model T with $N(18, 4.50)$

Sketch a picture of the Normal model for the total time, shading the region representing over 20 minutes.

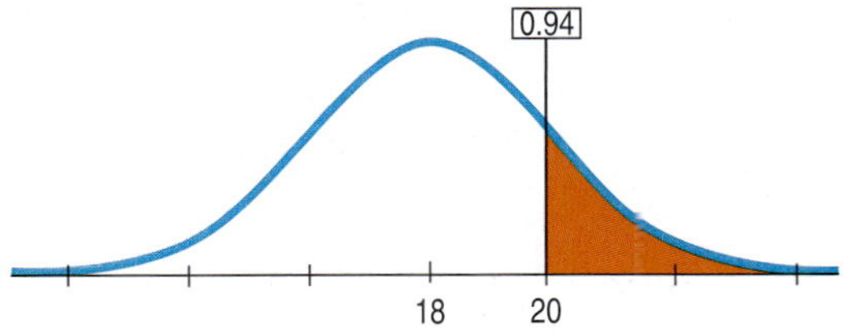

Find the z-score for 20 minutes.

$$z = \frac{20 - 18}{2.12} = 0.94$$

Use technology or a table to find the probability.

$$P(T > 20) = P(z > 0.94) = 0.1736$$

Tell

State your conclusion.

There's a little more than a 17% chance that it will take a total of over 20 minutes to pack two consecutive stereo systems.

Think

2. What percentage of the stereo systems take longer to pack than to box?

Define your variables.

Let P = time for packing a system

B = time for boxing a system

D = difference in times to pack and box a system

Write an appropriate equation.

$D = P - B$

What are we trying to find?

The probability that it takes longer to pack than to box a system is the probability that the difference $P - B$ is greater than zero.

Don't forget the conditions.

We are told that a Normal model applies, and we can assume the times it takes to pack and box these systems are independent.

Show

Find the expected value.

$E(D) = E(P - B)$
$= E(P) - E(B)$
$= 9 - 6 = 3$ minutes

For the difference of independent random variables, variances add.

Since the times are independent,
$Var(D) = Var(P - B)$
$= Var(P) + Var(B)$
$= 1.5^2 + 1^2$
$Var(D) = 3.25$

Find the standard deviation.

$SD(D) = \sqrt{3.25} \approx 1.80$ minutes

We model D with $N(3, 1.80)$

Sketch a picture of the Normal model for the difference in times and shade the region representing a difference greater than zero.

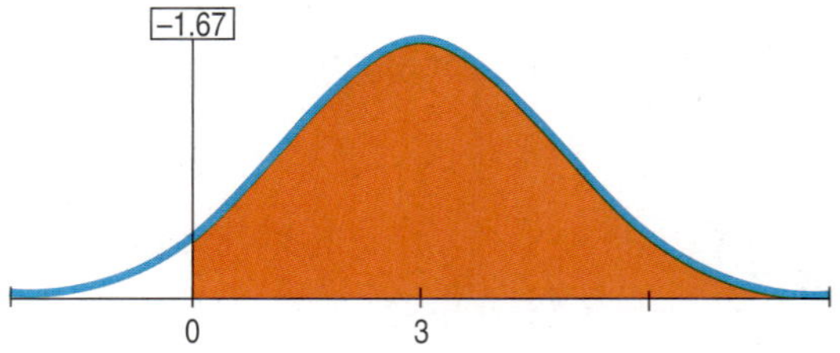

Find the z-score for 0 minutes, then use a table or technology to find the probability.

$$z = \frac{0 - 3}{1.80} = -1.67$$

$$P(D > 0) = P(z > -1.67) = 0.9525$$

Tell

State your conclusion.

About 95% of all the stereo systems will require more time for packing than for boxing.

What Can Go Wrong?

- ***Probability models are still just models.*** Models can be useful, but they are not reality. Think about the assumptions behind your models. Are your dice really perfectly fair? (They are probably pretty close.) But when you hear that the probability of a nuclear accident is 1/10,000,000 per year, is that likely to be a precise value? Question probabilities as you would data.
- ***If the model is wrong, so is everything else.*** Before you try to find the mean or standard deviation of a random variable, check to make sure the probability model is reasonable. As a start, the probabilities in your model should add up to 1. If not, you may have calculated a probability incorrectly, or left out a value of the random variable. For instance, in the insurance example, the description mentions only death and disability. Good health is by far the most likely outcome, not to mention the best for both you and the insurance company (who gets to keep your money). Don 't overlook that.

  To find the expected value of the sum or difference of random variables, we simply add or subtract means. Center is easy; spread is trickier. Watch out for some common traps.
- ***Watch out for variables that aren't independent.*** You can add expected values of *any* two random variables, but you can only add variances of independent random variables. Suppose a survey includes questions about the number of hours of sleep people get each night and also the number of hours they are awake each day. From their answers we find the mean and standard deviation of hours

asleep and hours awake. The expected total must be 24 hours; after all, people are either asleep or awake.[2] The means still add just fine. Since all the totals are exactly 24 hours, however, the standard deviation of the total will be 0. We can't add variances here because the number of hours you're awake depends on the number of hours you're sleep. Be sure to check for independence before adding variances.

- ***Variances of independent random variables add. Standard deviations don't.***
- ***Variances of independent random variables add, even when you're looking at the difference between them.***
- ***Don't write independent instances of a random variable with notation that looks like they are the same variables.*** Make sure you write each instance as a different random variable. Just because each random variable describes a similar situation doesn't mean that each random outcome will be the same. These are *random* variables, not the variables you saw in Algebra. Write $X_1 + X_2 + X_3$ rather than $X + X + X$.

Random Variables and the Computer

Statistics packages deal with data, not with random variables. Nevertheless, the calculations needed to find means and standard deviations of random variables are little more than weighted means. Most packages can manage that, but then they are just being overblown calculators. For technological assistance with these calculations, we recommend you pull out your calculator.

Connections

We've seen means, variances, and standard deviations of data. We know that they estimate parameters of models for these data. Now we're looking at the probability models directly. We only have parameters because there is no data to summarize.

It should be no surprise that expected values and standard deviations adjust to shifts and changes of units in the same way as the corresponding data summaries. The fact that we can add variances of independent random quantities is fundamental and will explain why a number of statistical methods work the way they do.

Key Concepts

Random variable A random variable assumes any of several different values as a result of some random event. Random variables are denoted by a capital letter such as *X*.

Discrete random variable A random variable that can take one of a finite number of distinct outcomes is called a discrete random variable.

[2] In spite of the fact that some students do manage to attain a state somewhere between sleeping and wakefulness during Statistics class.

Continuous random variable A random variable that can take any numeric value within a range of values. The range may be infinite or bounded at either or both ends.

Probability model The probability model is a function that associates a probability X with each value of a discrete random variable X, denoted $P(X = x)$, or with any interval of values of a continuous random variable.

Expected value The expected value of a random variable is its theoretical long-run average value, the center of its model. Denoted μ or $E(X)$, it is found by summing the products of variable values and probabilities:

$$\mu = E(X) = \sum x \cdot P(X = x).$$

Standard deviation The standard deviation of a random variable describes the spread in the model, and is the square root of the variance:

$$\sigma^2 = Var(X) = \sum (x - \mu)^2 \cdot P(X = x)$$

$$\sigma = SD(X) = \sqrt{Var(X)}$$

When changing a random variable by a constant:

$E(X \pm c) = E(X) \pm c$ $\quad Var(X \pm c) = Var(X)$

$E(aX) = aE(X)$ $\quad Var(aX) = a^2 Var(X)$

When adding or subtracting random variables:

$E(X \pm Y) = E(X) \pm E(Y)$

and *if X* and *Y are independent,* $Var(X \pm Y) = Var(X) + Var(Y)$

Skills

When you complete this lesson you should:

Think

- Be able to recognize random variables.
- Understand that random variables must be independent in order to determine the variability of their sum or difference by adding variances.

Show

- Be able to find the probability model for a random variable.
- Know how to find the mean (expected value) and the variance of a random variable.
- Always use the proper notation for these population parameters, μ or $E(X)$ for the mean, and σ, $SD(X)$, σ^2, or $Var(X)$ when discussing variability.
- Know how to determine the new mean and standard deviation after adding a constant, multiplying by a constant, or adding or subtracting two independent random variables.

Tell

- Be able to interpret the meaning of the expected value and standard deviation of a random variable in the proper context.

Exercises

1. Expected value. Find the expected value of each random variable:

a)

x	10	20	30
$P(X = x)$	0.3	0.5	0.2

b)

x	2	4	6	8
$P(X = x)$	0.3	0.4	0.2	0.1

2. Expected value. Find the expected value of each random variable:

a)

x	0	1	2
$P(X = x)$	0.2	0.4	0.4

b)

x	100	200	300	400
$P(X = x)$	0.1	0.2	0.5	0.2

3. Pick a card, any card. You draw a card from a deck. If you get a red card, you win nothing. If you get a spade, you win $5. For any club, you win $10 plus an extra $20 for the ace of clubs.

a) Create a probability model for the amount you win at this game.
b) Find the expected amount you'll win.
c) How much would you be willing to pay to play this game?

4. You bet! You roll a die. If it comes up a 6, you win $100. If not, you get to roll again. If you get a 6 the second time, you win $50. If not, you lose.

a) Create a probability model for the amount you win at this game.
b) Find the expected amount you'll win.
c) How much would you be willing to pay to play this game?

5. Kids. A couple plans to have children until they get a girl, but they agree that they will not have more than three children even if all are boys. (Assume boys and girls are equally likely.)

a) Create a probability model for the number of children they'll have.
b) Find the expected number of children.
c) Find the expected number of boys they'll have.

6. Carnival. A carnival game offers a $100 cash prize for anyone who can break a balloon by throwing a dart at it. It costs $5 to play, and you're willing to spend up to $20 trying to win. You estimate that you have about a 10% chance of hitting the balloon on any throw.

a) Create a probability model for this carnival game.
b) Find the expected number of darts you'll throw.
c) Find your expected winnings.

7. Software. A small software company bids on two contracts. It anticipates a profit of $50,000 if it gets the larger contract and a profit of $20,000 on the smaller contract. The company estimates there's a 30% chance it will get the larger contract and a 60% chance it will get the smaller contract. Assuming the contracts will be awarded independently, what's the expected profit?

8. Racehorse. A man buys a racehorse for $20,000, and enters it in two races. He plans to sell the horse afterward, hoping to make a profit. If the horse wins both races, its value will jump to $100,000. If it wins one of the races, it will be worth $50,000. If it loses both races, it will be worth only $10,000. The man believes there's a 20% chance that the horse will win the first race and a 30% chance it will win the second one. Assuming that the two races are independent events, find the man's expected profit.

9. Variation 1. Find the standard deviations of the random variables in Exercise 1.

10. Variation 2. Find the standard deviations of the random variables in Exercise 2.

11. Pick another card. Find the standard deviation of the amount you might win drawing a card in Exercise 3.

12. The die. Find the standard deviation of the amount you might win rolling a die in Exercise 4.

13. Kids. Find the standard deviation of the number of children the couple in Exercise 5 may have.

14. Darts. Find the standard deviation of your winnings throwing darts in Exercise 6.

15. Repairs. The probability model below describes the number of repair calls that an appliance repair shop may receive during an hour.

Repair Calls	0	1	2	3
Probability	0.1	0.3	0.4	0.2

a) How many calls should the shop expect per hour?
b) What is the standard deviation?

16. Red lights. A commuter must pass through five traffic lights on her way to work, and will have to stop at each one that is red. She estimates the probability model for the number of red lights she hits, as shown below.

X = # of red	0	1	2	3	4	5
$P(X = x)$	0.05	0.25	0.35	0.15	0.15	0.05

a) How many red lights should she expect to hit each day?
b) What's the standard deviation?

17. Defects. A consumer organization inspecting new cars found that many had appearance defects (dents, scratches, paint chips, etc.). While none had more than three of these defects, 7% had three, 11% two, and 21% one defect. Find the expected number of appearance defects in a new car, and the standard deviation.

18. Insurance. An insurance policy costs \$100, and will pay policyholders \$10,000 if they suffer a major injury (resulting in hospitalization) or \$3,000 if they suffer a minor injury (resulting in lost time from work). The company estimates that each year 1 in every 2,000 policyholders may have a major injury, and 1 in 500 a minor injury.

a) Create a probability model for the profit on a policy.
b) What's the company 's expected profit on this policy?
c) What's the standard deviation?

19. Contest. You play two games against the same opponent. The probability you win the first game is 0.4. If you win the first game, the probability you also win the second is 0.2. If you lose the first game, the probability that you win the second is 0.3.

a) Are the two games independent? Explain your answer.
b) What's the probability you lose both games?
c) What's the probability you win both games?
d) Let random variable X be the number of games you win. Find the probability model for X.
e) What are the expected value and standard deviation of X?

20. Contracts. Your company bids for two contracts. You believe the probability you get contract #1 is 0.8. If you get contract #1, the probability you also get contract #2 will be 0.2, and if you do not get #1, the probability you get #2 will be 0.3.

a) Are the two contracts independent? Explain.
b) Find the probability you get both contracts.
c) Find the probability you get no contract.
d) Let X be the number of contracts you get. Find the probability model for X.
e) Find the expected value and standard deviation of X.

21. Batteries. In a group of 10 batteries, 3 are dead. You choose 2 batteries at random.

a) Create a probability model for the number of good batteries you get.
b) What's the expected number of good ones you get?
c) What's the standard deviation?

22. Kittens. In a litter of seven kittens, three are female. You pick two kittens at random.

a) Create a probability model for the number of male kittens you get.
b) What's the expected number of males?
c) What's the standard deviation?

23. Random variables. Given independent random variables with means and standard deviations as shown, find the mean and standard deviation of each of these variables:

a) $3X$
b) $Y + 6$
c) $X + Y$
d) $X - Y$

	Mean	SD
X	10	2
Y	20	5

24. Random variables. Given independent random variables with means and standard deviations as shown, find the mean and standard deviation of each of these variables:

a) $X - 20$
b) $0.5Y$
c) $X + Y$
d) $X - Y$

	Mean	SD
X	80	12
Y	12	3

25. Random variables. Given independent random variables with means and standard deviations as shown, find the mean and standard deviation of each of these variables:

a) $0.8Y$
b) $2X - 100$
c) $X + 2Y$
d) $3X - Y$

	Mean	SD
X	120	12
Y	300	16

26. Random variables. Given independent random variables with means and standard deviations as shown, find the mean and standard deviation of each of these variables:

a) $2Y + 20$
b) $3X$
c) $0.25X + Y$
d) $X - 5Y$

	Mean	SD
X	80	12
Y	12	3

27. Eggs. A grocery supplier believes that in a dozen eggs, the mean number of broken ones is 0.6 with a standard deviation of 0.5 eggs. You buy 3 dozen eggs without checking them.

a) How many broken eggs do you expect to get?
b) What's the standard deviation?
c) What assumptions did you have to make about the eggs in order to answer this question?

28. Garden. A company selling vegetable seeds in packets of 20 estimates that the mean number of seeds that will actually grow is 18, with a standard deviation of 1.2 seeds. You buy 5 different seed packets.

a) How many bad seeds do you expect to get?
b) What's the standard deviation?
c) What assumptions did you make about the seeds? Do you think that assumption is warranted? Explain.

29. Repair calls. Find the mean and standard deviation of the number of repair calls the appliance shop in Exercise 15 should expect during an 8-hour day.

30. Stop! Find the mean and standard deviation of the number of red lights the commuter in Exercise 16 should expect to hit on her way to work during a 5-day work week.

31. Fire! An insurance company estimates that it should make an annual profit of $150 on each homeowner's policy written, with a standard deviation of $6000.
a) Why is the standard deviation so large?
b) If it writes only two of these policies, what are the mean and standard deviation of the annual profit?
c) If it writes 10,000 of these policies, what are the mean and standard deviation of the annual profit?
d) Do you think the company is likely to be profitable? Explain.
e) What assumptions underlie your analysis? Can you think of circumstances under which those assumptions might be violated? Explain.

32. Casino. A casino knows that people play the slot machines in hopes of hitting the jackpot, but that most of them lose their dollar. Suppose a certain machine pays out an average of $0.92, with a standard deviation of $120.
a) Why is the standard deviation so large?
b) If you play 5 times, what are the mean and standard deviation of the casino's profit?
c) If gamblers play this machine 1000 times in a day, what are the mean and standard deviation of the casino's profit?
d) Do you think the casino is likely to be profitable? Explain.

33. Cereal. The amount of cereal that can be poured into a small bowl varies with a mean of 1.5 ounces and a standard deviation of 0.3 ounces. A large bowl holds a mean of 2.5 ounces with a standard deviation of 0.4 ounces. You open a new box of cereal and pour one large and one small bowl.
a) How much more cereal do you expect to be in the large bowl?
b) What's the standard deviation of this difference?
c) If the difference follows a Normal model, what's the probability the small bowl contains more cereal than the large one?
d) What are the mean and standard deviation of the total amount of cereal in the two bowls?
e) If the total follows a Normal model, what's the probability you poured out more than 4.5 ounces of cereal in the two bowls together?
f) The amount of cereal the manufacturer puts in the boxes is a random variable with a mean of 16.3 ounces and a standard deviation of 0.2 ounces. Find the expected amount of cereal left in the box, and the standard deviation.

34. Pets. The American Veterinary Association claims that the annual cost of medical care for dogs averages $100 with a standard deviation of $30, and for cats averages $120 with a standard deviation of $35.
a) What's the expected difference in the cost of medical care for dogs and cats?
b) What's the standard deviation of that difference?
c) If the difference in costs can be described by a Normal model, what's the probability that medical expenses are higher for someone's dog than for her cat?

35. More cereal. In Exercise 33 we poured a large and a small bowl of cereal from a box. Suppose the amount of cereal that the manufacturer puts in the boxes is a random variable with mean 16.2 ounces, and standard deviation 0.1 ounces.
a) Find the expected amount of cereal left in the box.
b) What's the standard deviation?
c) If the weight of the remaining cereal can be described by a Normal model, what's the probability that the box still contains more than 13 ounces?

36. More pets. You're thinking about getting two dogs and a cat. Assume that annual veterinary expenses are independent and have a Normal model with the means and standard deviations described in Exercise 34.
a) Define appropriate variables and express the total annual veterinary costs you may have.
b) Describe the model for this total cost. Be sure to specify its name, expected value, and standard deviation.
c) What's the probability that your total expenses will exceed $400?

37. Medley. In the 4 × 100 medley relay event, four swimmers swim 100 yards, each using a different stroke. A college team preparing for the conference championship looks at the times their swimmers have posted and creates a model based on the following assumptions:
- The swimmers' performances are independent.
- Each swimmer's times follow a Normal model.
- The means and standard deviations of the times (in seconds) are as shown:

Swimmer	Mean	St. Dev.
1 (backstroke)	50.72	0.24
2 (breaststroke)	55.51	0.22
3 (butterfly)	49.43	0.25
4 (freestyle)	44.91	0.21

a) What are the mean and standard deviation for the relay team's total time in this event?
b) The team's best time so far this season was 3:19.48. (That's 199.48 seconds.) Do you think the team is likely to swim faster than this at the conference championship? Explain.

38. Bikes. Bicycles arrive at a bike shop in boxes. Before they can be sold, they must be unpacked, assembled, and tuned (lubricated, adjusted, etc.). Based on past experience, the shop manager makes the following assumptions about how long this may take:

- The times for each setup phase are independent.
- The times for each phase follow a Normal model.
- The means and standard deviations of the times (in minutes) are as shown:

Phase	Mean	St. Dev.
Unpacking	3.5	0.7
Assembly	21.8	2.4
Tuning	12.3	2.7

a) What are the mean and standard deviation for the total bicycle setup time?

b) A customer decides to buy a bike like one of the display models, but wants a different color. The shop has one, still in the box. The manager says they can have it ready in half an hour. Do you think the bike will be set up and ready to go as promised? Explain.

39. Farmers' market. A farmer has 100 lb of apples and 50 lb of potatoes for sale. The market price for apples (per pound) each day is a random variable with a mean of 0.5 dollars and a standard deviation of 0.2 dollars. Similarly, for a pound of potatoes, the mean price is 0.3 dollars and the standard deviation is 0.1 dollars. It also costs him 2 dollars to bring all the apples and potatoes to the market. The market is busy with eager shoppers, so we can assume that he'll be able to sell all of each type of produce at that day's price.

a) Define your random variables, and use them to express the farmer's net income.

b) Find the mean.

c) Find the standard deviation of the net income.

d) Do you need to make any assumptions in calculating the mean? How about the standard deviation?

40. Bike sale. The Exercise 38 bicycle shop will be offering 2 specially priced children's models at a sidewalk sale. The basic model will sell for $120 and the deluxe model for $150. Past experience indicates that sales of the basic model will have a mean of 5.4 bikes with a standard deviation of 1.2, and sales of the deluxe model will have a mean of 3.2 bikes with a standard deviation of 0.8 bikes. The cost of setting up for the sidewalk sale is $200.

a) Define random variables and use them to express the bicycle shop's net income.

b) What's the mean of the net income?

c) What's the standard deviation of the net income?

d) Do you need to make any assumptions in calculating the mean? How about the standard deviation?

Chapter 17

Probability Models

When we last saw our heroine, she was . . .

Oops! Wrong book. What we mean to say is that several chapters ago we simulated buying cereal boxes to get sports cards You remember the setup:

Suppose a cereal manufacturer puts pictures of famous athletes on cards in boxes of cereal, in the hope of increasing sales. The manufacturer announces that 20% of the boxes contain a picture of Tiger Woods, 30% a picture of Lance Armstrong, and the rest a picture of Serena Williams.

Now, instead of simulation, we can use probability.

Searching for Tiger

Tiger Woods. **Figure 17.1**

You've *got* to have the Tiger Woods picture, so you start madly opening boxes of cereal, hoping to find one. Assuming that the pictures are randomly distributed, there's a 20% chance you succeed on any box you open. We call the act of opening a box a "trial," and note that:

- There are only two possible outcomes (called *success* and *failure*) on each trial. Either you get Tiger's picture or you don't.
- The probability of success, denoted p, is the same on every trial. Here $p = 0.20$.
- The trials are independent. Finding Tiger in the first box does not change what might happen when you reach for the next box.

Situations like this occur often, and are called **Bernoulli trials.** Common examples of Bernoulli trials include tossing a coin, looking for defective products rolling off an assembly line, or even shooting free throws in a basketball game.

Daniel Bernoulli (1700–1782) was the nephew of Jakob, whom you saw in Chapter 14. He was the first to work out the mathematics for what we now call Bernoulli trials.
Figure 17.2

Back to Tiger. What's the probability you find his picture in the first box of cereal? It's 20%, of course. We could write P(#boxes = 1) = 0.20.

How about the probability that you don't find Tiger until the second box? Well, that means you fail on the first trial and then succeed on the second. With the probability of success 20%, the probability of failure, denoted q, is $1 - 0.2 = 80\%$. Since the trials are independent, the probability of getting your first success on the second trial is $P(\#\text{boxes} = 2) = (0.8)(0.2) = 0.16$.

Of course, you could have a run of bad luck. Maybe you won't find Tiger until the fifth box of cereal. What are the chances of that? You'd have to fail 4 straight times and then succeed, so $P(\#\text{boxes} = 5) = (0.8)^4(0.2) = 0.08192$.

How many boxes might you expect to have to open? We could reason that since Tiger's picture is in 20% of the boxes, or 1 in 5, we expect to find his picture, on average, in the fifth box; that is, $\mu = \dfrac{1}{0.2} = 5$ boxes. That's correct, but not easy to prove. See how in the Math Box.

The Geometric Model

A single Bernoulli trial is usually not all that interesting. We might not care about a particular cereal box. We are more likely to want to know how long it will take us to achieve a success. The model that tells us this probability is called the **Geometric probability model.** Geometric models are completely specified by one parameter, p, the probability of success, and are denoted Geom(p). Since achieving the first success on trial number X requires first experiencing $X - 1$ failures, the probabilities are easily expressed by a formula.

> **Geometric probability model for Bernoulli trials: Geom(p)**
>
> p = probability of success (and $q = 1 - p$ = probability of failure)
> X = number of trials until the first success occurs
>
> $$P(X = x) = q^{x-1}p$$
>
> Expected value: $\mu = \dfrac{1}{p}$
>
> Standard deviation: $\sigma = \sqrt{\dfrac{q}{p^2}}$

Math Box

We want to find the mean (expected value) of random variable X, using a geometric model with probability of success p.

First, write the probabilities:

x	1	2	3	4	...
$P(X=x)$	p	qp	q^2p	q^3p	...

The expected value is: $E(X) = 1p + 2qp + 3q^2p + 4q^3p + \cdots$

Let $p = 1 - q$: $= (1-q) + 2q(1-q) + 3q^2(1-q) + 4q^3(1-q) + \cdots$

Simplify: $= 1 - q + 2q - 2q^2 + 3q^2 - 3q^3 + 4q^3 - 4q^4 + \cdots$

That's an infinite geometric series, with first term 1 and common ratio q: $= 1 + q + q^2 + q^3 + \cdots$

$$= \frac{1}{1-q}$$

So, finally . . . $E(X) = \frac{1}{p}$.

Independence

One of the important requirements for Bernoulli trials is that the trials be independent. Sometimes that's a reasonable assumption. Is it true for our example? We said that whether we find a Tiger Woods card in one box has no effect on the probabilities in other boxes. This is *almost* true. If exactly 20% of the boxes have Tiger Woods cards, then when you find one, you've reduced the number of remaining Tiger Woods cards. With a few million boxes of cereal, the difference is hardly worth mentioning.

But if you knew there were 2 Tiger Woods cards hiding in the 10 boxes of cereal on the market shelf, then finding one in the first box you try would clearly change your chances of finding Tiger in the next box.

If we had an infinite number of boxes, there wouldn't be a problem. It's selecting from a finite population that causes the probabilities to change, making the trials not independent. Obviously, taking 2 out of 10 boxes changes the probability. Taking even a few hundred out of millions, though, makes very little difference. Fortunately, we have a rule of thumb for the in-between cases. If we've looked at less than 10% of the population, we can pretend that the trials are still independent.

The 10% condition

Bernoulli trials must be independent. If that assumption is violated, it is still okay to proceed as long as the sample is smaller than 10% of the population.

Working with a Geometric Model STEP-BY-STEP

People with O-negative blood are called "universal donors" because O-negative blood can be given to anyone else, regardless of the recipient's blood type. Only about 6% of people have O-negative blood. If donors line up at random for a blood drive, how many do you expect to examine before you find someone who has O-negative blood? What's the probability that the first O-negative donor found is one of the first four people in line?

Think

Check to see that these are Bernoulli trials.

- There are two outcomes:
  success = O-negative
  failure = other blood types
- The probability of success for each person is $p = 0.06$, because they have lined up at random.
- Trials are *not* independent, because the population is finite, *but* the donors lined up are fewer than 10% of all possible donors.

Define the random variable and specify the model.

Let X = number of donors until an O-negative is found.

We can model X with Geom(0.06).

Show

Find the mean.

$$E(X) = \frac{1}{0.06} \approx 16.7$$

Calculate the probability of success on one of the first four trials. That's the probability that $X = 1, 2, 3,$ *or* 4.

$$P(X \le 4) = P(X = 1) + P(X = 2) + P(X = 3) + P(X = 4)$$

$$= (0.06) + (0.94)(0.06) + (0.94)^2(0.06) + (0.94)^3(0.06)$$

$$\approx 0.2193$$

Tell

State your conclusion.

In blood drives such as this one, we expect to examine an average of 16.7 people to find a universal donor. About 22% of the time we'll find one within the first 4 people in line.

TI Tips

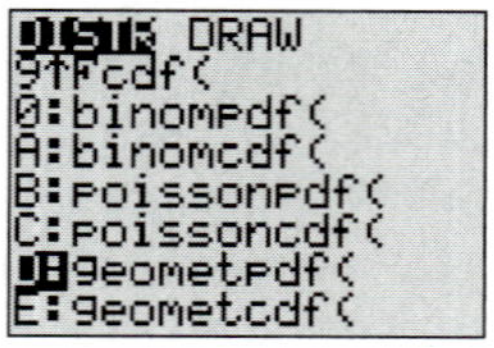

Your TI knows the geometric model. Just as you saw back in Chapter 6 with the Normal model, commands to calculate probability distributions are found in the **2nd DISTR** menu. Have a look. After many others (Don't drop the course yet!) you'll see two Geometric probability functions at the bottom of the list.

- **D:geometpdf(.**

  The "pdf" stands for "probability density function." This command allows you to find the probability of any *individual* outcome. You need only specify p, which defines the Geometric model, and x, which indicates the number of trials until you get a success. The format is **geometpdf(p,x)**.

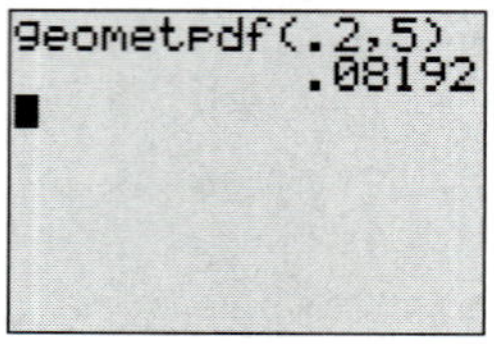

  For example, suppose we want to know the probability that we find our first Tiger Woods picture in the fifth box of cereal. Since Tiger is in 20% of the boxes, we use $p = 0.2$ and $x = 5$, entering the command **geometpdf(.2,5)**. The calculator says there's about an 8% chance.

- **E:geometcdf(.**

  This is the "cumulative density function," meaning that it finds the sum of the probabilities of several possible outcomes. In general, the command

`geometcdf(p,x)` calculates the probability of finding the first success *on or before* the *x*th trial.

Let's find the probability of getting a Tiger Woods picture by the time we open the fourth box of cereal—in other words, the probability our first success comes on the first box, or the second, or the third, or the fourth. Again we specify $p = 0.2$, and now use $x = 4$. The command `geometcdf(.2,4)` calculates all the probabilities and adds them. There's about a 59% chance that our quest for a Tiger Woods photo will succeed by the time we open the fourth box.

The Binomial Model

Same situation, different question. You buy 5 boxes of cereal. What's the probability you get *exactly* 2 pictures of Tiger Woods? Before, we asked how long it would take until our first success. Now we want to find the probability of getting 2 successes among the 5 trials. We are still talking about Bernoulli trials, but now we're asking a different question.

This time we're interested in the *number of successes* in the 5 trials. We want to find $P(\#\text{successes} = 2)$. This is an example of a binomial probability. It takes two parameters to define this **Binomial model;** the number of trials, n, and the probability of success, p. We denote this Binom(n, p). Here, $n = 5$ trials, and $p = 0.2$, the probability of finding a Tiger Woods card in any trial.

Exactly 2 successes in 5 trials means 2 successes and 3 failures. It seems logical that the probability should be $(0.2)^2(0.8)^3$. Too bad! It's not that easy. That calculation would give you the probability of finding Tiger in the first 2 boxes and not in the next 3—*in that order.* Still, you could find Tiger in the third and fifth boxes and still have 2 successes. The probability of those outcomes in that particular order is $(0.8)(0.8)(0.2)(0.8)(0.2)$. That's also $(0.2)^2(0.8)^3$. In fact, the probability will always be the same no matter what order the successes and failures occur in. Anytime we get 2 successes in 5 trials, no matter what the order, the probability will be $(0.2)^2(0.8)^3$. But we need to take account of all the possible orders in which the outcomes can occur.

Notice that these possible orders are *disjoint.* (For example, if your successes came on the first two trials, they couldn't come on the last two.) So we can use the Addition Rule and add up the probabilities for all the possible orderings. Since the probabilities are all the same, we only need to know how many orders are possible. For small numbers, we can just make a tree diagram and count the branches. For larger numbers this isn't practical, so we let the computer or calculator do the work.

Each different order in which we can have k successes in n trials is called a "combination." The total number of ways that can happen is written $\binom{n}{k}$ or ${}_nC_k$ and pronounced "n choose k."

$$\binom{n}{k} = {}_nC_k = \frac{n!}{k!(n-k)!} \text{ where } n! = n \times (n-1) \times \ldots \times 1$$

For 2 successes in 5 trials,

$$\binom{5}{2} = {}_5C_2 = \frac{5!}{2!(5-2)!} = \frac{5 \times 4 \times 3 \times 2 \times 1}{2 \times 1 \times 3 \times 2 \times 1} = \frac{5 \times 4}{2 \times 1} = 10.$$

So there are 10 ways to get 2 Tiger pictures in 5 boxes, and the probability of each is $(0.2)^2(0.8)^3$. Now we can find what we wanted:

$$P(\#\text{successes} = 2) = 10(0.2)^2(0.8)^3 = 0.2048.$$

In general, the probability of exactly k successes in n trials is $\binom{n}{k} p^k q^{n-k}$.

Using this formula, we could find the expected value by adding up $x \cdot P(X = x)$ for all values, but it would be a long, hard way to get an answer that you already know intuitively. What's the expected value? If we have 5 boxes, and Tiger's picture is in 20% of them, then we would expect to have $5(0.2) = 1$ success. If we had 100 trials with probability of success 0.2, how many successes would you expect? Can you think of any reason not to say 20? It seems so simple that most people wouldn't even think about it. You just multiply the probability of success by n. In other words, $E(X) = np$. Not fully convinced? We prove that in the next Math Box.

The standard deviation is less obvious; you can't just rely on your intuition. Fortunately, the formula for the standard deviation also boils down to something simple: $SD(X) = \sqrt{npq}$. If you're curious to know where that comes from, it's in the Math Box, too. Have a look.

In 100 boxes of cereal, we expect to find 20 Tiger Woods cards, with a standard deviation of $\sqrt{100 \times 0.8 \times 0.2} = 4$ pictures.

Time to summarize. A Binomial probability model describes the number of successes in a specified number of trials. It takes two parameters to specify this model: the number of trials n and the probability of success p.

Binomial probability model for Bernoulli trials: Binom(n, p)

n = number of trials

p = probability of success (and $q = 1 - p$ = probability of failure)

X = number of successes in n trials

$$P(X = x) = \binom{n}{x} p^x q^{n-x}, \text{ where } \binom{n}{x} = \frac{n!}{x!(n-x)!}$$

Mean: $\mu = np$

Standard deviation: $\sigma = \sqrt{npq}$

Math Box

To derive the formulas for the mean and standard deviation of a Binomial model we start with the most basic situation.

Consider a single Bernoulli trial with probability of success p. Let's find the mean and variance of the number of successes.

Here's the probability model for the number of successes:

x	0	1
$P(X = x)$	q	p

Find the expected value:

$$E(X) = 0q + 1p$$
$$E(X) = p$$

And now the variance:

$$\begin{aligned} Var(X) &= (0-p)^2 q + (1-p)^2 p \\ &= p^2 q + q^2 p \\ &= pq(p+q) \\ &= pq(1) \\ Var(X) &= pq \end{aligned}$$

What happens when there is more than one trial, though? A Binomial model simply counts the number of successes in a series of n independent Bernoulli trials. That makes it easy to find the mean and standard deviation of a binomial random variable, Y.

$$\begin{aligned} \text{Let } Y &= X_1 + X_2 + X_3 + \cdots + X_n \\ E(Y) &= E(X_1 + X_2 + X_3 + \cdots + X_n) \\ &= E(X_1) + E(X_2) + E(X_3) + \cdots + E(X_n) \\ &= p + p + p + \cdots + p \text{ (There are } n \text{ terms.)} \end{aligned}$$

So, as we thought, the mean is $E(Y) = np$.

And since the trials are independent, the variances add:

$$\begin{aligned} Var(Y) &= Var(X_1 + X_2 + X_3 + \cdots + X_n) \\ &= Var(X_1) + Var(X_2) + Var(X_3) + \cdots + Var(X_n) \\ &= pq + pq + pq + \cdots + pq \text{ (Again, } n \text{ terms)} \\ Var(Y) &= npq \end{aligned}$$

Voila! The standard deviation is $SD(Y) = \sqrt{npq}$.

Working with a Binomial Model STEP-BY-STEP

Suppose 20 donors come to the blood drive. What are the mean and standard deviation of the number of universal donors among them? What is the probability that there are 2 or 3 universal donors?

Think

Check to see that these are Bernoulli trials.

- There are two outcomes:
  success = O-negative
  failure = other blood types
- $p = 0.06$, because people have lined up at random.
- Trials are *not* independent, because the population is finite, *but* fewer than 10% of all possible donors are lined up.

Define the random variable and specify the model.

Let X = number of O-negative donors among $n = 20$ people

We can model X with Binom(20, 0.06).

Show Find the expected value and standard deviation.

$E(X) = np = 20(0.06) = 1.2$

$SD(X) = \sqrt{npq} = \sqrt{20(0.06)(0.94)} \approx 1.06$

Calculate the probability of 2 or 3 successes using technology.

$$P(X = 2 \text{ or } 3) = P(X = 2) + P(X = 3)$$
$$= \binom{20}{2}(0.06)^2(0.94)^{18} +$$
$$= \binom{20}{3}(0.06)^3(0.94)^{17}$$
$$\approx 0.2246 + 0.0860 = 0.3106$$

Tell State your conclusion.

In groups of 20 randomly selected blood donors, we expect to find an average of 1.2 universal donors, with a standard deviation of 1.06. About 31% of the time we'll find 2 or 3 universal donors among the 20 people.

TI Tips

Remember how the calculator handles Geometric probabilities? Well, the commands for finding Binomial probabilities are essentially the same. Again you'll find them in the `2nd DISTR` menu.

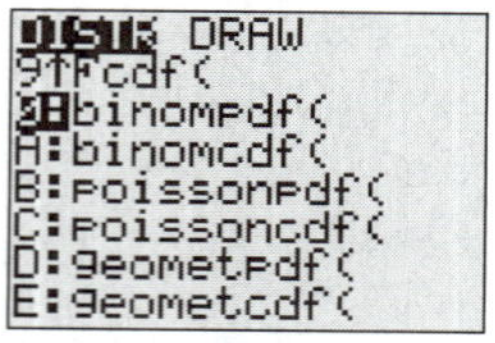

- `0:binompdf(`.

  This probability density function allows you to find the probability of an *individual* outcome. You need to define the Binomial model by specifying n and p, and then indicate the desired number of successes, x. The format is `binompdf(n,p,X)`.

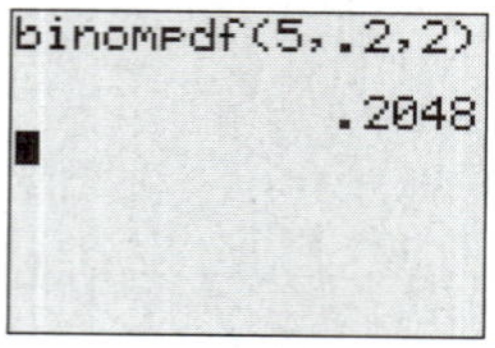

  For example, recall that Tiger Woods' picture is in 20% of the cereal boxes. Suppose that we want to know the probability of finding Tiger exactly twice among 5 boxes of cereal. We use $n = 5$, $p = 0.2$, and $x = 2$, entering the command `binompdf(5,.2,2)`. There's about a 20% chance of getting two pictures of Tiger Woods in five boxes of cereal.

- `A:binomcdf(`.

  Need to add several Binomial probabilities? To find the total probability of getting x or fewer successes among the n trials use the cumulative Binomial density function `A: binomcdf(n,p,X)`.

  For example, suppose we have ten boxes of cereal and wonder about the probability of finding up to 4 pictures of Tiger. That's the probability of 0, 1, 2, 3, or 4 successes, so we specify the command `binomcdf(10,.2,4)`. Pretty likely!

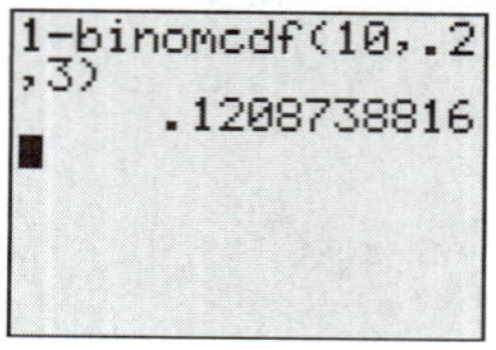

  Of course "up to 4" allows for the possibility that we end up with none. What's the probability we get at least 4 pictures of Tiger in 10 boxes? Well, "at least 4" means "not 3 or fewer." That's the complement of 0, 1, 2, or 3 successes. Have your TI evaluate `1 -binomcdf(10,.2,3)`. There's about a 12% chance we'll find at least four pictures of Tiger in 10 boxes of cereal.

The Normal Model to the Rescue!

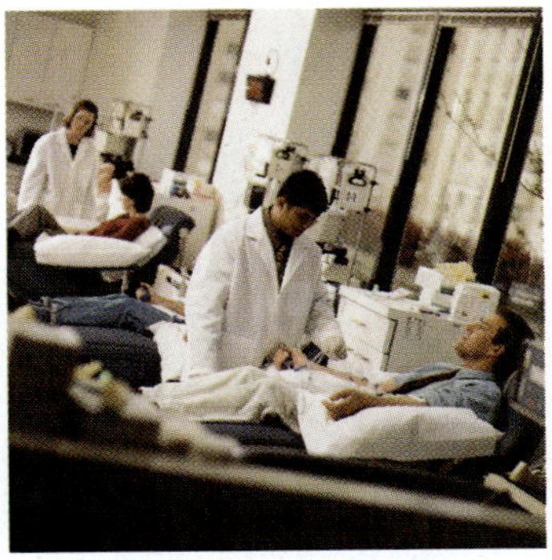

Suppose the Tennessee Red Cross anticipates the need for at least 1850 units of O-negative blood this year. It estimates that it will collect blood from 32,000 donors. How great is the risk that the Tennessee Red Cross will fall short of meeting its need? We've just learned how to calculate such probabilities. We can use the Binomial model with $n = 32{,}000$ and $p = 0.06$. The probability of getting *exactly* 1850 units of O-negative blood from 32,000 donors is ${}_{32000}C_{1850} \times 0.06^{1850} \times 0.94^{30150}$. No calculator on earth can calculate that first term (it has more than 100,000 digits).[1] And that's just the beginning. The problem said *at least* 1850, so we have to do it again for 1851, for 1852, and all the way up to 32,000.

When we're dealing with a large number of trials like this, making direct calculations of the probabilities becomes tedious (or outright impossible). Here an old friend—the Normal model—comes to the rescue.

The Binomial model has mean $np = 1920$ and standard deviation $\sqrt{npq} \approx 42.48$. We could try approximating its distribution with a Normal model, using the same mean and standard deviation. Remarkably enough, that turns out to be a very good approximation. (We'll see why in the next chapter.) With that approximation, we can find the probability:

$$P(X > 1850) = P\left(z > \frac{1850 - 1920}{42.48}\right) \approx P(z > -1.65) \approx 0.95.$$

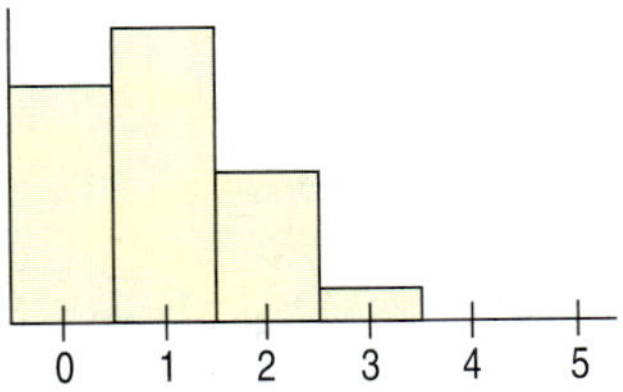

There seems to be about a 5% chance that this Red Cross chapter will run short of O-negative blood.

Can we always use a Normal model to make estimates of Binomial probabilities? No. Consider the Tiger Woods situation—pictures in 20% of the cereal boxes. If we buy five boxes, the actual Binomial probabilities that we get 0, 1, 2, 3, 4, or 5 pictures of Tiger are 33%, 41%, 20%, 5%, 1%, and 0.03%, respectively. The first histogram shows that this probability model is strongly skewed. That makes it clear that we should not try to estimate these probabilities by using a Normal model.

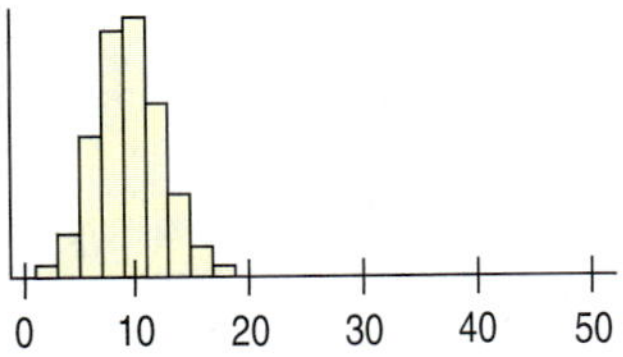

Now suppose we open 50 boxes of this cereal and count the number of Tiger Woods pictures we find. The second histogram shows this probability model. It is centered at $np = 50(0.2) = 10$ pictures, as expected, and it appears to be fairly symmetric around that center. Let's have a closer look.

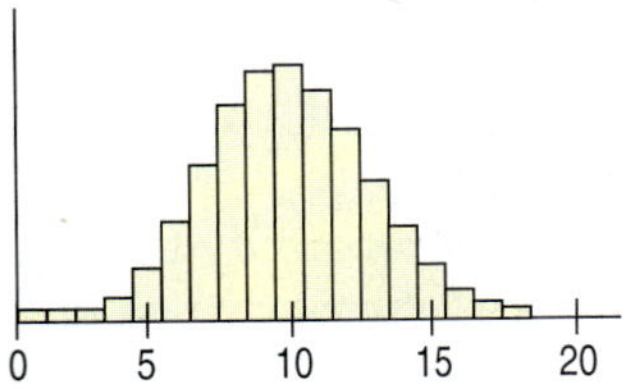

The third histogram again shows Binom(50, 0.2), this time magnified somewhat and centered at the expected value of 10 pictures of Tiger. It looks close to Normal, for sure. With this larger sample size, it appears that a Normal model might be a useful approximation.

We see that a Normal model is close enough only for a large enough number of trials. And what we mean by "large enough" depends on the probability of success. We need a larger sample if the probability of success is very low (or very high). It turns out that a Normal model works pretty well if we expect to see at least 10 successes and 10 failures. That is, we check the **success/failure condition:**

---

[1] If your calculator *can* find Binom(32000, 0.06), then it's smart enough to use an approximation. Read on to see how you can, too.

The success/failure condition

A Binomial model is approximately Normal if we expect at least 10 successes and 10 failures.

$$np \geq 10 \text{ and } nq \geq 10$$

Why 10? Well, actually it's 9, as revealed in the Math Box.

Math Box

It's easy to see where the magic number 10 comes from. You just need to remember how Normal models work. The problem is that a Normal model extends infinitely in both directions. But a Binomial model must have between 0 and n successes, so if we use a Normal to approximate a Binomial, we have to cut off its tails. That's not very important if the center of the Normal model is so far from 0 and n that the lost tails have only a negligible area. More than three standard deviations should do it because a Normal model has little probability past that.

So the mean needs to be at least 3 standard deviations from 0 and at least 3 standard deviations from n. Let's look at the 0 end.

We require:	$\mu - 3\sigma > 0$
Or, in other words:	$\mu > 3\sigma$
For a Binomial that's:	$np > 3\sqrt{npq}$
Squaring yields:	$n^2p^2 > 9npq$
Now simplify:	$np > 9q$
Since $q \leq 1$, we can require:	$np > 9$

For simplicity we usually demand that np (and nq for the other tail) be at least 10 to use the Normal approximation, the **success/failure condition.**

Continuous Random Variables

There's a problem with the Normal model; it can take on *any value.* That means we can no longer list all the possible outcomes and their probabilities, as we could for discrete random variables. Such random variables are called **continuous random variables.**

When we use the Normal model, we no longer calculate the probability that the random variable equals a *particular* value, but only that it lies *between* two values. We won't calculate the probability of getting exactly 1850 units of blood, but we have no problem approximating the probability of getting 1850 *or more,* which was, after all, what we really wanted.[2]

[2]If we really had been interested in a single value, we might have found the probability of getting between 1849.5 and 1850.5 units of blood.

What Can Go Wrong?

- ***Be sure you have Bernoulli trials.*** Be sure to check the requirements first: two outcomes per trial, a constant probability of success, and independence. Remember that the 10% condition provides a reasonable substitute for independence.
- ***Don't confuse Geometric and Binomial models.*** Both involve Bernoulli trials, but the questions are different. If you are repeating trials until your first success, that's a Geometric probability. You don't know in advance how many trials you'll need—theoretically, it could take forever. If you are counting the number of successes in a specified number of trials, that's a Binomial probability.
- ***Don't use the Normal approximation with small n.*** To use a Normal approximation in place of a Binomial model, there must be at least 10 expected successes and 10 expected failures.

The Binomial, the Geometric, and the Computer

Most statistics packages offer functions that compute Binomial probabilities, and many offer functions for Geometric probabilities as well. The only important differences among these functions is in what they are named and the order of their arguments.

Some technology solutions automatically use the Normal approximation for the Binomial when the exact calculations become unmanageable.

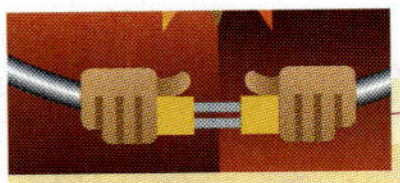

Connections

This chapter builds on what we know about random variables. We now have two more probability models to join the Normal model.

There are a number of "forward" connections from this chapter. We'll see the 10% condition and the success/failure condition often. And the facts about the Binomial distribution can help explain how proportions behave, as we'll see in the next chapter.

Key Concepts

Bernoulli trials, if . . .
1. there are two possible outcomes.
2. the probability of success is constant.
3. the trials are independent.

Geometric probability model A Geometric model is appropriate for a random variable that counts the number of Bernoulli trials until the first success.

Binomial probability model A Binomial model is appropriate for a random variable that counts the number of successes in a fixed number of Bernoulli trials.

Success/failure condition For a Normal model to be a good approximation to a Binomial distribution, we must expect at least 10 successes and 10 failures. That is, $np \geq 10$ and $nq \geq 10$.

Skills

When you complete this lesson you should:

Think

- Know how to tell if a situation involves Bernoulli trials.
- Be able to choose whether to use a Geometric or a Binomial model for a random variable involving Bernoulli trials.

Show

- Know the appropriate conditions for using a Geometric, Binomial, or Normal model.
- Know how to find the expected value of a Geometric model.
- Be able to calculate Geometric probabilities.
- Know how to find the mean and standard deviation of a Binomial model.
- Be able to calculate Binomial probabilities, perhaps with a Normal model.

Tell

- Be able to interpret means, standard deviations, and probabilities in the Bernoulli trial context.

Exercises

1. Bernoulli. Can we use probability models based on Bernoulli trials to investigate the following situations? Explain.

a) We roll 50 dice to find the distribution of the number of spots on the faces.

b) How likely is it that in a group of 120 the majority may have Type A blood, given that Type A is found in 43% of the population?

c) We deal 5 cards from a deck and get all hearts. How likely is that?

d) We wish to predict the outcome of a vote on the school budget, and poll 500 of the 3000 likely voters to see how many favor the proposed budget.

e) A company realizes that about 10% of its packages are not being sealed properly. In a case of 24, is it likely that more than 3 are unsealed?

2. Bernoulli 2. Can we use probability models based on Bernoulli trials to investigate the following situations? Explain.

a) You are rolling 5 dice and need to get at least two 6's to win the game.

b) We record the eye colors found in a group of 500 people.

c) A manufacturer recalls a doll because about 3% have buttons that are not properly attached. Customers return 37 of these dolls to the local toy store. Is the manufacturer likely to find any dangerous buttons?

d) A city council of 11 Republicans and 8 Democrats picks a committee of 4 at random. What's the probability they choose all Democrats?

e) A 2002 Rutgers University study found that 74% of high school students have cheated on a test at least once. Your local high school principal conducts a survey in homerooms and gets responses that admit to cheating from 322 of the 481 students.

3. Simulating the model. Think about the Tiger Woods picture search again. You are opening boxes of cereal one at a time looking for his picture, which is in 20% of the boxes. You want to know how many boxes you might have to open in order to find Tiger.

a) Describe how you would simulate the search for Tiger using random numbers.

b) Run at least 30 trials.

c) Based on your simulation, estimate the probabilities that you might find your first picture of Tiger in the first box, the second, etc.

d) Calculate the actual probability model.

e) Compare the distribution of outcomes in your simulation to the probability model.

4. Simulation II. You are one space short of winning a child's board game, and must roll a 1 on a die to claim victory. You want to know how many rolls it might take.

a) Describe how you would simulate rolling the die until you get a 1.

b) Run at least 30 trials.

c) Based on your simulation, estimate the probabilities that you might win on the first roll, the second, the third, etc.

d) Calculate the actual probability model.

e) Compare the distribution of outcomes in your simulation to the probability model.

5. Tiger again. Let's take one last look at the Tiger Woods picture search. You know his picture is in 20% of the cereal boxes. You buy five boxes to see how many pictures of Tiger you might get.
a) Describe how you would simulate the number of pictures of Tiger you might find in five boxes of cereal.
b) Run at least 30 trials.
c) Based on your simulation, estimate the probabilities that you get no pictures of Tiger, 1 picture, 2 pictures, etc.
d) Calculate the actual probability model.
e) Compare the distribution of outcomes in your simulation to the probability model.

6. Seatbelts. Suppose 75% of all drivers always wear their seatbelts. Let's investigate how many of the drivers might be belted among five cars waiting at a traffic light.
a) Describe how you would simulate the number of seatbelt-wearing drivers among the five cars.
b) Run at least 30 trials.
c) Based on your simulation, estimate the probabilities there are no belted drivers, exactly one, two, etc.
d) Calculate the actual probability model.
e) Compare the distribution of outcomes in your simulation to the probability model.

7. Hoops. A basketball player has made 80% of his foul shots during the season. Assuming the shots are independent, find the probability that in tonight's game he
a) misses for the first time on his fifth attempt.
b) makes his first basket on his fourth shot.
c) makes his first basket on one of his first 3 shots.

8. Chips. Suppose a computer chip manufacturer rejects 2% of the chips produced because they fail pre-sale testing.
a) What's the probability that the fifth chip you test is the first bad one you find?
b) What's the probability you find a bad one within the first 10 you examine?

9. More hoops. For the basketball player in Exercise 7, what's the expected number of shots until he misses?

10. Chips ahoy. For the computer chips described in Exercise 8, how many do you expect to test before finding a bad one?

11. Blood. Only 4% of people have Type AB blood.
a) On average, how many donors must be checked to find someone with Type AB blood?
b) What's the probability that there is a type AB donor among the first 5 people checked?
c) What's the probability that the first Type AB donor will be found among the first 6 people?
d) What's the probability that we won't find a Type AB donor before the tenth person?

12. Colorblindness. About 8% of males are colorblind. A researcher needs some colorblind subjects for an experiment, and begins checking potential subjects.
a) On average, how many men should the researcher expect to check to find one who is colorblind?
b) What's the probability that she won't find anyone colorblind among the first 4 men she checks?
c) What's the probability that the first colorblind man found will be the sixth person checked?
d) What's the probability that she finds someone who is colorblind before checking the tenth man?

13. Lefties. Assume that 13% of people are left-handed. If we select 5 people at random, find the probability of each outcome described below.
a) The first lefty is the fifth person chosen.
b) There are some lefties among the 5 people.
c) The first lefty is the second or third person.
d) There are exactly 3 lefties in the group.
e) There are at least 3 lefties in the group
f) There are no more than 3 lefties in the group.

14. Arrows. An Olympic archer is able to hit the bull's-eye 80% of the time. Assume each shot is independent of the others. If she shoots 6 arrows, what's the probability of each result described below.
a) Her first bull's-eye comes on the third arrow.
b) She misses the bull's-eye at least once.
c) Her first bull's-eye comes on the fourth or fifth arrow.
d) She gets exactly 4 bull's-eyes.
e) She gets at least 4 bull's-eyes.
f) She gets at most 4 bull's-eyes.

15. Lefties redux. Consider our group of 5 people from Exercise 13.
a) How many lefties do you expect?
b) With what standard deviation?
c) If we keep picking people until we find a lefty, how long do you expect it will take?

16. More arrows. Consider our archer from Exercise 14.
a) How many bull's-eyes do you expect her to get?
b) With what standard deviation?
c) If she keeps shooting arrows until she hits the bull's-eye, how long do you expect it will take?

17. Still more lefties. Suppose we choose 12 people instead of the 5 chosen in Exercise 13.
a) Find the mean and standard deviation of the number of right-handers in the group.
b) What's the probability that they're not all right-handed?
c) What's the probability that there are no more than 10 righties?
d) What's the probability that there are exactly 6 of each?
e) What's the probability that the majority is right-handed?

18. Still more arrows. Suppose our archer from Exercise 14 shoots 10 arrows.
a) Find the mean and standard deviation of the number of bull's-eyes she may get.

b) What's the probability that she never misses?
c) What's the probability that there are exactly 8 bull's-eyes?
d) What's the probability that there are no more than 8 bull's-eyes?
e) What's the probability that she hits the bull's-eye more often than she misses?

19. Tennis, anyone? A certain tennis player makes a successful first serve 70% of the time. Assume that each serve is independent of the others. If she serves 6 times, what's the probability she gets
a) all 6 serves in?
b) exactly 4 serves in?
c) at least 4 serves in?
d) no more than 4 serves in?

20. Frogs. A wildlife biologist examines frogs for a genetic trait he suspects may be linked to sensitivity to industrial toxins in the environment. Previous research had established that this trait is usually found in one of every 8 frogs. He collects and examines a dozen frogs. If the frequency of the trait has not changed, what's the probability he finds the trait in
a) none of the 12 frogs?
b) at least 2 frogs?
c) 3 or 4 frogs?
d) no more than 4 frogs?

21. And more tennis. Suppose the tennis player in Exercise 19 serves 80 times in a match.
a) What's the mean and standard deviation of the number of good first serves expected?
b) Verify that you can use a Normal model to approximate the distribution of the number of good first serves.
c) Use the 68-95-99.7 Rule to describe this distribution.
d) What's the probability she makes at least 65 first serves?

22. More arrows. The archer in Exercise 14 will be shooting 200 arrows in a large competition.
a) What are the mean and standard deviation of the number of bull's-eyes she might get?
b) Is a Normal model appropriate here? Explain.
c) Use the 68-95-99.7 Rule to describe the distribution of the number of bull's-eyes she may get.
d) Would you be surprised if she made only 140 bull's-eyes? Explain.

23. Frogs, part II. Based on concerns raised by his preliminary research, the biologist in Exercise 20 decides to collect and examine 150 frogs.
a) Assuming the frequency of the trait is still 1 in 8, determine the mean and standard deviation of the number of frogs with the trait he should expect to find in his sample.
b) Verify that he can use a Normal model to approximate the distribution of the number of frogs with the trait.
c) He found the trait in 22 of his frogs. Do you think this proves that the trait has become more common? Explain.

24. Apples. An orchard owner knows that he'll have to use about 6% of the apples he harvests for cider because they will have bruises or blemishes. He expects a tree to produce about 300 apples.
a) Describe an appropriate model for the number of cider apples that may come from that tree. Justify your model.
b) Find the probability there will be no more than a dozen cider apples.
c) Is it likely there will be more than 50 cider apples? Explain.

25. Lefties again. A lecture hall has 200 seats with folding arm tablets, 30 of which are designed for left-handers. The average size of classes that meet there is 188, and we can assume that about 13% of students are left-handed. What's the probability that a right-handed student in one of these classes is forced to use a lefty arm tablet?

26. No-shows. An airline, believing that 5% of passengers fail to show up for flights, overbooks (sell more tickets than there are seats). Suppose a plane will hold 265 passengers, and the airline sells 275 seats. What's the probability the airline will not have enough seats so someone gets bumped?

27. Annoying phone calls. A newly hired telemarketer is told he will probably make a sale on about 12% of his phone calls. The first week he called 200 people, but only made 10 sales. Should he suspect he was misled about the true success rate? Explain.

28. The euro. Shortly after the introduction of the euro coin in Belgium, newspapers around the world published articles claiming the coin is biased. The stories were based on reports that someone had spun the coin 250 times and gotten 140 heads—that's 56% heads. Do you think this is evidence that spinning a euro is unfair? Explain.

29. Seatbelts. Police estimate that 80% of drivers now wear their seatbelts. They set up a safety roadblock, stopping cars to check for seatbelt use.
a) How many cars do they expect to stop before finding a driver whose seatbelt is not buckled?
b) What's the probability that the first unbelted driver is in the 6th car stopped?
c) What's the probability that the first 10 drivers are all wearing their seatbelts?
d) If they stop 30 cars during the first hour, find the mean and standard deviation of the number of drivers expected to be wearing seatbelts.
e) If they stop 120 cars during this safety check, what's the probability they find at least 20 drivers not wearing their seatbelts?

30. Rickets. Vitamin D is essential for strong, healthy bones. Our bodies produce vitamin D naturally when sunlight falls upon the skin, or it can be taken as a dietary supplement. Although the bone disease rickets was largely eliminated in England during the 1950s, some people there are concerned that this generation of children is at increased risk because they are more likely to watch TV or play computer games than spend time outdoors. Recent research indicated that about 20% of British children are deficient in vitamin D. Suppose doctors test a group of elementary school children.

a) What's the probability that the first vitamin D–deficient child is the 8th one tested?

b) What's the probability that the first 10 children tested are all okay?

c) How many kids do they expect to test before finding one who has this vitamin deficiency?

d) They will test 50 students at the third grade level. Find the mean and standard deviation of the number who may be deficient in vitamin D?

e) If they test 320 children at this school, what's the probability that no more than 50 of them have the vitamin deficiency?

31. ESP. Scientists wish to test the mind-reading ability of a person who claims to "have ESP." They use five cards with different and distinctive symbols (square, circle, triangle, line, squiggle). Someone picks a card at random and thinks about the symbol. The "mind reader" must correctly identify which symbol was on the card. If the test consists of 100 trials, how many would this person need to get right in order to convince you that ESP may actually exist? Explain.

32. True-False. A true-false test consists of 50 questions. How many does a student have to get right to convince you that he is not merely guessing? Explain.

Review of Part IV Randomness and Probability

Quick Review

Here's a brief summary of the key concepts and skills in probability and probability modeling:

- The Law of Large Numbers says that the more times we try something the closer the results will come to theoretical perfection.
  - Don't mistakenly misinterpret the Law of Large Numbers as the "Law of Averages." There's no such thing.
- Basic rules of probability can handle most situations:
  - To find the probability that an event OR another event happens, add their probabilities and subtract the probability that both happen.
  - To find the probability that an event AND another independent event both happen, multiply probabilities.
  - Conditional probabilities tell you how likely one event is to happen, knowing that another event has happened.
  - Mutually exclusive events (also called "disjoint") cannot both happen at the same time.
  - Two events are independent if knowing that one happens doesn't change the probability that the other happens.
- A probability model for a random variable describes the theoretical distribution of outcomes.
  - The mean of a random variable is its expected value.
  - For independent random variables, variances add.
  - To estimate probabilities involving quantitative variables, you may be able to use a Normal model—but only if the distribution of the variable is unimodal and symmetric.
  - To estimate the probability you'll get your first success on a certain trial, use a Geometric model.
  - To estimate the probability you'll get a certain number of successes in a specified number of independent trials, use a Binomial model.

Ready? Here are some opportunities to check your understanding of these ideas.

Review Exercises

1. Quality control. A consumer organization estimates that 29% of new cars have a cosmetic defect such as a scratch or a dent when they are delivered to car dealers. This same organization believes that 7% have a functional defect—something that does not work properly—and that 2% of new cars have both kinds of problems.

a) If you buy a new car, what's the probability that it has some kind of defect?
b) What's the probability it has a cosmetic defect but no functional defect?
c) If you notice a dent on a new car, what's the probability it has a functional defect?
d) Are the two kinds of defects disjoint events? Explain.
e) Do you think the two kinds of defects are independent events? Explain.

2. Workers. A company's human resources officer reports a breakdown of employees by job type and gender, shown in the table.

Job Type	Male	Female
Management	7	6
Supervision	8	12
Production	45	72

a) What's the probability that a worker selected at random is
   i) female?
   ii) female or a production worker?
   iii) female, if the person works in production?
   iv) a production worker, if the person is female?
b) Do these data suggest that job type is independent of gender? Explain.

3. Airfares. Each year a company must send 3 officials to a meeting in China and 5 officials to a meeting in France. Airline ticket prices vary from time to time, but the company purchases all tickets for a country at the same price. Past experience has shown that tickets to China have a mean price of $1000 with a standard deviation of $150, while the mean airfare to France is $500 with a standard deviation of $100.

a) Define random variables and use them to express the total amount the company will have to spend to send these delegations to the two meetings.
b) Find the mean and standard deviation of this total cost.
c) Find the mean and standard deviation of the difference in price of a ticket to China and a ticket to France.
d) Do you need to make any assumptions in calculating these means? How about the standard deviations?

4. Bipolar. Psychiatrists estimate that about 1 in 100 adults suffers from bipolar disorder. What's the probability that in a city of 10,000 there are over 200 people with this condition? Be sure to verify that a Normal model can be used here.

5. A game. To play a game, you must pay $5 for each play. There is a 10% chance you will win $5, a 40% chance you will win $7, and a 50% chance you will win only $3.

a) What are the mean and standard deviation of your net winnings?
b) You play twice. Assuming the plays are independent events, what are the mean and standard deviation of your total winnings?

6. Emergency switch. Safety engineers must determine whether industrial workers can operate a machine's emergency shutoff device. Among a group of test subjects, 66% were successful with their left hands, 82% with their right hands, and 51% with both hands.

a) What percent of these workers could not operate the switch with either hand?
b) Are success with right and left hands independent events? Explain.
c) Are success with right and left hands mutually exclusive? Explain.

7. Twins. In the United States, the probability of having twins (usually about 1 in 90 births) rises to about 1 in 10 for women who have been taking the fertility drug Clomid. Among a group of 10 pregnant women, what's the probability that

a) at least one will have twins if none were taking a fertility drug?
b) at least one will have twins if all were taking Clomid?
c) at least one will have twins if half were taking Clomid?

8. Deductible. A car owner may buy insurance that will pay the full price of repairing the car after an accident, or save $12 a year by getting a policy with a $500 deductible. Her insurance company says that about 0.5% of drivers in her area have an at-fault auto accident during any given year. Based on this information, should she buy the policy with the deductible or not? How does the value of her car influence this decision?

9. More twins. A group of 5 women became pregnant while undergoing fertility treatments with the drug Clomid, discussed in Exercise 7. What's the probability that

a) none will have twins?
b) exactly 1 will have twins?
c) at least 3 will have twins?

10. At fault. The car insurance company in Exercise 8 believes that about 0.5% of drivers have an at-fault accident during a given year. Suppose the company insures 1355 drivers in that city.

a) What are the mean and standard deviation of the number who may have at-fault accidents?
b) Can you describe the distribution of these accidents with a Normal model? Explain.

11. Twins, part III. At a large fertility clinic, 152 women became pregnant while taking Clomid. (See Exercise 7.)

a) What are the mean and standard deviation of the number of twin births we might expect?
b) Can we use a Normal model in this situation? Explain.
c) What's the probability that no more than 10 of the women have twins?

12. Child's play. In a board game you determine the number of spaces you may move by spinning a spinner and rolling a die. The spinner has three regions: Half of the spinner is marked "5," and the other half is equally divided between "10"and "20." The six faces of the die show 0, 0, 1, 2, 3, and 4 spots. When it's your turn, you spin and roll, adding the numbers together to determine how far you may move.

a) Create a probability model for the outcome on the spinner.
b) Find the mean and standard deviation of the spinner results.
c) Create a probability model for the outcome on the die.
d) Find the mean and standard deviation of the die results.
e) Find the mean and standard deviation of the number of spaces you get to move.

13. Language. Neurological research has shown that in about 80% of people language abilities reside in the brain's left side. Another 10% display right-brain language centers, and the remaining 10% have 2-sided language control. (The latter two groups are mainly left-handers.) (*Science News*, 161 no. 24 [2002])

a) Assume that a freshman composition class contains 25 randomly selected people. What's the probability that no more than 15 of them have left-brain language control?

b) In a randomly assigned group of 5 of these students, what's the probability that no one has 2-sided language control?
c) In the entire freshman class of 1200 students, how many would you expect to find of each type?
d) What are the mean and standard deviation of the number of these freshmen who might be right-brained in language abilities?
e) If an assumption of normality is justified, use the 68-95-99.7 Rule to describe how many students in the freshman class might have right-brain language control.

14. Play again. If you land in a "penalty zone" on the game board described in Exercise 12, your move will be determined by subtracting the roll of the die from the result on the spinner. Now what are the mean and standard deviation of the number of spots you may move?

15. Beanstalks. In some cities tall people who want to meet and socialize with other tall people can join Beanstalk Clubs. To qualify, a man must be over 6′2″ tall, and a woman over 5′10.″ According to the National Health Survey, heights of adults may have a Normal model with mean heights of 69.1″ for men and 64.0″ for women. The respective standard deviations are 2.8″ and 2.5.″
a) You're probably not surprised to learn that men are generally taller than women, but what does the greater standard deviation for men's heights indicate?
b) Are men or women more likely to qualify for Beanstalk membership?
c) Beanstalk members believe that height is an important factor when people select their spouses. To investigate, we select at random a married man and, independently, a married woman. Define two random variables, and use them to express how many inches taller the man is than the woman.
d) What's the mean of this difference?
e) What's the standard deviation of this difference?
f) What's the probability that the man is taller than the woman (that the difference in heights is greater than 0)?
g) Suppose a survey of married couples reveals that 92% of the husbands were taller than their wives. Based on your answer to part f, do you believe that people chose spouses independent of height? Explain.

16. Stocks. Since the stock market began in 1872, stock prices have risen in about 73% of the years. Assuming that market performance is independent from year to year, what's the probability that
a) the market will rise for 3 consecutive years?
b) the market will rise 3 years out of the next 5?
c) the market will fall during at least 1 of the next 5 years?
d) the market will rise during a majority of years over the next decade?

17. Multiple choice. A multiple-choice test has 50 questions, with 4 answer choices each. You must get at least 30 correct to pass the test, and the questions are very difficult.
a) Are you likely to be able to pass by guessing on every question? Explain.
b) Suppose, after studying for a while, you believe you have raised your chances of getting each question right to 70%. How likely are you to pass now?
c) Assuming you are operating at the 70% level and the instructor arranges questions randomly, what's the probability that the third question is the first one you get right?

18. Stock strategy. Many investment advisors argue that after stocks have declined in value for 2 consecutive years, people should invest heavily because the market rarely declines 3 years in a row.
a) Since the stock market began in 1872, there have been two consecutive losing years eight times. In six of those cases, the market rose during the following year. Does this confirm the advice?
b) Overall, stocks have risen in value during 95 of the 130 years since the market began in 1872. How is this fact relevant in assessing the statistical reasoning of the advisors?

19. Insurance. A 65-year-old woman takes out a $100,000 term life insurance policy. The company charges an annual premium of $520. Estimate the company's expected profit on such policies if mortality tables indicate that only 2.6% of women aged 65 die within a year.

20. Teen smoking. The Centers for Disease Control say that about 30% of high school students smoke tobacco (down from a high of 38% in 1997). Suppose you randomly select high school students to survey them on their attitudes toward scenes of smoking in the movies. What's the probability that
a) none of the first 4 students you interview is a smoker?
b) the first smoker is the sixth person you choose?
c) there are no more than 2 smokers among 10 people you choose?

21. Passing stats. Molly's college offers two sections of Statistics 101. From what she has heard about the two professors listed, Molly estimates that her chances of passing the course are 0.80 if she gets Professor Scedastic and 0.60 if she gets Professor Kurtosis. The registrar uses a lottery to randomly assign the 120 enrolled students based on the number of available seats in each class. There are 70 seats in Professor Scedastic's class and 50 in Professor Kurtosis's class.
a) What's the probability that Molly will pass Statistics?
b) At the end of the semester, we find out that Molly failed. What's the probability that she got Professor Kurtosis?

22. Teen smoking II. Suppose that, as reported by the Centers for Disease Control, about 30% of high school students smoke tobacco. You randomly select 120 high school students to survey them on their attitudes toward scenes of smoking in the movies.
a) What's the expected number of smokers?
b) What's the standard deviation of the number of smokers?
c) The number of smokers among 120 randomly selected students will vary from group to group. Explain why that number can be described with a Normal model.
d) Using the 68-95-99.7 Rule, create and interpret a model for the number of smokers among your group of 120 students.

23. Random variables. Given independent random variables with means and standard deviations as shown, find the mean and standard deviation of each of these variables:
a) $X + 50$
b) $10Y$
c) $X + 0.5Y$
d) $X - Y$

	Mean	SD
X	50	8
Y	100	6

24. Merger. Explain why the facts you know about variances of independent random variables might encourage two small insurance companies to merge. (*Hint:* Think about the expected amount and potential variability in payouts for the separate and the merged companies.)

25. Youth survey. According to a recent Gallup survey 93% of teens use the Internet, but there are differences in how teen boys and girls say they use computers. The telephone poll found that 77% of boys had played computer games in the past week, compared with 65% of girls. On the other hand, 76% of girls said they had e-mailed friends in the past week, compared with only 65% of boys.
a) For boys, the cited percentages are 77% playing computer games and 65% using e-mail. That total is 142%, so there is obviously a mistake in the report. No? Explain.
b) Based on these results, do you think playing games and using e-mail are mutually exclusive? Explain.
c) Do you think e-mailing friends and gender are independent? Explain.
d) Suppose that in fact 93% of the teens in your area do use the Internet. You want to interview a few who do not, so you start contacting teenagers at random. What is the probability that you don't find someone who does not use the Internet until the 5th person you ask?

26. Meals. A college student on a seven-day meal plan reports that the amount of money he spends daily on food varies with a mean of \$13.50 and a standard deviation of \$7.
a) What are the mean and standard deviation of the amount he might spend in two consecutive days?
b) What assumption did you make in order to find that standard deviation? Are there any reasons you might question that assumption?
c) Estimate his average weekly food costs, and the standard deviation.
d) Do you think it likely he might spend less than \$50 in a week? Explain, including any assumptions you make in your analysis.

27. Travel to Kyrgyzstan. Your pocket copy of *Kyrgyzstan on 4237±360 Soms a Day* claims that you can expect to spend about 4237 soms each day with a standard deviation of 360 soms. How well can you estimate your expenses for the trip?
a) Your budget allows you to spend 90,000 soms. To the nearest day, how long can you afford to stay in Kyrgyzstan on average?
b) What's the standard deviation of your expenses for a trip of that duration?
c) You doubt that your total expenses will exceed your expectations by more than two standard deviations. How much extra money should you bring? On average, how much of a "cushion" will you have per day?

28. Picking melons. Two stores sell watermelons. At the first store the melons weigh an average of 22 pounds, with a standard deviation of 2.5 pounds. At the second store the melons are smaller, with a mean of 18 pounds and a standard deviation of 2 pounds. You select a melon at random at each store.
a) What's the mean difference in weights of the melons?
b) What's the standard deviation of the difference in weights?
c) If a Normal model can be used to describe the difference in weights, what's the probability that the melon you got at the first store is heavier?

29. Home sweet home. According to the 2000 Census, 66% of U.S. households own the home they live in. A mayoral candidate conducts a survey of 820 randomly selected homes in your city and finds only 523 owned by the current residents. The candidate then attacks the incumbent mayor, saying that there is an unusually low level of home ownership in the city. Do you agree? Explain.

30. Buying melons. The first store in Exercise 28 sells watermelons for 32 cents a pound. The second store is having a sale on watermelons—only 25 cents a pound. Find the mean and standard deviation of the difference in the price you may pay for melons randomly selected at each store.

31. Who's the boss? The 2000 Census revealed that 26% of all firms in the United States are owned by women. You call some firms doing business locally, assuming that the national percentage is true in your area
a) What's the probability that the first three you call are all owned by women?

b) What's the probability that none of your first four calls finds a firm that is owned by a woman?
c) Suppose none of your first five calls found a firm owned by a woman. What's the probability that your next call does?

32. Jerseys. A Statistics professor comes home to find that all four of his children got white team shirts from soccer camp this year. He concludes that this year, unlike other years, the camp must not be using a variety of colors. But then he finds out that in each child's age group there are 4 teams, only 1 of which wears white shirts. Each child just happened to get on the white team at random.
a) Why was he so surprised? If each age group uses the same 4 colors, what's the probability that all four kids would get the same color shirt?
b) What's the probability that all four would get white shirts?
c) We lied. Actually, in the oldest child's group there are 6 teams instead of the 4 teams in each of the other three groups. How does this change the probability you calculated in part b?

33. When to stop? In Exercise 27 of the Review Exercises for Part III, we posed this question:

You play a game that involves rolling a die. You can roll as many times as you want, and your score is the total for all the rolls. But . . . if you roll a 6 your score is 0 and your turn is over. What might be a good strategy for a game like this?

You attempted to devise a good strategy by simulating several plays to see what might happen. Let's try calculating a strategy.
a) On what roll would you expect to get a 6 for the first time?
b) So, roll *one time less* than that. Assuming all those rolls were not 6's, what's your expected score?
c) What's the probability that you can roll that many times without getting a 6?

34. Plan B. Here's another attempt at developing a good strategy for the dice game in Exercise 33. Instead of stopping after a certain number of rolls, you could decide to stop when your score reaches a certain number of points.
a) How many points would you expect a roll to *add* to your score?
b) In terms of your current score, how many points would you expect a roll to *subtract* from your score?
c) Based on your answers in parts a and b, at what score will another roll "break even"?
d) Describe the strategy this result suggests.

35. Technology on campus. Every five years the Conference Board of the Mathematical Sciences surveys college math departments. In 2000 the board reported that 51% of all undergraduates taking Calculus I were in classes that used graphing calculators and 31% were in classes that used computer assignments. Suppose that 16% used both calculators and computers.
a) What percent used neither kind of technology?
b) What percent used calculators but not computers?
c) What percent of the calculator users had computer assignments?
d) Based on this survey, do calculator and computer use appear to be independent events? Explain.

36. Dogs. A census by the county dog control officer found that 18% of homes kept one dog as a pet, 4% had two dogs, and 1% had three or more. If a salesman visits two homes selected at random, what's the probability he encounters
a) no dogs?
b) some dogs?
c) dogs in each home?
d) more than one dog in each home?

37. Socks. In your sock drawer you have 4 blue socks, 5 grey socks, and 3 black ones. Half asleep one morning, you grab 2 socks at random and put them on. Find the probability you end up wearing
a) 2 blue socks.
b) no grey socks.
c) at least 1 black sock.
d) a green sock.
e) matching socks.

38. Coins. A coin is to be tossed 36 times.
a) What are the mean and standard deviation of the number of heads?
b) Suppose the resulting number of heads is unusual, two standard deviations above the mean. How many "extra" heads were observed?
c) If the coin were tossed 100 times, would you still consider the same number of extra heads unusual? Explain.
d) In the 100 tosses, how many extra heads would you need to observe in order to say the results were unusual?
e) Explain how these results refute the "Law of Averages" but confirm the Law of Large Numbers.

39. The Drake equation. In 1961 astronomer Frank Drake developed an equation to try to estimate the number of extraterrestrial civilizations in our galaxy that might be able to communicate with us via radio transmissions. Now largely accepted by the scientific community, the Drake equation has helped spur efforts by radio astronomers to search for extraterrestrial intelligence.

Here is the equation:

$$N_c = N \cdot f_p \cdot n_e \cdot f_l \cdot f_i \cdot f_c \cdot f_L$$

OK, it looks a little messy, but here's what it means:

Factor	What It Represents	Possible Value
N	Number of stars in the Milky Way Galaxy	200–400 billion
f_p	Probability that a star has planets	20%–50%
n_e	Number of planets in a solar system capable of sustaining earth-type life	1? 2?
f_l	Probability that life develops on a planet with a suitable environment	1%–100%
f_i	Probability that life evolves intelligence	50%?
f_c	Probability that intelligent life develops radio communication	10%–20%
f_L	Fraction of the planet's life for which the civilization survives	$\frac{1}{1{,}000{,}000}$?
N_c	Number of extraterrestrial civilizations in our galaxy with which we could communicate	?

So, how many ETs are out there? That depends; values chosen for the many factors in the equation depend on ever-evolving scientific knowledge and one's personal guesses. But now, some questions.

a) What quantity is calculated by the first product $N \cdot f_p$?

b) What quantity is calculated by the product $N \cdot f_p \cdot n_e \cdot f_l$?

c) What probability is calculated by the product $f_l \cdot f_i$?

d) Which of the factors in the formula are conditional probabilities? Restate each in a way that makes the condition clear.

40. Recalls. In a car rental company's fleet, 70% of the cars are American brands, 20% are Japanese, and the rest are German. The company notes that manufacturers' recalls seem to affect 2% of the American cars, but only 1% of the others.

a) What's the probability that a randomly chosen car is recalled?

b) What's the probability that a recalled car is American?

41. Pregnant? Suppose that 70% of the women who, suspecting they may be pregnant and purchase an in-home pregnancy test, are actually pregnant. Further suppose that the test is 98% accurate. What's the probability that a woman whose test indicates that she is pregnant actually is?

42. Door prize. You are among 100 people attending a charity fundraiser at which a large-screen TV will be given away as a door prize. To determine who wins, 99 white balls and 1 red ball have been placed in a box and thoroughly mixed. The guests will line up and, one at a time, pick a ball from the box. Whoever gets the red ball wins the TV, but if the ball is white it is returned to the box. If none of the 100 guests gets the red ball, the TV will be auctioned off for additional benefit of the charity.

a) What's the probability that the first person in line wins the TV?

b) You are the third person in line. What's the probability that you win the TV?

c) What's the probability that the charity gets to sell the TV because no one wins?

d) Suppose you get to pick your spot in line. Where would you want to be in order to maximize your chances of winning?

e) After hearing some protest about the plan, the organizers decide to award the prize by not returning the white balls to the box, thus insuring that one of the 100 people will draw the red ball and win the TV. Now what position in line would you choose in order to maximize your chances?

Part V

From the Data at Hand to the World at Large

Chapter 18

Sampling Distribution Models

WHO	U.S. voters
WHAT	Presidential preference
WHEN	Oct. 27, 2000
WHERE	United States
WHY	Election prediction

On October 27, 2000, less than two weeks before the presidential election, an NBC news poll asked 1000 randomly selected registered voters whom they would likely vote for if the election were held that day. Forty-five percent said they'd choose Al Gore and 43% expressed a similar preference for George W. Bush. A CNN poll taken at the same time found 46% for Bush and only 42% for Gore. Was one poll "wrong"? Pundits claimed that the race was "too close to call." What's going on? Should we be surprised to find that we could get proportions this different from properly selected random samples drawn from the same population? You're probably used to seeing that observations vary, but how much variability among polls should we expect to see?

Why do sample proportions vary at all? How can surveys conducted at essentially the same time by the same organization asking the same questions get different results? The answer is at the heart of statistics. It's because each survey is based on a *different* sample of 1000 people. The proportions vary from sample to sample because the samples are composed of different people.

It's actually pretty easy to predict how much a proportion will vary under circumstances like this. When we can understand and predict the variability of our estimates, we've taken the essential step toward seeing past that variability so we can understand the world.

Modeling the Distribution of Sample Proportions

Imagine

Rather than showing real repeated samples, we can imagine what would happen if we were to actually draw many samples.

We've talked about think, show, and tell. Now we have to add *imagine.* We want to imagine the results from all the random samples of size 1000 that we didn't take. What would the histogram of all the sample proportions look like?

For Gore vs. Bush in October of 2000, where do you expect the center of the histogram to be? Of course, we don't *know* the answer to that (and probably never will). But we know that it will be at the true proportion in the population, and we can call that p. How about the *shape* of the histogram?

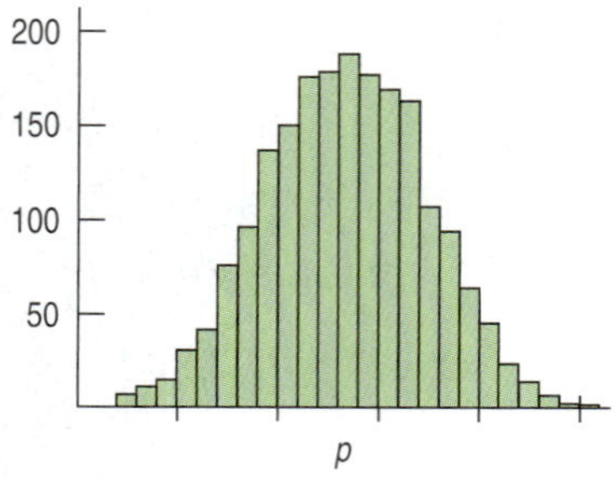

The distribution of observed proportions of voters supporting Bush in samples of 1000 simulated with $p = 0.46$. The histogram shows the proportions for 2000 simulated samples. **Figure 18.1**

We don't have to just imagine. We can simulate. We want to simulate a bunch of those random samples of 1000 that we didn't really take. To do that, we'll simulate many independent random samples of size 1000, keeping the same probability of success. We chose 0.46 for p as a reasonable value. Here's a histogram of the proportion saying they would vote for Bush for 2000 independent samples of 1000 voters when the true proportion is p. It should be no surprise that we don't get the same proportion for each sample we draw even though the underlying true value is the same for the population from which we've drawn the samples.

Does it surprise you that the histogram is unimodal? Symmetric? That it is centered at p? You probably don't find any of this shocking. Does the shape remind you of any model that we've discussed? It's an amazing and fortunate fact that a Normal model is just the right one for the histogram of sample proportions.

To use a Normal model, we need to specify its mean and standard deviation. Which Normal model is the right one? The center of the histogram is naturally at p, so we'll put μ, the mean of the normal, at p.

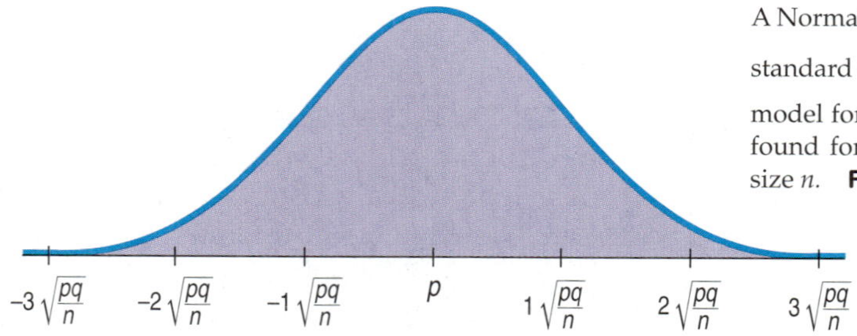

A Normal model centered at p with a standard deviation of $\sqrt{\frac{pq}{n}}$ is a good model for a collection of proportions found for many random samples of size n. **Figure 18.2**

What about the spread? Usually the mean gives us no information about the standard deviation. Suppose we told you that a batch of bike helmets had a mean diameter of 26 centimeters, and asked what the standard deviation was. If you said, "I have no idea," you'd be exactly right. There's no information about σ from knowing the value of μ.

NOTATION ALERT:

The letters p and q are the standard choice for proportions.

Be careful. We've already used capital P for probability, so we stick with lower-case p for proportions.

But there's a special fact about proportions. With proportions we get something for free. Once we know p, we automatically also know the standard deviation. We saw in the last chapter that for a Binomial model the standard deviation of the *number* of successes is $\sqrt{npq}$. Now we want the standard deviation of the *proportion* of successes, $\hat{p}$. The sample proportion $\hat{p}$ is the number of successes divided by the number of trials n, so the standard deviation is also divided by n:

$$\sigma(\hat{p}) = SD(\hat{p}) = \frac{\sqrt{npq}}{n} = \sqrt{\frac{pq}{n}}.$$

When we draw simple random samples of n individuals, the proportions we find will vary from sample to sample. We can model the distribution of these sample proportions with a probability model that is

$$N\left(p, \sqrt{\frac{pq}{n}}\right)$$

For the presidential election, we know what the true proportion favoring Bush was a week later, when the 2000 election actually took place. President Bush received 47.9% of the vote. On October 27, though, the true proportion very well may have been different. We'll never know what that true percentage was while the polls were being taken, but let's suppose it was 46%. Here's a picture of the Normal model for our simulation histogram:

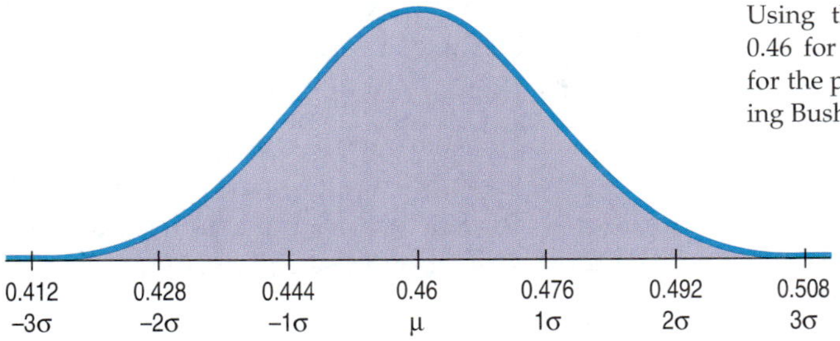

Using the observed proportion of 0.46 for p gives this Normal model for the proportion of voters supporting Bush. **Figure 18.3**

We put the center at $p = 0.46$, so the standard deviation is

$$\sqrt{\frac{pq}{n}} = \sqrt{\frac{(0.46)(0.54)}{1000}} = 0.016, \text{ or } 1.6\%.$$

Because we have a Normal model, we can use the 68-95-99.7 Rule. For example, we know that 95% of normally distributed values are within two standard deviations of the mean, so we should not be surprised if 95% of different polls gave results that were near 46% (0.46) but varied above and below that by 3.2% (0.032). The proportions supporting Bush found in the two polls—43% and 46%—are both *consistent* with a true proportion of 46%.

How Good Is the Normal Model?

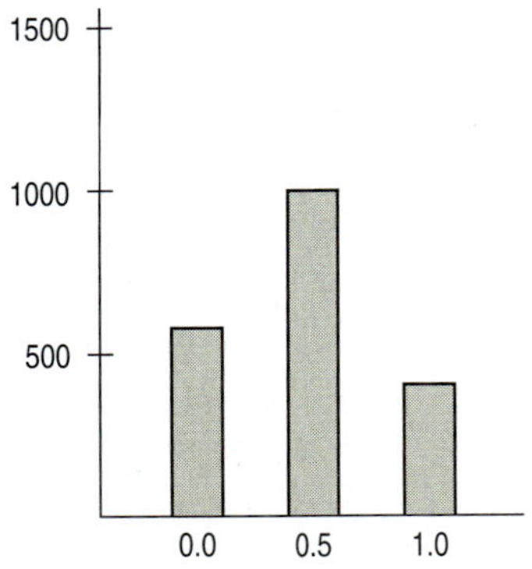

Proportions from samples of size 2 can take on only three possible values. A Normal model may not work well. **Figure 18.4**

Stop and think for a minute about what we've just said. It's a remarkable claim. We've said that if we draw repeated random samples of the same size, n, from some population and measure the proportion we get for each sample, then the collection of these proportions will pile up around the underlying population proportion, p, in such a way that a histogram of the sample proportions can be modeled well by a Normal model.

There must be a catch. Suppose the samples were of size 2, for example. Then the only possible proportion values would be 0, 0.5, and 1. There's no way the histogram could ever look like a Normal model with only three possible values for the variable.

Well, there *is* a catch. The claim is only approximately true. (But, that's OK. After all, models are only supposed to be approximately true.) And the model becomes a better and better representation of the distribution of the sample proportions as the sample size gets bigger.[1] Samples of size 1 or 2 just aren't going to work very well. But the distributions of proportions of many larger samples do have histograms that are remarkably close to a Normal model.

[1]Formally, we say the claim is true in the limit as n grows.

Assumptions and Conditions

Most models are useful only when specific assumptions are true. In the case of the model for the distribution of sample proportions, there are two assumptions:

1. The sampled values must be independent of each other.
2. The sample size, n, must be large enough.

Of course, assumptions are hard—often impossible—to check. That's why we *assume* them. But we should check to see whether the assumptions are reasonable. Fortunately, we can often check *conditions* that provide information about the assumptions. The corresponding conditions to check before using the Normal to model the distribution of sample proportions are:

1. **10% condition.** If sampling has not been made with replacement (that is, returning each sampled individual to the population before drawing the next individual), then the sample size, n, must be no larger than 10% of the population. For the polls, the total population is very large, so the 1000 that were sampled is a small *fraction* of the population. There are other ways in which samples can fail to be independent, but the only good protection from such failures is to think carefully about possible reasons for the data to fail to be independent. There are no simple conditions to check that guarantee independence.
2. **Success/failure condition.** The sample size has to be big enough so that both np and nq are greater than 10. If we label the outcome that has probability p a "success" and the outcome with probability $(1 - p) = q$ a "failure," then this condition says that we need to observe at least 10 successes and at least 10 failures to have enough data for sound conclusions. For the polls, a "success" might be voting for Bush. With $p = 0.479$, we expect $1000 \times 0.479 =$ 479 successes and $1000 \times 0.521 = 521$ failures. Both are greater than 10, so there are certainly enough successes and enough failures for the condition to be satisfied.

The terms "success" and "failure" for the outcomes that have probability p and q are common in Statistics. But they are arbitrary. When we say that a disease occurs with probability p, we certainly don't mean that getting sick is a "success" in the normal sense of the word.

These two conditions seem to contradict each other. Condition 2 wants a big sample size. How big depends on p. If p is near 0.5, we need a sample of only 20 or so. If p is only 0.01, however, we'd need 1000. But condition 1 says that the sample size can be no larger than 10% of the population. Fortunately, this isn't usually a problem in practice. Often, as in polls that sample from all U.S. adults, or industrial samples from a day's production, the populations are much larger than 10 times the sample size.

NOTATION ALERT:

Remember that we are using the "Greek letter pee," p, for the parameter value in our model and the "hatted" value $\hat{p}$ for the observed proportion in the data.

A Sampling Distribution Model for a Proportion

We simulated repeated samples and looked at the histogram of sample proportions. Then we modeled this with a Normal model. This let us make statements about how much proportions vary from sample to sample. We are going to want to talk about such variation for almost every statistic we come across. So we'll want to build models like this.

These **sampling distribution models** are strange because even though we depend on them, we never actually get to see them. We never actually take repeated samples from the same population and make a histogram. We only *imagine* or *simulate* them. But they're important because they act as a bridge from the real world of data to the imaginary model of the statistic and enable us to say something about the population when all we have is data from the real world.

Once we think of the idea of a sampling distribution model, it should be clear that we can find a sampling distribution model for any statistic we can compute on sampled data. Because we are sampling at random, we can imagine drawing random samples over and over and computing the statistic for each sample. The sampling distribution model is a model for the shape of a histogram of these values. Not surprisingly, the model works better and better as the sample size grows.

The sampling distribution model for a proportion

Provided that the sampled values are independent and the sample size is large enough, the sampling distribution of $\hat{p}$ is modeled by a Normal model with mean $\mu(\hat{p}) = p$, and standard deviation $SD(\hat{p}) = \sqrt{\frac{pq}{n}}$.

We have now answered the question raised at the start of the chapter. To know how variable a proportion is, we need to know the proportion and the size of the sample. That's all.

What isn't at all clear is whether these sampling distribution models will always be simple probability models like the Normal model. Fortunately, many of the statistics we work with do have simple sampling distribution models. Usually they need only a parameter or two to describe them.

Why do we really care about these distributions that we can never see? The answer is that once we have estimates for those parameters, we can use the model to help us understand how the statistic would have been distributed if we had drawn all those samples—but without the work and expense of actually drawing them. This will help us generalize from our data to the world at large. That's just the sort of thing models are good for.

Working with Sampling Distribution Models for Proportions STEP-BY-STEP

About 13% of the population is left-handed.[2] A 200-seat school auditorium has been built with 15 "leftie seats," seats that have the built-in desk on the left rather than the right arm of the chair. (For the right-handed readers among you, have you ever tried to take notes in a chair with the desk on the left side?) In a class of 90 students, what's the probability that there will not be enough seats for the left-handed students?

Think State what we want to know.

We want to find the probability that in a group of 90 students, more than 15 will be left-handed. Since 15 out of 90 is 16.7%, the question is equivalent to asking the probability of finding more than 16.7% left-handed students out of a sample of 90.

[2] Actually, it's quite difficult to get an accurate estimate of the proportion of lefties in the population. Estimates range from 8% to 15%.

Check the conditions.

✓ **10% condition:** The 90 students in the class can be taken to be a random sample of students and are surely less than 10% of the population of all students. (Even if the school itself is small, we're imagining the population of all *possible* students who could have gone to the school.)

✓ **Success/failure condition:**

$$np = 90(0.13) = 11.7 > 10$$

$$nq = 90(0.87) = 78.3 > 10$$

Show State the parameters and the sampling distribution model.

The population proportion is $p = 0.13$. The conditions allow us to use a Normal probability model to model the sampling distribution of $\hat{p}$. The mean of this Normal model is 0.13 and the standard deviation is

$$SD(\hat{p}) = \sqrt{\frac{pq}{n}} = \sqrt{\frac{(0.13)(0.87)}{90}} \approx 0.035.$$

Our model for $\hat{p}$ is $N(0.13, 0.035)$.

Make a picture. Sketch the model and shade the area we're interested in, in this case the area to the right of 16.7%.

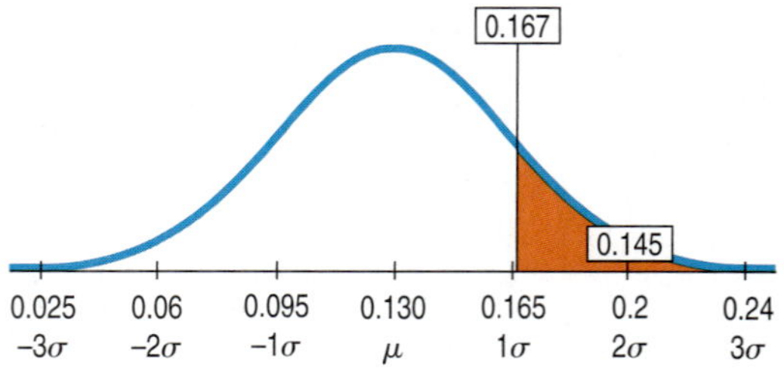

Use the standard deviation as a ruler to find the *z*-score of the cutoff proportion. We see that 16.7% lefties would be just over one standard deviation above the mean.

$$z = \frac{\hat{p} - p}{SD(\hat{p})} = \frac{0.167 - 0.13}{0.035} = 1.06$$

Find the resulting probability from a table of Normal probabilities, a computer program, or a calculator.

$$P(\hat{p} > 0.167) = P(z > 1.06) = 0.1446$$

Tell Discuss the probability in the context of the question.

There is a probability of about 14.5% that there will not be enough seats for the left-handed students in the class.

Means

Like any statistic computed from a random sample, a sample mean also has a sampling distribution. Let's use simulation to get a sense of what that sampling distribution might be.[3]

Here's a simple simulation. Let's start with one fair die. If we toss this die 10,000 times, what should the histogram of the numbers on the face of the die look like?

---

[3] Can you stand the tension?

Here are the results of a simulated 10,000 tosses:

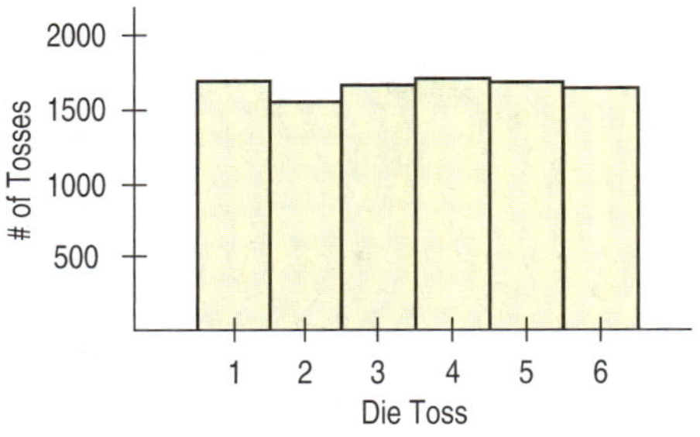

Now, what would happen if we toss a *pair* of dice 10,000 times, take the *average*, and plot the histogram of the average? Before you look, think a minute. Is getting an average of 1 on *two* dice as likely as getting an average of 3 or 3.5?

Let's see:

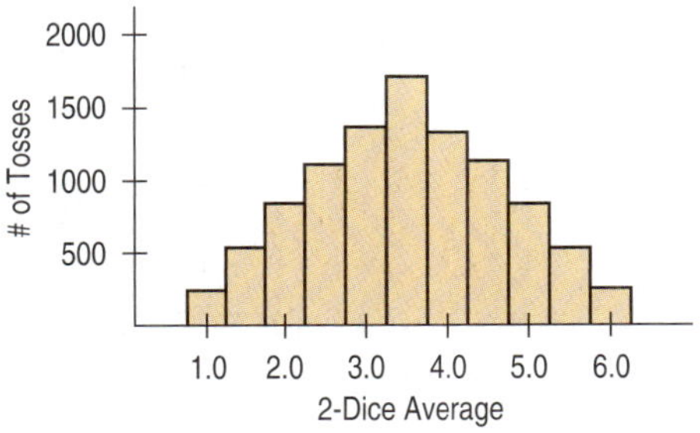

You're much more likely to get an average near 3.5 than you are to get one near 1 or 6. Without calculating those probabilities exactly, it's fairly easy to see that the *only* way to get an average of 1 is to get two 1's. To get a total of 7 (for an average of 3.5), though, there are many more possibilities. This distribution even has a name—the *triangular* distribution.

What if we average 3 dice? We'll simulate 10,000 tosses of 3 dice and taking their average:

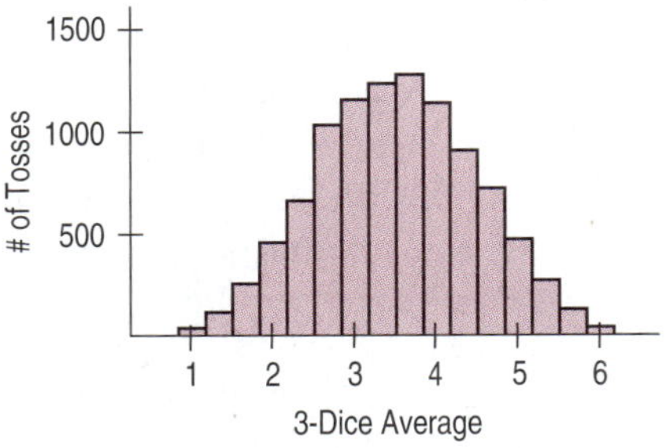

What's happening? First notice that it's getting harder to have averages near the ends. Getting an average of 1 or 6 with 3 dice requires all three to come up 1 or 6, respectively. That's less likely than for 2 dice to come up both 1 or both 6. The distribution is being pushed toward the middle. But what's happening to the shape? (This distribution doesn't have a name as far as we know.)

Let's continue this simulation to see what happens with larger samples. Here's a histogram of the averages for 10,000 tosses of 5 dice:

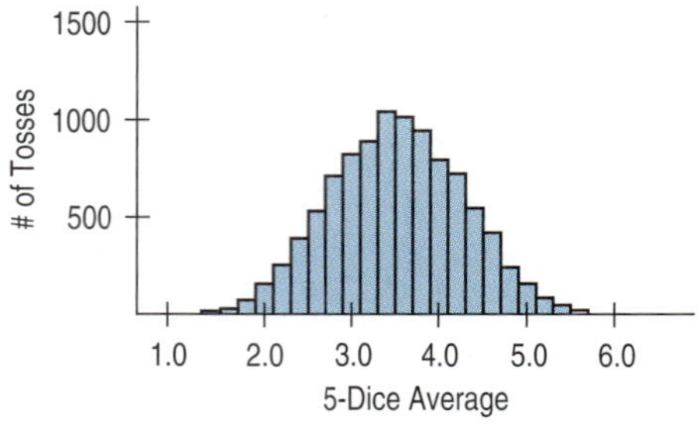

The pattern is becoming clearer. Two things continue to happen. The first fact we knew already from the Law of Large Numbers. It says that as the sample size (number of dice) gets larger, each sample average is more likely to be closer to the population mean. So, we see the shape continuing to tighten around 3.5. But the shape of the distribution is the surprising part. It's becoming bell-shaped. And not just bell-shaped; it's approaching the Normal model.

Are you convinced? Let's skip ahead and try 20 dice. The histogram of averages for throws of 20 dice looks like this:

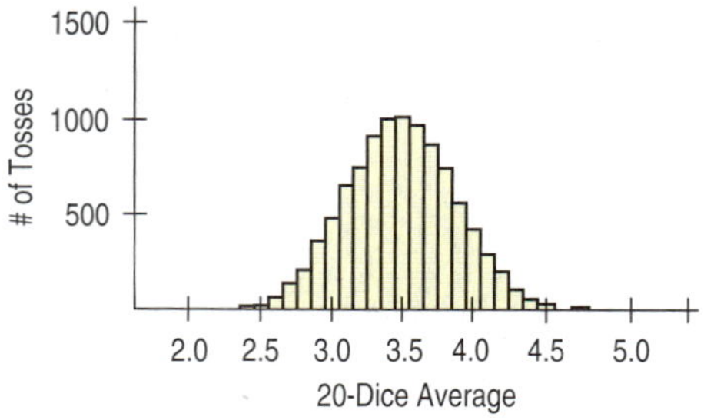

Now we can see the Normal shape very clearly (and notice how much smaller the spread is). But can we count on this happening for situations other than dice throws? What kinds of sample means have sampling distributions that we can model with a Normal model? It turns out that Normal models work well amazingly often.

The Fundamental Theorem of Statistics

Pierre-Simon Laplace 1749–1827
Figure 18.5

The dice simulation looks like a special situation. But what we saw with dice turns out to be true for means of *any* repeated random samples. The sampling distribution of *any* mean becomes Normal as the sample size grows. All we need is for the observations to be independent. We don't even care about the shape of the population distribution.[4] This surprising fact was proved in a fairly general form in 1810 by Pierre-Simon Laplace, and caused quite a stir (at least in Mathematics circles) because it is so unintuitive. It is called the **Central Limit Theorem**[5] (CLT).

[4] There is one technical condition. The variance of the population distribution must be finite. But that's true for almost all real populations, so we won't bother to check it.

[5] The word "Central" in the name of the theorem means "fundamental." It does not refer to the center of a distribution.

Be careful, though. Don't mistakenly think we just said that everything's Normal. Far from it.

Samples aren't Normal. A finite set of data can't ever be. And *sample distributions* do not always approach a Normal model as sample size increases. As samples get larger, we expect the distribution of the data to look more and more like the population from which it is drawn—skewed, bimodal, whatever.

The Central Limit Theorem does not talk about the distribution of data within a sample. It talks about the means of different samples drawn from the same population, called a sampling distribution model.[6] And it does not guarantee that this sampling distribution model is always Normal. If the population is skewed and the samples are small, the means won't be normally distributed. The Central Limit Theorem says that the sampling distribution approximates a Normal model when the samples are large enough. But that's still a very surprising and powerful result.

Why should the Normal model be so special as to pop up like this, seemingly out of nowhere? For once in this text, we're not going to try to persuade you that it is obvious, clear, simple, or straightforward. In fact, the CLT is surprising and a bit weird. Not only does the histogram of the sample means get closer and closer to the Normal model as the sample size grows, but *this is true regardless of the shape of the population distribution!* Even if we sample from a skewed or bimodal population, the Central Limit Theorem tells us that means of repeated samples will tend to follow a Normal model as the sample size grows. Of course, you won't be surprised to learn that it works *better* (and faster) the closer the population model is to a Normal itself. And it works better for larger samples. If the data come from a population that's exactly Normal to start with, you'll only need a sample of size 1 to get the mean to have a Normal distribution. If the population distribution is very skewed (the CEO data from Chapter 4, for example), it may take a mean of dozens or even hundreds of observations for the Normal approximation to work well.

The best and most convincing way to see this is to do a simulation yourself—by drawing many random samples repeatedly, finding their means, and making a histogram of the means. We know of no better way to convince yourself that the Central Limit Theorem is true.[7]

But Which Normal?

The CLT says that the sampling distribution of any mean is Normal. But which Normal model? We know that Normals are specified by their mean and standard deviation. We'd be shocked if the histogram of those means wasn't centered at the population mean. In fact, it is.

We also noticed in our dice simulation that the histograms got narrower as we averaged more and more dice together. This shouldn't be surprising. Means vary less than the individual observations. Think about it for a minute. Which would

[6]Think carefully here to avoid confusion between the distribution of a sample and the sampling distribution model for sample means. The two may sound kind of similar but they're very different beasts!

[7]In fact, the mathematical proof of the CLT, although quite straightforward, is not intuitively convincing. It's not one of those "Oh, that's obvious; I should have seen it myself" proofs. Simulation is much more convincing.

be more surprising, having *one* person in your Statistics class who is over 6′9″ tall or having the *mean* of 100 students taking the course be over 6′9″? The first event is fairly rare.[8] You may have seen somebody this tall in one of your classes sometime. But finding a class of 100 whose mean height is over 6′9″ tall just won't happen. Why? Because means have *smaller standard deviations than individuals.*

How much smaller? Well, we have good news and bad news. The good news is that the standard deviation falls as the sample size grows. The bad news is that it doesn't drop as fast as we might like. It only goes down by the *square root* of the sample size.

Why does it work that way? The Math Box will show you that the Normal model for the sampling distribution of means has a standard deviation equal to

$$\frac{\sigma}{\sqrt{n}}$$

The n's justify the means.
—Apocryphal statistical saying

where σ is the standard deviation of the population. We want to emphasize that it's a standard deviation parameter of the sampling distribution model for the mean, $\bar{y}$, so we write it as $\sigma(\bar{y})$ or $SD(\bar{y})$, pronounced "SD of y bar."

The CLT statement looks an awful lot like the sampling distribution model for a

The Central Limit Theorem(CLT)

As the sample size, n, increases, the mean of n independent values has a sampling distribution that tends toward a Normal model with mean $\mu(\bar{y})$ equal to the population mean, μ, and standard deviation $\sigma(\bar{y}) = SD(\bar{y}) = \frac{\sigma}{\sqrt{n}}$.

proportion. That's no coincidence. Proportions are really a special case of means,[9] but a very special one in which the standard deviation is linked to the mean. The CLT, then, covers proportions as well.

Math Box

We know that $\bar{y}$ involves a sum divided by n:

$$\bar{y} = \frac{y_1 + y_2 + y_3 + \cdots + y_n}{n}.$$

As we saw in Chapter 16, when a random variable is divided by a constant its variance is divided by the *square* of the constant:

$$Var(\bar{y}) = \frac{Var(y_1 + y_2 + y_3 + \cdots + y_n)}{n^2}.$$

[8] If students are a random sample of adults, fewer than 1 out of 10,000 should be taller than 6′9″. Why might college students not really be a random sample with respect to height? Even if they're not a perfectly random sample, a college student over 6′9″ tall is still rare.

[9] Let every success have the value "1" and every failure a "0"; then the proportion of 1's is just the mean of all the 0's and 1's. It turns out that $\sigma = \sqrt{pq}$, so $\sigma(\hat{p}) = \sqrt{pq}/\sqrt{n} = \sqrt{pq/n}$.

To get our sample, we draw the y's randomly, ensuring they are independent. For independent random variables, variances add:

$$Var(\bar{y}) = \frac{Var(y_1) + Var(y_2) + Var(y_3) + \cdots + Var(y_n)}{n^2}.$$

All n of the y's were drawn from our population, so they all have the same variance, σ^2:

$$Var(\bar{y}) = \frac{\sigma^2 + \sigma^2 + \sigma^2 + \cdots + \sigma^2}{n^2} = \frac{n\sigma^2}{n^2} = \frac{\sigma^2}{n}.$$

The standard deviation of $\bar{y}$ is the square root of this variance:

$$SD(\bar{y}) = \sqrt{\frac{\sigma^2}{n}} = \frac{\sigma}{\sqrt{n}}.$$

Assumptions and Conditions

The CLT requires remarkably few assumptions, so there are few conditions to check:

1. **Random sampling condition.** The values must be sampled randomly or the concept of a sampling distribution makes no sense.
2. **Independence assumption.** The sampled values must be mutually independent. There's no way to check in general whether the observations are independent. However, when the sample is drawn without replacement (as is usually the case), you should check the . . .

   10% condition. The sample size, n, is no more than 10% of the population.

Diminishing Returns

The standard deviation of the sampling distribution declines *only* with the square root of the sample size and not, for example, with $1/n$. The mean of a random sample of 4 has half $\left(\frac{1}{\sqrt{4}} = \frac{1}{2}\right)$ the standard deviation of an individual data value. To cut it in half again, we'd need a sample of 16, and a sample of 64 to halve it once more. In practice, random sampling works well, and means have smaller standard deviations than the individual data values that were averaged. This is the power of averaging.

It always seems that if only we could afford a much larger sample, we could get the standard deviation of the sampling distribution *really* under control so that the sample mean could tell us still more about the unknown population mean. As we shall see, that nasty square root limits how much we can make a sample tell about the population. This is an example of something that's known as the Law of Diminishing Returns.

Working with the Sampling Distribution Model for the Mean STEP-BY-STEP

Suppose that mean adult weight is 175 pounds with a standard deviation of 25 pounds and that a Normal model is appropriate. An elevator in our building has a weight limit of 10 persons or 2000 pounds. What's the probability that the 10 people who get on the elevator overload its weight limit?

Think State what we want to know.

Asking the probability that the total weight of a sample of 10 people exceeds 2000 pounds is equivalent to asking the probability that their *mean* weight is greater than 200 pounds.

Check the conditions.

✓ **Random sampling condition:** We will assume that the 10 people getting on the elevator are a random sample from the population.

✓ **Independence assumption:** It's reasonable to think that the weights of 10 randomly sampled people will be mutually independent (but there could be exceptions—for example, if they were all from the same family or if the elevator were in a building with a diet clinic!).

✓ **10% condition:** 10 people is surely less than 10% of the population of possible elevator riders.

Show State the parameters and the sampling distribution model.

We've assumed that the model for weights is Normal with a mean $\mu = 175$ and standard deviation, $\sigma = 25$.

The CLT tells us that we can model the sampling distribution of $\bar{y}$ with a Normal model with mean 175 and standard deviation

$$\sigma(\bar{y}) = \frac{\sigma}{\sqrt{n}} = \frac{25}{\sqrt{10}} \approx 7.91.$$

Make a picture. Sketch the model and shade the area we're interested in. Here the mean weight of 200 pounds appears to be far out the right tail of the curve.

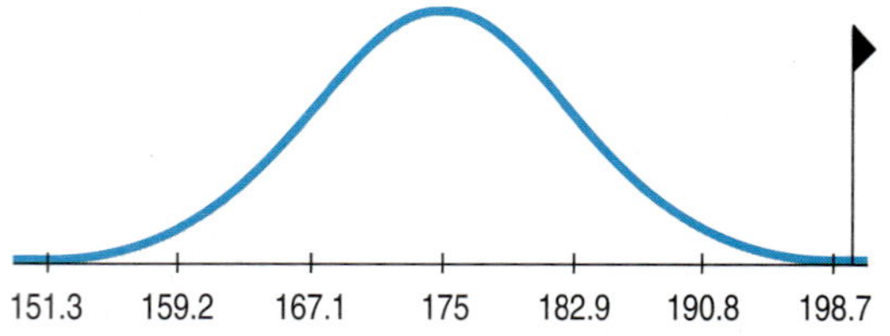

Use the standard deviation as a ruler to find the z-score of the cutoff mean weight. We see that an average of 200 pounds is more than 3 standard deviations above the mean.

$$z = \frac{\bar{y} - \mu}{SD(\bar{y})} = \frac{200 - 175}{7.91} = 3.16$$

Find the resulting probability from a table of Normal probabilities, a computer program, or a calculator.

$$P(\bar{y} > 200) = P(z > 3.16) = 0.0008$$

Tell State your conclusion in the proper context.

The chance that a random collection of 10 adults will exceed the elevator's weight limit is 0.0008. So, if they are a random sample, it is quite unlikely that 10 people will exceed the total weight allowed on the elevator.

Standard Error

Both of the sampling distributions we've looked at are Normal. We know for proportions,

$$SD(\hat{p}) = \sqrt{\frac{pq}{n}}$$

and for means,

$$SD(\bar{y}) = \frac{\sigma}{\sqrt{n}}.$$

These are great if we know, or can pretend that we know, p or σ, and sometimes we'll do that.

Often we know only the observed proportion, $\hat{p}$, or the sample standard deviation, s. So of course we just use what we know, and we estimate. That may not seem like a big deal, but it gets a special name. Whenever we estimate the standard deviation of a sampling distribution, we call it a **standard error.**[10]

For a proportion, the standard error of $\hat{p}$ is

$$SE(\hat{p}) = \sqrt{\frac{\hat{p}\hat{q}}{n}}.$$

For the sample mean, the standard error is

$$SE(\bar{y}) = \frac{s}{\sqrt{n}}.$$

You may see a "standard error" reported by a computer program in a summary or offered by a calculator. It's safe to assume that if no statistic is specified, what was meant is $SE(\bar{y})$, the standard error of the mean.

Sampling Distribution Models

Let's summarize what we've learned about sampling distributions. At the heart is the idea that *the statistic itself is a random quantity.* We can't know what our statistic will be because it comes from a random sample. It's just one instance of something that happened for our particular random sample. A different random sample would have given a different result. The sampling distribution shows us the distribution of possible values that the statistic could have had.

We could simulate that distribution by pretending to take lots of samples. Fortunately, for the mean and the proportion, the CLT tells us that we can model their sampling distribution directly with a Normal model.

The two basic truths about sampling distributions are:

1. Sampling distributions arise because samples vary. Each random sample will have different cases and, so, a different value of the statistic.

---

[10]This isn't such a great name because it isn't standard and nobody made an error. But it's much shorter and more convenient than saying, "the estimated standard deviation of the sampling distribution of the sample statistic."

2. Although we can always simulate a sampling distribution, the Central Limit Theorem saves us the trouble for means and proportions.

Here's a picture showing the process going into the sampling distribution model:

We start with a population model, which can have any shape. It can even be bimodal or skewed (as this one is). We label the mean of this model μ and its standard deviation, σ.

We draw one real sample (solid line) of size n and show its histogram and summary statistics. We *imagine* (or simulate) drawing many other samples (dotted lines), which have their own histograms and summary statistics.

We gather all the means into a histogram.

The CLT tells us we can model the shape of the histogram with a Normal model. The mean of this Normal is μ, and the standard deviation is $\frac{\sigma}{\sqrt{n}}$. When we don't know σ, we estimate it with the standard deviation of the one real sample. That gives us the *standard error*, $\frac{s}{\sqrt{n}}$.

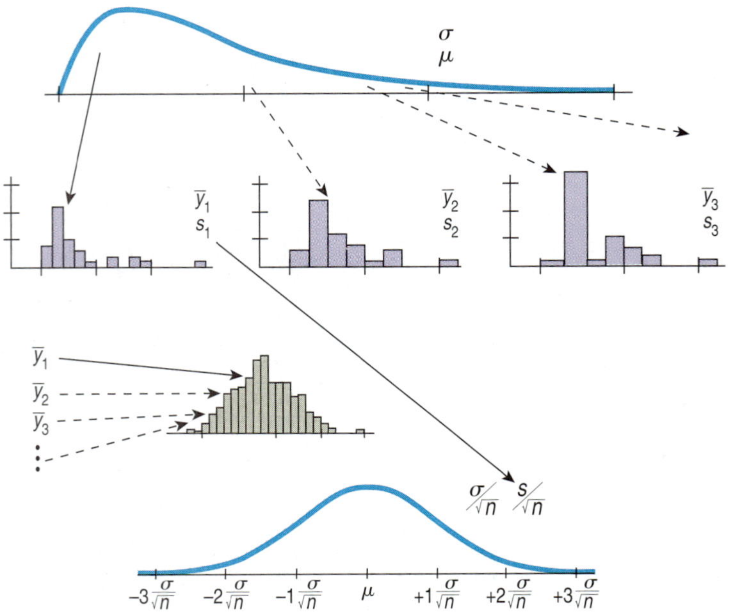

Figure 18.6

What Can Go Wrong?

- ***Beware of observations that are not independent.*** The CLT depends crucially on the assumption of independence. If our elevator riders are related, are all from the same school (for example, an elementary school), or in some other way aren't a random sample, then the statements we try to make about the mean are going to be wrong. Unfortunately, this isn't something you can check in your data. You have to think about how the data were gathered. Good sampling practice and well-designed randomized experiments assure independence.
- ***Watch out for small samples from skewed populations.*** The CLT assures us that the sampling distribution model is Normal if n is large enough. If the population is nearly Normal, even small samples work. If the population is very skewed, then n will have to be large before the Normal model will work well. If we sampled 15 or even 20 CEOs and tried to make a statement about the mean of all CEOs' compensation, we'd likely get into trouble because the underlying distribution model is so skewed. Unfortunately, there's no good rule of thumb.[11] It just depends on how skewed the population's distribution is. Always plot the data to check.

[11]For proportions, of course, there is a rule: the success/failure condition. It works for proportions because the standard deviation of a proportion is linked to the mean.

- ***Don't confuse the sampling distribution with the distribution of the sample.*** When you take a sample, you always look at the distribution of the values, usually with a histogram, and you may calculate summary statistics. Examining the distribution of the sample like this is wise. But that's not the sampling distribution. The sampling distribution models an imaginary collection of the values that a statistic might have taken from all the random samples that you didn't get. We use the sampling distribution model to make statements about how the statistic varies.

Connections

The concept of a sampling distribution connects to almost everything we have done. The fundamental connection is to the deliberate application of randomness in random sampling and randomized comparative experiments. If we didn't employ randomness to generate unbiased data, then repeating the data collection would just get the same data values again (with perhaps a few new measurement or recording errors). The *distribution* of statistic values arises directly because different *random* samples and randomized experiments would generate different statistic values.

Of course, the connection to the Normal distribution is obvious. We first introduced the Normal model before because it was "nice." As a unimodal, symmetric distribution with 99.7% of its area within three standard deviations of the mean, the Normal model is easy to work with. Now we see that the Normal holds a special place among distributions because we can use it to model the sampling distribution of the mean and the proportion.

We use simulation to understand sampling distributions. In fact, some important sampling distributions were discovered first by simulation.

Key Concepts

Sampling distribution model Different random samples give different values for a statistic. The sampling distribution model shows the behavior of the statistic over all the possible samples.

Sampling distribution model for a proportion If assumptions of independence and random sampling are met, and we expect at least 10 successes and 10 failures, then the sampling distribution of a proportion is modeled by a Normal model with a mean equal to the true proportion value, p, and a standard deviation equal to $\sqrt{\frac{p(1-p)}{n}}$.

Central Limit Theorem The Central Limit Theorem (CLT) states that the sampling distribution model of the sample mean (and proportion) is approximately Normal for large n, *regardless of the distribution of the population, as long as the observations are independent.*

Sampling distribution model for a mean If assumptions of independence and random sampling are met, and the sample size is large enough, the sampling distribution of the sample mean is modeled by a Normal model with a mean equal to the population mean, μ, and a standard deviation equal to $\frac{\sigma}{\sqrt{n}}$.

Standard error When we estimate the standard deviation of a sampling distribution using statistics found from the data, the estimate is called a standard error.

Skills

When you complete this lesson you should:

Think

- Understand that the variability of a statistic (as measured by the standard deviation of its sampling distribution) depends on the size of the sample. Statistics based on larger samples are less variable.
- Understand that the Central Limit Theorem gives the sampling distribution model of the mean for sufficiently large samples regardless of the underlying population.

Show

- Be able to demonstrate a sampling distribution by simulation.
- Be able to use a sampling distribution model to make simple statements about the distribution of a proportion or mean under repeated sampling.

Tell

- Be able to interpret a sampling distribution model as describing the values taken by a statistic in all possible realizations of a sample or randomized experiment under the same conditions.

Exercises

1. Coin tosses. In a large class of introductory Statistics students, the professor has each person toss a coin 16 times and calculate the proportion of his or her tosses that were heads. The students then report their results, and the professor plots a histogram of these several proportions.
a) What shape would you expect this histogram to be? Why?
b) Where do you expect the histogram to be centered?
c) How much variability would you expect among these proportions?
d) Explain why a Normal model should not be used here.

2. M&M's. The candy company claims that 10% of the M&M's it produces are green. Suppose that the candies are packaged at random in small bags containing about 50 M&M's. A class of elementary school students learning about percents opens several bags, counts the various colors of candies, and calculates the proportion that are green.
a) If we plot a histogram showing the proportions of green candies in the various bags, what shape would you expect it to have?
b) Can that histogram be approximated by a Normal model? Explain.
c) Where should the center of the histogram be?
d) What should the standard deviation of the proportion be?

3. More coins. Suppose the class in Exercise 1 repeats the coin tossing experiment.
a) The students toss the coins 25 times each. Use the 68-95-99.7 Rule to describe the sampling distribution model.
b) Confirm that you can use a Normal model here.
c) They increase the number of tosses to 64 each. Draw and label the appropriate sampling distribution model. Check the appropriate conditions to justify your model.
d) Explain how the sampling distribution model changes as the number of tosses increases.

4. Bigger bag. Suppose the class in Exercise 2 buys bigger bags of candy, with 200 M&Ms each. Again the students calculate the proportion of green candies they find.
a) Explain why it's appropriate to use a Normal model to describe the distribution of the proportion of green M&Ms they might expect.
b) Use the 68-95-99.7 Rule to describe how this proportion might vary from bag to bag.
c) How would this model change if the bags contained even more candies?

5. Just (un)lucky? One of the students in the introductory Statistics class in Exercise 3 claims to have tossed her coin 200 times and found only 42% heads. What do you think of this claim? Explain.

6. Too many green ones? In a really large bag of M&M's, the kids in Exercise 4 found 500 candies, and 12% of them were green. Is this an unusually large proportion of green M&Ms? Explain.

7. Speeding. State police believe that 70% of the drivers traveling on a major interstate highway exceed the speed limit. They plan to set up a radar trap and check the speeds of 80 cars.

a) Using the 68-95-99.7 Rule, draw and label the distribution of the proportion of these cars the police will observe speeding.

b) Do you think the appropriate conditions are met? Explain.

8. Smoking. Public health statistics indicate that 26.4% of American adults smoke cigarettes. Using the 68-95-99.7 Rule, describe the sampling distribution model for the proportion of smokers among a randomly selected group of 50 adults. Be sure to discuss your assumptions and conditions.

9. Loans. Based on past experience, a bank believes that 7% of the people who receive loans will not make payments on time. The bank has recently approved 200 loans.

a) What are the mean and standard deviation of the proportion of clients in this group who may not make timely payments?

b) What assumptions underlie your model? Are the conditions met? Explain.

c) What's the probability that over 10% of these clients will not make timely payments?

10. Contacts. Assume that 30% of students at a university wear contact lenses.

a) We randomly pick 100 students. Let $\hat{p}$ represent the proportion of students in this sample who wear contacts. What's the appropriate model for the distribution of $\hat{p}$? Specify the name of the distribution, the mean, and the standard deviation. Be sure to verify that the conditions are met.

b) What's the approximate probability that more than one third of this sample wear contacts?

11. Polling. Just before a referendum on a school budget, a local newspaper polls 400 voters in an attempt to predict whether the budget will pass. Suppose that the budget actually has the support of 52% of the voters. What's the probability the newspaper's sample will lead them to predict defeat? Be sure to verify that the assumptions and conditions necessary for your analysis are met.

12. Seeds. Information on a packet of seeds claims that the germination rate is 92%. What's the probability that more than 95% of the 160 seeds in the packet will germinate? Be sure to discuss your assumptions and check the conditions that support your model.

13. Apples. When a truckload of apples arrives at a packing plant, a random sample of 150 is selected and examined for bruises, discoloration, and other defects. The whole truckload will be rejected if more than 5% of the sample is unsatisfactory. Suppose that in fact 8% of the apples on the truck do not meet the desired standard. What's the probability that the shipment will be accepted anyway?

14. Genetic defect. It's believed that 4% of children have a gene that may be linked to juvenile diabetes. Researchers hoping to track 20 of these children for several years test 732 newborns for the presence of this gene. What's the probability that they find enough subjects for their study?

15. Nonsmokers. While some nonsmokers do not mind being seated in a smoking section of a restaurant, about 60% of the customers demand a smoke-free area. A new restaurant with 120 seats is being planned. How many seats should be in the nonsmoking area in order to be very sure of having enough seating there? Comment on the assumptions and conditions that support your model, and explain what "very sure" means to you.

16. Meals. A restaurateur anticipates serving about 180 people on a Friday evening, and believes that about 20% of the patrons will order the chef's steak special. How many of those meals should he plan on serving in order to be pretty sure of having enough steaks on hand to meet customer demand? Justify your answer, including an explanation of what "pretty sure" means to you.

17. Sampling. A sample is chosen randomly from a population that can be described by a Normal model.

a) What's the sampling distribution model for the sample mean? Describe shape, center, and spread.

b) If we choose a larger sample, what's the effect on this sampling distribution model?

18. Sampling, part II. A sample is chosen randomly from a population that was strongly skewed to the left.

a) Describe the sampling distribution model for the sample mean if the sample size is small.

b) If we make the sample larger, what happens to the sampling distribution model's shape, center, and spread?

c) As we make the sample larger, what happens to the expected distribution of the data in the sample?

19. GPAs. A college's data about the incoming freshmen indicates that the mean of their high school GPAs was 3.4 with a standard deviation of 0.35; the distribution was roughly mound-shaped and only slightly skewed. The students are randomly assigned to freshman writing seminars in groups of 25. What might the mean GPA of one of these seminar groups be? Describe the appropriate sampling distribution model—shape, center, and spread—with attention to assumptions and conditions. Make a sketch using the 68-95-99.7 Rule.

20. Home values. Assessment records indicate that the value of homes in a small city is skewed high, with a mean of \$140,000 and standard deviation of \$60,000. To check the accuracy of the assessment data, officials plan to conduct a detailed appraisal of 100 homes selected at random. Using the 68-95-99.7 Rule, draw and label an appropriate sampling model for the mean value of the homes selected.

21. Pregnancy. Assume that the duration of human pregnancies can be described by a Normal model with mean 266 days and standard deviation 16 days.

a) What percentage of pregnancies should last between 270 and 280 days?

b) At least how many days should the longest 25% of all pregnancies last?

c) Suppose a certain obstetrician is currently providing prenatal care to 60 pregnant women. Let $\bar{y}$ represent the mean length of their pregnancies. According to the Central Limit Theorem, what's the distribution of this sample mean, $\bar{y}$? Specify the model, mean, and standard deviation.

d) What's the probability that the mean duration of these patients' pregnancies will be less than 260 days?

22. Rainfall. Statistics from Cornell's Northeast Regional Climate Center indicate that Ithaca, NY, gets an average of 35.4″ of rain each year, with a standard deviation of 4.2″. Assume that a Normal model applies.

a) During what percentage of years does Ithaca get more than 40″ of rain?

b) Less than how much rain falls in the driest 20% of all years?

c) A Cornell University student is in Ithaca for 4 years. Let $\bar{y}$ represent the mean amount of rain for those 4 years. Describe the sampling distribution model of this sample mean, $\bar{y}$.

d) What's the probability that those four years average less than 30″ of rain?

23. Pregnant again. The duration of human pregnancies may not actually follow a Normal model, as described in Exercise 21.

a) Explain why it may be somewhat skewed to the left.

b) If the correct model is in fact skewed, does that change your answers to parts a, b, and c of Exercise 21? Explain why or why not for each.

24. At work. Some business analysts estimate that the length of time people work at a job has a mean of 6.2 years and a standard deviation of 4.5 years.

a) Explain why you suspect this distribution may be skewed to the right.

b) Explain why you could estimate the probability that 100 people selected at random had worked for their employers an average of 10 years or more, but you could not estimate the probability that an individual had done so.

25. Dice and dollars. You roll a die, winning nothing if the number of spots is odd, \$1 for a 2 or a 4, and \$10 for a 6.

a) Find the expected value and standard deviation of your prospective winnings.

b) You play twice. Find the mean and standard deviation of your total winnings.

c) You play 40 times. What's the probability that you win at least \$100?

26. New game. You pay \$10 and roll a die. If you get a 6, you win \$50. If not, you get to roll again. If you get a 6 this time, you get your \$10 back.

a) Create a probability model for this game.

b) Find the expected value and standard deviation of your prospective winnings.

c) You play this game five times. Find the expected value and standard deviation of your average winnings.

d) 100 people play this game. What's the probability the person running the game makes a profit?

27. Pollution. Carbon monoxide (CO) emissions for a certain kind of car vary with mean 2.9 gm/mi and standard deviation 0.4 gm/mi. A company has 80 of these cars in its fleet. Let $\bar{y}$ represent the mean CO level for the company's fleet.

a) What's the approximate model for the distribution of $\bar{y}$? Explain.

b) Estimate the probability that $\bar{y}$ is between 3.0 and 3.1 gm/mi.

c) There is only a 5% chance that the fleet's mean CO level is greater than what value?

28. Potato chips. The weight of potato chips in a medium-size bag is stated to be 10 ounces. The amount that the packaging machine puts in these bags is believed to have a Normal model with mean 10.2 ounces and standard deviation 0.12 ounces.

a) What fraction of all bags sold are underweight?

b) Some of the chips are sold in "bargain packs" of 3 bags. What's the probability that none of the 3 is underweight?

c) What's the probability that the mean weight of the 3 bags is below the stated amount?

d) What's the probability that the mean weight of a 24-bag case of potato chips is below 10 ounces?

29. Tips. A waiter believes the distribution of his tips has a model that is slightly skewed to the right, with a mean of \$9.60 and a standard deviation of \$5.40.

a) Explain why you cannot determine the probability that a given party will tip him at least \$20.

b) Can you estimate the probability that the next 4 parties will tip an average of at least \$15? Explain.

c) Is it likely that his 10 parties today will tip an average of at least \$15? Explain.

30. Groceries. Grocery store receipts show that customer purchases have a skewed distribution with a mean of \$32 and a standard deviation of \$20.

a) Explain why you cannot determine the probability that the next customer will spend at least \$40.

b) Can you estimate the probability that the next 10 customers will spend an average of at least $40? Explain.
c) Is it likely that the next 50 customers will spend an average of at least $40? Explain.

31. More tips. The waiter in Exercise 29 usually waits on about 40 parties over a weekend of work.
a) Estimate the probability that he will earn at least $500 in tips.
b) How much does he earn on the best 10% of such weekends?

32. More groceries. Suppose the store in Exercise 30 had 312 customers today.
a) Estimate the probability that the store's revenues were at least $10,000.
b) If in a typical day, the store serves 312 customers, how much does the store take in on the worst 10% of such days?

33. IQs. Suppose that IQs of East State University's students can be described by a Normal model with mean 130 and standard deviation 8 points. Also suppose that IQs of students from West State University can be described by a Normal model with mean 120 and standard deviation 10.
a) We select 1 student at random from East State. Find the probability that this student's IQ is at least 125 points.
b) We select 1 student at random from each school. Find the probability that the East State student's IQ is at least 5 points higher than the West State student's IQ.
c) We select 3 West State students at random. Find the probability that this group's average IQ is at least 125 points.
d) We also select 3 East State students at random. What's the probability that their average IQ is at least 5 points higher than the average for the three West Staters?

34. Milk. Although most of us buy milk by the quart or gallon, farmers measure daily production in pounds. Ayrshire cows average 47 pounds of milk a day, with a standard deviation of 6 pounds. For Jersey cows, the mean daily production is 43 pounds, with a standard deviation of 5 pounds. Assume that Normal models describe milk production for these breeds.
a) We select an Ayrshire at random. What's the probability that she averages more than 50 pounds of milk a day?
b) What's the probability that a randomly selected Ayrshire gives more milk than a randomly selected Jersey?
c) A farmer has 20 Jerseys. What's the probability that the average production for this small herd exceeds 45 pounds of milk a day?
d) A neighboring farmer has 10 Ayrshires. What's the probability that his herd average is at least 5 pounds higher than the average for the Jersey herd?

Chapter 19

Confidence Intervals for Proportions

Coral are in decline worldwide, possibly because of pollution or changes in sea temperature. The consequences of this decline are far-reaching. The death of coral reefs may be an early warning of climate change and could have far-reaching economic impact.

One spectacular kind of coral, the sea fan, looks like a plant growing from the sea floor, but it is actually an animal.[1] A sea fan of the size in the photo above may have taken 40 years to grow, but it can be killed quickly by pollution or disease. Sea fans in the Caribbean Sea have been under attack by the disease *aspergillosis.* In June of 2000, the sea fan disease team from Dr. Drew Harvell's lab randomly sampled some sea fans at the Las Redes Reef in Akumal, Mexico, at a depth of 40 feet. They found that 54 of the 104 sea fans they sampled were infected with the disease. What might this say about the prevalence of this disease among sea fans in general?

WHO	Sea fans
WHAT	Percent infected
WHEN	June 2000
WHERE	Las Redes Reef, Akumal, Mexico, 40 feet deep
WHY	Research

We have a sample proportion, which we write as $\hat{p}$, of 54/104, or 51.9%. Our first guess might be that this observed proportion is close to the population proportion, p. But we also know that because of natural sampling variability, if the researchers had drawn a second sample of 104 sea fans at roughly the same time, the proportion infected from that sample probably wouldn't have been exactly 51.9%.

What *can* we say about the population proportion, p? To start to answer this question, think about how different the sample proportion might have been if we'd taken another random sample from the same population. But wait. Remember—we aren't actually going to take more samples. We just want to *imagine* how the sample proportions might vary from sample to sample. In other words, we want to know about the *sampling distribution* of the sample proportion of infected sea fans.

[1]For purists, sea fans are actually colonies of genetically identical animals.

A Confidence Interval

Let's look at our model for the sampling distribution. What do we know about it? We know it's approximately Normal (under certain assumptions, which we should be careful to check) and that its mean is the proportion of all infected sea fans on the Las Redes Reef. Is the infected proportion of *all* sea fans 51.9%? No, that's just $\hat{p}$, our estimate. We don't know the proportion, p, of all the infected sea fans; that's what we're trying to find out. We do know, though, that the sampling distribution model of $\hat{p}$ is centered at p, and we know that the standard deviation of the sampling distribution is $\sqrt{\frac{pq}{n}}$.

NOTATION ALERT:

Remember that q is just shorthand for $1 - p$, and $\hat{q} = 1 - \hat{p}$.

Since we don't know p, we can't find the true standard deviation of the sampling distribution model. Instead we'll use $\hat{p}$ and find the standard error,

$$SE(\hat{p}) = \sqrt{\frac{\hat{p}\hat{q}}{n}} = \sqrt{\frac{(0.519)(0.481)}{104}} = 0.049 = 4.9\%.$$

Now we know that the sampling model for $\hat{p}$ should look like this:

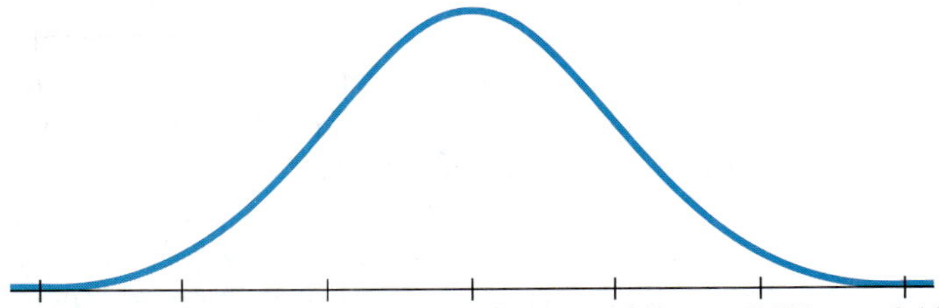

The sampling distribution model for $\hat{p}$ is Normal with a mean of p and a standard deviation of 0.049. **Figure 19.1**

Great. What does that tell us? Well, because it's Normal, it says that about 68% of all samples will have $\hat{p}$'s within 1 *SE*, 0.049, of p. And about 95% of all samples will be within $p \pm 2$ *SE*s. But where is *our* sample proportion in this picture? We still don't know!

We do know that for 95% of random samples, $\hat{p}$ will be no more than 2 *SE*s away from p. So let's look at this from $\hat{p}$'s point of view. If I'm $\hat{p}$, there's a 95% chance that p is no more than 2 *SE*s away from me. If I reach out 2 *SE*s, or 2×0.049, away from me on both sides, I'm 95% sure that p will be within my grasp. Now, I've got him! Probably.

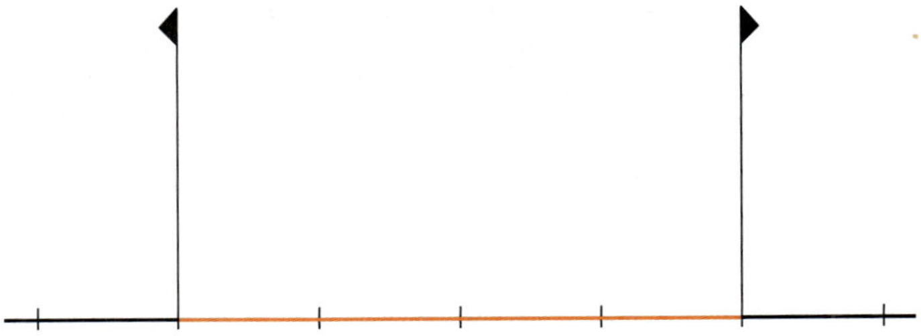

Reaching out 2 *SE*s either side of $\hat{p}$ gives a 95% chance of trapping the true proportion, p. **Figure 19.2**

So what can we really say about p? Here's a list of things we'd like to be able to say, in order of strongest to weakest and the reasons we can't say most of them:

1. **"51.9% of *all* sea fans on the Las Redes Reef are infected."** It would be nice to be able to make absolute statements about population values with certainty, but we just don't have enough information to do that. There's no way to be sure that the population proportion is the same as the sample proportion; in fact, it almost certainly isn't. Observations vary. Another sample would yield a different sample proportion.
2. **"It is *probably* true that 51.9% of all sea fans on the Las Redes Reef are infected."** No. In fact we can be pretty sure that whatever the true proportion is, it's not exactly 51.900%. So the statement is not true.
3. **"We don't know exactly what proportion of sea fans on the Las Redes Reef are infected but we *know* that it's within the interval 51.9% ± 2 × 4.9%. That is, it's between 42.1% and 61.7%."** This is getting closer, but we still can't be certain. We can't know *for sure* that the true proportion is in this range—or in any particular range.
4. **"We don't know exactly what proportion of sea fans on the Las Redes Reef are infected, but the interval from 42.1% and 61.7% *probably* contains the true proportion."** We've now fudged twice—first by giving an interval and second by admitting that we only think the interval "probably" contains the true value. And this statement is true.

"Far better an approximate answer to the right question, . . . than an exact answer to the wrong question."
—John W. Tukey

That last statement may be true, but it's a bit wishy-washy. We can tighten it up a bit by quantifying what we mean by "probably." We saw that 95% of the time when we reach out 2 *SE*s from $\hat{p}$ we capture p, *so we can be 95% confident that this is one of those times.* After putting a number on the probability that this interval covers the true proportion, we've given our best guess of where the parameter is and how certain we are that it's within some range.

5. **"We are 95% confident that between 42.1% and 61.7% of Las Redes sea fans are infected."** Statements like these are called **confidence intervals.** They're the best we can do.

Each confidence interval discussed in the book has a name. You'll see many different kinds of confidence intervals in the following chapters. Some will be about more than *one* sample, some will be about statistics other than *proportions*, some will use models other than the Normal. The interval calculated and interpreted here is sometimes called a **one-proportion *z*-interval.**[2]

Margin of Error: Certainty vs. Precision

We've just claimed that with a certain confidence we've captured the true proportion of all infected sea fans. Our confidence interval had the form

$$\hat{p} \pm 2\,SE(\hat{p})$$

[2]In fact, this confidence interval is so standard for a single proportion that you may see it simply called a "confidence interval for the proportion."

The extent of the interval on either side of $\hat{p}$ is called the **margin of error** *(ME)*. We'll want to use the same approach for many other situations besides estimating proportions. In general, confidence intervals look like this:

$$estimate \pm ME$$

The margin of error for our 95% confidence interval was 2 *SE*. What if we wanted to be more confident? To be more confident, we'll need to capture p more often, and to do that we'll need to make the interval wider. For example, if we want to be 99.7% confident, the margin of error will have to be 3 *SE*.

Figure 19.3

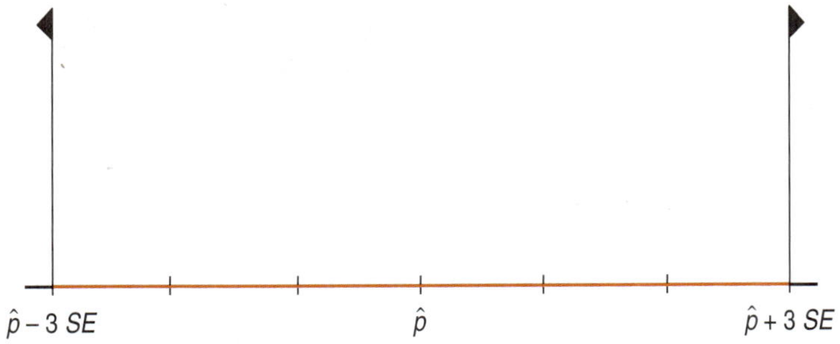

The more confident we want to be, the larger the margin of error must be. We could be 100% confident that the proportion of infected sea fans is between 0% and 100%, but this isn't likely to be very useful. On the other hand, we could give a confidence interval from 51.8% to 52.0%, but we can't be very confident about a precise statement like this. Every confidence interval is a balance between certainty and precision.

The tension between certainty and precision is always there. Fortunately, in most cases we can be both sufficiently certain and sufficiently precise to make useful statements. There is no simple answer to the conflict. You must choose a confidence level yourself. The data can't do it for you. The choice of confidence level is somewhat arbitrary. The most commonly chosen confidence levels are 90%, 95%, and 99%, but any percentage can be used. (In practice, using something like 92.9% or 97.2% is likely to make people think you're up to something.)

Critical Values

In our sea fans example we used 2 *SE* to give us a 95% confidence interval. We got the 2 from the informal 68–95–99.7% Rule. We could also look up a more exact value from a table or with technology and find that we really should use 1.96 instead of 2. We call 1.96 the **critical value** and denote it z^*. For any confidence level, we can find the corresponding critical value from a computer, a calculator, or a Normal probability table.

For a 90% confidence interval, the critical value is 1.645, because for a Normal model 90% of the values are within 1.645 standard deviations from the mean.

The bottom row of Table T gives the critical values, z^*, for commonly used levels of confidence.

Figure 19.4

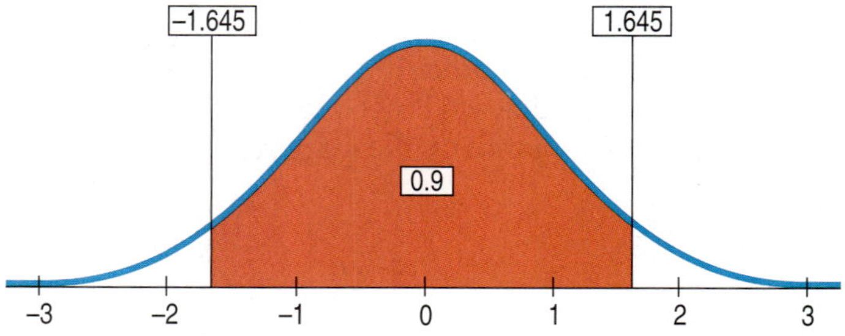

Assumptions and Conditions

We've just made some pretty sweeping statements about sea fans. Those statements were possible because we used a Normal model for the sampling distribution. But is that model appropriate?

Instead of saying "assume" maybe we should say "pretend." We'd do the same things, but the spirit would be a bit more honest. All statistical models depend upon **assumptions.** Different models depend upon different assumptions. If those assumptions are not true, not only might the model be inappropriate, but the conclusions based on it may be wrong.

You may find people claiming to test assumptions, but if you look closely, you'll find that they are just checking a related condition. You can never be certain that an assumption is true. However, you can often decide whether it is plausible by checking a related **condition.** Here are the assumptions and the corresponding conditions you must check before creating a confidence interval about a proportion.

Independence Assumption

The data values are assumed to be independent from each other. Independence is a fundamental property, but not one we can check in the data. Instead, we think about whether independence is reasonable and we check three conditions.

Plausible independence condition. Is there any reason to believe that the data values somehow affect each other? (For example, might the disease in sea fans be contagious?) This condition depends on your knowledge of the situation. It's not one you can check by looking at the data.

Randomization condition. Were the data sampled at random or generated from a properly randomized experiment? Proper randomization can help ensure independence.

10% condition. Samples are almost always drawn without replacement. If the sample exceeds 10% of the population, the probability of a success changes so much during the sampling that our Normal model may no longer be appropriate.

Sample Size Assumption

The model we use for inference is based on the Central Limit Theorem. The sample must be large enough to make the sampling model for the sample proportions approximately Normal. It turns out that we need more data as the proportion gets closer and closer to either extreme (0 or 1). This requirement is easy to check as the following condition.

Success/failure condition. We must expect at least 10 "successes" and at least 10 "failures." Recall that by tradition we arbitrarily label one alternative (usually the outcome being counted) as a "success" even if it's something bad (like a sick sea fan). The other alternative is, of course, then a "failure."

One-proportion *z*-interval

When the conditions are met, we are ready to find the confidence interval for the population proportion, p. Since the standard error of the proportion is estimated by $SE(\hat{p}) = \sqrt{\frac{\hat{p}\hat{q}}{n}}$, the confidence interval is $\hat{p} \pm z^* \times SE(\hat{p})$. The critical value, z^*, depends on the particular confidence level, C, that you specify.

A Confidence Interval for a Proportion STEP-BY-STEP

WHO	Adults in the United States
WHAT	Response to a question about the death penalty
WHEN	May 2002
WHERE	United States
HOW	537 adults were randomly sampled and asked by the Gallup Poll
WHY	Public opinion research

In May 2002, the Gallup Poll asked 537 randomly sampled adults the question "Generally speaking, do you believe the death penalty is applied fairly or unfairly in this country today?" Of these, 53% answered "Fairly" and 7% said they didn't know. What can we conclude from this survey?

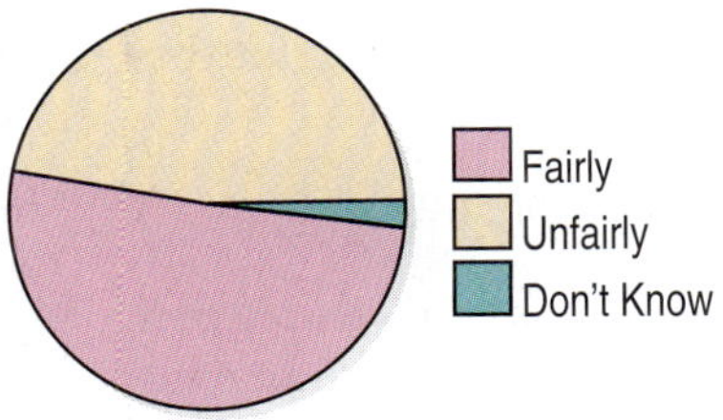

To answer this question we'll build a confidence interval for the proportion of all U.S. adults who believe the death penalty is applied fairly. There are four steps to building a confidence interval for proportions:

Parameter Identify the *parameter* you wish to estimate. This is the value we hope to catch within our confidence interval.

Choose and state a confidence level.

We wish to find an interval that is likely with 95% confidence to contain the true proportion, p, of U.S. adults who think the death penalty is applied fairly.

Plan Check the conditions. We often cannot check assumptions. The conditions are the practical aspects of the data that we *can* check to be assured that the Normal model can be applied.

✓ **Plausible independence condition:** Gallup phoned a random sample of U.S. adults. It is very unlikely that any of their respondents influenced each other.

✓ **Random condition:** Gallup drew a random sample from all U.S. adults. We do not have details of their randomization but we assume that we can trust it.

✓ **10% condition:** Although sampling was necessarily without replacement, there are many more U.S. adults than were sampled. The sample is certainly less than 10% of the population.

✓ **Success/failure condition:**
$n\hat{p} = 537(53.0\%) = 285 > 10$ and
$n\hat{q} = 537(47.0\%) = 252 > 10$,
so our sample is large enough.

State the sampling distribution model for the statistic.

Under these conditions the sampling distribution of the proportion can be modeled by a Normal model.

Choose your method.

We will find a **one-proportion z-interval.**

Show

Mechanics Construct the confidence interval.

We know $n = 537$, $\hat{p} = 0.53$, so

First find the standard error. (Remember: it's called the "standard error" because we don't know p and have to use $\hat{p}$ instead.)

$$SE(\hat{p}) = \sqrt{\frac{\hat{p}\hat{q}}{n}} = \sqrt{\frac{(0.53)(0.47)}{537}} = 0.022.$$

Because the sampling model is Normal, for a 95% confidence interval the critical value $z^* = 1.96$.

Next find the margin of error. We could informally use 2 for our critical value, but 1.96 is more accurate.

From these, we find the margin of error as

$$ME = z^* \times SE(\hat{p}) = 1.96(0.022) = 0.043.$$

Write the confidence interval.

So the 95% confidence interval is

$$0.53 \pm 0.043 \text{ or } (0.487, 0.573).$$

Reality Check The CI is centered at the sample proportion and about as wide as we might expect for a sample of 500.

Tell

Interpretation Tell what the confidence interval means, in the proper context.

We can be 95% confident that between 48.7% and 57.3% of all U.S. adults think that the death penalty is applied fairly.

TI Tips

It will come as no surprise that your TI-83 can calculate a confidence interval for a population proportion. Remember the sea fans? Of 104 seafans, 54 were diseased. To find the resulting confidence interval, we first take a look at a whole new menu.

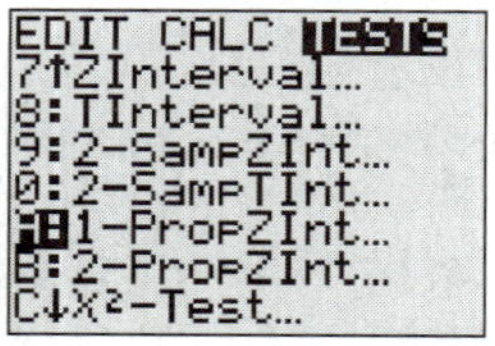

- Under `STAT` go to the `TESTS` menu. Quite a list! Commands are found here for most of the inference procedures you will learn through the coming chapters.
- We're using a Normal model to find a confidence interval for a proportion based on one sample. Scroll down the list and select `A:1-PropZInt`.

- Enter the number of successes observed and the sample size.
- Specify a confidence level and then **Calculate**.

And there it is! Note that the TI calculates the sample proportion for you, but the important result is the interval itself, 42% to 62%. The calculator did the easy part— just Show. Tell is harder. It's your job to interpret that interval correctly.

OK, now it's your turn. Try creating the confidence interval for the percentage of the population that thinks the death penalty is applied fairly. Recall that the Gallup folks polled 537 people and reported that 53% said "Yes."

Beware: You may run into a problem. When you enter the value of **x**, you need the *count* of "Yes" answers, not the percentage. The correct count is about 53% of 537. You can enter **x:.53*537** and the calculator will evaluate that as 284.61. Wrong. Unless you fix that result you'll get an error message. Think about it—the number of people who said the death penalty was fair must have been a whole number—evidently 285. When Gallup reported the results, they rounded off the actual percentage (285 ÷ 537 = 53.073%) to 53%. Simply change the value of **x** to 285 and you should be able to **Calculate** the correct interval.

What Can Go Wrong?

Confidence intervals are powerful tools. Not only do they tell what we know about the parameter value, but—more important—they also tell what we *don't* know. In order to use confidence intervals effectively, you must be clear about what you say about them.

Don't Misstate What the Interval Means

- ***Don't suggest that the parameter varies.*** A statement like "There is a 95% chance that the true proportion is between 42.7% and 51.3%" sounds as though you think the population proportion wanders around and sometimes happens to fall between 42.7% and 51.3%. When you interpret a confidence interval, make it clear that *you* know that the population parameter is fixed and that it is the *interval* that varies from sample to sample.
- ***Don't claim that other samples will agree with yours.*** Keep in mind that the confidence interval makes a statement about the true population proportion. An interpretation such as "In 95% of samples of U.S. adults the proportion who think marijuana should be decriminalized will be between 42.7% and 51.3%" is just wrong. The interval isn't about sample proportions, but about the population proportion.
- ***Don't be certain about the parameter.*** Saying "Between 42.1% and 61.7% of sea fans are infected" asserts that the population proportion cannot be outside that interval. Of course, we can't be absolutely certain of that. (Just pretty sure.)
- ***Don't forget: It's the parameter.*** Don't say, "I'm 95% confident that $\hat{p}$ is between 42.1% and 61.7%." Of course you are—in fact, we calculated that

$\hat{p} = 51.9\%$ of the fans in our sample were infected. So we already *know* the sample proportion. The confidence interval is about the (unknown) population parameter, p.

There are about 500 species of sea fans found on coral reefs throughout the world.

- ***Don't claim to know too much.*** Don't say, "I'm 95% confident that between 42.1% and 61.7% of all the sea fans in the world are infected." You didn't sample from all the sea fans in the world. Just those of this type on the Las Redes Reef.
- ***Do take responsibility.*** Confidence intervals are about *un*certainty. *You* are the one who is uncertain, not the parameter. You have to accept the responsibility and consequences of the fact that not all the intervals you compute will capture the true value. In fact, about 5% of the 95% confidence intervals you find will fail to capture the true value of the parameter. You *can* say, "I am 95% confident that between 42.1% and 61.7% of the sea fans on the Las Redes Reef are infected."[3]

Margin of Error Too Large to Be Useful

We know we can't be exact, but how precise do we need to be? A confidence interval that says that the percentage of infected sea fans is between 10% and 90% wouldn't be of much use. Most likely, you have some sense of how large a margin of error you can tolerate. What can you do?

One way to make the margin of error smaller is to reduce your level of confidence. But that may not be a useful solution. It's a rare study that reports confidence levels lower than 80%. Levels of 95% or 99% are more common.

The time to think about your margin of error to see whether it's small enough to be useful is when you design your study. Don't wait until you compute your confidence intervals. To get a narrower interval without giving up confidence, you need to have less variability in your sample proportion. How can you do that? Choose a larger sample.

Suppose a candidate is planning a poll and wants to estimate voter support within 3% with 95% confidence. How large a sample does she need?

Let's look at the margin of error:

$$ME = z^* \sqrt{\frac{\hat{p}\hat{q}}{n}}$$

$$0.03 = 1.96 \sqrt{\frac{\hat{p}\hat{q}}{n}}.$$

We want to find n, the sample size. To find n we need a value for $\hat{p}$. We don't have a sample yet, but we can probably guess a value for p. The worst case—the one that needs the largest sample size—is when p is 0.50, so if we use that value for $\hat{p}$, we'll certainly be safe. Our candidate probably expects to be near 50% anyway.

Our equation, then, is

$$0.03 = 1.96\sqrt{\frac{(0.5)(0.5)}{n}}.$$

[3] When we are being very careful we say, "95% of samples of this size will produce confidence intervals that capture the true proportion of infected sea fans on the Las Redes Reef."

To solve for n we first multiply both sides of the equation by $\sqrt{n}$ and then divide by 0.03:

$$0.03\sqrt{n} = 1.96\sqrt{(0.5)(0.5)}$$

$$\sqrt{n} = \frac{1.96\sqrt{(0.5)(0.5)}}{0.03} \approx 32.67$$

Notice that evaluating this expression tells us the *square root* of the sample size. We need to square that result to find n:

$$n \approx (32.67)^2 \approx 1067.1.$$

To be safe, we round up and conclude that we need at least 1068 respondents to keep the margin of error as small as 3% with a confidence level of 95%.

Unfortunately, bigger samples cost more money and more effort. Because the standard error declines only with the *square root* of the sample size, to cut the standard error (and thus the ME) in half, we must *quadruple* the sample size.

Public opinion polls often use a sample size of 1000, which gives an ME of 3% when $p = 0.5$. But businesses and nonprofit organizations often use much larger samples to estimate the response to a direct mailing campaign. Why? Because the proportion of people who respond to these mailings is very small, often below 5%. So a margin of error of 3% isn't going to be of much use.

Generally a margin of error of 5% or less is acceptable, but different circumstances call for different standards. For a pilot study, a margin of error of 10% may be fine, so a sample of 100 will do quite well. In a close election, a polling organization might want to get the margin of error down to 2%. Drawing a large sample to get a smaller ME, however, can run into trouble. It takes time to survey 2400 people, and a survey that extends over a week or more may be trying to hit a target that moves during the time of the survey. An important event can change public opinion in the middle of the survey process.

Keep in mind that the sample size for a survey is the number of respondents, not the number of people to whom questionnaires were sent. And keep in mind that a low response rate turns any study essentially into a voluntary response study, which is of little value for inferring population values. It's almost always better to spend resources on increasing the response rate than on surveying a larger group. A full or nearly full response by a modest-size sample can yield useful results.

Of course, surveys are not the only place where proportions pop up. Credit card banks sample huge mailing lists to find out what kind of response rate they're likely to get on a new type of credit card. Even pilot studies are likely to be mailed to 50,000 customers or more. In cases like these, the proportions are likely to be quite small, as will the margins of error needed to say anything useful. When p is small, very large samples are usually used. There's a catch-22 here, though. You need to know p to find the necessary sample size, but you need the sample to estimate p. We used $p = 0.50$ for our election poll calculation, but with such a low return rate expected the banks shouldn't do that. If they can make an educated guess for the value of p—suppose they know the response rate is usually around 4%—they will be better off using that value when setting up their equation to find the desired size for their mailing.

Violations of Assumptions

Confidence intervals and margins of error are often reported along with poll results and other analyses. But it's easy to misuse them, and wise to be aware of the ways things can go wrong.

- ***Watch out for biased samples.*** Don't forget about the potential sources of bias in surveys that we discussed in Chapter 12. Just because we have more statistical machinery now doesn't mean we can forget what we've already learned. A questionnaire that finds that 85% of people enjoy filling out surveys still suffers from nonresponse bias even though now we're able to put confidence intervals around this (biased) estimate.
- ***Think about independence.*** The assumption that the values in our sample are mutually independent is one that we usually cannot check. It always pays to think about it, though. For example, the disease affecting the sea fans might be contagious, so that fans growing near a diseased fan are more likely themselves to be diseased. Such contagion would violate the independence assumption and could severely affect our sample proportion. It could be that the proportion of infected sea fans on the entire reef is actually quite small and the researchers just happened to find an infected area. To avoid this, the researchers should be careful to sample sites far enough apart to make contagion unlikely.

Confidence Intervals for Proportions and the Computer

Confidence intervals for proportions are so easy and natural that many statistics packages don't offer special commands for them. Most statistics programs want the "raw data" for computations. For proportions, the raw data are the "success" and "failure" status for each case. Usually, these are given as 1 or 0, but they might be category names like "yes" and "no." But often we just know the proportion of successes, $\hat{p}$, and the total count, n. Computer packages don't usually deal with summary data like this easily, but the statistics routines found on many graphing calculators allow you to create confidence intervals from summaries of the data—usually all you need to enter are the number of successes and the sample size.

In some programs you can reconstruct variables of 0's and 1's with the given proportions. But even when you have (or can reconstruct) the raw data values, you may not get *exactly* the same margin of error from a computer package as you would find working by hand. The reason is that some packages make approximations or use other methods. The result is very close, but not exactly the same. But Statistics means never having to say you're certain, so the approximate result is good enough.

Connections

Now we can see a practical application of sampling distributions. To find a confidence interval, we lay out an interval measured in standard deviations. We're using the standard deviation as a ruler again. But now the standard deviation we need is the standard deviation of the sampling distribution. That's the one that tells how much the proportion varies. (And when we estimate it from the data, we call it a standard error.)

Key Concepts

Confidence interval A level C confidence interval for a model parameter is an interval of values usually of the form

$$\text{Estimate} \pm \text{margin of error}$$

found from data in such a way that C% of all random samples will yield intervals that capture the true parameter value.

One-proportion *z*-interval A confidence interval for the true value of a proportion. The confidence interval is

$$\hat{p} \pm z^* SE(\hat{p})$$

where z^* is a critical value from the Standard Normal model corresponding to the specified confidence level.

Margin of error In a confidence interval, the extent of the interval on either side of the observed statistic value is called the margin of error. A margin of error is typically the product of a critical value from the sampling distribution and a standard error from the data. A small margin of error corresponds to a confidence interval that pins down the parameter precisely. A large margin of error corresponds to a confidence interval that gives relatively little information about the estimated parameter.

Critical value The number of standard errors to move away from the mean of the sampling distribution to correspond to the specified level of confidence. The critical value is usually found from a table or with technology.

Assumptions Every model depends on assumptions. Although we may be able to think about whether an assumption is plausible, it remains something that we *assume* and cannot verify.

Conditions Although we cannot verify assumptions, often there are conditions about the data that we can check to see whether an assumption is at least reasonable.

Skills

When you complete this lesson you should:

Think

- Understand confidence intervals as a balance between the precision and the certainty of a statement about a model parameter.
- Understand that the margin of error of a confidence interval for a proportion changes with the sample size and the level of confidence.
- Know how to examine your data for violations of conditions that would make inference about a population proportion unwise or invalid.

Show

- Be able to construct a one-proportion *z*-interval.

Tell

- Be able to interpret a one-proportion *z*-interval in a simple sentence or two. Write such an interpretation so that it does not state or suggest that the parameter of interest is itself random, but rather that the bounds of the confidence interval are the random quantities about which we state our degree of confidence.

Exercises

1. **Margin of error.** A TV newsman reports the results of a poll of voters, and then says, "The margin of error is plus or minus 4%." Explain carefully what that means.

2. **Margin of error.** A medical researcher estimates the percentage of children who are exposed to lead-base paint, adding that he believes his estimate has a margin of error of about 3%. Explain what the margin of error means.

3. **Conditions.** Consider each situation described below. Identify the population and the sample, explain what p and $\hat{p}$ represent, and tell whether the methods of this chapter can be used to create a confidence interval.
   a) Police set up an auto checkpoint at which drivers are stopped and their cars inspected for safety problems. They find that 14 of the 134 cars stopped have at least one safety violation. They want to estimate the percentage of all cars that may be unsafe.
   b) A TV talk show asks viewers to register their opinions on prayer in schools by logging on to a Web site. Of the 602 people who voted, 488 favored prayer in schools. We want to estimate the level of support among the general public.
   c) A school is considering requiring students to wear uniforms. The PTA surveys parent opinion by sending a questionnaire home with all 1245 students; 380 surveys are returned, with 228 families in favor of the change.
   d) A college admits 1632 freshmen one year, and four years later 1388 of them graduate on time. The college wants to estimate the percentage of all their freshman enrollees who graduate on time.

4. **More conditions.** Consider each situation described below. Identify the population and the sample, explain what p and $\hat{p}$ represent, and tell whether the methods of this chapter can be used to create a confidence interval.
   a) A consumer group hoping to assess customer experiences with auto dealers surveys 167 people who recently bought new cars; 3% of them expressed dissatisfaction with the salesperson.
   b) What percent of college students have cell phones? 2883 students were asked as they entered a football stadium, and 243 indicated they had phones with them.
   c) 240 potato plants in a field in Maine are randomly checked and only 7 show signs of blight. How severe is the blight problem for the U.S. potato industry?
   d) 12 of the 309 employees of a small company suffered an injury on the job last year. What can the company expect in future years?

5. **Conclusions.** A catalog sales company promises to deliver orders placed on the Internet within 3 days. Follow-up calls to a few randomly selected customers show that a 95% confidence interval for the proportion of all orders that arrive on time is 88% ± 6%. What does this mean? Are these conclusions correct? Explain.
   a) Between 82% and 94% of all orders arrive on time.
   b) 95% of all random samples of customers will show that 88% of orders arrive on time.
   c) 95% of all random samples of customers will show that 82% to 94% of orders arrive on time.
   d) We are 95% sure that between 82% and 94% of the orders placed by the customers in this sample arrived on time.
   e) On 95% of the days, between 82% and 94% of the orders will arrive on time.

6. **More conclusions.** In January 2002, two students made worldwide headlines by spinning a Belgian euro 250 times and getting 140 heads—that's 56%. That makes the 90% confidence interval (51%, 61%). What does this mean? Are these conclusions correct? Explain.
   a) Between 51% and 61% of all euros are unfair.
   b) We are 90% sure that in this experiment this euro landed heads on between 51% and 61% of the spins.
   c) We are 90% sure that spun euros will land heads between 51% and 61% of the time.
   d) If you spin a euro many times, you can be 90% sure of getting between 51% and 61% heads.
   e) 90% of all euros will land heads between 51% and 61% of the time.

7. **Confidence intervals.** Several factors are involved in the creation of a confidence interval. Among them are the sample size, the level of confidence, and the margin of error. Which statements are true?
   a) For a given sample size, higher confidence means a smaller margin of error.
   b) For a specified confidence level, larger samples provide smaller margins of error.
   c) For a fixed margin of error, larger samples provide greater confidence.
   d) For a given confidence level, halving the margin of error requires a sample twice as large.

8. **Confidence intervals, again.** Several factors are involved in the creation of a confidence interval. Among them are the sample size, the level of confidence, and the margin of error. Which statements are true?
   a) For a given sample size, reducing the margin of error will mean lower confidence.
   b) For a certain confidence level, you can get a smaller margin of error by selecting a bigger sample.

c) For a fixed margin of error, smaller samples will mean lower confidence.
d) For a given confidence level, a sample 9 times as large will make a margin of error one third as big.

9. Cars. What fraction of cars are made in Japan? The computer output below summarizes the results of a random sample of 50 autos. Explain carefully what it tells you.

```
z-Interval for proportion
With 90.00% confidence,
0.29938661 < p(japan) < 0.46984416
```

10. Parole. A study of 902 decisions made by the Nebraska Board of Parole produced the following computer output. Assuming these cases are representative of all cases that may come before the Board, what can you conclude?

```
z-Interval for proportion
With 95.00% confidence,
0.56100658 < p(parole) < 0.62524619
```

11. Ghosts. A May 2000 Gallup Poll found that 38% of a random sample of 1012 adults said that they believe in ghosts.
a) Find the margin of error for this poll if we want 90% confidence in our estimate of the percent of American adults who believe in ghosts.
b) Explain what that margin of error means.
c) If we want to be 99% confident, will the margin of error be larger or smaller? Explain.
d) Find that margin of error.
e) In general, if all other aspects of the situation remain the same, will smaller margins of error involve greater or less confidence in the interval?

12. Cloning. A May 2002 Gallup Poll found that only 8% of a random sample of 1012 adults approved of attempts to clone a human.
a) Find the margin of error for this poll if we want 95% confidence in our estimate of the percent of American adults who approve of cloning humans.
b) Explain what that margin of error means.
c) If we only need to be 90% confident, will the margin of error be larger or smaller? Explain.
d) Find that margin of error.
e) In general, if all other aspects of the situation remain the same, would smaller samples produce smaller or larger margins of error?

13. Teenage drivers. An insurance company checks police records on 582 accidents selected at random and notes that teenagers were at the wheel in 91 of them.
a) Create a 95% confidence interval for the percentage of all auto accidents that involve teenage drivers.
b) Explain what your interval means.
c) Explain what "95% confidence" means.
d) A politician urging tighter restrictions on drivers' licenses issued to teens says, "In one of every 5 auto accidents a teenager is behind the wheel.' Does your confidence interval support or contradict this statement? Explain.

14. Junk mail. Direct mail advertisers send solicitations (a.k.a. "junk mail") to thousands of potential customers in the hope that some will buy the company's product. The response rate is usually quite low. Suppose a company wants to test the response to a new flyer, and sends it to 1000 people randomly selected from their mailing list of over 200,000 people. They get orders from 123 of the recipients.
a) Create a 90% confidence interval for the percentage of people the company contacts who may buy something.
b) Explain what this interval means.
c) Explain what "90% confidence" means.
d) The company must decide whether to now do a mass mailing. The mailing won't be cost-effective unless it produces at least a 5% return. What does your confidence interval suggest? Explain.

15. Safe food. Some food retailers propose subjecting food to a low level of radiation in order to improve safety, but sale of such "irradiated" food is opposed by many people. Suppose a grocer wants to find out what his customers think. He has cashiers distribute surveys at checkout and ask customers to fill them out and drop them in a box near the front door. He gets responses from 122 customers, of whom 78 oppose the radiation treatments. What can the grocer conclude about the opinions of all his customers?

16. Local news. The mayor of a small city has suggested that the state locate a new prison there, arguing that the construction project and resulting jobs will be good for the local economy. A total of 183 residents show up for a public hearing on the proposal, and a show of hands finds only 31 in favor of the prison project. What can the city council conclude about public support for the mayor's initiative?

17. Death penalty, again. In the survey on the death penalty you read about in the chapter, the Gallup Poll actually split the sample at random, asking 538 respondents the question quoted earlier, "Generally speaking, do you believe the death penalty is applied fairly or unfairly in this country today?" The other half were asked "Generally speaking, do you believe the death penalty is applied unfairly or fairly in this country today?" Seems like the same question, but sometimes the order of the choices matters. Suppose that for the second way of phrasing it, only 44% said they thought the death penalty was fairly applied.
a) Construct a 95% confidence interval for the true proportion of adults who approve of the way the death

penalty is currently applied, according to the responses for this second question.

b) Recall that 53% of the respondents in the other random half of the study said that the death penalty is applied fairly. Does a proportion of 0.53 fall inside the confidence interval you just found?

18. NHO Survey. A national health organization warns that 30% of middle school students nationwide have been intoxicated. Concerned, a local health agency randomly and anonymously surveys 110 of the 1212 middle school students in its city. Only 21 of them report having been intoxicated.

a) What proportion of the sample reported having been intoxicated?

b) Does this mean that this city's youth are not drinking as much as the national data would indicate? Explain.

c) Create a 95% confidence interval for the proportion of the city's middle school students who have been intoxicated.

d) Is there any reason to believe that the national level of 30% is not true of the middle school students in this city?

19. Death penalty poll, part III. In the chapter's example and again in Exercise 17 we have looked at a Gallup Poll investigating the public's attitude toward the death penalty. In response to one question, 53% thought it was fair, but when the question was phrased differently the proportion in favor dropped to 44%.

a) What kind of bias may be present here?

b) Each group consisted of 538 respondents. If we combine them, considering the overall group to be one larger random sample, what is a 95% confidence interval for the proportion of the general public that thinks the death penalty is being fairly applied?

c) How does the margin of error based on this pooled sample compare to the margins of error from the separate groups? Why?

20. Gambling. A city ballot includes a local initiative that would legalize gambling. The issue is hotly contested, and two groups decide to conduct polls to predict the outcome. The local newspaper finds that 53% of 1200 randomly selected voters plan to vote "yes," while a college Statistics class finds 54% of 450 randomly selected voters in support. Both groups will create 95% confidence intervals.

a) Without finding the confidence intervals, explain which one will have the larger margin of error.

b) Find both confidence intervals.

c) Which group concludes that the outcome is too close to call? Why?

21. Rickets. Vitamin D, whether ingested as a dietary supplement or produced naturally when sunlight falls upon the skin, is essential for strong, healthy bones. The bone disease rickets was largely eliminated in England during the 1950s, but now there is concern that a generation of children more likely to watch TV or play computer games than spend time outdoors is at increased risk. A recent study of 2700 children randomly selected from all parts of England found 20% of them deficient in vitamin D.

a) Find a 98% confidence interval.

b) Explain carefully what your interval means.

c) Explain what "98% confidence" means.

22. Pregnancy. In 1998 a San Diego reproductive clinic reported 49 births to 207 women under the age of 40 who had previously been unable to conceive.

a) Find a 90% confidence interval for the success rate at this clinic.

b) Interpret your interval in this context.

c) Explain what "90% confidence" means.

d) Would it be misleading for the clinic to advertise a 25% success rate? Explain.

23. Deer ticks. Wildlife biologists inspect 153 deer taken by hunters and find 32 of them carrying ticks that test positive for Lyme disease.

a) Create a 90% confidence interval for the percentage of deer that may carry such ticks.

b) If the scientists want to cut the margin of error in half, how many deer must they inspect?

c) What concerns do you have about this sample?

24. Pregnancy. The San Diego reproductive clinic in Exercise 22 wants to publish more definitive information on its success rate.

a) The clinic wants to cut the stated margin of error in half. How many patients' results must be used?

b) Do you have any concerns about this sample? Explain.

25. Graduation. It's believed that as many as 25% of adults over 50 never graduated from high school. We wish to see if this percentage is the same among the 25 to 30 age group.

a) How many of this younger age group must we survey in order to estimate the proportion of non-grads to within 6% with 90% confidence?

b) Suppose we want to cut the margin of error to 4%. What's the necessary sample size?

c) What sample size would produce a margin of error of 3%?

26. Hiring. In preparing a report on the economy, we need to estimate the percentage of businesses that plan to hire additional employees in the next 60 days.

a) How many randomly selected employers must we contact in order to create an estimate in which we are 98% confident with a margin of error of 5%?

b) Suppose we want to reduce the margin of error to 3%. What sample size will suffice?

c) Why might it not be worth the effort to try to get an interval with a margin of error of only 1%?

27. **Graduation, again.** As in Exercise 25, we hope to estimate the percentage of adults aged 25 to 30 who never graduated from high school. What sample size would allow us to increase our confidence level to 95% while reducing the margin of error to only 2%?

28. **Better hiring info.** Editors of the business report in Exercise 26 are willing to accept a margin of error of 4%, but want 99% confidence. How many randomly selected employers will they need to contact?

29. **Pilot study.** A state's environmental agency worries that many cars may be violating clean air emissions standards. The agency hopes to check a sample of vehicles in order to estimate that percentage with a margin of error of 3% and 90% confidence. To gauge the size of the problem, the agency first picks 60 cars and find 9 with faulty emissions systems. How many should be sampled for a full investigation?

30. **Another pilot study.** During routine screening, a doctor notices that 22% of her adult patients show higher than normal levels of glucose in their blood—a possible warning signal for diabetes. Hearing this, some medical researchers decide to conduct a large-scale study, hoping to estimate the proportion to within 4% with 98% confidence. How many randomly selected adults must they test?

31. **Approval rating.** A newspaper reports that the governor's approval rating stands at 65%. The article adds that the poll is based on a random sample of 972 adults and has a margin of error of 2.5%. What level of confidence did the pollsters use?

32. **Amendment.** A TV news reporter says that a proposed constitutional amendment is likely to win approval in the upcoming election because a poll of 1505 likely voters indicated that 52% would vote in favor. The reporter goes on to say that the margin of error for this poll was 3%.

a) Explain why the poll is actually inconclusive.

b) What confidence level did the pollsters use?

Chapter 20

Testing Hypotheses About Proportions

Ingots are huge pieces of metal, often weighing in excess of 20,000 pounds, made in a giant mold. They must be cast in one large piece for use in fabricating large structural parts for cars and planes. If they crack while being made, the crack may propagate into the zone required for the part, compromising its integrity. Airplane manufacturers insist that metal for their planes be defect-free, so the ingot must be made over if any cracking is detected.

Even though the metal from the cracked ingot is recycled, the scrap cost runs into the tens of thousands of dollars. Metal manufacturers would like to avoid cracking if at all possible. But the casting process is complicated and not everything is completely under control. In one plant, only about 80% of the ingots have been free of cracks. In an attempt to reduce the cracking proportion, the plant engineers and chemists recently tried out some changes in the casting process. Since then, 400 ingots have been cast and only 17% of them have cracked. Should management declare victory? Has the cracking rate really decreased or was 17% just due to luck?

We can treat the 400 ingots cast with the new method as a random sample. We know that each random sample will have a somewhat different proportion of cracked ingots. Is the 17% we observe merely a result of natural sampling variability, or is this lower cracking rate strong enough evidence to assure management that the true cracking rate now is really below 20%?

"Half the money I spend on advertising is wasted; the trouble is I don't know which half."
—John Wanamaker (attributed)

People want answers to questions like these all the time. Has the president's approval rating changed since last month? Has teenage smoking decreased in the past five years? Is the global temperature increasing? To answer such questions we test *hypotheses* about models.

Hypotheses

Hypothesis n.;
pl. {Hypotheses}.
A supposition; a proposition or principle which is supposed or taken for granted, in order to draw a conclusion or inference for proof of the point in question; something not proved, but assumed for the purpose of argument.
—*Webster's Unabridged Dictionary*, 1913

In Statistics, a hypothesis proposes a model for the world. Then we look at the data. If the data are consistent with that model, we have no reason to disbelieve the hypothesis. But if the facts are inconsistent with the model, what then? It depends. If the data are only slightly out of step with the model, we might stick with the model. If the data dramatically contradict the model, though, that's strong evidence that the model is incorrect.

Notice the difference between the two possibilities. If the facts are consistent with the model, they *lend support* to the hypothesis. Does this *prove* the hypothesis is true? No. Lending support is not the same as proving something. Many other models may also be consistent with the same set of facts. Even if a hypothesis is true, we can never really prove it.

When a hypothesis is false, however, we might be able to recognize that. When data are glaringly *inconsistent* with the hypothesis, it becomes clear that the hypothesis can't be right. Then we can reject it. This is the logic of traditional scientific thinking and one of the principal differences between scientific thinking and other kinds of reasoning.[1]

For hundreds of years it was assumed that the sun revolved around the earth. The fact that the sun appears to rise in the east every morning and set in the west every evening is *consistent* with this hypothesis and *seems* to lend support to it, but it certainly doesn't prove it. It may explain, however, why Copernicus, who believed that the earth revolves around the sun, had such a hard time convincing the world of his (correct) model.

This is also the logic of jury trials. To prove someone is guilty, we start by *assuming* they are innocent. We retain that hypothesis until the facts make it unlikely beyond a reasonable doubt. Then, and only then, we reject the hypothesis of innocence and declare the person guilty.

In statistical tests of hypotheses, we use the same logic. We begin by assuming that a hypothesis is true. Next we consider whether the data are consistent with the hypothesis. If they are, all we can do is retain the hypothesis we started with. If they are not, then like a jury, we ask whether they are unlikely beyond a reasonable doubt. The statistical twist is that we can quantify our level of doubt.

If the data are surprising, but we believe they're trustworthy, then we start to doubt the hypothesis. What do we mean by "surprising"? We can find the probability that data like these could occur based on our hypothesized model. If the results seem consistent with what we would expect from natural sampling variability, we'll **retain** the hypothesis. But if the probability of seeing results like our data is really low, we **reject** the hypothesis.

Of course, when the probability is very low, it may be that the hypothesis is actually true and we just witnessed something extremely unlikely. When it comes to data though, statisticians don't believe in miracles. Instead, they say that if the data are unlikely *enough*, they'll reject the hypothesis.

Testing Hypotheses

How can we state and test a hypothesis about ingot cracking? Remember that we start by *assuming* a hypothesis is true. What should we assume here? The cracking rate has been at 20% for years. To test whether the changes made by the engineers

[1]Throughout the book, when we talk about science and scientific thinking, we include the social sciences as well. Indeed, other disciplines, such as History, include works of scientific thinking. When we speak of "the scientist," we don't necessarily mean people in white lab coats; we'll mean any person thinking scientifically.

have improved the cracking rate, we assume that they have in fact made no difference. Our starting hypothesis, called the null hypothesis, is that the proportion of cracks is still 20%.

NOTATION ALERT:

Capital H is the standard letter for hypotheses, and H_0 always labels the null hypothesis.

The **null hypothesis,** which we denote H_0, specifies a population model parameter of interest and proposes a value for that parameter. Which value to take is often obvious from the context of the problem itself, from the *Who* and *What* of the data. But sometimes it takes a bit of thinking to translate the question we hope to answer into a hypothesis about a parameter of a particular model. Here we can write H_0: $p = 0.20$.

What would convince you that the cracking rate had actually gone down? Probably only if you observed a cracking rate *much lower* than 20% in your sample. If only 3 out of the next 400 ingots crack (0.75%), you'll probably be convinced the changes helped. If the sample cracking rate is only slightly lower than 20%, though, you might still be skeptical. After all, observations do vary, so we should not be surprised that natural sampling variability will result in small differences. How big must the difference be before we are convinced that the cracking rate has changed?

Whenever we ask how big a difference is, we think of the standard deviation. (You *did* think of the standard deviation, didn't you?) Let's start by finding the standard deviation of the sample cracking rate. The sample cracking rate is a proportion, so we already know how to find its standard deviation.

To remind us that the parameter value comes from the null hypothesis, it is sometimes written as p_0 and the standard deviation as

$$SD(\hat{p}) = \sqrt{\frac{p_0 q_0}{n}}$$

Since the change in process, 400 new ingots have been cast. The sample size of 400 is big enough to satisfy the success/failure condition. (We expect $0.20 \times 400 = 80$ ingots to crack.) We have no reason to think the ingots are not independent, so the Normal sampling distribution model should work well. The standard deviation of the sampling model is

$$SD(\hat{p}) = \sqrt{\frac{pq}{n}} = \sqrt{\frac{(0.20)(0.80)}{400}} = 0.02.$$

Why is this a standard deviation and not a standard error? Because we haven't estimated anything. Once we assume that the null hypothesis is true, it gives us a value for the model parameter p. With proportions, if we know p then we also automatically know its standard deviation. And because we find the standard deviation from the model parameter, this is a standard deviation and not a standard error. When we found a confidence interval for p, we could not assume that we knew its value, so we estimated the standard deviation from the sample value $\hat{p}$.

Now we know both parameters of the Normal sampling distribution model: $p = 0.20$ and $SD(\hat{p}) = 0.02$. So, we can find out how likely it would be to see the observed value of $\hat{p} = 17\%$. Since we are using a Normal model, we find the z-score:

$$z = \frac{0.17 - 0.20}{0.02} = -1.5$$

and we ask, "How likely is it to observe a value at least 1.5 standard deviations below the mean of a Normal model?" The answer (from a calculator, computer

Beyond a Reasonable Doubt
We ask whether the data were unlikely beyond a reasonable doubt. We've just calculated that probability. The probability that the observed statistic value (or an even more extreme value) could occur if the null model were true—in this case, 0.067—is called the P-value.

program, or the Normal table) is about 0.067. This is the probability of observing a cracking rate of 17% or less if the null model is true. Management now must decide whether an event that would happen 6.7% of the time by chance is strong enough evidence to conclude that the true cracking proportion has decreased.

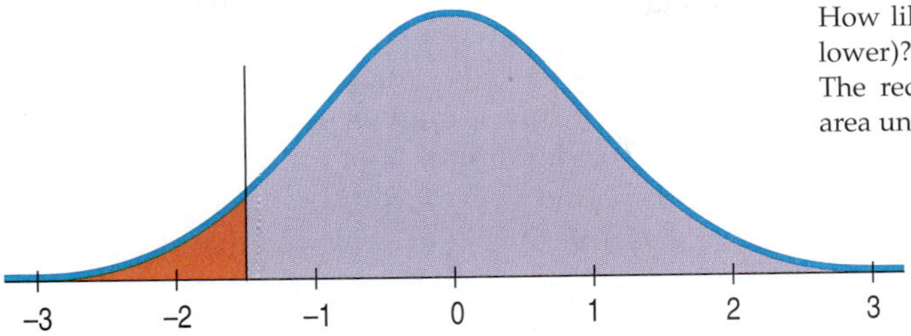

How likely is a z-score of −1.5 (or lower)? This is what it looks like. The red area is 0.067 of the total area under the curve. **Figure 20.1**

A Trial as a Hypothesis Test

We've said that hypothesis testing is very much like a court trial. To understand the logic better, let's push the analogy a little further. In our imagined trial, suppose the defendant has been accused of robbery. We wonder whether he is guilty or not. In British common law and those systems derived from it (including U.S. law), the null hypothesis is that the defendant is innocent. Instructions to juries are quite explicit about this.

We then marshal the evidence. For us, this means collecting data. In the trial the prosecutor presents evidence. This evidence takes the form of facts that seem to contradict the presumption of innocence. ("If the defendant were innocent, wouldn't it be remarkable that the police found him at the scene of the crime with a bag full of money in his hand, a mask on his face, and a getaway car parked outside?")

The next step is to judge the evidence. Evaluating the evidence is the responsibility of the jury in a trial, but it falls on your shoulders in hypothesis testing. The jury considers the evidence in light of the *presumption* of innocence and judges whether the evidence against him would be plausible *if the defendant were in fact innocent.*

Like the jury, we ask, "Could these data plausibly have happened by chance if the null hypothesis were true?" If they were very unlikely to have occurred, then the evidence raises reasonable doubt in our minds about the null hypothesis.

Ultimately, we must make a decision. The standard of "beyond a reasonable doubt" is wonderfully ambiguous because it leaves the jury to decide the degree to which the evidence contradicts the presumption of innocence. We have to ask the same question. How unlikely is unlikely? Some people advocate setting rigid standards, like 1 time out of 20 (.05) or 1 time out of 100 (.01). But if *you* have to make the decision, you must judge for yourself in any particular situation whether the probability is small enough to constitute "reasonable doubt."

What to Do with an "Innocent" Defendant

If the evidence is not strong enough to reject the defendant's presumption of innocence, what verdict does the jury return? They say "not guilty." Notice that they do not say that the defendant is innocent. Nor do they employ a standard of

"If the People fail to satisfy their burden of proof, you must find the defendant not guilty."
—NY state jury instructions

"reasonable certainty" in place of the standard of "reasonable doubt." All they say is that they have not seen sufficient evidence to convict, to reject innocence. The defendant may, in fact, be innocent, but the jury has no way to be sure.

Said statistically, the jury's null hypothesis is H_0: innocent defendant. If the evidence is too unlikely given this assumption, the jury rejects the null hypothesis and finds the defendant guilty. But—and this is an important distinction—if there is *insufficient evidence* to convict the defendant, the jury does not decide that H_0 is true and declare him innocent. Juries can only *fail to reject* the null hypothesis and declare the defendant "not guilty."

In the same way, if the data are not particularly unlikely under the assumption that the null hypothesis is true, then the most we can do is to "fail to reject" the null hypothesis. We never declare the null hypothesis to be true, because we simply do not know whether it's true or not. (After all, more evidence may come along later.) Sometimes in this case we say that the *null hypothesis has been retained.*

In the trial, the burden of proof is on the prosecution. In a hypothesis test the burden of proof is on the unusual claim. The null hypothesis is the ordinary state of affairs, so it's the alternative that we consider unusual and for which we must marshal evidence.

Imagine a clinical trial testing the effectiveness of a new headache remedy. We will most likely test it against a placebo, and the null hypothesis will be that the new drug is no more effective than the placebo. If we use only six people to test the drug, what are we likely to conclude? The results are likely *not to be clear* with only six people in the trial. We will be unable to reject the hypothesis. Does this mean the drug doesn't work? Of course not. It simply means that we don't have enough evidence to reject our assumption. That's why we don't start by assuming that the drug *is more effective.* If we were to do so, then we could test just a few people, find that the results aren't clear, and claim that we've been unable to reject our original assumption. The FDA is unlikely to be impressed by such an argument.

The Reasoning of Hypothesis Testing

Hypothesis tests follow a carefully structured path. To avoid getting lost as we navigate down it, we divide that path into four distinct sections.

1. Hypotheses

We've already talked about the null hypothesis. What should we believe if we reject the null? To perform a hypothesis test, we must specify an alternative hypothesis. Remember that we can never prove a null hypothesis, only reject it or retain it. If we reject it, we then accept the alternative. Often, the null hypothesis is the established belief, the *status quo.* If we have a new method that we think may work better, the null hypothesis will assume that it doesn't. The alternative hypothesis would then be that it does.

In statistical hypothesis testing, hypotheses are almost always about model parameters. To assess how unlikely our data may be, we need a null model. The null hypothesis specifies a parameter value to use in our model. The alternative hypothesis usually gives a range of other possible values.

Some folks pronounce the hypothesis labels "Ho!" and "Ha!" (but it makes them seem overexcitable). Others pronounce H_0 "H naught" (as in "all is for naught"). Nobody, it seems, says "H zero" or "H-Oh," so you probably shouldn't either.

The null hypothesis. To perform a hypothesis test, we must first translate our question of interest into a statement about model parameters. Suppose we want to see if people prefer Coke or Pepsi. How do we translate this into a null hypothesis we can test? We need to specify a parameter and a value for it. If we let p be the proportion of people who prefer Coke to Pepsi, we could let the null hypothesis be "H_0: $p = 0.50$." Now we can collect data and test this hypothesis. The key step is to take your question and translate it into a statement about the parameter of a model so that we can test it. In the usual shorthand, write H_0: *parameter* = *value*.

The alternative hypothesis. The **alternative hypothesis,** H_A, contains the values of the parameter we accept if we reject the null. If we reject the null hypothesis, then we accept the alternative hypothesis. In the Coke vs. Pepsi example, our null hypothesis is that $p = 0.50$. What's the alternative? We would be interested in learning that either cola was preferred. In terms of the parameter, we can write H_A: $p \neq 0.50$. If the data convince us that we should reject the null hypothesis, we would accept the alternative.

2. Plan

The sampling distribution model for $\hat{p}$ is Normal, and centered at the hypothesized proportion, p_0. We use p_0 to calculate its standard deviation, too:

$$SD(\hat{p}) = \sqrt{\frac{p_0 q_0}{n}}$$

To plan a statistical hypothesis test, specify the *model* you will use to test the null hypothesis and the parameter of interest. Of course, all models require assumptions, so you will need to state them and check any corresponding conditions. Your plan step should end with a statement such as

Because the conditions are satisfied, it is appropriate to model the sampling distribution of the proportion with a $N(p_0, SD(\hat{p}))$ model.

Each test we discuss in the book has a name. You should also include the name of the test you plan to perform. We'll see many tests in the following chapters. Some will be about more than one sample, some will involve statistics other than proportions, some will use models other than the Normal (and so will not use z-scores). We call this test about the value of a proportion a **one-proportion z-test.**[2]

3. Mechanics

Under "mechanics" we place the actual calculation of a test statistic from the data. Different tests we encounter will have different formulas. Usually, the mechanics are handled by a statistics program or calculator, but it's good to have the formulas recorded for reference and to know what's being computed. The ultimate goal of the calculation is to obtain a **P-value**—the probability that the observed statistic value (or an even more extreme value) could occur if the null model were correct. If the P-value is small enough, we'll reject the null hypothesis.

. . . They make things admirably plain,
But one hard question will remain:
If one hypothesis you lose,
Another in its place you choose . . .
—James Russell Lowell, *Credidimus Jovem Regnare*

4. Conclusion

The conclusion in a hypothesis test is always a statement about the null hypothesis. The conclusion must state either that we reject or that we fail to reject the null hypothesis. And, as always, the conclusion should be stated in context.

[2]It's also called the "one sample test for a proportion."

Formal tests of a null hypothesis base the decision of whether to reject the null hypothesis solely on the size of the P-value. But in real life, we want to evaluate the costs of our decisions as well. How much would you be willing to pay for a faster computer? Shouldn't your decision depend on how much faster? And on how much more it costs? Costs are not just monetary either. Would you use the same standard of proof for testing the safety of an airplane as for the speed of your new computer?

Your conclusion about the null hypothesis should never be the end of a testing procedure. Often there are actions to take or policies to change. In our ingot example, management must decide whether to continue the changes proposed by the engineers. The decision always includes the practical consideration of whether the new method is worth the cost. Suppose management decides to reject the null hypothesis of 20% cracking in favor of the alternative that it has been reduced. They must still evaluate how much the cracking rate has been reduced and how much it cost to accomplish it. The *size of the effect* is always a concern when we test hypotheses. A good way to look at the effect size is to examine a confidence interval.

One-proportion z-test

The conditions for the one-proportion *z*-test are the same as for the one-proportion *z*-interval. We test the hypothesis $H_0: p = p_0$ using the statistic $z = \frac{(\hat{p} - p_0)}{SD(\hat{p})}$. We use the hypothesized proportion to find the standard deviation, $SD(\hat{p}) = \sqrt{\frac{p_0 q_0}{n}}$.

When the conditions are met and the null hypothesis is true, this statistic follows the standard Normal model, so we can use that model to obtain a P-value.

Alternative Alternatives

In the Coke vs. Pepsi example, we were equally interested in proportions that deviate from 50% in *either* direction. So we wrote our alternative hypothesis as $H_A: p \neq 0.50$.

Such an alternative hypothesis is known as a **two-sided alternative** because we are equally interested in deviations on either side of the null hypothesis value. For two-sided alternatives, the P-value is the probability of deviating in *either* direction from the null hypothesis value.

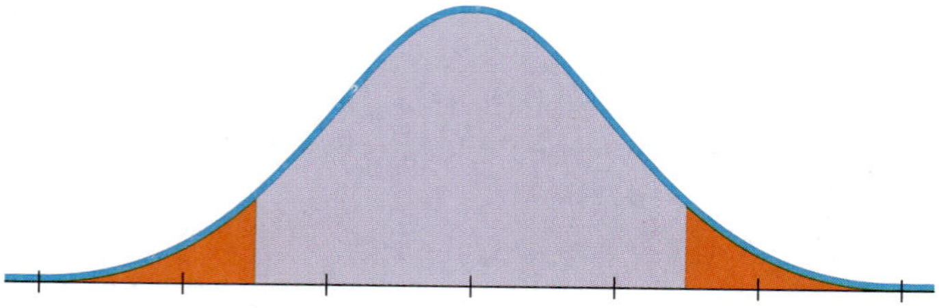

The P-value for a two-sided alternative adds the probabilities in both tails of the sampling distribution model outside the value that corresponds to the test statistic.

Figure 20.2

In the ingot example, management is particularly interested in *lowering* the cracking rate below 20%. Management probably doesn't want to pursue changes in the process that make the cracking rate worse. The only alternative of interest is that the cracking rate *decreases*. We would write our alternative hypothesis, then, as $H_A: p < 0.20$. An alternative hypothesis that focuses on deviations from the null hypothesis value in only one direction is called a **one-sided alternative.**

The P-value for a one-sided alternative considers only the probability of values beyond the test statistic value in the specified direction.

Figure 20.3

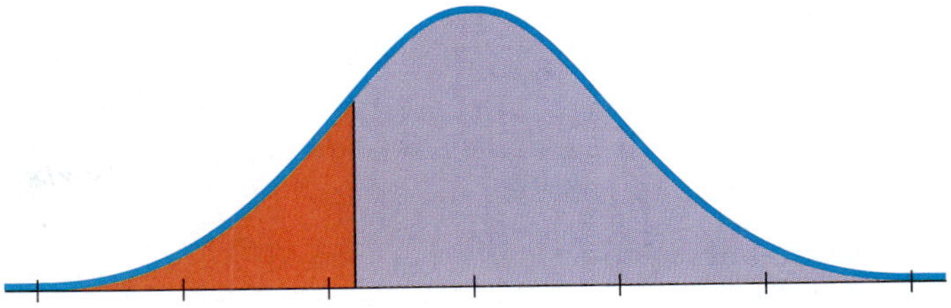

For one-sided alternatives, the P-value is the probability of deviating *only in the direction of the alternative* away from the null hypothesis value.

How do we know whether we want a one- or two-sided alternative? To answer this we return to the W's, and specifically to the *Why* of the study. In the ingot example, the data were collected to see whether the changes *improved* the cracking rate. When we test a hypothesis, we must specify both the null and the alternative. But the alternative is often the hypothesis that motivated the study.

In some social sciences, alternative hypotheses are called "research hypotheses" and are stated clearly at the beginning of research reports. Ask "why was this study done?" and you are likely to hear about the alternative hypothesis. Keep in mind, though, that you can't start by assuming that the alternative is true. To be able to do the test, you must specify and assume the null. The burden of proof is on the claim made by the research hypothesis. Without sufficient evidence otherwise, we retain the null.

Testing a Hypothesis STEP-BY-STEP

Doesn't Anyone Root for the Visitors?

Nelly Kelly loved baseball games,
Knew the players, knew all their names,
You could see her there ev'ry day,
Shout "Hurray" when they'd play.
Her boy friend by the name of Joe
Said, "To Coney Isle, dear, let's go,"
Then Nelly started to fret and pout,
And to him I heard her shout . . .

Don't look yet—do you know the next line?
What did Nelly tell her boyfriend?

"Take me out to the ball game,
Take me out with the crowd.
Buy me some peanuts and Cracker Jack,
I don't care if I never get back,
Let me **root, root, root for the home team,**
If they don't win it's a shame.
For it's one, two, three strikes, you're out,
At the old ball game."

Anyone who plays or watches sports has heard of the "home field advantage." Teams tend to win more often when they play at home. Or do they?

If there were no home field advantage, the home teams would win about half of all games played. In the 2002 major league baseball season, there were 2425 regular season games. It turns out that the home team won 1314 of the 2425 games, or 54.2% of the time. Could this deviation from 50% be explained just from natural sampling variability, or is this evidence to suggest that there really is a home field advantage, at least in professional baseball?

In testing the hypothesis that there is not a home field advantage, we are asking whether the observed rate of home team victories, 54.2%, is so much greater than 50% that we cannot explain it away as just chance variation.

There are four main steps to performing a hypothesis test—hypotheses, test, mechanics, and conclusion. Let's see what this will tell us about the home team's chances of winning a baseball game.

Think

Hypotheses State what we want to know.

We want to know whether the home team in professional baseball is more likely to win. The parameter of interest is the proportion of home team wins. With no advantage, we'd expect that proportion to be 0.50.

The null hypothesis makes the claim of no difference from what we'd expect.

We are interested only in a home field *advantage*, so the alternative hypothesis is one-tailed.

$$H_0: p = 0.50$$

$$H_A: p > 0.50$$

Plan

Check the conditions.

✓ **Independence assumption:** Generally, the outcome of one game has no effect on the outcome of another game. But this may not always be strictly true. For example, if a key player is injured, the probability that the team will win in the next couple of games may decrease slightly, but independence is still roughly true.

✓ **Random sampling condition:** We have results for all 2425 games of the 2002 season. But we aren't just interested in 2002. We'll consider those games, while not randomly selected, to be a reasonable representative sample of recent and future professional baseball games.

✓ **10% condition:** These 2425 games are less than 10% of all recent and future games.

Note that the success/failure condition is based on the *expected* outcomes of games if the hypothesis of no home field advantage is correct.

✓ **Success/failure condition:**

$$np_0 = 2425(0.50) = 1212.5 > 10$$

$$nq_0 = 2425(0.50) = 1212.5 > 10$$

Specify the sampling distribution; it's centered at the hypothesized proprotion.

Because the conditions are satisfied, it is appropriate to model the sampling distribution of the proportion with $N(p_0, SD(\hat{p}))$.

Tell what test you plan to use.

We can perform a **one-proportion z-test.**

Show

Mechanics

The null model gives us the mean, and (because we are working with proportions) the mean gives us the standard deviation. Note that this is *not* standard error—we don't have to use $\hat{p}$ in the calculation.

The null model is a Normal distribution with a mean of 0.50 and a standard deviation of

$$SD(\hat{p}) = \sqrt{\frac{p_0 q_0}{n}} = \sqrt{\frac{(0.5)(0.5)}{2425}} \approx 0.01015.$$

The sample proportion is $\hat{p} = 0.542$.

Make a picture. Sketch a Normal model centered at $p_0 = 0.50$. Because this is an upper tail test, shade the region to the right of the observed proportion.

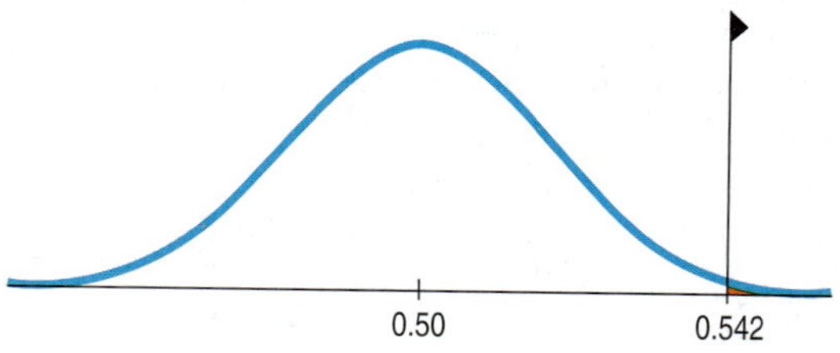

We next find the z-score for the observed proportion to find out how many standard deviations it is from the hypothesized proportion.

$$z = \frac{\hat{p} - p_0}{SD(\hat{p})} = \frac{0.542 - 0.5}{0.01015} = 4.14.$$

The sample proportion lies 4.14 standard deviations above the mean.

The P-value is the probability of observing a value this extreme (or more) if there is no home field advantage. We can find it using Table Z or technology.

$$P = P(z > 4.14) < 0.0001.$$

Tell

Conclusion

Your conclusion should link the P-value to a decision about the null hypothesis and then state a conclusion in the proper context (about the home field advantage in baseball, in other words).

The very small P-value says that if the true proportion of home team wins were 0.50, then the observed value of 0.542 or larger would occur in less than 1 out of 10,000 seasons. We reject the null hypothesis. This is strong evidence that the true proportion of home team wins is not 50%, and that there is a home field advantage.

OK, but how *big* is the home field advantage? Measuring the size of the effect involves a confidence interval. (Use your calculator.)

TI Tips

By now probably nothing surprises you about your TI-83. Of course it can help you with the mechanics of a hypothesis test. But that's not much. It cannot write the correct hypotheses, check the appropriate conditions, interpret the results, or state a conclusion. You have to do the tough stuff!

Let's do the mechanics of the Step-By-Step example about home field advantage in baseball. We hypothesized that home teams would win 50% of all games, but during this 2425-game season they actually won 54.2% of the time.

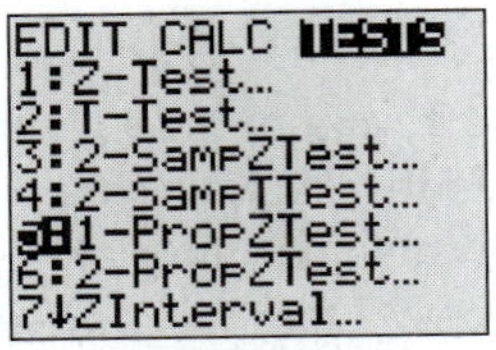

- Go to the `STAT TESTS` menu. Scroll down the list and select `5:1-Prop ZTest`.
- Specify the hypothesized proportion `P0`.
- Enter `x`, the observed number of wins: `.542*2425`. The calculator evaluates that as 1314.35—not possible, even with rain-shortened games. Round off to a whole number of wins.
- Specify the sample size.
- Since this is a one-tail upper tail test, indicate that you want to see if the observed proportion is significantly greater than what was hypothesized.
- `Calculate` the result.

OK, the rest is up to you. The calculator reports a z-score of 4.12 and a P-value (in scientific notation) of 1.88×10^{-5}, or about 0.00002. Such a small P-value indicates that the high percentage of home team wins is unlikely to be sampling error. State your conclusion in the appropriate context.

And how big is the advantage for the home team? In the last chapter you learned to create a 95% confidence interval. Try it here.

Looks like we can be 95% confident that in major league baseball games the home team wins between 52.2% and 56.2% of the time. Over a full season, that's an average of about two to five extra victories for a team in the 81 games they play at home.

P-Values and Decisions: What to Tell About a Hypothesis Test

Tell More

"Extraordinary claims require extraordinary proof."
—Carl Sagan

Hypothesis tests are particularly useful when we must make a decision. Is the defendant to be considered guilty or not? Should we choose print advertising or television? Questions like these cannot always be answered with the margins of error of confidence intervals. The absolute nature of the hypothesis test decision, however, makes some people (including the authors) uneasy. If possible, it's often a good idea to report the confidence interval for the parameter of interest as well.

How small should the P-value be in order for you to reject the null hypothesis? A jury needs enough evidence to show the defendant guilty "beyond a reasonable doubt." How does that translate to P-values? The answer is that it's highly context-dependent. When we're screening for a disease and want to be sure we treat all those who are sick, we may be willing to reject the null hypothesis of no disease with a fairly large P-value. But a longstanding hypothesis, believed by many to be true, needs stronger evidence (and a correspondingly small P-value) to reject it.

See if you require the same P-value to reject each of the following null hypotheses:

- A renowned musicologist claims that she can distinguish between the works of Mozart and Haydn simply by hearing a randomly selected 20 seconds of music from any work by either composer. What's the null hypothesis? If she's just guessing, she'll get 50% of the pieces correct on average. So our null hypothesis is that p is 50%. If she's for real, she'll get more than 50% correct. Now, we present her with 10 pieces of Mozart or Haydn chosen at random. She gets 9 out of 10 correct. It turns out that the P-value associated with that result is 0.011. (In other words, if you tried to just guess, you'd get at least 9 out of 10 correct only about 1% of the time.) What would *you* conclude? Most people would probably reject the null hypothesis and be convinced that she has some ability to do as she claims. Why? Because the P-value is small, and we don't have any particular reason to doubt the alternative.
- On the other hand, imagine a student who bets that he can make a flipped coin land the way he wants just by thinking hard. To test him, we flip a fair coin 10 times. Suppose he gets 9 out of 10 right. This also has a P-value of 0.011. Are you willing now to reject this null hypothesis? Are you convinced that he's not just lucky? What amount of evidence *would* convince you? We require more evidence when rejecting the null hypotheses would contradict longstanding beliefs or other scientific results. Of course, with sufficient evidence we would revise our opinions (and scientific theories). That's how science makes progress.

Another factor in choosing a P-value is the importance of the issue being tested. Consider the following two tests:

- A researcher claims that the proportion of college students who hold part-time jobs now is higher than the proportion known to hold such jobs a decade ago. You might be willing to believe the claim (and reject the null hypothesis of no change) with a P-value of 10%.
- An engineer claims that the proportion of rivets holding the wing on an airplane that are likely to fail is below the proportion at which the wing would fall off. What P-value would be small enough to get you to fly on that plane?

Your conclusion about any null hypothesis should be accompanied by the P-value of the test. If possible, it should also include a confidence interval for the parameter of interest. Don't just declare the null hypothesis rejected or not rejected. Report the P-value to show the strength of the evidence against the hypothesis. This will let each reader decide whether or not to reject the null hypothesis.

Tests and Intervals STEP-BY-STEP

Advances in medical care such as prenatal ultrasound examination now make it possible to determine a child's sex early in a pregnancy. There is a fear that in some cultures some parents may use this technology to select the gender of their children. A study from Punjab, India (E. E. Booth, M. Verma, R. S. Beri, "Fetal Sex Determination in Infants in Punjab, India: Correlations and Implications," *BMJ* 309 [12 November 1994]: 1259–1261) reports that in 1993 in one hospital 56.9% of the 550 live births that year were boys. It's a medical fact that male babies are slightly more common than female babies. The study's authors report a baseline for this region of 51.7% male live births.

Let's consider two related questions. First, we wonder what the sample proportion of 56.9% indicates. Could this deviation from the historical percentage of 51.7% be explained just from natural sampling variability, or is this evidence to suggest that there really has been a change in the percentage of male births?

We may also want to know how large the change might be, so we'll need a confidence interval, too. Tests and intervals are closely related, but for proportions, they are not quite identical calculations. Seeing them together step-by-step helps to show their similarities and differences.

Think

Hypotheses State what we want to know.

The null hypothesis makes the claim of no difference from the baseline.

Before seeing the data, we were interested in any change in male births, so the alternative hypothesis is two-sided.

We want to know whether the proportion of male births has changed from the established baseline of 51.7%. The parameter of interest is the proportion of male births.

$$H_0: p = 0.517$$

$$H_A: p \neq 0.517$$

Plan

Check the conditions.

✓ **Independence assumption:** There is no reason to think that the sex of one birth can affect the sex of other babies, so births can reasonably be assumed to be independent with regard to the sex of the child.

✓ **Random sampling condition:** The 550 live births are not a random sample. This may influence our ability to extend our conclusions beyond the births studied.

✓ **10% condition:** We would like to be able to make statements about births at this hospital or at similar hospitals in India. These 550 births are less than 10% of all of those births.

For testing proportions, the conditions are the same ones we had for making confidence intervals except that we check the success/failure condition with the *hypothesized* proportions rather than with the *observed* proportions.

✓ **Success/failure condition:** Both $np_0 = 550(.517) = 284.35$ and $nq_0 = 550(.483) = 265.65$ are greater than 10; we expect the births of more than 10 boys and more than 10 girls, so the sample is large enough.

Specify the sampling distribution.

Because the conditions are satisfied, it is appropriate to model the sampling distribution of the proportion with a $N(p_0, SD(\hat{p}))$ model.

Tell what test you plan to use.

We can perform a **one-proportion z-test.**

Show

Mechanics

The null model gives us the mean, and (because we are working with proportions) the mean gives us the standard deviation. Since we have p_0, we're able to find the standard deviation of $\hat{p}$.

The null model is a Normal distribution with a mean of 0.517 and a standard deviation of

$$SD(\hat{p}) = \sqrt{\frac{p_0 q_0}{n}}$$

$$= \sqrt{\frac{(0.517)(1 - 0.517)}{550}} = 0.0213$$

The observed proportion is $\hat{p} = 0.569$,

Make a picture. Sketch a Normal model centered at $p_0 = 0.517$. Shade the region to the right of the observed proportion, and because this is a two-tail test, also shade the corresponding region in the other tail.

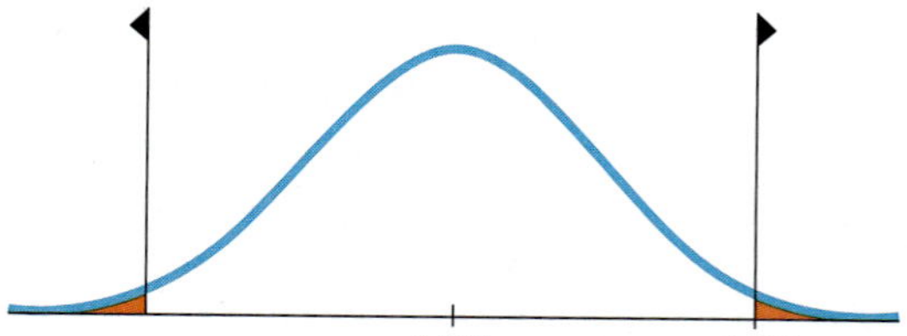

We next find the z-score for the observed proportion to find out how many standard deviations it is from the hypothesized proportion.

$$z = \frac{\hat{p} - p_0}{SD(\hat{p})} = \frac{0.569 - 0.517}{0.0213} = 2.44$$

so the sample proportion lies 2.44 standard deviations above the mean.

From the z-score we can find the P-value using a table or technology.

Because this is a two-tail test, the P-value is the probability of observing an outcome more than 2.44 standard deviations from the mean of a Normal model *in either direction.* We must therefore *double* the probability we find in the upper tail.

$$P = 2P(z > 2.44) = 2(0.0073) = 0.0146$$

Tell

Conclusion

Write the conclusion. Remember to link your decision about the null hypothesis to the P-value, and then state your conclusion in the correct context.

The P-value of 0.0146 says that if the true proportion of male babies were still at 51.7%, then an observed proportion as different as 56.9% male babies would occur at random only about 15 times in 1000. We reject the null hypothesis. This is strong evidence that the birth ratio of boys to girls is not equal to its natural level, but rather has increased.

We should be careful here not to jump to any conclusions. Our P-value is roughly at the level of 1 time in 70. We can't be sure how this deviation came about, whether this hospital is typical, or whether the time period studied was selected randomly.

Think Again

How big a difference are we talking about? Let's find a confidence interval for the percentage of male births.

Plan

Check the conditions.

The conditions are identical to those for the hypothesis test, with one difference. Now we are not given a hypothesized proportion, p_0, so we must instead work with the observed proportion $\hat{p}$.

✓ **Success/failure condition:** Both $n\hat{p} = 550(0.569) = 313$ and $n\hat{q} = 237$ are greater than 10.

Specify the sampling distribution. Notice that now the parameters are based on the observed proportion and its *standard error.*

Because the conditions are satisfied, it is appropriate to model the sampling distribution of the proportion with a $N(\hat{p}, SE(\hat{p}))$ model.

Tell what method you plan to use.

We can find a **one-proportion z-interval.**

Show More

Mechanics

We can't find the sampling model's standard deviation from the proportion we used in the null model. After all, we've just rejected it. Instead, we find the *standard error* of $\hat{p}$ from the *observed* proportions. Other than that substitution, the calculation looks the same as for the hypothesis test.

$$SE(\hat{p}) = \sqrt{\frac{\hat{p}\hat{q}}{n}}$$

$$= \sqrt{\frac{(0.569)(1 - 0.569)}{550}} = 0.0211$$

Use the SE and the critical value for a 95% confidence interval to find the margin of error.

The sampling model is Normal, so for a 95% confidence interval, the critical value $z^* = 1.96$.

$$ME = z^* \times SE(\hat{p})$$
$$= 1.96(0.0211) = 0.041$$

Create the confidence interval for p:

$$\hat{p} \pm ME$$

So the 95% confidence interval is

$$0.569 \pm 0.041$$
$$\text{or } (0.528, 0.610)$$

Tell All

Conclusion

Confidence intervals help us think about the size of the effect. Here we can see that the change from the baseline of 51.7% male births might be quite substantial.

We are 95% confident that the true proportion of male births is between 52.8% and 61%.

Here's a portion of a Normal table that includes the part that gives the probability we needed for the hypothesis test. At $z = 2.44$ the table gives the percentile as 0.9927. The upper tail probability (shaded red) is therefore $1 - 0.9927 = 0.0073$, so for our two-tailed test the P-value is $2(0.0073) = 0.0146$.

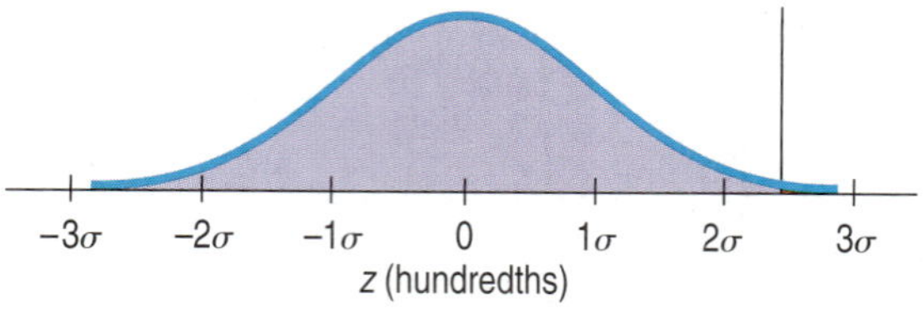

z	0.00	0.01	0.02	0.03	0.04	0.05
1.9	0.9713	0.9719	0.9726	0.9732	0.9738	0.9744
2.0	0.9772	0.9778	0.9783	0.9788	0.9793	0.9798
2.1	0.9821	0.9826	0.9830	0.9834	0.9838	0.9842
2.2	0.9861	0.9864	0.9868	0.9871	0.9875	0.9878
2.3	0.9893	0.9896	0.9898	0.9901	0.9904	0.9906
2.4	0.9918	0.9920	0.9922	0.9925	0.9927	0.9929
2.5	0.9938	0.9940	0.9941	0.9943	0.9945	0.9946
2.6	0.9953	0.9955	0.9956	0.9957	0.9959	0.9960

A portion of a Normal table with the look-up for $z = 2.44$ indicated. Since $1 - 0.9927 = 0.0073$, the P-value we want is $2(0.0073) = 0.0146$. **Figure 20.2**

A Better Confidence Interval for Proportions (Optional)

Confidence intervals and hypothesis tests for proportions use different standard deviation formulas because of the special property that links a proportion's value with its standard deviation. It turns out, however, that we can improve on the confidence interval for a proportion with a simple adjustment. The adjustment brings the standard deviations for the test and confidence interval into closer agreement.

First proposed by American statistician Edwin Wilson, this improved method is a little strange. It takes the original counts and adds four *phony* observations, two to the successes, two to the failures. So instead of the proportion $\hat{p} = \frac{y}{n}$, we use the adjusted proportion $\tilde{p} = \frac{y + 2}{n + 4}$ and, for convenience, we write $\tilde{n} = n + 4$. Wilson's method modifies the interval by using these adjusted values for both the center of the interval *and* the margin of error. The adjusted interval is

$$\tilde{p} \pm z^* \sqrt{\frac{\tilde{p}(1 - \tilde{p})}{\tilde{n}}}.$$

This adjusted form gives better performance overall[3] and works much better for proportions near 0 or 1. It has the additional advantage that we no longer need to check the success/failure condition that $n\hat{p}$ and $n\hat{q}$ are greater than 10.

What Can Go Wrong? Hypothesis tests are so widely used—and so widely misused—that we've devoted the next chapter to discussing the issues involved.

[3] By "better performance" we mean that a 95% confidence interval has more nearly a 95% chance of covering the true population proportion. Simulation studies have shown that our original, simpler confidence interval in fact is less likely than 95% to cover the true population proportion until the sample size gets much larger. (A. Agresti and B.A. Clull, "Approximate Is Better Than 'Exact' for Interval Estimation of Binomial Proportions," *The American Statistician*, 52 [1998]: 119–126.)

Hypothesis Tests for Proportions and the Computer

Hypothesis tests for proportions are so easy and natural that many statistics packages don't offer special commands for them. Most statistics programs want to know the "success" and "failure" status for each case. Usually these are given as 1 or 0, but they might be category names like "yes" and "no". Often we just know the proportion of successes, $\hat{p}$, and the total count, *n*. Computer packages don't usually deal naturally with summary data like this, but the statistics routines found on many graphing calculators do. These calculators allow you to test hypotheses from summaries of the data—usually all you need to enter are the number of successes and the sample size.

Connections

Hypothesis tests and confidence intervals share many of the same concepts. Both rely on sampling distribution models, and because the models are the same and require the same assumptions both check the same conditions. They also calculate many of the same statistics. Like confidence intervals, hypothesis tests use the standard deviation of the sampling distribution as a ruler, as we first saw in Chapter 6.

For testing, we find ourselves looking once again at *z*-scores, and we compute the P-value by finding the distance of our test statistic from the center of the null model. P-values are conditional probabilities. They give the probability of observing the result we have seen (or one even more extreme) *given* that the null hypothesis is true.

The standard Normal model is here again as our connection between *z*-score values and probabilities.

Key Concepts

Alternative hypothesis The alternative hypothesis proposes what we should conclude if we find the null hypothesis to be unlikely.

Null hypothesis The claim being assessed in a hypothesis test is called the null hypothesis. Usually, the null hypothesis is a statement of "no change from the traditional value," "no effect," "no difference," or "no relationship." For a claim to be a testable null hypothesis, it must specify a value for some population parameter that can form the basis for assuming a sampling distribution for a test statistic.

One-proportion *z*-test A test of the null hypothesis that the proportion of a single sample equals a specified value (H_0: $p = p_0$) by referring the statistic $z = \dfrac{\hat{p} - p_0}{SD(\hat{p})}$ to a standard Normal model.

One-sided alternative An alternative hypothesis is one-sided (H_A: $p > p_0$ or H_A: $p < p_0$) when we are interested in deviations in *only one* direction away from the hypothesized parameter value.

P-value The probability of observing a value for a test statistic at least as far from the hypothesized value as the statistic value actually observed if the null hypothesis is true. A small P-value indicates either that the observation is improbable or that the probability calculation was based on incorrect assumptions. The assumed truth of the null hypothesis is the assumption under suspicion.

Two-sided alternative An alternative hypothesis is two-sided (H_A: $p \neq p_0$) when we are interested in deviations in *either* direction away from the hypothesized parameter value.

Skills

When you complete this lesson you should:

Think

- Be able to state the null and alternative hypotheses for a one-proportion z-test.
- Know the conditions that must be true for a one-proportion z-test to be appropriate and how to examine your data for violations of those conditions.
- Be able to identify and use the alternative hypothesis when testing hypotheses. Understand how to choose between a one-sided and two-sided alternative hypothesis and know how to defend the choice of a one-sided alternative.

Show

- Be able to perform a one-proportion z-test.

Tell

- Be able to write a sentence interpreting the results of a one-proportion z-test.
- Know how to interpret the meaning of a P-value in nontechnical language, making clear that the probability claim is made about computed values under the assumption that the null model is true and not about the population parameter of interest.

Exercises

1. Hypotheses. Write the null and alternative hypotheses you would use to test each of the following situations.

a) A governor is concerned about his "negatives"—the percentage of state residents who express disapproval of his job performance. His political committee pays for a series of TV ads, hoping that they can keep the negatives below 30%. They will use follow-up polling to assess the ads' effectiveness.

b) Is a coin fair?

c) Only about 20% of people who try to quit smoking succeed. Sellers of a motivational tape claim that listening to the recorded messages can help people quit.

2. More hypotheses. Write the null and alternative hypotheses you would use to test each of the following situations.

a) In the 1950s only about 40% of high school graduates went on to college. Has the percentage changed?

b) 20% of cars of a certain model have needed costly transmission work after being driven between 50,000 and 100,000 miles. The manufacturer hopes that redesign of a transmission component has solved this problem.

c) We field test a new flavor soft drink, planning to market it only if we are sure that at least 60% of the people like the flavor.

3. Negatives. After the political ad campaign described in Exercise 1a, pollsters check the governor's negatives. They test the hypothesis that the ads produced no change against the alternative that the negatives are now below 30%, and find a P-value of 0.22. Which conclusion is appropriate?

a) There's a 22% chance that the ads worked.

b) There's a 78% chance that the ads worked.

c) There's a 22% chance that the poll they conducted is correct.

d) There's a 22% chance that poll results could be just natural sampling variation rather than a real change in public opinion.

4. Dice. The seller of a loaded die claims that it will favor the outcome 6. We don't believe that claim, and roll the die 200 times to test an appropriate hypothesis. Our P-value turns out to be 0.03. Which conclusion is appropriate?

a) There's a 3% chance that the die is fair.

b) There's a 97% chance that the die is fair.

c) There's a 3% chance that a loaded die could randomly produce the results we observed, so it's reasonable to conclude that the die is fair.

d) There's a 3% chance that a fair die could randomly produce the results we observed, so it's reasonable to conclude that the die is loaded.

5. Relief. A company's old antacid formula provided relief for 70% of the people who used it. The company tests a new formula to see if it is better, and gets a P-value of 0.27. Is it reasonable to conclude that the new formula and the old one are equally effective? Explain.

6. Cars. A survey investigating whether the proportion of today's high school seniors who own their own cars is higher than it was a decade ago finds a P-value of 0.017. Is it reasonable to conclude that more high schoolers have cars? Explain.

7. Blinking timers. Many people have trouble programming their VCRs, so a company has developed what it hopes will be easier instructions. The goal is to have at least 96% of customers succeed. The company tests the new system on 200 people, of whom 188 were successful. Is this strong evidence that the new system fails to meet the company's goal? A student's test of this hypothesis is shown below. How many mistakes can you find?

$H_0: \hat{p} = 0.96$

$H_A: \hat{p} \neq 0.96$

SRS, $0.96(200) > 10$

$$\frac{188}{200} = 0.94; \quad SD(\hat{p}) = \sqrt{\frac{(0.94)(0.06)}{200}} = 0.017$$

$$z = \frac{0.96 - 0.94}{0.017} = 1.18$$

$P = P(z > 1.18) = 0.12$

There is strong evidence that the new system does not work.

8. Got milk? In November 2001, The *Ag Globe Trotter* newsletter reported that 90% of adults drink milk. A regional farmers' organization planning a new marketing campaign across its multi-county area polls a random sample of 750 adults living there. In this sample, 657 people said that they drink milk. Do these responses provide strong evidence that the 90% figure is not accurate for this region? Correct the mistakes you find in a student's attempt to test an appropriate hypothesis.

$H_0: \hat{p} = 0.9$

$H_A: \hat{p} < 0.9$

SRS, $750 > 10$

$$\frac{657}{750} = 0.876; \quad SD(\hat{p}) = \sqrt{\frac{(0.88)(0.12)}{750}} = 0.012$$

$$z = \frac{0.876 - 0.94}{0.012} = -2$$

$P = P(z > -2) = 0.977$

There is more than a 97% chance that the stated percentage is correct for this region.

9. Dowsing. In a rural area only about 30% of the wells that are drilled find adequate water at a depth of 100 feet or less. A local man claims to be able to find water by "dowsing"—using a forked stick to indicate where the well should be drilled. You check with 80 of his customers and find that 27 have wells less than 100 feet deep. What do you conclude about his claim? (We consider a P-value of around 5% to represent strong evidence.)

a) Write appropriate hypotheses.
b) Check the necessary assumptions.
c) Perform the mechanics of the test. What is the P-value?
d) Explain carefully what the P-value means in this context.
e) What's your conclusion?

10. Autism. In the 1980s it was generally believed that autism affected about 5% of the nation's children. Some people believe that the increase in the number of chemicals in the environment has led to an increase in the incidence of autism. A recent study examined 384 children and found that 46 of them showed signs of some form of autism. Is this strong evidence that the level of autism has increased? (We consider a P-value of around 5% to represent strong evidence.)

a) Write appropriate hypotheses.
b) Check the necessary assumptions.
c) Perform the mechanics of the test. What is the P-value?
d) Explain carefully what the P-value means in this context.
e) What's your conclusion?
f) Do environmental chemicals cause autism?

11. Smoking. National data in the 1960s showed that about 44% of the adult population had never smoked cigarettes. In 1995 a national health survey interviewed a random sample of 881 adults and found that 52% had never been smokers.

a) Create a 95% confidence interval for the proportion of adults (in 1995) who had never been smokers.
b) Does this provide evidence of a change in behavior among Americans? Using your confidence interval, test an appropriate hypothesis and state your conclusion.

12. Satisfaction. A company hopes to improve customer satisfaction, setting as a goal no more than 5% negative comments. A random survey of 350 customers found only 10 with complaints.

a) Create a 95% confidence interval for the true level of dissatisfaction among customers.
b) Does this provide evidence that the company has reached its goal? Using your confidence interval, test an appropriate hypothesis and state your conclusion.

13. Pollution. A company with a fleet of 150 cars found that the emissions systems of 7 out of the 22 they tested failed to meet pollution control guidelines. Is this strong evidence that more than 20% of the fleet might be out of compliance? Test an appropriate hypothesis and state your conclusion. Be sure the appropriate assumptions and conditions are satisfied before you proceed.

14. Scratch and dent. An appliance manufacturer stockpiles washers and dryers in a large warehouse for shipment to retail stores. Sometimes in handling them the appliances get damaged. Even though the damage may be minor, the company must sell those machines at drastically reduced prices. The company goal is to keep the level of damaged machines below 2%. One day an inspector randomly checks 60 washers and finds that 5 of them have scratches or dents. Is this strong evidence that the warehouse is failing to meet the company goal? Test an appropriate hypothesis and state your conclusion. Be sure the appropriate assumptions and conditions are satisfied before you proceed.

15. Twins. In 2001 a national vital statistics report indicated that about 3% of all births produced twins. Data from a large city hospital found only 7 sets of twins were born to 469 teenage girls. Does that suggest that mothers under age 20 may be less likely to have twins? Test an appropriate hypothesis and state your conclusion. Be sure the appropriate assumptions and conditions are satisfied before you proceed.

16. Football. During the 2000 season, the home team won 138 of the 240 regular season National Football League games. Is this strong evidence of a home field advantage in professional football? Test an appropriate hypothesis and state your conclusion. Be sure the appropriate assumptions and conditions are satisfied before you proceed.

17. WebZine. A magazine is considering the launch of an online edition. The magazine plans to go ahead only if it's convinced that more than 25% of current readers would subscribe. The magazine contacts a simple random sample of 500 current subscribers, and 137 of those surveyed expressed interest. What should the company do? Test an appropriate hypothesis and state your conclusion. Be sure the appropriate assumptions and conditions are satisfied before you proceed.

18. Seeds. A garden center wants to store leftover packets of vegetable seeds for sale the following spring, but the center is concerned that the seeds may not germinate at the same rate a year later. The manager finds a packet of last year's green bean seeds and plants them as a test. Although the packet claims a germination rate of 92%, only 171 of 200 test seeds sprout. Is this evidence that the seeds have lost viability during a year in storage? Test an appropriate hypothesis and state your conclusion. Be sure the appropriate assumptions and conditions are satisfied before you proceed.

19. Women executives. A company is criticized because only 13 of 43 people in executive-level positions are women. The company explains that although this proportion is lower than it might wish, it's not surprising given that only 40% of all their employees are women. What do you think? Test an appropriate hypothesis and state your conclusion. Be sure the appropriate assumptions and conditions are satisfied before you proceed.

20. Jury. Census data for a certain county shows that 19% of the adult residents are Hispanic. Suppose 72 people are called for jury duty, and only 9 of them are Hispanic. Does this call into question the fairness of the jury selection system? Explain.

21. Dropouts. Some people are concerned that new tougher standards and high stakes tests adopted in many states may drive up the high school dropout rate. The National Center for Education Statistics reported that the high school dropout rate for the year 2000 was 10.9%. One school district, whose dropout rate has always been very close to the national average, reports that 210 of their 1782 students dropped out last year. Is their experience evidence that the dropout rate may be increasing? Explain.

22. Acid rain. A study of the effects of acid rain on trees in the Hopkins Forest shows that of 100 trees sampled, 25 of them exhibited some sort of damage from acid rain. This rate seemed to be higher than the 15% quoted in a recent *Environmetrics* article on the average proportion of damaged trees in the Northeast. Does the sample suggest that trees in the Hopkins Forest are more susceptible than the rest of the region? Comment, and write up your own conclusions based on an appropriate confidence interval as well as a hypothesis test. Include any assumptions you made about the data.

23. Lost luggage. An airline's public relations department says that the airline rarely loses Passengers' luggage. It further claims that on those occasions when luggage is lost, 90% is recovered and delivered to its owner within 24 hours. A consumer group who surveyed a large number of air travelers found that only 103 of 122 people who lost luggage on that airline were reunited with the missing items by the next day. Does this cast doubt on the airline's claim? Explain.

24. TV ads. A start-up company is about to market a new computer printer. It decides to gamble by running commercials during the Super Bowl. The company hopes that name recognition will be worth the high cost of the ads. The goal of the company is that at least 40% of the public recognize its brand name and associate it with computer equipment. The day after the game, a pollster contacts 420 randomly chosen adults, and finds that 181 of them know that this company manufactures printers. Would you recommend that the company continue to advertise during Super Bowls? Explain.

Chapter 21

More About Tests

WHO	Trials of TT practitioners attempting to detect a HEF.
WHAT	Success/failure
WHEN	1998 publication date
WHY	Test claim of HEF/debunk TT?

Therapeutic touch (TT), taught in many schools of nursing, is a therapy in which the practitioner moves her hands near, but not touching, a patient in an attempt to manipulate a "human energy field" (HEF). Therapeutic touch practitioners believe that by adjusting this field they can promote healing. However, no instrument has ever detected a human energy field and no experiment has ever shown that TT practitioners can detect such a field.

In 1998 the *Journal of the American Medical Association* published a paper reporting work by a then 9-year-old girl (L. Rosa, E. Rosa, L. Sarner, S. Barrett, "A Close Look at Therapeutic Touch," *JAMA* 279(13) [1 April 1998]:1005–1010). She had performed a simple experiment in which she challenged 15 TT practitioners to detect whether her unseen hand was hovering over their left or right hand (selected by a coin flip). The practitioners "warmed up" with a period during which they could see the experimenter's hand, and each said that they could detect the girl's human energy field. Then a screen was placed so that the practitioners could not see the girl's hand, and they attempted 10 trials each. Overall, of 150 trials, the TT practitioners were successful 70 times, for a success proportion of 46.7%. Is there evidence from this experiment that TT practitioners can successfully detect a "human energy field"?

Zero In on the Null

Null hypotheses have special requirements. In order to perform a statistical test of the hypothesis, the null must be a statement about the value of a parameter from a model. We use this value to compute the probability that the observed sample statistic—or something even farther from the null value—would occur.

How do we choose the null hypothesis? The appropriate null arises directly from the context of the problem. It is not dictated by the data, but instead by the situation.

One good way to identify both the null and alternative hypotheses is to think about the *Why* of the situation. A pharmaceutical company wanting to develop and market a new drug needs to show that the new drug is effective. The Food and Drug Administration (FDA) will not allow a new drug to be sold in the United States that has not been proven effective in a double-blind, randomized clinical trial. (Most countries have similar restrictions on the introduction of new medications.) The typical null hypothesis in this case is that the proportion of patients recovering after receiving the new drug is the same as we would expect of patients receiving a placebo. The alternative hypothesis is that the new drug cures a higher proportion. But a physician seeking the best treatment for her patients would probably prefer to see the new drug tested against a currently available treatment.

In the 1930s, a series of experiments was performed at Duke University in an attempt to see whether humans were capable of extrasensory perception, or ESP. A set of cards with 5 symbols, made famous in the movie *Ghostbusters,* was used.

In the experiment, the "sender" selects one of the 5 cards at random from a deck and then concentrates on it. The "receiver" tries to determine which card it is. If we let p be the proportion of correct responses, what's the null hypothesis? Since there are 5 possible responses, H_0 would be $p = 0.20$. What's the alternative? It seems that it should be $p > 0.20$, a one-sided alternative. But some ESP researchers have expressed the claim that if the proportion guessed were much *lower* than expected, that would show an "interference" and should be considered evidence for ESP as well. So they argue for a two-sided alternative.

To write a null hypothesis, you can't just choose any parameter value you like. The null must relate to the question at hand. Nor can you automatically interpret "null" to mean zero. A claim that the TT practitioners should guess correctly *none of the time* would be absurd. The null hypothesis in this case is that the proportion of correct responses is 0.5—what you'd expect from random guessing. You need to find the value for the parameter in the null hypothesis from the context of the problem.

There is a temptation to state your *claim* as the null hypothesis. As we have seen, however, you cannot prove a null hypothesis true any more than you can prove a defendant innocent. So, it makes more sense to use what you want to show as the *alternative.* This way, when you reject the null, you are left with what you want to show.

Another One-Proportion *z*-Test STEP-BY-STEP

Let's look at the therapeutic touch experiment with a one-proportion *z*-test.

Think

Hypotheses

The null hypothesis is that the TT practitioners are just guessing. Because there are two choices, if the practitioners are just guessing, they'll succeed about half the time.

A one-sided alternative hypothesis seems the natural one to test here. We wouldn't be interested in below-chance performance.

We want to know whether the TT practitioners could detect a "human energy field" (HEF) at better than chance levels. The parameter of interest is the proportion of successful identifications.

H_0: $p = 0.50$

H_A: $p > 0.50$

Plan

Check the conditions.

If some TT practitioners had been successful, their trials might not be independent, but the assumption only needs to hold if the null hypothesis is true. Under the null hypothesis that there is no HEF, each of these trials is an independent randomized guess.

✓ **Independence assumption:** The choice of hand was randomized with a coin flip. Under the null hypothesis, the trials should be independent.

✓ **Randomization:** The experiment was randomized by flipping a coin.

✓ **10% condition:** The experiment observes some of what could be an infinite number of trials.

✓ **Success/failure condition:** Both $np_0 = 150(0.5) = 75$ and $nq_0 = 150(0.5) = 75$ are greater than 10. We expect more than 10 successes and more than 10 failures, so enough trials were run.

State the null model.

Because the conditions are satisfied, it is appropriate to model the sampling distribution of the proportion with a $N(p_0, SD(\hat{p}))$ model.

Name the test.

We can perform a **one-proportion z-test.**

Show

Mechanics

Find the standard deviation of the sampling model using the hypothesized proportion, p_0.

The null model has a mean of 0.5 and a standard deviation of

$$SD(\hat{p}) = \sqrt{\frac{p_0q_0}{n}} = \sqrt{\frac{(0.5)(0.5)}{150}} \approx 0.041.$$

Observed proportion $\hat{p}$ is 0.467.

Make a picture. Sketch a Normal model centered at the hypothesized success rate of 50%. This is an upper tail test, so shade the region to the right of the observed success rate.

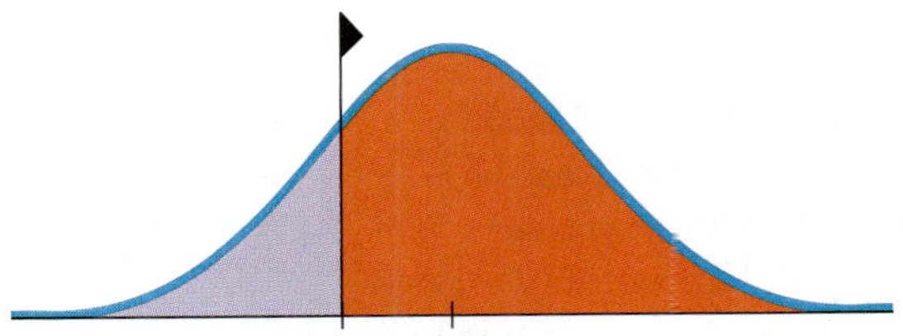

Find the z-score for the observed proportion.

$$z = \frac{\hat{p} - p_0}{SD(\hat{p})} = \frac{0.467 - 0.5}{0.41} = -0.805$$

Find the P-value by computer, calculator, or table (shown below). The P-value is the probability of observing a sample proportion at least as large as 0.467 if the true proportion were 0.5.

The observed success rate is 0.805 standard deviations below the hypothesized mean.

$$P = P(z > -0.805) = 0.788$$

Tell

Conclusion: Link the P-value to your decision about the null hypothesis, then state your conclusion in context.

The P-value of 0.788 says that if the true proportion of successful detections of a human energy field is 50%, then an observed proportion of 46.7% successes or more would occur at random about 8 times in 10. That's not a rare event, so we do not reject the null hypothesis.

If possible, propose a course of action. In the case of this study, the editor of the *Journal of the American Medical Association* suggested that insurance companies reconsider paying for therapeutic touch treatments. This, of course, raised a storm of protest letters from those who practice TT.

There is insufficient evidence to conclude that the practitioners are performing better than they would if they were just guessing.

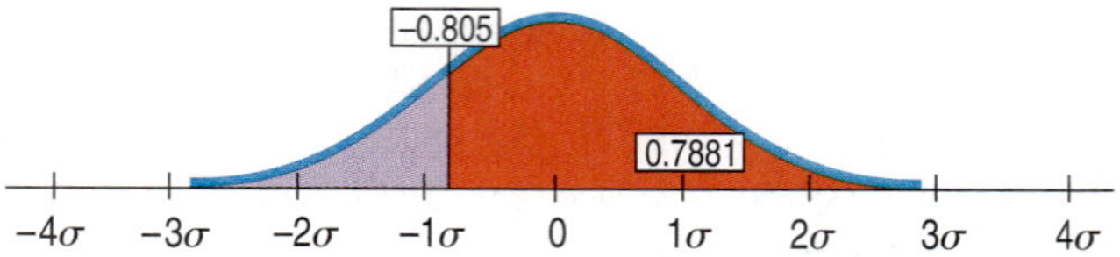

0.05	0.04	0.03	0.02	0.01	0.00	z
0.1711	0.1736	0.1762	0.1788	0.1814	0.1841	–0.9
0.1977	0.2005	0.2033	0.2061	0.2090	0.2119	–0.8
0.2266	0.2296	0.2327	0.2358	0.2389	0.2420	–0.7
0.2578	0.2611	0.2643	0.2676	0.2709	0.2743	–0.6
0.2912	0.2946	0.2981	0.3015	0.3050	0.3085	–0.5
0.3264	0.3300	0.3336	0.3372	0.3409	0.3446	–0.4
0.3632	0.3669	0.3707	0.3745	0.3783	0.3821	–0.3

A portion of the *z*-table corresponding to the test. The value -0.805 falls between -0.80 and -0.81. We'd have to interpolate to get from the table the accuracy we can get from technology. The P-value we want is the area of the right tail, so it's $1 - 0.2119 = 0.7881$. **Figure 21.1**

How to Think About P-values

A P-value is a conditional probability. It is the probability of the observed statistic *given* that the null hypothesis is true. To show this more clearly, we can write P-value = P (observed statistic value [or more extreme] $|\,H_0$).

Writing the P-value this way helps to make clear that the P-value is *not* the probability that the null hypothesis is true. It is a probability about the data. Let's say that again:

The P-value is not the probability that the null hypothesis is true.

The P-value is not even the probability that the null hypothesis is true *given* the data. We would write that probability as $P(H_0\,|$observed statistic value). This is the conditional probability in reverse. It would be nice to know this, but it's impossible to calculate without making additional assumptions. As we saw in Chapter 15, reversing the order in a conditional probability is difficult and the results can be counterintuitive.

Intuitively, smaller and smaller P-values lead us to doubt the null hypothesis more and more. But we cannot put a number on that doubt. We've agreed that extraordinary claims require stronger evidence. We've seen that we may not be willing to reject all claims with the same P-value. (Recall the example of the musicologist and the student claiming mental control over a coin flip.) Why was this? Because $P(H_0\,|\,\text{data})$ depends on our initial beliefs about $P(H_0)$. We have no way to quantify $P(H_0)$, however.

Suppose that as a political science major you are offered the chance to be a White House intern. There would be a very high probability that next summer you'll be in Washington, D.C. That is, *P*(Washington | Intern) would be high. But if we find a student in Washington, D.C., next summer, is it likely that he's a White House intern? Almost surely not; *P*(Intern | Washington) is low. You can't switch around conditional probabilities. The P-value is $P(\text{data}\,|\,H_0)$. We might like to report $P(H_0\,|\,\text{data})$, but these two quantities are NOT the same.

We can find the P-value, P(observed statistic value $|\,H_0$), because H_0 gives the parameter values that we need to find the required probability. But there's no direct way to find $P(H_0\,|$observed statistic value).[1] As tempting as it may be to say that a P-value of 0.03 means there's a 3% chance that the null hypothesis is true, that just isn't right. All we can say is that given the null hypothesis there's a 3% chance of observing the statistic value that we have actually observed (or one more unlike the null value).

[1]The approach to statistical inference known as Bayesian Statistics addresses the question in just this way, but it requires more advanced mathematics.

Alpha Levels

Sometimes we need to make a firm decision about whether or not to reject the null hypothesis. A jury must *decide* whether the evidence reaches the level of "beyond a reasonable doubt." A business must *select* a Web design. You need to decide which section of Statistics to enroll in.[2]

When the P-value is small, it tells us that our data are rare *given the null hypothesis*. As humans, we are suspicious of rare events. If the data are "rare enough," we just don't think that could have happened. Since the data *did* happen, something must be wrong. All we can do now is to reject the null hypothesis.

But how rare is "rare"?

We can define "rare event" arbitrarily by setting a threshold for our P-value. If our P-value falls below that point we'll reject the null hypothesis. We call such results **statistically significant.** The threshold is called an **alpha level.** Not surprisingly, it's labeled with the Greek letter α. Common alpha levels are .10, .05, and .01. You have the option—almost the *obligation*—to consider your alpha level carefully and choose an appropriate one for the situation. If you're assessing the safety of airbags, you'll want a low alpha level; even .01 might not be low enough. If you're just wondering whether folks prefer their pizza with or without pepperoni, you might be happy with $\alpha = .10$. It can be hard to justify your choice of α, though, so often we arbitrarily choose .05.

Sir Ronald Fisher (1890–1962) was one of the founders of modern Statistics. **Figure 21.2**

NOTATION ALERT:

The use of α to specify the threshold of statistical significance makes it unwise to use "α" for any other purpose in Statistics.

Of course, if the null hypothesis *is* true, no matter what alpha level you choose, you still have a probability α of rejecting the null hypothesis by mistake. This is the rare event we want to protect ourselves against. When we do reject the null hypothesis, no one ever thinks that *this* is one of those rare times. As statistician Stuart Hunter notes: *The statistician says "rare events do happen—but not to me!"*

Where did the value .05 come from? In 1931 in a famous book called *The Design of Experiments,* Sir Ronald Fisher discussed the amount of evidence needed to reject a null hypothesis. He said that it was *situation dependent,* but remarked, somewhat casually, that for many scientific applications, 1 out of 20 *might be* a reasonable value. Since then, some people—indeed some entire disciplines—have acted as if the number .05 is sacrosanct.

The alpha level is also called the **significance level.** When we reject the null hypothesis, we say that the test is "significant at that level." For example, we might say that we reject the null hypothesis "at the 5% level of significance." You must select the alpha level *before* you look at the data. Otherwise you can be accused of cheating by tuning your alpha level to suit the data.

What can you say if the P-value does not fall below α?

When you have not found sufficient evidence to reject the null according to the standard you have established, you should say that "The data have failed to provide sufficient evidence to reject the null hypothesis." Don't say that you "accept the null hypothesis." You certainly haven't proven or established it; it was assumed to begin with. You *can* say that you have *retained* the null hypothesis, or simply that you've failed to reject it.

Look again at the Step-by-Step example for therapeutic touch. The P-value was 0.795. This is so much larger than any reasonable alpha-level that we can't reject H_0. We concluded: "We fail to reject the null hypothesis. There is insufficient evidence to conclude that the practitioners are performing better than they would if they were just guessing."

[2] Is it too late to switch?

"The wise man proportions his belief to the evidence."
—David Hume, "Enquiry Concerning Human Understanding," 1748

The absolute nature of the reject/fail-to-reject decision when we use an alpha level may make you uncomfortable. If your P-value falls just slightly above your alpha level, you're not allowed to reject the null. Yet a P-value just barely below the alpha level leads to rejection. If this bothers you, you're in good company. Many statisticians think it better to report the P-value than to choose an alpha level and carry the decision through to a final reject/fail-to-reject verdict. So when you decide to declare a verdict, it's a good idea to report the P-value as an indication of the strength of the evidence.

It's in the stars

Some disciplines carry the idea further and code P-values by their size. In this scheme, a P-value between 0.05 and 0.01 gets highlighted by a *. One between 0.01 and 0.001 gets two **, and a P-value less than 0.001 gets ***. This can be a convenient summary of the weight of evidence against the null hypothesis if it's not taken too literally. But we warn you against taking the distinctions too seriously and against making a black-and-white decision near the boundaries. The boundaries are a matter of tradition, not science; there is nothing special about 0.05. A P-value of 0.051 should be looked at very seriously and not casually thrown away just because it's larger than 0.05, and one that's 0.009 is not very different from one that's 0.011.

Sometimes it's best to report that the conclusion is not yet clear and to suggest that more data be gathered. (In a trial, a jury may "hang" and be unable to return a verdict.) In these cases, it's still a good idea to report the P-value, since it's the best summary we have of what the data say or fail to say about the null hypothesis.

What Not to Say About Significance

A large insurance company mined its data and found a statistically significant ($P = 0.04$) difference between the mean value of policies sold in 2001 and 2002. The difference in the mean values was $9.83. Even though it was statistically significant, management did not see this as an important difference when a typical policy sold for more than $1000. On the other hand, even a clinically important improvement of 10% in cure rate with a new treatment is not likely to be statistically significant in a study of fewer than 225 patients. A small clinical trial would probably not be conclusive.

What do we mean when we say that a test is statistically significant? All we mean is that the test statistic had a P-value lower than our alpha-level. Don't be lulled into thinking that statistical significance carries with it any sense of practical importance or impact.

For large samples, even small, unimportant ("insignificant") deviations from the null hypothesis can be statistically significant. On the other hand, if the sample is not large enough, even large, financially or scientifically "significant" differences may not be statistically significant.

It's good practice to report the magnitude of the difference between the observed statistic value and the null hypothesis value (in the data units) along with the P-value on which we base statistical significance.

Critical Values Again

When making a confidence interval, we've found a **critical value** to correspond to our selected confidence level. Critical values can also be used as a shortcut for

If you need to make a decision on the fly with no technology, remember "2." That's our old friend from the 68-95-99.7 Rule corresponding to a 2-sided test at $\alpha = .05$. The exact critical value for z is 1.96, but 2 is close enough for most decisions.

hypothesis tests. Before computers and calculators were common, P-values were hard to find. It was easier to select a few common alpha levels (0.05, 0.01, 0.001, for example) and learn the corresponding critical values for the Normal model (that is, the critical values corresponding to confidence levels 0.95, 0.99, and 0.999, respectively). Rather than looking up your z-score in the table, you could just check it directly against these critical values. Any z-score larger in magnitude (that is, more extreme) than a particular critical value has to be less likely, so it will have a P-value smaller than the corresponding probability. If we are willing to settle for a flat reject/fail-to-reject decision, comparing an observed z-score with the critical value for a specified alpha level gives a shortcut path to that decision. With technology, though, P-values are easy to find. And since they give more information about the strength of the evidence, there's no reason not to report them.

Here are the traditional critical values from the Normal model[3]:

α	1-sided	2-sided
.05	1.645	1.96
.01	2.28	2.575
.001	3.09	3.29

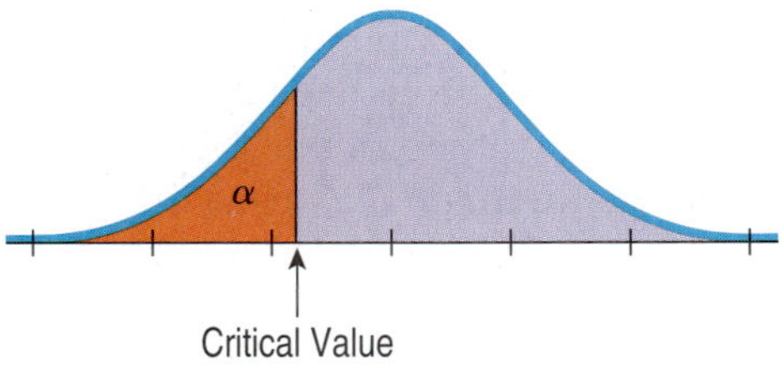

When the alternative is one-sided, the critical value puts all of α on one side. **Figure 21.3**

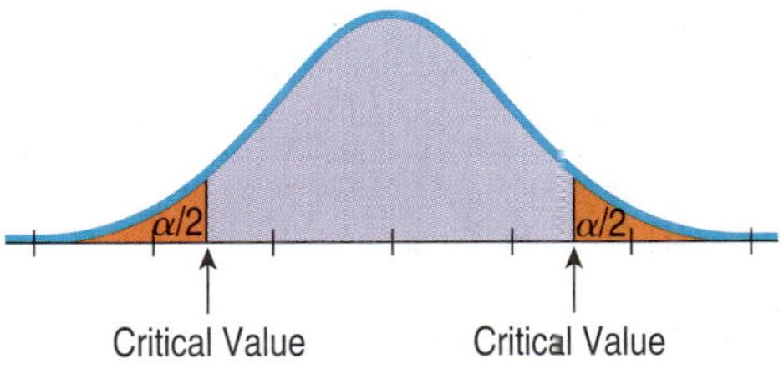

When the alternative is two-sided, the critical value splits α equally into two tails. **Figure 21.4**

Confidence Intervals and Hypothesis Tests

For the therapeutic touch example, a 90% confidence interval would give $0.47 \pm 1.65 \times 0.04 = (0.404, 0.536)$, or 40.4% to 53.6%. We could not reject H_0: $p = 0.50$ because 50% is a plausible value in the confidence interval. Indeed, *any* hypothesized value for the true proportion of successes in this interval is consistent with the data. For example, a success rate of 53% is a plausible value for the practitioners' true success rate. But we'd be pretty skeptical of a claim that TT practitioners can detect a human energy field 75% of the time. Any value outside the confidence interval would make a null hypothesis that we would reject, but we'd feel more strongly about values far outside the interval.

[3]In a sense, these are the flip side of the 68-95-99.7 Rule. There we chose simple statistical distances from the mean and recalled the areas of the tails. Here we select convenient tail areas (.05, .01, and .001, either on one side or adding both together) and record the corresponding statistical distances.

Confidence intervals and hypothesis tests are built from the same calculations.[4] They have the same assumptions and conditions. As we have just seen, you can approximate a hypothesis test by examining the confidence interval. Just ask whether the null hypothesis value is consistent with a confidence interval for the parameter at the corresponding confidence level. Because confidence intervals are naturally two-sided, they correspond to two-sided tests. For example, a 95% confidence interval corresponds to a two-sided hypothesis test at $\alpha = 5\%$. In general, a confidence interval with a confidence level of $C\%$ corresponds to a two-sided hypothesis test with an α level of $100 - C\%$.

The relationship between confidence intervals and one-sided hypothesis tests is a little more complicated. For a one-sided test with $\alpha = 5\%$, the corresponding confidence interval has a confidence level of 90%—that's 5% in each tail. In general, a confidence interval with a confidence level of $C\%$ corresponds to a one-sided hypothesis test with an α level of $\frac{1}{2}(100 - C)\%$.

Wear that Seatbelt! STEP-BY-STEP

The state police have embarked on a "Click It or Ticket" campaign with the goal of achieving at least 80% compliance with the law requiring all drivers to wear seatbelts. A local newspaper reports that a roadblock resulted in 33 tickets issued to 134 drivers who were unbelted when stopped for inspection. Does the fact that only $101/134 = 75.4\%$ of these drivers were wearing their seatbelts prove that the compliance rate among the driving public is below 80%?

Let's use a confidence interval to test a hypothesis.

Think

Hypotheses

If there's evidence that fewer than 80% of drivers are buckling up the "Click It or Ticket" campaign will continue.

We want to know whether the rate of compliance with the seatbelt law is less than 80%.

$$H_0: p = 0.80$$

$$H_A: p \neq 0.80$$

Plan

Check the conditions.

✓ **Independence assumption:** Drivers are not likely to influence one another when it comes to wearing a seatbelt.

✓ **Random sampling condition:** This wasn't a random sample, but we can assume these drivers are representative of the driving public.

[4] As we saw in Chapter 20, this is not *exactly* true for proportions. For a confidence interval, we estimate the standard deviation of $\hat{p}$ from $\hat{p}$ itself. Because we estimate it from the data, we have a *standard error.* For the corresponding hypothesis test, we use the model's standard deviation for $\hat{p}$, based on the null hypothesis value p_0. When $\hat{p}$ and p_0 are close, these calculations give very similar results. When they differ, you're likely to reject H_0 (because the observed proportion is far from your hypothesized value). In that case, you're better off building your confidence interval with a standard error estimated from the data.

✓ **10% condition:** The police stopped fewer than 10% of all drivers.

✓ **Success/failure condition:** There were 101 successes and 33 failures, both greater than 10. The sample is large enough.

State your method.

Under these conditions, the sampling model is Normal. We can create a **one-proportion z-interval.**

Show Write down the given information, and determine the sample proportion.

We know: $n = 134$, $x = 101$, so

$$\hat{p} = \frac{101}{134} = 0.754$$

To test the one-tailed hypothesis at the 5% level of significance, construct a 90% confidence interval. Determine the standard error of the sample proportion and the margin of error. The critical value is $z^* = 1.645$.

$$SE(\hat{p}) = \sqrt{\frac{\hat{p}\hat{q}}{n}} = \sqrt{\frac{(0.754)(0.246)}{134}} = 0.037$$

$$\begin{aligned} ME &= z^* \times SE(\hat{p}) \\ &= 1.645(0.037) = 0.061 \end{aligned}$$

The confidence interval is

estimate ± margin of error.

The 90% confidence interval is:

$$0.754 \pm 0.061 \text{ or } (0.693, 0.815).$$

Tell **Conclusion**

Link the confidence interval to your decision about the null hypothesis, then state your conclusion in context.

We can be 90% confident that between 69% and 81% of all drivers wear their seatbelts. Because the hypothesized rate of 80% is within this interval, we cannot reject the null hypothesis. There is insufficient evidence to conclude that fewer than 80% of all drivers are wearing seatbelts.

Making Errors

Nobody's perfect. Even with lots of evidence, we can still make the wrong decision. In fact, when we perform a hypothesis test, we can make mistakes in *two* ways:

I. The null hypothesis is true, but we mistakenly reject it.

II. The null hypothesis is false, but we fail to reject it.

These two types of errors are known as **Type I** and **Type II errors.** One way to keep the names straight is to remember that we start by assuming the null hypothesis is true, so a Type I error is the first kind of error we could make.

In medical disease testing, the null hypothesis is usually the assumption that a person is healthy. The alternative is that he or she has the disease we're testing for. So a Type I error is a **false positive;** a healthy person is diagnosed with the disease. A Type II error, in which an infected person is diagnosed as disease free, is a

Some false-positive results mean no more than an unnecessary chest X-ray. But for a drug test or a disease like AIDS, a false-positive result that is not kept confidential could have serious consequences.

false negative. These errors have other names, depending on the particular discipline and context.

Which type of error is more serious depends on the situation. In the jury trial, a Type I error occurs if the jury convicts an innocent person. A Type II error occurs if the jury fails to convict a guilty person. Which seems more serious? In medical diagnosis, a false negative could mean that a sick patient goes untreated. A false positive means that the person must undergo further tests. In a Statistics final exam (with H_0: the student has learned more than 60% of the material), a Type I error would be passing a student who in fact learned only 60% of the material, while a Type II error would be failing a student who knew enough to pass. Which of these errors seems more serious? It depends on the situation, the cost, and your point of view.

Here's an illustration of the situations:

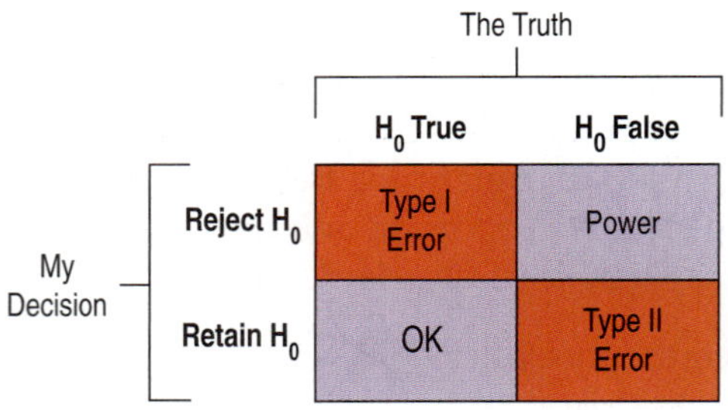

How often will a Type I error occur? It happens when the null hypothesis is true but we've had the bad luck to draw an unusual sample. To reject H_0, the P-value must fall below α. When H_0 is true, that happens *exactly* with probability α. So when you choose level α, you're setting the probability of a Type I error to α.

NOTATION ALERT:

This use of α and β can be confusing. In Statistics, α is almost always saved for the alpha level. But β's are sometimes used for linear model coefficients. Fortunately, it's usually quite clear which we mean.

What if H_0 is not true? Then we can't possibly make a Type I error. You can't get a false positive from a sick person. A Type I error can happen only when H_0 is true.

When H_0 is false and we reject it, we have done the right thing. Our ability to detect a false hypothesis is called the **power** of the test. In a jury trial, power is the ability of the criminal justice system to convict people who are guilty—a Good Thing! We'll have a lot more to say about power soon.

When H_0 is false and we fail to reject it, we have made a Type II error. We assign the letter β to the probability of this mistake. What's the value of β? That's harder to assess than α because we don't know *how false* H_0 is. When H_0 is true, we have a single parameter value. But when H_0 is false, we don't have one; we have many. We can compute the probability β for any parameter value in H_A. But which one should we choose?

We have seen ways to find a sample size by specifying the margin of error. Choosing the sample size to achieve a specified β (for a particular alternative value) is sometimes more appropriate, but the calculation is more complex and lies beyond the scope of this book.

There is no single value for β. In fact, we can think of a whole collection of β's, and display them as a curve, plotting each β against the corresponding parameter value in H_A. One way to focus our attention is by thinking about the *effect size.* That is, ask *"How big a difference would matter?"* Suppose a charity wants to test whether placing personalized address labels in the envelope along with a request for a donation increases the response rate above the baseline of 5%. If the minimum response that would pay for the address labels is 6%, we would calculate β for the alternative $p = 0.06$.

Of course, we can reduce β for *all* values in the alternative by increasing α. If we make it easier to reject the null, then we're more likely to reject it whether it's true or not. So we'd reduce β, but we'd make more Type I errors. This tension between Type I and Type II errors is inevitable. In the political arena, think of the ongoing debate between those who favor provisions to reduce Type I errors in the courts (Miranda rights, warrants required for wire taps, legal representation paid by the state if needed, etc.) and those who are concerned that Type II errors have become too common (admitting into evidence confessions made when no lawyer is present, eavesdropping on conferences with lawyers, restricting paths of appeal, etc.).

The only way to reduce *both* types of error is to collect more evidence or, in statistical terms, to collect more data. Otherwise, we just wind up trading off one kind of error against the other. Whenever you design a survey or experiment, it's a good idea to calculate β (for a reasonable α-level). Use a parameter value in the alternative that corresponds to an effect size that you would like to be able to detect. Too often, studies fail because their sample sizes are too small to detect the change they are looking for.

Power

When we failed to reject the null hypothesis about TT practitioners, did we prove that they were just guessing? No, it could be that they actually can discern a human energy field and we just couldn't tell. For example, suppose they really have the ability to get 53% of the trials right but just happened to get only 47% in our experiment. Our confidence interval shows that with these data we would have retained the null. And if we retained the null when the true proportion was actually greater than 50%, we would have made a Type II error in failing to detect their ability.

Remember, we can never prove a null hypothesis true. We can only fail to reject it. But when we fail to reject a null hypothesis, it's natural to wonder whether we looked hard enough. Might the null hypothesis actually be false and our test too weak to tell?

When the null hypothesis actually is false, we hope our test is strong enough to reject it. We'd like to know how likely we are to succeed. The power of the test gives us a way to think about that. The **power** of a test is the probability that it correctly rejects a false null hypothesis. When the power is high, we can be confident that we've looked hard enough. We know that β is the probability that a test *fails* to reject a false null hypothesis, so the power of the test is the complement, $1 - \beta$. We might have just written $1 - \beta$, but power is such an important concept that it gets its own name.

When a study fails to reject the null hypothesis, the test's power comes into question. Was the sample size big enough to detect an effect had there been one? Might we have missed an effect of an interesting size just because we failed to gather sufficient data or because there was too much variability in the data we could gather? The therapeutic touch experiment failed to reject the null hypothesis that the TT practitioners were just guessing. Might the problem be that the experiment simply lacked adequate power to detect their ability?

When we calculate power, we have to imagine that the null hypothesis is false. The value of the power depends on how far the truth lies from the null hypothesis value. We call the distance between the null hypothesis value, p_0, and the truth, p, the **effect size.** The power depends directly on the effect size. It's easier to see larger effects, so the farther p_0 is from p, the greater the power. If the therapeutic touch practitioners were in fact able to detect human energy fields 90% of the time, it should be easy to see that they aren't guessing. With an effect size this large, we'd have a powerful test. If their true success rate were only 53%, however, we'd need a larger sample size to have a good chance of noticing that (and rejecting H_0.)

How can we decide what power we need? Choice of power is more a financial or scientific decision than a statistical one because we must guess at the true parameter value. How sure do you need to be of detecting a particular effect size? For example, do you think that health insurance companies should pay for therapeutic touch if practitioners could detect a human energy field only 53% of the time—just slightly better than chance? That doesn't seem clinically useful.[5] How about 75% of the time? No therapy works all the time, and insurers might be quite willing to pay for such a success rate. Let's take 75% as a reasonably interesting effect size (keeping in mind that 50% is the level of guessing). With 150 trials, the TT experiment would have been able to detect such an ability with a power of 99.99%. So power was not an issue in this study. There is a very small chance that the study would have failed to detect a practitioner's ability had it existed. The sample size was clearly big enough.

A Picture Worth $\frac{1}{P(z > 3.09)}$ Words

It makes intuitive sense that the larger the effect size, the easier it should be to see it. Obtaining a larger sample size decreases the probability of a Type II error, so it increases the power. It also makes sense that the more we're willing to accept a Type I error, the less likely we will be to make a Type II error.

Here's a good way to visualize the relationships among these concepts. Suppose we are testing H_0: $p = p_0$ against the alternative H_A: $p > p_0$. We'll reject the null if the observed proportion, $\hat{p}$, is big enough. By big enough, we mean $\hat{p} > p^*$ for some critical value, p^* (shown as the red region in the right tail). For example, we might be willing to believe the ability of therapeutic touch practitioners if they were successful in 65% of our trials. This is what the upper curve shows. It's a picture of the sampling distribution model for the proportion when the null hypothesis is true. If the null were true, then this would be a picture of that truth. We'd make a Type I error whenever $\hat{p} > p^*$ because we would reject the (true) null hypothesis. And that would happen with probability α.

In reality, though, the null hypothesis is rarely *exactly* true. The lower probability model supposes that H_0 is not true. In particular, it supposes that the true

[5]On the other hand, a scientist might be interested in anything clearly different from the 50% guessing rate because that would suggest an entirely new Physics at work and could lead to a Nobel prize.

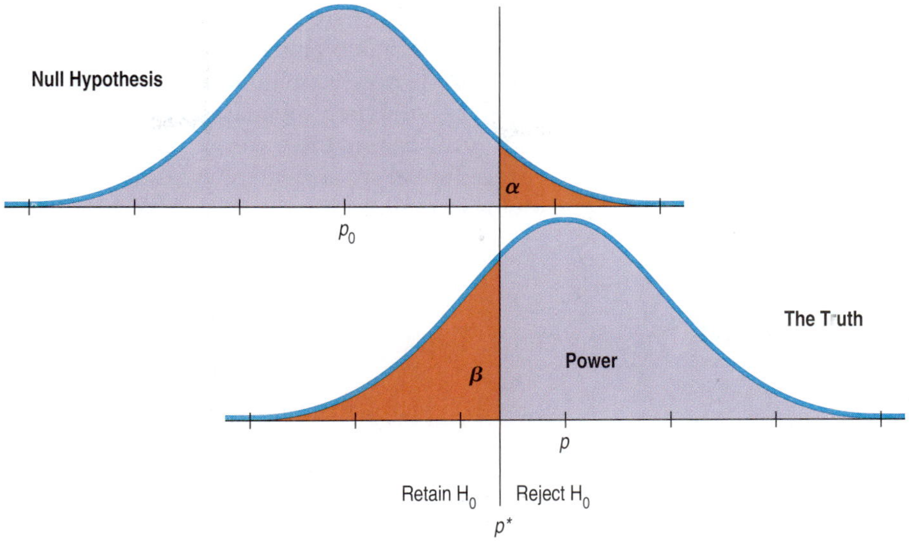

The power of a test is the probability that it rejects a false null hypothesis. The upper figure shows the null hypothesis model. We'd reject the null in a one-sided test if we observed a statistic value in the red region to the right of the critical value, p^*. But if the true value of p is greater than the hypothesized value, then the bottom figure shows that we're more likely to observe a value that exceeds the critical value, and make the correct decision to reject the null hypothesis. The power of the test is the blue region on the right of this figure. Of course, even drawing samples whose observed proportions are distributed around p, we'll sometimes get a value in the red region on the left and make a Type II error of failing to reject the null. **Figure 21.5**

value is p, not p_0. (Perhaps the TT practitioner really can detect the human energy field 72% of the time.) It shows a distribution of possible observed $\hat{p}$ values around this true value. Because of sampling variability, sometimes $\hat{p} < p^*$ and we fail to reject the (false) null hypothesis. Suppose a TT practitioner with a true ability level of 72% is actually successful on fewer than 65% of our tests. Then we'd make a Type II error. The area under the curve to the left of p^* in the bottom model represents how often this happens. The probability is β. In this picture, β is less than half, so most of the time we *do* make the right decision. The *power* of the test—the probability that we make the right decision—is shown as the region to the right of p^*. It's $1 - \beta$.

We calculate p^* based on the upper model because p^* depends only on the null model and the alpha level. No matter what the true proportion, no matter whether the practitioners can detect a human energy field 90%, 53%, or 2% of the time, p^* doesn't change. After all, we don't *know* the truth, so we can't use it to determine the critical value. But we always reject H_0 when $\hat{p} > p^*$.

How often we reject H_0 when it's *false* depends on the effect size. We can see from the picture that if the true proportion were farther from the hypothesized value, the bottom curve would shift to the right, making the power greater.

We can see several important relationships from this figure:

- *Power* $= 1 - \beta$.
- Reducing α to lower Type I error will move the critical value, p^*, to the right (in this example), and have the effect of increasing β, the probability of a Type II error, and correspondingly reducing the power.

- The larger the real difference between the hypothesized value, p_0, and the true population value, p, the smaller the chance of making a Type II error and the greater the power of the test. If the two proportions are very far apart, the two models will barely overlap, and we would not be likely to make any Type II errors at all—but then, we are unlikely to really need a formal hypothesis testing procedure to see such an obvious difference. If the TT practitioners were successful almost all the time, we'd be able to see that with even a small experiment.

Reducing Both Type I and Type II Error

Figure 21.5 seems to show that if we reduce Type I error, we automatically must increase Type II error. But there is a way to reduce both. Can you think of it?

If we can make both curves narrower, as shown in Figure 21.6, then both the probability of Type I errors and the probability of Type II errors will decrease, and the power of the test will increase.

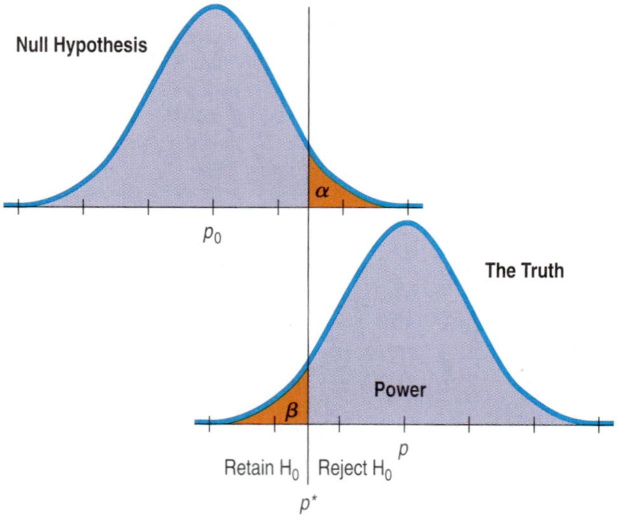

Making the standard deviations smaller increases the power without changing the alpha-level or corresponding critical value.

Figure 21.6

How can we accomplish that? The only way is to reduce the standard deviations by increasing the sample size. (Remember, these are pictures of sampling distribution models, not of data.) Increasing the sample size works regardless of the true population parameters. But recall the curse of diminishing returns. The standard deviation of the sampling distribution model decreases only as the *square root* of the sample size, so to halve the standard deviations we must *quadruple* the sample size.

What Can Go Wrong?

- ***Don't change your null hypothesis after you look at the data.*** You are not allowed to look at the data first and then adjust your null hypothesis so that it will be rejected. When your sample value $\hat{p}$ turns out to be 51.8% with a standard deviation of 1%, don't form a null hypothesis of the form H_0: $p = 49.8\%$, knowing that you can reject it. Use your understanding of the situation to form the null hypothesis *before* you look at the data.[6]

- ***Don't base your alternative hypothesis on the data either.*** You should decide whether to do a one- or two-tailed test based on what results would be of interest to you.
- ***Don't make what you want to show into your null hypothesis.*** Remember, you can reject the null, but you can never "accept" or "prove" the null hypothesis.
- ***Don't interpret the P-value as the probability that H_0 is true.*** The P-value is about the data, not the hypothesis. It's the probability of the data *given* that H_0 is true, not the other way around.
- ***Don't believe too strongly in arbitrary alpha levels.*** There's not really much difference between a P-value of 0.051 and a P-value of 0.049, but sometimes it's regarded as the difference between night (having to retain H_0) and day (being able to shout to the world that your results are "statistically significant"). It may just be better to report the P-value and a confidence interval and let the world decide along with you.
- ***Don't confuse practical and statistical significance.*** A large sample size can make it easy to discern even a trivial change from the null hypothesis value. On the other hand, an important difference can be missed if your test lacks sufficient power.
- ***In spite of all your care, you might make a wrong decision.*** We can never reduce the probability of a Type I error (α) or of a Type II error (β) to zero (but increasing the sample size helps).
- ***Always check the conditions.*** The reasoning of inference depends on randomization. No amount of care in calculating a test can recover from a biased sample. The probabilities we compute depend on the independence assumption.

Hypothesis Tests and the Computer

Reports about hypothesis tests generated by technologies don't follow a standard form. Most will name the test, provide the test statistic value, its standard deviation, and the P-value. But these elements may not be labeled clearly. For example, the expression "Prob $>|z|$" means the probability (the "Prob") of observing a test statistic whose magnitude (the absolute value tells us this) is larger than that of the one (the "z") found in the data (which, because it is written as "z," we know follows a Normal model). That is a fancy (and not very clear) way of saying P-value. In some packages you can specify that the test be one-sided. Others might report three P-values, covering the ground for both one-sided tests and the two-sided test.

Sometimes a confidence interval and hypothesis test are automatically given together. The CI ought to be for the corresponding confidence level: $1.0 - \alpha$.

Often, the standard deviation of the statistic is called the "standard error," and usually that's appropriate because we've had to estimate its value from the data. That's not the case for proportions, however. We get the standard deviation for a proportion from the null hypothesis value. Nevertheless, you may see the standard deviation called a "standard error" even for tests with proportions.

---

[6]It would be even better to form the hypotheses before collecting the data, but that isn't always practical if you are not collecting your own data.

It's common for statistics packages and calculators to report more digits of "precision" than could possibly have been found from the data. You can safely ignore them. Round values such as the standard deviation to one digit more than the number of digits reported in your data.

Here's the kind of results you might see. This is not from any program or calculator we know of, but it shows some of the things you might see in typical computer output.

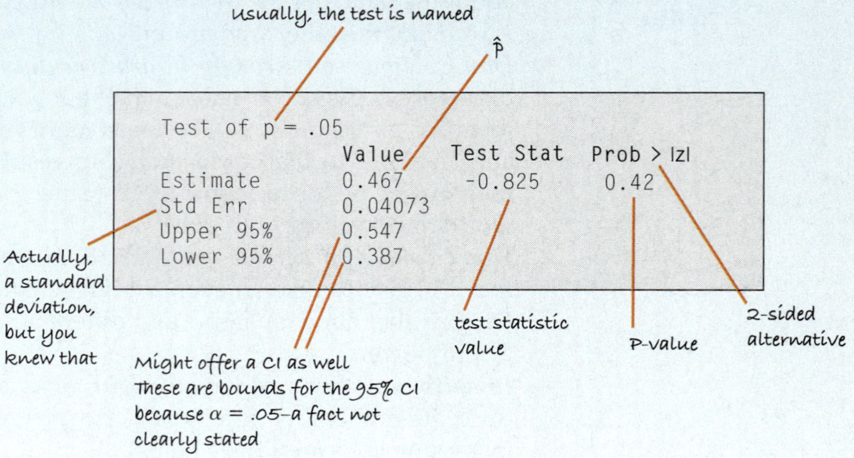

For information on hypothesis testing with particular statistics packages, see the table in Appendix B.

Connections

All of the hypothesis tests we'll see boil down to the same question: "Is the difference between two quantities large?" We always measure "how large" by finding a ratio of this difference to the standard deviation of the sampling distribution of the statistic. Using the standard deviation as our ruler for inference is one of the core ideas of statistical thinking.

We've discussed the close relationship between hypothesis tests and confidence intervals. They are two sides of the same coin.

This chapter also has natural links to the discussion of probability, to the Normal model, and to the two previous chapters on inference.

Key Concepts

Statistically significant When the P-value falls below the alpha level, we say that the test is "statistically significant" at that alpha level.

Alpha level The threshold P-value that determines when we reject a null hypothesis. If we observe a statistic whose P-value based on the null hypothesis is less than α, we reject that null hypothesis.

Significance level The alpha level is also called the significance level, most often in a phrase such as a conclusion that a particular test is "significant at the 5% significance level."

Critical value The value in the sampling distribution model of the statistic whose P-value is equal to the alpha level. Any statistic value farther from the null hypothesis value than the critical value will have a smaller P-value than α and will lead to rejecting the null hypothesis. The critical value is often denoted with an asterisk, as z^*, for example.

Type I error The error of rejecting a null hypothesis when in fact it is true (also called a "false positive"). The probability of a Type I error is α.

Type II error The error of failing to reject a null hypothesis when in fact it is false (also called a "false negative"). The probability of a Type II error is commonly denoted β.

Power The probability that a hypothesis test will correctly reject a false null hypothesis is the power of the test. To find power, we must specify a particular alternative parameter value as the "false" value. For a specific value in the alternative, the power is $1 - \beta$.

Effect size The difference between the null hypothesis value and true value of a model parameter is called the effect size.

Skills

When you complete this lesson you should:

Think

- Understand that statistical significance does not measure the importance or magnitude of an effect. Recognize when others misinterpret statistical significance as proof of practical importance.
- Understand the close relationship between hypothesis tests and confidence intervals.
- Be able to identify and use the alternative hypothesis when testing hypotheses. Understand how to choose between a one-sided and two-sided alternative hypothesis, and know how to defend the choice of a one-sided alternative.
- Understand how the critical value for a test is related to the specified alpha level.
- Understand that the power of a test gives the probability that it correctly rejects a false null hypothesis when a specified alternative is true.
- Understand that the power of a test depends in part on the sample size. Large sample sizes lead to greater power (and thus fewer Type II errors).

Show

- Know how to complete a hypothesis test for a population proportion.

Tell

- Be able to interpret the meaning of a P-value in nontechnical language.
- Understand that the P-value of a test does not give the probability that the null hypothesis is correct.
- Know that we do not "accept" a null hypothesis if we cannot reject it, but rather that we can only "fail to reject" or retain the hypothesis for lack of evidence against it.

Exercises

1. **P-value.** A medical researcher has tested a new treatment for poison ivy against the traditional ointment. With a P-value of 0.047, he concludes the new treatment is more effective. Explain what the P-value means in this context.

2. **Another P-value.** Have harsher penalties and ad campaigns increased seatbelt use among drivers and passengers? Observations of commuter traffic failed to find evidence of a significant change compared with three years ago. Explain what the study's P-value of 0.17 means in this context.

3. **Alpha.** A researcher developing scanners to search for hidden weapons at airports has concluded that a new device is significantly better than the current scanner. He made this decision based on a test using $\alpha = .05$. Would he have made the same decision at $\alpha = .10$? How about $\alpha = .01$? Explain.

4. **Alpha again.** Environmentalists concerned about the impact of high-frequency radio transmissions on birds found that there was no evidence of a higher mortality rate among hatchlings in nests near cell towers. They based this conclusion on a test using $\alpha = .05$. Would they have made the same decision at $\alpha = .10$? How about $\alpha = .01$? Explain.

5. **Significant?** Public health officials believe that 90% of children have been vaccinated against measles. A random survey of medical records at many schools across the country found that among more than 13,000 children only 89.4% had been vaccinated. A statistician would reject the 90% hypothesis with a P-value of $P = 0.011$.
   a) Explain what the P-value means in this context.
   b) The result is statistically significant, but is it important? Comment.

6. **Significant?** A new reading program may reduce the number of elementary students who read below grade level. The company that developed this program supplied materials and teacher training for a large-scale test involving nearly 8500 children in several different school districts. Statistical analysis of the results showed that the percentage of students who did not attain the grade level standard was reduced from 15.9% to 15.1%. The hypothesis that the new reading program produced no improvement was rejected with a P-value of 0.023.
   a) Explain what the P-value means in this context.
   b) Even though this reading method has been shown to be significantly better, why might you not recommend that your local school adopt it?

7. **Testing cars.** A clean air standard requires that vehicle exhaust emissions not exceed specified limits for various pollutants. Many states require that cars be tested annually to be sure they meet these standards. Suppose state regulators double check a random sample of cars that a suspect repair shop has certified as okay. They will revoke the shop's license if they find significant evidence that the shop is certifying vehicles that do not meet standards.
   a) In this context, what is a Type I error?
   b) In this context, what is a Type II error?
   c) Which type of error would the shop's owner consider more serious?
   d) Which type of error might environmentalists consider more serious?

8. **Quality control.** Production managers on an assembly line must monitor the output to be sure that the level of defective products remains small. They periodically inspect a random sample of the items produced. If they find a significant increase in the proportion of items that must be rejected, they will halt the assembly process until the problem can be identified and repaired.
   a) In this context, what is a Type I error?
   b) In this context, what is a Type II error?
   c) Which type of error would the factory owner consider more serious?
   d) Which type of error might customers consider more serious?

9. **Cars again.** As in Exercise 7, state regulators are checking up on repair shops to see if they are certifying vehicles that do not meet pollution standards.
   a) In this context, what is meant by the power of the test the regulators are conducting?
   b) Will the power be greater if they test 20 or 40 cars? Why?
   c) Will the power be greater if they use a 5% or a 10% level of significance? Why?
   d) Will the power be greater if the repair shop's inspectors are only a little out of compliance or a lot? Why?

10. **Production.** Consider again the task of the quality control inspectors in Exercise 8.
    a) In this context, what is meant by the power of the test the inspectors conduct?
    b) They are currently testing 5 items each hour. Someone has proposed they test 10 each hour instead. What are the advantages and disadvantages of such a change?
    c) Their test currently uses a 5% level of significance. What are the advantages and disadvantages of changing to an alpha level of 1%?
    d) Suppose that as a day passes one of the machines on the assembly line produces more and more items that are defective. How will this affect the power of the test?

11. Equal opportunity? A company is sued for job discrimination because only 19% of the newly hired candidates were minorities when 27% of all applicants were minorities. Is this strong evidence that the company's hiring practices are discriminatory?

a) Is this a one-tailed or a two-tailed test? Why?
b) In this context, what would a Type I error be?
c) In this context, what would a Type II error be?
d) In this context, describe what is meant by the power of the test.
e) If the hypothesis is tested at the 5% level of significance instead of 1%, how will this affect the power of the test?
f) The lawsuit is based on the hiring of 37 employees. Is the power of the test higher than, lower than, or the same as it would be if it were based on 87 hires?

12. Stop signs. Highway safety engineers test new road signs, hoping that increased reflectivity will make them more visible to drivers. Volunteers drive through a test course with several of the new and old style signs and rate which kind shows up the best.

a) Is this a one-tailed or a two-tailed test? Why?
b) In this context, what would a Type I error be?
c) In this context, what would a Type II error be?
d) In this context, describe what is meant by the power of the test.
e) If the hypothesis is tested at the 1% level of significance instead of 5%, how will this affect the power of the test?
f) The engineers hoped to base their decision on the reactions of 50 drivers, but time and budget constraints may force them to cut back to 20. How would this affect the power of the test? Explain.

13. Dropouts. A Statistics professor has observed that for several years about 13% of the students who initially enroll in his Introductory Statistics course withdraw before the end of the semester. A salesman suggests that he try a statistics software package that gets students more involved with computers, predicting that it will cut the dropout rate. The software is expensive, and the salesman offers to let the professor use it for a semester to see if the dropout rate goes down significantly. The professor will have to pay for the software only if he chooses to continue using it.

a) Is this a one-tailed or two-tailed test? Explain.
b) Write the null and alternative hypotheses.
c) In this context, explain what would happen if the professor makes a Type I error.
d) In this context, explain what would happen if the professor makes a Type II error.
e) What is meant by the power of this test?

14. Ads. A company is willing to renew its advertising contract with a local radio station only if the station can prove that more than 20% of the residents of the city have heard the ad and recognize the company's product. The radio station conducts a random phone survey of 400 people.

a) What are the hypotheses?
b) The station plans to conduct this test using a 10% level of significance, but the company wants the significance level lowered to 5%. Why?
c) What is meant by the power of this test?
d) For which level of significance will the power of this test be higher? Why?
e) They finally agree to use $\alpha = .05$, but the company proposes that the station call 600 people instead of the 400 initially proposed. Will that make the risk of Type II error higher or lower? Explain.

15. Dropouts, part II. Initially, 203 students signed up for the Stats course in Exercise 13. They used the software suggested by the salesman, and only 11 dropped out of the course.

a) Should the professor spend the money for this software? Support your recommendation with an appropriate test.
b) Explain carefully what your P-value means in this context.

16. Testing the ads. The company in Exercise 14 contacts 600 people selected at random, and only 133 remember the ad.

a) Should the company renew the contract? Support your recommendation with an appropriate test.
b) Explain carefully what your P-value means in this context.

17. Hoops. A basketball player with a poor foul-shot record practices intensively during the off-season. He tells the coach that he has raised his proficiency from 60% to 80%. Dubious, the coach asks him to take 10 shots, and is surprised when the player hits 9 out of 10. Did the player prove that he has improved?

a) Suppose the player really is no better than before—still a 60% shooter. What's the probability he could hit at least 9 of 10 shots anyway? (*Hint:* Use a Binomial model.)
b) If that is what happened, now the coach thinks the player has improved when he has not. Which type of error is that?
c) If the player really can hit 80% now, and it takes at least 9 out of 10 successful shots to convince the coach, what's the power of the test?
d) List two ways the coach and player could increase the power to detect any improvement.

18. Pottery. An artist experimenting with clay to create pottery with a special texture has been experiencing difficulty with these special pieces. About 40% break in the kiln during firing. Hoping to solve this problem, she buys some more expensive clay from another supplier.

She plans to make and fire 10 pieces, and will decide to use the new clay if at most one of them breaks.

a) Suppose the new expensive clay really is no better than her usual clay. What's the probability that this test convinces her to use it anyway? (*Hint:* Use a Binomial model.)
b) If she decides to switch to the new clay and it is no better, what kind of error did she commit?
c) If the new clay really could reduce breakage to only 20%, what's the probability that her test will not detect the improvement?
d) How can she improve the power of her test? Offer at least two suggestions.

19. Survey. A company has surveyed a stratified sample of its employees to find out how many might take advantage of a program to help people stop smoking. You may assume that the sampling strategy was properly random and that the data-gathering methodology avoided biases. The table below shows the results. For which of the groups could we use our methods of inference to determine a 95% confidence interval for the proportion of employees who would participate in the stop smoking program?

Group	Number of Employees	Number Surveyed	Percent to Participate
Laborers	6235	300	9%
Clerical	1520	200	7%
Management	342	25	8%

20. Fire safety. A city law requires all buildings to have a fire safety inspection at least once every three years. Concerned that some of these inspections are not being done, the mayor orders a survey to see what fraction of the city's buildings may be out of compliance. Results for the sample appear in the table below. For which of the building classifications could you use our methods of inference to create 95% confidence intervals for the proportion of buildings lacking the required inspection?

Class	Number of Buildings	Number Surveyed	Percent Not Inspected
Single-family home	7742	200	7%
Apartment building	205	20	10%
Commercal	407	70	16%

21. Little League. In a 1999–2000 longitudinal study of youth baseball, researchers found that 26% of 298 young pitchers complained of elbow pain after pitching.

a) Create a 90% confidence interval for the percentage of young players who may develop elbow pain after pitching.
b) A coach claims that only about 1 kid in 5 is at risk of arm injury from pitching. Is this claim consistent with your confidence interval?

22. News sources. In May of 2000 the Pew Research Foundation sampled 1593 respondents and asked how they obtain news. The foundation reports that 33% now say they obtain news from the Internet at least once a week. Pew reports a margin of error of ±3% for this result. It had generally been assumed, based on earlier polls, that only 25% got news from the Internet. Does the Pew result provide strong evidence that the percentage has increased? Use the confidence interval to test an appropriate hypothesis, and state your conclusion.

Chapter 22

Comparing Two Proportions

WHO	1026 U.S. adults
WHAT	Opinions on traits
WHY	Polling by Gallup Poll
WHEN	2001
WHERE	United States

Who are typically more intelligent, men or women? To find out what people think, the Gallup Poll selected a random sample of 520 women and 506 men. The pollsters showed them a list of personal attributes and asked them to indicate whether each attribute was "generally more true of men or of women." When asked about intelligence, 28% of the men thought men were generally more intelligent, but only 14% of the women agreed. Is there a gender gap in opinions about which sex is smarter? This is only a random sample. What would we estimate the true size of that gap to be?

Comparisons between two percentages are much more common than questions about isolated percentages. And they are more interesting. We often want to know how two groups differ, whether a treatment is better than a placebo control, or whether this year's results are better than last year's.

Y.A.S.D.

We know the *difference* between the proportions of our two random samples. It's 14%. That sounds like a lot, but is it the sort of difference that might just be due to random sampling? To decide about that, we need a ruler. For that we need Yet Another Standard Deviation (Y.A.S.D.)—the standard deviation of the sampling distribution. But what's the standard deviation of the difference between two sample proportions?

The answer comes to us from Chapter 16, where we saw that the secret to understanding the variability of the sum or difference of two random variables is to add their *variances.* Remember?

> ***The variance of the sum or difference of two independent random variables is the sum of their variances.***

For independent random variables, **variances add.**

This is such an important (and powerful) idea that it's worth pausing a moment to review the reasoning. Here's some intuition about why variation increases even when we subtract two random quantities.

Grab a full box of cereal. The box claims to contain 16 ounces of cereal. We know that's not exact: There's some small variation from box to box. Now pour a bowl of cereal. Of course, your 2-ounce serving will not be exactly 2 ounces. There'll be some variation there too. How much cereal would you guess was left in the box? Do you think your guess will be as close as your guess for the full box? *After* you pour your bowl, the amount of cereal in the box is still a random quantity (with a smaller mean than before), but it is even *more variable* because of the additional variation in the amount you poured.

According to our rule, the variance of the amount of cereal left in the box would now be the *sum* of the two *variances.*

We want a standard deviation, not a variance, but that's just a square root away. In the standard deviation form, we can write symbolically what we've just said (because it's too much bother to say it in words).

$$SD(X - Y) = \sqrt{Var(X) + Var(Y)}$$

Be careful, though—this simple formula applies only when X and Y are independent.

The Standard Deviation of the Difference Between Two Proportions

Fortunately, proportions observed in independent random samples are independent, so we can put the two proportions in for X and Y and add their variances. We just need to use careful notation to keep things straight.

When we have two samples, each can have a different size and proportion value, so we keep them straight with subscripts. Often we choose subscripts that remind us of the groups. For our example, we might use "$_M$" and "$_F$," but generically we'll just use "$_1$" and "$_2$." We will represent the two sample proportions as $\hat{p}_1$ and $\hat{p}_2$, and the two sample sizes as n_1 and n_2.

The standard deviations of the sample proportions are $SD(\hat{p}_1) = \sqrt{\frac{p_1q_1}{n_1}}$ and $SD(\hat{p}_2) = \sqrt{\frac{p_2q_2}{n_2}}$, so the variance of the difference in the proportions is

For independent random variables, variances add.

$$Var(\hat{p}_1 - \hat{p}_2) = \left(\sqrt{\frac{p_1q_1}{n_1}}\right)^2 + \left(\sqrt{\frac{p_2q_2}{n_2}}\right)^2.$$

The standard deviation is the square root of that variance:

$$SD(\hat{p}_1 - \hat{p}_2) = \sqrt{\frac{p_1q_2}{n_1} + \frac{p_2q_2}{n_2}}$$

We usually don't know the true values of p_1 and p_2, but when we have the sample proportions in hand from the data, we use them to estimate the variances. So the standard error is

$$SE(\hat{p}_1 - \hat{p}_2) = \sqrt{\frac{\hat{p}_1\hat{q}_1}{n_1} + \frac{\hat{p}_2\hat{q}_2}{n_2}}.$$

Before we look at our example, we need to check assumptions and conditions.

Assumptions and Conditions

Independence Assumptions

Within each group the data should be based on results for independent individuals. We can't check that for certain, but we *can* check the following:

Randomization condition. The data in each group should be drawn independently and at random from a homogeneous population or generated by a randomized comparative experiment.

The 10% condition. When the data are sampled without replacement, the sample should not exceed 10% of the population.

When we compare two groups in this way, we need an additional independence assumption. In fact, this is the most important of these assumptions. If it is violated, these methods just won't work. We check it with the independent samples condition.

Independent samples condition. The two groups we're comparing must also be independent *of each other.* Usually, the independence of the groups from each other is evident from the way the data were collected.

Why is this condition so important? If we compared husbands with their wives, or a group of subjects before and after some treatment, we can't just add the variances. Subjects' performance before a treatment might very well be *related* to their performance after the treatment. So the proportions are not independent and the variance formula does not hold. We'll see a way to compare nonindependent samples in a later chapter.

Sample Size Condition

Each of the samples must be big enough. As with individual proportions, we need larger samples to estimate proportions that are near 0% or 100%. We usually check the success/failure condition.

Success/failure condition for each sample. Both samples are big enough that at least 10 successes and at least 10 failures have been observed in each.

The Sampling Distribution

We're almost there. We just need one more fact about proportions. We know already that for large enough samples, each of our proportions has an approximately Normal sampling distribution. The same is true of their difference.

The sampling distribution model for a difference between two independent proportions

Provided that the sampled values are independent, the samples are independent, and the sample sizes are large enough, the sampling distribution of $\hat{p}_1 - \hat{p}_2$ is modeled by a Normal model with mean $\mu = p_1 - p_2$ and standard deviation

$$\sigma = SD(\hat{p}_1 - \hat{p}_2) = \sqrt{\frac{p_1 q_1}{n_1} + \frac{p_2 q_2}{n_2}}.$$

The sampling distribution model and the standard deviation give us all we need to find a margin of error for the difference in proportions.

Now we can make a confidence interval. Instead of hypothesized proportions, we have observed proportions, $\hat{p}_1$ and $\hat{p}_2$, so we'll use $SE(\hat{p}_1 - \hat{p}_2)$ to estimate the standard deviation. The rest is just like a one-proportion z-interval.

> **A two-proportion z-interval**
>
> When the conditions are met, we are ready to find the confidence interval for the difference of two proportions, $p_1 - p_2$. Using the standard error of the difference,
>
> $$SE(\hat{p}_1 - \hat{p}_2) = \sqrt{\frac{\hat{p}_1\hat{q}_1}{n_1} + \frac{\hat{p}_2\hat{q}_2}{n_2}}$$
>
> the interval is $(\hat{p}_1 - \hat{p}_2) \pm z^* \times SE(\hat{p}_1 - \hat{p}_2)$. The critical value z^* depends on the particular confidence level, C, that you specify.

A Two-Proportion z-Interval STEP-BY-STEP

Now we are ready to answer the question of how big a gap there is between the sexes in their opinions of whether men are intelligent. The question clearly calls for a confidence interval, so let's follow the four confidence interval steps. The method is called the **two-proportion z-interval.**

Think

Parameter Identify the parameter you wish to estimate.
(It usually doesn't matter in which direction we subtract, so for convenience we often choose the direction with a positive difference.)

We want to know the true difference in the population proportion, p_M, of American men who think that men can be described as "intelligent" and the proportion, p_F, of American women who think so. The parameter of interest is the difference, $p_M - p_F$.

Choose and state a confidence level.

We will find a 95% confidence interval for this parameter.

Plan
Check the conditions.

✓ **Randomization condition:** Gallup drew a random sample of U.S. adults.

✓ **10% condition:** Although sampling was necessarily without replacement, there are many more U.S. women and U.S. men than were sampled in each of the groups polled.

✓ **Independent samples condition:** The sample of women and the sample of men are independent of each other.

The success/failure condition must hold for each group.

✓ **Success/failure condition:**

$$n\hat{p}(\text{men}) = 506 \times 28.0\% = 142 > 10$$

$$n\hat{q}(\text{men}) = 506 \times 72.0\% = 364 > 10$$

$$n\hat{p}(\text{women}) = 520 \times 14.0\% = 73 > 10$$

$$n\hat{q}(\text{women}) = 520 \times 86.0\% = 447 > 10$$

Both samples exceed the minimum size.

State the sampling distribution model for the statistic.

Under these conditions, the sampling distribution of the difference between the sample proportions is approximately Normal with a mean of $p_M - p_F$, the true difference between the population proportions.

Choose your method.

We will find a **two-proportion z-interval.**

Show

Mechanics Construct the confidence interval.

We know:

$$n_M = 506,\ n_F = 520.$$

The observed sample proportions are

$$\hat{p}_M = 0.28,\ \hat{p}_F = 0.14.$$

As often happens, the key step in finding the confidence interval is estimating the standard deviation of the sampling distribution model of the statistic. Here the statistic is the difference in the proportions of men and women who think that men are intelligent. Substitute the data values into the formula.

We estimate $SD(\hat{p}_M - \hat{p}_F)$ as

$$SE(\hat{p}_M - \hat{p}_F) = \sqrt{\frac{\hat{p}_M\hat{q}_M}{n_M} + \frac{\hat{p}_F\hat{q}_F}{n_F}}.$$

$$= \sqrt{\frac{0.28(1 - 0.28)}{506} + \frac{0.14(1 - 0.14)}{520}}$$

$$= 0.025$$

The sampling distribution is Normal, so the critical value for a 95% confidence interval, z^*, is 1.96. The margin of error is the critical value times the SE.

$$ME = z^* \times SE(\hat{p}_M - \hat{p}_F)$$

$$= 1.96(0.025) = 0.049$$

The confidence interval is the statistic ± ME.

The observed difference in proportions is $(\hat{p}_M - \hat{p}_F) = 0.28 - 0.14 = 0.14$, so the 95% confidence interval is

$$0.14 \pm 0.049,$$

or 9% to 19%.

Tell

Interpretation Tell what the confidence interval means.

We are 95% confident that the proportion of American men who think that the attribute "intelligent" applies more to men than to women is between 9% and 19% more than the proportion of American women who think that.

TI Tips

You can use a routine in the `STAT TESTS` menu to create confidence intervals for the difference of two proportions. Remember, the calculator can do only the mechanics—checking conditions and writing conclusions are still up to you.

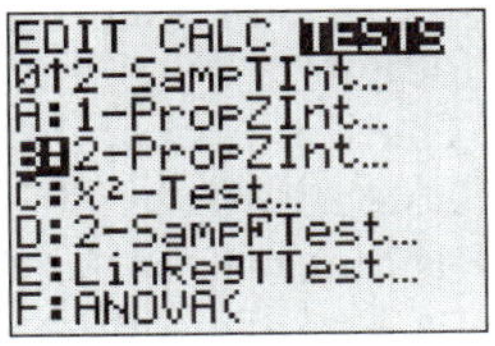

The Gallup Poll asked whether the attribute "intelligent" described men in general. The poll revealed that 28% of 506 men thought it did, but only 14% of 520 women agreed. We want to estimate the true size of the gender gap by creating a 95% confidence interval.

- Go to the `STAT TESTS` menu. Scroll down the list and select `B:2-PropZInt`.

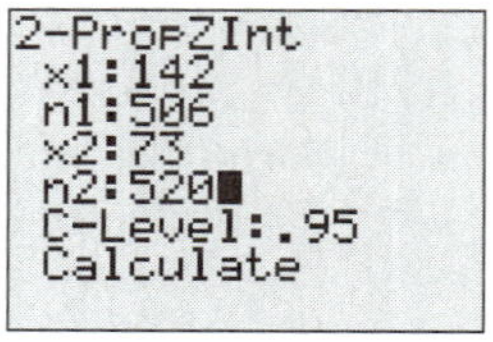

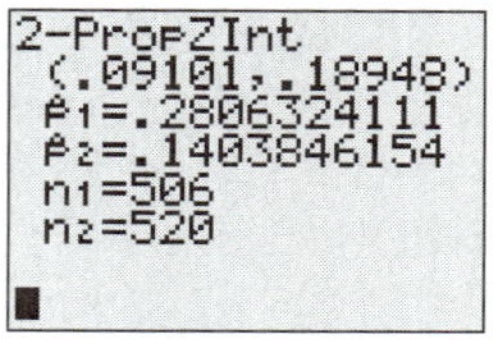

- Enter the observed number of males: **.28*506**. Remember that the actual number of males must be a whole number, so be sure to round off.
- Enter the sample size: **506** males.
- Repeat those entries for women: **.14*520** agreed, and the sample size was **520**.
- Specify the desired confidence level.
- **Calculate** the result.

And now explain what you see: we are 95% confident that the proportion of men who think the attribute "intelligent" describes males in general is between 9% and 19% higher than the proportion of women who think so.

Will I Snore When I'm 64?

WHO	Randomly selected U.S. adults over age 18
WHAT	Proportion who snore by age (less than 30, 30 or older)
WHEN	2001
WHERE	United States
WHY	To study sleep behaviors of U.S. adults

The National Sleep Foundation asked a random sample of 1010 U.S. adults questions about their sleep habits. The sample was selected in the fall of 2001 from random telephone numbers, stratified by region and sex, guaranteeing that an equal number of men and women were interviewed (2002 *Sleep in America Poll*, National Sleep Foundation, Washington, D.C.).

One of the questions asked about snoring. Of the 995 respondents, 37% of adults reported that they snored at least a few nights a week during the past year. Would you expect that percentage to be the same for all age groups? Split into two age categories, 26% of the 184 people under 30 snored, compared with 39% of the 811 in the older group. Is this difference of 13% real, or due only to natural fluctuations in the sample we've chosen?

The question calls for a hypothesis test. Now the parameter of interest is the true *difference* between the snoring rates of the two age groups.

What's the appropriate null hypothesis? That's easy here. We hypothesize that there is no difference in the proportions. This is such a natural null hypothesis that we rarely consider any other. But we usually express it in a slightly different way. To make it relate directly to the *difference*, we hypothesize that the difference in proportions is zero:

$$H_0: p_1 - p_2 = 0.$$

Everyone into the Pool

Our hypothesis is about a new parameter—the *difference* in proportions. We'll need a standard error for that. We know that the standard error of the difference in proportions is

$$SE(\hat{p}_1 - \hat{p}_2) = \sqrt{\frac{\hat{p}_1\hat{q}_1}{n_1} + \frac{\hat{p}_2\hat{q}_2}{n_2}}$$

and we could just plug in the numbers, but we can do better. The secret is that proportions and their standard deviations are linked. There are two proportions in the standard error formula—but look at the null hypothesis. It says that these proportions are equal. To do a hypothesis test, we *assume* that the null hypothesis is true. So there should be just a single value of $\hat{p}$ in the SE formula (and, of course, $\hat{q}$ is just $1 - \hat{p}$).

How would we do this for the snoring example? If the null hypothesis is true, the two groups have the same proportion. Overall, for all adults, we see $48 + 318 = 366$ snorers out of a total of $184 + 811 = 995$ adults who responded to this question. The overall proportion of snorers is $366/995 = 0.3678$.

Combining the counts like this to get an overall proportion is called **pooling.** (Whenever we combine data from different sources or different groups because we believe that they really came from the same underlying population, it is called *pooling.*)

When we have counts for each group, we can find the pooled proportion as

$$\hat{p}_{\text{pooled}} = \frac{Success_1 + Success_2}{n_1 + n_2}$$

where $Success_1$ is the number of successes in group 1 and $Success_2$ is the number of successes in group 2.

When we have only proportions and not the counts, as in the snoring example, we have to reconstruct the number of successes by multiplying the sample sizes by the proportions:

$$Success_1 = n_1\hat{p}_1 \text{ and } Success_2 = n_2\hat{p}_2.$$

Note that 48 is actually 26.1% of 184. We round back to the nearest whole number to find the count from a rounded percent.

If these calculations don't come out to whole numbers, round them first. There must have been a whole number of successes, after all. (This is the *only* time you should use rounded values in a calculation.)

We then put this pooled value into the formula, substituting it for *both* sample proportions in the standard error formula:

$$SE_{\text{pooled}}(\hat{p}_1 - \hat{p}_2) = \sqrt{\frac{\hat{p}_{\text{pooled}}\hat{q}_{\text{pooled}}}{n_1} + \frac{\hat{p}_{\text{pooled}}\hat{q}_{\text{pooled}}}{n_2}}$$

$$= \sqrt{\frac{0.3678 \times (1 - 0.3678)}{184} + \frac{0.3678 \times (1 - 0.3678)}{811}}$$

which comes out to 0.039375.

Compared to What?

Naturally, we'll reject our null hypothesis if we see a large enough difference in the two proportions. How can we decide whether the difference we see, $\hat{p}_1 - \hat{p}_2$, is large? The answer is simple. As always, we just compare it with its standard error.

Since the sampling distribution is Normal, we can divide the observed difference by its standard error to get a *z*-score. The *z*-score will tell us how many standard errors the observed difference is away from 0. We can then use the 68-95-99.7 Rule to decide whether this is large, or some technology to get an exact P-value. The result is a **two-proportion *z*-test.**

Two-proportion *z*-test

The conditions for the two-proportion *z*-test are the same as for the two-proportion *z*-interval. We are testing the hypothesis

$$H_0: p_1 = p_2.$$

Because we hypothesize that the proportions are equal, we pool them to find

$$\hat{p}_{pooled} = \frac{Success_1 + Success_2}{n_1 + n_2}$$

and use that pooled value to estimate the standard error.

$$SE_{pooled}(\hat{p}_1 - \hat{p}_2) = \sqrt{\frac{\hat{p}_{pooled}\hat{q}_{pooled}}{n_1} + \frac{\hat{p}_{pooled}\hat{q}_{pooled}}{n_2}}$$

Now we find the test statistic using the statistic,

$$z = \frac{\hat{p}_1 - \hat{p}_2}{SE_{pooled}(\hat{p}_1 - \hat{p}_2)}.$$

When the conditions are met and the null hypothesis is true, this statistic follows the standard Normal model, so we can use that model to obtain a P-value.

A Two-Proportion *z*-Test STEP-BY-STEP

Let's look at the snoring rates of the two groups.

Think

Hypotheses State what we want to know.

We want to know whether snoring rates differ for those under and over 30 years old.

The study simply broke down the responses by age, so there is no sense that either alternative was of interest. A two-sided alternative hypothesis is appropriate.

H_0: There is *no difference* in snoring rates between those who are 18 to 29 years old and those who are 30 years or older:

$$p_1 - p_2 = 0.$$

✓ **Reality Check** The observed difference is 13%. That seems like a big difference from 0 with sample sizes this large.

H_A: The rates are different: $p_1 - p_2 \neq 0$.

Plan
Check the conditions.

✓ **Randomization condition:** The patients were randomly selected by telephone number and stratified by sex and region.

✓ **10% condition:** The number of adults surveyed is certainly far less than 10% of the population.

✓ **Independent samples condition:** The two groups are independent of each other because the sample was selected at random.

✓ **Success/failure condition**[1]: In the younger age group, 48 snored and 136 didn't. In the older group, 318 snored and 493 didn't. The observed number of both successes and failures is much more than 10 for both groups.[2]

State the null model.

Because the conditions are satisfied, we can model the sampling distribution of the difference in proportions with a Normal model.

Choose your method.

We can perform a **two-proportion z-test.**

Show **Mechanics**

We know: $n_{young} = 184$, $n_{old} = 811$

$$\hat{p}_{young} = 0.261,\ \hat{p}_{old} = 0.392$$

The hypothesis is that the proportions are equal, so pool the sample data.

$$\hat{p}_{pooled} = \frac{x_{old} + x_{young}}{n_{old} + n_{young}} = \frac{318 + 48}{811 + 184} = 0.3678$$

Use the pooled SE to estimate $SD(p_{old} - p_{young})$.

$$SE_{pooled}(\hat{p}_{old} - \hat{p}_{young}) = \sqrt{\frac{\hat{p}_{pooled}\hat{q}_{pooled}}{n_{old}} + \frac{\hat{p}_{pooled}\hat{q}_{pooled}}{n_{young}}}$$

$$= \sqrt{\frac{(0.3678)(0.6322)}{811} + \frac{(0.3678)(0.6322)}{184}}$$

$$\approx 0.039375$$

The observed difference in sample proportions is $\hat{p}_{old} - \hat{p}_{young} = 0.392 - 0.261 = 0.131$.

Make a picture. Sketch a Normal model centered at the hypothesized difference of 0. Shade the region to the right of the observed difference, and because this is a two-tailed test, also shade the corresponding region in the other tail.

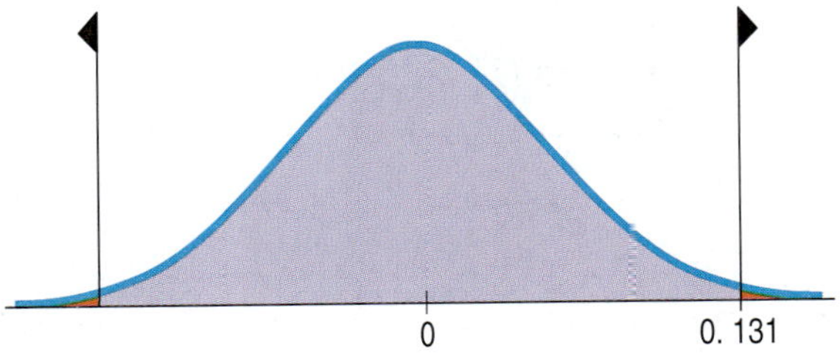

Find the z-score for the observed difference in proportions, 0.131.

$$z = \frac{(\hat{p}_{old} - \hat{p}_{young}) - 0}{SE(\hat{p}_{old} - \hat{p}_{young})} = \frac{0.131 - 0}{0.039375} = 3.33$$

Find the P-value using Table Z or technology. Because this is a two-tailed test, we must *double* the probability we find in the upper tail.

$$P = 2P(z \geq 3.33) = 0.0008$$

[1] Technically, this is the first time we've seen that the observed counts of successes and failures can be different from those we'd expect. We expect $n\hat{p}_{pooled}$ but observe $n\hat{p}$. Checking the observed counts is easy. But if your data just barely miss (say, you see 9 successes), check $n\hat{p}_{pooled}$ as well. If it passes the test, you're OK.

[2] This is one of those situations in which the traditional term "success" seems a bit weird. A success here could be that a person snores. We're using the terms "success" and "failure" as arbitrary labels left over from studies of gambling games.

Tell

Conclusion
Link the P-value to your decision about the null hypothesis, and state your conclusion in context.

The P-value of 0.0008 says that if there really were no difference in snoring rates between the two age groups, then the difference observed in this study would happen only 8 times in 10,000. This is rare enough for us to reject the null hypothesis of no difference and conclude that there is a difference in the rate of snoring between older adults and younger adults. It appears that older adults are more likely to snore.

TI Tips

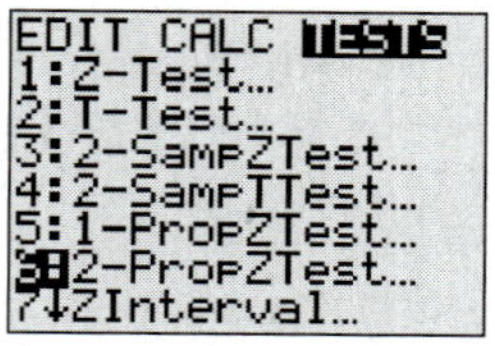

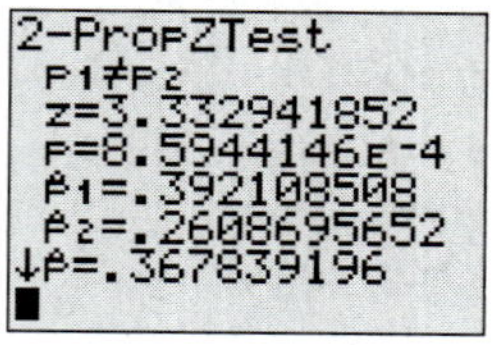

Yes, of course, there's a `STAT TESTS` routine to test a hypothesis about the difference of two proportions. Let's do the mechanics for the test about snoring. Of 811 people over 30 years old, 318 snored, while only 48 of the 184 people under 30 did.

- In the `STAT TESTS` menu select `6:2-PropZTest`.
- Enter the observed numbers of snorers and the sample sizes for both groups.
- Since this is a two-tailed test, indicate that you want to see if the proportions are unequal. When you choose this option, the calculator will automatically include both tails as it determines the P-value.
- `Calculate` the result. Don't worry; for this procedure the calculator will pool the proportions automatically.

Now it is up to you to interpret the result and state a conclusion. We see a *z*-score of 3.33 and the P-value is 0.0008. Such a small P-value indicates that the observed difference is unlikely to be sampling error. What does that mean about snoring and age?

What Can Go Wrong?

- ***Don't use two-sample proportion methods when the samples aren't independent.*** These methods give wrong answers when this assumption of independence is violated. Good random sampling is usually the best insurance of independent groups. Make sure there is no relationship between the two groups. For example, you can't compare the proportion of respondents who own SUVs with the proportion of those same respondents who think the tax on gas should be eliminated. The responses are not independent because you've asked the same people. To use these methods to estimate or test the difference, you'd need to survey two different groups of people.

  Alternatively, if you have a random sample, you can split your respondents according to their answers to one question and treat the two resulting groups as independent samples. So, you could estimate or test the difference in the proportions of respondents who favor eliminating the gas tax between SUV owners and non-SUV owners.

- ***Don't apply inference methods when you don't have random samples.*** If the data do not come from representative random samples, then the inference about the difference in proportions will be wrong.
- ***Don't interpret a significant difference in proportions causally.*** It turns out that people with higher incomes are more likely to snore. Does money affect sleep patterns? Probably not. We have seen that older people are more likely to snore, and they are also likely to earn more. In a prospective or retrospective study, there is always the danger that other lurking variables not accounted for are the real reason for an observed difference. Be careful not to jump to conclusions about causality.

Inferences for the Difference Between Two Proportions and the Computer

It is so common to test against the null hypothesis of no difference between the two true proportions that most statistics programs simply assume this null hypothesis. And most will automatically use the pooled standard deviation. If you wish to test a different null (say that the true difference is 0.3), you may have to search for a way to do it.

Many statistics packages don't offer special commands for inference for differences between proportions. As with inference for single proportions, most statistics programs want the "success" and "failure" status for each case. Usually these are given as 1 or 0, but they might be category names like "yes" and "no." Often we just know the proportions of successes, $\hat{p}_1$ and $\hat{p}_2$, and the counts, n_1 and n_2. Computer packages don't usually deal with summary data like these easily. Calculators typically do a better job.

Connections

In Chapter 3 we looked at contingency tables for two categorical variables. Differences in proportions are just 2 × 2 contingency tables. You'll often see data presented in this way. For example, the snoring data could be shown as

	18–29	30 and over	Total
Snore	48	318	366
Don't snore	136	493	629
Total	184	811	995

We tested whether the column percentages of snorers were the same for the two age groups.

This chapter gives the first examples we've seen of inference methods for a parameter other than a simple proportion. Although we have a different standard error, the step-by-step procedures are almost identical. In particular, once again we divide the statistic (the difference in proportions) by its standard error and get a z-score. You should feel right at home.

Key Concepts

Variances of independent random variables add

The variance of a sum or difference of independent random variables is the sum of the variances of those variables.

Sampling distribution of the difference between two proportions

The sampling distribution of $\hat{p}_1 - \hat{p}_2$ is, under appropriate assumptions, modeled by a Normal model with mean $\mu = p_1 - p_2$ and standard deviation $SD(\hat{p}_1 - \hat{p}_2) = \sqrt{\frac{p_1 q_1}{n_1} + \frac{p_2 q_2}{n_2}}$.

Two-proportion *z*-interval

A two-proportion *z*-interval gives a confidence interval for the true difference in proportions, $p_1 - p_2$, in two independent groups.

The confidence interval is $(\hat{p}_1 - \hat{p}_2) \pm z \times SE(\hat{p}_1 - \hat{p}_2)$, where z^* is a critical value from the standard Normal model corresponding to the specified confidence level.

Pooling

When we have data from different sources that we believe are homogeneous, we can get a better estimate of the common proportion and its standard deviation. We can combine, or pool, the data into a single group for the purpose of estimating the common proportion. The resulting pooled standard error is based on more data and is thus more reliable (if the null hypothesis is true and the groups are truly homogeneous).

Two-proportion *z*-test

Test the null hypothesis H_0: $p_1 = p_2$ by referring the statistic

$$z = \frac{\hat{p}_1 - \hat{p}_2}{SE_{pooled}(\hat{p}_1 - \hat{p}_2)}$$

to a standard Normal model.

Skills

When you complete this lesson you should:

Think

- Be able to state the null and alternative hypotheses for testing the difference between two population proportions.
- Know how to examine your data for violations of conditions that would make inference about the difference between two population proportions unwise or invalid.
- Understand that the formula for the standard error of the difference between two independent sample proportions is based on the principle that when finding the sum or difference of two independent random variables, their variances add.

Show

- Know how to find a confidence interval for the difference between two proportions.
- Be able to perform a significance test of the natural null hypothesis that two population proportions are equal.

Tell

- Know how to write a sentence describing what is said about the difference between two population proportions by a confidence interval.
- Know how to write a sentence interpreting the results of a significance test of the null hypothesis that two population proportions are equal.
- Be able to interpret the meaning of a P-value in nontechnical language, making clear that the probability claim is made about computed values and not about the population parameter of interest.
- Know that we do not "accept" a null hypothesis if we fail to reject it.

Exercises

1. **Arthritis.** The Centers for Disease Control report a survey of randomly selected Americans age 65 and older, which found that 411 of 1012 men and 535 of 1062 women suffered from some form of arthritis.
   a) Are the assumptions and conditions necessary for inference satisfied? Explain.
   b) Create a 95% confidence interval for the difference in the proportions of senior men and women who have this disease.
   c) Interpret your interval in this context.
   d) Does this confidence interval suggest that arthritis is more likely to afflict women than men? Explain.

2. **Graduation.** In October 2000 the U.S. Department of Commerce reported the results of a large-scale survey on high school graduation. Researchers contacted more than 25,000 Americans aged 24 years to see if they had finished high school; 84.9% of the 12,460 males and 88.1% of the 12,678 females indicated that they had high school diplomas.
   a) Are the assumptions and conditions necessary for inference satisfied? Explain.
   b) Create a 95% confidence interval for the difference in graduation rates between males and females.
   c) Interpret your confidence interval.
   d) Does this provide strong evidence that girls are more likely than boys to complete high school? Explain.

3. **Pets.** In 1991, researchers at the National Cancer Institute released the results of a study that investigated the effect of weed-killing herbicides on house pets. They examined 827 dogs from homes where an herbicide was used on a regular basis, diagnosing malignant lymphoma in 473 of them. Of the 130 dogs from homes where no herbicides were used, only 19 were found to have lymphoma.
   a) What's the standard error of the difference in the two proportions?
   b) Construct a 95% confidence interval for this difference.
   c) State an appropriate conclusion.

4. **Carpal tunnel.** The painful wrist condition called carpal tunnel syndrome can be treated with surgery or less invasive wrist splints. In September 2002, *Time Magazine* reported on a study of 176 patients. Among the half that had surgery, 80% showed improvement after three months, but only 54% of those who used the wrist splints improved.
   a) What's the standard error of the difference in the two proportions?
   b) Construct a 95% confidence interval for this difference.
   c) State an appropriate conclusion.

5. **Prostate cancer.** There has been debate among doctors over whether surgery can prolong life among men suffering from prostate cancer, a type of cancer that typically develops and spreads very slowly. In the summer of 2003, *The New England Journal of Medicine* published results of some Scandanavian research. Men diagnosed with prostate cancer were randomly assigned to either undergo surgery or not. Among the 347 men who had surgery, 16 eventually died of prostate cancer, compared with 31 of the 348 men who did not have surgery.
   a) Was this an experiment or an observational study? Explain.
   b) Create a 95% confidence interval for the difference in rates of death for the two groups of men.
   c) Based on your confidence interval, is there evidence that surgery may be effective in preventing death from prostate cancer? Explain.

6. **Race and smoking.** In 1995, 24.8% of 550 white adults surveyed reported that they smoked cigarettes, while 25.7% of the 550 black adults surveyed were smokers.
   a) Create a 90% confidence interval for the difference in the percentages of smokers among black and white American adults.
   b) Does this survey indicate a race-based difference in smoking among American adults? Explain, using your confidence interval to test an appropriate hypothesis.

7. **Politics.** A poll checking on the level of public support for proposed antiterrorist legislation reported that 68% of the respondents were in favor. The pollsters reported a sampling error of ±3%. When the responses were broken down by party affiliation, support was 2% higher among Republican respondents than Democrats. The pollsters said the margin of error for this difference was ±4%.
   a) Why is the margin of error larger for the difference in support between the parties than for the overall level of support?
   b) Based on these results, can we conclude that support is significantly higher among Republicans? Explain.

8. **War.** In September 2002, a Gallup Poll found major differences of opinion based on political affiliation over whether Congress should give President Bush authority to take military action in Iraq. Overall, about 50% of the 1010 respondents were in favor, with a reported margin of error of ±3%. Opinion differed greatly among Republicans, Democrats, and Independents, as seen in the bar graph.
   a) How large did this poll estimate the difference in support between Republicans and Democrats to be?

b) Was the margin of error for that difference equal to, greater than, or less than 3%? Explain.

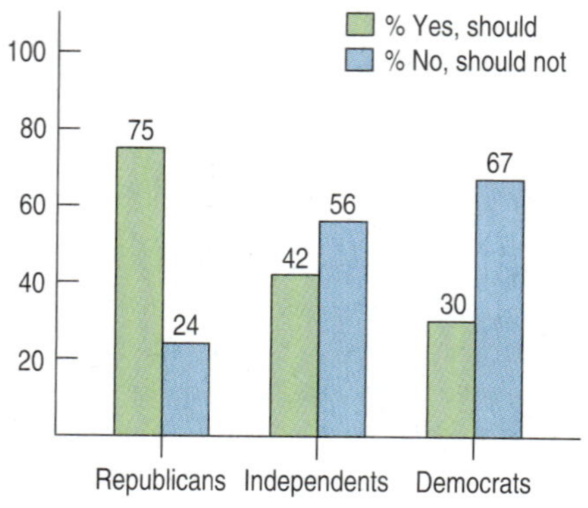

9. Teen smoking, part I. A Vermont study published in December 2001 by the American Academy of Pediatrics examined parental influence on teenagers' decisions to smoke. A group of students who had never smoked were questioned about their parents' attitudes toward smoking. These students were questioned again two years later to see if they had started smoking. The researchers found that among the 284 students who indicated that their parents disapproved of kids smoking, 54 had become established smokers. Among the 41 students who initially said their parents were lenient about smoking, 11 became smokers. Do these data provide strong evidence that parental attitude influences teenagers' decisions about smoking?

a) What kind of design did the researchers use?
b) Write appropriate hypotheses.
c) Are the assumptions and conditions necessary for inference satisfied?
d) Test the hypothesis and state your conclusion.
e) Explain in this context what your P-value means.
f) If that conclusion is actually wrong, which type of error did you commit?

10. Depression. A study published in the *Archives of General Psychiatry* in March 2001 examined the impact of depression on a patient's ability to survive cardiac disease. Researchers identified 450 people with cardiac disease, evaluated them for depression, and followed the group for 4 years. Of the 361 patients with no depression, 67 died. Of the 89 patients with minor or major depression, 26 died. Among people who suffer from cardiac disease, are depressed patients more likely to die than nondepressed ones?

a) What kind of design was used to collect these data?
b) Write appropriate hypotheses.
c) Are the assumptions and conditions necessary for inference satisfied?
d) Test the hypothesis and state your conclusion.
e) Explain in this context what your P-value means.
f) If your conclusion is actually incorrect, which type of error did you commit?

11. Teen smoking, part II. Consider again the Vermont study discussed in Exercise 9.

a) Create a 95% confidence interval for the difference in proportion of children who may smoke and have approving parents and those who may smoke and have disapproving parents.
b) Interpret your interval in this context.
c) Carefully explain what "95% confidence" means.

12. Depression revisited. Consider again the study of the association between depression and cardiac disease survivability in Exercise 10.

a) Create a 95% confidence interval for the difference in survival rates.
b) Interpret your interval in this context.
c) Carefully explain what "95% confidence" means.

13. Pregnancy. In 1998, a San Diego reproductive clinic reported 42 live births to 157 women under the age of 38, but only 7 live births for 89 clients aged 38 and older. Is this strong evidence of a difference in the effectiveness of the clinic's methods for older women?

a) Test an appropriate hypothesis and state your conclusion.
b) If you concluded there was a difference, estimate that difference with a confidence interval and interpret your interval in context.

14. Birthweight. In 2003 the Journal of the American Medical Association reported a study examining the possible impact of air pollution caused by the 9/11 attack on New York's World Trade Center on the weight of babies. Researchers found that 8% of 182 babies born to mothers who were exposed to heavy doses of soot and ash on September 11 were classified as having low birthweight. Only 4% of 2300 babies born in another New York City hospital whose mothers had not been near the site of the disaster were similarly classified. Does this indicate a possibility that air pollution might be linked to a significantly higher proportion of low weight babies?

a) Test an appropriate hypothesis and state your conclusion.
b) If you concluded there is a difference, estimate that difference with a confidence interval and interpret that interval in context.

15. Politics and sex. One month before the election, a poll of 630 randomly selected voters showed 54% planning to vote for a certain candidate. A week later it became known that he had had an extramarital affair, and a new poll showed only 51% of 1010 voters supporting him. Do these results indicate a decrease in voter support for his candidacy?

a) Test an appropriate hypothesis and state your conclusion.
b) If you concluded there was a difference, estimate that difference with a confidence interval and interpret your interval in context.

16. Retirement. The Employee Benefit Research Institute reports that 27% of males anticipate having enough money to live comfortably in retirement, but only 18% of females express that confidence. If these results were based on samples of 250 people of each gender, would you consider this strong evidence that men and women have different outlooks?

a) Test an appropriate hypothesis and state your conclusion.

b) If you concluded there was a difference, estimate that difference with a confidence interval and interpret your interval in context.

17. Twins. In 2001, one county reported that among 3132 white women who had babies, 94 were multiple births. There were also 20 multiple births to 606 black women. Does this indicate any racial difference in the likelihood of multiple births?

a) Test an appropriate hypothesis and state your conclusion.

b) If your conclusion is incorrect, which type of error did you commit?

18. Shopping. A survey of 430 randomly chosen adults found that 21% of the 222 men and 18% of the 208 women had purchased books online.

a) Is there evidence that men are more likely than women to make online purchases of books? Test an appropriate hypothesis and state your conclusion in context.

b) If your conclusion in fact proves to be wrong, did you make a Type I or Type II error?

19. Mammograms. It's widely believed that regular mammogram screening may detect breast cancer early, resulting in fewer deaths from that disease. One study that investigated this issue over a period of 18 years was published during the 1970s. Among 30,565 women who had never had mammograms, 196 died of breast cancer, while only 153 of 30,131 who had undergone screening died of breast cancer.

a) Do these results suggest that mammograms may be an effective screening tool to reduce breast cancer deaths?

b) If your conclusion is incorrect, what type of error have you committed?

20. Mammograms redux. In 2001, the conclusion of the study outlined in Exercise 19 was questioned. A new 9-year study was conducted in Sweden, comparing 21,088 women who had mammograms with 21,195 who did not. Of the women who underwent screening, 63 died of breast cancer, compared with 66 deaths among the control group. (*New York Times*, Dec 9, 2001)

a) Do these results support the effectiveness of regular mammograms in preventing deaths from breast cancer?

b) If your conclusion is incorrect, what kind of error have you committed?

21. Pain. Researchers comparing the effectiveness of two pain medications randomly selected a group of patients who had been complaining of a certain kind of joint pain. They randomly divided these people into two groups, then administered the pain killers. Of the 112 people in the group who received medication A, 84 said this pain reliever was effective. Of the 108 people in the other group, 66 reported that pain reliever B was effective.

a) Write a 95% confidence interval for the percent of people who may get relief from this kind of joint pain by using medication A. Interpret your interval.

b) Write a 95% confidence interval for the percent of people who may get relief by using medication B. Interpret your interval.

c) Do the intervals for A and B overlap? What do you think this means about the comparative effectiveness of these medications?

d) Find a 95% confidence interval for the difference in the proportions of people who may find these medications effective. Interpret your interval

e) Does this interval contain zero? What does that mean?

f) Why do the results in parts c and e seem contradictory? If we want to compare the effectiveness of these two pain relievers, which is the correct approach? Why?

22. Gender gap. Candidates for political office realize that different levels of support among men and women may be a crucial factor in determining the outcome of the election. One candidate finds that 52% of 473 men polled say they will vote for him, but only 45% of the 522 women in the poll express support.

a) Write a 95% confidence interval for the percent of male voters who may vote for our candidate. Interpret your interval.

b) Write a 95% confidence interval for the percent of female voters who may vote for him. Interpret your interval.

c) Do the intervals for males and females overlap? What do you think this means about the gender gap?

d) Find a 95% confidence interval for the difference in the proportions of males and females who will vote for this candidate. Interpret your interval.

e) Does this interval contain zero? What does that mean?

f) Why do the results in parts c and e seem contradictory? If we want to see if there is a gender gap among voters with respect to this candidate, which is the correct approach? Why?

Review of Part V From the Data at Hand to the World at Large

Quick Review

What do samples really tell us about the populations from which they are drawn? Are the results of an experiment meaningful, or are they just sampling error? Statistical inference based on our understanding of sampling models can help answer these questions. Here's a brief summary of the key concepts and skills:

- Sampling models describe the variability of sample statistics using a remarkable result called the Central Limit Theorem.
  - When the number of trials is sufficiently large, proportions found in different samples vary according to an approximately Normal model.
  - When samples are sufficiently large, the means of different samples vary, with an approximately Normal model.
  - The variability of sample statistics decreases as sample size increases.
  - Statistical inference procedures are based on the Central Limit Theorem.
  - No inference procedure is valid unless the underlying assumptions are true. Always check the conditions before proceeding.
- A confidence interval uses a sample statistic (such as a proportion) to estimate a range of plausible values for the parameter of a population model.
  - All confidence intervals involve an estimate of the parameter, a margin of error, and a level of confidence.
  - For confidence intervals based on a given sample, the greater the margin of error the higher the confidence.
  - At a given level of confidence, the larger the sample the smaller the margin of error.
- A hypothesis test proposes a model for the population, then examines the observed statistics to see if that model is plausible.
  - A null hypothesis suggests a parameter value for the population model. Usually, we assume there is nothing interesting, unusual, or different about the sample results.
  - The alternative hypothesis states what we will believe if the sample results turn out to be inconsistent with our null model.
  - We compare the difference between statistic and hypothesized value with the standard error of the statistic. It's the sampling distribution of this ratio that gives us a P-value.
  - The P-value of the test is the probability that the null model could produce results at least as extreme as those observed in the sample or the experiment just as a result of sampling error.
  - A low P-value provides evidence that the null model is probably incorrect. Then we reject the null model.
  - A high P-value indicates that the sample results are not inconsistent with the null model, so we cannot reject it. However, this does not prove the null model is true.
  - Sometimes we will mistakenly reject the null hypothesis even though it's actually true—that's called a Type I error. If we fail to reject a false null hypothesis, we commit a Type II error.
  - The power of a test is its ability to detect a false null hypothesis.
  - You can lower the risk of a Type I error by requiring a higher standard of proof (lower P-value) before rejecting the null hypothesis. But this will raise the risk of a Type II error and decrease the power of the test.
  - The only way to increase the power of a test while decreasing the chance of committing either error is to design a study based on a larger sample.

And now for some opportunities to review these concepts and skills . . .

Review Exercises

1. **Herbal cancer.** A report in the *New England Journal of Medicine* (June 6, 2000) notes growing evidence that the herb *Aristolochia fangchi* can cause urinary tract cancer in those who take it. Suppose you are asked to design an experiment to study this claim. Imagine that you have data on urinary tract cancers in subjects who have used this herb and similar subjects who have not used it and that you can measure incidences of cancer and precancerous lesions in these subjects. State the null and alternative hypotheses you would use in your study.

2. **Colorblind.** Medical literature says that about 8% of males are colorblind. A university's introductory psychology course is taught in a large lecture hall. Among the students there are 325 males. Each semester when the professor discusses visual perception, he shows the class a test for colorblindness. The percentage of males who are colorblind varies from semester to semester.
   a) Is the sampling distribution model for the sample proportion likely to be Normal? Explain.
   b) What are the mean and standard deviation of this sampling distribution model?
   c) Sketch the sampling model using the 68-95-99.7 Rule.
   d) Write a few sentences explaining what the model says about this professor's class.

3. **Birth days.** During a 2-month period in 2002, 72 babies were born at the Tompkins Community Hospital in upstate New York. The table shows how many babies were born on each day of the week.

Day	Births
Mon.	7
Tues.	17
Wed.	8
Thurs.	12
Fri.	9
Sat.	10
Sun.	9

   a) If births are uniformly distributed across all days of the week, how many would you expect on each day?
   b) Only 7 births occurred on a Monday. Does this indicate that women might be less likely to give birth on a Monday? Explain.
   c) Are the 17 births on Tuesdays unusually high? Explain.
   d) Can you think of any reasons why births may not occur completely at random?

4. **Polling.** In the 1992 U.S. presidential election, Bill Clinton received 43% of the vote compared with 38% for George Bush, and 19% for Ross Perot. Suppose we had taken a random sample of 100 voters in an exit poll and asked them for whom they had voted.
   a) Would you always get 43 votes for Clinton, 38 for Bush, and 19 for Perot in a sample of 100? Why or why not?
   b) In 95% of such polls, our sample proportion of voters for Clinton should be between what two values?
   c) In 95% of such polls, the sample proportion of Perot votes should be between what two numbers?
   d) Would you expect the sample proportion of Perot votes to vary more, less, or about the same as the sample proportion of Bush votes? Why?

5. **Leaky gas tanks.** Nationwide it is estimated that 40% of service stations have gas tanks that leak to some extent. A new program in California is designed to lessen the prevalence of these leaks. We want to assess the effectiveness of the program by seeing if the percentage of service stations whose tanks leak has decreased. To do this, we randomly sample 27 service stations in California and determine whether there is any evidence of leakage. In our sample, only 7 of the stations exhibit any leakage. Is there evidence that the new program is effective?
   a) What are the null and alternative hypotheses?
   b) Check the assumptions necessary for inference.
   c) Test the null hypothesis.
   d) What do you conclude (in plain English)?
   e) If the program actually works, have you made an error? What kind?
   f) What two things could you do to decrease the probability of making this kind of error?
   g) What are the advantages and disadvantages of taking those two courses of action?

6. **Surgery and germs.** Joseph Lister (for whom Listerine is named!) was a British physician who was interested in the role of bacteria in human infections. He suspected that germs were involved in transmitting infection, and so he tried using carbolic acid as an operating room disinfectant. In 75 amputations, he used carbolic acid 40 times. Of the 40 amputations using carbolic acid, 34 of the patients lived. In the 35 amputations without carbolic acid, 19 lived. The question of interest is whether carbolic acid is effective in increasing the chances of surviving an amputation.
   a) What kind of a study is this?
   b) What do you conclude? Support your conclusion by testing an appropriate hypothesis.
   c) What reservations do you have about the design of the study?

7. **Scrabble.** Using a computer to play many simulated games of Scrabble, researcher Charles Robinove found that the letter "A" occurred in 54% of the hands. This study had a margin of error of ± 10%. (*Chance*, 15, no. 1 [2002])
   a) Explain what the margin of error means in this context.
   b) Why might the margin of error be so large?
   c) Probability theory predicts that the letter "A" should appear in 63% of the hands. Does this make you concerned that the simulation might be faulty? Explain.

8. **Dice.** When one die is rolled, the number of spots showing has a mean of 3.5 and a standard deviation of 1.7. Suppose you roll 10 dice. What's the approximate proba-

bility that your total is between 30 and 40 (that is, the average for the 10 dice is between 3 and 4)? Specify the model you use and the assumptions and conditions that justify your approach.

9. News sources. In May of 2000, the Pew Research Foundation sampled 1593 respondents and asked how they obtain news. In Pew's report, 33% of respondents say that they now obtain news from the Internet at least once a week.

a) Pew reports a margin of error of ±3% for this result. Explain what the margin of error means.

b) Pew also asked about investment information, and 21% of respondents reported that the Internet is their main source of this information. When limited to the 780 respondents who identified themselves as investors, the percent who rely on the Internet rose to 28%. How would you expect the margin of error for this statistic to change in comparison with the margin of error for the percentage of all respondents?

c) When restricted to the 239 active traders in the sample, Pew reports that 45% rely on the Internet for investment information. Find a confidence interval for this statistic.

d) How does the margin of error for your confidence interval compare with the values in parts a and b? Explain why.

10. Death penalty. In May of 2002, the Gallup Organization asked a random sample of 537 American adults this question:

If you could choose between the following two approaches, which do you think is the better penalty for murder, the death penalty or life imprisonment, with absolutely no possibility of parole?

Of those polled, 52% chose the death penalty.

a) Create a 95% confidence interval for the percentage of all American adults who favor the death penalty.

b) Based on your confidence interval, is it clear that the death penalty has majority support? Explain.

c) If pollsters wanted to follow up on this poll with another survey that could determine the level of support for the death penalty to within 2% with 98% confidence, how many people should they poll?

11. Bimodal. We are sampling randomly from a distribution known to be bimodal.

a) As our sample size increases, what's the expected shape of the sample's distribution?

b) What's the expected value of our sample's mean? Does the size of the sample matter?

c) How is the variability of this sample's mean related to the standard deviation of the population? Does the size of the sample matter?

d) How is the shape of the sampling distribution model affected by the sample size?

12. Vitamin D. In July 2002 the *American Journal of Clinical Nutrition* reported that 42% of 1546 African American women studied had vitamin D deficiency. The data came from a national nutrition study conducted by the Centers for Disease Control in Atlanta.

a) Do these data meet the assumptions necessary for inference? What would you like to know that you don't?

b) Create a 95% confidence interval.

c) Interpret the interval in this context.

d) Explain in this context what "95% confidence" means.

13. Archery. A champion archer can generally hit the bull's-eye 80% of the time. Suppose she shoots 200 arrows during competition. Let $\hat{p}$ represent the percentage of bull's-eyes she gets (the sample proportion).

a) What are the mean and standard deviation of the sampling distribution model for $\hat{p}$?

b) Is a Normal model appropriate here? Explain.

c) Sketch the sampling model using the 68-95-99.7 Rule.

d) What's the probability she gets at least 85% bull's-eyes?

14. Free throws. During the 2000–2001 NBA season, San Antonio Spurs player Tim Duncan made 409 of 662 free throws he attempted. During the 2001–2002 season, he made 460 of his 568 free throws.

a) Write a 95% confidence interval for the increase in percent of foul shots he can make.

b) Based on your confidence interval, is there strong evidence that he has become a better foul shooter? Explain.

15. Twins. There is some indication in medical literature that doctors may have become more aggressive in inducing labor or doing preterm cesarean sections when a woman is carrying twins. Records at a large hospital show that of the 43 sets of twins born in 1990, 20 were delivered before the 37th week of pregnancy. In 2000, 26 of 48 sets of twins were born preterm. Does this indicate an increase in the incidence of early births of twins? Test an appropriate hypothesis and state your conclusion.

16. Eclampsia. It's estimated that 50,000 pregnant women worldwide die each year of eclampsia, a condition involving elevated blood pressure and seizures. A research team from 175 hospitals in 33 countries investigated the effectiveness of magnesium sulfate in preventing the occurrence of eclampsia in at-risk patients. Results are summarized below. (*Lancet,* June 1, 2002)

Treatment	Total subjects	Reported side effects	Developed eclampsia	Deaths
Magnesium sulfide	4999	1201	40	11
Placebo	4993	228	96	20

a) Write a 95% confidence interval for the increase in the proportion of women who may develop side effects from this treatment. Interpret your interval.
b) Is there evidence that the treatment may be effective in preventing the development of eclampsia? Test an appropriate hypothesis and state your conclusion.

17. Eclampsia. Refer again to the research summarized in Exercise 16. Is there any evidence that when eclampsia does occur the magnesium sulfide treatment may help prevent the woman's death?
a) Write an appropriate hypothesis.
b) Check the assumptions and conditions.
c) Find the P-value of the test.
d) What do you conclude about the magnesium sulfide treatment?
e) If your conclusion is wrong, which type of error have you made?
f) Name two things you could do to increase the power of this test.
g) What are the advantages and disadvantages of those two options?

18. Eggs. The ISA Babcock Company supplies poultry farmers with hens, advertising that a mature B300 Layer produces eggs with a mean weight of 60.7 grams. Suppose that egg weights follow a Normal model with standard deviation 3.1 grams.
a) What fraction of the eggs produced by these hens weigh more than 62 grams?
b) What's the probability that a dozen randomly selected eggs average more than 62 grams?
c) Using the 68-95-99.7 Rule, sketch a model of the total weights of a dozen eggs.

19. Polling disclaimer. A newspaper article that reported the results of an election poll included the following explanation.

The Associated Press poll on the 2000 presidential campaign is based on telephone interviews with 798 randomly selected registered voters from all states except Alaska and Hawaii. The interviews were conducted June 21–25 by ICR of Media, Pa.

The results were weighted to represent the population by demographic factors such as age, sex, region and education.

No more than one time in 20 should chance variations in the sample cause the results to vary by more than 4 percentage points from the answers that would be obtained if all Americans were polled.

The margin of sampling error is larger for responses of subgroups, such as income categories or those in political parties. There are other sources of potential error in polls, including the wording and order of questions.

a) Did they describe the 5 W's well?
b) What kind of sampling design could take into account the several demographic factors listed?
c) What was the margin of error of this poll?
d) What was the confidence level?
e) Why is the margin of error larger for subgroups?
f) Which kinds of potential bias did they caution readers about?

20. Enough eggs? One of the important issues for poultry farmers is the production rate—the percentage of days on which a given hen actually lays an egg. Ideally, that would be 100% (an egg every day), but realistically hens tend to lay eggs on about 3 of every 4 days. ISA Babcock wants to advertise the production rate for the B300 Layer (see Exercise 18) as a 95% confidence interval with a margin of error of ±2%. How many hens must they collect data on?

21. Teen deaths. Traffic accidents are the leading cause of death among people aged 15 to 20. In May 2002, the National Highway Traffic Safety Administration reported that even though only 6.8% of licensed drivers are between 15 and 20 years old, they were involved in 14.3% of all fatal crashes. Insurance companies have long known that teenage boys were high risks, but what about teenage girls? One insurance company found that the driver was a teenage girl in 44 of the 388 fatal accidents they investigated. Is this strong evidence that the accident rate is lower for girls than for teens in general?
a) Test an appropriate hypothesis and state your conclusion.
b) Explain what your P-value means in this context.

22. Perfect pitch. A recent study on perfect pitch tested 2700 students in American music conservatories. It found that 7% of non-Asian and 32% of Asian students have perfect pitch. A test of the difference in proportions resulted in a P-value of < 0.0001.
a) What are the researchers' null and alternative hypotheses?
b) State your conclusion.
c) Explain in this context what the P-value means.
d) The researchers claimed that the data prove that genetic differences between the two populations cause a difference in the frequency of occurrence of perfect pitch. Do you agree? Why or why not?

23. Largemouth bass. Organizers of a fishing tournament believe that the lake holds a sizable population of largemouth bass. They assume that the weights of these fish have a model that is skewed to the right with a mean of 3.5 pounds and a standard deviation of 2.2 pounds.
a) Explain why a skewed model makes sense here.
b) Explain why you cannot determine the probability that a largemouth bass randomly selected ("caught") from the lake weighs over 3 pounds.
c) Each fisherman in the contest catches 5 fish each day. Can you determine the probability that someone's catch averages over 3 pounds? Explain.

d) The 12 fishermen competing each caught the limit of 5 fish. What's the probability that the total catch of 60 fish averaged more than 3 pounds?

24. Cheating. A Rutgers University study released in 2002 found that many high school students cheat on tests. The researchers surveyed a random sample of 4500 high school students nationwide; 74% of them said they had cheated at least once.

a) Create a 90% confidence interval for the level of cheating among high school students. Don't forget to check the appropriate conditions.
b) Interpret your interval.
c) Explain what "90% confidence" means.
d) Would a 95% confidence interval be wider or narrower? Explain without actually calculating the interval.

25. Language. Neurological research has shown that in about 80% of people, language abilities reside in the brain's left side. Another 10% display right-brain language centers, and the remaining 10% have two-sided language control. (The latter two groups are mainly left-handers.) (*Science News*, 161, no. 24 [2002])

a) We select 60 people at random. Is it reasonable to use a Normal model to describe the possible distribution of the proportion of the group that has left-brain language control? Explain.
b) What's the probability that our group has at least 75% left-brainers?
c) If the group had consisted of 100 people, would that probability be higher, lower, or about the same? Explain why, without actually calculating the probability.
d) How large a group would almost certainly guarantee at least 75% left-brainers? Explain.

26. Cigarettes. In 1999 the Centers for Disease Control estimated that about 34.8% of high school students smoked cigarettes. They established a national health goal of reducing that figure to 16% by the year 2010. To that end, they hoped to achieve a reduction to 30% by the end of 2001. Early in 2002 they released a research study in which only 28.5% of a random sample of 10,204 high school students said they were current smokers. Is this evidence that progress toward the goal is on track?

a) Write appropriate hypotheses.
b) Verify that the appropriate assumptions are satisfied.
c) Find the P-value of this test.
d) Explain what the P-value means in this context.
e) State an appropriate conclusion.
f) Of course, your conclusion may be incorrect. If so, which kind of error did you commit?

27. Crohn's disease. In 2002 the medical journal *Lancet* reported that 335 of 573 patients suffering from Crohn's disease responded positively to injections of the arthritis-fighting drug infliximab.

a) Create a 95% confidence interval for the effectiveness of this drug.
b) Interpret your interval in context.
c) Explain carefully what "95% confidence" means in this context.

28. Teen smoking. The Centers for Disease Control say that about 30% of teenagers smoke tobacco (down from a high of 38% in 1997). A college has 522 students in its freshmen class. Is it likely that more than 40% of them may be smokers? Explain.

29. Alcohol abuse. Growing concern about binge drinking among college students has prompted one large state university to conduct a survey to assess the size of the problem on its campus. The university plans to randomly select students and ask how many have been drunk during the past week. If the school hopes to estimate the true proportion among all its students with 90% confidence and a margin of error of ±4%, how many students must be surveyed?

30. Errors. An auto parts company advertises that its special oil additive will make the engine "run smoother, cleaner, longer, with fewer repairs." An independent laboratory decides to test part of this claim. It arranges to use a taxicab company's fleet of cars. The cars are randomly divided into two groups. The company's mechanics will use the additive in one group of cars but not in the other. At the end of a year the laboratory will compare the percentage of cars in each group that required engine repairs.

a) What kind of a study is this?
b) Will they do a one-tailed or a two-tailed test?
c) Explain in this context what a Type I error would be.
d) Explain in this context what a Type II error would be.
e) Which type of error would the additive manufacturer consider more serious?
f) If the cabs with the additive do indeed run significantly better, can the company conclude it is an effect of the additive? Can they generalize this result and recommend the additive for all cars? Explain.

31. Preemies. Among 242 Cleveland area children born prematurely at low birth weights between 1977 and 1979, only 74% graduated from high school. Among a comparison group of 233 children of normal birth weight, 83% were high school graduates. ("Outcomes in Young Adulthood for Very-Low-Birth-Weight Infants," *New England Journal of Medicine*, 346, no. 3 [2002])

a) Create a 95% confidence interval for the difference in graduation rates between children of normal and very low birth weights. Be sure to check the appropriate assumptions and conditions.
b) Does this provide evidence that premature birth may be a risk factor for not finishing high school? Use your confidence interval to test an appropriate hypothesis.
c) Suppose your conclusion is incorrect. Which type of error did you make?

32. Safety. Observers in Texas watched children at play in eight communities. Of the 814 children seen biking, roller skating, or skateboarding, only 14% wore a helmet.

a) Create and interpret a 95% confidence interval.
b) What concerns do you have about this study that might make your confidence interval unreliable?
c) Suppose we want to do this study again, picking various communities and locations at random, and hope to end up with a 98% confidence interval having a margin of error of ±4%. How many kids must we observe?

33. Fried PCs. A computer company recently experienced a disastrous fire that ruined some of its inventory. Unfortunately, during the panic of the fire, some of the damaged computers were sent to another warehouse where they were mixed with undamaged computers. The engineer responsible for quality control would like to check out each computer in order to decide if it's undamaged or damaged. Each computer undergoes a series of 100 tests. The number of tests it fails will be used to make the decision. If it fails more than a certain number, it will be classified as damaged, and then scrapped. From past history, the distribution of the number of tests failed is known for both undamaged and damaged computers. The probabilities associated with each outcome are listed in the table below:

Number of tests failed	0	1	2	3	4	5	>5
Undamaged (%)	80	13	2	4	1	0	0
Damaged (%)	0	10	70	5	4	1	10

The table indicates, for example, that 80% of the undamaged computers have no failures, while 70% of the damaged computers have 2 failures.

a) To the engineers this is a hypothesis-testing situation. State the null and alternative hypotheses.
b) Someone suggests classifying a computer as damaged if it fails any of the tests. Discuss the advantages and disadvantages of this test plan.
c) What number of tests would a computer have to fail in order to be classified as damaged if the engineers want to have the probability of a Type I error equal to 5%.
d) What's the power of the test plan in part c?
e) A colleague points out that by increasing α just 2%, the power can be increased substantially. Explain.

34. Power. We are replicating an experiment. How will each of the following changes affect the power of our test? Indicate whether it will increase, decrease, or remain the same, assuming all other aspects of the situation remain unchanged.

a) We increase the number of subjects from 40 to 100.
b) We require a higher standard of proof, changing from $\alpha = .05$ to $\alpha = .01$.

Part VI

Learning About the World

Chapter 23

Inferences About Means

WHO	Vehicles on Triphammer Road
WHAT	Speed
UNITS	Miles per hour
WHEN	April 11, 2000, 1 p.m.
WHERE	A small town in the northeastern United States
WHY	Concern over impact on residential neighborhood

Motor vehicle crashes are the leading cause of death for people of every age between 4 and 33 years old. In the year 2000, motor vehicle accidents claimed the lives of 41,821 people in the United States, up from 41,717 the year before. This means that, on average, motor vehicle crashes resulted in 115 deaths each day, or 1 death every 13 minutes.

Speeding is a contributing factor in 29% of all fatal accidents. Not only were 12,350 lives lost in speeding-related crashes during 2000, but the economic cost of such crashes is estimated to be about $27.4 billion per year (National Highway Traffic Safety Administration).

Triphammer Road is a busy street that passes through a residential neighborhood. Residents there are concerned that vehicles traveling on Triphammer often exceed the posted speed limit of 30 miles per hour. The local police sometimes place a radar speed detector by the side of the road; as a vehicle approaches, this detector displays the vehicle's speed to its driver. The police hope that drivers will slow down if they are reminded of their speed.

The local residents are not convinced that such a passive method is helping the problem. They wish to persuade the village to add extra police patrols to encourage drivers to observe the speed limit. To help their case, a resident stood where he could see the detector and recorded the speed of vehicles passing it during a 15-minute period one day. When clusters of vehicles went by, he noted only the speed of the front vehicle. Here are the data:

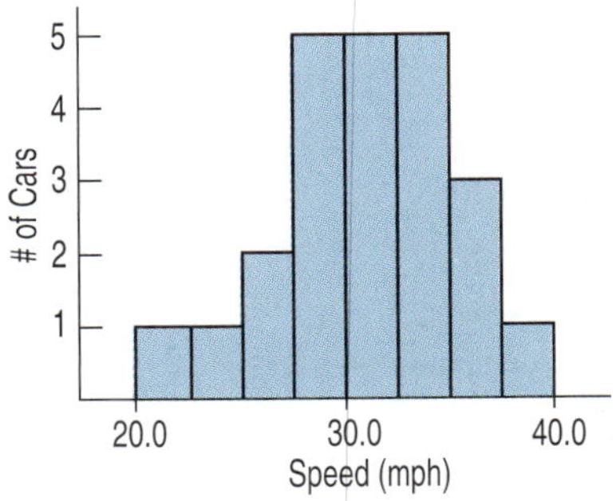

The speeds of cars on Triphammer Road seem to be unimodal and symmetric, at least at this scale.

Figure 23.1

Speed		
29	29	24
34	34	34
34	32	36
28	31	31
30	27	34
29	37	36
38	29	21
31	26	

We're interested both in estimating the true mean speed and in testing whether it exceeds the posted speed limit. Although the sample of vehicles is a convenience sample, not a truly random sample, there's no compelling reason to believe that vehicles at one time of day are driving faster or slower than vehicles at another time of day,[1] so we can take the sample to be representative.

These data differ from data on proportions in one important way. Proportions are usually reported as summaries. After all, individual responses are just "success" and "failure" or "1" and "0." Quantitative data though, usually report a value for each individual. When you have a value for each individual, you should remember the three rules of data analysis and plot the data, as we have done here.

We have quantitative data, so we summarize with means and standard deviations. Because we want to do inference, we'll think about sampling distributions, too, but we already know most of the facts we need.

Getting Started

When we estimate the standard deviation of the sampling model from the data, it's called the *standard error.* We'll use that term and the $SE(\bar{y})$ notation. Remember, though, that it's just the estimated standard deviation of the sampling model.

You've learned how to create confidence intervals and test hypotheses about proportions (if you haven't, this would be a really good time for a quick review). Now we want to do the same thing for means. Just as we did before, we will base both our confidence interval and our hypothesis test on the sampling model. And the Central Limit Theorem tells us that the sampling model we need is still the Normal. This is true for means no matter what shape population the data come from (at least for large samples).

We also know that the standard deviation of the model is $SD(\bar{y}) = \frac{\sigma}{\sqrt{n}}$.

For proportions, we knew that $SD(\hat{p}) = \sqrt{\frac{pq}{n}}$, so we used $SE(\hat{p}) = \sqrt{\frac{\hat{p}\hat{q}}{n}}$ to estimate the standard deviation. Because they are linked, we could find the standard deviation from $\hat{p}$. For means, knowing $\bar{y}$ doesn't tell us *anything* about $SD(\bar{y})$. So what should we do? We do what any sensible person would do: We estimate σ with s, the sample standard deviation. The resulting standard error is $SE(\bar{y}) = \frac{s}{\sqrt{n}}$.

A century ago, people used the Normal model with this standard error, assuming it would work. After all, a similar estimate worked fine for proportions. And for large sample sizes it *did* work reasonably well.

However, people began to notice problems for smaller samples. The trouble is that $SE(\bar{y})$ is based on the sample statistic, s, which varies from sample to sample independently of the sample-to-sample variation of $\bar{y}$. This extra variation can mess up the margin of error and P-value, especially for a small sample. Somehow, we have to allow for the extra variation.

The plot is thicker than that. Not only is there extra variation in $SE(\bar{y})$, but even the *shape* of its sampling model changes. The model is no longer Normal—and the shape alters more for small samples than for larger ones.

William S. Gosset, the man who first realized this fact, transformed Statistics, but most people who use his work don't even know his name.

[1]Except, perhaps, at rush hour. But at that time, traffic is slowed. Our concern is with ordinary traffic during the day.

Gosset's *t*

To find the sampling distribution of $\frac{\bar{y}}{s/\sqrt{n}}$, Gosset simulated it *by hand.* He drew paper slips of small samples from a hat *hundreds of times* and computed the means and standard deviations with a mechanically cranked calculator. Today you could repeat in seconds on a computer the experiment that took him over a year. Gosset's work was so meticulous that not only did he get the shape of the new histogram approximately right, but he even figured out the exact *formula* for it from his sample. The formula was not confirmed mathematically until years later by Sir R. A. Fisher. **Figure 23.2**

Gosset had a job that made him the envy of many. He was the quality control engineer for the Guinness Brewery in Dublin, Ireland. His job was to make sure that the stout (a thick, dark beer) leaving the brewery was of high enough quality to meet the demands of the brewery's many discerning customers. It's easy to imagine, when testing stout, why a large sample with many observations might be undesirable, not to mention dangerous to one's health. So Gosset often used small samples of 3 or 4. But he noticed that with samples of this size, his tests for quality weren't quite right. He knew this because when the batches that he rejected were sent back to the laboratory for more extensive testing, too often they turned out to be OK.

Gosset checked the stout's quality by performing hypothesis tests. He knew that the test would make some Type I errors and reject about 5% of the *good* batches of stout. However, the lab told him that he was in fact rejecting about 15% of the good batches. Gosset knew something was wrong, and it bothered him.

Gosset took time off to study the problem (and earn a graduate degree in the emerging field of Statistics). He figured out that when he used the estimated standard error, $\frac{s}{\sqrt{n}}$, the shape of the sampling model changed. He even figured out what the new model should be and called it a *t*-distribution.

The Guinness Company didn't give Gosset a lot of support for his work. In fact, it had a policy against publishing results. Gosset had to convince the company that he was not publishing an industrial secret, and (as part of getting permission to publish) had to use a pseudonym. The pseudonym he chose was "Student," and ever since, the model he found has been known as **Student's *t*.**

The shape of Gosset's model changes with different sample sizes. So the Student's *t*-models form a whole *family* of related distributions that depend on a parameter known as **degrees of freedom.** We often denote degrees of freedom as *df*, and the model as t_{df}, with the degrees of freedom as a subscript.

What Does This Mean for Means?

To make confidence intervals or test hypotheses for means, we need to use Gosset's model. Which one? Well, for means, it turns out the right value for degrees of freedom is $df = n - 1$.

NOTATION ALERT:

Ever since Gosset, *t* has been reserved in Statistics for his distribution.

A sampling distribution for means

When the conditions are met, the standardized sample mean,

$$t = \frac{\bar{y} - \mu}{SE(\bar{y})},$$

follows a Student's *t*-model with $n - 1$ degrees of freedom. We estimate the standard error with

$$SE(\bar{y}) = \frac{s}{\sqrt{n}}.$$

When Gosset corrected the model for the extra uncertainty, the margin of error got bigger, as you might have guessed. When you use Gosset's model instead of the Normal model, your confidence intervals will be just a bit wider and your P-values just a bit larger. That's the correcting you need. By using the *t*-model, you've compensated for the extra variability in precisely the right way.

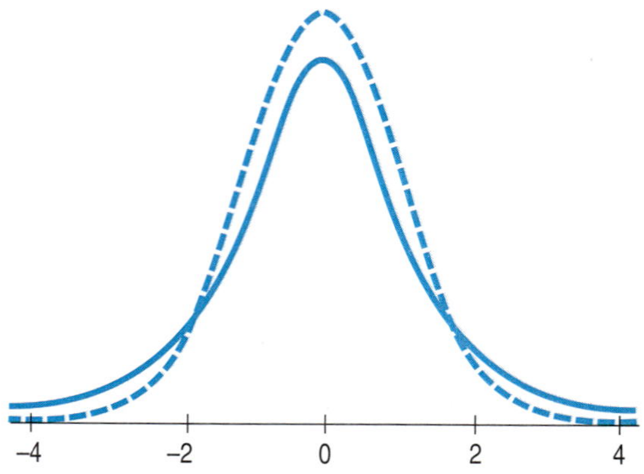

The t-model on 2 degrees of freedom has fatter tails than the Normal model. So the 68-95-99.7 Rule doesn't work for t-models with only a few degrees of freedom.
Figure 23.3

Student's t-models are unimodal, symmetric, and bell shaped, just like the Normal. But t-models with only a few degrees of freedom have much fatter tails than the Normal. (That's what makes the margin of error bigger.) As the degrees of freedom increase, the t-models look more and more like the Normal. In fact, the t-model with infinite degrees of freedom is exactly Normal.[2] This is great news if you happen to have an infinite number of data values. Unfortunately, that's not practical. Fortunately, above a few hundred degrees of freedom it's very hard to tell the difference.

For this reason, many books present rules for when to switch from t to Normal as the model for the sampling distribution. With technology, there's no need to do this. The one exception is when we have a model that gives us a value for σ. If we *know* σ, it would be foolish not to use that information. And if we don't have to estimate s, then we can use the Normal model.

z or t?

If you know σ, use z. (That's rare!)

Whenever you use s to estimate σ, use t. (Almost always.)

When σ is known

Administrators of a hospital were concerned about the prenatal care given to mothers in their part of the city. To study this, they examined the gestation times of babies born there. They drew a sample of 25 babies born in their hospital in the previous 6 months. Human gestation times for healthy pregnancies are known to be well modeled by a Normal with a mean of 266 days and a standard deviation of 16 days. The hospital administrators wanted to test the mean gestation time of their sample of babies against the known standard. For this test, they should use the established value for the standard deviation, 16 days, rather than estimating the standard deviation from their sample. Because they use model parameter values, they should base their test on the Normal model rather than Student's t.

Finding t-Values by Hand

The Student's t-model is different for each value of degrees of freedom. We might print a table like the old Normal tables for each degrees of freedom value, but that's a lot of pages, and not likely to be a bestseller. One way to shorten the book is to admit that while it might be nice to be able to get a critical value for a 93.4% confidence interval, in practice we usually limit ourselves to 90%, 95, 99%, and

[2]Formally, in the limit as n goes to infinity.

As degrees of freedom increase, the shape of Student's *t*-models changes more gradually. Table T at the back of the book includes degrees of freedom between 100 and 1000 selected so that you can pin down the probability value for just about any df. If your df's aren't listed, take the cautious approach by using the next lower value.

99.9% confidence levels. So Statistics books usually have one table of *t*-model critical values for selected confidence levels. (This one does, too; see Appendix T). The tables run down the page for as many degrees of freedom as can fit, and they are actually much easier to use than the Normal tables.

Then they get to the bottom of the page and run out of room. Of course, for *enough* degrees of freedom, the *t*-model gets closer and closer to the Normal, so the tables give a final row with the critical values from the Normal model and label it "∞ df."

Or we could use technology. Any graphing calculator or statistics program can give critical values for a *t*-model for any number of degrees of freedom and for any confidence level you please. And they can go straight to P-values when we test a hypothesis. You can also find tables on the Internet. (Search for terms like "statistical tables *z*, *t*.")

TI Tips

You already know how to use your TI to find probabilities for Normal models using *z*-scores and **normalcdf**. What about *t*-models? Yes, the calculator can work with them, too.

You know from your experience with confidence intervals that $z = 1.645$ cuts off the upper 5% in a Normal model. Use the TI to check that. From the **DISTR** menu, enter **normalcdf(1.645,99)**. Only 0.04998? Close enough for statisticians!

We might wonder about the probability of observing a *t*-value greater than 1.645, but we can't find that. There's only one Normal model, but there are many *t*-models, depending on the number of degrees of freedom. We need to be more specific.

Let's find the probability of observing a *t*-value greater than 1.645 when there are 12 degrees of freedom. That we can do. Look in the **DISTR** menu again. See it? Yes, **tcdf**. That function works essentially like **normalcdf**, but after you enter the left and right cutoffs you must also specify the number of degrees of freedom. Try **tcdf(1.645,99,12)**.

The upper tail probability for t_{12} is 0.063, higher than the Normal model's 0.05. That should make sense to you—remember, *t*-models are a bit fatter in the tails, so more of the distribution lies beyond the 1.645 cutoff. (That means we'll have to go a little wider to make a 90% confidence interval.)

Check out what happens when there are more degrees of freedom, say, 25. The command **tcdf(1,645,99,25)** yields a probability of 0.056. That's closer to 0.05, for a good reason: *t*-models look more and more like the Normal model as the number of degrees of freedom increases.

Use your calculator to play around with **tcdf(** a bit. Try to develop a clear understanding of how *t*-models compare to the more familiar Normal model. That will help you as you learn to use *t*-models to make inferences about means.

Assumptions and Conditions

Gosset found the *t*-model by simulation. Years later, when Sir Ronald A. Fisher showed mathematically that Gosset was right, he needed to make some assumptions to make the proof work. These are the assumptions we need to use the Student's *t*-models.

Independence Assumption

The data values should be mutually independent. There's really no way to check independence from the data, but we should think about whether the assumption is reasonable.

Randomization condition. The data arise from a random sample or suitably randomized experiment. Randomly sampled data—and especially data from an SRS—are ideal.

When a sample is drawn without replacement, technically we ought to check the following:

10% condition. The sample is no more than 10% of the population. When we made inferences about proportions, this condition was crucial. For means, though, it is rarely a problem in practice. We can estimate means more reliably than proportions, so we almost never need to take that large a fraction of the population as our sample. We won't mention it often for means—but don't forget about it if you have a small population, or a very large sample.

Normal Population Assumption

To use a Student's t-model, we are formally required to assume that the data are from a population that follows a Normal model. Practically speaking, there's no way to be certain this is true.

And it's almost certainly *not* true. Models are idealized; real data are, well, real. The good news, however, is that even for small samples, it's sufficient to check the following:

Nearly Normal condition. The data come from a distribution that is unimodal and symmetric. Verify this by making a histogram or Normal probability plot. The importance of Normality for Student's t depends on the sample size. Just our luck; it matters most when it's hardest to check.[3]

For very small samples ($n < 15$ or so), the data should follow a Normal model pretty closely. Of course, with so little data, it's rather hard to tell. But you do find outliers or strong skewness, you should not use these methods.

For moderate sample sizes (n between 15 and 40 or so), the t methods will work well as long as the data are unimodal and reasonably symmetric. Make a histogram.

When the sample size is larger than 40 or 50, the t methods are safe to use even if the data are skewed. Make a histogram anyway. If you find outliers in the data, it's always a good idea to remove them and report results with and without them, even for large samples. They may well hold additional information about the data that deserves special attention. If you find multiple modes, consider analyzing each one separately.

One-sample t-interval

When the conditions are met, we are ready to find the confidence interval for the population mean, μ. Since the standard error of the mean is

$$SE(\bar{y}) = \frac{s}{\sqrt{n}},$$

the interval is $\bar{y} \pm t^*_{n-1} \times SE(\bar{y})$. The critical value t^*_{n-1} depends on the particular confidence level, C, that you specify and on the number of degrees of freedom, $n - 1$, which we get from the sample size.

[3]There are formal tests of Normality, but they don't really help. When we have a small sample—just when we really care about checking Normality—these tests have very little power. So it doesn't make much sense to use them in deciding whether to perform a t-test. We don't recommend that you use them.

A One-Sample *t*-Interval for the Mean STEP-BY-STEP

Let's build a 90% confidence interval for the mean speed of all vehicles traveling on Triphammer Road. The interval that we'll make is called the **one-sample *t*-interval.**

Think

Parameter Identify the parameter you wish to estimate.

Choose and state a confidence level.

Of course, we start by looking at the data.

We wish to find a 90% confidence interval for the mean speed, μ, of vehicles driving on Triphammer Road.

Here's a histogram of the 23 observed speeds.

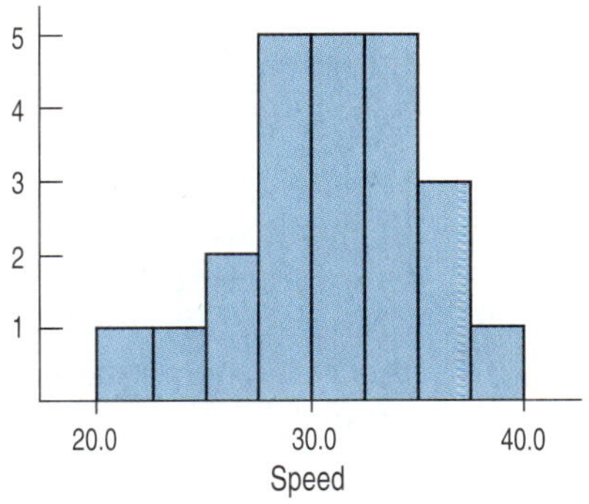

Reality Check The histogram centers around 30 mph, and the data lie between 20 and 40 mph. We'd expect a confidence interval to place the population mean within a few mph of 30.

Plan Check the conditions.

✓ **Randomization condition:** Not really met. We have a convenience sample, but we have reason to believe that it is representative.

✓ **10% condition:** The cars we observed were fewer than 10% of all cars that travel Triphammer Road.

✓ **Nearly Normal condition:** The histogram of the speeds is unimodal and symmetric.

State the sampling distribution model for the statistic.

Under these conditions the sampling distribution of the mean can be modeled by a Student's t model with

$$(n - 1) = 22 \text{ degrees of freedom.}$$

Choose your method.

We will use a **one-sample *t*-interval for the mean.**

Show

Mechanics Construct the confidence interval.

Be sure to include the units along with the statistics.

We know:

$$n = 23 \text{ cars}$$
$$\bar{y} = 31.0 \text{ mph}$$
$$s = 4.25 \text{ mph}$$

We estimate the standard error of $\bar{y}$:

$$SE(\bar{y}) = \frac{s}{\sqrt{n}} = \frac{4.25}{\sqrt{23}} = 0.886 \text{ mph.}$$

The critical value we need to make a 90% interval comes from a Student's t table, a

The 90% critical value is $t^*_{22} = 1.717$. (See the table on the next page.)

computer program, or a calculator. We have 23 − 1 = 22 degrees of freedom. The selected confidence level says that we want 90% of the probability to be caught in the middle, so we exclude 5% in *each* tail, for a total of 10%. The degrees of freedom and 5% tail probability are all we need to know to find the critical value.

From these, we find that the margin of error is

$$ME = t^*_{22} \times SE(\bar{y}) \\ = 1.717(0.886) \\ = 1.521 \text{ mph.}$$

So the 90% confidence interval for the mean speed is

$$31.0 \pm 1.5 \text{ mph}, \quad \text{or} \quad (29.5 \text{ mph}, 32.5 \text{ mph}).$$

✓ Reality Check The result looks plausible and in line with what we thought.

Tell

Interpretation Tell what the confidence interval means.

We are 90% confident that the true mean speed of all vehicles on Triphammer Road is between 29.5 and 32.5 miles per hour.

When we construct confidence intervals in this way, we expect 90% of them to cover the true mean and 10% to miss the true value. This particular interval is one constructed in this way, so, in this sense, it has a 90% chance of covering the true mean.

Caveat: This was not a random sample of vehicles. It was a convenience sample taken at one time on one day. And the participants were not blinded. Drivers could see the police device, and some may have slowed down. We'd be reluctant to extend our inference to other situations.

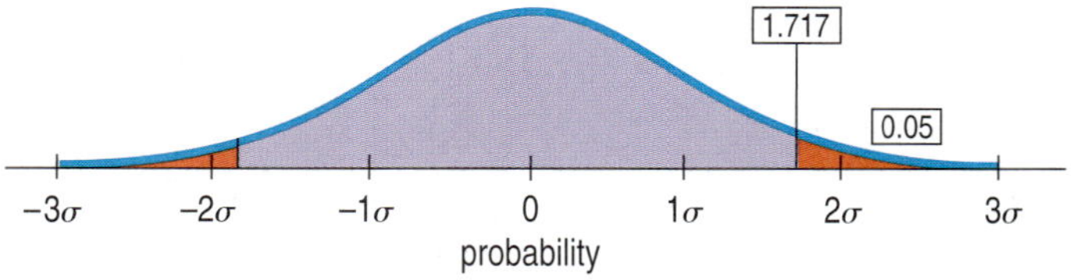

	0.25	0.2	0.15	0.1	0.05	0.025	0.02
19	.6876	.8610	1.066	1.328	1.729	2.093	2.205
20	.6870	.8600	1.064	1.325	1.725	2.086	2.197
21	.6864	.8591	1.063	1.323	1.721	2.080	2.189
22	.6858	.8583	1.061	1.321	1.717	2.074	2.183
23	.6853	.8575	1.060	1.319	1.714	2.069	2.177
24	.6848	.8569	1.059	1.318	1.711	2.064	2.172
25	.6844	.8562	1.058	1.316	1.708	2.060	2.167
26	.6840	.8557	1.058	1.315	1.706	2.056	2.162
27	.6837	.8551	1.057	1.314	1.703	2.052	2.158
C				80%	90%	95%	

Here's the part of the Student's *t* table that gives the critical value we needed. Table T is in the back of the book.

To find a critical value, locate the row of the table corresponding to the degrees of freedom and the column corresponding to the confidence level you want. The value in the table at that intersection is the critical value we need: 1.717.

TI Tips

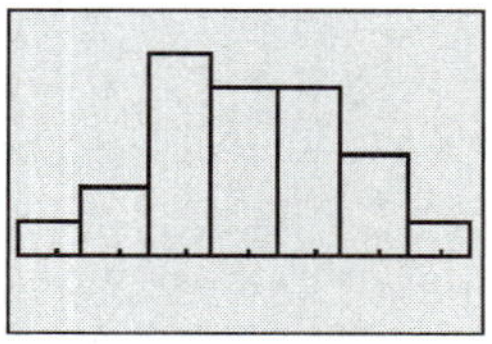

Yes, your calculator can create a confidence interval for a mean. And it's so easy we'll do two!

Find a confidence interval given a set of data.

- Type the speeds of the 23 Triphammer cars into `L1`. Go ahead; we'll wait.

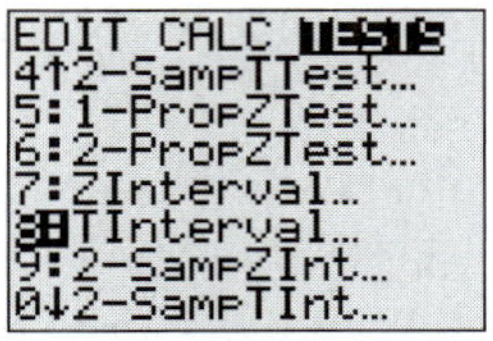

29	34	34	28	30	29	38	31	29	34	32	31
27	37	29	26	24	34	36	31	34	36	21	

- Set up a STATPLOT to create a histogram of the data so you can check the nearly Normal condition. Looks okay—unimodal and roughly symmetric.
- Under STAT TESTS choose 8:Tinterval.
- Choose Inpt:Data, then specify that your data is List:L1.
- For these data the frequency is 1. (If your data have a frequency distribution stored in another list, you would specify that.)
- Choose the confidence level you want.
- Calculate the interval.

There's the 90% confidence interval. That was easy—but remember, the calculator only does the Show. Now you have to Tell what it means.

No data? Find a confidence interval given the sample's mean and standard deviation.

Sometimes instead of the original data you just have the summary statistics. For instance, suppose a random sample of 53 lengths of fishing line had a mean strength of 83 pounds and standard deviation of 4 pounds. Let's make a 95% confidence interval for the mean strength of this kind of fishing line.

- Without the data you can't check the nearly Normal condition. But 83 is a moderately large sample, so assuming there were no outliers, it's okay to proceed. You need to say that.
- Go back to STAT TESTS and choose 8:Tinterval again. This time indicate that you wish to enter the summary statistics. To do that, select Stats, then hit ENTER.
- Specify the sample mean, standard deviation, and sample size
- Choose a confidence level and Calculate the interval.
- If (repeat, IF . . .) strengths of fishing lines follow a Normal model, we are 95% confident that this kind of line has a mean strength between 81.9 and 84.1 pounds.

Another Caution About Interpreting Confidence Intervals

Confidence intervals for means offer new tempting wrong interpretations. Here are some things you *shouldn't* say:

- ***Don't say,*** *"90% of all the vehicles* on Triphammer Road drive at a speed between 29.5 and 32.5 mph." The confidence interval is about the *mean* speed, not about the actual speeds of individual vehicles.
- ***Don't say,*** "We are 90% confident that *a randomly selected vehicle* will have a speed between 29.5 and 32.5 mph." This false interpretation is also about individual vehicles rather than about the *mean* of the speeds. We are 90% confident that the *mean* speed of all vehicles on Triphammer Road is between 29.5 and 32.5 mph.
- ***Don't say,*** "The mean speed of the vehicles is 31.0 mph 90% *of the time.*" That's about means, but still wrong. It implies that the true mean varies, when in fact

it is the confidence interval that would have been different had we gotten a different sample.

- Finally, ***don't say,*** "90% *of all samples* will have mean speeds between 29.5 and 32.5 mph." That statement suggests that *this* interval somehow sets a standard for every other interval. In fact, this interval is no more (or less) likely to be correct than any other. You could say that 90% of all possible samples will produce intervals that actually do contain the true mean speed. (The problem is that because we'll never know where the true mean speed really is we can't know if our sample was one of those 90%.)

Make a Picture, Make a Picture, Make a Picture

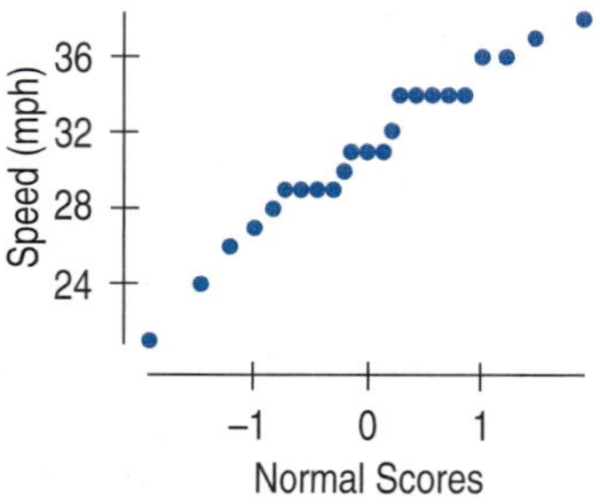

A Normal probability plot of speeds looks reasonably straight.
Figure 23.4

The only reasonable way to check the nearly Normal condition is with graphs of the data. Make a histogram of the data and verify that its distribution is unimodal and symmetric and that it has no outliers. You may also want to make a Normal probability plot to see that it's reasonably straight. You'll be able to spot deviations from the Normal model more easily with a Normal probability plot, but it's easier to understand the particular nature of the deviations from a histogram.

If you have a computer or graphing calculator doing the work, there's no excuse not to look at *both* displays as part of checking the nearly Normal condition.

A Test for the Mean

The residents along Triphammer Road have a more specific concern. It appears that the mean speed along the road is higher than it ought to be. To get the police to patrol more frequently, though, they'll need to show that the true mean speed is in fact greater than the 30 mph speed limit. This calls for a hypothesis test called the **one-sample-*t*-test for the mean.**

You already know enough to construct this test. The test statistic looks just like the others we've seen. It compares the difference between the observed statistic and a hypothesized value to the standard error of the observed statistic. We already know that for means, the appropriate probability model to use for P-values is Student's t with $n - 1$ degrees of freedom.

We're ready to go:

One-sample *t*-test for the mean

The conditions for the one-sample *t*-test for the mean are the same as for the one-sample *t*-interval. We test the hypothesis $H_0: \mu = \mu_0$ using the statistic

$$t_{n-1} = \frac{\bar{y} - \mu_0}{SE(\bar{y})}.$$

The standard error of $\bar{y}$ is $SE(\bar{y}) = \frac{s}{\sqrt{n}}$.

When the conditions are met and the null hypothesis is true, this statistic follows a Student's t model with $n - 1$ degrees of freedom. We use that model to obtain a P-value.

A One-Sample *t*-Test for the Mean STEP-BY-STEP

Let's apply the one-sample *t*-test to the Triphammer Road car speeds. The residents would like to know whether the mean speed exceeds the posted speed limit. The speed limit is 30 mph, so we'll use that as the null hypothesis value.

Think

Hypotheses State what we want to know. Make clear what the population and parameter are.

The null hypothesis is that the true mean speed is equal to the limit. Because we're interested in whether the vehicles are speeding, the alternative is one sided.

We want to know whether the mean speed of vehicles on Triphammer Road exceeds the posted speed limit of 30 mph.

H_0: Mean speed, $\mu = 30$ mph

H_A: Mean speed, $\mu > 30$ mph

✓ Reality Check The histogram of the observed speeds is clustered around 30, so we'd be surprised to find that the mean was much higher than that. (The fact that 30 is within the confidence interval that we've just found confirms this suspicion.)

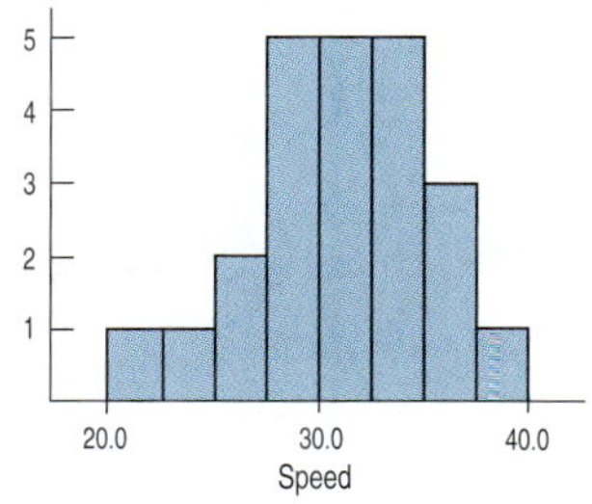

Plan State the null model.

Check the conditions.

✓ **Randomization condition:** Although we have a convenience sample, we have reason to believe that it is a representative sample.

✓ **Nearly Normal condition:** The histogram of the speeds is unimodal and reasonably symmetric. This is close enough to Normal for our purposes.

State the sampling distribution.

Under these conditions, the sampling distribution of the mean can be modeled by Student's *t* with $(n - 1) = 22$ degrees of freedom.

Choose your method.

We will use a **one-sample *t*-test for the mean.**

Show

Mechanics Be sure to include the units when you write down what you know from the data.

We know:

$n = 23$ cars
$\bar{y} = 31.0$ mph
$s = 4.25$ mph

$$SE(\bar{y}) = \frac{s}{\sqrt{n}} = \frac{4.25}{\sqrt{23}} = 0.886 \text{ mph.}$$

We use the null model to find the P-value. Make a picture of the *t*-model centered at $\mu = 30$. Since this is an upper tail test, shade the region to the right of the observed mean speed.

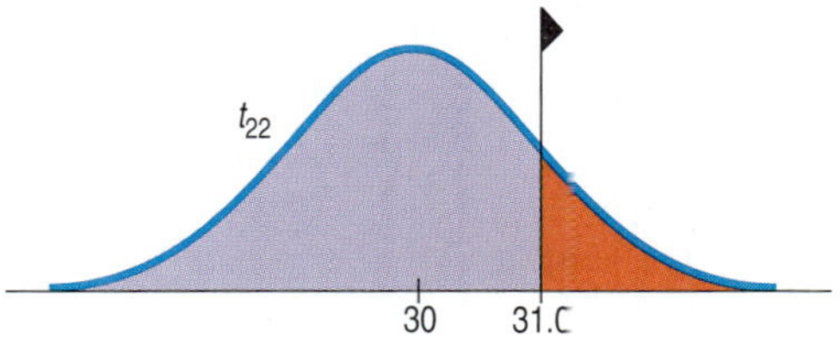

The *t*-statistic calculation is just a standardized value, like *z*. We subtract the hypothesized mean and divide by the standard error.

$$t = \frac{\bar{y} - \mu_0}{SE(\bar{y})} = \frac{31.0 - 30.0}{0.886} = 1.13$$

The P-value is the probability of observing a sample mean as large as 31.0 (or larger) *if* the true mean were 30.0, as the null hypothesis states. We can find this P-value from a table, calculator, or computer program.

(The observed mean is 1.13 standard errors above the hypothesized value.)

$$P = P(t_{22} > 1.13) = 0.136$$

✓ Reality Check We're not surprised that the difference isn't statistically significant.

Tell

Conclusion Link the P-value to your decision about H_0, and state your conclusion in context.

Unfortunately for the residents, there is no course of action associated with failing to reject this particular null hypothesis.

The P-value of 0.136 says that if the true mean speed of vehicles on Triphammer Road were 30 mph, samples of 23 vehicles can be expected to have an observed mean of at least 31.0 mph 13.6% of the time. That P-value is not small enough for us to reject the hypothesis that the true mean is 30 mph at any reasonable alpha level. We conclude that there is not enough evidence to say the average speed is too high.

Significance and Importance

Recall that "statistically significant" does not mean "actually important" or "meaningful," even though it sort of sounds that way. In this example, it does seem that speeds may be a bit above 30 miles per hour. Possibly a larger sample would show statistical significance.

But would that be the right decision? The difference between 31 miles per hour and 30 miles per hour doesn't seem meaningful, and rejecting the null hypothesis wouldn't change that. Even with a statistically significant result, it would be hard to convince the police that vehicles on Triphammer Road were driving at dangerously fast speeds. It would probably also be difficult to persuade the town that spending more money to lower the average speed on Triphammer Road would be a good use of the town's resources. Looking at the confidence interval, we can say that, with 90% confidence, the mean speed is somewhere between 29.5 and 32.5 mph. Even in the worst case, if the mean speed is 32.5 mph, would this be a bad enough situation to convince the town to spend more money? Probably not. It's always a good idea when we test a hypothesis to check the confidence interval and think about the likely values for the mean.

TI Tips

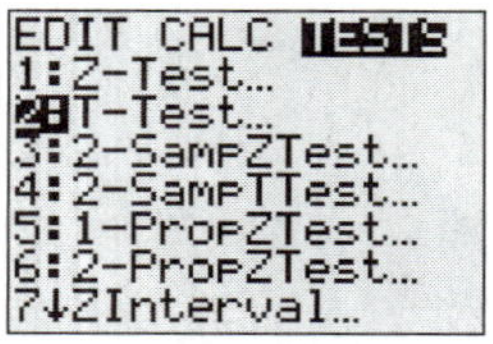

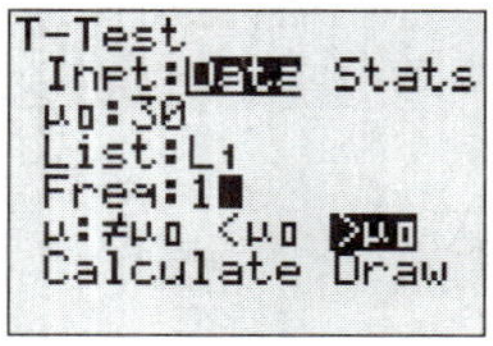

Testing a Hypothesis About a Given Set of Data

Still have the Triphammer Road auto speeds in `L1`? Good. Let's use the TI to see if the mean is significantly higher than 30 mph (you've already checked the histogram to verify the nearly Normal condition, of course).

- Go to the `STAT TESTS` menu and choose `2:T-Test`.
- Tell it you want to use the stored `Data`.
- Enter the mean of the null model, and indicate where the data are.
- Since this is an upper tail test, choose the $>\mu_0$ option.
- `Calculate`.

There's everything you need to know: the summary statistics, the calculated value of *t*, and the P-value of 0.126. (*t* and *P* differ slightly from the values in our worked example because when we did it by hand we rounded off the mean and standard deviation. No harm done.)

As always, the Tell is up to you.

Testing a Hypothesis Given the Sample's Mean and Standard Deviation

Don't have the actual data? Just summary statistics? No problem, assuming you can verify the necessary conditions. In the last TI Tips we created a confidence interval for the strength of fishing line. We had test results for a random sample of 53 lengths of line showing a mean strength of 83 pounds and standard deviation of 4 pounds. Is there evidence that this kind of fishing line exceeds the "80-lb test" as labeled on the package?

We bet you know what to do even without our help. Try it before you read on.

- Go back to `2:T-Test`.
- You're entering `Stats` this time.
- Specify the hypothesized mean and the sample statistics.
- Choose the alternative being tested (upper tail here).
- `Calculate`.

The results of the calculator's mechanics show a large *t* and a really small P-value (0.0000007). We have very strong evidence that the mean breaking strength of this kind of fishing line is over the 80 pounds claimed by the manufacturer.

Intervals and Tests

The 90% confidence interval for the mean speed was 31.0 mph ± 1.5, or (29.5 mph, 32.5 mph). If someone hypothesized that the mean speed was really 30 mph, how would you feel about it? How about 35 mph?

Because the confidence interval included the speed limit of 30 mph, it certainly looked like 30 mph might be a plausible value for the true mean speed of the vehicles on Triphammer Road. In fact, 30 mph gave a P-value of 0.136, too large to reject the null hypothesis. We should have seen this coming. The hypothesized mean of 30 mph lies *within the confidence interval.* It's one of the reasonable values for the mean.

Confidence intervals and significance tests are built from the same calculations. In fact, they are really complementary ways of looking at the same question. Here's the connection: The confidence level contains all the null hypothesis values you can't reject.

More precisely, a level C confidence interval contains *all* of the possible null hypothesis values that would be retained by a two-sided hypothesis test at α-level $1 - C$.

Confidence intervals are naturally two sided, so they match exactly with two-sided hypothesis tests. When, as in our example, the hypothesis is one sided, the corresponding α-level is $(1 - C)/2$.

Our 90% confidence interval was 29.5 to 32.5 mph. If any of these values had been the null hypothesis for the mean, then the corresponding hypothesis test at $\alpha = .05$ (because $\frac{1 - 0.90}{2} = .05$) would not have been able to reject the null. That is, the corresponding one-sided P-value for our observed mean of 31 mph would be greater than .05. So, we would retain any hypothesized value between 29.5 and 32.5 mph.

Sample Size

How large a sample do we need? The simple answer is "more." But more data cost money, effort, and time, so how much is enough? Suppose your computer takes 2 hours on average to download a movie. You hear about a program that claims to download movies in less than an hour. You're interested enough to spend $29.95 for it, but only if it really delivers. So you get the free evaluation copy and test it by downloading 10 different movies. Of course, the mean download time is not exactly 1 hour as claimed. Observations vary. If the margin of error was 8 minutes, though, you'd probably be able to decide whether the software is worth the money. Doubling the sample size would require another 10 hours of testing and would reduce your margin of error to a bit under 6 minutes. You'd need to decide whether that was worth the effort.

As we make plans to collect data, we should have some idea of how large a margin of error we need to be able to draw a conclusion or detect a difference we want to see. If the size of the effect we're studying is large, then we may be able to tolerate a larger *ME*. If we need great precision, however, we'll want a smaller *ME*, and, of course, that means a larger sample size.

Armed with the *ME* and confidence level, we can find the sample size we'll need. Almost.

We know that for a mean, $ME = t^*_{n-1} \times SE(\bar{y})$ and that $SE(\bar{y}) = \frac{s}{\sqrt{n}}$, so we can determine the sample size by solving this equation for *n*:

$$ME = t^*_{n-1} \frac{s}{\sqrt{n}}.$$

The good news is that we have an equation; the bad news is that we don't know most of the values we need to solve it.

When we thought about sample size for proportions back in Chapter 19, we ran into a similar problem. There we had to guess a working value for *p* to compute a sample size. Here, we need to know *s*. We don't know *s* until we get some data, but we want to calculate the sample size *before* collecting the data. We might be able to make a good guess, and that is often good enough for this purpose. If we have no idea what the standard deviation might be, or if the sample size really matters (for

Doing sample size calculations by hand

Let's give the sample size formula a spin. Suppose we want an *ME* of 8 minutes and we think the standard deviation of download times is about 10 minutes. Using a 95% confidence interval, and $z^* = 1.96$, we solve:

$$8 = 1.96\frac{10}{\sqrt{n}}$$

$$\sqrt{n} = \frac{1.96 \times 10}{8} = 2.45$$

$$n = (2.45)^2 = 6.0025$$

That's a small sample size, so we use $(6 - 1) = 5$ degrees of freedom to substitute an appropriate t^* value. At 95%, $t^*_5 = 2.571$. Now solve the equation one more time:

$$8 = 2.571\frac{10}{\sqrt{n}}$$

$$\sqrt{n} = \frac{2.571 \times 10}{8} \approx 3.214$$

$$n = (3.214)^2 \approx 10.33$$

To make sure the *ME* is no larger than you want, you should always round *up*, which gives $n = 11$ runs. So, to get an *ME* of 8 minutes, we should find the downloading times for $n = 11$ movies.

example, because each additional individual is very expensive to sample or experiment on), it might be a good idea to run a small *pilot study* to get some feeling for the standard deviation.

That's not all. Without knowing n, we don't know the degrees of freedom and we can't find the critical value, t^*_{n-1}. One common approach is to use the corresponding z^* value from the Normal model. If you've chosen a 95% confidence level, then just use 2, following the 68-95-99.7 Rule. If your estimated sample size is, say, 60 or more, you can work with that. If it's smaller than that, you may want to add a step, using z^* at first, finding n, and then replacing z^* with the corresponding t^*_{n-1} and calculating the sample size once more.

Sample size calculations are *never* exact. The margin of error you find *after* collecting the data won't match exactly the one you used to find n. The sample size formula depends on quantities that you won't have until you collect the data, but using it is an important first step. Before you collect data, it's always a good idea to know whether the sample size is large enough to give you a good chance of being able to tell you what you want to know.

Degrees of Freedom

Some calculators offer an alternative button for standard deviation that divides by n instead of $n - 1$. Why don't you stick a wad of gum over that button so you won't be tempted to use it? Use $n - 1$.

The number of degrees of freedom, $(n - 1)$, might have reminded you of the value we divide by to find the standard deviation of the data (since, in fact, it's the same number). We promised back when we introduced that formula to say a bit more about why we divide by $n - 1$ rather than by n. The reason is closely tied to the reasoning of the t-distribution.

If only we knew the true population mean, μ, we would find the sample standard deviation as

$$s = \sqrt{\frac{\Sigma(y - \mu)^2}{n}}. \qquad \text{(Equation 23.1)}^4$$

We use $\bar{y}$ instead of μ, though, and that causes a problem. For any sample, the data values will generally be closer to their own sample mean than to the true population mean, μ. Why is that? Imagine that we take a random sample of 10 high school seniors. The mean SAT verbal score is 500 in the United States. But the sample mean, $\bar{y}$, for *these* 10 seniors won't be exactly 500. Are the 10 seniors' scores closer to 500 or $\bar{y}$? They'll always be closer to their own $\bar{y}$. If we used $\Sigma(y - \bar{y})^2$ instead of $\Sigma(y - \mu)^2$ in Equation 23.1 to calculate s, our standard deviation estimate would be too small. How can we fix it? The amazing mathematical fact is that we can compensate for the smaller sum exactly by dividing by $n - 1$ instead of by n. So that's all the $n - 1$ is doing in the denominator of s. And we call $n - 1$ the degrees of freedom.

[4]Statistics textbooks usually have equation numbers so they can talk about equations by name. We haven't needed equation numbers yet, but we admit it's useful here, so this is our first.

What Can Go Wrong?

Ways to Not Be Normal

Student's *t* methods work only when the Normality assumption is true. Naturally, many of the ways things can go wrong turn out to be different ways that the Normality assumption can fail. It's always a good idea to look for the most common kinds of failure. It turns out that you can even fix some of them.

- ***Beware multimodality.*** The nearly Normal condition clearly fails if a histogram of the data has two or more modes. When you see this, look for the possibility that your data come from two groups. If so, your best bet is to try to separate the data into its separate groups. (Use the variables to help distinguish the modes if possible. For example, if the modes seem to be mostly men in one and women in the other, split the data according to sex.) Then analyze each group separately.
- ***Beware skewed data.*** Make a Normal probability plot and a histogram of the data. If the data are very skewed, you might try re-expressing the variable. Re-expressing may yield a distribution that is unimodal and symmetric, more appropriate for the inference methods for means. Re-expression cannot help if the sample distribution is not unimodal. Some people may object to re-expressing the data, but unless your sample is very large, you just can't use the methods of this chapter on skewed data.

As tempting as it is to get rid of annoying values, you can't just throw away outliers and not discuss them. It isn't appropriate to lop off the highest or lowest values just to improve your results.

- ***Set outliers aside.*** The nearly Normal condition also fails if the data have outliers. If you find outliers in the data, you may want to set them aside before using Student's *t* methods. Once they are singled out, you should look at them carefully. Sometimes, it's obvious that a data value is wrong and the justification for removing or correcting it is clear. When there's no clear justification for removing outliers, you might want to run the analysis both with and without the outliers and note any differences in your conclusions. Any time data values are set aside, you *must* report on them individually. Often they will turn out to be the most informative part of your report on the data.[5]

. . . And of Course

- ***Watch out for bias.*** Measurements of all kinds can be biased. If your observations differ from the true mean in a systematic way, your confidence interval may not capture the true mean. And there is no sample size that will save you. A bathroom scale that's 5 pounds off will be 5 pounds off even if you weigh yourself 100 times and take the average. We've seen several sources of bias in surveys, but any measurements can be biased. Be sure to think about possible sources of bias in your measurements.
- ***Make sure data are independent.*** Student's *t* methods also require the sampled values to be mutually independent. We check for random sampling and the

[5]This suggestion may be controversial in some disciplines. Setting aside outliers is seen by some as "cheating" because the result is likely to be a narrower confidence interval or a smaller P-value. But an analysis of data with outliers left in place is *always* wrong. The outliers violate the nearly Normal condition and also the implicit assumption of a homogeneous population, so they invalidate inference procedures. An analysis of the non-outlying points, along with a separate discussion of the outliers, is often much more informative, and can reveal important aspects of the data.

10% condition. You should also think hard about whether there are likely violations of independence in the data collection method. If there are, be very cautious about using these methods.

- ***Make sure that data are from an appropriately randomized sample.*** Ideally, all data that we analyze are drawn from a simple random sample or generated by a randomized experiment. When they're not, be careful about making inferences from them. You may still compute a confidence interval correctly, or get the mechanics of the P-value right, but this might not save you from making a serious mistake in inference.

Inference for Means and the Computer

Statistics packages offer convenient ways to make histograms of the data. Even better for assessing near-Normality is a Normal probability plot. When you work on a computer, there is simply no excuse for skipping the step of plotting the data to check that it is nearly Normal. Beware: Statistics packages don't agree on whether to place the Normal score on the *x*-axis (as we have done) or the *y*-axis. Read the axis labels.

Any standard statistics package can complete a hypothesis test. Here's what the package output might look like in general (although no package we know gives the results in exactly this form):

Null hypothesis

Alternative hypothesis

```
Test Ho: μ(speed) = 30 vs Ha: μ(speed) > 30
Sample Mean = 31.043478
t = 1.178 w/22 df
P-value = 0.1257
```

The t-statistic (and its degrees of freedom)

The P-value is usually given last

The package computes the sample mean and sample standard deviation of the variable and finds the P-value from the *t*-distribution based on the appropriate number of degrees of freedom. All modern statistics packages report P-values. The package may also provide additional information such as the sample mean, sample standard deviation, *t*-statistic value, and degrees of freedom. These are useful for interpreting the resulting P-value and telling the difference between a meaningful result and one that is merely statistically significant. Statistics packages that report the estimated standard deviation of the sampling distribution usually label it "standard error" or "SE."

Inference results are also sometimes reported in a table. You may have to read carefully to find the values you need. Often, test results and the corresponding confidence interval bounds are given together. And often you must read carefully to find the alternative hypotheses. Here's an example of that kind of output:

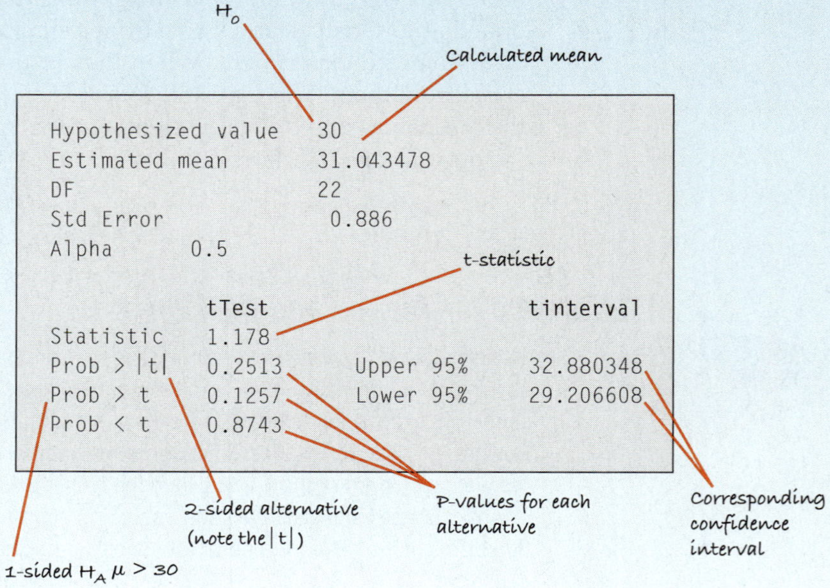

Connections

The steps for finding a confidence interval or hypothesis test are identical to the corresponding steps for proportions. Even the form of the calculations is similar. The *t*-statistic, like the *z*-statistic for proportions, tells us how many standard errors our statistic is from the hypothesized mean. For means, though, we have to estimate the standard error separately from the mean. This added uncertainty changes the model for the sampling distribution from *z* to *t*.

As with all of our inference methods, the randomization applied in drawing a random sample or in randomizing a comparative experiment is what generates the sampling distribution. Randomization is what makes inference in this way possible at all.

The new concept of degrees of freedom connects back to the denominator of the sample standard deviation calculation, as shown earlier.

There's just no escaping histograms and Normal probability plots. The Nearly Normal Condition required to use Student's *t* can be checked best by making appropriate displays of the data. Back when we first used histograms, we looked at their shape and in particular checked whether they were unimodal and symmetric and whether they showed any outliers. Those are just the features we check for here. The Normal probability plot zeros in on the Normal model a little closer.

Key Concepts

Student's *t*-distribution
Degrees of freedom

A family of distributions indexed by their degrees of freedom. The *t*-models are unimodal, symmetric, and bell shaped, but generally have fatter tails and a narrower center than the Normal model. As the degrees of freedom increase, *t*-distributions approach the Normal.

One-sample *t*-interval

A one-sample *t*-interval for the population mean is $\bar{y} \pm t^*_{n-1} \times SE(\bar{y})$ where

$$SE(\bar{y}) = \frac{s}{\sqrt{n}}.$$

The critical value t^*_{n-1} depends on the particular confidence level, *C*, that you specify and on the number of degrees of freedom, $n - 1$.

One-sample *t*-test for the mean

The one-sample *t*-test for the mean tests the hypothesis H_0: $\mu = \mu_0$ using the statistic

$$t_{n-1} = \frac{\bar{y} - \mu_0}{SE(\bar{y})}.$$

The standard error of $\bar{y}$ is

$$SE(\bar{y}) = \frac{s}{\sqrt{n}}.$$

Skills

When you complete this lesson you should:

Think

- Know the assumptions required for *t*-tests and *t*-based confidence intervals.
- Know how to examine your data for violations of conditions that would make inference about the population mean unwise or invalid.
- Understand that a confidence interval and a hypothesis test are essentially equivalent. You can do a two-tailed hypothesis test at level of significance α with a $1 - \alpha$ confidence interval, or a one-tailed test with a $1 - 2\alpha$ confidence interval.

Show

- Be able to compute and interpret a *t*-test for the population mean using a statistics package or working from summary statistics for a sample.
- Be able to compute and interpret a *t*-based confidence interval for the population mean using a statistics package or working from summary statistics for a sample.

Tell

- Be able to explain the meaning of a confidence interval for a population mean. Make clear that the randomness associated with the confidence level is a statement about the interval bounds and not about the population parameter value.
- Understand that a 95% confidence interval does not trap 95% of the sample values.
- Be able to interpret the result of a test of a hypothesis about a population mean.
- Know that we do not "accept" a null hypothesis if we cannot reject it. We can fail to reject it, or we can say that we "retain" it.
- Understand that P-value of a test does not give the probability that the null hypothesis is correct.

Exercises

1. t-models, part I. Using the *t* tables, software, or a calculator, estimate

a) the critical value of *t* for a 90% confidence interval with df = 17.

b) the critical value of *t* for a 98% confidence interval with df = 88.

c) the P-value for $t \geq 2.09$ with 4 degrees of freedom.

d) the P-value for $|t| > 1.78$ with 22 degrees of freedom.

2. t-models, part II. Using the *t* tables, software, or a calculator, estimate

a) the critical value of *t* for a 95% confidence interval with df = 7.

b) the critical value of t for a 99% confidence interval with df = 102.
c) the P-value for $t \leq 2.19$ with 41 degrees of freedom.
d) the P-value for $|t| > 2.33$ with 12 degrees of freedom.

3. t-models, part III. Describe how the shape, center, and spread of t-models change as the number of degrees of freedom increases.

4. t-models, part IV (last one!). Describe how the critical value of t for a 95% confidence interval changes as the number of degrees of freedom increases.

5. Cattle. Livestock are given a special feed supplement to see if it will promote weight gain. The researchers report that the 77 cows studied gained an average of 56 pounds, and that a 95% confidence interval for the mean weight gain this supplement produces has a margin of error of ±11 pounds. Some students wrote the following conclusions. Did anyone interpret the interval correctly? Explain any misinterpretations.

a) 95% of the cows studied gained between 45 and 67 pounds.
b) We're 95% sure that a cow fed this supplement will gain between 45 and 67 pounds.
c) We're 95% sure that the average weight gain among the cows in this study was between 45 and 67 pounds.
d) The average weight gain of cows fed this supplement will be between 45 and 67 pounds 95% of the time.
e) If this supplement is tested on another sample of cows, there is a 95% chance that their average weight gain will be between 45 and 67 pounds.

6. Teachers. Software analysis of the salaries of a random sample of 288 Nevada teachers produced the confidence interval shown below. Which conclusion is correct? What's wrong with the others?

t-Interval for μ: with 90.00% Confidence, $38944 < \mu(\text{TchPay}) < 42893$

a) If we took many random samples of Nevada teachers, about 9 out of 10 of them would produce this confidence interval.
b) If we took many random samples of Nevada teachers, about 9 out of 10 of them would produce a confidence interval that contained the mean salary of all Nevada teachers.
c) About 9 out of 10 Nevada teachers earn between $38,944 and $42,893.
d) About 9 out of 10 of the teachers surveyed earn between $38,944 and $42,893.
e) We are 90% confident that the average teacher salary in the United States is between $38,944 and $42,893.

7. Pulse rates. A medical researcher measured the pulse rates (beats per minute) of a sample of randomly selected adults and found the following Student's t-based Confidence Interval:

With 95.00% Confidence,
$70.887604 < \mu(\text{Pulse}) < 74.497011$

a) Explain carefully what the software output means.
b) What's the margin of error for this interval?
c) If the researcher had calculated a 99% confidence interval, would the margin of error be larger or smaller? Explain.

8. Crawling. Data collected by child development scientists produced this confidence interval for the average age (in weeks) at which babies begin to crawl.

t-Interval for μ (95.00% Confidence): $29.202 < \mu(\text{age}) < 31.844$

a) Explain carefully what the software output means.
b) What is the margin of error for this interval?
c) If the researcher had calculated a 90% confidence interval, would the margin of error be larger or smaller? Explain.

T **9. Normal temperature.** The researcher described in Exercise 7 also measured the body temperatures of that randomly selected group of adults. The data he collected are summarized below. We wish to estimate the average (or "normal") temperature among the adult population.

Summary of	Temp.
Count	52
Mean	98.2846
Median	98.2000
MidRange	98.6000
StdDev	0.682379
Range	2.80000
IntQRange	1.05000

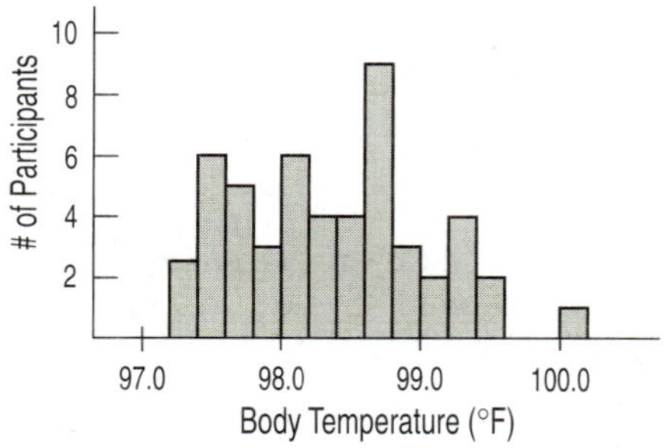

a) Are the necessary conditions for a t-interval satisfied? Explain.
b) Find a 98% confidence interval for mean body temperature.
c) Explain the meaning of that interval.
d) Explain what "98% confidence" means in this context.
e) 98.6 degrees is commonly assumed to be "normal." Do these data suggest otherwise? Explain.

10. Parking. Hoping to lure more shoppers downtown, a city builds a new public parking garage in the central business district. The city plans to pay for the structure through parking fees. During a two-month period (44 weekdays), daily fees collected averaged \$126 with a standard deviation of \$15.

a) What assumptions must you make in order to use these statistics for inference?
b) Write a 90% confidence interval for the mean daily income this parking garage will generate.
c) Explain in context what this confidence interval means.
d) Explain what "90% confidence" means in this context.
e) The consultant who advised the city on this project predicted that parking revenues would average \$130 per day. Based on your confidence interval, do you think the consultant could have been correct? Why?

11. Normal temperatures, part II. Consider again the statistics about human body temperature in Exercise 9.

a) Would a 90% confidence interval be wider or narrower than the 98% confidence interval you calculated before? Explain. (You should not need to compute the new interval.)
b) What are the advantages and disadvantages of the 98% confidence interval?
c) If we conduct further research, this time using a sample of 500 adults, how would you expect the 98% confidence interval to change? Explain.
d) How large a sample would you need to estimate the mean body temperature to within 0.1 degrees with 98% confidence?

12. Parking II. Suppose that for budget planning purposes the city in Exercise 10 needs a better estimate of the mean daily income from parking fees.

a) Someone suggests that the city use its data to create a 95% confidence interval instead of the 90% interval first created. How would this interval be better for the city? (You need not actually create the new interval.)
b) How would the 95% interval be worse for the planners?
c) How could they achieve an interval estimate that would better serve their planning needs?
d) How many days' worth of data must they collect to have 95% confidence of estimating the true mean to within \$3?

13. Hot dogs. A nutrition laboratory tests 40 "reduced sodium" hot dogs, finding that the mean sodium content is 310 mg with a standard deviation of 36 mg.

a) Find a 95% confidence interval for the mean sodium content of this brand of hot dog.
b) What assumptions have you made in this inference? Are the appropriate conditions satisfied?
c) Explain clearly what your interval means.

14. Speed of light. In 1882 Michelson measured the speed of light (usually denoted "*c*" as in the famous statement $e = mc^2$). His values are in km/sec and have 299,000 subtracted from them. He reported the results of 23 trials with a mean of 756.22 and a standard deviation of 107.12.

a) Find a 95% confidence interval for the true speed of light from these statistics.
b) State in words what this interval means. Keep in mind that the speed of light is a physical constant that, as far as we know, has a value that is true throughout the universe.
c) What assumptions must you make in order to use your method?

15. Second dog. The nutrition lab in Exercise 13 tests the hot dogs again, this time using a sample of 60 "reduced sodium" frankfurters. The new sample produces a mean of 318 mg of sodium, and the standard deviation is 32 mg.

a) Should this larger sample of hot dogs produce a more accurate estimate of the mean sodium content? Explain.
b) What is the standard error of the mean sodium content?
c) Find and interpret a 95% confidence interval.
d) Food labeling regulations require that any food identified as "reduced sodium" must have at least 30% less sodium than its regular counterpart. If regular franks average 465 mg of sodium, should this brand be labeled "reduced"? Explain, using your confidence interval.

16. Better light. After his first attempt to determine the speed of light (described in Exercise 14), Michelson conducted an "improved" experiment. In 1897 he reported results of 100 trials with a mean of 852.4 and a standard deviation of 79.0.

a) What is the standard error of the mean for these data?
b) Without computing it, how would you expect a 95% confidence interval for the second experiment to differ from the confidence interval for the first? Note at least three specific reasons why they might differ, and indicate the ways in which these differences would change the interval.
c) According to Stigler (who reports these values), the true speed of light is 299,710.5 km/sec, corresponding to a value of 710.5 for Michelson's 1897 measurements. What does this indicate about Michelson's two experiments? Explain, using your confidence interval.

17. TV safety. The manufacturer of a metal stand for home TV sets must be sure that its product will not fail under the weight of the TV. Since some larger sets weigh nearly 300 pounds, the company's safety inspectors have set a standard of ensuring that the stands can support an average of over 500 pounds. Their inspectors regularly subject a random sample of the stands to increasing weight until they fail. They test the hypothesis H_0: $\mu = 500$ against H_a: $\mu > 500$, using the level of significance

$\alpha = .01$. If the sample of stands fail to pass this safety test, the inspectors will not certify the product for sale to the general public.

a) Is this an upper-tail or lower-tail test? In the context of the problem, why do you think this is important?
b) Explain what will happen if the inspectors commit a Type I error.
c) Explain what will happen if the inspectors commit a Type II error.

18. Catheters. During an angiogram, heart problems can be examined via a small tube (a catheter) threaded into the heart from a vein in the patient's leg. It's important that the company who manufactures the catheter maintain a diameter of 2.00 mm. (The standard deviation is quite small.) Each day, quality control personnel make several measurements to test H_0: $\mu = 2.00$ against H_a: $\mu \neq 2.00$ at a significance level of $\alpha = .05$. If they discover a problem, they will stop the manufacturing process until it is corrected.

a) Is this a one-sided or two-sided test? In the context of the problem, why do you think this is important?
b) Explain in this context what happens if the quality control people commit a Type I error.
c) Explain in this context what happens if the quality control people commit a Type II error.

19. TV safety revisited. The manufacturer of the metal TV stands in Exercise 17 is thinking of revising its safety test.

a) If the company's lawyers are worried about being sued for selling an unsafe product, should they increase or decrease the value of α? Explain.
b) In this context, what is meant by the power of the test?
c) If the company wants to increase the power of the test, what options does it have? Explain the advantages and disadvantages of each option.

20. Catheters again. The catheter company in Exercise 18 is reviewing its testing procedure.

a) Suppose the significance level is changed to $\alpha = .01$. Will the probability of Type II error increase, decrease, or remain the same?
b) What is meant by the power of the test the company conducts?
c) Suppose the manufacturing process is slipping out of proper adjustment. As the actual mean diameter of the catheters produced gets farther and farther above the desired 2.00 mm, will the power of the quality control test increase, decrease, or remain the same?
d) What could they do to improve the power of the test?

21. Marriage. In 1960, census results indicated that the age at which American men first married had a mean of 23.3 years. It is widely suspected that young people today are waiting longer to get married. We want to find out if the mean age of first marriage has increased during the past 40 years.

a) Write appropriate hypotheses.
b) We plan to test our hypothesis by selecting a random sample of 40 men who married for the first time last year. Do you think the necessary assumptions for inference are satisfied? Explain.
c) Describe the approximate sampling distribution model for the mean age in such samples.
d) The men in our sample married at an average age of 24.2 years with a standard deviation of 5.3 years. What's the P-value for this result?
e) Explain (in context) what this P-value means.
f) What's your conclusion?

22. Fuel economy. A company with a large fleet of cars hopes to keep gasoline costs down, and sets a goal of attaining a fleet average of at least 26 miles per gallon. To see if the goal is being met, they check the gasoline usage for 50 company trips chosen at random, finding a mean of 25.02 mpg and a standard deviation of 4.83 mpg. Is this strong evidence that they have failed to attain their fuel economy goal?

a) Write appropriate hypotheses.
b) Are the necessary assumptions to perform inference satisfied?
c) Describe the sampling distribution model of mean fuel economy for samples like this.
d) Find the P-value.
e) Explain what the P-value means in this context.
f) State an appropriate conclusion.

23. Ruffles. Students investigating the packaging of potato chips purchased 6 bags of Lay's Ruffles marked with a net weight of 28.3 grams. They carefully weighed the contents of each bag, recording the following weights (in grams): 29.3, 28.2, 29.1, 28.7, 28.9, 28.5.

a) Do these data satisfy the assumptions for inference? Explain.
b) Find the mean and standard deviation of the observed weights.
c) Create a 95% confidence interval for the mean weight of such bags of chips.
d) Explain in context what your interval means.
e) Comment on the company's stated net weight of 28.3 grams.

24. Doritos. The students also checked 6 bags of Doritos marked with a net weight of 28.3 grams. They carefully weighed the contents of each bag, recording the following weights (in grams): 29.2, 28.5, 28.7, 28.9, 29.1, 29.5.

a) Do these data satisfy the assumptions for inference? Explain.
b) Find the mean and standard deviation of the observed weights.
c) Create a 95% confidence interval for the mean weight of such bags of chips.
d) Explain in context what your interval means.
e) Comment on the company's stated net weight of 28.3 grams.

25. Cars. One of the important factors in auto safety is the weight of the vehicle. Insurance companies are interested in knowing the average weight of cars currently licensed in the United States; they believe it is 3000 pounds. To see if that estimate is correct, they checked a random sample of 91 cars. For that group the mean weight was 2919 pounds, with a standard deviation of 531.5 pounds. Is this strong evidence that the mean weight of all cars is not 3000 pounds?

26. Portable phones. A manufacturer claims that a new design for a portable phone has increased the range to 150 feet, allowing many customers to use the phone throughout their homes and yards. An independent testing laboratory found that a random sample of 44 of these phones worked over an average distance of 142 feet, with a standard deviation of 12 feet. Is there evidence that the manufacturer's claim is false?

27. Chips ahoy. In 1998, as an advertising campaign, the Nabisco Company announced a "1000 Chips Challenge," claiming that every 18-ounce bag of their Chips Ahoy cookies contained at least 1000 chocolate chips. Dedicated Statistics students at the Air Force Academy (no kidding) purchased some randomly selected bags of cookies, and counted the chocolate chips. Some of their data are given below. (*Chance,* 12, no. 1 [1999])

1219	1214	1087	1200	1419	1121	1325	1345
1244	1258	1356	1132	1191	1270	1295	1135

a) Check the assumptions and conditions for inference. Comment on any concerns you have.
b) Create a 95% confidence interval for the average number of chips in bags of Chips Ahoy cookies.
c) What does this evidence say about Nabisco's claim? Use your confidence interval to test an appropriate hypothesis and state your conclusion.

28. Yogurt. *Consumer Reports* tested 14 brands of vanilla yogurt and found the following numbers of calories per serving:

160	200	220	230	120	180	140
130	170	190	80	120	100	170

a) Check the assumptions and conditions for inference.
b) Create a 95% confidence interval for the average calorie content of vanilla yogurt.
c) A diet guide claims that you will get 120 calories from a serving of vanilla yogurt. What does this evidence indicate? Use your confidence interval to test an appropriate hypothesis and state your conclusion.

29. Maze. Psychology experiments sometimes involve testing the ability of rats to navigate mazes. The mazes are classified according to difficulty, as measured by the mean length of time it takes rats to find the food at the end. One researcher needs a maze that will take rats an average of about one minute to solve. He tests one maze on several rats, collecting the data at the right.

Time (sec)	
38.4	57.6
46.2	55.5
62.5	49.5
38.0	40.9
62.8	44.3
33.9	93.8
50.4	47.9
35.0	69.2
52.8	46.2
60.1	56.3
55.1	

a) Plot the data. Do you think the conditions for inference are satisfied? Explain.
b) Test the hypothesis that the mean completion time for this maze is 60 seconds. What is your conclusion?
c) Eliminate the outlier, and test the hypothesis again. What is your conclusion?
d) Do you think this maze meets the "one-minute average" requirement? Explain.

30. Braking. A tire manufacturer is considering a newly designed tread pattern for its all-weather tires. Tests have indicated that these tires will provide better gas mileage and longer treadlife. The last remaining test is for braking effectiveness. The company hopes the tire will allow a car traveling at 60 mph to come to a complete stop within an average of 125 feet after the brakes are applied. They will adopt the new tread pattern unless there is strong evidence that the tires do not meet this objective. The distances (in feet) for 10 stops on a test track were 129, 128, 130, 132, 135, 123, 102, 125, 128, and 130. Should the company adopt the new tread pattern? Test an appropriate hypothesis and state your conclusion. Explain how you dealt with the outlier, and why you made the recommendation you did.

Chapter 24

Comparing Means

WHO	AA alkaline batteries
WHAT	Length of battery life while playing a CD continuously
UNITS	Minutes
WHY	Class project
WHEN	1998

Should you buy generic rather than brand-name batteries? A statistics student designed an experiment to test battery life. He wanted to know whether there was any real difference between brand-name batteries and a generic brand. To estimate the difference in mean lifetimes, he kept a battery-powered CD player with the same CD running continuously, fixing the volume control at 5, and measured the time until no more music was heard through the headphones. (He ran an initial trial to find out approximately how long that would take, so that he didn't have to spend the first 3 hours of each run listening to the same CD.) For the experiment, he used six pairs of AA alkaline batteries from two major battery manufacturers: a well-known brand name and a generic brand. In the language of experiments, battery brand was his factor. The brand names were the two levels of his factor. His response variable was the time in minutes until the sound stopped. To account for changes in the CD player's performance over time, he randomized the run order by choosing pairs of batteries at random.

Here are his data (times in minutes):

Brand Name	Generic
194.0	190.7
205.5	203.5
199.2	203.5
172.4	206.5
184.0	222.5
169.5	209.4

Experiments that compare two groups are common throughout both science and industry. We might want to compare the effects of a new drug with the traditional therapy, the fuel efficiency of two car engine designs, or the sales of new product in two different test cities. In fact, battery manufacturers perform such experiments themselves.

Plot the Data

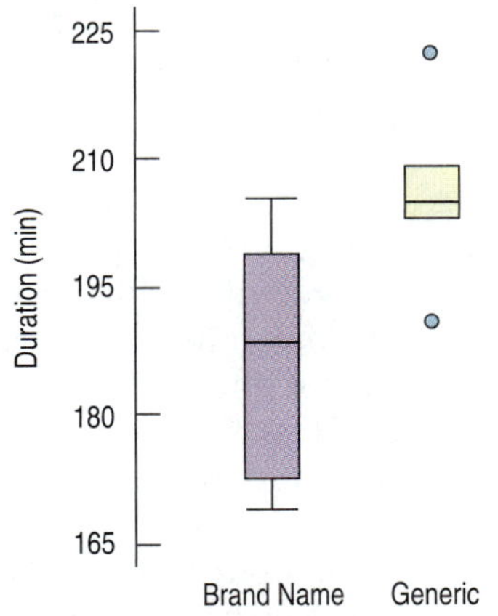

Boxplots comparing the brand name and generic data suggest a difference in duration. **Figure 24.1**

The natural display for comparing two groups is boxplots of the data for the two groups, placed side-by-side. Although we can't make a confidence interval or test a hypothesis from the boxplots themselves, you should always start with boxplots when comparing groups. Let's look at the boxplots of the battery test data.

It sure looks like the generic batteries lasted longer. And we can see that they were also more consistent. But is the difference large enough to change our battery-buying behavior? Can we be confident that the difference is more than just random fluctuation? That's why we need statistical inference.

The boxplot for the generic data identifies two possible outliers. That's interesting, but with only six measurements in each group, the outlier nomination rule is not very reliable. Both of the extreme values are plausible results and the range of the generic values is smaller than the range of the brand-name values even with the outliers. So we're probably better off just leaving these values in the data.

Comparing Two Means

Comparing two means is not very different from comparing two proportions. In fact, it's not different in concept from any of the methods we've seen. Now, the population model parameter of interest is the difference between the *mean* battery lifetimes of the two brands, $\mu_1 - \mu_2$.

The rest is the same as before. The statistic of interest is the difference in the two observed means, $\bar{y}_1 - \bar{y}_2$. We'll start with this statistic to build our confidence interval, but we'll need to know its standard deviation and its sampling model. Then we can build confidence intervals and find P-values for hypothesis tests.

We know that for independent random variables, variances add. It worked for proportions; it works for means. To find the standard deviation of the difference between the two sample means, we add their variances and then take a square root:

$$SD(\bar{y}_1 - \bar{y}_2) = \sqrt{Var(\bar{y}_1) + Var(\bar{y}_2)}$$
$$= \sqrt{\left(\frac{\sigma_1}{\sqrt{n_1}}\right)^2 + \left(\frac{\sigma_2}{\sqrt{n_2}}\right)^2}$$
$$= \sqrt{\frac{\sigma_1^2}{n_1} + \frac{\sigma_2^2}{n_2}}$$

z or t?

If you know σ, use z. (That's rare!)

Whenever you use s to estimate σ, use t. (Almost always.)

Of course, we still don't know the true standard deviations of the two groups, σ_1 and σ_2, so as usual, we'll use the estimates, s_1 and s_2. Using the estimates gives us the *standard error,*

$$SE(\bar{y}_1 - \bar{y}_2) = \sqrt{\frac{s_1^2}{n_1} + \frac{s_2^2}{n_2}}.$$

We'll use the standard error to see how big the difference really is. Because we are working with means and estimating the standard error of their difference using the data, we shouldn't be surprised that the sampling model is a Student's t.

The confidence interval we build is called a **two-sample *t*-interval** (for the difference in means). The corresponding hypothesis test is called a **two-sample *t*-test.** The interval looks just like all the others we've seen—the statistic plus or minus an estimated margin of error:

$$(\bar{y}_1 - \bar{y}_2) \pm ME$$

$$\text{where } ME = t^* \times SE(\bar{y}_1 - \bar{y}_2)$$

Compare this formula with the one for the confidence interval for the difference of two proportions we saw in Chapter 22. The formulas are almost the same. It's just that here we use a Student's *t*-model instead of a Normal model to find the appropriate critical t^* value corresponding to our chosen confidence.

What are we missing? Only the degrees of freedom for the Student's *t*-model. Unfortunately, *that* formula is strange.

The deep, dark secret is that the sampling model isn't *really* Student's *t*, but only something close. The trick is that by using a special, adjusted degrees of freedom value, we can make it so close to a Student's *t*-model that nobody can tell the difference. The adjustment formula is straightforward but doesn't help us understand anything, so we leave it to the computer or calculator. (If you are curious and really want to see the formula, look in the footnote.)[1]

An Easier Rule?

The formula for the degrees of freedom of the sampling distribution of the difference between two means is long, so some books teach an easier rule: The number of degrees of freedom is always at *least* the smaller of the two *n*'s, minus 1 and at most $n_1 + n_2 - 2$. The problem is that if you need to use a two-sample *t* and don't have the formula at hand to find the correct degrees of freedom, you have to be conservative and use the lower value. And *that* approximation can be a poor choice because it can give less than *half* the degrees of freedom you're entitled to from the correct formula.

A sampling distribution for the difference between two means

When the conditions are met, the standardized sample difference between the means of two independent groups,

$$t = \frac{(\bar{y}_1 - \bar{y}_2) - (\mu_1 - \mu_2)}{SE(\bar{y}_1 - \bar{y}_2)},$$

can be modeled by a Student's *t*-model with a number of degrees of freedom found with a special formula. We estimate the standard error with

$$SE(\bar{y}_1 - \bar{y}_2) = \sqrt{\frac{s_1^2}{n_1} + \frac{s_2^2}{n_2}}.$$

Assumptions and Conditions

Now we've got everything we need. Before we can make a two-sample *t*-interval or perform a two-sample *t*-test, though, we have to check the assumptions and conditions.

Independence Assumption

The data in each group must be drawn independently and at random from a homogeneous population, or generated by a randomized comparative experiment.

1

$$df = \frac{\left(\frac{s_1^2}{n_1} + \frac{s_2^2}{n_2}\right)^2}{\frac{1}{n_1 - 1}\left(\frac{s_1^2}{n_1}\right)^2 + \frac{1}{n_2 - 1}\left(\frac{s_2^2}{n_2}\right)^2}$$

Are you sorry you looked? This formula usually doesn't even give a whole number. If you are using a table, you'll need a whole number, so round down to be safe. If you are using technology, it's even easier. The approximation formulas that computers and calculators use for the Student's *t*-distribution can deal with fractional degrees of freedom, so it's OK to pass the fractional degrees of freedom from this formula through to those formulas.

We can't expect that the data, taken as one big group, come from a homogeneous population, because that's what we're trying to check. But without randomization of some sort, there are no sampling distribution models and no inference. We can check two conditions:

Randomization condition. Were the data collected with suitable randomization? For surveys, are they a representative random sample? For experiments, was the experiment randomized?

10% condition. We use this condition to make sure we have not violated the independence assumption by sampling too large a fraction of the population. This is a less common violation for means than it was for proportions.

Normal Population Assumption

As we did before with Student's t-models, we should check the assumption that the underlying populations are *each* Normally distributed. We check the following:

Nearly Normal condition. We must check this for *both* samples; a violation by either one violates the condition. As we saw for single sample means, the Normality assumption matters most when sample sizes are small. For samples of $n < 15$ in either group, you should not use these methods if the histogram or normal probability plot shows severe skewness. For samples of $n < 40$, a mildly skewed histogram is OK, but you should remark on any outliers you find and not work with severely skewed data. When both samples are bigger than 40, the Central Limit Theorem starts to kick in no matter how the data are distributed, so the nearly Normal condition for the data matters less. Even in large samples, however, you should still be on the lookout for outliers and multiple modes because they may provide useful information.

Independent Groups Assumption

To use the two-sample t methods, the two groups we are comparing must be independent of each other. In fact, this test is sometimes called the two *independent samples* t-test. No statistical test can verify this assumption. You have to think about how the data were collected. The assumption would be violated, for example, if one sample were comprised of husbands and the other sample, their wives. Whatever we measure on couples might naturally be related. Similarly, if we compared subjects' performances before some treatment with their performances afterward, we'd expect a relationship of each "before" measurement with its corresponding "after" measurement. In cases such as these, where the observational units in the two groups are related or matched, *the two-sample methods of this chapter can't be applied.* When this happens we need a different procedure, as we'll see in the next chapter.

Two-sample t-interval

When the conditions are met, we are ready to find the confidence interval for the difference between means of two independent groups, $\mu_1 - \mu_2$. Since the standard error of the difference is

$$SE(\bar{y}_1 - \bar{y}_2) = \sqrt{\frac{s_1^2}{n_1} + \frac{s_2^2}{n_2}},$$

the interval is $(\bar{y}_1 - \bar{y}_2) \pm t^*_{df} \times SE(\bar{y}_1 - \bar{y}_2)$. The critical value t^*_{df} depends on the particular confidence level, C, that you specify and on the number of degrees of freedom, which we get from the sample sizes and a special formula.

A Two-Sample *t*-Interval STEP-BY-STEP

Judging from the boxplot, the generic batteries seem to have lasted about 20 minutes longer than the brand-name batteries. Before we change our buying habits, what should we expect to happen with the next batteries we buy? How much longer might the generics last? Let's make a confidence interval for the differences of the means.

Think

Parameter Identify the *parameter* you wish to estimate. In this case the parameter is the difference in the means of the populations to which the two groups belong.

Choose and state a confidence level.

We wish to find an interval that is likely with 95% confidence to contain the true difference $\mu_G - \mu_B$ between the mean lifetime of the generic brand AA batteries and the mean lifetime of the brand-name batteries.

✓ Reality Check From the boxplots, it appears our confidence interval should be centered near a difference of 20 minutes. We don't have a lot of intuition about how far the interval should extend on either side of 20.

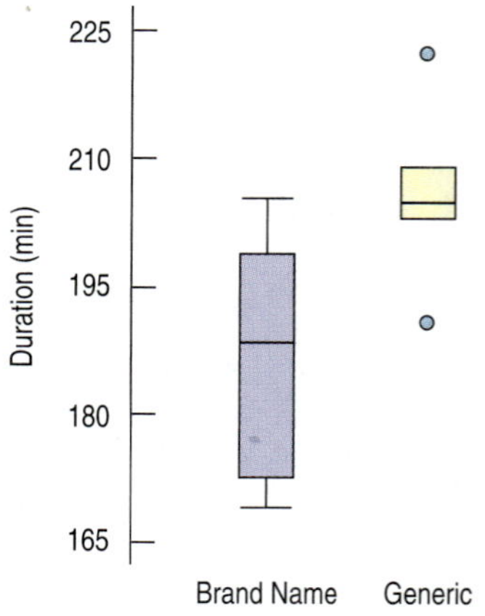

Plan Check the conditions.

✓ **Independent groups assumption:** Batteries manufactured by two different companies from separate packages should be independent.

✓ **Randomization condition:** The batteries were selected at random from those available for sale. Not exactly an SRS, but a reasonably representative random sample. The batteries do come in packs, however, so they may not be independent. For example, a storage problem might affect all the batteries in the same pack. To make our case stronger, we might want to repeat the experiment for several different packs of batteries.

✓ **10% condition:** Although sampling was necessarily without replacement, there are many more batteries than were sampled.

✓ **Nearly Normal condition:** The samples are small, but histograms look unimodal and symmetric:

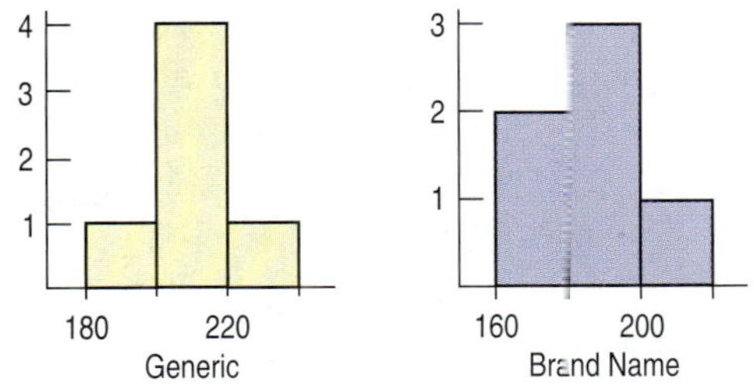

State the sampling distribution model for the statistic. Here the degrees of freedom come from the approximation formula.

Choose your method.

Under these conditions, the sampling model of the difference in the sample means can be modeled by a Student's t-model with about 9 degrees of freedom.

We will use a **two-sample t-interval.**

Show

Mechanics Construct the confidence interval.

Be sure to include the units along with the statistics.

Use the sample standard deviations to find the standard error of the sampling distribution.

We know:

$$n_1 = 6 \qquad n_2 = 6$$

$$\bar{y}_1 = 206.0 \text{ min} \qquad \bar{y}_2 = 137.4 \text{ min}$$

$$s_1 = 10.3 \text{ min} \qquad s_2 = 14.6 \text{ min}$$

Because we think the Independence condition is OK, we can say that:

$$SE(\bar{y}_1 - \bar{y}_2) = \sqrt{SE^2(\bar{y}_1) + SE^2(\bar{y}_2)}$$

$$= \sqrt{\frac{s_1^2}{n_1} + \frac{s_2^2}{n_2}}$$

$$= \sqrt{\frac{10.3^2}{6} + \frac{14.6^2}{6}}$$

$$= \sqrt{\frac{106.09}{6} + \frac{213.16}{6}}$$

$$= \sqrt{53.208}$$

$$= 7.29$$

We have three choices for degrees of freedom. The best alternative is to let the computer or calculator use the approximation formula. This gives a fractional degree of freedom (here df = 8.98), but the technology can find a corresponding critical value. In this case, it is $t^* = 2.263$.

Or we could round the approximation formula's df value down to an integer so we can use a t table. That gives 8 df and a critical value, $t^* = 2.306$.

The sampling model has 8.98 degrees of freedom (from the approximation formula).

The corresponding critical value for a 95% confidence level from a Student's t-model on 8.98 df is $t^* = 2.263$.

From these, we find the margin of error:

$$ME = t^* \times SE(\bar{y}_1 - \bar{y}_2)$$

$$= 2.263(7.29)$$

$$= 16.50$$

The easy rule says to use only $6 - 1 = 5$ df. That gives a critical value $t^* = 2.571$. The corresponding confidence interval is about 14% wider—a high price to pay for a small savings in effort.

So the 95% confidence interval is:

$$(206.0 - 187.4) \pm 16.5 \text{ minutes}$$

$$\text{or } 18.6 \pm 16.5 \text{ minutes}$$

$$= (2.1, 35.1) \text{ minutes.}$$

Tell

Interpretation Tell what the confidence interval means.

We are 95% confident that the mean useful life of the generic batteries is between 2.1 minutes and 35.1 minutes longer than the mean useful life of the brand-name batteries for this task. If generic batteries are cheaper, there seems little reason not to use them. If it is more trouble or costs more to buy them, then you should consider whether the additional performance is worth it.

Another One Just Like the Other Ones?

Yes. That's been our point all along. Once again we see a statistic plus or minus the margin of error. And the ME is just a critical value times the standard error. Just look out for that crazy degrees of freedom formula.

TI Tips

If you have been successful using your TI to make confidence intervals for proportions and 1-sample means, then you probably can already use the 2-sample function just fine. But humor us while we do one. Please?

Find a confidence interval for the difference in means, given data from two independent samples.

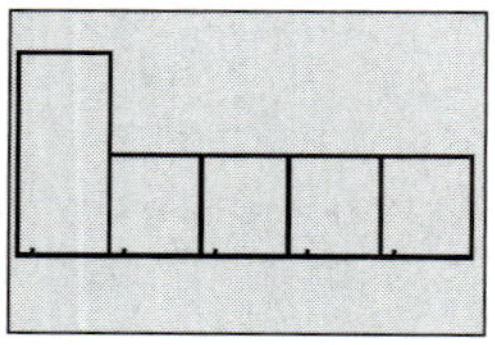

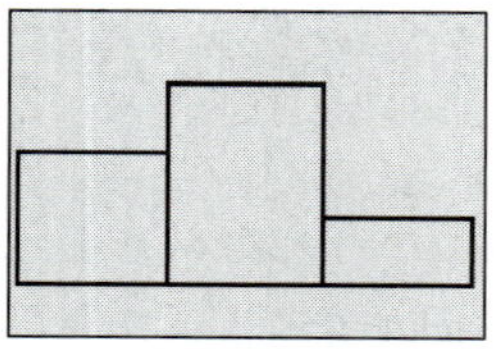

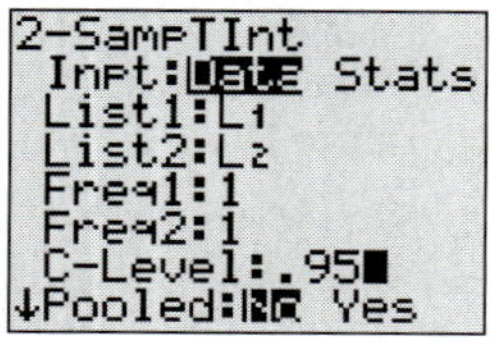

- Let's do the batteries. Always think about whether the samples are independent. If not, stop right here. These procedures are appropriate only for independent groups.
- Enter the data into two lists.

NameBrand in `L1`:	194.0	205.5	199.2	172.4	184.0	169.5
Generic in `L2`:	190.7	203.5	203.5	206.5	222.5	209.4

- Make histograms of the data to check the nearly Normal condition. We see that `L1`'s histogram doesn't look so good. But remember—this is a very small data set. The bars represent only one or two values each. It's not unusual for the histogram to look a little ragged. Try resetting the `WINDOW` to a range of 160 to 220 with `XScl=20`, and `Ymax=4`. Redraw the `GRAPH`. Looks better.
- It's your turn to try this. Check `L2`. Go on, do it.
- Under `STAT TESTS` choose `0:2-SampTInt`.
- Specify that you are using the `Data` in `L1` and `L2`, specify 1 for both frequencies, and choose the confidence level you want.

- `Pooled`? We'll discuss this issue later in the chapter, but the easy advice is: Just Say `No`.
- To `Calculate` the interval, you need to scroll down one more line.

Now you have the 95% confidence interval. See `df`? The calculator did that messy degrees of freedom calculation for you. You have to love that!

Notice that the interval bounds are negative. That's because the TI is doing $\mu_1 - \mu_2$, and the generic batteries (`L2`) lasted longer. No harm done—you just need to be careful to interpret that result correctly when you Tell what the confidence interval means.

No data? Find a confidence interval using the sample statistics.

In many situations we don't have the original data, but must work with the summary statistics from the two groups. As we saw in the last chapter you can still have your TI create the confidence interval with `0:2-SampTInt` by choosing the `Inpt:Stats` option. Enter both means, standard deviations, and sample sizes, then `Calculate`. We show you the details in the next TI Tips.

Testing the Difference Between Two Means

If you bought a used camera in good condition from a friend, would you pay the same as you would if you bought the same item from a stranger? A researcher at Cornell University (J. J. Halpern, "The Transaction Index: A Method for Standardizing Comparisons of Transaction Characteristics Across Different Contexts," *Group Decision and Negotiation,* 6, no. 6[1997]: 557–572) wanted to know how friendship might affect simple sales such as this. She randomly divided subjects into two groups and gave each group descriptions of items they might want to buy. One group was told to imagine buying from a friend whom they expected to see again. The other group was told to imagine buying from a stranger.

Here are the prices they offered for a used camera in good condition:

WHO	University students
WHAT	Prices offered for a used camera
UNITS	Dollars
WHY	Study of the effects of friendship on transactions
WHEN	1990s
WHERE	Cornell University

PRICE OFFERED FOR A USED CAMERA ($)

Buying from a Friend	Buying from a Stranger
275	260
300	250
260	175
300	130
255	200
275	225
290	240
300	

It looks like there's a difference. Here are the boxplots:

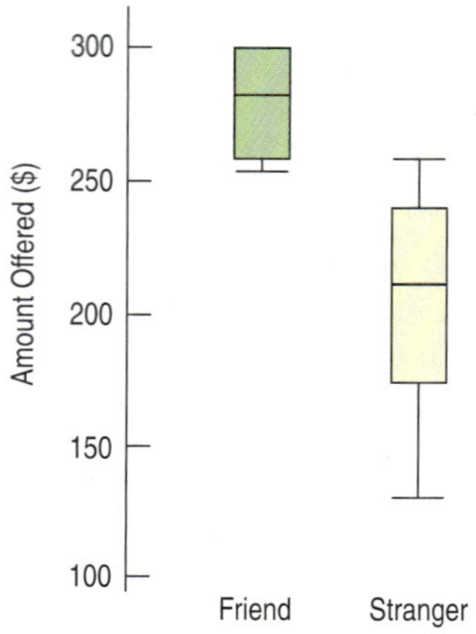

Boxplots suggest a difference between prices offered to friends and prices offered to strangers, but is the difference just random fluctuation? **Figure 24.2**

Is the difference statistically significant? Should we really be careful when buying items from a friend? Let's perform a hypothesis test.

A Test for the Difference Between Two Means

The researcher who designed this study had a specific concern. Previous theories had doubted that friendship had a measurable effect on pricing. She hoped to find an effect of friendship. This calls for a hypothesis test—in this case a **two-sample *t*-test for means.**

You already know enough to construct this test. The test statistic looks just like the others we've seen. It finds the difference between the observed group means and compares this with a hypothesized value for that difference. We'll call that hypothesized difference Δ_0 ("delta naught"). It's so common for that hypothesized difference to be zero that we often just assume $\Delta_0 = 0$. We then compare the difference in the means with the standard error of that difference. We already know that for a difference between independent means, we can find P-values from a Student's *t*-model on that same special number of degrees of freedom.

We're ready to go:

Two-sample *t*-test for the difference between the means of two independent groups

The conditions for the two-sample *t*-test for the difference between the means of two independent groups are the same as for the two-sample *t*-interval. We test the hypothesis

$$H_0: \mu_1 - \mu_2 = \Delta_0,$$

where the hypothesized difference is almost always 0, using the statistic

$$t = \frac{(\bar{y}_1 - \bar{y}_2) - \Delta_0}{SE(\bar{y}_1 - \bar{y}_2)}.$$

The standard error of $\bar{y}_1 - \bar{y}_2$ is

$$SE(\bar{y}_1 - \bar{y}_2) = \sqrt{\frac{s_1^2}{n_1} + \frac{s_2^2}{n_2}}.$$

When the conditions are met and the null hypothesis is true, this statistic can be closely modeled by a Student's *t*-model with a number of degrees of freedom given by a special formula. We use that model to obtain a P-value.

A Two-Sample *t*-test for the Difference Between Two Means STEP-BY-STEP

The usual null hypothesis is that there's no difference. That's just the right null hypothesis for the camera purchase prices.

Think

Hypotheses State what we want to know.

The research claim is that friendship changes what people are willing to pay[2]. The natural null hypothesis is that friendship makes no difference.

We didn't start with any knowledge of whether friendship might increase or decrease the price, so we choose a two-sided alternative.

We want to know whether people are likely to offer a different amount for a used camera when buying from a friend than when buying from a stranger.

H_0: The difference in mean price offered to friends and the mean price offered to strangers is zero;

$$\mu_F - \mu_S = 0.$$

H_A: The difference in mean prices is not zero:

$$\mu_F - \mu_S \neq 0.$$

Reality Check Looks like the prices are higher if you buy from a friend, but it's hard to be sure. The two ranges barely overlap, so we'd be pretty surprised if we don't reject the null hypothesis.

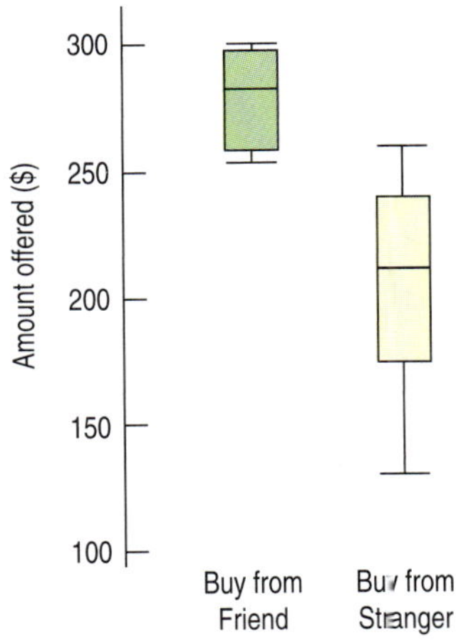

Plan State the null model.

Check the conditions.

✓ **Independent groups assumption:** Randomizing the experiment gives us independent groups.

✓ **Randomization condition:** The experiment was randomized. Subjects were assigned to treatment groups at random.

✓ **10% condition:** This is a randomized experiment, so this condition doesn't apply.

✓ **Nearly Normal condition:** Histograms of the two sets of prices are unimodal and symmetric:

[2]This claim is a good example of what is called a "research hypothesis" in many social sciences. The only way to check it is to deny that it's true and see where the resulting null hypothesis leads us.

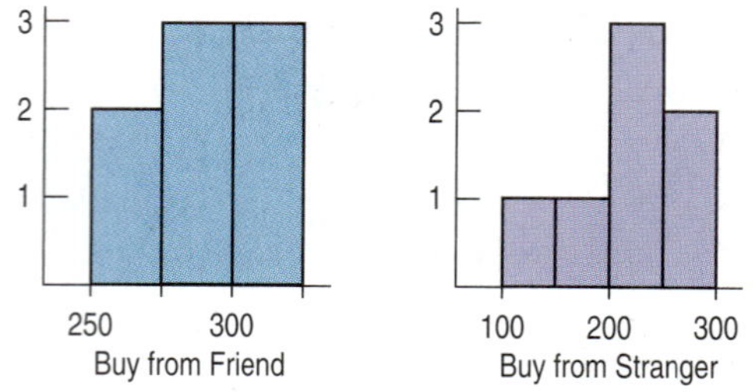

State the sampling distribution model of the statistic.

Because the conditions are satisfied, it is appropriate to model the sampling distribution of the difference in the means with a Student's t-model.

Choose your method.

We will perform a **two-sample t-test.**

Show

Mechanics

We know:

$n_1 = 8$	$n_2 = 7$
$\bar{y}_1 = \$281.88$	$\bar{y}_2 = \$211.43$
$s_1 = \$18.31$	$s_2 = \$46.43$

We use the null model to find the P-value. First determine the standard error of the difference between sample means.

Because the independence condition appears to be satisfied, we can say that

$$SE(\bar{y}_1 - \bar{y}_2) = \sqrt{SE^2(\bar{y}_1) + SE^2(\bar{y}_2)}$$

$$= \sqrt{\frac{s_1^2}{n_1} + \frac{s_2^2}{n_2}}$$

$$= \sqrt{\frac{18.31^2}{8} + \frac{46.43^2}{7}}$$

$$= \sqrt{349.87}$$

$$= 18.70$$

Make a picture. Sketch the t-model centered at the hypothesized difference of zero. Because this is a two-tail test, shade the region to the right of the observed difference and the corresponding region in the other tail.

The observed difference is

$$(\bar{y}_1 - \bar{y}_2) = 281.88 - 211.43 = \$70.45.$$

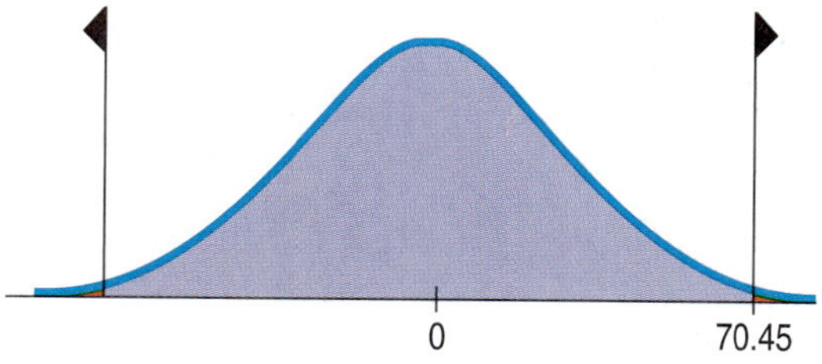

Find the t-value.

A statistics program or graphing calculator can find the P-value using the fractional degrees of freedom from the approximation formula. If you are doing a test like this without software, you could use the smaller sample size to determine degrees of freedom. In this case $n_2 - 1 = 6$.

$$t = \frac{(\bar{y}_1 - \bar{y}_2) - (0)}{SE(\bar{y}_1 - \bar{y}_2)} = \frac{70.45}{18.70} = 3.77.$$

The sampling distribution model has 7.62 degrees of freedom.

$P = 2P(t > 3.77) = 0.006$

Tell

Conclusion Link the P-value to your decision about the null hypothesis and state the conclusion in context.

The P-value tells us that if there were no difference in the mean prices, the difference we have observed would occur only 6 times in 1000. That's too rare for most folks to believe, so we reject the null hypothesis and conclude that people are likely to pay a friend for a used camera a different amount than they'd pay a stranger (and possibly for other similar items).

We should be cautious about generalizing to items whose prices are outside the range of those in this study.

If possible, propose a course of action.

We may want to take special care not to pay too much when buying an item such as this from a friend.

TI Tips

Now let's use the TI to do a hypothesis test for the difference of two means—independent, of course! (Have we said that enough times yet?)

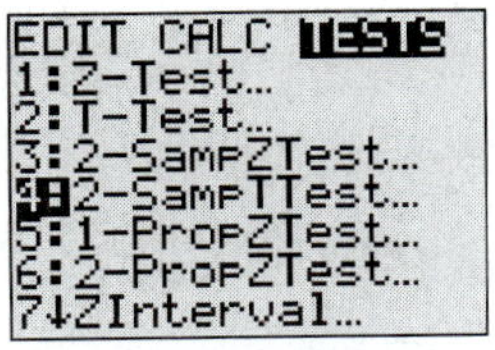

Test a hypothesis when you know the sample statistics.

We'll demonstrate by using the statistics from the camera-pricing example. A sample of 8 people suggested they'd sell the camera to a friend for an average price of \$281.88 with standard deviation \$18.31. An independent sample of 7 other people would charge a stranger an average of \$211.43 with standard deviation \$46.43. Does this represent a significant difference in prices?

- From the `STAT TESTS` menu select `4:2-SampTTest`.
- Specify `Inpt:Stats`, and enter the appropriate sample statistics.
- You have to scroll down to complete the specifications. This is a two-tailed test, so choose alternative $\neq$ `μ2`.
- `Pooled`? Just say `No`. (We did promise to explain that and we will, coming up next.)
- Ready . . . set . . . `Calculate`!

The TI reports a calculated value of $t = 3.77$ and a P-value of 0.006. It's hard to tell who your real friends are.

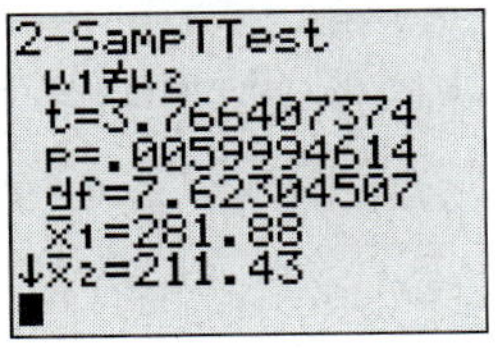

By now we probably don't have to tell you how to do a `2-SampTTest` starting with data in lists.

So we won't.

Back into the Pool

Remember that when we know a proportion, we know its standard deviation. When we tested the null hypothesis that two proportions were equal, that link meant we could assume their variances were equal as well. This led us to pool our data for the hypothesis test. (Of course, we couldn't pool for the confidence interval because confidence intervals work with the observed proportions and don't assume they are equal.)

For means, there is also a pooled *t*-test. Like the two-proportions *z*-test, this test assumes that the variances in the two groups are equal. But be careful. Means don't have any link between their value and their variance. Knowing the mean doesn't tell you anything about the variance. And knowing that two means are equal doesn't say anything about whether their variances are equal. If we are willing to *assume* that their variances are equal, though, we can pool the data from two groups to estimate the common variance and make the degrees of freedom formula much simpler.

We are still estimating the pooled standard deviation from the data, so we use Student's *t*-model, and the test is called a **pooled t-test.**

Equal Variance Assumption

To use the pooled *t*-test, we need to assume that the variances of the two populations from which the samples have been drawn are equal. That is, $\sigma_1^2 = \sigma_2^2$. (Of course, we can think about the standard deviations being equal instead.)

If we can assume equal variances, then we can estimate this common variance from the numbers we already have:

$$s_{\text{pooled}}^2 = \frac{(n_1 - 1)s_1^2 + (n_2 - 1)s_2^2}{(n_1 - 1) + (n_2 - 1)}$$

(If the two sample sizes are equal, this is just the average of the two variances.)

Now we just substitute this pooled variance for each of the variances in the standard error formula. Remember, the standard error formula for the difference of two independent means is:

$$SE(\bar{y}_1 - \bar{y}_2) = \sqrt{\frac{s_1^2}{n_1} + \frac{s_2^2}{n_2}}.$$

After substituting the common pooled variance for each of the two variances in this formula, the pooled standard error formula is much simpler:

$$SE_{\text{pooled}}(\bar{y}_1 - \bar{y}_2) = \sqrt{\frac{s_{\text{pooled}}^2}{n_1} + \frac{s_{\text{pooled}}^2}{n_2}}.$$

The formula for degrees of freedom for the Student's *t*-model is simpler too. It was so complicated for the two-sample t that we stuck it in a footnote[3]. Now it's just $n_1 + n_2 - 2$.

[3]See footnote 1, page 468.

Pooled variance *t*-test and confidence interval for the difference between two independent means

The conditions for the pooled *t*-test for the difference between the means of two independent groups (commonly called a "pooled *t*-test") are the same as for the two-sample *t*-test with the additional assumption that the variances of the two groups are the same. We test the hypothesis

$$H_0: \mu_1 - \mu_2 = \Delta_0,$$

where the hypothesized difference is almost always 0, using the statistic

$$t = \frac{(\bar{y}_1 - \bar{y}_2) - \Delta_0}{SE_{pooled}(\bar{y}_1 - \bar{y}_2)}.$$

The standard error of $\bar{y}_1 - \bar{y}_2$ is

$$SE_{pooled}(\bar{y}_1 - \bar{y}_2) = \sqrt{\frac{s^2_{pooled}}{n_1} + \frac{s^2_{pooled}}{n_2}}$$

where the pooled variance is

$$s^2_{pooled} = \frac{(n_1 - 1)s_1^2 + (n_2 - 1)s_2^2}{(n_1 - 1) + (n_2 - 1)}.$$

When the conditions are met and the null hypothesis is true, this statistic follows a Student's *t*-model with $(n_1 - 1) + (n_2 - 1)$ degrees of freedom. We use that model to obtain a P-value.

The corresponding confidence interval is

$$(\bar{y}_1 - \bar{y}_2) \pm t^*_{df} \times SE_{pooled}(\bar{y}_1 - \bar{y}_1),$$

where the critical value t^* depends on the confidence level and is found with $(n_1 - 1) + (n_2 - 1)$ degrees of freedom.

Substitute the pooled-*t* estimate of the standard error and its degrees of freedom into the steps of the confidence interval or hypothesis test and you'll be using the pooled-*t* method. Of course, if you decide to use a pooled-*t* method, you must defend your assumption that the variances of the two groups are equal.

How can we defend an assumption like that? We're testing whether the means are equal, so we admit that we don't *know* whether they are equal. Doesn't it seem a bit much to just *assume* that the variances are equal?

Is the Pool All Wet?

So when *should* you use pooled-*t* methods rather than two-sample *t* methods?

Never.

What, never?

Well, hardly ever.

You see, when the variances of the two groups are in fact equal, the two methods give pretty much the same result. Pooled methods have a small advantage (slightly narrower confidence intervals, slightly more powerful tests) mostly because their degrees of freedom formula is usually a bit bigger, but the advantage is slight.

Because the advantages of pooling are small, and you are allowed to pool only rarely (when the equal variances assumption is met), ***don't.***

It's never wrong ***not*** to pool.

When the variances are *not* equal, the pooled methods are just not valid, and can give poor results. You have to use the two-sample methods instead.

As the sample sizes get bigger, the advantages that come from a few more degrees of freedom make less and less difference. So the advantage (such as it is) of the pooled method is greatest when the samples are small—just when it's hardest to check the conditions. And the difference in the degrees of freedom is greatest when the variances are not equal—just when you can't use the pooled method anyway. Our advice is to use the two-sample t methods to compare means.

Why did we devote a whole section to a method that we don't recommend using? Good question. The answer is that pooled methods are actually very important in Statistics. We'll see important pooled methods in coming chapters. It's just that the simplest of the pooled methods—those for comparing two means—have good alternatives in the two-sample methods that don't require the extra assumption. Without the burden of the equal variances assumption, the two-sample methods apply to more situations and are safer to use.

Why Not Test the Condition That the Variances Are Equal?

There is a hypothesis test that would do this. However, it is very sensitive to failures of the assumptions and works poorly for small sample sizes—just the situation in which we might care about a difference in the methods. When the choice between two-sample t and pooled-t methods makes a difference (that is, when the sample sizes are small), the test for whether the variances are equal hardly works at all.

Is There Ever a Time When Assuming Equal Variances Makes Sense?

Yes. In a randomized comparative experiment, we start by assigning our experimental units to treatments at random. We know that at the start of the experiment each treatment group is a random sample from the same population[4], so each treatment group begins with the same population variance. In this case, assuming equal variances is equivalent to assuming that the treatment doesn't change the variance. When we test the difference between the means, the null hypothesis is almost always that the true means are equal. If we're willing to stretch that idea to say that the treatments made no difference *at all* (for example, that the treatment is no different from the placebo offered as a control), then we might be willing to assume that the variances have remained equal. It's still an assumption and there are conditions that need to be checked (make the boxplots, make the boxplots, make the boxplots), but at least it's a plausible assumption.

This line of reasoning is important. The methods used to analyze comparative experiments *do* pool variances in exactly this way and defend the pooling with a version of this argument.

[4]That is, the population of experimental subjects. Remember that to be valid, experiments do not need a representative sample drawn from a population because we are not trying to estimate a population model parameter.

Tukey's Quick Test (Optional)

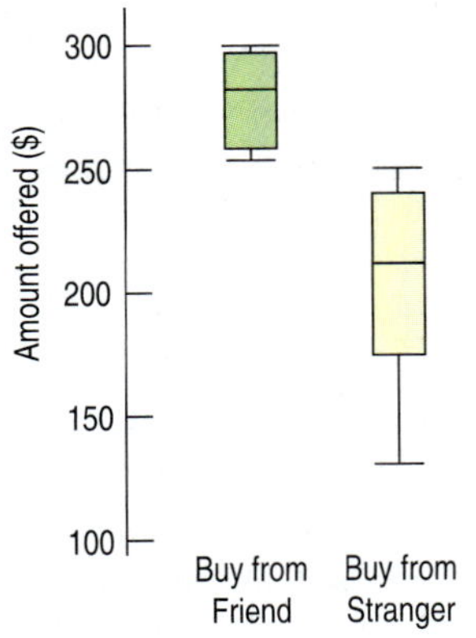

Buying from a Friend	Buying from a Stranger
$275	$260
300	250
260	175
300	130
255	200
275	225
290	240
300	

The famous statistician John Tukey[5] was once challenged to come up with a simpler alternative to the two-sample t-test that, like the 68-95-99.7 Rule, had critical values that could be easily remembered. The test he came up with asks you only to count and to remember three numbers: 7, 10, and 13.

When you first looked at the boxplots of the price data, you might have noticed that they didn't overlap very much. That's the basis for Tukey's test.

To use Tukey's test, one group must have the highest value and the other, the lowest. We just count how many values in the high group are higher than all the values of the lower group. Add to this the number of values in the low group that are lower than *all* the values of the higher group. (You can count ties as 1/2.) Now if this total is 7 or more, we can reject the null hypothesis of equal means at $\alpha =$ .05. The "critical values" of 10 and 13 give us α's of .01 and .001.

Let's try it. The "Friend" group has the highest value ($300) and the "Stranger" group has the lowest ($130). Six of the values in the Friend group are higher than the highest value of the Stranger group ($260) and one is a tie. Six of the Stranger values are lower than the lowest value for Friends. That's a total of 12 1/2 values. That's more than 10, but less than 13. So the P-value is between .01 and .001—just what we found with the two-sample *t*.

This is a remarkably good test. The only assumption it requires is that the two samples are independent. And it's so simple to do that there's no reason not to do one to check your two-sample *t* results. If they disagree, check the assumptions. Tukey's quick test, however, is not as widely known or accepted as the two-sample *t* test, so you still need to know and use the two-sample *t*.

What Can Go Wrong?

- ***Watch out for paired data.*** The independent groups assumption deserves special attention. Some designs *deliberately* violate the independent groups assumption. For example, suppose you wanted to test a diet program. You select 10 people at random to take part in your diet. You measure their weights at the beginning of the diet and after 10 weeks of the diet. So, you have two columns of weights, one for *before* and one for *after*. Can you use these methods to test whether the mean has gone down? No! The data are related; each "after" weight goes naturally with the "before" weight for the *same* person.
  If the samples are not independent, you can't use two-sample methods. This is probably the main thing that can go wrong when using these two-sample methods. Certainly, someone's weight before and after the 10 weeks will be related (whether the diet works or not). The methods of this chapter can be used *only* if the observations in the two groups are *independent*. Matched-pairs designs in which the observations are deliberately related arise often and are important. The next chapter deals with them.

[5]You know some of his other work. Tukey originated the stem-and-leaf display and the boxplot in the form we use here, and published theoretical work on data re-expression that justifies the recommendations of Chapter 10. He also coined the term "bit" for binary digit.

- ***Look at the plots.*** The usual (by now) cautions about checking for outliers and non-normal distributions apply, of course.
  The simple defense is to make and examine boxplots. You may be surprised how often this simple step saves you from the wrong or even absurd conclusions that can be generated by a single undetected outlier. You don't want to conclude that two methods have very different means just because one observation is atypical.

Do what we say, not what we do . . .

Precision machines used in industry often have a bewildering number of parameters that have to be set, so experiments are performed in an attempt to try to find the best settings. Such was the case for a hole-punching machine used by a well-known computer manufacturer to make printed circuit boards. The data were analyzed by one of the authors, but because he was in a hurry, he didn't look at the boxplots first and just performed *t*-tests on the experimental factors. When he found extremely small P-values even for factors that made no sense, he plotted the data. Sure enough, there was one observation 1,000,000 times bigger than the others. It turns out that it had been recorded in microns (millionths of an inch), while all the rest were in inches.

Two-Sample Methods and the Computer

Here's some typical computer package output with comments:

May just say "difference of means"

```
2-Sample t-Test of μ1-μ2

Difference Between Means = 0.99145299 t-Statistic = 1.540
w/196 df
Fail to reject Ho at Alpha = 0.05
P = 0.9374
```

Test Statistic

Some programs will draw a conclusion about the test. Others just give the P-value and let you decide for yourself.

df found from approximation formula

Many programs give far too many digits. Ignore the excess ones.

Most statistics packages compute the test statistic for you and report a P-value corresponding to that statistic. And, of course, statistics packages make it easy to examine the boxplots of the two groups, so you have no excuse for skipping this important check.

Some statistics software automatically tries to test whether the variances of the two groups are equal. Some automatically offer both the two-sample *t* and pooled-*t* results. Ignore the test for the variances; it has little power in any situation in which its results could matter. If the pooled and two-sample methods differ in any important way, you should stick with the two-sample method. Most likely, the equal variance assumption needed for the pooled method has failed.

The degrees of freedom approximation usually gives a fractional value. Most packages seem to round the approximate value down to the next smallest integer (although they may actually compute with the fractional value, gaining a tiny amount of power).

Connections

The two-sample t-test for means is essentially the same as the two-proportion z-test. Much of the reasoning is the same. But because means don't have the link between their value and their variance, we must estimate the standard deviations separately. That leads us to use the Student's t-model rather than the Normal for the sampling distribution.

We first learned about side-by-side boxplots in Chapter 5. There we made general statements about the shape, center, and spread of each group. When we compared groups, we asked whether their centers looked different compared with how spread out the distributions were. Here we've made that kind of thinking precise with confidence intervals for the difference and tests of whether the means are the same.

We use Student's t as we did for single sample means, and for the same reasons. We are using standard deviations from the data to estimate the standard deviation of the sampling model. As before, to work with Student's t-models we need to check the nearly Normal condition. Histograms and Normal probability plots are the best methods for such checks.

As always, we've decided whether a statistic is large by comparing it with its standard error. In this case, our statistic is the difference in means.

We pooled data to find a standard deviation when we tested the hypothesis of equal proportions. For that test, the assumption of equal variances was a consequence of the null hypothesis that the proportions were equal, so it didn't require an extra assumption. When two proportions are equal, so are their variances. But means don't have a linkage with their corresponding variances, so to use pooled t methods, we must make the additional assumption of equal variances. When we can make the assumption, the pooled variance calculations are very similar to those for proportions, combining the squared deviations of each group from its own mean to find a common variance.

Key Concepts

Two-sample t methods
Two-sample t methods allow us to draw conclusions about the difference between the means of two independent groups. The two-sample methods make relatively few assumptions about the underlying populations, so they are usually the method of choice for comparing two sample means. However, the Student's t-models are only approximations for their true sampling distribution. To make that approximation work well, the two-sample t methods have a special rule for estimating degrees of freedom.

Two-sample t-interval
A confidence interval for the difference in the means of two independent groups found as

$$(\bar{y}_1 - \bar{y}_2) \pm t^*_{df} \times SE(\bar{y}_1 - \bar{y}_2), \text{ where}$$

$$SE(\bar{y}_1 - \bar{y}_2) = \sqrt{\frac{s_1^2}{n_1} + \frac{s_2^2}{n_2}}$$

and the number of degrees of freedom is given by a special formula (see footnote 1 if you really want the formula).

Two-sample t-test
A hypothesis test for the difference in the means of two independent groups. It tests the null hypothesis

$$H_0: \mu_1 - \mu_2 = \Delta_0,$$

where the hypothesized difference is almost always 0, using the statistic

$$t = \frac{(\bar{y}_1 - \bar{y}_2) - \Delta_0}{SE(\bar{y}_1 - \bar{y}_2)}$$

with the number of degrees of freedom given by the special formula.

Pooling Data from two or more populations may sometimes be combined, or *pooled,* to estimate a statistic (typically a pooled variance) when we are willing to assume that the estimated value is the same in both populations. The resulting larger sample size may lead to an estimate with lower sample variance. However, pooled estimates are appropriate only when the required assumptions are true.

Pooled-*t* Methods Pooled-*t* methods provide inference about the difference between the means of two independent populations under the assumption that both populations have the same standard deviation. When the assumption is justified, pooled-*t* methods generally produce slightly narrower confidence intervals and more powerful significance tests than two-sample *t* methods. When the assumption is not justified, they generally produce worse results—sometimes substantially worse.

We recommend that you use two-sample *t* methods instead.

Pooled *t*-interval A confidence interval for the difference in the means of two independent groups used when we are willing and able to make the additional assumption that the variances of the groups are equal. It is found as

$$(\bar{y}_1 - \bar{y}_2) \pm t^*_{df} \times SE_{\text{pooled}}(\bar{y}_1 - \bar{y}_2),$$

$$\text{where } SE_{\text{pooled}}(\bar{y}_1 - \bar{y}_2) = \sqrt{\frac{s^2_{\text{pooled}}}{n_1} + \frac{s^2_{\text{pooled}}}{n_2}}.$$

The pooled variance is

$$s^2_{\text{pooled}} = \frac{(n_1 - 1)s_1^2 + (n_2 - 1)s_2^2}{(n_1 - 1) + (n_2 - 1)}$$

and the number of degrees of freedom is $(n_1 - 1) + (n_2 - 1)$.

Pooled *t*-test A hypothesis test for the difference in the means of two independent groups when we are willing and able to assume that the variances of the groups are equal. It tests the null hypothesis

$$H_0: \mu_1 - \mu_2 = \Delta_0,$$

where the hypothesized difference is almost always 0, using the statistic

$$t_{df} = \frac{(\bar{y}_1 - \bar{y}_2) - \Delta_0}{SE_{\text{pooled}}(\bar{y}_1 - \bar{y}_2)}$$

where the pooled standard error is defined as for the pooled interval and the degrees of freedom is $(n_1 - 1) + (n_2 - 1)$.

Skills

When you complete this lesson you should:

Think

- Be able to recognize situations in which we want to do inference on the difference between the means of two independent groups.
- Know how to examine your data for violations of conditions that would make inference about the difference between two population means unwise or invalid.
- Be able to recognize when a pooled-*t* procedure might be appropriate and be able to explain why you decided to use a two-sample method anyway.

Show

- Be able to perform a two-sample *t*-test using a statistics package or calculator (at least for finding the degrees of freedom).
- Be able to perform a pooled *t*-test using a statistics package or calculator.

Tell

- Be able to interpret a test of the null hypothesis that the means of two independent groups are equal. (If the test is a pooled *t*-test, your interpretation should include a defense of your assumption of equal variances.)

Exercises

1. Learning math. The Core Plus Mathematics Project (CPMP) is an innovative approach to teaching mathematics that engages students in group investigations and mathematical modeling. After field tests in 36 high schools over a three-year period, researchers compared the performances of CPMP students with those taught using a traditional curriculum. In one test, students had to solve applied algebra problems using calculators. Scores for 320 CPMP students were compared with those of a control group of 273 students in a traditional math program. Computer software was used to create a confidence interval for the difference in mean scores. (*Journal for Research in Mathematics Education*, 31, no. 3 [2000])

Conf level: 95%   Variable: Mu(CPMP) – Mu(Ctrl)
Interval: (5.573, 11.427)

a) What's the margin of error for this confidence interval?
b) If we had created a 98% CI, would the margin of error be larger or smaller?
c) Explain what the calculated interval means in this context.
d) Does this result suggest that students who learn mathematics with CPMP will have significantly higher mean scores in algebra than those in traditional programs? Explain.

2. Stereograms. Stereograms appear to be composed entirely of random dots. However, they contain separate images that a viewer can "fuse" into a three-dimensional (3D) image by staring at the dots while defocusing the eyes. An experiment was performed to determine whether knowledge of the form of the embedded image affected the time required for subjects to fuse the images. One group of subjects (group NV) received no information or just verbal information about the shape of the embedded object. A second group (group VV) received both verbal information and visual information (specifically, a drawing of the object). The experimenters measured how many seconds it took for the subject to report that he or she saw the 3D image.

2-Sample t-Interval for $\mu1 - \mu2$ df = 70
Conf level = 90%
μ(NV) – μ(VV) interval: (0.55, 5.47)

a) Interpret your interval in context.
b) Does it appear that viewing a picture of the image helps people "see" the 3D image in a stereogram?
c) What's the margin of error for this interval?
d) Explain carefully what the 90% confidence level means.
e) Would you expect a 99% confidence level to be wider or narrower? Explain.
f) Might that change your conclusion in part b? Explain.

3. CPMP, again. During the study described in Exercise 1, students in both CPMP and traditional classes took another algebra test that did not allow them to use calculators. The table below shows the results. Are the mean scores of the two groups significantly different? Test an appropriate hypothesis and state your conclusion.

Math program	n	Mean	SD
CPMP	312	29.0	18.8
Traditional	265	38.4	16.2

Performance on Algebraic Symbolic Manipulation Without Use of Calculators

a) Write an appropriate hypothesis.
b) Do you think the assumptions for inference are satisfied? Explain.
c) Here is computer output for this hypothesis test. Explain what the P-value means in this context.

2-Sample t-Test of $\mu1 - \mu2 \neq 0$
t-Statistic = –6.496 w/583 df
P < 0.0001

d) State a conclusion about the CPMP program.

4. CPMP and word problems. The study of the new CPMP mathematics methodology described in Exercise 1 also tested students' abilities to solve word problems. This table shows how the CPMP and traditional groups performed. What do you conclude?

Math program	n	Mean	SD
CPMP	320	57.4	32.1
Traditional	273	53.9	28.5

5. Commuting. A man who moves to a new city sees that there are two routes he could take to work. A neighbor who has lived there a long time tells him Route *A* will average 5 minutes faster than Route *B*. The man decides to experiment. Each day he flips a coin to determine which way to go, driving each route 20 days. He finds that Route *A* takes an average of 40 minutes with standard deviation 3 minutes, and Route *B* takes an average of 43 minutes with standard deviation 2 minutes. Histograms of travel times for the routes are roughly symmetric and show no outliers.

a) Find a 95% confidence interval for the difference in average commuting time for the two routes.
b) Should the man believe the old-timer's claim that he can save an average of 5 minutes a day by always driving Route A? Explain.

6. Pulse rates. A researcher wanted to see whether there is a significant difference in resting pulse rates for men and women. The data she collected are displayed in the boxplots and summarized below.

	Gender	
	Male	Female
Count	28	24
Mean	72.75	72.625
Median	73	73
StdDev	5.37225	7.69987
Range	20	29
IQR	9	12.5

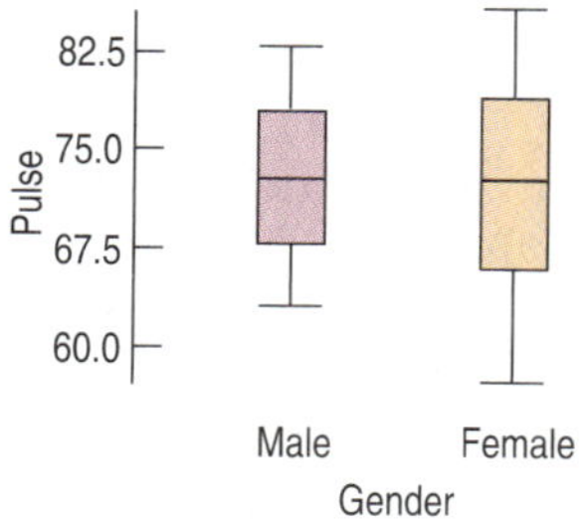

a) What do the boxplots suggest about any gender differences in pulse rates?
b) Is it appropriate to analyze these data using the methods of inference discussed in this chapter? Explain.
c) Create a 90% confidence interval for the difference in mean pulse rates.
d) Does the confidence interval confirm your answer to part a? Explain.

T 7. Cereal. The data below show the sugar content (as a percentage of weight) of several national brands of children's and adults' cereals. Create and interpret a 95% confidence interval for the difference in mean sugar content. Be sure to check the necessary assumptions and conditions.

Children's cereals: 40.3, 55, 45.7, 43.3, 50.3, 45.9, 53.5, 43, 44.2, 44, 47.4, 44, 33.6, 55.1, 48.8, 50.4, 37.8, 60.3, 46.6

Adults' cereals: 20, 30.2, 2.2, 7.5, 4.4, 22.2, 16.6, 14.5, 21.4, 3.3, 6.6, 7.8, 10.6, 16.2, 14.5, 4.1, 15.8, 4.1, 2.4, 3.5, 8.5, 10, 1, 4.4, 1.3, 8.1, 4.7, 18.4

T 8. Egyptians. Some archaeologists theorize that ancient Egyptians interbred with several different immigrant populations over thousands of years. To see if there is any indication of changes in body structure that might have resulted, they measured 30 skulls of male Egyptians dated from 4000 B.C.E. and 30 others dated from 200 B.C.E. (A. Thomson and R. Randall-Maciver, *Ancient Races of the Thebaid,* Oxford: Oxford University Press, 1905.)

a) Are these data appropriate for inference? Explain.
b) Create a 95% confidence interval for the difference in mean skull breadth between these two eras.
c) Do these data provide evidence that the mean breadth of males' skulls changed over this time period? Explain.

Maximum Skull Breadth

4000 B.C.E.	4000 B.C.E.	200 B.C.E.	200 B.C.E.
131	131	141	131
125	135	141	129
131	132	135	136
119	139	133	131
136	132	131	139
138	126	140	144
139	135	139	141
125	134	140	130
131	128	138	133
134	130	132	138
129	138	134	131
134	128	135	136
126	127	133	132
132	131	136	135
141	124	134	141

9. Reading. An educator believes that new reading activities for elementary school children will improve reading comprehension scores. She randomly assigns third graders to an eight-week program in which some will use these activities and others will experience traditional teaching methods. At the end of the experiment, both groups take a reading comprehension exam. Their scores are shown in the back-to-back stem-and-leaf display. Do these results suggest that the new activities are better? Test an appropriate hypothesis and state your conclusion.

New Activities		Control
	1	07
4	2	068
3	3	377
96333	4	122238
9876432	5	355
721	6	02
1	7	
	8	5

10. Streams. Researchers collected samples of water from streams in the Adirondack Mountains to investigate the effects of acid rain. They measured the pH (acidity) of the water and classified the streams with respect to the kind of substrate (type of rock over which they flow). A lower pH means the water is more acidic. Here is a plot of the pH of the streams by substrate (limestone, mixed, or shale):

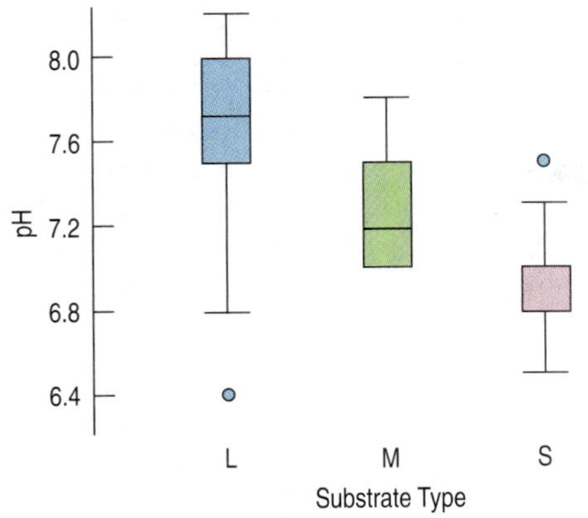

Here are selected parts of a software analysis comparing the pH of streams with limestone and shale substrates:

2-Sample t-Test of $\mu1 - \mu2$
Difference Between Means = 0.735
t-Statistic = 16.30 w/133 df
$p \leq 0.0001$

a) State the null and alternative hypotheses for this test.
b) From the information you have, do the assumptions and conditions appear to be met?
c) What conclusion would you draw?

11. Hurricanes. The data below show the number of hurricanes recorded annually before and after 1970. Create an appropriate visual display and determine whether these data are appropriate for testing whether there has been a change in the frequency of hurricanes.

1944–1969	1970–2000
3, 2, 1, 2, 4, 3, 7, 2, 3, 3, 2, 5, 2, 2, 4, 2, 2, 6, 0, 2, 5, 1, 3, 1, 0, 3	2, 1, 0, 1, 2, 3, 2, 1, 2, 2, 2, 3, 1, 1,1, 3, 0, 1, 3, 2, 1, 2, 1, 1, 0, 5, 6, 1, 3, 5, 3

12. Memory. Does ginkgo biloba enhance memory? In an experiment to find out, subjects were assigned randomly to take ginkgo biloba supplements or a placebo. Their memory was tested to see whether it improved. Here are boxplots comparing the two groups and some computer output from a two-sample t-test computed for the data.

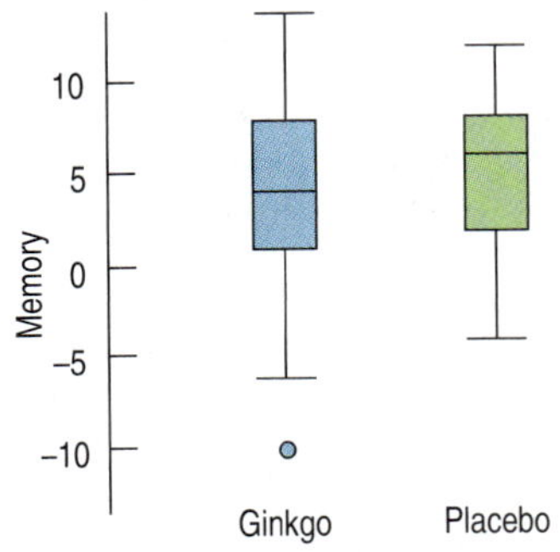

2-Sample t-Test of $\mu_G - \mu_P > 0$
Difference Between Means = −0.9914
t-Statistic = −1.540 w/196 df
P = 0.9374

a) Explain in this context what the P-value means.
b) State your conclusion about the effectiveness of ginkgo biloba.
c) Proponents of ginkgo biloba continue to insist that it works. What type of error do they claim your conclusion makes? Explain.

13. Baseball. American League baseball teams play their games with the designated hitter rule, meaning that pitchers do not bat. The league believes that replacing the pitcher, traditionally a weak hitter, with a another player in the batting order produces more runs and generates more interest among fans. Below are the average numbers of runs scored in American League and National League stadiums for the first half of the 2001 season.

American				National			
11.1	10.8	10.8	10.3	14.0	11.6	10.4	10.3
10.3	10.1	10.0	9.5	10.2	9.5	9.5	9.5
9.4	9.3	9.2	9.2	9.5	9.1	8.8	8.4
	9.0	8.3		8.3	8.2	8.1	7.9

a) Create an appropriate display of these data. What do you see?
b) With a 95% confidence interval, estimate the mean number of runs scored in American League games.
c) What concerns do you have about making a similar confidence interval for National League games? What could you do?
d) Coors Field, in Denver, stands a mile above sea level, an altitude far greater than that of any other major league ball park. Some believe that the thinner air makes it harder for pitchers to throw curve balls and easier for batters to hit the ball a long way. Do you think the 14 runs scored per game at Coors is unusual? Explain.
e) Explain why you should not use two separate confidence intervals to decide whether the two leagues differ in average number of runs scored.

14. Handy. A factory hiring people to work on an assembly line gives job applicants a test of manual agility. This test counts how many strangely shaped pegs the applicant can fit into matching holes in a one-minute period. The table below summarizes the data by gender of the job applicant. Assume that all conditions necessary for inference are met.

	Male	Female
Number of subjects	50	50
Pegs placed:		
Mean	19.39	17.91
Std Dev	2.52	3.39

a) Find 95% confidence intervals for the average number of pegs that males and females can each place.

b) Those intervals overlap. What does this suggest about any gender-based difference in manual agility?
c) Find a 95% confidence interval for the difference in the mean number of pegs that could be placed by men and women.
d) What does this interval suggest about any gender-based difference in manual agility?
e) The two results seem contradictory. Which method is correct: doing two-sample inference, or doing one-sample inference twice?
f) Why don't the results agree?

15. Double header. Do the data in Exercise 13 suggest that the American League's designated hitter rule may lead to more runs?
a) Using a 95% confidence interval, estimate the difference between the mean number of runs scored in American and National League games.
b) Interpret your interval.
c) Does that interval suggest that the two leagues may differ in average number of runs scored per game?
d) Does omitting the 14 runs scored per game at Coors Field affect your decision?

16. Hard water. In an investigation of environmental causes of disease, data were collected on the annual mortality rate (deaths per 100,000) for males in 61 large towns in England and Wales. In addition, the water hardness was recorded as the calcium concentration (parts per million, ppm) in the drinking water. The data set also notes for each town whether it was south or north of Derby. Is there a significant difference in mortality rates in the two regions? Here are the summary statistics.

Summary of: **mortality**
For categories in: **Derby**

Group	Count	Mean	Median	StdDev
North	34	1631.59	1631	138.470
South	27	1388.85	1369	151.114

a) Test appropriate hypotheses and state your conclusion.
b) The boxplots of the two distributions show an outlier among the data north of Derby. What effect might that have had on your test?

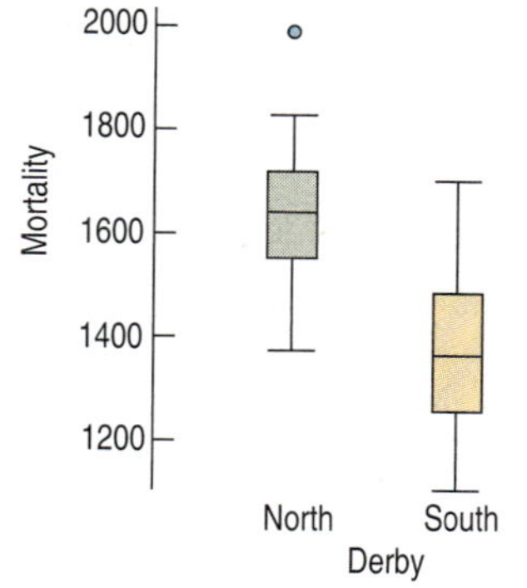

17. Job satisfaction. A company institutes an exercise break for its workers to see if this will improve job satisfaction, as measured by a questionnaire that assesses worker-s'satisfaction. Scores for 10 randomly selected workers before and after implementation of the exercise program are shown. The company wants to assess the effectiveness of the exercise program Explain why you can't use the methods discussed in this chapter to do that. (Don't worry, we'll give you another chance to do this the right way.)

Worker number	Job Satisfaction Index	
	Before	After
1	34	33
2	28	36
3	29	50
4	45	41
5	26	37
6	27	41
7	24	39
8	15	21
9	15	20
10	27	37

18. Summer school. Having done poorly on their math final exams in June, six students repeat the course in summer school, then take another exam in August. If we consider these students representative of all students who might attend this summer school in other years, do these results provide evidence that the program is worthwhile?

June	54	49	68	66	62	62
Aug.	50	65	74	64	68	72

19. Sex and violence. In June 2002, the *Journal of Applied Psychology* reported on a study that examined whether the content of TV shows influenced the ability of viewers to recall brand names of items featured in the commercials. The researchers randomly assigned volunteers to watch one of three programs, each containing the same nine commercials. One of the programs had violent content, another sexual content, and the third neutral content. After the shows ended the subjects were asked to recall the brands of products that were advertised. Results are summarized below.

	Program Type		
	Violent	Sexual	Neutral
No. of subjects	108	108	108
Brands recalled			
Mean	2.08	1.71	3.17
St. Dev	1.87	1.76	1.77

a) Do these results indicate that viewer memory for ads may differ depending on program content? A test of the hypothesis that there is no difference in ad memory between programs with sexual content and those with violent content has a P-value of 0.136. State your conclusion.

b) Is there evidence that viewer memory for ads may differ between programs with sexual content and those with neutral content? Test an appropriate hypothesis and state your conclusion.

20. Ad campaign. You are a consultant to the marketing department of a business preparing to launch an ad campaign for a new product. The company can afford to run ads during one TV show, and has decided not to sponsor a show with sexual content. You read the study described in Exercise 19, then use a computer to create a confidence interval for the difference in mean number of brand names remembered between the groups watching violent shows and those watching neutral shows.

```
TWO-SAMPLE T
95% CI FOR MU viol - MU neut: (-1.578, -0.602)
```

a) At the meeting of the marketing staff, you have to explain what this output means. What will you say?

b) What advice would you give the company about the upcoming ad campaign?

21. Sex and violence II. In the study described in Exercise 19, the researchers also contacted the subjects again, 24 hours later, and asked them to recall the brands advertised. Results are summarized below.

	Program Type		
	Violent	Sexual	Neutral
No. of subjects	101	106	103
Brands recalled			
Mean	3.02	2.72	4.65
St. Dev	1.61	1.85	1.62

a) Is there a significant difference in viewers' abilities to remember brands advertised in shows with violent vs. neutral content?

b) Find a 95% confidence interval for the difference in mean number of brand names remembered between the groups watching shows with sexual content and those watching neutral shows. Interpret your interval in this context.

22. Ad recall. In Exercises 19 and 21, we see the number of advertised brand names people recalled immediately after watching TV shows and 24 hours later. Strangely enough, it appears that they remembered more about the ads the next day. Should we conclude this is true in general about people's memory of TV ads?

a) Suppose one analyst conducts a two-sample hypothesis test to see if memory of brands advertised during violent TV shows is higher 24 hours later. The P-value of his test is 0.00013. What might he conclude?

b) Explain why his procedure was inappropriate. Which of the assumptions for inference was violated?

c) How might the design of this experiment have tainted these results?

d) Suggest a design that could compare immediate brand name recall with recall one day later.

23. Lower scores? Newspaper headlines recently announced a decline in science scores among high school seniors. In 2000, 15,109 seniors tested by The National Assessment in Education Program (NAEP) scored a mean of 147 points. Four years earlier, 7537 seniors had averaged 150 points. The standard error of the difference in the mean scores for the two groups was 1.22.

a) Have the science scores declined significantly? Cite appropriate statistical evidence to support your conclusion.

b) The sample size in 2000 was almost double that in 1996. Does this make the results more convincing, or less? Explain.

24. The Internet. The NAEP report described in Exercise 23 compared science scores for students who had home Internet access with the scores of those who did not, as shown in the graph. They report that the differences are statistically significant.

a) Explain what "statistically significant" means in this context.

b) If their conclusion is incorrect, which type of error did the researchers commit?

c) Does this prove that using the Internet at home can improve a student's performance in science?

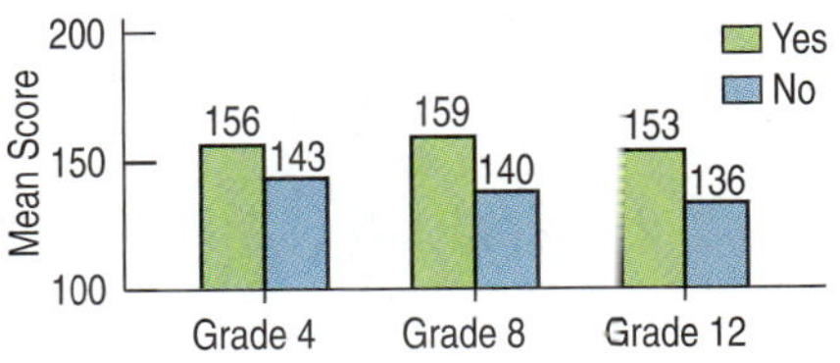

25. Statistics journals. When a professional statistician has information to share with colleagues, he or she will submit an article to one of several Statistics journals for publication. This can be a lengthy process; typically, the article must be circulated for "peer review" and perhaps edited before being accepted for publication. Then the article must wait in line with other articles before actually appearing in print. In the Winter 1998 issue of *Chance* magazine, Eric Bradlow and Howard Wainer reported on this delay for several journals between 1990 and 1994. For 288 articles published in *The American Statistician*, the mean length of time between initial submission and publication was 21 months, with a standard deviation of 8 months. For 209 *Applied Statistics* articles, the mean time to publication was 31 months with a standard deviation of 12 months. Create and interpret a 90% confidence interval for the difference in mean delay, and comment on the assumptions that underlie your analysis.

26. Music and memory. Is it a good idea to listen to music when studying for a big test? In a study conducted by some Statistics students, 62 people were randomly assigned to listen to rap music, music by Mozart, or no music while attempting to memorize objects pictured on a page. They were then asked to list all the objects they could remember. Here are summary statistics for each group:

	Rap	Mozart	No Music
Count	29	20	13
Mean	10.72	10.0	12.77
StDev	3.99	3.19	4.73

a) Does it appear that it is better to study while listening to Mozart than to rap music? Test an appropriate hypothesis and state your conclusion.

b) Create a 90% confidence interval for the mean difference in memory score between students who study to Mozart and those who listen to no music at all. Interpret your interval.

27. Rap. Using the results of the experiment described in Exercise 26, does it matter whether one listens to rap music while studying, or is it better to study without music at all?

a) Test an appropriate hypothesis and state your conclusion.

b) If you concluded there is a difference, estimate the size of that difference with a confidence interval and explain what your interval means.

28. Cuckoos. Cuckoos lay their eggs in the nests of other (host) birds. The eggs are then adopted and hatched by the host birds. But the potential host birds lay eggs of different sizes. Does the cuckoo change the size of her eggs for different foster species? These are lengths (in mm) of cuckoo eggs found in nests of three different species of other birds. The data are drawn from the work of O. M. Latter in 1902 and were used in a fundamental textbook on statistical quality control by L. H. C. Tippett (1902–1985), one of the pioneers in that field.

CUCKOO EGG LENGTH (MM)

Foster Parent Species		
Sparrow	Robin	Wagtail
20.85	21.05	21.05
21.65	21.85	21.85
22.05	22.05	21.85
22.85	22.05	21.85
23.05	22.05	22.05
23.05	22.25	22.45
23.05	22.45	22.65
23.05	22.45	23.05
23.45	22.65	23.05
23.85	23.05	23.25
23.85	23.05	23.45
23.85	23.05	24.05
24.05	23.05	24.05
25.05	23.05	24.05
	23.25	24.85
	23.85	

Investigate the question of whether the mean length of cuckoo eggs is the same for different species and state your conclusion.

Chapter 25

Paired Samples and Blocks

WHO	11 Healthcare workers
WHAT	Annual mileage driven
WHEN	1993-1994
WHERE	Illinois
WHY	Experiment to see whether change in work week increased efficiency

Do flexible schedules reduce the demand for resources? The Lake County, IL, Health Department experimented with a flexible four-day work week. For a year, the department recorded the mileage driven by 11 field workers on an ordinary five-day work week. Then it changed to a flexible four-day work week and recorded mileage for another year. (Charles S. Catlin, "Four-day Work Week Improves Environment," *Journal of Environmental Health,* Denver, 59 [March 1997]:7.)

Here are the data:

Name	5-Day mileage	4-Day mileage
Jeff	2798	2914
Betty	7724	6112
Roger	7505	6177
Tom	838	1102
Aimee	4592	3281
Greg	8107	4997
Larry G.	1228	1695
Tad	8718	6606
Larry M.	1097	1063
Leslie	8089	6392
Lee	3807	3362

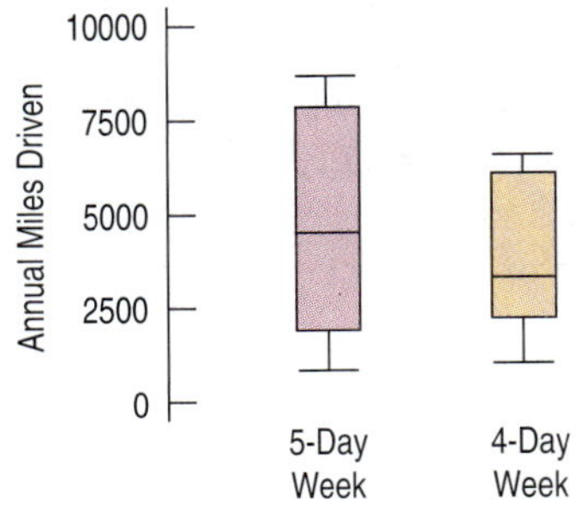

Using boxplots to compare 5-day-week driving with 4-day-week driving shows little because it ignores the natural pairing. Those who drive a lot continue to do so. **Figure 25.1**

Boxplots of the mileages don't show much. We can't tell whether the 4-day work week was successful in reducing miles driven. A two-sample *t*-test wouldn't help much either. (It would find a P-value of 0.4, clearly not evidence of a difference.) But wait a minute. The two-sample *t* test is not valid here. We have 11 individuals, and we know their mileage *before and after* the change in schedule. These data are not independent.

Paired Data

Data such as these are called **paired.** We have each worker's mileage both before and after the work schedule change. Pairing isn't a problem; it's an opportunity. The independence assumption is violated, but we can actually do much better than the two-sample *t*-test. After all, we should be focusing on the *changes* in driving mileage.

Paired data arise in a number of ways. Perhaps the most common is to compare subjects with themselves before and after a treatment. When pairs arise from an experiment, the pairing is a type of *blocking*. When they arise from an observational study, it is a form of *matching*.

If you know the data are paired, you can take advantage of that fact—in fact, you *must* take advantage of it. You *may not* use the two-sample and pooled methods of the previous chapter when the data are paired. You must decide whether the data are paired from understanding how they were collected and what they mean (check the W's). There is no test to determine whether the data are paired.

Once we recognize that the mileage data are matched pairs, it makes sense to consider the change in annual miles driven for each worker as the work schedule changed. So we look at the collection of *pairwise* differences:

Name	5-Day mileage	4-Day mileage	Difference
Jeff	2798	2914	−116
Betty	7724	6112	1612
Roger	7505	6177	1328
Tom	838	1102	−264
Aimee	4592	3281	1311
Greg	8107	4997	3110
Larry G.	1228	1695	−467
Tad	8718	6606	2112
Larry M.	1097	1063	34
Leslie	8089	6392	1697
Lee	3807	3362	445

Jeff actually increased his mileage under the 4-day plan, so his difference is negative. But Greg (who started out driving a far greater distance) reduced his mileage substantially, saving over 3100 miles under the new plan. Because it is the *differences* we care about, we'll treat them as if *they* were the data, ignoring the original two columns. Now that we have only one column of values to consider, we can use a simple one-sample *t*-test. Mechanically, a **matched pairs *t*-test** is just a one-sample *t*-test for the means of these pairwise differences. The sample size is the number of pairs.

So much for Show.

Assumptions and Conditions

Paired Data Assumption

The data must be paired. You can't just decide to pair data when in fact the samples are independent. When you have two groups with the same number of observations, it may be tempting to match them up.

Don't, unless you are prepared to justify your claim that the data are paired.

On the other hand, be sure to recognize paired data when you have it. Remember, two-sample *t* methods aren't valid without independent groups, and paired groups aren't independent.

Independence Assumption

If the data are paired, the *groups* are not independent. For these methods, it's the *differences* that must be independent of each other. In our example, the fact that Jeff drove farther doesn't affect how far Betty drove. (If Jeff and Betty carpooled for part of the year, this wouldn't be true and the assumption would be violated.)

Randomization condition. Randomness can arise in one of two ways. The individuals may be a random sample. In an experiment, the order of the two treatments may be randomly assigned, or the treatments may be randomly assigned to one member of each pair. In a before-and-after study, we may believe that the observed differences are a representative sample from a population of interest. If we have any doubts, we'll need to include a control group to be able to draw conclusions. What we want to know usually focuses our attention on where the randomness should be.

In our example, our main concern is testing whether a 4-day work week reduces mileage. The randomness comes from all the many random driving events that make up the annual totals. If we were to repeat the experiment in two other years, we would find different mileage totals, but (we hope) the same overall pattern of change.

If we also wanted to claim that this change would be typical of all state employees, *then* we might be concerned with how the workers were selected. Are they a random sample of Illinois workers? Was this department selected randomly? If not, our inference may be restricted only to these 11 individuals.

10% condition. When the inference is about a population from which the paired individuals are drawn, we must be sure that we have sampled no more than 10% of that population. If we hoped to generalize our conclusions to all state healthcare workers, we'd want to verify that these 11 were not more than 10% of that group.

Normal Population Assumption

We need to assume that the population of differences follows a Normal model. We don't need to check the individual columns.

Nearly Normal condition. This condition can be checked with a histogram or Normal probability plot of the differences. As with the one-sample *t*-methods, this assumption matters less as we have more pairs to consider. You may be pleasantly surprised when you check this condition. Even if your original measurements are skewed or bimodal, the differences may be nearly Normal. After all, the individual who was way out in the tail on an initial measurement is likely to still be out there on the second one, giving a perfectly ordinary difference.

A paired t-test for the mean difference between two groups

When the conditions are met, we are ready to test whether the paired differences differ significantly from zero. We test the hypothesis

$$H_0: \mu_d = \Delta_0,$$

where the d's are the pairwise differences and Δ_0 is almost always 0.

We use the statistic,

$$t_{n-1} = \frac{\bar{d} - \Delta_0}{SE(\bar{d})},$$

where n is the number of *pairs* and

$$SE(\bar{d}) = \frac{s_d}{\sqrt{n}}.$$

$SE(\bar{d})$ is the ordinary standard error for the mean applied to the differences.

When the conditions are met and the null hypothesis is true, this statistic follows a Student's t-model on $n - 1$ degrees of freedom, so we can use that model to obtain a P-value.

A Paired *t*-Test STEP-BY-STEP

The steps of testing a hypothesis for paired differences are very much like the steps for a one-sample t-test for a mean. Only now we first take the difference of each pair and work with them as our data values.

Think

Hypothesis The parameter is the mean difference in the mileage driven.

Although we hope for a reduction in miles driven, we have no reason to suppose that the difference must be in that direction, so we'd better test a two-sided alternative.

H_0: The mileage driven by each health department worker during a four-day work week is the same as his or her mileage under the original five-day work week; the mean difference is zero: $\mu_d = 0$.

H_A: The mean difference is different from zero: $\mu_d \neq 0$.

✓ Reality Check The individual differences are all in the hundreds to low thousands of miles. We should expect the mean difference to be comparable in magnitude.

Plan Check the conditions.

State why you think the data are paired. Simply having the same number of individuals in each group, displaying them in side-by-side columns, doesn't make them paired.

✓ **Paired data assumption:** The data are paired because they are measurements on the same individuals before and after a change in work schedule.

✓ **Independence assumption:** The behavior of any individual is independent of the behavior of the others, so the differences are mutually independent.

Think about what we hope to learn and where the randomization comes from. Here, the randomization comes from the random events that happen to each driver during the study.

✓ **Randomization condition:** The measured values are the sums of individual trips, each of which experienced random events that arose while driving. Repeating the experiment in two new years would give randomly different values.

We would need to check the 10% condition if we hoped to extend our inference to, for example, all state health workers.

✓ **10% condition:** Our inference is about driving amounts, not about the workers, so we don't need to check this condition here.

For paired data we work with the differences, so it's the Normality of the differences that we care about. The distributions of the individual measurements don't matter for this method—only the distribution of the differences.

✓ **Nearly Normal condition:** The histogram of the differences is unimodal and symmetric.

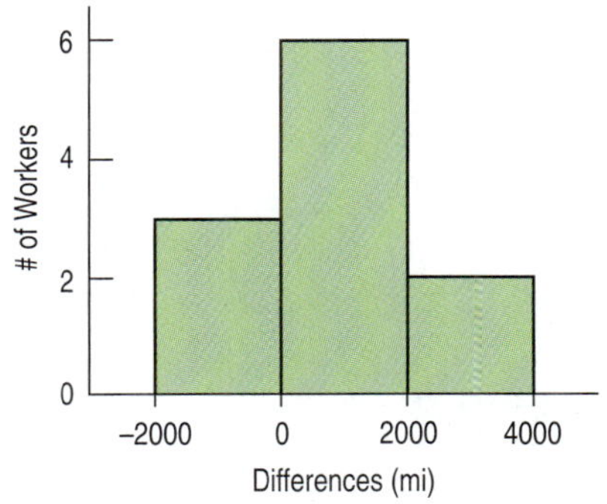

Specify the sampling distribution.

Under these conditions the sampling distribution of the differences can be modeled by a Student's t-model with $(n - 1) = 10$ degrees of freedom.

Choose the method.

We will use a **paired t-test.**

Show

Mechanics

$\bar{d}$ is the mean difference.

s_d is the standard deviation of the differences.

n is the number of *pairs;* in this case, the number of workers.

We find from the data:

$n = 11$ pairs

$\bar{d} = 982$ miles

$s_d = 1139.6$ miles

Make a picture. Sketch a t-model centered at the hypothesized mean of 0. Because this is a two-tail test, shade both the region to the right of the observed mean difference of 982 miles and the corresponding region in the lower tail.

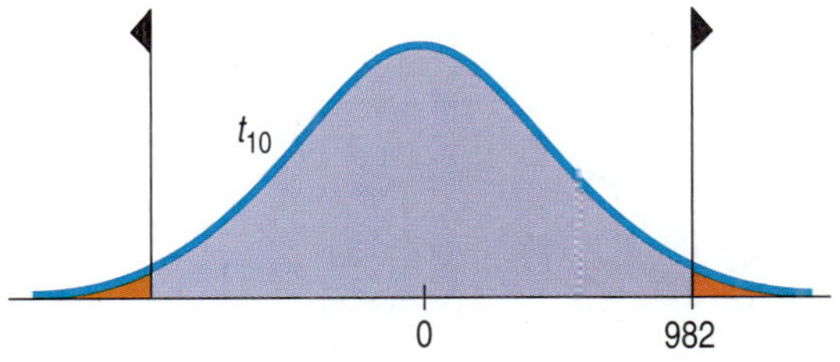

Find the standard error, and the t-score of the observed mean difference. There is nothing new in the mechanics of the paired-t methods. These are the mechanics of the t-test for a mean applied to the differences. Find the P-value, using technology.

We estimate the standard deviation of $\bar{d}$ using:

$$SE(\bar{d}) = \frac{s_d}{\sqrt{n}} = \frac{1139.6}{\sqrt{11}} = 343.6.$$

$$t_{10} = \frac{\bar{d} - 0}{SE(\bar{d})} = \frac{982.0}{343.6} = 2.86.$$

$$P = 2P(t_{10} > 2.86) = 0.017.$$

The P-value is 0.017.

✓ Reality Check

The mean difference is 982 miles. That's more than twice the SE of 344, so it looks like the change is real. The t-value of 2.86 and P-value of 0.017 are consistent with that.

Tell **Interpretation** Link the P-value to your decision about H_0, and state your conclusion in context.

With a P-value this small, we can reject the null hypothesis. We conclude that the change in work week did lead to a change in driving mileage.

If possible, propose a course of action.

Without a confidence interval, it's hard to know whether the difference in mileage is important in the sense of reducing air pollution or cost, or is merely statistically significant. So we should look at a confidence interval. If the difference in mileage proves to be large in a practical sense, then we might recommend a change in schedule for the rest of the department.

TI Tips

Since the inference procedures for matched data are essentially just the one-sample *t* procedures, you already know what to do . . . once you have the list of paired differences, that is. That list is not hard to create.

Test a hypothesis about the mean of paired differences.

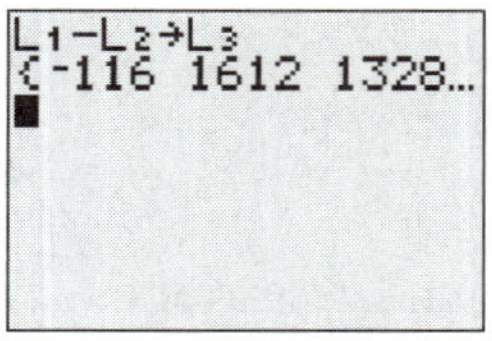

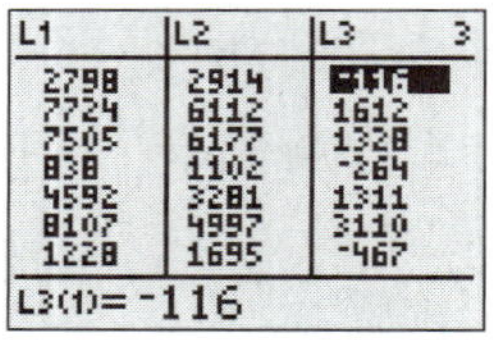

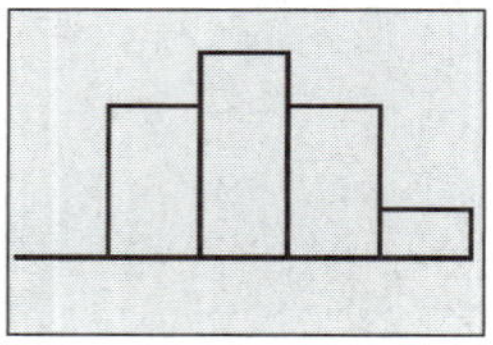

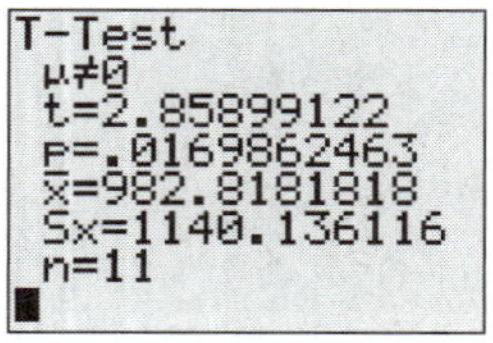

- Think: Are the samples independent or paired. Independent? Go back to the last chapter! Paired? Read on.
- Enter the driving data from page 491 into two lists, say 5-day mileage in `L1`, 4-day mileage in `L2`.
- Create a list of the differences. We want to take each value in `L1`, subtract the corresponding value in `L2`, and store the paired difference in `L3`. The command is `L1-L2→L3`. (The arrow is the `STO` button.) Now take a look at `L3`. See—it worked!
- Make a histogram of the differences, `L3`, to check the nearly Normal condition. Notice that we do not look at the histograms of the 5-day mileage or the 4-day mileage. Those are not the data that we care about now that we are using a paired procedure. Note also that the calculator's first histogram is not close to Normal. More work to do . . .
- As you have seen before, small samples often produce ragged histograms, and these may look very different after a change in bar width. Reset the `WINDOW to Xmin=-3000`, `Xmax=4500`, and `Xscl=1500`. The new histogram looks okay.
- Under `STAT TESTS` simply use `2:T-Test`, as you've done before for hypothesis tests about a mean.
- Specify that the hypothesized difference is 0, you're using the `Data` in `L3`, and it's a two-tailed test.
- `Calculate`.

The small P-value shows strong evidence that the change in the work week reduces the number of miles workers drive.

Confidence Intervals for Matched Pairs

WHO	170 Randomly sampled couples
WHAT	Ages
WHEN	Recently
WHERE	Britain

In developed countries, the average age of women is generally higher than that of men. After all, women tend to live longer. But if we look at *married couples,* husbands tend to be slightly older than wives. How much older on average are husbands? We have data from a random sample of 200 British couples, the first 16 of which are shown below. Only 170 couples provided ages for both husband and wife, so we can work only with that many pairs. Let's form a confidence interval for the mean difference of husband's and wife's age for these 170 couples. Here are the first 16 pairs:

Wife's Age	Husband's Age
43	49
28	25
30	40
57	52
52	58
27	32
52	43
43	47
23	31
25	26
39	40
32	35
35	35
33	35
43	47
35	38
⋮	⋮

These data are obviously paired. The survey selected couples at random, not individuals. We're interested in the mean age difference within couples. How would we construct a confidence interval for the true mean difference in ages?

Paired *t*-interval

When the conditions are met, we are ready to find the confidence interval for the mean of the paired differences. Since the standard error of the mean difference is

$$SE(\bar{d}) = \frac{s_d}{\sqrt{n}},$$

the confidence interval is $\bar{d} \pm t^*_{n-1} \times SE(\bar{d})$. The critical value t^* depends on the particular confidence level, C, that you specify and on the degrees of freedom, $n - 1$, which is based on the number of pairs, n.

A Paired *t*-Interval STEP-BY-STEP

Making confidence intervals for matched pairs follows exactly the steps for a one-sample *t*-interval.

Think

Parameter Identify the parameter you wish to estimate.

For a paired analysis, the parameter of interest is the mean of the differences. The population of interest is the population of differences.

✓ Reality Check The histogram shows husbands are often older than wives (because most of the differences are greater than 0). The mean difference seen here of about 2 years is reasonable.

We wish to find an interval that is likely with 95% confidence to contain μ_d, the true mean difference in ages of husbands and wives.

Plan Check the conditions.

✓ **Paired data assumption:** The data are paired because they are on members of married couples.

✓ **Randomization condition:** These couples were randomly sampled.

✓ **10% condition:** The sample is less than 10% of the population of married couples in Britain.

✓ **Nearly Normal condition:** The histogram of the husband-wife differences is unimodal and symmetric.

State the sampling distribution model for the statistic.

Under these conditions the sampling distribution of the differences can be modeled by a Student's *t*-model with $(n - 1) = 169$ degrees of freedom.

Choose your method.

We will find a **paired *t*-interval.**

Show

Mechanics

n is the number of *pairs*, here, the number of couples.

$\bar{d}$ is the mean difference.

s_d is the standard deviation of the differences.

$n = 170$ couples

$\bar{d} = 2.2$ years

$s_d = 4.1$ years

We estimate the standard error of $\bar{d}$ as:

$$SE(\bar{d}) = \frac{s_d}{\sqrt{n}} = \frac{4.1}{\sqrt{170}} = 0.31 \text{ years.}$$

Be sure to include the units along with the statistics.

The *df* for the *t*-model is $n - 1 = 169$

The 95% critical value for t_{169} (from the table) is 1.97

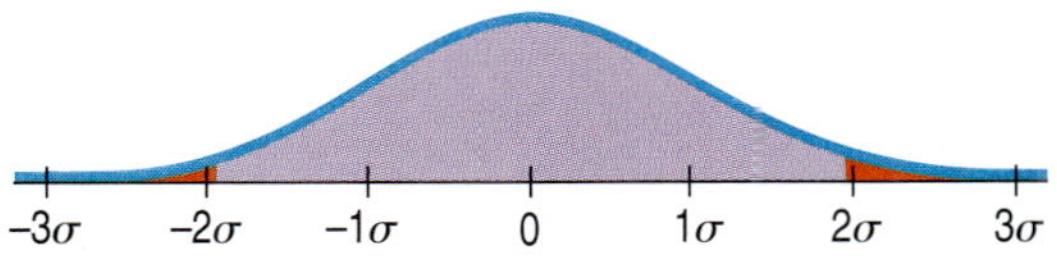

The critical value we need to make a 95% interval comes from a Student's *t* table, a computer program, or a calculator.

From these, we find the margin of error to be

$$ME = t^*_{169} \times SE(\bar{d}) = 1.97(0.31) = 0.61$$

So the 95% confidence interval is:

$$2.2 \pm 0.6 \text{ years,}$$

or an interval of (1.6, 2.8) years.

✓ Reality Check This result makes sense. Our everyday experience confirms that an age difference of about 2 years is reasonable.

Tell

Interpretation Tell what the confidence interval means.

We are 95% confident that in married couples in Britain, the husband is, on average, between 1.6 and 2.8 years older than his wife.

TI Tips

Now let's get the TI to create a confidence interval for the mean of paired differences.

We'll demonstrate by using the statistics about the ages of the British married couples. (If we had all the data, we could enter that, of course. All 170 couples? Um, no thanks.) The husbands in the sample were an average of 2.2 years older than their wives, with a standard deviation of 4.1 years. We've already seen that the data are paired, and that a histogram of the differences satisfies the nearly Normal condition. (With a sample this large, we could proceed with inference even if we didn't have the actual data and were unable to make the histogram.)

- Once again, we treat the paired differences just like data from one sample. A confidence interval for the mean difference, then, like that for a mean, uses the `STAT TESTS` one-sample procedure `8:TInterval`.
- Specify `Inpt:Stats` and enter the statistics for the paired differences.
- `Calculate`.

Done. Finding the interval was the easy part. Now it's time for you to Tell what it means. Don't forget to talk about married couples in Britain.

Blocking

Because the sample includes both older and younger couples, there's a lot of variation in the ages of the men and in the ages of the women. In fact, that variation is so great that a boxplot of the two groups would show no difference. But that would be the wrong plot. It's the difference we care about. Pairing removes the extra variation and allows us to focus on the individual differences. In experi-

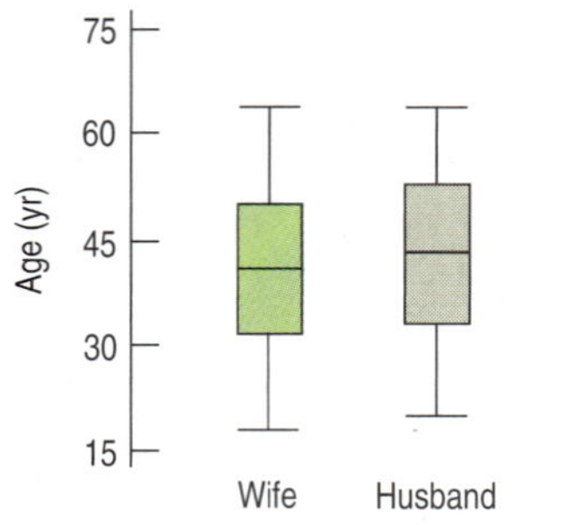

This display is worthless. It does no good to compare all the wives as a group with all the husbands. We care about the paired differences.

Figure 25.2

ments, we block to separate the variability between the experimental units from the variability in the response.

When we pair, we have roughly half the degrees of freedom of a two-sample test. You may see discussions that suggest that in "choosing" a paired analysis we "give up" these degrees of freedom. This isn't really true, though. If the data are paired, then there never were additional degrees of freedom, and we have no "choice." The fact of the pairing determines how many degrees of freedom are available.

Matching pairs generally removes so much extra variation that it more than compensates for having only half the degrees of freedom. Of course, inappropriate matching when the groups are in fact independent (say, by matching on the first letter of the last name of subjects) would cost degrees of freedom without the benefit of reducing the variance. When you design a study or experiment, you should use a paired design if possible.

What Can Go Wrong?

- ***Don't use a two-sample t-test for paired data.*** See the What Can Go Wrong discussion in Chapter 24.
- ***Don't use a paired-t method when the samples aren't paired.*** When two groups don't have the same number of values, it's pretty easy to see that they can't be paired. But just because two groups have the same number of observations doesn't mean they can be paired even if they are shown side-by-side in a table. We might have 25 men and 25 women in our study, but they might be completely independent of one another. If they were siblings or spouses, we might consider them paired. Remember that you cannot *choose* which method to use based on your preferences. If the data are from two independent samples, use two-sample t methods. If the data are from an experiment in which observations were paired, you must use a paired method. If the data are from an observational study, you must be able to defend your choice to use matched pairs.
- ***Don't forget outliers.*** The outliers we care about now are in the differences. A subject who is extraordinary both before and after a treatment may still have a perfectly typical difference. But one outlying difference can completely distort your conclusions. Be sure to plot the differences (even if you also plot the data).
- ***Don't look for the difference in side-by-side boxplots.*** The point of the paired analysis is to remove extra variation. The boxplots of each group still contain that variation. Comparing them is likely to be misleading. A scatterplot of the two variables can sometimes be helpful.

Paired t and the Computer

Most statistics programs can compute paired t analyses. Some may want you to find the differences yourself and use the one-sample t methods. Those that perform the entire procedure will need to know the two variables to compare. The computer, of course, cannot verify that the variables are naturally paired. Most programs will check whether the two variables have the same number of observations, but some stop there, and that can cause trouble. (See the comments on individual packages for details.) Most programs will automatically omit any pair that is missing a value for either variable (as we did with the British couples). You must look carefully to see whether that has happened.

Computers make it easy to examine the boxplots of the two groups[1] and the histogram of the differences—both important steps. Some programs offer a scatterplot of the two variables. That can be helpful. In terms of the scatterplot, a paired *t*-test is about whether the points tend to be above or below the 45° line $y = x$.

As we've seen with other inference results, some packages stack a lot of information into a simple table, but you must locate what you want for yourself. Here's a generic example with comments:

Could be called "Matched Pair" or "Paired-t" analysis

Individual group means

Mean of the differences and its SE

Paired t-statistic

```
Matched Pairs

Group 1 Mean      42.6231     t-Ratio      7.151783
Group 2 Mean      40.6824     DF           169
Mean Difference   2.23529     Prob > |t|   <0.0001
Std Error         0.31255     Prob > t     <0.0001
Upper 95%         2.85230     Prob < t     1.0000
Lower 95%         1.61829
N                 170
Correlation       0.93858
```

Its df

P-values for: Two-sided One-sided alternatives

Corresponding confidence interval bounds on the mean difference.

Correlation is often reported. Be careful. We have not checked for nonlinearity or outlying pairs. Either could make the correlation meaningless, even though the paired t was still appropriate.

Other packages try to be more descriptive. It may be easier to find the results, but you may get less information from the output table:

Groups may be missing values. Only cases with both values present are used. You may not learn that from some packages.

Even simple tables can have superfluous numbers such as these.

```
Paired T for hAge-Wage

                      N     Mean    Std Dev   SE(Mean)

hAge                 199    42.62   11.646    0.8255
wAge                 170    40.68   11.414    0.8254
Paired Difference    170     2.235   4.0752   0.31255

95% CI for mean difference: (1.618, 2.852)
T-Test of mean difference = 0(vs ≠ 0): T-Value = 7.1518 P-Value < 0.0001
```

CI corresponds to specified α.

Some packages let you specify the alternative and report only results for that alternative.

t-statistic and its P-value

(You may need to calculate $n_d - 1$ for yourself to get the df.)

[1] Even though our concern is with the differences of the pairs, you should examine the boxplots of the two groups separately so you are aware of any outliers.

Connections

The most important connection is to the concept of blocking that we first discussed when we considered designed experiments in Chapter 13. Pairing is a basic and very effective form of blocking.

Of course, the details of the mechanics for both tests and intervals are identical to those for the one-sample *t* methods. Everything we know about those methods applies here.

The connection to the two-sample and pooled methods of the previous chapter is that when the data are naturally paired, those methods are not appropriate because paired data fail the required condition of independence.

Key Concepts

Paired data

Data are paired when the observations are collected in pairs or the observations in one group are naturally related to observations in the other.

The simplest form of pairing is to measure each subject twice—often before and after a treatment is applied. More sophisticated forms of pairing in experiments are a form of blocking and arise in other contexts.

Paired *t*-test

A hypothesis test for the mean of the pairwise differences of two groups. It tests the null hypothesis

$$H_0: \mu_d = \Delta_0,$$

where the hypothesized difference is almost always 0, using the statistic

$$t = \frac{\bar{d} - \Delta_0}{SE(\bar{d})}$$

with $n - 1$ degrees of freedom, where

$$SE(\bar{d}) = \frac{s_d}{\sqrt{n}} \text{ and } n \text{ is the number of pairs.}$$

Paired-*t* confidence interval

A confidence interval for the mean of the pairwise differences between independent groups found as

$$\bar{d} \pm t^*_{n-1} \times SE(\bar{d}), \text{ where } SE(\bar{d}) = \frac{s_d}{\sqrt{n}} \text{ and } n \text{ is the number of pairs.}$$

Skills

When you complete this lesson you should:

Think

- Be able to recognize whether a design that compares two groups is paired or not.

Show

- Be able to find a paired confidence interval, recognizing that it is mechanically equivalent to doing a one-sample *t*-interval applied to the differences.
- Be able to perform a paired *t*-test, recognizing that it is mechanically equivalent to a one-sample *t*-test applied to the differences.

Tell

- Be able to interpret a paired *t*-test, recognizing that the hypothesis tested is about the mean of the differences between paired values rather than about the differences between the means of two independent groups.

Exercises

1. More eggs? Can a food additive increase egg production? Agricultural researchers want to design an experiment to find out. They have 100 hens available. They have two kinds of feed—the regular feed and the new feed with the additive. They plan to run their experiment for a month, recording the number of eggs each hen produces.

a) Design an experiment that will require a two-sample t-procedure to analyze the results.

b) Design an experiment that will require a matched-pairs t-procedure to analyze the results.

c) Which experiment would you consider the stronger design? Why?

2. MTV. Some students do homework with the TV on. (Anyone come to mind?) Some researchers want to see if people can work as effectively with as without distraction. The researchers will time some volunteers to see how long it takes them to complete some relatively easy crossword puzzles. During some of the trials, the room will be quiet, during other trials in the same room, a TV will be on, tuned to MTV.

a) Design an experiment that will require a two-sample t-procedure to analyze the results.

b) Design an experiment that will require a matched-pairs t-procedure to analyze the results.

c) Which experiment would you consider the stronger design? Why?

3. Women. Values for the labor force participation rate of women (LFPR) are published by the U.S. Bureau of Labor Statistics. We are interested in whether there was a difference between female participation in 1968 and 1972, a time of rapid change for women. We check LFPR values for 19 randomly selected cities for 1968 and 1972. Shown below is software output for two possible tests.

Paired t-Test of μ(1 − 2)
Test Ho: μ(1972-1968) = 0 vs Ha: μ(1972-1968) ≠ 0
Mean of Paired Differences = 0.0337
t-Statistic = 2.458 w/18 df
p = 0.0244

2-Sample t-Test of μ1 − μ2
Ho: μ1 − μ2 = 0 Ha: μ1 − μ2 ≠ 0
Test Ho: μ(1972) − μ(1968) = 0 vs
Ha: μ(1972) − μ(1968) ≠ 0
Difference Between Means = 0.0337
t-Statistic = 1.496 w/35 df
p = 0.1434

a) Which of these tests is appropriate for these data? Explain.

b) Using the test you selected, state your conclusion.

4. BST. Many dairy cows now receive injections of BST, a hormone intended to spur greater milk production. After the first injection, a test herd of 60 Ayrshire cows increased their mean daily production from 47 pounds to 61 pounds of milk. The standard deviation of the increases was 5.2 pounds. We want to estimate the mean increase a farmer could expect in his own cows.

a) Check the assumptions and conditions for inference.

b) Write a 95% confidence interval.

c) Explain what your interval means in this context.

d) Given the cost of BST, a farmer believes he cannot afford to use it unless he is sure of attaining at least a 25% increase in milk production. Based on your confidence interval, what advice would you give him?

5. Rain. Simpson, Alsen, and Eden (*Technometrics* 1975) report the results of trials in which clouds were seeded and the amount of rainfall recorded. The authors report on 26 seeded and 26 unseeded clouds in order of the amount of rainfall, largest amount first. Here are two possible tests to study the question of whether cloud seeding works. Which test is appropriate for these data? Explain your choice. Using the test you select, state your conclusion.

Paired t-Test of μ(1 − 2)
Mean of Paired Differences = −277.39615
t-Statistic = −3.641 w/25 df
p = 0.0012

2-Sample t-Test of μ1 − μ2
Difference Between Means = −277.4
t-Statistic = −1.998 w/33 df
p = 0.0538

a) Which of these tests is appropriate for these data? Explain.

b) Using the test you selected, state your conclusion.

6. BST II. In the experiment about hormone injections in cows described in Exercise 4, a group of 52 Jersey cows increased average milk production from 43 pounds to 52 pounds per day, with a standard deviation of 4.8 pounds. Is this evidence that the hormone may be more effective in one breed than the other? Test an appropriate hypothesis and state your conclusion. Be sure to discuss any assumptions you make.

T **7. Temperatures.** The table below gives the average high temperatures in January and July for several European cities. Write a 90% confidence interval for the mean temperature difference between summer and winter in

Europe. Be sure to check conditions for inference, and clearly explain what your interval means.

MEAN HIGH TEMPERATURES (°F)

City	Jan.	July
Vienna	34	75
Copenhagen	36	72
Paris	42	76
Berlin	35	74
Athens	54	90
Rome	54	88
Amsterdam	40	69
Madrid	47	87
London	44	73
Edinburgh	43	65
Moscow	21	76
Belgrade	37	84

T **8. Marathons.** Shown are the winning times (in minutes) for men and women in the New York City Marathon between 1978 and 1998. Assuming that performances in the Big Apple resemble performances elsewhere, we can think of these data as a sample of performance in marathon competitions. Create a 90% confidence interval for the mean difference in winning times for male and female marathon competitors. (*Chance*, 12, no. 4, [1999])

Year	Men	Women
1978	132.2	152.5
1979	131.7	147.6
1980	129.7	145.7
1981	128.2	145.5
1982	129.5	147.2
1983	129.0	147.0
1984	134.9	149.5
1985	131.6	148.6
1986	131.1	148.1
1987	131.0	150.3
1988	128.3	148.1
1989	128.0	145.5
1990	132.7	150.8
1991	129.5	147.5
1992	129.5	144.7
1993	130.1	146.4
1994	131.4	147.6
1995	131.0	148.1
1996	129.9	148.3
1997	128.2	148.7
1998	128.8	145.3

9. Push-ups. Every year the students at Gossett High School take a physical fitness test during their gym classes. One component of the test asks them to do as many push-ups as they can. Results for one class are shown below, according to gender. Assuming that students at Gossett are assigned to gym classes at random, create a 90% confidence interval for how many more pushups boys can do than girls, on average, at that high school.

Boys	17	27	31	17	25	32	28	23	25	16	11	34
Girls	24	7	14	16	2	15	19	25	10	27	31	8

10. Exercise. An August 2001 article in the journal *Medicine and Science in Sports and Exercise* compared how long it would take men and women to burn 200 calories during light or heavy workouts on various kinds of exercise equipment. The results summarized in the table are the average times for a group of physically active young men and women whose performances were measured on each type of equipment.

a) On average, how many minutes longer than a man must a woman exercise at a light exertion rate in order to burn 200 calories? Give a 95% confidence interval.

b) Estimate the average number of minutes longer a woman must work out at light exertion than at heavy exertion to get the same benefit. Give a 95% confidence interval.

c) These data are actually averages rather than individual times. How might this affect the margins of error in these confidence intervals?

AVERAGE MINUTES TO BURN 200 CALORIES

Machine Type	Hard Exertion		Light Exertion	
	Men	Women	Men	Women
Treadmill	12	17	14	22
X-C skier	12	16	16	23
Stair climber	13	18	20	37
Rowing machine	14	16	21	25
Exercise rider	22	24	27	36
Exercise bike	16	20	29	44

11. Job satisfaction. (When you first read about this exercise break plan in Chapter 24 you did not have an inference method that would work. Try again now.) A company institutes an exercise break for its workers to see if this will improve job satisfaction, as measured by a questionnaire that assesses workers'satisfaction. Scores for 10 randomly selected workers before and after the implementation of the exercise program are shown.

a) Identify the procedure you would use to assess the effectiveness of the exercise program, and check to see if the conditions allow use of that procedure.
b) Test an appropriate hypothesis and state your conclusion.

Worker number	Job satisfaction index	
	Before	After
1	34	33
2	28	36
3	29	50
4	45	41
5	26	37
6	27	41
7	24	39
8	15	21
9	15	20
10	27	37

12. Summer school. (When you first read about the summer school issue in Chapter 24 you did not have an inference method that would work. Try again now.) Having done poorly on their math final exams in June, six students repeat the course in summer school and take another exam in August. If we consider these students to be representative of all students who might attend this summer school in other years, do these results provide evidence that the program is worthwhile?

June	54	49	68	66	62	62
Aug.	50	65	74	64	68	72

13. Sleep. W. S. Gosset (Student) refers to data recording the number of hours of additional sleep gained by 10 patients from the use of *laevohysocyamine hydrobromide*. We want to see if there is strong evidence that the herb can help people get more sleep.
a) State the null and alternative hypotheses clearly.
b) A t-test of the null hypothesis of no gain has a t-statistic of 3.680 with 9 degrees of freedom. Find the P-value.
c) Interpret this result by explaining the meaning of the P-value.
d) State your conclusion regarding the hypotheses.
e) This conclusion, of course, may be incorrect. If so, which type of error was made?

14. Gasoline. Many drivers of cars that can run on regular gas actually buy premium in the belief that they will get better gas mileage. To test that belief, we use 10 cars in a company fleet in which all the cars run on regular gas. Each car is filled first with either regular or premium gasoline, decided by a coin toss, and the mileage for that tankful recorded. Then the mileage is recorded again for the same cars for a tankful of the other kind of gasoline. We don't let the drivers know about this experiment. Here are the results (miles per gallon):

Car #	1	2	3	4	5	6	7	8	9	10
Regular	16	20	21	22	23	22	27	25	27	28
Premium	19	22	24	24	25	25	26	26	28	32

a) Is there evidence that cars get significantly better fuel economy with premium gasoline?
b) How big might that difference be? Check a 90% confidence interval.
c) Even if the difference is significant, why might the company choose to stick with regular gasoline?
d) Suppose you had done a Bad Thing. (We're sure you didn't.) Suppose you had mistakenly treated these data as two independent samples instead of matched pairs. What would the significance test have found? Carefully explain why the results are so different.

15. Yogurt. Do these data suggest that there is a significant difference in calories between servings of strawberry and vanilla yogurt? Test an appropriate hypothesis and state your conclusion. Don't forget to check assumptions and conditions!

CALORIES PER SERVING

Brand	Strawberry	Vanilla
America's Choice	210	200
Breyer's Lowfat	220	220
Columbo	220	180
Dannon Light 'n Fit	120	120
Dannon Lowfat	210	230
Dannon laCreme	140	140
Great Value	180	80
La Yogurt	170	160
Mountain High	200	170
Stonyfield Farm	100	120
Yoplait Custard	190	190
Yoplait Light	100	100

16. Caffeine. A student experiment investigating the potential impact of caffeine on studying for a test involved 30 subjects, randomly divided into two groups. Each group took a memory test. The subjects then each drank two cups of regular (caffeinated) cola or caffeine-free cola. Thirty minutes later they each took another version of the memory test, and the changes in their scores were noted. Among the 15 subjects who drank caffeine, scores fell an average of -0.933 points, with a standard deviation of 2.988 points. Among the no-caffeine group, scores went up an average of 1.429 points with a standard deviation of 2.441 points. Assumptions of Normality were deemed reasonable based on histograms of differences in scores.

a) Did scores change significantly for the group who drank caffeine? Test an appropriate hypothesis and state your conclusion.
b) Did scores change significantly for the no-caffeine group? Test an appropriate hypothesis and state your conclusion.
c) Does this indicate that some mystery substance in noncaffeinated soda may aid memory? What other explanation is plausible?

17. Braking. In a test of braking performance, a tire manufacturer measured the stopping distance for one of its tire models. On a test track, a car made repeated stops from 60 miles per hour. The test was run on both dry and wet pavement, with results as shown in the table. (Note that actual *braking distance,* which takes into account the driver's reaction time, is much longer, typically nearly 300 feet at 60 mph!)

a) Write a 95% confidence interval for the mean dry pavement stopping distance. Be sure to check the appropriate assumptions and conditions, and explain what your interval means.
b) Write a 95% confidence interval for the mean increase in stopping distance on wet pavement. Be sure to check the appropriate assumptions and conditions, and explain what your interval means.

STOPPING DISTANCE (FT)

Dry pavement	Wet pavement
145	211
152	191
141	220
143	207
131	198
148	208
126	206
140	177
135	183
133	223

18. Brain waves. An experiment was performed to see whether sensory deprivation over an extended period of time has any effect on the alpha-wave patterns produced by the brain. To determine this, 20 subjects, inmates in a Canadian prison, were randomly split into two groups. Members of one group were placed in solitary confinement. Those in the other group were allowed to remain in their own cells. Seven days later, alpha-wave frequencies were measured for all subjects, as shown in the following table (P. Gendreau et al., "Changes in EEG Alpha Frequency and Evoked Response Latency During Solitary Confinement," *Journal of Abnormal Psychology* 79 [1972]: 54–59):

Nonconfined	Confined
10.7	9.6
10.7	10.4
10.4	9.7
10.9	10.3
10.5	9.2
10.3	9.3
9.6	9.9
11.1	9.5
11.2	9.0
10.4	10.9

a) What are the null and alternative hypotheses? Be sure to define all the terms and symbols you use.
b) Are the assumptions necessary for inference met?
c) Perform the appropriate test, indicating the formula you used, the calculated value of the test statistic, and the P-value.
d) State your conclusion.

19. Braking, test 2. For another test of the tires in Exercise 17, the company tried them on 10 different cars, recording the stopping distance for each car on both wet and dry pavement. Results are shown in the table.

STOPPING DISTANCE (FT)

Car #	Dry pavement	Wet pavement
1	150	201
2	147	220
3	136	192
4	134	146
5	130	182
6	134	173
7	134	202
8	128	180
9	136	192
10	158	206

a) Write a 95% confidence interval for the mean dry pavement stopping distance. Be sure to check the appropriate assumptions and conditions, and explain what your interval means.
b) Write a 95% confidence interval for the mean increase in stopping distance on wet pavement. Be sure to check the appropriate assumptions and conditions, and explain what your interval means.

20. Tuition. How much more do public colleges and universities charge out-of-state students for tuition per semester? A random sample of 19 public colleges and universities listed in the *Information Please Almanac* found the data shown below. Tuition figures per semester are rounded to the nearest hundred dollars.

Institution	Resident	Nonresident
U Akron (OH)	3200	7900
Athens State (GA)	3800	7500
Ball State (IN)	3000	7800
Bloomsburg U (PA)	3700	8500
UC Irvine (CA)	4300	12,000
Central State (OH)	2900	6400
Clarion U (PA)	3900	8600
Dakota State	2500	4600
Fairmont State (WV)	1800	4500
Johnson State (VT)	4000	8600
Lock Haven U (PA)	7400	12,100
New College of S. Fla.	2000	7900
Oakland U (MI)	3100	8700
U Pittsburgh	5400	11,200
Savannah State (GA)	2000	5200
SW Louisiana	1900	4900
W Liberty State (WV)	1900	4500
W Texas State	1600	6000
Worcester State (MA)	2700	6200

a) Create a 90% confidence interval for the mean difference in cost. Be sure to justify the procedure you use.
b) Interpret your interval in context.
c) A national magazine claims that public institutions charge state residents an average of $4000 less for tuition each semester. What does your confidence interval indicate about the validity of this assertion?

21. Strikes. Advertisements for an instructional video claim that the techniques will improve the ability of Little League pitchers to throw strikes, and that, after undergoing the training, players will be able to throw strikes on at least 60% of their pitches. To test this claim, we have 20 Little Leaguers throw 50 pitches each, and we record the number of strikes. After the players participate in the training program, we repeat the test. The table shows the number of strikes each player threw before and after the training.
a) Is there evidence that after training players can throw strikes more than 60% of the time?
b) Is there evidence that the training is effective in improving a player's ability to throw strikes?

Number of strikes (out of 50)		Number of strikes (out of 50)	
Before	**After**	**Before**	**After**
28	35	33	33
29	36	33	35
30	32	34	32
32	28	34	30
32	30	34	33
32	31	35	34
32	32	36	37
32	34	36	33
32	35	37	35
33	36	37	32

22. Uninsured. During the economic recession of 2000–2001, unemployment increased and job benefits were scaled back. The table shows the percentage of people in each state who lacked health insurance during the years '99-'00 and '00-'01, as reported by the U.S. Census Bureau. Is there any evidence that more people were without health insurance during the recession?

State	'99–'00	'00–'01	State	'99–'00	'00–'01
AL	13.3	13.2	MT	17.3	15.2
AK	18.6	17.3	NE	17.7	16.5
AZ	18.6	17.3	NV	17.7	16.5
AR	14.4	15.2	NH	8.7	8.9
CA	19.0	19.0	NJ	12.1	12.6
CO	14.9	14.9	NM	24.4	22.4
CT	9.4	10.0	NY	15.9	15.9
DE	9.6	9.2	NC	14.0	14.0
DC	14.1	13.4	ND	11.5	10.5
FL	17.6	17.9	OH	10.7	11.2
GA	14.7	15.5	OK	17.7	18.6
HI	9.8	9.5	OR	13.3	12.7
ID	16.8	15.7	PA	8.5	9.0
IL	13.6	13.7	RI	6.9	7.6
IN	10.3	11.5	SC	13.8	12.2
IA	8.2	8.2	SD	10.9	10.2
KS	11.4	11.1	TN	10.6	11.1
KY	13.4	13.0	TX	22.7	23.2
LA	19.9	18.7	UT	13.0	13.7
ME	10.8	10.6	VT	9.8	9.1
MD	10.8	11.3	VA	12.4	11.3
MA	9.0	8.5	WA	13.7	13.3
MI	9.7	9.8	WV	14.7	13.6
MN	7.8	8.1	WI	8.9	7.6
MS	14.6	15.0	WY	15.4	15.8
MO	8.1	9.9			

Review of Part VI Learning About the World

Quick Review

We continue to explore how to answer questions about the statistics we get from samples and experiments. In this Part, those questions have been about means—means of one sample, two independent samples, or matched pairs. Here's a brief summary of the key concepts and skills:

- A confidence interval uses a sample statistic to estimate a range of possible values for the parameter of a population model.
- A hypothesis test proposes a model for the population, then examines the observed statistics to see if the model is plausible.
- Statistical inference procedures for proportions are based on the Central Limit Theorem. We can make inferences about a single proportion or the difference of two proportions using Normal models.
- Statistical inference procedures for means are also based on the Central Limit Theorem, but we don't usually know the population standard deviation. Student's *t*-models take the additional uncertainty of independently estimating the standard deviation into account.
    - We can make inferences about one mean, the difference of two independent means, or the mean of paired differences using *t*-models.
    - No inference procedure is valid unless the underlying assumptions are true. Always check the conditions before proceeding.
    - Because *t*-models assume that samples are drawn from Normal populations, data in the sample should appear to be nearly normal. Skewness and outliers are particularly problematic.
    - When there are two variables, you must think carefully about how the data were collected. You may use two-sample *t* procedures only if the groups are independent.
    - Unless there is some obvious reason to suspect that two independent populations have the same standard deviation, you should not pool the variances. It is never wrong to use unpooled *t* procedures.
    - If the two groups are somehow paired, the data are *not* from independent groups. You must use matched-pairs *t* procedures.

Now for some opportunities to review these concepts. Be careful. You have a lot of thinking to do. These review exercises mix questions about proportions and means. You have to determine which of our inference procedures is appropriate in each situation. Then you have to check the proper assumptions and conditions. Keeping track of those can be difficult, so first we summarize the many procedures (including, for completeness, some we'll see in the next two chapters) with their corresponding assumptions and conditions on the next page. Look them over carefully . . . then, on to the Exercises!

Assumptions for Inference	And the Conditions That Support or Override Them
Proportions (z)	
• **One sample**	
1. Individuals are independent.	1. SRS and < 10% of the population.
2. Sample is sufficiently large.	2. Successes and failures ≥ 10.
• **Two sample**	
1. Samples are independent.	1. (Think about how the data were collected.)
2. Data in each sample are independent.	2. Both are SRSs and < 10% of populations OR random allocation.
3. Both samples are sufficiently large.	3. Successes and failures ≥ 10 for both.
Means (t)	
• **One sample** (df = $n - 1$)	
1. Individuals are independent.	1. SRS and < 10% of the population.
2. Population has a Normal model.	2. Histogram is unimodal and symmetric*.
• **Matched pairs** (df = $n - 1$)	
1. Data are matched.	1. (Think about the design.)
2. Individuals are independent.	2. SRS and < 10% OR random allocation.
3. Population of differences is Normal.	3. Histogram of differences is unimodal and symmetric.
• **Two independent samples** (df from technology)	
1. Samples are independent.	1. (Think about the design.)
2. Data in each sample are independent.	2. SRSs and < 10% OR random allocation.
3. Both populations are Normal.	3. Both histograms are unimodal and symmetric.*
(Coming soon in Chapters 26 and 27)	
Distributions/Association (χ^2)	
• **Goodness of fit** (df = # of cells − 1; one variable, one sample compared with population model)	
1. Data are counts.	1. (Are they?)
2. Data in sample are independent.	2. SRS and < 10% of the population.
3. Sample is sufficiently large.	3. All expected counts ≥ 5.
• **Homogeneity** [df = $(r - 1)(c - 1)$; samples from many populations compared on one variable]	
1. Data are counts.	1. (Are they?)
2. Data in samples are independent.	2. SRSs and < 10% OR random allocation.
3. Samples are sufficiently large.	3. all expected counts ≥5.
• **Independence** [df = $(r - 1)(c - 1)$; sample from one population classified on two variables]	
1. Data are counts.	1. (Are they?)
2. Data are independent.	2. SRSs and < 10% of the population.
3. Sample is sufficiently large.	3. All expected counts ≥ 5.
Regression (t, df = $n - 2$)	
• **Association** between two measurement variables ($\beta = 0$?)	
1. Form of relationship is linear.	1. Scatterplot looks approximately linear.
2. Errors are independent.	2. No apparent pattern in residuals plot.
3. Variability of errors is constant.	3. Residuals plot has consistent spread.
4. Errors have a Normal model.	4. Histogram of residuals is approximately unimodal and symmetric, or Normal probability plot reasonably straight.*

(*less critical as n increases)

Review Exercises

1. Crawling. A study published in 1993 found that babies born at different times of the year may develop the ability to crawl at different ages! The author of the study suggested that these differences may be related to the temperature at the time the infant is 6 months old. (Benson and Janette, *Infant Behavior and Development* [1993])

a) The study found that 32 babies born in January crawled at an average age of 29.84 weeks, with a standard deviation of 7.08 weeks. Among 21 July babies, crawling ages averaged 33.64 weeks with a standard deviation of 6.91 weeks. Is this difference significant?

b) For 26 babies born in April, the mean and standard deviation were 31.84 and 6.21 weeks, while for 44 October babies the mean and standard deviation of crawling ages were 33.35 and 7.29 weeks. Is this difference significant?

c) Are these results consistent with the researcher's claim? (We'll examine these data in more detail in a later chapter.)

2. Mazes and smells. Can pleasant smells improve learning? Researchers timed 21 subjects as they tried to complete paper-and-pencil mazes. Each subject attempted a maze both with and without the presence of a floral aroma. Subjects were randomized with respect to whether they did the scented trial first or second. Some of the data collected are shown in the table. Is there any evidence that the floral scent improved the subjects' ability to complete the mazes? (A. R. Hirsch and L. H. Johnston, "Odors and Learning." Chicago: Smell and Taste Treatment and Research Foundation)

TIME TO COMPLETE THE MAZE (SEC)

Unscented	Scented
25.7	30.2
41.9	56.7
51.9	42.4
32.2	34.4
64.7	44.8
31.4	42.9
40.1	42.7
43.2	24.8
33.9	25.1
40.4	59.2
58.0	42.2
61.5	48.4
44.6	32.0
35.3	48.1
37.2	33.7
39.4	42.6
77.4	54.9
52.8	64.5
63.6	43.1
56.6	52.8
58.9	44.3

3. Women. The U.S. Census Bureau reports that 26% of all U.S. businesses are owned by women. A Colorado consulting firm surveys a random sample of 410 businesses in the Denver area and finds that 115 of them have women owners. Should the firm conclude that its area is unusual? Test an appropriate hypothesis and state your conclusion.

4. Drugs. In a full-page ad that ran in many U.S. newspapers in August 2002, a Canadian discount pharmacy listed costs of drugs that could be ordered from a Web site in Canada. The table compares prices (in US$) for commonly prescribed drugs.

COST PER 100 PILLS

Drug Name	United States	Canada	Percent Savings
Cardizem	131	83	37
Celebrex	136	72	47
Cipro	374	219	41
Pravachol	370	166	55
Premarin	61	17	72
Prevacid	252	214	15
Prozac	263	112	57
Tamoxifen	349	50	86
Vioxx	243	134	45
Zantac	166	42	75
Zocor	365	200	45
Zoloft	216	105	51

a) Give a 95% confidence interval for the average savings in dollars.

b) Give a 95% confidence interval for the average savings in percent.

c) Which analysis do you think is more appropriate? Why?

d) In small print the newspaper ad says, "Complete list of all 1500 drugs available on request." How does this comment affect your conclusions above?

5. Pottery. Archaeologists can use the chemical composition of clay found in pottery artifacts to determine whether different sites were populated by the same ancient people. They collected five samples of Romano-British pottery from each of two sites in Great Britain—the Ashley Rails site and the New Forest site—and measured the percentage of aluminum oxide in each. Based on these data, do you think the same people used these two kiln sites? Base your conclusion on a 95% confidence interval for the difference in aluminum oxide content of pottery made at the sites. (A. Tubb, A. J. Parker, and G. Nickless, "The Analysis of Romano-British Pottery by Atomic Absorption Spectrophotometry." *Archaeometry*, 22[1980]: 153–171)

Ashley Rails	19.1	14.8	16.7	18.3	17.7
New Forest	20.8	18.0	18.0	15.8	18.3

6. Streams. Researchers in the Adirondack Mountains collect data on a random sample of streams each year. One of the variables recorded is the substrate of the stream—the type of soil and rock over which they flow. The researchers found that 69 of the 172 sampled streams had a substrate of shale. Construct a 95% confidence interval for the proportion of Adirondack streams with a shale substrate. Clearly interpret your interval in this context.

7. Gehrig. Ever since Lou Gehrig developed amyotrophic lateral sclerosis (ALS), this deadly condition has been commonly known as Lou Gehrig's disease. Some believe that ALS is more likely to strike athletes or the very fit. Columbia University neurologist Lewis P. Rowland recorded personal histories of 431 patients he examined between 1992 and 2002. He diagnosed 280 as having ALS; 38% of them had been varsity athletes. The other 151 had other neurological disorders, and only 26% of them had been varsity athletes. (*Science News*, Sept. 28 [2002])

a) Is there evidence that ALS is more common among athletes?

b) What kind of study is this? How does that affect the inference you made in part (a)?

8. Teen drinking. A study of the health behavior of school-aged children asked a sample of 15-year-olds in several different countries if they had been intoxicated at least twice. The results are shown in the table, by gender. Give a 95% confidence interval for the difference in the rates for males and females. Be sure to check the assumptions that support your chosen procedure, and explain what your interval means. (*Health and Health Behavior Among Young People.* Copenhagen: World Health Organization, 2000)

PERCENT OF 15-YEAR-OLDS DRUNK AT LEAST TWICE

Country	Female	Male
Denmark	63	71
Wales	63	72
Greenland	59	58
England	62	51
Finland	58	52
Scotland	56	53
No. Ireland	44	53
Slovakia	31	49
Austria	36	49
Canada	42	42
Sweden	40	40
Norway	41	37
Ireland	29	42
Germany	31	36
Latvia	23	47
Estonia	23	44
Hungary	22	43
Poland	21	39
USA	29	34
Czech Rep.	22	36
Belgium	22	36
Russia	25	32
Lithuania	20	32
France	20	29
Greece	21	24
Switzerland	16	25
Israel	10	18

9. Babies. The National Perinatal Statistics Unit of the Sydney Children's Hospital reports that the mean birth weight of all babies born in Australia in 1999 was 3360 grams—about 7.41 pounds. A Missouri hospital reports that the average weight of 112 babies born there last year was 7.68 pounds, with a standard deviation of 1.31 pounds. If we believe the Missouri babies fairly represent American newborns, is there any evidence that U.S. babies and Australian babies do not weigh the same amount at birth?

10. Petitions. To get a voter initiative on a state ballot, petitions that contain at least 250,000 valid voter signatures must be filed with the Elections Commission. The board then has 60 days to certify the petitions. A group wanting to create a statewide system of universal health insurance has just filed petitions with a total of 304,266 signatures. As a first step in the process, the Board selects an SRS of 2000 signatures and checks them against local voter lists. Only 1772 of them turn out to be valid.

a) What percent of the sample signatures were valid?

b) What percent of the petition signatures submitted must be valid in order to have the initiative certified by the Elections Commission?

c) What will happen if the Elections Commission commits a Type I error?

d) What will happen if the Elections Commission commits a Type II error?

e) Does the sample provide evidence in support of certification? Explain.

f) What could the Elections Commission do to increase the power of the test?

11. Feeding fish. In the midwestern United States, a large aquaculture industry raises largemouth bass. Researchers wanted to know whether the fish would grow better if fed a natural diet of fathead minnows or an artificial diet of food pellets. They stocked six ponds with bass fingerlings weighing about 8 grams. For one year, the fish in three of the ponds were fed minnows, and the others were fed the commercially prepared pellets. The fish were then harvested, weighed, and measured. The bass fed a natural food source had a higher average length (19.6 cm) and weight (95.9 g) than those fed the commercial fish food (17.3 cm and 72.0 g, respectively). The researchers reported P-values for both measurements to be less than 0.001.

a) Explain to someone who has not studied Statistics what the P-values mean here.

b) What advice should the researchers give the people who raise largemouth bass?

c) If that advice turns out to be incorrect, what type of error occurred?

12. Risk. A study of auto safety determined the number of driver deaths per million vehicle sales for the model years 1995–1999, classified by type of vehicle. The data below are for 6 midsize models and 6 SUVs. We wonder if there is evidence that drivers of SUVs are safer, hoping to create a 95% confidence interval for the difference in driver death rates for the two types of vehicles. Are these data appropriate for this inference? Explain. (Ross and Wenzel, *An Analysis of Traffic Deaths by Vehicle Type and Model,* March 2002)

Midsize	47	54	64	76	88	97
SUV	55	60	62	76	91	109

13. Age. In a study of how depression may impact one's ability to survive a heart attack, the researchers reported the ages of the two groups they examined. The mean age of 2397 patients without cardiac disease was 69.8 years (SD = 8.7 years), while for the 450 patients with cardiac disease the mean and standard deviation of the ages were 74.0 and 7.9, respectively.

a) Create a 95% confidence interval for the difference in mean ages of the two groups.

b) How might an age difference confound these research findings about the relationship between depression and ability to survive a heart attack?

14. Smoking. In the depression and heart attack research described in Exercise 13, 32% of the diseased group were smokers, compared with only 23.7% of those free of heart disease.

a) Create a 95% confidence interval for the difference in the proportions of smokers in the two groups.

b) Is this evidence that the two groups in the study were different? Explain.

c) Could this be a problem in analyzing the results of the study? Explain.

15. Computer use. A Gallup telephone poll of 1240 teens conducted in 2001 found that boys were more likely than girls to play computer games, by a margin of 77% to 65%. An equal number of boys and girls were surveyed.

a) What kind of sampling design was used?

b) Give a 95% confidence interval for the difference in game playing by gender.

c) Does your confidence interval suggest that among all teens a higher percentage of boys than girls play computer games?

16. Recruiting. In September 2002, CNN reported on a method of grad student recruiting by the Haas School of Business at U.C.-Berkeley. The school notifies applicants by formal letter that they have been admitted, and also emails the accepted students a link to a Web site that greets them with personalized balloons, cheering, and applause. The director of admissions says this extra effort at recruiting has really worked well. The school accepts 500 applicants each year, and the percentage who actually choose to enroll at Berkeley has increased from 52% the year before the Web greeting to 54% this year.

a) Create a 95% confidence interval for the change in enrollment rates.

b) Based on your confidence interval, are you convinced that this new form of recruiting has been effective? Explain.

17. Hearing. Fitting someone for a hearing aid requires assessing the patient's hearing ability. In one method of assessment, the patient listens to a tape of 50 English words. The tape is played at low volume, and the patient is asked to repeat the words. The patient's hearing ability score is the number of words perceived correctly. Four tapes of equivalent difficulty are available so that each ear can be tested with more than one hearing aid. These lists were created to be equally difficult to perceive in silence, but hearing aids must work in the presence of background noise. Researchers had 24 subjects with normal hearing compare two of the tapes when a background noise was present, with the order of the tapes randomized. Is it reasonable to assume that the two lists are still equivalent for purposes of the hearing test when there is background noise? Base your decision on a confidence interval for the mean difference in the number of words people might misunderstand. (Faith Loven, *A Study of the Interlist Equivalency of the CID W-22 Word List Presented in Quiet and in Noise.* University of Iowa [1981])

Subject	List A	List B
1	24	26
2	32	24
3	20	22
4	14	18
5	32	24
6	22	30
7	20	22
8	26	28
9	26	30
10	38	16
11	30	18
12	16	34
13	36	32
14	32	34
15	38	32
16	14	18
17	26	20
18	14	20
19	38	40
20	20	26
21	14	14
22	18	14
23	22	30
24	34	42

18. Cesareans. Some people fear that differences in insurance coverage can affect healthcare decisions. A survey of several randomly selected hospitals found that 16.6% of 223 recent births in Vermont involved cesarean deliveries, compared with 18.8% of 186 births in New Hampshire. Is this evidence that the rate of cesarean births in the two states is different?

19. Newspapers. Who reads the newspaper more, men or women? Eurostat, an agency of the European Union (EU), conducts surveys on several aspects of daily life in EU countries. Recently, the agency asked samples of 1000 respondents in each of 14 European countries whether they read the newspaper on a daily basis. Below are the data by country and gender.

% Reading a Newspaper Daily

Country	Men	Women
Belgium	56.3	45.5
Denmark	76.8	70.3
Germany	79.9	76.8
Greece	22.5	17.2
Spain	46.2	24.8
Ireland	58.0	54.0
Italy	50.2	29.8
Luxembourg	71.0	67.0
Netherlands	71.3	63.0
Austria	78.2	74.1
Portugal	58.3	24.1
Finland	93.0	90.0
Sweden	89.0	88.0
UK	32.6	30.4

a) Examine the differences in the percentages for each country. Which of these countries seem to be outliers? What do they have in common?

b) After eliminating the outliers, is there evidence that in Europe men are more likely than women to read the newspaper?

20. Meals. A college student is on a "meal program." His budget allows him to spend an average of $10 per day for the semester. He keeps track of his daily food expenses for 2 weeks; the data are given in the table. Is there strong evidence that he will overspend his food allowance? Explain.

Date	Cost ($)
7/29	15.20
7/30	23.20
7/31	3.20
8/1	9.80
8/2	19.53
8/3	6.25
8/4	0
8/5	8.55
8/6	20.05
8/7	14.95
8/8	23.45
8/9	6.75
8/10	0
8/11	9.01

21. Wall Street. In September of 2000, the Harris Poll organization asked 1002 randomly sampled American adults whether they agreed or disagreed with the following statement:

> Most people on Wall Street would be willing to break the law if they believed they could make a lot of money and get away with it.

Of those asked, 60% said they agreed with this statement. We know that if we could ask the entire population of American adults, we would not find that exactly 60% think that Wall Street workers would be willing to break the law to make money. Construct a 95% confidence interval for the true percentage of American adults who agree with the statement.

22. Teach for America. Several programs attempt to address the shortage of qualified teachers by placing uncertified instructors in schools with acute needs—often in inner cities. A 1999–2000 study compared students taught by certified teachers with others taught by undercertified teachers in the same schools. Reading scores of the students of certified teachers averaged 35.62 points with standard deviation 9.31. The scores of students instructed by undercertified teachers had mean 32.48 points with standard deviation 9.43 points on the same test. There were 44 students in each group. The appropriate t procedure has 86 degrees of freedom. Is there evidence of lower scores with uncertified teachers? Discuss. (*The Effectiveness of "Teach for America" and Other Under-certified Teachers on Student Academic Achievement: A Case of Harmful Public Policy*. Education Policy Analysis Archives [2002])

23. Legionnaires' disease. In 1974, the Bellevue-Stratford Hotel in Philadelphia was the scene of an outbreak of what later became known as legionnaires' disease. The cause of the disease was finally discovered to be bacteria that thrived in the air-conditioning units of the hotel. Owners of the Rip Van Winkle Motel, hearing about the Bellevue-Stratford, replace their air-conditioning system. The following data are the bacteria counts, in the air of eight rooms, before and after a new air-conditioning system was installed (measured in colonies per cubic foot of air). The objective is to find out whether the new system has succeeded in lowering the bacterial count. You are the statistician assigned to report to the hotel whether the strategy has worked. Base your analysis on a confidence interval. Be sure to list all your assumptions, methods, and conclusions.

Room Number	Before	After
121	11.8	10.1
163	8.2	7.2
125	7.1	3.8
264	14	12
233	10.8	8.3
218	10.1	10.5
324	14.6	12.1
325	14	13.7

24. Teach for America, Part II. The study described in Exercise 22 also looked at scores in mathematics and language. Here are software outputs for the appropriate tests. Explain what they show.

Mathematics

T-TEST OF Mu(1) − Mu(2) = 0

Mu(Cert) − Mu(NoCert) = 4.53   t (86) = 2.95   p = 0.002

Language

T-TEST OF Mu(1) − Mu(2) = 0

Mu(Cert) − Mu(NoCert) = 2.13   t (84) = 1.71   p = 0.045

25. Bipolar kids. The June 2002 *American Journal of Psychiatry* reported that researchers used medication and psychotherapy to treat children aged 7 to 16 who exhibit bipolar symptoms. After 2 years, symptoms had cleared up in only 26 of the 89 children involved in the study.

a) Write a 95% confidence interval, and interpret it in this context.

b) If researchers subsequently hope to produce an estimate of treatment effectiveness for bipolar disorder that has a margin of error of only 6%, how many patients should they study?

26. Online testing. The Educational Testing Service is now administering several of its standardized tests online, the CLEP and GMAT exams, for example. Since taking a test on a computer is different from taking a test with pencil and paper, one wonders if the scores will be the same. To investigate this question, researchers created two versions of an SAT-type test and got 20 volunteers to participate in an experiment. Each volunteer took both versions of the test, one with pencil and paper and the other online. Subjects were randomized with respect to the order in which they sat for the tests (online/paper) and which form they took (Test A, Test B) in which environment. The scores (out of a possible 20) are summarized in the table.

Subject	Paper	Online
	Test A	Test B
1	14	13
2	10	13
3	16	8
4	15	14
5	17	16
6	14	11
7	9	12
8	12	12
9	16	16
10	7	14
	Test B	Test A
11	8	13
12	11	13
13	15	17
14	11	13
15	13	14
16	9	9
17	15	9
18	14	15
19	16	12
20	8	10

a) Were the two forms (A/B) of the test equivalent in terms of difficulty? Test an appropriate hypothesis and state your conclusion.

b) Is there evidence that testing environment (paper/on-line) matters? Test an appropriate hypothesis and state your conclusion.

27. Bread. Clarksburg Bakery is trying to predict how many loaves to bake. In the last 100 days, the bakery has sold between 95 and 140 loaves per day. Here are a histogram and the summary statistics for the number of loaves sold for the last 100 days.

Summary of Sales

Mean	103
Median	100
StdDev	9.000
Min	95
Max	140
Lower 25th %tile	97
Upper 25th %tile	105.5

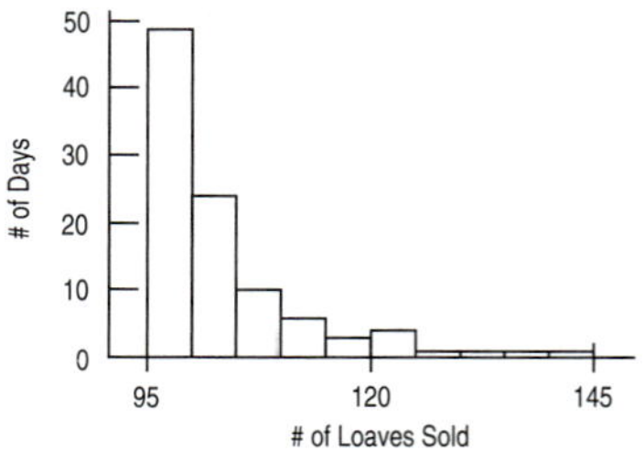

a) Can you use these data to estimate the number of loaves sold on the busiest 10% of all days? Explain.

b) Explain why you can use these data to construct a 95% confidence interval for the mean number of loaves sold per day.

c) Calculate a 95% confidence interval and carefully interpret what that confidence interval means.

d) If the bakery would have been satisfied with a confidence interval whose margin of error was twice as wide, how many days' data could they have used?

e) When the bakery opened, the owners estimated that they would sell an average of 100 loaves per day. Does your confidence interval provide strong evidence that this estimate was incorrect? Explain.

28. Irises. Can measurements of the petal length of flowers be of value when you need to determine the species a certain flower? Here are the summary statistics from measurements of the petals of two species of irises. (R. A. Fisher, "The Use of Multiple Measurements in Axonomic Problems." *Annals of Eugenics* 7 [1936]:179–188)

	Species	
	Versicolor	Virginica
Count	50	50
Mean	55.52	43.22
Median	55.50	44
StdDev	5.51895	5.36158
Min	45	30
Max	69	56
Lower Quartile	51	40
Upper Quartile	59	47

a) Make parallel boxplots of petal lengths for the two species.
b) Describe the differences seen in the boxplots.
c) Write a 95% confidence interval for this difference.
d) Explain what your interval means.
e) Based on your confidence interval, is there evidence of a difference in petal length? Explain.

29. Insulin and diet. A study published in the *Journal of the American Medical Association* examined people to see if they showed any signs of IRS (insulin resistance syndrome) involving major risk factors for Type 2 diabetes and heart disease. Among 102 subjects who consumed dairy products more than 35 times per week, 24 were identified with IRS. In comparison, IRS was identified in 85 of 190 individuals with the lowest dairy consumption, fewer than 10 times per week.
a) Is this strong evidence that IRS risk is different in people who frequently consume dairy products than in those who do not?
b) Does this prove that dairy consumption influences the development of IRS? Explain.

30. Speeding. A newspaper report in August 2002 raised the issue of racial bias in the issuance of speeding tickets. The following facts were noted:
- 16% of drivers registered in New Jersey are black.
- Of the 324 speeding tickets issued in one month on a 65 mph section of the New Jersey Turnpike, 25% went to black drivers.

a) Is the percentage of speeding tickets issued to blacks unusually high compared with the state's registration information?
b) Does this prove that racial profiling may be present?
c) What other statistics would you like to know about this situation?

31. Rainmakers? In an experiment to determine whether seeding clouds with silver iodide increases rainfall, 52 clouds were randomly assigned to be seeded or not. The amount of rain they generated was then measured (in acre-feet). Create a 95% confidence interval for the average amount of additional rain created by seeding clouds. Explain what your interval means.

Variable	Count	Mean	Median	StdDev
Unseeded clouds	26	164.588	44.2000	278.426
Seeded clouds	26	441.985	221.600	650.787

Variable	IntQRange	25 %ile	75 %ile
Unseeded clouds	138.600	24.4000	163
Seeded clouds	337.600	92.4000	430

32. Fritos. As a project for an introductory statistics course, students checked 6 bags of Fritos marked with a net weight of 35.4 grams. They carefully weighed the contents of each bag, recording the following weights (in grams): 35.5, 35.3, 35.1, 36.4, 35.4, 35.5. Is there evidence that the mean weight of bags of Fritos is less than advertised?
a) Write appropriate hypotheses.
b) Do these data satisfy the assumptions for inference? Explain.
c) Test your hypothesis using all 6 weights.
d) Retest your hypothesis with the one unusually high weight removed.
e) What would you conclude about the stated net weight?

33. Color or text? In an experiment, 32 volunteer subjects are briefly shown seven cards, each displaying the name of a color printed in a different color (example: red, blue, and so on). The subject is asked perform one of two tasks: memorize the order of the words or memorize the order of the colors. Researchers record the number of cards remembered correctly. Then the cards are shuffled and the subject is asked to perform the other task. The tables display the results for each subject. Is there any evidence that either the color or the written word dominates perception?
a) What role does randomization play in this experiment?
b) State appropriate hypotheses.
c) Are the assumptions necessary for inference reasonable here?
d) Perform the test.
e) State your conclusion.

Subject	Color	Word	Subject	Color	Word
1	4	7	17	4	3
2	1	4	18	7	4
3	5	6	19	4	3
4	1	6	20	0	6
5	6	4	21	3	3
6	4	5	22	3	5
7	7	3	23	7	3
8	2	5	24	3	7
9	7	5	25	5	6
10	4	3	26	3	4
11	2	0	27	3	5
12	5	4	28	1	4
13	6	7	29	2	3
14	3	6	30	5	3
15	4	6	31	3	4
16	4	7	32	6	7

34. And it means? Every statement about a confidence interval contains two parts—the level of confidence and the interval. Suppose that an insurance agent estimating the mean loss claimed by clients after home burglaries created the 95% confidence interval ($1644, $2391).

a) What's the margin of error for this estimate?
b) Carefully explain what the interval means.
c) Carefully explain what the 95% confidence level means.

35. Batteries. We work for the "Watchdog for the Consumer" consumer advocacy group. We've been asked to look at a battery company that claims its batteries last an average of 100 hours under normal use. There have been several complaints that the batteries don't last that long, so we decide to test them. To do this we select 16 batteries and run them until they die. They lasted a mean of 97 hours, with a standard deviation of 12 hours.

a) One of the editors of our newsletter (who does not know statistics) says that 97 hours is a lot less than the advertised 100 hours, so we should reject the company's claim. Explain to him the problem with doing that.
b) What are the null and alternative hypotheses?
c) What assumptions must we make in order to proceed with inference?
d) At a 5% level of significance, what do you conclude?
e) Suppose that, in fact, the average life of the company's batteries is only 98 hours. Has an error been made in part d? If so, what kind?

36. Hamsters. How large are hamster litters? Among 47 golden hamster litters recorded, there were an average of 7.72 baby hamsters, with a standard deviation of 2.5 hamsters per litter.

a) Create and interpret a 90% confidence interval.
b) Would a 98% confidence interval have a larger or smaller margin of error? Explain.
c) How many litters must be used to estimate the average litter size to within 1 baby hamster with 95% confidence?

Part VII

Inference When Variables Are Related

Chapter 26

Comparing Counts

Does your zodiac sign determine how successful you will be in later life? *Fortune* magazine collected the zodiac signs of 256 heads of the largest 400 companies. Here are the number of births for each sign:

Births	Sign
23	Aries
20	Taurus
18	Gemini
23	Cancer
20	Leo
19	Virgo
18	Libra
21	Scorpio
19	Sagittarius
22	Capricorn
24	Aquarius
29	Pisces

Birth totals by sign for 256 Forbes 400 executives.

WHO	Executives of Fortune-400 Companies
WHAT	Zodiac birth sign
WHY	Curiosity?

We can see some variation in the number of births per sign and there *are* more Pisces, but is it enough to claim that successful people are more likely to be born under some signs than others?

Goodness-of-Fit

"All creatures have their determined time for giving birth and carrying fetus, only a man is born all year long, not in determined time, one in the seventh month, the other in the eighth, and so on till the beginning of the eleventh month."

—Aristotle

If births were distributed uniformly across the year, we would expect about 1/12 of them to occur under each sign of the zodiac. That suggests 256/12, or about 21.3 births per sign. How closely do the observed numbers of births per sign fit this simple "null" model?

A hypothesis test to address this question is called a test of "**goodness-of-fit.**" The name suggests a certain badness-of-grammar, but it is quite standard. After all, we are asking whether the model that births are uniformly distributed over the signs fits the data good, . . . er, well. Goodness-of-fit involves testing a hypothesis. We have specified a model for the distribution and want to know whether it fits. There is no single parameter to estimate, so a confidence interval wouldn't make much sense.

If the question were about only one astrological sign (For example, "Are Pisces more likely to be executives?"[1]), we could use a one-proportion z-test and ask if the true proportion of executives with that sign is equal to 1/12. However, here we have 12 hypothesized proportions, one for each sign. We need a test that considers all of them together and gives an overall idea of whether the observed distribution differs from the hypothesized one.

Assumptions and Conditions

These data are organized in tables as we saw in Chapter 3, and the assumptions and conditions reflect that. Rather than having an observation for each individual, we typically work with summary counts in categories. In our example, we don't know the birth signs of each of the 256 executives, only the totals for each sign.

Counted Data Condition

The first condition is just to check that the data are *counts* for the categories of a categorical variable. This might seem a simplistic, even silly condition. But many kinds of values can be assigned to categories, and it is unfortunately common to find the methods of this chapter applied incorrectly to proportions or amounts. So check to be sure you really have counts.

Independence Assumption

The easiest case is when the individuals who are counted in the cells are sampled independently from some population. That's what we'd like to have if we want to draw conclusions about that population. Randomness can arise in other ways, though. For example, if we care only about Forbes 400 executives, we might still think that the birth date of a particular executive is randomly distributed through the year. If we want to generalize to a large population, we should check the randomization condition.

Randomization condition. The individuals who have been counted and whose counts are available for analysis should be a random sample from some population.

[1]A question actually asked us by someone who was undoubtedly a Pisces.

Sample Size Assumption

We must have enough data for the methods to work. That turns out not to be a simple question. We usually check the following:

Expected cell frequency condition: We should expect to see at least 5 individuals in each cell.

The expected cell frequency condition sounds like—and is, in fact, quite similar to—the condition that np and nq be greater than 10 when we tested proportions.

Calculations

NOTATION ALERT:

We compare the counts observed in each cell with the counts we expect to observe. The usual notation uses O's and E's or abbreviations such as those we've used here. The way the expected counts are found depends on the model.

We have observed a count in each category from the data, and have an expected count for each category from the hypothesized proportions. We wonder, are the differences just natural sampling variability, or are they so large that they indicate something important? Naturally enough, we look at the *differences* between these observed and expected counts, denoted (*Obs* − *Exp*). We'd like to think about the total of the differences, but just adding them won't work because some differences are positive, others negative. We've been in this predicament before—once when we looked at deviations from the mean and again when we dealt with residuals. In fact, these are residuals. They're just the differences between the observed data and the counts given by the (null) model. We'll handle these residuals in essentially the same way we did in regression: We square them. That makes everything positive, and focuses attention on those categories with large differences from what we expected. Because the differences between observed and expected counts generally get larger the more data we have, we also need to divide by something to get an idea of the *relative* sizes of the differences.

The test statistic, called **chi-square** (or chi-squared) **statistic,** is found by adding up the sum of the squares of the deviations between the observed and expected counts divided by the expected counts:

$$\chi^2 = \sum_{all\ cells} \frac{(Obs - Exp)^2}{Exp}.$$

NOTATION ALERT:

The Greek letter χ's only use in Statistics is to represent this statistic and the associated sampling distribution. This is another violation of our "rule" that Greek letters represent population parameters. Here we are using a Greek letter simply to name a family of distribution models and a statistic.

The chi-square statistic is denoted χ^2 where χ is the Greek letter chi (pronounced "ki" as in "sky"). It refers to a family of sampling distribution models we have not seen before called (remarkably enough) the chi-square models.

This family of models, like the Student's t-models, differ only in the number of degrees of freedom. As with Student's t, the number of degrees of freedom for a goodness-of-fit test is $n - 1$. Here, however, n is *not* the sample size, but instead is the number of categories. For the zodiac example, we have 12 signs, so our χ^2 statistic has 11 degrees of freedom.

One-Sided or Two-Sided?

The chi-square statistic is used only for testing, not for constructing confidence intervals. If the observed counts don't match the expected, the statistic will be large. And it can't be "too small." That would just mean that our data *really* fit the hypothesis well. So the chi-square test is always one-sided. If the calculated statistic value is large enough, we'll reject the null hypothesis. What could be simpler?

Even though it behaves like a one sided test, conceptually a chi-square test is two-sided. When we reject the null hypothesis, we really don't know *how* our data differ from the null model. By squaring the differences, we made everything positive whether our observed counts were higher or lower than what we expected. There's no direction to the rejection of the null model. We just know that it doesn't fit.

A Chi-Square Test for Goodness-of-Fit STEP-BY-STEP

We have counts of 256 executives in 12 zodiac sign categories. The natural null hypothesis is that birth dates of executives are divided equally among all the zodiac signs. The test statistic looks at how closely the observed data match this idealized situation.

Think

Hypotheses State what we want to know.

We want to know whether births of successful people are uniformly distributed across the signs of the zodiac.

H_0: Births are uniformly distributed over zodiac signs.[2]

H_A: Births are not uniformly distributed over zodiac signs.

Plan Check the conditions.

✓ **Counted data condition:** We have counts of the number of executives in categories.

✓ **Randomization condition:** We have a convenience sample of executives, but no reason to suspect bias.

✓ **Expected cell frequency condition:** The null hypothesis expects that 1/12 of the 256 births, or 21.333, should occur in each sign. These expected values are all greater than 5, so the condition is satisfied.

State the statistic and sampling distribution.

Under these conditions, the sampling distribution of the test statistic is χ^2 with $12 - 1 = 11$ degrees of freedom.

Name the test you will use.

We will do a **chi-square goodness-of-fit test.**

---

[2] It may seem that we have broken our rule of thumb that null hypotheses should specify parameter values. If you want to get formal about it, the null hypothesis is that

$$p_{\text{Aries}} = p_{\text{Taurus}} = \ldots = p_{\text{Pisces}}.$$

That is, we hypothesize that the true proportions of births of CEOs under each sign are equal. The role of the null hypothesis is to specify the values we need so that we can compute the test statistic. That's what this one does.

Show

Mechanics Each cell contributes an $\frac{(Obs - Exp)^2}{Exp}$ value, to the chi-square sum. We add up these components for each zodiac sign. If you do it by hand, it can be helpful to do the calculation as a table. We show that after the Step-by-Step.

The expected value for each zodiac sign is 21.333.

$$\chi^2 = \sum \frac{(Obs - Exp)^2}{Exp} = \frac{(23 - 21.333)^2}{21.333} + \frac{(20 - 21.333)^2}{21.333} + \ldots$$

$= 5.094$ for all 12 signs.

The χ^2 models are skewed to the high end, and change shape depending on the degrees of freedom. The P-value considers only the right tail. Large χ^2 statistic values correspond to small P-values, which lead us to reject the null hypothesis.

The P-value is the area in the upper tail of the χ^2 model for $12 - 1 = 11$ degrees of freedom above the computed χ^2 value.

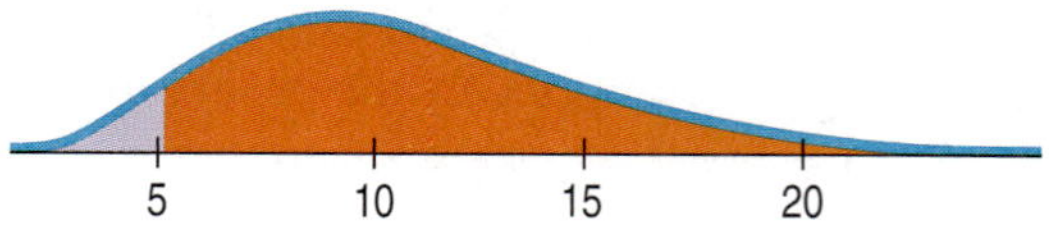

$P = P(\chi^2 > 5.094) = 0.926$

Tell

Conclusion

Remember to state the conclusion in terms of what the data mean rather than just making a statement about the distribution of counts.

The P-value of 0.926 says that if the zodiac signs of executives were in fact distributed uniformly, an observed chi-square value of 5.09 or higher would occur about 93% of the time. We conclude that these data show virtually no evidence of nonuniform distribution of zodiac signs among executives.

The Chi-Square Calculation

Let's make the chi-square procedure very clear. Here are the steps:

1. **Find the expected values.** These come from the null hypothesis model. Every model gives a hypothesized proportion for each cell. The expected value is the product of the total number of observations times this proportion.

   For our example, the null model hypothesizes *equal* proportions. With 12 signs, there should be 1/12 of the 256 executives in each sign. The expected number for each sign is 21.333.
2. **Compute the residuals.** Once you have expected values for each cell, find the residuals, *Observed* − *Expected*.
3. **Square the residuals.**
4. **Compute the components.** Now find the component, $\frac{(Observed - Expected)^2}{Expected}$, for each cell.
5. **Find the sum of the components.** That's the chi-square statistic.
6. **Find the degrees of freedom.** It's equal to the number of cells minus one. For the zodiac signs, that's $12 - 1 = 11$ degrees of freedom.
7. **Test the hypothesis.** Large chi-square values mean lots of deviation from the hypothesized model, so they give small P-values. Look up the critical value from a table of chi-square values, or use technology to find the P-value directly.

The steps of the chi-square calculations are often laid out in tables. Use one row for each category, and columns for observed counts, expected counts, residuals, squared residuals, and the contributions to the chi-square total like this:

Sign	Observed	Expected	Residual = (*Obs* − *Exp*)	$(Obs - Exp)^2$	Component = $\frac{(Obs - Exp)^2}{Exp}$
Aries	23	21.333	1.667	2.7788890	0.130262
Taurus	20	21.333	−1.333	1.7768890	0.083293
Gemini	18	21.333	−3.333	11.108889	0.520737
Cancer	23	21.333	1.667	2.7788890	0.130262
Leo	20	21.333	−1.333	1.7768890	0.083293
Virgo	19	21.333	−2.333	5.4428890	0.255139
Libra	18	21.333	−3.333	11.108889	0.520737
Scorpio	21	21.333	−0.333	0.11088900	0.005198
Sagittarius	19	21.333	−2.333	5.4428890	0.255139
Capricorn	22	21.333	0.667	0.44488900	0.020854
Aquarius	24	21.333	2.667	7.1128890	0.333422
Pisces	29	21.333	7.667	58.782889	2.755491
					$\sum = 5.094$

TI Tips

Well, it had to happen sometime. By now you must be convinced that your TI can do anything. Sorry. It doesn't do the chi-square goodness-of-fit test.

Oh, sure, if you look in the STAT TESTS menu you will see C: χ^2-Test, but that's not it. There are other kinds of chi-square tests that you will learn about later in this chapter, and the calculator's statistics package *will* do those for you. But goodness-of-fit you'll have to learn to do yourself. Fortunately that's not very hard.

If there are only a few cells, you can just write out the formula and use the calculator to do the arithmetic. That's probably the easiest approach. But if you are clever with the calculator, you can run through the procedure step by step, using lists to create a table like the one above. We'll demonstrate with the zodiac data.

Calculating Chi-square for a goodness-of-fit-test, TI Style:

- Enter the counts of executives born under each star sign in L1. Those counts were: 23 20 18 23 20 19 18 21 19 22 24 29.
- Enter the expected percentages (or fractions, here 1/12) in L2. In this example they are all the same value, but that's not always the case.

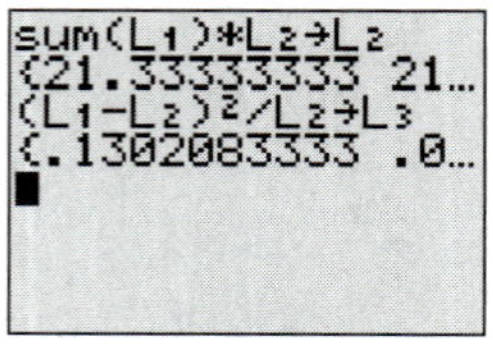

- Convert the expected percentages to expected counts by multiplying each of them by the total number of observations. We use the calculator's summation command in the `LIST MATH` menu to find the total count of the data in `L1`, and multiply that sum by the percentages in `L2` to produce the expected counts. The command is `sum(L1)*L2→L2`. (We don't ever need the percentages again, so we replace them by storing the expected counts in `L2` instead.)

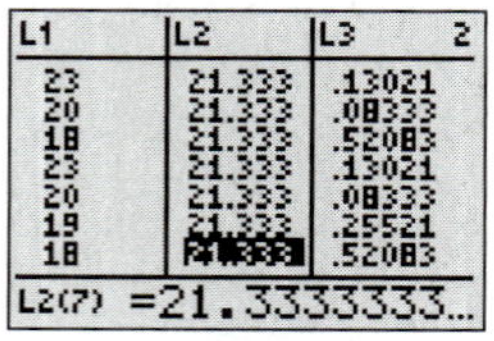

- Now calculate the chi-square components and store them in the next column: `(L1-L2)²/L2→L3`.
- Finally, find the `sum` of the components in `L3`.

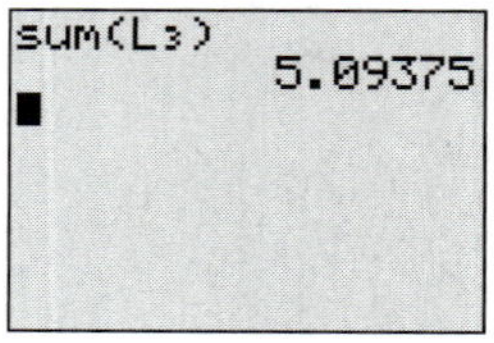

There's your calculated value of χ^2.

Finding a P-value:
The P-value is the probability of observing a χ^2 value at least as high as the one you calculated from these data. As you probably expect, that's akin to `normalcdf` and `tcdf`. You can find what you need in the `DISTR` menu at `7:`χ^2`cdf`. You just need to specify the left and right boundaries and the number of degrees of freedom.

- Enter χ^2`cdf(5.09375,999,11)`, as shown. (Why 999? Unlike *t* and *z*, chi-square values can get pretty big, especially when there are many cells. You may need to go a long way to the right to get to where the tail becomes essentially meaningless. You can see what we mean by looking at Table C, showing chi-square values.)

And there's the P-value, a whopping 0.93! There's nothing at all unusual about these data. (So much for the zodiac's predictive power.)

But I Believe the Model . . .

Goodness-of-fit tests are likely to be performed by people who have a theory of what the proportions *should* be in each category, and who believe their theory to be true. Unfortunately, the only *null* hypothesis available for a goodness-of-fit test is that the theory is true. And as we know, the hypothesis testing procedure allows us only to *reject* the null or *fail to reject* it. We can never confirm that a theory is in fact true, which is often what people want to do.

Unfortunately, they're stuck. At best, we can point out only that the data are consistent with the proposed theory. But this doesn't *prove* the theory. The data could be consistent with the model even if the theory is wrong. In that case, we fail to reject the null hypothesis, but can't conclude anything for sure about whether the theory is true.

And we can't fix the problem by turning things around. Suppose we try to make our favored hypothesis the alternative. Then it is impossible to pick a single null. For example, suppose, as a doubter of astrology, you want to prove that the distribution of executive births is uniform. If you choose uniform as the null hypothesis, you can only *fail* to reject it. So you'd like uniformity to be your alternative hypothesis. Which particular violation of equally distributed births would you choose as your null? The problem is that the model can be wrong in many, many ways. There's no way to frame a null hypothesis the other way around. There's just no way to prove that a favored model is true.

Why can't we prove the null?

A biologist wants to show that her inheritance theory about fruit flies is valid. It says that 10% of the flies should be type 1, 70% type 2, and 20% type 3. After her students collected data on 100 flies, she did a goodness-of-fit test and found a P-value of 0.07. She started celebrating, since her null hypothesis was retained—that is, until her students collected data on 100 more flies. With 200 flies, the P-value dropped to 0.02. Although she knew the answer was probably no, she asked the statistician hopefully if she could just ignore half the data and stick with the original 100. By this reasoning we could always "prove the null" just by not collecting much data. With only a little data, the chances are good that they'll be consistent with almost anything. But they also have little chance of disproving anything either. In this case, we say the test has no "power." Don't let yourself be lured into this scientist's reasoning. More data is always better. You just can't ever prove the null hypothesis is true.

Comparing Observed Distributions

Many high schools survey graduating classes to determine the plans of the graduates. We might wonder whether the plans of students have stayed roughly the same over past decades or whether they have changed. Here is a summary table from one high school. Each **cell** of the table shows how many students from a particular graduating class (the column) made a certain choice (the row).

WHO	High school graduates
WHAT	Postgraduation activities
WHEN	1980, 1990, 2000
WHY	Regular survey for general information

	1980	1990	2000	Total
College/Post-HS education	320	245	288	853
Employment	98	24	17	139
Military	18	19	5	42
Travel	17	2	5	24
Total	453	290	315	1058

Activities of graduates of a high school reported a year after graduation, by graduation year. (Source: IHS) **Table 26.1**

We might wonder about changes in the choice of military service as a post–high school activity. The numbers for 1980 and 1990 look similar, until you notice the class sizes are quite different. The 18 seniors in 1980 who chose military service were only about 4% of the graduating class. In 1990, the 19 seniors making the same choice represented 6.6% of the class. Because the class sizes change so much, we're probably better off examining the proportions for each class rather than the counts:

	1980	1990	2000	Total
College	70.6	84.5	91.4	80.6
Employment	21.6	8.28	5.40	13.1
Military	3.97	6.55	1.59	3.97
Travel	3.75	0.690	1.59	2.27
Total	100	100	100	100

Activities of graduates of a high school reported a year after graduation, as percentage of the class.
Table 26.2

We already know how to test whether *two* proportions are the same. For example, we could consider whether the proportion of students choosing military service was the same between 1980 and 1990 with a two-proportion z-test. But now we have more than two groups. We want to test whether the students' choices are the same across all three graduating classes. The z-test for two proportions generalizes to a **chi-square test of homogeneity.**

Why chi-square? It turns out that the statistic is *identical* to the chi-square statistic for goodness-of-fit that we just saw. (How similar can you get?) Why a different name, then? The goodness-of-fit test compared counts with a model. But here we're asking whether choices have changed, so we have no model. We find the expected counts for each category directly from the data. As a result, we count the degrees of freedom slightly differently as well.

The term "homogeneity" means that things are the same. Here, we ask whether the post–high school choices made by students are the *same* for these three graduating classes.

Assumptions and Conditions

The assumptions and conditions are the same as for the chi square test for goodness-of-fit. The **counted data condition** says that these data must be counts. You can't do a test of homogeneity on proportions, so we have to work with the counts of graduates given in the first table. Also, you can't do a chi-square test on measurements. For example, if we had recorded GPAs for these same groups over the same time span, we wouldn't be able to test whether the mean GPAs had changed using this test.[3]

Often when we test for homogeneity, we aren't interested in some larger population, so we don't really need a random sample. (We would need one if we wanted to draw a more general conclusion—say, about the choices made by all high school students in these graduation years.) Don't we need *some* randomness, though? Fortunately, the null hypothesis can be thought of as a model in which the counts in the table are distributed as if each student chose a plan randomly according to the overall proportions of the choices, regardless of the student's class. As long as we don't want to generalize, we don't have to check the **randomization condition.**

We still must be sure we have enough data for this method to work. The **expected cell frequency condition** says that the expected count in each cell must be at least 5. We'll confirm that as we do the calculations.

Calculations

The null hypothesis says that the proportions of graduates choosing each alternative should be the same for all three classes. So the expected proportions for each choice are just the overall proportion of students making that choice. The expected counts are those proportions applied to the number of students in each graduating class.

[3]To do that, you'd use a method called Analysis of Variance. Stay tuned.

For example, overall, 139, or about 13.138%, of the 1058 students covered by these three surveys were employed. If the distributions are homogeneous (as the null hypothesis asserts), then 13.138% of the 453 students in the class of 1980 (or about 59.52 students) should be employed. Similarly, 13.138% of the 290 students in the class of 1990 (or about 38.1) should be employed.

Working in this way, we (or, more likely, the computer) can fill in expected values for each cell. Because these are theoretical values, there is no requirement that they be integers. The expected values look like this:

	1980	1990	2000	Total
College	365.226	233.809	253.965	853
Employment	59.5151	38.1002	41.3847	139
Military	17.9830	11.5123	12.5047	42
Travel	10.2760	6.57845	7.14556	24
Total	453	290	315	1058

Expected values for the high school graduates. **Table 26.3**

Now check the **expected cell frequency condition.** Indeed, there are at least 5 individuals expected in each cell.

Following the pattern of the goodness-of-fit test, we compute the component for each cell of the table. For the first cell, 1980 college-bound students, that's

$$\frac{(Obs - Exp)^2}{Exp} = \frac{(320 - 365.226)^2}{365.226} = 5.600.$$

Summing these components across all cells gives

$$\chi^2 = \sum_{all\ cells} \frac{(Obs - Exp)^2}{Exp} = 72.77.$$

How about the degrees of freedom? We don't really need to calculate all of the expected values in the table. We know there are 853 college-bound students, so once we find the expected values for 1980 and 1990, we can determine the expected number of college-bound students for 2000 by just subtracting. Similarly, we know how many students graduated in each class, so after filling in three rows, we can fill in the expected values for Travel by subtracting. To fill out the table, we need to know the counts in only $R - 1$ rows and $C - 1$ columns. So we say that the table has $(R - 1)(C - 1)$ degrees of freedom.

In our example, we need to calculate only 3 choices in each column and counts for 2 classes, for a total of $3 \times 2 = 6$ degrees of freedom. We'll need the degrees of freedom to find a P-value for the chi-square statistic.

A Chi-Square Test for Homogeneity STEP-BY-STEP

We have counts of 1058 students observed in three different years a decade apart and categorized according to their postgraduation activities.

Think

Hypotheses State what we want to know.

We want to know whether the choices made by high school graduates in what they do after high school have changed across the three graduating classes.

State the hypotheses.

The homogeneity test comes with a built-in null hypothesis. We hypothesize that the distribution does not change from group to group. The test looks for differences large enough to step beyond what we might expect from random sample-to-sample variation. It can reveal a large deviation in a single category or small but persistent differences over all the categories—or anything in between.

H_0: The post–high school choices made by the classes of 1980, 1990, and 2000 have the same distribution (are homogeneous).

H_A: The post–high school choices made by the classes of 1980, 1990, and 2000 do not have the same distribution.

Plan Check the conditions.

✓ **Counted data condition:** We have counts of the number of students in categories.

✓ **Randomization condition:** We don't want to draw inferences to other high schools or other classes, so there is no need to check for a random sample.

✓ **Expected cell frequency condition:** The expected values (shown below) are all at least 5.

State the statistic and sampling distribution.

Under these conditions, the sampling distribution of the test statistic is χ^2 with $(4 - 1) \times (3 - 1) = 6$ degrees of freedom.

Name the test you will use.

We will perform a **chi-square test of homogeneity.**

Show

Mechanics Show the expected counts for each cell of the data table. You could make separate tables for the observed and expected counts, or put both counts in each cell as shown here. While observed counts must be whole numbers, expected counts rarely are—don't be tempted to round those off.

	1980	1990	2000
Coll.	320 / 365.23	245 / 233.81	288 / 253.97
Emp.	98 / 59.515	24 / 38.10	17 / 41.38
Mil.	18 / 17.98	19 / 11.51	5 / 12.50
Trav.	17 / 10.28	2 / 6.58	5 / 7.15

Calculate χ^2.

$$\chi^2 = \sum_{\text{all cells}} \frac{(Obs - Exp)^2}{Exp} = 72.77.$$

The shape of a χ^2 model depends on the degrees of freedom. A χ^2 model with 6 df is skewed to the high end.

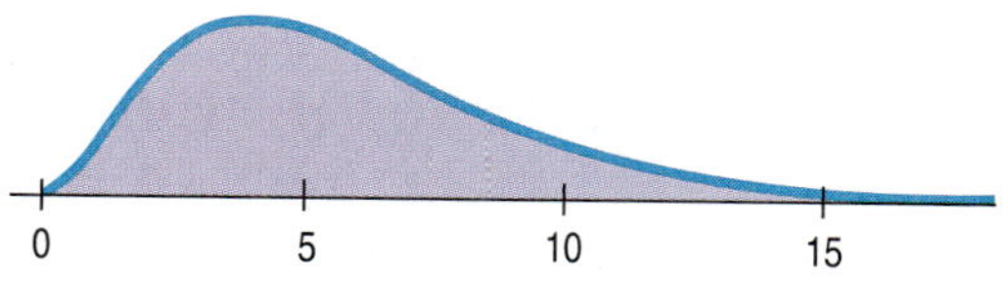

The P-value considers only the right tail. In this case the statistic value is off the scale, so the P-value is quite small.

$P = P(\chi^2 > 72.77) < 0.0001$

Tell

Conclusion

State your conclusion in terms of the data. It should specifically talk about whether the distributions for the groups appear to be different.

The P-value is very small, indicating that the pattern we see would be very unlikely to occur by chance were post–high school choices homogeneous. We reject the null hypothesis, and conclude that the choices made by high school graduates have indeed changed over the two decades examined.

If you find that simply rejecting the hypothesis of homogeneity is a bit unsatisfying, you're in good company. It's hardly a shock that high school students made different choices in 2000 than in 1980. What we'd really like to know is how big the differences were, where they were greatest, and where they were smallest. The test for homogeneity doesn't answer these interesting questions, but it does provide some evidence that can help us.

Examining the Residuals

When we reject the null hypothesis, it's always a good idea to examine residuals. (We don't need to when we fail to reject because when the χ^2 value is small, all of its components must have been small.) For chi-square tests, we want to compare residuals for cells that may have very different counts. So we're better off standardizing the residuals. We know the mean residual is zero,[4] but we need to know each residual's standard deviation. When we tested proportions, we saw a link between the expected proportion and its standard deviation. For counts there's a similar link. To standardize a cell's residual, we just divide by the square root of its expected value.

$$c = \frac{(Obs - Exp)}{\sqrt{Exp}}$$

Notice that these **standardized residuals** are just the square roots of the **components** we calculated for each cell, with the + or the − sign indicating whether we observed more cases than we expected, or fewer.

The standardized residuals give us a chance to think about the underlying patterns and to consider the ways in which the distribution may have changed from class to class. Now that we've subtracted the mean (zero) and divided by their standard deviations, these are *z*-scores. If the null hypothesis were true, we could even appeal to the Central Limit Theorem, think of the Normal model, and use the 68-95-99.7 Rule to judge how extraordinary the large ones are.

[4]Residual = observed − expected. Because the total of the expected values is set to be the same as the observed total, the residuals must sum to zero.

Here are the standardized residuals for the high school data:

Standardized residuals can help show how the table differs from the null hypothesis pattern. **Table 26.4**

	1980	1990	2000
College	−2.366	0.732	2.136
Employment	4.989	−2.284	−3.791
Military	0.004	2.207	−2.122
Travel	2.098	−1.785	−0.803

The row for Employment immediately attracts our attention. It holds the largest (in magnitude) two standardized residuals, and they're both big. It looks like employment was a more common choice for the class of 1980 and a less common choice for the classes of 1990 and 2000. This trend may have been influenced by changes in the economy or by a growing sense that college might be a better choice. We can see an opposite but less dramatic trend in the College row, from moderate negative residual to moderate positive residual across the three classes, indicating that going to college has become more common.

Independence

A study from the University of Texas Southwestern Medical Center examined whether the risk of hepatitis C was related to whether people had tattoos and to where they got their tattoos. Hepatitis C causes about 10,000 deaths each year in the United States, but often lies undetected for years after infection.

The data from this study can be summarized in a two-way table, as follows:

WHO	Patients being treated for non–blood-related disorders
WHAT	Tattoo status and hepatitis C status
WHEN	1991, 1992
WHERE	Texas

	Hepatitis C	No Hepatitis C	Total
Tattoo, parlor	17	35	52
Tattoo, elsewhere	8	53	61
None	22	491	513
Total	47	579	626

Counts of patients classified by their hepatitis C test status according to whether they had a tattoo from a tattoo parlor, from another source, or no tattoo. **Table 26.5**

These data differ from the kinds of data we've considered before in this chapter because they categorize subjects from a single group on two categorical variables rather than on only one. The categorical variables here are hepatitis C status ("Hepatitis C" or "No Hepatitis C") and Tattoo status ("Parlor," "Elsewhere," "None"). We've seen counts classified by two categorical variables displayed like this in Chapter 3, so we know such tables are called contingency tables. **Contingency tables** categorize counts on two (or more) variables so that we can see whether the distribution of counts on one variable is contingent on the other.

The natural question to ask of these data is whether the chance of having hepatitis C is *independent* of tattoo status. Recall that for events **A** and **B** to be independent, $P(\mathbf{A})$ must equal $P(\mathbf{A} \mid \mathbf{B})$. Here, this means the probability that a randomly selected patient has hepatitis C should not change conditional on learning the patient's tattoo status. We examined the question of independence in just this way back in Chapter 15, but we lacked a way to test it. The rules for independent events are much too precise and absolute to work well with real data. A **chi-square test for independence** is the test called for here.

If hepatitis status is independent of tattoos, we'd expect the proportion of people testing positive for hepatitis to be the same for the three levels of tattoo status. This sounds a lot like the test of homogeneity. In fact, the calculation is identical.

The only difference between the test for homogeneity and the test for independence is in what you . . .

The difference is that now we have two categorical variables measured on a single population. For the homogeneity test, we have a single categorical variable measured independently on two or more populations. And we ask different questions: "Are the variables independent?" rather than "Are the groups homogeneous?" These are subtle differences, but they can be important when we draw conclusions.

Assumptions and Conditions

Of course, we still need counts and enough data so that the expected values are at least 5 in each cell.

If we're interested in the independence of variables, we usually want to generalize from the data to some population. In that case, we'll need to check that the data are a representative random sample from that population.

A Chi-Square Test for Independence STEP-BY-STEP

We have counts of 626 individuals categorized according to their "tattoo status" and their "hepatitis status."

Hypotheses State what we want to know.

We perform a test of independence when we suspect the variables may not be independent. We are on the familiar ground of making a claim (in this case, that knowing tattoo status will change probabilities for hepatitis C status), by testing the null hypothesis that it is *not* true.

We want to know whether the categorical variables "tattoo status" and "hepatitis status" are statistically independent.

H_0: Tattoo status and hepatitis status are independent.[5]

H_A: Tattoo status and hepatitis status are not independent.

Plan Check the conditions.

✓ **Counted data condition:** We have counts of individuals in categories of two categorical variables.

✓ **Randomization condition:** These data are from a retrospective study of patients being treated for something unrelated to hepatitis. Although they are not an SRS, they were selected to avoid biases and should be representative of the general population.

[5]Once again, parameters are hard to find. The hypothesis of independence itself tells us how to find expected values for each cell of the contingency table. That's all we need.

Warning: Be very wary of proceeding when there are small expected counts. If we see expected counts that fall far short of 5, or if many cells violate the condition, we should not use χ^2. (We discuss ways you can fix the problem next!) If you do continue, always check the residuals to be sure those cells did not have a major influence on your result.

Note that this table shows both the observed and expected counts for each cell.

✓ **Expected cell frequency condition:** The expected values do not meet the condition that all are bigger than 5. We will return to this later.

	Hepatitis C	No Hepatitis C	Total
Tattoo, parlor	17 3.904	35 48.096	52
Tattoo, elsewhere	8 4.580	53 56.420	61
None	22 38.516	491 474.48	513
Total	47	579	626

State the null model.

Under these conditions, the sampling distribution of the test statistic is χ^2 with $(3-1) \times (2-1) = 2$ df.

Name the test you will use.

We will perform a **chi-square test of independence.**

Show

Mechanics Calculate χ^2.

$$\chi^2 = \sum_{\text{all cells}} \frac{(Obs - Exp)^2}{Exp} = 57.91.$$

The shape of a chi-square model depends on its degrees of freedom. With 2 df, the model looks quite different, as you can see here. We still care only about the right tail.

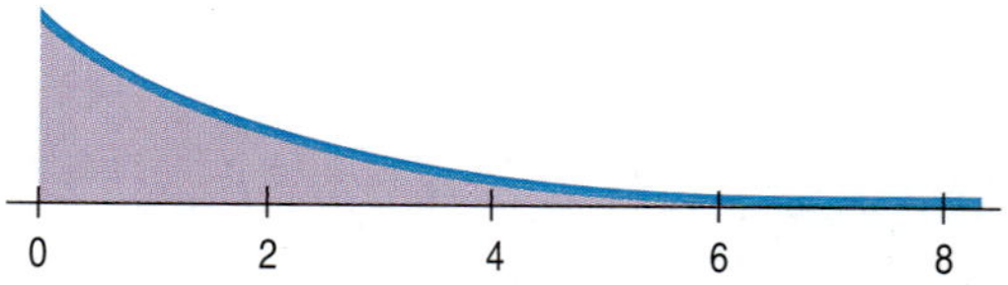

$P = P(\chi^2 > 57.91) < 0.0001$

Tell

Conclusion

State your conclusion about the independence of the two variables.

(Notice that we are *not* sure of this conclusion because of the small expected counts. A complete solution must include the additional analysis, recalculation, and final conclusion discussed below.)

The P-value is very small, indicating that if these variables were independent the pattern we have seen would be very unlikely to occur by chance. We conclude that the hepatitis status is not independent of tattoo status. But we'll want to check that the two cells with small expected counts did not influence our result too greatly.

Examine the Residuals

Each cell of the contingency table contributes a term to the chi-square sum. As we did earlier, we should examine the residuals because we have rejected the null hypothesis. In this instance, we have an additional concern that the cells with small expected frequencies not be the ones that make the chi-square statistic large.

Our concern with the data arises from the potential for improving public health. If patients with tattoos are more likely to test positive for hepatitis C, perhaps physicians should be advised to suggest blood tests for such patients.

The standardized residuals look like this:

Think Again

	Hepatitis C	No Hepatitis C
Tattoo, parlor	6.628	−1.888
Tattoo, elsewhere	1.598	−0.455
None	−2.661	0.758

Standardized residuals for the hepatitis and tattoos data. Are any of them particularly large in magnitude?
Table 26.6

The chi-square value of 57.91 is the sum of the squares of these six values. The cell for patients with tattoos obtained in a tattoo parlor who have hepatitis C is large and positive, indicating there are more patients in that cell than the null hypothesis of independence would predict. This result suggests that a principal source of infection may be tattoo parlors.

The second largest component is a negative value for those with no tattoos who test positive for hepatitis C. A negative value says that there are fewer patients in this cell than independence would expect. That is, those who have no tattoos are less likely to be infected with hepatitis C than we might expect from a simple hypothesis of independence.

What about the cells with small expected counts? The formula for the chi-square standardized residuals divides by the square root of the expected frequency. Too small an expected frequency can arbitrarily inflate the residual, and lead to an inflated chi-square statistic. Any expected count close to the arbitrary minimum of 5 calls for checking that cell's standardized residual to be sure it is not particularly large. In this case, the standardized residual for the Hepatitis C and Tattoo, no parlor cell is not particularly large, but the standardized residual for the Hepatitis C and Tattoo parlor cell is large.

Show More

We might choose not to report the results because of concern with the small expected frequency. Alternatively, we could include a warning along with our report of the results. Yet another approach is to combine appropriate categories to get a larger sample size and correspondingly larger expected frequencies. Here, we might naturally combine the two rows for tattoos, obtaining a 2×2 table:

	Hepatitis C	No Hepatitis C	Total
None	22	491	**513**
Tattoo	25	88	**113**
Total	**47**	**579**	**626**

Combining the two tattoo categories gives a table with all expected counts greater than 5. **Table 26.7**

This table has expected values greater than 5 in every cell and a chi-square value of 42.42 on 1 degree of freedom. The corresponding P-value is ≤ 0.0001.

We conclude that tattoo status and hepatitis C status are not independent. The data *suggest* that tattoo parlors may be a particular problem, but we haven't enough data to draw that conclusion.

TI Tips

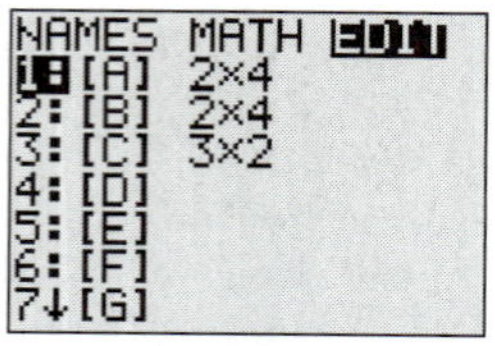

And now some good news: The TI *will* do chi-square tests of homogeneity and independence. Let's use the tattoo data. Here goes.

Test a hypothesis of homogeneity or independence

Stage 1: You need to enter the data as a matrix. A "matrix" is just a formal mathematical term for a table of numbers.

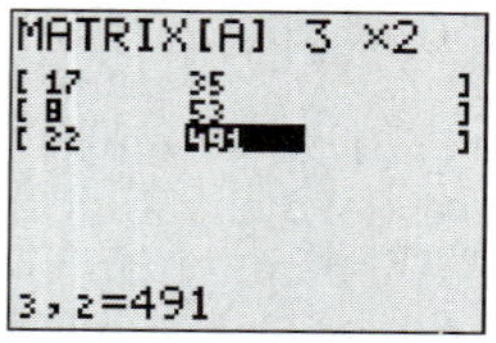

- Push the `MATRIX` button, and choose to `EDIT` matrix `[A]`.
- First specify the dimensions of the table, rows × columns.
- Enter the appropriate counts, one cell at a time. The calculator automatically asks for them row by row.

Stage 2: Do the test.

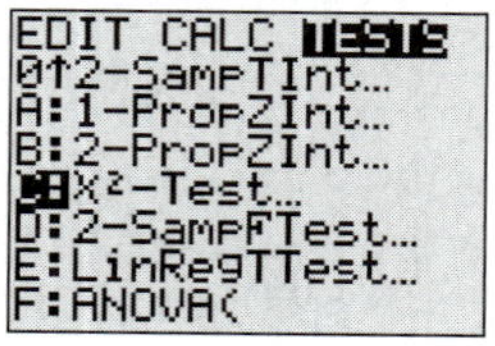

- In the `STAT TESTS` menu choose `C:`χ^2`-Test`.
- The TI now confirms that you have placed the observed frequencies in `[A]`. It also tells you that when it finds the expected frequencies it will store those in `[B]` for you. Now `Calculate` the mechanics of the test.

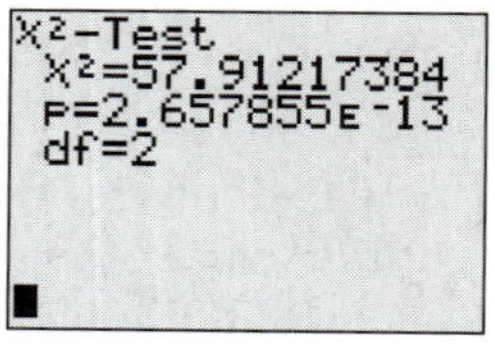

The TI reports a calculated value of $\chi^2 = 57.91$ and an exceptionally small P-value.

Stage 3: Check the expected counts.

- Go back to `MATRIX EDIT` and choose `[B]`.

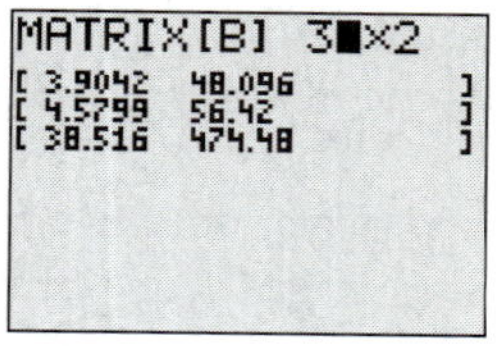

Notice that two of the cells fail to meet the condition that expected counts be at least 5. This problem enters into our analysis and conclusions.

Stage 4: And now some bad news. There's no easy way to calculate the standardized residuals. Look at the two matrices, `[A]` and `[B]`. Large residuals will happen when the corresponding entries differ greatly, especially when the expected count in `[B]` is small (because you will divide by the square root of the entry in `[B]`). The first cell is a good candidate, so we show you the calculation of its standardized residual.

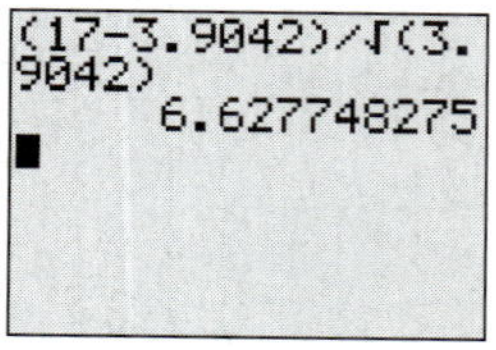

A residual of over 6 is pretty large—possibly an indication that you're more likely to get hepatitis in a tattoo parlor, but the expected count is smaller than 5. We're pretty sure that hepatitis status is not independent of having a tattoo, but we should be wary of saying anything more. Probably the best approach is to combine categories to get cells with expected counts above 5.

Chi-Square and Causation

Chi-square tests are common. Tests for independence are especially widespread. Unfortunately, many people interpret a small P-value as proof of causation. We know better. Just as correlation between quantitative variables does not demonstrate causation, a failure of independence between two categorical variables does not show a cause-and-effect relationship between them. And for the same reasons.

The chi-square test for independence treats the two variables symmetrically. There is no way to differentiate the direction of any possible causation from one variable to the other. In our example, it is unlikely that having hepatitis causes one to crave a tattoo, but other examples are not so clear.

Of course, there's never any way to eliminate the possibility that a lurking variable is responsible for the observed lack of independence. For example, it might be that people who have body piercings or those who inject drugs are both more likely to get tattooed and more likely to contract hepatitis C. Even a small subpopulation of drug users among those with tattoos might be enough to create the observed result.

In some sense, a failure of independence between two categorical variables is less impressive than a strong, consistent, linear association between quantitative variables. Two categorical variables can fail the test of independence in many ways, including ways that show no consistent pattern of failure. Examination of the chi-square standardized residuals can help you think about the underlying patterns.

What Can Go Wrong?

- ***Don't use chi-square methods unless you have counts.*** All three of the chi-square tests apply only to counts. Other kinds of data can be arrayed in two-way tables. Just because numbers are in a two-way table doesn't make them suitable for chi-square analysis. Data reported as proportions or percentages can be suitable for chi-square procedures, *but only after they are converted to counts.* If you try to do the calculations without first finding the counts, your results will be wrong.
- ***Beware large samples.*** Beware *large* samples?! That's not the advice you're used to hearing. The chi-square tests, however, are unusual. You should be wary of chi-square tests performed on very large samples. No hypothesized distribution fits perfectly, no two groups are exactly homogeneous, and no two variables are completely independent. The degrees of freedom for chi-square tests don't grow with the sample size. With a sufficiently large sample size, a chi-square test can always reject the null hypothesis. But we have no measure of how far the data are from the null model. There are no confidence intervals to help us judge the effect size.

Chi-Square and the Computer

Most statistics packages associate chi-square tests with contingency tables. Often chi-square is available as an option only when you make a contingency table. This organization can make it hard to locate the chi-square test and may confuse the three different roles that the chi-square test can take. In particular, chi-square tests for goodness-of-fit may be hard to find or missing entirely. Chi-square tests for homogeneity are computationally the same as chi-square tests for independence, but you may have to perform them as tests of independence.

Most statistics packages work with data on individuals rather than with the summary counts. If the only information you have is the table of counts, you may find it more difficult to get a statistics package to compute chi-square. Some packages offer a way to reconstruct the data from the summary counts so that they can then be passed back through the chi-square calculation, finding the cell counts again (hey, whatever works). Many package offer chi-square standardized residuals (although they may be called something else).

Connections

Chi-square methods relate naturally to inference methods for proportions. We can think of a test of homogeneity as stepping from a comparison of two proportions to a question of whether three or more proportions are equal. The standard deviations of the residuals in each cell are linked to the expected counts much like the standard deviations we found for proportions.

Independence is, of course, a fundamental statistics concept. But chi-square tests do not offer a general way to check on independence for all those times when we have had to assume it.

Stacked bar charts or side-by-side pie charts can help us think about patterns in two-way tables. A histogram or boxplot of the standardized residuals can help locate extraordinary values.

Key Concepts

Two-way table Each *cell* of a two-way table shows counts of individuals. One way classifies a sample according to a categorical variable. The other way can classify different groups of individuals according to the same variable or classify the same individuals according to a different categorical variable.

Cell A cell of a two-way table is one element of the table corresponding to a specific row and a specific column. Table cells can hold counts, percentages, or measurements on other variables. Or they can hold several values.

Contingency table A two-way table that classifies individuals according to two categorical variables is called a *contingency table.*

Chi-square models Chi-square models are skewed to the right. They are parameterized by their degrees of freedom, and become less skewed with increasing degrees of freedom.

Chi-square statistic The chi-square statistic is found by summing the chi-square components. Chi-square tests can be used to test goodness-of-fit, homogeneity, or independence.

Chi-square component The components of a chi-square calculation are

$$\frac{(Observed - Expected)^2}{Expected},$$

found for each cell of the table.

Standardized residual In each cell of a two-way table, a standardized residual is the square root of the chi-square component for that cell with the sign of the Observed − Expected difference. When we reject a chi-square test, an examination of the standardized residuals can sometimes reveal more about how the data deviate from the null model.

Goodness-of-fit A test of whether the distribution of counts in one categorical variable matches the distribution predicted by a model is called a test of goodness-of-fit. A chi-square test of goodness-of-fit finds

$$\chi^2 = \sum_{all\ cells} \frac{(Obs - Exp)^2}{Exp}$$

where the expected counts come from the predicting model. It finds a P-value from a chi-square model with $k - 1$ degrees of freedom, where k is the number of categories in the categorical variable.

Homogeneity A test comparing the distribution of counts for two or more groups on the same categorical variable is called a test of *homogeneity.* A chi-square test of homogeneity finds

$$\chi^2 = \sum_{all\ cells} \frac{(Obs - Exp)^2}{Exp}$$

where the expected counts are the overall counts, adjusted for the totals in each group. We find a P-value from a chi-square distribution with (*#Rows* − 1) × (*#Cols* − 1) degrees of freedom, where *#Rows* gives the number of categories and *#Cols* gives the number of independent groups.

Independence A test of whether two categorical variables are independent examines the distribution of counts for one group of individuals classified according to both variables. A chi-square test of *independence* uses the same calculation as a test of homogeneity. We find a P-value from a chi-square distribution with (*#Rows* − 1) × (*#Cols* − 1) degrees of freedom, where *#Rows* gives the number of categories in one variable and *#Cols* gives the number of categories in the other.

Skills

When you complete this lesson you should:

Think

- Be able to recognize when a test of goodness-of-fit, a test of homogeneity, or a test of independence would be appropriate for a table of counts.
- Understand that the degrees of freedom for a chi-square test depend on the dimensions of the table and not on the sample size. Understand that this means that increasing the sample size increases the ability of chi-square procedures to reject the null hypothesis.

Show

- Be able to display and interpret counts in a two-way table.
- Know how to use the chi-square tables to perform chi-square tests.
- Know how to compute a chi-square test using your statistics software or calculator.
- Be able to examine the standardized residuals to explain the nature of the deviations from the null hypothesis.

Tell

- Know how to interpret chi-square as a test of goodness-of-fit in a few sentences.
- Know how to interpret chi-square as a test of homogeneity in a few sentences.
- Know how to interpret chi-square as a test of independence in a few sentences.

Exercises

1. Dice. After getting trounced by your little brother in a children's game, you suspect the die he gave you to roll may be unfair. To check, you roll it 60 times, recording the number of times each face appears. Do these results cast doubt on the die's fairness?

a) If the die is fair, how many times would you expect each face to show?

b) To see if these results are unusual, will you test goodness-of-fit, homogeneity, or independence?

c) State your hypotheses.

d) Check the conditions.

e) How many degrees of freedom are there?

f) Find χ^2 and the P-value.

g) State your conclusion.

Face	Count
1	11
2	7
3	9
4	15
5	12
6	6

2. M&Ms. As noted in an earlier chapter, the Masterfoods Company says that until very recently yellow candies made up 20% of its milk chocolate M&M's, red another 20%, and orange, blue, and green are each 10%. The rest are brown. On his way home from work the day he was writing these exercises, one of the authors bought a bag of plain M&M's. He got 29 yellow ones, 23 red, 12 orange, 14 blue, 8 green, and 20 brown. Is this sample consistent with the company's stated proportions? Test an appropriate hypothesis and state your conclusion.

a) If the M&M's are packaged in the stated proportions, how many of each color should the author have expected to get in his bag?
b) To see if his bag was unusual, should he test goodness-of-fit, homogeneity, or independence?
c) State the hypotheses.
d) Check the conditions.
e) How many degrees of freedom are there?
f) Find χ^2 and the P-value.
g) State a conclusion.

3. Nuts. A company says its premium mixture of nuts contains 10% Brazil nuts, 20% cashews, 20% almonds, and 10% hazelnuts, and the rest are peanuts. You buy a large can and separate the various kinds of nuts. Upon weighing them, you find there are 112 grams of Brazil nuts, 183 grams of cashews, 207 grams of almonds, 71 grams of hazelnuts, and 446 grams of peanuts. You wonder whether your mix is significantly different from what the company advertises.

a) Explain why the chi-square goodness-of-fit test is not an appropriate way to find out.
b) What might you do instead of weighing the nuts in order to use a χ^2 test?

4. Mileage. A salesman who is on the road visiting clients thinks that on average he drives the same distance each day of the week. He keeps track of his mileage for several weeks and discovers that he averages 122 miles on Mondays, 203 miles on Tuesdays, 176 miles on Wednesdays, 181 miles on Thursdays, and 108 miles on Fridays. He wonders if this evidence contradicts his belief in a uniform distribution of miles across the days of the week. Explain why it is not appropriate to test his hypothesis using the chi-square goodness-of-fit test.

5. NYPD and race. Census data for New York City indicate that 29.2% of the under-18 population is white, 28.2% black, 31.5% latino, 9.1% Asian, and 2% other ethnicities. The New York Civil Liberties Union points out that of 26,181 police officers, 64.8% are white, 14.5% black, 19.1% Hispanic, and 1.4% Asian. Do the police officers reflect the ethnic composition of the city's youth? Test an appropriate hypothesis and state your conclusion.

6. Violence against women. In its study *When Men Murder Women*, the Violence Policy Center reported that 2129 women were murdered by men in 1996. Of these victims, a weapon could be identified for 2013 of them. Of those for whom a weapon could be identified, 1139 were killed by guns, 372 by knives or other cutting instruments, 158 by other weapons, and 344 by personal attack (battery, strangulation, etc.). The FBI's Uniform Crime Report says that among all murders nationwide the weapon use rates were as follows: guns 63.4%, knives 13.1%, other weapons, 16.8%, personal attack 6.7%. Is there evidence that violence against women involves different weapons than other violent attacks in the United States?

7. Fruit flies. Offspring of certain fruit flies may have yellow or ebony bodies and normal wings or short wings. Genetic theory predicts that these traits will appear in the ratio 9:3:3:1 (9 yellow, normal: 3 yellow, short: 3 ebony, normal: 1 ebony, short). A researcher checks 100 such flies and finds the distribution of the traits to be 59, 20, 11, and 10, respectively.

a) Are the results this researcher observed consistent with the theoretical distribution predicted by the genetic model?
b) If the researcher had examined 200 flies and counted exactly twice as many in each category—118, 40, 22, 20—what conclusion would he have reached?
c) Why is there a discrepancy between the two conclusions?

8. Pi. Many people know the mathematical constant π is approximately 3.14. But that's not exact. To be more precise, here are 20 decimal places: 3.14159265358979323846. Still not exact, though. In fact, the actual value is irrational, a decimal that goes on forever without any repeating pattern. But notice that there are no 0's and only one 7 in the 20 decimal places above. Does that pattern persist, or do all the digits show up with equal frequency? The table shows the number of times each digit appears in the first million digits. Test the hypothesis that the digits 0 through 9 are uniformly distributed in the decimal representation of π.

The first million digits of π ...

Digit	Count
0	99959
1	99758
2	100026
3	100229
4	100230
5	100359
6	99548
7	99800
8	99985
9	100106

9. *Titanic*. Here is a table showing who survived the sinking of the *Titanic* based on whether they were crew members, or passengers booked in first-, second-, or third-class staterooms:

	Crew	First	Second	Third	Total
Alive	212	202	118	178	710
Dead	673	123	167	528	1491
Total	885	325	285	706	2201

a) If we draw an individual at random from this table, what's the probability that we will draw a member of the crew?
b) What's the probability of randomly selecting a third-class passenger who survived?
c) What's the probability of a randomly selected passenger surviving, given that the passenger was a first-class passenger?
d) If someone's chances of surviving were the same regardless of their status on the ship, how many members of the crew would you expect to have lived?
e) State the null and alternative hypotheses we would test here.
f) Give the degrees of freedom for the test.
g) The chi-square value for the table is 187.8, and the corresponding P-value is barely greater than 0. State your conclusions about the hypotheses.

10. NYPD and gender. The table below shows the rank attained by male and female officers in the New York City Police Department. Do these data indicate that men and women are equitably represented at all levels of the department?

Rank	Male	Female
Officer	21,900	4,281
Detective	4,058	806
Sergeant	3,898	415
Lieutenant	1,333	89
Captain	359	12
Higher ranks	218	10

a) What's the probability that a police officer selected at random from the NYPD is a female?
b) What's the probability that a police officer selected at random is a detective?
c) Assuming no bias in promotions, how many female detectives would you expect the NYPD to have?
d) To see if there is evidence of differences in ranks attained by males and females, will you test goodness-of-fit, homogeneity, or independence?
e) State the hypotheses.
f) Test the conditions.
g) How many degrees of freedom are there?
h) Find χ^2 and the P-value.
i) State your conclusion.
j) If you concluded that the distributions are not the same, analyze the differences using the standardized residuals of your calculations.

11. Cranberry juice. It's common folk wisdom that drinking cranberry juice can help prevent urinary tract infections in women. In 2001 the *British Medical Journal* reported the results of a Finnish study in which three groups of 50 women were monitored for these infections over 6 months. One group drank cranberry juice daily, another group drank a lactobacillus drink, and the third drank neither of those beverages, serving as a control group. In the control group, 18 women developed at least one infection compared with 20 of those who consumed the lactobacillus drink and only 8 of those who drank cranberry juice. Does this study provide supporting evidence for the value of cranberry juice in warding off urinary tract infections?
a) Is this a survey, a retrospective study, a prospective study, or an experiment? Explain.
b) Will you test goodness-of-fit, homogeneity, or independence?
c) State the hypotheses.
d) Test the conditions.
e) How many degrees of freedom are there?
f) Find χ^2 and the P-value.
g) State your conclusion.
h) If you concluded that the groups are not the same, analyze the differences using the standardized residuals of your calculations.

12. Cars. A random survey of autos parked in student and staff lots at a large university classified the brands by country of origin, as seen in the table. Are there differences in the national origins of cars driven by students and staff?

	Driver	
Origin	**Student**	**Staff**
American	107	105
European	33	12
Asian	55	47

a) Is this a test of independence or homogeneity?
b) Write appropriate hypotheses.
c) Check the necessary assumptions and conditions.
d) Find the P-value of your test.
e) State your conclusion and analysis.

13. Montana. A 1992 poll conducted by the University of Montana classified respondents by gender and political party, as shown in the table. We wonder if there is evidence of an association between gender and party affiliation

	Democrat	Republican	Independent
Male	36	45	24
Female	48	33	16

a) Is this a test of homogeneity or independence?
b) Write an appropriate hypothesis.
c) Are the conditions for inference satisfied?
d) Find the P-value for your test.
e) State a complete conclusion.

14. Fish diet. Medical researchers followed 6272 Swedish men for 30 years to see if there was any association between the amount of fish in their diet and prostate cancer. ("Fatty Fish Consumption and Risk of Prostate Cancer," *Lancet* [June 2001])

Fish Consumption	Total Subjects	Prostate Cancers
Never/seldom	124	14
Small part of diet	2621	201
Moderate part	2978	209
Large part	549	42

a) Is this a survey, a retrospective study, a prospective study, or an experiment? Explain.
b) Is this a test of homogeneity or independence?
c) Do you see evidence of an association between the amount of fish in a man's diet and his risk of developing prostate cancer?
d) Does this study prove that eating fish does not prevent prostate cancer? Explain.

15. Montana revisited. The poll described in Exercise 13 also investigated the respondents' party affiliations based on what area of the state they lived in. Test an appropriate hypothesis about this table, and state your conclusions.

	Democrat	Republican	Independent
West	39	17	12
Northeast	15	30	12
Southeast	30	31	16

16. Working parents. In July 1991 and again in April 2001 the Gallup Poll asked random samples of 1015 adults about their opinions on working parents. The table summarizes responses to the question "Considering the needs of both parents and children, which of the following do you see as the ideal family in today's society?"

	1991	2001
Both work full time	142	131
One works full time, other part time	274	244
One works, other works at home	152	173
One works, other stays home for kids	396	416
No opinion	51	51

a) Is this a survey, a retrospective study, a prospective study, or an experiment? Explain.
b) Will you test goodness-of-fit, homogeneity, or independence?
c) Based on these results, do you think there was a change in people's attitudes during the 10 years between these polls?.

17. Grades. Two different professors teach an introductory Statistics course. The table shows the distribution of final grades they reported. We wonder whether one of these professors is an "easier" grader.

	Prof. Alpha	Prof. Beta
A	3	9
B	11	12
C	14	8
D	9	2
F	3	1

a) Will you test goodness-of-fit, homogeneity, or independence?
b) Write appropriate null hypotheses.
c) Find the expected counts for each cell, and explain why the chi-square procedures are not appropriate for this table.

18. Full moon. Some people believe that a full moon elicits unusual behavior in people. The table shows the number of arrests made in a small town during weeks of six full moons and six other randomly selected weeks during the same year. We wonder if there is evidence of a difference in the types of illegal activity that takes place.

Offense	Full Moon	Not Full
Violent (murder, assault, rape, etc)	2	3
Property (burglary, vandalism, etc)	17	21
Drugs/Alcohol	27	19
Domestic Abuse	11	14
Other offenses	9	6

a) Will you test goodness-of-fit, homogeneity, or independence?
b) Write appropriate null hypotheses.
c) Find the expected counts for each cell, and explain why the chi-square procedures are not appropriate for this table.

19. Grades again. In some situations where the expected cell counts are too small, as in the case of the grades given by Professors Alpha and Beta in Exercise 17, we can complete an analysis anyway. We can often proceed after combining cells in some way that both makes sense and produces a table in which the conditions are satisfied. Here we create a new table displaying the same data, but calling D's and F's "Below C", as shown.

	Prof. Alpha	Prof. Beta
A	3	9
B	11	12
C	14	8
Below C	12	3

a) Find the expected counts for each cell in this new table, and explain why a chi-square procedure is now appropriate.
b) With this change in the table, what has happened to the number of degrees of freedom?
c) Test your hypothesis about the two professors, and state an appropriate conclusion.

20. Full moon, next phase. In Exercise 18 you found that the expected cell counts failed to satisfy the conditions for inference.
a) Find a sensible way to combine some cells that will make the expected counts acceptable.
b) Test a hypothesis about the full moon and state your conclusion.

21. Racial steering. A subtle form of racial discrimination in housing is "racial steering." Racial steering occurs when real estate agents show prospective buyers only homes in neighborhoods already dominated by that family's race. This violates the Fair Housing Act of 1968. According to an article in *Chance* magazine (Vol. 14, no. 2 [2001]), tenants at a large apartment complex recently filed a lawsuit alleging racial steering. The complex is divided into two parts, Section A and Section B. The plaintiffs claimed that white potential renters were steered to Section A, while African Americans were steered to Section B. The table displays the data that were presented in court to show the locations of recently rented apartments. Do you think there is evidence of racial steering?

	New Renters		
	White	Black	Total
Section A	87	8	95
Section B	83	34	117
Total	170	42	212

22. *Titanic,* redux. Newspaper headlines at the time, and traditional wisdom in the succeeding decades, have held that women and children escaped the *Titanic* in greater proportion than men. Here's a table with data by gender. Do you think that survival was independent of gender? Defend your conclusion.

	Female	Male	Total
Alive	343	367	710
Dead	127	1364	1491
Total	470	1731	2201

23. Steering revisited. You could have checked the data in Exercise 21 for evidence of racial steering using two-proportion z procedures.
a) Find the z–value for this approach and show that when you square z you get the value of χ^2 you calculated in Exercise 21.
b) Show that the resulting P-values are the same.

24. Survival and gender, one more time. In Exercise 22 you could have checked for a difference in the chances of survival for men and women using two-proportion z procedures.
a) Find the z–value for this approach.
b) Show that the square of your calculated value of z is the value of χ^2 you calculated in Exercise 22.
c) Show that the resulting P-values are the same.

25. Race and education. Data from the U.S. Census Bureau show levels of education a sample of U.S. residents attained by age 30.

	Not HS Grad	HS Diploma	College Grad	Adv. Degree
White	810	6429	4725	1127
Black	263	1598	549	117
Hispanic	1031	1269	412	99
Other	66	341	305	197

a) Do these data highlight significant differences in education levels attained by these groups?

26. Pregnancies. Most pregnancies result in live births, but some end in miscarriages or stillbirths. A June 2001 National Vital Statistics Report examined those outcomes in the United States during 1997, broken down by the age of the mother. The table shows counts consistent with that report. Is there evidence that the distribution of outcomes is not the same for these age groups?

Age of mother	Live births	Fetal losses
Under 20	49	13
20–29	201	41
30–34	88	21
35 or over	49	21

27. Race and education, part 2. Consider only the people who have graduated from high school from Exercise 25. Do these data suggest there are significant differences in opportunities for black and Hispanic Americans who have completed high school to pursue college or advanced degrees?

	H.S. diploma	College grad	Adv. degree
Black	1598	549	117
Hispanic	1269	412	99

28. Education by age. Use the survey results in the table to investigate differences in education level attained among different age groups in the United States.

	Age Group				
Education Level	25–34	35–44	45–54	55–64	≥ 65
Not H.S. grad	27	50	52	71	101
H.S.	82	19	88	83	59
1–3 years college	43	56	26	20	20
≥ 4 years college	48	75	34	26	20

Chapter 27

Inferences for Regression

WHO	250 Male subjects
WHAT	Body fat and waist size
UNITS	%Body fat, and inches
WHEN	1990s
WHERE	United States
WHY	Scientific research

Three percent of a man's body is essential fat. (For a woman, the percentage is more like 12.5%.) As the name implies, essential fat is necessary for a normal, healthy body. Fat is stored in small amounts throughout your body. Too much body fat, however can be dangerous to your health. For men between 18 and 39 years old, a healthy percent body fat ranges from 8% to 19%. (For women of the same age, it's 21% to 32%.)

Measuring body fat can be tedious and expensive. The "standard reference" measurement is by dual-energy X-ray absorptiometry (DEXA), which involves two low-dose X-ray generators and takes from 10 to 20 minutes.

How close can we get to a useable prediction of body fat from easily measurable variables such as height, weight or waist size? Here's a scatterplot of the %body fat plotted against waist size for a sample of 250 males of various ages.

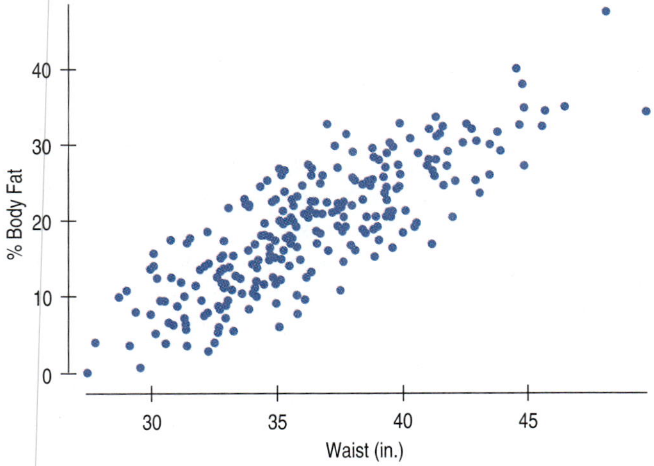

Percent body fat vs. waist size for 250 men of various ages. The scatterplot shows a strong, positive, linear relationship. **Figure 27.1**

The least squares line for these data has the following equation:

$$\widehat{\%Body\ Fat} = -42.7 + 1.7\ Waist$$

The slope says that, on average, %body fat grows at a rate of 1.7 percent for each added inch around the waist.

How useful is this model? We learned in Chapter 8 how to calculate these coefficients. Now we'd like to know what the regression model can tell us beyond the data at hand, in this case the 250 men in this study. To do that, we'll need to make confidence intervals and test hypotheses about the slope and intercept of the regression line.

The Population and the Sample

What do we mean by inference for regression? We know better than to think that even if we knew every population value, the data would line up perfectly on a straight line. After all, even in our sample, not all men who have 38-inch waists have the same %body fat. In fact, there's a whole distribution of %body fat for these men:

The distribution of %body fat for men with a waist size of 38 inches is unimodal and symmetric. **Figure 27.2**

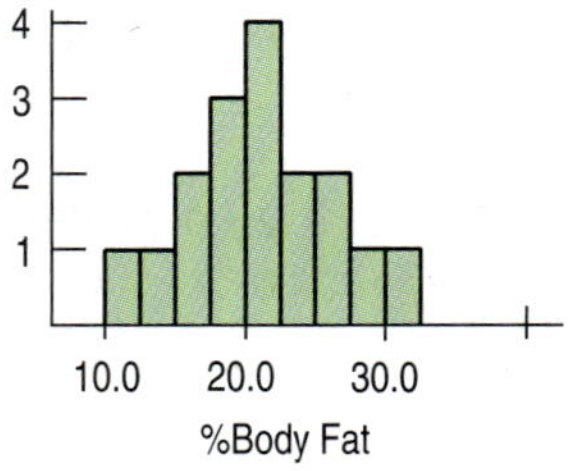

Of course, the same is true at each waist size. We could depict the distribution of %body fat at different waist sizes like this:

There's a distribution of %body fat for *each* value of waist size. We'd like the means of these distributions to line up. **Figure 27.3**

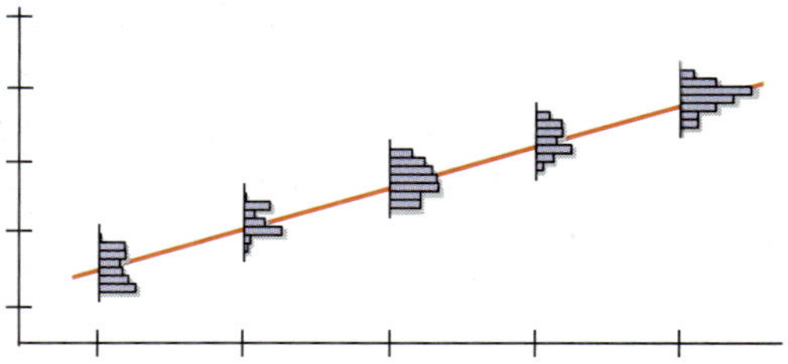

But we want to *model* the relationship between %body fat and waist size for all men. To do that, we imagine an idealized regression line. This model assumes that the means of the distributions of %body fat for each waist size fall along the line even though the individuals are scattered around it. We know that this model is not a perfect description of how the variables are associated, but it may be useful for predicting %body fat and understanding how it's related to waist size.

NOTATION ALERT:

This time we only used up one Greek letter for two things. Lower-case Greek β (beta) is the natural choice to correspond to the b's in the regression equation. We used β before for the probability of a Type II error, but there's little chance of confusion here.

If we had all the values in the population, we could find the slope and intercept of this *idealized regression line* explicitly by using least squares. Following our usual conventions, we write the idealized line with Greek letters and consider the coefficients to be *parameters:* β_0 is the intercept and β_1 is the slope. Corresponding to our fitted line of $\hat{y} = b_0 + b_1x$, we write

$$\mu_y = \beta_0 + \beta_1 x.$$

Why μ_y insead of $\hat{y}$? Because this is a model. The model says there is a distribution of %body fat for each waist size, and places the *mean %body fat* for each *waist size* on the same straight line.

Of course, not all the individual *y's* are at these means. (That's why the equation uses μ.) Some individuals lie above and some below the line, so, like all models, this one makes **errors.** Lots of them. In fact, one at each point. These errors can be positive or negative, depending on which side of the line the data fall (or even zero if the line happens to pass right through the point). We denote the errors by ε and write $\varepsilon = y - \mu_y$ for each data point (x, y).

When we put the errors into the equation, we can talk about individual y's instead of means:

$$y = \beta_0 + \beta_1 x + \varepsilon.$$

This equation is now true for each data point (since the individual ε's soak up the deviations) and gives a value of y for any value of x.

For the body fat data, an idealized model such as this provides a summary of the relationship between %body fat and waist size. Like all models, it simplifies the real situation. We know there is more to predicting body fat than waist size alone. But the advantage of models is that the simplification might help us to think about the situation and assess how well %body fat can be predicted from simpler measurements.

We estimate the β's by finding a regression line, $\hat{y} = b_0 + b_1 x$, as we did in Chapter 8. The residuals, $e = y - \hat{y}$, are the sample-based versions of the errors ε. We'll use them to help us assess the regression model.

We know that least squares regression will give reasonable estimates of the parameters of this model from a random sample of data. Our challenge is to account for our uncertainty in how well they do. For that, we need to make some assumptions about the model and the errors.

Assumptions and Conditions

Back in Chapter 8 when we fit lines to data, we needed to check only the straight enough condition. Now, when we want to make inferences about the coefficients of the line, we'll have to make more assumptions. Fortunately, we can check conditions to help us judge whether these assumptions are reasonable for our data. And as we've done before, we'll make some checks *after* we find the regression equation.

Also, we need to be careful about the order in which we check conditions. If our initial assumptions are not true, it makes no sense to check the later ones. So now we number the assumptions to keep them in order.

1. Linearity Assumption

Check the scatterplot. The shape must be linear or we can't use regression at all.

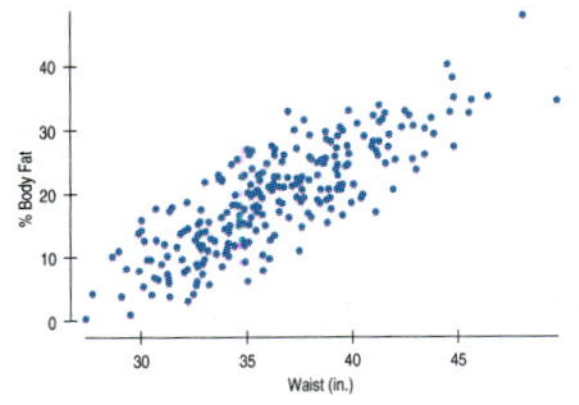

If the true relationship is far from linear and we use a straight line to fit the data, our entire analysis may be useless, so we always check this first.

The **straight enough condition** is satisfied if a scatterplot looks straight. It's generally not a good idea to draw a line through the scatterplot when checking. That can fool your eye into seeing the plot as more straight. Sometimes it's easier to see violations of the straight enough condition by looking at a scatterplot of the residuals against the predicted values, $\hat{y}$. That plot has a horizontal direction and should have no pattern.

If the scatterplot is straight enough, we can go on to some assumptions about the errors. If not, stop here, or consider re-expressing the data (see Chapter 10) to make the scatterplot more nearly linear. For the %body fat data, the scatterplot is beautifully linear.

Check the residual plot (1). The residuals should appear to be randomly scattered.

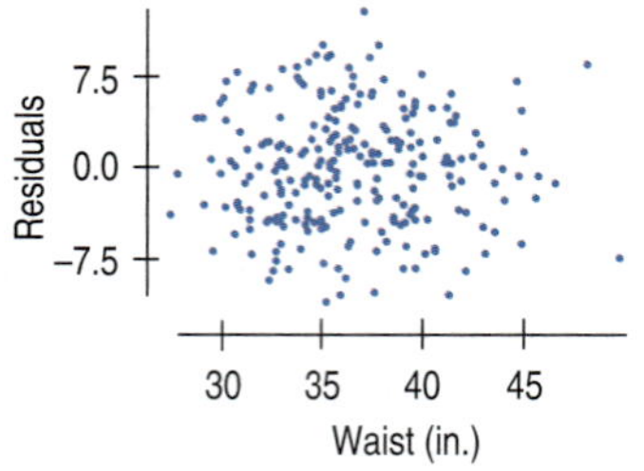

The residuals show only random scatter when plotted against waist size. **Figure 27.4**

Check the residual plot (2). The spread of the residuals should be uniform.

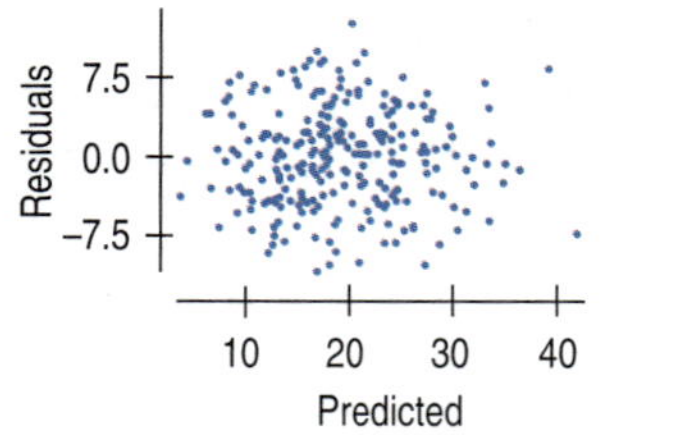

A scatterplot of residuals against predicted values can help check for plot thickening. Note that this plot looks identical to the plot of residuals against waist size. For a regression of one response variable on one predictor, these plots differ only in the labels on the *x*-axis. **Figure 27.5**

Check a histogram of the residuals. The distribution of the residuals should be unimodal and symmetric.

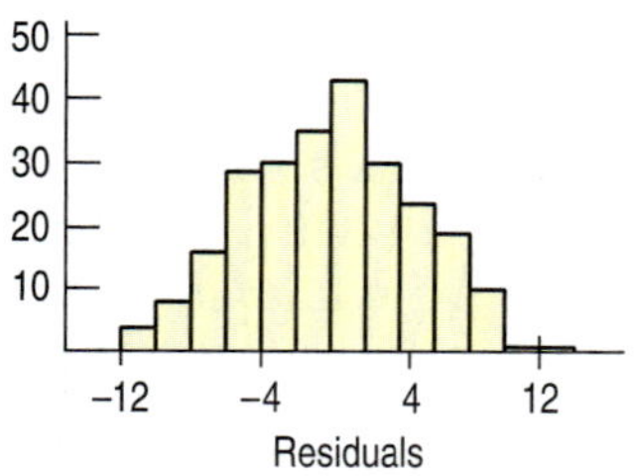

A histogram of the residuals is one way to check whether they are nearly Normal. Alternatively, we can look at a Normal probability plot. **Figure 27.6**

2. Independence Assumption

The errors in the true underlying regression model (the ε's) must be mutually independent. As usual, there's no way to be sure that the independence assumption is true.

Usually when we care about inference for the regression parameters it's because we think our regression model might apply to a larger population. In such cases, we can check a **randomization condition,** that the individuals are a representative sample from that population.

We can also check displays of the regression residuals for evidence of patterns, trends, or clumping, any of which would suggest a failure of independence. In the special case when the x-variable is related to time, a common violation of the independence assumption is for the errors to be correlated. (The error our model makes today may be similar to the one it made for yesterday.) This violation can be checked by plotting the residuals against the x-variable and looking for patterns.

The %body fat data were collected on a sample of men taken to be representative. The subjects were not related in any way, so we can be pretty sure that their measurements are independent. The residual plot shows no pattern.

3. Equal Variance Assumption

The variability of y should be about the same for all values of x. In Chapter 8 we looked at the standard deviation of the residuals (s_e) to measure the size of the scatter. Now we'll need this standard deviation to build confidence intervals and test hypotheses. The standard deviation of the residuals is the building block for the standard errors of all the parameters. But it only makes sense if the scatter of the residuals is the same everywhere. In effect, the standard deviation of the residuals is a "pooled" estimate, and pooled estimates are appropriate only when the variance is constant.

Practically, what we can check is the **Does the plot thicken? condition.** A scatterplot of y against x offers a visual check. Fortunately, we've already made one. Make sure the spread around the line is nearly constant. Be alert for a "fan" shape or other tendency for the variability to grow or shrink in one part of the scatterplot. Often it is better to plot the residuals against x or against the predicted values, $\hat{y}$. With the slope of the line removed, it's easier to see patterns. For the body fat data, the spread of %body fat around the line is remarkably constant across waist sizes from 30 inches to about 45 inches.

If the plot is straight enough, the data are independent, and the plot doesn't thicken, you can now move on to the final assumption.

4. Normality Assumption

We assume the errors around the idealized regression line at each value of x follow a Normal model. We need this assumption so that we can use a Student's t-model for inference.

As with other times when we've used Student's t, we'll settle for the residuals satisfying the **nearly Normal condition.** Look at a histogram or normal probability plot of the residuals.

The histogram of residuals in the %body fat regression (next page) certainly looks nearly Normal. As we have noted before, the Normality assumption becomes less important as the sample size grows because the model is about means and the Central Limit Theorem takes over.

If all four assumptions are true, the idealized regression model looks like this:

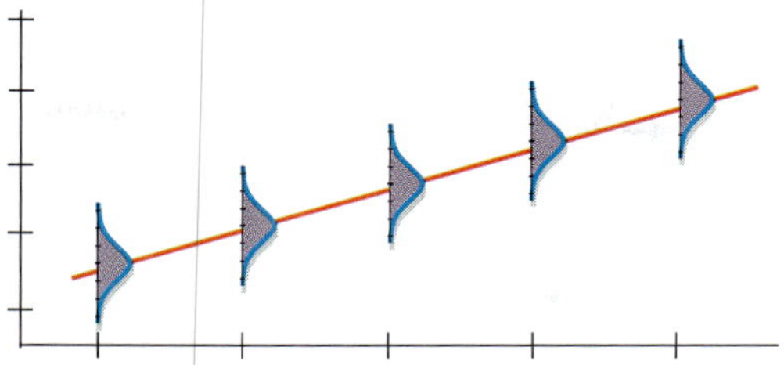

The regression model has a distribution of y-values for each x-value. These distributions follow a Normal model with means lined up along the line and the same standard deviations. **Figure 27.7**

At each value of x there is a distribution of y-values that follows a Normal model, and each of these Normal models is centered on the line and has the same standard deviation.

Which Come First: the Conditions or the Residuals?

"Truth will emerge more readily from error than from confusion."
—Francis Bacon (1561–1626)

In regression, there's a little catch. The best way to check many of the conditions is with the residuals, but we get the residuals only *after* we compute the regression model. To compute the regression model, however, we should check the conditions.

So we work in this order:

- Make a scatterplot of the data to check the straight enough condition. (If the relationship isn't straight, try re-expressing the data. Or stop.)
- If the data are straight enough, fit a regression model and find the residuals, e, and predicted values, $\hat{y}$.
- Make a scatterplot of the residuals against the predicted values. This plot should have no pattern. Check in particular for any bend (which would suggest that the data weren't all that straight after all), for any thickening (or thinning), and, of course, for any outliers.
- If the data are measured over time, plot the residuals against time to check for evidence of patterns that might suggest they are not independent.
- If the scatterplots look OK, then make a histogram and Normal probability plot of the residuals to check the nearly Normal condition.
- If all the conditions seem to be satisfied, go ahead with inference.

Regression Inference STEP-BY-STEP

If our data can jump through all these hoops, we're ready to do regression inference. Let's try one on the body fat data.

Think

Variables Name the variables, report the W's, and specify the questions of interest.

We have body measurements on 250 adult males from the BYU Human Performance Research Center. We want to understand the relationship between %body fat and waist size.

Plan Check the conditions.

✓ **Straight enough condition:** There's no obvious bend in the original scatterplot of the data or in the plot of residuals against predicted values.

✓ **Independence assumption:** These data are not collected over time and there's no reason to think that the %body fat of one man influences the %body fat of another.

(We've looked at the plots already. See Figures 27.5 and 27.6.)

✓ **Does the plot thicken? condition:** Neither the original scatterplot nor the residual scatterplot shows any changes in the spread about the line.

✓ **Nearly Normal condition:** A histogram of the residuals is unimodal and symmetric. The Normal probability plot of the residuals is quite straight, indicating that the Normal model is reasonable for the errors.

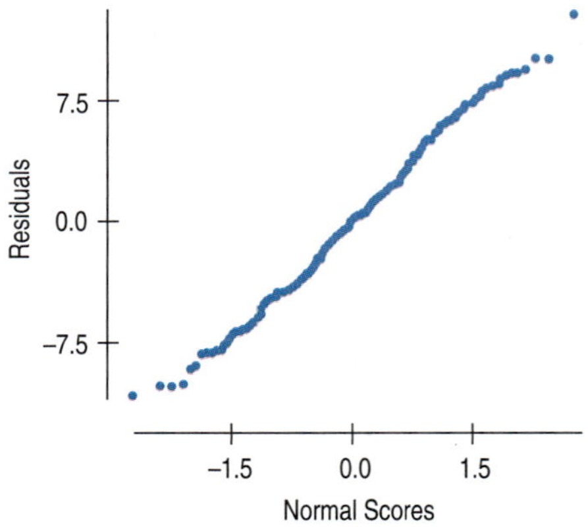

Under these conditions the regression model is appropriate.

Choose your method.

We will use the **regression model.**

Show

Mechanics Let's just "push the button" and see what the regression looks like.

The formula for the regression equation can be found in Chapter 8, and the standard error formulas will be shown a bit later, but regressions are almost always found from a computer program or calculator.

Computer output for this regression might look in part like this:

Dependent variable is: %BF

R-squared = 67.8%

s = 4.713 with 250 − 2 = 248 degrees of freedom

Variable	Coeff	SE(Coeff)	t-ratio	prob
Constant	−42.734	2.717	−15.7	≤0.0001
Waist	1.70	0.0743	22.9	≤0.0001

The estimated regression equation is

$$\widehat{\%Body\ Fat} = -42.73 + 1.70\ Waist.$$

Tell

Interpretation

The R^2 for the regression is 67.8%. Waist size seems to account for about 2/3 of the %body fat variation in men. The regression equation indicates that each inch in waist size results in about a 1.7 increase in %body fat.

More Interpretation We haven't worked it out in detail yet, but the output gives us numbers labeled as t-statistics and corresponding P-values, and we have a general idea of what those mean.

The standard error of 0.07 for the slope is much smaller than the slope itself, so it looks like the estimate is reasonably precise. And there are a couple of t-ratios and P-values given. Because the P-values are small, it appears that some null hypotheses can be rejected.

(Time to learn more about regression inference so we can figure out what the rest of the output means.)

Intuition About Regression Inference

Wait a minute! We've just pulled a fast one. We've pushed the "regression button" on our computer or calculator, but haven't discussed where the standard errors for the slope or intercept come from. We know that if we had collected similar data on a different random sample of men, the slope and intercept would be different. Each sample would have produced its own regression line with slightly different b_0's and b_1's. There's only one regression model; each sample regression is trying to estimate the same parameters, β_0 and β_1. This sample-to-sample variation is what generates the sampling distributions for the coefficients.

We expect any sample to produce a b_1 whose expected value is the true slope, β_1. What about its standard deviation? What aspects of the data affect how much the slope and intercept vary from sample to sample?

- **Spread around the line.** Here are two situations in which we might do regression. Which situation would yield the more consistent slope? That is, if we were to sample over and over from these two underlying populations and compute all the slopes, which group of slopes would vary less?

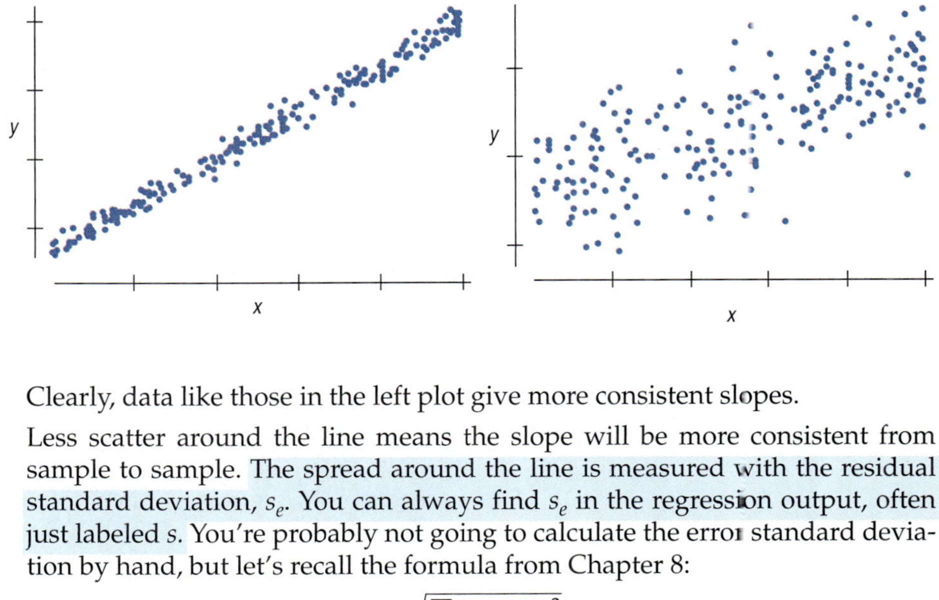

Which of these scatterplots shows a situation that would give the more consistent regression slope estimate if we were to sample repeatedly from the underlying population?
Figure 27.8

Clearly, data like those in the left plot give more consistent slopes.

Less scatter around the line means the slope will be more consistent from sample to sample. The spread around the line is measured with the residual standard deviation, s_e. You can always find s_e in the regression output, often just labeled s. You're probably not going to calculate the error standard deviation by hand, but let's recall the formula from Chapter 8:

$$s_e = \sqrt{\frac{\sum(y - \hat{y})^2}{n - 2}}.$$

n − 2?

Remember why we divide by $n - 2$? Well, for the standard deviation in Chapter 5, we divided by $n - 1$ because we didn't know the true mean and had to estimate it. Now it's later in the course and we know even less. Here we don't know *two* things: the slope and the intercept. If we knew them both, we'd divide by n and have n degrees of freedom. When we estimate both, however, we adjust by subtracting 2, so we divide by $n - 2$ and (as we will see soon) lose 2 degrees of freedom.

The smaller the error standard deviation, the less scatter around the line and the stronger the relationship between x and y.

Some people prefer to assess the strength of a regression by looking at s_e rather than R^2. After all, s_e has the same units as y and because it's the standard deviation of the errors around the line, it tells you how close the data are to our model. By contrast, R^2 is the proportion of the variation of y accounted for by x. Why not look at both?

- **Spread of the x's:** Here are two more situations. Which of these would yield more consistent slopes?

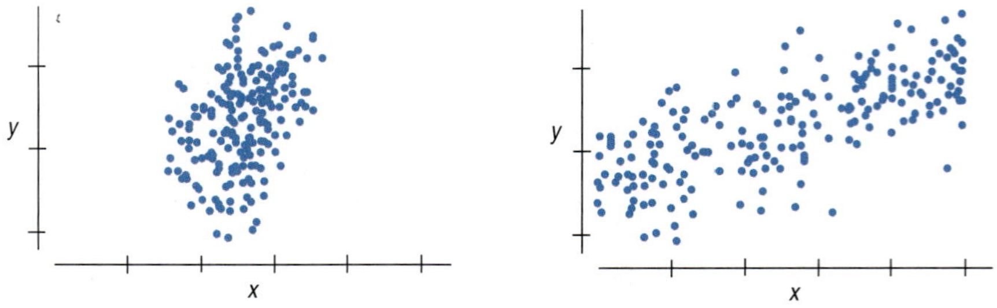

Which of these scatterplots shows a situation that would give the more consistent regression slope estimate if we were to sample repeatedly from the underlying population? **Figure 27.9**

A plot like the one on the right has a broader range of x-values, so it gives a more stable base for the slope. We'd expect the slope of a regression from those data to vary less from sample to sample. A large standard deviation of x, s_x provides a more stable regression.

- **Sample size.** Here we go again. What about these two?

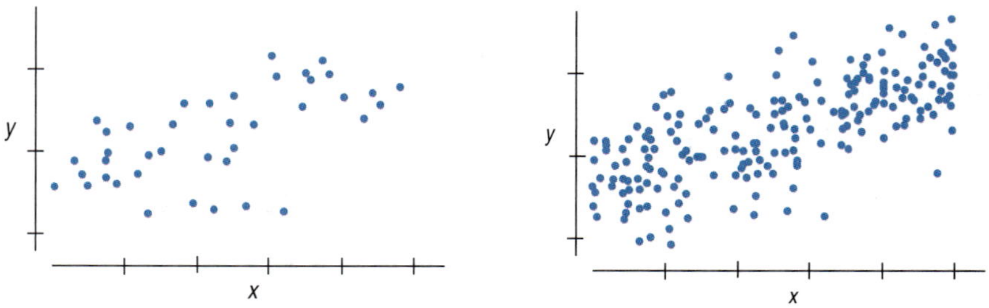

Which of these scatterplots shows a situation that would give the more consistent regression slope estimate if we were to sample repeatedly from the underlying population? **Figure 27.10**

It shouldn't be a surprise that having a larger sample size, n, gives more consistent estimates.

Standard Error for the Slope

Three aspects of the scatterplot, then, affect the standard error of the regression slope:

- Spread around the line: s_e
- Spread of x values: s_x
- Sample size: n

These are in fact the *only* things that affect the standard error of the slope. Although you'll probably never have to calculate it by hand, the formula for the standard error is:

$$SE(b_1) = \frac{s_e}{\sqrt{n-1}\, s_x}.$$

The error standard deviation, s_e is in the *numerator,* since spread around the line *increases* the slope's standard error. The denominator has both a sample size term($\sqrt{n-1}$) and s_x because increasing either of these *decreases* the slope's standard error.

We know the b_1's vary from sample to sample. As you'd expect, their sampling distribution model is centered at β_1, the slope of the idealized regression line. Now we can estimate its standard deviation with $SE(b_1)$. What about its shape? Here the Central Limit Theorem and "Wild Bill" Gossett come to the rescue again. When we standardize the slopes by subtracting the model mean and dividing by their standard error, we get a Student's t-model, this time with $n - 2$ degrees of freedom:

$$\frac{b_1 - \beta_1}{SE(b_1)} \sim t_{n-2}.$$

A sampling distribution for regression slopes

When the conditions are met, the standardized estimated regression slope,

$$t = \frac{b_1 - \beta_1}{SE(b_1)}$$

follows a Student's t-model with $n - 2$ degrees of freedom. We estimate the standard error with

$SE(b_1) = \frac{s_e}{\sqrt{n-1}\, s_x}$, where $s_e = \sqrt{\frac{\sum(y-\hat{y})^2}{n-2}}$, n is the number of data values, and s_x is the ordinary standard deviation of the x-values.

What About the Intercept?

The same reasoning applies for the intercept. We can write

$$\frac{b_0 - \beta_0}{SE(b_0)} \sim t_{n-2}$$

but we rarely use this fact for anything. The intercept usually isn't interesting. Most hypothesis tests and confidence intervals for regression are about the slope. But in case you really want to see the formula for the standard error of the intercept, we've parked it in a footnote.[1]

[1] $SE(b_0) = s_e\sqrt{\frac{1}{n} + \frac{\bar{x}^2}{\sum(x_i - \bar{x})^2}}$

Regression Inference

What if the Slope Were 0?
If the slope of the regression were zero, the equation would collapse to $\hat{y} = b_0$. Now x is nowhere in sight. And b_0 would turn out to be just $\bar{y}$.

Now that we have the standard error of the slope and its sampling distribution, we can test a hypothesis about it and make confidence intervals. The usual null hypothesis about the slope is that it's equal to 0. Why? Well, a slope of zero would say that y doesn't tend to change at all when x changes—in other words, that there is no association between the two variables. If the slope were zero, there wouldn't be much left of our regression equation.

So a null hypothesis of a zero slope questions the entire claim of a linear relationship between the two variables—and often that's just what we want to know. In fact, every software package or calculator that does regression simply assumes that you want to test the null hypothesis that the slope is really zero.

To test H_0: $\beta_1 = 0$ we find

$$t = \frac{b_1 - 0}{SE(b_1)}.$$

This is just like every t-test we've seen: a difference between the statistic and its hypothesized value divided by its standard error.

For our body fat data, the computer found the slope (1.7), its standard error (0.0743), and the ratio of the two: $\frac{1.7 - 0}{0.0743} = 22.9$ (see p. 533). Nearly 23 standard errors from the hypothesized value certainly seems big. The P-value (<0.0001) confirms that a t-ratio this large would be very unlikely to occur if the true slope were zero.

Maybe the standard null hypothesis isn't all that interesting here. Did you have any doubts that %body fat is related to waist size? A more sensible use of these same values might be to make a confidence interval for the slope instead.

We can build a confidence interval in the usual way, as an estimate plus or minus a margin of error. As always, the margin of error is just the product of the standard error and a critical value. Here the critical value comes from the t distribution with $n - 2$ degrees of freedom, so a 95% confidence interval for β is

$$b_1 \pm t^*_{n-2} \times SE(b_1).$$

For the body fat data, $t^*_{248} = 1.970$, so that comes to $1.7 \pm 1.97 \times 0.074$, or an interval from 1.55 to 1.85 %body fat per inch of waist size.

Another Example

Every spring, Nenana, Alaska, hosts a contest in which participants try to guess the exact minute that a wooden tripod placed on the frozen Tanana River will fall through the breaking ice. The contest started in 1917 as a diversion for railroad engineers with a jackpot of $800 for the closest guess. It has grown into an event in which hundreds of thousands of entrants enter their guesses on the Internet[2] and vie for more than $300,000.

Because so much money and interest depends on the time of breakup, it has been recorded to the nearest minute with great accuracy ever since 1917. And because a standard measure of breakup has been used

[2]Search for "Nenana Ice Classic."

throughout this time, the data are consistent. An article in *Science* ("Climate Change in Nontraditional Data Sets." *Science* 294 [26 October 2001]: 811) used the data to investigate global warming—whether greenhouse gasses and other human actions have been making the planet warmer. Others might just want to make a good prediction of next year's breakup time.

Of course, we can't use regression to tell the *causes* of any change. But we can estimate the *rate* of change (if any) and use it to make better predictions.

Here are some of the data:

WHO	Years
WHAT	Year, day, and hour of ice breakup
UNITS	Years since 1900. Day and hour as days and fraction of days after midnight Jan. 1 of the year. Unit is "days."
WHEN	1917 – present
WHERE	Nenana, Alaska
WHY	Wagering, but proposed to look at global warming

Year (since 1900)	Breakup date (days after Jan. 1)	Year (since 1900)	Breakup date (days after Jan. 1)
17	119.4792	30	127.7938
18	130.3979	31	129.3910
19	122.6063	32	121.4271
20	131.4479	33	127.8125
21	130.2792	34	119.5882
22	131.5556	35	134.5639
23	128.0833	36	120.5403
24	131.6319	37	131.8361
25	126.7722	38	125.8431
26	115.6688	39	118.5597
27	131.2375	40	110.6437
28	126.6840	41	122.0764
29	124.6535	⋮	⋮

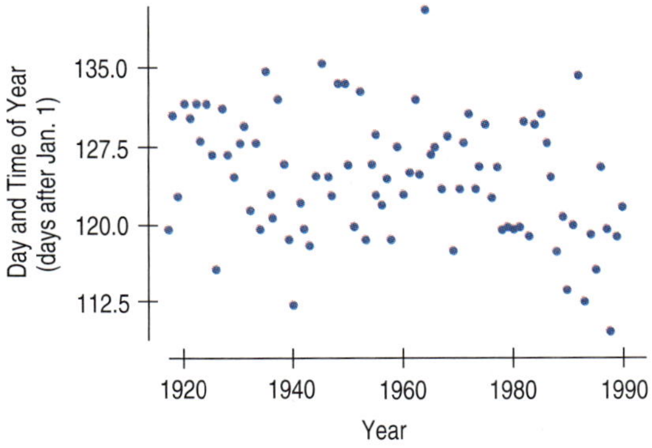

Has the time of ice breakup on the Tanana River changed since 1917, when record keeping began? Earlier breakup times might be a sign of global warming. **Figure 27.11**

A Regression Slope *t*-Test STEP-BY-STEP

The slope of the regression gives the change in breakup date per year. Let's test the hypothesis that the slope is zero.

Think

Hypotheses

State what we want to know.

(Hypotheses on the intercept are not particularly interesting for these data.)

We wonder whether the time of ice breakup has become earlier.

H_0: There is no change in the date of ice breakup $\beta_1 = 0$

H_A: Yes, there is: $\beta_1 \neq 0$

Plan Check the conditions.

✓ **Straight enough condition:** There is no obvious bend in the scatterplot.

✓ **Independence assumption:** These data are a time series, which raises our suspicions that they may not be independent. We'll check the residuals plot:

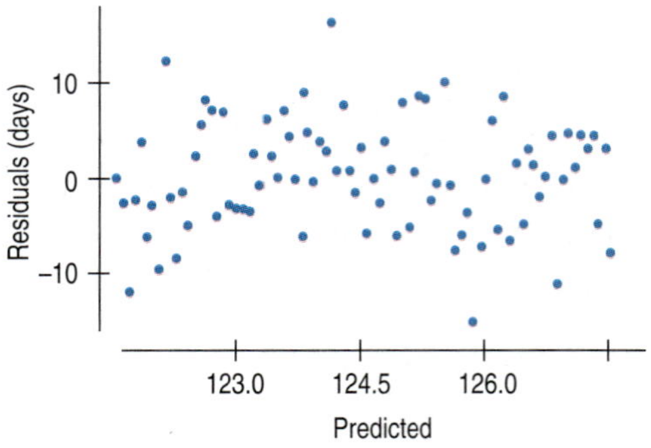

There is no clear evidence of dependence in the data above, although there may be some hint that the date oscillates up and down over time. The data are not a random sample, so we should be reluctant to extend our conclusions beyond this river and these years.

✓ **Does the plot thicken? condition:** The residuals plot shows no obvious trends in the spread.

✓ **Nearly Normal condition:** A histogram of the residuals is unimodal and symmetric.

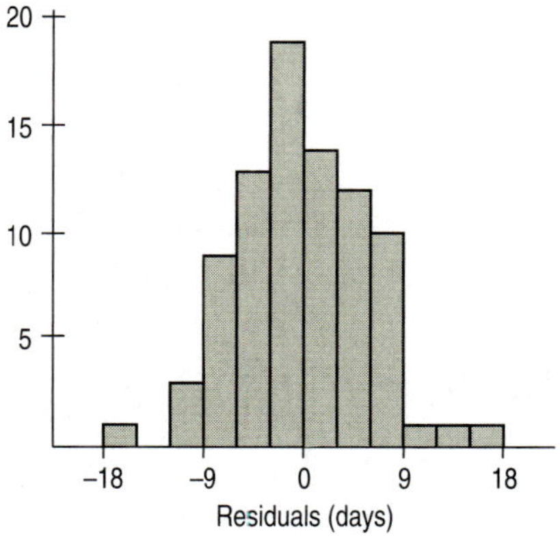

State the sampling distribution.

Under these conditions, the sampling distribution of the regression slope can be modeled by a Student's *t*-model with $(n - 2) = 82$ degrees of freedom.

Choose your method.

We will use a **regression slope *t*-test.**

Show

Mechanics

The regression equation can be found from the formulas we saw in Chapter 8, but regressions are almost always found from a computer program or calculator.

The P-values given in the regression output table are from the Student's t distribution on $(n - 2) = 82$ degrees of freedom. They are appropriate for two-sided alternatives.

Computer output for this regression looks in part like this:

Dependent variable is: breakupday

R-squared = 8.6%

s = 5.747 with 84 − 2 = 82 degrees of freedom

Variable	Coeff	SE(Coeff)	t-ratio	Prob
Constant	128.753	1.638	78.6	≤0.000
Year	−0.071961	0.0259	−2.78	0.00671

The estimated regression equation is

$$\widehat{Breakupday} = 128.8 - 0.07\ year.$$

Tell

Conclusion

State the conclusion.

The P-value of 0.0067 means that the association we see in the data is unlikely to have occurred by chance. We reject the null hypothesis, and conclude that there is strong evidence that, on average, the ice breakup is occurring earlier each year. But the oscillation pattern in the residuals requires further investigation.

Show More

Create a confidence interval for the true slope

A 95% confidence interval for β_1 is:

$$b_1 \pm t^*_{82} \times SE(b_1)$$
$$-0.072 \pm (1.99)(0.0259)$$

or (−0.12, −0.02) days.

Tell More

Interpret the interval

Simply rejecting the standard null hypothesis doesn't guarantee that the size of the effect is large enough to be important. Whether we want to know the breakup time to the nearest minute or are interested in global warming, a change measured in hours each year is big enough to be interesting.

We are 95% confident that the ice has been breaking up, on average, between 0.02 days (about a half-hour) and 0.12 days (about 3 hours) earlier each year since 1900.

TI Tips

°F	Min
44	142.7
46	142.1
47	143.4
50	143.6
51	144.0
52	143.4
54	142.4
55	143.1
57	143.7
60	143.4
65	143.4

The TI will easily do almost everything you need for inference for regression: scatterplots, residual plots, histograms of residuals, and the t-test for slope of the regression line. OK, it won't do confidence intervals, but it will tell you enough information to easily figure out $SE(b)$ so you can create the interval yourself. Not bad.

As an example we'll use data from *Chance* magazine (Vol. 12, No. 4, 1999), giving times and temperatures for 11 of the top performances in women's marathons during the 1990s. Let's examine the influence of temperature on the performance of elite runners in marathons.

Test a Hypothesis About the Association

- Enter the temperatures (nearest degree Fahrenheit) in L1 and the runners' times (nearest tenth of a minute) in L2.

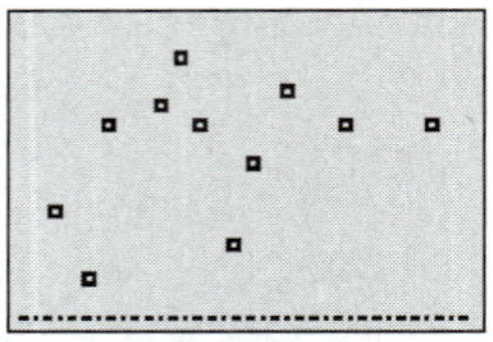

- Check the scatterplot. It's not obviously nonlinear, so go ahead.
- Under `STAT TESTS` choose `E:LinRegTTest`.
- Specify the two data lists (with `Freq:1`).
- Choose the two-tailed option. (We are interested in whether higher temperatures enhance or interfere with a runner's performance.)
- Tell it to store the regression equation in `Y1` (`VARS, Y-VARS, Function` . . . remember?), then `Calculate`.

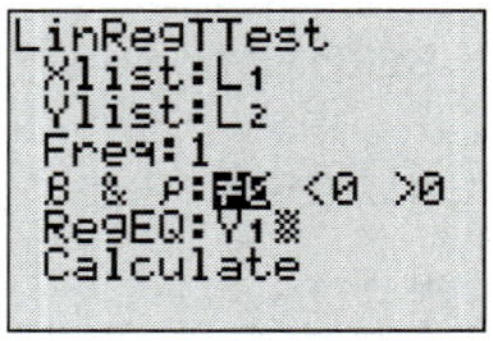

The TI creates so much information you have to scroll down to see it all! Look what's there.

- The calculated value of `t`, and the `P`-value.
- The coefficients of the regression equation, `a` and `b`.
- The value of `s`, our sample estimate of the common standard deviation of errors around the true line.
- The values of `r`^{2} and `r`.

Wait, where's *SE*(*b*)? You also need to know that in order to create confidence intervals. It's not there. No problem—you can figure it out. Remember that the *t*-value is *b* divided by *SE*(*b*). So *SE*(*b*) must be *b* divided by *t*. Here $SE(b) = 0.0325 \div 1.1358 = 0.0286$.

Checking Conditions

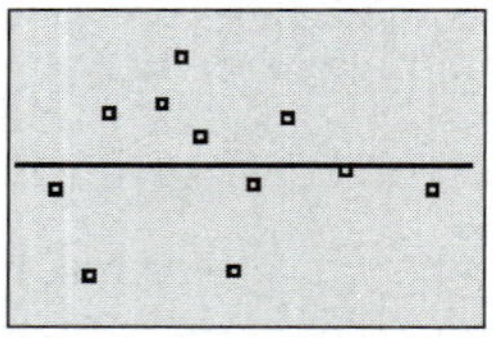

Beware!!! Before you try to interpret any of this, you must check the conditions to see if inference for regression is allowed.

- We already looked at the scatterplot; it was reasonably linear.
- To create the residuals plot, set up another scatterplot with `RESID` (from `LIST NAMES`) as your `Ylist`. Ok, it looks fairly random.
- The residuals plot may show a slight hint of diminishing scatter, but with so few data values it's not very clear.
- The histogram of the residuals is unimodal and roughly symmetric.

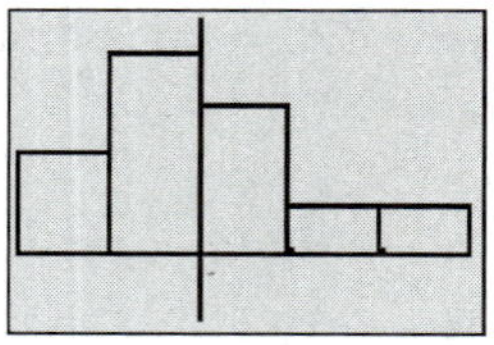

What Does It All Mean?

Because the conditions check out ok, we can try to summarize what we have learned? With a P-value over 28%, it's quite possible that any perceived relationship could be just sampling error. Based on these 11 races there appears to be little evidence of an association between temperature and women's performances in the marathon.

Standard Errors for Predicted Values (Optional)

Once we have a useful regression model, how can we indulge our natural desire to predict, without being irresponsible? We know how to compute predicted values of *y* for any value of *x*. We first did that in Chapter 8. This predicted value would be our best estimate, but it's still just an informed guess.

Now, however, we have standard errors. We can use those to construct a confidence interval for the predictions, smudging the results in the right way to report our uncertainty honestly.

From our model of %body fat and waist size, we might want to use waist size to get a reasonable estimate of %body fat. A confidence interval can tell us how precise that prediction will be. The precision depends on the question we ask, however, and there are two questions. Do we want to know the mean %body fat for *all* men with a waist size of, say, 38 inches? Or do we want to estimate the %body fat for a particular man with a 38-inch waist without making him climb onto the X-ray table?

What's the difference between the two questions? The predicted %body fat is the same, but one question leads to an answer much more precise than the other. We can predict the *mean* %body fat for *all* men whose waist size is 38 inches with a lot more precision than we can predict the %body fat of a *particular individual* whose waist size happens to be 38 inches. Both are interesting questions.

We start with the same prediction in both cases. We are predicting the value for a new individual, one that was not part of the original data set. To emphasize this, we'll call his x-value "x sub new" and write it x_ν.[3] Here, x_ν is 38 inches. The regression model predicts %body fat as $\hat{y}_\nu = b_0 + b_1 x_\nu$.

Now that we have the predicted value, we construct both intervals around this same number. Both intervals take the form

$$\hat{y}_\nu \pm t^*_{n-2} \times SE.$$

Even the t^* value is the same for both. It's the critical value (from a t-table or computer program) for $n - 2$ degrees of freedom and the specified confidence level. The difference between the two intervals is all in the standard errors. Our choice of ruler depends on which interval we want.

The standard errors for prediction depend on the same kinds of things as the coefficients' standard errors. If there is more spread around the line, we'll be less certain when we try to predict the response. Of course, if we're less certain of the slope, we'll be less certain of our prediction. If we have more data, our estimate will be more precise. And there's one more piece. If we're farther from the center of our data, our prediction will be less precise. The last factor is new, but makes intuitive sense. It's a lot easier to predict a data point near the middle of the data set than to extrapolate far from the center.

Each of these factors contributes uncertainty—that is, variability—to the estimate. Because the factors are independent of each other, we can add their variances to find the total variability. The resulting formula for the standard error of the *mean* predicted value explicitly takes into account each of the factors:

For the Nenana Ice Classic, someone who planned to place a bet would want to predict this year's breakup time. By contrast, scientists interested in global warming are likely to be more interested in the mean breakup time. Unfortunately for those who want to gamble, the variability is greater for predicting for a single year.

$$SE(\hat{\mu}_\nu) = \sqrt{SE^2(b_1) \times (x_\nu - \bar{x})^2 + \frac{s_e^2}{n}}$$

Individual values vary more than means, so the standard error for a single predicted value has to be larger than the standard error for the mean. In fact, the standard error of a single predicted value has an *extra* source of variability: the variation of individuals around the predicted mean. That appears as the extra variance term, s_e^2, at the end under the square root:

$$SE(\hat{y}_\nu) = \sqrt{SE^2(b_1) \times (x_\nu - \bar{x})^2 + \frac{s_e^2}{n} + s_e^2}$$

[3]Yes, this is a bilingual pun. The Greek letter ν is called "nu." Don't blame me; my co-author suggested this.

Remember to keep this distinction between the two kinds of standard errors when looking at computer output. The smaller one is for the mean predicted value, and the larger one is for an individual predicted value[4].

Confidence Intervals for Predicted Values (Optional)

Now that we have standard errors we can ask how well our analysis can predict the mean %body fat for men with 38-inch waists. The regression output table provides most of the numbers we need:

$s_e = 4.713$
$n = 250$
$SE(b_1) = 0.074$, and from the data we need to know that
$\bar{x} = 36.3$

The regression model gives a predicted value at $x_\nu = 38$ of

$$\hat{y}_\nu = -42.7\% + 1.7 \times 38 = 21.9\%.$$

Let's find the 95% confidence interval for the mean %body fat for all men with 38-inch waists. We find the standard error from the formula:

$$SE(\hat{\mu}_\nu) = \sqrt{0.074^2 \times (38 - 36.3)^2 + \frac{4.713^2}{250}} = 0.32\%.$$

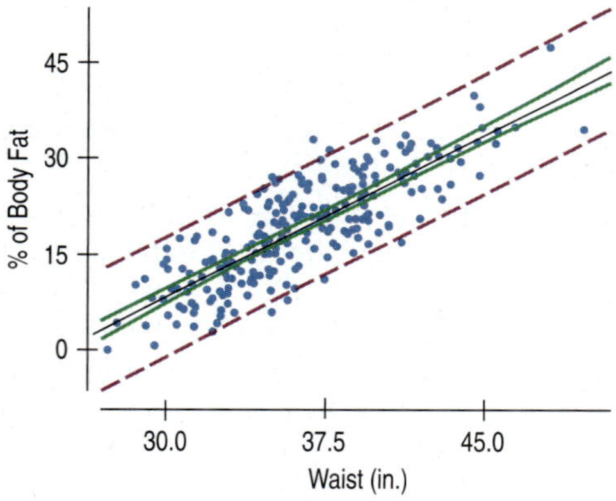

A scatterplot of %body fat vs. waist size with a least squares regression line. The solid green lines near the regression line show the extent of the 95% confidence interval for *mean* body fat at each waist size. The dashed red lines show the prediction interval. Most of the points are contained within the *prediction intervals,* but not within the confidence intervals. **Figure 27.12**

The t^* value that excludes 2.5% in either tail with $250 - 2 = 248$ df is (according to the tables) 1.97.

Putting it all together, we find the margin of error as

$$ME = 1.97 \times 0.32 = 0.63\%.$$

So, we are 95% confident that the mean %body fat for men with 38-inch waists is

$$21.9\% \pm 0.63\%.$$

Suppose, instead, we want to predict the %body fat for an individual man with a 38-inch waist. We need the larger standard error:

$$SE(\hat{y}_\nu) = \sqrt{0.074^2 \times (38 - 36.3)^2 + \frac{4.713^2}{250} + 4.713^2} = 4.72\%.$$

The corresponding margin of error is

$$ME = 1.97 \times 4.72 = 9.30\ \%,$$

so the prediction interval is:

$$21.9\% \pm 9.30\%.$$

[4]You may see the standard error expressions written in other equivalent ways. The most common alternatives are

$$SE(\hat{\mu}_\nu) = s_e\sqrt{\frac{1}{n} + \frac{(x_\nu - \bar{x})^2}{\sum(x - \bar{x})^2}} \quad \text{and} \quad SE(\hat{y}_\nu) = s_e\sqrt{1 + \frac{1}{n} + \frac{(x_\nu - \bar{x})^2}{\sum(x - \bar{x})^2}}.$$

We can think of this interval as having a 95% chance of capturing the true %body fat of a randomly selected man whose waist is 38 inches.[5] Notice how much wider this interval is than the previous one. As we've known since Chapter 18, the mean is much less variable than a randomly selected individual value.

Keep in mind this distinction between the two kinds of confidence intervals. The narrower interval is a **confidence interval for the mean predicted value** at x_ν, and the wider interval is a **prediction interval for an individual** with that x-value.

What Can Go Wrong?

In this chapter we've added inference to the regression explorations that we did in Chapters 8 and 9. Everything covered in those chapters that could go wrong with regression can still go wrong. It's probably a good time to review Chapter 9. We'll let you do that.

With inference, we've put numbers on our estimates and predictions, but these numbers are only as good as the model. Here are the main things to watch out for:

- ***Don't fit a linear regression to data that aren't straight.*** This is the most fundamental assumption. If the relationship between x and y isn't approximately linear, there's no sense in fitting a straight line to it.

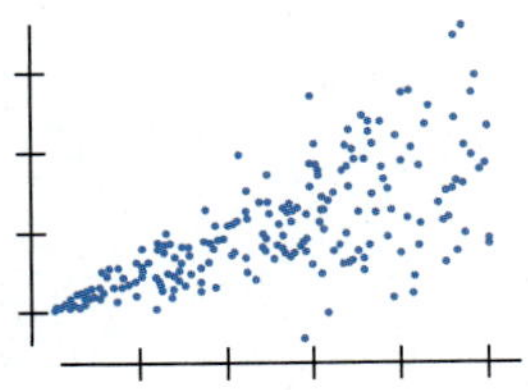

- ***Watch out for the plot thickening.*** The common part of confidence and prediction intervals is the estimate of the error standard deviation, the spread around the line. If it changes with x, the estimate won't make sense. Imagine making a prediction interval for these data.

  When x is small, we can predict y precisely, but as x gets larger, it's much harder to pin y down. Unfortunately, if the spread changes, the single value of s_e won't pick that up. The prediction interval will use the average spread around the line with the result that we'll be too pessimistic about our precision for low x-values and too optimistic for high x-values. A re-expression of y is often a good fix for changing spread.
- ***Make sure the errors are normal.*** When we make a prediction interval for an individual, the Central Limit Theorem can't come to our rescue. For us to believe the prediction interval, the errors must be from the Normal model. Check the histogram and Normal probability plot of the residuals to see if this assumption looks reasonable.
- ***Watch out for extrapolation.*** It's tempting to think that because we have prediction *intervals*, they'll take care of all of our uncertainty so we don't have to worry about extrapolating. Wrong. The interval is only as good as the model. The uncertainty our intervals predict is only correct if our model is true. There's no way to adjust for wrong models. That's why it's always dangerous to predict for x-values that lie far from the center of the data.
- ***Watch out for high influence points and outliers.*** We always have to be on the lookout for a few points that have undue influence on our model—and regression is certainly no exception.

[5]Technically, it's a little more complicated, but it's very close to this.

Regression Analysis and the Computer

All statistics packages make a table of results for a regression. These tables differ slightly from one package to another, but all are essentially the same. We've seen two examples of such tables already.

All packages offer analyses of the residuals. With some, you must request plots of the residuals as you request the regression. Others let you find the regression first and then analyze the residuals afterward. Either way, your analysis is not complete if you don't check the residuals with a histogram or Normal probability plot and a scatterplot of the residuals against *x* or the predicted values.

You should, of course, always look at the scatterplot of your two variables (make a picture, make a picture, . . .) before computing a regression. In Chapter 8 we showed how to go conveniently from a scatterplot to regression for many packages, but some of those regressions gave only the regression equation and not the *t*-statistics or P-values.

Here we show the direct path from the data to a regression table. Some packages, however, don't generate the plots you need automatically when you just ask for a regression.

Can we trust you to make the scatterplots yourself? (We knew we could.)

Regressions are almost always found with a computer or calculator. The calculations are too long to do conveniently by hand for data sets of any reasonable size. No matter how the regression is computed, the results are usually presented in a table that has a standard form. Here's a portion of a typical regression results table along with annotations showing where the numbers come from:

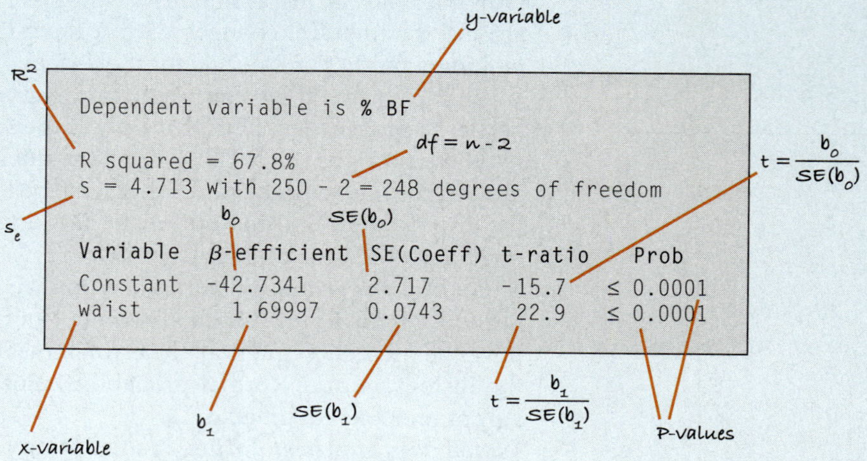

The regression table gives the coefficients (once you find them in the middle of all this other information), so we can see that the regression equation is

$$\widehat{\%BF} = -42.17 + 1.7\ waist$$

and that the R^2 for the regression is 67.8%. (Is accounting for 68% of the variation in %body fat good enough to be useful? Is a prediction *ME* of more than 9% good enough? Health professionals might not be satisfied.)

The column of *t*-ratios gives the test statistics for the respective null hypotheses that the true values of the coefficients are zero. The corresponding P-values are also usually reported.

Connections

We would never consider a regression analysis without first making a scatterplot. And the aspects of scatterplots that we always look for relate directly to regression. We can't use regression methods unless the *form* of the relationship is linear. The *direction* of the relationship gives the sign of the regression slope. The *scatter* in the plot is measured by the standard deviation of the residuals—which plays a central role in the inference calculations. It's also reflected in the R^2 statistic, which gives the fraction of the variability of y accounted for by the regression model and is the square of the correlation.

Regression inference is connected to just about every inference method we have seen for measured data. The assumption that the spread of data about the line is constant is essentially the same as the assumption of equal variances required for the pooled-t methods. Our use of all the residuals together to estimate their standard deviation is a form of pooling.

Inference for regression is closely related to inference for means, so your understanding of means transfers pretty directly to your understanding of regression. Here's a table that displays the similarities:

	Means	Regression Slope
Parameter	μ	β_1
Statistic	$\bar{y}$	b_1
Population spread estimate	$s_y = \sqrt{\frac{\sum(y-\bar{y})^2}{n-1}}$	$s_e = \sqrt{\frac{\sum(e-0)^2}{n-2}}$
Standard error of the statistic	$SE(\bar{y}) = \frac{s_y}{\sqrt{n}}$	$SE(b_1) = \frac{s_e}{s_x\sqrt{n-1}}$
Test statistic	$\frac{\bar{y}-\mu_0}{SE(\bar{y})} \sim t_{n-1}$	$\frac{b_1-\beta_1}{SE(b_1)} \sim t_{n-2}$
Margin of error	$ME = t^*_{n-1} \times SE(\bar{y})$	$ME = t^*_{n-2} \times SE(b_1)$

Key Concepts

Conditions for inference in regression (and checks for some of them)

- Linearity. (Check that the scatterplot of y against x has linear form and that the scatterplot of residuals against predicted values has no obvious pattern.)
- Independent residuals. (Think about the nature of the data. Check a residuals plot.)
- Constant variance. (Check that the scatterplot shows consistent spread across the range of the x-variable, and that the residuals plot has constant variance too. A common problem is increasing spread with *increasing* predicted values—the *plot thickens!*)
- Normality of the residuals. (Check a histogram of the residuals.)

Residual standard deviation

The spread of the data around the regression line is measured with the residual standard deviation, s_e.

$$s_e = \sqrt{\frac{\sum(y-\hat{y})^2}{n-2}} = \sqrt{\frac{\sum e^2}{n-2}}$$

t-test for the regression slope When the assumptions are satisfied, we can perform a test for the slope coefficient. We usually test the null hypothesis that the true value of the slope is zero against the alternative that it is not. A zero slope would indicate a complete lack of linear relationship between y and x.

$$\text{To test } H_0\text{: } \beta_1 = 0 \text{ we find: } t = \frac{b_1 - 0}{SE(b_1)}$$

where

$$SE(b_1) = \frac{s_e}{\sqrt{n-1}\, s_x}, \quad s_e = \sqrt{\frac{\sum(y - \hat{y})^2}{n-2}}$$

n is the number of cases, and s_x is the standard deviation of the x-values. We find the P-value from the Student's t model with $n - 2$ degrees of freedom.

Confidence interval for the regression slope When the assumptions are satisfied, we can find a confidence interval for the slope parameter from $b_1 \pm t^*_{n-2} \times SE(b_1)$. The critical value, t^*_{n-2} depends on the confidence interval specified and on Student's t-model with $n - 2$ degrees of freedom.

Confidence interval for a mean predicted value Different samples will give different estimates of the regression model and so, different predicted values for the same value of x. We find a confidence interval for the mean of these predicted values at a specified x-value, x_ν, as $\hat{y}_\nu \pm t^*_{n-2} \times SE(\hat{\mu}_\nu)$ where

$$SE(\hat{\mu}_\nu) = \sqrt{SE^2(b_1) \times (x_\nu - \bar{x})^2 + \frac{s_e^2}{n}}.$$

The critical value, t^*_{n-2} depends on the specified confidence level and the Student's t model with $n - 2$ degrees of freedom.

Prediction interval for an individual Different samples will give different estimates of the regression model and so, different predicted values for the same value of x. We can make a confidence interval to capture a certain percentage of the entire distribution of predicted values. This makes it much wider than the corresponding confidence interval for the mean. The confidence interval takes the form $\hat{y}_\nu \pm t^*_{n-2} \times SE(\hat{y}_\nu)$, where

$$SE(\hat{y}_\nu) = \sqrt{SE^2(b_1) \times (x_\nu - \bar{x})^2 + \frac{s_e^2}{n} + s_e^2}.$$

The critical value, t^*_{n-2} depends on the specified confidence level and the Student's t model with $n - 2$ degrees of freedom.

Skills

When you complete this lesson you should:

Think

- Understand that the "true" regression line does not fit the population data perfectly, but rather is an idealized summary of that data.
- Know how to examine your data and a scatterplot of y vs. x for violations of assumptions that would make inference for regression unwise or invalid.
- Know how to examine displays of the residuals from a regression to double-check that the conditions required for regression have been met. In particular, know how to judge linearity and constant variance from a scatterplot of residuals against predicted values. Know how to judge Normality from a histogram and Normal probability plot.
- Remember to be especially careful to check for failures of the independence assumption when working with data recorded over time. To search for patterns, examine scatterplots both of x against time and of the residuals against time.

Show

- Know how to test the standard hypothesis that the true regression slope is zero. Be able to state the null and alternative hypotheses. Know where to find the relevant numbers in standard computer regression output.
- Be able to find a confidence interval for the mean of the predicted y-values and a prediction interval for a particular *y*-value based on the summary statistics for *x* and the values reported in a standard regression output table. Know how to interpret these intervals in terms of the regression.

Tell

- Be able to summarize a regression in words. In particular, be able to state the meaning of the true regression slope, the standard error of the estimated slope, and the standard deviation of the errors.
- Be able to interpret the P-value of the *t*-statistic for the slope to test the standard null hypothesis and to interpret a confidence interval for the slope.
- Be able to interpret a prediction interval for a predicted *y*-value for a given *x*-value and a confidence interval for the mean of *y*-values for a given x-value.

Exercises

1. Ms. President? In Chapter 7 we saw data collected by the Gallup organization. They have, over six decades, periodically asked the following question:

If your party nominated a generally well-qualified person for president who happened to be a woman, would you vote for that person?

Here is a scatterplot of the percentage answering "yes" vs. the year of the century (37 = 1937):

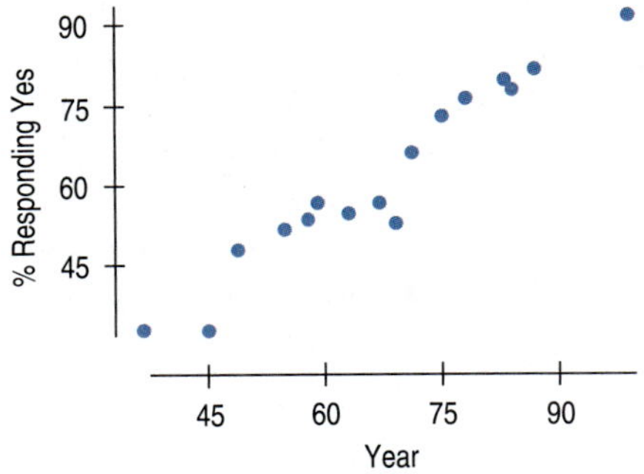

In Chapter 7 we could describe the relationship only in general terms. Now we can learn more. Here is the regression analysis:

Dependent variable is: Yes
R-squared = 94.2%
s = 4.274 with 16 − 2 = 14 degrees of freedom

Variable	Coefficient	SE(Coeff)	t-ratio	Prob
Constant	−5.58269	4.582	−1.22	0.2432
Year	0.999373	0.0661	15.1	≤0.0001

a) Explain in words and numbers what the regression says.
b) State the hypothesis about the slope (both numerically and in words) that describes how voters' thoughts have changed about voting for a woman.
c) Assuming that the assumptions for inference are satisfied, perform the hypothesis test and state your conclusion. Be sure to state it in terms of voters' opinions.
d) Explain what the *R*-squared in this regression means.

2. Drug use. The *European School Study Project on Alcohol and Other Drugs*, published in 1995, investigated the use of marijuana and other drugs. Data from 11 countries are summarized in the scatterplot and regression analysis below. They show the association between the percentage of a country's ninth graders who report having smoked marijuana and who have used other drugs such as LSD, amphetamines, and cocaine.

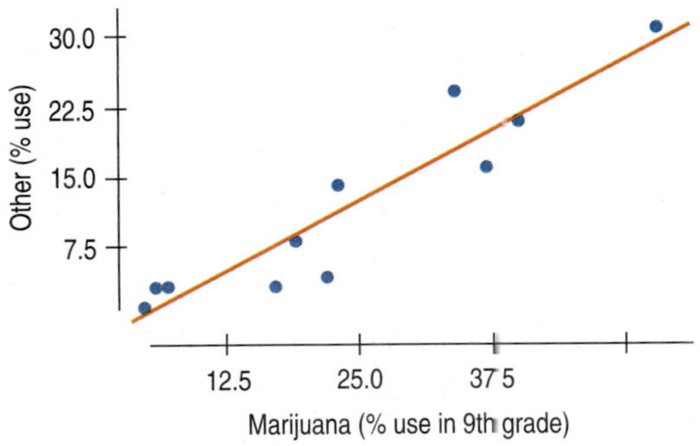

Dependent variable is: Other
R-squared = 87.3%
s = 3.853 with 11 − 2 = 9 degrees of freedom

Variable	Coefficient	SE(Coeff)	t-ratio	Prob
Constant	−3.06780	2.204	−1.39	0.1974
Marijuana	0.615003	0.0784	7.85	0.0001

a) Explain in words and numbers what the regression says.
b) State the hypothesis about the slope (both numerically and in words) that describes how use of marijuana is associated with other drugs.
c) Assuming that the assumptions for inference are satisfied, perform the hypothesis test and state your conclusion in context.
d) Explain what the R-squared in this regression means.
e) Do these results indicate that marijuana use leads to the use of harder drugs? Explain.

3. No opinion. Here's a regression of the percentage of respondents whose response to the question about voting for a woman president was "no opinion." We wonder if the percentage of the public who have no opinion on this issue has changed over the years. Assume that the conditions for inference are satisfied.

Dependent variable is: No Opinion
R-squared = 9.5%
s = 2.280 with 16 − 2 = 14 degrees of freedom

Variable	Coefficient	SE(Coeff)	t-ratio	Prob
Constant	7.69262	2.445	3.15	0.0071
Year	−0.042708	0.0353	−1.21	0.2458

a) State the appropriate hypothesis for the slope.
b) Test your hypothesis and state your conclusion in the proper context.
c) Below is the scatterplot corresponding to the regression for No Opinion. How does the scatterplot change your opinion of the trend in "no opinion" responses? Do you think the true slope is negative? Does this change the conclusion of your hypothesis test of part b? Explain.

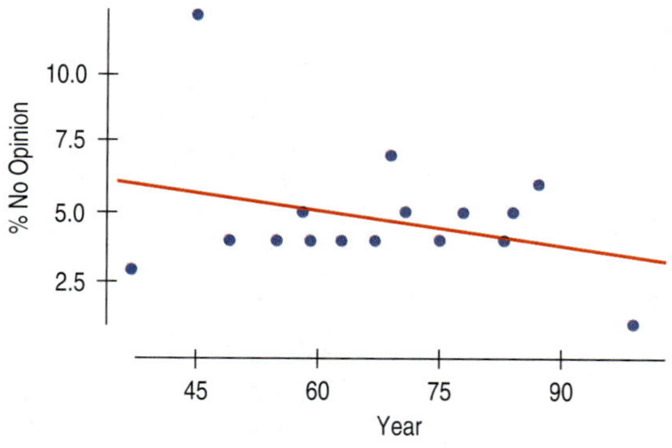

4. Cholesterol. Does a person's cholesterol level tend to increase with age? Data collected in Framingham, MA, from 294 adults aged 45 to 62 produced the regression analysis shown. Assuming that the data satisfy the conditions for inference, examine the association between age and cholesterol level.

Dependent variable is: Chol

Variable	Coefficient	SE(Coeff)	t-ratio	Prob
Constant	196.619	33.21	5.92	≤0.0001
Age	0.745779	0.6075	1.23	0.2206

a) State the appropriate hypothesis for the slope.
b) Test your hypothesis and state your conclusion in the proper context.

5. Marriage age. The scatterplot suggests a decrease in the difference in ages at first marriage for men and women since 1975. We want to examine the regression to see if this decrease is significant.

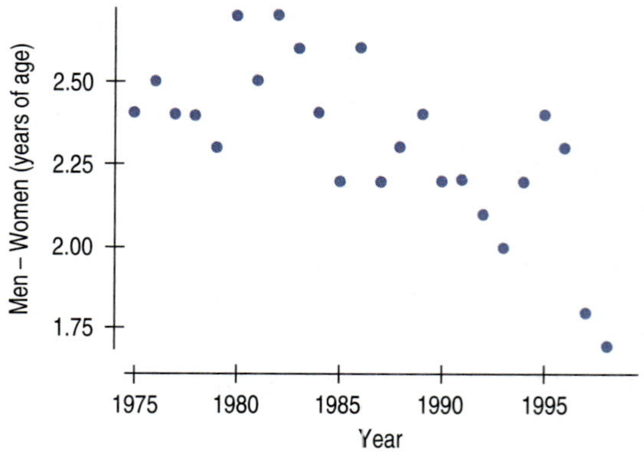

Dependent variable is: Men − Women
R-squared = 46.3%
s = 0.1866 with 24 − 2 = 22 degrees of freedom

Variable	Coefficient	SE(Coeff)	t-ratio	Prob
Constant	49.9021	10.93	4.56	0.0002
Year	−0.023957	0.0055	−4.35	0.0003

a) Write appropriate hypotheses.
b) Here are the residuals plot and a histogram of the residuals. Do you think the conditions for inference are satisfied? Explain.

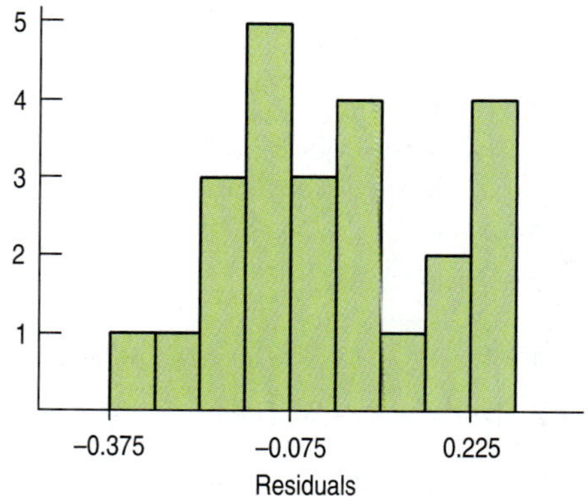

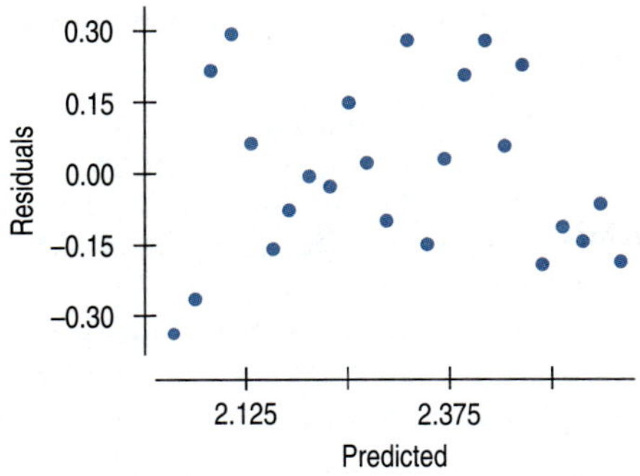

c) Test the hypothesis and state your conclusion about the trend in age at first marriage.
d) Give a 95% confidence interval for the rate at which the age gap is closing. Clearly explain what your confidence interval means.

6. Used cars. Classified ads in a newspaper offered several used Toyota Corollas for sale. Listed below are the ages of the cars and the advertised prices.

Age (yr)	Prices advertised ($)
1	12,995; 10,950
2	10,495
3	10,995; 10,995
4	6,995; 7,990
5	8,700; 6,995
6	5,990; 4,995
9	3,200; 2,250; 3,995
11	2,900; 2,995
13	1,750

a) Make a scatterplot for these data.
b) Do you think a linear model is appropriate? Explain.
c) Find the equation of the regression line.
d) Check the residuals to see if the conditions for inference are met.
e) Create a 95% confidence interval for the slope of the regression line.
f) Explain what your confidence interval means.

7. Fuel economy. A consumer organization has reported test data for 50 car models. We will examine the association between the weight of the car (in thousands of pounds) and the fuel efficiency (in miles per gallon). Shown are the summary statistics, scatterplot, and regression analysis:

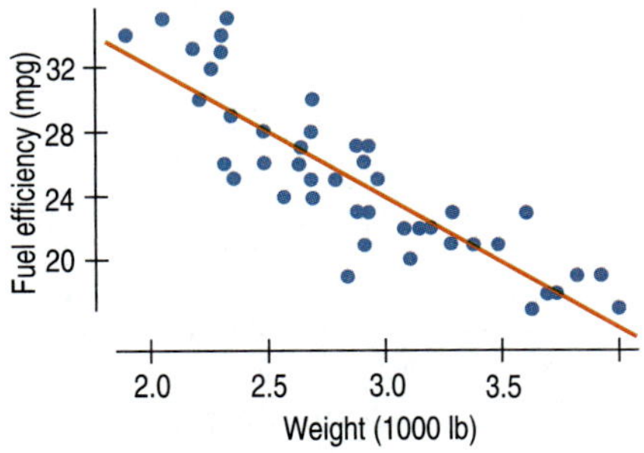

Variable	Count	Mean	StdDev
MPG	50	25.0200	4.83394
wt/1000	50	2.88780	0.511656

Dependent variable is: MPG
R-squared = 75.6%
s = 2.413 with 50 − 2 = 48 df

Variable	Coefficient	SE(Coeff)	t-ratio	Prob
Constant	48.7393	1.976	24.7	≤0.0001
Weight	−8.21362	0.6738	−12.2	≤0.0001

a) Is there strong evidence of an association between the weight of a car and its gas mileage? Write an appropriate hypothesis.
b) Are the assumptions for regression satisfied?

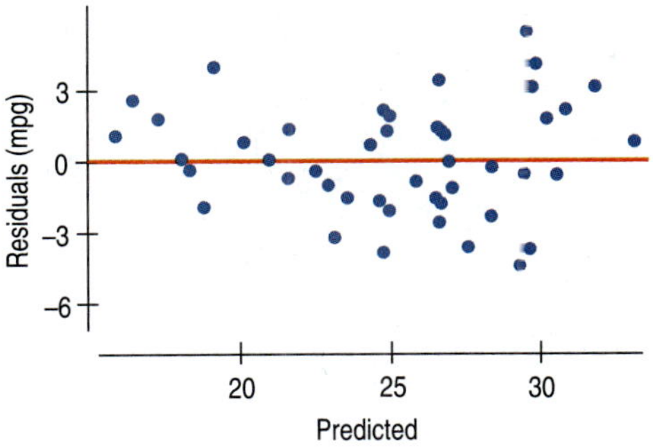

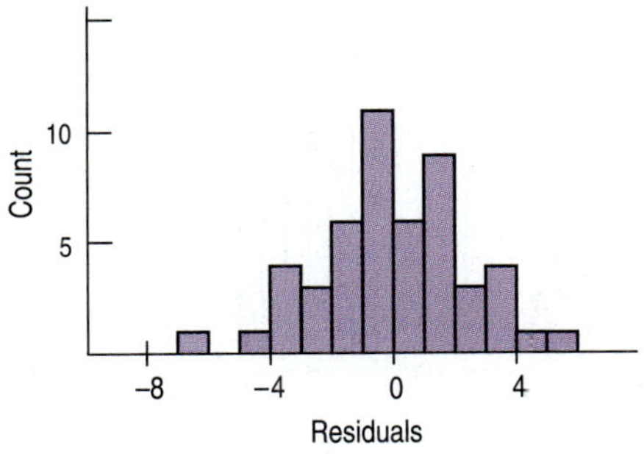

c) Test your hypothesis and state your conclusion.

8. SAT scores. How strong is the association between student scores on the Math and Verbal sections of the SAT? Scores on this exam range from 200 to 800, and are widely used by college admissions offices. Here are summaries and plots of the scores for a recent graduating class at Ithaca High School.

Variable	Count	Mean	Median	StdDev	Range	IntQRange
Verbal	162	596.296	610	99.5199	490	140
Math	162	612.099	630	98.1343	440	150

Dependent variable is: Math
R-squared = 46.9%
s = 71.75 with 162 − 2 = 160 df

Variable	Coefficient	SE(Coeff)	t-ratio	Prob
Constant	209.554	34.35	6.10	≤0.0001
Verbal	0.675075	0.0568	11.9	≤0.0001

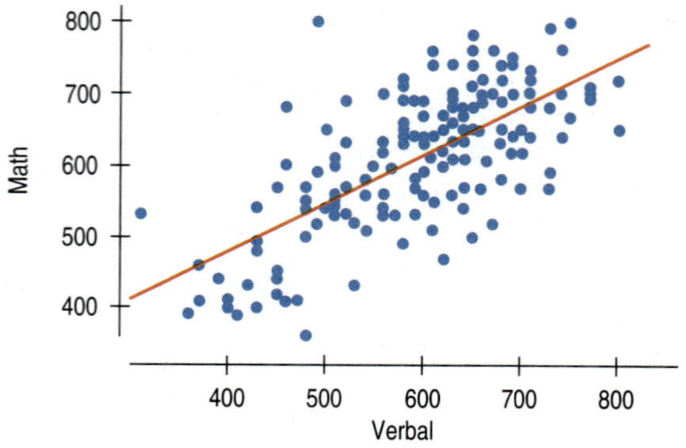

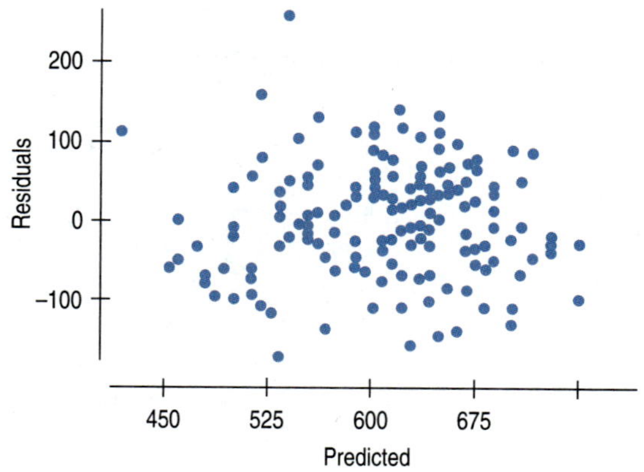

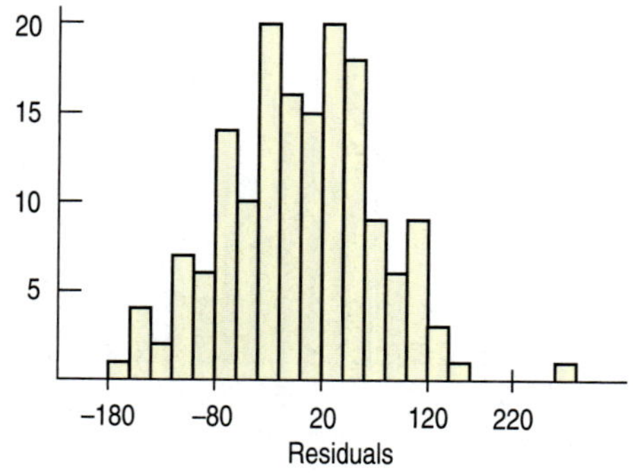

a) Is there evidence of an association between math and verbal scores? Write an appropriate hypothesis.
b) Discuss the assumptions for inference.
c) Test your hypothesis and state an appropriate conclusion.

9. Fuel economy, part II. Consider again the data in Exercise 7 about the gas mileage and weights of cars.
a) Create a 95% confidence interval for the slope of the regression line.
b) Explain in this context what your confidence interval means.

10. SATs, part II. Consider the high school SAT scores data from Exercise 8.
a) Find a 90% confidence interval for the slope of the true line describing the association between math and verbal scores.
b) Explain in this context what your confidence interval means.

11. MPG revisited. Consider again the data in Exercise 7 about the gas mileage and weights of cars.
a) Create a 95% confidence interval for the average fuel economy among cars weighing 2500 pounds, and explain what your interval means.
b) Create a 95% prediction interval for the gas mileage you might get driving your new 3450-pound SUV, and explain what that interval means.

12. SATs again. Consider the high school SAT scores data from Exercise 8 once more.
a) Find a 90% confidence interval for the mean SAT-Math score for all students with an SAT-Verbal score of 500.
b) Find a 90% prediction interval for the Math score of the senior class president, if you know she scored 710 on the Verbal section.

13. Cereal. A healthy cereal should be low in both calories and sodium. Data for 77 cereals were examined and judged acceptable for inference. The 77 cereals had between 50 and 160 calories per serving and between 0 and 320 mg of sodium per serving. The regression analysis is shown.

Dependent variable is: Sodium
R-squared = 9.0%
s = 80.49 with 77 − 2 = 75 degrees of freedom

Variable	Coefficient	SE(Coeff)	t-ratio	Prob
Constant	21.4143	51.47	0.416	0.6786
Calories	1.29357	0.4738	2.73	0.0079

a) Is there an association between the number of calories and the sodium content of cereals? Explain.
b) Do you think this association is strong enough to be useful? Explain.

14. Brain size. Does your IQ depend on the size of your brain? A group of female college students took a test that measured their verbal IQs and also underwent an MRI scan to measure the size of their brains (in 1000s of pixels). The scatterplot and regression analysis are shown, and the assumptions for inference were satisfied.

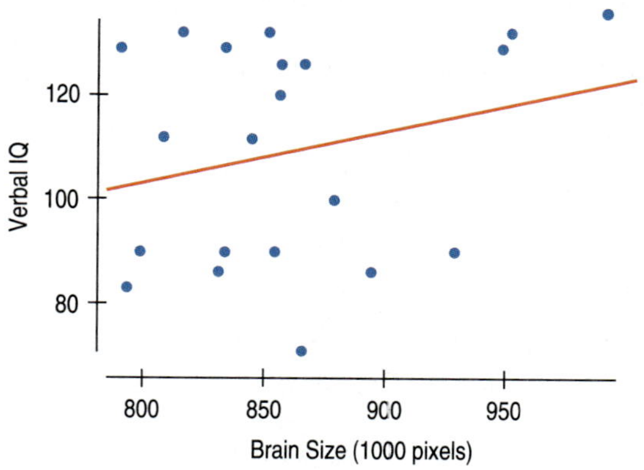

Dependent variable is: IQ_Verbal
R-squared = 6.5%

Variable	Coefficient	SE(Coeff)
Constant	24.1835	76.38
Size	0.098842	0.0884

a) Test an appropriate hypothesis about the association between brain size and IQ.
b) State your conclusion about the strength of this association.

15. Another bowl. Further analysis of the data for the breakfast cereals in Exercise 13 looked for an association between fiber content and calories by attempting to construct a linear model. Several graphs are shown. Which of the assumptions for inference are violated? Explain.

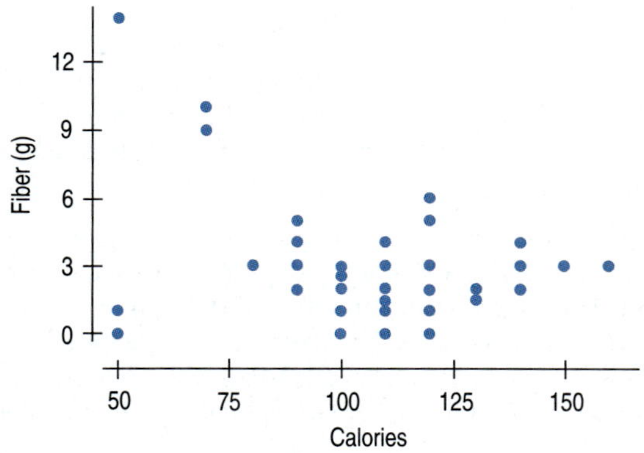

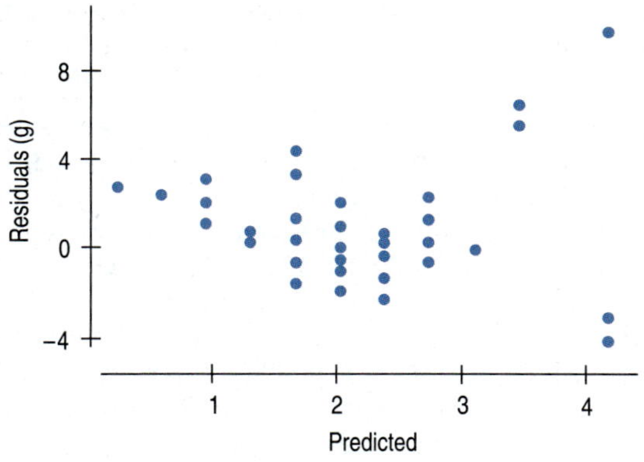

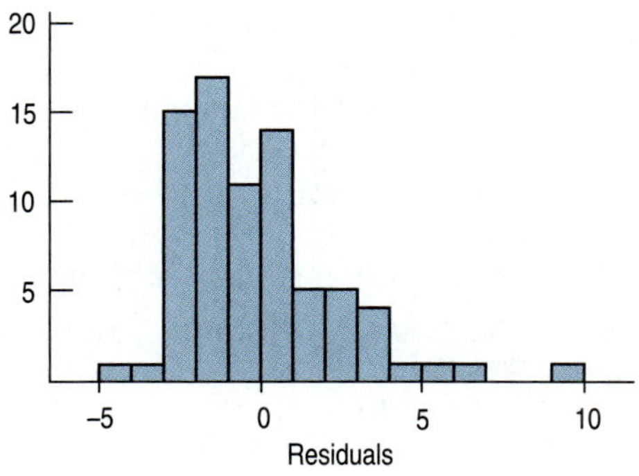

16. Winter. The output shows an attempt to model the association between average January temperature (in degrees Fahrenheit) and latitude (in degrees north of the equator) for 59 U.S. cities. Which of the assumptions for inference do you think are violated? Explain.

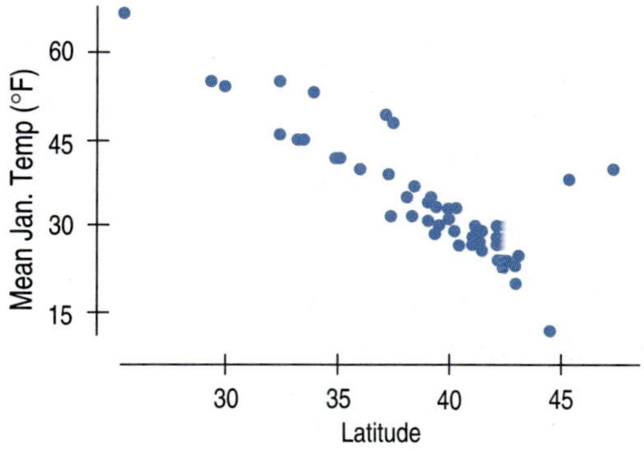

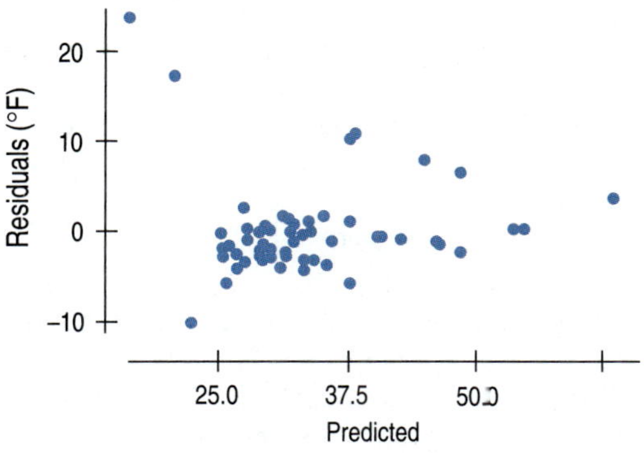

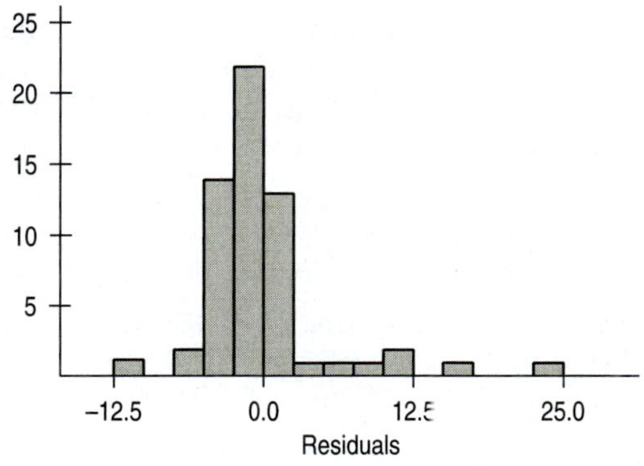

17. Acid rain. Biologists studying the effects of acid rain on wildlife collected data from 163 streams in the Adirondack Mountains. They recorded the pH (acidity) of the water and the BCI, a measure of biological diversity. Following is a scatterplot of BCI against pH.

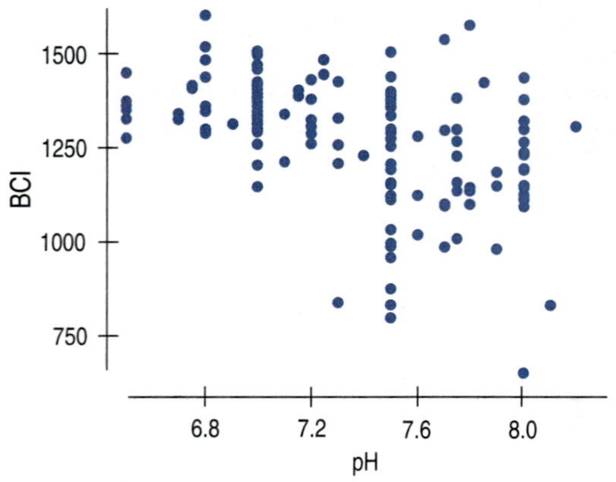

And here is part of the regression analysis:

Dependent variable is: BCI
R-squared = 27.1%
s = 140.4 with 163 − 2 = 161 degrees of freedom

Variable	Coefficient	SE(Coeff)
Constant	2733.37	187.9
pH	−197.694	25.57

a) State the null and alternative hypotheses under investigation.
b) Assuming that the assumptions for regression inference are reasonable, find the t and P-value for the test.
c) State your conclusion.

18. El Niño. Concern over the weather associated with El Niño has increased interest in the possibility that the climate on earth is getting warmer. The most common theory relates an increase in atmospheric levels of carbon dioxide (CO_2), a greenhouse gas, to increases in temperature. Here is part of a regression analysis of the mean annual CO_2 concentration in the atmosphere measured in parts per million (ppm) at the top of Mauna Loa in Hawaii and the mean annual air temperature over both land and sea across the globe, in degrees Celsius. The scatterplots and residuals plots indicated that the data were appropriate for inference.

Dependent variable is: Temp
R-squared = 33.4%
s = 0.0809 with 37 − 2 = 35 degrees of freedom

Variable	Coefficient	SE(Coeff)
Constant	15.3066	0.3139
CO2	0.004	0.0009

a) Write the equation of the regression line.
b) Is there evidence of an association between CO_2 level and global temperature?
c) Do you think predictions made by this model will be very accurate? Explain.

19. Ozone. The Environmental Protection Agency is examining the relationship between the ozone level (in parts per million) and the population (in millions) of U.S. cities. Part of the regression analysis is shown.

Dependent variable is: Ozone
R-squared = 84.4%
s = 5.454 with 16 − 2 = 14 df

Variable	Coefficient	SE(Coeff)
Constant	18.892	2.395
Pop	6.650	1.910

a) We suspect that the greater the population of a city the higher its ozone level. Is the relationship significant? Assuming the conditions for inference are satisfied, test an appropriate hypothesis and state your conclusion in context.
b) Give a 90% confidence interval for the approximate increase in ozone level associated with each additional million city inhabitants.
c) For the cities studied, the mean population was 1.7 million people. The population of Boston is approximately 0.6 million people. Predict the mean ozone level for cities of that size with an interval in which you have 90% confidence.

20. Sales and profits. A business analyst was interested in the relationship between a company's sales and its profits. She collected data (in millions of dollars) from a random sample of Fortune 500 companies, and created the regression analysis and summary statistics shown. The assumptions for regression inference appeared to be satisfied.

	Profits	Sales
Count	79	79
Mean	209.839	4178.29
Variance	635,172	49,163,000
Std Dev	796.977	7011.63

Dependent variable is: Profits
R-squared = 66.2% s = 466.2

Variable	Coefficient	SE(Coeff)
Constant	−176.644	61.16
Sales	0.092498	0.0075

a) Is there a significant association between sales and profits? Test an appropriate hypothesis and state your conclusion in context.
b) Explain, in context, the meaning of R-squared.
c) Find a 95% confidence interval for the slope of the regression line. Interpret your interval in context.
d) Last year the drug manufacturer Eli Lilly, Inc. reported gross sales of $9 billion (that's $9,000 million). Create a 95% prediction interval for the company's profits, and interpret your interval in context.

21. Start the car! In October 2002, *Consumer Reports* listed the price (in dollars) and power (in cold cranking amps) of auto batteries. We want to know if more expensive batteries are generally better in terms of starting power. Here are several software displays.

Dependent variable is: Power
R-squared = 25.2%
s = 116.0 with 33 − 2 = 31 degrees of freedom

Variable	Coefficient	SE(Coeff)	t-ratio	P-value
Constant	384.594	93.55	4.11	0.0003
Cost	4.14649	1.282	3.23	0.0029

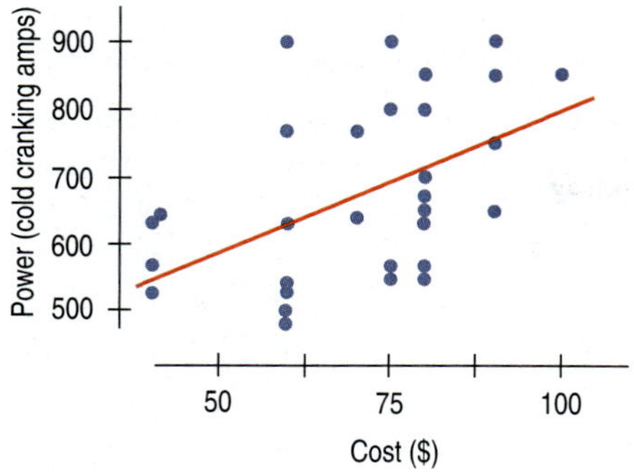

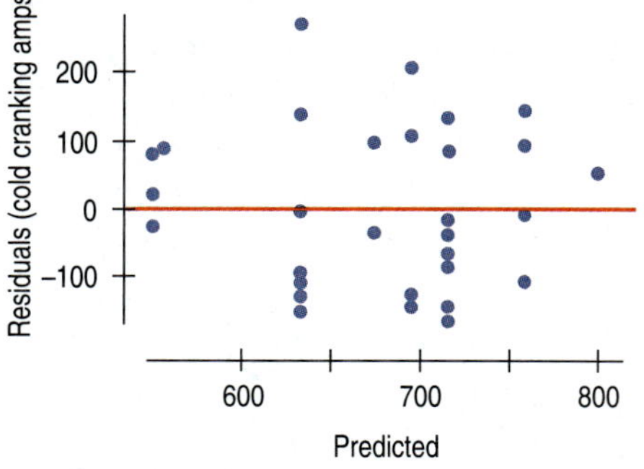

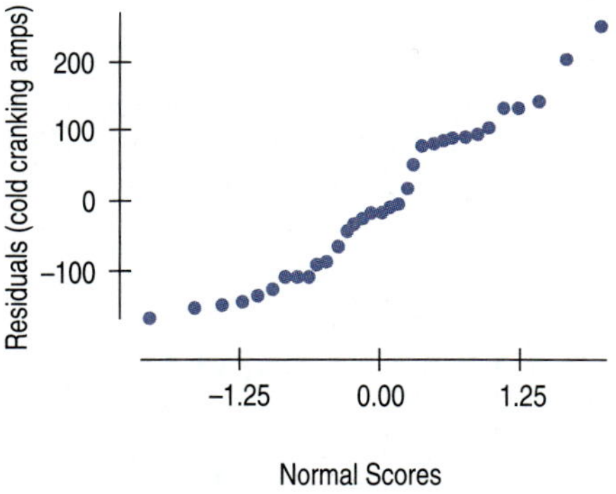

a) How many batteries were tested?
b) Are the conditions for inference satisfied? Explain.
c) Is there evidence of an association between the cost and cranking power of auto batteries? Test an appropriate hypothesis and state your conclusion.
d) Is the association strong? Explain.
e) What is the equation of the regression line?
f) Create a 90% confidence interval for the slope of the true line.
g) Interpret your interval in this context.

T **22. Crawling.** Researchers at the University of Denver Infant Study Center wondered if temperature might influence the age at which babies learn to crawl. Perhaps the extra clothing that babies wear in cold weather would restrict movement and delay the age at which they started crawling. Data were collected on 208 boys and 206 girls. Parents reported the month of the baby's birth and the age (in weeks) at which their child first crawled. The table gives the average temperature (°F) when the babies were 6 months old and average crawling age (in weeks) for each month of the year. Make the plots and compute the analyses necessary to answer the following questions.

Birth Month	6-Month Temperature	Average Crawling Age
Jan.	66	29.84
Feb.	73	30.52
Mar.	72	29.70
April	63	31.84
May	52	28.58
June	39	31.44
July	33	33.64
Aug.	30	32.82
Sept.	33	33.83
Oct.	37	33.35
Nov.	48	33.38
Dec.	57	32.32

a) Would this association appear to be weaker, stronger, or the same if data had been plotted for individual babies instead of using monthly averages? Explain.
b) Is there evidence of an association between temperature and crawling age? Test an appropriate hypothesis and state your conclusion. Don't forget to check the assumptions.
c) Create and interpret a 95% confidence interval for the slope of the true relationship.

T **23. Printers.** In March 2002, *Consumer Reports* reviewed several models of inkjet printers. Shown are the speed of the printer (in pages per minute) and the cost per page printed. Is there evidence of an association between speed and cost? Test an appropriate hypothesis and state your conclusion.

Speed (ppm)	Cost (cents/page)
4.6	12.0
5.5	8.5
4.5	6.2
3.8	3.4
4.6	2.6
3.7	4.0
4.7	5.8
4.7	8.1
4.0	9.4
3.1	14.9
1.9	2.6
2.2	4.3
1.8	4.6
2.0	14.8
2.0	4.4

T 24. Strike two. Remember the Little League instructional video discussed in Chapter 25? Ads claimed that the techniques would improve the performances of Little League pitchers. To test this claim, 20 Little Leaguers threw 50 pitches each, and we recorded the number of strikes. After the players participated in the training program, we repeated the test. The table shows the number of strikes each player threw before and after the training. A test of paired differences failed to show that this training was effective in improving a player's ability to throw strikes. Is there any evidence that the effectiveness of the video depends on the player's initial ability to throw strikes? Test an appropriate hypothesis and state your conclusion.

Number of Strikes (out of 50)

Before	After	Before	After
28	35	33	33
29	36	33	35
30	32	34	32
32	28	34	30
32	30	34	33
32	31	35	34
32	32	36	37
32	34	36	33
32	35	37	35
33	36	37	32

T 25. Body fat. Do the data shown in the table indicate an association between waist size and %body fat?

a) Test an appropriate hypothesis and state your conclusion.

b) Give a 95% confidence interval for the mean %body fat found in people with 40-inch waists.

Waist (in.)	Weight (lb)	Body Fat (%)	Waist (in.)	Weight (lb)	Body Fat (%)
32	175	6	33	188	10
36	181	21	40	240	20
38	200	15	36	175	22
33	159	6	32	168	9
39	196	22	44	246	38
40	192	31	33	160	10
41	205	32	41	215	27
35	173	21	34	159	12
38	187	25	34	146	10
38	188	30	44	219	28

T 26. Body fat, again. Use these data to examine the association between weight and %body fat.

a) Find a 90% confidence interval for the slope of the regression line of %body fat on weight.

b) Interpret your interval in context.

c) Give a 95% prediction interval for the %body fat of an individual who weighs 165 pounds.

27. Education and mortality. The software output below is based on the mortality rate (deaths per 100,000 people) and the education level (average number of years in school) for 58 U.S. cities.

Variable	Count	Mean	StdDev
Mortality	58	942.501	61.8490
Education	58	11.0328	0.793480

Dependent variable is: Mortality
R-squared = 41.0%
s = 47.92 with 58 − 2 = 56 degrees of freedom

Variable	Coefficient	SE(Coeff)
Constant	1493.26	88.48
Education	-49.9202	8.000

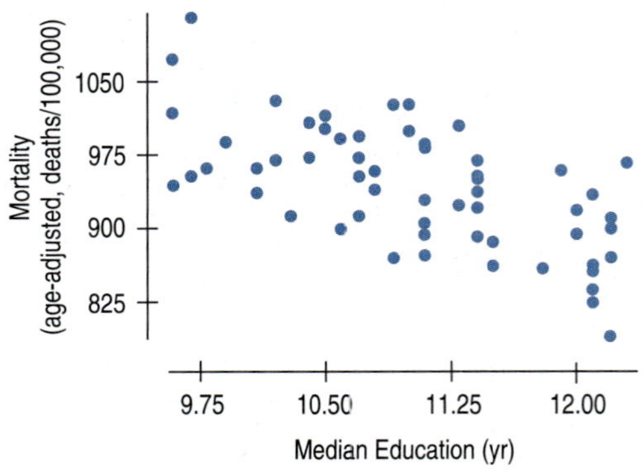

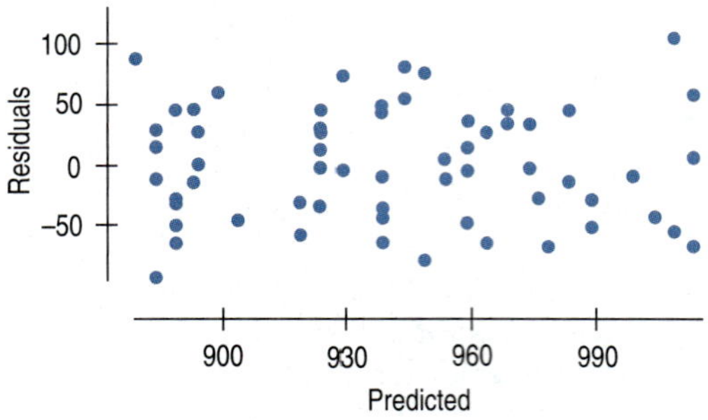

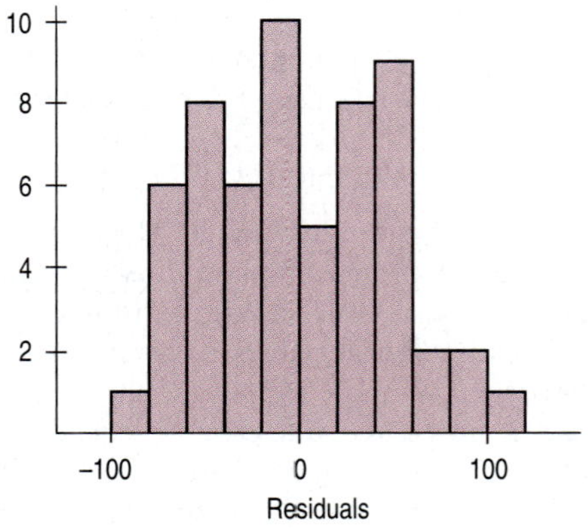

a) Comment on the assumptions for inference.
b) Is there evidence of a strong association between the level of education in a city and the mortality rate? Test an appropriate hypothesis and state your conclusion.
c) Find a 95% confidence interval for the slope of the true relationship.
d) Explain what your interval means.
e) Find a 95% confidence interval for the average mortality rate in cities where the adult population completed an average of 12 years of school.

28. Property assessments. The software outputs below provide information about the size (in square feet) of 18 homes in Ithaca, NY, and the city's assessed valuation of those homes.

Variable	Count	Mean	StdDev	Range
SqFt	18	2003.39	264.727	890
Asse$$	18	60946.7	5527.62	19710

Dependent variable is: Asse$$
R-squared = 32.5%
s = 4682 with 18 − 2 = 16 degrees of freedom

Variable	Coefficient	SE(Coeff)
Constant	37108.8	8664
SqFt	11.8987	4.290

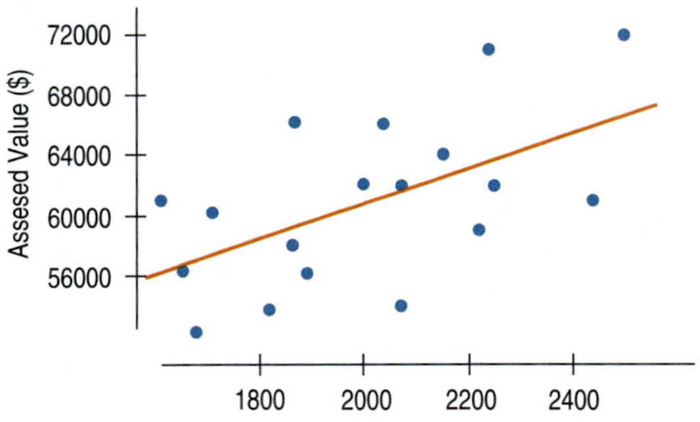

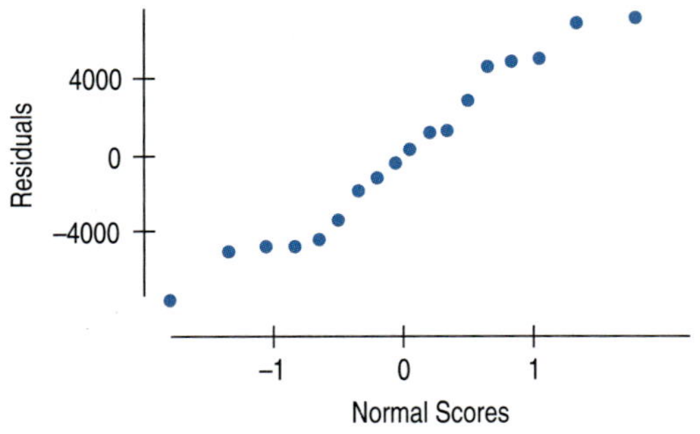

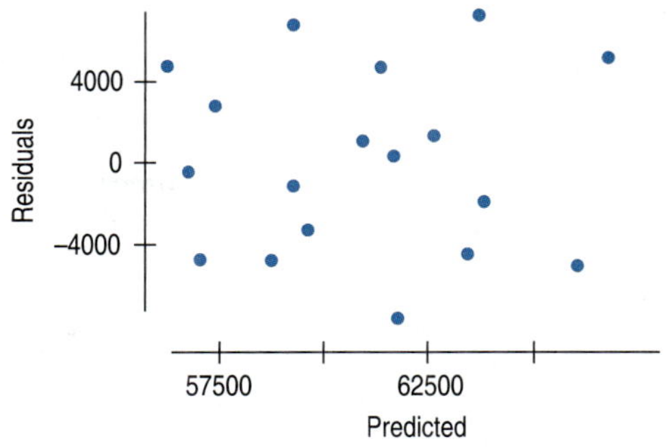

a) Explain why inference for linear regression is appropriate with these data.
b) Is there a significant association between the size of a home and its assessed value? Test an appropriate hypothesis and state your conclusion.
c) What percentage of the variability in assessments is explained by this model?
d) Give a 90% confidence interval for the slope of the true regression line, and explain its meaning in the proper context.
e) The owner of a home measuring 2100 square feet files an appeal, claiming that the $70,200 assessed value is too high. Do you agree? Explain your reasoning.

Review of Part VII Inference When Variables Are Related

Quick Review

With these last two chapters you have added important analytical tools to your ways of looking at data. Here's a brief summary of those key concepts and skills, as well as an overview of statistical inference:

- Inference about distributions of counts uses chi-square models.
  - To see if an observed distribution is consistent with a proposed model, use a goodness-of-fit test.
  - To see if two or more observed distributions could have arisen from populations with the same model use a test of homogeneity.
- Inference about association between two variables tests the hypothesis that it is plausible to consider the variables independent.
  - If the variables are categorical, display the data in a contingency table and use a chi-square test of independence.
  - If the variables are quantitative, display them with a scatterplot. You may use a linear regression *t*-test if there appears to be a linear association for which the residuals are random, consistent in terms of spread, and approximately Normal.
- You can now use statistical inference to answer questions about means, proportions, distributions, and associations.
  - No inference procedure is valid unless the underlying assumptions are true. Always check the conditions before proceeding.
  - You can make inferences about a single proportion or the difference of two proportions using Normal models.
  - You can make inferences about one mean, the difference of two independent means, or the mean of paired differences using *t*-models.
  - You can make inferences about distributions using chi-square models.
  - You can make inferences about association between categorical variables using chi-square models.
  - You can make inferences about linear association between quantitative variables using *t*-models.

Remember (have we said this often enough yet?): Never use any inference procedure without first checking the assumptions and conditions. We summarized those in the previous part review; have another look. On the next page we summarize the various types of inference procedures and the corresponding formulas. And then, of course, come more opportunities to practice using these concepts and skills . . . .

Quick Guide to Inference

Think			Show				Tell?
Inference about?	**One sample or two?**	**Procedure**	**Model**	**Parameter**	**Estimate**	**SE**	**Chapter**
Proportions	One sample	1-Proportion z-Interval	z	p	$\hat{p}$	$\sqrt{\frac{\hat{p}\hat{q}}{n}}$	19
		1-Proportion z-test				$\sqrt{\frac{p_0 q_0}{n}}$	20, 21
	Two independent samples	2-Proportion z-Interval	z	$p_1 - p_2$	$\hat{p}_1 - \hat{p}_2$	$\sqrt{\frac{\hat{p}_1\hat{q}_1}{n_1} + \frac{\hat{p}_2\hat{q}_2}{n_2}}$	22
		2-Proportion z-test				$\sqrt{\frac{\hat{p}\hat{q}}{n_1} + \frac{\hat{p}\hat{q}}{n_2}}, \; \hat{p} = \frac{y_1 + y_2}{n_1 + n_2}$	22
Means	One sample	t-Interval t-Test	t df $= n - 1$	μ	$\bar{y}$	$\frac{s}{\sqrt{n}}$	23
	Two independent samples	2-Sample t-test 2-Sample t-Interval	t df from technology	$\mu_1 - \mu_2$	$\bar{y}_1 - \bar{y}_2$	$\sqrt{\frac{s_1^2}{n_1} + \frac{s_2^2}{n_2}}$	24
	Matched pairs	Paired t-test Paired t-interval	t df $= n - 1$	μ_d	$\bar{d}$	$\frac{s_d}{\sqrt{n}}$	25
Distributions (one categorical variable)	One sample	Goodness of fit	χ^2 df $= cells - 1$			$\sum \frac{(\text{obs} - \text{exp})^2}{\text{exp}}$	26
	Many independent samples	Homogeneity χ^2 test	χ^2 df $= (r - 1)(c - 1)$				
Independence (two categorical variables)	One sample	Independence χ^2 test					
Association (two quantitative variables)	One sample	Linear Regression t-Test or Confidence Interval for β	t df $= n - 2$	β_1	b_1	$\frac{s_e}{s_x\sqrt{n-1}}$ (compute with technology)	27
		Confidence Interval for μ_ν		μ_ν	$\hat{y}_\nu$	$\sqrt{SE^2(b_1) \cdot (x_\nu - \bar{x})^2 + \frac{s_e^2}{n}}$	
		Prediction Interval for y_ν		y_ν	$\hat{y}_\nu$	$\sqrt{SE^2(b_1) \cdot (x_\nu - \bar{x})^2 + \frac{s_e^2}{n} + s_e^2}$	
Inference about?	**One sample or two?**	**Procedure**	**Model**	**Parameter**	**Estimate**	**SE**	**Chapter**

Review Exercises

1. Genetics. Two human traits controlled by a single gene are the ability to roll one's tongue and whether one's ear lobes are free or attached to the neck. Genetic theory says that people will have neither, one, or both of these traits in the ratio 1:3:3:9 (1—attached, noncurling; 3—attached, curling; 3—free, noncurlung; 9—free, curling). An Introductory Biology class of 122 students collected the data shown. Are they consistent with the genetic theory? Test an appropriate hypothesis and state your conclusion.

	Trait			
	Attached, noncurling	Attached, curling	Free, noncurling	Free, curling
Count	10	22	31	59

2. Tableware. Nambe Mills manufactures plates, bowls, and other tableware made from an alloy of several metals. Each item must go through several steps, including polishing. To better understand the production process and its impact on pricing, the company checked the polishing time (in minutes) and the retail price (in US$) of these items. The regression analysis is shown below. The scatterplot showed a linear pattern, and residuals were deemed suitable for inference.

Dependent variable is: Price
R-squared = 84.5%
s = 20.50 with 59 − 2 = 57 degrees of freedom

Variable	Coefficient	SE(Coeff)
Constant	−2.89054	5.730
Time	2.49244	0.1416

a) How many different products were included in this analysis?
b) What fraction of the variation in retail price is explained by the polishing time?
c) Create a 95% confidence interval for the slope of this relationship.
d) Interpret your interval in this context.

3. Hard water. In an investigation of environmental causes of disease, data were collected on the annual mortality rate (deaths per 100,000) for males in 61 large towns in England and Wales. In addition, the water hardness was recorded as the calcium concentration (parts per million, or ppm) in the drinking water. Here are the scatterplot and regression analysis of the relationship between mortality and calcium concentration.

Dependent variable is: mortality
R-squared = 43%
s = 143.0 with 61 − 2 = 59 degrees of freedom

Variable	Coefficient	SE(Coeff)
Constant	1676	29.30
calcium	−3.23	0.48

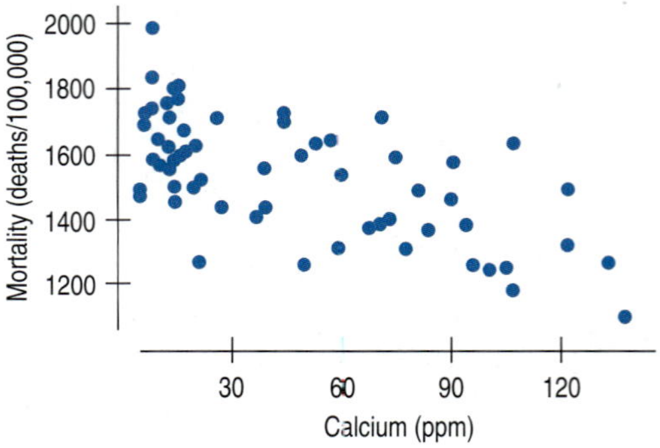

a) Is there an association between the hardness of the water and the mortality rate? Write the appropriate hypothesis.
b) Assuming the assumptions for regression inference are met, what do you conclude?
c) Create a 95% confidence interval for the slope of the true line relating calcium concentration and mortality.
d) Interpret your interval in context.

4. Mutual funds. In March 2002, *Consumer Reports* listed the rate of return for several large cap mutual funds over the previous 3-year and 5-year periods. ("Large cap" refers to companies worth over $10 billion.)
a) Create a 95% confidence interval for the difference in rate of return for the 3- and 5-year periods covered by these data. Clearly explain what your interval means.
b) It's common for advertisements to carry the disclaimer that "past returns may not be indicative of future performance," but do these data indicate that there was an association between 3-year and 5-year rates of return?

Annualized Returns (%)

Fund Name	3-year	5-year
Ameristock	7.9	17.1
Clipper	14.1	18.2
Credit Suisse Strategic Value	5.5	11.5
Dodge & Cox Stock	15.2	15.7
Excelsior Value	13.1	16.4
Harbor Large Cap Value	6.3	11.5
ICAP Discretionary Equity	6.6	11.4
ICAP Equity	7.6	12.4
Neuberger Berman Focus	9.8	13.2
PBHG Large Cap Value	10.7	18.1
Pelican	7.7	12.1
Price Equity Income	6.1	10.9
USAA Cornerstone Strategy	2.5	4.9
Vanguard Equity Income	3.5	11.3
Vanguard Windsor	11.0	11.0

5. Resume fraud. In 2002 the Veritas Software company found out that its chief financial officer did not actually have the MBA he had listed on his resume. They fired him, and the value of the company's stock dropped 19%. Kroll, Inc., a firm that specializes in investigating such matters, said that they believe as many as 25 percent of background checks might reveal false information. How many such random checks would they have to do to estimate the true percentage of people who misrepresent their backgrounds to within ±5% with 98% confidence?

6. Paper airplanes. In preparation for a regional paper airplane competition, a student tried out her latest design. The distances her plane traveled (in feet) in 11 trial flights are given here. (The world record is an astounding 193.01 feet!) The data were 62, 52, 68, 23, 34, 45, 27, 42, 83, 56, and 40 feet.
Here are some summaries:

Count	11
Mean	48.3636
Median	45
StdDev	18.0846
StdErr	5.45273
IntQRange	25
25th %tile	35.5000
75th %tile	60.5000

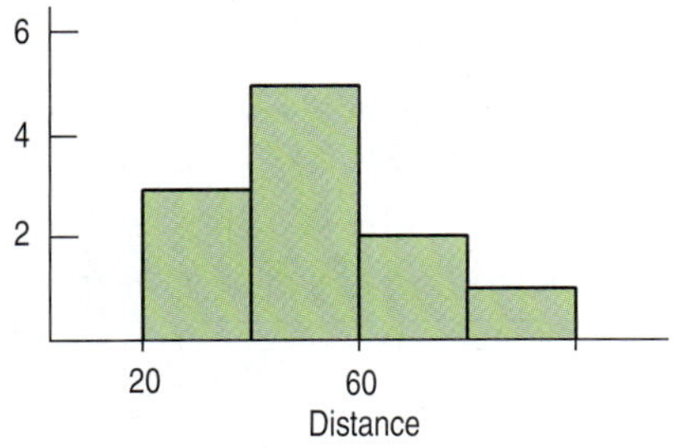

a) Construct a 95% confidence interval for the true distance.

b) Based on your confidence interval, is it plausible that the mean distance is 40 ft? Explain.

c) How would a 99% confidence interval for the true distance differ from your answer in part a? Explain briefly, without actually calculating a new interval.

d) How large a sample size would the student need to get a confidence interval half as wide as the one you got in part a, at the same confidence level?

7. Back to Montana. The respondents to the Montana poll described in Exercise 13 in Chapter 26 were also classified by income level: low (under $20,000), middle ($20,000–$35,000), or high (over $35,000). Is there any evidence that party enrollment there is associated with income? Test an appropriate hypothesis about this table, and state your conclusions.

	Democrat	Republican	Independent
Low	30	16	12
Middle	28	24	22
High	26	38	6

8. Wild horses. Large herds of wild horses can become a problem on some federal lands in the West. Researchers hoping to improve the management of these herds collected data to see if they could predict the number of foals that would be born based on the size of the current herd. Their attempt to model this herd growth is summarized in the output shown.

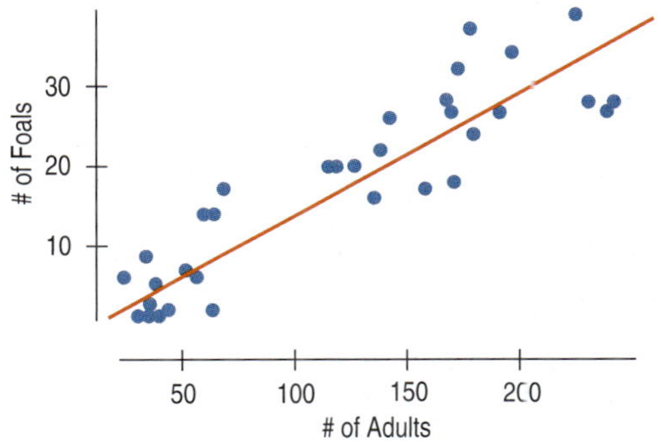

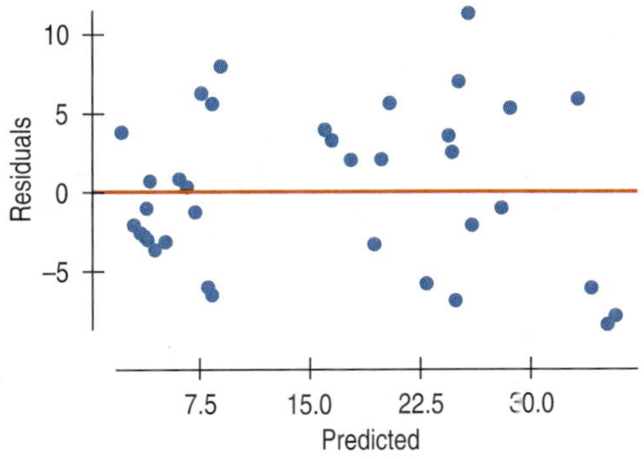

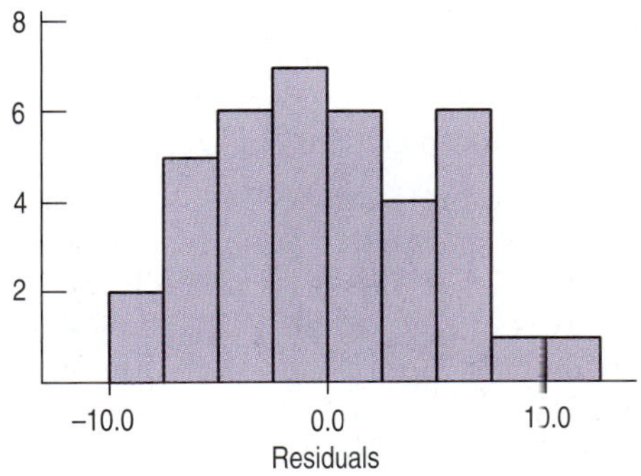

Variable	Count	Mean	StdDev
Adults	38	110.237	71.1809
Foals	38	15.3947	11.9945

Dependent variable is: Foals
R-squared = 83.5%
s = 4.941 with 38 − 2 = 36 degrees of freedom

Variable	Coefficient	SE(Coeff)	t-ratio	Prob
Constant	−1.57835	1.492	−1.06	0.2970
Adults	0.153969	0.0114	13.5	≤0.0001

a) How many herds of wild horses were studied?
b) Are the conditions necessary for inference satisfied? Explain.
c) Create a 95% confidence interval for the slope of this relationship.
d) Explain in this context what that slope means.
e) Suppose that a new herd with 80 adult horses is located. Estimate, with a 90% prediction interval, the number of foals that may be born.

9. Lefties and music. In an experiment to see if left- and right-handed people have different abilities in music, subjects heard a tone and were then asked to identify which of several other tones matched the first. Of 76 right-handed subjects, 38 were successful in completing this test, compared with 33 of 53 lefties. Is this strong evidence of a difference in musical abilities based on handedness?

10. AP Statistics scores. In 2001, more than 41,000 Statistics students nationwide took the Advanced Placement Examination in Statistics. The national distribution of scores and the results at Ithaca High School are shown in the table.

Score	National distribution	Ithaca High School: Number of boys	Ithaca High School: Number of girls
5	11.5%	13	13
4	23.4%	21	15
3	24.9%	6	13
2	19.1%	7	3
1	21.1%	4	2

a) Is the distribution of scores at this high school significantly different from the national results?
b) Was there a significant difference between the performances of boys and girls at this school?

11. Polling. How accurate are pollsters in predicting the outcomes of Congressional elections? The table shows the actual number of Democrat seats in the House of Representatives and the number predicted by the Gallup organization for nonpresidential election years since World War II.

a) Is there a significant difference between the number of seats predicted for the Democrats and the number they actually held? Test an appropriate hypothesis and state your conclusions.

Democrat Congressmen

Year	Predicted	Actual
1946	190	188
1950	235	234
1954	232	232
1958	272	283
1962	259	258
1966	247	248
1970	260	255
1974	292	291
1978	277	277
1982	275	269
1986	264	258
1990	260	267
1994	201	204
1998	211	211

b) Is there a strong association between the pollsters' predictions and the outcomes of the elections? Test an appropriate hypothesis and state your conclusions.

12. Twins. In 2000, the *Journal of American Medical Association* published a study that examined a sample of pregnancies that resulted in the birth of twins. Births were classified as preterm with intervention (induced labor or cesarean), preterm without such procedures, or term or postterm. Researchers also classified the pregnancies by the level of prenatal medical care the mother received (inadequate, adequate, or intensive). The data, from the years 1995–97, are summarized in the table below. Figures are in thousands of births. (*JAMA* 284[2000]: 335–341)

TWIN BIRTHS 1995–1997 (IN THOUSANDS)

Level of Prenatal Care	Preterm (induced or Cesarean)	Preterm (without procedures)	Term or postterm	Total
Intensive	18	15	28	61
Adequate	46	43	65	154
Inadequate	12	13	38	63
Total	76	71	131	278

Is there evidence of an association between the duration of the pregnancy and the level of care received by the mother?

13. Twins, again. After reading of the *JAMA* study in Exercise 12, a large city hospital examined their records of twin births for several years, and found

the data summarized in the table below. Is there evidence that the way the hospital deals with pregnancies involving twins may have changed?

Outcome of Pregnancy	1990	1995	2000
Preterm (induced or cesarean)	11	13	19
Preterm (without procedures)	13	14	18
Term or postterm	27	26	32

14. Preemies. Do the effects of being born prematurely linger into adulthood? Researchers examined 242 Cleveland area children born prematurely between 1977 and 1979, and compared them with 233 children of normal birth weight; 24 of the "preemies" and 12 of the other children were described as being of "subnormal height" as adults. Is this evidence that babies born with a very low birth weight are more likely to be smaller than normal adults? ("Outcomes in Young Adulthood for Very-Low-Birth-Weight Infants," *New England Journal of Medicine*, 346, no. 3 [January 2002])

15. LA rainfall. The Los Angeles Almanac Web site reports recent annual rainfall (in inches), as shown in the table.

a) Create a 90% confidence interval for the mean annual rainfall in LA.

b) If you wanted to estimate the mean annual rainfall with a margin of error of only 2 inches, how many years' data would you need?

c) Do these data suggest any change in annual rainfall as time passes? Check for an association between rainfall and year.

Year	Rain (in.)	Year	Rain (in.)
1980	8.96	1991	21.00
1981	10.71	1992	27.36
1982	31.28	1993	8.14
1983	10.43	1994	24.35
1984	12.82	1995	12.46
1985	17.86	1996	12.40
1986	7.66	1997	31.01
1987	12.48	1998	9.09
1988	8.08	1999	11.57
1989	7.35	2000	17.94
1990	11.99	2001	4.42

16. Age and party. The Gallup Poll conducted a representative telephone survey during the first quarter of 1999. Among the reported results was the following table concerning the preferred political party affiliation of respondents and their ages. Is there evidence of age-based differences in party affiliation in the United States?

Age	Republican	Democratic	Independent	Total
18–29	241	351	409	1001
30–49	299	330	370	999
50–64	282	341	375	998
65+	279	382	343	1004
Total	1101	1404	1497	4002

a) Will you conduct a test of homogeneity or independence? Why?

b) Test an appropriate hypothesis.

c) State your conclusion, including an analysis of differences you find (if any).

17. Eye and hair color. A survey of 1021 school-age children was conducted by randomly selecting children from several large urban elementary schools. Two of the questions concerned eye and hair color. In the survey, the following codes were used:

Hair Color	Eye Color
1 = Blond	1 = Blue
2 = Brown	2 = Green
3 = Black	3 = Brown
4 = Red	4 = Grey
5 = Other	5 = Other

The Statistics students analyzing the data were asked to study the relationship between eye and hair color.

a) One group of students produced the output shown below. What kind of analysis is this? What are the null and alternative hypotheses? Is the analysis appropriate? If so, summarize the findings, being sure to include any assumptions you've made and/or limitations to the analysis. If it's not an appropriate analysis, explicitly state why not.

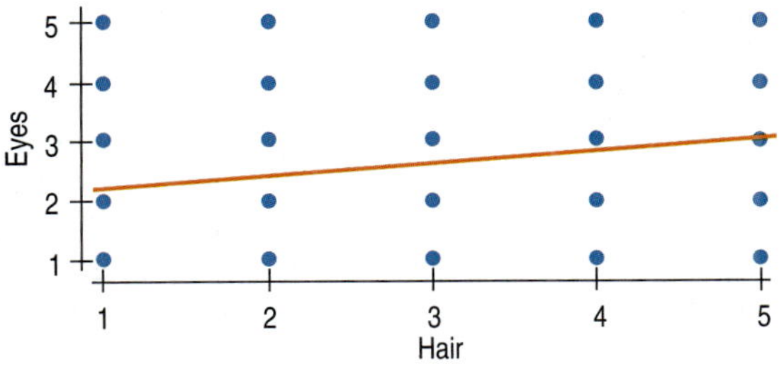

Dependent variable is: Eyes
R-squared = 3.7%
s = 1.112 with 1021 − 2 = 1019 degrees of freedom

Variable	Coefficient	SE(Coeff)	t-ratio	Prob
Constant	1.99541	0.08346	23.9	≤0.0001
Hair	0.211809	0.03372	0.28	≤0.0001

b) A second group of students used the same data to produce the output shown below. What kind of analysis is this? What are the null and alternative hypotheses? Is the analysis appropriate? If so, summarize the findings, being sure to include any assumptions you've made and/or limitations to the analysis. If it's not an appropriate analysis, explicitly state why not.

Table contents: Counts
Standardized Residuals

Eye Color

Hair Color	1	2	3	4	5
1	143 7.6754	30 0.417988	58 −5.88169	15 −0.63925	12 −0.314506
2	90 −2.57141	45 0.290189	215 1.72235	30 0.491885	20 −0.0824592
3	28 −5.39425	15 −2.3478	190 6.28154	10 −1.76376	10 −0.803818
4	30 2.06116	15 2.71589	10 −4.0554	10 2.37402	5 0.759931
5	10 −0.521945	5 0.332621	15 −0.941918	5 1.36326	5 2.07578

$$\sum\frac{(observed - expected)^2}{expected} = 223.6 \quad \text{P-value} < 0.00001$$

18. Depression and the Internet. The September 1998 issue of the *American Psychologist* published an article reporting on an experiment examining "the social and psychological impact of the Internet on 169 people in 73 households during their first 1 to 2 years on-line." In the experiment, a sample of households was offered free Internet access for one or two years in return for allowing their time and activity online to be tracked. The members of the households who participated in the study were also given a battery of tests at the beginning and again at the end of the study. One of the tests measured the subjects' levels of depression on a 4-point scale, with higher numbers meaning the person was more depressed. Internet usage was measured in average number of hours per week. The regression analysis examines the association between the subjects' depression levels and the amounts of Internet use. The conditions for inference were satisfied.

Dependent variable is: Depression After
R-squared = 4.6%
s = 0.4563 with 162 - 2 = 160 degrees of freedom

Variable	Coefficient	SE(coeff)	t-ratio	Prob
Constant	0.565485	0.0399	14.2	≤ 0.0001
Intr_use	0.019948	0.0072	2.76	0.0064

a) Do these data indicate that there is an association between Internet use and depression? Test an appropriate hypothesis and state your conclusion clearly.

b) One conclusion of the study was that those who spent more time online tended to be more depressed at the end of the experiment. News headlines said that too much time on the internet can lead to depression. Does the study support this conclusion? Explain.

c) As noted, the subjects' depression levels were tested at both the beginning and the end of this study; higher scores indicated the person was more depressed. Results are summarized in the table. Is there evidence that the depression level of the subjects changed during this study?

Depression Level
162 subjects

Variable	Mean	StdDev
DeprBfore	0.730370	0.487817
DeprAfter	0.611914	0.461932
Difference	-0.118457	0.552417

19. Pregnancy. In 1998 a San Diego reproductive clinic reported 42 live births to 157 women under the age of 38, but only 7 successes for 89 clients aged 38 and older. Is this evidence of a difference in the effectiveness of the clinic's methods for older women?

a) Test the appropriate hypotheses using the 2-proportion *z*-procedure.

b) Repeat the analysis using an appropriate chi-square procedure.

c) Explain how the two results are equivalent.

20. Family planning. A 1954 study of 1438 pregnant women examined the association between the woman's education level and the occurrence of unplanned pregnancies, producing these data:

	Education Level		
	<3 yr HS	3+ yr HS	Some college
Number of pregnancies	591	608	239
% unplanned	66.2%	55.4%	42.7%

Do these data provide evidence of an association between family planning and education level? (*Fertility Planning and Fertility Rates by Socio-Economic Status*, Social and Psychological Factors Affecting Fertility, 1954)

21. Old Faithful. As you saw in an earlier chapter, Old Faithful isn't all that faithful. Eruptions do not occur at uniform intervals, and may vary greatly. Can we improve our chances of predicting the time of the next eruption if we know how long the previous eruption lasted?

a) Describe what you see in this scatterplot.

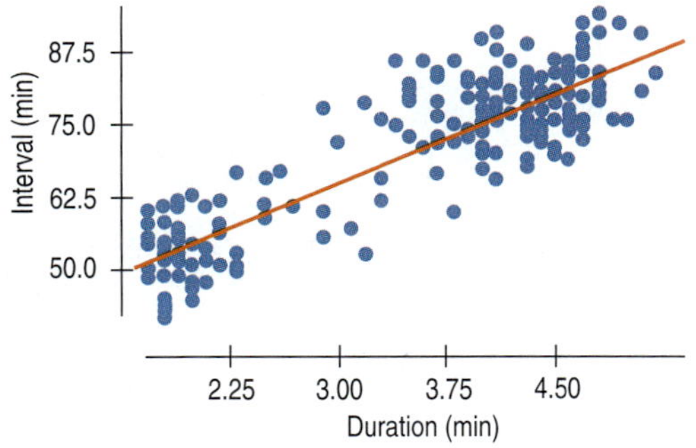

b) Write an appropriate hypothesis.

c) Here are a histogram of the residuals and the residuals plot. Do you think the assumptions for inference are met? Explain.

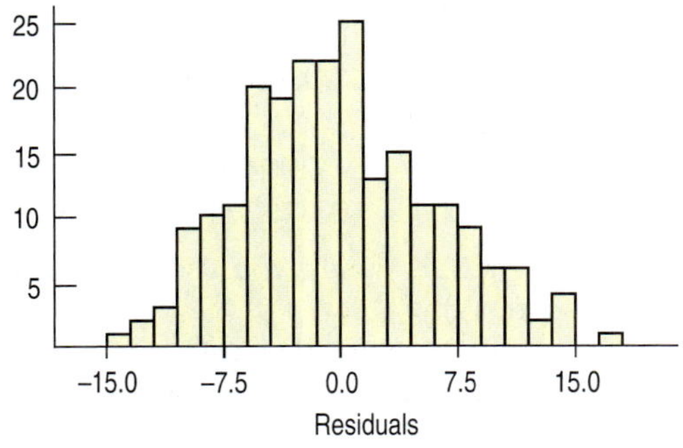

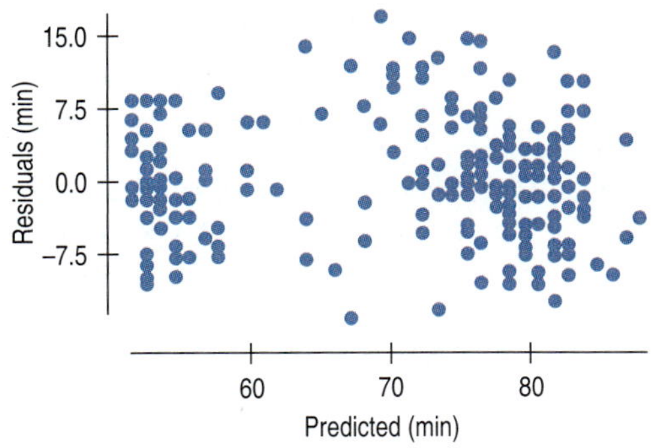

d) State a conclusion based on this regression analysis:

Dependent variable is: Interval
R-squared = 77.0%
s = 6.159 with 222 − 2 = 220 degrees of freedom

Variable	Coefficient	SE(Coeff)	t-ratio	Prob
Constant	33.9668	1.428	23.8	≤0.0001
Duration	10.3582	0.3822	27.1	≤0.0001

Variable	Mean	StdDev
Duration	3.57613	1.08395
Interval	71.0090	12.7992

e) The second table shows the summary statistics for the two variables. Create a 95% confidence interval for the mean length of time that will elapse following a 2-minute eruption.

f) You arrive at Old Faithful just as eruption ends. Witnesses say it lasted 4 minutes. Create a 95% prediction interval for the length of time you will wait to see the next eruption.

22. Togetherness. Are good grades in high school associated with family togetherness? A simple random sample of 142 high school students was asked how many meals per week their families ate together. Their responses produced a mean of 3.78 meals per week, with a standard deviation of 2.2. Researchers then matched these responses against the students' grade point averages. The scatterplot appeared to be reasonably linear, so they went ahead with the regression analysis, seen below. No apparent pattern emerged in the residuals plot.

Dependent variable: GPA
R-squared = 11.0%
s = 0.6682 with 142 − 2 = 140 df

Variable	Coefficient	SE(Coeff)
Constant	2.7288	0.1148
Meals/wk	0.1093	0.0263

a) Is there evidence of an association? Test an appropriate hypothesis and state your conclusion.

b) Do you think this association would be useful in predicting a student's grade point average? Explain.

c) Are your answers to parts a and b contradictory? Explain.

23. Learning math. Developers of a new math curriculum called "Accelerated Math" compared performances of students taught by their system with control groups of students in the same schools who were taught using traditional instructional methods and materials. Statistics about pretest and posttest scores are shown in the table. (J. Ysseldyke and S. Tardrew, *Differentiating Math Instruction*, Renaissance Learning, 2002)

a) Did the groups differ in average math score at the start of this study?

b) Did the group taught using the Accelerated Math program show a significant improvement in test scores?

c) Did the control group show significant improvement in test scores?

d) Were gains significantly higher for the Accelerated Math group than for the control group?

		Instructional Method	
		Acc. math	**Control**
Number of students		**231**	**245**
Pretest	**Mean**	560.01	549.65
	St. Dev	84.29	74.68
Posttest	**Mean**	637.55	588.76
	St. Dev	82.9	83.24
Individual gain	**Mean**	77.53	39.11
	St. Dev.	78.01	66.25

24. Pesticides. A study published in 2002 in the journal *Environmental Health Perspectives* examined the gender ratios of children born to workers exposed to dioxin in Russian pesticide factories. The data covered the years 1961 to 1988 in the city of Ufa, Bashkortostan, Russia. Of 227 children born to workers exposed to dioxin, only 40% were male. Overall in the city of Ufa the proportion of males was 51.2%. Is this evidence that human exposure to dioxin may result in the birth of more girls? (An interesting note: It appeared that paternal exposure was most critical; 51% of babies born to mothers exposed to the chemical were boys.)

25. Dairy sales. Peninsula Creameries sells both cottage cheese and ice cream. The CEO recently noticed that in months when the company sells more cottage cheese, it seems to sell more ice cream as well. Two of his aides were assigned to test whether this is true or not. The first aide's plot and analysis of sales data for the past 12 months (in millions of pounds for cottage cheese and for ice cream) appears below.

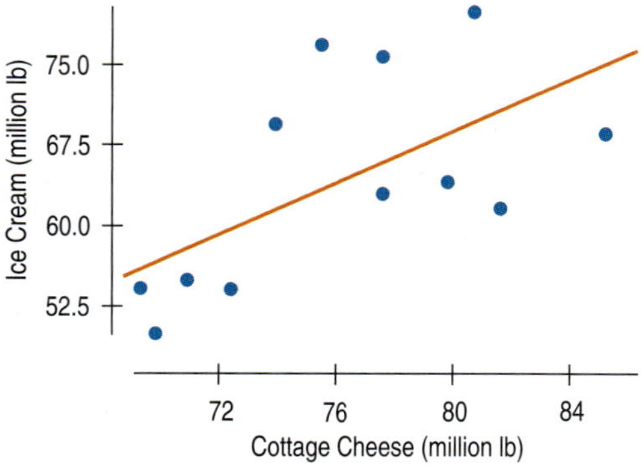

Dependent variable is: Ice cream
R-squared = 36.9%
s = 8.320 with 12 − 2 = 10 degrees of freedom

Variable	Coefficient	SE(Coeff)	t-ratio	Prob
Constant	−26.5306	37.68	−0.704	0.4975
Cottage C ...	1.19334	0.4936	2.42	0.0362

The other aide looked at the differences in sales of ice cream and cottage cheese for each month, and created the following output:

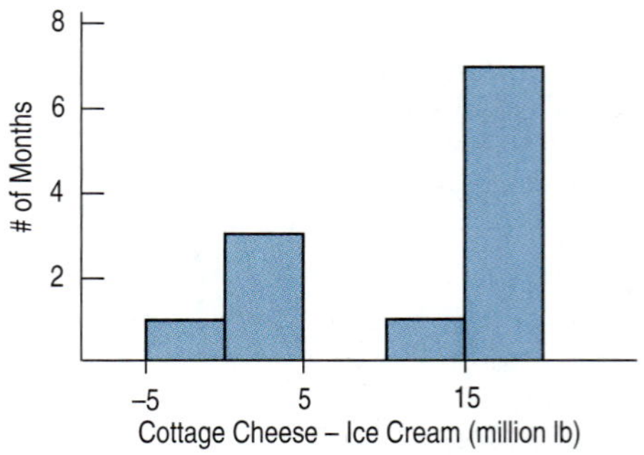

Cottage Cheese-Ice Cream

Count	12
Mean	11.8000
Median	15.3500
StdDev	7.99386
IntQRange	14.3000
25th %tile	3.20000
75th %tile	17.5000

Test H0: μ(CC − IC) = 0 vs Ha: μ(CC − IC) ≠ 0
Sample Mean = 11.800000 t-Statistic = 5.113 w/11 df
Prob = 0.0003
Lower 95% bound = 6.7209429
Upper 95% bound = 16.879057

a) Which analysis would you use to answer the CEO's question? Why?
b) What would you tell the CEO?
c) Which analysis would you use to test whether the company sells more cottage cheese or ice cream in a typical year? Why?
d) What would you tell the CEO about this other result?
e) What assumptions are you making in the analysis you chose in part a? What assumptions are you making in the analysis in part c?
f) Next month's cottage cheese sales are 82 million pounds. Ice cream sales are not yet available. How much ice cream do you predict Peninsula Creameries will sell?
g) Give a 95% confidence interval for the true slope of the regression equation of ice cream sales by cottage cheese sales.
h) Explain what your interval means.

26. Infliximab. In an article appearing in the journal *Lancet* in 2002, medical researchers reported on the experimental use of the arthritis drug infliximab in treating Crohn's disease. In a trial, 573 patients were given initial 5-mg injections of the drug. Two weeks later 335 had responded positively. These patients were then randomly assigned to three groups. Group I received continued injections of a placebo, Group II continued with 5 mg of infliximab, and Group III received 10 mg of the drug. After 30 weeks, 23 of 110 Group I patients were in remission, compared with 44 of 113 Group II and 50 of 112 Group III patients. Do these data indicate that continued treatment with infliximab is of value for Crohn's disease patients who exhibit a positive initial response to the drug?

27. Weight loss. A weight loss clinic advertises that its program of diet and exercise will allow clients to lose 10 pounds in one month. A local reporter investigating weight reduction gets permission to interview a randomly selected sample of clients who report the given weight losses during their first month in this program. Create a confidence interval to test the clinic's claim that typical weight loss is 10 pounds.

Pounds Lost	
9.5	9.5
13	9
9	8
10	7.5
11	10
9	7
5	8
9	10.5
12.5	10.5
6	9

28. Education vs. income. The information below examines the median income and education level (years in school) for several U.S. cities.

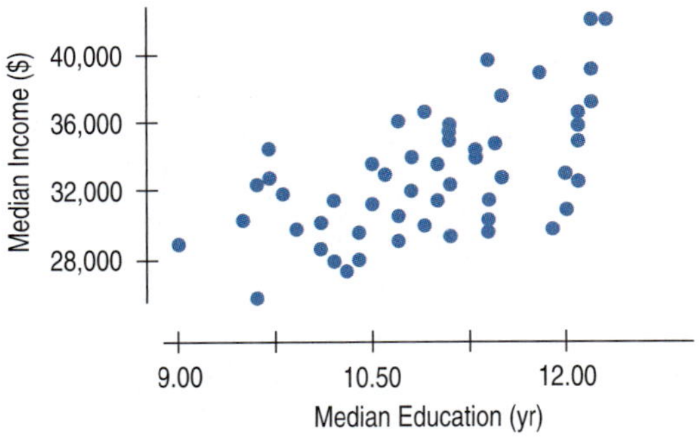

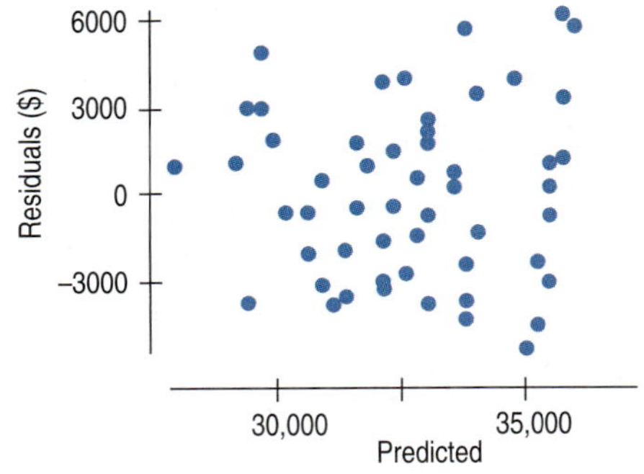

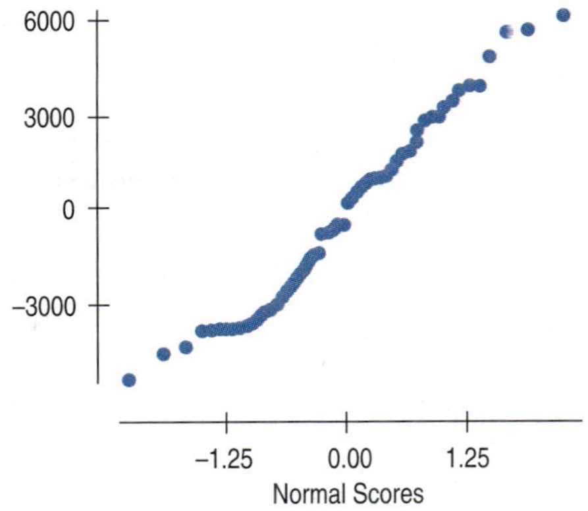

Variable	Count	Mean	StdDev
Education	57	10.9509	0.848344
income	57	32742.6	3618.01

Dependent variable is: Income
R-squared = 32.9%
s = 2991 with 57 − 2 = 55 degrees of freedom

Variable	Coefficient	SE(Coeff)	t-ratio	prob
Constant	5970.05	5175	1.15	0.2537
Education	2444.79	471.2	5.19	≤ 0.0001

a) Do you think the assumptions for inference are met? Explain.

b) Does there appear to be an association between education and income levels in these cities.

c) Would this association appear to be weaker, stronger, or the same if data were plotted for individual people rather than for cities in aggregate? Explain.

d) Create and interpret a 95% confidence interval for the slope of the true line that describes the association between income and education.

e) Predict the median income for cities where residents spent an average of 11 years in school. Describe your estimate with a 90% confidence interval, and interpret that result.

29. Diet. Thirteen overweight women volunteered for a study to determine whether eating specially prepared crackers before a meal could help them lose weight. The subjects were randomly assigned to eat crackers with different types of fiber (bran fiber, gum fiber, both, and a control cracker). Unfortunately, some of the women developed uncomfortable bloating and upset stomachs. Researchers suspected that some of the crackers might be at fault. The contingency table of "Cracker" versus "Bloat" shows the relationship between the four different types of crackers and the reported bloating. The study was paid for by the manufacturers of the gum fiber. What would you recommend to them about the prospects for marketing their new diet cracker?

		Bloat	
		Little/None	Moderate/Severe
Cracker	Bran	11	2
	Gum	4	9
	Combo	7	6
	Control	8	4

30. Cramming. Students in two basic Spanish classes were required to learn 50 new vocabulary words. One group of 45 students received the list on Monday and studied the words all week. Statistics summarizing this group's scores on Friday's quiz are given. The other group of 28 students did not get the vocabulary list until Thursday. They also took the quiz on Friday after "cramming" Thursday night. Then, when they returned to class the following Monday they were retested—without advance warning. Both sets of test scores for these students are shown.

Group 1

Fri.
Number of students = 45
Mean = 43.2 (of 50)
StDev = 3.4
Students passing (score ≥ 40) = 33%

a) Did the week-long study group have a mean score significantly higher than that of the overnight crammers?
b) Was there a significant difference in the percentages of students who passed the quiz on Friday?
c) Is there any evidence that when students cram for a test their "learning" does not last for 3 days?
d) Use a 95% confidence interval to estimate the mean number of words that might be forgotten by crammers.
e) Is there any evidence that how much students forget depends on how much they "learned" to begin with?

Group 2

Fri.	Mon.	Fri.	Mon.
42	36	50	47
44	44	34	34
45	46	38	31
48	38	43	40
44	40	39	41
43	38	46	32
41	37	37	36
35	31	40	31
43	32	41	32
48	37	48	39
43	41	37	31
45	32	36	41
47	44		

Appendixes

Appendix A: Formulas

$Range = Max - Min$
$IQR = Q3 - Q1$
Outlier Rule-of-Thumb: $y < Q1 - 1.5 \times IQR$ or $y > Q3 + 1.5 \times IQR$

$$\bar{y} = \frac{\sum y}{n}$$

$$s = \sqrt{\frac{\sum (y - \bar{y})^2}{n - 1}}$$

$$z = \frac{y - \mu}{\sigma} \text{ (model based)}$$

$$z = \frac{y - \bar{y}}{s} \text{ (data based)}$$

$$r = \frac{\sum z_x z_y}{n - 1}$$

$$\hat{y} = b_0 + b_1 x \qquad \text{where } b_1 = \frac{r s_y}{s_x} \text{ and } b_0 = \bar{y} - b_1 \bar{x}$$

$P(\mathbf{A}) = 1 - P(\mathbf{A}^C)$

$P(\mathbf{A} \cup \mathbf{B}) = P(\mathbf{A}) + P(\mathbf{B}) - P(\mathbf{A} \cap \mathbf{B})$

$P(\mathbf{A} \cap \mathbf{B}) = P(\mathbf{A}) \times P(\mathbf{B}|\mathbf{A})$

$$P(\mathbf{B}|\mathbf{A}) = \frac{P(\mathbf{A} \cap \mathbf{B})}{P(\mathbf{A})}$$

If **A** and **B** are independent, $P(\mathbf{B}|\mathbf{A}) = P(\mathbf{B})$

$E(X) = \mu = \sum x \cdot P(x)$	$Var(X) = \sigma^2 = \sum (x - \mu)^2 P(x)$
$E(X \pm c) = E(X) \pm c$	$Var(X \pm c) = Var(X)$
$E(aX) = aE(X)$	$Var(aX) = a^2 Var(X)$
$E(X \pm Y) = E(X) \pm E(Y)$	$Var(X \pm Y) = Var(X) + Var(Y)$ if X and Y are independent

Geometric:	$P(x) = q^{x-1}p$	$\mu = \frac{1}{p}$	$\sigma = \sqrt{\frac{q}{p^2}}$
Binomial:	$P(x) = \binom{n}{x} p^x q^{n-x}$	$\mu = np$	$\sigma = \sqrt{npq}$

$$\hat{p} = \frac{x}{n} \qquad \mu(\hat{p}) = p \qquad SD(\hat{p}) = \sqrt{\frac{pq}{n}}$$

Sampling distribution of $\bar{y}$:
(CLT) As n grows, the sampling distribution approaches the Normal model with

$$\mu(\bar{y}) = \mu_y \qquad SD(\bar{y}) = \frac{\sigma}{\sqrt{n}}$$

Inference:

Confidence interval for parameter = ***statistic ± critical value × SD(statistic)***

$$\text{Test statistic} = \frac{statistic - parameter}{SD(statistic)}$$

Parameter	Statistic	*SD*(statistic)	*SE*(statistic)
p	$\hat{p}$	$\sqrt{\frac{pq}{n}}$	$\sqrt{\frac{\hat{p}\hat{q}}{n}}$
$p_1 - p_2$	$\hat{p}_1 - \hat{p}_2$	$\sqrt{\frac{p_1q_1}{n_1} + \frac{p_2q_2}{n_2}}$	$\sqrt{\frac{\hat{p}_1\hat{q}_1}{n_1} + \frac{\hat{p}_2\hat{q}_2}{n_2}}$
μ	$\bar{y}$	$\frac{\sigma}{\sqrt{n}}$	$\frac{s}{\sqrt{n}}$
$\mu_1 - \mu_2$	$\bar{y}_1 - \bar{y}_2$	$\sqrt{\frac{\sigma_1^2}{n_1} + \frac{\sigma_2^2}{n_2}}$	$\sqrt{\frac{s_1^2}{n_1} + \frac{s_2^2}{n_2}}$
μ_d	$\bar{d}$	$\frac{\sigma_d}{\sqrt{n}}$	$\frac{s_d}{\sqrt{n}}$
μ_ν	$\hat{y}_\nu$		$\sqrt{SE^2(b_1)\cdot(x_\nu - \bar{x})^2 + \frac{s_e^2}{n}}$
y_ν	$\hat{y}_\nu$		$\sqrt{SE^2(b_1)\cdot(x_\nu - \bar{x})^2 + \frac{s_e^2}{n} + s_e^2}$

Pooling:

Whenever testing that there is no difference between proportions (H_0: $p_1 - p_2 = 0$), use $\hat{p}_{pooled} = \frac{x_1 + x_2}{n_1 + n_2}$

For testing difference between means *only if* populations are known to have equal variances, use $s_p = \sqrt{\frac{(n_1 - 1)s_1^2 + (n_2 - 1)s_2^2}{n_1 + n_2 - 2}}$

Substitute these pooled estimates in the respective SE formulas for both groups when assumptions and conditions are met.

Chi-square: $\chi^2 = \sum \frac{(obs - exp)^2}{exp}$

Appendix B: Guide to Statistical Software

Chapter 3 Displaying and Describing Categorical Data

DATA DESK

To make a bar chart or pie chart, select the variable.

In the **Plot** menu choose **Bar Chart** or **Pie Chart**.

To make a frequency table, in the **Calc** menu choose **Frequency Table**.

Comments

These commands treat the data as categorical even if they are numerals. If you select a quantitative variable by mistake, you'll see an error message warning of too many categories.

EXCEL

First make a pivot table (Excel's name for a frequency table).

From the **Data** menu choose **Pivot Table** and **Pivot Chart Report**.

When you reach the Layout window, drag your variable to the row area and drag your variable again to the data area. This tells Excel to count the occurrences of each category.

Once you have an Excel pivot table, you can construct bar charts and pie charts.

Click inside the Pivot Table.

Click the Pivot Table Chart Wizard button. Excel creates a bar chart.

A longer path leads to a pie chart; see your Excel documentation.

Comments

Excel uses the pivot table to specify the category names and find counts within each category. If you already have that information, you can proceed directly to the Chart Wizard.

JMP

JMP makes a bar chart and frequency table together.

From the **Analyze** menu, choose **Distribution**.

In the Distribution dialog, drag the name of the variable into the empty variable window beside the label "Y, Columns"; click **OK**.

To make a pie chart choose **Chart** from the **Graph** menu.

In the Chart dialog, select the variable name from the Columns list, click on the button labeled "Statistics," and select "N" from the drop-down menu.

Click the "X, Level" button to assign the same variable name to the X-axis.

Under Options, click on the top button—labeled "Vertical"—and select "Pie" from the drop-down menu. Click **OK**.

MINITAB

To make a bar chart choose **Chart** from the **Graph** menu.

In the Chart dialog, enter the name of the variable that you wish to graph in the first row of the "Graph variables" table under the column marked X. In the "Data display" table, make sure that the first row reads "Display: Bar" and "For each: Graph", click **OK**.

To make a pie chart choose **Pie Chart** from the **Graph** menu.

In the Pie Chart dialog, make sure that the button next to the words "Chart data in:" is selected.

Enter the name of the variable to plot in the empty box to the right. Click **OK**.

SPSS

To make a bar chart choose **Bar** from the **Graphs** menu.

From the Bar Charts Dialog, choose **Simple** and indicate the nature of the data.

In the Define Simple Bar dialog, select the variable name from the source list and click on the **Category Axis** arrow.

Click the **OK** button to create the display.

A similar path makes a pie chart by choosing **Pie** rather than Bar from the **Graphs** menu.

TI-89

The TI-89 won't do displays for categorical variables.

Chapter 4 Displaying Quantitative Data

DATA DESK

- Select the variable to display.
- In the **Plot** menu choose **Histogram.**

EXCEL

Excel cannot make histograms or dotplots without a third-party add-in.

Comments

Excel's Data Analysis add-in does offer something called a histogram, but it just makes a crude frequency table, and the Chart Wizard cannot then create a statistically appropriate histogram.

JMP

- Choose **Distribution** from the **Analyze** menu.
- In the **Distribution** dialog, drag the name of the variable that you wish to analyze into the empty window beside the label "**Y, Columns.**"
- Click **OK.**

MINITAB

- Choose **Histogram** from the **Graph** menu.
- In the **Plot** dialog, assign the name of a quantitative variable to the first row of the box labeled "X."
- Click **OK.**

SPSS

- Choose **Interactive** from the **Graphs** menu.
- From the **Interactive Graphs** submenu, choose **Histogram.**
- In the **Create Histogram** dialog, drag a variable from the source list into the target. SPSS creates a variable called Counts and places it in the vertical axis target automatically to indicate making a frequency histogram. You can specify a relative frequency histogram with the "Percentage" variable name instead.
- Click **OK.**

(continued)

TI-89

- Select [F2] (Plots), then 1: Plot Setup, select a plot and press [F1] to define it.
- Select plot type 4: Histogram. Use VAR-LINK to select the data list.
- Enter a number for the histogram bucket (bar) width.
- Press [ENTER] to complete the plot definition. Press [F5] to display the histogram.
- Press [♦][F2] to adjust the window appropriately, then press [♦][F3] (Graph).

Comments

If the data are stored as a frequency table (say, with data values in list1 and frequencies in list2) change Use Freq and Categories to YES and use VAR-LINK to select list2 as the frequency variable on the plot definition screen.

Chapter 5 Describing Distributions Numerically

DATA DESK

Select the variable(s) to summarize. In the **Calc** menu open the **Summaries** submenu. **Options** offer separate tables, a single unified table, and other formats.

EXCEL

Click on an empty cell. Type an equals sign and choose **"Average"** from the popup list of functions that appears to the left of the text editing box. Enter the data range in the box that says **"Number 1."** Click the **OK** button.

To compute the standard deviation of a column of data directly, use the **STDEV** from the popup list of functions in the same way.

Comments

Excel's STDEV function should not be used for data values larger in magnitude than 100,000 or for lists of more than a few thousand values. It is programmed with an unstable formula that can generate rounding errors when these limits are exceeded.

JMP

Choose **Distribution** from the **Analyze** menu. In the **Distribution** dialog, drag the name of the variable that you wish to analyze into the empty window beside the label "Y, Columns." Click **OK.** JMP computes standard summary statistics along with displays of the variable.

MINITAB

Choose **Basic Statistics** from the **Stat** menu. From the **Basic Statistics** submenu, choose **Display Descriptive Statistics.** Assign variables from the variable list box to the Variables box. MINITAB makes a Descriptive Statistics table.

SPSS

Choose **Descriptive Statistics** from the **Analyze** menu and then choose **Explore. . . .** In the **Explore** dialog, assign one or more variables from the source list to the Dependent List and click the **OK** button. SPSS will generate several plots and tables.

TI-89

- To compute summary statistics press [F4] (Calc). Input the name of the list using VAR-LINK. Press Enter. Use the down arrow to scroll through the output.
- To create a box plot press [F2] (Plots) then [ENTER]. Select a plot to define and press [F1]. Select either 3: Box Plot or 4: Mod Box Plot (to identify outliers). Select the mark type of your choice (for outliers). Press [ENTER] to finish. Press [F5] to display the graph.

Comments

If the data are stored as a frequency table (say, with data values in list1 and frequencies in list2), use VAR-LINK to select list2 as the frequency variable in 1-Var Stats.

For the plot, change Use Freq and Categories to YES and use VAR-LINK to select list2 as the frequency variable on the plot definition screen.

Chapter 6 The Standard Deviation as a Ruler and the Normal Model

DATA DESK

To make a "Normal Probability Plot" in Data Desk,

- Select the Variable.
- Choose **Normal Prob Plot** from the **Plot** menu.

Comments

Data Desk places the ordered data values on the vertical axis and the Normal scores on the horizontal axis.

EXCEL

Excel offers a "Normal probability plot" as part of the Regression command in the Data Analysis extension, but (as of this writing) it is not a correct Normal probability plot and should not be used.

JMP

To make a "Normal Quantile Plot" in JMP,

- Make a histogram using **Distributions** from the **Analyze** menu.
- Click on the drop-down menu next to the variable name.
- Choose **Normal Quantile Plot** from the drop-down menu.
- JMP opens the plot next to the histogram.

Comments

JMP places the ordered data on the vertical axis and the Normal scores on the horizontal axis. The vertical axis aligns with the histograms axis, a useful feature.

MINITAB

To make a "Normal Probability Plot" in MINITAB,

- Choose **Probability Plot** from the **Graph** menu.
- Assign the variable to be displayed to the Variables box.
- Click the **OK** button.

Comments

MINITAB places the ordered data on the horizontal axis and the Normal scores on the vertical axis.

SPSS

To make a Normal "P-P plot" in SPSS,

- Choose **P-P** from the **Graphs** menu.
- Select the variable to be displayed in the source list.
- Click the arrow button to move the variable into the target list.
- Click the **OK** button.

Comments

SPSS places the ordered data on the horizontal axis and the Normal scores on the vertical axis. You may safely ignore the options in the P-P dialog.

(continued)

TI-89

- To create a "Normal Probability Plot" press [F2] and select choice 2: Norm Prob Plot. Select a plot number and use VAR-LINK to enter the data list. Select X or Y for the data axis. Press [ENTER] to calculate the *z*-scores.
- Press [F2] and select choice 1: Plot Setup. Turn off any undesired plots (either [F3] (Clear) or [F4](√)). Press [F5] to display the plot.
- To find what percent of a normal model lies between two *z*-scores, press [F5] (Distr), then select 4: Normal Cdf. Enter the lower and upper *z*-scores, specify mean 0 and standard deviation 1 and press [ENTER].
- To find the *z*-score for a given percentile, press [F5] (Distr), then arrow down to 2: Inverse press the right arrow to see the sub menu and select 1: Inverse Normal. Enter the area to the left of the desired point, mean 0 and standard deviation 1 and press [ENTER].

Comments

Normal models strictly go to infinity on either end, which is 1EE99 on the calculator. In practice, any "large" number will work. For example, the percentage of the normal model over two standard deviations above the mean can use Lower Value 2 and Upper Value 999. To find area more than two standard deviations below the mean, use Lower Value −999, and Upper value −2.

Chapter 7 Scatterplots, Associations, and Correlation

DATA DESK

To make a scatterplot of two variables, select one variable as Y and the other as X and choose **Scatterplot** from the **Plot** menu. Then find the correlation by choosing **Correlation** from the scatterplot's HyperView menu.

Alternatively, select the two variables and choose **Pearson Product-Moment** from the **Correlations** submenu of the **Calc** menu.

Comments

We prefer that you look at the scatterplot first and then find the correlation. But if you've found the correlation first, click on the correlation value to drop down a menu that offers to make the scatterplot.

EXCEL

To make a Scatterplot with the Excel Chart Wizard:

- Click on the **Chart Wizard** Button in the menu bar. Excel opens the Chart Wizard's Chart Type Dialog window.
- Make sure the **Standard Types** tab is selected, and select ***XY* (Scatter)** from the choices offered.
- Specify the **scatterplot without lines** from the choices offered in the Chart sub-type selections. The **Next** button takes you to the Chart Source Data dialog.
- If it is not already frontmost, click on the **Data Range** tab, and enter the data range in the space provided.
- By convention, we always represent variables in columns. The Chart Wizard refers to variables as Series. Be sure the **Column** option is selected.
- Excel places the leftmost column of those you select on the *x*-axis of the scatterplot. If the column you wish to see on the *x*-axis is not the leftmost column in your spreadsheet, click on the **Series** tab and edit the specification of the individual axis series.
- Click the **Next** button. The Chart Options dialog appears.
- Select the **Titles** tab. Here you specify the title of the chart and names of the variables displayed on each axis.
- Type the chart title in the **Chart title:** edit box.
- Type the *x*-axis variable name in the **Value (X) Axis:** edit box. Note that you must name the columns correctly here. Naming another variable will not alter the plot, only mislabel it.
- Type the *y*-axis variable name in the **Value (Y) Axis:** edit box.
- Click the **Next** button to open the chart location dialog.
- Select the **As new sheet:** option button.
- Click the **Finish** button.

Often, the resulting scatterplot will not be useful. By default, Excel includes the origin in the plot even when the data are far from zero. You can adjust the axis scales.

To change the scale of a plot axis in Excel:

- Double-click on the axis. The **Format Axis Dialog** appears.
- If the **scale tab** is not the frontmost, select it.

EXCEL

- Enter new minimum or new maximum values in the spaces provided. You can drag the dialog box over the scatterplot as a straightedge to help you read the maximum and minimum values on the axes.
- Click the **OK** button to view the rescaled scatterplot.
- Follow the same steps for the *x*-axis scale.

Compute a correlation in Excel with the **CORREL** function from the drop-down menu of functions. If CORREL is not on the menu, choose **More Functions** and find it among the statistical functions in the browser.

In the dialog that pops up, enter the range of cells holding one of the variables in the space provided.

Enter the range of cells for the other variable in the space provided.

JMP

To make a scatterplot and compute correlation, choose **Fit Y by X** from the **Analyze** menu.

In the Fit Y by X dialog, drag the Y variable into the "**Y, Response**" box, and drag the X variable into the "**X, Factor**" box. Click the **OK** button.

Once JMP has made the scatterplot, click on the red triangle next to the plot title to reveal a menu of options. Select **Density Ellipse** and select .95. JMP draws an ellipse around the data and reveals the **Correlation** tab. Click the blue triangle next to Correlation to reveal a table containing the correlation coefficient.

MINITAB

To make a scatterplot, choose **Plot** from the **Graph** menu. In the Plot dialog, click on the **Y** cell for Graph 1 in the Graph variables box to specify the *y*-variable. Then assign the *y*-variable from the Variable list box. Click on the **X** cell for the graph and assign the *x*-variable from the Variable list box. Click the **OK** button to view the scatterplot.

To compute a correlation coefficient, choose **Basic Statistics** from the **Stat** menu.

From the Basic Statistics submenu, choose **Correlation.** Click on the **Variables** box and assign variables from the Variable List box. Click the **OK** button to compute the correlation table.

SPSS

To make a scatterplot, choose **Interactive** from the **Graphs** menu. From the Interactive Graphs submenu, choose **Scatterplot.** In the Create Scatterplot dialog, drag variable names from the source list into the targets on the right. Each target describes a specific part or aspect of the plot. For example, drag a variable name to the *y*-axis target to specify the variable to display on the *y*-axis.

Similarly, the *x*-axis target gets the name of the variable to display on the *x*-axis.

To compute a correlation coefficient, choose **Correlate** from the **Analyze** menu. From the Correlate submenu, choose **Bivariate.** In the Bivariate Correlations dialog, use the arrow button to move variables between the source and target lists.

Make sure the **Pearson** option is selected in the Correlation Coefficients field.

TI-89

To create a scatterplot, press [F2] (Plots). Select choice 1: Plot Setup. Select a plot to define and press [F1]. Select Plot Type 1: Scatter. Select a mark type. Specify the lists where the data are stored as Xlist and Ylist using VAR-LINK. Press [ENTER] to finish. Press [F5] to display the plot.

To find the correlation, press [F4] (Calc), then arrow to 3: Regressions press the right arrow and select **1:LinReg(a+bx).** Then specify the lists where the data are stored. You can also select a y-function to store the equation of the line.

Comments

Notice that if you **TRACE** (press [F3]) the scatterplot the calculator will tell you the X and Y value at each point.

Chapter 8 Linear Regression

DATA DESK

Select the *y*-variable and the *x*-variable. In the **Plot** menu choose **Scatterplot.** From the scatterplot HyperView menu choose **Add Regression Line** to display the line. From the HyperView menu choose **Regression** to compute the regression.

Comments

Alternatively, find the regression first with the **Regression** command in the **Calc** menu. Click on the *x*-variable's name to open a menu that offers the scatterplot.

EXCEL

Make a scatterplot of the data. With the scatterplot frontmost, select **Add Trendline . . .** from the **Chart** menu. Click the **Options** tab and select **Display Equation on Chart.** Click **OK.**

Comments

The computer grid for Chapter 7 shows how to make a scatterplot. We don't repeat those steps here.

JMP

Choose **Fit Y by X** from the **Analyze** menu. Specify the *y*-variable in the Select Columns box and click the "**Y, Response**" button. Specify the *x*-variable and click the "**X, Factor**" button. Click **OK** to make a scatterplot. In the scatterplot window, click on the red triangle beside the heading labeled "Bivariate Fit . . ." and choose "**Fit Line.**" JMP draws the least squares regression line on the scatterplot and displays the results of the regression in tables below the plot.

MINITAB

Choose **Regression** from the **Stat** menu. From the Regression submenu, choose **Fitted Line Plot.** In the Fitted Line Plot dialog, click in the **Response Y** box, and assign the *y*-variable from the Variable list. Click in the **Predictor X** box, and assign the *x*-variable from the Variable list. Make sure that the Type of Regression Model is set to Linear. Click the **OK** button.

SPSS

Choose **Interactive** from the **Graphs** menu. From the Interactive Graphs submenu, choose **Scatterplot.** In the Create Scatterplot dialog, drag the *y*-variable into the **y-axis target,** and the *x*-variable into the **x-axis target.** Click on the **Fit** tab. Choose **Regression** from the **Method** popup menu. Click the **OK** button.

TI-89

To find the equation of the regression line (and add the line to a scatterplot) choose **LinReg(a+bx)** from the **Calc Regressions** menu, tell it the list names, and a function to store the equation. To make a residuals plot, define a **PLOT** as a scatterplot.

Specify your explanatory datalist as Xlist. For Ylist find the list name resid from VAR-LINK by arrowing to the STATVARS portion, then press [2] (r) and locate the list. Press [ENTER] to finish the plot definition and [F5] to display the plot.

Comments

Each time you execute a **LinReg** command, the calculator automatically computes the residuals and stores them in a data list named RESID. If you don't want to see this (or any other calculator-generated list) any more, press [F1] (Tools) and select choice 3: Setup Editor. Leaving the box for lists to display blank will reset the calculator to show only lists 1 through 6.

Chapter 9 Regression Wisdom

DATA DESK

Click on the **HyperView** menu on the **Regression** output table. A menu drops down to offer scatterplots of residuals against predicted values, normal probability plots of residuals, or just

Comments

If you change any of the variables in the regression analysis, Data Desk will offer to update the plots of residuals.

the ability to save the residuals and predicted values.
Click on the name of a predictor in the regression table to be offered a scatterplot of the residuals against that predictor.

EXCEL

The Data Analysis add-in for Excel includes a Regression command. The dialog box it shows offers to make plots of residuals.

Comments
Do not use the Normal probability plot offered in the regression dialog. It is not what it claims to be and is wrong.

JMP

From the **Analyze** menu choose **Fit Y by X.** Select **Fit Line.** Under Linear Fit, Select **Plot Residuals.** You can also choose to **Save Residuals.** Subsequently, from the **Distribution** menu choose **Normal quantile plot** or **histogram** for the residuals.

MINITAB

From the **Stat** menu choose **Regression.** In the Regression dialog click **Storage.** Check **Fits** and **Residuals.**

From the Regression submenu choose **Residual Plots.** Indicate the columns where you saved the fits and residuals and click **OK.**

SPSS

From the **Analyze** menu choose **Regression.** From the Regression submenus choose **Linear.** After assigning variables to their roles in the regression, click the **Plots . . .** button.
In the Plots dialog you can specify a normal probability plot of residuals and scatterplots of various versions of standardized residuals and predicted values.

Comments
A plot of ***ZRESID** against ***PRED** will look most like the residual plots we've discussed. SPSS standardizes the residuals by dividing by their standard deviation. (There's no need to subtract their mean; it must be zero.) The standardization doesn't affect the scatterplot.

TI-89

To make a residuals plot, define a Plot as a scatter plot. Specify your explanatory datalist as Xlist. For Ylist find the list name resid from VAR-LINK by arrowing to the STATVARS portion, then press [2] (r) and locate the list. Press [ENTER] to finish the plot definition and [F5] to display the plot.

Comments
Each time you execute a **LinReg** command, the calculator automatically computes the residuals and stores them in a data list named RESID. If you don't want to see this (or any other calculator-generated list) any more, press [F1] (Tools) and select choice 3: Setup Editor. Leaving the box for lists to display blank will reset the calculator to show only lists 1 through 6.

Chapter 10 Re-expressing Data: It's Easier Than You Think

DATA DESK

To re-express a variable in Data Desk, select the variable and Choose the function to re-express it from the **Manip** > **Transform** menu. Square root, log, reciprocal, and reciprocal root are immediately available. For others, make a derived variable and type the function. Data Desk makes a new derived variable that holds the re-expressed values. Any value changed in the original variable will immediately be re-expressed in the derived variable.

Comments
Or choose **Manip** > **Transform** > **Dynamic** > **Box-Cox** to generate a continuously changeable variable and a slider that specifies the power. Set plots to **Automatic Update** in their HyperView menus and watch them change dynamically as you drag the slider.

(continued)

EXCEL

To re-express a variable in Excel, use Excel's built-in functions as you would for any calculation. Changing a value in the original column will change the re-expressed value.

JMP

To re-express a variable in JMP, double-click to the right of the last column of data to create a new column. Name the new column and select it. Choose **Formula** from the **Cols** menu. In the Formula dialog, choose the transformation and variable that you wish to assign to the new column. Click the **OK** button. JMP places the re-expressed data in the new column.

Comments

The log and square root re-expressions are found in the **Transcendental** menu of functions in the formula dialog.

MINITAB

To re-express a variable in MINITAB, Choose **Calculator** from the **Calc** menu. Type a name for the new re-expressed variable. Use the **Function List** and **Variables list** box to build the expression. Click the **OK** button.

SPSS

To re-express a variable in SPSS, Choose **Compute** from the **Transform** menu. Enter a name in the Target Variable field. Use the calculator and Function List to build the expression. Move a variable to be re-expressed from the source list to the Numeric Expression field. Click the **OK** button.

TI-89

To re-express data stored in a list, perform the re-expression on the whole list and store it in another list. For example, to use the common (base 10) logarithms of the data in list1, on the home screen, enter the command **log(list1)** [STO▸] **list2.**

Comments

- To find the log command press [CATALOG] then [4] (L) arrow to log(and press [ENTER].
- Natural logs are LN (press [2nd][X]).
- For square roots, press [2nd][×]

Chapter 11 Understanding Randomness

DATA DESK

Generate random numbers in Data Desk with the **Generate Random Numbers . . .** command in the **Manip** menu. A dialog guides you in specifying the number of variables to fill, the number of cases, and details about the values. For most simulations, generate random uniform values.

Comments

Bernoulli Trials generate random values that are 0 or 1 with a specified chance of a 1.

Binomial Experiments automatically generate a specified number of Bernoulli trials and count the number of 1's.

EXCEL

The **RAND** function generates a random value between 0 and 1. You can multiply to scale it up to any range you like and use the INT function to turn the result into an integer.

Comments

Published tests of Excel's random number generation have declared it to be inadequate. However, for simple simulations, it should be OK. Don't trust it for important large simulations.

JMP

In a new column, in the **Cols** menu choose **Column Info . . .** In the dialog, click the **New Property** button, and choose **Formula** from the drop-down menu.

Click the **Edit Formula** button and in the **Functions(grouped)** window, click on **Random. Random Integer (10),** for example, will generate a random integer between 1 and 10.

MINITAB

In the **Calc** menu choose **Random Data . . .**
In the Random Data submenu choose **Uniform . . .**

A dialog guides you in specifying details of range and number of columns to generate.

SPSS

The **RV.UNIFORM(min, max)** function returns a random value that is equally likely between the min and max limits.

TI-89

To generate random numbers, move the cursor to highlight the name of a blank list. Use **5:RandInt** from the [F4] (Calc) Probability menu. This command will produce any number of random integers in the specified range.

Comments

Some examples:
RandInt(0,10) randomly chooses a 0 or a 1. This is an effective simulation of ten coin tosses.
RandInt(1,6,2) randomly returns two integers between 1 and 6. This is a good way to simulate rolling two dice.
RandInt(0,57,3) produces three random integers between 0 and 57, a nice way to simulate the chapter's dorm room lottery.

Chapter 16 Random Variables

TI-89

To calculate the mean and standard deviation of a discrete random variable, enter the probability model in two lists:

- In one list (say, list1) enter the *x* values of the variable.
- In a second list (say, list2) enter the associated probabilities $P(X = x)$.
- From the **STAT CALC** ([F4]) menu select **1-VarStats.** Use VAR-LINK to enter the list name list1 in the List box and list2 in the Freq box.

Comments

You can enter the probabilities as fractions; the calculator will change them to decimals for you.
Notice that the calculator knows enough to only compute the standard deviation σ, but mistakenly uses $\bar{x}$ when it should say μ. Make sure you don't make that mistake!

Chapter 17 Probability Models

DATA DESK

BinomDistr(*x, n, prob*) (pdf)
CumBinomDistr(*x, n, prob*) (cdf)

Comments

Data Desk does not compute Geometric probabilities.
These functions work in derived variables or in scratchpads.

(continued)

EXCEL

Binomdist(*x, n, prob, cumulative*)

Comments

Set cumulative = true for cdf, false for pdf.
Excel's function fails when x or n is large.
Possibly, it does not use the Normal approximation.
Excel does not compute Geometric probabilities.

JMP

Binomial Probability (*prob, n, x*) (pdf)
Binomial Distribution (*prob, n, x*) (cdf)

Comments

JMP does not compute Geometric probabilities.

MINITAB

Choose **Probability Distributions** from the **Calc** menu.
Choose **Binomial** from the Probability Distributions submenu.
To calculate the probability of getting x success in n trials, choose **Probability.**
To calculate the probability of getting x or fewer successes among n trials, choose **Cumulative Probability.**

Comments

Minitab does not compute Geometric probabilities.

SPSS

PDF.GEOM(*x, prob*)
CDF.GEOM(*x, prob*)

PDF.BINOM(*x, n, prob*)
CDF.BINOM(*x, n, prob*)

TI-89

Find the commands under the [F5] (Distributions) menu.

- F: Geometric Pdf will ask for p and x. It returns the probability of the first success occurring on the xth trial.
- G: Geometric Cdf will ask for p and the upper and lower values of interest, say a and b. It returns $P(a \leq X \leq b)$, the probability the first success occurs between the ath and b^{th} trials, inclusive.
- A:Binomial Pdf asks for n, p, and x.
- B: Binomial Cdf asks for n, p, and the lower and upper values of interest.

Comments

- For Geometric variables, when finding $P(X \geq a)$ specify an upper value of infinity, 1[EE]99, or a very large number.
- For Binomial variables, when finding $P(X \geq a)$ the upper value is n.

Chapter 19 Confidence Intervals for Proportions

DATA DESK

Data Desk does not offer built-in methods for inference with proportions.

Comments

For summarized data, open a Scratchpad to compute the standard deviation and margin of error by typing the calculation.

EXCEL

Inference methods for proportions are not part of the standard Excel tool set.

Comments

For summarized data, type the calculation into any cell and evaluate it.

JMP

For a **categorical** variable that holds category labels, the **Distribution** platform includes tests and intervals of proportions.

For summarized data, put the category names in one variable and the frequencies in an adjacent variable. Designate the frequency column to have the **role** of **frequency.** Then use the **Distribution** platform.

Comments

JMP uses slightly different methods for proportion inferences than those discussed in this text. Your answers are likely to be somewhat different.

MINITAB

Choose **Basic Statistics** from the **Stat** menu.

- Choose **1Proportion** from the Basic Statistics submenu.
- If the data are category names in a variable, assign the variable from the variable list box to the **Samples in columns** box. If you have summarized data, click the **Summarized Data** button and fill in the number of trials and the number of successes.
- Click the **Options** button and specify the remaining details.
- If you have a large sample, check **Use test and interval based on normal distribution.**

Click the **OK** button.

Comments

When working from a variable that names categories, MINITAB treats the last category as the "success" category. You can specify how the categories should be ordered.

SPSS

SPSS does not find confidence intervals for proportions.

TI-89

To calculalate a confidence interval for a population proportion:

- Go to the **Ints** menu ([2nd][F2]) and select **5:1-PropZInt.**
- Enter the number of succeses observed and the sample size.
- Specify a confidence level.
- Calculate the interval.

Comments

Beware: When you enter the value of *x*, you need the count, not the percentage. The count must be a whole number. If the number of successes are given as a percentage, you must first multiply *np* and round the result.

Chapter 20 Testing Hypotheses About Proportions

DATA DESK

Data Desk does not offer built-in methods for inference with proportions. The **Replicate Y by X** command in the **Manip** menu will "reconstruct" summarized count data so you can display it.

Comments

For summarized data, open a Scratchpad to compute the standard deviation and margin of error by typing the calculation.

(continued)

EXCEL

Inference methods for proportions are not part of the standard Excel tool set.

Comments

For summarized data, type the calculation into any cell and evaluate it.

JMP

For a **categorical** variable that holds category labels, the **Distribution** platform includes tests and intervals of proportions. For summarized data, put the category names in one variable and the frequencies in an adjacent variable. Designate the frequency column to have the **role** of **frequency.** Then use the **Distribution** platform.

Comments

JMP uses slightly different methods for proportion inferences than those discussed in this text. Your answers are likely to be slightly different.

MINITAB

Choose **Basic Statistics** from the **Stat** menu.

- Choose **1Proportion** from the Basic Statistics submenu.
- If the data are category names in a variable, assign the variable from the variable list box to the **Samples in columns** box.
- If you have summarized data, click the **Summarized Data** button and fill in the number of trials and the number of successes.
- Click the **Options** button and specify the remaining details.
- If you have a large sample, check **Use test and interval based on Normal distribution.**
- Click the **OK** button.

Comments

When working from a variable that names categories, MINITAB treats the last category as the "success" category. You can specify how the categories should be ordered.

SPSS

SPSS does not find hypothesis tests for proportions.

T1-89

To do the mechanics of a hypothesis test for a proportion,

- Select **5:1-PropZTest** from the **STAT Tests** ([2nd][F1]) menu.
- Specify the hypothesized proportion.
- Enter the observed value of *x*.
- Specify the sample size.
- Indicate what kind of test you want: one-tail lower tail, two-tail, or one-tail upper tail.
- Specify whether to calculate the result or draw (a normal curve with p-value area shaded) the result.

Comments

Beware: When you enter the value of *x*, you need the *count,* not the percentage. The count must be a whole number. If the number of successes are given as a percent, you must first multiply *np* and round the result to obtain *x*.

Chapter 22 Comparing Two Proportions

DATA DESK

Data Desk does not offer built-in methods for inference with proportions. Use **Replicate Y by X** to construct data corresponding to given proportions and totals.

Comments

For summarized data, open a Scratchpad to compute the standard deviations and margin of error by typing the calculation.

EXCEL

Inference methods for proportions are not part of the standard Excel tool set.

Comments

For summarized data, type the calculation into any cell and evaluate it.

JMP

For a **categorical** variable that holds category labels, the **Distribution** platform includes tests and intervals of proportions.

For summarized data put the category names in one variable and the frequencies in an adjacent variable. Designate the frequency column to have the **role** of **frequency**. Then use the **Distribution** platform.

Comments

JMP uses slightly different methods for proportion inferences than those discussed in this text. Your answers are likely to be slightly different.

MINITAB

To find a hypothesis test for a proportion, Choose **Basic Statistics** from the **Stat** menu.

Choose **2Proportions. . .** from the Basic Statistics submenu.

If the data are organized as category names in one column and case IDs in another, assign the variables from the variable list box to the **Samples in one column** box. If the data are organized as two separate columns of responses, click on **Samples in different columns:** and assign the variables from the variable list box. If you have summarized data, click the **Summarized Data** button and fill in the number of trials and the number of successes for each group.

Click the **Options** button and specify the remaining details. Remember to click the **Use pooled estimate of *p* for test** box when testing the null hypothesis of no difference between proportions.

Click the **OK** button.

Comments

When working from a variable that names categories, MINITAB treats the last category as the "success" category. You can specify how the categories should be ordered

SPSS

SPSS does not find hypothesis tests for proportions.

TI-89

To calculate a confidence interval for the difference between two population proportions:

- Select **6:2-PropZInt** from the **STAT Ints** menu.
- Enter the observed counts and the sample sizes for both samples.
- Specify a confidence level.
- Calculate the interval.

To do the mechanics of a hypothesis test for equality of population proportions:

- Select **6:2-PropZTest** from the **STAT Tests** menu.
- Enter the observed counts and sample sizes.
- Indicate what kind of test you want: one-tail upper tail, lower tail, or two-tail.
- Specify if results should simply be calculated or displayed with the area corresponding to the *p*-value of the test shaded.

Comments

Beware: when you enter the value of x, you need the *count,* not the percentage. The count must be a whole number. If the number of successes are given as a percent, you must first multiply np and round the result to obtain x.

Chapter 23 Inferences About Means

DATA DESK

Select variables.
From the **Calc** menu, choose **Estimate** for confidence intervals or **Test** for hypothesis tests. Select the interval or test from the drop-down menu and make other choices in the dialog.

EXCEL

Specify formulas. Find t* with the TINV(alpha, df) function.

Comments
Not really automatic. There's no easy way to find P-values in Excel.

JMP

From the **Analyze** menu select **Distribution.** For a confidence interval, scroll down to the "Moments" section to find the interval limits. For a hypothesis test, click the red triangle next to the variable's name and choose **Test Mean** from the menu, then fill in the resulting dialog.

Comments
"Moment" is a fancy statistical term for means, standard deviations, and other related statistics.

MINITAB

From the **Stat** menu choose the **Basic Statistics** submenu. From that menu, choose **1-sample t . . .** Then fill in the dialog.

Comments
The dialog offers a clear choice between confidence interval and test.

SPSS

From the **Analyze** menu choose the **Compare Means** submenu. From that, choose the **One-Sample t-test** command.

Comments
The commands suggest neither a single mean nor an interval. But the results provide both a test and an interval.

TI-89

Finding a confidence interval:
In the **STAT Ints** menu choose **2:TInterval.** Specify whether you are using data stored in a list or if you will enter the mean, standard deviation, and sample size. You must also specify the desired level of confidence.

Testing a hypothesis:
In the **STAT Tests** menu choose **2:T-Test.** You must specify whether you are using data stored in a list or if you will enter the mean, standard deviation, and size of your sample. You must also specify the hypothesized model mean and whether the test is to be two-tail, lower tail, or upper tail. Select whether the test is to be simply computed or whether to display the distribution curve and highlight the area corresponding to the *p*-value of the test.

Chapter 24 Comparing Means

DATA DESK

Select variables
From the **Calc** menu, choose **Estimate** for confidence intervals or **Test** for hypothesis tests. Select the interval or test from the drop-down menu and make other choices in the dialog.

Comments
Data Desk expects the two groups to be in separate variables.

EXCEL

From the **Tools** menu, choose **Data Analysis.** From the **Data Analysis** menu, choose **t-test: two-sample assuming unequal variances.**
Fill in the cell ranges for the two groups, the hypothesized difference, and the alpha level.

Comments

Excel expects the two groups to be in separate cell ranges. Notice that, contrary to Excel's wording, we do not need to assume that the variances are *not* equal; we simply choose not to assume that they *are* equal.

JMP

From the **Analyze** menu select **Fit y by x.** Select variables: a **Y, Response** variable that holds the data and an **X, Factor** variable that holds the group names. JMP will make a dotplot. Click the **red triangle** in the dotplot title, and choose **Unequal variances.** The *t*-test is at the bottom of the resulting table. Find the P-value from the Prob>F section of the table (they are the same).

Comments

JMP expects data in one variable and category names in the other.

MINITAB

From the **Stat** menu choose the **Basic Statistics** submenu. From that menu, choose **2-sample t...** Then fill in the dialog.

Comments

The dialog offers a choice of data in two variables or data in one variable and category names in the other.

SPSS

From the **Analyze** menu choose the **Compare Means** submenu. From that, choose the **Independent-Samples t-test** command. Specify the data variable and "group variable." Then type in the labels used in the group variable. SPSS offers both the two-sample and pooled-*t* results in the same table.

Comments

SPSS expects the data in one variable and group names in the other. If there are more than two group names in the group variable, only the two that are named in the dialog box will be compared.

TI-89

For a confidence interval:
In the **STAT Ints** menu choose **4:2-SampTInt.** You must specify if you are using data stored in two lists or if you will enter the means, standard deviations, and sizes of both samples. You must also indicate whether to pool the variances (when in doubt, say no) and specify the desired level of confidence.

To test a hypothesis:
In the **STAT Tests** menu choose
4:2-SampTTest. You must specify if you are using data stored in two lists or if you will enter the means, standard deviations, and sizes of both samples. You must also indicate whether to pool the variances (when in doubt, say no) and specify whether the test is to be two-tail, lower-tail, or upper-tail.

Chapter 25 Paired Samples and Blocks

DATA DESK

Select variables.
From the **Calc** menu, choose **Estimate** for confidence intervals or **Test** for hypothesis tests. Select the interval or test from the drop-down menu and make other choices in the dialog.

Comments

Data Desk expects the two groups to be in separate variables and in the same "Relation"—that is, about the same cases.

(continued)

EXCEL

From the **Tools** menu, choose **Data Analysis.** From the **Data Analysis** menu, choose **t-test: paired two-sample for Means.** Fill in the cell ranges for the two groups, the hypothesized difference, and the alpha level.

Comments

Excel expects the two groups to be in separate cell ranges.
Warning: Do not compute this test in Excel without checking for missing values. If there are any missing values (empty cells), Excel will usually give a wrong answer. Excel compacts each list, pushing values up to cover the missing cells and then checks only that it has the same number of values in each list. The result is mismatched pairs and an entirely wrong analysis.

JMP

From the **Analyze** menu select **Matched Pairs.** Specify the columns holding the two groups in the **Y Paired Response** Dialog. Click **OK.**

MINITAB

From the **Stat** menu choose the **Basic Statistics** submenu. From that menu, choose **Paired t...** Then fill in the dialog.

Comments

Minitab takes "First sample" minus "Second sample."

SPSS

From the **Analyze** menu, choose the **Compare Means** submenu. From that, choose the **Paired-Samples t-test** command. Select pairs of variables to compare and click the arrow to add them to the selection box.

Comments

You can compare several pairs of variables at once. Options include the choice to exclude cases missing in any pair from all tests.

TI-89

If the data are stored in two lists, say, list1 and list2, create a list of the differences: Move the cursor to the name of an empty list, then use VAR-LINK to enter the command list1-list2. Press [ENTER] to perform the subtraction.

Since inference for paired differences uses one-sample *t* procedures, select **2:T-Test** or **2:TInterval** from the **STAT Tests** or **Ints** menu. Specify as your data the list of differences you just created and apply the procedure.

Chapter 26 Comparing Counts

DATA DESK

Select variables.
From the **Calc** menu, choose **Contingency Table.** From the table's HyperView menu choose **Table Options.** (Or Choose **Calc** > **Calculation Options** > **Table Options.**) In the dialog, check the boxes for **Chi Square** and for **Standardized Residuals.** Data Desk will display the chi-square and its P-value below the table, and the standardized residuals within the table.

Comments

Data Desk automatically treats variables selected for this command as categorical variables even if their elements are numerals.

The **Compute Counts** command in the table's HyperView menu will make variables that hold the table contents (as selected in the Table Options dialog) including the standardized residuals.

EXCEL

Excel offers the function **CHITEST(actual_range,expected_range),** which computes a chi-square value for homogeneity. Both ranges are of the form UpperleftCell:LowerRightCell, specifying two rectangular tables that must hold counts (although Excel will not check for integer values). The two tables must be of the same size and shape.

Comments

Excel's documentation claims this is a test for independence and labels the input ranges accordingly, but Excel offers no way to find expected counts, so the function is not particularly useful for testing independence. You can only use this function if you already know both tables of counts or are willing to program additional calculations.

JMP

From the **Analyze** menu select **Fit Y by X.** Select variables: a Y, Response variable that holds responses for one variable, and an X, Factor variable that holds responses for the other. Both selected variables must be Nominal or Ordinal. JMP will make a plot and a contingency table. Below the contingency table, JMP offers a **Tests** panel. In that panel the Chi Square for independence is called a **Pearson ChiSquare.** The table also offers the P-value.

Click on the Contingency Table title bar to drop down a menu that offers to include a **Deviation** and **Cell Chi square** in each cell of the table.

Comments

JMP will choose a chi-square analysis for a **Fit Y by X** if both variables are nominal or ordinal (marked with an N or O), but not otherwise. Be sure the variables have the right type.
Deviations are the observed − expected differences in counts.
Cell chi-squares are the squares of the standardized residuals.
Refer to the deviations for the sign of the difference.
Look under **Distributions** in the **Analyze** menu to find a chi-square test for goodness-of-fit.

MINITAB

From the **Stat** menu choose the **Tables** submenu. From that menu, choose **Chi Square Test . . . .** In the dialog identify the columns that make up the table. Minitab will display the table and print the chi-square value and its P-value.

Comments

Alternatively, select the **Cross Tabulation . . .** command to see more options for the table, including expected counts and standardized residuals.

SPSS

From the **Analyze** menu choose the **Descriptive Statistics** submenu. From that submenu, choose **Crosstabs . . .** In the Crosstabs dialog, assign the row and column variables from the variable list. Both variables must be categorical. Click the **Cells** button to specify that standardized residuals should be displayed. Click the **Statistics** button to specify a chi-square test.

Comments

SPSS presents only variables that it knows to be categorical in the variable list for the Crosstabs dialog. If the variables you want are missing, check that they have the right type.

TI-89

To test goodness-of-fit, enter the observed counts in a list and the expected counts in another list. Expected counts can be entered as n*p and the calculator will compute them for you.
From the **STAT Tests** menu select **7:Chi2 GOF.** Enter the list names using VAR-LINK and the degrees of freedom, k-1, where k is the number of categories. Select whether to simply calculate or display the result with the area corresponding to the p-value highlighted.

To test a hypothesis of homogeneity or independence, you need to enter the data as a matrix. From the home screen, press [APPS] and select **6:Data/Matrix Editor,** then select **3:New.** Specify type as Matrix and name the matrix in the **Variable** box. Specify the number of rows and columns. Type the entries, pressing [ENTER] after each. Press [2nd][ESC] to leave the editor.

To do the test, choose **8:Chi2 2-way** from the **STAT Tests** menu.

Chapter 27 Inferences for Regression

DATA DESK

- Select *Y* and *X* variables.
- From the **Calc** menu, choose **Regression.**
- Data Desk displays the regression table.
- Select plots of residuals from the Regression table's HyperView menu.

Comments

You can change the regression by dragging the icon of another variable over either the *Y* or *X* variable name in the table and dropping it there. The regression will re-compute automatically.

EXCEL

- From the **Tools** menu, select Data Analysis.
- Select Regression from the **Analysis Tools** list.
- Click the **OK** button.
- Enter the data range holding the Y-variable in the box labeled "Y-range".
- Enter the range of cells holding the X-variable in the box labeled "X-range."
- Select the **New Worksheet Ply** option.

Select **Residuals** options. Click the **OK** button.

Comments

The Y and X ranges do not need to be in the same rows of the spreadsheet, although they must cover the same number of cells. But it is a good idea to arrange your data in parallel columns as in a data table.

Although the dialog offers a Normal probability plot of the residuals, the data analysis add-in does not make a correct probability plot, so don't use this option.

JMP

- From the **Analyze** menu select **Fit Y by X.**
- Select variables: a Y, Response variable, and an X, Factor variable. Both must be continuous (quantitative).
- JMP makes a scatterplot.
- Click on the red triangle besides the heading labeled **Bivariate Fit...** and choose **Fit Line.** JMP draws the least squares regression line on the scatterplot and displays the results of the regression in tables below the plot.
- The portion of the table labeled "Parameter Estimates" gives the coefficients, their standard errors, *t*-ratios, and P-values.

Comments

JMP chooses a regression analysis when both variables are "Continuous." If you get a different analysis, check the variable types.

The Parameter table does not include the residual standard deviation s_e. You can find that as Root Mean Square Error in the Summary of Fit panel of the output.

MINITAB

- Choose **Regression** from the **Stat** menu.
- Choose **Regression...** from the **Regression** submenu.
- In the Regression dialog, assign the Y-variable to the Response box and assign the X-variable to the Predictors box.
- Click the **Graphs** button.
- In the Regression-Graphs dialog, select **Standardized residuals,** and check **Normal plot of residuals** and **Residuals versus fits.**
- Click the **OK** button to return to the Regression dialog.
- Click the **OK** button to compute the regression.

Comments

You can also start by choosing a Fitted Line plot from the **Regression** submenu to see the scatterplot first—usually good practice.

SPSS

- **Choose Regression** from the **Analyze** menu.
- Choose **Linear** from the **Regression** submenu.
- In the Linear Regression dialog that appears, select the Y variable and move it to the dependent target. Then move the X-variable to the independent target.
- Click the **Plots** button.
- In the Linear Regression Plots dialog, choose to plot the *SRESIDs against the *ZPRED values.
- Click the **Continue** button to return to the Linear Regression dialog.
- Click the **OK** button to compute the regression.

TI-89

Under **STAT Tests** choose **A:LinRegTTest.** Specify the two lists where the data are stored and (usually) choose the two-tail option. Select an equation name to store the resulting line. In addition to reporting the calculated value of t and the P-value, the calculator will tell you the coefficients of the regression equation (a and b), the values of r^2 and r, the value of s used in prediction and confidence intervals, and the standard error of the slope. For 95% prediction and confidence intervals choose **7:LinRegTInt** from the **STAT Ints** menu. Specify the two lists where the data are stored and select an equation name to store the resulting line. Select for an interval for the slope or for a response. If for a response, enter the x value.

Appendix C: Answers

Here are the "answers" to the exercises for the chapters and the unit reviews. As we said in Chapter 1, the answers are outlines of the complete solution. Your solution should follow the model of the Step-by-Step examples, where appropriate. You should explain the context, show your reasoning and calculations, and draw conclusions. For some problems, what you decide to include in an argument may differ somewhat from the answers here. But, of course, the numerical part of your answer should match the numbers in the answers shown.

CHAPTER 2

1. Answers will vary.

2. *Who*—30 similar companies
Cases—Each of the 30 companies is a case.
What—401(k) employee participation rates
When—Sometime after1992
Where—United States
Why—The company in question is concerned that their employee participation rate is lower than the rates of similar companies.
How—Companies were "sampled," using an unspecified method.
Variable—401(k) participation rate
Type—Quantitative
Units—Percent
Concerns—How was the sample of companies selected?

3. *Who*—50 recent oil spills
Cases—Each of the 50 recent oil spills is a case.
What—Spillage amount and cause of puncture
When—Reported in 1995
Where—United States
Why—To use in designing new tankers
How—Not specified
Variable—Spillage amount
Type—Quantitative
Units—Not specified
Variable—Cause of puncture
Type—Categorical

4. *Who*—Winners of Best Actor or Best Actress Oscars
Cases—Each actor or actress is an individual.
What—Age at the time they won award
Where—United States
Why—To compare age distributions of actors and actresses
How—Census of all award winners
Variables—Age
Type—Quantitative
Units—Years

5. *Who*—54 bears
Cases—Each bear is a case
What—Weight, neck size, length and sex
When—Not specified
Where—Not specified
Why—To estimate weight from easier to measure variables
How—Researchers collected data on 54 bears they were able to catch.
Variable—Weight
Type—Quantitative
Units—Not specified
Variable—Neck Size
Type —Quantitative
Units—Not specified
Variable—Length
Type—Quantitative
Units—Not specified
Variable—Sex
Type—Categorical

6. *Who*—10 crankshafts
Cases—Each crankshaft is a case.
What—The pouring of molten iron
When—Reported in 1995
Where—Cleveland Casting Plant in Cleveland, Ohio.
Why—Quality control
How—Random sampling
Variable—Pouring temperature
Type—Quantitative
Units—Degrees Fahrenheit

7. *Who*—Arby's sandwiches
Cases—Each sandwich is a case.
What—Type of meat, number of calories, and serving size
When—Not specified
Where—Arby's restaurants
Why—To assess nutritional value of sandwiches
How—Census of all sandwiches at Arby's restaurants
Variable—Type of meat
Type—Categorical
Variable—Number of calories
Type—Quantitative
Units—Calories
Variable—Serving size
Type—Quantitative
Units—Ounces

8. *Who*—Shipboard firefighters
Cases—Each firefighter is an individual.
What—Pulling force, weight, and gender
When—Reported in 1982
Where—Not specified
Why—The researchers wanted to compare the abilities of men and women.
How—Not specified
Variable—Pulling force
Type—Quantitative
Units—Newtons
Variable—Weight
Type—Quantitative

Units—Not specified, probably pounds
Variable—Gender
Type—Categorical

9. *Who*—882 births
Cases—Each of the 882 births is a case.
What—Mother's age, length of pregnancy, type of birth, level of prenatal care, birth weight of baby, gender of baby, and baby's health problems
When—1998-2000
Where—Large city hospital
Why—Researchers were investigating the impact of prenatal care on newborn health.
How—Not specified exactly, but probably from hospital records.
Variable—Mother's age
Type—Quantitative
Units—Probably years
Variable—Length of pregnancy
Type—Quantitative
Units—Weeks
Variable—Birth weight of baby
Type—Quantitative
Units—Not specified, probably pounds and ounces
Variable—Type of birth
Type—Categorical
Variable—Level of prenatal care
Type—Categorical
Variable—Gender
Type—Categorical
Variable—Baby's health problems
Type—Categorical

10. *Who*—385 species of flowers
Cases—Each of the 385 species at each of the 47 years is a case, for a total of 18,095 cases.
What—Date of first flowering
When—Not specified
Where—Southern England
Why—The researchers believe that this indicates a warming of the overall climate.
How—Not specified
Variables—Date of first flowering
Type—Quantitative
Units—Days

11. *Who*—25,892 men
Cases—Each of the 25,892 men was an individual.
What—Fitness level and cause of death
When—Over a 10-year period prior to the article being published in May 2002
Where—Not specified
Why—To establish an association between fitness level and death from cancer
How—Researchers tracked the group of men over a 10-year period.
Variable—Fitness level
Type—Categorical
Variable—Cause of death
Type—Categorical

12. *Who*—Students
Cases—Each student is an individual.
What—Age, race or ethnicity, number of absences, grade level, reading score, math score and disabilities/special needs
When—Current
Where—Not specified
Why—Keeping this information is a state requirement.
How—The information is collected and stored as part of school records.
Variable—Age
Type—Quantitative
Units—not specified, probably years (perhaps years, months)
Variable—Race or ethnicity
Type—Categorical
Variable—Days absent
Type—Quantitative
Units—Number of days
Variable—Current grade level
Type—Categorical (ordinal)
Variable—Standardized reading score
Type—Quantitative
Units—Not specified
Variable—Standardized math score
Type—Quantitative
Units—Not specified
Variable—Disability/special needs
Type—Categorical

13. *Who*—Experiment volunteers
Cases—Each volunteer is an individual.
What—herbal cold remedy or sugar solution, and cold severity
When—Not specified
Where—Major pharmaceutical firm
Why—To test efficacy of herbal remedy on common cold.
How—The scientists set up a controlled experiment.
Variable—Type of treatment
Type—Categorical
Variable—Severity rating
Type—Quantitative (perhaps ordinal categorical)
Units—Scale from 0 to 5
Concerns—The severity of a cold seems subjective and difficult to quantify. Scientists may feel pressure to report negative findings of herbal product.

14. *Who*—Customers of a start-up company
Cases—Each customer is an individual.
What—Customer name, ID number, region of the country, date of last purchase, amount of purchase, and item purchased
When—Now
Where—United States?
Why—The company is building a database of sales information.
How—From company database
Variable—Customer name
Type—Categorical
Variable—Customer ID number
Type—Categorical
Variable –Region of country
Type—Categorical
Variable—Date of last purchase
Type—Quantitative
Units—Days, years
Variable—Amount of purchase
Type—Quantitative
Units—Not specified (dollars?)
Variable—Item purchased
Type—Categorical

15. *Who*—Automobiles
Cases—Each car is a case.

What—Make, country of origin, type of vehicle, and age of vehicle
When—Not specified
Where—A large university
Why—Not specified.
How—A survey was taken in campus parking lots.
Variable—Make
Type—Categorical
Variable—Country of origin
Type—Categorical
Variable—Type of vehicle
Type—Categorical
Variable –Age of vehicle
Type—Quantitative
Units—Years

16. *Who*—American vineyards
Cases—Each vineyard is a case.
What—Size of vineyard, number of years in existence, state, varieties of grapes grown, average case price, gross sales, and percent profit
When—Not specified
Where—United States
Why—To provide information for American wine producers
How—Not specified
Variable—Size
Type—Quantitative
Units—Acres
Variable—Number of years in existence
Type—Quantitative
Units—Number
Variable—State
Type—Categorical
Variable—Varieties of grapes grown
Type—Categorical
Variable—Average case price
Type—Quantitative
Units—Dollars?
Variable—Gross sales
Type—Quantitative
Units—Dollars?
Variable—Percent profit
Type—Quantitative
Units—Percent

17. *Who*—Streams
Cases—Each stream is a case.
What—Name of stream, substrate of the stream, acidity of the water, temperature, BCI
When—Not specified
Where—Upstate New York
Why—To study ecology of streams
How—Not specified
Variable—Stream name
Type—Categorical
Variable—Substrate
Type—Categorical
Variable—Acidity of water
Type—Quantitative
Units—pH
Variable—Temperature
Type—Quantitative
Units—Degrees Celsius
Variable—BCI
Type—Quantitative
Units—Not specified

18. *Who*—1180 Americans
Cases—Each of the 1180 Americans surveyed is an individual in this poll.
What—Region, age, political affiliation, and whether or not the person voted in the 1998 midterm Congressional election.
When—First quarter of 1999
Where—United States
Why—The information was gathered for presentation in a Gallup public opinion poll.
How—Phone survey
Variable—Region
Type—Categorical
Variable—Age
Type—Quantitative
Units—Not specified (years?)
Variable—Party affiliation
Type—Categorical
Variable—Voted in last election?
Type—Categorical

19. *Who*—All airline flights in the United States
Cases—Each flight is a case.
What—Type of aircraft, number of passengers, whether departures and arrivals were on schedule, and mechanical problems
When—Current
Where—United States
Why—Required by the Federal Aviation Administration
How—Data are collected from airline flight information
Variable—Type
Type—Categorical
Variable—Number of passengers
Type—Quantitative
Units—Number
Variable—Departed on time?
Type—Categorical
Variable—Arrived on time?
Type—Categorical
Variable—Mechanical problems?
Type— Categorical

20. *Who*—Every model of automobile in the United States
Cases—Each vehicle model is a case.
What—Vehicle manufacturer, vehicle type, weight, horsepower, and gas mileage for city and highway driving
When—Current
Where—United States
Why—By the Environmental Protection Agency to track fuel economy of vehicles
How—The data is collected from the manufacturer of each model
Variable—Manufacturer
Type—Categorical
Variable—Vehicle type
Type—Categorical
Variable—Weight
Type—Quantitative
Units—Not specified (pounds)
Variable—Horsepower
Type—Quantitative
Units—Not specified (horsepower)

Variable—Gas mileage, city
Type—Quantitative
Units—Miles per gallon
Variable—Gas mileage, highway
Type—Quantitative
Units—Miles per gallon
Concerns—Do manufacturers ratings of their own vehicles gas mileage reflect customer experience?

21. *Who*—41 refrigerators
Cases—Each of the 41 refrigerators is a case.
What—Brand, cost, size , type, estimated annual energy cost, overall rating, and repair history
When—2002
Where—United States
Why—To provide information to the readers of *Consumer Reports*
How—Not specified
Variable—Brand
Type—Categorical
Variable—Cost
Type—Quantitative
Units—Not specified (dollars)
Variable—Size
Type—Quantitative
Units—Cubic feet
Variable—Type
Type—Categorical
Variable—Estimated annual energy cost
Type—Quantitative
Units—Not specified (dollars)
Variable—Overall rating
Type—Categorical (ordinal)
Variable—Percent requiring repair in last 5 years
Type—Quantitative
Units—Percent

CHAPTER 3

1. Answers will vary.
2. Answers will vary.
3. Answers will vary.
4. Answers will vary.

5. a) Yes. We can add because these categories do not overlap (each person is assigned only one cause of death).
b) $100 - (30.3 + 23.0 + 8.4 + 7.9 + 4.1) = 26.3\%$
c) Either a bar chart or pie chart with "other" added would be appropriate. A bar chart is shown.

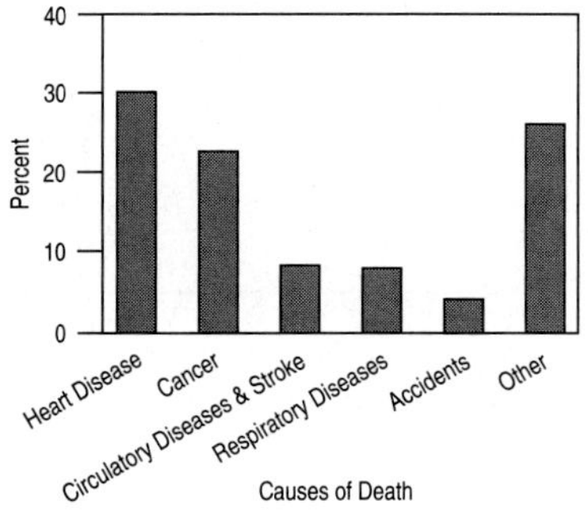

6. The majority of people surveyed either did not graduate from high school or graduated from high school and did not attend college. Fewer than 20% received 2-year degrees or higher.

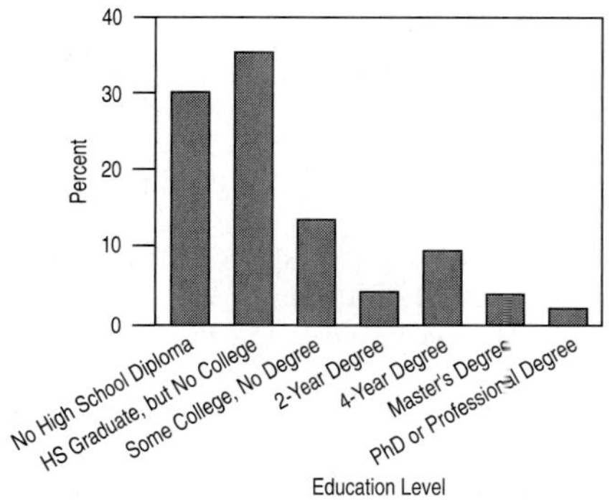

7. a) Individuals must have been able to select more than one phenomenon. Because of this, it is not reasonable to add those percents.
b) No, there may be people who believe in more than one of these, or none. We can't tell from these percentages.
c) The total of the percents is more than 100%, since individuals were able to select more than one phenomenon.

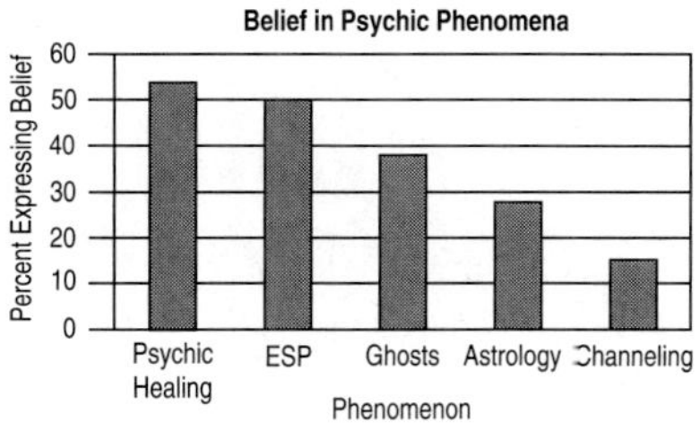

8. a) *Who*—Illegal gun trafficking cases
What—Types of violation
Where—United States
When—July 1996 through December 1998
Why—Study by US BATF
How—Survey of 1530 investigations
b) They total more than 100%. Either a case may be assigned to more than one category, or one or more of these numbers are wrong.
c) The percent of Types of Violation totals more than 100%.

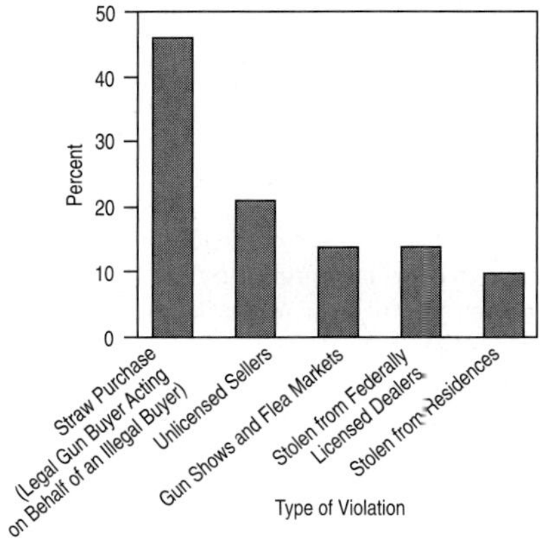

d) For example: Nearly half of the illegal gun trafficking cases were due to straw purchases (legal gun buyer acting on behalf of an illegal buyer). Unlicensed sellers accounted for 21%. The data are in question, since the percents sum to more than 100%, which should not happen if each case was assigned to only 1 of the 5 violations. (Other answers may vary.)

e) The percentages would be quite different if we had based them on the number of firearms instead of cases. Some cases had many firearms associated with them.

9. The bar chart shows that grounding is the most frequent cause of oil spills, although the other three sources—collision, fire, and hull failure—are nearly as common. Very few have unknown causes. A pie chart seems appropriate as well. One can see that the four types of causes are nearly evenly split.

10. a) There are too many categories to make a meaningful bar chart or pie chart.

b) One way to reduce the number of categories is to collect many of the countries that didn't win many medals into an "other" category. Here we've put every country with fewer than 6 medals into "Others."

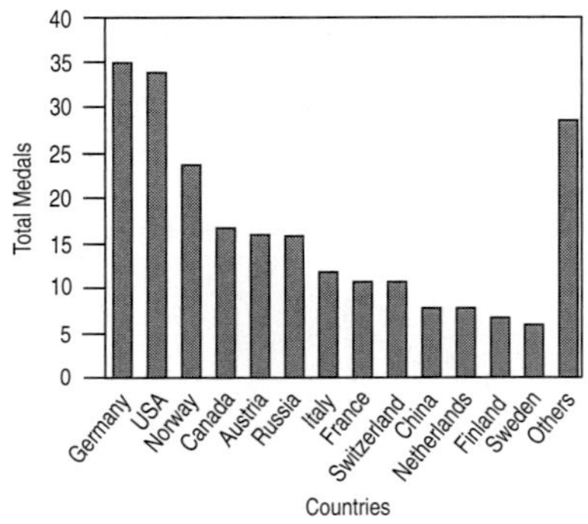

11. a) 67% − 46% = 21% (approximately)

b) No, the chart makes it look like about 3 times as much.

c) To maintain equivalent intervals, the vertical axis should begin at 0, not near 30%.

d)

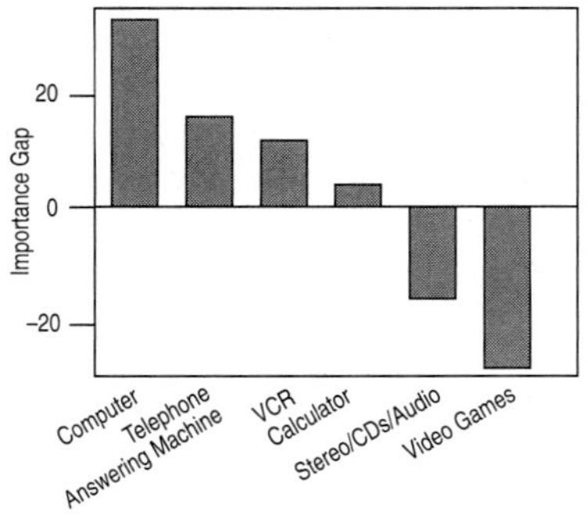

e) Teens tend to think that some technologies are critically important to own, although they don't use them every day. On the other hand, some technologies that are less important they use very often. The importance gap highlights this difference.

12. The 3-dimensional display distorts the percentages. The percentages don't add up to 100%. Not all the percentages seem to correspond to the areas of the pie (especially 85%, which looks smaller than 67%). The display is not well labeled.

13. a)

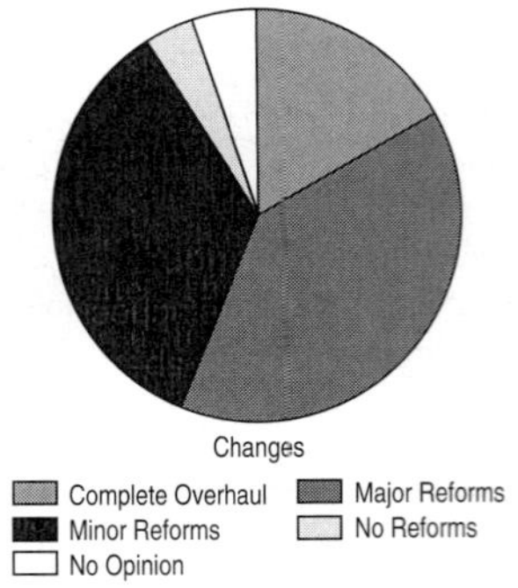

b) The bar chart makes comparisons of percentages easier and keeps the order of the response.

c) The vast majority favor some type of reform. While only 17% of the American adults surveyed recommended a complete overhaul, 74% of the respondents recommended either major or minor reforms in the way that corporations are audited.

14. a) Foreign cars are defined as non-American. There are 45 + 102 = 147 non-American cars or 147/359 = 40.95%.

b) There are 212 American cars of which 107 or 107/212 = 50.47% were owned by students.

c) There are 195 students of whom 107 or 107/195 = 54.87% owned American cars.

d)

		Totals	Percentages
Origin	American	212	59.05%
	European	45	12.53%
	Asian	102	28.41%

e) For students, the origin distribution is

		Driver	
		Student	Percentages
Origin	American	107	54.87%
	European	33	16.92%
	Asian	55	28.21%
	Totals	195	100.00%

For staff, it is

		Driver	
		Staff	Percentages
Origin	American	105	64.02%
	European	12	7.32%
	Asian	47	28.66%
	Totals	164	100.00%

f) No, the marginal distributions look slightly different. Bar charts or pie charts could be used to compare.

15. a) 82.5% b) 12.9% c) 11.1 %
d) 13.4% e) 85.7%

f) Many charts are possible. Here is a side-by-side bar chart.

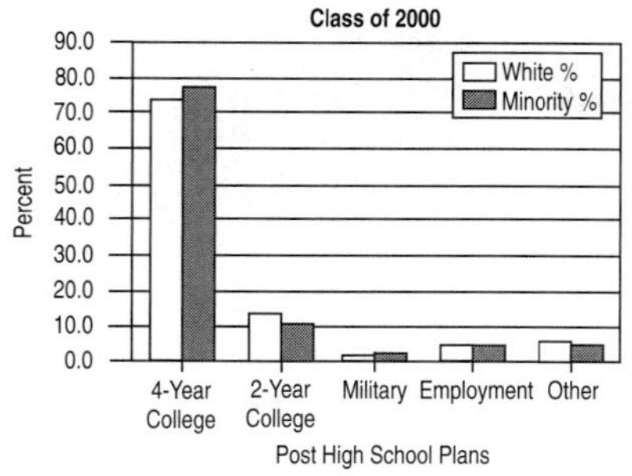

g) The white and minority students' plans are very similar. The small differences should be interpreted with caution because the total number of minority students is small. There is little evidence of an association between race and plans.

16. a) 3.96% b) 42.5% c) 3.00% d) 32.1%

e)

What Graduates Did	Total	%
Continuing education	905	64.0
Employed	338	23.9
In the military	56	4.0
Other	116	8.2

f)

What Graduates Did	1959	%
Continuing education	197	59.2%
Employed	103	30.9%
In the military	20	6.0%
Other	13	3.9%

g) The percentage in continuing education increased from 59.2% to 66.5%, while the percentage for employed decreased from 30.9% to 20.4%. The percentage for the military decreased from 1959 to 1970, while the other category increased significantly.

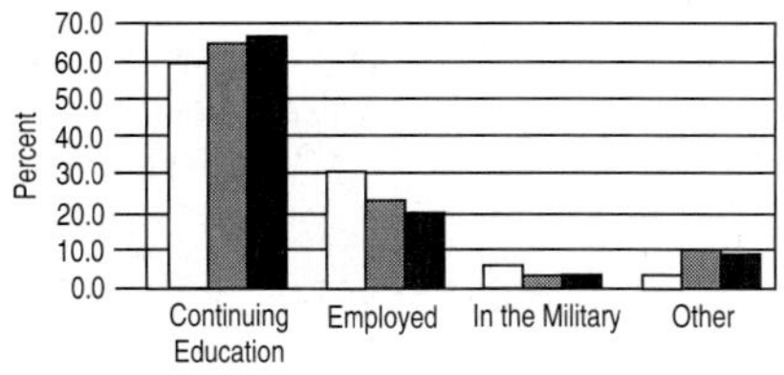

17. a) 67.1 % b) 31.3 % c) 93.9% d) 74.1 %
e) No, the percent of Canadian citizens overall speaking French is 31.3%, whereas the percent of citizens of Quebec speaking French is 93.9%. These percentages are very different and should be the same if language knowledge and province of residence are independent.

18. There seems to be a strong association between having a tattoo done and contracting hepatitis C. There appears to be a much greater risk for tattoos done in commercial parlors, less for tattoos done elsewhere, and very little risk for those with no tattoos.

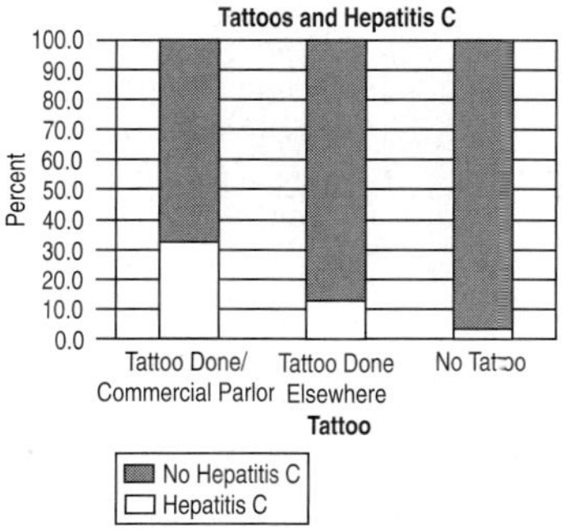

19. a) 9.3% b) 24.7% c) 80.8%
d) Yes, there is a strong association between weather and ability to forecast weather. On days he forecast rain, he was correct 30% of the time. When he forecast no rain, he was correct 97.5%.

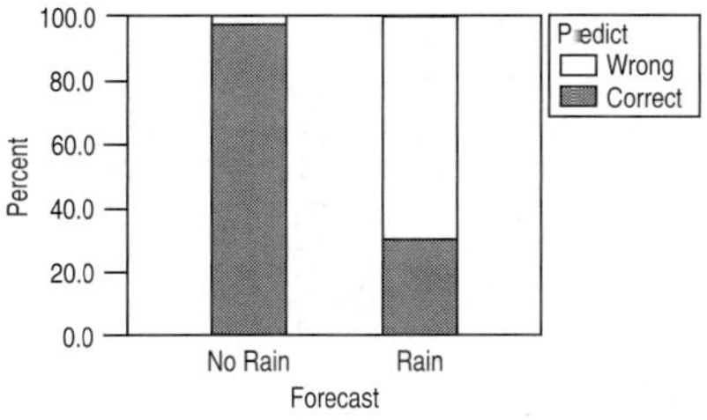

20. a) There was an 88% increase in the number of inmates from 1990 to 1998. The number of drug offenses more than doubled, but the percentage increased only moderately. Increases in public order violations were similar. The number of violent and property offenses increased only a small amount, but as shown in the bar chart, these actually decreased in percent.

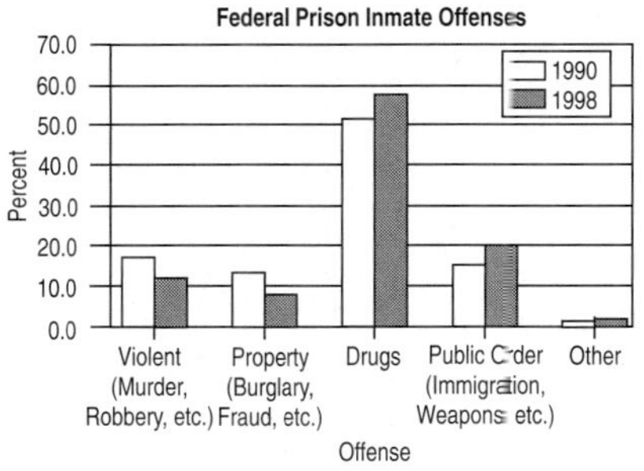

b) It shows that both the number and the *percentage* of drug cases among federal prisoners went up. However, it may not be reflective of drug use. There may have been a more concerted effort to prosecute such offenses.

21. The change in attitude in 10 years was fairly small. There was a slight decrease in the response "One works full time, other part time," and there seems to be a similar increase in the response "One works, other works at home."

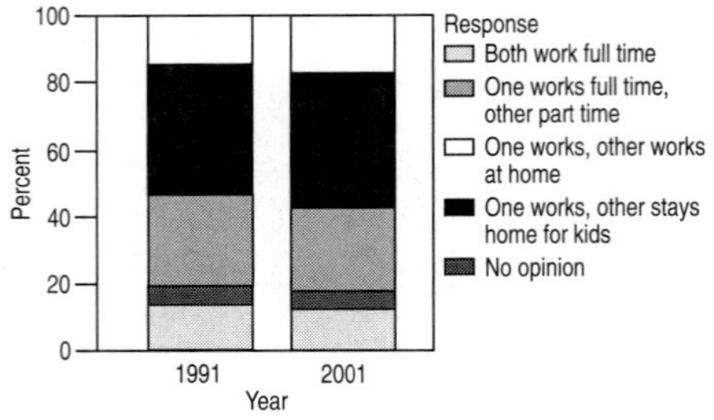

22. a) 22.7% b) 52.9% c) 39.7%

d)

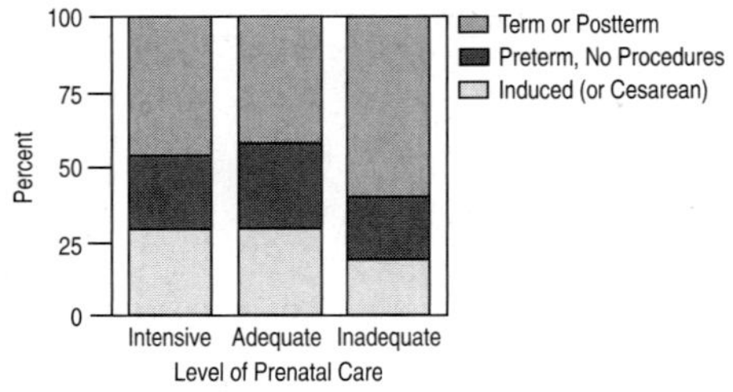

e) It appears that inadequate care leads to more term or post-term births and fewer induced or cesarean births.

23. a)

Blood Pressure		Total	Percent
	Low	95	20.0%
	Normal	232	48.9%
	High	147	31.0%

b)

Blood Pressure		Under 30	Percent
	Low	27	27.6%
	Normal	48	49.0%
	High	23	23.5%

Blood Pressure		30–49	Percent
	Low	37	20.7%
	Normal	91	50.8%
	High	51	28.5%

Blood Pressure		Over 50	Percent
	Low	31	15.7%
	Normal	93	47.2%
	High	73	37.1%

c)

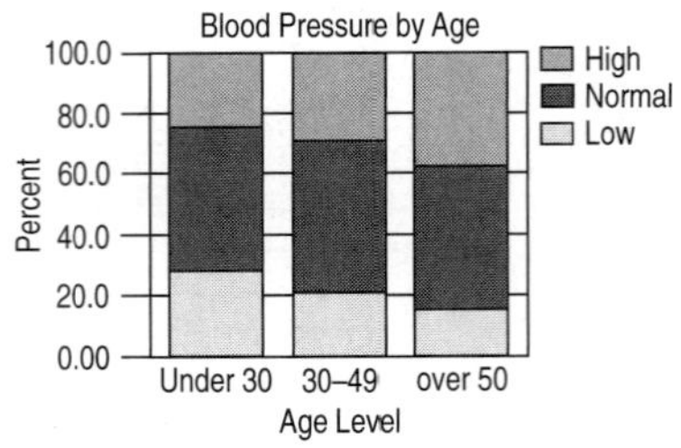

d) As age increases, the percent of adults with high blood pressure increases. On the other hand, the percent of adults with low blood pressure decreases.

e) No, but it gives an indication that it might. There might be additional reasons that explain the differences in blood pressures.

24. a) For each classification of BMI (column), participants' self-reported exercise levels. These are column percentages. The percentages sum to 100% in each column, *not* across each row.

b)

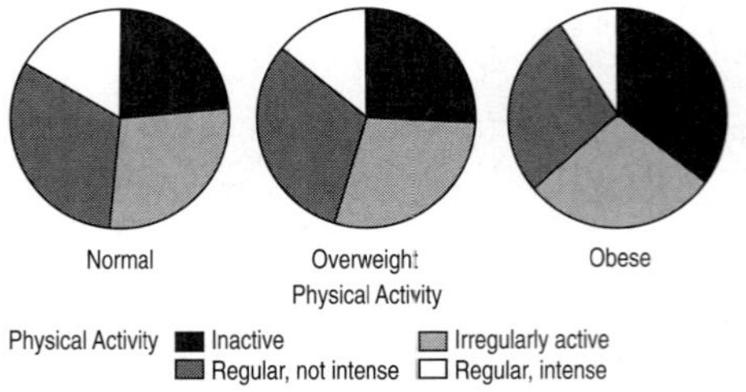

c) No. The graphical displays provide strong evidence that lack of exercise and BMI are not independent. While it may seem logical that lack of exercise causes obesity, the causality could run the other way, or a lurking variable may be the cause of the link between the variables.

25. No, it could be related to other socioeconomic variables. Perhaps women who became mothers were less likely to continue their educations.

26. a) No. I would suspect horse owners to be more affluent than other pet owners. Horses and their care are much more expensive than the other pets listed.

b) These are column percentages. Each column totals 100%.

c) Yes. Among horse owners, there are relatively fewer households in the lowest income bracket and relatively more households in the highest income bracket. In the middle income ranges, the percentages are about the same for each of the different types of pets.

27. a) 34.1% b) 5.7%

c) In Europe, a greater percentage of toys are sold in toy chains, toy, hobby, and game retailers, as well as department stores. Those distribution channels account for 75% of the sales in Europe. In North America, general merchandise and food, drug, and miscellaneous outlets and toy chains have the highest percentages, totaling 86% of the toy sales.

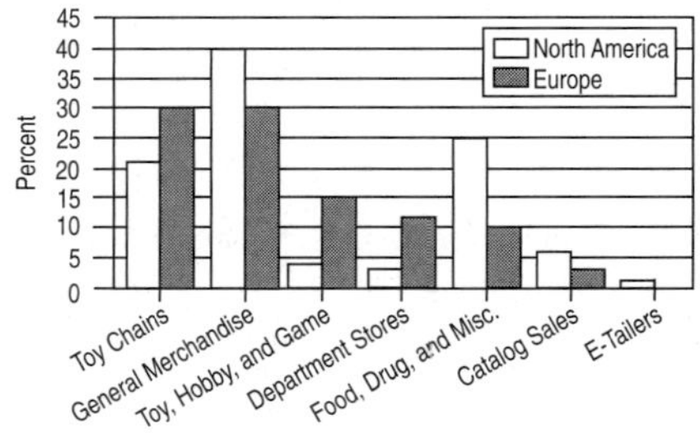

d) The distribution channel varies by region, although general merchandise stores are either the most important or a close second in all regions. Toy chains are especially important in Europe and toy and hobby shops are significant in Asia. Only in North America are a sizable percentage of toys sold in general food and drug stores. E-tailing of toys was relatively unimportant in the year 1999.

28. a) 5.11% b) 50.3%

c) There are about 50% of each sex in each age group, but it ranges from 48.4% female in the youngest group to 53.3% for the oldest. As the age increases, there is a slight increase in the percentage of female drivers.

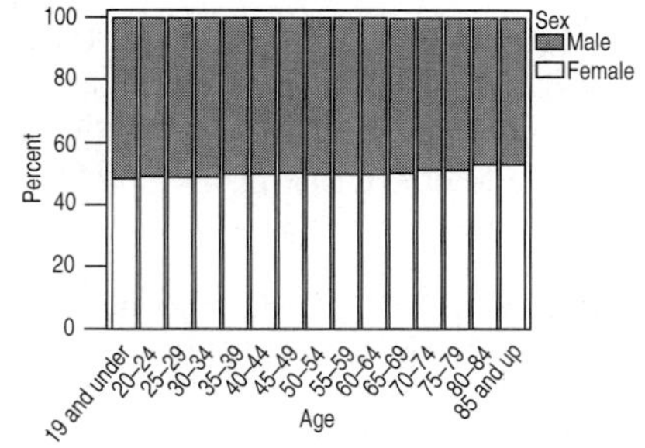

d) There is a slight association. As the age increases, there is a small increase in the percent of female drivers.

29. a) 160 of 1300, or 12.3%

b) Yes. Major surgery: 15.3% vs. minor surgery: 6.7%

c) Large hospital: 13%, small hospital: 10%

d) Large hospital: Major 15% vs. minor 5%
Small hospital: Major 20% vs. minor 8%

e) No. Smaller hospitals have a higher rate for both kinds of surgery, even though it's lower "overall."

f) The small hospital has a larger percentage of minor surgeries (83.3%) than the large hospital (20%). Minor surgeries have a lower delay rate, so the small hospital looks better "overall."

30. a) Overall, Pack Rats are late 5.6% of the time. Boxes R Us is late 6.0% of the time.

b) Pack Rats have 3% late rate on regular and 16% on overnight. Boxes R Us have 2% late rate on regular and 7% on overnight, so they are better on both.

c) Simpson's paradox

31. a) 42.6%

b) A higher percentage of males than females were admitted: Males: 47.2% to females: 30.9%

c) Program 1: Males 61.9%, women 82.4%
Program 2: Males 62.8%, women 68.0%
Program 3: Males 33.7%, women 35.2%
Program 4: Males 5.9%, women 7.0%

d) The comparisons in c) show that males have a *lower* admittance rate in every program, even though the overall rate shows males with a higher rate of admittance. This is an example of Simpson's paradox.

CHAPTER 4

1. Answers will vary. **2.** Answers will vary.

3. a) Unimodal (near 0) and skewed. Many seniors will have 0 or 1 speeding tickets. Some may have several, and a few may have more than that.

b) Probably unimodal and slightly skewed to the right. It is easier to score 15 strokes over the mean than 15 strokes under the mean.

c) Probably unimodal and symmetric. Weights may be equally likely to be over or under the average.

d) Probably bimodal. Men's and women's distributions may have different modes. It may also be skewed to the right, since it is possible to have very long hair, but hair length can't be negative.

4. a) Bimodal because you have players and parents. It may also be skewed to the right, since parents' ages can be larger than the mean more easily than lower.

b) Unimodal and skewed to the right. There are probably many students with 0 or 1 sibling and some with 2 or more.

c) Unimodal and symmetric. It will be unusual to have either very high or low pulse rates.

d) Uniform. Each face of the die has the same chance of coming up, so the number of times should be about the same for each face.

5. Skewed to right. Bimodal. One mode near 1, another near 8. All data between 1 and 35. Some outliers on the high end.

6. Skewed to the right. Mode near 1. One outlier very far from rest of data. Spread fairly small. Most of data less than 5.

7. a) Bimodal. Looks like two groups. Modes are near 6% and 46%. No real outliers.

b) Looks like two groups of cereals, a low-sugar and a high-sugar group.

8. a) Looks bimodal, one mode near 65 inches, one near 71 inches. Could be two groups that look fairly symmetric within each group.

b) Probably the mix of men and women in the group.

9. a) 75%

b) Skewed to the right with at least one high outlier. Most of the wineries are less than 75 acres with a few high ones. The mode is between 25 and 50 acres.

10. Skewed to the right, centered at around 30 to 31 minutes, with most observations between 29 and 32 minutes. Skewed to the right because it is easier to run much slower than usual, but hard to run the same amount *faster* than usual.

11. Skewed to the right, mode in low 30s. Three low outliers, then a gap from 9 to 22.

12. a)

Stem	Leaf
22	8
21	
20	66
19	
18	136
17	578
16	0022367
15	23367

15|2 = 152 Species

b) Skewed to the right; several high outliers. Center near 163.

13. This distribution is nearly uniform. Values range from 65 to 155 horsepower. The center is near 105.

Stem	Leaf
15	05
14	2
13	0358
12	0559
11	00555
10	359
9	00577
8	0058
7	01158
6	55889

6|5 = 65 horsepower

14. NE/MW states are tightly clustered near 5%. S/W states are bimodal with modes near 14 and 22. The S/W states have outliers as well. Around all the modes, the distributions are fairly symmetric.

15. a)

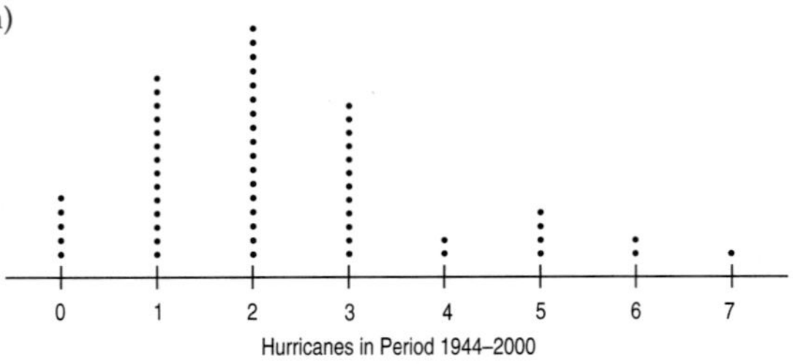

b) Slightly skewed to the right. Unimodal, mode near 2. Possibly a second mode near 5. No outliers.

16. The second set is centered lower, and is more skewed. Spreads are about equal.

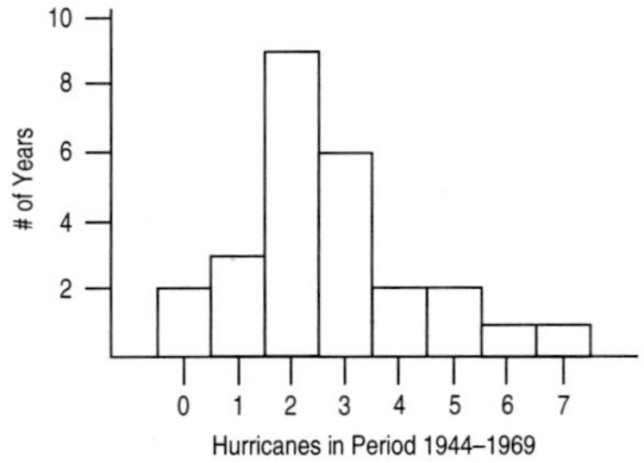

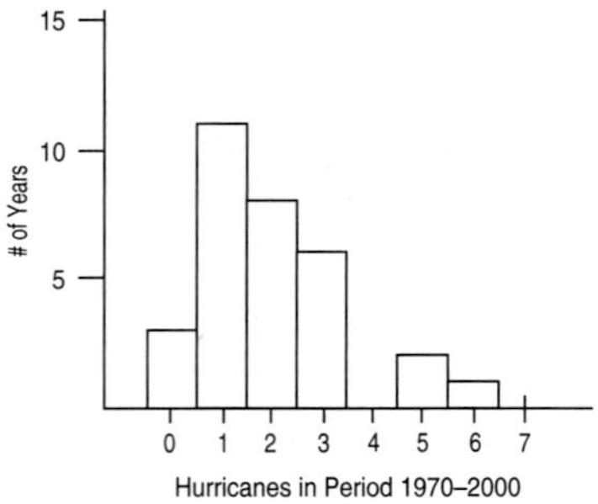

17. Skewed to the right, possibly bimodal with one fairly symmetric group near 4.4, another at 5.6. Two outliers in middle seem not to belong to either group.

Stem	Leaf
57	8
56	27
55	1
54	
53	
52	9
51	
50	8
49	
48	2
47	3
46	034
45	267
44	015
43	0199
42	669
41	22

41|2 = 4.12 pH

18. Unimodal with center around 10, but with several countries reporting percentages over 20. This makes the distribution look skewed to the right, but it may be two different groups.

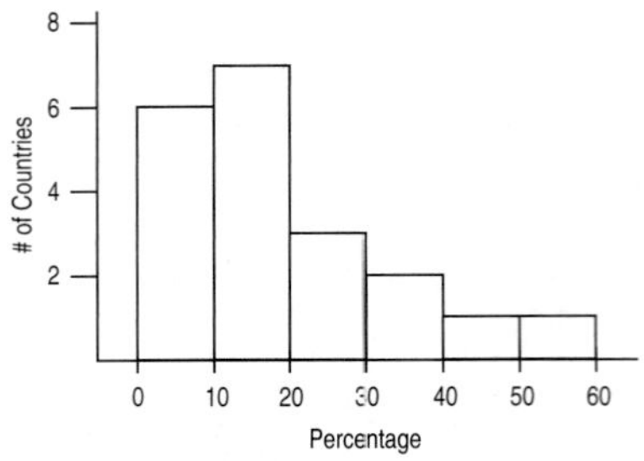

19. a) They should be put on the same scale, from 0 to 20 days.
b) Men have a mode at 1 day then tapering off from there. Women have a mode near 5 days with a sharp drop afterward.
c) A possible reason is childbirth.

20. Whites' death ages are more skewed, clustering nearer the top with a mode in the 75 to 84 age group. Blacks' death ages are more spread out, peak earlier (in the 65–74 age bracket) and are more symmetric. There is also a larger infant death rate among blacks.

21. Histogram bin widths are too wide to be useful.

22. a) Histogram bins are too narrow to be useful.
b) Skewed to the left, mode near 170, several outliers below 100. Fairly tightly clustered except for outliers.

23. Neither appropriate nor useful. Zip codes are categorical data, not quantitative. But they do contain *some* information. The leading digit gives a rough East to West placement in the United States. So we see that they have almost no customers in the Northeast, but a bar chart by leading digit would be more appropriate.

24. a) The codes are integers and the width of a bin is less than 1. But the question doesn't make sense, since the codes are categorical, not quantitative.
b) Question doesn't make sense, since the display is inappropriate.
c) Display is not appropriate. Data are categorical. He should use a bar chart.

25. What is the x-axis? What units does productivity have here?

26. The axes aren't labeled. It is not clear what units either productivity or wages are in or whether they were measured at the same (time?) points.

27. a)

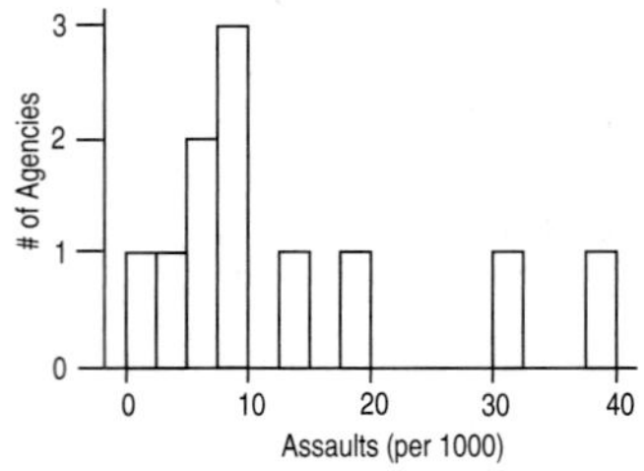

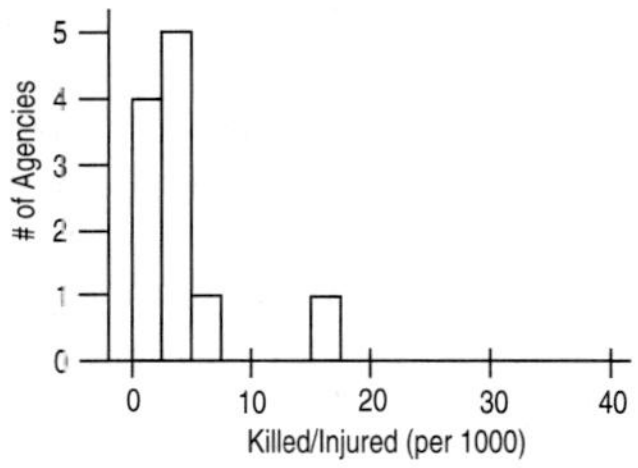

b) Assaults have a much more spread-out distribution. Both are skewed to the right. Killed/Injured has a center near 4, assaults near 10. There are high outliers in both distributions.
c) Outliers are BATF and National Park Service in assaults and National Park Service in number killed/injured.

28. Smokers' distribution is less symmetric, slightly higher with a mode near 200. Ex-smokers have a mode near 250 and are more symmetric. There was an outlier in the smoker's group at 350.

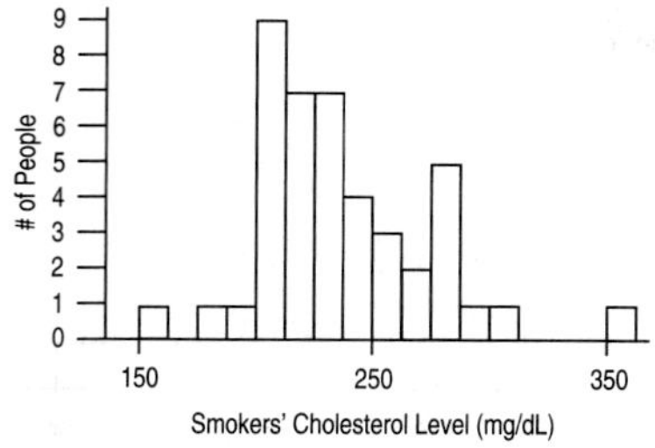

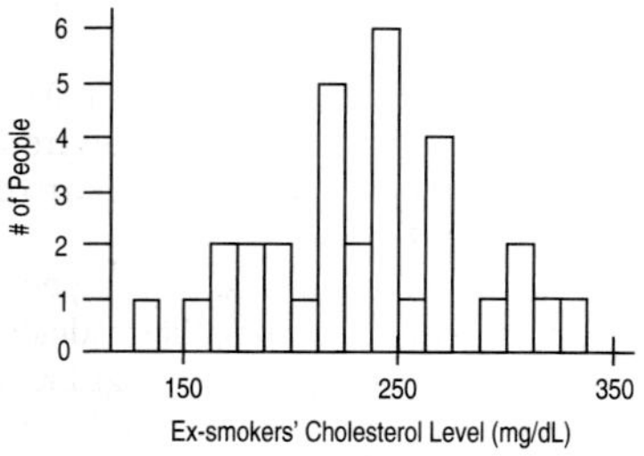

29. a) Rounding the data values and splitting each stem into five groups gives: (other answers are possible)

Stem and Leaf

U.S. Cars		Others
	3	7
44	3	45
	3	222
10	3	01
98	2	8
777	2	7
	2	
2	2	222
11	2	0
999888	1	
7776	1	67

1|6 means 16 mpg

b) Data for U.S. car mileage have a lower center and are skewed to the right with a mode near 19 mpg. Perhaps bimodal with a second mode near 28 mpg. Others have more of the cars at a higher mode near 32 and only a few with lower mode near 22.

30. a)

Stem and Leaf

American		National
	14	0
	13	
	12	
1	11	6
883310	10	234
543220	9	15555
3	8	12348
	7	9

7|9 means 79 runs

b) National League scores fewer runs in general, but with much more spread. The mode is around 9.5 runs per game. There are two outliers on the high end. American League runs scored are more tightly clustered, with a center around 9.5.

c) Yes, it looks like an outlier.

31. a)

Stem	Leaf
8	0148
7	9
6	023
5	6
4	
3	25
2	8

2|8 = 28 thousand $

b) Left skewed with some gaps

c)

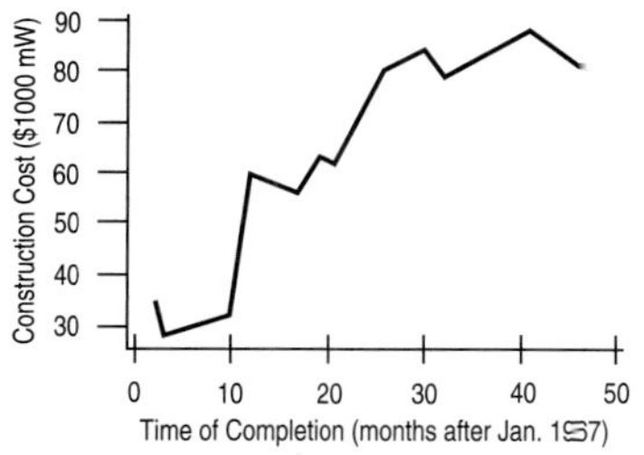

d) Costs are generally increasing over time.

32. a)

Stem	Leaf
25	2
24	0
23	6668
22	047
21	
20	
19	9
18	
17	2259
16	005677

16|0 = 16.0 thousand deaths

b)

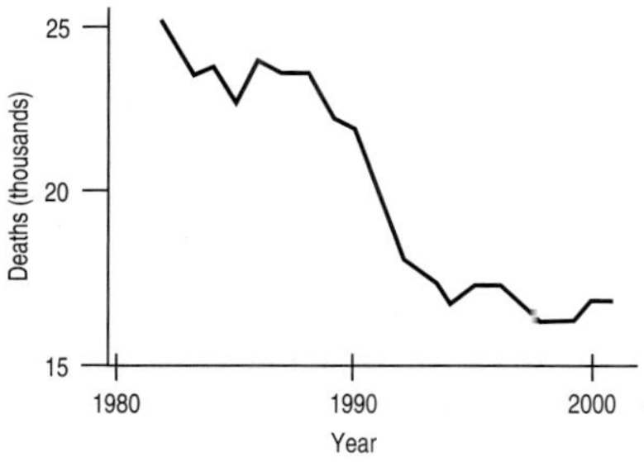

c) Before 1990, deaths by drunk driving clustered near a mode of about 23,000 per year. Since then, there has been a sharp dropoff, and now deaths from drunk driving are clustered near 17,000 per year.

33. a) Most of the data are found in the far left of this histogram. The distribution is very skewed to the right.

b) The logarithm makes the histogram more unimodal and symmetric. It is easy to see that the center is around 3.5 in log assets.

c) That has a value of around 2,500 million dollars.

d) That has a value of around 1,000 million dollars.

34. a) The numbers are manageable (each acre-foot is about 320,000 gallons).

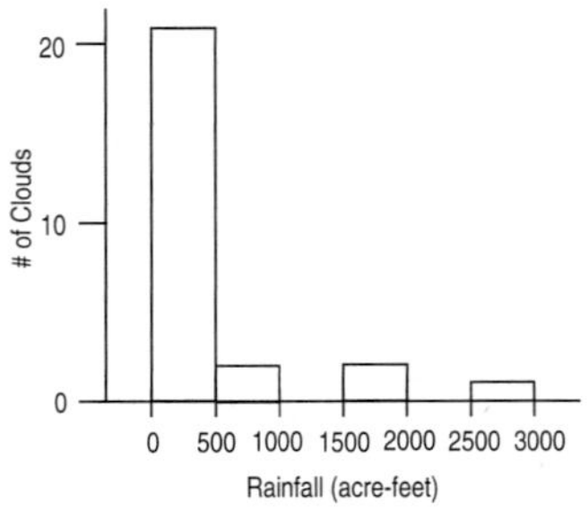

b) The distribution is very skewed to the right.

c)

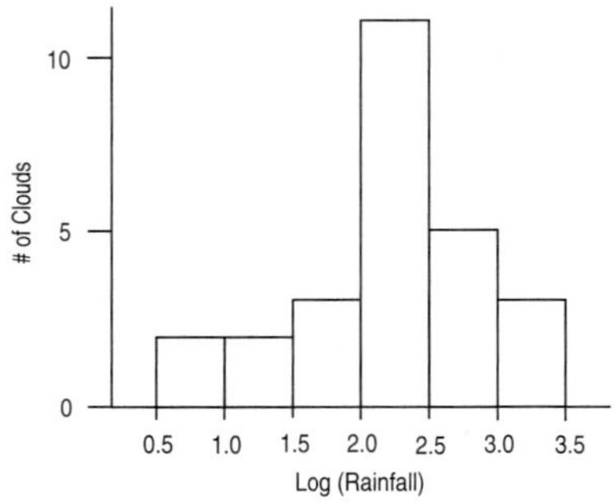

d) Log(10) is the exponent of 10, which results in the original value. For example, $10^3 = 1000$, so log(10) of 1000 is 3.

CHAPTER 5

1. Answers will vary. **2.** Answers will vary.

3. a) \$1001.50 b) 1025, 850, 1200 c) 835, 350

4. a) 56.3 b) 40, 36, 68 c) 105, 32

5. a) Median will probably be unaffected. The mean will be larger.
b) The range and standard deviation will increase; IQR will be unaffected.

6. The company is using the **mean** of 7 days, while the union negotiators are using the **median** of 3 days. There may be high outliers, or a distribution of sick days that is generally skewed to the right.

7. a) Mean \$525, median \$450
b) 2 employees earn more than mean.
c) The median because of the outlier.
d) The IQR will be least sensitive to the outlier of \$1200, so it would be the best to report.

8. a) 60, 65, 66, 70, 76
b)

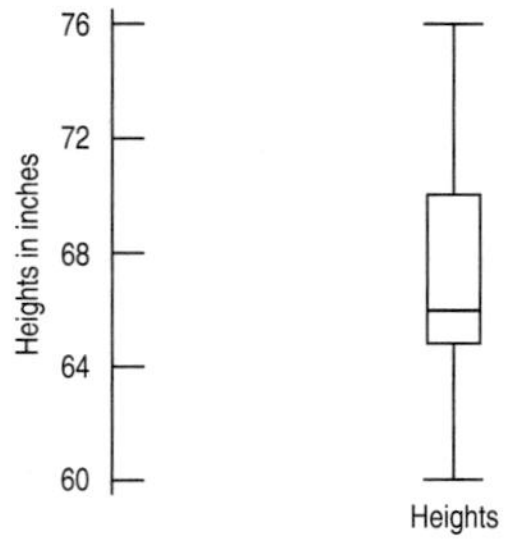

c) Mean 67.12 inches. SD 3.79 inches.

d)

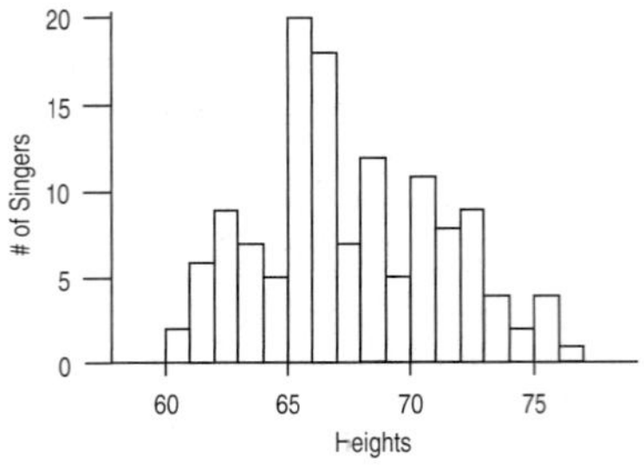

e) The distribution is centered near 67 in., with median 66 in. and mean 67.12 in. The IQR is 15 in., with the middle 50% of heights between 65 and 70 in. The distribution appears to be bimodal, probably due to differences in heights of men and women.

9. a) The standard deviation will be larger for set 2, since they are more spread out. SD (set 1) = 2.2, SD(set 2) = 3.2.
b) The standard deviation will be larger for set 2, since 11 and 19 are farther from 15 than are 14 and 16. Other numbers are the same. SD(set 1) = 3.6, SD(set 2) = 4.5.
c) The standard deviation will be the same for both sets, since the values in the second data set are just the values in the first data set + 80. The spread has not changed. SD(set 1) = 4.2. SD(set 2) = 4.2.

10. a) Set 2 will have a larger SD because 6 and 8 in set 2 are farther from 7 than 7 and 7 in set 1. The other numbers are the same. SD(set 1) = 2.1, SD(set 2) = 2.2.
b) The standard deviation will be the same for both sets, since the values in set 1 are just the values in set 2 + 90. The spread remains the same. SD(set 1) = 36.1, SD(set 2) = 36.1
c) Set 2 has a wider range and will have a larger SD. SD(set 1) = 6.0, SD(set 2) = 7.2.

11. According to the fence rule, 61 is not technically an outlier. The median is 24.5. The two quartiles are 14 and 33, so the IQR is 19. That means 1.5 IQRs is 26.5. Adding 26.5 to the upper quartile of 33 gives a fence of 61.5. So, 61 is just within the fence and not an outlier by that definition. But it certainly looks unusual compared with the other 9 seasons!

12. a) The distribution is strongly skewed to the right, so use the median and IQR.
b) The IQR is 50, so the upper fence is the upper quartile + 1.5 IQRs; that is, 78 + 75 = 153. There appear to be 4 to 5 parks that should be considered as outliers with more than 153 camp sites.
c)

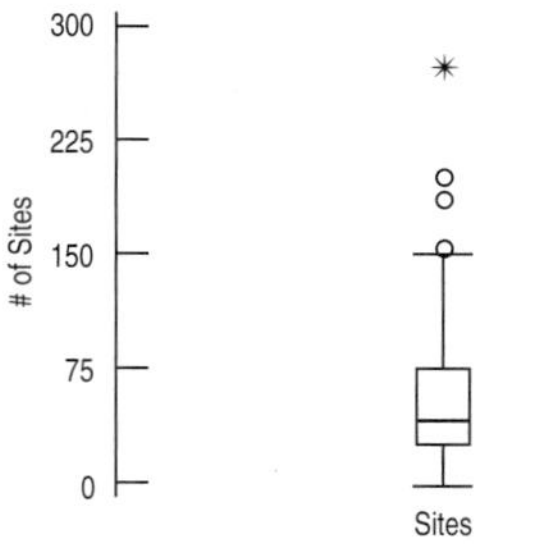

d) The distribution is unimodal with a strong skew to the right. There are several outliers past the 1.5 × IQR upper fence of 153 camp sites. The median number of camp sites is 43.5 sites. The mean is 62.8 sites. The mean is larger than the median because it has been influenced by the strong skew and the outliers.

13. Women appear to marry about 3 years younger than men, but the two distributions are very similar in shape and spread.

14. Both fuel economy and its spread decrease from 4 to 6 to 8 cylinders (not enough data to compare 5-cylinder cars). The lower 50% of MPGs for the 8-cylinder cars corresponds roughly to the bottom 25% of MPGs for the 6-cylinder cars. All of the 8-cylinder cars get less mileage than all of the 4-cylinder cars.

15. a) Seneca. b) Seneca. c) Keuka.
d) The Cayuga and Seneca wineries have about same average price; the boxplots show similar medians and similar IQRs, even though Seneca's range is larger. Keuka has consistently higher prices except for one low outlier, and a more consistent pricing as shown by the smaller IQR. Distributions for all three appear to be roughly symmetric around their centers.

16. a) April b) February c) August
d) The median ozone level in June is slightly higher than January, but June's readings are much more consistent. June does show two outliers, one low and one high.
e) Strong seasonal pattern with low consistent ozone concentrations in later summer/early fall and high variable concentrations in early spring. The medians follow a cyclic pattern rising from January to April, then falling to October and rising again from October to December.

17. a) Because the mean is larger than the median, we might suppose that the distribution is right skewed. An outlier or outliers might explain why the SD is so much larger than the IQR.
b) The differences in the statistics could be due to skewness or to outliers on the high end.
c) The distribution of times in the men's 100-m swim in Sydney is unimodal, with most times between 48 and 53 minutes. There is a slight skew to the right, with three times between 58 and 63 and one very extreme outlier at about 113 minutes.

18. Since the mean or average is the balance point for the data, having 223 areas below the average and only 99 above the average indicates that the distribution of unemployment rates must be skewed to the right.

19. a) Class 3
b) Class 3
c) Class 3 because it is skewed. Median would be higher than the mean because it is skewed to the left.
d) Class 1
e) Class 1

20. a) Class 3. Highest median and almost 75% of class 3 scored at or above the medians of 1 and 2.
b) Fairly symmetric (except class 3). Quite spread out, ranging from about 30 to near 100.
c) The class A is 1, class B is 2 and class C is 3.

21. a) Essentially symmetric, very slightly skewed to the right with two high outliers at 36 and 48. Most victims are between the ages of 16 and 24.
b) The slight increase between ages 22 and 24 is apparent in the histogram but not in the boxplot. It may be a second mode.
c) The median would be the most appropriate measure of center because of the slight skew and the extreme outliers.
d) The IQR would be the most appropriate measure of spread because of the slight skew and the extreme outliers.

22. a) 1611 yd
b) Between 5585.75 yd and 6131 yd
c) Mean and SD, since this is roughly unimodal and symmetric.
d) The distribution is fairly symmetric and unimodal. Because of the symmetry, the mean of 5892.91 yd and median of 5928 yd are nearly the same, showing a center near 5900 yd. The standard deviation of the lengths is 386.59 yd. The range is 1611 yd from a minimum 5185 yd to a maximum 6796 yd?

23. a) Probably slightly left skewed. The mean is slightly below the median and the 25th percentile is farther from the median than the 75th percentile.
b) No, all data are within the fences.
c)

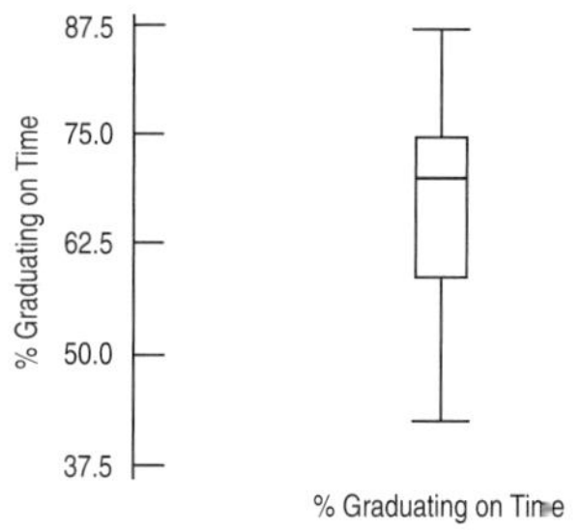

d) The 48 universities graduate about 68% of freshman in 4 years on average, with percents ranging from 43% to 87%. The middle 50% of these universities graduate between 59% and 75% of their freshman in 4 years.

24. a) Skewed to the right, since the mean is much larger than the median and the upper quartile is farther from the median than the lower quartile.
b) The IQR is about 36, so fences are below 0 and at 109. Since the range is 244 and the minimum is 6, the maximum is 250, which is certainly an outlier. Without knowing the data points, we are not sure of other outliers, but the standard deviation of 47.8 makes us suspect there are others.
c) We don't know if there are other outliers above the upper fence, but the boxplot may look something like this:

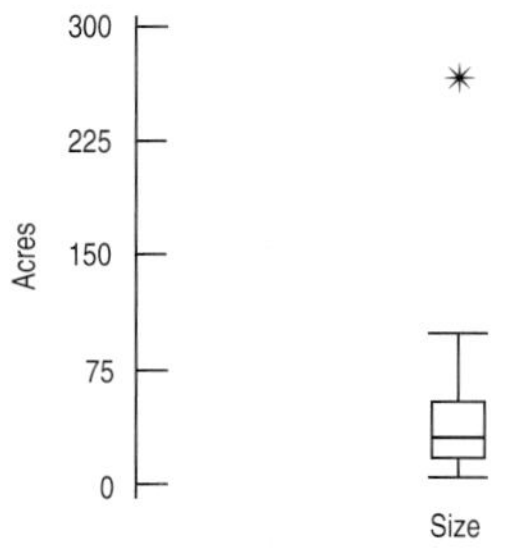

d) The vineyards range in size from 6 to 250 acres. The median size of the 36 vineyards is 33.5 acres, so half are larger and half are smaller. The middle 50% of the vineyards have sizes between 18.5 and 55 acres. The distribution of sizes is skewed to the right, with at least one outlier.

25. a) *Who:* Student volunteers
What: Memory test
Where, when: Not specified
How: Students took memory test 2 hours after drinking caffeine-free, half-dose caffeine, or high-caffeine soda.
Why: To see if caffeine makes you more alert and aids memory retention.

b) Drink: Categorical test score: quantitative.
c)

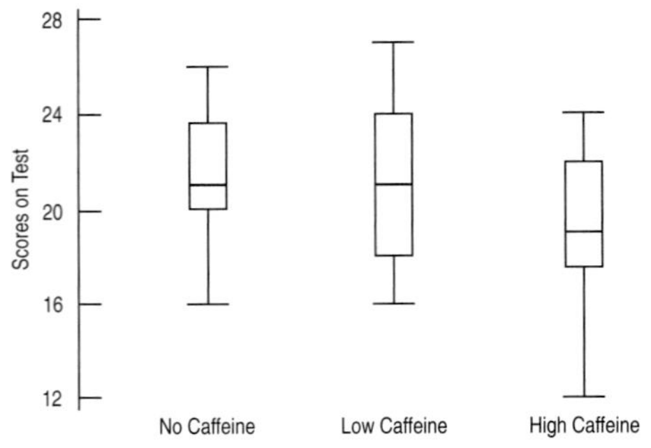

d) The participants scored about the same with no caffeine and low caffeine. The medians for both were 21 points, with slightly more variation for the low-caffeine group. The high-caffeine group generally scored lower than other two groups on all measures of the five-number summary: min, lower quartile, median, upper quartile, and max. It is not clear if the differences are significant.

26. a) The median and IQR because the means are much larger than the median and the SDs are much larger than the IQR, indicating either right skewness and/or outliers.
b) Since the median rainfall for seeded clouds is more than 4 times that for unseeded clouds, it appears that seeding clouds may be effective.

27. a) Since these data are strongly skewed to the right, the median and IQR are the best statistics to report.
b) The mean will be larger than the median because the data are skewed to the right.
c) Median 4 million. The IQR is 4.5 million (UQ = 6 million, LQ =1.5 million).
d) The distribution of populations of the states and Washington, D.C., is unimodal and skewed to the right. The median population is 4 million. One state is an outlier with a population of 34 million.

28. The southern and western states appear to have significantly higher growth rates between 1990 and 2000 than the northeastern and midwestern states.

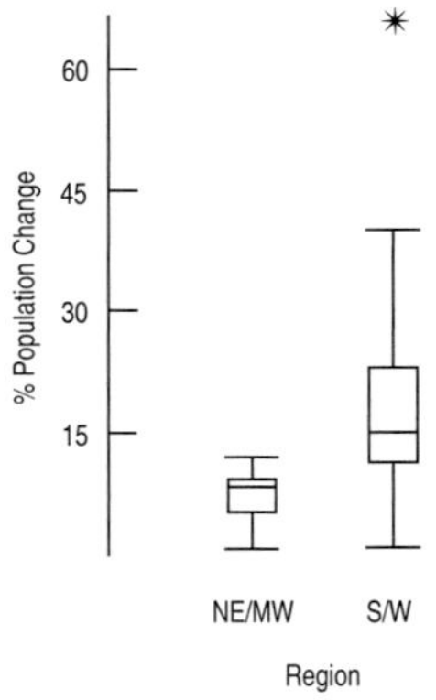

29. a) About 36 mph
b) LQ about 34.5 mph and UQ about 36.5 mph
c) The range appears to be 7 mph from about 31 to 38 mph. The IQR is about 2 mph.
d) We can't know exactly, but the boxplot may look something like this:

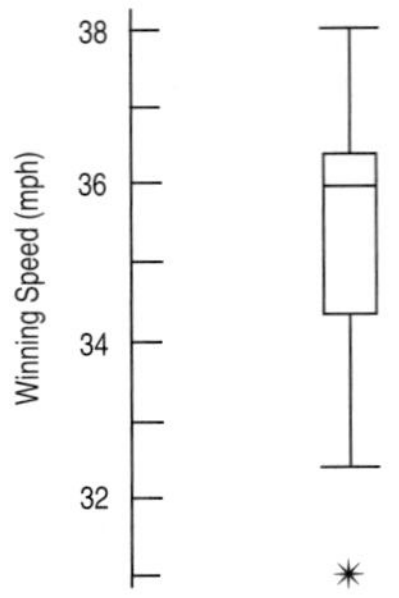

e) The median winning speed has been about 36 mph, with a max of about 38 and a min of about 31 mph. The middle 50% of the speeds appeared to range from between 34.5 and 36.5 mph for an IQR of 2 mph. The middle 20% of the data appear to be tightly clustered around 36. Only 10% of the Kentucky Derby winners raced at speeds above about 37 mph.

30. Distribution is essentially symmetric with median near 225. The IQR is about 100 points. Extremes are about 80 and 380.

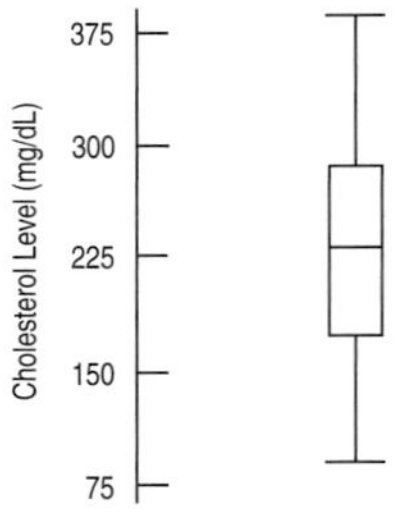

31. a) Boys b) Boys c) Girls
d) The boys appeared to have more skew, as their scores were less symmetric between quartiles. The girls' quartiles are the same distance from the median, although the left tail stretches a bit farther to the left.
e) Girls. Their median and upper quartiles are larger. The lower quartile is slightly lower, but close.
f) $[14(4.2) + 11(4.6)]/25 = 4.38$

32. a)

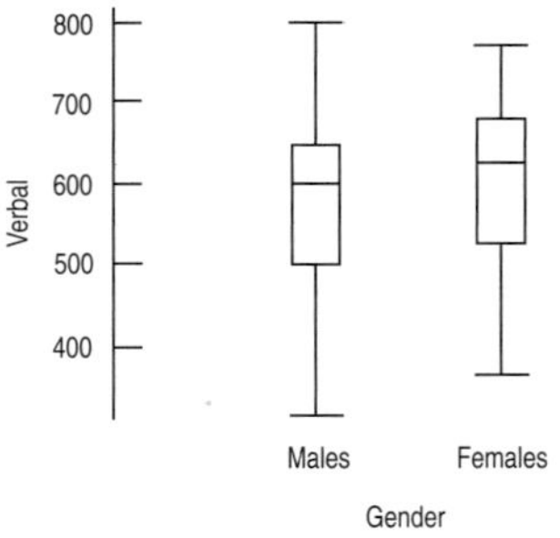

b) Median score by females at 625 points is 25 points higher than that by males. Female mean is higher by 12. The middle 505 of females scored between 530 and 680, while the middle 50% of males scored between 515 and 650. The males did have a larger range, from 310 to 800, the highest score for both genders. Both distributions are slightly skewed to the left.

33. a)

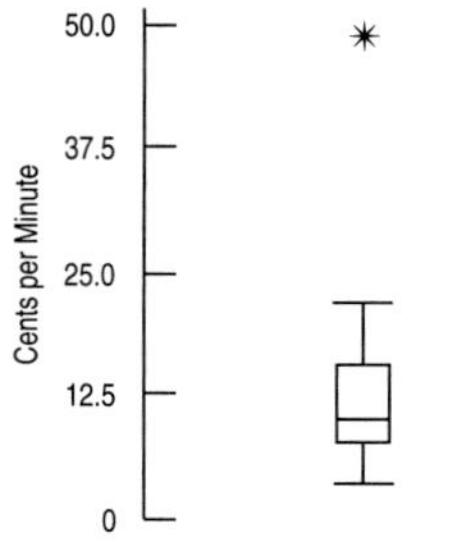

b) The mean cost per minute for Net2Phone rates is 13.7 cents. The median cost per minute is 9.9 cents per minute. Because of the outliers, the median is the more appropriate measure of center to use.

c) The IQR for the cost per minute of the phone calls is 7.6 cents. The standard deviation is 11.8 cents per minute. Again, due to the outliers, the better choice for measure of spread is the IQR.

d) Yes, both India and Pakistan are outliers. They each lie more than 1.5 times the IQR above the UQ.

e) The distribution of the long-distance rates for Net2Phone is unimodal and symmetric except for two outliers, India and Pakistan at 49 cents per minute. The median cost is 9.9 cents per minute. The middle 50% of costs per minute are between 7.9 and 15.5 cents per minute for an IQR of 7.6 cents per minute.

f) These data represent only 24 of the 250 countries that Net2Phone offers service to. These might not be representative of the entire group.

34. a) Either the boxplot or the histogram would be appropriate displays of the data.

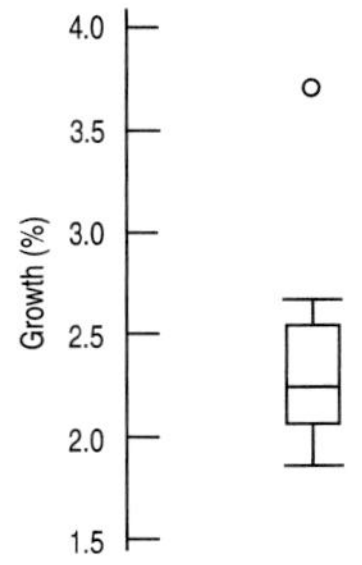

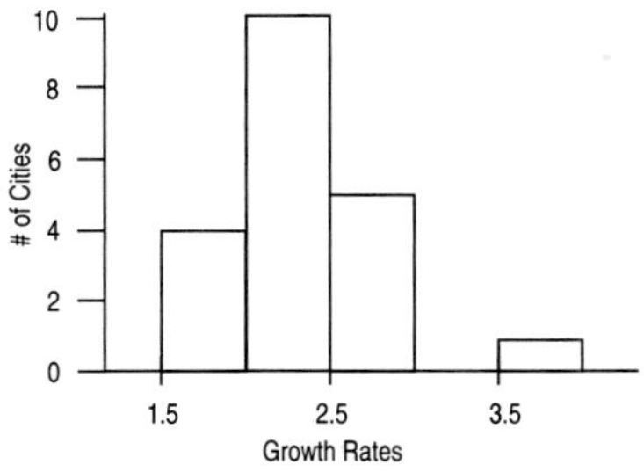

b) Mean 2.317%, median 2.235%. Mean is higher because of the outlier.

c) The median because of the outlier.

d) IQR 0.515%, std dev 0.427%.

e) The standard deviation is also influenced by the outlier. The better measure of spread is the IQR.

f) Mean and median would be 1.2% lower. SD and IQR would not change.

g) Median and IQR won't change very much. The middle value and the two quartiles will shift at most one data value. The mean and SD will decrease.

h) The distribution of growth rates for the cities is unimodal and symmetric except for the one outlier, Las Vegas, at 3.72%. The median growth rate for these cities is 2.235%. The middle 50% of the cities had growth rates between 2.045% and 2.560% for an interquartile range of 0.515%. The median and IQR are the best statistics to report when a distribution has outliers, but if the outlier were omitted, the average growth rate would be 2.24% with a standard deviation of 0.28%.

35. a) Five number summary: 275, 448, 499, 531, 604
IQR: 83
Mean: 487.2
Std dev: 72.3

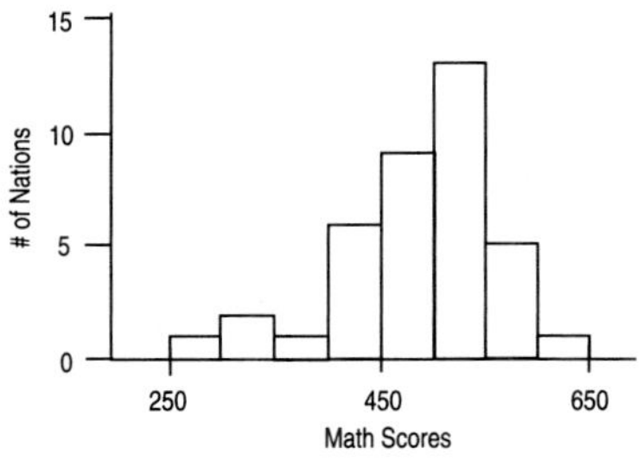

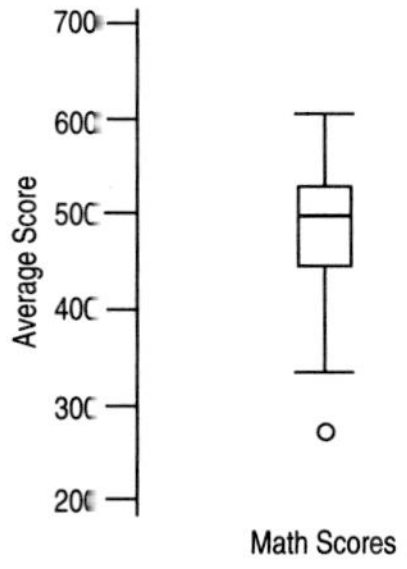

b) The distribution is unimodal and skewed to the left. As shown in the boxplot, there is one outlier, an average score of 275. The median was 499 while the mean was 502, slightly above the median score. The middle 50% of the nations scored between 448 and 531 for an IQR of 83 points.

36. a)

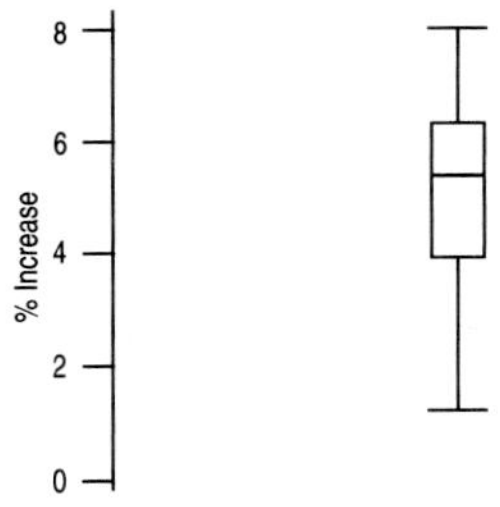

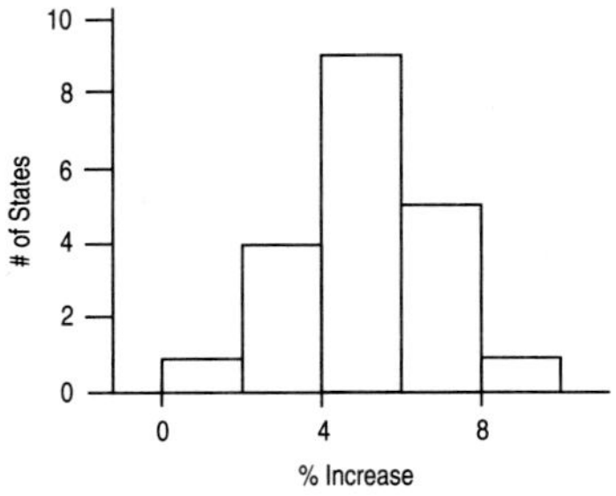

b) Mean 5.08%, SD 1.79%. Five number summary: 1.3, 3.95, 5.4, 6.35, 8 (%).

c) The distribution is unimodal and symmetric. There are no outliers. The mean percent increase was 5.08% with a standard deviation of 1.79%.

37. In the year 2000, per capita gasoline use by state in the United States averaged around 500 gallons per person (mean 488, median 502). States varied in their consumption with a standard deviation of 62 gallons, ranging from a min of 297 (NC) to a max of 587 (TN). The two low outliers were NC and HI. The IQR of

82 gallons reflects the fact that 50% of the states varied from 453 to 533 gallons per capita.

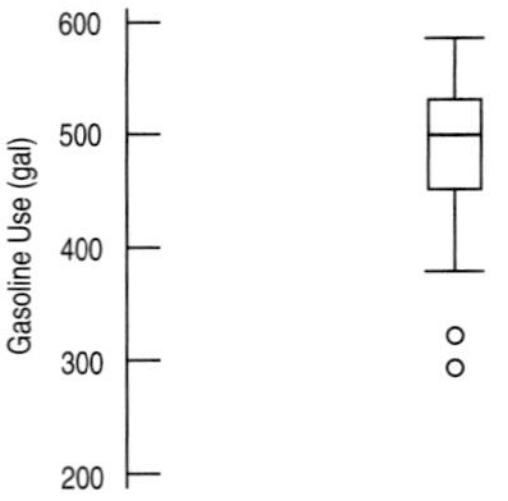

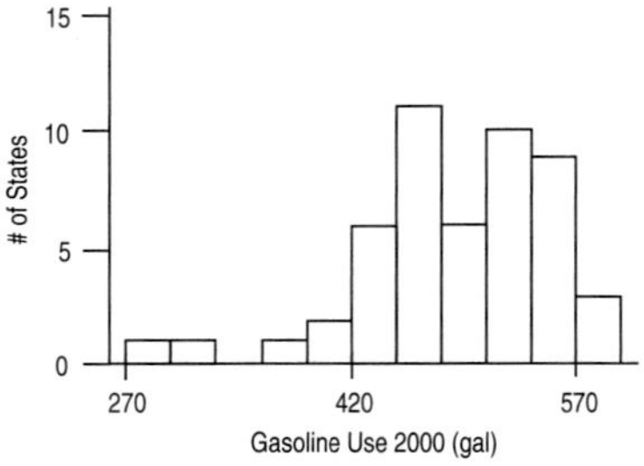

38.

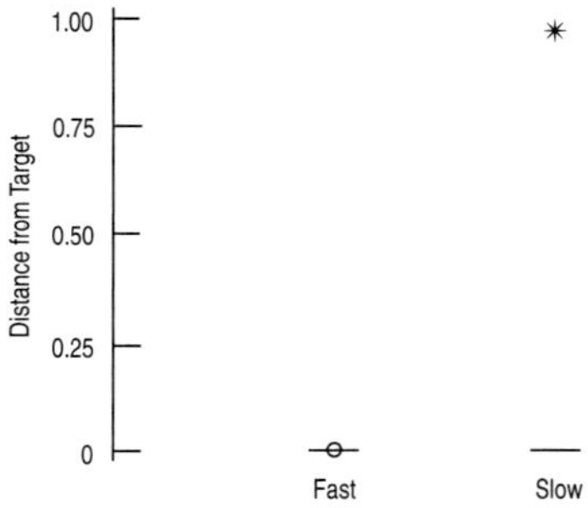

There appears to be an outlier! This point should be investigated. We'll proceed by redoing the plots with the outlier omitted:

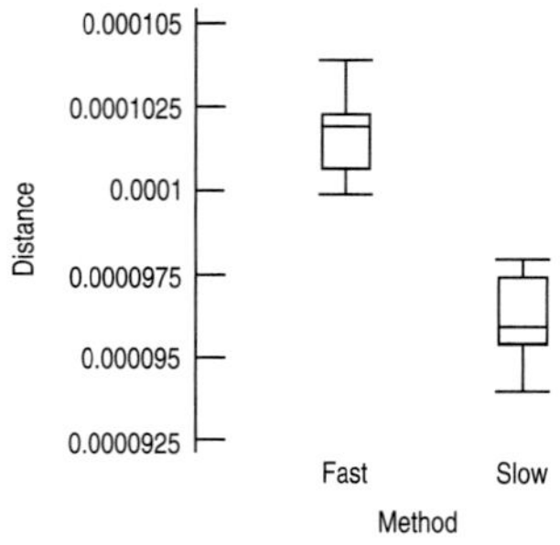

It appears that slow speed provides much greater accuracy. But the outlier should be investigated. It is possible that slow speed can induce an infrequent very large distance.

39. a) Although numeric codes have been assigned to the different titles, these data are categorical, not quantitative. The mean of 54.41 is meaningless.
b) The typical reasons are skewness and/or outliers.
c) No. Here the numbers are just codes. Most of the people probably had titles of Mr. or Mrs., making the "median" 1, but these summary statistics are meaningless.

40. a) Neither. These are not quantitative data.
b) Neither. These are not quantitative data.
c) Not very much, since zip codes are categorical. However, there is *some* information in the first digit of zip codes. They indicate a general East (0–1) to West (8–9) direction. So, the distribution shows that a large portion of their sales occurs in the West and another in the 32000 area. But a bar chart of the first digits might be a better display of this.

41. No, boxplots are for quantitative data, and these are categorical, although coded as numbers. The numbers used for hair color and eye color are arbitrary, so the boxplot and any accompanying statistics for eye color make no sense.

42. a) Fusion time and group.
b) Fusion time is quantitative (units = seconds). Group is categorical.
c) Both distributions are skewed to the right with high outliers. The boxplot indicates that verbal information may reduce fusion time. The median for the Verbal/Visual group seems to be about the same as the lower quartile of the No/Verbal group.

43. The analysis would probably be improved by using the log-transformed data. The distributions are more symmetric, and it's easier to compare the groups. The outliers are eliminated.

44. The reciprocal re-expression has gone too far. The distributions for the reciprocals show the same skewness as the original data, but now there are no outliers. Of the three choices, the log re-expression appears to be the best.

CHAPTER 6

1. a) Skewed to the right; mean is higher than median.
b) $350 and $950.
c) Minimum $350. Mean $750. Median $550. Range $1200. IQR $600. Q1 $400. SD $400.
d) Minimum $330. Mean $770. Median $550. Range $1320. IQR $660. Q1 $385. SD $440.

2. a) Range 3.30 pounds. IQR 0.95 pounds.
b) Slightly skewed to the left because the mean is lower than the median and the first quartile is farther from the median than the third quartile.
c) Mean 96 oz. SD 10.4 oz. Q1 89.6 oz. Q3 104.8 oz. Median 99.2 oz. IQR 15.2 oz. Range 52.8 oz.
d) Mean 126 oz. SD 10.4 oz. Q1 119.6 oz. Q3 134.8 oz. Median 129.2 oz. IQR 15.2 oz. Range 52.8 oz.
e) Median, IQR.

3. Lowest score = 910 Mean = 1230 Standard deviation = 120
Top 25% above 1350 Median = 1270 IQR = 240

4. Maximum temperature = 51.8°F Range = 59.4°F
Mean = 33.8°F Standard deviation = 12.6°F
Median = 35.6°F IQR = 28.8°F

5. In January, a high of 55 is not quite 2 standard deviations above the mean, whereas in July a high of 55 is more than 2 standard deviations lower than the mean. So it's less likely to happen in July.

6. In French she scored 1.25 standard deviations higher than the mean. On the math exam she scored 1.50 standard deviations higher than the mean, so she did "better" on the math exam.

7. a) Megan b) Anna

8. a) To know something about their consistency and the chances they will last a certain amount of time.
b) RockReady. Mean is larger and SD smaller.

c) 16 hours is 2.5 SD higher than DuraTunes's mean, and 2.67 SD higher than RockReady's mean. So, although neither battery has much chance of lasting 16 hours, DuraTunes's chance is greater.

9. College professors can have between 0 and maybe 40 (or possibly 50) years experience. A standard deviation of 1/2 year is impossible, because many professors would be 10 or 20 SDs away from the mean, whatever it is. An SD of 16 years would mean that 2 SDs on either side of the mean is plus or minus 32, for a range of 64 years. That's too high. So, the SD must be 6 years.

10. Probably 2000, but it could be 20000 if they played to a few really large audiences (like sold-out stadiums).

11. a)

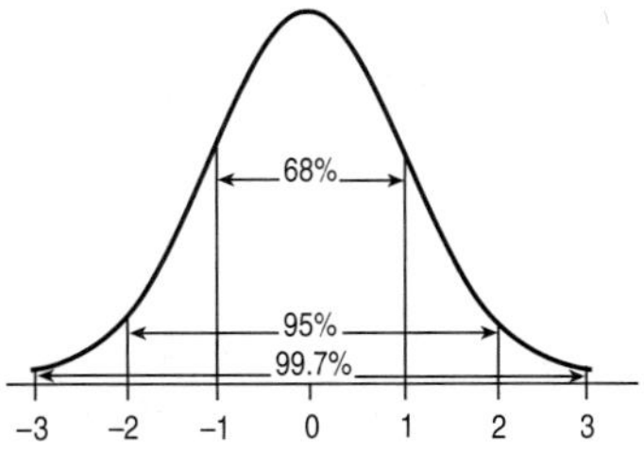

b) 18.6 to 31.0 mpg c) 16%
d) 13.5% e) less than 12.4 mpg

12. a)

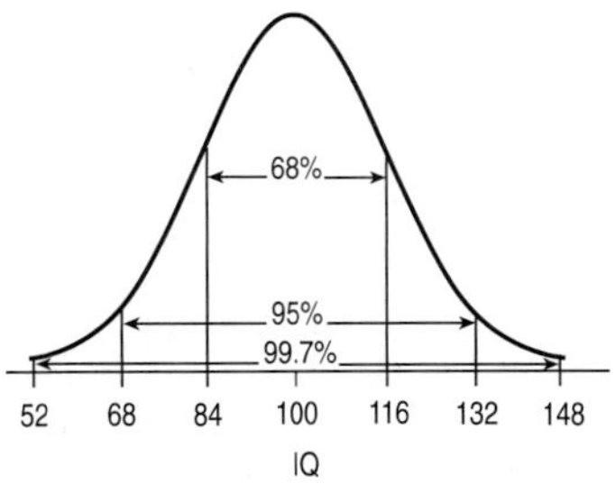

b) 68 to 132 IQ points c) 16% d) 13.5% e) 2.5%

13. a) 16% b) 5.7%
c) Because the Normal model doesn't fit well.
d) Distribution is skewed to the right with an outlier on the high side.

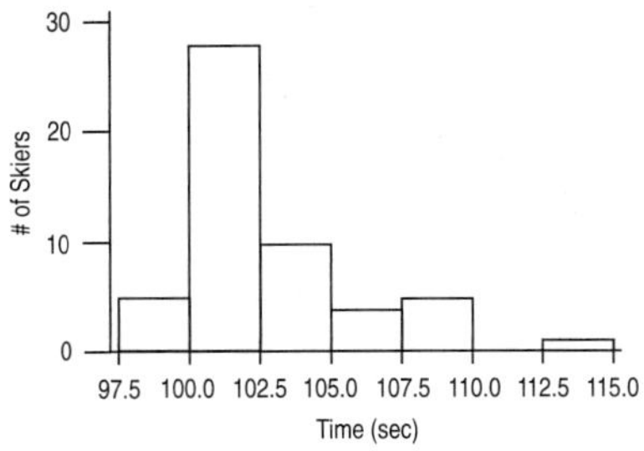

14. a)

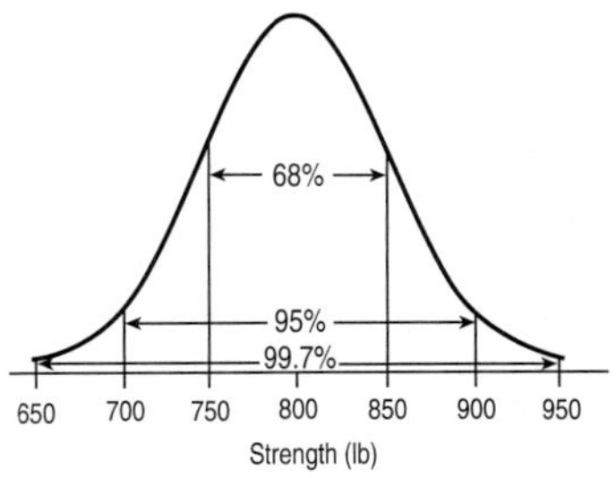

b) Chances are 84% that the strength is at least 750 pounds. That means 16% of the time it will be below. Seems like much too high a percentage.
c) 97.5%
d) In the extreme case, I would want a very small probability of failure, maybe less than 1 out of a million. For this I'd need to be sure that 800 was 6 SDs higher than my limit. So I might not use the rivets if I needed them to have shear strength more than 500 pounds.

15. a)

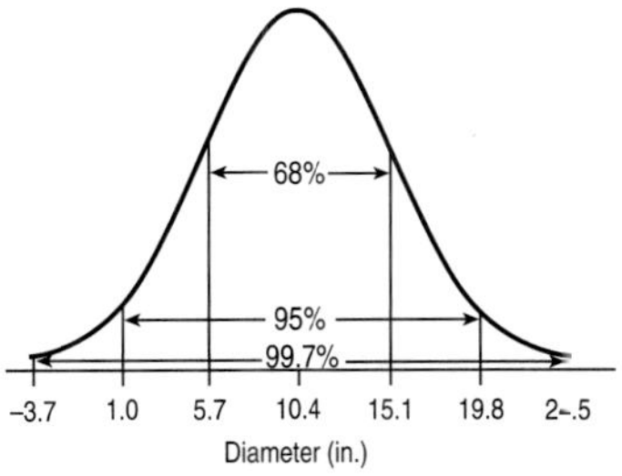

b) Between 1.0 and 19.8 inches
c) 2.5% d) 34% e) 16%

16. Since the histogram is not unimodal and symmetric, it is not wise to have faith in numbers from the Normal model.

17. a) 16%
b) 16% of the students should be watching less than −1.27 hours a week, but no one can watch less than 0 hours, so the model doesn't fit well.
c) Data are strongly skewed to the right, not symmetric.

18. a) Median because the distribution is so skewed to the left.
b) IQR. Distribution is skewed.
c) 68%
d) More than 75%
e) Normal model is not appropriate. Data are strongly skewed.

19. a) 6.68% b) 98.78% c) 71.63% d) 61.71%

20. a) 97.98% b) 37.07% c) 7.91% d) 79.95%

21. a) 0.842 b) −0.675 c) −1.881 d) −1.645 to 1.645

22. a) −1.175 b) 0.524 c) 1.476 d) −0.675 to 0.675

23. a) 79.55 b) 18.50 c) 95.79 d) −2.77

24. a) 129.77 b) 0.05 c) 10.64 d) 615.77

25. a)

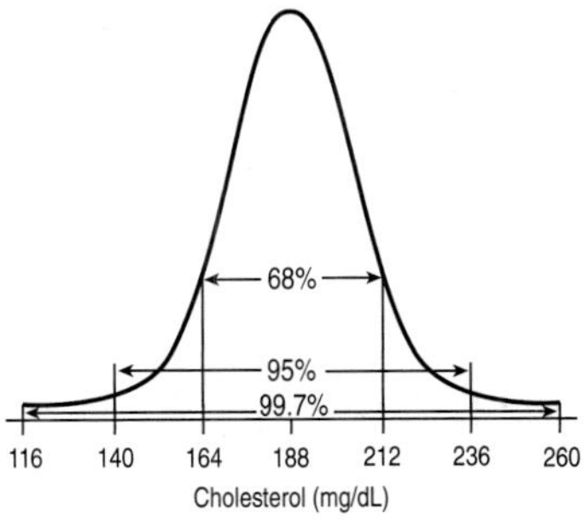

b) 30.85% c) 17.00% d) 32 points e) 212.9 points

26. a) No, that's more than 3 SDs above the mean.
b) 21.2% c) 67.3%
d) Quartiles at 30,314 and 33,686 miles, so 3,372 miles
e) 27,623 miles

27. a) 11.1% b) (35.9, 40.5) inches c) 40.5 inches

28. a) Based on the Normal model, we expect 95% to be between 96.8 and 99.6 degrees.
b) 28.4% c) 97.6 degrees

29. Mean 12.1 months, SD 1.3 months
30. Mean 3 lb, SD 1.3 lb
31. a) 5.3 grams b) 6.4 grams
c) Younger because SD is smaller.
d) Mean 62.7 grams, SD 6.2 grams
32. a) 3.26 grams b) 75.70 grams c) 2.86 grams
d) The new tomatoes are more consistent in their weights.

PART I REVIEW

1. a)

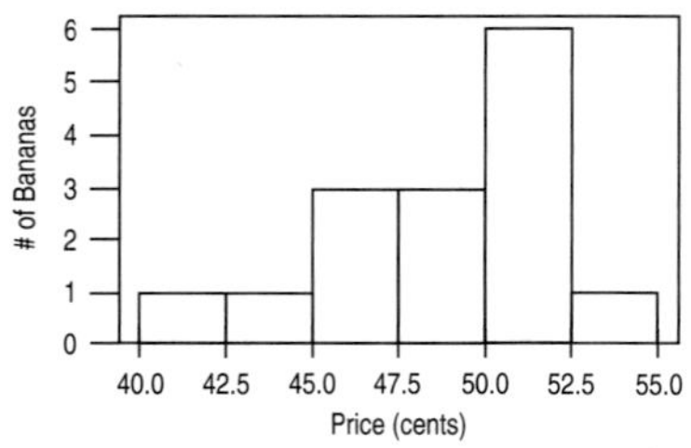

b) Median 49 cents, IQR 6 cents
c) The distribution is unimodal and left skewed. The center is near 50 cents; values range from 41 cents to 53 cents.

2. a) It is (rounded to 1 decimal place), but there's no reason it should be unless the number of women receiving each type of care was roughly the same.
b) Yes, but they do not prove that adequate prenatal care is important for pregnant women. The mortality rate is quite a bit lower for women with adequate care than for other women, but there may be a lurking variable.
c) Intensive care is given for emergency conditions. The data do *not* suggest that the care is the *cause* of the higher mortality.

3. a) If enough sopranos have a height of 65 inches, this can happen.
b) The distribution of heights for each voice part is roughly symmetric. The basses are slightly taller than the tenors. The sopranos and altos have about the same median height. Heights of basses and sopranos are more consistent than those of altos and tenors.

4. With only 3 cases, probably no display is appropriate.

5. a) It means their heights are also more variable.
b) The *z*-score for women to qualify is 2.40 compared with 1.75 for men, so it is harder for women to qualify.

6. a) The distribution is unimodal and skewed to the right. The mode is near 100, and values range from 95 to 145.
b) The mean will be larger than the median, since the distribution is right skewed.
c) Create a boxplot with quartiles at 97 and 105.5, median at 100. The IQR is 8.5 so the upper fence is at $(1.5 \times 8.5) + 105.5 = 118.25$. There are several outliers to the right. There are no outliers to the left because the minimum at 95 lies well within the left fence at $97 - (1.5 \times 8.5) = 84.25$.
d) No, the Normal model is not appropriate for these data. They are unimodal but not symmetric.

7. a) *Who*—People who live near Watsamatta University
What—Age, attended college? Favorable opinion of Watsamatta?
When—Not stated
Where—region around Watsamatta U.
Why—To report to the university's directors
How—Sampled and phoned 850 local residents

b) Age—quantitative (years); attended college?—categorical; favorable opinion?—categorical.
c) The fact that the respondents know they are being interviewed by the university's staff may influence answers.

8. a)

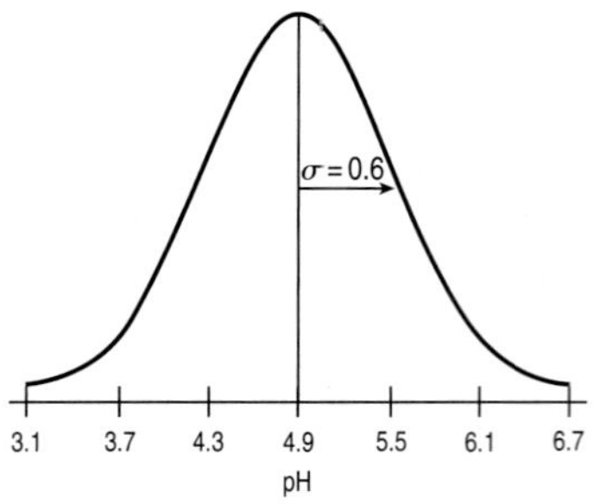

b) 3.3% c) 6.7% d) pH 4.40 e) pH 5.89
f) Quartiles at 4.50 and 5.30, so IQR is 0.80

9. a) These are categorical data, so mean and standard deviation are meaningless.
b) Not appropriate. Even if it fits well, the Normal model is meaningless for categorical data.

10. a) Stream name—categorical; substrate—categorical; pH—quantitative; temperature—quantitative (°C); BCI—quantitative units missing.
b) Bar chart or pie chart

11. a)

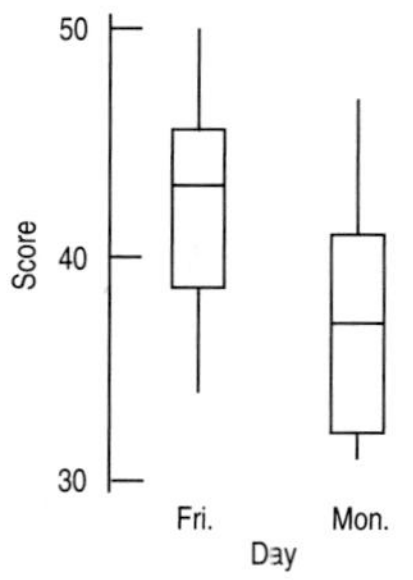

b) The scores on Friday were higher by about 5 points. This is a drop of more than 10% of the average score and shows that students fared worse on Monday after preparing for the test on Friday. The spreads are about the same, but the scores on Monday are a bit skewed to the right.
c)

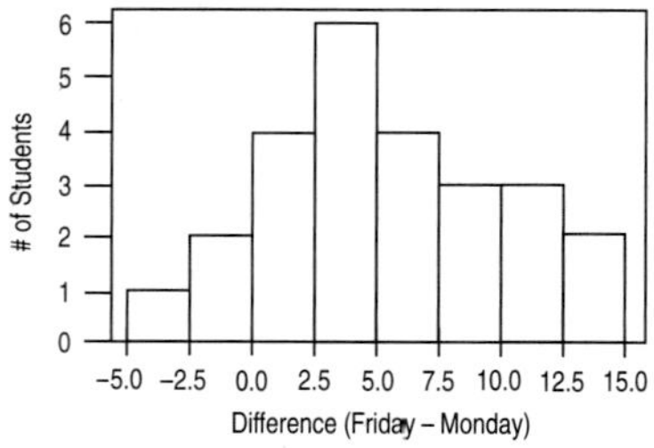

d) The changes (Friday − Monday) are unimodal and centered near 4 points with a spread of about 5 (SD). They are fairly symmetric, but slightly skewed to the right. Only 3 students did better on Monday (had a negative difference).

12. No, you can't add these, since the groups are not disjoint.

13. a) Categorical
b) Go fish. All you need to do is match the denomination. The denominations are not ordered. (Answers will vary.)

c) Gin rummy. All cards are worth their value in points (face cards are 10 points). (Answers will vary.)

14. a)

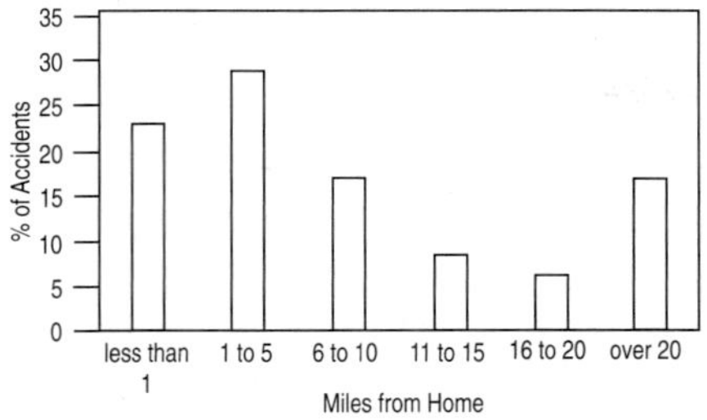

b) We are given no information about how many miles are driven in each of these categories, so we have no idea how many accidents to *expect*. We also have no information about how many accidents were involved in compiling the data.

15. a) Annual mortality rate for males (quantitative) in deaths per 100,000 and water hardness (quantitative) in parts per million.

b) Calcium is bimodal. There looks to be a mode down near 12 ppm that is the center of a fairly tight symmetric distribution and another mode near 62.5 ppm that is the center of a much more spread out, symmetric (almost uniform) distribution. Mortality, however, appears unimodal and symmetric with the mode near 1500 deaths per 100,000.

16. a) Overall mean is $(34 \times 1631.59 + 27 \times 1388.85)/(34+27) = 1524.15$ deaths per 100,000.

b) Yes. The distribution for the Northern towns is higher than that for the South. Fully half of the towns in the South have mortality rates lower than *any* of the Northern towns. Some Northern towns have rates higher than all of the Southern towns. It seems clear that mortality is higher, in general, in the North.

17. a) They are on different scales.

b) January's values are lower and more spread out.

c) Roughly symmetric but slightly skewed to the left. There are more low outliers than high ones. Center is around 40 degrees with an IQR of around 7.5 degrees.

18. Bimodal with modes around 50 and 80 minutes. Fairly symmetric around each mode.

19. a) Bimodal with modes near 2 and 4.5 minutes. Fairly symmetric around each mode.

b) Because there are two modes, which probably correspond to two different groups of eruptions, an average might not make sense.

c) The intervals between eruptions are longer for long eruptions. There is very little overlap. More than 75% of the short eruptions had intervals less than about an hour (62.5 minutes), while more than 75% of the long eruptions had intervals longer than about 75 minutes. Perhaps the interval could even be used to predict whether the next eruption will be long or short.

20. The chance of an accident is not the same for different age groups. The distribution of ages for drivers involved in fatal crashes is not the same as that for other drivers. So, the two variables are not independent.

21. a)

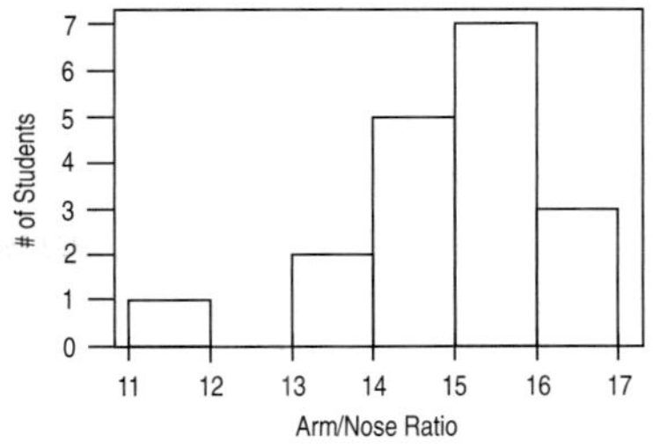

The distribution is left skewed with a center of about 15. It has an outlier near 11.

b) Even though the distribution is somewhat skewed, the mean and median are close. The mean is 15.0 and the SD is 1.25.

c) Yes. 11.8 is already an outlier. 9.3 is more than 4.5 SDs below the mean. It is a *very* low outlier.

22. a) About 38%

b) 6%

c) Data are bimodal, and the Normal model is inappropriate.

23. If we look only at the overall statistics, it appears that the follow-up group is insured at a much lower rate than those not traced (11.1% of the time as compared with 16.6%). But most of the follow-up group were black, who have a lower rate of being insured. When broken down by race, the follow-up group actually has a higher rate of being insured for both blacks and whites. So the overall statistic is misleading and due to the difference in race makeup of the two groups.

24. a) 3, 25.5, 36, 50.5, 70

b) Because the IQR is so large, none are technically outliers, but the seasons with fewer than 20 homeruns stand out as a separate group.

c)

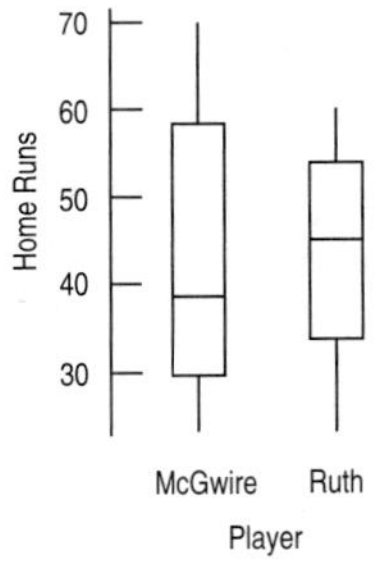

d) Without the injured seasons, McGwire and Ruth's home run production distributions look similar. (Ruth's seasons as a pitcher were not included as well.) Ruth's median is a little higher, and he was a little more consistent (less spread), but McGwire had the two highest season totals.

e)

Stem and Leaf

McGwire	Stem	Ruth
0	7	
5	6	0
82	5	449
92	4	1166679
9932	3	45
2	2	25

7|0 = 70 home runs

f) Now we can see how much more consistent Ruth was. Most of Ruth's seasons had home run totals in the 40s or 50s. McGwire's seasons are much more spread out (not even including the three at the bottom).

25. a)

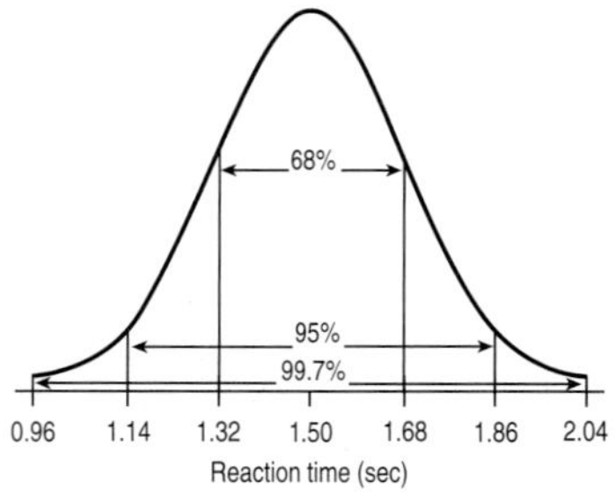

b) According to the model, reaction times are symmetric with center at 1.5 seconds. 95% of all reaction times are between 1.14 and 1.86 seconds.
c) 8.2%
d) 24.1%
e) Quartiles are 1.38 and 1.62 seconds, so the IQR is 0.24 seconds.
f) The slowest 1/3 of all drivers have reaction times of 1.58 seconds or more.

26. a) *Who*—62 people
What—Number of objects correctly memorized
When—Not stated
Where—Not stated
Why—To see if music affects memorization ability
How—Randomized experiment
b) Type of music (categorical) and number of items remembered (quantitative)
c) Because we do not have all the data, we can't know exactly how the boxplots look, but we do know that the minimums are all within the fences and that two groups have at least one outlier on the high side.

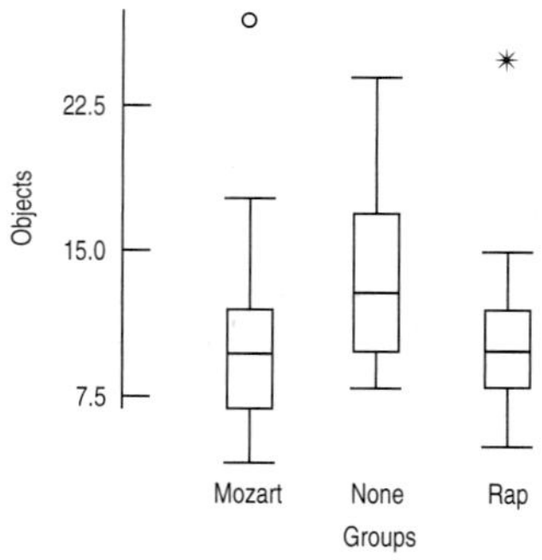

d) All three distributions are right skewed. Mozart and rap had very similar distributions. The scores for the None groups are, if anything, slightly higher than those for the other two groups. It is clear that groups listening to music did not score higher than those who heard none.

27. a)

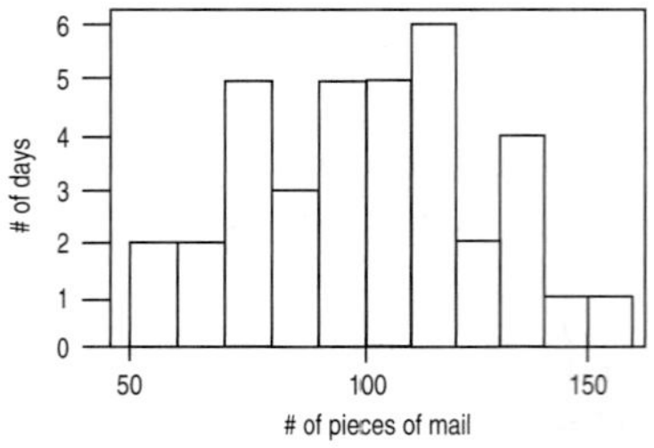

b) Mean 100.25, SD 25.54 pieces of mail.
c) The distribution is somewhat symmetric and unimodal, but the center is rather flat, almost uniform.
d) 64%. The Normal model seems to work reasonably well.

28. Chief executives have a mean salary less than the median, so the distribution is likely to be skewed to the left. General and operations managers have a mean salary larger than the median, so their distribution are likely to be skewed to the right.

29. a) 38 cars
b) Possibly, the distribution is skewed to the right.
c) Center—median is 148.5 cubic inches. Spread—IQR is 126 cubic inches.
d) No. It's bigger than average, but smaller than more than 25% of cars. The upper quartile is at 231 inches.
e) No. 1.5 IQR is 189, and 105 − 189 is negative, so there can't be any low outliers. 231 + 189 = 420. There aren't any cars with engines bigger than this, since the maximum has to be at most 105 (the lower quartile) + 275 (the range) = 380.
f) Because the distribution is skewed to the right, this is probably not a good approximation.
g) Mean, median, range, quartiles, IQR, SD all get multiplied by 16.4.

30. a) Fairly symmetric, almost uniform except for the right tail.
b) 47 horses
c) IQR is 47, so fences are at 7.5 and 195.5. Since the range is only 90, we know there can't be any observations lower than 35 (upper quartile − range) or greater than 168 (lower quartile + range), so no.
d) Distribution is very roughly unimodal and symmetric, so the approximation might be reasonable.
e) 22 of 38, or about 58%
f) Mean, median, and quartiles would increase by 10. SD, IQR, and range will not change.

31. a) 27.5%
b) If this were a random sample of all voters, yes.
c) 50.1% d) 10.2% e) 27.3% f) 40.9%

32. a) Republican—1101, Democrat—1404, Independent—1497; or Republican—27.5%, Democrat—35.1%, Independent—37.4%
b)

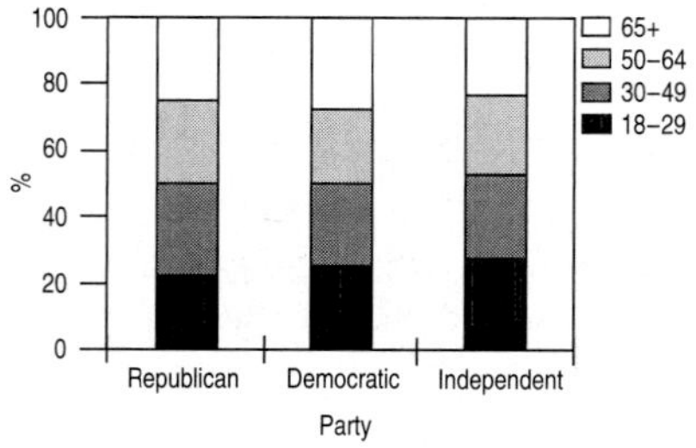

c) Age distributions are similar along party lines, with independents having slightly more young voters and Republicans having slightly fewer. Age groups are fairly evenly distributed, with each party having about 25% of each age group.

d) Nearly independent with exceptions noted in part c.

33. a) *Who*—100 health food store customers
What—Have you taken a cold remedy?, and Effectiveness (scale 1 to 10)
When—not stated
Where—not stated
Why—promotion of herbal medicine
How—in-person interviews

b) Have you taken a cold remedy?—categorical. Effectiveness—categorical or ordinal.

c) No. Customers are not necessarily representative, and the council had an interest in promoting the herbal remedy.

34. a) The differences are 3% or more. This is too large for rounding. Perhaps some responded that they knew of her, but their opinion was neither favorable nor unfavorable. The poll should have included this option.

b) There are different people in each poll, so proportions will vary.

c)

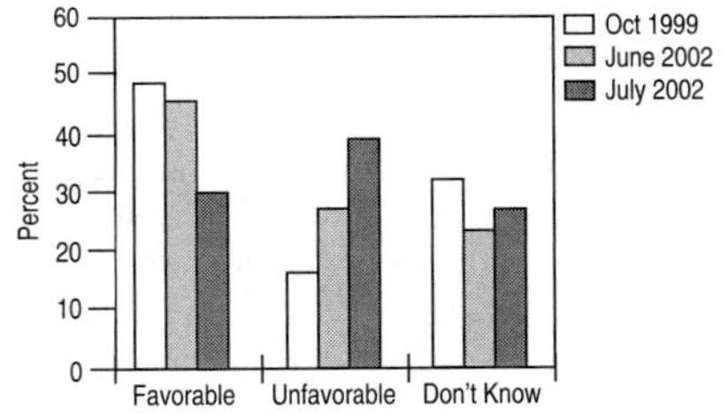

d)

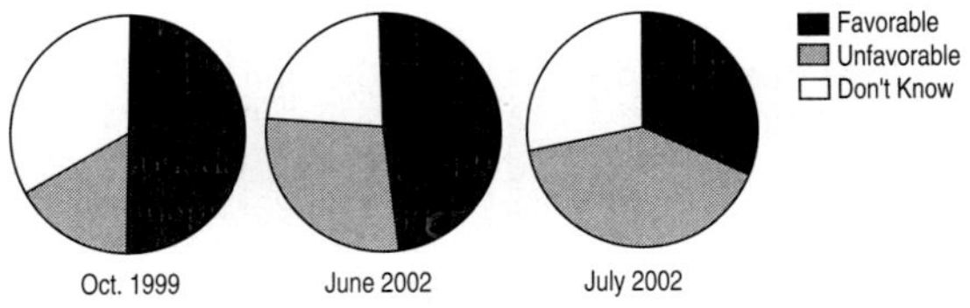

e)

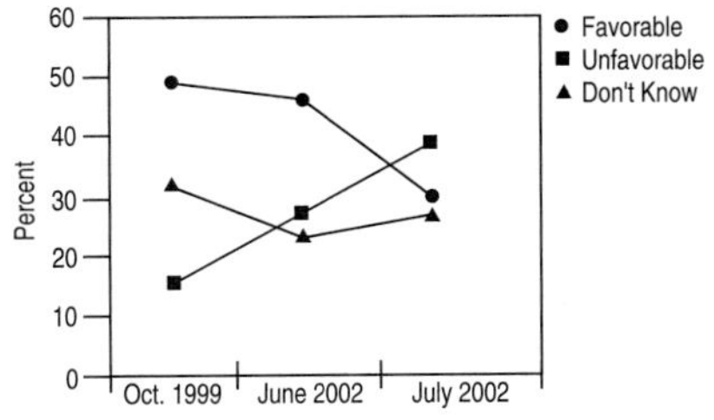

f) The bar chart, when split by time period, shows the drop-off in favorable ratings fairly well. The time plot is probably clearest (but note that the time periods are not evenly spaced.) All three plots have something to say.

g) Her unfavorable ratings went up dramatically between June and July 2002.

35. a) *Who*—Years from 1991 to 2000
What—Bicycle injuries reported
When—1991 to 2000
Where—Massachusetts
Why—To study trends in bicycle safety
How—Safety bureau reports

b)

Stem	Leaf
17	6
16	
15	2
14	5
13	1478
12	8
11	2
10	3

10 | 3 = 1030 injuries

c)

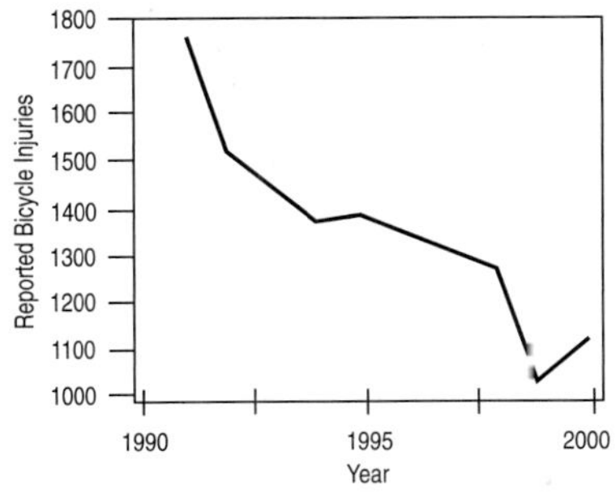

d) In the stemplot, it is clear that some years may be unusual.

e) The downward trend is visible in the timeplot.

f) In the decade 1991 to 2000, reported bicycle injuries decreased steadily from about 1800 per year to around 1100 per year.

36. a) −9, 1, 4, 9, 25

b)

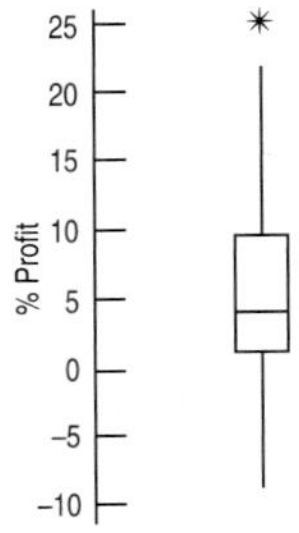

c) Mean 4.72% of sales, SD 7.55% of sales

d) Fairly symmetric and unimodal, centered around 4% of sales. 50% of the companies report % profit between 1% and 9%. There is one outlier at 25% of sales.

37. a) Mean 1.29 hours, SD 0.43 hours

b) 1.4 hours

c) 0.89 hours (or 53.4 minutes)

d) Survey results vary, and the mean and the SD may have changed.

38. a) The homicide rate rose sharply from 1900 to 1930, then declined dramatically until the early 40s. It started increasing quickly in the early 60s to around 1980, where it remained fairly stable until 1990, when it started declining again.

b) Executions rose sharply from 1900 to 1940, then fell as quickly, reaching near 0 in the decade 1970–1979. The last two decades have shown increase.

c) Not possible to reach cause-and-effect conclusion from two timeplots. There could be lurking variables.

CHAPTER 7

1. a) Weight in ounces: explanatory; Weight in grams: response. (Could be other way around.) To predict the weight in grams based on ounces. Scatterplot: positive, linear, no scatter (perfectly linear relationship).
b) Circumference: explanatory. Weight: response. To predict the weight based on the circumference. Scatterplot: positive, linear, somewhat scattered.
c) Shoe size: explanatory; GPA: response. To try to predict GPA from shoe size. Scatterplot: no direction, null, very scattered.
d) Miles driven: explanatory; Gallons remaining: response. To predict the gallons remaining in the tank based on the miles driven since filling up. Scatterplot: negative, linear, some scatter.

2. a) Price: explanatory; Number sold: response. To predict the number sold based on the price. Scatterplot: negative, linear, some scatter.
b) Water pressure: explanatory; Depth: response. To predict water pressure based on depth. Scatterplot: positive, linear, very little scatter.
c) Visibility: explanatory; Depth: response. To predict depth based on visibility (although predicting visibility based on depth is also possible). Scatterplot: negative, linear?, very scattered.
d) Weight: explanatory; Reading score: response. To predict reading test scores based on weight. Scatterplot: positive, possibly linear, significant scatter.

3. a) Altitude: explanatory; Temperature: response. (Other way around possible as well.) To predict the temperature based on the altitude. Scatterplot: negative, possibly linear, very scattered.
b) Ice cream cone sales: explanatory. Air conditioner sales: response—although the other direction would work as well. To predict one from the other. Scatterplot: positive, linear, some scatter.
c) Age: explanatory; Grip strength: response. To predict the grip strength based on age. Scatterplot: negative, somewhat linear, fairly scattered.
d) Reaction time: explanatory; Blood alcohol level: response. To predict blood alcohol level from reaction time test. (Other way around is possible). Scatterplot: positive, nonlinear, some scatter.

4. a) Time: explanatory; Cost: response. To predict cost based on time. Scatterplot: positive, linear?, some scatter.
b) Time delay: explanatory; Distance: response. To predict the distance from the lightning based on the time delay of the thunder. Scatterplot: positive, linear, little scatter.
c) Brightness: explanatory; Distance: response. To predict distance based on apparent brightness. Scatterplot: negative, nonlinear, somewhat scattered.
d) Weight of car: explanatory; Age of owner: response. To predict the age of the owner based on the weight of the car. (Or other way around.) Scatterplot: no direction, null, very scattered.

5. a) None b) 3 and 4 c) 2, 3, and 4 d) 1 and 2 e) 3 and possibly 1

6. a) 1 b) 4 c) 2 and 4 d) 3 e) 2 and 4

7. There seems to be a very weak—or possibly no—relation between brain size and performance IQ.

8. Nonlinear form. Small to moderate scatter. The rate has not been constant; the rate of increase from the beginning to about 1950 is steeper than from 1950 to the present.

9. a)

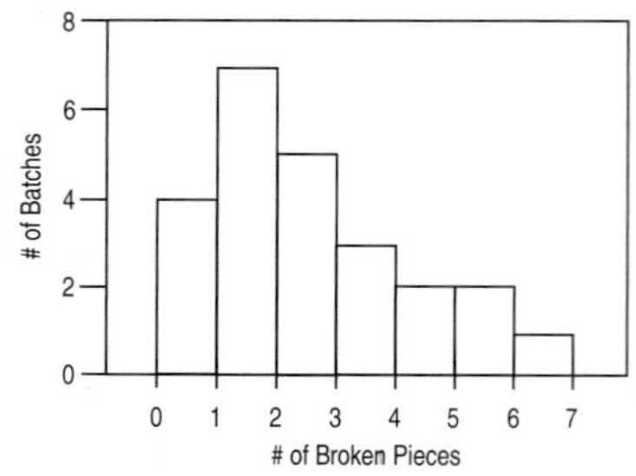

b) Unimodal, skewed to the right. The skew.
c) The positive, somewhat linear relation between batch number and broken pieces.

10. a)

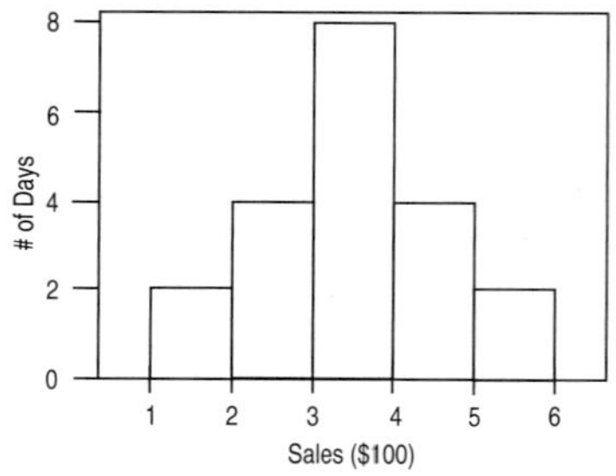

b) Positive linear relation, so sales are increasing.
c) Unimodal, symmetric sales; average sales around $350.

11. a) 0.006 b) 0.777 c) −0.923 d) −0.487

12. a) −0.977 b) 0.736 c) 0.951 d) −0.021

13. a) −0.649
b) The correlation will not change. Correlation does not change with change of units.
c) There is a moderately strong negative linear association between number of calories consumed and time at the table for toddlers. Longer times are associated with fewer calories.
d) There appears to be a relation between time at the table and calories consumed, but there is no reason to believe increased time *causes* decreased calorie consumption. There may be a lurking variable.

14. a)

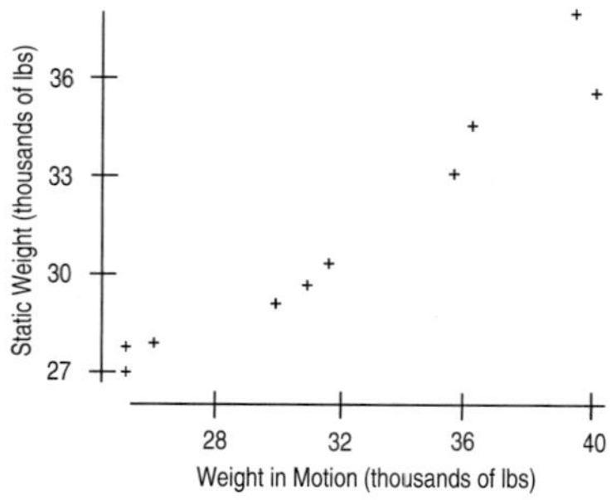

b) Positive, linear, very strong.
c) The new scale is able to predict the static weight fairly well, except possibly at the high end. It may be possible to predict the static weight from the new scale accurately enough to be useful.
d) 0.965.
e) The correlation would not change.
f) At the higher end of the weight-in-motion scale, there is one point where the weight in motion is much higher than the static weight. The line does not seem to go through the points where x and y are equal. The new scale may have to be recalibrated.

15. a)

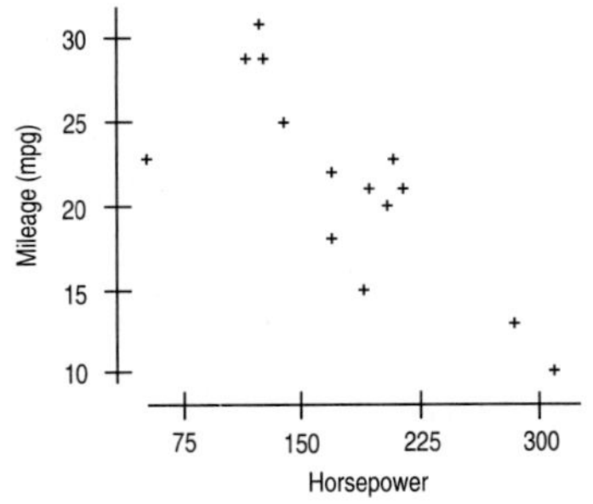

b) Negative, linear, strong.
c) −0.878
d) There is a strong linear relation in a negative direction between horsepower and mpg. As the horsepower increases, the fuel economy decreases. There is also an outlier that should be investigated.

16. a)

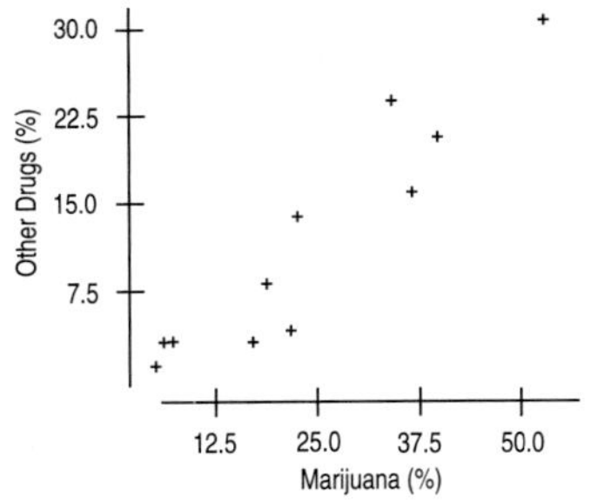

b) 0.934
c) There is a strong linear relation in a positive direction between the percent of teens using marijuana and the percent of teens using other drugs.
d) There is no indication of causality. There could be lurking variables.

17.

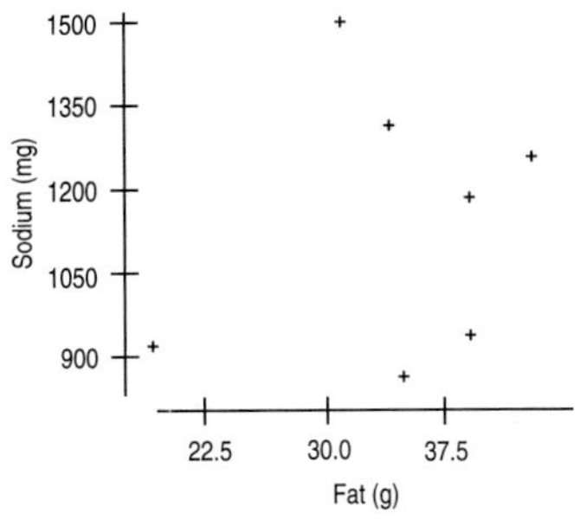

(Plot could have explanatory and predictor variables swapped.) Correlation is 0.199. There does not appear to be a relation between sodium and fat content in burgers, especially without the low-fat low-sodium item. The correlation of 0.199 shows a weak relationship, even with the outlier included.

18. a)

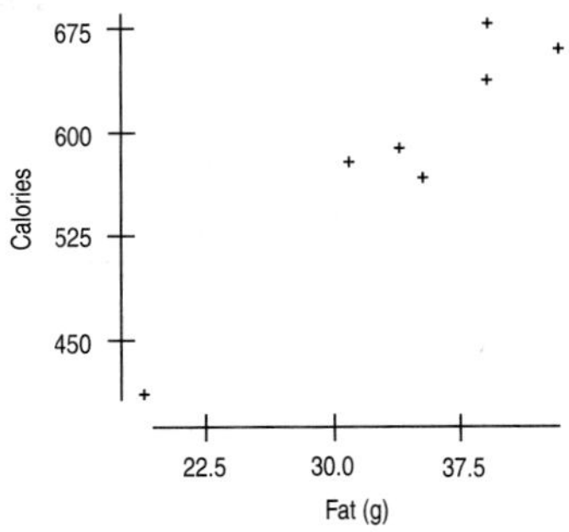

b) 0.961.
c) There appears to be a strong linear relation in a positive direction. The correlation of 0.961 supports the conclusion of a strong relation. There is an outlier at 410 calories with 19 grams of fat that makes the correlation stronger.

19. a) Yes, the scatterplot appears to be somewhat linear.
b) As the number of runs increases, the attendance also increases.
c) There is a positive association, but it does not *prove* that more fans will come if the number of runs increases. Association does not indicate causality.

20. a) There appears to be a weak relationship between the number of wins and attendance. The points show significant scattering. The correlation of 0.577 is not very strong.
b) Runs. There does appear to be more of a linear relation for runs and attendance than for winning and attendance. The correlation is higher for runs vs. attendance (0.740) than for wins vs. attendance (0.577).
c) The correlation between runs and wins is 0.680. The correlation is not as strong as between runs and attendance.

21. There may be an association but not a correlation unless the variables are quantitative. There could be a correlation between average number of hours of TV watched per week per person and the number of crimes committed per year. Even if there is a relationship, it doesn't mean one causes the other.

22. The relation might be nonlinear, resulting in a correlation close to 0 even though the association is strong.

23. a) Assuming the relation is linear, a correlation of −0.772 shows a strong relation in a negative direction.
b) Continent is a categorical variable. Correlation does not apply.
c) Correlation cannot be greater than 1. There is an error.
d) Assuming the relation is linear, the strong correlation shows a relation, but it does not show *causality*

24. The source of data is categorical. The correlation is meaningless.

25. This is categorical data even though it is represented by numbers. The correlation is meaningless.

26. a) 0.117
b) No, the low correlation is due to the fact that the relation is not linear.

27. a)

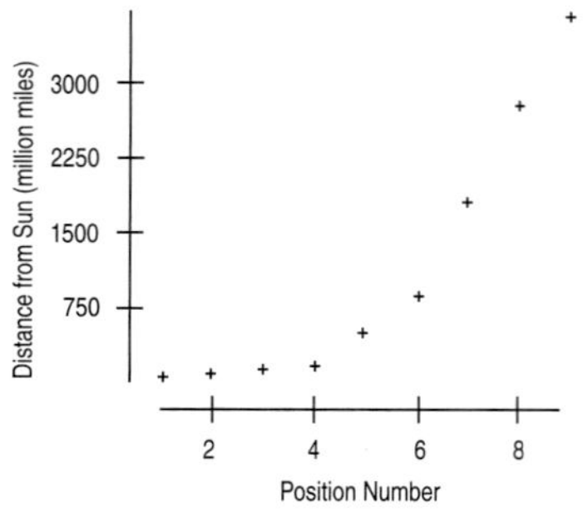

The relation between position and distance is nonlinear with a positive direction. There is very little scatter from the trend.

b) The relation is not linear.

c)

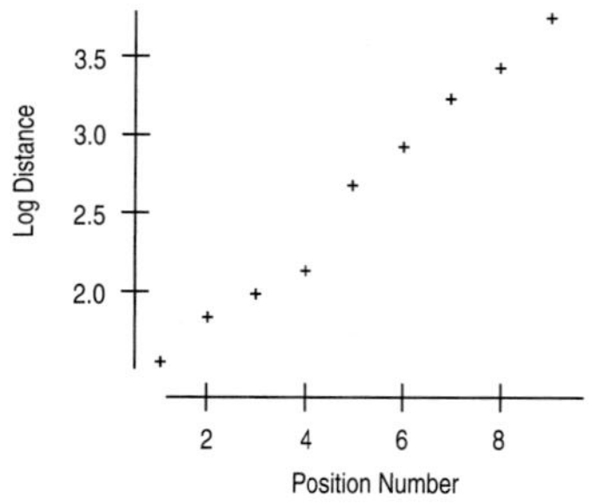

The relation between position number and log of distance appears to be linear.

28. a)

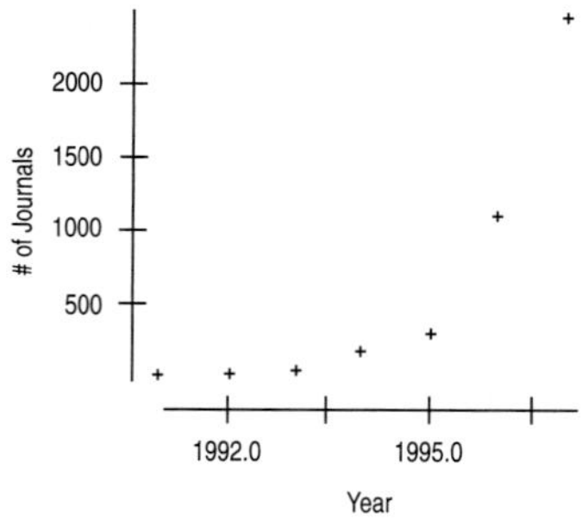

The association is positive and very strong but not linear.

b)

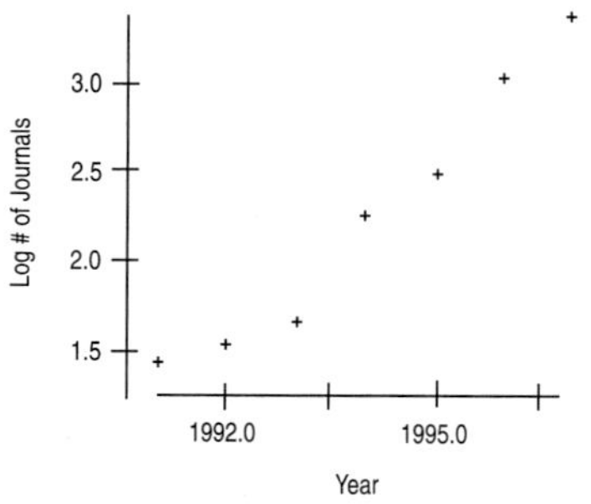

Taking the log of the number of journals makes the relation more linear in form.

CHAPTER 8

1.

$\bar{x}$	s_x	$\bar{y}$	s_y	r	$\hat{y} = b_0 + b_1x$
a) 10	2	20	3	0.5	$\hat{y} = 12.5 + 0.75x$
b) 2	0.06	7.2	1.2	−0.4	$\hat{y} = 23.2 - 8x$
c) 12	6	**152**	**30**	−0.8	$\hat{y} = 200 - 4x$
d) 2.5	1.2	**25**	100	**0.6**	$\hat{y} = -100 + 50x$

2.

$\bar{x}$	s_x	$\bar{y}$	s_y	r	$\hat{y} = b_0 + b_1x$
a) 30	4	18	6	−0.2	$\hat{y} = 27 - 0.3x$
b) 100	18	60	10	0.9	$\hat{y} = 10 + 0.5x$
c) **4**	0.8	50	15	**0.8**	$\hat{y} = -10 + 15x$
d) **6**	**1.2**	18	4	−0.6	$\hat{y} = 30 - 2x$

3. a) Model is appropriate.
b) Model is not appropriate. Relationship is nonlinear.
c) Model may not be appropriate. Spread is changing.

4. a) Model is not appropriate. Relationship is nonlinear.
b) Model may not be appropriate. Spread is changing.
c) Model is appropriate.

5. The line $\hat{y} = 7.0 + 1.1x$ minimizes the sum of squared vertical distances from the points to the line.

6. The line $\hat{y} = 1975 - 0.45x$ minimizes the sum of squared vertical distances from the points to the line.

7. a) Price (in thousands of dollars) is y and size (in square feet) is x. Slope is thousands of \$ per square foot.
b) Size explains 71.4% of the variation in home prices.
c) Positive. Larger homes should cost more.
d) 0.845
e) Price should be 0.845 SDs above the mean in price.
f) Price should be 1.690 SDs below the mean in price.

8. a) Yes, the relationship is not very strong, but it's reasonably straight.
b) The number of wins explains 33.3% of the variation in attendance.
c) 0.577
d) 1.154 SDs above the average.
e) 0.577 SDs below the average.

9. a) Every square foot increase in size increases the average price \$0.061 × 1000, or \$61.00.
b) 230.82 thousand, or \$230,820.
c) \$115,020; \$6000 is the residual.

10. a) Predicted attendance = 5773.27 + 517.609 × wins.
b) 31,653.72 people.
c) Every win adds an average 517.609 people in attendance.
d) It means the team's average attendance is lower than the average for a team with as many wins.
e) 10,957.54 attendees. This means that the Cardinals averaged nearly 11,000 more attendees than one would predict for a team with 43 wins.

11. 300 pounds/foot. If a "typical" car is 15 feet long, all of 3, 30, and 3000 would give ridiculous weights.

12. 1 ft/inch. If a typical circumference is around 20 inches, then other slopes give ridiculous heights.

13. a) R^2 does not tell whether the model is appropriate, but measures the strength of the linear relationship. High R^2 could also be due to an outlier.
b) Predictions based on a regression line are for average values of y for a given x. The actual wingspan will vary around the prediction.

14. a) R^2 measures the amount of variation accounted for. It does not imply that x determines the values of y. Here, literacy rate *accounts for* 64% of the *observed* variation in life expectancy.
b) This interpretation is implying a causal relationship. Just because two variables are related does not mean one causes another. Here, one could say that an increase of 5% in literacy rate is associated with an average 2-year improvement in life expectancy.

15. a) Probably not. Your score is better than about 97.5% of people, assuming scores follow the Normal model. Your next score is likely to be closer to the mean.
b) The friend probably should retake the test. His score is better than only about 16% of people. His score is likely to be closer to the mean.

16. People on the cover are usually there for outstanding performances. Because they are so far from the mean, the performance in the next year is likely to be closer to the mean.

17. a) Moderately strong, fairly straight, and positive. Possibly some outliers (higher than expected math scores).
b) The student with 500 verbal and 800 math.
c) Positive, fairly strong linear relationship. 46.9% of variation in math scores is explained by verbal scores.
d) Predicted math = 217.7 + 0.662 × verbal.
e) Every point of verbal score adds an average 0.662 points to the predicted math score.
f) 548.5 points.
g) 53.0 points.

18. a) Predicted GPA = −1.215 + 0.0032 × SAT.
b) One could say that a person with a 0 SAT score would have a −1.212 GPA, but a score of 0 on the SAT is impossible, as is a negative GPA. So the y-intercept serves only to adjust the height of the line and is meaningless by itself.
c) The expected GPA increases by 0.0032 points for every combined SAT point scored.
d) 3.224
e) SAT is probably only somewhat useful, since R^2 is only 0.221. There are many other factors that influence GPA.
f) Positive. My GPA would be higher than expected for my SAT score.

19. a) 0.685
b) Predicted verbal = 162.1 + 0.71 × math.
c) The observed verbal score is higher than predicted from the math score.
d) 516.7 points.
e) 559.6 points.
f) Regression to the mean. Someone whose math score is below average is predicted to have a verbal score below average, but not as far (in SDs). So if we use *that* verbal score to predict math, they will be even closer to the mean in predicted math score than their observed math score.If we kept cycling back and forth, eventually we would predict the mean of each and stay there.

20. 1245.7 points.

21. a)

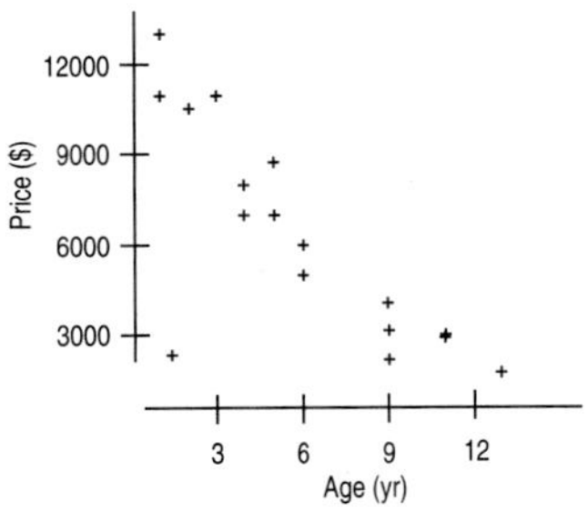

b) Negative, linear, strong.
c) Yes.
d) −0.946
e) Age accounts for 89.4% of the variation in advertised prices.
f) Other factors contribute—options, condition, mileage, etc.

22. a) Yes. Plot shows positive, linear, fairly strong relationship.
b) Marijuana use accounts for 87.3% of variation in use of other drugs.
c) Percentage of other drug use = −4.0 + 0.82 × marijuana use percentage.
d) Each additional percent of teens using marijuana adds 0.82 percent to the percentage of teens using other drugs.
e) The results do not *confirm* marijuana as a gateway drug. They do indicate an *association* between marijuana and other drug use.

23. a) Predicted price = 12319.6 − 924 × years.
b) Every extra year of age decreases average value by $924.
c) The average new Corolla costs $12,319.60.
d) $5851.60
e) Negative residual. Its price is below the predicted value for its age.
f) −$1579.60
g) No. After age 13, the model predicts negative prices. The relationship is no longer linear.

24. a) 20.4 g
b) −10.4 g. Veggie burgers have less fat than typical menu items.
c) Answers will vary—should mention the predicted fat content, the observed fat content, and the residual.

25. a)

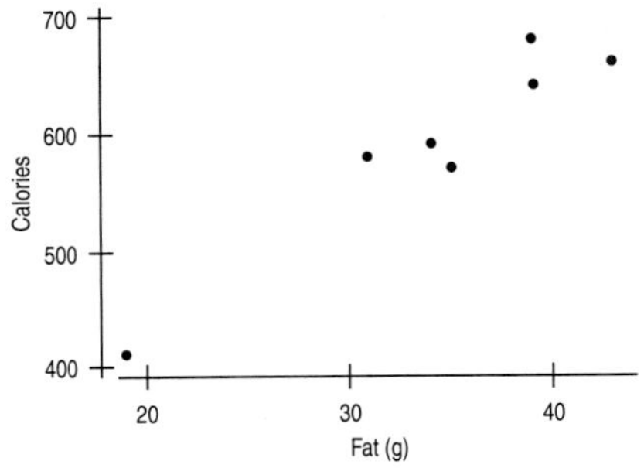

b) 92.3% of the variation in calories can be accounted for by the fat content.
c) Predicted calories = 211.0 + 11.06 × calories/fat gram.

d)

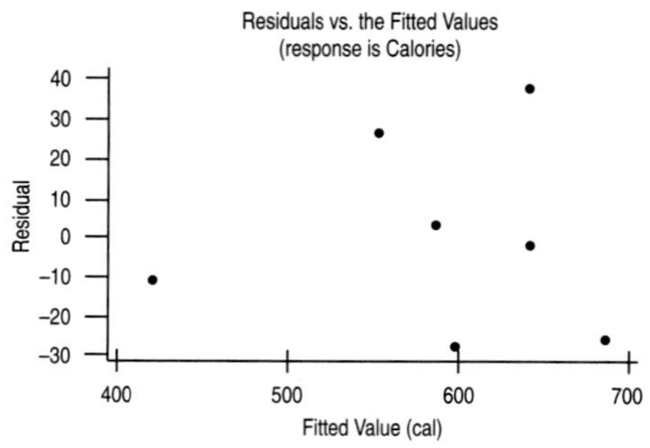

Residuals show no clear pattern, so the model seems appropriate.

e) Could say a fat-free burger still has 211.0 calories, but this is extrapolation (no data close to 0).

f) Every gram of fat adds 11.06 calories, on average.

g) 553.5 calories.

26. a) Yes.

b) Strong.

c) Predicted calories = 185.7 + 13.93 calories/fat gram.

d) Every extra fat gram adds 13.93 calories, on average.

e) A fat-free sandwich would have 185.7 calories, but this is extrapolation.

f) The sandwich has fewer calories than average for its grams of fat.

g) The chicken sandwich.

h) The calorie content of the fish sandwich is less than expected for burgers (498.4 calories) but much less than expected for chicken (547.9 calories). It seems more in line with burgers than chicken.

27. a) The regression was for predicting calories from fat, not the other way around.

b) Predicted fat grams = −15.0 + 0.083 grams/calories. Predict 34.8 grams of fat.

28. a) Fairly linear, positive, and quite strong. Appears to be more variability with higher costs of living.

b) The cost of living in 2000 accounts for 91.6% of the variation in cost of living in 2001.

c) 13.1%

d) Moscow's cost of living is 13.1% higher than expected from the model.

29. a) 82.9 minutes.

b) The linear relationship is strong, but without seeing the data we don't know if the model is appropriate.

c) Every extra minute of digital time adds 0.44 minutes of analog time, on average.

d) It lasts longer in analog mode than predicted for its number of digital minutes.

30. Predicted candy sales = −178.0992 + 0.0900 × year.
2.1523 million dollars.
Relationship is strong and linear with little scatter, so faith in prediction is strong with the caveat that we assume the linear model continues to be appropriate.

31. a) 0.578

b) CO_2 levels account for 33.4% of the variation in mean temperature.

c) Predicted mean temperature = 15.3066 + 0.004 × CO_2.

d) Each part per million of CO_2 adds 0.004 degrees to mean temperature (Celsius).

e) One *could* say that with no CO_2 in the atmosphere, there would be a temperature of 15.3066 degrees Celsius, but this is extrapolation.

f) No.

g) Predicted 16.7626 degrees C.

32. a)

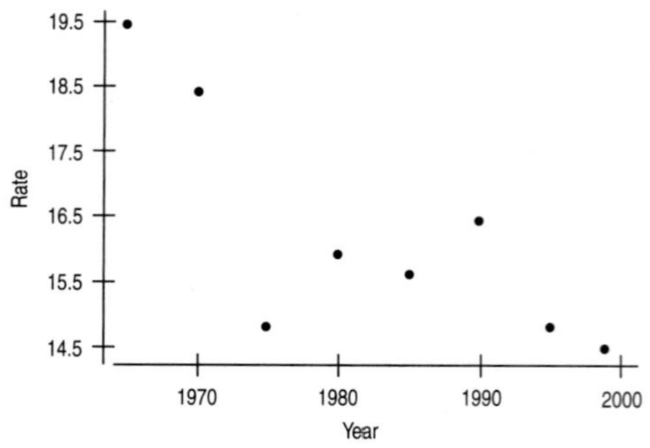

Decreasing trend, but possibly not linear.

b) Predicted birth rate = 246.05 − 0.12 × year.

c)

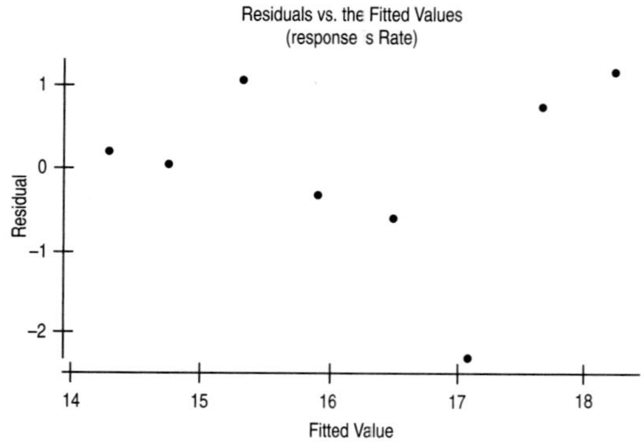

Difficult to tell with only 8 points, but positive on the ends and negative in the middle may indicate a curve in the data.

d) Every year, the number of live births is decreasing 0.12 per 1000 women, on average.

e) 16.73 live births per 1000 women.

f) Model predicts 1.73 live births per 1000 women too high.

g) 13.60 live births per 1000 women. Seems a little low, but we are extrapolating.

h) 11.86 live births per 1000 women. Extrapolating this far is dangerous.

33. a) Predicted body fat % = −27.4 + 0.25 × weight.

b) Residuals look randomly scattered around 0, so conditions are satisfied.

c) For each pound of weight, average body fat increases 0.25 percent.

d) Reliable is relative. R^2 is 48.5%, but residuals have a standard deviation of 7%, so variation around the line is large.

e) 0.9 percent.

34. Predicted body fat % = −62.6 + 2.22 × waist.
R^2 is 78.7%, and the standard deviation of the residuals is smaller (4.5%) so this model should be better able to predict.

35. a) As calcium levels increase, mortality rate decreases. Relationship is fairly strong, negative, and linear.

b) Predicted mortality = 1676.0 − 3.23 × calcium.

c) Mortality decreases 3.23 deaths per 100,000, on average, for each part per million of calcium. The intercept indicates a baseline mortality of 1676 deaths per 100,000 with no calcium, but this is extrapolation.

d) Exeter has 348.6 fewer deaths per 100,000 than the model predicts.

e) 1353 deaths per 100,000.

f) Calcium concentration explains 43.0% of the variation in death rate per 100,000 people.

36. a) Yes—length is easier to judge from a picture than weight.

b) 0.914

c) Predicted weight = −393.0 + 5.9 × length.

d) Every inch of length adds an average 5.9 pounds.

e) Fairly accurate. The R^2 value is 83.6%. The standard deviation of the residuals is 54.01 pounds. I would like to see a scatterplot and residual plots to assess the regression conditions before having too much faith in this model.

37.

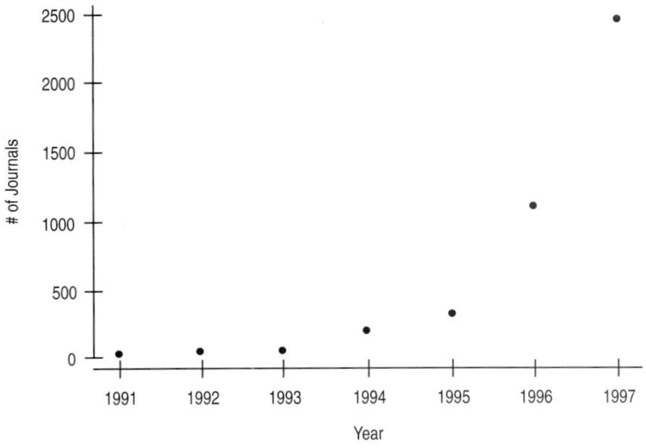

The growth is not linear. Need to re-express y or x first.

38. a) Predicted oil production = −3,706,193 million barrels + 3289. 6 million barrels/year × year.

b) 2,876,296.6 million barrels.

c) Looks much higher than values have been for a long time.

d)

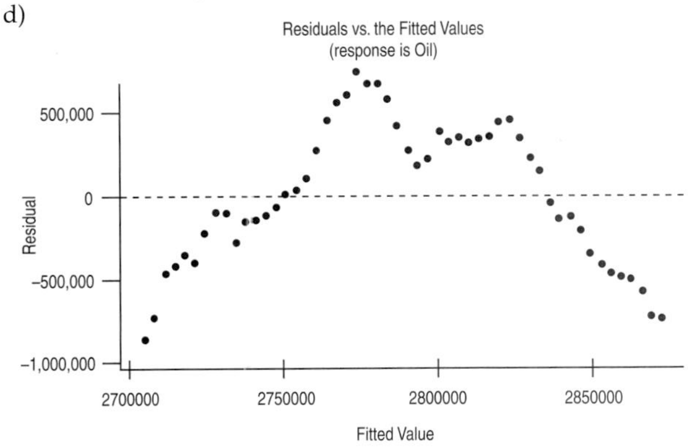

From the residual plot, the data fail the straight enough condition. The linear model is not appropriate.

CHAPTER 9

1. a) The trend appears to be somewhat linear up to about 1940, but from 1940 to about 1970 the trend appears to be nonlinear. From 1975 or so, to present, the trend appears to be linear.

b) Relatively strong for certain time periods.

c) No, as a whole, the graph is clearly nonlinear. Within certain time periods the correlation is high (1975 to the present).

d) Overall, no. You could fit a linear model to the time period 1975 to 1995, but why? You don't need to interpolate, since every year is reported and extrapolation seems very dangerous.

2. a) −0.846

b) For each increase of 10 years, the difference in average age at first marriage is decreasing by about 0.16 years.

c) About 1.81 years.

d) The latest data point is before the year 2000. Extrapolating for 2010 is risky because it depends on the assumption that the trend will continue in the same manner.

3. a) Answers may vary. Using the data for 1955–1995, the scatterplot is relatively linear with some curvature. The residual plot shows a definite trend, indicating that the data are not linear. If you used the line, for 2005, the predicted age is 25.3 years.

b) Not much since, the data are not truly linear, and 2005 is 10 years from the last data point (extrapolating is risky).

c) No, that extrapolation of more than 50 years would be absurd. There's no reason to believe the trend from 1955 to 1995 will continue.

4. a) The data from the late 1800s to 1950 are high leverage points. Since they follow generally the same linear trend as the 1975–1998 data, those data points increase the correlation and the R^2 value.

b) Yes, although there are a couple of unusual residual values in the bottom left corner of the residual graph.

c) For each increase of 10 years, the average age difference drops about 0.24 years.

d) These data begin with $X = 1975$. The y-intercept is the predicted difference in age at the year $X = 0$, quite an extrapolation.

5. a) No. We need to see the scatterplot first to see if the conditions are satisfied.

b) No, the linear model might not fit the data at all.

6. a) No, it just means that the model doesn't explain more than 13% of the variation of the response variable.

b) She should look at s to see accuracy of predictions. R^2 is not a direct measure of accuracy.

7. a) The graph shows that on average, students progress at about one reading level per year. This graph shows averages for each grade. The linear trend has been increased by using averages.

b) Very close to 1.

c) The individual data points would show much more scatter, and the correlation would be lower.

d) A slope of 1 would indicate that for each 1-year grade level increase, the average reading level is increasing by 1 year.

8. The graph has a positive trend, showing that increased SAT score is associated with increased GPA. However, the graph is based on averages, not individual data. While SAT may be a fair predictor of GPA on average, there may also be lurking variables.

9. a) As the temperature increases by 1°F, the cost decreases by \$2.13. So warmer temperatures indicate lower costs.

b) For a temperature of 0°F, the cost is \$133.

c) Too high; the residuals (observed − predicted) around 0 degrees are negative, showing that the model overestimates the costs.

d) $111.70
e) About $105.70
f) No, the residuals show a definite curved pattern. The data are probably not linear.
g) No, there would be no difference. The relationship does not depend on the units.

10. a) The slope indicates that as the speed increases by 1 mph, the fuel economy decreases by 0.1 mpg; for every 10 mph of increase in speed, the fuel economy decreases by 1 mpg.
b) The intercept is the mileage at 0 mph, which doesn't make any sense.
c) The residuals are negative, so the model is overestimating the mpg.
d) 27 mpg.
e) 28.5 mpg.
f) The association is strong, but not linear.
g) No, the residuals indicate a clear nonlinear relationship.

11. a) 1) Yes, an outlier.
2) No, not influential for the slope.
3) Correlation would decrease because outlier has large z_x and z_y, increasing correlation.
4) Slope wouldn't change because the outlier is in line with other points.
b) 1) Yes, an outlier.
2) Yes, influential.
3) Correlation would weaken and become less negative.
4) Slope would increase toward 0, since outlier makes it negative.
c) 1) Yes, outlier.
2) Yes, somewhat influential.
3) Correlation would increase, since scatter would decrease.
4) Slope would increase slightly.
d) 1) Yes, outlier.
2) No, not influential.
3) Correlation would become stronger and become more negative because scatter would decrease.
4) Slope would increase and get a little less negative.

12. a) 1) Yes, an outlier.
2) Yes, influential.
3) Correlation would become stronger and increase because scatter would decrease.
4) Slope would become stronger and increase because outlier pulls the line toward 0.
b) 1) Yes, an outlier.
2) Yes, influential.
3) Correlation would become weaker because outlier has high z_x and z_y values, increasing correlations.
4) Slope would decrease because outlier pulls the line from nearly flat to a positive slope.
c) 1) Yes, an outlier.
2) No, not influential.
3) Correlation would become stronger because scatter would decrease.
4) About the same; slope may decrease slightly.
d) 1) Yes, an outlier.
2) No, not influential.
3) Correlation would become weaker and become less negative because outlier has large negative $z_x \times z_y$ value.
4) Slope would stay about the same because outlier is consistent with slope determined by other points.

13. 1) e 2) d 3) c 4) b 5) a

14. 1) d 2) e 3) c 4) b 5) a

15. a) Stronger. Both slope and correlation would increase.
b) Restricting the study to nonhuman animals would justify it.
c) Moderately strong.
d) For every year increase in life expectancy, the gestation period increases by about 15.5 days, on average.
e) About 270.5 days.

16. a) Removing hippos would make the association stronger, since hippos are more of a departure from the pattern.
b) Increase.
c) No, there must be a good reason for removing data points.
d) Yes, removing it lowered the slope from 15.5 to 11.6 days per year.

17. No. There is one high leverage outlier, National Park Service. With that point, R-squared is 46.2%; without that point, R-squared is 0.

18. There seem to be two distinct relations in this data, one for the years 1965 to 1985 and another for 1990 to 1998:
1965 to 1985: $\hat{Y} = 2521.62 - 1.256X$
1990 to 1998: $\hat{Y} = -1152.14 + 0.592X$

19. Answers may vary. There seem to be two time periods. From 1980 to 1993 or so, there was a consistent increase of about 1% a year. A regression of those years shows
Predicted illegitimate percentage = −1988.94 + 1.014 year
with an R^2 of 98.9%. The years from 1994 to 1998 are nearly flat. A model of those years shows:
Predicted illegitimate percentage = −87.28 + 0.060 year
with an R^2 of 17.3%.
How to use the data depends on the purpose of the study.

20.

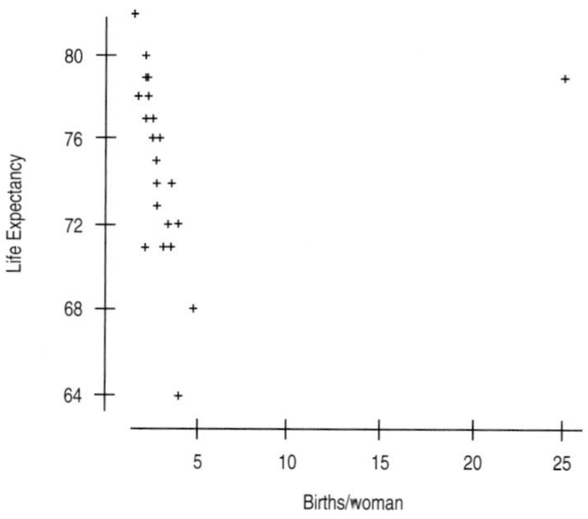

a) Except for the outlier, Costa Rica, the data appear to have a linear form in a negative direction.
b) The outlier is Costa Rica, whose data appears to be wrong, with 25 births per woman. That's impossible.
c) With Costa Rica, $r = 0.081$, R-squared = 0.7%, indicating that 0.7% of the variation in life expectancy is explained by the variation in births per woman. Without Costa Rica, $r = -0.815$, R-squared = 66.4%, indicating that 66.4% of the variation in life expectancy is explained by the variation in births/woman.
d) With Costa Rica, $\hat{Y} = 74.2 + 0.08X$; without Costa Rica, $\hat{Y} = 86.8 - 4.4X$.
e) The model with Costa Rica is not appropriate. The residual plot shows a distinct outlier, which is Costa Rica. Removing

Costa Rica gives better residuals plots, suggesting that the linear equation is more appropriate.

f) With Costa Rica, the slope is near 0, suggesting that the linear relation is not very useful. The y-intercept suggests that with no births, the life expectancy is about 74 years. Without Costa Rice, the slope is -4.36, indicating that an average increase of one child per woman predicts a lower life expectancy of 4.36 years, on average. The y-intercept indicates that a country with no birth rate would have a life expectancy of 86.8 years. This is extrapolation.

g) No, while there is an association, there is no reason to expect causality. Lurking variables may be involved.

21. a) The scatterplot is clearly nonlinear; however, the last few years, say from 1972 on, do appear to be linear.

b) Using the data from 1972 to 2000 gives $r = 0.998$ and Predicted CPI $= -9247.62 + 4.710$ X. Predicted CPI in 2010 $= 219.72$.

c) The stock market crash and World War II are clearly visible in their impact on CPI.

CHAPTER 10

1. a) 2.8
b) 16.44
c) 7.84
d) 0.36
e) 2.09

2. a) 1.44
b) 630.96
c) 2.33
d) 0.77
e) 6.6

3. a) Fairly linear, negative, strong.
b) Gas mileage decreases an average 7.652 mpg for each thousand pounds of weight.
c) No. Residuals show a curved pattern.
d) Residuals are more randomly spread around 0, with some low outliers.
e) Predicted gallons per 100 miles $= 0.625 + 1.178 \times$ Weight.
f) For each additional 1000 pounds of weight, an additional 1.178 gallons will be needed to drive 100 miles.
g) 21.06 miles per gallon.

4.

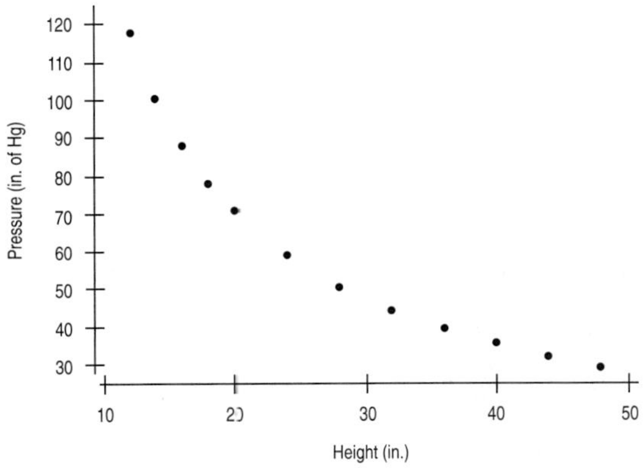

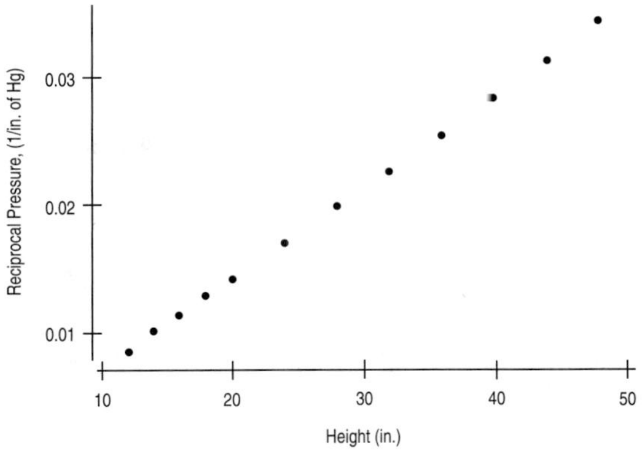

1/Pressure is an exact relationship. R^2 is 100%.

Predicted reciprocal pressure $= -0.000077 + 0.000713$ height

Predictor	Coeff	SE Coeff	T	P
Constant	−0.00007670	0.00007813	−0.98	0.349
Height	0.00071307	0.00000260	274.30	0.000

s = 0.0001057 R − Sq = 100.0% R − Sq(adj) = 100.0%

or $\log(\widehat{\text{pressure}}) = 3.15 - 1.001 \log(\text{height})$

5. a)

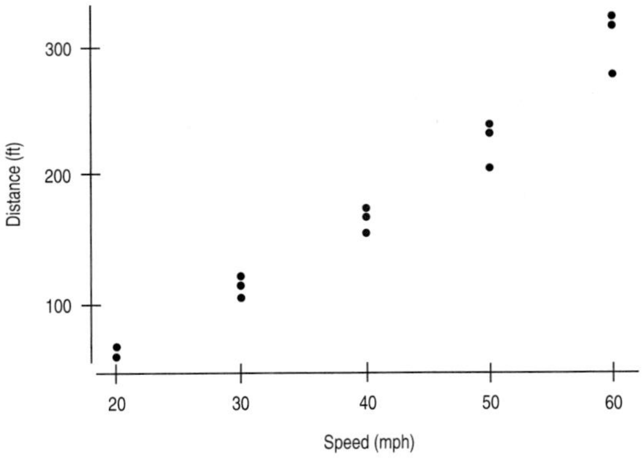

Predicted distance $= -65.9 + 5.98$ speed.
But residuals have a curved shape, so linear model is not appropriate.

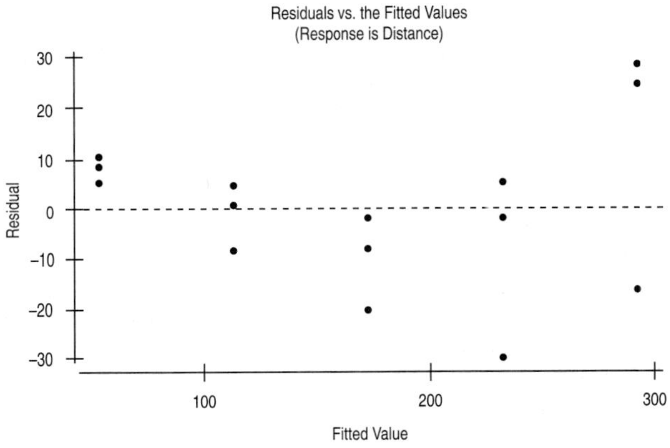

b)

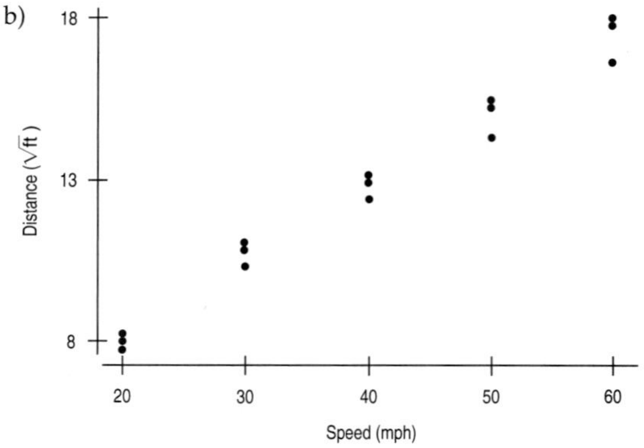

$\sqrt{\text{Distance}}$ linearizes the plot.

c) Predicted $\sqrt{\text{Distance}} = 3.30 + 0.235 \times$ Speed.

d) 263.4 feet.

e) 390.2 feet.

f) Fairly confident, since $R^2 = 98.4\%$, and s is small.

6. a)

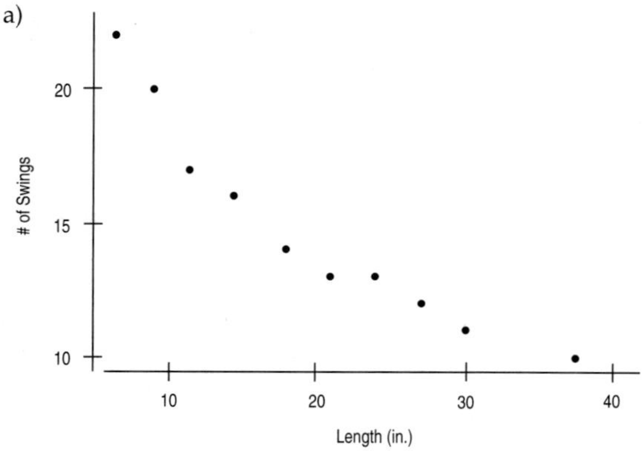

Relationship is curved, not straight.

b)

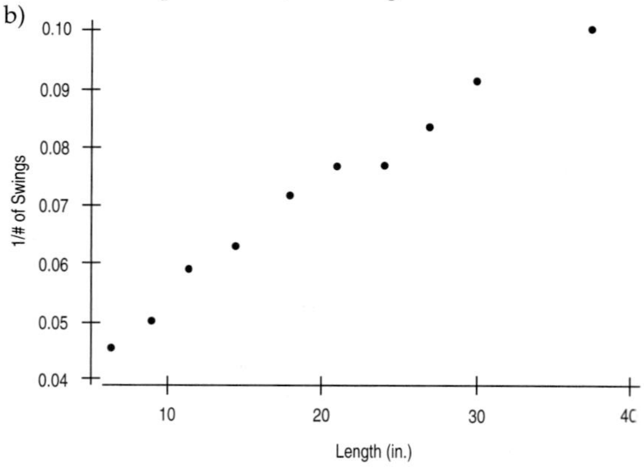

1/Swings makes the plot more linear.

c) Predicted $1/\text{Swings} = 0.0367 + 0.00176 \times$ Length.
or $\log(\widehat{\text{swings}}) = 1.721 - 0.453 \log(\text{length})$

d) 22.9 swings. e) 8.3 swings.

f) Fairly confident. These values are outside the data range, but not by a lot. Also, $R^2 = 98.1\%$.

7. a) Log Salary works well.

b) Predicted Log(Salary) $= -113.47 + 0.057 \times$ Year.

c) 31.18 million dollars.

8. a)

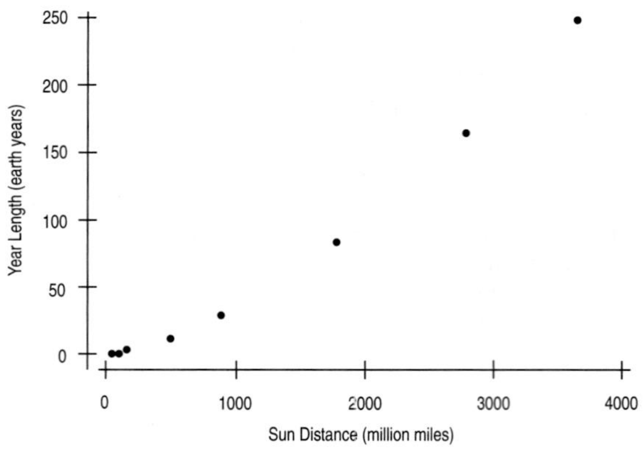

Concave upward curve.

b)

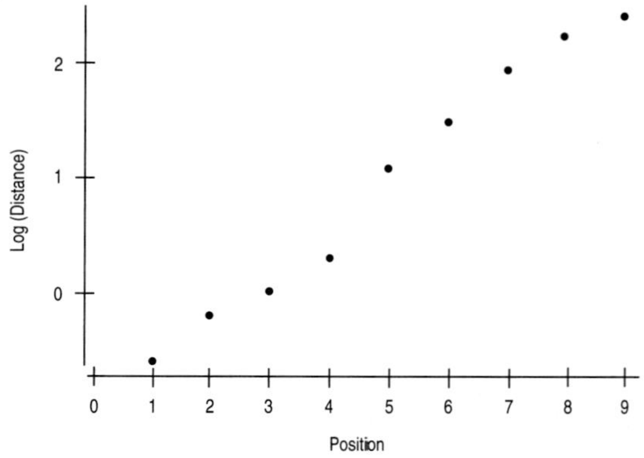

Taking log of both variables linearizes the plot.
Predicted log (length) $= -2.955 + 1.501$ log (Distance).

c) Fits perfectly. $R^2 = 1$.

9. a)

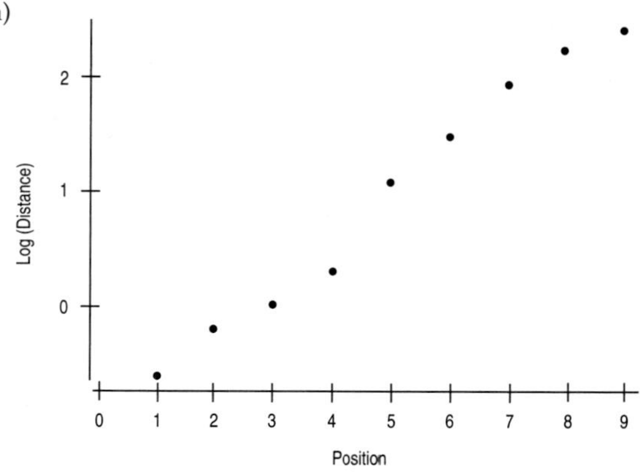

Log(Distance) against-position works pretty well.
Predicted log (Distance) $= 1.245 + 0.271 \times$ Position number.

b) Pluto's residual is not especially larger in the log scale. However, a model without Pluto predicts the 9th planet should be 5741 million miles. Pluto, at "only" 3666 million miles doesn't fit very well, giving support to the argument that Pluto doesn't behave like a planet.

10. Predicted log (Distance) = 1.306 + 0.233 × New Position. The linear relationship is very strong (R^2 = 99.4%). The new position works better for modeling log (Distance), since the other model had R^2 = 98.2%.

11. a) Predicted log (Distance) = 3.635. Pluto's log (Distance) is 3.564, and Quaoar's is 3.602. Quaoar is better predicted.
b) Predicted log (Distance) = 1.299 + 0.235 New Position. The R^2 has gone up to 99.5%. It's a slightly better fit.

12. Both models have high R^2, but Exercise 8 model has $R^2 = 1$. That indicates that perhaps we have found a physical law. If we find another system with the same pattern, it would add evidence for Titius-Bode "law"; otherwise, we would discount the law.

13. (Exercise 4) $\widehat{pressure} = 1413.3(height)^{-1.001}$

14. (Exercise 5) $\widehat{dist} = 0.05(speed)^2 + 1.96(speed) + 4.4$

15. (Exercise 6) $\widehat{swings} = 52.547(length)^{-0.453}$

16. (Exercise 7) $\widehat{sal} = (0.0000297)(1.14)^{year}$

17. (Exercise 8) $\widehat{year} = 0.00111(dist)^{1.501}$

18. (Exercise 9) $\widehat{dist} = 17.59(1.866)^{position}$

19. a)

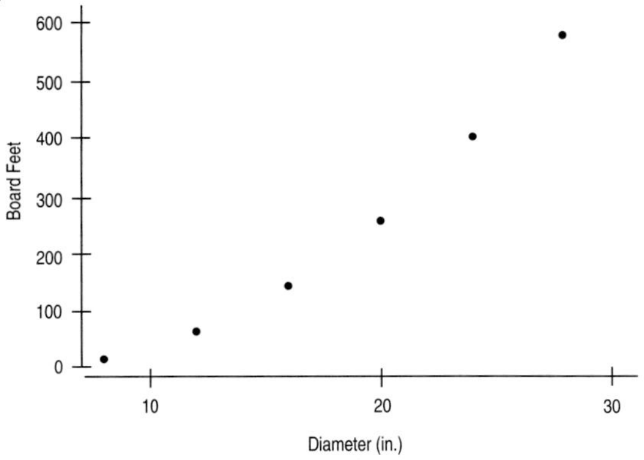

$\sqrt{\widehat{bdft}} = -4 + diam$ or $\widehat{bdft} = (diam)^2 - 8(diam) + 16.$
The model is exact.
b) 36 board feet
c) 1024 board feet

20. a) $\widehat{lift} = 179.92 + 2.4(class)$
b)

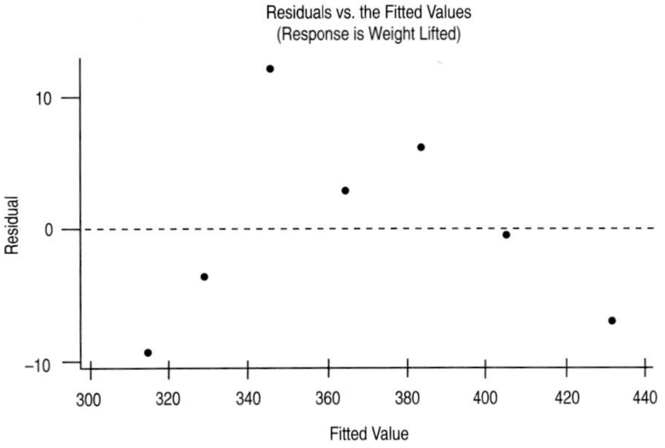

Residuals show a curved pattern; need a different model.
c) $\widehat{lift} = -0.025(\text{class})^2 + 6.42(\text{class}) + 25.59$
d) Less pattern in the residuals plot
e) Boevski's large positive residual indicates he lifted much more than expected.
f) $\widehat{lift} = -0.02(class)^2 + 5.8(class) + 45.5$
g) 346.47 kg.
h) He lifted 11 kg more than the model predicted.

21.

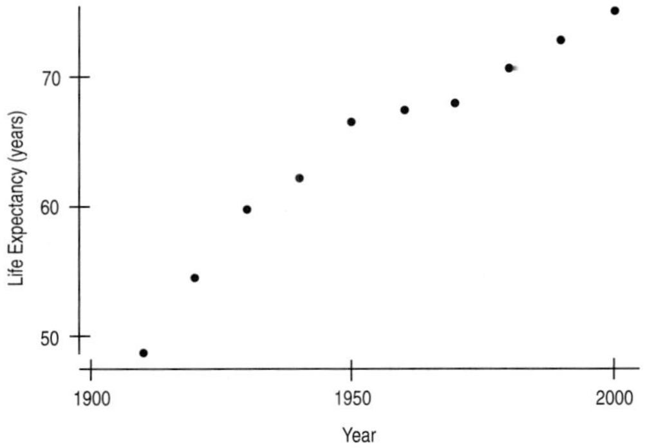

With the bend in the middle, a linear model may be okay. Predicted Life Expectancy = −454.94 + 0.266 × Year. Or try $\widehat{life} = 0.0000524(year)^3 - 0.310(year)^2 + 609.9(year) - 4000604.4$, though a cubic model seems unduly complicated and may not be justifiable here.

22. a) The linear model:
Predicted Diameter = 1.97 + 0.463 × Age
gives R^2 = 98%, but there is a clear pattern in the residuals.
A cubic model seems okay, but such models are risky.
$\widehat{diam} = 0.0023(age)^3 - 0.083(age)^2 + 1.31(age) - 0.197$
b) Less strong, since averages are less variable than individuals.

23. a) $\widehat{mpg} = -0.0114(speed)^2 + 1.158(speed) - 0.419$
b) Somewhat; the residuals seem reasonably scattered.
c) R-sq = 96%
d) No. People don't drive at consistent speeds.

24. a) $\widehat{\dfrac{1}{ave.\ wt}} = 1.603 + 0.00112(oranges)$

25. a) $\sqrt{\widehat{left}} = 8.39 - 0.070(age)$
or $\widehat{left} = .0052(age)^2 - 1.21(age) + 71.57$
b) 68.8 years or 69.5 years (depending on the model)

26. Not successfully. Relationship curves up and down; is not linearizable by methods of this chapter.

27. a) $\widehat{\log(journals)} = -686.76 + 0.346(year)$
b) 21497.04 journals.
c) Seems too high. Internet growth has exploded, but the model is unlikely to be very accurate.

PART II REVIEW

1. *% Large Classes*, 0.69.
% Under 20, −0.71.
% Graduating on Time, −0.51.
% Full time Faculty, 0.09.

2. a) If no meals are eaten together, the GPA is 2.73.
b) For each increase of 1 meal, the GPA increases by 0.11.
c) 3.15
d) The predicted GPA was higher than the observed value.

e) There is no indication that there is a causal relation. There may be lurking variables.

3. a) There does not appear to be a linear relationship.
b) Nothing, there is no reason to believe that the results for the Finger Lakes region are representative of the vineyards of the world.
c) Predicted Case Price= $92.77 + 0.567 \times$ Years.
d) Only 2.7% of the variation in case price is accounted for by the ages of vineyards. Most of that is due to two outliers. We are better off using the mean price rather than this model.

4. a) No, no apparent relationship.
b) There is one very large leverage point.
c) Increase. The cross point is extreme in the x direction and low on the y-axis, causing the correlation to weaken (become closer to 0).
d) The slope of the line would increase.

5. a) Predicted Twin Births $= -4316980 + 2214.19 \times$ Year.
b) For each 1-year increase in time, the number of twins born in a year increases by approximately 2214.2.
c) 115,835.2 births. The scatterplot appears to be somewhat linear, but there is some curvature in the pattern. There is no reason to believe that the increase will continue to be linear 5 years out from the data.
d) The residuals plot shows a definite curved pattern, so the relation is not linear.

6. a) 0.811
b) Predicted DJIA $= -603335 + 305.471 \times$ Year.
c) For each 1-year increase, the DOW increased by about 305.5 points on average.
d) The relationship does not appear to be linear, as the residuals have a definite pattern. The residuals do not appear to be independent.

7. a) -0.520
b) Negative, not strong, somewhat linear, but with more variation as pH increases.
c) The BCI would also be average.
d) The predicted BCI will be 1.56 SDs of BCI below the mean BCI.

8. a) Number of motorboat registrations.
b) The association is fairly strong linear, and has a positive direction.
c) 0.924
d) 85.4% of the variation in manatees killed is explained by the variation in powerboat registrations.
e) No, there is no reason to assign causality.

9. a) Predicted Manatee Deaths $= -45.9 + 0.132 \times$ Powerboat Registrations (in 1000s).
b) For each increase of 10,000 motorboat registrations, the number of manatees killed increases by 1.32.
c) If there were 0 motorboat registrations, the number of manatee deaths would be -45.9. This is obviously a silly extrapolation.
d) The predicted number is 67.4 deaths. The actual number of deaths was 81. The residual is $81 - 67.4 = 13.6$. The model underestimated the number of deaths by 13.6.
e) Negative residuals would suggest that the actual number of deaths was lower than the predicted number.
f) Over time the number of motorboat registrations has increased, and the number of manatee kills has increased. The trend may continue.

10. a) 73 points. b) 7 points. c) $r = 0.75$. d) 100 points.
e) The regression equation is designed to predict final exam scores based on midterm exam scores. You would need to find the regression equation to predict midterm scores based on final exam scores.
f) -85 points.
g) Increase. The point is unusual and has a high negative residual that would decease the correlation; removing it would increase the correlation and the R^2 value.
h) Slope will increase.

11. a) -0.984. b) 96.9%. c) 32.95 mph. d) 1.66 mph.
e) Slope will increase.
f) Correlation will weaken (become less negative).
g) Correlation is the same, regardless of units.

12. a) 0.473.
b) A weak linear association in a positive direction.
c) The actual score was higher than the predicted value for Monday.
d) The predicted Monday score would be (0.473) SDs or 2.37 points below the mean for Monday, or 34.9 points.
e) Predicted Monday Score $= 14.6 + 0.54 \times$ Friday Score.
f) 36.0 points.

13. a) Weight (but unable to verify linearity).
b) The direction of the relation is negative.
c) Weight accounts for 81.5% of the variation in mileage.

14. a) Displacement and Weight (but unable to verify linearity).
b) No. Large engines (higher displacement) weigh more, so the engine itself may influence the weight somewhat. More likely, heavy cars are equipped with larger engines because their added weight needs a larger engine (higher displacement) to drive.
c) The change in units will not affect the correlation.
d) The predicted fuel economy will be 0.786 SDs below the mean fuel economy.

15. a) Predicted Horsepower $= 3.50 + 34.314 \times$ Weight.
b) Thousands. For the equation to have predicted values between 60 and 160, the X values would have to be in thousands of pounds.
c) Yes. The residual plot does not show any pattern.
d) 115.0 horsepower.

16. Gender and colorblindness are both categorical variables, not quantitative. Correlation is meaningless for them, so we say the variables are associated.

17. a) The scatterplot shows a fairly strong linear relation in a positive direction. There seem to be two distinct clusters of data.
b) Predicted Interval $= 33.967 + 10.358 \times$ Duration.
c) As the duration of the previous eruption increases by 1 minute, the time between eruptions increases by about 10.4 minutes on average.
d) Since 77% of the variation in interval is accounted for by duration, and the error standard deviation is 6.16 minutes, the prediction will be relatively accurate.
e) 75.4 minutes.
f) A residual is the observed value minus the predicted value. So the residual $= 79 - 75.4 = 3.6$ minutes, indicating that the model underestimated the interval in this case.

18. a) Yes, the R^2 values indicate that 97.2% of the Indian crocodile length and 98% of the Australian crocodile length is explained by the head size.
b) The slopes of the regression equations are similar, as are the R^2 values.
c) The two models have different y-intercepts. It means that the Indian crocodile is smaller.

d) Predicted body length for the Indian crocodile is 389.4 cm but is 458.2 cm for the Australian croc. The skeleton was probably from an Indian crocodile.

19. a) $r = 0.888$. Although r is high, you must look at the scatterplot and verify that the relation is linear in form.

b)

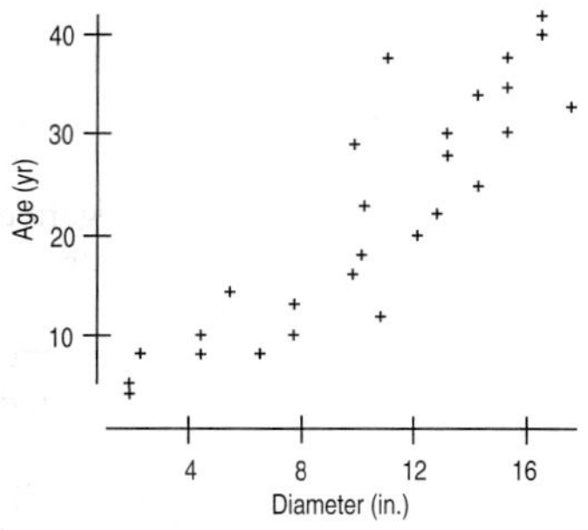

The association between diameter and age appears to be strong, somewhat linear, and positive.

c) Predicted Age $= -0.97 + 2.21 \times$ Diameter.

d)

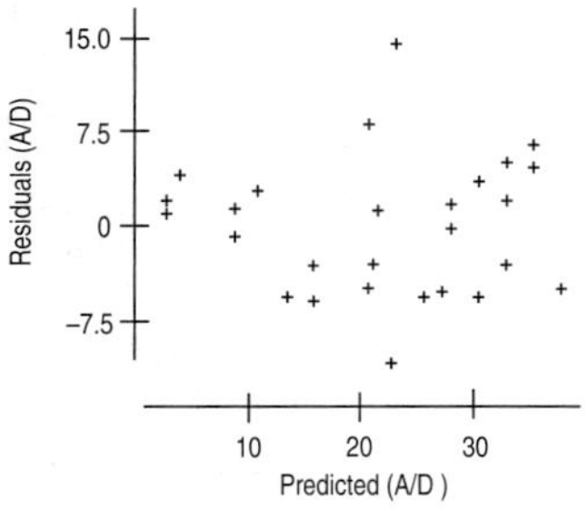

The residuals show a curved pattern (and two outliers).

e) The residuals for five of the seven largest trees (15 in. or larger) are positive, indicating that the predicted values underestimate the age.

20. a) Yes.

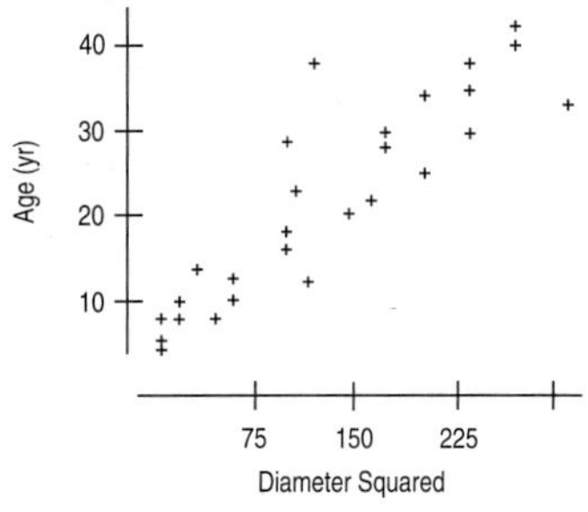

b) Predicted Age $= 7.24 + 0.11 \times$ Diameter Squared.

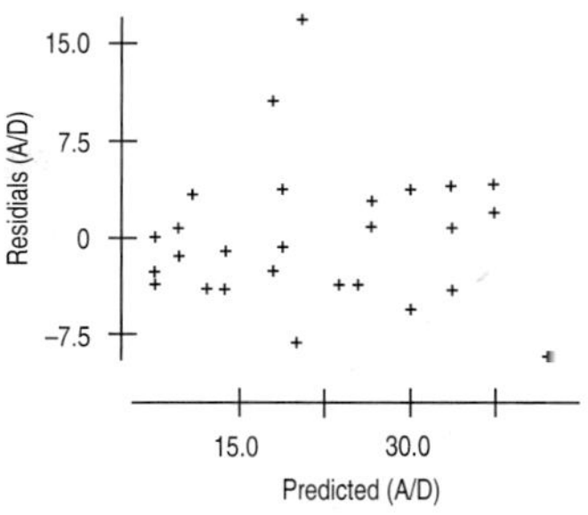

c) The residuals appear to be more randomly scattered and have less of a pattern. But there are still some points with large residuals.

d) 43.9 years old.

21. Most houses have areas between 1000 and 5000 square feet. Increasing 1000 square feet would result in either $1000(.008) = 8$ thousand dollars, $1000(.08) = 80$ thousand dollars, $1000(.8) = 800$ thousand dollars, or $1000(8) = 8000$ thousand dollars. Only \$80,000 is reasonable so the slope must be 0.08.

22.

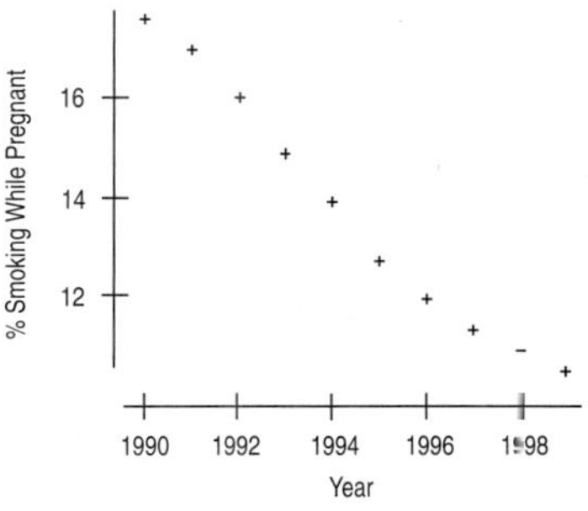

a) The association is very strong, somewhat linear, and negative. However, there is some curvature to the scatterplot.

b) -0.991.

c) Averaging increases the strength of the correlation making it more negative.

d) Predicted Percentage $= 1745.84 - 0.868 \times$ Year. For each year increase, the average percent of women smoking while pregnant decreases by 0.87%.

23. a) The model predicts % smoking from year, not the other way around.

b) Predicted Year $= 2009.9 - 1.130 \times$ % Smoking.

c) The smallest % smoking given is 10.4, and an extrapolation for $X = 0$ is probably too far from the given data. The prediction is not very reliable in spite of the strong correlation.

24. a) There is a very weak linear relationship between quality of service and tip size.

b) $R^2 = 1.21\%$, indicating that the variation in quality of service accounts for only about 1% of the variation in tip percentages.

25. The relation shows a negative direction, with a somewhat linear form, but perhaps with some slight curvature. There are several model outliers.

26. a) Latitude, since the correlation -0.848 is stronger (but unable to verify linearity).

b) The same.

c) The same. Changes in units do not change the shape of the association nor correlation of the data.
d) The predicted average January temperature would be 0.738 SDs below the mean average January temperature.

27. a) 71.9%.
b) As latitude increases, the January temperature decreases.
c) Predicted January Temperature = 108.80 − 2.111 × Latitude.
d) As the latitude increases by 1 degree, the average January temperature drops by about 2.11 degrees on average.
e) The y-intercept would indicate that the average January temperature is 108.8 when the latitude is 0. However, this is extrapolation and may not be meaningful.
f) 24.4 degrees.
g) The equation underestimates the average January temperature.

28. No. First, the R^2 indicates that only 4.6% of the variation in depression is accounted for by Internet use. That is a very low percentage. Even if it were higher, there may be lurking variables that explain the increase in both.

29. a) The scatterplot shows a strong, linear, positive association.
b) There is an association, but it is likely that training and technique have increased over time and affected both jump performances.
c) Neither; the change in units does not affect the correlation.
d) The long jumper would jump 0.92 SDs above the mean long jump on average.

30. a) Predicted High Jump = −17.93 + 0.321 × Long Jump.
b) As the long jump increases by 1 inch, the high jump increases by 0.32 inches on average.
c) 91.21 inches.
d) This equation is designed to predict high jump based on long jump. To predict the long jump, you would need the equation predicting long jump based on high jump.
e) Predicted Long Jump = 96.88 + 2.616 × High Jump.

31. a) No relation; the correlation would probably be close to 0.
b) The relation would have a positive direction and the correlation would be strong, assuming students were studying French in each grade level. Otherwise, no correlation.
c) No relation; correlation close to 0.
d) The relation would have a positive direction and the correlation would be strong, since vocabulary would increase with each grade level.

32. a) There is a strong, fairly linear, positive trend for the data; as the year of birth increases, the preterm birth rate increases.
b) The highest preterm birth rate is for mothers receiving adequate prenatal care utilization, and the lowest preterm birth rate is for mothers receiving inadequate prenatal care utilization. The slope is about the same for these relations. Mothers receiving intensive prenatal care utilization had more preterm births than mothers receiving inadequate prenatal care and fewer preterm births than mothers receiving adequate prenatal care; however, their rate of increase is higher.
c) No, there is undoubtedly an underlying variable explaining these differences. Perhaps the level of prenatal care was determined by the complications the mothers experienced during the pregnancy.

33. Predicted Calories = 560.7 − 3.08 × Time.
Each minute extra at the table results in 3.08 fewer calories being consumed on average. Perhaps the hungry children eat fast and eat more.

34. a) Predicted Gallons = 12451.2 − 6.2 × Year.
b) The model is designed to predict gallons based on the year. That question asks to predict the year based on the gallons.
c) Predicted Year = 2008.2 −0.16 × Gallons (in 1000s). Prediction is 2008.
d) The prediction in the wrong direction is close because the relationship is so strong. The line that minimizes the y-residuals also does a pretty good job at minimizing the x-residuals.

35. There seems to be a strong, positive, linear relationship with one high leverage point (Northern Ireland) that makes the overall R^2 quite low. Without that point, the R^2 increases to 61.5%. Of course, these data are averaged across thousands of households, and so the correlation appears to be higher than individuals would be. Any conclusions about individuals would be suspect.

36. a) Predicted Weight = −1971.26 + 1.091 × Year.
b) The scatterplot appears to have a linear trend in a positive direction; however, since the weights are averages, the linear trend would be stronger than for individual players.
c) 214.75 pounds. Possibly, but it is a 10-year extrapolation from a range of only 20 years.
d) 323.88 pounds. No, this is an extrapolation of 110 years, and the average weight seems absurd.
e) 1306.11 pounds. Absolutely ridiculous to have an average weight of over 1000 pounds. The prediction is an extrapolation of 1010 years.

37. a) 3.842 b) 501.187 c) 4.0

38. a) Predicted Weight = −1121.66 + 0.673×Year.
b) 2032.
c) No. That seems to be too much extrapolation for the model.

39. a) 30,818 pounds.
b) 1302 pounds.
c) 31,187.6 pounds.
d) I would be concerned about using this relation if we needed accuracy closer than 1000 pounds or so, as the residuals are more than ± 1000 pounds.
e) Negative residuals will be more of a problem, as the predicted weight would overestimate the weight of the truck; trucking companies might be inclined to take the ticket to court.

40. a) Symmetric distributions of x and y may help ensure that the residuals around a line through the data will be more symmetric and normally distributed. The re-expressed data will not have extreme outliers as well.
b) Yes. The scatterplot shows a linear trend in a positive direction. It has some moderate outliers in the x direction. The residuals plot shows some moderate residuals in the negative direction and some curvature, but the model using re-expressed data is surely better than the original data.
c) Predicted Log Profit = −0.11 + 0.648 × Log(Sales).
d) $124.43 million.

41. The original data are nonlinear with a significant curvature. Using reciprocal square root of diameter gave a scatterplot that is nearly linear.

$$1/\sqrt{\text{drain time}} = 0.0024 + 0.219 \text{ diameter.}$$

42. The scatterplot of Cost per Chip vs. Chips Produced has a significant curvature. Taking the log of Chips Produced and the log of Cost per-chip provided a nearly linear scatterplot.

log Predicted Cost per Chip = 2.67 − 0.502 × log Chips Produced.

43. The predicted values are (12, 774), (24, 738), (36, 702), (48, 666).
The residuals are (12, 26), (24, −58), (36, 38), (48, −6).
The squared residuals are (12, 676), (24, 3364), (36, 1444), (48, 36).

The "least squares" regression equation minimizes the sum of the squares of the residuals.

CHAPTER 11

1. Yes. You cannot predict the outcome beforehand.
2. The outcomes cannot be predicted beforehand. Each of the individual outcomes, numbers 00 through 36, should be equally likely.
3. A machine pops up numbered balls. If it were truly random, the outcome could not be predicted and the outcomes would be equally likely. It is random only if the balls generate numbers in equal frequencies.
4. Answers may vary. **Rolling one die or two dice:** If the dice are fair, then each outcome, 1 through 6, should be equally likely. **Spinning a spinner:** Each outcome should be equally likely requiring, but the spinner might be more likely to land on one outcome than another due to friction or design. **Shuffling cards and dealing a hand:** If the cards are shuffled adequately (7 times for riffle shuffling), the cards will be approximately equally likely.
5. a) The outcomes are not equally likely; for example, tossing 5 heads does not have the same probability as tossing 0 or 9 heads, but the simulation assumes they are equally likely.
   b) The even-odd assignment assumes that the player is equally likely to score or miss the shot. In reality, the likelihood of making the shot depends on the player's skill.
   c) Suppose a hand has 4 aces. This might be represented by 1, 1, 1, 1, and any other number. The likelihood for the first ace in the hand is not the same as for the second or third or fourth. But with this simulation, the likelihood is the same for each.
6. a) The numbers would represent the sums, but the sums are not all equally likely. The simulation assumes they are equally likely.
   b) The number of boys in a family of 5 children is not equally likely; for example, having a total of 5 boys is less likely than having 3 boys out of 5 children. The simulation assigns the same likelihood to each event.
   c) The likelihoods for out, single, double, triple, and home run are not the same, but the simulation assumes they are.
7. The conclusion should indicate that the simulation *suggests* that the average length of the line would be 3.2 people. Future results might not match the simulated results exactly.
8. The simulation *suggests* that 24% of the people might contract the disease. The simulation does not represent what happened but what might have happened.
9. Answers will vary, but average answer will be about 51.5%.
10. Answers will vary, but average answer will be about 5 boxes.
11. Answers will vary, but average answer will be about 26%.
12. Answers will vary, but few simulations will have any runs getting all 6 correct, leading us to conclude that the probability is very small. (The true probability is 0.00024.)
13. Answers will vary, but average answer will be about 1.9 tests.
14. Answers will vary, but average answer will be about 18%.
15. Answers will vary, but average answer will be about 1.24 points.
16. Answers will vary, but average answer will be 6.8 people.
17. Do the simulation in two steps. First simulate the payoffs. Then count until $500 is reached. Answers will vary, but average should be near 10.2 customers.
18. Answers will vary, but average answer will be about $37.
19. Answers will vary, but average answer will be about 3 children.
20. Answers will vary, but average answer will be slightly less than 6 children.
21. Answers will vary, but average answer will be about 7.5 rolls.
22. Answers will vary, but average answer will be about 2.7 rolls.
23. No, it will happen about 40% of the time.
24. Answers will vary, but average answer will be about 39%.
25. Answers will vary, but average answer will be about 37.5%.
26. Answers will vary, but average answer will be about 37.5%.
27. 3 women will be selected about 7.8% of the time.
28. Answers will vary, but average answer will be about 38.5%.
29. Answers will vary, but average answer will be about 28 envelopes.

CHAPTER 12

1. a) Population—Human resources directors of Fortune 500 companies.
   b) Parameter—Proportion who don't feel surveys intruded on their work day.
   c) Sampling Frame—list of HR directors at Fortune 500 companies.
   d) Sample—23% who responded.
   e) Method—Questionnaire mailed to all (nonrandom).
   f) Bias—Nonresponse. Hard to generalize because who responds is related to the question itself.
2. a) Population—U.S. adults.
   b) Parameter—Proportion who feel marijuana should be legalized for medicinal purposes.
   c) Sampling Frame—None given; potentially all people with access to Web site.
   d) Sample—Those visiting the Web site who responded.
   e) Method—Voluntary response (no randomization employed).
   f) Bias—Voluntary response sample. Those who visit the Web site and respond may be predisposed to a particular answer.
3. a) Population—All U.S. adults.
   b) Parameter—Proportion who have used and benefited from alternative medicine.
   c) Sampling Frame—all Consumer's Union subscribers.
   d) Sample—Those who responded (random).
   e) Method—Questionnaire to all (nonrandom).
   f) Bias—Nonresponse. Those who respond may have strong feelings one way or another.
4. a) Population—U. S. citizens.
   b) Parameter—Type of content that bothers most on TV.
   c) Sampling Frame—All U.S. adults.
   d) Sample—1423 randomly selected citizens.
   e) Method—Not clear.
   f) Bias—probably not biased. Conclusions could be generalized.
5. a) Population—Adults .
   b) Parameter—Proportion who think drinking and driving is a serious problem.
   c) Sampling Frame—Bar patrons.
   d) Sample—Every 10th person leaving the bar.
   e) Method—Systematic sampling.

f) Bias—Those interviewed had just left a bar. They probably think drinking and driving is less of a problem than do adults in general.

6. a) Population—City voters.
b) Parameter—Not clear; percentages of voters favoring various issues?
c) Sampling Frame—All city residents.
d) Sample—Cluster sample; one block from each district.
e) Method—Convenience sample within each cluster.
f) Bias—Parameter(s) of interest not clear. Sampling within clusters is not random and may bias results.

7. a) Population—Soil around a former waste dump.
b) Parameter—Concentrations of toxic chemicals.
c) Sampling Frame—Accessible soil around the dump.
d) Sample—16 soil samples.
e) Method—Not clear.
f) Bias—Don't know if soil samples were randomly chosen. If not, may be biased toward more or less polluted soil.

8. a) Population—Cars.
b) Parameter—Proportion with up-to-date registration, insurance, and safety inspections.
c) Sampling Frame—All cars on that road.
d) Sample—Those actually stopped by roadblock.
e) Method—Cluster sample of location; census within cluster.
f) Bias—Time of day and location may not be representative of all cars. Other than that, should be able to estimate proportion of all cars.

9. a) Population—Snack food bags.
b) Parameter—Weight of bags, proportion passing inspection.
c) Sampling Frame—All bags produced each day.
d) Sample—Bags in 10 randomly selected cases, 1 bag from each case for inspection
e) Method—Multistage sampling.
f) Bias—Should be unbiased.

10. a) Population—Dairy farms.
b) Parameter—Proportion passing inspection.
c) Sampling Frame—All dairy farms?
d) Sample—Not clear. Perhaps a random sample of farms, and then milk within each farm?
e) Method—Multistage sampling.
f) Bias—Should be unbiased if farms and milk at each farm are randomly selected.

11. a) Voluntary response. Only those who both see the ad *and* feel stongly enough will respond.
b) Cluster sampling. One school may not be typical of all.
c) Attempted census. Will have nonresponse bias.
d) Stratified sampling with follow-up. Should be unbiased.

12. a) Voluntary response. Only those who see the show *and* feel strongly will call.
b) Possibly more representative than part a, but only strongly motivated parents go to PTA meetings.
c) Multistage sampling with cluster sample within each school. Probably a good design if most of the parents in the class respond.
d) Systematic sampling. Probably a reasonable design.

13. a) Answers will definitely differ. Question 1 will probably get many "No" answers, while Question 2 will get many "Yes" answers. This is wording bias.
b) "Do you think standardized tests are appropriate for deciding whether a student should be promoted to the next grade?" (Other answers will vary.)

14. a) Biased toward yes because of "pollute." "Should companies be responsible for any costs of environmental clean-up?"
b) Biased towards no because of "old enough to serve in the military." "Do you think the drinking age should be lowered from 21?"
c) Seems unbiased.
d) Biased toward yes because of "great tradition." Better to ask, "Do you favor continued funding for the space program?"

15. a) Not everyone has an equal chance. People with unlisted numbers, people without phones, and those at work cannot be reached.
b) Generate random numbers and call at random times.
c) Under the original plan, those families in which one person stays home are more likely to be included. Under the second plan, many more are included. People without phones are still excluded.
d) It improves the chance of selected households being included.
e) This takes care of phone numbers. Time of day may be an issue. People without phones are still excluded.

16. Cell phones are more likely to be used by higher income individuals. This will cause an undercoverage bias. As cell phones grow in use, this problem will be lessened.

17. a) Answers will vary.
b) Your own arm length. Parameter is your own arm length; population is all possible measurements of it.
c) Population is now the arm lengths of your friends. The average estimates the mean of these lengths.
d) Probably not. Friends are likely to be of the same age, and not very diverse, or representative of the larger population.

18. a) Mean gas mileage for the last six fill-ups.
b) Mean gas mileage for the vehicle.
c) Conditions of late may not be typical.
d) Mean gas mileage for all cars of this make and model.

19. a) Assign numbers 001 to 120 to each order. Use random numbers to select 10 transactions to examine.
b) Sample proportionately within each type. (Do a stratified random sample.)

20. a) Most likely that all laborers are selected, no managers, and few foremen. Bias may be introduced because the company itself is conducting the survey.
b) Assign a number from 001 to 439 to each employee. Use a random number table or software to select the sample.
c) Still heavily favors the laborers.
d) Stratify by job type (proportionately to the members in each).
e) Answers will vary. Assign numbers 01 to 14 to each person; use a random number table or software to do the selection.

21. a) Select three cases at random, then select one jar randomly from each case.
b) Use random numbers to choose 3 cases from numbers 61 through 80; then use random numbers between 1 and 12 to select the jar from each case.
c) No. Multistage sampling.

22. What conclusions they may be able to make will depend on whether fish with discolored scales are equally likely to be caught as those without. It also depends on the level of compliance by fisherman. If fish are not equally likely to be caught, or fishermen are more disposed to bring discolored fish, the results will be biased.

23. a) Depends on the yellow page listings used. If from regular (line) listings, this is fair if all doctors are listed. If from ads, probably not, as those doctors may not be typical.

b) Not appropriate. This cluster sample will probably contain listings for only one or two business types.

24. a) Petition may bias people to say they support the playground. Also, many may not be home on Saturday afternoon.
b) If the food at the largest cafeteria is representative, this should be OK. However, those who really don't like the food won't be eating there.

CHAPTER 13

1. a) Experiment.
b) Bipolar disorder patients.
c) Omega-3 fats from fish oil, two levels.
d) 2 treatments.
e) Improvement (fewer symptoms?).
f) Design not specified.
g) Blind (due to placebo), unknown if double-blind.
h) Individuals with bipolar disease improve with high-dose omega-3 fats from fish oil.

2. a) Experiment.
b) Men aged 60 to 75.
c) Exercise (1 level).
d) 1 treatment, 16-week, high-intensity resistance training twice a week.
e) Strength levels pre- and postexercise program.
f) Pre- and posttest–matched design.
g) Not blinded.
h) Applies only to men 60 to 75 who participate in similar exercise programs. However, since there is no random assignment, other factors might have explained the difference in strength.

3. a) Observational study.
b) Prospective.
c) Men and women with moderately high blood pressure and normal blood pressure, unknown selection process.
d) Memory and reaction time.
e) As there is no random assignment, there is no way to know that high blood pressure *caused* subjects to do worse on memory and reaction time tests. A lurking variable may also be the cause.

4. a) Observational study.
b) Prospective.
c) Disabled women aged 65 and older with and without a vitamin B12 deficiency, unknown selection process.
d) Suffering severe depression.
e) As there is no random assignment, there is no way to know that the deficiency caused the severe depression.

5. a) Observational study.
b) Retrospective.
c) Swedish men, unknown selection process;
d) Risk of kidney cancer.
e) As there is no random assignment, there is no way to know that the overweight or high blood pressure caused the higher risk for kidney cancer.

6. a) Experiment.
b) 459 subjects.
c) Diet with 3 levels.
d) 3 treatments (3 groups—but only one diet and one control group were described).
e) Systolic blood pressure.
f) Completely randomized.
g) Not blinded.
h) Indicates that the DASH diet appears to lower systolic blood pressure.

7. a) Experiment.
b) Postmenopausal women.
c) Alcohol—2 levels; blocking variable—estrogen supplements (2 levels).
d) 2 treatments $\times$ 2 blocking levels.
e) Increase in estrogen levels.
f) Blocked.
g) Not blind.
h) Indicates that alcohol comsumption *for those taking estrogen supplements* may increase estrogen levels.

8. a) Experiment.
b) People suffering from insomnia.
c) 2 factors: desserts and exercise (2 levels each).
d) 4 treatments.
e) Improvement in ability to sleep.
f) Completely randomized.
g) Not blind.
h) Insomniacs who exercise and refrain from desserts will experience improved ability to sleep.

9. a) Experiment.
b) Locations in a garden.
c) 1 factor: traps (2 levels).
d) 2 treatments.
e) Number of bugs in the trap.
f) Blocked by location.
g) Not blind.
h) One type of trap is more effective than the other.

10. a) Observational study.
b) Retrospective.
c) Women exposed to dioxin from an industrial accident.
d) Risk of breast cancer.
e) As there is no random assignment, there is no way to know that the dioxin levels caused the increase in breast cancer; there may have been lurking variables that were not identified.

11. a) Observational study.
b) Retrospective.
c) Women in Finland, unknown selection process with data from church records.
d) Lifespans.
e) As there is no random assignment, there is no way to know that having sons or daughters shortens or lengthens the lifespan of mothers.

12. a) Observational study.
b) Retrospective.
c) Women; unknown selection process with information taken from work histories.
d) Risk of breast cancer.
e) As there is no random assignment, there is no way to know that working nights caused breast cancer; there may be confounding variables not identified in the study.

13. a) Observational.
b) Prospective.
c) People with or without depression, unknown selection process.
d) Crying response to sad situations.
e) There is no apparent difference in crying response (to sad movies) for depressed and nondepressed groups.

14. a) Experiment.
b) People exposed to cold virus.

c) 1 factor: herbal treatment (2 levels).
d) 2 treatments.
e) Severity of cold symptoms.
f) No discussion of randomness.
g) Blind, as subjects did not know if they received the herbal treatment or the placebo. Not clear if it was double-blind.
h) There is no indication that the herbal treatment is effective.

15. a) Experiment.
b) Rats.
c) 1 factor: sleep deprivation; four levels.
d) 4 treatments.
e) Glycogen content in the brain.
f) No discussion of randomness.
g) Blinding is not discussed.
h) The conclusion could be that rats deprived of sleep have significantly lower glycogen levels and may need sleep to restore that brain energy fuel. Extrapolating to humans would be very speculative.

16. a) Experiment.
b) Racing greyhounds.
c) 1 factor, diet with 3 levels.
d) 3 treatments.
e) Speed.
f) Random assignment to order of diets; matched design before and after diet.
g) No blinding.
h) Greyhounds who eat diets high in vitamin C run more slowly.

17. a) Experiment.
b) People experiencing migraines.
c) 2 factors (pain reliever and water temperature), 2 levels each.
d) 4 treatments.
e) Level of pain relief.
f) Completely randomized over 2 factors.
g) Blind, as subjects did not know if they received the pain medication or the placebo, but not blind, as the subjects will know if they are drinking regular or ice water.
h) It may indicate whether pain reliever alone or in combination with ice water gives pain relief, but patients are not blinded to ice water, so placebo effect may also be the cause of any relief seen due to ice water.

18. a) Experiment.
b) Inactive dogs.
c) 1 factor: dog food (assuming amount of food to be determined by weight or size of dog)(2 levels).
d) 2 treatments.
e) Weight.
f) Blocked by size of breed.
g) Blinded, assuming dog owners do not know which food the dog is receiving.
h) Assuming the dog owners followed the prescribed feeding levels, there could be a conclusion as to whether or not the dog food helped maintain healthy weight.

19. Answers may vary. Use a random number generator to randomly select 24 numbers from 1 to 24 without replication. Assign the first 8 numbers to the first group, the second 8 numbers to the second group, and the third group of 8 numbers to the third group.

20. Answers may vary. Use a random number generator to randomly select 24 numbers from 1 to 24 without replication. Assign the first group of 4 numbers to the first treatment (no fertilizer, natural watering), the second group of 4 numbers to the second treatment (no fertilizer, daily water), the third group of 4 numbers to the third treatment (half fertilizer, natural watering), and so on to the sixth treatment.

21. a) The differences among the Mozart and quiet groups were more than would have been expected from ordinary sampling variation.
b)

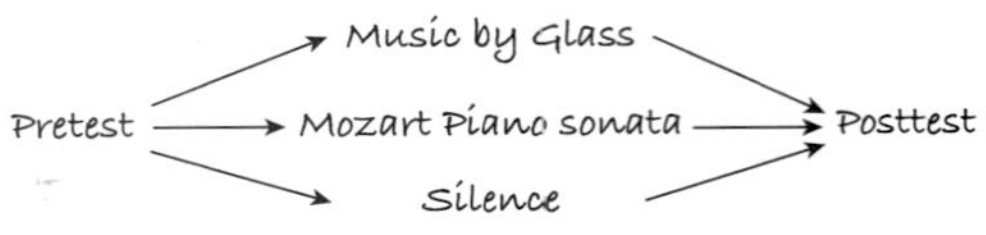

c) The Mozart group seems to have the smallest median difference and thus the *least* improvement, but there does not appear to be a significant difference.
d) No, if anything there is less improvement, but the difference does not seem significant compared with the usual variation.

22. Answers may vary. Suppose you select the next 12 batches of sake for the experiment. Divide the yeast into two parts. For each batch, play Mozart for half the yeast and no Mozart for the other half. When the sake is done, have trained sake testers (who don't know the which experimental treatment was applied) taste samples from each group and rate the sake. Compare the ratings for the Mozart and the non-Mozart sake. Try to keep as many other variables as possible under control (type of yeast, size of batch, etc.)

23. a) Observational. Randomly select a group of children, ages 10 to 13, have them taste the cereal, and ask if they like the cereal.
b) Answers may vary. Get volunteers age 10 to 13. Each volunteer will taste both cereals, randomizing the order in which they taste them. Compare the percentage of favorable ratings for each cereal.

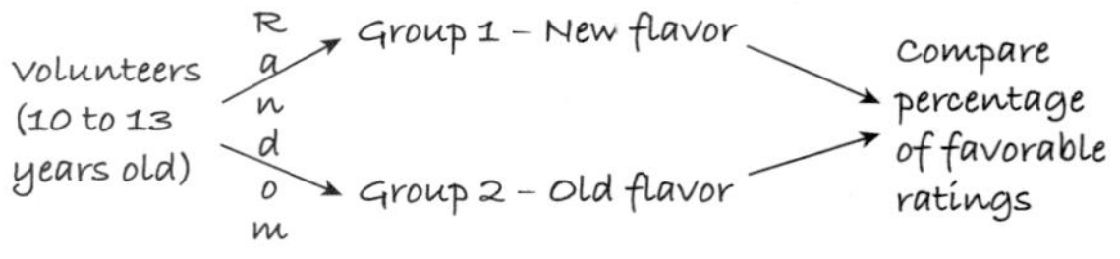

c) Answers may vary. From the volunteers, identify the children who watch Frump and identify the children who do not watch Frump. Use a blocked design to reduce variation in cereal preference that may be associated with watching the Frump cartoon.

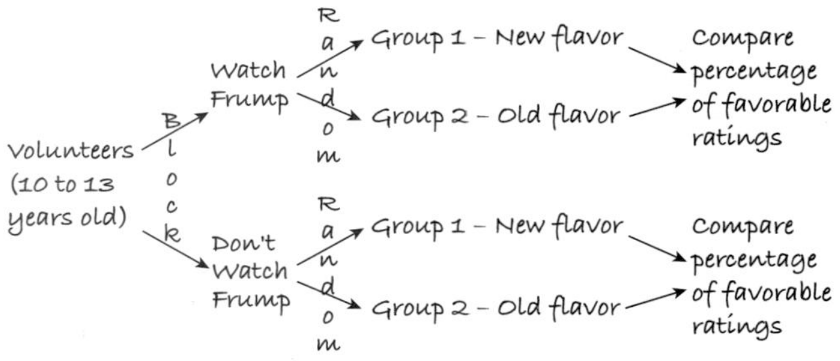

24. Use a retrospective observational study. For example, collect records from a random selection of police and emergency room logs for the past 3 years. Find the number of cases for the days when there is a full moon, when there is a waxing moon, a waning moon, and when the moon is nearly dark. Compare the numbers for each group.

25. a) Observational, prospective study.
b) The supposed relation between health and wine consumption

might be explained by the confounding variables of income and education.

c) None of these. While the variables have a relation, there is no causality indicated for the relation.

26. a) The difference in the depression rates for the two groups is greater than would be expected by natural sampling variation.

b) Observational study. There was no experimental treatment.

c) The difference could be explained by lurking variables. Perhaps swimmers are more affluent (can afford a membership at the Y or have access to a pool), or perhaps depressed people tend to swim less.

d) Answers may vary. Give the subjects a test to measure depression. Then randomly assign the 120 subjects to one of three groups: the control group (no exercise program), the anaerobic exercise group, and the aerobic exercise group. Monitor subjects' exercise (have them report to a particular gym or pool). At the end of 12 weeks, administer the depression test again. Compare the postexercise and preexercise depression scores.

27. a) Arrange the 20 containers in 20 separate locations. Use a random number generator to identify the 10 containers that should be filled with water.

b) Guessing, the dowser should be correct about 50% of the time. A record of 60% (12 out of 20) does not appear to be significantly different.

c) Answers may vary. You would need to see a high level of success—say, 90% to 100%, that is, 18 to 20 correct.

28. Answers may vary. Randomly select half of the patients who agree to the study to get large doses of vitamin E after surgery. Give the other half a similar-looking placebo pill. Monitor their progress, recording the time until they have reached an easily agreed upon level of healing. Have the evaluating doctor blinded to whether the patient received the placebo or not. Compare the number of days until recovery of the two groups.

29. Randomly assign half the reading teachers in the district to use each method. Students should be randomly assigned to teachers as well. Make sure to block both by school and grade (or control grade by using only one grade). Construct an appropriate reading test to be used at the end of the year and compare scores.

30.

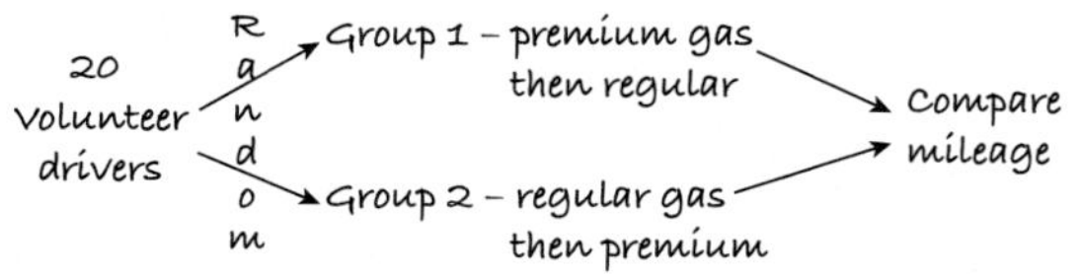

Answers may vary. This experiment has 1 factor (type of gasoline), at 2 levels (premium and regular), resulting in two treatments. The response variable is gas mileage. An experiment diagram for a matched design appears above. Have each of the volunteers use each kind of gas for a month. Randomly assign 10 of them to use regular first, the other 10 to use premium first. Ask them to keep driving logs (the number of miles driven and the gallons of gasoline) for each month. Compare the differences in the fuel economy for the two kinds of gasoline.

31. a) They mean that the difference is higher than they would expect from normal sampling variability.

b) An observational study.

c) No. Perhaps the differences are due to some confounding variable (like people are more likely to engage in riskier behaviors on the weekend) rather than due to the day of admission.

d) Perhaps people have more serious accidents and traumas on weekends and are thus more likely to die as a result.

32. a) Answers may vary. Randomly assign the eight patients to either the current medication or the new medication. Have nurses assess the degree of shingles involvement for the patient. Ask patients to rate their pain levels. Administer the medications for a prescribed time. Have nurses reassess the degree of shingles involvement. Ask patients to rate their pain levels post medication. Compare the improvement levels for each group.

b) 41098 18329 78458 31685 55259

Let A = 1, B = 2 . . . H = 8.

Assign the first four randomly selected to the first group, the remainder to the second. So Group 1 is D, A, H, C and Group 2 is B, E, F, G.

c) Assuming that the ointments look alike, it would be possible to blind the experiment for the subject and for the administrator of the treatment.

d) A block design with factors for gender and for ointment would be appropriate. Subjects would be randomly assigned to each treatment group in the blocked design.

33. Answers may vary. This experiment has 1 factor (pesticide), at 3 levels (pesticide A, pesticide B, no pesticide), resulting in 3 treatments. The response variable is the number of beetle larvae found on each plant. Randomly select a third of the plots to be sprayed with pesticide A, a third with pesticide B, and a third to be sprayed with no pesticide (since the researcher also wants to know whether the pesticides even work at all). To control the experiment, the plots of land should be as similar as possible, with regard to amount of sunlight, water, proximity to other plants, etc. If not, plots with similar characteristics should be blocked together. If possible, use some inert substance as a placebo pesticide on the control group, and do not tell the counters of the beetle larvae which plants have been treated with pesticides. After a given period of time, count the number of beetle larvae on each plant and compare the results.

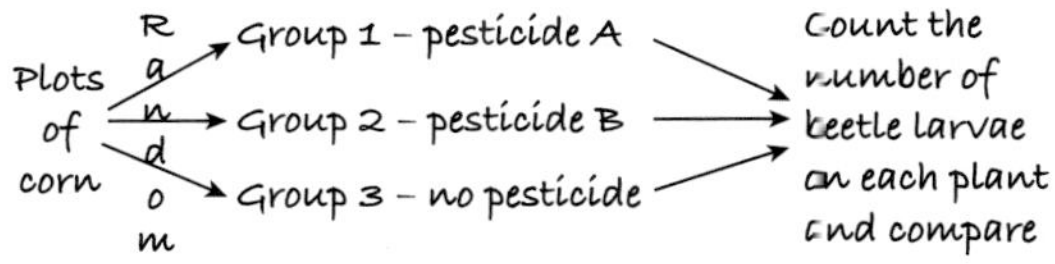

34. a) The students were not randomly assigned. Those who signed up for the prep course may be a special group whose scores would have improved anyway.

b) Answers may vary. Find a group of volunteers who are willing to participate. Give all volunteers the SAT exam. Randomly assign the subjects to the review or no review group. Give the tutoring to the one group. After a reasonable time, retest both groups. Check to see that the tutored group had a significant improvement in scores when compared with the no review group.

c) After the volunteers have taken the first SAT exam, separate the volunteers into blocks of low, average, and high SAT exam score performance. Now assign half of each block to the review and half to the no review groups. Give the tutoring. Now retest all groups. Compare the differences between treatments for each block.

35. Answers may vary. Find a group of volunteers. Each volunteer will be required to shut off the machine with his or her left hand and the right hand. Randomly assign the left or right hand to be used first. Complete the first attempt for the whole group. Now repeat the experiment with the alternate hand. Check the differences in time for the left and right hands.

36. Answers may vary. There are two factors: temperature of the water and wash cycle. Since each factor has 2 levels, there are 4 treatment groups (hot-reg., cold-reg., hot-del., cold-del.). It would be nice to have 32 shirts, but equal numbers of shirts in each group is not necessary. Randomly assign shirts to each of the 4 treatment groups. Rate the level of cleaning for the grass-stained shirts. Compare the 4 groups and determine the best use of the product.

PART III REVIEW

1. Observational prospective study. Indications of behavior differences can be seen in the two groups. May show a link between premature birth and behavior, but there may be lurking variables involved.
2. Observational retrospective study. Can conclude there *may* be a link between tea drinking and survival after a heart attack. But lurking variables may also be involved.
3. Experiment, matched by gender and weight, randomization within blocks of two pups of same gender and weight. Factor is type of diet. Treatments are low-calorie diet and allowing the dog to eat all it wants. Response variable is length of life. Can conclude that, on average, dogs with a lower-calorie diet live longer.
4. Random sample. Population is all homes on the property tax list. Parameter is level of radon contamination. Procedure is probably a stratified random sample. May make inference from sample to general population about radon levels.
5. Observational prospective study. Indicates folate *may* help in reducing colon cancer for those with family histories of the disease.
6. Observational retrospective study. Indicates that during past 47 years first flowering has gotten earlier.
7. Sampling. Probably a simple random sample, although may be stratified by type of firework. Population is all fireworks produced each day. Parameter is proportion of duds. Can determine if the day's production is ready for sale.
8. Experiment, though there is no indication of a control group or differing treatments. Cosmetics *may* damage male reproductive systems in laboratory animals. Extrapolating to humans is risky.
9. Observational retrospective study. Living near strong electromagnetic fields may be associated with more leukemia than normal. Lurking variables, such as socioeconomic level, may be involved.
10. Observational retrospective study. Indicates no long-term risk of prostate cancer due to vasectomy.
11. Experiment. Blocked by sex of rat. Randomization is not specified. Factor is type of hormone given. Treatments are leptin and insulin. Response variable is lost weight. Can conclude that hormones can help suppress appetites in rats, and the type of hormone varies by gender.
12. Experiment. Factors are glaze type and temperature. Treatments are combinations of 4 glaze types and 3 temperatures. Response is age appearance of the pottery. Assuming an unbiased evaluator, can make a conclusion about best combination of glaze and temperature.
13. Experiment. Factor is gene therapy. Hamsters were randomized to treatments. Treatments were gene therapy or not. Response variable is heart muscle condition. Can conclude that gene therapy is beneficial (at least in hamsters).
14. Observational study (neither retrospective nor prospective). There seems to be a relationship between eye size and time of singing.
15. Sampling. Population is all oranges on the truck. Parameter is proportion of unsuitable oranges. Procedure is probably simple random sampling. Can conclude whether or not to accept the truckload.
16. Sampling. Population is all bottle cap seals. Parameter is proportion with inadequate seals. Procedure is probably simple random sampling. Can conclude if the bottling process is all right or needs to be adjusted.
17. Observational prospective study. Physically fit men may have a lower risk of death from cancer.
18. Experiment. Subjects blocked by calculus or not for analysis. Probably no randomization (students self-select into sections). Factor is software usage. Treatments are use of software or not. Response variable is final exam score. Can decide if computer software is beneficial, and if so, is there a difference between the calculus and the noncalculus groups.
19. Answers will vary. This is a simulation problem. Using a random digits table or software, call 0–4 a loss, and 5–9 a win for the gambler on a game. Use blocks of 5 digits to simulate a week's pick.
20. a) Answers will vary. This is a simulation problem. Using a random digits table or software, obtain 3 numbers between 01 and 20 for your pick, then 5 others between 0 and 20. Count how many matches.
    b) With more numbers to choose from, the odds of winning go down dramatically.
21. Answers will vary.
22. a) Experiment. Treatments were actively imposed, rats were randomized, there was control (rats with no radio wave exposure), and they used many rats.
    b) The differences in brain tumors were small enough that they could be explained by sampling variability.
    c) May cause bias of some sort, intended or not.
23. a) Experiment. Actively manipulated candy giving, diners were randomly assigned treatments, control group was those with no candy, lots of dining parties.
    b) It depends on when the decision was made. If early in the meal, the server may give better treatment to those who will receive candy—biasing the results.
    c) A difference in response so large it cannot be attributed to natural sampling variability.
24. a)

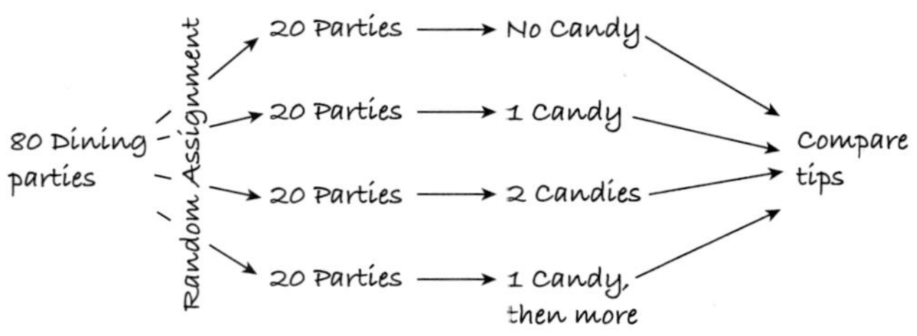

    b) One factor (candy) with 4 levels (none, one, two, or one then another).
    c) 4.
    d) Tip percentage.
    e) Probably blinded (diners probably weren't aware they were in an experiment), but not double blinded.

f) If "randomization" is done early in the meal, she may treat some better than others.

25. a) Voluntary response. Only those who feel strongly will pay for the 900 phone call.
b) "If it would help future generations live a longer, healthier life, would you be in favor of human cloning?"

26. a) Water (quality and temperature) and material can vary. Results may be influenced by these confounding variables.
b) Unrealistic conditions. This won't say how Sparklekleen works in normal situations.
c) Might work, but if all the swatches were stained at the same time, the stains on the later swatches will have more time to "set in," causing bias against Sparklekleen.
Other variables (changes in water temperature or pressure) won't be randomized.
d) No guarantee that conditions are comparable.

27. a) Simulation results will vary. Average will be around 5.8 points.
b) Simulation results will vary. Average will also be around 5.8 points.
c) Answers will vary.

28. a) 10.6% chance to break at 900 pounds or less.
b) Simulation results will vary. Use groups of three digits to simulate each rivet. For every one that is less than "106" denote as a failed rivet. Count how many rivets you need until 3 failures are reached.

29. a) Yes.
b) No. Residences without phones are excluded. Residences with more than one phone had a higher chance.
c) No. People who respond to the survey may be of age but not be registered voters.
d) No. Households who answered the phone may be more likely to have someone at home when the phone call was generated. These may not be representative of all households.

30. a) A difference in response so large it cannot be attributed to natural sampling variability.
b) More likely, younger looking individuals are more sexually active than older ones. We have no means of comparison (different levels of sexual activity in people of the same age, for example).

31. a) Does not prove it. There may be other confounding variables. Only way to prove this would be to do a controlled experiment.
b) Alzheimer's usually shows up late in life. Perhaps smokers have died of other causes before Alzheimer's can be seen.
c) An experiment would be unethical. One could design a prospective study in which groups of smokers and nonsmokers are followed for many years and the incidence of Alzheimer's is tracked.

32. a) Randomized block experiment.
b) No—in an experiment we are looking for differences in response to treatments, not trying to generalize to all adults.
c) A sugar pill may affect digestion, confounding the experiment.

33.

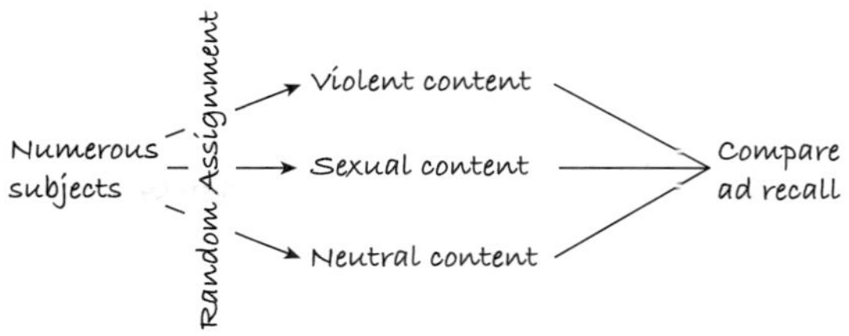

Numerous subjects will be randomly assigned to see shows with violent, sexual or neutral content. They will see the same commercials. After the show, they will be interviewed for their recall of brand names in the commercials.

34. a) *Who*—900 Englishmen. *What*—reasons they go to a pub. *Why*—Kaliber alcohol-free beer wants to know. *When*—not stated. *Where*—England. *How*—survey (sampling method not specified).
b) Englishmen.
c) How those interviewed were chosen.
d) Probably convenience samples of those in pubs.
e) The study was financed by an alcohol-free beer.

35. a) May have been a simple random sample, but given the relative equality in age groups, may have been stratified.
b) 35.1%.
c) We don't know. Perhaps cell phones or unlisted numbers were excluded and Democrats have more (or fewer) of those. Probably OK, though.
d) Do party affiliations differ for different age groups?

36. a) Nonresponse bias by conservatives.
b) U.S. adults.
c) Results do not total 100%.
d) Observed differences are of the same size one might expect from natural sampling variability.

37. The factor in the experiment will be type of bird control. I will have three treatments: scarecrow, netting, and no control. I will randomly assign several different areas in the vineyard to one of the treatments, taking care that there is sufficient separation that the possible effect of the scarecrow will not be confounded. At the end of the season, the response variable will be the proportion of bird-damaged grapes.

38. Since players vary in their ability to hit the ball, I will have each batter hit with both types of bats several times in a randomly chosen order. For each batter, calculate the average difference in distance, metal or wood as the response variable.

39. a) We want all subjects treated as alike as possible. If there were no "placebo surgery," subjects would know this and perhaps behave differently.
b) The experiment was intended to see if there was a difference in the effectiveness of the two treatments. (If we wanted to generalize, we would need to assume that the results for these volunteers is the same as on all patients who might need this operation.
c) Statistically significant means a difference in results so large it cannot be explained by natural sampling variability.

40. Results will vary.
(Use a random number table or software to do the simulation. Numbers 1 to 11 will represent the "worst" team, 12 to 21 the second worst, 22 to 30 your third-place team, 31 to 66 the others. Obtain random numbers in the range, ignoring any duplications of the team who gets to pick first. Count the number of times the third-place team picks first or second out of the total number of trials.)

41. a) Use stratified sampling to select 2 first-class passengers and 12 from coach.
b) Number passengers alphabetically, 01 = Bergman to 20 = Testut. Read in blocks of two, ignoring any numbers more than 20. This gives 65, 43, 67, 11 (selects Fontana), 27, 04 (selects Castillo).
c) Number passengers alphabetically 001 to 120. Use the random number table to find three-digit numbers in this range until 12 have been selected.

42. Simulation results will vary. Theoretically, the chance is about 15%. (Select four numbers between 01 and 20 to represent the Middle Easterners. Count the number of times in several repetitions where both to be searched are among the selected four numbers.)

43. Simulation results will vary.
(Use integers 00 to 99 as a basis. Use integers 0 to 69 to represent a tee shot on the fairway. If on the fairway, use digits 00 to 79 to represent on the green. If off the fairway, use 00 to 39 to represent getting on the green. If not on the green, use digits 00 to 89 to represent landing on the green. For the first putt, use digits 00 to 19 to represent making the shot. For subsequent putts, use digits 00 to 89 to represent making the shot.)

44. a) Answers may vary. A component in this simulation is a shot. Use pairs of random digits 00 to 99 to represent a shot. The way in which this component is simulated depends on the type of shot. For the first shot, let pairs of digits 01 to 80 represent hitting the fairway, and let pairs of digits 81 to 99, and 00, represent not hitting the fairway. If the first simulated shot hits the fairway, let 01 to 80 represent landing on the green on the second shot, and let 81 to 99, and 00, represent not landing on the green on the second shot. If the first simulated shot does not hit the fairway, let 01 to 40 represent landing on the green on the second shot, and let 41 to 99, and 00, represent not landing on the green on the second shot. If the second simulated shot does not land on the green, let 01 to 90 represent landing on the green, and 91 to 99, and 00, represent not landing on the green. Keep simulating shots until the shot lands on the green. Once on the green, let 01 to 20 represent sinking the putt on the first putt, and let 21 to 99, and 00, represent not sinking the putt on the first putt. If second putts are required, continue simulating putts until a putt goes in, with 01 to 90 representing making the putt, and 91 to 99, and 00, representing not making the putt. A run consists of following the guidelines above until the final putt is made. The response variable is the number of shots required until the final putt is made. The simulated average score on the hole is the total number of shots required divided by the total number of runs. According to 20 runs of this simulation, a pretty good golfer can be expected to average about 3.7 strokes per hole. Your simulation results may vary.
b) Answers may vary. The simulation is set up identically to part a), with the exception of the second shot. Now, let 01 to 10 represent hitting the green, and let 11 to 99, and 00, represent not hitting the green. According to 20 runs of this simulation, a pretty good golfer can be expected to average about 5.3 strokes per hole. Your simulation results may vary.
c) Answers may vary.

CHAPTER 14

1. In this context "truly random" should mean that every number is equally likely to occur and knowing one outcome will not affect the next.

2. In circumstances "like this," rain occurs 25% of the time.

3. If events are independent, there is no "law of averages." She would be wrong to think they are "due" for a harsh winter.

4. He's referring to the "law of averages," which is false for independent events. If rain in the fall and winter are independent of each other, a nice fall will have no bearing on winter rains.

5. There is no "law of averages" for independent events. His chance for a hit does not change based on recent successes or failures.

6. a) There is no "law of averages" for independent events. If crashes are independent, it makes no difference. If crashes were due to problems with the aircraft, another crash may be more likely; however, increased maintenance vigilance may *lessen* the chance of another crash.
b) A good safety record may be due to competence rather than luck. In any event, if events are independent, the probability of a crash has not changed.

7. a) There is a small chance you would have to pay out much more than the $300.
b) Many customers pay for insurance. The small risk for any one customer is spread among all.

8. a) Almost all people make bets without winning the jackpot.
b) This creates publicity—more people may be attracted to play. (And, of course, it's not a loss. We assume that they take in more than they pay out.)

9. a) Legitimate.
b) Legitimate.
c) Not legitimate (sum more than 1).
d) Legitimate.
e) Not legitimate (can't have negatives or values more than 1).

10. a) Not legitimate (sum less than 1).
b) Not legitimate (sum greater than 1).
c) Legitimate.
d) Not legitimate (can't have negatives).
e) Legitimate.

11. a) **1.** 0.72 **2.** 0.89 **3.** 0.28
b) **1.** 0.5184 **2.** 0.0784

12. a) **1.** 0.45 **2.** 0.87
b) **1.** 0.3025 **2.** 0.2025 **3.** 0.243

13. a) **1.** 0.30 **2.** 0.30 **3.** 0.90 **4.** 0.0
b) **1.** 0.027 **2.** 0.128 **3.** 0.512 **4.** 0.271

14. a) **1.** 0.04 **2.** 0.51 **3.** 0.55
b) **1.** 0.041 **2.** 0.849 **3.** 0.9744 **4.** 0.373

15. a) Disjoint (can't be both red and orange).
b) Independent.
c) No. Once you know that one of a pair of disjoint events has occurred, the other is impossible.

16. a) Disjoint.
b) Independent (unless they are related).
c) No. Once you know that one of a pair of disjoint events has occurred, the other is impossible.

17. a) 0.0046 b) 0.125 c) 0.296 d) 0.421 e) 0.995

18. a) 0.027 b) 0.125 c) 0.001 d) 0.729 e) 0.784

19. a) 0.027 b) 0.063 c) 0.973 d) 0.014

20. a) 0.0225 b) 0.092 c) 0.00008 d) 0.556

21. a) 0.024 b) 0.250 c) 0.543

22. a) 0.148 b) 0.600 c) 0.3439

23. 0.078

24. 0.469

25. a) For any day with a valid three-digit date, the chance is 0.00, or 1 in 1000. For many dates in October through December, the probability is 0. (No three digits will make 10/15, for example.)

b) There are 65 days when the chance to match is 0. (Oct 10–31, Nov. 10–30, and Dec. 10–31.) The chance for no matches on the remaining 300 days is 0.741
c) 0.259
d) 0.049

CHAPTER 15

1. a) S = {HH, HT, TH, TT}, equally likely
b) S = {0,1,2,3}, not equally likely
c) S = {H,TH,TTH, TTT}, not equally likely
d) S = {1, 2, 3, 4, 5, 6}, not equally likely
2. a) S = {2, 3, 4, 5, 6, 7, 8, 9, 10, 11, 12}, not equally likely.
b) S = {BBB, BBG, BGB, BGG, GBB, GBG, GGB, GGG}, equally likely.
c) S = {0, 1, 2, 3, 4}, not equally likely.
d) S = {0, 1, 2, 3, 4, 5, 6, 7, 8, 9, 10}, not equally likely.
3. a) 0.68 b) 0.32 c) 0.04
4. a) 0.14 b) 0.23 c) 0.77
5. a) 0.31 b) 0.48 c) 0.31
6. a) 0.06 b) 0.50 c) 0.94
7. a) 0.50 b) 1.00 c) 0.077 d) 0.333
8. a) 0.333 b) 0.429 c) 0.667
9. a) 0.11 b) 0.27 c) 0.407 d) 0.344
10. a) 0.62 b) 0.867 c) 0.194 d) 0.66
11. 0.21
12. 0.08
13. a) 0.145 b) 0.118 c) 0.414 d) 0.217
14. a) 0.783 b) 0.013 c) 0.127 d) 0.586
15. a) 0.318 b) 0.955 c) 0.071 d) 0.009
16. a) 0.632 b) 0.140 c) 0.003 d) 0.624
17. a) 32%
b) 0.135
c) No, 7% of juniors have taken both.
d) No, the probability that a junior has taken a computer course is 0.23. The probability that a junior has taken a computer course *given* he or she has taken a Statistics course is 0.135.
18. a) 0.25 b) 0.875
c) No, 68% of all workers have health insurance. Of those with retirement plans, 87.5% have health insurance. These are not equal.
d) No, 49% of the people have both.
19. a) 0.266
b) No, 26.6 % of homes with garages have pools; 21% of homes overall have pools.
c) No, 17% of homes have both.
20. a) 0.444
b) No, 4% of U.S. residents have been to both.
c) No, 18% of U.S. residents have been to Canada; 44.4% of U.S. residents who have been to Mexico have been to Canada. If independent, these would be equal.
21. Yes, $P(\text{Ace}) = 1/13$. $P(\text{Ace}|\text{Spade}) = 1/13$.
22. Yes, 1/3 of the Dogs are Male and 1/3 of the Cats are Male.
23. No, 28.8% of men with OK blood pressure have high cholesterol, but 40.7% of those with High blood pressure do.
24. No, 86.7% of Republicans favor the death penalty, but only 33.3% of Democrats favor it.
25. a) No, the probability that the luggage arrives on time depends on whether the flight is on time. The probability is 95% if the flight is on time and only 65% if not.
b) 0.695
26. a) Yes, the percentage who graduate depends on what kind of school they attend. The graduation rate is 75% for public school students and 90% for others.
b) 79.5%
27. 0.975
28. 66.0%
29. a) No, the probability of missing work for day shift employees is 0.01. It is 0.02 for night shift employees. The probability depends on whether they work day or night shift.
b) 1.4%
30. a) Rates of the lung condition are different for smokers and nonsmokers, 57% and 13%, respectively. If independent, these would be the same.
b) 0.231
31. 57.1%
32. 0.567
33. a) 0.20 b) 0.272 c) 0.353 d) 0.033
34. 0.814
35. 0.563
36. 0.467

CHAPTER 16

1. a) 19 b) 4.2
2. a) 1.2 b) 280
3. a)

Win	\$0	\$5	\$10	\$30
P(amount won)	$\frac{26}{52}$	$\frac{13}{52}$	$\frac{12}{52}$	$\frac{1}{52}$

b) \$4.13
c) \$4 or less (answers may vary)
4. a)

Win	\$100	\$50	\$0
P(amount won)	$\frac{1}{6}$	$\frac{5}{36}$	$\frac{25}{36}$

b) \$23.61
c) \$23 or less (answers may vary)
5. a)

Kids	0	0	3
P(kids)	0.5	0.25	0.25

b) 1.75
c) 0.875

Boys	0	1	2	3
P(boys)	0.5	0.25	0.125	0.125

6. a)

Won	\$95	\$90	\$85	\$80	−\$20
P(amount won)	0.10	0.09	0.081	0.073	0.656

b) 3.44
c) \$17.20
7. \$27,000
8. \$10,600
9. a) 7 b) 1.89
10. a) 0.75 b) 87.18
11. \$5.44
12. \$38.16

13. 0.83
14. \$51.48
15. a) 1.7 b) 0.9
16. a) 2.25 b) 1.26
17. $\mu = 0.64, \sigma = 0.93$
18. a)

Profit	\$100	−\$9900	−\$2900
P(profit)	0.9975	0.0005	0.002

b) \$89.00
c) \$260.54

19. a) No. The probability of winning the second depends on the outcome of the first.
b) 0.42
c) 0.08
d)

Games won	0	1	2
P(games won)	0.42	0.50	0.08

e) $\mu = 0.66, \sigma = 0.62$

20. a) No. The chance to get the second contract depends on whether your company got the first.
b) 0.16
c) 0.14
d)

Contracts won	0	1	2
P(contracts won)	0.14	0.70	0.16

e) $\mu = 1.02, \sigma = 0.55$

21. a)

Number good	0	1	2
P(number good)	0.067	0.467	0.466

b) 1.40
c) 0.61

22. a)

Number males	0	1	2
P(number males)	0.143	0.571	0.286

b) 1.14
c) 0.64

23. a) $\mu = 30, \sigma = 6$ b) $\mu = 26, \sigma = 5$
c) $\mu = 30, \sigma = 5.39$ d) $\mu = -10, \sigma = 5.39$
24. a) $\mu = 60, \sigma = 12$ b) $\mu = 6, \sigma = 1.50$
c) $\mu = 92, \sigma = 12.37$ d) $\mu = 68, \sigma = 12.37$
25. a) $\mu = 240, \sigma = 12.80$ b) $\mu = 140, \sigma = 24$
c) $\mu = 720, \sigma = 34.18$ d) $\mu = 60, \sigma = 39.40$
26. a) $\mu = 44, \sigma = 6$ b) $\mu = 240, \sigma = 36$
c) $\mu = 32, \sigma = 4.24$ d) $\mu = 20, \sigma = 19.21$
27. a) 1.8
b) 0.87
c) Cartons are independent of each other.
28. a) 10
b) 2.68
c) Packets are independent of each other. OK if different types of seeds; if all the same type (and lot), assumption would probably not be valid.
29. $\mu = 13.6, \sigma = 2.55$ (assuming the hours are independent of each other).
30. $\mu = 11.25, \sigma = 2.82$
31. a) There will be many gains of \$150 with a few large losses.
b) $\mu = \$300, \sigma = \$8485.28$
c) $\mu = \$1{,}500{,}000, \sigma = \$600{,}000$
d) Yes. \$0 is 2.5 SD below the mean for 10,000 policies.
e) Losses are independent of each other. A major catastrophe with many policies in an area would violate the assumption.
32. a) Gamblers lose a relatively small amount most of the time, but there are a few large payouts.
b) $\mu = \$0.40, \sigma = \$268.33$
c) $\mu = \$80.00, \sigma = 3794.73$
d) If the machine is played only 1000 times a day, the chance of being profitable will be slightly more than 50%, since \$80 is about 0.02 SDs above 0. But if the casino has many slot machines, the chances of being profitable will go up.
33. a) 1 oz b) 0.5 oz c) 0.023
d) $\mu = 4$ oz, $\sigma = 0.5$ oz
e) 0.159
f) $\mu = 12.3$ oz, $\sigma = 0.54$ oz
34. a) −\$20 b) \$46.10 c) 0.332
35. a) 12.2 oz b) 0.51 oz c) 0.058
36. a) X = cost for a dog; Y = cost for a cat; total costs = $X_1 + X_2 + Y$
b) Normal, $\mu = \$320, \sigma = \$55$
c) 0.073
37. a) $\mu = 200.57$ sec, $\sigma = 0.46$ sec
b) No, $Z = \dfrac{199.48 - 200.57}{0.461} = -2.36$. There is only 0.009 probability of swimming that fast or faster.
38. a) $\mu = 37.6$ min, $\sigma = 3.7$ min
b) No, 30 min is more than 2 SDs below the mean.
39. a) A = price of a pound of apples; P = price of a pound of potatoes; Profit = $100A + 50P - 2$
b) \$63.00
c) \$20.62
d) Mean—no; SD—yes (independent sales prices).
40. a) B = number basic; D = number deluxe; Net = $120B + 150D - 200$
b) \$928.00
c) \$187.45
d) Mean—no; SD—yes (sales are independent).

CHAPTER 17

1. a) No. More than two outcomes are possible.
b) Yes, assuming the people are unrelated to each other.
c) No. The chance of a heart changes as cards are dealt.
d) No, 500 is more than 10% of 3000.
e) If packages in a case are independent of each other, yes; otherwise, no.
2. a) Yes. Outcomes are {at least two 6's} and {fewer than two 6's}.
b) No. More than two outcomes are possible.
c) If the dolls were manufactured independently of each other, yes.
d) No. The chance of a Democrat (or Republican) changes depending on who has already been picked.
e) Yes, assuming responses (and cheating) are independent among the students.

3. a) Use single random digits. Let 0, 1 = Tiger. Count the number of random numbers until a 0 or 1 occurs.
c) Results will vary.
d)

x	1	2	3	4	5	6	7	8	≥9
P(x)	0.2	0.16	0.128	0.102	0.082	0.066	0.052	0.042	0.168

4. a) Use random digits 1–6, ignoring 0, 7–9. Count the number of random numbers until a 1 occurs.
c) Results will vary.
d)

x	1	2	3	4	5	6	7	8	≥9
P(x)	0.167	0.139	0.116	0.096	0.080	0.067	0.056	0.047	0.233

5. a) Use single random digits. Let 0, 1 = Tiger. Examine random digits in groups of five, counting the number of 0's and 1's.
c) Results will vary.
d)

x	0	1	2	3	4	5
P(x)	0.33	0.41	0.20	0.05	0.01	0.0

6. a) Use pairs of random digits. Let 00–74 represent that a seatbelt is worn, 75–99 that it is not. Examine random digits in groups of five, counting the number of seatbelts.
c) Results will vary.
d)

x	0	1	2	3	4	5
P(x)	0.0	0.01	0.09	0.26	0.40	0.24

7. a) 0.0819 b) 0.0064 c) 0.992
8. a) 0.0184 b) 0.183
9. 5
10. 50
11. a) 25 b) 0.185 c) 0.217 d) 0.693
12. a) 12.5 b) 0.716 c) 0.0527 d) 0.528
13. a) 0.0745 b) 0.502 c) 0.211 d) 0.0166
e) 0.0179 f) 0.9987
14. a) 0.032 b) 0.738 c) 0.00768 d) 0.901
e) 0.246 f) 0.345
15. a) 0.65 b) 0.75 c) 7.69 picks
16. a) 4.8 b) 0.98 c) 1.25 shots
17. a) $\mu = 10.44, \sigma = 1.16$
b) 0.812 c) 0.475 d) 0.00193 e) 0.998
18. a) $\mu = 8, \sigma = 1.26$
b) 0.107 c) 0.624 d) 0.967 e) 0.302
19. a) 0.118 b) 0.324 c) 0.744 d) 0.580
20. a) 0.201 b) 0.453 c) 0.171 d) 0.989
21. a) $\mu = 56, \sigma = 4.10$
b) Yes, $np = 56 > 10$, $n(1 - p) = 24 > 10$.
c) In a match with 80 serves, approximately 68% of the time she will have between 51.9 and 60.1 good serves, approximately 95% of the time she will have between 47.8 and 64.2 good serves, and approximately 99.7% of the time she will have between 43.7 and 68.3 good serves.
d) Normal, approx.: 0.014; Binomial, exact: 0.016
22. a) $\mu = 160, \sigma = 5.66$
b) Yes, $np = 160 > 10$, $nq = 40 > 10$.
c) In matches with 200 arrows, about 68% of the time she will have between 154.34 and 165.66 bull's-eyes, about 95% of the time between 148.68 and 171.32 bull's eyes, and about 99.7% of the time between 143.02 and 176.98 bull's eyes.
d) Yes, that's more than 3 SDs below the mean. Probability is less than 0.0015.
23. a) $\mu = 18.75, \sigma = 4.05$
b) Yes, $np = 18.75 > 10$, $nq = 131.25 > 10$.
c) No, 22 is only 0.8 SD above the mean; this is likely to happen by natural sampling variability.
24. a) Assuming apples fall and become blemished independently of each other, Binom(300, 0.06) is appropriate. Since $np > 10$ and $nq > 10$, $N(18, 4.11)$ is also appropriate
b) Normal, approx.: 0.072; Binomial, exact: 0.085
c) No, 50 is 7.8 SDs above the mean.
25. Normal, approx.: 0.053; Binomial, exact: 0.061
26. Normal, approx.: 0.094; Binomial, exact: 0.116
27. The mean number of sales should be 24 with SD 4.60. Ten sales is more than 3.0 SDs below the mean. He was probably misled.
28. If the coin is fair, expect 125 heads, with SD 7.91; 140 is 1.9 SDs above the mean. From the Normal approximation, the chance of 140 or more heads is 2.9%. That's pretty unlikely to happen.
29. a) 5 b) 0.066 c) 0.107
d) $\mu = 24, \sigma = 2.19$
e) Normal, approx.: 0.819; Binomial, exact: 0.848
30. a) 0.042 b) 0.107 c) 5 d) $\mu = 10, \sigma = 2.83$
e) Normal, approx.: 0.025; Binomial, exact: 0.027
31. $\mu = 20, \sigma = 4$. I'd want *at least* 32 (3 SDs above the mean). (Answers will vary.)
32. $\mu = 25, \sigma = 3.54$. I'd want *at least* 36 (3 SDs above the mean). (Answers will vary.)

PART IV REVIEW

1. a) 0.34
b) 0.27
c) 0.069
d) No, 2% of cars have both types of defects.
e) Of all cars with cosmetic defects, 6.9% have functional defects. Of cars without cosmetic defects, 7.0% have functional defects. The probabilities here are estimates, so these are probably close enough to say the defects are independent.
2. a) i) 0.60 ii) 0.90 iii) 0.615 iv) 0.80
b) No. Fewer than half of the managers are female, but 60% of all workers are female.
3. a) C = Price to China; F = Price to France; Total = $3C + 5F$
b) $\mu = \$5500, \sigma = \$672.68$
c) $\mu = \$500, \sigma = \$180.28$
d) Means—no. Standard deviations—yes, ticket prices must be independent of each other for different countries, but all tickets to the same country are at the same price.
4. $np = 100 > 10$ and $nq = 9900 > 10$, so Success/Failure Condition is verified. Also, we assume that cases are independent. $\mu = 100$, $\sigma = 9.95$. Over 200 would be more than 10 SDs above the mean. Probability is essentially 0.
5. a) $\mu = -\$0.20, \sigma = \$1.89$
b) $\mu = -\$0.40, \sigma = \$2.67$
6. a) 3%

b) No, 62% of those who can do it with their right hand can do it with their left, but 83.3% of those who can't do it with their right hand can do it with their left.
c) No, 51% can use both hands.

7. a) 0.106
b) 0.651
c) 0.442

8. Expected (extra) cost of the cheaper policy with the deductible is \$2.50, much less than the \$12 for the no deductible surcharge, so on average she will save money by going with the deductible. But she should consider standard deviation as well (\$35.27). Value of the car shouldn't influence the decision.

9. a) 0.590
b) 0.328
c) 0.00856

10. a) $\mu = 6.775, \sigma = 2.60$
b) No, since $np = 6.78 < 10$.

11. a) $\mu = 15.2, \sigma = 3.70$
b) Yes. $np > 10$ and $nq > 10$
c) Normal, approx.: 0.080; Binomial, exact: 0.097

12. a)

Spaces	5	10	20
P(spaces)	0.5	0.25	0.25

b) $\mu = 10, \sigma = 6.12$
c)

Spaces	0	1	2	3	4
P(spaces)	1/3	1/6	1/6	1/6	1/6

d) $\mu = 1.67, \sigma = 1.49$
e) $\mu = 11.67, \sigma = 6.30$

13. a) 0.0173
b) 0.591
c) Left: 960; right: 120; both: 120
d) $\mu = 120, \sigma = 10.39$
e) About 68% chance of between 109 and 130; about 95% between 99 and 141; about 99.7% between 89 and 151.

14. $\mu = 8.33, \sigma = 6.30$

15. a) Men's heights are more variable than women's.
b) Men
c) M = Man's height; W = Woman's height; $M - W$ is how much taller the man is.
d) 5.1″
e) 3.75″
f) 0.913
g) If independent, it should be about 91.3%. We are told 92%. This difference seems small and may be due to natural sampling variability.

16. a) 0.389 b) 0.284 c) 0.793 d) 0.896

17. a) No. The chance is 1.6×10^{-7}.
b) 0.952
c) 0.063

18. a) No, this does not confirm the advice. If you follow the advice, it seems that the chances of its going up are 0.75.
b) It actually has risen in 73% of all years. Not much difference from their strategy.

19. −\$2080.00

20. a) 0.240 b) 0.050 c) 0.383

21. a) 0.717 b) 0.588

22. a) 36 b) 5.02
c) Because both $np = 36 \geq 10$ and $nq = 84 \geq 10$.
d) There is a 68% chance between 30.98 and 41.02 (31 and 41 students); 95% chance between 25.96 and 46.04 (26 and 46 students); 99.7% chance between 20.94 and 51.06 (21 and 51 students).

23. a) $\mu = 100, \sigma = 8$
b) $\mu = 1000, \sigma = 60$
c) $\mu = 100, \sigma = 8.54$
d) $\mu = -50, \sigma = 10$

24. Assuming policies are independent, we add the profit variances. The resulting standard deviation of total profit is less than the sum of the SDs of individual profits. This means the profit for the large company will be less variable than the total of profits for the smaller companies.

25. a) Many do both, so the two categories can total more than 100%.
b) No. They can't be disjoint. If they were, the total would be 100% or less.
c) No. Probabilities are different for boys and girls.
d) 0.0524

26. a) $\mu = \$27.00, \sigma = \$9.90$
b) Spending on different days is independent. This might not be reasonable, since a student may be more likely to spend less on a day after he had spent a lot.
c) $\mu = \$94.50, \sigma = \$18.52$
d) No. \$50 is 2.4 SDs below the mean. We assumed independence of costs each day.

27. a) 21 days
b) 1649.73 soms
c) 3300 soms extra. About 157 soms "cushion" each day.

28. a) 4 lb
b) 3.20 lb
c) 0.894

29. No, you'd expect 541.2 homeowners, with an SD of 13.56. 523 is 1.34 SDs below the mean; not unusual.

30. $\mu = \$2.54, \sigma = \$0.94$

31. a) 0.018 b) 0.300 c) 0.26

32. a) 0.0156
b) 0.0039
c) Answer a Would become 0.0104. Answer b would become 0.0026.

33. a) 6 b) 15 c) 0.402

34. a) 3
b) X = current score; expect to lose $X/6$ points.
c) 18
d) Roll until you score 18 points, then stop.

35. a) 34%
b) 35%
c) 31.4%
d) 31.4% of classes that used calculators used computer assignments, while in classes that didn't use calculators, 30.6% used computer assignments. These are close enough to think the choice is probably independent.

36. a) 0.5929 b) 0.407 c) 0.053 d) 0.0025

37. a) 1/11 b) 7/22 c) 5/11 d) 0 e) 19/66

38. a) $\mu = 18, \sigma = 3$
b) 6
c) No, σ is now 5.
d) 10 or more
e) What appears "surprising" in the short run becomes expected in a large number of trials.

39. a) Expected number of stars with planets.
b) Expected number of planets with intelligent life.
c) Probability of a planet with a suitable environment having intelligent life.
d) f_l : If a planet has a suitable environment, the probability that life develops.
f_i: If a planet develops life, the probability that the life evolves intelligence.
f_c: If a planet has intelligent life, the probability that it develops radio communication.

40. a) 0.017
b) 0.824

41. 0.991

42. a) 0.01 b) 0.0098
c) 0.366 d) First
e) The chance of winning is 0.01 anywhere in line, so position does not matter.

CHAPTER 18

1. a) Symmetric, because probability of heads and tails is equal.
b) 0.5
c) 0.125
d) $np = 8 < 10$

2. a) Probably skewed right.
b) No. $np = 5 < 10$
c) 0.10
d) 0.042

3. a) About 68% should have proportions between 0.4 and 0.6, about 95% between 0.3 and 0.7, and about 99.7% between 0.2 and 0.8.
b) $np = 12.5$, $nq = 12.5$; both are > 10.
c)

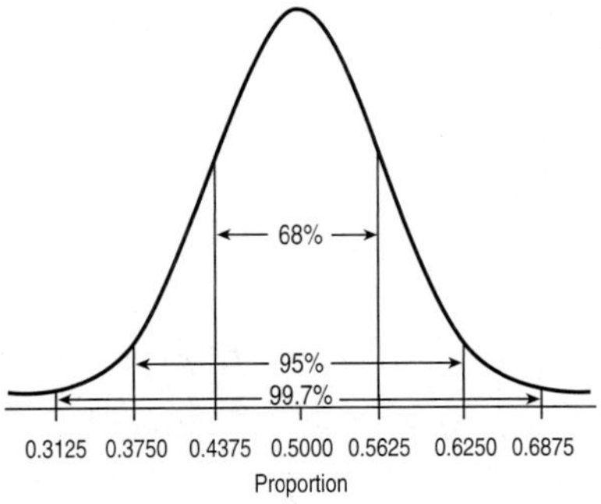

$np = nq = 32$; both are > 10.
d) Becomes narrower (less spread around 0.5).

4. a) $np = 20$, $nq = 180$; both are > 10.
b) About 68% will be between 7.9% and 12.1%, about 95% will be between 5.8% and 14.2%, and about 99.7% should be between 3.7% and 16.3%.
c) Same center, less spread.

5. This is a fairly unusual result: about 2.26 SDs below the mean. The probability of that is about 0.012. So, in a class of 100 this is certainly a reasonable possibility.

6. No. It's only 1.49 SDs above the mean.

7. a)

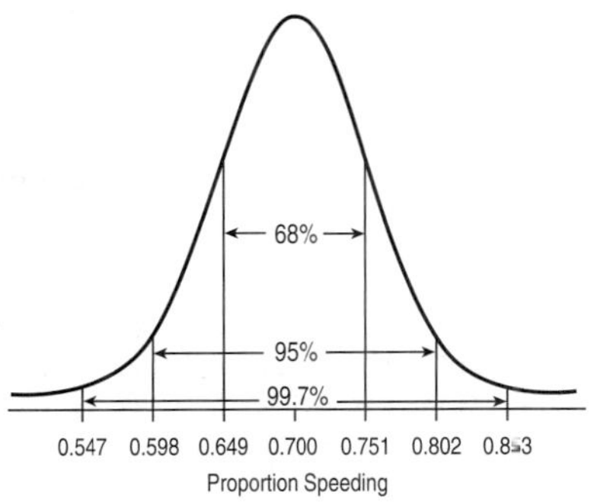

b) Both $np = 56$ and $nq = 24 > 10$. Drivers *may* be independent of each other, but if flow of traffic is very fast, they may not be. Or weather conditions may affect all drivers. In these cases they may get more or fewer speeders than they expect.

8. There is a 68% chance that between 20.2% and 32.6% are smokers, 95% chance between 14% and 38.8%, and 99.7% chance between 7.8% and 45%. The 50 adults would have to be a random sample whose choice to smoke is independent of the others in the sample. The success/failure condition is satisfied, $np = 13.2$, and $nq = 36.8$. Both are > 10.

9. a) $\mu = 7\%$, $\sigma = 1.8\%$
b) Assume that clients pay independently of each other that we have a random sample of all possible clients, and that these represent less than 10% of all possible clients. $np = 14$ and $nq = 186$ are both greater than 10.
c) 0.048

10. a) Normal, $\mu = 30\%$, $\sigma = 4.6\%$; SRS, $np = 30$, $nq = 70$.
b) 0.234

11. 0.212. Reasonable that those polled are independent of each other and represent less than 10% of all potential voters. We assume the sample was selected at random. Success/Failure Condition met: $np = 208$, $nq = 192$. Both > 10.

12. 0.081. Assume the seeds are a random sample, germinate independently of each other, and represent less than 10% of all seeds of this type. Since the seeds are in the same pack, they may not be independent of each other, or be a random sample. Success/Failure Condition met: $np = 147.2$, $nq = 12.8$. Both > 10.

13. 0.088 using $N(0.08, 0.022)$, model.

14. 0.960 using $N(0.04, 0.007)$ model.

15. Answers will vary. Using $\mu + 3\sigma$ for "very sure," the restaurant should have 89 nonsmoking seats. Assumes customers at any time are independent of each other, a random sample, and represent less than 10% of all potential customers. $np = 72$, $nq = 48$, so Normal model is reasonable ($\mu = 0.60$, $\sigma = 0.045$).

16. Answers will vary. Using $\mu + 2\sigma$ for "pretty sure,"he should plan on having at least 47 steak specials ($\mu = 0.20$, $\sigma = 0.030$).

17. a) Normal, center at μ, standard deviation $\sigma / \sqrt{n}$.
b) Standard deviation will be smaller. Center will remain the same.

18. a) Skewed left, center at μ, standard deviation $\sigma / \sqrt{n}$.
b) Becomes more Normal, center at μ, standard deviation $\sigma / \sqrt{n}$.
c) Becomes more like the population—skewed to the left.

19.

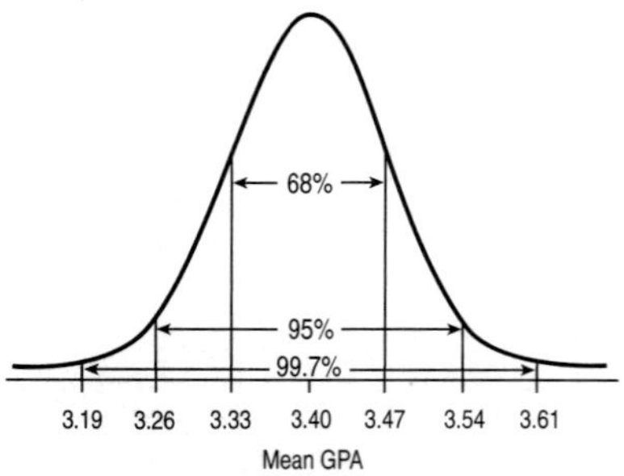

Normal, $\mu = 3.4$, $\sigma = 0.07$. We assume that the students are randomly assigned to the seminars, represent less 10% of all possible students, and that individual's GPAs are independent of one another.

20.

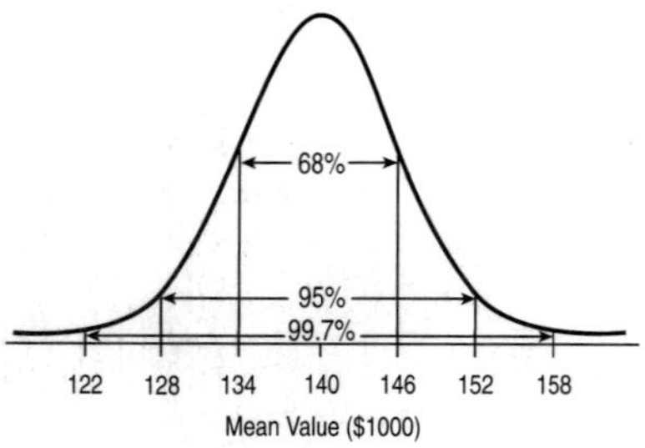

21. a) 21.1%
b) 276.8 days or more
c) $N(266, 2.07)$
d) 0.002

22. a) 13.7%
b) 31.9″
c) $N(35.4, 2.1)$
d) 0.005

23. a) There are more premature births than very long pregnancies. Modern practice of medicine stops pregnancies at about 2 weeks past normal due date.
b) Parts a and b—yes—we can't use Normal model if it's very skewed. Part c—no—CLT guarantees a Normal model for this large sample size.

24. a) Some people work far longer than the mean + 2 or 3 SDs.
b) The CLT says $\bar{y}$ is approximately Normal for large sample sizes, but not for samples of size 1 (individuals).

25. a) $\mu = \$2.00$, $\sigma = \$3.61$
b) $\mu = \$4.00$, $\sigma = \$5.10$
c) 0.191. Model is $N(80, 22.83)$.

26. a)

Amount won	40	0	−10
P(amount won)	1/6	5/36	25/36

b) $\mu = -\$0.28$, $\sigma = \$18.33$
c) $\mu = -\$1.40$, $\sigma = \$40.99$
d) 0.56

27. a) $N(2.9, 0.045)$
b) 0.0131
c) 2.97 gm/mi

28. a) 0.0478 b) 0.863 c) 0.0019
d) Essentially 0

29. a) Can't use a Normal model to estimate probabilities. The distribution is skewed right—not Normal.
b) 4 is probably not a large enough sample to say the average follows the Normal model.
c) No. This is 3.16 SDs above the mean.

30. a) Can't use a Normal model to estimate probabilities. The distribution is skewed right—not Normal.
b) Probably not. 10 is not a large sample. It depends on the amount of skewness of the distribution.
c) No. With 50 customers, $\bar{y}$ is $N(32, 2.83)$. The probability is 0.0023.

31. a) 0.0003. Model is $N(384, 34.15)$.
b) $427.77 or more

32. a) 0.482. Model is $N(9984, 353.27)$.
b) $9531.27 or less

33. a) 0.734
b) 0.652. Model is $N(10, 12.81)$.
c) 0.193. Model is $N(120, 5.774)$.
d) 0.751. Model is $N(10, 7.394)$.

34. a) 0.309
b) 0.696. Model is $N(4, 7.810)$.
c) 0.037. Model is $N(43, 1.118)$.
d) 0.325. Model is $N(4, 2.202)$.

CHAPTER 19

1. He believes the true proportion is within 4% of his estimate, with some (probably 95%) degree of confidence.

2. He believes the true proportion is within 3% of his estimate, with some (probably 95%) degree of confidence.

3. a) Population—all cars; sample—those actually stopped at the checkpoint; p—proportion of all cars with safety problems; $\hat{p}$—proportion actually seen with safety problems (10.4%); if sample (a cluster sample) is representative, then the methods of this chapter will apply.
b) Population—general public; sample—those who logged onto the Web site; p—population proportion of those who favor prayer in school; $\hat{p}$—proportion of those who voted in the poll who favored prayer in school (81.1%); can't use methods of this chapter—sample is biased and nonrandom.
c) Population—parents at the school; sample—those who returned the questionnaire; p—proportion of all parents who favor uniforms; $\hat{p}$—proportion of respondents who favor uniforms (60%); have to use caution with methods of this chapter, since nonresponse may bias results.
d) Population—students at the college; sample—the 1632 students who entered that year; p—proportion of all students who will graduate on time; $\hat{p}$—proportion of that year's students who graduate on time (85.0%); can use methods of this chapter if that year's students (a cluster sample) are viewed as a representative sample of all possible students at the school.

4. a) Population—people who recently bought new cars; sample—167 people surveyed; p—proportion of all new car buyers who are dissatisfied with the salesperson; $\hat{p}$—proportion of those surveyed who are unsatisfied (3%); can't use methods of this chapter because only 5 people were dissatisfied.
b) Population—college students; sample—2883 students who were asked about cell phones; p—proportion of college students with cell phones; $\hat{p}$—proportion of those asked who

have cell phones (8.4%); use methods of this chapter with caution—students entering the football stadium may not reflect all students.

c) Population—potato plants in the United States; sample—240 plants checked; p—proportion of all plants in the field with blight; $\hat{p}$—proportion of the 240 plants checked with blight (2.9%); can't use methods of this chapter—fewer than 10 "successes."

d) Population—employees at the company; sample—all employees that year; p—proportion of all employees who will have an injury on the job in a year; $\hat{p}$—proportion of that year's employees with an injury (3.9%); can use methods of this chapter if that year's employees are viewed as a random sample of all possible employees.

5. a) Not correct. This implies certainty.
b) Not correct. Different samples will give different results. Many fewer than 95% will have 88% on-time orders.
c) Not correct. The interval is about the population proportion, not the sample proportion in different samples.
d) Not correct. In this sample, we *know* 88% arrived on time.
e) Not correct. The interval is about the parameter, not about the days.

6. a) Not correct. The interval is about the proportion of heads, not individual coins.
b) Not correct. We know in this sample that 56% of the spins were heads.
c) Not correct. The interval is about the parameter, not about individual spins.
d) Not correct. The interval is about the proportion of heads, not about individual spins.
e) Not correct. The interval is about the proportion of heads, not about the percentage of euros.

7. a) False b) True c) True d) False

8. a) True b) True c) True d) True

9. On the basis of this sample, we are 90% confident that the proportion of Japanese cars is between 29.9% and 47.0%.

10. On the basis of this sample, we are 95% confident that the proportion of paroles granted by the Nebraska Board of Parole is between 56.1% and 62.5%.

11. a) 2.5%
b) The pollsters are 90% confident the true proportion of adults who believe in ghosts is within 2.5% of the estimated 38%.
c) Larger. More confidence for a given sample requires a wider interval.
d) 3.9%
e) A smaller margin of error will imply less confidence.

12. a) 1.7% (0.017)
b) The pollsters are 95% confident that the true proportion of adults who approve of attempts to clone humans is within 1.7% of the estimated 8%.
c) Smaller. Less confidence allows a narrower interval.
d) 1.4%
e) Larger

13. a) (12.7%, 18.6%)
b) We are 95% confident, based on this sample, that the proportion of all auto accidents that involve teenage drivers is between 12.7% and 18.6%.
c) About 95% of all random samples will produce confidence intervals that contain the true population proportion.
d) Contradicts. The interval is completely below 20%.

14. a) (10.6%, 14.0%)
b) We are 90% confident, based on this sample, that the proportion of people contacted who may buy something is between 10.6% and 14.0%.
c) About 90% of all random samples will produce confidence intervals that contain the true population proportion.
d) Do the mass mailing. The interval is considerably above 5%.

15. Probably nothing. Those who bothered to fill out the survey may be a biased sample.

16. Nothing. Those who showed up for the meeting are probably a biased group. In addition, a show-of-hands vote may influence people, making the votes nonindependent.

17. a) (39.9%, 48.2%)
b) No

18. a) 19.1%
b) Maybe. The proportion is significantly lower than 30%, but this is just one estimate.
c) (11.7%, 26.4%)
d) Yes, 30% is above the interval.

19. a) Wording
b) (45.5%, 51.5%)
c) Smaller—the sample size was larger.

20. a) The class' interval will be larger, since its sample size is smaller.
b) Newspaper: (50.2%, 55.8%) class: (49.4%, 58.6%).
c) Students because 50% is in their interval.

21. a) (18.2%, 21.8%)
b) We are 98% confident, based on the sample, that between 18.2% and 21.8% of English children are deficient in vitamin D.
c) About 98% of all random samples will produce a confidence interval that contains the true proportion.

22. a) (18.8%, 28.5%)
b) We are 90% confident, based on this sample, that between 18.8% and 28.5% of women under 40 who are helped at this clinic will become pregnant and give birth.
c) About 90% of all random samples will produce intervals that contain the true proportion.
d) No, 25% is in the interval.

23. a) (15.5%, 26.3%) b) 612
c) Sample may not be random or representative. Deer that may legally be hunted may not be representative of all sexes and ages.

24. a) 828 women
b) This large a sample might be larger than 10% of the population.

25. a) 141 b) 318 c) 564

26. a) 542, assuming $p = 0.50$.
b) ~~1503~~ 1504
c) Would need 13,526 employers.

27. 1801

28. 1037

29. 384 total, using $p = 0.15$.

30. 581

31. 90%

32. a) 50% is in the interval.
b) 98%

CHAPTER 20

1. a) $H_0: p = 0.30; H_A: p < 0.30$
b) $H_0: p = 0.50; H_A: p \neq 0.50$
c) $H_0: p = 0.20; H_A: p > 0.20$

2. a) H_0: $p = 0.40$; H_A: $p \neq 0.40$
b) H_0: $p = 0.20$; H_A: $p < 0.20$
c) H_0: $p = 0.60$; H_A: $p > 0.60$

3. Statement d is correct.

4. Statement d is correct.

5. No, we can say only that there is a 27% chance of seeing the observed effectiveness just from natural sampling variation. There is no *evidence* that the new formula is more effective, but we can't conclude that they are equally effective.

6. Yes. If there is no difference, there is only a 1.7% chance of seeing such a high sample proportion just from natural sampling variation.

7. 1) Use p in hypotheses, not $\hat{p}$.
2) The question was about failing to meet the goal, so H_A should be $p < 0.96$.
3) Did not check $0.04(200) = 8$. Since $nq < 10$, the success/failure condition is violated.
4) $188/200 = 0.94$: $SD(\hat{p}) = \sqrt{\frac{(0.96)(0.04)}{200}} = 0.014$
5) z is incorrect; should be $z = \frac{0.94 - 0.96}{0.014} = -1.43$.
6) $P = P(z < -1.43) = 0.076$
7) There is only weak evidence that the new system does not work.

8. 1) Use p in hypotheses, not $\hat{p}$.
2) The question asks, *"not accurate,"* so H_A should be two sided: $p \neq 0.9$.
3) The correct conditions are SRS, $(0.9)(750) > 10$, and $(0.10)(750) > 10$.
4) $\hat{p} = 657/750 = 0.876$; $SD(\hat{p}) = \sqrt{\frac{(0.9)(0.1)}{750}} = 0.011$
5) z is incorrect; should be $z = \frac{0.876 - 0.9}{0.011} = -2.18$.
6) $P = 2P(z < -2.18) = 0.029$
7) There is only a 2.9% chance of observing a $\hat{p}$ as far from 0.90 by sampling variation, so we believe the proportion of adults who drink milk here is different from the claimed 90%.

9. a) H_0: $p = 0.30$; H_A: $p > 0.30$
b) Possibly an SRS; we don't know if the sample is less than 10% of his customers but could be viewed as less than 10% of all possible customers; $(0.3)(80) > 10$ and $(0.7)(80) > 10$. Wells are independent only if customers don't have farms on the same underground springs.
c) $z = 0.73$; P-value $= 0.232$
d) If his dowsing is no different from standard methods, there is more than a 23% chance of seeing results as good as those of the dowsers, or better, by natural sampling variation.
e) These data provide no evidence that the dowser's chance of finding water is any better than normal drilling.

10. a) H_0: $p = 0.05$; H_A: $p > 0.05$
b) SRS (not clear from information provided), <10% of all children, $(0.05)(384) > 10$, and $(0.95)(384) > 10$.
c) $z = 6.28$, $P = 2 \times 10^{-10}$
d) If the autism rate has not increased, the chance of observing at least 46 autistic children in a sample of 384 is 2×10^{-10} (almost 0).
e) Reject H_0. These data show the rate of autism is now more than 5%.
f) We do not know that chemicals cause autism, only that the rate is higher now than in the past.

11. a) Based on these data, we are 95% confident the proportion of adults in 1995 who had never smoked cigarettes is between 48.7% and 55.3%.
b) H_0: $p = 0.44$; H_A: $p \neq 0.44$. Since 44% is not in the confidence interval, we will reject H_0 and conclude the proportion of adults in 1995 who had never smoked was more than in the 1960s.

12. a) Based on these data, we are 95% confident the proportion of dissatisfied customers is between 1.1% and 4.6%.
b) H_0: $p = 0.05$; H_A: $p < 0.05$. Since 5% is not in the 95% confidence interval, we will reject H_0 at $\alpha = .025$ and conclude the proportion of dissatisfied customers is less than 5%, so the company has met its goal.

13. H_0: $p = 0.20$; H_A: $p > 0.20$. SRS (not clear from information provided); 22 is more than 10% of the population of 150; $(0.20)(22) < 10$. Do not proceed with a test.

14. H_0: $p = 0.02$; H_A: $p > 0.02$. SRS; less than 10% of all washers and dryers made by the company; $(0.02)(60) < 10$. Do not proceed with a test.

15. H_0: $p = 0.03$; H_A: $p < 0.03$. $\hat{p} = 0.015$. One mother having twins will not impact another, so observations are independent; not an SRS; sample is less than 10% of all births. However, the mothers at this hospital may not be representative of all teenagers; $(0.03)(469) = 14.07 > 10$; $(0.97)(469) > 10$. $z = -1.91$; P-value $=$ 0.0278. With a P-value this low, reject H_0. These data show evidence that the rate of twins born to teenage girls at this hospital is less than the national rate of 3%. It is not clear whether this can be generalized to all teenagers.

16. H_0: $p = 0.50$; H_A: $p > 0.50$. Results of one game should not impact another, so games are independent; data are all results for one season, which should be representative of all seasons; sample is less than 10% of all games; $(0.50)(240) > 10$; $(0.50)(240) > 10$. $z = 2.32$; P-value $= 0.0101$. With a P-value this low, reject H_0. These data show strong evidence that the home team does have an advantage; they win more than 50% of games at home.

17. H_0: $p = 0.25$; H_A: $p > 0.25$. SRS; sample is less than 10% of all potential subscribers; $(0.25)(500) > 10$; $(0.75)(500) > 10$. $z = 1.24$; P-value $= 0.1076$. The P-value is high, so do not reject H_0. These data do not show that more than 25% of current readers would subscribe; the company should not go ahead with the WebZine on the basis of these data.

18. H_0: $p = 0.92$; H_A: $p < 0.92$. Seeds in a single packet may not be independent of each other. This is a cluster sample of all seeds in the packet. We may view this cluster as representative of all year-old seeds, in which case the sample is less than 10% of all seeds; $(0.92)(200) > 10$; $(0.08)(200) > 10$. $z = -3.39$; P-value $= 0.0004$. Because the P-value is very low, we reject H_0. There is strong evidence that these seeds have lost viability; their germination rate is less than 92%.

19. H_0: $p = 0.40$; H_A: $p < 0.40$. Data are for all executives in this company and may not be able to be generalized to all companies; $(0.40)(43) > 10$; $(0.60)(43) > 10$. $z = -1.31$; P-value $=$ 0.0955. Because the P-value is high, we fail to reject H_0. These data do not show that the proportion of women executives is less than the 40% women in the company in general.

20. H_0: $p = 0.19$; H_A: $p < 0.19$. $\hat{p} = 0.125$. $z = -1.41$; P-value $= 0.0793$. Because the P-value is high, we fail to reject H_0. These data do not show convincing evidence that Hispanics are represented in the jury pool at less than their 19% proportion in the population in general, but indicates that it is below what was expected.

21. H_0: $p = 0.109$; H_A: $p > 0.109$. $\hat{p} = 0.118$; $z = 1.198$; P-value $= 0.115$. Because the P-value is high, we fail to reject H_0. These data do not show the dropout rate has increased from 10.9%.

22. H_0: $p = 0.15$; H_A: $p > 0.15$. $\hat{p} = 0.25$; $z = 2.80$; P-value $= 0.0026$. The 95% confidence interval is (0.165, 0.335). We must assume the trees sampled are a SRS of the trees in the area and are less than 10% of all trees in the forest. The results are generalizable only to the Hopkins forest (or nearby if the forest is viewed as representative). Because the P-value is so low, we reject H_0. There is strong evidence that the proportion of trees damaged by acid rain in the Hopkins forest is higher than the 15% average for the Northeast.

23. H_0: $p = 0.90$; H_A: $p < 0.90$. $\hat{p} = 0.844$; $z = -2.05$; P-value $=$ 0.0201. Because the P-value is so low, we reject H_0. There is strong evidence that the actual rate at which passengers with lost luggage are reunited with it within 24 hours is less than the 90% claimed by the airline.

24. H_0: $p = 0.40$; H_A: $p > 0.40$. $\hat{p} = 0.431$; $z = 1.29$; P-value $= 0.0977$. Because the P-value is high, we fail to reject H_0. These data do not show that at least 40% of the public recognizes the brand; I would not recommend they continue to advertise during Super Bowls on the basis of these data.

CHAPTER 21

1. If there is no difference in effectiveness, the chance of seeing an observed difference this large or larger is 4.7% by natural sampling variation.

2. If harsher penalties and ad campaigns have made no difference in seatbelt use, there is a 17% chance of seeing an observed difference this large or larger by natural sampling variation.

3. $\alpha = .10$: Yes. The P-value is < 0.05, so it's less than 0.10. But to reject H_0 at $\alpha = .01$, the P-value must be below 0.01, which isn't necessarily the case.

4. At $\alpha = .10$ they reach the same decision only if the P-value is > 0.10. We know only that it's > 0.05. But we know that it's > 0.01, so at $\alpha = .01$ they reach the same decision.

5. a) There is only a 1.1% chance of seeing a sample proportion as low as 89.4% vaccinated by natural sampling variation if 90% have really been vaccinated.
b) We conclude that p is below 0.9, but a 95% confidence interval would show that the true proportion is between (0.889, 0.899). Most likely, a decrease from 90% to 89.9% would not be considered important. On the other hand, with 1,000,000 children a year vaccinated, even 0.1% represents about 1000 kids—so this may very well be important.

6. a) There is only a 2.3% chance of seeing a sample proportion of 15.1% of students not attaining grade level by natural sampling variation if 15.9% is the true population value.
b) Under old methods, 1352 students would not be expected to read at grade level. With the new program, 1284 did not. This is only a decrease of 68 students. It would depend on the costs of switching to the new program.

7. a) It is decided the shop is not meeting standards when it is.
b) The shop is certified as meeting standards when it is not.
c) Type I
d) Type II

8. a) Deciding there has been an increase in defective items when there has not.
b) Deciding the number of defectives is small, when it has increased.
c) Probably Type II, depending on the costs of shutting the line down. Generally, because of warranty costs and lost customer loyalty, defects that are caught in the factory are much cheaper to fix than defects found after items are sold.
d) Type II

9. a) The probability of detecting the shop is not meeting standards when it is not.
b) 40 cars. Larger n.
c) 10%. More chance to reject H_0.
d) A lot. Larger differences are easier to detect.

10. a) The probability of deciding there are too many defectives when this is true.
b) Advantage: more power. Disadvantage: more work testing.
c) Advantage: smaller Type I error chance. Disadvantage: less power.
d) Increases because the effect size increases.

11. a) One-tailed. The company wouldn't be sued if "too many" minorities were hired.
b) Deciding the company is discriminating when it is not.
c) Deciding the company is not discriminating when it is
d) The probability of correctly detecting discrimination when it exists.
e) Increases power.
f) Lower, since n is smaller.

12. a) One-tailed because we are interested only in whether they are more visible. If the new design is less visible, we don't care how much less visible it is.
b) Deciding the signs are more visible when they are not.
c) Failing to decide new signs are more visible when they are.
d) Ability (probability) to detect that a more visible sign works.
e) It will decrease power, because you'll need more evidence to reject H_0.
f) It will decrease power because it will make the SD larger.

13. a) One-tailed. Software is supposed to decrease the dropout rate.
b) H_0: $p = 0.13$; H_A: $p < 0.13$
c) He buys the software when it doesn't help students.
d) He doesn't buy the software when it does help students.
e) The probability of correctly deciding the software is helpful.

14. a) H_0: $p = 0.20$; H_A: $p > 0.20$
b) The company wants more "proof" the ad is effective before deciding it is.
c) The probability of correctly deciding that more than 20% have heard the ad and recognize the product when it's true.
d) 10%. More chance to reject H_0.
e) Lower. Larger n has more power and smaller Type II error probability.

15. a) $z = -3.21$, $p = 0.0007$. The change is statistically significant. A 95% confidence interval is (2.3%, 8.5%). This is clearly lower than 13%. If the cost of the software justifies it, the professor should consider buying the software.
b) The chance of observing 11 or fewer dropouts in a class of 203 is only 0.07% if the dropout rate is really 13%.

16. a) $z = 1.33$, $p = 0.0923$. The company should not renew the contract.
b) There is a 9.23% chance of having 133 or more of 600 people in a random sample remember the ad if in fact 20% of people do.

17. a) 0.0464
b) Type I
c) 37.6%
d) Increase the number of shots. Or keep the number of shots at 10 but increase alpha by declaring that 8, 9, or 10 will be deemed as having improved.

18. a) 0.0464
b) Type I
c) 0.6242
d) Increase the number of pieces tested, or keep the number of pieces tested at 10, but increase the number of "acceptable broken pieces" from 1 to 2.

19. Laborers only.

20. Single-family home only.

21. a) (21.8%, 30.2%)
b) No, 20% is below the low end of the interval.

22. H_0: $p = 0.25$; H_A: $p > 0.25$. The confidence interval is from 30% to 36%. Because the original proportion of 25% is far from the interval, we have strong evidence to suggest that the proportion of people who obtain news from the Internet has increased.

CHAPTER 22

1. a) Yes. Random sample; less than 10% of the population; samples are independent; more than 10 successes and failures in each sample.
b) (0.055, 0.140)
c) We are 95% confident, based on these samples, that the proportion of American women age 65 and older who suffer from arthritis is between 5.5% and 14.0% more than the proportion of American men of the same age who suffer from arthritis.
d) Yes; the entire interval lies above 0.

2. a) Yes. Random sample; less than 10% of the population; samples are independent; more than 10 successes and failures in each sample.
b) (0.024, 0.040)
c) We are 95% confident, based on these samples, that the proportion of 24-year-old American women who have graduated from high school is between 2.4% and 4.0% more than that of 24-year-old American men.
d) Yes; the entire interval lies above 0.

3. a) 0.035
b) (0.356, 0.495)
c) We are 95% confident, based on these data, that the proportion of pets with a malignant lymphoma in homes where herbicides are used is between 35.6% and 49.5% higher than the proportion of pets with lymphoma in homes where no pesticides are used.

4. a) 0.068
b) (0.126,0.394)
c) We are 95% confident, based on these data, that the proportion of patients who show improvement in carpal tunnel syndrome with surgery is between 12.6% and 39.4% more than the proportion who show improvement with wrist splints.

5. a) Experiment. Men were randomly assigned to have surgery or not.
b) (0.006, 0.080)
c) Since the entire interval lies above 0, there is evidence that surgery may be effective in preventing death from prostate cancer.

6. a) (−0.034, 0.052)
b) H_0: $p_1 - p_2 = 0$; H_A: $p_1 - p_2 \neq 0$. Since 0 is in the interval, this survey does not provide evidence of a race-based difference in smoking percentages.

7. a) Differences have a larger standard error than single samples.
b) No. The confidence interval 2% ± 4% includes 0.

8. a) 45%
b) Greater. Differences have standard errors larger than single samples.

9. a) Prospective study
b) H_0: $p_1 - p_2 = 0$; H_A: $p_1 - p_2 \neq 0$ where p_1 is the proportion of students whose parents disapproved of smoking who became smokers and p_2 is the proportion of students whose parents are lenient about smoking who became smokers.
c) Yes. We assume the students were randomly selected; they are less than 10% of the population; samples are independent; more than 10 successes and failures in each sample.
d) $z = -1.17$, P-value = 0.2422. These samples do not show evidence that parental attitudes influence teens' decisions to smoke.
e) If there is no difference in the proportions, there is about a 24% chance of seeing the observed difference or larger by natural sampling variation.
f) Type II

10. a) Prospective study
b) H_0: $p_1 - p_2 = 0$; H_A: $p_1 - p_2 < 0$ where p_1 is the proportion of people without depression who died within the 4 years and p_2 is the proportion of depressed people who died within the same time period.
c) Yes. We assume the patients were representative; they are less than 10% of the population; samples are independent; more than 10 successes and failures in each sample.
d) $z = -2.22$, P-value = 0.0131. With a P-value this low, we reject H_0. This study indicates that the death rate for patients with heart disease who die within 4 years is less in nondepressed patients than in depressed patients.
e) If there is no difference in the proportions, we will see an observed difference this large or larger only about 1.3% of the time by natural sampling variation.
f) Type I

11. a) (−0.065, 0.221)
b) We are 95% confident that the proportion of teens whose parents disapprove of smoking who will eventually smoke is between 6.5% less and 22.1% more than for teens with parents who are lenient about smoking.
c) 95% of all random samples will produce intervals that contain the true difference.

12. a) (0.004, 0.209)
b) We are 95% confident, based on these data, that the proportion of heart disease patients who die within 4 years is between 0.4% and 20.9% higher for depressed patients than for nondepressed patients.
c) 95% of all random samples will produce intervals that contain the true value.

13. a) H_0: $p_1 - p_2 = 0$; H_A: $p_1 - p_2 \neq 0$. $z = 3.56$, P-value = 0.0004. With a P-value this low, we reject H_0. There is a significant difference in the clinic's effectiveness. Younger mothers have a higher birth rate than older mothers. Note that the success/failure condition is met based on the pooled estimate of p.
b) We are 95% confident, based on these data, that the proportion of successful live births at the clinic is between 10.0%

and 27.8% higher for mothers under 28 than in those 38 and older. However, the Success/Failure Condition is not met for the older women, since #successes < 10. We should be cautious in interpreting the level of the confidence interval.

14. a) $H_0: p_1 - p_2 = 0$; $H_A: p_1 - p_2 \neq 0$. $z = 3.56$, P-value = 0.0004. With a P-value this low, we reject H_0. This study shows a significant difference in the rate of teen suicides. Adopted teens are more likely to attempt suicide.
b) We are 95% confident, based on this study, that the proportion of teens who will attempt suicide is between 0.8% and 7.9% higher in adopted teens than in those who were not adopted.

15. $H_0: p_1 - p_2 = 0$; $H_A: p_1 - p_2 > 0$. $z = 1.18$, P-value = 0.118. With a P-value this high, we fail to reject H_0. These data do not show evidence of a decrease in the voter support for the candidate.

16. a) $H_0: p_1 - p_2 = 0$; $H_A: p_1 - p_2 \neq 0$. $z = 2.41$, P-value = 0.0160. With a P-value this low, we reject H_0. This is moderately strong evidence that men and women have different outlooks.
b) We are 95% confident that between 12% and 24% more men than women expect to have enough money in retirement.

17. a) $H_0: p_1 - p_2 = 0$; $H_A: p_1 - p_2 \neq 0$. $z = -0.39$, P-value = 0.6951. With a P-value this high, we fail to reject H_0. There is no evidence of racial differences in the likelihood of multiple births, based on these data.
b) Type II

18. a) $H_0: p_1 - p_2 = 0$; $H_A: p_1 - p_2 > 0$. $z = 0.78$, P-value = 0.2166. With a P-value this high, we fail to reject H_0. There is no evidence, based on this information, that men are more likely than women to make online purchases of books.
b) Type II

19. a) $H_0: p_1 - p_2 = 0$; $H_A: p_1 - p_2 > 0$. $z = 2.17$, P-value = 0.0148. With a P-value this low, we reject H_0. These data do suggest that mammograms may reduce breast cancer deaths.
b) Type I

20. a) $H_0: p_1 - p_2 = 0$; $H_A: p_1 - p_2 > 0$. $z = 0.24$, P-value = 0.4068. With a P-value this high, we fail to reject H_0. These data do not suggest that mammograms are effective in reducing breast cancer deaths.
b) Type II

21. a) We are 95% confident, based on this study, that between 67.0% and 83.0% of patients with joint pain will find medication A effective.
b) We are 95% confident, based on this study, that between 51.9% and 70.3% of patients with joint pain will find medication B effective.
c) Yes, they overlap. This might indicate no difference in the effectiveness of the medications, although this is not a proper test.
d) We are 95% confident that the proportion of patients with joint pain who will find medication A effective is between 1.7% and 26.1% higher than the proportion who will find medication B effective.
e) No. There is a difference in the effectiveness of the medications.
f) To estimate the variability in the difference of proportions, we must add variances. The two one-sample intervals do not. The 2-sample method is the correct approach.

22. a) We are 95% confident, based on the data, that between 47.5% and 56.5% of male voters will vote for the candidate.
b) We are 95% confident, based on the data, that between 40.7% and 49.3% of female voters will vote for the candidate.
c) Yes, they overlap. There appears to be no discernible gender gap, but this is not the proper approach.
d) We are 95% confident, based on the data, that the proportion of men who will vote for the candidate is between 0.8% and 13.2% higher than the proportion of female voters who will vote for him.
e) No. There is a gender gap.
f) To estimate the variability in the difference of proportions, we must add variances. The two one-sample intervals do not. The 2-sample method is the correct approach.

PART V REVIEW

1. H_0: There is no difference in cancer rates, $p_1 - p_2 = 0$
H_A: The cancer rate in those who use the herb is higher, $p_1 - p_2 > 0$.

2. a) Yes, $0.08 \times 325 = 26$, so we expect more than 10 successes and 10 failures.
b) $\mu = .08$, $\sigma = 0.015$
c)

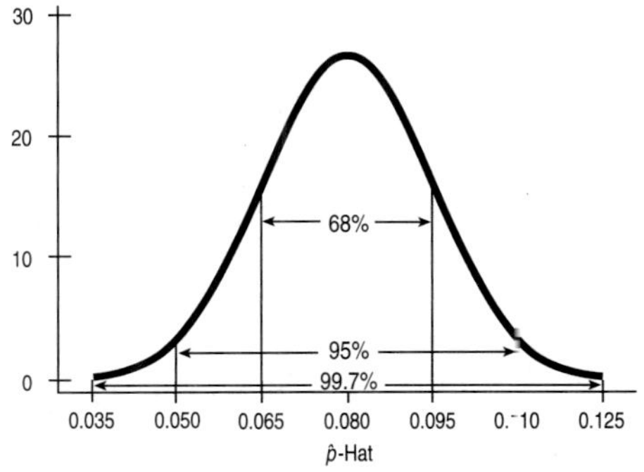

d) There is about a 68% chance of observing between 6.5% and 9.5% of colorblind males in a class of this size, a 95% chance of having between 5% and 11% colorblind males. Almost all classes of this size will have a percentage between 3.5% and 12.5% colorblind males.

3. a) 10.29
b) Not really. The z-score is −1.11. Not any evidence to suggest that the proportion for Monday is low.
c) Yes. The z-score is 2.26 with a P-value of 0.024 (two-sided).
d) Some births are scheduled for the convenience of the doctor and/or the mother.

4. a) No. There is always natural sampling variation.
b) 33.3% and 52.7% (using 1.96 SD's)
c) 11.3% and 26.7%
d) Less. Proportions farther from 0.5 have smaller standard deviations.

5. a) $H_0: p = 0.40$; $H_A: p < 0.40$
b) Random sample; less than 10% of all California gas stations, $0.4(27) = 10.8$, $0.6(27) = 16.2$. Assumptions and conditions are met.
c) $z = -1.49$, P-value = 0.0677
d) With a P-value this high, we fail to reject H_0. These data do not provide evidence that the proportion of leaking gas tanks is less than 40% (or that the new program is effective in decreasing the proportion).
e) Yes, Type II.
f) Increase α, increase the sample size
g) Increasing α—increases power, lowers chance of Type II error, but increases chance of Type I error.
Increasing sample size—increases power, costs more time and money

6. a) An experiment.
b) H_0: There is no difference, $p_1 - p_2 = 0$
H_A: Patients with carbolic acid are more likely to live, $p_1 - p_2 > 0$
$z = 2.91$, P-value $= 0.0018$; with a P-value so low, we reject H_0. These data show that carbolic acid is effective in increasing the chances of surviving an amputation.
c) We are not told whether the patients were randomized to the treatments. We are not told whether the experiment was double blinded or even blinded at all. This could have biased the results toward a more favorable outcome.

7. a) The researcher believes that the true proportion of "A"'s is within 10% of the estimated 54%, namely, between 44% and 64%.
b) Small sample
c) No, 63% is contained in the interval.

8. 0.647
$\bar{y} \sim N(3.5, 0.538)$. Rolls are independent.

9. a) Pew believes that the true proportion is within 3% of the 33% from the sample; that is, between 30% and 36%.
b) Larger, since its a smaller sample.
c) We are 95% confident that the proportion of active traders who rely on the Internet for investment information is between 38.7% and 51.3%, based on this sample.
d) Larger, since it's a smaller sample.

10. a) 47.8% to 56.2%
b) Since the interval extends below 50%, it is not clear the death penalty has majority support.
c) About 3382 people

11. a) Bimodal!
b) μ, the population mean. Sample size does not matter.
c) $\sigma/\sqrt{n}$; sample size does matter.
d) It becomes closer to a Normal model and narrower as the sample size increases.

12. a) Individuals were probably independent of one another, they are less than 10% of all African American women, and there were clearly more than 10 successes and 10 failures. Is the sample a random sample from the population of African-American women?
b) (39.5% to 44.5%)
c) We are 95% confident, based on this study, that between 39.5% and 44.5% of African American women have a vitamin D deficiency.
d) 95% of all such random samples will produce intervals that contain the true proportion.

13. a) $\mu = 0.80$ $\sigma = 0.028$
b) Yes. 0.8(200) = 160, 0.2(200) = 40. Both > 10.
c)

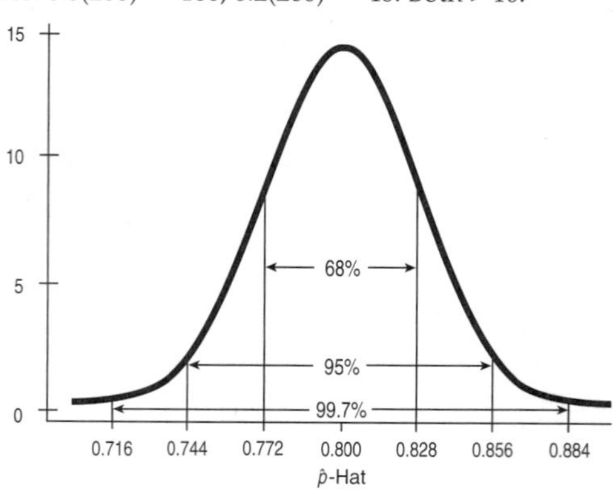

d) 0.039

14. a) $H_0: p_1 - p_2 = 0$ $H_A: p_1 - p_2 > 0$. $z = 2.71$, P= .003
With a P-value this low we reject H_0. This study shows significantly higher rate of low-weight babies born to mothers exposed to high levels of air pollution during pregnancy.
b) We are 90% confident that the proportion of low birthweight babies will be between 0.8% and 7.6% higher for mothers exposed to high levels of air pollution than those who were not.

15. H_0: There is no difference, $p_1 - p_2 = 0$ H_A: Early births have increased, $p_1 - p_2 < 0$. $z = -0.729$, P-value $= 0.2329$. Because the P-value is so high, we do not reject H_0. These data do not show an increase in the incidence of early birth of twins.

16. a) We are 95% confident that the increase in the proportion of women who may develop side effects from magnesium sulfide is between 18.1% and 20.8%.
b) H_0: There is no difference, $p_1 - p_2 = 0$. H_A: Treatment prevents eclampsia, $p_1 - p_2 < 0$. $z = -4.84$, P-value $= 6.4 \times 10^{-7}$
Because the P-value is so low, we reject H_0. This study shows evidence that treatment with magnesium sulfide is effective in preventing eclampsia.

17. a) H_0: There is no difference, $p_1 - p_2 < 0$. H_A: Treatment prevents deaths from eclampsia, $p_1 - p_2 < 0$.
b) Samples are random and independent; less than 10% of all pregnancies (or eclampsia cases); more than 10 successes and failures in each group.
c) 0.8008
d) There is not sufficient evidence to conclude that magnesium sulfide is effective in preventing eclampsia deaths.
e) Type II
f) Increase the sample size, increase α.
g) Increasing sample size: decreases variation in the sampling distribution, is costly. Increasing α: Increases likelihood of rejecting H_0, increases chance of Type I error.

18. a) 33.7% b) 0.073
c)

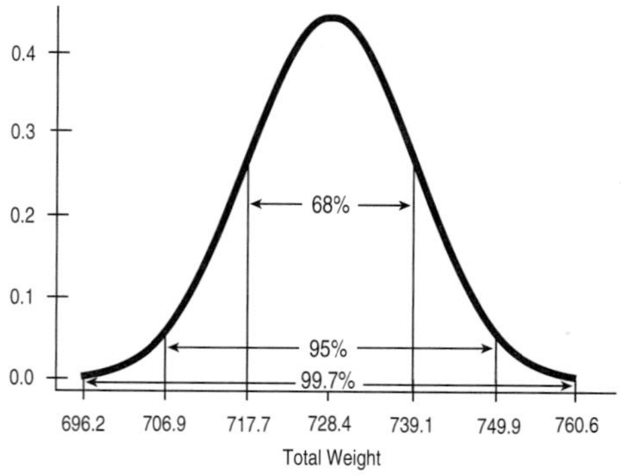

19. a) It is not clear What the pollster asked. Otherwise they did fine.
b) Stratified sampling. c) 4%
d) 95% e) Smaller sample size
f) Wording and order of questions (response bias)

20. About 1800

21. a) H_0: There is no difference, p = 0.143. H_A: The fatal accident rate is lower in girls, p < 0.143. $z = -1.67$, P-value $= 0.0479$. Because the P-value is low, we reject H_0. These data give some evidence that the fatal accident rate is lower for girls than for teens in general.
b) If the proportion is really 14.3%, we will see the observed proportion (11.3%) or lower 4.8% of the time by sampling variation.

22. a) H_0: There is no difference, $p_1 - p_2 = 0$. H_A: There is a difference, $p_1 - p_2 \neq 0$

b) There is a difference in the proportion of students with perfect pitch; more Asians are likely to have it.
c) If there is no difference, the observed 25% difference will be seen by sampling variation less than about 1 time in 10,000.
d) The data do not "prove" anything about genetic differences *causing* differences in perfect pitch—merely that Asian students are more likely to have it.

23. a) One would expect many small fish, with a few large ones.
b) We don't know the exact distribution, but we know it's not Normal.
c) Probably not. With a skewed distribution, a sample size of 5 is not a large enough sample to say the mean is approximately Normal.
d) 0.961

24. a) Random sample; less than 10% of all high school students; many more than 10 successes and 10 failures. 90% confidence interval for proportion who cheat: (72.9 to 75.1%).
b) Based on this information, we are 90% confident the proportion of all high school students who have cheated at least once on a test is between 72.9% and 75.1%.
c) 90% of all such random samples will produce confidence intervals that contain the true proportion of students who cheat.
d) Wider. More confidence means a larger margin of error.

25. a) Yes. $0.8(60) = 48$, $0.2(60) = 12$. Both are > 10.
b) 0.834
c) Higher. Bigger sample means smaller standard deviation for $\hat{p}$.
d) Answers will vary. A sample size of 500 makes the probability 0.997.

26. a) H_0: The goal is not on track, $p = 0.3$. H_A: The goal is on track, $p < 0.3$.
b) Random sample; less than 10% of all high school students; Many more than 10 failures and successes.
c) 0.00047
d) If the proportion were still 30%, the probability of seeing a value as low as (or lower than) 28.5% in a random sample this large is about 0.00047.
e) By 2001, the rate of cigarette smoking in high school students was lower than the target of 30%.
f) Type I

27. a) 54.4 to 62.5%
b) Based on this study, with 95% confidence the proportion of Crohn's disease patients who will respond favorable to infliximab is between 54.4% and 62.5%.
c) 95% of all such random samples will produce confidence intervals that contain the true proportion of patients who respond favorably.

28. No. The probability of 40% or more is very, very small: 3.1×10^{-7}.

29. At least 423, assuming that p is near 50%.

30. a) An experiment
b) A one-sided test, since they are interested only in a decrease in percentage needing repairs.
c) Deciding the additive reduces the number of repairs needed when there really is no difference.
d) Deciding the additive makes no difference when it really does reduce the number of repairs needed.
e) Type II
f) Given that the two groups received roughly same use and care, yes. They can't necessarily claim it will work for all cars, only cars similar to their fleet.

31. a) Random sample (?); certainly less than 10% of all preemies and normal babies; more than 10 failures and successes in each group. 1.7% to 16.3% greater for normal-birth-weight children.
b) Since 0 is not in the interval, there is evidence that preemies have a lower high school graduation rate than children of normal birth weight.
c) Type I, since we rejected the null hypothesis.

32. a) We are 95% confident that between 11.6% and 16.4% of Texas children wear helmets when biking, roller skating, or skateboarding, based on these data.
b) The data might not be a random sample.
c) About 408 using the previous 14% as $\hat{p}$.

33. a) H_0: The computer is undamaged. H_A: The computer is damaged.
b) 20% of good PCs will be classified as damaged (bad), while all damaged PCs will be detected (good).
c) 3 or more
d) 20%
e) By switching to 2 or more as the rejection criterion, 7% of the good PCs will be misclassified, but only 10% of the bad ones will, increasing the power from 20% to 90%.

34. a) Increase
b) Decrease

CHAPTER 23

1. a) 1.74 b) 2.37 c) 0.0524 d) 0.0889

2. a) 2.37 b) 2.36 c) 0.9829 d) 0.0381

3. Shape and center do not change; spread becomes narrower.

4. The critical value becomes smaller, approaching 1.96.

5. a) The confidence interval is for the population mean, not the individual cows in the study.
b) The confidence interval is not for individual cows.
c) We *know* the average gain in this study was 56 pounds!
d) The average weight gain of all cows does not vary. It's what we're trying to estimate.
e) No. There is not a 95% chance for another sample to have an average weight gain between 45 and 67 pounds. There is a 95% chance that another sample will have its average weight gain within two standard errors of the true mean.

6. a) Nine out of 10 intervals will contain the true mean salary; different samples will produce different intervals.
b) This is correct.
c) The interval is for the population mean, not individual teachers.
d) The interval is for the mean, not individual teachers.
e) The interval addresses only Nevada teachers, not the entire country.

7. a) Based on this sample, we can say, with 95% confidence, that the mean pulse rate of adults is between 70.9 and 74.5 beats per minute.
b) 1.8 beats per minute
c) Larger

8. a) Based on this sample, we can say, with 95% confidence, that the mean age at which babies begin to crawl is between 29.2 and 31.8 weeks.
b) 1.3 c) Smaller

9. a) Yes. Randomly selected group; less than 10% of the population; the histogram is not unimodal and symmetric, but it is not highly skewed and there are no outliers, so with a sample size of 52, the CLT says $\bar{y}$ is approximately normal.
b) (98.06, 98.51) degrees F
c) We are 98% confident, based on the data, that the average body temperature for an adult is between 98.05°F and 98.51°F.

d) 98% of all such random samples will produce intervals containing the true mean temperature.
e) These data suggest that the true normal temperature is somewhat less than 98.6°F.

10. a) The data are a representative sample of less than 10% of all days; $n = 44$ is a large sample.
b) (\$122.20, \$129.80)
c) We are 90% confident the mean daily income for the parking garage is between \$122.20 and \$129.80, based on this sample.
d) 90% of all such samples will produce intervals that contain the true mean daily fee.
e) No. The interval is below \$130.

11. a) Narrower. We need fewer values to be less confident.
b) Advantage: more chance of including the true value. Disadvantage: wider interval.
c) Narrower; due to the larger sample, the SE will be smaller.
d) About 252

12. a) More chance the interval contains the true mean.
b) The interval would be wider.
c) More data would result in a narrower interval at same confidence level.
d) About 99

13. a) (298.5, 321.5)
b) Normal population, random sample, less than 10% of all hot dogs. These seem reasonable here—but we would need to check the nearly Normal condition.
c) With 95% confidence, the mean sodium content in these "reduced sodium" hot dogs is between 298.5 mg and 321.5 mg, based on this sample.

14. a) (709.90, 802.54)
b) With 95% confidence, based on these data, the speed of light is between 299,709.9 and 299,802.5 km/sec.
c) Normal model for the distribution, independent measurements, less than 10% of all possible measurements. These seem reasonable here, but it would be nice to see if the nearly Normal condition held for the data.

15. a) Yes. Larger sample, smaller SE.
b) 4.1 mg sodium
c) With 95% confidence, the mean sodium content of all hot dogs is between 309.7 mg and 326.3 mg, based on this sample.
d) $0.7(465) = 325.5$. Since the confidence interval extends above this, it is possible these should not be labeled as "reduced sodium."

16. a) 7.9 km/sec
b) Should be narrower. Different mean will change the center of the interval. Larger sample size and smaller standard deviation will reduce the SE. Since the t-critical value is also smaller, the margin of error will be smaller.
c) New interval: (836.72, 868.08) km/sec. This experiment is worse than the first, which included 710.5. This interval is considerably above that value. There may have been a bias in this experiment's measurements.

17. a) Upper-tail. We want to show it will hold 500 pounds (or more) easily.
b) They will decide the stands are safe, when they're not.
c) They will decide the stands are unsafe, when they are in fact safe.

18. a) Two-sided. If they're too big, they won't fit through the vein. If they're too small, they probably won't work well.
b) The catheters are rejected when in fact the diameters are fine, and the manufacturing process is needlessly stopped.
c) Catheters that do not meet specifications are allowed to be produced and sold.

19. a) Decrease α. This means a smaller chance of declaring the stands safe, if they are not.
b) The probability of correctly detecting that the stands are capable of holding more than 500 pounds.
c) Decrease the standard deviation—probably costly. Increase the sample size—takes more time for testing and is costly. Increase α—more Type I errors. Increase the "design load" to be well above 500 pounds—again, costly.

20. a) Increase
b) The probability of correctly detecting deviations from 2 mm in diameter.
c) Increase
d) Increase the sample size or increase α.

21. a) H_0: $\mu = 23.3$; H_A: $\mu > 23.3$
b) We have a random sample that comprises less than 10% of the population. Population may not be normally distributed, as it would be easier to have a few much older men at their first marriage than some very young men. However, with a sample size of 40, $\bar{y}$ should be approximately Normal. We should check the histogram for severity of skewness and possible outliers.
c) $t_{39}(23.3, s/\sqrt{40})$
d) 0.1447
e) If the average age at first marriage is still 23.3 years, there is a 14.5% chance of getting a sample mean of 24.2 years or older simply from natural sampling variation.
f) We have not shown that the average age at first marriage has increased from the mean of 23.3 years.

22. a) H_0: $\mu = 26$; H_A: $\mu < 26$
b) We have a representative sample, less than 10% of all trips, and a large enough sample that skewness should not be a problem.
c) $t_{49}(25.02, 4.83/\sqrt{50})$
d) 0.0789
e) If the average fuel economy is 26 mpg, the chance of obtaining a sample mean of 25.02 or less by natural sampling variation is 8%.
f) Since $0.05 < P < 0.10$, there is some evidence that the company may not be achieving the fuel economy goal.

23. a) Probably a representative sample, less than 10% of all Ruffles bags; the nearly Normal condition seems reasonable from a Normal probability plot. The histogram is nearly uniform, with no outliers or skewness.
b) $\bar{y} = 28.78$, $s = 0.40$
c) (28.36, 29.21) grams
d) Based on this sample, we are 95% confident the average weight of the content of Ruffles bags is between 28.36 and 29.21 grams.
e) The company is erring on the safe side, as it appears that, on average, it is putting in slightly more chips than stated.

24. a) Probably a representative sample, less than 10% of all Doritos bags; the nearly Normal condition seems reasonable from a Normal probability plot. The data are fairly symmetric with no apparent outliers.
b) $\bar{y} = 28.98$, $s = 0.36$
c) (28.61, 29.36) grams
d) With 95% confidence, the average weight of the content of Doritos bags is between 28.61 and 29.36 grams, based on this sample.

e) The company is erring on the safe side, as it appears that, on average, it is putting in slightly more chips than stated.

25. No. Based on this large random sample, $t = -1.45$; P-value = 0.1494. Because the P-value is high, we fail to reject H_0. These data do not provide evidence to support the claim that the average weight of all cars is not 3000 pounds. We retain the null hypothesis that the mean is 3000 pounds.

26. Yes. Based on this large random sample, $t = -4.42$, P-value = 3.29×10^{-5}. Because the P-value is low, we reject H_0. These data show that the range of these phones is not 150 feet; in fact, it is less.

27. a) Random sample; less than 10% of all Chips Ahoy bags; the nearly Normal condition seems reasonable from a Normal probability plot. The histogram is roughly unimodal and symmetric with no outliers.
b) (1187.9, 1288.4) chips
c) Based on this sample, the mean number of chips in an 18-ounce bag is between 1187.9 and 1288.4, with 95% confidence.The *mean* number of chips is clearly greater than 1000. However, if the claim is about individual bags, then it's not necessarily true. If the mean is 1188 and the SD deviation is near 94, then 2.5% of the bags will have fewer than 1000 chips using the Normal model. If in fact the mean is 1288, the proportion below 1000 will be less than 0.3%, but the claim is still false.

28. a) Random sample; this is less than 10% of all vanilla yogurt brands. Nearly Normal condition is reasonable by examining a Normal probability plot. The histogram is roughly unimodal (although somewhat uniform) and symmetric with no outliers.
b) (132.0, 183.7) calories
c) Based on this sample, the mean number of calories in a serving of vanilla yogurt is between 132 and 183.7, with 95% confidence. We conclude that the diet guide's claim of 120 calories is too low.

29. a) The Normal probability plot is relatively straight, with one outlier at 93.8 sec. Without the outlier, the conditions seem to be met. The histogram is roughly unimodal and symmetric with no other outliers.
b) $t = -2.63$, P-value = 0.0160. With the outlier included, we might conclude that the mean completion time for the maze is not 60 seconds; in fact, it is less.
c) $t = -4.46$, P-value = 0.0003. Because the P-value is so small, we reject H_0. Without the outlier, we conclude that the average completion time for the maze is not 60 seconds; in fact, it is less. The outlier here did not change the conclusion.
d) The maze does not meet the "one-minute average" requirement. Both tests rejected a null hypothesis of a mean of 60 seconds.

30. The data value of 102 feet is an outlier. When this is removed, the Normal probability plot is relatively straight. The Nearly Normal Condition seems satisfied. With the outlier removed, the histogram is roughly unimodal and symmetric with no other outliers. H_0: $\mu = 125$; H_A: $\mu > 125$ feet. With the outlier eliminated, $\bar{y} = 128.89$, $t = 3.29$, P-value = 0.01. With a P-value this low, we reject H_0. There is strong evidence to suggest that the tires will not bring the car to a complete stop within 125 feet. On the basis of these data, the company should not adopt the new tread pattern. Only 2 out of the 10 data values were less than the desired 125 feet, and 1 of these was an outlier.

CHAPTER 24

1. a) 2.927
b) Larger
c) Based on this sample, we are 95% confident that students who learn math using the CPMP method will score on average between 5.57 and 11.43 points better on a test solving applied algebra problems with a calculator than students who learn by traditional methods.
d) Yes; 0 is not in the interval.

2. Based on this sample, we are 90% confident that people who receive either no or only verbal information about the image in a stereogram will take between 0.55 and 5.47 seconds longer, on average, to report they saw the image than people who receive both verbal and visual information.
b) Yes, since 0 is not in the interval.
c) 2.46
d) 90% of all random samples will produce intervals that contain the true value of the mean difference between the times for these two groups.
e) Wider. More confidence means less precision.
f) Possibly. The wider interval may contain 0.

3. a) H_0: $\mu_C - \mu_T = 0$ vs. H_A: $\mu_C - \mu_T \neq 0$
b) Yes. Groups are independent, though we don't know if students were randomly assigned to the programs. Sample sizes are large, so CLT applies.
c) If the means for the two programs are really equal, there is less than a 1 in 10,000 chance of seeing a difference as large as or larger than the observed difference just from natural sampling variation.
d) On average, students who learn with the CPMP method do significantly worse on algebra tests that do not allow them to use calculators than students who learn by traditional methods.

4. H_0: $\mu_C - \mu_T = 0$; H_A: $\mu_C - \mu_T \neq 0$. $t = 1.406$ df = 590.05, P-value = 0.1602. Because of the large P-value, we fail to reject H_0. Based on this sample, there is no evidence of a difference in mean scores on a test of word problems, whether students learned with CPMP or traditional methods.

5. a) (1.36, 4.64)
b) No; 5 minutes is beyond the high end of the interval.

6. a) The mean rates are roughly equal, but females are more variable.
b) Yes; boxplots look symmetric.
c) (−3.025, 3.275)
d) Yes; 0 is in the interval.

7.

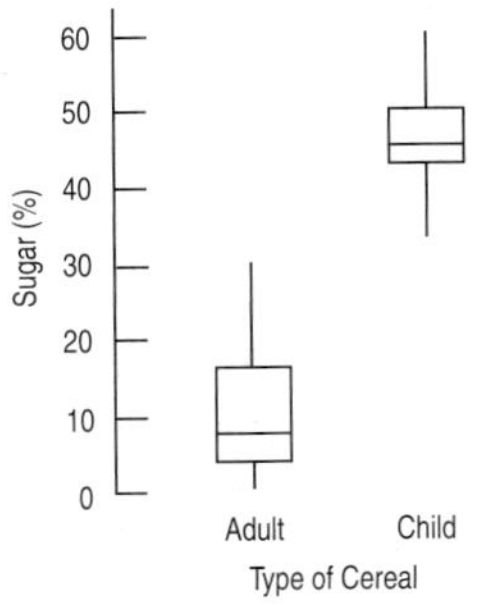

Random sample—questionable, but probably representative, independent samples, less than 10% of all cereals; boxplot shows no outliers—not exactly symmetric, but these are reasonable sample sizes. Based on these samples, with 95% confidence, children's cereals average between 32.49% and 40.80% more sugar content than adult's cereals.

8. a) Random sample (we assume), less than 10% of all Egyptians at those times, independent samples, boxplots look symmetric.

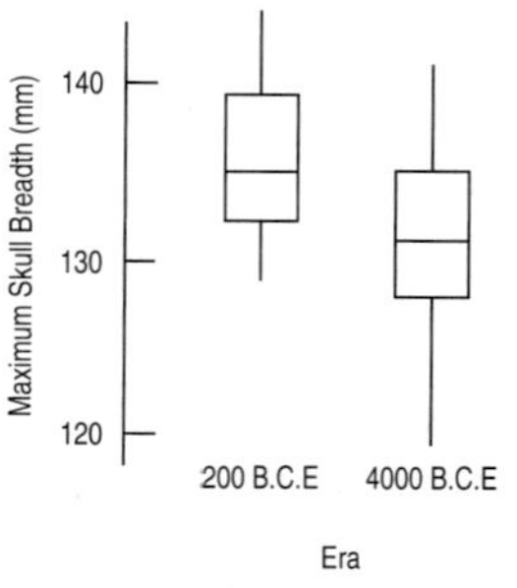

b) (1.88, 6.66) mm

c) These data provide evidence that mean maximum skull breadth in Egyptians in 200 B.C.E. was between 1.88 and 6.66 mm larger than that in 4000 B.C.E.

9. H_0: $\mu_N - \mu_C = 0$ vs. H_A: $\mu_N - \mu_C > 0$. $t = 2.076$ P-value = 0.0228 df = 33.4. Because of the small P-value, we reject H_0. These data do suggest that new activities are better. The mean reading comprehension score for the group with new activities is significantly (at $\alpha = 0.05$) higher than the mean score for the control group.

10. a) H_0: $\mu_L - \mu_S = 0$ vs. H_A: $:\mu_L - \mu_S \neq 0$

b) Don't know if the streams were a random sample, or whether they are less than 10 % of all Adirondack streams. Boxplots show outliers and Shale may be skewed (median is equal to Q1 or Q3), but samples are large.

c) Based on these data, it appears that water flowing over limestone is less acidic, on average, than water flowing over shale.

11.

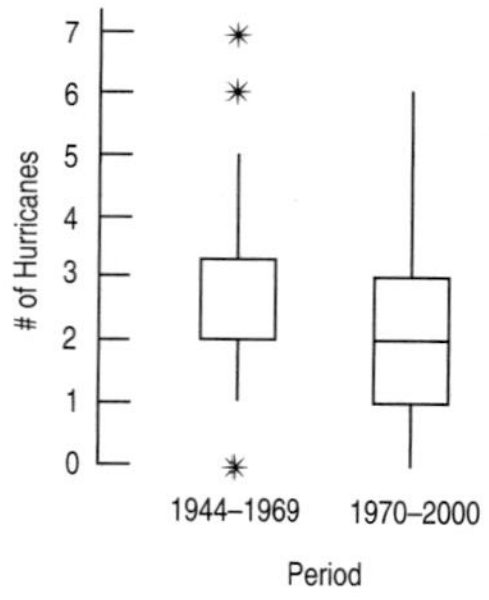

There are several concerns here. First, we don't have a random sample. We have to assume that the actual number of hurricanes in a given year is a random sample of the hurricanes that might occur under similar weather conditions. Also, the data for 1944–1969 are not symmetric and have three outliers. The outliers will tend to make the average for the period 1944–1969 larger. These data are not appropriate for inference. The boxplots provide little evidence of a change in the mean number of hurricanes in the two periods.

12. a) If there is no difference between ginkgo and the placebo, there is a 93.74% chance of seeing a difference as large or larger as that observed, just from natural sampling variation.

b) There is no evidence based on this study that ginkgo biloba improves memory, as the difference in mean memory score was not significant.

c) Type II

13. a)

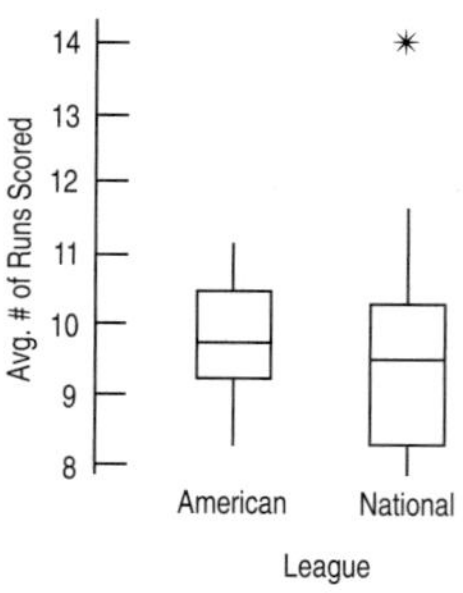

Both are reasonably symmetric, except for the outlier in the National League.

b) Based on these data, the average number of runs in an American League stadium is between 9.34 and 10.27, with 95% confidence.

c) There is an outlier. It could be deleted, and mentioned separately.

d) Yes. The boxplot indicates it is an outlier.

e) We want to work directly with the average difference. The two separate confidence intervals do not answer questions about the difference. The difference has a different standard deviation.

14. a) Males: (18.67, 20.11) pegs; females: (16.95, 18.87) pegs.

b) It suggests that there is no evidence of a difference, but the method is incorrect.

c) (0.29, 2.67) pegs

d) There is a difference—males do better on average by between 0.29 and 2.67 pegs.

e) Two-sample inference

f) If we examine the gap between the means using two separate confidence intervals, we are essentially adding the margins of error, which are based on standard deviations. To be correct we must instead add variances. That's exactly what happens when we create the confidence interval for the difference in means—the proper approach.

15. a) $(-0.69, 1.14)$

b) Based on these data, with 95% confidence, American League stadiums average between –0.69 and 1.14 more runs than National League stadiums.

c) No; 0 is in the interval.

d) No. The interval is now $(-0.19, 1.23)$. It still contains 0.

16. a) H_0: $\mu_N - \mu_S = 0$ vs. H_A: $\mu_N - \mu_S \neq 0$. $t = 6.47$, df = 53.49, P-value = 3.2×10^{-8}. Because the P-value is low, we reject H_0. On the basis of these data, there is clear evidence that mortality rates are different. The mean rate in the north is significantly higher.

b) It will raise $\bar{y}$ for the north, but from looking at the boxplots and the fact that the mean and median are nearly the same, it probably will not change the conclusion of the test.

17. These are not two independent samples. These are before and after scores for the same individuals.

18. These are before and after scores for the same individuals, not independent samples.

19. a) These data do not show a difference in ad recall between shows with sexual content and violent content.

b) H_0: $\mu_S - \mu_N = 0$ vs.H_A: $\mu_S - \mu_N \neq 0$. $t = -6.08$, df = 213.99, P-value = 5.5×10^{-9}. Because the P-value is low, we reject H_0. These data show that ad recall between shows with sexual and neutral content is different; those who saw shows with neutral content had higher average recall.

20. a) With 95% confidence, those who watch shows with violent content remembered an average of between 1.6 and 0.6 fewer brand names than those who saw shows with neutral content.

b) If they want viewers to remember their brand, advise that they consider advertising in shows with neutral content in preference to those with violent content. Of course, costs of the ad should be considered.

21. a) H_0: $\mu_V - \mu_N = 0$ vs H_A: $\mu_V - \mu_N \neq 0$. $t = -7.21$, df = 201.96, P-value = 1.1×10^{-11}. Because of the very small P-value, we reject H_0. There is a significant difference in mean ad recall between shows with violent content and neutral content; viewers of shows with neutral content remember more brand names, on average.

b) With 95% confidence, the average number of brand names remembered 24 hours later is between 1.46 and 2.40 higher for viewers of neutral content shows than for viewers of sexual content shows, based on these data.

22. a) He would conclude that recall is higher 24 hours later.

b) The samples are not independent. They are the same people asked at two time periods.

c) The first inquiry might influence people.

d) Use two different groups for each type of show. Interview one group immediately, the other 24 hours later.

23. a) The 95% confidence interval for the difference is (0.61, 5.39). 0 is not in the interval, so scores in 1996 were significantly higher. (Or the t, with more than 7500 df, is 2.459 for a P-value of 0.0069)

b) Since both samples were very large, there shouldn't be a difference.

24. a) The observed differences are too large to attribute to chance or natural sampling variation.

b) Type I

c) No. There may be many other factors.

25. The 90% confidence interval for the difference in mean number of months to publication between *Applied Statistics* and *The American Statistician* is (8.43,11.57) months. We assume that the articles are a random sample of the kinds of articles typically submitted to these two journals, and that they represent fewer than 10% of all articles that could have been submitted. Both samples are large.

26. a) H_0: $\mu_M - \mu_R = 0$ vs. H_A: $\mu_M - \mu_R > 0$. $t = -0.70$, df = 45.88, P-value = 0.7563. Because the P-value is so large, we do not reject H_0. These data provide no evidence that listening to Mozart while studying is better than listening to rap.

b) With 90% confidence, the average difference in score is between (0.189 and 5.357) objects more for those who listen to no music while studying, based on these samples.

27. a) H_0: $\mu_R - \mu_N = 0$ vs. H_A: $\mu_R - \mu_N < 0$. $t = -1.36$, df = 20.00, P-value = 0.944. Because the P-value is large, we fail to reject H_0. These data show no evidence of a difference in mean number of objects recalled between listening to rap or no music at all.

b) Didn't conclude a difference.

28.

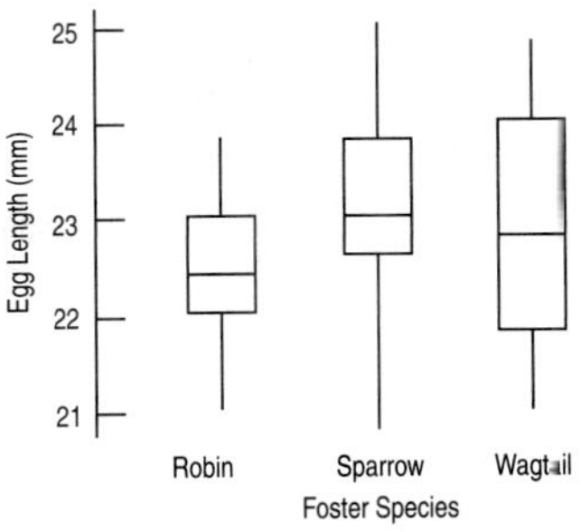

H_0: $\mu_S - \mu_R = 0$ vs. H_A: $\mu_S - \mu_R \neq 0$.
$t = 1.641$, df = 21.60, P-value = 0.115.
Since P > 0.05, fail to reject H_0. There is no evidence of a difference in mean cuckoo egg length between robin and sparrow foster parents.

H_0: $\mu_S - \mu_W = 0$ vs. H_A: $\mu_S - \mu_W \neq 0$
t= 0.549, df = 26.86, P-value = 0.587.
Since P > 0.05, fail to reject H_0. There is no evidence of a difference in mean cuckoo egg length between sparrow and wagtail foster parents.

H_0: $\mu_R - \mu_W = 0$ vs. H_S: $\mu_R - \mu_W \neq 0$
$t = -1.012$, df = 23.60, P-value = 0.322.
Since P > 0.05, fail to reject H_0. There is no evidence of a difference in mean cuckoo egg length between robin and wagtail foster parents.

In general,we should be wary of doing 3 t-tests on the same data. Our Type I error rate is not the same for doing 3 tests as it is for one test. However, because none of the tests showed significant differences, this is less of a concern here.

CHAPTER 25

1. a) Randomly assign 50 hens to each of the two kinds of feed. Compare production at the end of the month.

b) Give all 100 hens the new feed for 2 weeks and the old food for 2 weeks, randomly selecting which feed the hens get first. Analyze the differences in production for all 100 hens.

c) Matched pairs. Because hens vary in egg production, the matched-pairs design will control for that.

2. a) Randomly assign half the volunteers to do the puzzles in a quiet room, half to do them with MTV on. Compare the times.

b) Randomly assign half the volunteers to do a puzzle in a quiet room, half to do a puzzle with MTV on. Then have each do a puzzle under the other condition. Look at the differences in completion times.

c) Matched pairs. People vary in their ability to do crossword puzzles.

3. a) Matched pairs—same cities in different time periods.

b) There is a significant difference (P-value = 0.0244) in the labor force participation rate for women in these cities; women's participation increased between 1968 and 1972.

4. a) Same cows before and after injection; the cows should be representative of others of their breed; cows are independent of each other; less than 10% of all cows; don't know about Nearly Normal differences.

b) (12.66, 15.34)

c) Based on this sample, with 95% confidence, the average increase in milk production for Ayrshire cows given BST is between 12.66 and 15.34 pounds per day.

d) 0.25(47) = 11.75. The average increase is much more than this, so we would recommend he go to the extra expense.

5. a) 2-sample. Clouds are independent of one another.

b) Based on these data, there is some evidence of a difference (P-value 0.0538) in the amount of rain between seeded and unseeded clouds.

6. H_0: $\mu_A - \mu_J = 0$ vs. H_A: $\mu_A - \mu_J \neq 0$. $t = 5.29$, df = 109.55, P-value = 6.4×10^{-7}. Because P < 0.01, reject H_0. These data show that the average increase for the two kinds of cows is different, Ayrshire cows have a greater increase in milk production with BST. We need to assume these two groups of cows are representative of their breeds.

7.

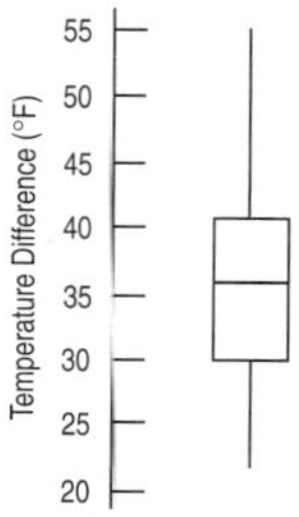

Data are paired for each city; cities are independent of each other; less than 10% of all European cities; boxplot shows the temperature differences are symmetric with no outliers. This is probably not a random sample, so we might be wary of inferring that this difference applies to all European cities. Based on these data, we are 90% confident that the average temperature in European cities in July is between 32.3° and 41.3°F higher than in January.

8. We are 90% confident that the average women's winning marathon time is between 16.86 and 18.06 minutes higher than the men's based on this sample.

9. Based on these data we are 90% confident that boys, on average, can do between 1.6 and 13.0 more push-ups than girls. (independent samples—not paired).

10. a) (4.8,15.2) minutes

b) (4.9, 20.4) minutes

c) Margin of error for raw data will be higher.

11. a) Paired sample test. Data are before/after for the same workers; workers randomly selected; assume less than 10% of all this company's workers; boxplot of differences shows them to be symmetric with no outliers.

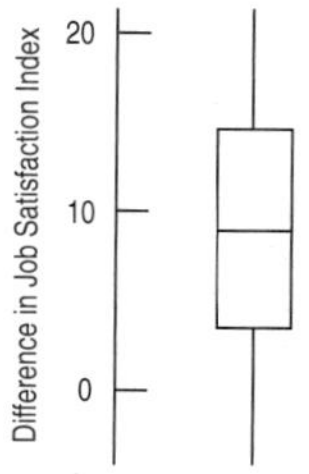

b) H_0: $\mu_D = 0$ vs. H_A: $\mu_D > 0$. $t = 3.60$, P-value = 0.0029. Because P < 0.01, reject H_0. These data show that average job satisfaction has increased after implementation of the exercise program.

12. H_0: $\mu_D = 0$ vs. H_A: $\mu_D > 0$. $t = 1.75$, P-value = 0.0699. Because P > 0.05, we fail to reject H_0. These data do not provide enough evidence to conclude that the summer school program is worthwhile, at $\alpha = .05$.

13. a) H_0: $\mu_D = 0$ vs. H_A: $\mu_D > 0$

b) 0.0025

c) If there is no gain of additional hours of sleep with the herb, the chance of seeing a mean difference as large or larger than the one observed is about one-quarter percent.

d) The data provide evidence that the herb is helpful in gaining additional sleep.

e) Type I

14. a) H_0: $\mu_D = 0$ vs. H_A: $\mu_D > 0$. $t = 4.47$, P-value = 0.0008. Because of the very small P-value, we reject H_0. These data provide strong evidence that cars get significantly better mileage, on average with premium than with regular gasoline.

b) (1.18, 2.82) miles per gallon

c) Premium gasoline costs more than regular.

d) t = 1.25, P-value is 0.1144. Would have decided no difference. The variation in the cars' performances is larger than the differences.

15. H_0: $\mu_D = 0$ vs. H_A: $\mu_D \neq 0$. Data are paired by brand; brands are independent of each other; less than 10% of all yogurts (questionable); boxplot of differences shows an outlier (100) for Great Value

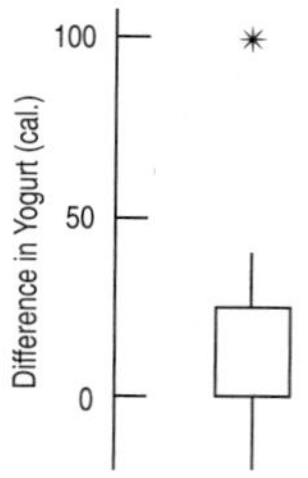

With the outlier included, the mean difference (Strawberry−Vanilla) is 12.5 calories with a t-stat of 1.332 with 11 df, for a P-value of 0.2098. Deleting the outlier, the difference is even smaller, 4.55 calories with a t-stat of only 0.833 and a P-value of 0.4241. With P-values so large, we do not reject H_0. We conclude that the data do not provide evidence of a difference in mean calories.

16. a) H_0: $\mu_D = 0$ vs. H_A: $\mu_D \neq 0$. $t = -1.21$, P-value = 0.2466. Since P > 0.05, fail to reject H_0. There is no evidence that the mean score will change after using caffeine.

b) H_0: $\mu_D = 0$ vs. H_A: $\mu_D \neq 0$. $t = 2.27$, P-value = 0.0397. Since P < 0.05, reject H_0. There is evidence that the mean score will increase when no caffeine is used.

c) No. Might be variation due to the people in the two groups that produced a Type I error. (Answers will vary.)

17. a) Not a simple random sample, but most likely representative; stops most likely independent of each other; less than 10% of all possible stops; boxplot is symmetric with no outliers.

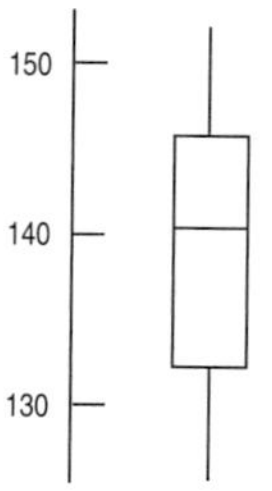

Based on these data, with 95% confidence, the average braking distance for these tires on dry pavement is between 133.6 and 145.2 feet.

b) Not a simple random sample, but most likely representative; stops most likely independent of each other; less than 10% of all possible wet stops; a normal probability plot is relatively straight.
Based on these data, with 95% confidence, the average increase in distance for these tires on wet pavement is between 57.4 and 74.6 feet.

18. a) H_0: $\mu_{NC} - \mu_C = 0$ vs. H_A: $\mu_{NC} - \mu_C \neq 0$; μ_{NC} is the mean for nonconfined inmates, μ_C is the mean for inmates confined to solitary.

b) Groups are independent of each other, not paired; random assignment to groups, less than 10% of all inmates, boxplot shows no outliers in either group.

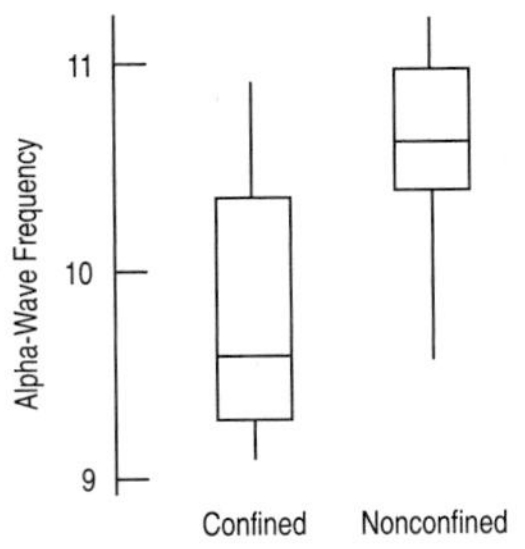

c) 2-sample t-test statistic: 3.357, P-value = 0.0038

d) Because the P-value is so small, we reject H_0. Solitary confinement makes a difference in mean alpha-wave frequencies; those subjected to confinement have lower frequencies.

19. a) Cars were probably not a simple random sample, but may be representative in terms of stopping distance; they represent fewer than 10% of all cars who might use these tires; Boxplot does not show outliers, but does indicate right skewness. A 95% confidence interval for the mean stopping distance on dry pavement is (131.8,145.6) feet.

b) Data are paired by car; cars were probably not randomly chosen, but representative; less than 10% of all cars who might use these tires; boxplot shows an outlier (car 4) with a difference of 12. With deletion of that car, a Normal probability plot of the differences is relatively straight.

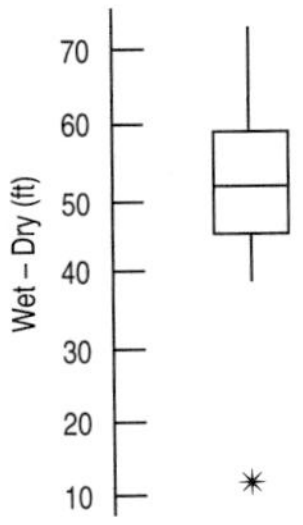

Having deleted an outlier difference of 12 feet, we estimate with 95% confidence that the average braking distance is between 47.2 and 62.8 feet more on wet pavement than on dry, based on this sample. (With the outlier, the confidence interval is 38.8 to 62.6 feet.)

20. a) Data are paired by college.

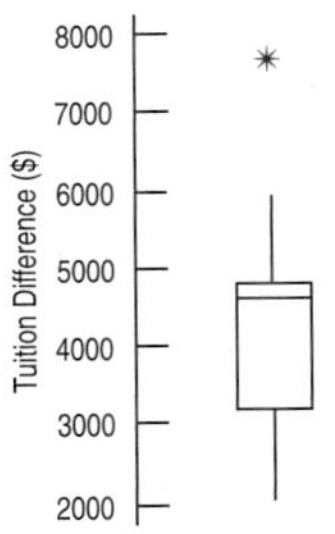

UC Irvine is an outlier. Without UC Irvine the 90% confidence interval for the mean difference in nonresident and resident tuition is ($3662.65 to $4592.91). With UC Irvine included, it is $3769.30 to $4862.30.

b) Having deleted the observation for UC Irvine, whose difference of $7700 was an outlier, we are 90% confident based on the remaining data, that nonresidents pay, on average, between $3662.60 and $4592.90 more than residents. With UC Irvine, the interval is $3769.30 to $4862.30.

c) Assertion is reasonable; $4000 is in the confidence interval.

21. a) 60% is 30 strikes; H_0: $\mu = 30$ vs. H_A: $\mu > 30$; $t = 6.07$, P-value $= 3.92 \times 10^{-6}$. With a very small P-value, we reject H_0. There is very strong evidence that players can throw more than 60% strikes after training, based on this sample.

b) H_0: $\mu_D = 0$ vs. H_A: $\mu_D > 0$. $t = 0.135$, P-value = 0.4472. With such a high P-value, we do not reject H_0. These data provide no evidence that the program has improved pitching in these Little League players.

22. H_0: $\mu_D = 0$ vs. H_A: $\mu_D > 0$. $t = -1.74$, P-value = 0.956. These data show no evidence that more people were without health insurance during the recession of 2000–2001 than in 1999–2000. In fact, the mean for 2000-2001 was lower than the mean for 1999–2000.

PART VI REVIEW

1. a) H_0: $\mu_{Jan} - \mu_{Jul} = 0$; H_A: $\mu_{Jan} - \mu_{Jul} \neq 0$. $t = -1.94$, df = 43.68, P-value = 0.0590. Since $P < 0.10$, reject the null. These data show a significant difference in mean age to crawl between January and July babies.

b) H_0: $\mu_{Apr} - \mu_{Oct} = 0$; H_A: $\mu_{Apr} - \mu_{Oct} \neq 0$. $t = -0.92$; df = 59.40; P-value = 0.3610. Since $P > 0.10$, do not reject the null; these data do not show a significant difference between April and October with regard to the mean age at which crawling begins.

c) These results are not consistent with the claim.

2. H_0: $\mu_D = 0$; H_A: $\mu_D > 0$. $t = 1.36$; df = 20; P-value = 0.0949. Because the P-value is high, we do not reject H_0. These data do not show that floral scent improved the average maze completion time between scented and unscented.

3. H_0: $p = 0.26$; H_A: $p \neq 0.26$. $z = 0.946$; P-value = 0.3443. Because the P-value is high, we do not reject H_0. These data do not show that the Denver area is different from the national rate in the proportion of businesses with women owners.

4. a) Based on these data we are 95% confident the average savings in Canada for prescription drugs is between $77.57 and $174.43.

b) Based on these data we are 95% confident that the average savings in Canada for prescription drugs is between 40.1% and 64.2%.
c) Using percents makes the histogram more unimodal and symmetric.
d) Probably would change. The pharmacy may have listed only the 12 drugs with the "best" savings.

5. Based on these data we are 95% confident that the mean difference in aluminum oxide content is between –3.37 and 1.65. The means in aluminum oxide content of the pottery made at the two sites could reasonably be the same.

6. Based on these data we are 95% confident that the proportion of streams in the Adirondacks with shale substrates is between 32.8% and 47.4%.

7. a) H_0: $p_{ALS} - p_{Other} = 0$; H_A: $p_{ALS} - p_{Other} > 0$. $z = 2.52$; P-value $= 0.0058$. With such a low P-value, we reject H_0. This is strong evidence that there is a higher proportion of varsity athletes among ALS patients than those with other disorders.
b) Observational retrospective study. To make the inference one must assume the patients studied are representative.

8. Paired samples; boxplots show no strong skewness or outliers. One might wonder how the individuals in the study were selected. We are 95% confident that average percentage of 15-year-old males who have been drunk is between 4.5% and 11.4% more than 15-year-old females for these countries. We cannot infer that these percentages are true for other countries.

9. H_0: $\mu = 7.41$; H_A: $\mu \neq 7.41$. $t = 2.18$; df $= 111$; P-value $= 0.0313$. With such a low P-value, we reject H_0. Assuming that Missouri babies fairly represent the United States, these data show that American babies are different from Australian babies in birth weight; American babies are heavier, on average.

10. a) 88.6%
b) 82.2%
c) The petition would be certified when there are not enough valid signatures.
d) A correct petition is not certified.
e) H_0: $p = 0.822$; H_A: $p > 0.822$. $z = 7.48$; P-value $= 3.64 \times 10^{-14}$ With such a low P-value, we reject H_0. This sample provides sufficient evidence for certification of the petition.
f) Increase sample size.

11. a) If there is no difference in the average fish sizes, the chance of seeing an observed difference this large just by natural sampling variation is 0.1%.
b) If cost justified, feed them a natural diet.
c) Type I

12. We have two independent samples, but we don't know how these vehicles were chosen. Even if we consider them representative, the samples are small, and the data for SUVs are skewed to the right. These data are not appropriate for inferences.

13. a) Assuming the conditions are met, from these data we are 95% confident that patients with cardiac disease average between 3.39 and 5.01 years older than those without cardiac disease.
b) Older patients are at greater risk from a variety of other health issues, and perhaps more depressed.

14. a) We are 95% confident that the proportion of smokers is between 3.67% and 12.93% more in patients with heart disease than in those without heart disease, based on this information.
b) Yes. The interval lies completely above 0.
c) Could be a confounding variable. The smokers are at even greater risk for heart attack.

15. a) Stratified sample survey
b) We are 95% confident that boys are between 7.0% and 17.0% more likely to play computer games than girls, based on the survey.
c) Yes. The entire interval lies above 0.

16. a) Based on the data, we are 95% confident that the difference in recruiting is between −4.2% and 8.2%.
b) No. The interval contains 0 and negative values—it may actually be the case that the new strategy lowers acceptance rates.

17. Based on the data, we are 95% confident that the mean difference in words misunderstood is between −3.76 and 3.10. Because 0 is in the confidence interval, we would conclude that the two tapes are equivalent.

18. H_0: $p_{VT} - p_{NH} = 0$; H_A: $p_{VT} - p_{NH} \neq 0$. $z = -0.59$; P-value $= 0.5563$. With such a high P-value, we do not reject H_0. These data show no evidence of a difference in the rates of cesarean deliveries between Vermont and New Hampshire.

19. a)

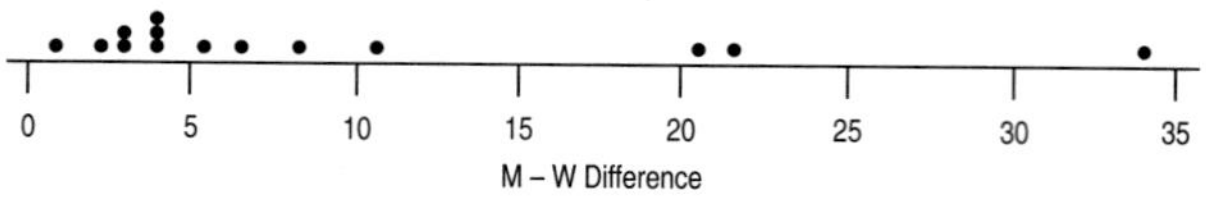

The countries that appear to be outliers are Spain, Italy, and Portugal. They are all Mediterranean countries.
b) H_0: $\mu_D = 0$; H_A: $\mu_D > 0$.
$t = 5.56$; df $= 10$; P-value $= 0.0001$. With such a low P-value, we reject H_0. These data show that European men are more likely than women to read newspapers.

20. H_0: $\mu = \$10$; H_A: $\mu > \$10$. $t = 0.66$; df $= 13$; P-value $= 0.26$. With such a high P-value, we do not reject H_0. These data do not provide evidence that he is likely to overspend his budget of $10 per day.

21. Based on the survey, we are 95% confident that the proportion of the American adults who would agree with the statement is between 57.0% and 63.0%.

22. H_0: $\mu_{Cert} - \mu_{UC} = 0$; H_A: $\mu_{Cert} - \mu_{UC} > 0$. $t = 1.57$; df $= 86$; P-value $= 0.0598$. The P-value is low enough to reject H_0. These data provide evidence that students of certified teachers achieve higher mean reading scores than students of uncertified teachers.

23. Data are matched pairs (before and after for the same rooms); less than 10% of all rooms in a large hotel; uncertain how these rooms were selected (are they representative?). Histogram shows that differences are roughly unimodal and symmetric with no outliers. A 95% confidence interval for the difference, before − after is (0.58, 2.65) counts. Since the entire interval is above 0, these data show that the new air-conditioning system was effective in reducing average bacteria counts.

24. There is a significant difference in Math performance; students of certified teachers do better. There is a significant difference in language performance at $\alpha = .05$ between students of certified teachers and those of undercertified teachers.

25. a) We are 95% confident that between 19.77% and 38.66% of children with bipolar symptoms will be helped with medication and psychotherapy, based on this study.
b) 221 children

26. a) H_0: $\mu_D = 0$; H_A: $\mu_D \neq 0$. $t = 0.381$; df $= 19$; P-value $= 0.7078$. With a high P-value, we do not reject H_0. There is no evidence that the tests differ in mean difficulty.
b) H_0: $\mu_D = 0$; H_A: $\mu_D \neq 0$. The boxplot of the differences shows three outliers, but they are symmetric. A paired t-test with

them included shows $t = -0.2531$ with 16 df and a P-value of 0.8029, showing no evidence of a difference in mean scores. With the three outliers removed, the t-test shows $t = -1.1793$ with 16 df and a P-value of 0.2555—still no evidence of a difference in means. We conclude the testing environment does not affect mean score.

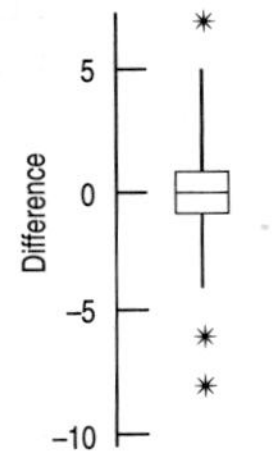

27. a) From this histogram, about 115 loaves or more. (Not Normal.)
b) Large sample size; CLT says $\bar{y}$ will be approximately Normal.
c) From the data, we are 95% confident that the bakery will sell between 101.2 and 104.8 loaves of bread on an average day.
d) 25
e) Yes, 100 loaves per day is too low—the entire confidence interval is above that.

28. a)

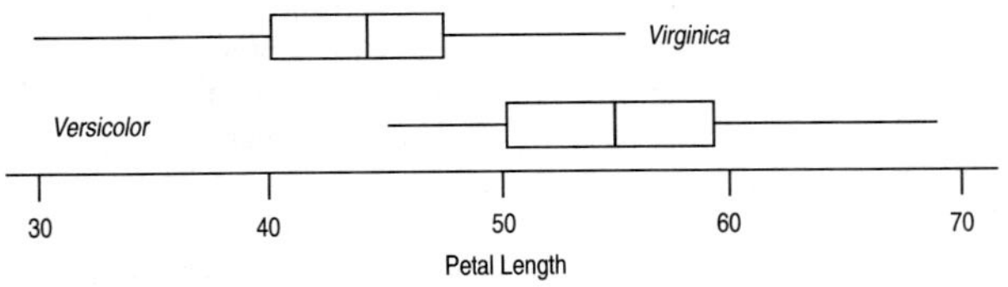

b) *Versicolor* generally has longer petals than *virginica.*
c) (10.14, 14.46)
d) We are 95% confident, based on the information given, that the average petal length for *versicolor* irises is between 10.14 and 14.46 mm longer than that of *virginica* irises.
e) Yes. The entire interval is above 0.

29. a) H_0: $p_{High} - p_{Low} = 0$; H_A: $p_{High} - p_{Low} \neq 0$. $z = -3.57$; P-value $= 0.0004$. Because the P-value is so low, we reject H_0. These data show the IRS risk is different in the two groups; people who consume dairy products often have a lower risk on average.
b) Doesn't prove it; this is not an experiment.

30. a) H_0: $p = 0.16$ H_A: $p > 0.16$. $z = 4.42$; P-value $= 5 \times 10^{-6}$. Because the P-value is so low, we reject H_0. These data show the proportion of tickets given to blacks on this section of the New Jersey Turnpike is unusually high.
b) Doesn't prove it; there may be other factors.
c) Answers will vary. Possibly what proportion of drivers on this highway are black?

31. Based on these data, we are 95% confident that seeded clouds will produce an average of between -4.76 and 559.56 more acre-feet of rain than unseeded clouds. Since the interval contains negative values, it may be that seeding is unproductive.

32. a) H_0: $\mu = 35.4$; H_A: $\mu < 35.4$
b) There is one high value, but it is technically not an outlier. Otherwise the histogram appears roughly unimodal and symmetric (only 6 values).
c) $t = 0.726$; P-value $= 0.7497$. With such a large P-value, we do not reject H_0. The data do not show that the average weight is less than claimed.
d) $t = -0.53$; p-value $= 0.3107$. Without the high outlier, the data still do not show that the average weight is significantly less than claimed.
e) The stated weight seems legitimate based on these 6 bags.

33. a) Randomizing order of the tasks helps avoid bias and memory effects. Randomizing the cards helps avoid bias as well.
b) H_0: $\mu_D = 0$; H_A: $\mu_D > 0$
c)

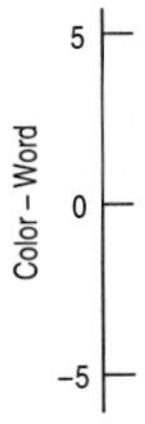

Boxplot of the differences looks symmetric with no outliers.
d) $t = -1.70$; P-value $= 0.0999$; do not reject H_0 because $P > 0.05$.
e) The data do not provide evidence that the color or written word dominates.

34. a) \$373.50
b) They are 95% confident that the average loss in a home burglary is between \$1644 and \$2391, based on their sample.
c) 95% of all random samples will produce confidence intervals that contain the true mean loss.

35. a) Different samples give different means; this is a fairly small sample. The difference may be due to natural sampling variation.
b) H_0: $\mu = 100$; H_A: $\mu < 100$
c) Batteries selected are a SRS (representative); less than 10% of the company's batteries; lifetimes are approximately Normal.
d) $t = -1.0$; p-value $= 0.1666$; do not reject H_0. This sample does not show that the average life of the batteries is significantly less than 100 hours.
e) Type II.

36. a) Based on these data, we are 90% confident that the average hamster litter will have between 7.11 and 8.33 babies.
b) Larger—to be more confident we need a wider interval.
c) About 27 (based on t^*_{24}).

CHAPTER 26

1. a) 10
b) Goodness-of-fit
c) H_0: The die is fair (all faces have $p = 1/6$).
H_A: The die is not fair.
d) Count data; rolls are random and independent; expected frequencies all bigger than 5.
e) 5
f) $\chi^2 = 5.600$, P-value $= 0.3471$
g) Because the P-value is high, do not reject H_0. The data show no evidence that the die is unfair.

2. a) Yellow and red: 21.2, orange, blue and green: 10.6, brown: 31.8
b) Goodness-of-fit
c) H_0: The distribution is as specified by the company.
H_A: The distribution is not as specified.
d) Count data; Bag may not be a random sample, but most likely representative; Expected counts are all bigger than 5.

e) 5
f) $\chi^2 = 9.315$, P-value = 0.0972
g) Because the P-value is high, do not reject H_0. These data do not provide evidence that the distribution is other than specified.

3. a) Weights are quantitative, not counts.
b) Count the number of each kind of nut, assuming the company's percentages are based on counts rather than weights.

4. Data are averages, not counts.

5. H_0: The police force represents the population (29.2% white, 28.2% black, etc.). H_A: The police force is not representative of the population. $\chi^2 = 16516.88$, df = 4, P-value = 0.0000. Because the P-value is so low, we reject H_0. These data show that the police force is not representative of the population. In particular, there are too many white officers in relationship to their membership in the community.

6. H_0: Murders among women have the same causes as all murders (63.4% guns, etc). H_A: Murder among women have different causes than all murders. $\chi^2 = 479.508$, df = 3, P-value < 0.0001. Because the P-value is so low, we reject H_0. Women's murders do not follow the same pattern of cause as all murders nationwide. Women are much less likely to be killed by other weapons and more likely to be killed by personal attack.

7. a) $\chi^2 = 5.671$, df = 3, P-value = 0.1288. With a P-value this high, we fail to reject H_0. Yes, these data are consistent with those predicted by genetic theory.
b) $\chi^2 = 11.342$, df = 3, P-value = 0.0100. Because of the low P-value, we reject H_0. These data provide evidence that the distribution is not as specified by genetic theory.
c) With small samples, many more data sets will be consistent with the null hypothesis. With larger samples, small discrepancies will show evidence against the null hypothesis.

8. H_0: Digits are all equally likely (all occur with frequency 1/10). H_A: Digits are not all equally likely. $\chi^2 = 5.509$, df = 9, P-value = 0.7879. Because the P-value is large, we do not reject H_0. These data provide no evidence that the digits in pi are not all equally likely.

9. a) 40.2% b) 8.1%
c) 62.2% d) 285.48
e) H_0: Survival was independent of status on the ship. H_A: Survival depended on the status
f) 3
g) We reject the null hypothesis. Survival depended on status. We can see that first-class passengers were more likely to survive than any other class.

10. a) 15.0%
b) 13.0%
c) 729.6
d) Independence
e) H_0: Rank is independent of gender. H_A: Rank and gender are not independent.
f) Count data; not a random sample, but all NYPD officers; expected counts all greater than 5.
g) 5
h) $\chi^2 = 290.131$, P-value <0.0001
i) Because the P-value is so low, we reject H_0. Gender and rank in the NYPD are not independent.
j) Standardized residuals are

	Male	Female
Officer	−2.3434	5.5747
Detective	−1.1759	2.7973
Sergeant	3.8429	−9.1421
Lieutenant	3.5824	−8.5223
Captain	2.4617	−5.8563
Higher ranks	1.7412	−4.1423

Women are overrepresented at the lower ranks and underrepresented at every rank from sergeant up.

11. a) Experiment—actively imposed treatments (different drinks)
b) Homogeneity
c) H_0: The rate of urinary tract infection is the same for all three groups. H_A: The rate of urinary tract infection is different among the groups.
d) Count data; random assignment to treatments; all expected frequencies larger than 5.
e) 2
f) $\chi^2 = 7.776$, P-value = 0.020
g) With a P-value this low, we reject H_0. These data provide reasonably strong evidence there is a difference in urinary tract infection rates between cranberry juice drinkers, lactobacillus drinkers, and the control group.
h) The standardized residuals are

	Cranberry	Lactobacillus	Control
Infection	−1.87276	1.191759	0.681005
No Infection	1.245505	−0.79259	−0.45291

From the standardized residuals (and the sign of the residuals), it appears those who drank cranberry juice were less likely to develop urinary tract infections; those who drank lactobacillus were more likely to have infections.

12. a) Homogeneity
b) H_0: The distribution of car origin is the same for students and staff. H_A: The distribution of car origin is different for students and staff.
c) Count data; random survey of cars in lots (probably can't generalize to other universities); expected frequencies greater than 5.
d) $\chi^2 = 7.828$, df = 2, P-value = 0.020.
e) With a P-value this low, we reject H_0. The distribution of car origins differs between students and staff. Examination of the residuals shows that students are more likely to drive European cars than staff and less likely than staff to drive American cars.

13. a) Independence
b) H_0: Political affiliation is independent of gender. H_A: There is a relationship between political affiliation and gender.
c) Count data; probably a random sample, but can't extend results to other states; all expected frequencies greater than 5.
d) $\chi^2 = 4.851$, df = 2, P-value = 0.0884
e) Because of the high P-value, we do not reject H_0. These data do not provide evidence of a relationship between political affiliation and gender.

14. a) Prospective study; individuals were selected and then subsequently followed.
b) Independence
c) $\chi^2 = 3.677$, df = 3, P-value = 0.2985. Because of the high P-value, we do not reject H_0. These data do not provide evidence of a relationship between the amount of fish in the diet and prostate cancer. (Data are for totals and cancer, not non-cancer and cancer.)
d) No. There may be many other factors involved.

15. H_0: Political affiliation is independent of region. H_A: There is a relationship between political affiliation and region. $\chi^2 = 13.849$, df = 4, P-value = 0.0078. With a P-value this low, we reject H_0. Political affiliation and region are related. Examination of the residuals shows that those in the West are more likely to be Democrat than Republican; those in the Northeast are more likely to be Republican than Democrat.

16. a) Survey
b) Homogeneity
c) $\chi^2 = 4.030$, df = 4, P-value = 0.4019. Because the P-value is so high, we fail to reject H_0. These data do not show evidence of a change in attitudes about the ideal family between 1991 and 2001.

17. a) Homogeneity
b) H_0: The grade distribution is the same for both professors. H_A: The grade distributions are different.
c)

	Dr. Alpha	Dr. Beta
A	6.667	5.333
B	12.778	10.222
C	12.222	9.778
D	6.111	4.889
F	2.222	1.778

Three cells have expected frequencies less than 5.

18. a) Homogeneity
b) H_0: The types of crime are not related to the phase of the moon.
H_A: The types of crime are different for the different moon phases.
c) Expected counts:

	Full Moon	Not Full
Violent	2.558	2.442
Property	19.442	18.558
Drugs/alcohol	23.535	22.465
Domestic abuse	12.791	12.209
Other offenses	7.674	7.326

Two cells have expected counts less than 5.

19. a)

	Dr. Alpha	Dr. Beta
A	6.667	5.333
B	12.778	10.222
C	12.222	9.778
Below C	8.333	6.667

All expected frequencies are now larger than 5.
b) Decreased from 4 to 3.
c) $\chi^2 = 9.306$, P-value = 0.0255. Because the P-value is so low, we reject H_0. The grade distributions for the two professors are different. Dr. Alpha gives fewer A's and more grades below C than Dr. Beta.

20. a) Combine Violent and Domestic Abuse into one category (or Violent and Other).
b) $\chi^2 = 2.877$, df = 3, P-value = 0.4109. Because the P-value is so high, we do not reject H_0. These data do not provide any evidence of a difference in type of illegal activity in different moon phases.

21. $\chi^2 = 14.058$, df = 1, P-value = 0.0002. With a P-value this low, we reject H_0. There is a evidence of racial steering. Blacks are much less likely to rent in Section A than Section B.

22. $\chi^2 = 453.476$, df = 1, P-value <0.0001. With a P-value this low, we reject H_0. Survival was related to gender. Females were much more likely than males to survive (72.98% to 21.20%).

23. a) $z = 3.74936$, $z^2 = 14.058$.
b) P-value (z) = 0.0002 (same as in Exercise 21).

24. a) $z = 21.29498$.
b) $z^2 = 453.476$.
c) Both P-values are near 0.

25. $\chi^2 = 2815.968$, df = 9, P-value <0.0001. Because the P-value is so low, we reject H_0. There are definite differences in education levels attained by the groups. The largest component indicates that Hispanics are more likely to not have high school diplomas. The next largest residual indicates that fewer whites than expected do not have a high school diploma.

26. $\chi^2 = 5.89$, df = 3, P = 0.117. With P > 0.05, these data show no evidence of an association between the mother's age group and the outcome of the pregnancy.

27. $\chi^2 = 0.870$, df = 2, P-value = 0.6471. Because the P-value is so large, we do not reject H_0. These data show no evidence of a difference in higher education opportunities between blacks and Hispanics.

28. $\chi^2 = 178.453$, df = 12, P-value < 0.0001. Because the P-value is so low, we reject H_0. There is a difference in education level among the different age groups. The largest component indicates those 35 to 44 were less likely to have only a high school diploma. The second largest indicates the same age group is more likely than other age groups to have at least four years of college.

CHAPTER 27

1. a) % Yes = −5.583 + 0.999 × Year. The percentage who would vote for a woman has been increasing about 1% per year.
b) H_0: There has been no change in percentage of voters who would vote for a woman candidate for president, $\beta_1 = 0$.
H_A: There has been a change, $\beta_1 > 0$.
c) t =15.1, P-value <0.0001. With such a low P-value, we reject H_0. There has been a significant change. Voters are increasingly willing to vote for a woman for president.
d) 94.2% of the variation in percentage willing to vote for a woman is accounted for by the regression on year.

2. a) Percent using other drugs = −3.068 + 0.615 × percent using marijuana . The percentage of ninth graders in these countries who have used other drugs is estimated to increase 0.615% for each 1% increase in the percentage of ninth graders who have used marijuana.

b) H_0: There is no (linear) relationship between marijuana use and use of other drugs, $\beta_1 = 0$. H_A: There is a relationship, $\beta_1 \neq 0$.
c) $t = 7.85$, P-value = 0.0001. With such a low P-value, we reject H_0. Percentage of teens using other drugs is positively related to percentage using marijuana.
d) Percentage using marijuana accounts for 87.3% of the variation in other drug usage for ninth graders in these countries.
e) The use of other drugs is associated with marijuana use, but there is no proof of causality. There may be lurking variables.

3. a) H_0: There has been no change in the percentage expressing no opinion about voting for a woman president, $\beta_1 = 0$. H_A: There has been a change, $\beta_1 \neq 0$.
b) $t = -1.21$, P-value = 0.2458. Because the P-value is so large, we do not reject H_0. These data do not indicate the percentage of "no opinion" responses has changed.
c) The plot indicates no real trend. The high value in 1945 and low value in 1990 are influential. True slope does not appear to be negative after discounting influential points at the ends. Answer to the last question remains the same because we did not reject H_0 in b.

4. a) H_0: There is no linear relationship between age and cholesterol level, $\beta_1 = 0$. H_A: Cholesterol levels increase with age, $\beta_1 > 0$.
b) $t = 1.23$, P-value = 0.1103. Because the P-value is so large, we do not reject H_0. These data show no significant relationship between age and cholesterol levels.
The data show no (linear) relationship between age and cholesterol. The P-value of 0.1103 indicates over a 11% chance of a slope as large as 0.746 or higher just from natural sampling variation. The plot should be examined to see if a nonlinear relationship is present.

5. a) H_0: Difference in age at first marriage has not been decreasing, $\beta_1 = 0$. H_A: Difference in age at first marriage has been decreasing, $\beta_1 < 0$.
b) Residual plot shows no obvious pattern; histogram is not particularly Normal, but shows no obvious skewness or outliers.
c) $t = -4.35$, P-value = 0.0001. With such a low P-value, we reject H_0. These data show evidence that difference in age at first marriage is decreasing.
d) Based on these data, we are 95% confident that the average difference in age at first marriage is changing at a rate between −0.035 and −0.013 years per year.

6. a)

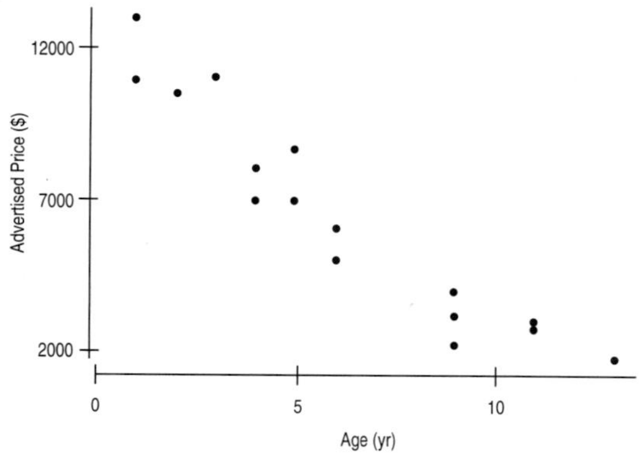

b) Yes, the plot seems linear.
c) Predicted advertised price = 12319.59 − 924.00 × age
d)

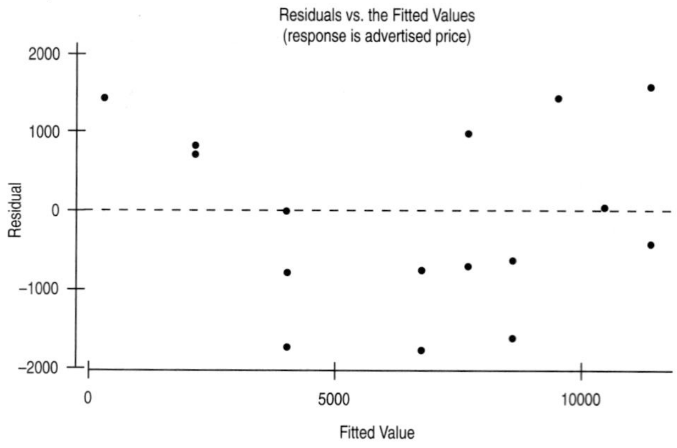

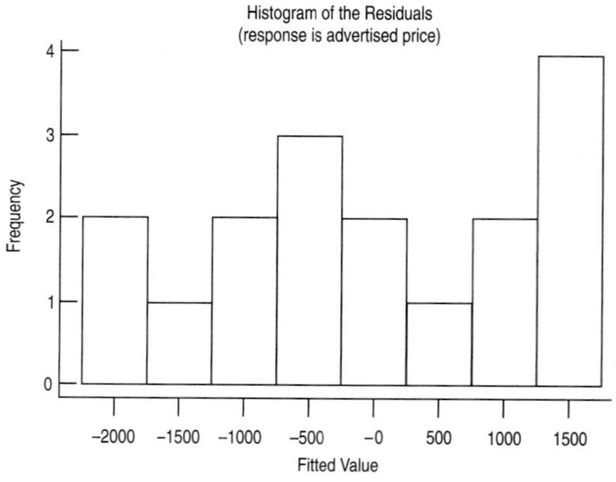

The residual plot shows some possible curvature. The histogram of the residuals is not particularly Normal. Inference may not be valid here, but we will proceed (with caution).
e) (−1099.4, −748.6)
f) Based on these data, we are 95% confident that a used car's value decreases between \$748.60 and \$1099.40 per year.

7. a) H_0: Fuel economy and weight are not (linearly) related, $\beta_1 = 0$. H_A: Fuel economy changes with weight, $\beta_1 \neq 0$. P-value < 0.0001, indicating strong evidence of an association.
b) Yes, the conditions seem satisfied. Histogram of residuals is unimodal and symmetric; residual plot looks OK, but some "thickening" of the plot with increasing values.
c) $t = -12.2$, P-value < 0.0001. These data show evidence that gas mileage decreases with the weight of the car.

8. a) The scatterplot suggests a positive linear relatioship. H_0: There is no (linear) relationship between SAT Verbal and Math scores, $\beta_1 = 0$. H_A: There is a relationship, $\beta_1 \neq 0$.
b) Assumptions seem reasonable, since conditions are satisfied. Residual plot shows no patterns (one outlier); histogram is unimodal and roughly symmetric.
c) $t = 11.9$; P-value < 0.0001. These data show evidence of a positive relationship between SAT Verbal and Math scores.

9. a) (−9.57, −6.86) mpg per 1000 pounds.
b) Based on these data we are 95% confident that fuel mileage decreases between 6.86 and 9.57 miles per gallon on average for each additional 1000 pounds of weight.

10. a) (0.581, 0.769)
b) Based on the sample, we are 90% confident that average

Math SAT scores increase between 0.58 and 0.769 points for each additional point scored on the Verbal test.

11. a) Based on this regression, we are 95% confident that 2500-pound cars will average between 27.44 and 28.97 miles per gallon.
b) Based on the regression, a 3450-pound car will get between 16.00 and 24.81 miles per gallon, with 95% confidence.

12. a) Based on the regression, we are 90% confident that the mean Math score for students with a Verbal score of 500 is between 534.0 and 560.18.
b) Based on the regression, we are 90% confident that the Math score for the valedictorian will be between 569 and 800 (SAT scores cannot be higher than 800).

13. a) Yes. $t = 2.73$, P-value $= 0.0079$. With a P-value so low, we reject H_0. There is a positive relationship between calories and sodium content.
b) No. $R^2 = 9\%$ and s appears to be large, although without seeing the data it is a bit hard to tell.

14. a) H_0: No linear relationship between brain size and IQ, $\beta_1 = 0$. H_A: There is evidence of a relationship, $\beta_1 \neq 0$. $t = 1.12$; this will not be significant.
b) With $R^2 = 6.5\%$, the relationship is very weak. There seem to be three students with large brains who also scored high. Without them, there seems to be no association at all.

15. Plot of calories against fiber does not look linear; this is borne out in the residuals plot, which also shows increasing variance as predicted values get large. The histogram of residuals is right skewed.

16. Scatterplot of temperature with latitude shows curvature (downward). Histogram of residuals is right skewed; residual plot shows decreasing variance as predicted values increase.

17. a) H_0: No (linear) relationship between BCI and pH, $\beta_1 = 0$. H_A: There is a relationship, $\beta_1 \neq 0$.
b) $t = -7.73$ with 161 df; P-value <0.0001
c) There is a negative relationship; BCI decreases as pH increases at an average of 197.7 BCI units per increase of 1 pH.

18. a) $Temp = 15.31 + 0.004 \times CO_2$
b) Yes; $t = 4.44$, P-value $= 8.5 \times 10\text{-}5$
c) The standard deviation of the residuals is 0.0809 ppm, so we don't expect the model to predict to an accuracy greater than about $\pm$ 0.16 ppm.

19. a) H_0: No linear relationship between population and ozone, $\beta_1 = 0$. H_A: Ozone increases with population, $\beta_1 > 0$. $t = 3.48$, P-value $= 0.0018$. With a P-value so low, we reject H_0. These data show evidence that ozone does increase with population.
b) Based on this regression, each additional million residents is expected to increase average ozone level by between 3.29 and 10.01 ppm, with 90% confidence.
c) Based on the regression, the mean ozone level for cities with 600,000 people is between 18.47 and 27.29 ppm, with 90% confidence.

20. a) H_0: No linear relationship between sales and profit, $\beta_1 = 0$. H_A: There is a relationship, $\beta_1 \neq 0$. $t = 12.33$; P-value ~ 0. There is a significant positive relationship between sales and profit.
b) In these data, sales explains 66.2% of the observed variation in profits.
c) Based on this regression, average profits increase between 0.078 and 0.107 million dollars ($78,000 and $107,000) for every million dollars in sales, with 95% confidence.
d) Based on the regression, the profit for Eli Lilly, Inc. should be between −281.1 and 1592.8 million dollars (−$281,100,000 and $1,592,800,000) with 95% confidence. This interval is so wide it's really useless.

21. a) 33 batteries.
b) Data plot is roughly linear with lots of scatter; plot of residuals vs. predicted values shows no overt patterns; Normal probability plot of residuals is reasonably straight.
c) H_0: No linear relationship between cost and cranking amps, $\beta_1 = 0$. H_A: Cranking amps increase with cost, $\beta_1 > 0$. $t = 3.23$; P-value $= 0.0029$. With a P-value so low, we reject H_0. These data provide evidence that more expensive batteries do have more cranking amps.
d) No. $R^2 = 25.2\%$ and $s = 116$ amps. Considering that the range of amperage is only about 400 amps, an s of 116 is not very useful.
e) Cranking amps $= 384.59 + 4.15 \times$ Cost.
f) (1.97, 6.32) cold cranking amps per dollar.
g) Cranking amps increase, on average, between 1.97 and 6.32 with every dollar of battery cost increase, with 90% confidence.

22.

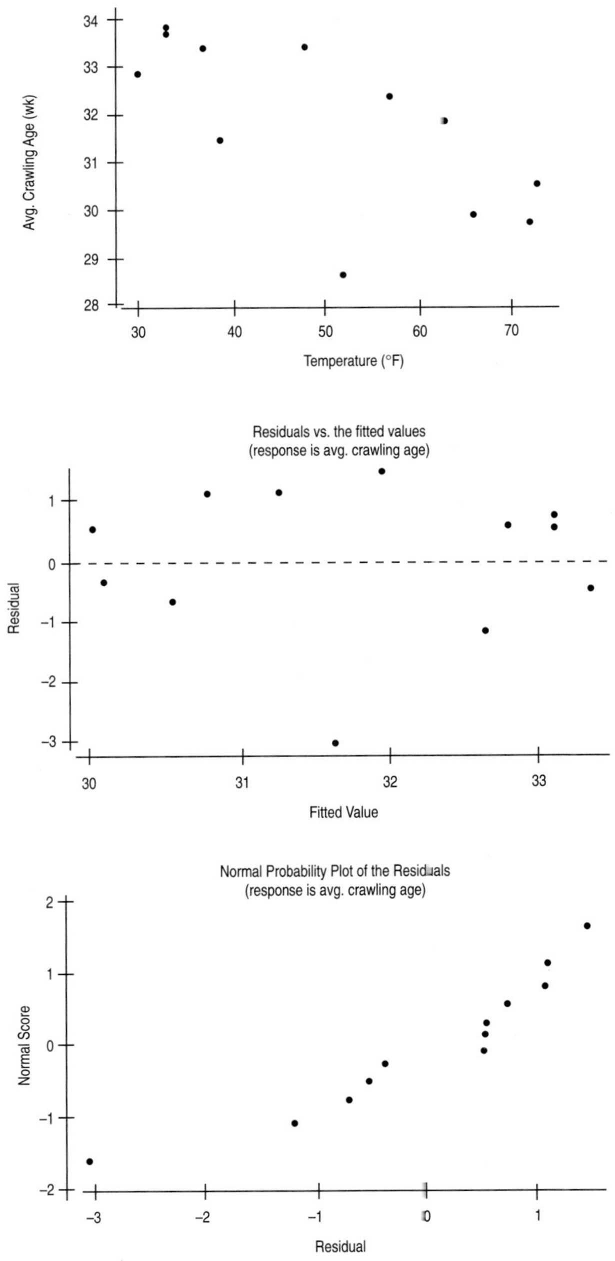

a) Weaker. Individuals are more variable than averages.

b) The residuals plot shows a large negative outlier; the Normal probability plot is not very straight, but the sample size is small. We will proceed with the inference with caution.
H_0: No linear relationship between 6-month temperature and crawling age, $\beta_1 = 0$. H_A: Relationship between 6-month temperature and crawling age, $\beta_1 \neq 0$. t with 10 df is -3.10 with P-value 0.0113. With a P-value so low, we reject H_0. There does seem to be a negative relationship between temperature and crawling age.

c) $(-0.134, -0.022)$ weeks per °F.

23.

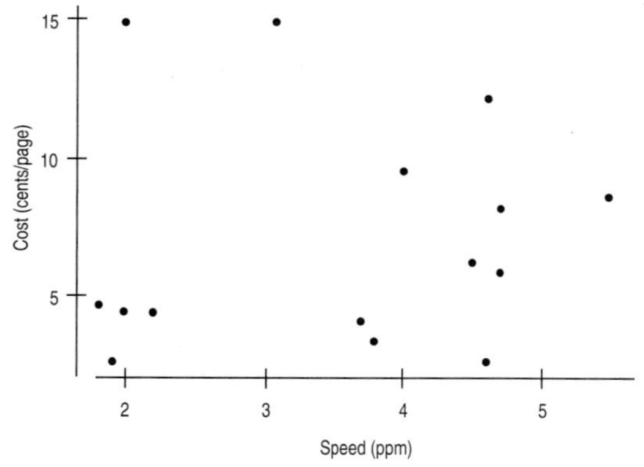

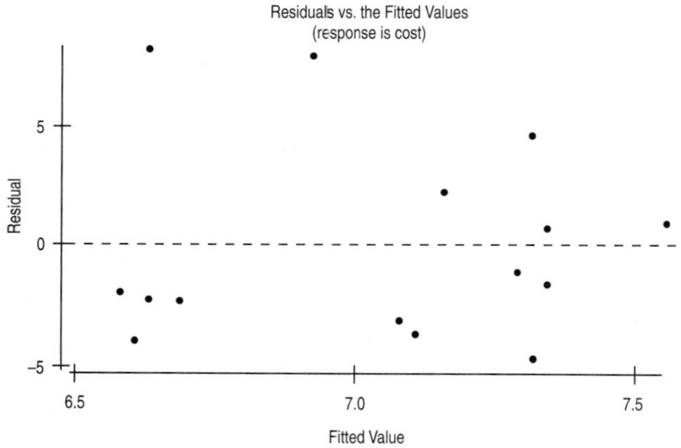

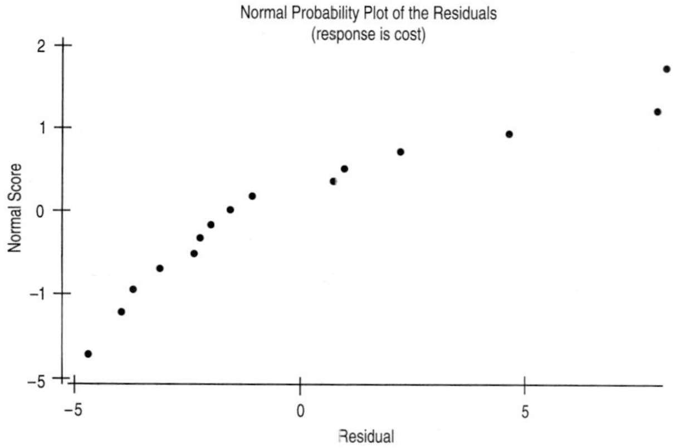

Data plot does not show any indication of a linear relationship. There may be a curvilinear relationship. Normal probability plot of the residuals is not linear (residuals not normal). Inference for linear regression is not valid here.

24.

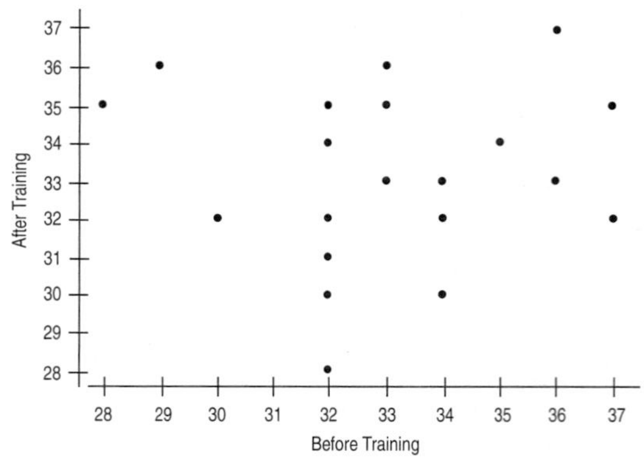

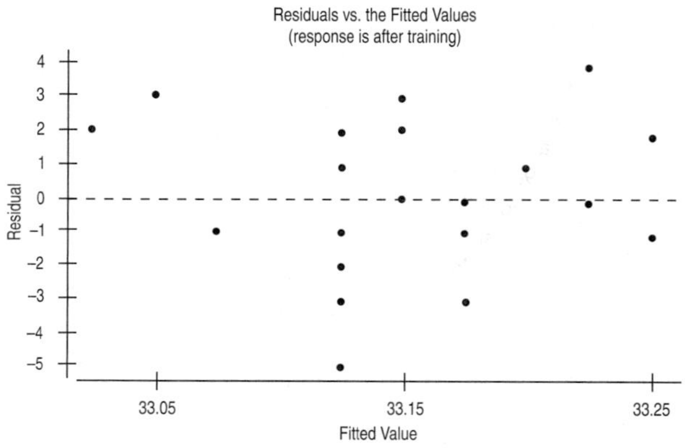

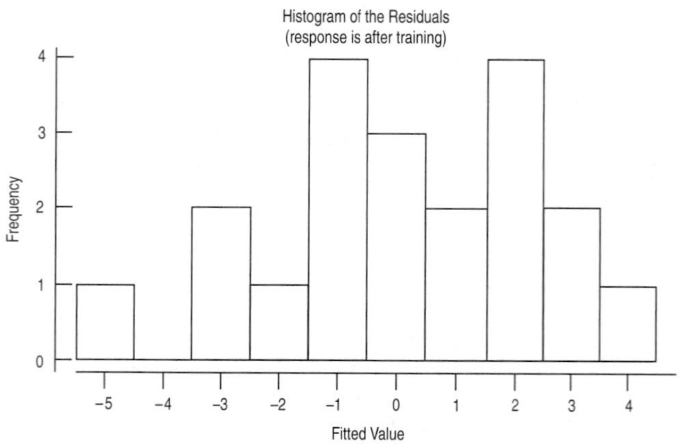

Data plot does not show a linear relationship. Histogram of residuals is reasonable.
H_0: No relationship between initial ability and effectiveness, $\beta_1 = 0$. H_A: There is a relationship, $\beta_1 \neq 0$. $t = 0.11$; P-value $= 0.912$. Because P is high, we do not reject H_0.

This regression shows no evidence of a relationship between initial ability and effectiveness of the video.

25. a) H_0: No linear relationship between waist size and %body fat, $\beta_1 = 0$. H_A: Body fat increases with waist size, $\beta_1 > 0$. $t = 8.14$; P-value < 0.0001. Body fat seems to increase with waist size.
b) With 95% confidence, mean percent body fat for people with 40-inch waists is between 23.58 and 29.02, based on this regression.

26. a) (0.145, 0.355) % per pound.
b) Based on the regression, average body fat increases between 0.145% and 0.355% for each pound of weight.
c) With 95% confidence, a person weighing 165 pounds will have between 0% (−1.61%) and 29.32% body fat, based on this regression.

27. a) Data plot looks linear; no overt pattern in residuals; histogram of residuals roughly symmetric and unimodal.
b) H_0: No linear relationship between education and mortality, $\beta_1 = 0$. H_A: People with more education live longer, $\beta_1 < 0$. $t = -6.24$; P-value <0.001. There is evidence that people with more education do live longer.
c) (−65.95, −33.89) deaths per 100,000 people.
d) Deaths per 100,000 people decrease on average between 33.89 and 65.95 for each year of average education, based on the regression.
e) Based on the regression, the average mortality rate for cities with an average of 12 years of school will be between 874.239 and 914.196 deaths per 100,000 people.

28. a) Data plot looks linear; no obvious pattern in residuals; Normal plot of residuals roughly linear.
b) H_0: No linear relationship between square footage and assessed value, $\beta_1 = 0$. H_A: Larger houses have higher assessed values, $\beta_1 > 0$. $t = 2.77$; P-value $= 0.0068$. With the very low P-value, we reject H_0. There is evidence that larger houses do have higher assessed values.
c) 32.5%
d) Based on this regression, average assessed value will increase between $4.58 and $19.22 for each square foot.
e) No. A 95% confidence interval for the average price of a 2100-square-foot house is $45,619 to $78,572.

PART VII REVIEW

1. H_0: The proportions are as specified by the ratio 1:3:3:9; H_A: The proportions are not as stated. $\chi^2 = 5.01$; df $= 3$; P-value $= 0.1711$. Since $P > 0.05$, we fail to reject H_0. These data do not provide evidence to indicate that the proportions are other than 1:3:3:9.

2. a) 59 products
b) 84.5%
c) (2.21, 2.78) dollars per minute
d) Based on this regression, average price increases between $2.21 and $2.78 for each minute of polishing time, with 95% confidence.

3. a) H_0: Mortality and calcium concentration in water are not linearly related, $\beta_1 = 0$; H_A: They are related, $\beta_1 \neq 0$.
b) $t = -6.73$; P-value <0.0001. There is a significant negative relationship between calcium in drinking water and mortality.
c) (−4.19, −2.27) deaths per 100,00 for each ppm calcium.
d) Based on the regression, we are 95% confident that mortality (deaths per 100,000) decreases on average between 2.27 and 4.19 for each part per million of calcium in drinking water.

4. a) Based on these data, with 95% confidence 5-year yields are between 3.15 and 5.93% higher than 3-year yields on average (paired data).
b) Yes (at least for this data set). The regression line is 5-year = 6.93 + 0.719 3-year. H_0: $\beta_1 = 0$ against H_A: $\beta_1 \neq 0$ has $t = 4.27$; P-value $= 0.0009$. Since P is so small, we reject H_0. There is evidence of an association. (But we don't know that this was an SRS or even a representative sample of large cap funds.)

5. 404 checks

6. a) (36.21, 60.51) feet.
b) Yes, 40 is in the interval.
c) Wider; we'd need to have a wider interval to be more confident.
d) Roughly 4 times as big—44 flights.

7. H_0: Income and party are independent. H_A: Income and party are not independent. $\chi^2 = 17.19$; P-value $= 0.0018$. With such a small P-value, we reject H_0. These data show evidence that income level and party are not independent. Examination of components shows Democrats are most likely to have low-incomes; Independents are most likely to have middle incomes, and Republicans most likely to have high incomes.

8. a) 38
b) Data plot looks linear; residuals plot shows random scatter; histogram of residuals approximately Normal.
c) (0.131, 0.177) foals per adult.
d) Based on this regression, we have 95% confidence that for every adult horse an average of between 0.131 and 0.177 foals will be born.
e) A herd with 80 adult horses will have between 2.27 and 19.21 foals, with 90% confidence.

9. H_0: $p_L - p_R = 0$; H_A: $p_L - p_R \neq 0$. $z = 1.38$; P-value $= 0.1683$. Since $P > 0.05$, we do not reject H_0. These data do not provide evidence of a difference in musical abilities between right- and left-handed people.

10. a) Combining boys and girls, $\chi^2 = 42.80$; P-value < 0.0001. Reject H_0. These data show evidence that the distribution of scores at this school is significantly different from national results.
b) (Pooling those with scores of 2 or 1) $\chi^2 = 5.59$, P-value $= 0.1336$. There is no significant difference in the distribution of scores for boys and girls.

11. a) H_0: $\mu_D = 0$; H_A: $\mu_D \neq 0$.
Boxplot of the differences indicates a strong outlier (1958). With the outlier kept in, the t-stat is 0, with a P-value of 1.00 (two sided). There is no evidence of a difference (on average) of actual and that predicted by Gallup. With the outlier taken out, the t-stat is still only −0.8525 with a P-value of 0.4106, so the conclusion is the same.
b) H_0: There is no (linear) relationship between predicted and actual number of Democratic seats won ($\beta_1 = 0$). H_A: There is a relationship ($\beta_1 \neq 0$). The relationship is very strong, with an R^2 of 97.7%. The t-stat is 22.56. Even with only 12 df, this is clearly significant (P-value <.0001). There is an outlying residual (1958), but without it, the regression is even stronger.

12. $\chi^2 = 6.14$; P-value $= 0.1887$. Since $P > 0.05$, we do not reject H_0. These data do not provide evidence of an association between duration of pregnancy and level of care.

13. $\chi^2 = 0.69$; P-value $= 0.9526$. Since $P > 0.05$, we do not reject H_0. These data provide no evidence to show that the way the hospital deals with twin pregnancies has changed.

14. H_0: $p_P - p_N = 0$; H_A: $p_P - p_N > 0$. $z = 1.96$; P-value $= 0.0249$. With such a small P-value, we reject H_0. These data provide moderately strong evidence to suggest that preemies are more likely than babies of normal weight to be of "subnormal height" as adults.

15. a) Based on these data, the average annual rainfall in LA is between 11.65 and 17.39 inches, with 90% confidence.
b) About 46 years
c) No. The regression equation is Rain $= -51.684 + 0.033 \times$ Year. $R^2 = 0.1\%$. The t-stat for the slope is 0.12 with a P-value of 0.9029.

16. a) Independence—individuals classified on two variables.
b) H_0: No relationship between age and party; H_A: There is a relationship. $\chi^2 = 16.66$; P-value $= 0.0106$. With such a small P-value, we reject H_0. These data indicate a relationship between age and party.
c) There is a relationship between age and party—the "largest" standardized residual is for Republicans 18 to 29 (−2.07). The next largest is for Independents in the same age group (1.79). These data indicate that young people are much more likely to be Independents than Republicans. We also see that the oldest group is more likely to be Democrat (1.57).

17. a) This is a linear regression that is meaningless—the data are categorical.
b) This is a two-way table, that is appropriate. H_0: eye and hair color are independent H_A: Eye and hair color are not independent. However, four cells have expected counts less than 5, so the χ^2 analysis is not valid unless cells are merged. However with a χ^2 value of 223.6 with 16 df and a P-value of <0.0001, the results are not likely to change if we merge appropriate eye colors.

18. a) H_0: There is no (linear) relationship between depression and Internet usage. $\beta_1 = 0$. H_A: There is a linear relationship. $\beta_1 \neq 0$. $t = 2.76$; P-value $= 0.0064$. With such a small P-value, we reject H_0. These data provide strong evidence of a relationship between internet use and depression.
b) The study says nothing about causality. Many other factors may be involved.
c) H_0: $\mu_D = 0$; H_A: $\mu_D > 0$. $t = -2.73$; P-value $= 0.0071$. With such a small P-value, we reject H_0. These data indicate that mean depression level actually got better (decreased) during the study.

19. a) H_0: $p_Y - p_O = 0$; H_A: $p_Y - p_O \neq 0$. $z = 3.56$; P-value $= 0.0004$. With such a small P-value, we reject H_0. We conclude there is evidence of a difference in effectiveness; it appears the methods are not as good for older women.
b) $\chi^2 = 12.70$; P-value $= 0.0004$. Same conclusion.
c) The P-values are the same; $z^2 = (3.563944)^2 = 12.70 = \chi^2$.

20. $\chi^2 = 40.715$; P-value <0.0001. These data do indicate an association between education and family planning. More educated women have fewer unplanned pregnancies.

21. a) Positive direction, generally linear trend; moderate scatter.
b) H_0: There is no linear relationship between interval and duration. $\beta_1 = 0$. H_A: There is a linear relationship $\beta_1 \neq 0$.
c) Yes; histogram is unimodal and roughly symmetric; residuals plot shows random scatter.
d) $t = 27.1$; P-value ≤ 0.001. With such a small P-value, we reject H_0. There is a significant positive linear relationship between duration and time to next eruption of Old Faithful.
e) Based on this regression, the average time to next eruption after a 2-minute eruption is between 53.24 and 56.12 minutes, with 95% confidence.
f) Based on this regression, we will have to wait between 63.23 and 87.57 minutes after a 4-minute eruption, with 95% confidence.

22. a) H_0: $\beta_1 = 0$; H_A: $\beta_1 \neq 0$. $t = 4.16$, P-value <0.0001. These data show evidence of a positive relationship between number of meals eaten together and grades.
b) No. R^2 is small and $s = 0.66$ points. So we could predict only to within 1.32 grade points at best.
c) No. The slope is clearly not 0, but that doesn't mean the relationship is strong or the predictions are useful.

23. a) $t = 1.42$, P-value $= 0.1574$. Since $P > 0.05$, we do not reject H_0. The two groups did not differ in ability at the start of the study.
b) $t = 15.11$; P-value < 0.0001. The group taught using the accelerated Math program showed a significant improvement.
c) $t = 9.24$; P-value < 0.0001. The control group showed a significant improvement in test scores.
d) $t = 5.78$; P-value < 0.0001. The Accelerated Math group had significantly higher gains than the control group.

24. H_0: $p = 0.512$; H_A: $p < 0.512$. $z = -3.35$; P-value $= 0.0004$. With such a small P-value, we reject H_0. These data provide evidence that exposure to dioxin reduces the rate of male births.

25. a) The regression—he wanted to know about association.
b) There is a moderate relationship between cottage cheese and ice cream sales; for every million pounds of cottage cheese, 1.19 million pounds of ice cream are sold on average.
c) Testing if the mean difference is 0.(matched t-test). Regression won't answer this question.
d) The company sells more cottage cheese than ice cream, on average.
e) part a—linear relationship; residuals have a Normal distribution; residuals are independent with equal variation about the line. c—Observations are independent; differences are approximately Normal; less than 10% of all possible months' data.
f) About 71.32 million pounds.
g) (0.09, 2.29)
h) From this regression, every million pounds of cottage cheese sold is associated with an increase in ice cream sales of between 0.09 and 2.29 million pounds.

26. $\chi^2 = 14.96$; P-value $= 0.0006$. With such a small P-value, we reject H_0. These data provide evidence that continued treatment with inflixamab is of value.

27. Based on these data, the average weight loss for the clinic is between 8.24 and 10.06 pounds, with 95% confidence. The clinic's claim is plausible.

28. a) Yes. Data plot is linear; residuals plot shows random scatter; histogram of residuals is roughly normal.
b) Yes; $t = 5.19$; P-value ≤ 0.0001.
c) Weaker. Individuals are more variable than averages.

d) Based on this regression, every extra year of median education in a city is associated with an increase of between \$1500.48 and \$3389.10 in median income.

e) Based on the regression, median income for cities where residents spent an average of 11 years in school is between \$32,198.81 and \$33,526.67, with 90% confidence.

29. $\chi^2 = 8.23$; P-value $= 0.0414$. There is evidence of an association between cracker type and bloating. Standardized residuals for the gum cracker are -1.32 and 1.58. Prospects for marketing this cracker are not good.

30. a) H_0: $\mu_1 - \mu_2 = 0$; H_A: $\mu_1 - \mu_2 > 0$. $t = 0.98$; P-value $= 0.1864$. Since $P > 0.05$, we do not reject H_0. Week-long study scores were not significantly higher.

b) H_0: $p_1 - p_2 = 0$; H_A: $p_1 - p_2 \neq 0$. $z = -3.10$, P-value $= 0.0019$. With such a small P-value, we reject H_0. There is evidence of a difference in proportion for passing on Friday; it appears that cramming may be more effective.

c) H_0: $\mu_D = 0$; H_A: $\mu_D > 0$. $t = 5.17$, P-value < 0.0001. These data show evidence that learning does not last for 3 days because mean score declined.

d) Based on these data, the average number of words forgotten by crammers is between 3.03 and 7.05 with 95% confidence.

e) Yes. Regression equation is Monday $= 14.5 + 0.536 \times$ Friday. $t = 2.57$; P-value $= 0.0170$.

Appendix D: Photo Acknowledgments

Page 1 © Joseph Sohm; ChromoSohm Inc./Corbis **Page 2** © AP/Wide World Photos **Page 3** FRAZZ reprinted by permission of United Feature Syndicate, Inc. **Page 6** © Dorling Kindersley **Page 6** Courtesy of Amber Chand, EZIBA **Page 8** © Dorling Kindersley **Page 10** © Bettman/Corbis **Page 15** © AP/Wide World Photos **Page 16** Courtesy of the Florence Nightingale Museum **Page 19** © Stephen J. Carrera/Associated Press AP **Page 23** © Stone/Getty Images **Page 36** ©Reuters NewMedia, Inc./Corbis **Page 40** © Corbis Sygma **Page 57** © PhotoDisc **Page 75** © AFP/Corbis **Page 83** © lundt Dimitri/Corbis Sygma **Page 84** © Pete Saloutos/ Corbis **Page 85** Royalty Free/Corbis **Page 114** © PhotoDisc **Page 115** © AP/ Wide World Photo **Page 117** © Corbis **Page 137** © Dorling Kindersley **Page 140** **Page 162** © PhotoDisc © Corbis **Page 165** © 2002 Bill Amend. Reprinted with permission of UNIVERSAL PRESS SYNDICATE. All rights reserved. **Page 167** © AFP/CORBIS **Page 167** © AP/Wide World Photos **Page 181** © Corbis **Page 214** Courtesy of Beth Anderson **Page 215** © PhotoDisc **Page 216** © United Feature Syndicate, Inc. **Page 218** (Tiger Woods) © 2002 Getty Images **Page 218** (Serena Williams, Lance Armstrong) © Corbis **Page 226** © Michael Newman/ PhotoEdit **Page 227** (George Gallup) © AP/Wide World Photos **Page 236** © 1993 Watterson. Reprinted with permission of UNIVERSAL PRESS SYNDICATE. All rights reserved. **Page 239** © Creators Syndicate **Page 246** © Courtesy of Beth Anderson **Page 248** (Gustav Fechner/C.S. Peirce) © St. Andrew's University History of Mathematics Archive **Page 249** © United Press Syndicate **Page 250** © Dorling Kindersley **Page 273** © PhotoDisc **Page 274** © Courtesy of Beth Anderson **Page 277** © St. Andrew's University History of Mathematics Archive **Page 288** © Getty News and Sport **Page 289** © Corbis **Page 290** © St. Andrew's University History of Mathematics Archive **Page 309** © Digital Vision **Page 315** © University of Texas **Page 325** © Stephen Mallon/Imagebank/Getty Images **Page 316** © Courtesy of Beth Anderson **Page 325** © 2002 Getty Images **Page 326** © St. Andrew's University History of Mathematics Archive **Page 326** © 1993 Watterson. Reprinted with permission of UNIVERSAL PRESS SYNDICATE. All rights reserved. **Page 333** © PhotoDisc **Page 344** © Courtesy of Dick DeVeaux **Page 346** © Courtesy of Beth Anderson **Page 346** © AFP/Corbis **Page 354** © St. Andrew's University History of Mathematics Archive **Page 366** © Stuart Westmoreland/Corbis **Page 369** © 'Paws, Inc. Reprinted with permission of UNIVERSAL PRESS SYNDICATE. All rights reserved. **Page 382** © Digital Vision **Page 401** © Courtesy of Beth Anderson **Page 405** © University of York Department of Mathematics **Page 408** Massachusetts Governor's Highway Safety Bureau **Page 421** © Stone/Getty Images **Page 426** © PhotoDisc **Page 442** © Royalty-Free/Corbis **Page 443** © Courtesy of Beth Anderson **Page 445** © University of York Department of Mathematics **Page 466** © Courtesy of Beth Anderson **Page 491** © Courtesy of Dave Bock **Page 517** © PhotoDisc **Page 518** © Royalty-Free/Corbis **Page 543** © Stone/Getty **Page 552** © Nenana Ice Classic **Page 576** © Courtesy of Dave Bock

Appendix E: Index

Page numbers in italic indicate material in the Step-by-Step features; *n* indicates footnote.

D

E

Q

R

S

T

Appendix F: Index of TI Tips

Appendix G: Tables

Row	TABLE OF RANDOM DIGITS									
1	96299	07196	98642	20639	23185	56282	69929	14125	38872	94168
2	71622	35940	81807	59225	18192	08710	80777	84395	59563	86280
3	03272	41230	81739	74797	70406	18564	69273	72532	78340	36699
4	46376	58596	14365	63685	56555	42974	72944	96463	63533	24152
5	47352	42853	42903	97504	56655	70355	88606	61406	38757	70657
6	20064	04266	74017	79319	70170	96572	08523	56025	89077	57678
7	73184	95907	05179	51002	83374	52297	07769	99792	78365	93487
8	72753	36216	07230	35793	71907	65571	66784	25548	91861	15725
9	03939	30763	06138	80062	02537	23561	93136	61260	77935	93159
10	75998	37203	07959	38264	78120	77525	86481	54986	33042	70648
11	94435	97441	90998	25104	49761	14967	70724	67030	53887	81293
12	04362	40989	69167	38894	00172	02999	97377	33305	60782	29810
13	89059	43528	10547	40115	82234	86902	04121	83889	76208	31076
14	87736	04666	75145	49175	76754	07884	92564	80793	22573	67902
15	76488	88899	15860	07370	13431	84041	69202	18912	83173	11983
16	36460	53772	66634	25045	79007	78518	73580	14191	50353	32064
17	13205	69237	21820	20952	16635	58867	97650	82983	64865	93298
18	51242	12215	90739	36812	00436	31609	80333	96606	30430	31803
19	67819	00354	91439	91073	49258	15992	41277	75111	67496	68430
20	09875	08990	27656	15871	23637	00952	97818	64234	50199	05715
21	18192	95308	72975	01191	29958	09275	89141	19558	50524	32041
22	02763	33701	66188	50226	35813	72951	11638	01876	93664	37001
23	13349	46328	01856	29935	80563	03742	49470	67749	08578	21956
24	69238	92878	80067	80807	45096	22936	64325	19265	37755	69794
25	92207	63527	59398	29818	24789	94309	88380	57000	50171	17891
26	66679	99100	37072	30593	29665	84286	44458	60180	81451	58273
27	31087	42430	60322	34765	15757	53300	97392	98035	05228	68970
28	84432	04916	52949	78533	31666	62350	20584	56367	19701	60584
29	72042	12287	21081	48426	44321	58765	41760	43304	13399	02043
30	94534	73559	82135	70260	87936	85162	11937	18263	54138	69564
31	63971	97198	40974	45301	60177	35604	21580	68107	25184	42810
32	11227	58474	17272	37619	69517	62964	67962	34510	12607	52255
33	28541	02029	08068	96656	17795	21484	57722	76511	27849	61738
34	11282	43632	49531	78981	81980	08530	08629	32279	29478	50228
35	42907	15137	21918	13248	39129	49559	94540	24070	88151	36782
36	47119	76651	21732	32364	58545	50277	57558	30390	18771	72703
37	11232	99884	05087	76839	65142	19994	91397	29350	83852	04905
38	64725	06719	86262	53356	57999	50193	79936	97230	52073	94467
39	77007	26962	55466	12521	48125	12280	54985	26239	76044	54398
40	18375	19310	59796	89832	59417	18553	17238	05474	33259	50595

Table Z
Areas under the standard normal curve

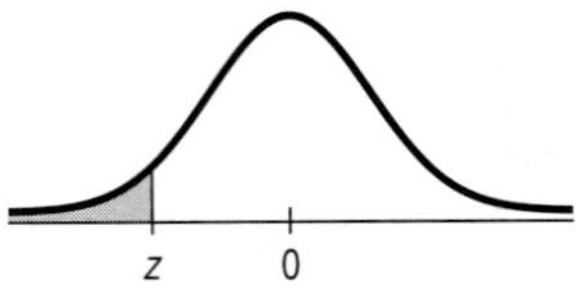

Second decimal place in z										
0.09	0.08	0.07	0.06	0.05	0.04	0.03	0.02	0.01	0.00	z
									0.0000†	−3.9
0.0001	0.0001	0.0001	0.0001	0.0001	0.0001	0.0001	0.0001	0.0001	0.0001	−3.8
0.0001	0.0001	0.0001	0.0001	0.0001	0.0001	0.0001	0.0001	0.0001	0.0001	−3.7
0.0001	0.0001	0.0001	0.0001	0.0001	0.0001	0.0001	0.0001	0.0002	0.0002	−3.6
0.0002	0.0002	0.0002	0.0002	0.0002	0.0002	0.0002	0.0002	0.0002	0.0002	−3.5
0.0002	0.0003	0.0003	0.0003	0.0003	0.0003	0.0003	0.0003	0.0003	0.0003	−3.4
0.0003	0.0004	0.0004	0.0004	0.0004	0.0004	0.0004	0.0005	0.0005	0.0005	−3.3
0.0005	0.0005	0.0005	0.0006	0.0006	0.0006	0.0006	0.0006	0.0007	0.0007	−3.2
0.0007	0.0007	0.0008	0.0008	0.0008	0.0008	0.0009	0.0009	0.0009	0.0010	−3.1
0.0010	0.0010	0.0011	0.0011	0.0011	0.0012	0.0012	0.0013	0.0013	0.0013	−3.0
0.0014	0.0014	0.0015	0.0015	0.0016	0.0016	0.0017	0.0018	0.0018	0.0019	−2.9
0.0019	0.0020	0.0021	0.0021	0.0022	0.0023	0.0023	0.0024	0.0025	0.0026	−2.8
0.0026	0.0027	0.0028	0.0029	0.0030	0.0031	0.0032	0.0033	0.0034	0.0035	−2.7
0.0036	0.0037	0.0038	0.0039	0.0040	0.0041	0.0043	0.0044	0.0045	0.0047	−2.6
0.0048	0.0049	0.0051	0.0052	0.0054	0.0055	0.0057	0.0059	0.0060	0.0062	−2.5
0.0064	0.0066	0.0068	0.0069	0.0071	0.0073	0.0075	0.0078	0.0080	0.0082	−2.4
0.0084	0.0087	0.0089	0.0091	0.0094	0.0096	0.0099	0.0102	0.0104	0.0107	−2.3
0.0110	0.0113	0.0116	0.0119	0.0122	0.0125	0.0129	0.0132	0.0136	0.0139	−2.2
0.0143	0.0146	0.0150	0.0154	0.0158	0.0162	0.0166	0.0170	0.0174	0.0179	−2.1
0.0183	0.0188	0.0192	0.0197	0.0202	0.0207	0.0212	0.0217	0.0222	0.0228	−2.0
0.0233	0.0239	0.0244	0.0250	0.0256	0.0262	0.0268	0.0274	0.0281	0.0287	−1.9
0.0294	0.0301	0.0307	0.0314	0.0322	0.0329	0.0336	0.0344	0.0351	0.0359	−1.8
0.0367	0.0375	0.0384	0.0392	0.0401	0.0409	0.0418	0.0427	0.0436	0.0446	−1.7
0.0455	0.0465	0.0475	0.0485	0.0495	0.0505	0.0516	0.0526	0.0537	0.0548	−1.6
0.0559	0.0571	0.0582	0.0594	0.0606	0.0618	0.0630	0.0643	0.0655	0.0668	−1.5
0.0681	0.0694	0.0708	0.0721	0.0735	0.0749	0.0764	0.0778	0.0793	0.0808	−1.4
0.0823	0.0838	0.0853	0.0869	0.0885	0.0901	0.0918	0.0934	0.0951	0.0968	−1.3
0.0985	0.1003	0.1020	0.1038	0.1056	0.1075	0.1093	0.1112	0.1131	0.1151	−1.2
0.1170	0.1190	0.1210	0.1230	0.1251	0.1271	0.1292	0.1314	0.1335	0.1357	−1.1
0.1379	0.1401	0.1423	0.1446	0.1469	0.1492	0.1515	0.1539	0.1562	0.1587	−1.0
0.1611	0.1635	0.1660	0.1685	0.1711	0.1736	0.1762	0.1788	0.1814	0.1841	−0.9
0.1867	0.1894	0.1922	0.1949	0.1977	0.2005	0.2033	0.2061	0.2090	0.2119	−0.8
0.2148	0.2177	0.2206	0.2236	0.2266	0.2296	0.2327	0.2358	0.2389	0.2420	−0.7
0.2451	0.2483	0.2514	0.2546	0.2578	0.2611	0.2643	0.2676	0.2709	0.2743	−0.6
0.2776	0.2810	0.2843	0.2877	0.2912	0.2946	0.2981	0.3015	0.3050	0.3085	−0.5
0.3121	0.3156	0.3192	0.3228	0.3264	0.3300	0.3336	0.3372	0.3409	0.3446	−0.4
0.3483	0.3520	0.3557	0.3594	0.3632	0.3669	0.3707	0.3745	0.3783	0.3821	−0.3
0.3859	0.3897	0.3936	0.3974	0.4013	0.4052	0.4090	0.4129	0.4168	0.4207	−0.2
0.4247	0.4286	0.4325	0.4364	0.4404	0.4443	0.4483	0.4522	0.4562	0.4602	−0.1
0.4641	0.4681	0.4721	0.4761	0.4801	0.4840	0.4880	0.4920	0.4960	0.5000	−0.0

†For $z \leq 3.90$, the areas are 0.0000 to four decimal places.

Table *Z* (cont.)
Areas under the standard normal curve

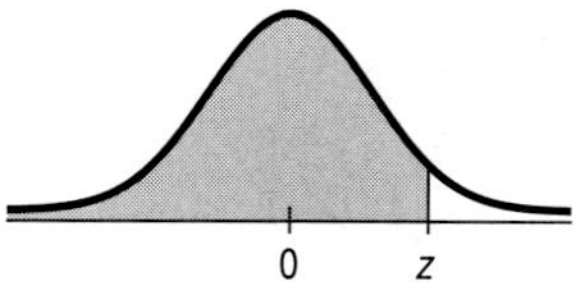

z	0.00	0.01	0.02	0.03	0.04	0.05	0.06	0.07	0.08	0.09
0.0	0.5000	0.5040	0.5080	0.5120	0.5160	0.5199	0.5239	0.5279	0.5319	0.5359
0.1	0.5398	0.5438	0.5478	0.5517	0.5557	0.5596	0.5636	0.5675	0.5714	0.5753
0.2	0.5793	0.5832	0.5871	0.5910	0.5948	0.5987	0.6026	0.6064	0.6103	0.6141
0.3	0.6179	0.6217	0.6255	0.6293	0.6331	0.6368	0.6406	0.6443	0.6480	0.6517
0.4	0.6554	0.6591	0.6628	0.6664	0.6700	0.6736	0.6772	0.6808	0.6844	0.6879
0.5	0.6915	0.6950	0.6985	0.7019	0.7054	0.7088	0.7123	0.7157	0.7190	0.7224
0.6	0.7257	0.7291	0.7324	0.7357	0.7389	0.7422	0.7454	0.7486	0.7517	0.7549
0.7	0.7580	0.7611	0.7642	0.7673	0.7704	0.7734	0.7764	0.7794	0.7823	0.7852
0.8	0.7881	0.7910	0.7939	0.7967	0.7995	0.8023	0.8051	0.8078	0.8106	0.8133
0.9	0.8159	0.8186	0.8212	0.8238	0.8264	0.8289	0.8315	0.8340	0.8365	0.8389
1.0	0.8413	0.8438	0.8461	0.8485	0.8508	0.8531	0.8554	0.8577	0.8599	0.8621
1.1	0.8643	0.8665	0.8686	0.8708	0.8729	0.8749	0.8770	0.8790	0.8810	0.8830
1.2	0.8849	0.8869	0.8888	0.8907	0.8925	0.8944	0.8962	0.8980	0.8997	0.9015
1.3	0.9032	0.9049	0.9066	0.9082	0.9099	0.9115	0.9131	0.9147	0.9162	0.9177
1.4	0.9192	0.9207	0.9222	0.9236	0.9251	0.9265	0.9279	0.9292	0.9306	0.9319
1.5	0.9332	0.9345	0.9357	0.9370	0.9382	0.9394	0.9406	0.9418	0.9429	0.9441
1.6	0.9452	0.9463	0.9474	0.9484	0.9495	0.9505	0.9515	0.9525	0.9535	0.9545
1.7	0.9554	0.9564	0.9573	0.9582	0.9591	0.9599	0.9608	0.9616	0.9625	0.9633
1.8	0.9641	0.9649	0.9656	0.9664	0.9671	0.9678	0.9686	0.9693	0.9699	0.9706
1.9	0.9713	0.9719	0.9726	0.9732	0.9738	0.9744	0.9750	0.9756	0.9761	0.9767
2.0	0.9772	0.9778	0.9783	0.9788	0.9793	0.9798	0.9803	0.9808	0.9812	0.9817
2.1	0.9821	0.9826	0.9830	0.9834	0.9838	0.9842	0.9846	0.9850	0.9854	0.9857
2.2	0.9861	0.9864	0.9868	0.9871	0.9875	0.9878	0.9881	0.9884	0.9887	0.9890
2.3	0.9893	0.9896	0.9898	0.9901	0.9904	0.9906	0.9909	0.9911	0.9913	0.9916
2.4	0.9918	0.9920	0.9922	0.9925	0.9927	0.9929	0.9931	0.9932	0.9934	0.9936
2.5	0.9938	0.9940	0.9941	0.9943	0.9945	0.9946	0.9948	0.9949	0.9951	0.9952
2.6	0.9953	0.9955	0.9956	0.9957	0.9959	0.9960	0.9961	0.9962	0.9963	0.9964
2.7	0.9965	0.9966	0.9967	0.9968	0.9969	0.9970	0.9971	0.9972	0.9973	0.9974
2.8	0.9974	0.9975	0.9976	0.9977	0.9977	0.9978	0.9979	0.9979	0.9980	0.9981
2.9	0.9981	0.9982	0.9982	0.9983	0.9984	0.9984	0.9985	0.9985	0.9986	0.9986
3.0	0.9987	0.9987	0.9987	0.9988	0.9988	0.9989	0.9989	0.9989	0.9990	0.9990
3.1	0.9990	0.9991	0.9991	0.9991	0.9992	0.9992	0.9992	0.9992	0.9993	0.9993
3.2	0.9993	0.9993	0.9994	0.9994	0.9994	0.9994	0.9994	0.9995	0.9995	0.9995
3.3	0.9995	0.9995	0.9995	0.9996	0.9996	0.9996	0.9996	0.9996	0.9996	0.9997
3.4	0.9997	0.9997	0.9997	0.9997	0.9997	0.9997	0.9997	0.9997	0.9997	0.9998
3.5	0.9998	0.9998	0.9998	0.9998	0.9998	0.9998	0.9998	0.9998	0.9998	0.9998
3.6	0.9998	0.9998	0.9999	0.9999	0.9999	0.9999	0.9999	0.9999	0.9999	0.9999
3.7	0.9999	0.9999	0.9999	0.9999	0.9999	0.9999	0.9999	0.9999	0.9999	0.9999
3.8	0.9999	0.9999	0.9999	0.9999	0.9999	0.9999	0.9999	0.9999	0.9999	0.9999
3.9	1.0000†									

Second decimal place in z

†For $z \geq 3.90$, the areas are 1.0000 to four decimal places.

Table T

Values of t_{α}

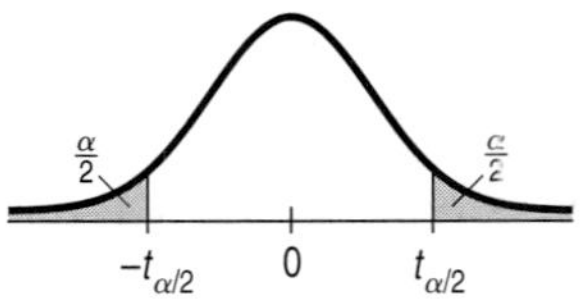

Two tails

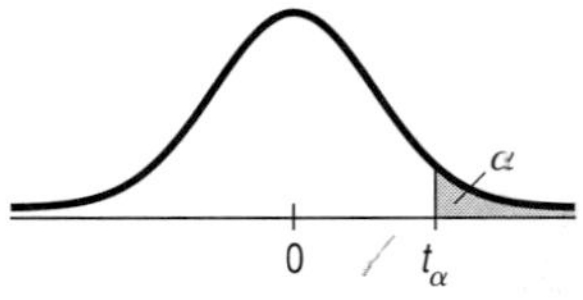

One tail

	Two tail probability	0.20	0.10	0.05	0.02	0.01	
	One tail probability	0.10	0.05	0.025	0.01	0.005	
	df						df
	1	3.078	6.314	12.706	31.821	63.657	1
	2	1.886	2.920	4.303	6.965	9.925	2
	3	1.638	2.353	3.182	4.541	5.841	3
	4	1.533	2.132	2.776	3.747	4.604	4
	5	1.476	2.015	2.571	3.365	4.032	5
	6	1.440	1.943	2.447	3.143	3.707	6
	7	1.415	1.895	2.365	2.998	3.499	7
	8	1.397	1.860	2.306	2.896	3.355	8
	9	1.383	1.833	2.262	2.821	3.250	9
	10	1.372	1.812	2.228	2.764	3.169	10
	11	1.363	1.796	2.201	2.718	3.106	11
	12	1.356	1.782	2.179	2.681	3.055	12
	13	1.350	1.771	2.160	2.650	3.012	13
	14	1.345	1.761	2.145	2.624	2.977	14
	15	1.341	1.753	2.131	2.602	2.947	15
	16	1.337	1.746	2.120	2.583	2.921	16
	17	1.333	1.740	2.110	2.567	2.898	17
	18	1.330	1.734	2.101	2.552	2.878	18
	19	1.328	1.729	2.093	2.539	2.861	19
	20	1.325	1.725	2.086	2.528	2.845	20
	21	1.323	1.721	2.080	2.518	2.831	21
	22	1.321	1.717	2.074	2.508	2.819	22
	23	1.319	1.714	2.069	2.500	2.807	23
	24	1.318	1.711	2.064	2.492	2.797	24
	25	1.316	1.708	2.060	2.485	2.787	25
	26	1.315	1.706	2.056	2.479	2.779	26
	27	1.314	1.703	2.052	2.473	2.771	27
	28	1.313	1.701	2.048	2.467	2.763	28
	29	1.311	1.699	2.045	2.462	2.756	29
	30	1.310	1.697	2.042	2.457	2.750	30
	32	1.309	1.694	2.037	2.449	2.738	32
	35	1.306	1.690	2.030	2.438	2.725	35
	40	1.303	1.684	2.021	2.423	2.704	40
	45	1.301	1.679	2.014	2.412	2.690	45
	50	1.299	1.676	2.009	2.403	2.678	50
	60	1.296	1.671	2.000	2.390	2.660	60
	75	1.293	1.665	1.992	2.377	2.643	75
	100	1.290	1.660	1.984	2.364	2.626	100
	120	1.289	1.658	1.980	2.358	2.617	120
	140	1.288	1.656	1.977	2.353	2.611	140
	180	1.286	1.653	1.973	2.347	2.603	180
	250	1.285	1.651	1.969	2.341	2.596	250
	400	1.284	1.649	1.966	2.336	2.588	400
	1000	1.282	1.646	1.962	2.330	2.581	1000
	∞	1.282	1.645	1.960	2.326	2.576	∞
confidence levels		80%	90%	95%	98%	99%	

Table X
Values of χ^2_α

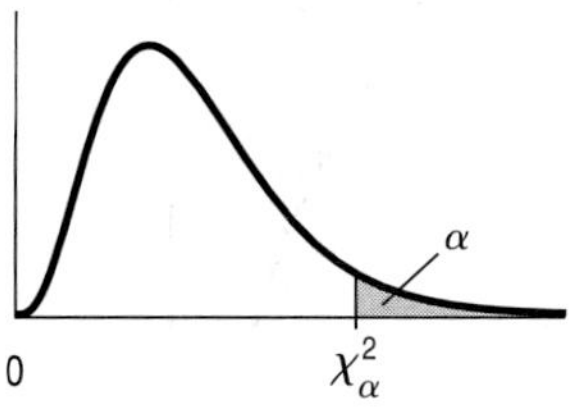

Right tail probability df	0.10	0.05	0.025	0.01	0.005
1	2.706	3.841	5.024	6.635	7.879
2	4.605	5.991	7.378	9.210	10.597
3	6.251	7.815	9.348	11.345	12.838
4	7.779	9.488	11.143	13.277	14.860
5	9.236	11.070	12.833	15.086	16.750
6	10.645	12.592	14.449	16.812	18.548
7	12.017	14.067	16.013	18.475	20.278
8	13.362	15.507	17.535	20.090	21.955
9	14.684	16.919	19.023	21.666	23.589
10	15.987	18.307	20.483	23.209	25.188
11	17.275	19.675	21.920	24.725	26.757
12	18.549	21.026	23.337	26.217	28.300
13	19.812	22.362	24.736	27.688	29.819
14	21.064	23.685	26.119	29.141	31.319
15	22.307	24.996	27.488	30.578	32.801
16	23.542	26.296	28.845	32.000	34.267
17	24.769	27.587	30.191	33.409	35.718
18	25.989	28.869	31.526	34.805	37.156
19	27.204	30.143	32.852	36.191	38.582
20	28.412	31.410	34.170	37.566	39.997
21	29.615	32.671	35.479	38.932	41.401
22	30.813	33.924	36.781	40.290	42.796
23	32.007	35.172	38.076	41.638	44.181
24	33.196	36.415	39.364	42.980	45.559
25	34.382	37.653	40.647	44.314	46.928
26	35.563	38.885	41.923	45.642	48.290
27	36.741	40.113	43.195	46.963	49.645
28	37.916	41.337	44.461	48.278	50.994
29	39.087	42.557	45.722	59.588	52.336
30	40.256	43.773	46.979	50.892	53.672
40	51.805	55.759	59.342	63.691	66.767
50	63.167	67.505	71.420	76.154	79.490
60	74.397	79.082	83.298	88.381	91.955
70	85.527	90.531	95.023	100.424	104.213
80	96.578	101.879	106.628	112.328	116.320
90	107.565	113.145	118.135	124.115	128.295
100	118.499	124.343	129.563	135.811	140.177

Assumptions for Inference	And the Conditions That Support or Override Them
Proportions (z)	
• **One sample**	
1. Individuals are independent.	1. SRS and $< 10\%$ of the population.
2. Sample is sufficiently large.	2. Successes and failures ≥ 10.
• **Two sample**	
1. Samples are independent.	1. (Think about how the data were collected.)
2. Data in each sample are independent.	2. Both are SRSs and $< 10\%$ of populations OR random allocation.
3. Both samples are sufficiently large.	3. Successes and failures ≥ 10 for both.
Means (t)	
• **One Sample** (df $= n - 1$)	
1. Individuals are independent.	1. SRS and $< 10\%$ of the population.
2. Population has a Normal model.	2. Histogram is unimodal and symmetric*.
• **Matched pairs** (df $= n - 1$)	
1. Data are matched.	1. (Think about the design.)
2. Individuals are independent.	2. SRS and $< 10\%$ OR random allocation.
3. Population of differences is Normal.	3. Histogram of differences is unimodal and symmetric.
• **Two independent samples** (df from technology)	
1. Samples are independent.	1. (Think about the design.)
2. Data in each sample are independent.	2. SRSs and $< 10\%$ OR random allocation.
3. Both populations are Normal.	3. Both histograms are unimodal and symmetric.*
Distributions/Association (χ^2)	
• **Goodness of fit** (df = # of cells − 1; one variable, one sample compared with population model)	
1. Data are counts.	1. (Are they?)
2. Data in sample are independent.	2. SRS and $< 10\%$ of the population.
3. Sample is sufficiently large.	3. All expected counts ≥ 5.
• **Homogeneity** [df $= (r - 1)(c - 1)$; samples from many populations compared on one variable]	
1. Data are counts.	1. (Are they?)
2. Data in samples are independent.	2. SRSs and $< 10\%$ OR random allocation.
3. Samples are sufficiently large.	3. All expected counts ≥ 5.
• **Independence** [df $= (r - 1)(c - 1)$; sample from one population classified on two variables]	
1. Data are counts.	1. (Are they?)
2. Data are independent.	2. SRSs and $< 10\%$ of the population.
3. Sample is sufficiently large.	3. All expected counts ≥ 5.
Regression (t, df $= n - 2$)	
• **Association** between two measurement variables ($\beta = 0$?)	
1. Form of relationship is linear.	1. Scatterplot looks approximately linear.
2. Errors are independent.	2. No apparent pattern in residuals plot.
3. Variability of errors is constant.	3. Residuals plot has consistent spread.
4. Errors have a Normal model.	4. Histogram of residuals is approximately unimodal and symmetric, or normal probability plot reasonably straight.*
	(*less critical as n increases)